Lecture Notes in Computer Science 14604

The series Lecture Notes in Computer Science (LNCS), including its subseries Lecture Notes in Artificial Intelligence (LNAI) and Lecture Notes in Bioinformatics (LNBI), has established itself as a medium for the publication of new developments in computer science and information technology research, teaching, and education.

LNCS enjoys close cooperation with the computer science R & D community, the series counts many renowned academics among its volume editors and paper authors, and collaborates with prestigious societies. Its mission is to serve this international community by providing an invaluable service, mainly focused on the publication of conference and workshop proceedings and postproceedings. LNCS commenced publication in 1973.

Qiang Tang · Vanessa Teague
Editors

Public-Key Cryptography – PKC 2024

27th IACR International Conference on Practice and Theory of Public-Key Cryptography Sydney, NSW, Australia, April 15–17, 2024 Proceedings, Part IV

Springer

Editors
Qiang Tang
The University of Sydney
Sydney, NSW, Australia

Vanessa Teague
The Australian National University
Acton, ACT, Australia

ISSN 0302-9743 ISSN 1611-3349 (electronic)
Lecture Notes in Computer Science
ISBN 978-3-031-57727-7 ISBN 978-3-031-57728-4 (eBook)
https://doi.org/10.1007/978-3-031-57728-4

This Springer imprint is published by the registered company Springer Nature Switzerland AG
The registered company address is: Gewerbestrasse 11, 6330 Cham, Switzerland

Paper in this product is recyclable.

Preface

The 27th International Conference on Practice and Theory of Public-Key Cryptography (PKC 2024) was held in Sydney, Australia, on April 15–17, 2024. It was sponsored by the International Association for Cryptologic Research (IACR) and is the main IACR-sponsored conference with an explicit focus on public-key cryptography. PKC 2024 authors represented 24 different countries, bringing a vibrant international community of cryptography researchers to Australia.

The conference received 176 submissions, reviewed by the Program Committee of 68 cryptography experts (including four area chairs) working with 183 external reviewers. The reviewing process took two months and selected 54 papers to appear in PKC 2024. Papers were reviewed in the usual double-blind fashion with an average of just over three reviews per paper. Program committee members and general chairs were limited to 3 submissions (4 if all with students), and their submissions were scrutinized more closely. The two program chairs were not allowed to submit papers. PKC 2024 was the first major cryptography conferences to accept SoK papers.

PKC 2024 welcomed Nadia Heninger (University of California, San Diego) and Aggelos Kiayias (University of Edinburgh) as the invited speakers. The Program Committee also selected two best papers: *An algorithm for efficient detection of (N, N)-splittings and its application to the isogeny problem in dimension 2* by Maria Corte-Real Santos, Craig Costello and Sam Frengley, and *Quantum CCA-Secure PKE, Revisited* by Navid Alamati and Varun Maram.

The award committee (Masayuki Abe, Alexandra Boldyreva, Qiang Tang, Vanessa Teague, Moti Yung) also chose the PKC Test of Time Award for 2024.

PKC is a remarkable undertaking, possible only through the hard work and significant contributions of many people. We would like to express our sincere gratitude to all the authors, as well as to the Program Committee and external reviewers, session chairs and presenters. Special thanks to the area chairs: Steven Galbraith, Giuseppe Persiano, Kazue Sako and Vassilis Zikas. Their specialist knowledge and good judgement were critical for making good decisions.

Additionally, we would like to thank Willy Susilo, Fuchun Guo and the team at the University of Wollongong for making the general arrangements such a success. Also, as always, Kay McKelly and Kevin McCurley provided invaluable support for all things technical behind the scenes.

All of this happens against a backdrop in which even some democratic governments are working to undermine encrypted communications in the name of "safety." In Australia, exporting a new encryption algorithm without a permit can be punished with years in jail. Open, scientific, internationally collaborative research in cryptography is more important than ever.

We hope you enjoyed the conference and the warm welcome of Sydney.

April 2024

Qiang Tang
Vanessa Teague

Organization

General Chairs

Fuchun Guo	University of Wollongong, Australia
Willy Susilo	University of Wollongong, Australia

Program Committee Chairs

Qiang Tang	The University of Sydney, Australia
Vanessa Teague	Democracy Developers Ltd., The Australian National University and Thinking Cybersecurity Pty. Ltd., Australia

Steering Committee

Masayuki Abe	NTT, Japan
Alexandra Boldyreva	Georgia Tech, USA
Jung Hee Cheon	Seoul National University, South Korea
Yvo Desmedt	University of Texas at Dallas, USA
Goichiro Hanaoka	National Institute of Advanced Industrial Science and Technology, Japan
Tibor Jager	University of Wuppertal, Germany
Aggelos Kiayias	University of Edinburgh, UK
Vladimir Kolesnikov	Georgia Tech, USA
Tanja Lange	Eindhoven University of Technology, The Netherlands
Jiaxin Pan	NTNU, Norway & University of Kassel, Germany
David Pointcheval	École Normale Supérieure Paris, France
Qiang Tang	The University of Sydney, Australia
Vanessa Teague	Democracy Developers Ltd., The Australian National University and Thinking Cybersecurity Pty. Ltd., Australia
Moti Yung (Secretary)	Google Inc. & Columbia University, USA
Yuliang Zheng (Chair)	University of Alabama at Birmingham, USA

Area Chairs

Steven Galbraith	The University of Auckland, Aotearoa-New Zealand *Post-quantum cryptography, quantum cryptography, Math & Attacks*
Giuseppe Persiano	University of Salerno, Italy and Google, USA *Theoretical Foundations & Advanced Primitives*
Kazue Sako	Waseda University, Japan *Applied Cryptography, SNARKs & Verifiable Computation*
Vassilis Zikas	Purdue University, USA *Multiparty computation & consensus*

Program Committee

Divesh Aggarwal	National University of Singapore, Singapore
Christian Badertscher	Input Output Global, Switzerland
Foteini Baldimtsi	George Mason University, USA
Sofia Celi	Brave, Portugal
Suvradip Chakraborty	Visa Research, USA
Long Chen	Chinese Academy of Sciences, China
Yilei Chen	Tsinghua University, China
Rongmao Chen	National University of Defense Technology, China
Jung Hee Cheon	Seoul National University, Republic of Korea
Amy Corman	RMIT University, Australia
Luca De Feo	IBM Research Europe, Switzerland
Yi Deng	Chinese Academy of Sciences, China
Xiong Fan	Rutgers University, USA
Hanwen Feng	The University of Sydney, Australia
Rishab Goyal	University of Wisconsin-Madison, USA
Debayan Gupta	Ashoka University, India
Thomas Haines	The Australian National University, Australia
Goichiro Hanaoka	AIST, Japan
Cheng Hong	Ant Research, China
Tibor Jager	University of Wuppertal, Germany
Zhengzhong Jin	MIT, USA
Dmitry Khovratovich	Ethereum Foundation, Luxembourg
Fuyuki Kitagawa	NTT Social Informatics Laboratories, Japan

Chelsea Komlo	University of Waterloo, Canada
Markus Krausz	Ruhr University Bochum, Germany
Péter Kutas	University of Birmingham, UK and Eötvös Loránd University, Hungary
Tanja Lange	Eindhoven University of Technology, The Netherlands
Feng-Hao Liu	Washington State University, USA
Chen-da Liu-Zhang	HSLU and Web3 Foundation, Switzerland
Julian Loss	CISPA Helmholtz Center for Information Security, Germany
Mohammad Mahmoody	University of Virginia, USA
Daniel Masny	Meta, USA
Pratyay Mukherjee	Supra Research, India
Khoa Nguyen	University of Wollongong, Australia
Miyako Ohkubo	NICT, Japan
Omkant Pandey	Stony Brook University, USA
Krzysztof Pietrzak	IST Austria, Austria
David Pointcheval	ENS, Paris, France
Amin Sakzad	Monash University, Australia
Rebecca Schwerdt	Karlsruhe Institute of Technology, Germany
abhi shelat	Northeastern University, USA
Mark Simkin	Ethereum Foundation, Denmark
Yifan Song	Tsinghua University, China
Yongsoo Song	Seoul National University, Republic of Korea
Fang Song	Portland State University, USA
Shravan Srinivasan	Lagrange Labs, USA
Ron Steinfeld	Monash University, Australia
Sri Aravinda Krishnan Thyagarajan	NTT Research, USA and The University of Sydney, Australia
Prashant Nalini Vasudevan	National University of Singapore, Singapore
Daniele Venturi	Sapienza University of Rome, Italy
Xiaoyun Wang	Tsinghua University, China
Huaxiong Wang	Nanyang Technological University, Singapore
Benjamin Wesolowski	CNRS and ENS de Lyon, France
Jiayu Xu	Oregon State University, USA
Rupeng Yang	University of Wollongong, Australia
Kevin Yeo	Google and Columbia University, USA
Yu Yu	Shanghai Jiao Tong University, China
Thomas Zacharias	University of Glasgow, UK
Cong Zhang	Zhejiang University, China
Zhenfeng Zhang	Chinese Academy of Sciences, China
Bingsheng Zhang	Zhejiang University, China

Jiaheng Zhang — National University of Singapore, Singapore
Dominique Schroeder — Friedrich-Alexander University of Erlangen-Nürnberg, Germany
Wessel van Woerden — University of Bordeaux, France

Additional Reviewers

Aydin Abadi
Behzad Abdolmaleki
Masayuki Abe
Miguel Ambrona
Arathi Arakala
Sven Argo
Benedikt Auerbach
Renas Bacho
Weihao Bai
Shi Bai
Fabio Banfi
Andrea Basso
Fabrice Benhamouda
Olivier Bernard
Daniel J. Bernstein
Siddhartha Bhoi
Alex Bienstock
Katharina Boudgoust
Charles Bouillaguet
Pedro Branco
Fabian Buschkowski
Rohit Chatterjee
Binyi Chen
Hyeongmin Choe
Arka Rai Choudhuri
Hao Chung
Michele Ciampi
Valerio Cini
Alexandru Cojocaru
Pierrick Dartois
Poulami Das
Koen de Boer
Paola de Perthuis
Benne de Weger
Giovanni Deligios
Lalita Devadas
Jesus Diaz
Jelle Don
Léo Ducas
Pranjal Dutta
Keita Emura
Daniel Escudero
Muhammed F. Esgin
Thomas Espitau
Prastudy Fauzi
Danilo Francati
Daniele Friolo
Yao Jiang Galteland
Gayathri Garimella
Riddhi Ghosal
Aarushi Goel
Lenaick Gouriou
Anna Guinet
Hui Guo
Kyoohyung Han
Lucjan Hanzlik
Charlotte Hoffmann
Alex Hoover
Yao-Ching Hsieh
David Hu
Zhicong Huang
Andreas Hülsing
Nikai Jagganath
Aayush Jain
Xiaoyu Ji
Haodong Jiang
Haohao Jiang
Ioanna Karantaidou
Sabyasachi Karati
Handan Kilinc Alper
Suhri Kim
Dongwoo Kim
Seongkwang Kim
Sungwook Kim

Miran Kim
Kamil Kluczniak
Anders Konrig
Swastik Kopparty
Alexis Korb
Abhiram Kothapalli
Elisabeth Krahmer
Sabrina Kunzweiler
Kaoru Kurosawa
Qiqi Lai
Georg Land
Changmin Lee
Yun Li
Yanan Li
Xiao Liang
Yao-Ting Lin
Qipeng Liu
Zeyu Liu
Weiran Liu
Fengrun Liu
Wen-jie Lu
Varun Madathil
Lorenzo Magliocco
Monosij Maitra
Easwar Mangipudi
Elisaweta Masserova
Takahiro Matsuda
Daniel McVicker
Simon-Philipp Merz
Ruiqi Mi
Peihan Miao
Arash Mirzaei
Anuja Modi
Johannes Mono
Ethan Mook
Kirill Morozov
Marta Mularczyk
Ky Nguyen
Ryo Nishimaki
Alice Pellet-Mary
Nikhil Pappu
Jeongeun Park
Guillermo Pascual Perez
Alain Passelegue
Rutvik Patel
Sihang Pu
Ludo Pulles
Octavio Pérez Kempner
Wei Qi
Tian Qiu
Wenjie Qu
Willy Quach
Ahmadreza Rahimi
Omar Renawi
Mahshid Riahinia
Jan Richter-Brockmann
Guilherme Rito
Damien Robert
Maxime Roméas
Lawrence Roy
Luigi Russo
Sagnik Saha
Yusuke Sakai
Robert Schaedlich
Sven Schäge
Jacob Schuldt
Mahdi Sedaghat
Sruthi Sekar
Joon Young Seo
Jun Jie Sim
Yongha Son
Bruno Sterner
Atsushi Takayasu
Gang Tang
Guofeng Tang
Yuhao Tang
Khai Hanh Tang
Stefano Tessaro
Junichi Tomida
Monika Trimoska
Yiannis Tselekounis
Akhil Vanukuri
Benedikt Wagner
Hendrik Waldner
Han Wang
Yuchen Wang
Li-Ping Wang
Zhedong Wang
Yi Wang
Jiabo Wang

Charlotte Weitkämper
Chenkai Weng
Jie Xu
Anshu Yadav
Aayush Yadav
Shota Yamada
Takashi Yamakawa
Dan Yamamoto
Zhaomin Yang
Yusuke Yoshida
Zuoxia Yu
Shang Zehua
Xinyu Zhang
Liangfeng Zhang
Raymond K. Zhao
Hong-Sheng Zhou
Tanping Zhou
Zidi Zhuang

One-Shot Signatures: Applications and Design Directions (Invited Talk)

Aggelos Kiayias

School of Informatics, University of Edinburgh, UK and IOG
aggelos.kiayias@ed.ac.uk

Abstract. More than 50 years ago, Stephen Wiesner envisioned how the uncertainty principle could be harnessed to create oblivious transfer quantum channels and unforgeable quantum money. This seminal work lead to a number of developments widening the impact of quantum enhanced protocols in cryptography. Recently, following the blossoming of this research domain, one-shot signatures were introduced by Amos, Georgiou, Kiayias, and Zhandry (STOC 2020). This cryptographic primitive enables digital signatures with classical public-key verification and a quantum signing algorithm that self-destructs after being used once. This impossible property to achieve in the classical setting (barring hardware assumptions) has a number of far reaching applications that include key-evolving signatures without erasures, provably secret signing keys, secure proof-of-stake blockchains without erasing keys or economic penalties as well as non-interactive publicly verifiable proofs of quantumness and min-entropy. Known design approaches for one-shot signatures rely on the one side of so called win-win results regarding the "collapsing" features of hash functions and commitments in the quantum setting. Specifically, while being collapsing is a desirable property of such primitives from a post-quantum security perspective, a failure to collapse combined with retaining a degree of security, may enable useful quantum enhanced primitives including one-shot signatures. In this talk we overview applications and the currently known design approaches for one-shot signatures as well as point to directions for future research.

Keywords: One-shot signatures · Digital Signatures · Quantum cryptography · Blockchain protocol security · Post-quantum security

Contents – Part IV

Encryption

Homomorphic Encryption

Encryption

More Efficient Public-Key Cryptography with Leakage and Tamper Resilience

Shuai Han[1,2], Shengli Liu[2,3(✉)], and Dawu Gu[1,3]

[1] School of Cyber Science and Engineering, Shanghai Jiao Tong University, Shanghai 200240, China
{dalen17,dwgu}@sjtu.edu.cn

[2] State Key Laboratory of Cryptology, P.O. Box 5159, Beijing 100878, China

[3] Department of Computer Science and Engineering, Shanghai Jiao Tong University, Shanghai 200240, China
slliu@sjtu.edu.cn

Abstract. In this paper, we study the design of efficient signature and public-key encryption (PKE) schemes in the presence of both leakage and tampering attacks. Firstly, we formalize the strong leakage and tamper-resilient (sLTR) security model for signature, which provides strong existential unforgeability, and deals with bounded leakage and restricted tampering attacks, as a counterpart to the sLTR security introduced by Sun et al. (ACNS 2019) for PKE. Then, we present direct constructions of signature and chosen-ciphertext attack (CCA) secure PKE schemes in the sLTR model, based on the matrix decisional Diffie-Hellman (MDDH) assumptions (which covers the standard symmetric external DH (SXDH) and k-Linear assumptions) over asymmetric pairing groups. Our schemes avoid the use of heavy building blocks such as the true-simulation extractable non-interactive zero-knowledge proofs (tSE-NIZK) proposed by Dodis et al. (ASIACRYPT 2010), which are usually needed in constructing schemes with leakage and tamper-resilience. Especially, our SXDH-based signature and PKE schemes are more efficient than the existing schemes in the leakage and tamper-resilient setting: our signature scheme has only 4 group elements in the signature, which is about $5\times\sim 8\times$ *shorter*, and our PKE scheme has only 6 group elements in the ciphertext, which is about $1.3\times\sim 3.3\times$ *shorter*. Finally, we note that our signature scheme is the *first* one achieving strong existential unforgeability in the leakage and tamper-resilient setting, where strong existential unforgeability has important applications in building more complex primitives such as signcryption and authenticated key exchange.

1 Introduction

Traditionally, when analyzing and proving security of cryptographic schemes, it is always assumed that the only way for an adversary to get information about the secret keys is through *black-box access* to the cryptographic devices. In reality, however, an adversary may go far beyond black-box access, and obtain secret key information by directly accessing/tampering with the memory or the internal computation of the devices. To deal with these threats, *leakage and*

Q. Tang and V. Teague (Eds.): PKC 2024, LNCS 14604, pp. 3–34, 2024.
https://doi.org/10.1007/978-3-031-57728-4_1

tamper-resilient cryptography emerges with the aim of designing provably secure cryptographic schemes in such scenarios.

Leakage-Resilient Security. The motivation for leakage-resilient cryptography is the increasing popularity of various side-channel attacks [23,28,29], including timing measurements, power analysis, electromagnetic measurements and microwave attacks, through which an adversary can recover partial information about the secret keys. Such a capability is usually formulated by a leakage oracle, which allows the adversary to specify arbitrary leakage functions L and obtain the results $L(sk)$ of applying L to the secret key sk. Leakage-resilient security requires that the cryptographic schemes remain secure even for the adversary who has access to the leakage oracle. In this work, we focus on the bounded leakage-resilient security [1,32], where the total amount $|L(sk)|$ of leakage information is less than the whole secret key $|sk|$ and in particular bounded.

Tamper-Resilient Security. The attacks that leakage-resilient cryptography considers are in fact *passive* attacks, while the adversary may also launch *active* attacks such as fault injection and memory tampering attacks [6,19], through which the adversary can force the cryptographic devices to operate under a different but related secret key, and observe the input-output behaviour of the device under the modified secret key. The theoretical treatment of such attacks was initiated by Bellare and Kohno [3], where the capability of adversaries is modeled by a class of tampering functions $\mathcal{T}$ on the secret key space. Tamper-resilient security stipulates that the cryptographic schemes remain secure even for the adversary who has access to the schemes executed under the related keys $T(sk)$, with $T \in \mathcal{T}$ chosen by the adversary.

As observed by Gennaro et al. [21], it is *impossible* to achieve tamper-resilient security against any polynomial number of arbitrary tampering queries, without making further assumptions, such as *key-updating* or *self-destruct* mechanism[1].

Leakage and Tamper-Resilient Public-Key Cryptography. In light of the fact that physical attacks in the real world include both passive and active attacks, Kalai et al. [26] initiate the study of designing public-key cryptographic schemes that are resilient to *both* leakage and tampering attacks.

Up to now, there are several models for leakage and tamper-resilient security. The first model is proposed by Kalai et al. [26] and considers *continual tampering and leakage (i.e., the CTL model).* This model provides a very strong security guarantee, but at the price of inevitably relying on *key-updating* or *self-destruct* mechanism. Kalai et al. [26] construct a signature scheme in the CTL model using a true-simulation extractable non-interactive zero-knowledge (tSE-NIZK) proof system [12] as a building block. As shown in [12], tSE-NIZK can be built generically from a chosen-ciphertext attack (CCA) secure public-key encryption (PKE) and a regular NIZK. However, even using the efficient Groth-Sahai NIZK [22], it would lead to a tSE-NIZK with proof consisting of at least 20 group

[1] Key-updating mechanism enables the secret key to be periodically updated. Self-destruct mechanism enables the cryptographic device to blow up and erase all internal states, including sk, once a tampering attempt is detected.

elements, and so does the signature of the resulting signature scheme. Kalai et al. [26] also present a PKE scheme with chosen-plaintext attack (CPA) secure in the CTL model, meaning that the adversary is not allowed to observe the effect of tampering on the decryption oracle. Fujisaki et al. [18] further investigate how to construct CCA-secure PKE in the CTL model, and present a scheme based on the one-time lossy filter technique [33]. The ciphertext of their PKE scheme consists of about 8 group elements.

The second model is introduced by Damgård et al. [10] and considers *both bounded leakage and bounded tampering (i.e., the BLT model).* Here bounded tampering means that the adversary is only allowed to make a limited number of tampering queries, and consequently, it does not need key-updating or self-destruct mechanisms. To achieve BLT security, they propose a novel approach which reduces tampering to leakage. The benefit of this approach is that it could achieve tampering-resilience against arbitrary function class $\mathcal{T}$. However, the approach suffers from two disadvantages, one being that the amount of leakage tolerated by the leakage-resilience is largely decreasing, and the other being that for PKE it does not allow "post-challenge" tampering queries[2]. Under this approach, Damgård et al. [10] propose a signature scheme from Σ-protocol via the Fiat-Shamir heuristic [17] in the random oracle model and a CCA-secure PKE scheme from tSE-NIZK [12]. Faonio et al. [15] also follow the approach, and prove that the leakage-resilient signature scheme in [12] and the leakage-resilient CCA-secure PKE scheme in [33] are secure in the BLT model. However, the signature scheme also uses tSE-NIZK, and its signature consists of more than 34 group elements. Their PKE scheme avoids the use of NIZK, but the ciphertext is over composite order groups and has a length of more than 5000 bits at the 128-bit security level, which corresponds to about 19 group elements in typical prime order groups (where each group element is about 256 bits).

The third model is formalized by Sun et al. [36] and is called *the leakage and tampering-resilient (LTR) model.* This model also considers bounded leakage, but for tampering, it allows an unbounded number of tampering queries, while the tampering functions are restricted in a predefined function class $\mathcal{T}$, the same as the tampering-resilient security introduced by Bellare and Kohno [3]. Similar to the BLT model, the LTR model does not need key-updating or self-destruct mechanisms, and not only that, it also allows "post-challenge" tampering queries for PKE. Subsequently, Sun et al. [35] strengthen the LTR model to *the strong LTR (sLTR) model,* by imposing only minimal restrictions on the adversary's decryption queries. These two works [35,36] focus on PKE, and construct CCA-secure PKE schemes from tSE-NIZK and new variants of hash proof systems [9] in the LTR model and the sLTR model, respectively. Their schemes achieve tamper-resilience against affine function class. However, due to the inefficiency of tSE-NIZK, the ciphertext of their schemes would consist of at least 20 group elements. Accordingly, Sun et al. [35] leave the construction of CCA-secure PKE in the sLTR model *without using tSE-NIZK* as an interesting future work.

---

[2] Namely, the adversary is not allowed to make any tampering queries after it receives the challenge ciphertext.

The fourth model is due to Chakraborty and Rangan [7] and extends the BLT model in the presence of *split-state mechanism*[3]. This model is called the *post-challenge BLT (pcBLT) model*, since it serves as an alternative way to make "post-challenge" tampering (and also leakage) queries for PKE possible. Chakraborty and Rangan [7] also focus on PKE and construct a CCA-secure PKE scheme from tSE-NIZK in the pcBLT model. Similarly, the ciphertext of their scheme would consist of at least 20 group elements.

There are also other models such as the line of research which protects cryptosystems against leakage and tampering attacks by leveraging (leakage-resilient) non-malleable codes [13,16,25,30]. However, these works usually rely on hardware requirements such as key-updating, self-destruct or split-state mechanisms, and the proposed schemes are more like feasibility results and less efficient.

Our Contributions. In this work, we study the design of efficient signature and PKE schemes in the sLTR model, without using tSE-NIZK (or other heavy building blocks). Our contributions are three-fold.

- We formalize the strong LTR (sLTR) model for signature schemes, as a counterpart to the sLTR model for PKE introduced in [35]. Here "strong" means the strong existential unforgeability of signatures, which even guarantees that the adversary cannot forge a new signature for an already signed message. Moreover, for the adversary to win, we impose only minimal restrictions on the forgery produced by the adversary, thus our security provides a very strong guarantee (see Remark 1 for more discussions).
- We give direct constructions of signature and CCA-secure PKE schemes in the sLTR model. Both of the schemes are designed in the standard model, over asymmetric pairing groups and without using tSE-NIZK, thus accomplishing the interesting future work left by Sun et al. [35].

  Both of our schemes are proven secure based on the standard matrix decisional Diffie-Hellman (MDDH) assumptions [14], which cover the standard symmetric external DH (SXDH)[4] and k-Linear assumptions. Our signature scheme achieves leakage-resilience with leakage rate[5] $\frac{1}{4} - o(1)$ and our PKE scheme with leakage rate $\frac{1}{3} - o(1)$. Both of our schemes achieve tamper-resilience against affine function class, the same as the existing schemes [35,36] in the (s)LTR model.

  Our SXDH-based schemes are more efficient than the existing schemes in the leakage and tamper-resilient setting (i.e., no matter in the CTL, BLT, LTR, sLTR, or pcBLT model) [7,10,15,18,26,35,36]. More precisely, our signature scheme has only 4 group elements in the signature, which is about

[3] Split-state mechanism ensures that the secret key is split into two (or more) disjoint parts and the adversary can obtain leakages from each of the secret key parts independently and tamper each of the parts independently.

[4] SXDH is a standard assumption that simply requires the DDH assumption to hold in both source groups $\mathbb{G}_1$ and $\mathbb{G}_2$ of the asymmetric pairing groups.

[5] Leakage rate is defined as the ratio of the leakage amount that can be tolerated to the secret key size.

5×∼8× *shorter*, and our PKE scheme has only 6 group elements in the ciphertext, which is about 1.3×∼3.3× *shorter*. We refer to Remark 2 and Remark 4 for a detailed efficiency analysis of our schemes.
- To our best knowledge, our signature scheme is the *first* one achieving strong existential unforgeability in the leakage and tamper-resilient setting. We note that strong existential unforgeability has important applications in building more complex primitives such as signcryption [2] and authenticated key exchange (AKE) [11], where it can help signcryption to achieve ciphertext integrity [4] and AKE to achieve strong notion of "matching conversations" security [5]. We also stress that the Generalized Boneh-Shen-Waters (GBSW) transform [34], which converts a (non-strongly) secure signature scheme to a strongly secure one with the help of chameleon hash, does *not* work in the presence of leakage and tampering. The reason is, the resulting signature scheme contains the trapdoor of chameleon hash in its secret key, thus the leakage and tampering of secret key means the leakage and tampering of trapdoor, which is not supported by the security of chameleon hash.

2 Preliminaries

Notations. Let $\lambda \in \mathbb{N}$ denote the security parameter throughout the paper, and all algorithms, distributions, functions and adversaries take 1^λ as an implicit input. If x is defined by y or the value of y is assigned to x, we write $x := y$. For a set $\mathcal{X}$, denote by $x \leftarrow_\$ \mathcal{X}$ the procedure of sampling x from $\mathcal{X}$ uniformly at random. If $\mathcal{D}$ is distribution, $x \leftarrow_\$ \mathcal{D}$ means that x is sampled according to $\mathcal{D}$. All our algorithms are probabilistic unless stated otherwise. We use $y \leftarrow_\$ \mathcal{A}(x)$ to define the random variable y obtained by executing algorithm $\mathcal{A}$ on input x. If $\mathcal{A}$ is deterministic we write $y \leftarrow \mathcal{A}(x)$. "PPT" abbreviates probabilistic polynomial-time. Denote by negl some negligible function. By $\Pr_i[\cdot]$ we denote the probability of a particular event occurring in game G_i.

For two random variables X and Y, the min-entropy of X is defined as $\mathbf{H}_\infty(X) := -\log(\max_x \Pr[X = x])$, and the statistical distance between X and Y is defined as $\Delta(X, Y) := \frac{1}{2} \cdot \sum_x |\Pr[X = x] - \Pr[Y = x]|$.

Lemma 1 (Leftover Hash Lemma [24]). *Let $\mathcal{H} = \{H : \mathcal{X} \to \mathcal{Y}\}$ be a family of universal hash functions, i.e., for any $x_1 \neq x_2 \in \mathcal{X}$, $\Pr[H(x_1) = H(x_2)] \leq 1/|\mathcal{Y}|$, where $H \leftarrow_\$ \mathcal{H}$. Then for any random variable X on $\mathcal{X}$, it holds that $\Delta((H, H(X)), (H, U)) \leq \sqrt{|\mathcal{Y}| \cdot 2^{-\mathbf{H}_\infty(X)}}$, where $H \leftarrow_\$ \mathcal{H}$ and $U \leftarrow_\$ \mathcal{Y}$.*

2.1 Digital Signatures

Definition 1 (SIG). *A digital signature (SIG) scheme* $\mathsf{SIG} = (\mathsf{Setup}, \mathsf{Gen}, \mathsf{Sign}, \mathsf{Vrfy})$ *with message space $\mathcal{M}$ consists of four PPT algorithms:*

- $\mathsf{pp} \leftarrow_\$ \mathsf{Setup}$*: The setup algorithm outputs a public parameter* pp*, which serves as an implicit input of other algorithms.*

- $(vk, sk) \leftarrow_{\$} \mathsf{Gen}(\mathsf{pp})$: *Taking* pp *as input, the key generation algorithm outputs a pair of verification key and signing key* (vk, sk).
- $\sigma \leftarrow_{\$} \mathsf{Sign}(sk, m)$: *Taking as input a signing key* sk *and a message* $m \in \mathcal{M}$, *the signing algorithm outputs a signature* σ.
- $0/1 \leftarrow \mathsf{Vrfy}(vk, m, \sigma)$: *Taking as input a verification key* vk, *a message* $m \in \mathcal{M}$ *and a signature* σ, *the deterministic verification algorithm outputs a bit indicating whether* σ *is a valid signature for* m *w.r.t.* vk.

Correctness requires that for all $\mathsf{pp} \leftarrow_{\$} \mathsf{Setup}$, $(vk, sk) \leftarrow_{\$} \mathsf{Gen}(\mathsf{pp})$ *and* $m \in \mathcal{M}$, *it holds that* $\Pr\left[\sigma \leftarrow_{\$} \mathsf{Sign}(sk, m) : \mathsf{Vrfy}(vk, m, \sigma) = 1\right] \geq 1 - \mathsf{negl}(\lambda)$.

2.2 Public-Key Encryption

Definition 2 (PKE). *A public-key encryption (PKE) scheme* $\mathsf{PKE} = (\mathsf{Setup}, \mathsf{Gen}, \mathsf{Enc}, \mathsf{Dec})$ *with message space* $\mathcal{M}$ *consists of four PPT algorithms:*

- $\mathsf{pp} \leftarrow_{\$} \mathsf{Setup}$: *The setup algorithm outputs a public parameter* pp, *which serves as an implicit input of other algorithms.*
- $(pk, sk) \leftarrow_{\$} \mathsf{Gen}(\mathsf{pp})$: *Taking* pp *as input, the key generation algorithm outputs a pair of public key and secret key* (pk, sk).
- $ct \leftarrow_{\$} \mathsf{Enc}(pk, m)$: *Taking as input a public key* pk *and a message* $m \in \mathcal{M}$, *the encryption algorithm outputs a ciphertext* ct.
- $m/\bot \leftarrow \mathsf{Dec}(sk, ct)$: *Taking as input a secret key* sk *and a ciphertext* ct, *the deterministic decryption algorithm outputs either a message* $m \in \mathcal{M}$ *or a special symbol* $\bot$ *indicating the failure of decryption.*

Correctness requires that for all $\mathsf{pp} \leftarrow_{\$} \mathsf{Setup}$, $(pk, sk) \leftarrow_{\$} \mathsf{Gen}(\mathsf{pp})$ *and* $m \in \mathcal{M}$, *it holds that* $\Pr\left[ct \leftarrow_{\$} \mathsf{Enc}(pk, m) : \mathsf{Dec}(sk, ct) = m\right] \geq 1 - \mathsf{negl}(\lambda)$.

2.3 Collision-Resistant Hash Functions

Definition 3 (Collision-resistant hash functions). *A family of hash functions* $\mathcal{H}$ *is collision-resistant, if for any PPT adversary* $\mathcal{A}$, *it holds that*

$$\mathsf{Adv}^{\mathsf{cr}}_{\mathcal{H},\mathcal{A}}(\lambda) := \Pr[H \leftarrow_{\$} \mathcal{H}, (x_1, x_2) \leftarrow_{\$} \mathcal{A}(H) : x_1 \neq x_2 \wedge H(x_1) = H(x_2)] \leq \mathsf{negl}(\lambda).$$

2.4 Pairing Groups and MDDH Assumptions

Let PGGen be a PPT algorithm outputting a description of pairing group $\mathsf{gpar} = (\mathbb{G}_1, \mathbb{G}_2, \mathbb{G}_T, p, e, P_1, P_2, P_T)$, where $\mathbb{G}_1$, $\mathbb{G}_2$ and $\mathbb{G}_T$ are additive cyclic groups of prime order $p > 2^{2\lambda}$, $e : \mathbb{G}_1 \times \mathbb{G}_2 \longrightarrow \mathbb{G}_T$ is a non-degenerated bilinear pairing, and P_1, P_2, P_T are generators of $\mathbb{G}_1, \mathbb{G}_2, \mathbb{G}_T$, respectively, with $P_T := e(P_1, P_2)$. We assume that the operations in $\mathbb{G}_1$, $\mathbb{G}_2$, $\mathbb{G}_T$ and the pairing e are efficiently computable. We consider *Type-III asymmetric pairing group*, where $\mathbb{G}_1 \neq \mathbb{G}_2$ and there is no efficient homomorphism between them. We require gpar to be an implicit input of other algorithms.

We use implicit representation of group elements as in [14]. For $s \in \{1, 2, T\}$ and $a \in \mathbb{Z}_p$, denote by $[a]_s = aP_s \in \mathbb{G}_s$ as the implicit representation of a in

$\mathbb{G}_s$. Similarly, for a matrix $\mathbf{A} = (a_{i,j}) \in \mathbb{Z}_p^{n\times m}$ we define $[\mathbf{A}]_s$ as the implicit representation of $\mathbf{A}$ in $\mathbb{G}_s$. $\mathsf{Span}(\mathbf{A}) := \{\mathbf{Ar}|\mathbf{r} \in \mathbb{Z}_p^m\} \subseteq \mathbb{Z}_p^n$ denotes the linear span of $\mathbf{A}$, and similarly $\mathsf{Span}([\mathbf{A}]_s) := \{[\mathbf{Ar}]_s|\mathbf{r} \in \mathbb{Z}_p^m\} \subseteq \mathbb{G}_s^n$. Note that given $\mathbf{A}$, $[\mathbf{B}]_s$, $[\mathbf{C}]_s$ and $\mathbf{D}$ with matching dimensions, one can efficiently compute $[\mathbf{AB}]_s$, $[\mathbf{B}+\mathbf{C}]_s$, $[\mathbf{CD}]_s$, and given $[\mathbf{A}]_1$ and $[\mathbf{B}]_2$, we let $e([\mathbf{A}]_1, [\mathbf{B}]_2) := [\mathbf{AB}]_T$.

Let $\ell, k \in \mathbb{N}$ be integers with $\ell > k$. A probabilistic distribution $\mathcal{D}_{\ell,k}$ is called a *matrix distribution*, if it outputs matrices in $\mathbb{Z}_p^{\ell\times k}$ of full rank k in polynomial time. Without loss of generality, we assume that the first k rows of $\mathbf{A} \leftarrow_{\$} \mathcal{D}_{\ell,k}$ form an invertible matrix. Let $\mathcal{D}_k := \mathcal{D}_{k+1,k}$. Denote by $\mathcal{U}_{\ell,k}$ the *uniform distribution* over all matrices in $\mathbb{Z}_p^{\ell\times k}$. Let $\mathcal{U}_k := \mathcal{U}_{k+1,k}$.

Definition 4 ($\mathcal{D}_{\ell,k}$-MDDH Assumption). *Let $s \in \{1,2\}$. The $\mathcal{D}_{\ell,k}$-MDDH assumption holds over group $\mathbb{G}_s$, if for any PPT adversary $\mathcal{A}$, it holds that* $\mathsf{Adv}^{\mathsf{mddh}}_{\mathcal{D}_{\ell,k},\mathbb{G}_s,\mathcal{A}}(\lambda) := \big|\Pr[\mathcal{A}([\mathbf{A}]_s, [\mathbf{Aw}]_s) = 1] - \Pr[\mathcal{A}([\mathbf{A}]_s, [\mathbf{u}]_s) = 1]\big| \le \mathsf{negl}(\lambda)$, *where the probability is over $\mathbf{A} \leftarrow_{\$} \mathcal{D}_{\ell,k}$, $\mathbf{w} \leftarrow_{\$} \mathbb{Z}_p^k$ and $\mathbf{u} \leftarrow_{\$} \mathbb{Z}_p^\ell$.*

MDDH assumption covers many well-studied assumptions, such as the DDH and the k-Linear (k-LIN) assumptions, by specifying the matrix distribution as $\mathcal{LIN}_1$ and $\mathcal{LIN}_k$ respectively [14], where $\mathcal{LIN}_k:\ \mathbf{A} = \begin{pmatrix} a_1 & & \\ & \ddots & \\ & & a_k \\ 1 & \cdots & 1 \end{pmatrix} \in \mathbb{Z}_p^{(k+1)\times k}$. MDDH also covers the standard symmetric external DH (SXDH) assumption, which simply requires the DDH assumption to hold both in $\mathbb{G}_1$ and $\mathbb{G}_2$.

Several relations among MDDH assumptions parameterized by different matrix distributions were established in [14, 20].

Lemma 2 ($\mathcal{D}_{\ell,k}$-MDDH $\Rightarrow$ $\mathcal{U}_k$-MDDH) [14] $\Rightarrow$ $\mathcal{U}_{\ell',k}$-MDDH [20]. *For any PPT adversary $\mathcal{A}$, there exists a PPT $\mathcal{B}$ s.t.* $\mathsf{Adv}^{\mathsf{mddh}}_{\mathcal{U}_k,\mathbb{G}_s,\mathcal{A}}(\lambda) \le \mathsf{Adv}^{\mathsf{mddh}}_{\mathcal{D}_{\ell,k},\mathbb{G}_s,\mathcal{B}}(\lambda)$.

For any PPT $\mathcal{A}$, there exists a PPT $\mathcal{B}$ s.t. $\mathsf{Adv}^{\mathsf{mddh}}_{\mathcal{U}_{\ell',k},\mathbb{G}_s,\mathcal{A}}(\lambda) \le \mathsf{Adv}^{\mathsf{mddh}}_{\mathcal{U}_k,\mathbb{G}_s,\mathcal{B}}(\lambda)$.

Consequently, for any $\ell > k$, $\mathcal{U}_{\ell,k}$-MDDH assumption is tightly implied by the k-LIN assumption (i.e., $\mathcal{LIN}_k$-MDDH).

We also define the $\mathcal{D}_{\ell,k}$-Kernel Matrix DH ($\mathcal{D}_{\ell,k}$-KerMDH) assumption according to [31] which is a natural search variant of the $\mathcal{D}_{\ell,k}$-MDDH assumption.

Definition 5 ($\mathcal{D}_{\ell,k}$-KerMDH Assumption). *Let $s \in \{1,2\}$. The $\mathcal{D}_{\ell,k}$-KerMDH assumption holds over group $\mathbb{G}_s$, if for any PPT adversary $\mathcal{A}$, it holds that* $\mathsf{Adv}^{\mathsf{kmdh}}_{\mathcal{D}_{\ell,k},\mathbb{G}_s,\mathcal{A}}(\lambda) := \Pr\big[[\mathbf{x}]_{3-s} \in \mathbb{G}_{3-s}^\ell \leftarrow_{\$} \mathcal{A}([\mathbf{A}]_s) : \mathbf{x}^\top\mathbf{A} = \mathbf{0} \land \mathbf{x} \neq \mathbf{0}\big] \le \mathsf{negl}(\lambda)$, *where the probability is over $\mathbf{A} \leftarrow_{\$} \mathcal{D}_{\ell,k}$.*

The following lemma shows that the $\mathcal{D}_{\ell,k}$-KerMDH assumption is implied by the $\mathcal{D}_{\ell,k}$-MDDH assumption, since one can use a non-zero $[\mathbf{x}]_{3-s}$ satisfying $\mathbf{x}^\top\mathbf{A} = \mathbf{0}$ to test membership in $\mathsf{Span}([\mathbf{A}]_s)$.

Lemma 3 ($\mathcal{D}_{\ell,k}$-MDDH $\Rightarrow$ $\mathcal{D}_{\ell,k}$-KerMDH [31]). *For any PPT adversary $\mathcal{A}$, there exists a PPT $\mathcal{B}$ s.t.* $\mathsf{Adv}^{\mathsf{kmdh}}_{\mathcal{D}_{\ell,k},\mathbb{G}_s,\mathcal{A}}(\lambda) \le \mathsf{Adv}^{\mathsf{mddh}}_{\mathcal{D}_{\ell,k},\mathbb{G}_s,\mathcal{B}}(\lambda) + 1/(p-1)$.

3 More Efficient SIG with Leakage and Tamper-Resilience

In this section, we present a direct and efficient construction of signature scheme with leakage and tamper-resilience, over asymmetric pairing groups based on the MDDH assumptions.

Concretely, in Subsect. 3.1, we formalize the leakage and tamper-resilient security for signature schemes, i.e., the *strong* LTR-CMA (sLTR-CMA) security, and then in Subsect. 3.2 and Subsect. 3.3, we present our signature scheme and its security proof, respectively.

3.1 Definition of sLTR-CMA Security

The standard security notion for signatures is existential unforgeability under chosen-message attacks (EUF-CMA). Here we extend it to $(\kappa, \mathcal{T})$-sLTR-CMA, parameterized by an integer κ and a function set $\mathcal{T}$: it additionally considers *leakages attacks*, where the total amount of leakage is bounded by κ bits, and *tampering attacks*, where the tampering functions are chosen from $\mathcal{T}$. Moreover, it provides *strong* existential unforgeability which further guarantees that the adversary cannot even forge a new signature for a message that it has ever queried. Below we present the formal definition of $(\kappa, \mathcal{T})$-sLTR-CMA security.

Definition 6 (sLTR-CMA Security for SIG). *Let* $\kappa = \kappa(\lambda) \in \mathbb{N}$, *and* $\mathcal{T}$ *be a set of functions from* $\mathcal{SK}$ *to* $\mathcal{SK}$ *where* $\mathcal{SK}$ *is the secret key space. A signature scheme* $\mathsf{SIG} = (\mathsf{Setup}, \mathsf{Gen}, \mathsf{Sign}, \mathsf{Vrfy})$ *is* $(\kappa, \mathcal{T})$-sLTR-CMA *secure, if for any PPT adversary* $\mathcal{A}$, *it holds that* $\mathsf{Adv}^{\mathsf{sltr\text{-}cma}}_{\mathsf{SIG},\mathcal{A},\kappa,\mathcal{T}}(\lambda) := \Pr[\mathsf{Exp}^{\mathsf{sltr\text{-}cma}}_{\mathsf{SIG},\mathcal{A},\kappa,\mathcal{T}} \Rightarrow 1] \le \mathsf{negl}(\lambda)$, *where the experiment* $\mathsf{Exp}^{\mathsf{sltr\text{-}cma}}_{\mathsf{SIG},\mathcal{A},\kappa,\mathcal{T}}$ *is defined in Fig. 1.*

$\mathsf{Exp}^{\mathsf{sltr\text{-}cma}}_{\mathsf{SIG},\mathcal{A},\kappa,\mathcal{T}}$:	$\mathcal{O}_{\text{SIGN}}(T, m)$:
$\mathsf{pp} \leftarrow_{\$} \mathsf{Setup}$, $(vk, sk) \leftarrow_{\$} \mathsf{Gen}(\mathsf{pp})$	If $T \notin \mathcal{T}$: Return $\perp$
$\mathcal{Q}_{\mathsf{id}} := \emptyset$ //Record the signing queries //under the identity function	$\sigma \leftarrow_{\$} \mathsf{Sign}(T(sk), m)$
	If $T = \mathsf{id}$: $\mathcal{Q}_{\mathsf{id}} := \mathcal{Q}_{\mathsf{id}} \cup \{(m, \sigma)\}$
$\ell := 0$ //Record the leakage length	Return σ
$(m^*, \sigma^*) \leftarrow_{\$} \mathcal{A}^{\mathcal{O}_{\text{SIGN}}(\cdot,\cdot), \mathcal{O}_{\text{LEAK}}(\cdot)}(\mathsf{pp}, vk)$	$\mathcal{O}_{\text{LEAK}}(L)$: //at most κ leakage bits
If $((m^*, \sigma^*) \notin \mathcal{Q}_{\mathsf{id}}) \wedge (\mathsf{Vrfy}(vk, m^*, \sigma^*) = 1)$:	If $\ell + \lvert L(sk) \rvert > \kappa$: Return $\perp$
Return 1;	$\ell := \ell + \lvert L(sk) \rvert$
Else: Return 0	Return $L(sk)$

Fig. 1. The $(\kappa, \mathcal{T})$-sLTR-CMA security experiment $\mathsf{Exp}^{\mathsf{sltr\text{-}cma}}_{\mathsf{SIG},\mathcal{A},\kappa,\mathcal{T}}$ for SIG, where id denotes the identity function and $\lvert L(sk) \rvert$ denotes the bit-length of $L(sk)$.

Remark 1 (On the formalization of sLTR-CMA security). In the experiment $\mathsf{Exp}^{\mathsf{sltr\text{-}cma}}_{\mathsf{SIG},\mathcal{A},\kappa,\mathcal{T}}$ defined in Fig. 1, oracle $\mathcal{O}_{\text{SIGN}}$ captures the ability of the adversary to implement tampering attacks and obtain signatures under tampered signing keys $T(sk)$ with $T \in \mathcal{T}$, and oracle $\mathcal{O}_{\text{LEAK}}$ captures the ability of the adversary to implement leakage attacks and obtain bounded leakage information $L(sk)$ about the signing key.

For the adversary to win, the condition $(m^*, \sigma^*) \notin \mathcal{Q}_{\mathsf{id}}$ is the minimal restriction on the adversary's forgery, since otherwise the adversary can query $\mathcal{O}_{\text{SIGN}}(\mathsf{id}, m^*)$ for an arbitrary message m^* to obtain a signature σ^* and simply output (m^*, σ^*) as the forgery, and as a result, the adversary would trivially win and it is impossible to achieve the above security.

If we replace the condition $(m^*, \sigma^*) \notin \mathcal{Q}_{\mathsf{id}}$ with a stronger one, namely requiring m^* to be different from all messages that the adversary has queried $\mathcal{O}_{\text{SIGN}}$, we call it (non-strong) LTR-CMA security with standard existential unforgeability. Furthermore, if $\mathcal{T}$ contains only the identity function id, we obtain the leakage-resilience security, while if $\kappa = 0$, we obtain the tamper-resilience security. If both $\mathcal{T} = \{\mathsf{id}\}$ and $\kappa = 0$, we recover the standard EUF-CMA security.

3.2 Construction of SIG from MDDH

Now we present our direct construction of sLTR-CMA secure SIG scheme over asymmetric pairing groups based on the MDDH assumptions. Let $\mathcal{D}_k$ be a matrix distribution with $k \in \mathbb{N}$, and let $\mathcal{H}$ be a family of collision resistant hash functions from $\{0,1\}^*$ to $\mathbb{Z}_p$. Our SIG scheme $\mathsf{SIG} = (\mathsf{Setup}, \mathsf{Gen}, \mathsf{Sign}, \mathsf{Vrfy})$ is shown in Fig. 2, where the message space is $\mathcal{M} = \{0,1\}^*$ and the secret key space is $\mathcal{SK} = \mathbb{Z}_p^{(k+1)\times(k+1)}$. Correctness of SIG follows by inspection: for any honestly generated signature $\sigma = ([\mathbf{c}]_1, [\mathbf{d}]_1)$, we have $[\mathbf{c}]_1 = [\mathbf{U}]_1\mathbf{w}$ with $\mathbf{w} \leftarrow_{\$} \mathbb{Z}_p^k$ and $[\mathbf{d}]_1 = \mathbf{K}[\mathbf{c}]_1 + [(\mathbf{K}_0 + \tau\mathbf{K}_1)\mathbf{U}]_1\mathbf{w} = [(\mathbf{K} + \mathbf{K}_0 + \tau\mathbf{K}_1)\mathbf{c}]_1$, which directly implies

$$e([\mathbf{c}^\top]_1, [(\mathbf{K}^\top + \mathbf{K}_0^\top + \tau\mathbf{K}_1^\top)\mathbf{A}]_2) = e([\mathbf{c}^\top(\mathbf{K}^\top + \mathbf{K}_0^\top + \tau\mathbf{K}_1^\top)]_1, [\mathbf{A}]_2) = e([\mathbf{d}^\top]_1, [\mathbf{A}]_2).$$

Moreover, since $\mathbf{U}$ output by $\mathcal{D}_k$ is of full rank, $[\mathbf{c}]_1 = [\mathbf{U}]_1\mathbf{w} \neq [\mathbf{0}]_1$ holds as long as $\mathbf{w} \neq \mathbf{0}$ holds, which happens with overwhelming probability $1 - 1/p^k$.

Next, we show its $(\kappa, \mathcal{T}_{\mathsf{aff}})$-sLTR-CMA security under $\kappa \leq \log p - \Omega(\lambda)$ bits of leakage information and under the set of affine functions

$$\mathcal{T}_{\mathsf{aff}} = \{T_{(a,\mathbf{B})} : \mathbf{K} \in \mathcal{SK} \mapsto a\mathbf{K} + \mathbf{B} \in \mathcal{SK} \mid a \in \mathbb{Z}_p, \mathbf{B} \in \mathcal{SK}\}. \tag{1}$$

Theorem 1 ($(\kappa, \mathcal{T}_{\mathsf{aff}})$-sLTR-CMA Security of SIG). *Let $\kappa \leq \log p - \Omega(\lambda)$ and let $\mathcal{T}_{\mathsf{aff}}$ be the set of affine functions defined in (1). Assume that the $\mathcal{D}_k$-MDDH assumption holds over both $\mathbb{G}_1$ and $\mathbb{G}_2$, and $\mathcal{H}$ is collision-resistant. Then the* SIG *scheme in Fig. 2 is $(\kappa, \mathcal{T}_{\mathsf{aff}})$-sLTR-CMA secure.*

Concretely, for any PPT adversary $\mathcal{A}$ who makes at most Q times of $\mathcal{O}_{\text{SIGN}}$ queries, there exist PPT $\mathcal{B}_1, \cdots, \mathcal{B}_5$, such that $\mathsf{Adv}^{\mathsf{sltr\text{-}cma}}_{\mathsf{SIG},\mathcal{A},\kappa,\mathcal{T}_{\mathsf{aff}}}(\lambda) \leq \mathsf{Adv}^{\mathsf{mddh}}_{\mathcal{D}_k,\mathbb{G}_2,\mathcal{B}_1}(\lambda) + \mathsf{Adv}^{\mathsf{cr}}_{\mathcal{H},\mathcal{B}_2}(\lambda) + \mathsf{Adv}^{\mathsf{mddh}}_{\mathcal{D}_k,\mathbb{G}_2,\mathcal{B}_3}(\lambda) + Q \cdot (\mathsf{Adv}^{\mathsf{mddh}}_{\mathcal{D}_k,\mathbb{G}_1,\mathcal{B}_4}(\lambda) + \mathsf{Adv}^{\mathsf{mddh}}_{\mathcal{D}_k,\mathbb{G}_1,\mathcal{B}_5}(\lambda)) + 2^{-\Omega(\lambda)}$.

The proof of Theorem 1 is postponed to Subsect. 3.3. Before presenting the formal proof, we give a detailed efficiency analysis and explain the main intuitions of our SIG construction in the following two remarks, respectively.

$\mathsf{pp} \leftarrow_\$ \mathsf{Setup}$:
$\mathsf{gpar} = (\mathbb{G}_1, \mathbb{G}_2, \mathbb{G}_T, p, e, P_1, P_2, P_T) \leftarrow_\$ \mathsf{PGGen}$.
$\mathbf{U}, \mathbf{A} \leftarrow_\$ \mathcal{D}_k$, where $\mathbf{U}, \mathbf{A} \in \mathbb{Z}_p^{(k+1)\times k}$.
$\mathbf{K}_0, \mathbf{K}_1 \leftarrow_\$ \mathbb{Z}_p^{(k+1)\times(k+1)}$.
$H \leftarrow_\$ \mathcal{H}$.
Return $\mathsf{pp} := (\mathsf{gpar}, [\mathbf{U}]_1, [\mathbf{K}_0\mathbf{U}]_1, [\mathbf{K}_1\mathbf{U}]_1, [\mathbf{A}]_2, [\mathbf{K}_0^\top\mathbf{A}]_2, [\mathbf{K}_1^\top\mathbf{A}]_2, H)$.

$(vk, sk) \leftarrow_\$ \mathsf{Gen}(\mathsf{pp})$:
$sk := \boxed{\mathbf{K}} \leftarrow_\$ \mathbb{Z}_p^{(k+1)\times(k+1)}$.
$vk := \boxed{[\mathbf{K}^\top\mathbf{A}]_2} \in \mathbb{G}_2^{(k+1)\times k}$.
Return (vk, sk).

$\sigma \leftarrow_\$ \mathsf{Sign}(sk, m)$:
$vk := [\mathbf{K}^\top\mathbf{A}]_2$.
$\mathbf{w} \leftarrow_\$ \mathbb{Z}_p^k$, $[\mathbf{c}]_1 := [\mathbf{U}]_1\mathbf{w} \in \mathbb{G}_1^{k+1}$.
$\tau := H(vk, m, [\mathbf{c}]_1) \in \mathbb{Z}_p$.
$[\mathbf{d}]_1 := \boxed{\mathbf{K}[\mathbf{c}]_1} + [(\mathbf{K}_0 + \tau\mathbf{K}_1)\mathbf{U}]_1\mathbf{w} \in \mathbb{G}_1^{k+1}$.
Return $\sigma := ([\mathbf{c}]_1, [\mathbf{d}]_1) \in \mathbb{G}_1^{k+1} \times \mathbb{G}_1^{k+1}$.

$0/1 \leftarrow \mathsf{Vrfy}(vk, m, \sigma)$:
Parse $\sigma = ([\mathbf{c}]_1, [\mathbf{d}]_1)$.
$\tau := H(vk, m, [\mathbf{c}]_1) \in \mathbb{Z}_p$.
If $e([\mathbf{c}^\top]_1, [(\boxed{\mathbf{K}^\top} + \mathbf{K}_0^\top + \tau\mathbf{K}_1^\top)\mathbf{A}]_2) = e([\mathbf{d}^\top]_1, [\mathbf{A}]_2)$
$\boxed{\wedge\ [\mathbf{c}]_1 \neq [\mathbf{0}]_1}$: Return 1.
Else: Return 0.

Fig. 2. Construction of $\mathsf{SIG} = (\mathsf{Setup}, \mathsf{Gen}, \mathsf{Sign}, \mathsf{Vrfy})$ based on MDDH, where the framed boxes and the gray boxes are used to help explain the intuitions behind the construction in Remark 3.

Remark 2 (Efficiency of our SIG). Let $x \cdot \mathbb{G}$ denote x elements in a group $\mathbb{G}$. Our SIG scheme in Fig. 2 is parameterized by the MDDH parameter $k \in \mathbb{N}$, and has public parameter $\mathsf{pp} : (3k^2 + 3k) \cdot \mathbb{G}_1 + (3k^2 + 3k) \cdot \mathbb{G}_2$, verification key $vk : (k^2 + k) \cdot \mathbb{G}_2$, signing key $sk : (k^2 + 2k + 1) \cdot \mathbb{Z}_p$ and signature $\sigma : (2k + 2) \cdot \mathbb{G}_1$. The verification involves $(2k^2 + 2k)$ pairing operations.

For $k = 1$, we get an efficient SIG scheme with $\mathsf{pp} : 6 \cdot \mathbb{G}_1 + 6 \cdot \mathbb{G}_2$, verification key $vk : 2 \cdot \mathbb{G}_2$, signing key $sk : 4 \cdot \mathbb{Z}_p$ and signature $\sigma : 4 \cdot \mathbb{G}_1$, and the verification involves only 4 pairing operations. The resulting SIG scheme is $(\kappa, \mathcal{T}_{\mathsf{aff}})$-sLTR-CMA secure based on the standard SXDH assumption, and supports $\kappa = \log p - \Omega(\lambda)$ bits key leakage. The leakage rate (i.e., κ/bit-length of sk) is $\frac{\log p - \Omega(\lambda)}{4 \log p} = \frac{1}{4} - o(1)$ asymptotically as p grows.

Remark 3 (Intuitions of our SIG). On a high level, our SIG in Fig. 2 can be parsed as two components: the terms in framed boxes (which are related to $\mathbf{K}$) and the terms in gray boxes (which are related to $\mathbf{K}_0$ and $\mathbf{K}_1$).

Our first idea is to let $sk = \boxed{\mathbf{K}}$ involve only term of the first component. With such a design, to achieve sLTR-CMA security, we only need to analyze the first component in the leakage and tampering-resilient setting, while for the second component we can analyze it without being disturbed by the leakage and tampering attacks on it.

Our second idea is to integrate the two components carefully during the generation (and verification) of signatures, such that the terms $[(\mathbf{K}_0 + \tau\mathbf{K}_1)\mathbf{U}]_1\mathbf{w}$ in the second component can trigger randomness of certain forms to hide (partial information of) the terms $\boxed{\mathbf{K}[\mathbf{c}]_1}$ in the first component, so that the signatures generated under *tampered* signing keys do not leak much information about $sk = \mathbf{K}$ beyond vk to the adversary in the sLTR-CMA security experiment. Consequently, the signing oracle is of no use to the adversary, and the sLTR-CMA security of our SIG essentially reduces to the security against no-message attacks (i.e., where the adversary obtains no signatures) in the *key leakage* setting, which is much easier to achieve and is mainly guaranteed by the first component.

Below we explain the intuitions behind these two components in more detail.

<u>INTUITIONS BEHIND THE FIRST COMPONENT.</u> Intuitively, $\boxed{\text{the terms in}}$ $\boxed{\text{framed}}$ $\boxed{\text{boxes}}$ can be viewed as a *publicly verifiable* function on $\mathbb{G}_1^{k+1}$:

- the function is defined by $sk = \boxed{\mathbf{K}}$, and it maps $[\mathbf{c}]_1 \in \mathbb{G}_1^{k+1}$ to $\boxed{\mathbf{K}[\mathbf{c}]_1}$;
- given $vk = \boxed{[\mathbf{K}^\top \mathbf{A}]_2}$, one can verify the correctness of function value

$$[\mathbf{d}]_1 = \boxed{\mathbf{K}[\mathbf{c}]_1} \tag{2}$$

  publicly via pairing equations:

$$\boxed{e([\mathbf{c}^\top]_1, [\mathbf{K}^\top \mathbf{A}]_2)} = e([\mathbf{d}^\top]_1, [\mathbf{A}]_2). \tag{3}$$

  Observe that (2) and (3) are equivalent under the $\mathcal{D}_k$-KerMDH assumption on $[\mathbf{A}]_2$ (which is further implied by the $\mathcal{D}_k$-MDDH assumption according to Lemma 3), since otherwise $[\mathbf{c}^\top \mathbf{K}^\top - \mathbf{d}^\top]_1$ constitutes a non-zero vector in the kernel of $[\mathbf{A}]_2$, which is hard to find under the $\mathcal{D}_k$-KerMDH assumption.

This publicly verifiable function enjoys a useful property:

- in the presence of *only* $vk = \boxed{[\mathbf{K}^\top \mathbf{A}]_2}$, the function value $\boxed{\mathbf{K}[\mathbf{c}]_1}$ of any $\boxed{[\mathbf{c}]_1 \neq [\mathbf{0}]_1}$ retains enough entropy from $\mathbf{K}$, so that it is information-theoretically hard to produce $([\mathbf{c}]_1, [\mathbf{d}]_1)$ satisfying (2) (and thus computationally hard to satisfy (3) under MDDH assumption).

To see why this property holds more concretely, we can let $\mathbf{a}^\perp \in \mathbb{Z}_p^{k+1}$ be a non-zero vector in the kernel of $\mathbf{A} \in \mathbb{Z}_p^{(k+1)\times k}$ such that $(\mathbf{a}^\perp)^\top \mathbf{A} = \mathbf{0}$, and sample $sk = \mathbf{K} \leftarrow_\$ \mathbb{Z}_p^{(k+1)\times(k+1)}$ equivalently via

$$\mathbf{K} := \widetilde{\mathbf{K}} + \boxed{\mathbf{a}^\perp \mathbf{k}^\top}$$

where $\widetilde{\mathbf{K}} \leftarrow_\$ \mathbb{Z}_p^{(k+1)\times(k+1)}$ and $\mathbf{k} \leftarrow_\$ \mathbb{Z}_p^{k+1}$. On the one hand, note that $\mathbf{k}$ is completely hidden in vk since $vk = [\mathbf{K}^\top \mathbf{A}]_2 = [(\widetilde{\mathbf{K}}^\top + \boxed{\mathbf{k}(\mathbf{a}^\perp)^\top})\mathbf{A}]_2 = [\widetilde{\mathbf{K}}^\top \mathbf{A}]_2$. On the other hand, for any $[\mathbf{c}]_1 \neq [\mathbf{0}]_1$, its function value is

$$\mathbf{K}[\mathbf{c}]_1 = (\widetilde{\mathbf{K}} + \mathbf{a}^\perp \mathbf{k}^\top)[\mathbf{c}]_1 = \widetilde{\mathbf{K}}[\mathbf{c}]_1 + [\boxed{\mathbf{a}^\perp(\mathbf{k}^\top \mathbf{c})}]_1,$$

where the term $\boxed{\mathbf{a}^\perp(\mathbf{k}^\top \mathbf{c})}$ is uniformly distributed over $\mathsf{Span}(\mathbf{a}^\perp) = \{\gamma \mathbf{a}^\perp | \gamma \in \mathbb{Z}_p\}$ due to the randomness of $\mathbf{k}$ and non-zero of $\mathbf{c}$. So the function value $\boxed{\mathbf{K}[\mathbf{c}]_1}$

has $\log p$ bits of entropy conditioned on vk, as shown by the term $\mathbf{a}^{\perp}(\mathbf{k}^{\top}\mathbf{c})$, and consequently it is hard to produce $([\mathbf{c}]_1, [\mathbf{d}]_1)$ satisfying (2) and (3).

INSUFFICIENCY OF THE FIRST COMPONENT AND ARISING OF THE SECOND. The first component and the aforementioned useful property serve as the basis for the security of our SIG. In particular, if the adversary $\mathcal{A}$ does not obtain any signatures in the security experiment, then it is hard for $\mathcal{A}$ to forge a signature satisfying (3), since the function value $\boxed{\mathbf{K}[\mathbf{c}]_1}$ has enough entropy (i.e., $\log p$ bits entropy) conditioned on vk. Moreover, the argument holds even if the adversary obtains bounded leakage information about $sk = \mathbf{K}$, as long as the amount of leakage κ satisfies $\log p - \kappa \geq \Omega(\lambda)$ so that there are still $\log p - \kappa \geq \Omega(\lambda)$ bits entropy left in $\boxed{\mathbf{K}[\mathbf{c}]_1}$. This shows the security against no-message attacks in the *leakage setting* of our SIG.

However, in the sLTR-CMA security experiment, $\mathcal{A}$ can obtain signatures as many as it wants, under *tampered* signing keys $T_{(a,\mathbf{B})}(sk) = a\mathbf{K} + \mathbf{B}$. So $\mathcal{A}$ will obtain multiple $\boxed{(a\mathbf{K} + \mathbf{B})[\mathbf{c}]_1}$ contained in the signatures $\sigma = ([\mathbf{c}]_1, [\mathbf{d}]_1)$, which would leak additional information about $sk = \mathbf{K}$ beyond vk.

To rescue the above arguments, we resort to the terms in gray boxes. Roughly speaking, we use $[(\mathbf{K}_0 + \tau\mathbf{K}_1)\mathbf{U}]_1\mathbf{w}$ to hide (partial information of) $\boxed{(a\mathbf{K} + \mathbf{B})[\mathbf{c}]_1}$ in the generation of $[\mathbf{d}]_1$:

$$[\mathbf{d}]_1 = \boxed{(a\mathbf{K} + \mathbf{B})[\mathbf{c}]_1} + [(\mathbf{K}_0 + \tau\mathbf{K}_1)\mathbf{U}]_1\mathbf{w}, \tag{4}$$

so that $\mathcal{A}$ will not learn much information about $sk = \mathbf{K}$ beyond vk from the obtained signatures, and then we can use the above arguments to show the security of our SIG.

MORE EXPLANATIONS ABOUT THE SECOND COMPONENT. It remains to give the intuitions of the terms in gray boxes in more detail, and in particular, explain how $[(\mathbf{K}_0 + \tau\mathbf{K}_1)\mathbf{U}]_1\mathbf{w}$ hide $\boxed{(a\mathbf{K} + \mathbf{B})[\mathbf{c}]_1}$ in the generation of $[\mathbf{d}]_1$ in (4).

From a high-level perspective, the terms in gray boxes can be viewed as the one-time simulation-sound (OTSS) NIZK scheme proposed by Kiltz and Wee [27],Section 3.3, and they essentially prove that $[\mathbf{c}]_1 = [\mathbf{U}]_1\mathbf{w}$ belongs to the linear subspace $\mathsf{Span}([\mathbf{U}]_1)$: in the signing algorithm Sign of our SIG, the term $[(\mathbf{K}_0 + \tau\mathbf{K}_1)\mathbf{U}]_1\mathbf{w}$ corresponds to the generation of OTSS-NIZK proof; in the verification algorithm Vrfy, the term $e([\mathbf{c}^{\top}]_1, [(\mathbf{K}_0^{\top} + \tau\mathbf{K}_1^{\top})\mathbf{A}]_2)$ corresponds to the verification of OTSS-NIZK proof.

- On the one hand, the generation and verification of OTSS-NIZK proofs do not involve any secret key, so they do not introduce additional elements to sk. This is very helpful in the key leakage and tampering-resilient setting, since the leakage and tampering of sk do not affect the terms in gray boxes, and we can use properties of this component without the need of considering any leakage and tampering.

- However, the OTSS property is insufficient for our purpose, since in the security experiment of SIG, the adversary can obtain multiple NIZK proofs $[(\mathbf{K}_0 + \tau\mathbf{K}_1)\mathbf{U}]_1\mathbf{w}$ contained in the multiple signatures $\sigma = ([\mathbf{c}]_1, [\mathbf{d}]_1)$, rather than a single NIZK proof allowed in the OTSS property.

Instead, we resort to another property about the second component $[(\mathbf{K}_0 + \tau\mathbf{K}_1)\mathbf{U}]_1\mathbf{w}$, namely it can trigger randomness of certain forms in a computationally indistinguishable way, as observed in [27]. To be more concrete, we can prove that the multiple pairs of

$$([\mathbf{c}]_1 = [\mathbf{U}]_1\mathbf{w},\ \ [(\mathbf{K}_0 + \tau\mathbf{K}_1)\mathbf{U}]_1\mathbf{w}\ )$$

contained in the signatures that $\mathcal{A}$ obtains are computationally indistinguishable from

$$([\mathbf{c}]_1 = [\mathbf{U}]_1\mathbf{w},\ \ [(\mathbf{K}_0 + \tau\mathbf{K}_1)\mathbf{U}]_1\mathbf{w} + \boxed{[\gamma\mathbf{a}^\perp]_1}), \tag{5}$$

where $\gamma \leftarrow_\$ \mathbb{Z}_p$ are randomnesses independently chosen for each pair, and $\mathbf{a}^\perp \in \mathbb{Z}_p^{k+1}$ is a non-zero vector in the kernel of $\mathbf{A} \in \mathbb{Z}_p^{(k+1)\times k}$ such that $(\mathbf{a}^\perp)^\top\mathbf{A} = \mathbf{0}$, even conditioned on a single pair

$$([\mathbf{c}^*]_1,\ \ [(\mathbf{K}_0 + \tau^*\mathbf{K}_1)\mathbf{c}^*]_1\ )$$

contained in $\mathcal{A}$'s forgery $(m^*, \sigma^* = ([\mathbf{c}^*]_1, [\mathbf{d}^*]_1))$ *in the case of* $\tau^* \neq \tau$. Jumping ahead, this corresponds to the game sequence $\{\mathsf{G}_{4.\eta.0} - \mathsf{G}_{4.\eta.4}\}_{0\le\eta\le Q-1}$ and $\mathsf{G}_{4.Q.0}$ in our security proof in Subsect. 3.3. This property is different from OTSS and is enjoyed by this specific NIZK scheme (in other words, other OTSS-NIZK schemes may not enjoy this property).

However, this property holds only *in the case of* $\tau^* \neq \tau$, i.e., when the following bad event never occurs.

- TagColl: the tag $\tau^* = H(vk, m^*, [\mathbf{c}^*]_1)$ involved in $\mathcal{A}$'s forgery $(m^*, \sigma^* = ([\mathbf{c}^*]_1, [\mathbf{d}^*]_1))$ is *identical* to the tag $\tau = H(vk' = [(a\mathbf{K} + \mathbf{B})^\top\mathbf{A}]_2, m, [\mathbf{c}]_1)$ involved in some signatures that $\mathcal{A}$ obtains under *tampered* signing keys.

So to apply this property, we need to first show that the event TagColl can hardly occur. This might be the most technical part of our security proof in Subsect. 3.3 and corresponds to Claim 2 therein. Roughly speaking, we divide TagColl into three sub-cases and analyze them individually to show that they all rarely occur, by utilizing the concrete algebraic structures of our construction, based on the collision resistance of H and on the MDDH assumption.

Consequently, we can apply the above property, and show that the terms $\boxed{[\gamma\mathbf{a}^\perp]_1}$ triggered by $[(\mathbf{K}_0 + \tau\mathbf{K}_1)\mathbf{U}]_1\mathbf{w}$ in (5) can be used to hide the partial information of $\boxed{(a\mathbf{K} + \mathbf{B})[\mathbf{c}]_1}$ in the generation of $[\mathbf{d}]_1$ in (4). To see this more concretely, again, we sample $sk = \mathbf{K}$ equivalently via

$$\mathbf{K} := \widetilde{\mathbf{K}} + \boxed{\mathbf{a}^\perp\mathbf{k}^\top}$$

where $\widetilde{\mathbf{K}} \leftarrow_{\$} \mathbb{Z}_p^{(k+1)\times(k+1)}$ and $\mathbf{k} \leftarrow_{\$} \mathbb{Z}_p^{k+1}$, and then we have

$$\begin{aligned}
[\mathbf{d}]_1 &= \boxed{(a\mathbf{K}+\mathbf{B})[\mathbf{c}]_1} + [\mathbf{K}_0 + \tau\mathbf{K}_1)\mathbf{U}]_1\mathbf{w} \\
&\overset{c}{\approx} \boxed{(a\mathbf{K}+\mathbf{B})[\mathbf{c}]_1} + [\mathbf{K}_0 + \tau\mathbf{K}_1)\mathbf{U}]_1\mathbf{w} + [\gamma\mathbf{a}^\perp]_1 \\
&= \boxed{(a(\widetilde{\mathbf{K}} + \mathbf{a}^\perp\mathbf{k}^\top) + \mathbf{B})[\mathbf{c}]_1} + [\mathbf{K}_0 + \tau\mathbf{K}_1)\mathbf{U}]_1\mathbf{w} + [\gamma\mathbf{a}^\perp]_1 \\
&= \boxed{(a\widetilde{\mathbf{K}} + \mathbf{B})[\mathbf{c}]_1} + [\mathbf{K}_0 + \tau\mathbf{K}_1)\mathbf{U}]_1\mathbf{w} + [\boxed{a\mathbf{a}^\perp(\mathbf{k}^\top\mathbf{c})} + \gamma\mathbf{a}^\perp]_1.
\end{aligned}$$

Note that the term $\gamma\mathbf{a}^\perp$ perfectly hides $\boxed{a\mathbf{a}^\perp(\mathbf{k}^\top\mathbf{c})} = (a\mathbf{k}^\top\mathbf{c})\mathbf{a}^\perp$ by the randomness of $\gamma \leftarrow_{\$} \mathbb{Z}_p$, thus the information of $\mathbf{k}$ is perfectly hidden in the multiple signatures generated under tampered signing keys.

<u>PUTTING TWO COMPONENTS TOGETHER.</u> Overall, the two components enjoy specific properties and we carefully integrate the two components in our SIG construction to achieve sLTR-CMA security: the terms $[(\mathbf{K}_0 + \tau\mathbf{K}_1)\mathbf{U}]_1\mathbf{w}$ in the second component can trigger randomness in the form of $[\gamma\mathbf{a}^\perp]_1$, which can then be used to hide the terms $\boxed{(a\mathbf{K}+\mathbf{B})[\mathbf{c}]_1}$ in the first component, so that the signatures generated under *tampered* signing keys do not leak much information about $sk = \mathbf{K}$ beyond vk to the adversary, and finally the sLTR-CMA security of our SIG follows from the useful property of the first component in the *key leakage* setting.

3.3 Proof of Theorem 1

Now we present the formal proof of Theorem 1. Let $\mathcal{A}$ be any PPT adversary against the $(\kappa, \mathcal{T}_{\mathsf{aff}})$-sLTR-CMA security of SIG, where $\mathcal{A}$ makes Q times of $\mathcal{O}_{\text{SIGN}}$ queries. We prove the theorem via a sequence of games $\mathsf{G}_0 - \mathsf{G}_3$, $\{\mathsf{G}_{4.\eta.0} - \mathsf{G}_{4.\eta.4}\}_{0\le\eta\le Q-1}$ and $\mathsf{G}_{4.Q.0}$, where G_0 is the $(\kappa, \mathcal{T}_{\mathsf{aff}})$-sLTR-CMA experiment (cf. Fig. 1), and in $\mathsf{G}_{4.Q.0}$, $\mathcal{A}$ has a negligible advantage. A brief description of differences between adjacent games is summarized in Table 1.

<u>**Game G_0:**</u> This is the $(\kappa, \mathcal{T}_{\mathsf{aff}})$-sLTR-CMA experiment (cf. Fig. 1).

Let $\mathsf{pp} = (\mathsf{gpar}, [\mathbf{U}]_1, [\mathbf{K}_0\mathbf{U}]_1, [\mathbf{K}_1\mathbf{U}]_1, [\mathbf{A}]_2, [\mathbf{K}_0^\top\mathbf{A}]_2, [\mathbf{K}_1^\top\mathbf{A}]_2, H)$ and $(vk = [\mathbf{K}^\top\mathbf{A}]_2, sk = \mathbf{K})$. In this game, when answering an $\mathcal{O}_{\text{SIGN}}$ query $(T_{(a,\mathbf{B})} \in \mathcal{T}_{\mathsf{aff}}, m)$, the challenger computes the tampered key $sk' = \mathbf{K}' := T_{(a,\mathbf{B})}(sk) = a\mathbf{K} + \mathbf{B}$ and $vk' := [\mathbf{K}'^\top\mathbf{A}]_2$, samples $\mathbf{w} \leftarrow_{\$} \mathbb{Z}_p^k$, and computes $[\mathbf{c}]_1 := [\mathbf{U}]_1\mathbf{w}$, $\tau := H(vk', m, [\mathbf{c}]_1)$ and $[\mathbf{d}]_1 := \mathbf{K}'[\mathbf{c}]_1 + [(\mathbf{K}_0 + \tau\mathbf{K}_1)\mathbf{U}]_1\mathbf{w}$ using the tampered key $sk' = \mathbf{K}'$. Then, the challenger returns $\sigma := ([\mathbf{c}]_1, [\mathbf{d}]_1)$ to $\mathcal{A}$, and further puts (m, σ) to set $\mathcal{Q}_{\mathsf{id}}$ if $T_{(a,\mathbf{B})}$ is the identity function id. For an $\mathcal{O}_{\text{LEAK}}$ query L, the challenger returns $L(sk)$ to $\mathcal{A}$ if the total leakage length is bounded by κ.

At the end of the game, $\mathcal{A}$ outputs a forgery $(m^*, \sigma^* = ([\mathbf{c}^*]_1, [\mathbf{d}^*]_1))$. Let Win denote the event that

$$(m^*, \sigma^*) \notin \mathcal{Q}_{\mathsf{id}} \wedge e([\mathbf{c}^{*\top}]_1, [(\mathbf{K}^\top + \mathbf{K}_0^\top + \tau^*\mathbf{K}_1^\top)\mathbf{A}]_2) = e([\mathbf{d}^{*\top}]_1, [\mathbf{A}]_2) \wedge [\mathbf{c}^*]_1 \neq [\mathbf{0}]_1,$$

Table 1. Brief Description of Games $\mathsf{G}_0 - \mathsf{G}_3$, $\{\mathsf{G}_{4.\eta.0} - \mathsf{G}_{4.\eta.4}\}_{0\le\eta\le Q-1}$ and $\mathsf{G}_{4.Q.0}$ for the $(\kappa, \mathcal{T}_{\mathsf{aff}})$-sLTR-CMA security proof of SIG, where the differences between adjacent games are highlighted in gray boxes. Here column "$\mathcal{O}_{\rm SIGN}(T_{(a,\mathbf{B})} \in \mathcal{T}_{\mathsf{aff}}, m)$" suggests how a signature $\sigma = ([\mathbf{c}]_1, [\mathbf{d}]_1)$ is generated: sub-column "$[\mathbf{c}]_1 \leftarrow_{\$}$ " refers to the space from which $[\mathbf{c}]_1$ is chosen; sub-column "$[\mathbf{d}]_1 =$" shows the computation of $[\mathbf{d}]_1$, where $sk' = \mathbf{K}' = T_{(a,\mathbf{B})}(sk) = a\mathbf{K} + \mathbf{B}$ denotes the tampered signing key. Column "$\mathcal{O}_{\rm LEAK}$" shows the output returned by $\mathcal{O}_{\rm LEAK}$. Column "Win's additional check for forgery $(m^*, \sigma^* = ([\mathbf{c}^*]_1, [\mathbf{d}^*]_1))$" describes the additional check that $\mathcal{A}$'s forgery wins, besides the routine check $(m^*, \sigma^*) \notin \mathcal{Q}_{\mathsf{id}} \wedge e([\mathbf{c}^{*\top}]_1, [(\mathbf{K}^\top + \mathbf{K}_0^\top + \tau^*\mathbf{K}_1^\top)\mathbf{A}]_2) = e([\mathbf{d}^{*\top}]_1, [\mathbf{A}]_2) \wedge [\mathbf{c}^*]_1 \neq [\mathbf{0}]_1$, where $\mathcal{Q}_{\mathsf{tag}}$ denotes the set of τ generated in $\mathcal{O}_{\rm SIGN}$ queries.

	$\mathcal{O}_{\rm SIGN}(T_{(a,\mathbf{B})} \in \mathcal{T}_{\mathsf{aff}}, m)$		$\mathcal{O}_{\rm LEAK}(L)$	Win's additional check for forgery $(m^*, \sigma^* = ([\mathbf{c}^*]_1, [\mathbf{d}^*]_1))$	Justification/Assumption
	$[\mathbf{c}]_1 \leftarrow_{\$}$	$[\mathbf{d}]_1 =$			
G_0	$\mathsf{Span}([\mathbf{U}]_1)$	$\mathbf{K}'[\mathbf{c}]_1 + [(\mathbf{K}_0 + \tau\mathbf{K}_1)\mathbf{U}]_1\mathbf{w}$	$L(sk)$		$(\kappa, \mathcal{T}_{\mathsf{aff}})$-sLTR-CMA experiment
G_1	$\mathsf{Span}([\mathbf{U}]_1)$	$(\mathbf{K}' + \mathbf{K}_0 + \tau\mathbf{K}_1)[\mathbf{c}]_1$	$L(sk)$		$\mathsf{G}_0 = \mathsf{G}_1$
G_2	$\mathsf{Span}([\mathbf{U}]_1)$	$(\mathbf{K}' + \mathbf{K}_0 + \tau\mathbf{K}_1)[\mathbf{c}]_1$	$L(sk)$	$[\mathbf{d}^*]_1 = [(\mathbf{K} + \mathbf{K}_0 + \tau^*\mathbf{K}_1)\mathbf{c}^*]_1$	$\mathcal{D}_k$-KerMDH on $[\mathbf{A}]_2$
G_3	$\mathsf{Span}([\mathbf{U}]_1)$	$(\mathbf{K}' + \mathbf{K}_0 + \tau\mathbf{K}_1)[\mathbf{c}]_1$	$L(sk)$	$[\mathbf{d}^*]_1 = [(\mathbf{K} + \mathbf{K}_0 + \tau^*\mathbf{K}_1)\mathbf{c}^*]_1$, $\tau^* \notin \mathcal{Q}_{\mathsf{tag}}$	Collision-resistance of $\mathcal{H}$ & $\mathcal{D}_k$-KerMDH on $[\mathbf{A}]_2$
$\mathsf{G}_{4.\eta.0}$	$\mathsf{Span}([\mathbf{U}]_1)$	$\begin{cases}(\mathbf{K}' + \mathbf{K}_0 + \tau\mathbf{K}_1)[\mathbf{c}]_1 + [\gamma\mathbf{a}^\perp]_1 \text{ with } \gamma \leftarrow_{\$} \mathbb{Z}_p, \text{ for the first } \eta \text{ queries}\\ (\mathbf{K}' + \mathbf{K}_0 + \tau\mathbf{K}_1)[\mathbf{c}]_1, \text{ for other queries}\end{cases}$	$L(sk)$	$[\mathbf{d}^*]_1 = [(\mathbf{K} + \mathbf{K}_0 + \tau^*\mathbf{K}_1)\mathbf{c}^*]_1, \tau^* \notin \mathcal{Q}_{\mathsf{tag}}$	$\mathsf{G}_3 = \mathsf{G}_{4.0.0}$
$\mathsf{G}_{4.\eta.1}$	$\begin{cases}\mathbb{G}_1^{k+1}, \text{ for the } (\eta+1)\text{-th query}\\ \mathsf{Span}([\mathbf{U}]_1), \text{ for other queries}\end{cases}$	$\begin{cases}(\mathbf{K}' + \mathbf{K}_0 + \tau\mathbf{K}_1)[\mathbf{c}]_1 + [\gamma\mathbf{a}^\perp]_1 \text{ with } \gamma \leftarrow_{\$} \mathbb{Z}_p, \text{ for the first } \eta \text{ queries}\\ (\mathbf{K}' + \mathbf{K}_0 + \tau\mathbf{K}_1)[\mathbf{c}]_1, \text{ for other queries}\end{cases}$	$L(sk)$	$[\mathbf{d}^*]_1 = [(\mathbf{K} + \mathbf{K}_0 + \tau^*\mathbf{K}_1)\mathbf{c}^*]_1, \tau^* \notin \mathcal{Q}_{\mathsf{tag}}$	$\mathcal{D}_k$-MDDH on $[\mathbf{U}]_1$
$\mathsf{G}_{4.\eta.2}$	$\begin{cases}\mathbb{G}_1^{k+1}, \text{ for the } (\eta+1)\text{-th query}\\ \mathsf{Span}([\mathbf{U}]_1), \text{ for other queries}\end{cases}$	$\begin{cases}(\mathbf{K}' + \mathbf{K}_0 + \tau\mathbf{K}_1)[\mathbf{c}]_1 + [\gamma\mathbf{a}^\perp]_1 \text{ with } \gamma \leftarrow_{\$} \mathbb{Z}_p, \text{ for the first } \eta \text{ queries}\\ (\mathbf{K}' + \mathbf{K}_0 + \tau\mathbf{K}_1)[\mathbf{c}]_1, \text{ for other queries}\end{cases}$	$L(sk)$	$[\mathbf{d}^*]_1 = [(\mathbf{K} + \mathbf{K}_0 + \tau^*\mathbf{K}_1)\mathbf{c}^*]_1, \tau^* \notin \mathcal{Q}_{\mathsf{tag}}$, $[\mathbf{c}^*]_1 \in \mathsf{Span}([\mathbf{U}]_1)$	Statistical arguments using the leftover entropy in $\mathbf{K}_0, \mathbf{K}_1$
$\mathsf{G}_{4.\eta.3}$	$\begin{cases}\mathbb{G}_1^{k+1}, \text{ for the } (\eta+1)\text{-th query}\\ \mathsf{Span}([\mathbf{U}]_1), \text{ for other queries}\end{cases}$	$\begin{cases}(\mathbf{K}' + \mathbf{K}_0 + \tau\mathbf{K}_1)[\mathbf{c}]_1 + [\gamma\mathbf{a}^\perp]_1 \text{ with } \gamma \leftarrow_{\$} \mathbb{Z}_p, \text{ for the first } \eta+1 \text{ queries}\\ (\mathbf{K}' + \mathbf{K}_0 + \tau\mathbf{K}_1)[\mathbf{c}]_1, \text{ for other queries}\end{cases}$	$L(sk)$	$[\mathbf{d}^*]_1 = [(\mathbf{K} + \mathbf{K}_0 + \tau^*\mathbf{K}_1)\mathbf{c}^*]_1, \tau^* \notin \mathcal{Q}_{\mathsf{tag}}$, $[\mathbf{c}^*]_1 \in \mathsf{Span}([\mathbf{U}]_1)$	Statistical arguments using the leftover entropy in $\mathbf{K}_0, \mathbf{K}_1$
$\mathsf{G}_{4.\eta.4}$	$\begin{cases}\mathbb{G}_1^{k+1}, \text{ for the } (\eta+1)\text{-th query}\\ \mathsf{Span}([\mathbf{U}]_1), \text{ for other queries}\end{cases}$	$\begin{cases}(\mathbf{K}' + \mathbf{K}_0 + \tau\mathbf{K}_1)[\mathbf{c}]_1 + [\gamma\mathbf{a}^\perp]_1 \text{ with } \gamma \leftarrow_{\$} \mathbb{Z}_p, \text{ for the first } \eta+1 \text{ queries}\\ (\mathbf{K}' + \mathbf{K}_0 + \tau\mathbf{K}_1)[\mathbf{c}]_1, \text{ for other queries}\end{cases}$	$L(sk)$	$[\mathbf{d}^*]_1 = [(\mathbf{K} + \mathbf{K}_0 + \tau^*\mathbf{K}_1)\mathbf{c}^*]_1, \tau^* \notin \mathcal{Q}_{\mathsf{tag}}$, ~~$[\mathbf{c}^*]_1 \in \mathsf{Span}([\mathbf{U}]_1)$~~	Statistical arguments using the leftover entropy in $\mathbf{K}_0, \mathbf{K}_1$
$\mathsf{G}_{4.\eta+1.0}$	$\mathsf{Span}([\mathbf{U}]_1)$	$\begin{cases}(\mathbf{K}' + \mathbf{K}_0 + \tau\mathbf{K}_1)[\mathbf{c}]_1 + [\gamma\mathbf{a}^\perp]_1 \text{ with } \gamma \leftarrow_{\$} \mathbb{Z}_p, \text{ for the first } \eta+1 \text{ queries}\\ (\mathbf{K}' + \mathbf{K}_0 + \tau\mathbf{K}_1)[\mathbf{c}]_1, \text{ for other queries}\end{cases}$	$L(sk)$	$[\mathbf{d}^*]_1 = [(\mathbf{K} + \mathbf{K}_0 + \tau^*\mathbf{K}_1)\mathbf{c}^*]_1, \tau^* \notin \mathcal{Q}_{\mathsf{tag}}$	$\mathcal{D}_k$-MDDH on $[\mathbf{U}]_1$
$\mathsf{G}_{4.Q.0}$	$\mathsf{Span}([\mathbf{U}]_1)$	$(\mathbf{K}' + \mathbf{K}_0 + \tau\mathbf{K}_1)[\mathbf{c}]_1 + [\gamma\mathbf{a}^\perp]_1$ with $\gamma \leftarrow_{\$} \mathbb{Z}_p$	$L(sk)$	$[\mathbf{d}^*]_1 = [(\mathbf{K} + \mathbf{K}_0 + \tau^*\mathbf{K}_1)\mathbf{c}^*]_1, \tau^* \notin \mathcal{Q}_{\mathsf{tag}}$	$\Pr[\mathsf{Win}] = \mathsf{negl}$: statistical arguments using the leftover entropy in $\mathbf{K}$

where $\tau^* := H(vk, m^*, [\mathbf{c}^*]_1)$. By definition, $\mathsf{Adv}^{\mathsf{sltr\text{-}cma}}_{\mathsf{SIG},\mathcal{A},\kappa,\mathcal{T}_{\mathsf{aff}}}(\lambda) = \Pr_0[\mathsf{Win}]$.

Game G_1: It is the same as G_0, except that, when answering $\mathcal{O}_{\rm SIGN}$ queries, the challenger computes $[\mathbf{d}]_1 := (\mathbf{K}' + \mathbf{K}_0 + \tau\mathbf{K}_1)[\mathbf{c}]_1$ directly from $[\mathbf{c}]_1$, τ and $(\mathbf{K}', \mathbf{K}_0, \mathbf{K}_1)$, without using the vector $\mathbf{w}$ for $[\mathbf{c}]_1 = [\mathbf{U}]_1\mathbf{w}$.

Since $[\mathbf{c}]_1 = [\mathbf{U}]_1\mathbf{w}$, this change is conceptual and $\Pr_0[\mathsf{Win}] = \Pr_1[\mathsf{Win}]$.

Game G_2: It is the same as G_1, except that, the event Win is now defined as

$$(m^*, \sigma^*) \notin \mathcal{Q}_{\mathsf{id}} \ \wedge \ [\mathbf{d}^*]_1 = [(\mathbf{K} + \mathbf{K}_0 + \tau^*\mathbf{K}_1)\mathbf{c}^*]_1 \ \wedge \ [\mathbf{c}^*]_1 \neq [\mathbf{0}]_1.$$

Claim 1. $\left|\Pr_1[\mathsf{Win}] - \Pr_2[\mathsf{Win}]\right| \le \mathsf{Adv}^{\mathsf{mddh}}_{\mathcal{D}_k,\mathbb{G}_2,\mathcal{B}_1}(\lambda) + 1/(p-1)$ *for a PPT adversary* $\mathcal{B}_1$ *against the* $\mathcal{D}_k$*-MDDH assumption on* $[\mathbf{A}]_2$.

Proof. By VrfyBad denote the event that $\mathcal{A}$'s forgery $(m^*, \sigma^* = ([\mathbf{c}^*]_1, [\mathbf{d}^*]_1))$ satisfying $e([\mathbf{c}^{*\top}]_1, [(\mathbf{K}^\top + \mathbf{K}_0^\top + \tau^*\mathbf{K}_1^\top)\mathbf{A}]_2) = e([\mathbf{d}^{*\top}]_1, [\mathbf{A}]_2)$ but $[\mathbf{d}^*]_1 \neq [(\mathbf{K} + \mathbf{K}_0 + \tau^*\mathbf{K}_1)\mathbf{c}^*]_1$. Clearly, G_2 is identical to G_1 unless VrfyBad occurs, thus $\left|\Pr_1[\mathsf{Win}] - \Pr_2[\mathsf{Win}]\right| \le \Pr_2[\mathsf{VrfyBad}]$. To bound $\Pr_2[\mathsf{VrfyBad}]$, observe that VrfyBad implies that

$$e(\underbrace{[\mathbf{d}^{*\top}]_1 - [\mathbf{c}^{*\top}(\mathbf{K}^\top + \mathbf{K}_0^\top + \tau^*\mathbf{K}_1^\top)]_1}_{\neq [\mathbf{0}]_1}, [\mathbf{A}]_2) = [0]_T,$$

i.e., $[\mathbf{d}^{*\top}]_1 - [\mathbf{c}^{*\top}(\mathbf{K}^\top + \mathbf{K}_0^\top + \tau^*\mathbf{K}_1^\top)]_1$ is a non-zero vector in the kernel of $[\mathbf{A}]_2$. Thus $\mathsf{VrfyBad}$ rarely occurs under the $\mathcal{D}_k$-KerMDH assumption on $[\mathbf{A}]_2$, which is further implied by the $\mathcal{D}_k$-MDDH assumption on $[\mathbf{A}]_2$ according to Lemma 3. Consequently, $\Pr_2[\mathsf{VrfyBad}] \leq \mathsf{Adv}^{\mathsf{mddh}}_{\mathcal{D}_k,\mathbb{G}_2,\mathcal{B}_1}(\lambda) + 1/(p-1)$ and Claim 1 follows. ∎

Game G_3: It is the same as G_2, except that, when answering $\mathcal{O}_{\text{SIGN}}$ queries, the challenger also puts τ to a set $\mathcal{Q}_{\mathsf{tag}}$, and for the forgery $(m^*, \sigma^* = ([\mathbf{c}^*]_1, [\mathbf{d}^*]_1))$ output by $\mathcal{A}$, the event Win is now defined as

$$(m^*, \sigma^*) \notin \mathcal{Q}_{\mathsf{id}} \ \wedge \ [\mathbf{d}^*]_1 = [(\mathbf{K} + \mathbf{K}_0 + \tau^*\mathbf{K}_1)\mathbf{c}^*]_1 \ \wedge \ [\mathbf{c}^*]_1 \neq [\mathbf{0}]_1 \ \wedge \ \tau^* \notin \mathcal{Q}_{\mathsf{tag}}.$$

Claim 2. $\left|\Pr_2[\mathsf{Win}] - \Pr_3[\mathsf{Win}]\right| \leq \mathsf{Adv}^{\mathsf{cr}}_{\mathcal{H},\mathcal{B}_2}(\lambda) + \mathsf{Adv}^{\mathsf{mddh}}_{\mathcal{D}_k,\mathbb{G}_2,\mathcal{B}_3}(\lambda) + 1/(p-1) + 2^{-\Omega(\lambda)}$ *for PPT adversaries $\mathcal{B}_2$ against the collision-resistance of $\mathcal{H}$ and $\mathcal{B}_3$ against the $\mathcal{D}_k$-MDDH assumption on $[\mathbf{A}]_2$.*

Proof. By $\mathsf{TagColl}$ denote the event that $\mathcal{A}$'s forgery $(m^*, \sigma^* = ([\mathbf{c}^*]_1, [\mathbf{d}^*]_1))$ satisfying

$$(m^*, \sigma^*) \notin \mathcal{Q}_{\mathsf{id}} \ \wedge \ [\mathbf{d}^*]_1 = [(\mathbf{K} + \mathbf{K}_0 + \tau^*\mathbf{K}_1)\mathbf{c}^*]_1 \ \wedge \ [\mathbf{c}^*]_1 \neq [\mathbf{0}]_1 \ \wedge \ \tau^* \in \mathcal{Q}_{\mathsf{tag}}.$$

Clearly, G_2 and G_3 are the same until $\mathsf{TagColl}$ occurs, thus $\left|\Pr_2[\mathsf{Win}] - \Pr_3[\mathsf{Win}]\right| \leq \Pr_3[\mathsf{TagColl}]$.

To bound $\Pr_4[\mathsf{TagColl}]$, we divide $\mathsf{TagColl}$ into the following three cases:

- **Case 1:** There exists an $\mathcal{O}_{\text{SIGN}}$ query $(T_{(a,\mathbf{B})} \in \mathcal{T}_{\mathsf{aff}}, m)$, such that

$$\begin{aligned} &\tau^* = H(vk, m^*, [\mathbf{c}^*]_1) = H(vk', m, [\mathbf{c}]_1) = \tau \in \mathcal{Q}_{\mathsf{tag}} \\ \text{but} \quad &(vk, m^*, [\mathbf{c}^*]_1) \neq (vk', m, [\mathbf{c}]_1), \end{aligned}$$

  where vk' is the tampered verification key involved in this $\mathcal{O}_{\text{SIGN}}$ query.
  Clearly, Case 1 suggests a collision of H, thus $\Pr_3[\textbf{Case 1}] \leq \mathsf{Adv}^{\mathsf{cr}}_{\mathcal{H},\mathcal{B}_2}(\lambda)$.
- **Case 2:** There exists an $\mathcal{O}_{\text{SIGN}}$ query $(T_{(a,\mathbf{B})} \in \mathcal{T}_{\mathsf{aff}}, m)$, such that

$$\begin{aligned} &\tau^* = H(vk, m^*, [\mathbf{c}^*]_1) = H(vk', m, [\mathbf{c}]_1) = \tau \in \mathcal{Q}_{\mathsf{tag}} \\ \text{but} \quad &(vk, m^*, [\mathbf{c}^*]_1) = (vk', m, [\mathbf{c}]_1) \ \wedge \ T_{(a,\mathbf{B})} = \mathsf{id}, \end{aligned}$$

  where id denotes the identity function.
  Since $T_{(a,\mathbf{B})} = \mathsf{id}$, the tampered signing key $sk' = \mathbf{K}'$ is in fact the original key $sk = \mathbf{K}$, and the tuple $(m, \sigma = ([\mathbf{c}]_1, [\mathbf{d}]_1))$ involved in this $\mathcal{O}_{\text{SIGN}}$ query is added to $\mathcal{Q}_{\mathsf{id}}$.
  Now we show that this case can never occur. On the one hand, $\mathsf{TagColl}$ requires $(m^*, \sigma^* = ([\mathbf{c}^*]_1, [\mathbf{d}^*]_1)) \notin \mathcal{Q}_{\mathsf{id}}$ and this case requires $(m^*, [\mathbf{c}^*]_1) = (m, [\mathbf{c}]_1)$, so it follows that $[\mathbf{d}^*]_1 \neq [\mathbf{d}]_1$. On the other hand, $\mathsf{TagColl}$ requires $[\mathbf{d}^*]_1 = [(\mathbf{K} + \mathbf{K}_0 + \tau^*\mathbf{K}_1)\mathbf{c}^*]_1$ and this case requires $\tau^* = \tau$, so we have $[\mathbf{d}^*]_1 = [(\mathbf{K} + \mathbf{K}_0 + \tau^*\mathbf{K}_1)\mathbf{c}^*]_1 = [(\mathbf{K}' + \mathbf{K}_0 + \tau\mathbf{K}_1)\mathbf{c}]_1 = [\mathbf{d}]_1$, which leads to a contradiction. Therefore, this case can never occur, i.e., $\Pr_3[\textbf{Case 2}] = 0$.

- **Case 3:** There exists an $\mathcal{O}_{\text{SIGN}}$ query $(T_{(a,\mathbf{B})} \in \mathcal{T}_{\mathsf{aff}}, m)$, such that

$$\begin{aligned} \tau^* = H(vk, m^*, [\mathbf{c}^*]_1) = H(vk', m, [\mathbf{c}]_1) = \tau \in \mathcal{Q}_{\mathsf{tag}} \\ \text{but} \quad (vk, m^*, [\mathbf{c}^*]_1) = (vk', m, [\mathbf{c}]_1) \ \wedge \ T_{(a,\mathbf{B})} \neq \mathsf{id}. \end{aligned}$$

Note that $vk' = vk$ means that $[\mathbf{K}'^\top \mathbf{A}]_2 = [\mathbf{K}^\top \mathbf{A}]_2$, where $sk' = \mathbf{K}' = T_{(a,\mathbf{B})}(sk) = a\mathbf{K} + \mathbf{B}$ is the tampered signing key. By rearranging terms, it follows that $[((a-1)\mathbf{K}^\top + \mathbf{B}^\top)\mathbf{A}]_2 = [\mathbf{0}]_2$. This shows that $(a-1)\mathbf{K}^\top + \mathbf{B}^\top$ is a matrix in the kernel of $[\mathbf{A}]_2$. We claim that $(a-1)\mathbf{K}^\top + \mathbf{B}^\top$ is a non-zero matrix with overwhelming probability $1 - 2^{-\Omega(\lambda)}$, which will be shown later. Thus by the $\mathcal{D}_k$-KerMDH assumption on $[\mathbf{A}]_2$ (which is further implied by the $\mathcal{D}_k$-MDDH assumption on $[\mathbf{A}]_2$ according to Lemma 3), this case can rarely occurs, and we have $\Pr_3[\textbf{Case 3}] \leq \mathsf{Adv}^{\mathsf{mddh}}_{\mathcal{D}_k,\mathbb{G}_2,\mathcal{B}_3}(\lambda) + 1/(p-1) + 2^{-\Omega(\lambda)}$.
It remains to show the claim that the matrix $(a-1)\mathbf{K}^\top + \mathbf{B}^\top$ is non-zero with overwhelming probability $1 - 2^{-\Omega(\lambda)}$. By the fact that $T_{(a,\mathbf{B})} \neq \mathsf{id}$, there are two sub-cases. The first sub-case is $a = 1$ and $\mathbf{B} \neq \mathbf{0}$. In this sub-case, we have $(a-1)\mathbf{K}^\top + \mathbf{B}^\top = \mathbf{B}^\top$, which is clearly non-zero. The second sub-case is $a \neq 1$. In this sub-case, we will show that $sk = \mathbf{K}$ contains enough entropy from $\mathcal{A}$'s view, so that the matrix $(a-1)\mathbf{K}^\top + \mathbf{B}^\top$ is non-zero with overwhelming probability. To see this, let $\mathbf{u}^\perp \in \mathbb{Z}_p^{k+1}$ (resp., $\mathbf{a}^\perp \in \mathbb{Z}_p^{k+1}$) be an arbitrary non-zero vector in the kernel of $\mathbf{U}$ (resp., $\mathbf{A}$) such that $(\mathbf{u}^\perp)^\top \mathbf{U} = \mathbf{0}$ (resp., $(\mathbf{a}^\perp)^\top \mathbf{A} = \mathbf{0}$). For the convenience of our analysis, we sample $sk = \mathbf{K} \leftarrow_\$ \mathbb{Z}_p^{(k+1)\times(k+1)}$ equivalently via

$$\mathbf{K} := \widetilde{\mathbf{K}} + \mu \mathbf{a}^\perp (\mathbf{u}^\perp)^\top$$

where $\widetilde{\mathbf{K}} \leftarrow_\$ \mathbb{Z}_p^{(k+1)\times(k+1)}$ and $\mu \leftarrow_\$ \mathbb{Z}_p$. Below we analyze the information about μ that $\mathcal{A}$ may obtain in G_3.

 - Firstly, the verification key vk is

$$[\mathbf{K}^\top \mathbf{A}]_2 = [(\widetilde{\mathbf{K}}^\top + \mu \mathbf{u}^\perp (\mathbf{a}^\perp)^\top)\mathbf{A}]_2 = [\widetilde{\mathbf{K}}^\top \mathbf{A}]_2,$$

 thus μ is completely hidden.
 - In $\mathcal{O}_{\text{SIGN}}$ queries, the tampered verification key vk' is

$$\begin{aligned} [\mathbf{K}'^\top \mathbf{A}]_2 = [(a\mathbf{K}^\top + \mathbf{B}^\top)\mathbf{A}]_2 &= [(a(\widetilde{\mathbf{K}}^\top + \mu \mathbf{u}^\perp (\mathbf{a}^\perp)^\top) + \mathbf{B}^\top)\mathbf{A}]_2 \\ &= [(a\widetilde{\mathbf{K}}^\top + \mathbf{B}^\top)\mathbf{A}]_2, \end{aligned}$$

 thus μ is completely hidden. Moreover, since $[\mathbf{c}]_1 = [\mathbf{U}]_1 \mathbf{w}$ with $\mathbf{w} \leftarrow_\$ \mathbb{Z}_p^k$, we have

$$\begin{aligned} [\mathbf{d}]_1 = (\mathbf{K}' + \mathbf{K}_0 + \tau \mathbf{K}_1)[\mathbf{c}]_1 &= (a\mathbf{K} + \mathbf{B} + \mathbf{K}_0 + \tau \mathbf{K}_1)[\mathbf{U}]_1 \mathbf{w} \\ &= \big(a(\widetilde{\mathbf{K}} + \mu \mathbf{a}^\perp (\mathbf{u}^\perp)^\top) + \mathbf{B} + \mathbf{K}_0 + \tau \mathbf{K}_1\big)[\mathbf{U}]_1 \mathbf{w} \\ &= (a\widetilde{\mathbf{K}} + \mathbf{B} + \mathbf{K}_0 + \tau \mathbf{K}_1)[\mathbf{U}]_1 \mathbf{w}, \end{aligned}$$

 thus μ is also completely hidden.

– From $\mathcal{O}_{\text{LEAK}}$ queries, $\mathcal{A}$ obtains at most κ bits information $L(sk) = L(\mathbf{K}) = L(\widetilde{\mathbf{K}} + \mu\mathbf{a}^{\perp}(\mathbf{u}^{\perp})^{\top})$ about sk, and also about μ.

Overall, the information about μ that $\mathcal{A}$ learns in G_3 is at most κ bits. Thus, there are still $\log p - \kappa \geq \Omega(\lambda)$ bits of entropy left in μ, and also in $sk = \mathbf{K} = \widetilde{\mathbf{K}} + \mu\mathbf{a}^{\perp}(\mathbf{u}^{\perp})^{\top}$. Consequently, the probability that the matrix $(a-1)\mathbf{K}^{\top} + \mathbf{B}^{\top}$ is non-zero is $\Pr[(a-1)\mathbf{K}^{\top} + \mathbf{B}^{\top} \neq \mathbf{0}] = 1 - \Pr[(a-1)\mathbf{K}^{\top} + \mathbf{B}^{\top} = \mathbf{0}] = 1 - \Pr[\mathbf{K} = (1-a)^{-1}\mathbf{B}] \geq 1 - 2^{-\Omega(\lambda)}$ and the claim follows.

Putting the above three cases together, we have $\Pr_3[\mathsf{TagColl}] \leq \mathsf{Adv}^{\mathsf{cr}}_{\mathcal{H},\mathcal{B}_2}(\lambda) + \mathsf{Adv}^{\mathsf{mddh}}_{\mathcal{D}_k,\mathbb{G}_2,\mathcal{B}_3}(\lambda) + 1/(p-1) + 2^{-\Omega(\lambda)}$, and Claim 2 follows. ∎

Next, we consider a sequence of games $\{\mathsf{G}_{4.\eta.0} - \mathsf{G}_{4.\eta.4}\}_{0 \leq \eta \leq Q-1}$ and $\mathsf{G}_{4.Q.0}$.

Game $\mathsf{G}_{4.\eta.0}$, $0 \leq \eta \leq Q$: It is the same as G_3, except that, at the beginning of the game, the challenger picks a non-zero vector $\mathbf{a}^{\perp} \in \mathbb{Z}_p^{k+1}$ in the kernel of $\mathbf{A}$ such that $(\mathbf{a}^{\perp})^{\top}\mathbf{A} = \mathbf{0}$. Moreover, when answering the first η $\mathcal{O}_{\text{SIGN}}$ queries, the challenger computes $[\mathbf{d}]_1 := (\mathbf{K}' + \mathbf{K}_0 + \tau\mathbf{K}_1)[\mathbf{c}]_1 + [\gamma\mathbf{a}^{\perp}]_1$ with $\gamma \leftarrow_{\$} \mathbb{Z}_p$ chosen uniformly and independently for each query. As for the remaining $Q - \eta$ $\mathcal{O}_{\text{SIGN}}$ queries, the challenger still computes $[\mathbf{d}]_1 := (\mathbf{K}' + \mathbf{K}_0 + \tau\mathbf{K}_1)[\mathbf{c}]_1$.

It is clearly that $\mathsf{G}_{4.0.0}$ is identical to G_3, thus $\Pr_3[\mathsf{Win}] = \Pr_{4.0.0}[\mathsf{Win}]$.

Game $\mathsf{G}_{4.\eta.1}$, $0 \leq \eta \leq Q-1$: It is the same as $\mathsf{G}_{4.\eta.0}$, except that, when answering the $(\eta+1)$-th $\mathcal{O}_{\text{SIGN}}$ query, the challenger samples $[\mathbf{c}]_1 \leftarrow_{\$} \mathbb{G}_1^{k+1}$ uniformly at random, instead of computing $[\mathbf{c}]_1 := [\mathbf{U}]_1\mathbf{w}$ with $\mathbf{w} \leftarrow_{\$} \mathbb{Z}_p^k$.

It is clearly that $\mathsf{G}_{4.\eta.0}$ and $\mathsf{G}_{4.\eta.1}$ are computationally indistinguishable to $\mathcal{A}$, under the $\mathcal{D}_k$-MDDH assumption on $[\mathbf{U}]_1$. Therefore, we have $\left|\Pr_{4.\eta.0}[\mathsf{Win}] - \Pr_{4.\eta.1}[\mathsf{Win}]\right| \leq \mathsf{Adv}^{\mathsf{mddh}}_{\mathcal{D}_k,\mathbb{G}_1,\mathcal{B}_4}(\lambda)$ for a PPT adversary $\mathcal{B}_4$.

Game $\mathsf{G}_{4.\eta.2}$, $0 \leq \eta \leq Q-1$: It is the same as $\mathsf{G}_{4.\eta.1}$, except that, the event Win is now defined as

$$(m^*, \sigma^*) \notin \mathcal{Q}_{\mathsf{id}} \wedge [\mathbf{d}^*]_1 = [(\mathbf{K} + \mathbf{K}_0 + \tau^*\mathbf{K}_1)\mathbf{c}^*]_1 \wedge [\mathbf{c}^*]_1 \neq [\mathbf{0}]_1 \wedge \tau^* \notin \mathcal{Q}_{\mathsf{tag}} \wedge \boxed{[\mathbf{c}^*]_1 \in \mathsf{Span}([\mathbf{U}]_1)}\,.$$

Claim 3. $\left|\Pr_{4.\eta.1}[\mathsf{Win}] - \Pr_{4.\eta.2}[\mathsf{Win}]\right| \leq 1/p$.

Proof. By CBad denote the event that $\mathcal{A}$'s forgery $(m^*, \sigma^* = ([\mathbf{c}^*]_1, [\mathbf{d}^*]_1))$ satisfying

$$(m^*, \sigma^*) \notin \mathcal{Q}_{\mathsf{id}} \wedge [\mathbf{d}^*]_1 = [(\mathbf{K} + \mathbf{K}_0 + \tau^*\mathbf{K}_1)\mathbf{c}^*]_1 \wedge [\mathbf{c}^*]_1 \neq [\mathbf{0}]_1 \wedge \tau^* \notin \mathcal{Q}_{\mathsf{tag}} \wedge [\mathbf{c}^*]_1 \notin \mathsf{Span}([\mathbf{U}]_1).$$

Clearly, $\mathsf{G}_{4.\eta.1}$ and $\mathsf{G}_{4.\eta.2}$ are the same until CBad occurs, thus $\left|\Pr_{4.\eta.1}[\mathsf{Win}] - \Pr_{4.\eta.2}[\mathsf{Win}]\right| \leq \Pr_{4.\eta.2}[\mathsf{CBad}]$.

Next, we analyze $\Pr_{4.\eta.2}[\mathsf{CBad}]$. Let $\mathbf{u}^{\perp} \in \mathbb{Z}_p^{k+1}$ be a non-zero vector in the kernel of $\mathbf{U}$ such that $(\mathbf{u}^{\perp})^{\top}\mathbf{U} = \mathbf{0}$ but $(\mathbf{u}^{\perp})^{\top}\mathbf{c}^* \neq 0$. For the convenience of our analysis, we sample $\mathbf{K}_0, \mathbf{K}_1 \leftarrow_{\$} \mathbb{Z}_p^{(k+1)\times(k+1)}$ equivalently via $\mathbf{K}_0 := \widetilde{\mathbf{K}_0} + \mu_0\mathbf{a}^{\perp}(\mathbf{u}^{\perp})^{\top}$, $\mathbf{K}_1 := \widetilde{\mathbf{K}_1} + \mu_1\mathbf{a}^{\perp}(\mathbf{u}^{\perp})^{\top}$, where $\widetilde{\mathbf{K}_0}, \widetilde{\mathbf{K}_1} \leftarrow_{\$} \mathbb{Z}_p^{(k+1)\times(k+1)}$ and $\mu_0, \mu_1 \leftarrow_{\$} \mathbb{Z}_p$. Below we analyze the information about μ_0 and μ_1 that $\mathcal{A}$ may obtain in $\mathsf{G}_{4.\eta.2}$.

- Firstly, the public parameter pp contains $[\mathbf{K}_0\mathbf{U}]_1, [\mathbf{K}_1\mathbf{U}]_1, [\mathbf{K}_0^\top\mathbf{A}]_2, [\mathbf{K}_1^\top\mathbf{A}]_2$. Due to the facts that $(\mathbf{u}^\perp)^\top\mathbf{U} = \mathbf{0}$ and $(\mathbf{a}^\perp)^\top\mathbf{A} = \mathbf{0}$, it is easy to see that $[\mathbf{K}_0\mathbf{U}]_1 = [\widetilde{\mathbf{K}_0}\mathbf{U}]_1, [\mathbf{K}_1\mathbf{U}]_1 = [\widetilde{\mathbf{K}_1}\mathbf{U}]_1, [\mathbf{K}_0^\top\mathbf{A}]_2 = [\widetilde{\mathbf{K}}_0^\top\mathbf{A}]_2, [\mathbf{K}_1^\top\mathbf{A}]_2 = [\widetilde{\mathbf{K}}_1^\top\mathbf{A}]_2$. Thus μ_0 and μ_1 are completely hidden. Moreover, the verification key vk does not involve $\mathbf{K}_0$ and $\mathbf{K}_1$, so μ_0 and μ_1 are also completely hidden.
- In $\mathcal{O}_{\text{SIGN}}$ queries, the tampered verification key vk' does not involve $\mathbf{K}_0$ and $\mathbf{K}_1$, thus also does not involve μ_0 and μ_1. Next we analyze the information about μ_0 and μ_1 contained in $[\mathbf{d}]_1$.
  * For the first η $\mathcal{O}_{\text{SIGN}}$ queries, we have $[\mathbf{d}]_1 = (\mathbf{K}' + \mathbf{K}_0 + \tau\mathbf{K}_1)[\mathbf{c}]_1 + [\gamma\mathbf{a}^\perp]_1 = (\mathbf{K}' + \widetilde{\mathbf{K}_0} + \tau\widetilde{\mathbf{K}_1} + (\mu_0 + \tau\mu_1)\mathbf{a}^\perp(\mathbf{u}^\perp)^\top)[\mathbf{c}]_1 + [\gamma\mathbf{a}^\perp]_1$. Due to fact that $[\mathbf{c}]_1 = [\mathbf{U}]_1\mathbf{w}$ with $\mathbf{w} \leftarrow_\$ \mathbb{Z}_p^k$, we have $[\mathbf{d}]_1 = (\mathbf{K}' + \widetilde{\mathbf{K}_0} + \tau\widetilde{\mathbf{K}_1})[\mathbf{c}]_1 + [\gamma\mathbf{a}^\perp]_1$. Therefore, μ_0 and μ_1 are completely hidden.
  * For the $(\eta+1)$-th $\mathcal{O}_{\text{SIGN}}$ query, we have $[\mathbf{d}]_1 = (\mathbf{K}' + \mathbf{K}_0 + \tau\mathbf{K}_1)[\mathbf{c}]_1 = (\mathbf{K}' + \widetilde{\mathbf{K}_0} + \tau\widetilde{\mathbf{K}_1} + (\mu_0 + \tau\mu_1)\mathbf{a}^\perp(\mathbf{u}^\perp)^\top)[\mathbf{c}]_1$, so the information of μ_0 and μ_1 contained in $[\mathbf{d}]_1$ is limited in $(\mu_0 + \tau\mu_1)$.
  * For the remaining $(Q - \eta - 1)$ $\mathcal{O}_{\text{SIGN}}$ queries, we also have $[\mathbf{d}]_1 = (\mathbf{K}' + \mathbf{K}_0 + \tau\mathbf{K}_1)[\mathbf{c}]_1 = (\mathbf{K}' + \widetilde{\mathbf{K}_0} + \tau\widetilde{\mathbf{K}_1} + (\mu_0 + \tau\mu_1)\mathbf{a}^\perp(\mathbf{u}^\perp)^\top)[\mathbf{c}]_1$. Due to fact that $[\mathbf{c}]_1 = [\mathbf{U}]_1\mathbf{w}$ with $\mathbf{w} \leftarrow_\$ \mathbb{Z}_p^k$, we have $[\mathbf{d}]_1 = (\mathbf{K}' + \widetilde{\mathbf{K}_0} + \tau\widetilde{\mathbf{K}_1})[\mathbf{c}]_1$. Therefore, μ_0 and μ_1 are completely hidden.
- From $\mathcal{O}_{\text{LEAK}}$ queries, $\mathcal{A}$ obtains leakage information about $sk = \mathbf{K}$. It does not involve $\mathbf{K}_0$ and $\mathbf{K}_1$, thus also does not involve μ_0 and μ_1.

Overall, the information that $\mathcal{A}$ might learn about μ_0 and μ_1 is limited in $(\mu_0 + \tau\mu_1)$.

For CBad to occur, $\mathcal{A}$'s forgery $(m^*, \sigma^* = ([\mathbf{c}^*]_1, [\mathbf{d}^*]_1))$ should satisfy $(m^*, \sigma^*) \notin \mathcal{Q}_{\mathsf{id}}$, $[\mathbf{c}^*]_1 \neq [\mathbf{0}]_1$, $\tau^* \notin \mathcal{Q}_{\mathsf{tag}}$, $[\mathbf{c}^*]_1 \notin \mathsf{Span}([\mathbf{U}]_1)$, and

$$[\mathbf{d}^*]_1 = [(\mathbf{K} + \mathbf{K}_0 + \tau^*\mathbf{K}_1)\mathbf{c}^*]_1 = [(\mathbf{K} + \widetilde{\mathbf{K}_0} + \tau^*\widetilde{\mathbf{K}_1})\mathbf{c}^* + (\mu_0 + \tau^*\mu_1)\mathbf{a}^\perp(\mathbf{u}^\perp)^\top\mathbf{c}^*]_1.$$

Below we argue that $\mathcal{A}$ can hardly compute such $[\mathbf{d}^*]_1$. Since $\tau^* \notin \mathcal{Q}_{\mathsf{tag}}$, the term $(\mu_0 + \tau^*\mu_1)$ is pairwise independent from the information $(\mu_0 + \tau\mu_1)$ that $\mathcal{A}$ might learn, thus $(\mu_0 + \tau^*\mu_1)$ is uniformly distributed over $\mathbb{Z}_p$ from $\mathcal{A}$'s view. Moreover, $\mathbf{u}^\perp \in \mathbb{Z}_p^{k+1}$ is chosen to satisfy $(\mathbf{u}^\perp)^\top\mathbf{c}^* \neq 0$ since $[\mathbf{c}^*]_1 \notin \mathsf{Span}([\mathbf{U}]_1)$. Therefore, $(\mu_0 + \tau^*\mu_1)\mathbf{a}^\perp(\mathbf{u}^\perp)^\top\mathbf{c}^*$ is uniformly distributed over $\mathsf{Span}(\mathbf{a}^\perp) = \{\gamma^*\mathbf{a}^\perp | \gamma^* \in \mathbb{Z}_p\}$ from $\mathcal{A}$'s view, and consequently, $\mathcal{A}$ can compute such $[\mathbf{d}^*]_1$ with probability at most $1/p$. This shows that $\Pr_{4.\eta.2}[\mathsf{CBad}] \leq 1/p$ and Claim 3 follows. ∎

Game $\mathsf{G}_{4.\eta.3}$, $0 \leq \eta \leq Q-1$: It is the same as $\mathsf{G}_{4.\eta.2}$, except that, when answering the $(\eta+1)$-th $\mathcal{O}_{\text{SIGN}}$ query, the challenger computes $[\mathbf{d}]_1 := (\mathbf{K}' + \mathbf{K}_0 + \tau\mathbf{K}_1)[\mathbf{c}]_1 + [\gamma\mathbf{a}^\perp]_1$ with $\gamma \leftarrow_\$ \mathbb{Z}_p$, instead of $[\mathbf{d}]_1 := (\mathbf{K}' + \mathbf{K}_0 + \tau\mathbf{K}_1)[\mathbf{c}]_1$.

Claim 4. $\left|\Pr_{4.\eta.2}[\mathsf{Win}] - \Pr_{4.\eta.3}[\mathsf{Win}]\right| \leq 1/p$.

Proof. We will show that $\mathsf{G}_{4.\eta.2}$ and $\mathsf{G}_{4.\eta.3}$ are identically distributed, except with probability $1/p$. To see this, let $\mathbf{u}^\perp \in \mathbb{Z}_p^{k+1}$ be a non-zero vector in the kernel of $\mathbf{U}$ such that $(\mathbf{u}^\perp)^\top\mathbf{U} = \mathbf{0}$. Similar to the proof of Claim 3, we sample

$\mathbf{K}_0, \mathbf{K}_1 \leftarrow_{\$} \mathbb{Z}_p^{(k+1)\times(k+1)}$ equivalently via $\mathbf{K}_0 := \widetilde{\mathbf{K}_0} + \mu_0 \mathbf{a}^\perp (\mathbf{u}^\perp)^\top$ and $\mathbf{K}_1 := \widetilde{\mathbf{K}_1} + \mu_1 \mathbf{a}^\perp (\mathbf{u}^\perp)^\top$, where $\widetilde{\mathbf{K}_0}, \widetilde{\mathbf{K}_1} \leftarrow_{\$} \mathbb{Z}_p^{(k+1)\times(k+1)}$ and $\mu_0, \mu_1 \leftarrow_{\$} \mathbb{Z}_p$. Recall that in the proof of Claim 3, we observe that μ_0 and μ_1 are completely hidden in the public parameter pp, the verification key vk, all $\mathcal{O}_{\text{SIGN}}$ queries except the $(\eta+1)$-th $\mathcal{O}_{\text{SIGN}}$ query, and $\mathcal{O}_{\text{LEAK}}$ queries. Moreover, due to the game change in $\mathsf{G}_{4.\eta.2}$, the event Win checks $[\mathbf{d}^*]_1 = [(\mathbf{K} + \mathbf{K}_0 + \tau^* \mathbf{K}_1)\mathbf{c}^*]_1$ only if $[\mathbf{c}^*]_1 \in \mathsf{Span}([\mathbf{U}]_1)$, and when $[\mathbf{c}^*]_1 \in \mathsf{Span}([\mathbf{U}]_1)$, the check becomes

$$\begin{aligned}[\mathbf{d}^*]_1 = [(\mathbf{K} + \mathbf{K}_0 + \tau^* \mathbf{K}_1)\mathbf{c}^*]_1 &= [(\mathbf{K} + \widetilde{\mathbf{K}_0} + \tau^* \widetilde{\mathbf{K}_1})\mathbf{c}^* + (\mu_0 + \tau^* \mu_1)\mathbf{a}^\perp (\mathbf{u}^\perp)^\top \mathbf{c}^*]_1 \\ &= [(\mathbf{K} + \widetilde{\mathbf{K}_0} + \tau^* \widetilde{\mathbf{K}_1})\mathbf{c}^*]_1,\end{aligned}$$

where μ_0 and μ_1 are also completely hidden. Therefore, the only place that involves μ_0 and μ_1 lies in the computation of $[\mathbf{d}]_1$ in the $(\eta+1)$-th $\mathcal{O}_{\text{SIGN}}$ query, where in $\mathsf{G}_{4.\eta.2}$, we have

$$[\mathbf{d}]_1 = (\mathbf{K}' + \mathbf{K}_0 + \tau \mathbf{K}_1)[\mathbf{c}]_1 = (\mathbf{K}' + \widetilde{\mathbf{K}_0} + \tau \widetilde{\mathbf{K}_1})[\mathbf{c}]_1 + [(\mu_0 + \tau \mu_1)\mathbf{a}^\perp (\mathbf{u}^\perp)^\top \mathbf{c}]_1, \tag{6}$$

while in $\mathsf{G}_{4.\eta.3}$, we have

$$\begin{aligned}[\mathbf{d}]_1 &= (\mathbf{K}' + \mathbf{K}_0 + \tau \mathbf{K}_1)[\mathbf{c}]_1 + [\gamma \mathbf{a}^\perp]_1 \\ &= (\mathbf{K}' + \widetilde{\mathbf{K}_0} + \tau \widetilde{\mathbf{K}_1})[\mathbf{c}]_1 + [(\mu_0 + \tau \mu_1)\mathbf{a}^\perp (\mathbf{u}^\perp)^\top \mathbf{c} + \gamma \mathbf{a}^\perp]_1,\end{aligned} \tag{7}$$

with $\gamma \leftarrow_{\$} \mathbb{Z}_p$. Note that due to the game change in $\mathsf{G}_{4.\eta.1}$, in the $(\eta+1)$-th $\mathcal{O}_{\text{SIGN}}$ query, $[\mathbf{c}]_1$ is chosen uniformly from $\mathbb{G}_1^{k+1}$, thus except with probability $1/p$, we have $(\mathbf{u}^\perp)^\top \mathbf{c} \neq 0$, and in this case, both the term $(\mu_0 + \tau \mu_1)\mathbf{a}^\perp (\mathbf{u}^\perp)^\top \mathbf{c}$ in (6) and the term $(\mu_0 + \tau \mu_1)\mathbf{a}^\perp (\mathbf{u}^\perp)^\top \mathbf{c} + \gamma \mathbf{a}^\perp$ in (7) are uniformly distributed over $\mathsf{Span}(\mathbf{a}^\perp) = \{\gamma^* \mathbf{a}^\perp | \gamma^* \in \mathbb{Z}_p\}$, due to the randomness of μ_0 and μ_1. Consequently, $\mathsf{G}_{4.\eta.2}$ (which computes $[\mathbf{d}]_1$ in the $(\eta+1)$-th $\mathcal{O}_{\text{SIGN}}$ query according to (6)) and $\mathsf{G}_{4.\eta.3}$ (which computes $[\mathbf{d}]_1$ in the $(\eta+1)$-th $\mathcal{O}_{\text{SIGN}}$ query according to (7)) are identically distributed, except with probability $1/p$. This shows that $|\Pr_{4.\eta.2}[\mathsf{Win}] - \Pr_{4.\eta.3}[\mathsf{Win}]| \leq 1/p$, and Claim 4 follows. ▌

Game $\mathsf{G}_{4.\eta.4}$, $0 \leq \eta \leq Q-1$: It is the same as $\mathsf{G}_{4.\eta.3}$, except that, the event Win is changed back to

$$(m^*, \sigma^*) \notin \mathcal{Q}_{\mathsf{id}} \wedge [\mathbf{d}^*]_1 = [(\mathbf{K} + \mathbf{K}_0 + \tau^* \mathbf{K}_1)\mathbf{c}^*]_1 \wedge [\mathbf{c}^*]_1 \neq [\mathbf{0}]_1 \wedge \tau^* \notin \mathcal{Q}_{\mathsf{tag}} \wedge \cancel{[\mathbf{c}^*]_1 \in \mathsf{Span}([\mathbf{U}]_1)}.$$

The transition from $\mathsf{G}_{4.\eta.3}$ to $\mathsf{G}_{4.\eta.4}$ is reverse to the transition from $\mathsf{G}_{4.\eta.1}$ to $\mathsf{G}_{4.\eta.2}$. Similar to Claim 3, we have the following claim.

Claim 5. $|\Pr_{4.\eta.3}[\mathsf{Win}] - \Pr_{4.\eta.4}[\mathsf{Win}]| \leq 1/p$.

Now we analyze the difference between $\mathsf{G}_{4.\eta.4}$ and $\mathsf{G}_{4.\eta+1.0}$. The only difference is the distribution of $[\mathbf{c}]_1$ in the $(\eta+1)$-th $\mathcal{O}_{\text{SIGN}}$ query, where in $\mathsf{G}_{4.\eta.4}$, $[\mathbf{c}]_1 \leftarrow_{\$} \mathbb{G}_1^{k+1}$ is chosen uniformly at random, while in $\mathsf{G}_{4.\eta+1.0}$, $[\mathbf{c}]_1 := [\mathbf{U}]_1 \mathbf{w}$

with $\mathbf{w} \leftarrow_\$ \mathbb{Z}_p^k$. It is clearly that $\mathsf{G}_{4.\eta.4}$ and $\mathsf{G}_{4.\eta+1.0}$ are computationally indistinguishable to $\mathcal{A}$, under the $\mathcal{D}_k$-MDDH assumption on $[\mathbf{U}]_1$. Therefore, we have $\left| \Pr_{4.\eta.4}[\mathsf{Win}] - \Pr_{4.\eta+1.0}[\mathsf{Win}] \right| \leq \mathsf{Adv}^{\mathsf{mddh}}_{\mathcal{D}_k,\mathbb{G}_1,\mathcal{B}_5}(\lambda)$ for a PPT adversary $\mathcal{B}_5$.

Finally, we arrive at $\mathsf{G}_{4.Q.0}$, which is restated as follows.

Game $\mathsf{G}_{4.Q.0}$: It is the same as G_3, except that, at the beginning of the game, the challenger picks a non-zero vector $\mathbf{a}^\perp \in \mathbb{Z}_p^{k+1}$ in the kernel of $\mathbf{A}$ such that $(\mathbf{a}^\perp)^\top \mathbf{A} = \mathbf{0}$. Moreover, when answering *all* $\mathcal{O}_{\text{SIGN}}$ queries, the challenger computes $[\mathbf{d}]_1 := (\mathbf{K}' + \mathbf{K}_0 + \tau\mathbf{K}_1)[\mathbf{c}]_1 + [\gamma\mathbf{a}^\perp]_1$ with $\gamma \leftarrow_\$ \mathbb{Z}_p$ chosen uniformly and independently for each query.

We have the following claim regarding $\Pr_{4.Q.0}[\mathsf{Win}]$.

Claim 6. $\Pr_{4.Q.0}[\mathsf{Win}] \leq 2^{-\Omega(\lambda)}$.

Proof. For the convenience of our analysis, we sample $sk = \mathbf{K} \leftarrow_\$ \mathbb{Z}_p^{(k+1)\times(k+1)}$ equivalently via $\mathbf{K} := \widetilde{\mathbf{K}} + \mathbf{a}^\perp\mathbf{k}^\top$ where $\widetilde{\mathbf{K}} \leftarrow_\$ \mathbb{Z}_p^{(k+1)\times(k+1)}$ and $\mathbf{k} \leftarrow_\$ \mathbb{Z}_p^{k+1}$. Below we analyze the information about $\mathbf{k}$ that $\mathcal{A}$ may obtain in $\mathsf{G}_{4.Q.0}$.

- Firstly, the verification key vk is $[\mathbf{K}^\top\mathbf{A}]_2 = [(\widetilde{\mathbf{K}}^\top + \mathbf{k}(\mathbf{a}^\perp)^\top)\mathbf{A}]_2 = [\widetilde{\mathbf{K}}^\top\mathbf{A}]_2$, thus $\mathbf{k}$ is completely hidden.
- In $\mathcal{O}_{\text{SIGN}}$ queries, the tampered verification key vk' is $[\mathbf{K}'^\top\mathbf{A}]_2 = [(a\mathbf{K}^\top + \mathbf{B}^\top)\mathbf{A}]_2 = [(a(\widetilde{\mathbf{K}}^\top + \mathbf{k}(\mathbf{a}^\perp)^\top) + \mathbf{B}^\top)\mathbf{A}]_2 = [(a\widetilde{\mathbf{K}}^\top + \mathbf{B}^\top)\mathbf{A}]_2$, thus $\mathbf{k}$ is completely hidden. Moreover, due to the game change in $\mathsf{G}_{4.Q.0}$, we have $[\mathbf{d}]_1 = (\mathbf{K}' + \mathbf{K}_0 + \tau\mathbf{K}_1)[\mathbf{c}]_1 + [\gamma\mathbf{a}^\perp]_1 = (a\mathbf{K} + \mathbf{B} + \mathbf{K}_0 + \tau\mathbf{K}_1)[\mathbf{c}]_1 + [\gamma\mathbf{a}^\perp]_1 = (a(\widetilde{\mathbf{K}} + \mathbf{a}^\perp\mathbf{k}^\top) + \mathbf{B} + \mathbf{K}_0 + \tau\mathbf{K}_1)[\mathbf{c}]_1 + [\gamma\mathbf{a}^\perp]_1 = (a\widetilde{\mathbf{K}} + \mathbf{B} + \mathbf{K}_0 + \tau\mathbf{K}_1)[\mathbf{c}]_1 + [a\mathbf{a}^\perp\mathbf{k}^\top\mathbf{c} + \gamma\mathbf{a}^\perp]_1$. Since $\gamma \leftarrow_\$ \mathbb{Z}_p$, the term $\gamma\mathbf{a}^\perp$ perfectly hides $a\mathbf{a}^\perp\mathbf{k}^\top\mathbf{c} = (a\mathbf{k}^\top\mathbf{c})\mathbf{a}^\perp$. Consequently, $\mathbf{k}$ is also completely hidden.
- From $\mathcal{O}_{\text{LEAK}}$ queries, $\mathcal{A}$ obtains at most κ bits information $L(sk) = L(\mathbf{K}) = L(\widetilde{\mathbf{K}} + \mathbf{a}^\perp\mathbf{k}^\top)$ about sk, and also about $\mathbf{k}$.

Overall, the information about $\mathbf{k}$ that $\mathcal{A}$ learns in $\mathsf{G}_{4.Q.0}$ is at most κ bits.

For Win to occur, $\mathcal{A}$'s forgery $(m^*, \sigma^* = ([\mathbf{c}^*]_1, [\mathbf{d}^*]_1))$ should satisfy $(m^*, \sigma^*) \notin \mathcal{Q}_{\mathsf{id}}$, $[\mathbf{c}^*]_1 \neq [\mathbf{0}]_1$, $\tau^* \notin \mathcal{Q}_{\mathsf{tag}}$, and

$$[\mathbf{d}^*]_1 = [(\mathbf{K} + \mathbf{K}_0 + \tau^*\mathbf{K}_1)\mathbf{c}^*]_1 = [(\widetilde{\mathbf{K}} + \mathbf{K}_0 + \tau^*\mathbf{K}_1)\mathbf{c}^* + \mathbf{a}^\perp\mathbf{k}^\top\mathbf{c}^*]_1.$$

Below we argue that such $[\mathbf{d}^*]_1$ has high entropy so that $\mathcal{A}$ can hardly compute it. We first analyze the entropy of $[\mathbf{d}^*]_1$ in the case $\kappa = 0$, i.e., there is no leakage at all. In this case, $\mathbf{k}$ is uniformly distributed over $\mathbb{Z}_p^{k+1}$ from $\mathcal{A}$'s view, and by $[\mathbf{c}^*]_1 \neq [\mathbf{0}]_1$, it follows that $\mathbf{k}^\top\mathbf{c}^*$ is uniformly distributed over $\mathbb{Z}_p$ from $\mathcal{A}$'s view. Therefore, $\mathbf{a}^\perp\mathbf{k}^\top\mathbf{c}^*$ is uniformly distributed over $\mathsf{Span}(\mathbf{a}^\perp) = \{\gamma^*\mathbf{a}^\perp | \gamma^* \in \mathbb{Z}_p\}$ from $\mathcal{A}$'s view, and consequently, such $[\mathbf{d}^*]_1$ has $\log p$ bits of entropy from $\mathcal{A}$'s view. Next, we analyze the entropy of $[\mathbf{d}^*]_1$ for any $\kappa \leq \log p - \Omega(\lambda)$. Even in the presence of κ bits leakage information, $[\mathbf{d}^*]_1$ still has entropy at least $\log p - \kappa \geq \Omega(\lambda)$ bits from $\mathcal{A}$'s view. Consequently, $\mathcal{A}$ can compute such $[\mathbf{d}^*]_1$ with probability at most $2^{-\Omega(\lambda)}$. This shows that $\Pr_{4.Q.0}[\mathsf{Win}] \leq 2^{-\Omega(\lambda)}$ and

Claim 6 follows. ∎

Taking all things together, Theorem 1 follows. □

4 More Efficient PKE with Leakage and Tamper-Resilience

In this section, we present a direct and efficient construction of public-key encryption (PKE) scheme with leakage and tamper-resilience, over asymmetric pairing groups based on the MDDH assumptions.

Concretely, in Subsect. 4.1, we formalize the leakage and tamper-resilient security for PKE, i.e., the *strong* LTR-CCA (sLTR-CCA) security, according to [35], and then in Subsect. 4.2 and Subsect. 4.3, we present our PKE scheme and its security proof, respectively.

4.1 Definition of sLTR-CCA Security

Below we recall the sLTR-CCA security for PKE defined in [35].

Definition 7 (sLTR-CCA Security for PKE). *Let* $\kappa = \kappa(\lambda) \in \mathbb{N}$, *and* $\mathcal{T}$ *be a set of functions from* $\mathcal{SK}$ *to* $\mathcal{SK}$ *where* $\mathcal{SK}$ *is the secret key space. A PKE scheme* $\mathsf{PKE} = (\mathsf{Setup}, \mathsf{Gen}, \mathsf{Enc}, \mathsf{Dec})$ *is* $(\kappa, \mathcal{T})$-sLTR-CCA *secure, if for any PPT adversary* $\mathcal{A}$, *it holds that* $\mathsf{Adv}^{\mathsf{sltr\text{-}cca}}_{\mathsf{PKE},\mathcal{A},\kappa,\mathcal{T}}(\lambda) := \left|\Pr[\mathsf{Exp}^{\mathsf{sltr\text{-}cca}}_{\mathsf{PKE},\mathcal{A},\kappa,\mathcal{T}} \Rightarrow 1] - \frac{1}{2}\right| \leq \mathsf{negl}(\lambda)$, *where the experiment* $\mathsf{Exp}^{\mathsf{sltr\text{-}cca}}_{\mathsf{PKE},\mathcal{A},\kappa,\mathcal{T}}$ *is defined in Fig. 3.*

$\mathsf{Exp}^{\mathsf{sltr\text{-}cca}}_{\mathsf{PKE},\mathcal{A},\kappa,\mathcal{T}}$:	$\mathcal{O}_{\mathrm{DEC}}(T, ct)$:
$\mathsf{pp} \leftarrow_\$ \mathsf{Setup}$, $(pk, sk) \leftarrow_\$ \mathsf{Gen}(\mathsf{pp})$	If $T \notin \mathcal{T}$: Return $\bot$
$\ell := 0$ //Record the leakage length	If $(T, ct) = (\mathsf{id}, ct^*)$: Return $\bot$
$(m_0, m_1, st) \leftarrow_\$ \mathcal{A}^{\mathcal{O}_{\mathrm{DEC}}(\cdot,\cdot), \mathcal{O}_{\mathrm{LEAK}}(\cdot)}(\mathsf{pp}, pk)$	Return $\mathsf{Dec}(T(sk), ct)$
If $\lvert m_0\rvert \neq \lvert m_1\rvert$: Return $\bot$	
$\beta \leftarrow_\$ \{0,1\}$ //Challenge bit	$\mathcal{O}_{\mathrm{LEAK}}(L)$: //at most κ leakage
$ct^* \leftarrow_\$ \mathsf{Enc}(pk, m_\beta)$	If $\ell + \lvert L(sk)\rvert > \kappa$: Return $\bot$
$\beta' \leftarrow_\$ \mathcal{A}^{\mathcal{O}_{\mathrm{DEC}}(\cdot,\cdot)}(st, ct^*)$	$\ell := \ell + \lvert L(sk)\rvert$
If $\beta' = \beta$: Return 1; Else: Return 0	Return $L(sk)$

Fig. 3. The $(\kappa, \mathcal{T})$-sLTR-CCA security experiment $\mathsf{Exp}^{\mathsf{sltr\text{-}cca}}_{\mathsf{PKE},\mathcal{A},\kappa,\mathcal{T}}$ for PKE, where id denotes the identity function and $\lvert L(sk)\rvert$ denotes the bit-length of $L(sk)$.

In the experiment $\mathsf{Exp}^{\mathsf{sltr\text{-}cca}}_{\mathsf{PKE},\mathcal{A},\kappa,\mathcal{T}}$ defined in Fig. 3, it imposes only minimal restrictions on the $\mathcal{O}_{\mathrm{DEC}}$ queries that $\mathcal{A}$ can make, i.e., $(T, ct) \neq (\mathsf{id}, ct^*)$. This is formulated in [35], as a strengthening of the (non-strong) LTR-CCA security defined in [36] where (T, ct) is subject to $ct \neq ct^*$.

4.2 Construction of PKE from MDDH

Now we present our direct construction of sLTR-CCA secure PKE scheme over asymmetric pairing groups based on the MDDH assumptions. Let $\mathcal{D}_k$ be a matrix distribution with $k \in \mathbb{N}$, let $\mathcal{U}_{k+2,k}$ be the uniform distribution, and let $\mathcal{H}$ be a family of collision resistant hash functions from $\{0,1\}^*$ to $\mathbb{Z}_p$. Our PKE scheme $\mathsf{PKE} = (\mathsf{Setup}, \mathsf{Gen}, \mathsf{Enc}, \mathsf{Dec})$ is shown in Fig. 4, where the message space is $\mathcal{M} = \mathbb{G}_1$ and the secret key space is $\mathcal{SK} = \mathbb{Z}_p^{k+2}$. It is routine to check the correctness of PKE.

<u>$\mathsf{pp} \leftarrow_\$ \mathsf{Setup}$:</u>
$\mathsf{gpar} = (\mathbb{G}_1, \mathbb{G}_2, \mathbb{G}_T, p, e, P_1, P_2, P_T) \leftarrow_\$ \mathsf{PGGen}$.
$\mathbf{U} \leftarrow_\$ \mathcal{U}_{k+2,k}$, where $\mathbf{U} \in \mathbb{Z}_p^{(k+2)\times k}$.
$\mathbf{A} \leftarrow_\$ \mathcal{D}_k$, where $\mathbf{A} \in \mathbb{Z}_p^{(k+1)\times k}$.
$\mathbf{K}_0, \mathbf{K}_1 \leftarrow_\$ \mathbb{Z}_p^{(k+1)\times(k+2)}$.
$H \leftarrow_\$ \mathcal{H}$.
Return $\mathsf{pp} := (\mathsf{gpar}, [\mathbf{U}]_1, [\mathbf{K}_0\mathbf{U}]_1, [\mathbf{K}_1\mathbf{U}]_1, [\mathbf{A}]_2, [\mathbf{K}_0^\top \mathbf{A}]_2, [\mathbf{K}_1^\top \mathbf{A}]_2, H)$.

<u>$(pk, sk) \leftarrow_\$ \mathsf{Gen}(\mathsf{pp})$:</u>
$sk := \boxed{\mathbf{k}} \leftarrow_\$ \mathbb{Z}_p^{k+2}$.
$pk := \boxed{[\mathbf{k}^\top \mathbf{U}]_1} \in \mathbb{G}_1^{1\times k}$.
Return (pk, sk).

<u>$ct \leftarrow_\$ \mathsf{Enc}(pk, m \in \mathbb{G}_1)$:</u>
$\mathbf{w} \leftarrow_\$ \mathbb{Z}_p^k$, $[\mathbf{c}]_1 := [\mathbf{U}]_1\mathbf{w} \in \mathbb{G}_1^{k+2}$.
$[d]_1 := \boxed{[\mathbf{k}^\top \mathbf{U}]_1 \mathbf{w}} + m \in \mathbb{G}_1$.
$\tau := H(pk, [\mathbf{c}]_1, [d]_1) \in \mathbb{Z}_p$.
$[\mathbf{e}]_1 := [(\mathbf{K}_0 + \tau \mathbf{K}_1)\mathbf{U}]_1 \mathbf{w} \in \mathbb{G}_1^{k+1}$.
Return $ct := ([\mathbf{c}]_1, [d]_1, [\mathbf{e}]_1) \in \mathbb{G}_1^{k+2} \times \mathbb{G}_1 \times \mathbb{G}_1^{k+1}$.

<u>$m/\perp \leftarrow \mathsf{Dec}(sk, ct)$:</u>
Parse $ct = ([\mathbf{c}]_1, [d]_1, [\mathbf{e}]_1)$.
$pk := \boxed{[\mathbf{k}^\top \mathbf{U}]_1}$.
$\tau := H(pk, [\mathbf{c}]_1, [d]_1) \in \mathbb{Z}_p$.
If $e([\mathbf{c}^\top]_1, [(\mathbf{K}_0^\top + \tau \mathbf{K}_1^\top)\mathbf{A}]_2) = e([\mathbf{e}^\top]_1, [\mathbf{A}]_2)$:
  Return $m := [d]_1 - \boxed{\mathbf{k}^\top [\mathbf{c}]_1} \in \mathbb{G}_1$.
Else: Return $\perp$.

Fig. 4. Construction of $\mathsf{PKE} = (\mathsf{Setup}, \mathsf{Gen}, \mathsf{Enc}, \mathsf{Dec})$ based on MDDH, where the framed boxes and the gray boxes are used to help explain the intuitions behind the construction in Remark 5.

Next, we show its $(\kappa, \mathcal{T}_{\mathsf{aff}})$-sLTR-CCA security under $\kappa \le \log p - \Omega(\lambda)$ bits of leakage information and under the set of affine functions

$$\mathcal{T}_{\mathsf{aff}} = \{T_{(a,\mathbf{b})} : \mathbf{k} \in \mathcal{SK} \mapsto a\mathbf{k} + \mathbf{b} \in \mathcal{SK} \mid a \in \mathbb{Z}_p, \mathbf{b} \in \mathcal{SK}\}. \tag{8}$$

Theorem 2 ($(\kappa, \mathcal{T}_{\mathsf{aff}})$-sLTR-CCA Security of PKE). *Let $\kappa \le \log p - \Omega(\lambda)$ and let $\mathcal{T}_{\mathsf{aff}}$ be the set of affine functions defined in (8). Assume that the $\mathcal{D}_k$-MDDH assumption holds over both $\mathbb{G}_1$ and $\mathbb{G}_2$, and $\mathcal{H}$ is collision-resistant. Then the PKE scheme in Fig. 4 is $(\kappa, \mathcal{T}_{\mathsf{aff}})$-sLTR-CCA secure.*

Concretely, for any PPT adversary $\mathcal{A}$, there exist PPT adversaries $\mathcal{B}_1, \cdots, \mathcal{B}_4$, such that $\mathsf{Adv}^{\mathsf{sltr\text{-}cca}}_{\mathsf{PKE},\mathcal{A},\kappa,\mathcal{T}}(\lambda) \le \mathsf{Adv}^{\mathsf{mddh}}_{\mathcal{D}_k,\mathbb{G}_2,\mathcal{B}_1}(\lambda) + \mathsf{Adv}^{\mathsf{cr}}_{\mathcal{H},\mathcal{B}_2}(\lambda) + \mathsf{Adv}^{\mathsf{mddh}}_{\mathcal{U}_{k+2,k},\mathbb{G}_1,\mathcal{B}_3}(\lambda) + \mathsf{Adv}^{\mathsf{mddh}}_{\mathcal{U}_{k+2,k},\mathbb{G}_1,\mathcal{B}_4}(\lambda) + 2^{-\Omega(\lambda)}$.

The proof of Theorem 2 is postponed to Subsect. 4.3. Before presenting the formal proof, we give a detailed efficiency analysis and explain the main intuitions of our PKE construction in the following two remarks, respectively.

Remark 4 (Efficiency of our PKE). Let $x \cdot \mathbb{G}$ denote x elements in a group $\mathbb{G}$. Our PKE scheme in Fig. 4 is parameterized by the MDDH parameter $k \in \mathbb{N}$, and has public parameter $\mathsf{pp} : (3k^2 + 4k) \cdot \mathbb{G}_1 + (3k^2 + 5k) \cdot \mathbb{G}_2$, public key $pk : k \cdot \mathbb{G}_1$, secret key $sk : (k + 2) \cdot \mathbb{Z}_p$ and ciphertext $ct : (2k + 4) \cdot \mathbb{G}_1$. The decryption involves $(2k^2 + 3k)$ pairing operations.

For $k = 1$, we get an efficient PKE scheme with $\mathsf{pp} : 7 \cdot \mathbb{G}_1 + 8 \cdot \mathbb{G}_2$, public key $pk : 1 \cdot \mathbb{G}_2$, secret key $sk : 3 \cdot \mathbb{Z}_p$ and ciphertext $ct : 6 \cdot \mathbb{G}_1$, and the decryption involves only 5 pairing operations. The resulting PKE scheme is $(\kappa, \mathcal{T}_{\mathsf{aff}})$-sLTR-CCA secure based on the standard SXDH assumption, and supports $\kappa = \log p - \Omega(\lambda)$ bits key leakage. The leakage rate is $\frac{\log p - \Omega(\lambda)}{3 \log p} = \frac{1}{3} - o(1)$ asymptotically as p grows.

Remark 5 (Intuitions of our PKE). Similar to our SIG scheme proposed in Subsect. 3.2, our PKE in Fig. 4 can also be parsed as two components: the terms in framed boxes (which are related to $\mathbf{k}$) and the terms in gray boxes (which are related to $\mathbf{K}_0$ and $\mathbf{K}_1$).

Our first idea is to let $sk = \boxed{\mathbf{k}}$ involve only term of the first component, similar to our SIG scheme, so that we only need to analyze the first component in the leakage and tampering-resilient setting.

Our second idea is to use the first component to mask the message during the generation of ciphertext, while use the second component to prove the well-formedness of ciphertext. More concretely, the first component can be viewed as the CPA-secure variant of the Cramer-Shoup PKE scheme [8] (which corresponds to the $[\mathbf{c}]_1, [d]_1$ in our ct), and the second component can be viewed as the one-time simulation-sound (OTSS) NIZK scheme proposed by Kiltz and Wee [27] (which corresponds to the $[\mathbf{e}]_1$ in our ct and essentially proves that $[\mathbf{c}]_1$ belongs to the linear subspace $\mathsf{Span}([\mathbf{U}]_1)$). The efficiency of our PKE scheme benefits from the efficiency of their schemes. For example, the Kiltz-Wee OTSS-NIZK has a very short proof, which is much shorter than the tSE-NIZK [12] usually required when constructing schemes in the leakage and tamper-resilient setting. However, the sLTR-CCA security of our PKE scheme does not simply follow from the CPA-security of the Cramer-Shoup PKE variant and the OTSS of the Kiltz-Wee NIZK. In fact, our sLTR-CCA security proof also relies on the concrete algebraic structures of the schemes and involves many subtleties similar to the sLTR-CMA security proof of our SIG scheme in Subsect. 3.2, as explained later.

Below we explain the intuitions behind these two components in more detail.

<u>Intuitions behind The First Component.</u> Intuitively, the terms in framed boxes can be viewed as the CPA-secure variant of the Cramer-Shoup PKE scheme [8]:

- the secret key is $sk = \boxed{\mathbf{k}}$ and the public key is $pk = \boxed{[\mathbf{k}^\top \mathbf{U}]_1}$;
- the ciphertext of message $m \in \mathbb{G}_1$ is simply

$$([\mathbf{c}]_1 = [\mathbf{U}]_1 \mathbf{w},\ [d]_1 = \boxed{[\mathbf{k}^\top \mathbf{U}]_1 \mathbf{w}} + m), \quad \text{with } \mathbf{w} \leftarrow_{\$} \mathbb{Z}_p^k, \tag{9}$$

and the decryption simply computes $m = [d]_1 - \boxed{\mathbf{k}^\top [\mathbf{c}]_1}$.

It is worthwhile to briefly recall why this component is CPA secure. Its CPA security proof consists of two main steps.

- Firstly, we change the generation of the challenge ciphertext as follows

$$([\mathbf{c}^*]_1 \leftarrow_{\$} \mathbb{G}_1^{k+2},\ [d^*]_1 = \boxed{[\mathbf{k}^\top \mathbf{c}^*]_1} + m). \tag{10}$$

  Observe that (10) is computationally indistinguishable from (9) under the $\mathcal{U}_{k+2,k}$-MDDH assumption on $[\mathbf{U}]_1$ (which is further implied by the $\mathcal{D}_k$-MDDH assumption according to Lemma 2).
- Since $[\mathbf{c}^*]_1 \leftarrow_{\$} \mathbb{G}_1^{k+2}$ is uniformly chosen, the mapping$\mathbf{k} \mapsto \boxed{[\mathbf{k}^\top \mathbf{c}^*]_1}$ indexed by $[\mathbf{c}^*]_1$ is a universal hash function.

  Note that in the presence of *only* $pk = \boxed{[\mathbf{k}^\top \mathbf{U}]_1}$, where $\mathbf{U} \in \mathbb{Z}_p^{(k+2)\times k}$, $sk = \boxed{\mathbf{k}}$ retains $2\log p$ bits of entropy, so it can be extracted by the universal hash function to yield a (statistically close to) uniform element $\boxed{[\mathbf{k}^\top \mathbf{c}^*]_1} \in \mathbb{G}_1$ in (10) (according to the leftover hash lemma, i.e., Lemma 1). Consequently, the term $\boxed{[\mathbf{k}^\top \mathbf{c}^*]_1}$ in (10) hides the message m.

<u>INSUFFICIENCY OF THE FIRST COMPONENT AND ARISING OF THE SECOND.</u> The first component and its CPA security proof serve as the basis for the security of our PKE. Moreover, the first component is in fact resilient to bounded key leakage, as noted by Naor and Segev in [32]. This is because the above argument for CPA security holds even if the adversary obtains bounded leakage information about $sk = \mathbf{k}$, as long as the amount of leakage κ satisfies $\log p - \kappa \geq \Omega(\lambda)$ so that there are still $2\log p - \kappa \geq \log p + \Omega(\lambda)$ bits entropy left in $\boxed{\mathbf{k}}$ to extract a uniform group element $\boxed{[\mathbf{k}^\top \mathbf{c}^*]_1} \in \mathbb{G}_1$. This shows the CPA security in the *leakage setting* of our PKE.

However, in the sLTR-CCA security experiment, $\mathcal{A}$ has also access to a decryption oracle, through which $\mathcal{A}$ can obtain the decryption results of multiple ciphertexts, under *tampered* secret keys $T_{(a,\mathbf{b})}(sk) = a\mathbf{k} + \mathbf{b}$. So the decryption oracle would leak additional information about $sk = \mathbf{k}$ beyond pk.

To rescue the above arguments, we resort to the terms in gray boxes. Roughly speaking, we use $[(\mathbf{K}_0 + \tau\mathbf{K}_1)\mathbf{U}]_1\mathbf{w}$ as a OTSS-NIZK, as shown in [27], to prove the well-formedness of ciphertexts. This guarantees that the decryption result of a ciphertext $ct = ([\mathbf{c}]_1, [d]_1, [\mathbf{e}]_1)$ is not $\perp$, i.e., $[\mathbf{e}]_1$ satisfies $e([\mathbf{c}^\top]_1, [(\mathbf{K}_0^\top + \tau\mathbf{K}_1^\top)\mathbf{A}]_2) = e([\mathbf{e}^\top]_1, [\mathbf{A}]_2)$, only when one of the following two cases occur:

- **Case 1**: $[\mathbf{c}]_1 \in \mathsf{Span}([\mathbf{U}]_1)$, *or*

- **Case 2**: the tag $\tau = H(pk' = [(a\mathbf{k}+\mathbf{b})^\top \mathbf{U}]_1, [\mathbf{c}]_1, [d]_1)$ is *identical* to the tag $\tau^* = H(pk = [\mathbf{k}^\top \mathbf{U}]_1, [\mathbf{c}^*]_1, [d^*]_1)$ involved in the challenge ciphertext $ct^* = ([\mathbf{c}^*]_1, [d^*]_1, [\mathbf{e}^*]_1)$.

If **Case 1** occurs, i.e., $[\mathbf{c}]_1 = [\mathbf{U}]_1\mathbf{w}$ for some $\mathbf{w} \in \mathbb{Z}_p^k$, then the decryption result under *tampered* secret key $T_{(a,\mathbf{b})}(sk) = a\mathbf{k} + \mathbf{b}$ would be $m = [d]_1 - \boxed{(a\mathbf{k}^\top + \mathbf{b}^\top)[\mathbf{c}]_1} = [d]_1 - \boxed{(a[\mathbf{k}^\top \mathbf{U}]_1\mathbf{w} + \mathbf{b}^\top[\mathbf{c}]_1)}$, which leaks no information about $sk = \mathbf{k}$ beyond $pk = \boxed{[\mathbf{k}^\top \mathbf{U}]_1}$ to $\mathcal{A}$.

However, for all decryption queries made by $\mathcal{A}$, the OTSS property can only ensure *either* **Case 1** *or* **Case 2** occur. So, it is important for us to prove that **Case 2** can hardly occur and it is always **Case 1** that occurs, then we can use the above argument to show that the decryption oracle does not leak any information about sk beyond pk to $\mathcal{A}$.

To show that **Case 2** hardly occurs, we can use similar techniques as the analysis of TagColl in the security proof of our SIG, i.e., dividing **Case 2** into three sub-cases and analyzing them individually to show that they all rarely occur, by utilizing the concrete algebraic structures of our construction, based on the collision resistance of H and on the MDDH assumption.

PUTTING TWO COMPONENTS TOGETHER. Overall, we carefully design our PKE construction so that the two components interplay with each other properly and help us to achieve sLTR-CCA security: the terms $[(\mathbf{K}_0 + \tau\mathbf{K}_1)\mathbf{U}]_1\mathbf{w}$ in the second component ensure that the decryption oracle under *tampered* secret keys do not leak any information about $sk = \boxed{\mathbf{k}}$ beyond pk to the adversary, so that the decryption oracle is of no use to the adversary, and then the sLTR-CCA security of our PKE follows from the CPA security of the first component in the *key leakage* setting.

4.3 Proof of Theorem 2

Now we present the formal proof of Theorem 2. Let $\mathcal{A}$ be any PPT adversary against the $(\kappa, \mathcal{T}_{\mathsf{aff}})$-sLTR-CCA security of PKE, where $\mathcal{A}$ makes Q times of $\mathcal{O}_{\mathrm{DEC}}$ queries. We prove the theorem via a sequence of games $\mathsf{G}_0 - \mathsf{G}_6$, where G_0 is the $(\kappa, \mathcal{T}_{\mathsf{aff}})$-sLTR-CCA experiment, and in G_6, $\mathcal{A}$ has no advantage. A brief description of differences between adjacent games is summarized in Table 2.

Game G_0: This is the $(\kappa, \mathcal{T}_{\mathsf{aff}})$-sLTR-CCA experiment (cf. Fig. 3). Let Win denote the event that $\beta' = \beta$. By definition, $\mathsf{Adv}^{\mathsf{sltr\text{-}cca}}_{\mathsf{PKE},\mathcal{A},\kappa,\mathcal{T}}(\lambda) = |\Pr_0[\mathsf{Win}] - \frac{1}{2}|$.

Let $\mathsf{pp} = (\mathsf{gpar}, [\mathbf{U}]_1, [\mathbf{K}_0\mathbf{U}]_1, [\mathbf{K}_1\mathbf{U}]_1, [\mathbf{A}]_2, [\mathbf{K}_0^\top\mathbf{A}]_2, [\mathbf{K}_1^\top\mathbf{A}]_2, H)$ and $(pk = [\mathbf{k}^\top\mathbf{U}]_1, sk = \mathbf{k})$. In this game, the challenge ciphertext ct^* that encrypts m_β is generated as follows. The challenger samples $\mathbf{w}^* \leftarrow_\$ \mathbb{Z}_p^k$, computes $[\mathbf{c}^*]_1 := [\mathbf{U}]_1\mathbf{w}^*$, $[d^*]_1 := [\mathbf{k}^\top\mathbf{U}]_1\mathbf{w}^* + m_\beta$, $\tau^* := H(pk, [\mathbf{c}^*]_1, [d^*]_1) \in \mathbb{Z}_p$, $[\mathbf{e}^*]_1 := [(\mathbf{K}_0 + \tau^*\mathbf{K}_1)\mathbf{U}]_1\mathbf{w}^*$, and returns the challenge ciphertext $ct^* := ([\mathbf{c}^*]_1, [d^*]_1, [\mathbf{e}^*]_1)$ to $\mathcal{A}$. Upon an $\mathcal{O}_{\mathrm{DEC}}$ query $(T_{(a,\mathbf{b})} \in \mathcal{T}_{\mathsf{aff}}, ct = ([\mathbf{c}]_1, [d]_1, [\mathbf{e}]_1))$, the challenger computes the tampered key $sk' = \mathbf{k}' := T_{(a,\mathbf{b})}(sk) = a\mathbf{k} + \mathbf{b}$ and $pk' := [\mathbf{k}'^\top\mathbf{U}]_1$,

Table 2. Brief Description of Games G_0 – G_6 for the $(\kappa, \mathcal{T}_{\mathsf{aff}})$-sLTR-CCA security proof of PKE, where the differences between adjacent games are highlighted in gray boxes. Here column "Challenge ciphertext ct^*" suggests how the challenge ciphertext $ct^* = ([\mathbf{c}^*]_1, [d^*]_1, [\mathbf{e}^*]_1)$ is generated: sub-column "$[\mathbf{c}^*]_1 \leftarrow_\$$ " refers to the space from which $[\mathbf{c}^*]_1$ is chosen; sub-columns "$[d^*]_1 =$" and "$[\mathbf{e}^*]_1 =$" show the computation of $[d^*]_1$ and $[\mathbf{e}^*]_1$ respectively, where $\tau^* := H(pk, [\mathbf{c}^*]_1, [d^*]_1)$. Column "$\mathcal{O}_{\mathrm{DEC}}$'s additional check" describes the additional check made by $\mathcal{O}_{\mathrm{DEC}}$ upon a decryption query $(T_{(a,\mathbf{b})} \in \mathcal{T}_{\mathsf{aff}}, ct = ([\mathbf{c}]_1, [d]_1, [\mathbf{e}]_1))$, besides the routine check $(T_{(a,\mathbf{b})}, ct) \neq (\mathsf{id}, ct^*) \wedge e([\mathbf{c}^\top]_1, [(\mathbf{K}_0^\top + \tau\mathbf{K}_1^\top)\mathbf{A}]_2) = e([\mathbf{e}^\top]_1, [\mathbf{A}]_2)$; $\mathcal{O}_{\mathrm{DEC}}$ outputs $\perp$ if the check fails. Column "$\mathcal{O}_{\mathrm{LEAK}}$" shows the output returned by $\mathcal{O}_{\mathrm{LEAK}}$. Recall that $\mathcal{A}$ is not allowed to query $\mathcal{O}_{\mathrm{LEAK}}$ after receiving the challenge ciphertext.

	Challenge ciphertext ct^*			$\mathcal{O}_{\mathrm{DEC}}(T_{(a,\mathbf{b})} \in \mathcal{T}_{\mathsf{aff}}, ct = ([\mathbf{c}]_1, [d]_1, [\mathbf{e}]_1))$'s additional check	$\mathcal{O}_{\mathrm{LEAK}}(L)$	Justification/Assumption
	$[\mathbf{c}^*]_1 \leftarrow_\$$	$[d^*]_1 =$	$[\mathbf{e}^*]_1 =$			
G_0	$\mathsf{Span}([\mathbf{U}]_1)$	$[\mathbf{k}^\top \mathbf{U}]_1 \mathbf{w}^* + m_\beta$	$[(\mathbf{K}_0 + \tau^*\mathbf{K}_1)\mathbf{U}]_1 \mathbf{w}^*$		$L(sk)$	$(\kappa, \mathcal{T}_{\mathsf{aff}})$-sLTR-CCA experiment
G_1	$\mathsf{Span}([\mathbf{U}]_1)$	$\mathbf{k}^\top [\mathbf{c}^*]_1 + m_\beta$	$(\mathbf{K}_0 + \tau^*\mathbf{K}_1)[\mathbf{c}^*]_1$		$L(sk)$	$\mathsf{G}_0 = \mathsf{G}_1$
G_2	$\mathsf{Span}([\mathbf{U}]_1)$	$\mathbf{k}^\top [\mathbf{c}^*]_1 + m_\beta$	$(\mathbf{K}_0 + \tau^*\mathbf{K}_1)[\mathbf{c}^*]_1$	$[\mathbf{e}]_1 = [(\mathbf{K}_0 + \tau\mathbf{K}_1)\mathbf{c}]_1$	$L(sk)$	$\mathcal{D}_k$-KerMDH on $[\mathbf{A}]_2$
G_3	$\mathsf{Span}([\mathbf{U}]_1)$	$\mathbf{k}^\top [\mathbf{c}^*]_1 + m_\beta$	$(\mathbf{K}_0 + \tau^*\mathbf{K}_1)[\mathbf{c}^*]_1$	$[\mathbf{e}]_1 = [(\mathbf{K}_0 + \tau\mathbf{K}_1)\mathbf{c}]_1$, $\tau \neq \tau^*$	$L(sk)$	Collision-resistance of $\mathcal{H}$ & $\mathcal{U}_{k+2,k}$-KerMDH on $[\mathbf{U}]_1$
G_4	$\mathbb{G}_1^{k+2}$	$\mathbf{k}^\top [\mathbf{c}^*]_1 + m_\beta$	$(\mathbf{K}_0 + \tau^*\mathbf{K}_1)[\mathbf{c}^*]_1$	$[\mathbf{e}]_1 = [(\mathbf{K}_0 + \tau\mathbf{K}_1)\mathbf{c}]_1, \tau \neq \tau^*$	$L(sk)$	$\mathcal{U}_{k+2,k}$-MDDH on $[\mathbf{U}]_1$
G_5	$\mathbb{G}_1^{k+2}$	$\mathbf{k}^\top [\mathbf{c}^*]_1 + m_\beta$	$(\mathbf{K}_0 + \tau^*\mathbf{K}_1)[\mathbf{c}^*]_1$	$[\mathbf{e}]_1 = [(\mathbf{K}_0 + \tau\mathbf{K}_1)\mathbf{c}]_1, \tau \neq \tau^*$, $[\mathbf{c}]_1 \in \mathsf{Span}([\mathbf{U}]_1)$	$L(sk)$	Statistical arguments using the leftover entropy in $\mathbf{K}_0, \mathbf{K}_1$
G_6	$\mathbb{G}_1^{k+2}$	random	$(\mathbf{K}_0 + \tau^*\mathbf{K}_1)[\mathbf{c}^*]_1$	$[\mathbf{e}]_1 = [(\mathbf{K}_0 + \tau\mathbf{K}_1)\mathbf{c}]_1, \tau \neq \tau^*, [\mathbf{c}]_1 \in \mathsf{Span}([\mathbf{U}]_1)$	$L(sk)$	Statistical arguments using the leftover entropy in $\mathbf{K}$ $\Pr[\mathsf{Win}] = \frac{1}{2}$ in G_6

computes $\tau := H(pk', [\mathbf{c}]_1, [d]_1)$, and checks whether $(T_{(a,\mathbf{b})}, ct) \neq (\mathsf{id}, ct^*) \wedge e([\mathbf{c}^\top]_1, [(\mathbf{K}_0^\top + \tau\mathbf{K}_1^\top)\mathbf{A}]_2) = e([\mathbf{e}^\top]_1, [\mathbf{A}]_2)$ holds. If the check passes, the challenger computes $m := [d]_1 - \mathbf{k}'^\top [\mathbf{c}]_1$ using the tampered key $sk' = \mathbf{k}'$ and returns m to $\mathcal{A}$; otherwise, the challenger returns $\perp$. For an $\mathcal{O}_{\mathrm{LEAK}}$ query L, the challenger returns $L(sk)$ to $\mathcal{A}$ if the total leakage length is bounded by κ. Recall that $\mathcal{A}$ can query $\mathcal{O}_{\mathrm{DEC}}$ throughout the game, but is only allowed to query $\mathcal{O}_{\mathrm{LEAK}}$ before receiving the challenge ciphertext.

Game G_1: It is the same as G_0, except that, when generating the challenge ciphertext ct^*, the challenger computes $[d^*]_1 := \mathbf{k}^\top[\mathbf{c}^*]_1 + m_\beta$ and $[\mathbf{e}^*]_1 := (\mathbf{K}_0 + \tau^*\mathbf{K}_1)[\mathbf{c}^*]_1$ directly from $[\mathbf{c}^*]_1$, m_β, τ^* and $(\mathbf{k}, \mathbf{K}_0, \mathbf{K}_1)$, without using the vector $\mathbf{w}^*$ for $[\mathbf{c}^*]_1 = [\mathbf{U}]_1\mathbf{w}^*$.

Since $[\mathbf{c}^*]_1 = [\mathbf{U}]_1\mathbf{w}^*$, the changes are conceptual and $\Pr_0[\mathsf{Win}] = \Pr_1[\mathsf{Win}]$.

Game G_2: It is the same as G_1, except that, when answering $\mathcal{O}_{\mathrm{DEC}}(T_{(a,\mathbf{b})} \in \mathcal{T}_{\mathsf{aff}}, ct = ([\mathbf{c}]_1, [d]_1, [\mathbf{e}]_1))$, the challenger returns $\perp$ to $\mathcal{A}$ directly if the following check fails:

$$(T_{(a,\mathbf{b})}, ct) \neq (\mathsf{id}, ct^*) \ \wedge \ [\mathbf{e}]_1 = [(\mathbf{K}_0 + \tau\mathbf{K}_1)\mathbf{c}]_1 .$$

Claim 7. $\left|\Pr_1[\mathsf{Win}] - \Pr_2[\mathsf{Win}]\right| \leq \mathsf{Adv}^{\mathsf{mddh}}_{\mathcal{D}_k, \mathbb{G}_2, \mathcal{B}_1}(\lambda) + 1/(p-1)$ *for a PPT adversary* $\mathcal{B}_1$ *against the* $\mathcal{D}_k$*-MDDH assumption on* $[\mathbf{A}]_2$.

Proof sketch. The proof is similar to the proof of Claim 1. Clearly, G_2 is identical to G_1 unless that $\mathcal{A}$ ever makes a $\mathcal{O}_{\mathrm{DEC}}$ query such that

$$e([\mathbf{c}^\top]_1, [(\mathbf{K}_0^\top + \tau\mathbf{K}_1^\top)\mathbf{A}]_2) = e([\mathbf{e}^\top]_1, [\mathbf{A}]_2) \ \wedge \ [\mathbf{e}]_1 \neq [(\mathbf{K}_0 + \tau\mathbf{K}_1)\mathbf{c}]_1.$$

We denote such an event by DecBad. Similar to the proof of Claim 1, DecBad rarely happens under the $\mathcal{D}_k$-KerMDH assumption on $[\mathbf{A}]_2$ (which is further implied by the $\mathcal{D}_k$-MDDH assumption on $[\mathbf{A}]_2$ according to Lemma 3). Consequently, Claim 7 follows. ∎

Game G_3: It is the same as G_3, except that, when answering $\mathcal{O}_{\text{DEC}}(T_{(a,\mathbf{b})} \in \mathcal{T}_{\mathsf{aff}}, ct = ([\mathbf{c}]_1, [d]_1, [\mathbf{e}]_1))$, the challenger now returns $\perp$ to $\mathcal{A}$ directly if the following check fails:

$$(T_{(a,\mathbf{b})}, ct) \neq (\mathsf{id}, ct^*) \ \wedge \ [\mathbf{e}]_1 = [(\mathbf{K}_0 + \tau\mathbf{K}_1)\mathbf{c}]_1 \ \wedge \ \tau \neq \tau^* ,$$

where $\tau := H(pk', [\mathbf{c}]_1, [d]_1)$ and $\tau^* := H(pk, [\mathbf{c}^*]_1, [d^*]_1)$ are the tags involved in this $\mathcal{O}_{\text{DEC}}$ query and in the challenge ciphertext ct^*, respectively.

Claim 8. $\left|\Pr_2[\mathsf{Win}] - \Pr_3[\mathsf{Win}]\right| \leq \mathsf{Adv}^{\mathsf{cr}}_{\mathcal{H},\mathcal{B}_2}(\lambda) + \mathsf{Adv}^{\mathsf{mddh}}_{\mathcal{U}_{k+2,k},\mathbb{G}_1,\mathcal{B}_3}(\lambda) + 1/(p-1) + 2^{-\Omega(\lambda)}$ *for PPT adversaries $\mathcal{B}_2$ against the collision-resistance of $\mathcal{H}$ and $\mathcal{B}_3$ against the $\mathcal{U}_{k+2,k}$-MDDH assumption on $[\mathbf{U}]_1$.*

Proof sketch. The proof is similar to the proof of Claim 2. Clearly, G_3 is identical to G_2 unless that $\mathcal{A}$ ever makes a $\mathcal{O}_{\text{DEC}}$ query such that

$$(T_{(a,\mathbf{b})}, ct) \neq (\mathsf{id}, ct^*) \ \wedge \ [\mathbf{e}]_1 = [(\mathbf{K}_0 + \tau\mathbf{K}_1)\mathbf{c}]_1 \ \wedge \ \tau = \tau^*.$$

We denote such an event by $\mathsf{TagColl}$. Similar to the proof of Claim 2, we can divide the event $\mathsf{TagColl}$ into three cases, analyze them individually and finally obtain Claim 8. ∎

Game G_4: It is the same as G_2, except that, when generating the challenge ciphertext ct^*, the challenger samples $[\mathbf{c}^*]_1 \leftarrow_{\$} \mathbb{G}_1^{k+2}$ uniformly at random, instead of computing $[\mathbf{c}^*]_1 := [\mathbf{U}]_1\mathbf{w}^*$ with $\mathbf{w}^* \leftarrow_{\$} \mathbb{Z}_p^k$.

By the $\mathcal{U}_{k+2,k}$-MDDH assumption on $[\mathbf{U}]_1$, G_3 and G_4 are computationally indistinguishable, and we have $\left|\Pr_3[\mathsf{Win}] - \Pr_4[\mathsf{Win}]\right| \leq \mathsf{Adv}^{\mathsf{mddh}}_{\mathcal{U}_{k+2,k},\mathbb{G}_1,\mathcal{B}_4}(\lambda)$ for a PPT adversary $\mathcal{B}_4$.

Game G_5: It is the same as G_4, except that, when answering $\mathcal{O}_{\text{DEC}}(T_{(a,\mathbf{b})} \in \mathcal{T}_{\mathsf{aff}}, ct = ([\mathbf{c}]_1, [d]_1, [\mathbf{e}]_1))$, the challenger now returns $\perp$ to $\mathcal{A}$ directly if the following check fails:

$$(T_{(a,\mathbf{b})}, ct) \neq (\mathsf{id}, ct^*) \ \wedge \ [\mathbf{e}]_1 = [(\mathbf{K}_0 + \tau\mathbf{K}_1)\mathbf{c}]_1 \ \wedge \ \tau \neq \tau^* \ \wedge \ [\mathbf{c}]_1 \in \mathsf{Span}([\mathbf{U}]_1) .$$

Claim 9. $\left|\Pr_4[\mathsf{Win}] - \Pr_5[\mathsf{Win}]\right| \leq Q/p.$

Proof sketch. The proof is similar to the proof of Claim 3. Clearly, G_5 is identical to G_4 unless that $\mathcal{A}$ ever makes a $\mathcal{O}_{\text{DEC}}$ query such that

$$(T_{(a,\mathbf{b})}, ct) \neq (\mathsf{id}, ct^*) \ \wedge \ [\mathbf{e}]_1 = [(\mathbf{K}_0 + \tau\mathbf{K}_1)\mathbf{c}]_1 \ \wedge \ \tau \neq \tau^* \ \wedge \ [\mathbf{c}]_1 \notin \mathsf{Span}([\mathbf{U}]_1).$$

We denote such an event by CBad. Similar to the proof of Claim 3, we can analyze the information about $\mathbf{K}_0$ and $\mathbf{K}_1$ that $\mathcal{A}$ may obtain in G_5, and use the leftover entropy in $\mathbf{K}_0$ and $\mathbf{K}_1$ to show that CBad occurs in a particular $\mathcal{O}_{\text{DEC}}$ query with probability at most $1/p$. Consequently, by a union bound over Q times of $\mathcal{O}_{\text{DEC}}$ queries, Claim 9 follows. ∎

Game G_6: It is the same as G_5, except that, when generating the challenge ciphertext ct^*, the challenger samples $[d^*]_1 \leftarrow_\$ \mathbb{G}_1$ uniformly at random, instead of computing $[d^*]_1 := \mathbf{k}^\top[\mathbf{c}^*]_1 + m_\beta$.

Claim 10. $\left|\Pr_5[\mathsf{Win}] - \Pr_6[\mathsf{Win}]\right| \leq 2^{-\Omega(\lambda)}$.

Proof. We will show that the $[d^*]_1 := \mathbf{k}^\top[\mathbf{c}^*]_1 + m_\beta$ in G_5 is statistically close to the $[d^*]_1 \leftarrow_\$ \mathbb{G}_1$ in G_6, with statistical distance at most $2^{-\Omega(\lambda)}$.

For the convenience of our analysis, we sample $sk = \mathbf{k} \leftarrow_\$ \mathbb{Z}_p^{k+2}$ equivalently via $\mathbf{k} := \widetilde{\mathbf{k}} + \mathbf{U}^\perp \cdot \mathbf{r}$, where $\widetilde{\mathbf{k}} \leftarrow_\$ \mathbb{Z}_p^{k+2}$ and $\mathbf{r} \leftarrow_\$ \mathbb{Z}_p^2$ are uniformly sampled, and $\mathbf{U}^\perp \in \mathbb{Z}_p^{(k+2)\times 2}$ is a non-zero vector in the kernel of $\mathbf{U} \in \mathbb{Z}_p^{(k+2)\times k}$ such that $(\mathbf{U}^\perp)^\top \cdot \mathbf{U} = \mathbf{0}$. Below we analyze the information about $\mathbf{r}$ that $\mathcal{A}$ may obtain in G_5 (except for the challenge ciphertext ct^*).

- Firstly, the public key pk is $[\mathbf{k}^\top\mathbf{U}]_1 = [(\widetilde{\mathbf{k}}^\top + \mathbf{r}^\top \cdot (\mathbf{U}^\perp)^\top)\mathbf{U}]_1 = [\widetilde{\mathbf{k}}^\top\mathbf{U}]_1$, thus $\mathbf{r}$ is completely hidden.
- In $\mathcal{O}_{\text{DEC}}$ queries, the tampered public key pk' is $[\mathbf{k}'^\top\mathbf{U}]_1 = [(a\mathbf{k}^\top + \mathbf{b}^\top)\mathbf{U}]_1 = [(a(\widetilde{\mathbf{k}}^\top + \mathbf{r}^\top \cdot (\mathbf{U}^\perp)^\top) + \mathbf{b}^\top)\mathbf{U}]_1 = [(a\widetilde{\mathbf{k}}^\top + \mathbf{b}^\top)\mathbf{U}]_1$, thus $\mathbf{r}$ is completely hidden. Moreover, due to the game change in G_5, the challenger will not output $m := [d]_1 - \mathbf{k}'^\top[\mathbf{c}]_1$ unless $[\mathbf{c}]_1 \in \mathsf{Span}([\mathbf{U}]_1)$, and for $[\mathbf{c}]_1 \in \mathsf{Span}([\mathbf{U}]_1)$, we have $m = [d]_1 - \mathbf{k}'^\top[\mathbf{c}]_1 = [d]_1 - (a\mathbf{k}^\top + \mathbf{b}^\top)[\mathbf{c}]_1 = [d]_1 - \big(a(\widetilde{\mathbf{k}}^\top + \mathbf{r}^\top \cdot (\mathbf{U}^\perp)^\top) + \mathbf{b}^\top\big)[\mathbf{c}]_1 = [d]_1 - (a\widetilde{\mathbf{k}}^\top + \mathbf{b}^\top)[\mathbf{c}]_1$, thus $\mathbf{r}$ is also completely hidden.
- From $\mathcal{O}_{\text{LEAK}}$ queries, $\mathcal{A}$ obtains at most κ bits information $L(sk) = L(\mathbf{k}) = L(\widetilde{\mathbf{k}} + \mathbf{U}^\perp \cdot \mathbf{r})$ about sk, and also about $\mathbf{r}$.

Overall, the information about $\mathbf{r}$ that $\mathcal{A}$ learns in G_5 (except for the challenge ciphertext ct^*) is at most κ bits. Thus, there are still $2\log p - \kappa = \log p + (\log p - \kappa) \geq \log p + \Omega(\lambda)$ bits of entropy left in $\mathbf{r}$, and also in $sk = \mathbf{k} = \widetilde{\mathbf{k}} + \mathbf{U}^\perp \cdot \mathbf{r}$.

On the other hand, for the challenge ciphertext ct^*, note that $[\mathbf{c}^*]_1$ is uniformly chosen from $\mathbb{G}_1^{k+2}$ due to the game change in G_4, thus the mapping $\mathbf{k} \mapsto \mathbf{k}^\top[\mathbf{c}^*]_1$ indexed by $[\mathbf{c}^*]_1$ is a universal hash function. By the leftover hash lemma (i.e., Lemma 1), $\mathbf{k}^\top[\mathbf{c}^*]_1$ is statistically close to the uniform distribution over $\mathbb{G}_1$, with statistical distance at most $\sqrt{p \cdot 2^{-(\log p + \Omega(\lambda))}} = \sqrt{2^{-\Omega(\lambda)}}$, which is also $2^{-\Omega(\lambda)}$. Consequently, the $[d^*]_1 := \mathbf{k}^\top[\mathbf{c}^*]_1 + m_\beta$ in G_5 is also statistically close to the uniform distribution, with statistical distance at most $2^{-\Omega(\lambda)}$. Therefore, G_5 and G_6 are statistically indistinguishable to $\mathcal{A}$, and Claim 10 follows. ∎

Finally in G_6, $[d^*]_1$ is uniformly chosen regardless of the value of β, thus the challenge bit β is completely hidden to $\mathcal{A}$. Then $\Pr_6[\mathsf{Win}] = \frac{1}{2}$.

Taking all things together, and noting that by Lemma 2, the $\mathcal{U}_{k+2,k}$-MDDH assumption is implied by the $\mathcal{D}_k$-MDDH assumption, Theorem 2 follows. □

Acknowledgment. We would like to thank the reviewers for their valuable comments. Shuai Han and Shengli Liu were partially supported by National Natural Science Foundation of China (Grant Nos. 62372292, 61925207), the National Key R&D Program of China under Grant 2022YFB2701500, Guangdong Major Project of Basic and Applied Basic Research (2019B030302008), and Young Elite Scientists Sponsorship Program by China Association for Science and Technology (YESS20200185). Dawu Gu was partially supported by the National Key R&D Program of China under Grant 2020YFA0712302.

References

1. Akavia, A., Goldwasser, S., Vaikuntanathan, V.: Simultaneous hardcore bits and cryptography against memory attacks. In: Reingold, O. (ed.) TCC 2009. LNCS, vol. 5444, pp. 474–495. Springer, Heidelberg (2009). https://doi.org/10.1007/978-3-642-00457-5_28
2. An, J.H., Dodis, Y., Rabin, T.: On the security of joint signature and encryption. In: Knudsen, L.R. (ed.) EUROCRYPT 2002. LNCS, vol. 2332, pp. 83–107. Springer, Heidelberg (2002). https://doi.org/10.1007/3-540-46035-7_6
3. Bellare, M., Kohno, T.: A theoretical treatment of related-key attacks: RKA-PRPs, RKA-PRFs, and applications. In: Biham, E. (ed.) EUROCRYPT 2003. LNCS, vol. 2656, pp. 491–506. Springer, Heidelberg (2003). https://doi.org/10.1007/3-540-39200-9_31
4. Bellare, M., Namprempre, C.: Authenticated encryption: relations among notions and analysis of the generic composition paradigm. In: Okamoto, T. (ed.) ASIACRYPT 2000. LNCS, vol. 1976, pp. 531–545. Springer, Heidelberg (2000). https://doi.org/10.1007/3-540-44448-3_41
5. Bellare, M., Rogaway, P.: Entity authentication and key distribution. In: Stinson, D.R. (ed.) CRYPTO 1993. LNCS, vol. 773, pp. 232–249. Springer, Heidelberg (1994). https://doi.org/10.1007/3-540-48329-2_21
6. Biham, E., Shamir, A.: Differential fault analysis of secret key cryptosystems. In: Kaliski, B.S. (ed.) CRYPTO 1997. LNCS, vol. 1294, pp. 513–525. Springer, Heidelberg (1997). https://doi.org/10.1007/BFb0052259
7. Chakraborty, S., Rangan, C.P.: Public key encryption resilient to post-challenge leakage and tampering attacks. In: Matsui, M. (ed.) CT-RSA 2019. LNCS, vol. 11405, pp. 23–43. Springer, Cham (2019). https://doi.org/10.1007/978-3-030-12612-4_2
8. Cramer, R., Shoup, V.: A practical public key cryptosystem provably secure against adaptive chosen ciphertext attack. In: Krawczyk, H. (ed.) CRYPTO 1998. LNCS, vol. 1462, pp. 13–25. Springer, Heidelberg (1998). https://doi.org/10.1007/BFb0055717
9. Cramer, R., Shoup, V.: Universal hash proofs and a paradigm for adaptive chosen ciphertext secure public-key encryption. In: Knudsen, L.R. (ed.) EUROCRYPT 2002. LNCS, vol. 2332, pp. 45–64. Springer, Heidelberg (2002). https://doi.org/10.1007/3-540-46035-7_4
10. Damgård, I., Faust, S., Mukherjee, P., Venturi, D.: Bounded tamper resilience: how to go beyond the algebraic barrier. In: Sako, K., Sarkar, P. (eds.) ASIACRYPT 2013, Part II. LNCS, vol. 8270, pp. 140–160. Springer, Heidelberg (2013). https://doi.org/10.1007/978-3-642-42045-0_8

11. Diemert, D., Gellert, K., Jager, T., Lyu, L.: More efficient digital signatures with tight multi-user security. In: Garay, J.A. (ed.) PKC 2021, Part II. LNCS, vol. 12711, pp. 1–31. Springer, Cham (2021). https://doi.org/10.1007/978-3-030-75248-4_1
12. Dodis, Y., Haralambiev, K., López-Alt, A., Wichs, D.: Efficient public-key cryptography in the presence of key leakage. In: Abe, M. (ed.) ASIACRYPT 2010. LNCS, vol. 6477, pp. 613–631. Springer, Heidelberg (2010). https://doi.org/10.1007/978-3-642-17373-8_35
13. Dziembowski, S., Pietrzak, K., Wichs, D.: Non-malleable codes. In: Yao, A.C.C. (ed.) ICS 2010. pp. 434–452. Tsinghua University Press, January 2010
14. Escala, A., Herold, G., Kiltz, E., Ràfols, C., Villar, J.: An algebraic framework for Diffie-Hellman assumptions. In: Canetti, R., Garay, J.A. (eds.) CRYPTO 2013, Part II. LNCS, vol. 8043, pp. 129–147. Springer, Heidelberg (2013). https://doi.org/10.1007/978-3-642-40084-1_8
15. Faonio, A., Venturi, D.: Efficient public-key cryptography with bounded leakage and tamper resilience. In: Cheon, J.H., Takagi, T. (eds.) ASIACRYPT 2016, Part I. LNCS, vol. 10031, pp. 877–907. Springer, Heidelberg (2016). https://doi.org/10.1007/978-3-662-53887-6_32
16. Faust, S., Mukherjee, P., Nielsen, J.B., Venturi, D.: Continuous non-malleable codes. In: Lindell, Y. (ed.) TCC 2014. LNCS, vol. 8349, pp. 465–488. Springer, Heidelberg (2014). https://doi.org/10.1007/978-3-642-54242-8_20
17. Fiat, A., Shamir, A.: How to prove yourself: practical solutions to identification and signature problems. In: Odlyzko, A.M. (ed.) CRYPTO 1986. LNCS, vol. 263, pp. 186–194. Springer, Heidelberg (1987). https://doi.org/10.1007/3-540-47721-7_12
18. Fujisaki, E., Xagawa, K.: Public-key cryptosystems resilient to continuous tampering and leakage of arbitrary functions. In: Cheon, J.H., Takagi, T. (eds.) ASIACRYPT 2016, Part I. LNCS, vol. 10031, pp. 908–938. Springer, Heidelberg (2016). https://doi.org/10.1007/978-3-662-53887-6_33
19. Gandolfi, K., Mourtel, C., Olivier, F.: Electromagnetic analysis: concrete results. In: Koç, Ç.K., Naccache, D., Paar, C. (eds.) CHES 2001. LNCS, vol. 2162, pp. 251–261. Springer, Heidelberg (2001). https://doi.org/10.1007/3-540-44709-1_21
20. Gay, R., Hofheinz, D., Kiltz, E., Wee, H.: Tightly CCA-secure encryption without pairings. In: Fischlin, M., Coron, J.-S. (eds.) EUROCRYPT 2016, Part I. LNCS, vol. 9665, pp. 1–27. Springer, Heidelberg (2016). https://doi.org/10.1007/978-3-662-49890-3_1
21. Gennaro, R., Lysyanskaya, A., Malkin, T., Micali, S., Rabin, T.: Algorithmic tamper-proof (ATP) security: theoretical foundations for security against hardware tampering. In: Naor, M. (ed.) TCC 2004. LNCS, vol. 2951, pp. 258–277. Springer, Heidelberg (2004). https://doi.org/10.1007/978-3-540-24638-1_15
22. Groth, J., Sahai, A.: Efficient non-interactive proof systems for bilinear groups. In: Smart, N. (ed.) EUROCRYPT 2008. LNCS, vol. 4965, pp. 415–432. Springer, Heidelberg (2008). https://doi.org/10.1007/978-3-540-78967-3_24
23. Halderman, J.A., et al.: Lest we remember: cold boot attacks on encryption keys. In: van Oorschot, P.C. (ed.) USENIX Security 2008, pp. 45–60. USENIX Association, July/August 2008
24. Håstad, J., Impagliazzo, R., Levin, L.A., Luby, M.: A pseudorandom generator from any one-way function. SIAM J. Comput. **28**(4), 1364–1396 (1999). https://doi.org/10.1137/S0097539793244708

25. Jafargholi, Z., Wichs, D.: Tamper detection and continuous non-malleable codes. In: Dodis, Y., Nielsen, J.B. (eds.) TCC 2015, Part I. LNCS, vol. 9014, pp. 451–480. Springer, Heidelberg (2015). https://doi.org/10.1007/978-3-662-46494-6_19
26. Kalai, Y.T., Kanukurthi, B., Sahai, A.: Cryptography with tamperable and leaky memory. In: Rogaway, P. (ed.) CRYPTO 2011. LNCS, vol. 6841, pp. 373–390. Springer, Heidelberg (2011). https://doi.org/10.1007/978-3-642-22792-9_21
27. Kiltz, E., Wee, H.: Quasi-adaptive NIZK for linear subspaces revisited. In: Oswald, E., Fischlin, M. (eds.) EUROCRYPT 2015, Part II. LNCS, vol. 9057, pp. 101–128. Springer, Heidelberg (2015). https://doi.org/10.1007/978-3-662-46803-6_4
28. Kocher, P.C.: Timing attacks on implementations of Diffie-Hellman, RSA, DSS, and other systems. In: Koblitz, N. (ed.) CRYPTO 1996. LNCS, vol. 1109, pp. 104–113. Springer, Heidelberg (1996). https://doi.org/10.1007/3-540-68697-5_9
29. Kocher, P., Jaffe, J., Jun, B.: Differential power analysis. In: Wiener, M. (ed.) CRYPTO 1999. LNCS, vol. 1666, pp. 388–397. Springer, Heidelberg (1999). https://doi.org/10.1007/3-540-48405-1_25
30. Liu, F.-H., Lysyanskaya, A.: Tamper and leakage resilience in the split-state model. In: Safavi-Naini, R., Canetti, R. (eds.) CRYPTO 2012. LNCS, vol. 7417, pp. 517–532. Springer, Heidelberg (2012). https://doi.org/10.1007/978-3-642-32009-5_30
31. Morillo, P., Ràfols, C., Villar, J.L.: The kernel matrix Diffie-Hellman assumption. In: Cheon, J.H., Takagi, T. (eds.) ASIACRYPT 2016. LNCS, vol. 10031, pp. 729–758. Springer, Heidelberg (2016). https://doi.org/10.1007/978-3-662-53887-6_27
32. Naor, M., Segev, G.: Public-key cryptosystems resilient to key leakage. In: Halevi, S. (ed.) CRYPTO 2009. LNCS, vol. 5677, pp. 18–35. Springer, Heidelberg (2009). https://doi.org/10.1007/978-3-642-03356-8_2
33. Qin, B., Liu, S.: Leakage-resilient chosen-ciphertext secure public-key encryption from hash proof system and one-time lossy filter. In: Sako, K., Sarkar, P. (eds.) ASIACRYPT 2013, Part II. LNCS, vol. 8270, pp. 381–400. Springer, Heidelberg (2013). https://doi.org/10.1007/978-3-642-42045-0_20
34. Steinfeld, R., Pieprzyk, J., Wang, H.: How to strengthen any weakly unforgeable signature into a strongly unforgeable signature. In: Abe, M. (ed.) CT-RSA 2007. LNCS, vol. 4377, pp. 357–371. Springer, Heidelberg (2006). https://doi.org/10.1007/11967668_23
35. Sun, S.-F., Gu, D., Au, M.H., Han, S., Yu, Yu., Liu, J.: Strong leakage and tamper-resilient PKE from refined hash proof system. In: Deng, R.H., Gauthier-Umaña, V., Ochoa, M., Yung, M. (eds.) ACNS 2019. LNCS, vol. 11464, pp. 486–506. Springer, Cham (2019). https://doi.org/10.1007/978-3-030-21568-2_24
36. Sun, S., Gu, D., Parampalli, U., Yu, Y., Qin, B.: Public key encryption resilient to leakage and tampering attacks. J. Comput. Syst. Sci. **89**, 142–156 (2017). https://doi.org/10.1016/j.jcss.2017.03.004

SoK: Public Key Encryption with Openings

Carlo Brunetta[1], Hans Heum[2](✉), and Martijn Stam[1]

[1] Simula UiB, Bergen, Norway
{carlob,martijn}@simula.no
[2] NTNU - Norwegian University of Science and Technology, Trondheim, Norway
hans.heum@ntnu.no

Abstract. When modelling how public key encryption can enable secure communication, we should acknowledge that secret information, such as private keys or the encryption's randomness, could become compromised. Intuitively, one would expect unrelated communication to remain secure, yet formalizing this intuition has proven challenging. Several security notions have appeared that aim to capture said scenario, ranging from the multi-user setting with corruptions, via selective opening attacks (SOA), to non-committing encryption (NCE). Remarkably, how the different approaches compare has not yet been systematically explored.

We provide a novel framework that maps each approach to an underlying philosophy of confidentiality: indistinguishability versus simulatability based, each with an a priori versus an a posteriori variant, leading to four distinct philosophies. In the absence of corruptions, these notions are largely equivalent; yet, in the presence of corruptions, they fall into a hierarchy of relative strengths, from IND-CPA and IND-CCA at the bottom, via indistinguishability SOA and simulatability SOA, to NCE at the top. We provide a concrete treatment for the four notions, discuss subtleties in their definitions and asymptotic interpretations and identify limitations of each. Furthermore, we re-cast the main implications of the hierarchy in a concrete security framework, summarize and contextualize other known relations, identify open problems, and close a few gaps.

Keywords: Selective Opening Attacks · Multi-User Security · Non-Committing Encryption · Corruptions

1 Introduction

A group of crypto friends want to exchange their latest ideas with each other. Obviously, they want to do so confidentially and, being slightly old-fashioned, imagine they use public key encryption to secure their communication. Yet, an adversary, mistakenly reckoning our friends are all about the other crypto, sets out to break into the devices used by some of the cryptographers, recovering a number of private keys in the hope of a big score. Ideally, the communication

Work by Hans Heum partially performed as part of his PhD studies at Simula UiB.

Q. Tang and V. Teague (Eds.): PKC 2024, LNCS 14604, pp. 35–68, 2024.
https://doi.org/10.1007/978-3-031-57728-4_2

that wasn't intended for the compromised bunch remains secure, so our somewhat disillusioned adversary cannot scoop their research ideas.

Scenarios similar to the one above, involving public key encryption (PKE) with multiple, say κ, users some of whom may be corrupted, have been used to motivate a range of different security notions for PKE above and beyond the now classical left-or-right indistinguishability under chosen ciphertext attacks (IND-CCA). These novel notions range from multi-user indistinguishability with corruptions, via various flavours of selective opening attacks (SOA), to (non-interactive) non-committing encryption (NCE). Given the plethora of theoretical notions based on very similar, practical motivations, the question arises what are the pros and cons of the various notions, and whether some notions should be preferred over others. In addition to leaking keys, similar notions have also studied security when the randomness used for encryption leaks, or when both keys and randomness leak. Thus we end up with a host of notions, and a sizeable literature exploring how they relate and how each may be achieved. Navigating this literature can be a daunting task for the uninitiated, particularly given diverging formalisms, subtle variations in security definitions (which may or not turn out consequential to any particular result), and even contradicting claims.

This is the situation that the present Systematization of Knowledge (SoK) aims to remedy. Our goal is *not* to provide a complete classification of all possible variations, but rather to provide a roadmap of the high level choices, and highlight possible pitfalls when designing security notions with openings. Our generalized definitions, given in Sect. 3, may serve as inspiration, yet we stress that for applications, utility of the definitions should be the guiding principle.

Our systematization identifies four philosophies underlying the notions of confidentiality of messages, using two orthogonal considerations: whether a notion is based on indistinguishability or simulation, and whether it is an a priori or a posteriori variant. Each notion then falls into one of the four categories: *a priori indistinguishability* for left-or-right indistinguishability-based (multi-user) notions (IND); *a posteriori indistinguishability* for indistinguishability SOA (ISO); *a posteriori simulatability* for simulation SOA (SSO); and *a priori simulatability* for non-committing encryption (NCE). Each notion furthermore comes in four variants depending on whether only keys leak (receiver opening, denoted $\star$), only messages and randomness leak (sender opening, denoted $\odot$), just messages (transmission opening, denoted $\diamond$), or all of the above (bi-opening, denoted $\circledast$); the exception is NCE, for which only sender, receiver, and bi-opening is defined. Finally, each notion comes in a CPA and a CCA variant, making for 30 notions of security in total—some of which are studied here for the first time. An overview of our notation is given in Table 1.

To begin with, we observe that the four philosophies of confidentiality, while polynomially equivalent sans openings, seem to fall into a strict hierarchy of strength whenever receiver and/or sender openings are accounted for, see Fig. 1. Transmission openings on the other hand are significantly weaker, and all but one of the main notions are known to be polynomially equivalent to IND-CPA resp.

Table 1. Overview of the different formalizations of capturing confidentiality, the auxiliary adversarial power, and the adversarial opening prowess, together with their relevant associated oracle(s): here, $\mathcal{E}$ are (challenge) encryption oracles, $\mathcal{C}$ is a challenge oracle, $\mathcal{D}$ is the decryption oracle, and $\mathcal{T}$, $\mathcal{S}$, and $\mathcal{R}$ are the transmission, sender, and receiver opening oracles, respectively (see Sect. 3.1).

Shorthand	Associated oracle(s)	Name
κ		number of users (receivers)
β		number of challenge bits
IND	$\mathcal{E}$	indistinguishability
ISO	$\mathcal{E}$ $\mathcal{C}$	indistinguishability-based selective opening
SSO	$\mathcal{E}$	simulation-based selective opening
NCE	$\mathcal{E}$	non-committing encryption
CPA		chosen plaintext attack
CCA	$\mathcal{D}$	chosen ciphertext attack
$\diamond$	$\mathcal{T}$	transmission opening
$\odot$	$\mathcal{S}$	sender opening
$\star$	$\mathcal{R}$	receiver opening
$\circledast$	$\mathcal{S}$ $\mathcal{R}$	bi-opening (sender + receiver)

IND-CCA when only transmission openings are included (with the remaining equivalence being conjectured, see Open Problem 8).

Findings. We give generalized definitions of the four main philosophies that all include multiple users, challenges, full adaptivity, and bi-openings; message samplers and simulators are all stateful, which simplifies (and in the case of message samplers, strengthens) the formalizations. In addition, we provide novel a priori indistinguishability notions of security in the presence of transmission, sender and bi-openings, which are notable for being equivalent to IND-CPA resp. IND-CCA, at a loss for sender openings (Theorem 1) and bi-openings (see the full version), but almost completely tightly in the case of transmission openings (Theorem 2).

While ideally we would give definite formalizations of each of the notions considered herein, there are a number of subtle definitional choices available with often no clear best one (for all contexts). We have leaned towards generality wherever possible, but some choices are less clear in terms of benefits and generality. For example, which inputs to a distinguisher should be provided by the game and which may be simulated (for SSO and NCE notions); specifically, whether the simulator may generate the parameters and public keys itself. We opted for a notion where the simulator generates the public keys but not the parameters, see Definition 5. As another contribution, we provide a concrete-security treatment of topics that have traditionally been studied asymptotically,

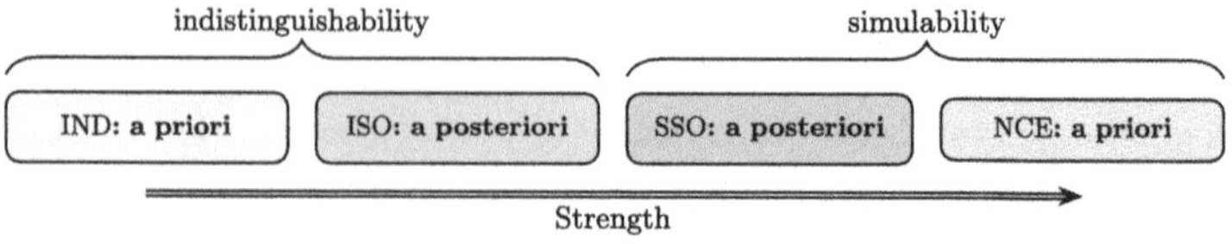

Fig. 1. The main hierarchy of philosophies, and their associated security notion with opening. The notions become stronger as we go up the hierarchy in the presence of sender or receiver opening (or both).

recasting several known implications in a concrete light, with asymptotic interpretations that connect to the literature (see Theorem 3–5).

Our systematization allowed us to uncover a number of open problems, which we highlight in Open Problem 1–Open Problem 8, with many more in the full version. Of particular interest are the many relations known for the CPA setting that remain open in the CCA setting (see Fig. 9). Surprisingly, it is unclear whether notions of SSO-CCA imply notions of ISO-CCA in the presence of openings, as a straightforward reduction runs into trouble with simulating the decryption oracle, see Open Problem 5.

Message samplers play a central role in definitions of SOA (the "a posteriori" philosophies), and here again we find a number of open problems. For example, for which (restricted) classes of message samplers do κ-ISO-CPA$\star$ and κ-ISO-CCA$\star$, like their sender opening counterparts ($\odot$), become equivalent to IND-CPA resp. IND-CCA (Open Problem 7)?

We hope that highlighting these open problems can serve as inspiration, and that the present systematization can help promote applying these security notions to protocol design, of which there are surprisingly few examples to date.

Future Directions. We limit our investigation to perfect correctness, as most of the literature cited does not consider imperfect correctness. With the rise of post-quantum cryptography, and lattice-based schemes in particular, the study of imperfect correctness is of increasing importance, and we view it as an important open problem to re-establish the relations studied herein in such a setting.

Besides confidentiality, related goals have also been studied in the presence of openings, such as non-malleability [36] and anonymity (key privacy) [35]. While beyond our present scope, we find it would be interesting and worthwhile to re-establish our hierarchy in these settings, and investigate the notions of security the four philosophies give rise to when combined with the various openings.

Full Version. Apart from the above-mentioned, the full version [11] contains much additional material, including but not limited to: historical context for the main notions; further relations; discussions on some related notions; a survey of constructions known to achieve the various notions; and proofs and asymptotic interpretations of the theorems contained in the main body.

2 Preliminaries

2.1 Notation

For a positive integer n, we let $[n]$ denote the set $\{1, \ldots, n\}$. For a bit string $x \in \{0,1\}^*$, $|x|$ denotes its length. For a finite set $\mathcal{X}$, $|\mathcal{X}|$ is the cardinality of $\mathcal{X}$. For a list $\mathtt{X}$, $\mathtt{X}[i]$ retrieves the ith element of the list, and, for an index set $\mathcal{I}$, $\mathtt{X}[\mathcal{I}]$ indicates the list $\mathtt{X}$ restricted to the elements whose indices are contained in $\mathcal{I}$.

We use code-based experiments, where by convention all sets, lists, and lazily sampled functions are initialized empty. We use $\Pr[\mathsf{Code} : \mathsf{Event} \mid \mathsf{Condition}]$ to denote the conditional probability of Event occurring when Code is executed, conditioned on Condition. We omit Code when it is clear from the context and Condition when it is not needed. In our experiments, we will assume that no oracle calls are made (by the adversary) with evidently out-of-bounds inputs (e.g. list indices or key handles). In our (pseudo)code, we denote with $x \leftarrow y$ the deterministic assignment of y to the variable x and use the shorthand $\mathcal{X} \stackrel{\cup}{\longleftarrow} x$ for the operation $\mathcal{X} \leftarrow \mathcal{X} \cup \{x\}$ and $\mathtt{X} \stackrel{\frown}{\longleftarrow} x$ for appending the element x to a list $\mathtt{X}$. Furthermore, we use the shorthand $x \leftarrow_{\$} \mathcal{X}$ to denote uniform sampling from the finite set $\mathcal{X}$ and $x \leftarrow_{\$} Y(\cdot)$ for assigning the output of the probabilistic algorithm Y to x. We can make the randomness r of Y explicit by writing $x \leftarrow Y(\cdot\,; r)$, for previously sampled r. We will also consider stateful algorithms, for instance when we write $m \leftarrow_{\$} \mathsf{M}_{\langle s \rangle}(\alpha)$ the algorithm M takes as state s and as input the value α and outputs m, but it may change its state s as part of its processing (code-snippet taken from Fig. 5).

2.2 PKE Syntax

A public-key encryption scheme PKE consists of five algorithms. The probabilistic parameter generation algorithm PKE.Pm on input a security parameter λ outputs shared, public system parameters pm (these might for instance be the description of an elliptic curve group with generator for an ECDLP-based system); we use the shorthand $\mathsf{PKE}[\lambda]$ for a concrete instantiation of the scheme for the given security parameter. The probabilistic key generation algorithm PKE.Kg on input pm outputs a public/private key pair $(\mathsf{pk}, \mathsf{sk})$; without loss of generality, we assume that any algorithm that receives pk implicitly receives pm as well, and any algorithm receiving sk also receives pk. The probabilistic algorithm PKE.Rnd on input pm samples random coins r for encryption. Subsequently, the deterministic encryption algorithm PKE.Enc on input a public key pk, a message $m \in \mathcal{M}$ and randomness r outputs a ciphertext c. We can also treat PKE.Enc as a probabilistic algorithm by folding in the randomness generation by PKE.Rnd, simply writing $c \leftarrow_{\$} \mathsf{PKE.Enc}_{\mathsf{pk}}(m)$. Finally, the typically deterministic decryption algorithm PKE.Dec on input a private key sk and a ciphertext c outputs either a message $m \in \mathcal{M}$ or some failure symbol $\perp$. Henceforth, we assume that the message space $\mathcal{M}$ consists of (a subset of) arbitrary, finite length bit strings, i.e. $\mathcal{M} \subseteq \{0,1\}^*$ (which includes fixed-length binary representations of an algebraic structure). In addition, ciphertexts are typically bit strings whose length depends on, and hence leaks, the message length.

We assume the schemes to be perfectly correct: for all parameters pm, all generated key pairs $(\mathsf{pk}, \mathsf{sk}) \leftarrow_{\$} \mathsf{PKE.Kg}(\mathsf{pm})$, and all messages $m \in \mathcal{M}$, it holds,

$$\Pr\left[r \leftarrow_{\$} \mathsf{PKE.Rnd}(\mathsf{pm}) \;:\; \mathsf{PKE.Dec}_{\mathsf{sk}}(\mathsf{PKE.Enc}_{\mathsf{pk}}(m; r)) = m\right] = 1$$

Remark 1. Some modern schemes, like LWE-based ones, allow a small probability of incorrectness, where decryption of an honestly generated ciphertext may occasionally return a wrong message or fail. Some classical schemes, such as hybrid KEM–DEM ones, may return distinct error messages (e.g. a KEM failure $\perp_{\mathsf{KEM}}$ versus a DEM failure $\perp_{\mathsf{DEM}}$). Other schemes might loosen the link between message length and ciphertext length to partially hide the former [22,47]. To deal with these more general scenarios, some of the security definitions might require some subtle changes (beyond pure syntactical ones) to best capture the changed reality; moreover, even when the definitions remain the same, security proofs might rely on perfect correctness. While we occasionally highlight specific challenges when faced with a more general scenario, we stress that results shown to hold for single-error, length-regular, perfectly correct schemes do not automatically port to either of those more general scenarios. Specifically, whether known results on SOA and NCE still hold in the imperfect correctness scenario is unclear and we leave open the challenge of re-establishing relations in a setting with imperfect correctness.

Open Problem 1. *How are known security definitions and their relations affected when lifted to a setting with imperfect correctness, multiple error messages, or deviations from length regularity?*

2.3 Security Notions

Most security notions can be phrased in terms of an adversarial goal and the adversary's powers. This separation in goals and powers is reflected in the notation GOAL-POWER, such as IND-CPA for indistinguishability under chosen plaintext attacks. We are primarily concerned with indistinguishability-style notions that task the adversary with guessing a single bit. These notions are modelled by a distinguishing experiment $\mathsf{Exp}^{\text{goal-power}}_{\mathsf{PKE}[\lambda],\ldots}(\mathbb{A})$ that, at the end of the game, either outputs true (if the adversary guesses correctly) or false (if not), leading to a distinguishing advantage (Definition 1). We will occasionally conflate the Boolean values true and false with the bits 1 and 0, respectively, and some games may manipulate the adversary's output prior to checking its guess, for instance to ensure that "bad" adversarial behaviour cannot be advantageous.

Definition 1 (Distinguishing advantage). *Let* $\mathsf{PKE}[\lambda]$ *be given and let the distinguishing experiment* $\mathsf{Exp}^{\text{goal-power}}_{\mathsf{PKE}[\lambda],\ldots}(\mathbb{A})$ *be given for notion* GOAL-POWER, *where dots represent other possible dependencies of the notion (e.g. simulators or message samplers). Then an adversary* $\mathbb{A}$*'s distinguishing advantage is*

$$\mathsf{Adv}^{\text{goal-power}}_{\mathsf{PKE}[\lambda],\ldots}(\mathbb{A}) := 2 \cdot \Pr\left[\mathsf{Exp}^{\text{goal-power}}_{\mathsf{PKE}[\lambda],\ldots}(\mathbb{A})\right] - 1\,.$$

Unless otherwise stated, all our notions, including single-user notions, are multi-challenge, modelled by one or more challenge oracles (that depend on the bit to be guessed). Their precise formalizations depend on the underlying philosophy related to capturing "nothing leaks" (see Sect. 3).

Many powers are associated with a helper oracle, like the decryption oracle $\mathcal{D}$ used to model chosen ciphertext attacks (CCA), or the various opening oracles (see Sect. 3.1). As part of the goal, we prefix notions by the number of users κ and/or challenge bits β, and as part of the powers we postfix notions by the opening oracles available to them ($\diamond$, $\odot$, $\star$ or $\circledast$), see Table 1. If κ resp. β is set to one we typically omit the prefix, and likewise the postfix absent openings.

Although our focus will be on CPA and CCA security, there are many other powers sitting in between in strength. Without going into details, these include plaintext checking attacks (PCA) [44], ciphertext verification attacks (CVA) [17, 39], constrained chosen ciphertext attacks (CCCA) [31], and replayable chosen ciphertext attacks (RCCA) [15]. In the context of selective opening attacks, the CPA and CCA worlds display some remarkable divergence, raising the question where the various intermediate notions would sit.

Most of the reductions we consider are black-box, in the sense that they treat the adversary they build upon as a black-box. Furthermore, for generality, we often state that our reductions are type-preserving, which means that the type of queries the reduction makes, matches those of the underlying adversary. Type-preserving reductions are convenient to show simultaneously that, for instance, both CCA security of one flavour implies CCA security of another flavour and CPA security of that one flavour implies CPA security of that other flavour.

We prefer the concrete security approach, but will sometimes revert to stating known results using the asymptotic language. We discuss and compare the concrete and asymptotic approaches to security in the full version [11].

3 Confidentiality with Openings

3.1 Four Kinds of Opening

In a system with many users, one would like a guarantee that uncompromised traffic remains confidential even if a subset of the users are compromised. We will address different confidentiality guarantees in the next section and first explore user compromises themselves. Typical deployment of PKE involves two distinct user roles: that of sender and that of receiver. Their compromises need to be modelled separately, leading to four distinct flavours of openings.

Transmission Openings. The weakest form of opening allows an adversary to open challenge ciphertexts to retrieve the underlying message. It differs from a chosen ciphertext attack as it specifically targets challenge ciphertexts, which are explicitly prohibited for a CCA-style decryption oracle. The notion is relatively rare, but we include it for completeness. We use the name transmission openings, denote the oracle as $\mathcal{T}$, and indicate its presence with the suffix $\diamond$.

Transmission openings can model partial compromises on both sender and receiver end: a sender might still have (a copy of) the message lying around, but have erased the ephemeral randomness used to encrypt; a receiver might take strong measures not to leak its long-term private key but might not care too much about the contents of a single message leaking. The added power of the transmission opening oracle to an adversary appears minimal, in contrast to the stronger sender and receiver openings that we will discuss next. Indeed, Bellare and Yilek [10] (henceforth BY12) showed transmission-SOA equivalent to IND-CPA in the context of simulation-based selective opening attacks (which we will consider as a posteriori simulatability in the next section), see Sect. 4. Similarly, for a priori indistinguishability, we show that the added power is minimal (see Theorem 2), while for a priori simulatability, a transmission opening oracle would not add anything to the notion (as the adversary already knows the plaintext, see Definition 6).

Sender Openings. Here an adversary can open any challenge ciphertext to receive both the message and underlying randomness; it models the compromise of a sender incapable of securely erasing said randomness. The study of SOA started out as a study of security in the presence of randomness reveals [18], as motivated by the setting of multi-party computation, where erasures are notoriously tricky [7]. Sender openings can be considered in a multiple-senders/single-receiver setting, so there is only one public–private key pair, yet the opening is per ciphertext. We let $\mathcal{S}$ denote the sender opening oracle, and indicate its presence with the suffix $\odot$. Compared to transmission openings, and depending on the formalism, sender openings are much harder to deal with formally: the core technical difficulty sits with the committing property of most encryption schemes, as any adversary receiving the randomness and message corresponding to a challenge ciphertext can re-encrypt to verify that challenges and openings are consistent.

Receiver Openings. An adversary who fully corrupts a receiver will obtain that user's private key. These kind of openings are found in both the multi-user literature [1,2,38] and the SOA literature [6,27,41].

For the latter, it is customary to reveal not just the private key, but also all the challenge messages that were encrypted under the corresponding public key. For us, receiver openings will only reveal the private key. For perfectly correct schemes, this choice is without loss of generality, as evidently, an adversary with access to both a ciphertext and the private key can simply run the decryption algorithm to obtain the originally encrypted message. When perfect correctness is not guaranteed, having one oracle that only reveals the private key and another that reveals the messages (cf. transmission openings) should result in a finer-grained notion. We denote the opening oracle as $\mathcal{R}$, and indicate its presence with the suffix $\star$. For receiver openings to be meaningful, one should consider multiple receivers; we let κ indicate the number of receivers (used as prefix for security notions). As for sender openings, the core difficulty of receiver openings is the adversary's ability to verify that challenges and openings are consistent.

Bi-openings. Finally, an adversary might be granted access to both sender and receiver opening oracles (and thus also transmission openings), as indicated by the suffix ⊛. Bi-openings have been the standard in the NCE setting from the get-go [3, 14], but only recently appeared in the SOA literature [41].

3.2 Four Philosophies of Confidentiality

To contrast and compare different confidentiality notions with openings, we first revisit four different philosophies to formalize confidentiality without. All four approaches aim to capture that an adversary "learns nothing" and hark back to Shannon's concept of perfect secrecy and its (near) equivalent notions [46]. The notions split in two, depending on whether they are indistinguishability versus simulatability based, and for both we consider an *a priori* and an *a posteriori* variant (Fig. 1). We describe each, going roughly in order of increasing strength.

A Priori Indistinguishability. In the information-theoretic, symmetric setting (where $\mathcal{M}$ consists of fixed-length bistrings) the idea is that, given any two messages, the same distribution over ciphertexts is induced, which can be formalized by stating that, for all m_0 and m_1 (and c),

$$\Pr[C = c|M = m_0] = \Pr[C = c|M = m_1]\,,$$

where the probability is primarily over the choice of the secret key. In the computational, public key setting, the formalization differs, leading to classic left-or-right indistinguishability: an adversary, given access to a single public key pk, selects two (equal length) messages m_0 and m_1, receives the encryption of one of them under pk, and needs to figure out which one. Generalizations to allow multiple challenges and multiple users [4] form the basis for multi-user indistinguishability with corruptions (κ-IND-CPA$\star$ and κ-IND-CCA$\star$, see Sect. 3.3).

A Posteriori Indistinguishability. Here the concept is that, given a ciphertext, any two messages are equally likely. In the information-theoretic setting, it can be formalized as

$$\Pr[M = m_0|C = c] = \Pr[M = m_1|C = c]\,,$$

which hides a dependency on the message distribution underlying M: the notion can only be satisfied iff the a priori distribution on the messages is uniform (in which case it is equivalent to a priori indistinguishability via Bayes's theorem).

For a computational PKE version, consider an experiment where an adversary specifies a message distribution M over $\mathcal{M} \subseteq \{0,1\}^*$. The game would sample a message m_0 according to M and encrypt m_0 to obtain ciphertext c. It would then sample a second message m_1 according to M, conditioned on $|m_0| = |m_1|$. Finally, the game returns (m_b, c) to the adversary, who has to guess b.

A posteriori indistinguishability is rather a rare notion for PKE, nonetheless it is the route taken for indistinguishability-based notions of selective opening attacks (ISO for short, see Sect. 3.4). In order for the notion to imply IND-CPA, however, the adversary should be allowed adaptive control over the distribution. In the concrete setting, we define the notion relative to a conditional resampler. In the asymptotic setting, this conditional resampler causes a bifurcation of the notion depending on whether said resampler can be efficiently implemented (effectively restricting the message samplers) or not.

A Posteriori Simulatability. Shannon's definition of perfect secrecy captured that, given a ciphertext c, each message m is as likely as it was before seeing c, or more formally

$$\Pr[M = m | C = c] = \Pr[M = m]\,;$$

again there is a dependency on the message distribution, but this time it can be arbitrary (so it is less troublesome than for a posteriori indistinguishability).

Perfect secrecy captures that, given a ciphertext, nothing should be leaked about the message. Goldwasser and Micali [24] famously captured this concept in a computational PKE setting as semantic security (SEM). Goldreich [23] later refined the notion by introducing a simulator: an adversary outputs a message distribution M, the game samples m according to M, encrypts m and returns the resulting ciphertext c to the adversary. Whatever the adversary subsequently computes, possibly using additional oracles, a simulator should be able to simulate. Some definitional variations are possible [48], based for instance on whether the adversary outputs only a single bit or an arbitrary output (to be simulated).

Like perfect secrecy, semantic security is arguably the most intuitive notion. Compared to a posteriori indistinguishability, there is no need to put any onerous restrictions on M, that is on how messages are sampled (although in the computational setting, it does need to be efficient). Simulation-based notions for selective opening attacks (SSO) follow this philosophy, see Sect. 3.5 for details.

A Priori Simulatability. Finally, we can require that the likelihood of observing a ciphertext c is independent of m, or

$$\Pr[C = c | M = m] = \Pr[C = c]\,.$$

In the information-theoretic setting, Shannon already showed this formalization equivalent to perfect secrecy. The concept can be reinterpreted to say that, given a message, nothing is learned about the ciphertexts that might result from encrypting it, which can be captured by saying one can produce, or simulate, fully convincing ciphertexts without access to the message (before an adversary even gets involved). Hence, a priori simulatability.

Restricting to chosen-plaintext attacks for PKE, a priori simulatability can be defined by allowing an adversary to obtain the public key, select a message m, and then either receive an encryption of m or a simulated ciphertext, with the simulator only given access to the public key and the length of the message. The most common incarnation of a priori simulatability in the PKE setting fixes the simulator to simply sample a message of matching length and encrypting it, and the resulting notion is known as real-or-random indistinguishability (ROR) [5].

Upgrading to chosen-ciphertext attacks, the decryption oracle might have to be simulated as well; precise formalizations of a priori simulatability can be found in the universal composability (UC) framework [13,40]. When allowing opening oracles, these need to be simulated as well; the resulting notion is known as (non-interactive) non-committing encryption (NCE), as discussed in Sect. 3.6.

Discussion. If we exclude a posteriori indistinguishability, then the remaining three notions are all equivalent in the information-theoretic setting, as already proven by Shannon. The same is true in the asymptotic computational setting: again excluding a posteriori indistinguishability, IND-CPA, SEM-CPA, and ROR-CPA are all polynomially equivalent [5,24], as are IND-CCA, SEM-CCA, and UC-CCA [32,48]. A posteriori indistinguishability appears not to have been studied for PKE without openings, although equivalence for message samplers satisfying conditional resamplability follows from Sect. 4.

3.3 A Priori Indistinguishability with Selective Openings (IND)

The multi-user setting [4] fits within the framework of a priori indistinguishability. Originally, openings were not considered, yet modelling multi-user security with receiver openings, also known as corruptions, has seen an uptick [1,25,29,42]. Several formalizations are possible, depending for instance on whether a single challenge bit is used across all κ public keys or whether each public key is allocated its own challenge bit. For receiver openings, we concentrate on the former, more standard approach (see Definition 2).

With only a single challenge bit, the opening of challenges would enable a trivial win and so must be disallowed. Thus, there is no meaningful notion of transmission or sender opening in such experiments. Generalizing to multiple challenge bits alleviates this issue: in the following, after recalling the canonical single-bit multi-user notion with receiver openings, we study a single-user multi-bit notion with sender openings, which to the best of our knowledge is studied here for the first time. In the full version, we collect the pieces and present the first notion of a priori indistinguishability with bi-openings, which, by allowing both multiple users and multiple challenge bits, strictly generalizes prior art.

Receiver Openings. As explained, our formalization of a priori indistinguishability with receiver openings matches canonical notions of multi-user indistinguishability with corruptions, and we adopt a recent formalization [29].

Experiment $\mathsf{Exp}^{\kappa\text{-ind-cca}\star}_{\mathsf{PKE}[\lambda]}(\mathbb{A})$

$b \leftarrow\!\!\$ \{0,1\}$

$\mathsf{pm} \leftarrow\!\!\$ \mathsf{PKE.Pm}(\lambda)$

$\forall_{i\in[\kappa]}(\mathsf{pk}_i, \mathsf{sk}_i) \leftarrow\!\!\$ \mathsf{PKE.Kg}(\mathsf{pm})$

$\hat{b} \leftarrow\!\!\$ \mathbb{A}^{\mathcal{E},\mathcal{D},\mathcal{R}}(\mathsf{pk}_1, \ldots, \mathsf{pk}_\kappa)$

if $\mathcal{K} \cap \mathcal{I} \neq \emptyset : \hat{b} \leftarrow\!\!\$ \{0,1\}$

return $b = \hat{b}$

Oracle $\mathcal{E}(i, m_0, m_1)$

if $|m_0| \neq |m_1|$: **return** $\lightning$

$\mathcal{K} \xleftarrow{\cup} i$

$c \leftarrow\!\!\$ \mathsf{PKE.Enc}_{\mathsf{pk}_i}(m_b)$

$\mathcal{C}_i \xleftarrow{\cup} c$

return c

Oracle $\mathcal{D}(i, c)$

if $c \in \mathcal{C}_i$: **return** $\lightning$

$m \leftarrow \mathsf{PKE.Dec}_{\mathsf{sk}_i}(c)$

return m

Oracle $\mathcal{R}(i)$

$\mathcal{I} \xleftarrow{\cup} i$

return sk_i

Fig. 2. A priori indistinguishability with receiver openings, also known as multi-user indistinguishability with corruptions.

Definition 2. *The* κ-IND-CCA$\star$ *advantage* $\mathsf{Adv}^{\kappa\text{-ind-cca}\star}_{\mathsf{PKE}[\lambda]}(\mathbb{A})$ *of an adversary* $\mathbb{A}$ *against public key encryption scheme* $\mathsf{PKE}[\lambda]$ *is the distinguishing advantage against the game* $\mathsf{Exp}^{\kappa\text{-ind-cca}\star}_{\mathsf{PKE}[\lambda]}(\mathbb{A})$ *(see Fig. 2).*

Uses and Limitations. By a straightforward hybrid argument, the multi-user setting with receiver openings is implied by the single-user setting with a κ tightness loss, which entails polynomial equivalence [4]. For concrete instantiations, there are schemes known to be tightly secure in the multi-user setting with corruptions in the programmable random oracle model (see the full version [11]). The notion furthermore benefits from ease of composition, e.g. in constructing tightly secure hybrid encryption from a KEM and a DEM [42].

The main limitation of the notion is its segregation of opening versus challenging: adversaries cannot gain any advantage through both challenging and opening a user, as enforced by overwriting the adversary's output with a uniform value in the final stage of $\mathsf{Exp}^{\kappa\text{-ind-cca}\star}_{\mathsf{PKE}[\lambda]}(\mathbb{A})$. This makes the notion inadequate for e.g. threshold security [45], for which security should hold as long as not too many challenges are opened.

Opening Challenges. Employing multiple challenge bits, opening challenges becomes a viable strategy, provided the adversary outputs an uncompromised bit handle and guess at the end. For receiver openings, each user may for instance be associated a challenge bit; so that users can now be both challenged and corrupted, as long as at least one uncompromised user remains by the end. A KEM version of this multiple-challenge-bit security notion suffices for a construction achieving tightly (multi-challenge-bit) secure authenticated key exchange [1].

However, having multiple challenge bits comes with its own set of challenges: in particular, it typically leads to lossy composition theorems [29,37]. The notion might also remain inadequate for e.g. threshold schemes, as having multiple challenge bits makes it hard to keep challenges consistent with each other.

Nonetheless, it facilitates the study of transmission and sender opening in the a priori indistinguishability setting (and therefore also bi-opening, see the full version [11]).

Experiment $\mathsf{Exp}^{\beta\text{-ind-cca}\odot}_{\mathsf{PKE}[\lambda]}(\mathbb{A})$

$\forall_{i \in [\beta]} b_i \leftarrow\!\!\$ \{0,1\}$

$\mathsf{pm} \leftarrow\!\!\$ \mathsf{PKE.Pm}(\lambda)$

$(\mathsf{pk}, \mathsf{sk}) \leftarrow\!\!\$ \mathsf{PKE.Kg}(\mathsf{pm})$

$(i, \hat{b}_i) \leftarrow\!\!\$ \mathbb{A}^{\mathcal{E},\mathcal{D},(\mathcal{T},)\mathcal{S}}(\mathsf{pk})$

if $i \in \mathcal{I} : \hat{b}_i \leftarrow\!\!\$ \{0,1\}$

return $b_i = \hat{b}_i$

Oracle $\mathcal{E}(i, m_0, m_1)$

if $|m_0| \neq |m_1|$: **return** $\lightning$

$r \leftarrow\!\!\$ \mathsf{PKE.Rnd}(\mathsf{pm})$

$c \leftarrow \mathsf{PKE.Enc}_{\mathsf{pk}}(m_{b_i}; r)$

$\mathtt{E} \xleftarrow{\frown} (i, m_{b_i}, r)$

$\mathcal{C} \xleftarrow{\cup} c$

return c

Oracle $\mathcal{D}(c)$

if $c \in \mathcal{C}$: **return** $\lightning$

$m \leftarrow \mathsf{PKE.Dec}_{\mathsf{sk}}(c)$

return m

Oracle $\mathcal{T}(j)$

$(i, m, r) \leftarrow \mathtt{E}[j]$

$\mathcal{I} \xleftarrow{\cup} i$

return m

Oracle $\mathcal{S}(j)$

$(i, m, r) \leftarrow \mathtt{E}[j]$

$\mathcal{I} \xleftarrow{\cup} i$

return (m, r)

Fig. 3. A multiple-challenge-bit a priori indistinguishability game with transmission and sender openings.

Sender Openings. We consider a single-receiver notion without receiver openings and define $\mathsf{Adv}^{\beta\text{-ind-cca}\odot}_{\mathsf{PKE}}(\mathbb{A})$ in the vein of Definition 2 using Fig. 3. At the start of the game, β challenge bits are drawn, representing β senders. The adversary can learn the value of a challenge bit by opening any challenge for which $m_0 \neq m_1$, which will no longer make for a valid guess. The notion is implied by the single-user notion (Theorem 1), essentially through a guessing argument, leading to a tightness loss linear in the number of challenge bits(see the full version [11] for the proof). A comparable loss, namely the κ security loss from IND-CCA to κ-IND-CCA$\star$, is known to be sharp both in the sense that there are schemes that meet the bound [4] and through meta-reduction showing that no black-box reduction can achieve a better bound [2]. One can wonder whether Theorem 1 is similarly sharp, as expressed in Open Problem 2.

Open Problem 2. *How sharp is the bound of Theorem 1?*

Theorem 1. *Let* $\mathsf{PKE}[\lambda]$ *be given. Then there is a type-preserving black-box reduction* $\mathbb{B}_{\text{ind}}$ *such that, for all* $\mathbb{A}_{\odot}$,

$$\mathsf{Adv}^{\beta\text{-ind-cca}\odot}_{\mathsf{PKE}[\lambda]}(\mathbb{A}_{\odot}) \leq \beta \cdot \mathsf{Adv}^{\text{ind-cca}}_{\mathsf{PKE}[\lambda]}(\mathbb{B}_{\text{ind}}) \,.$$

The runtime of $\mathbb{B}_{\text{ind}}$ *is upper bounded by that of* $\mathbb{A}_{\odot}$ *plus* q_e *encryptions and* q_d *decryptions, where* q_e *and* q_d *are* $\mathbb{A}_{\odot}$ *'s number of challenge oracle calls and decryption oracle calls respectively, and some small overhead.*

Transmission Openings. Figure 3 simultaneously serves to define advantages for the β-IND-CCA$\diamond$ and β-IND-CCA notions (by omitting $\mathcal{S}$ for the former and

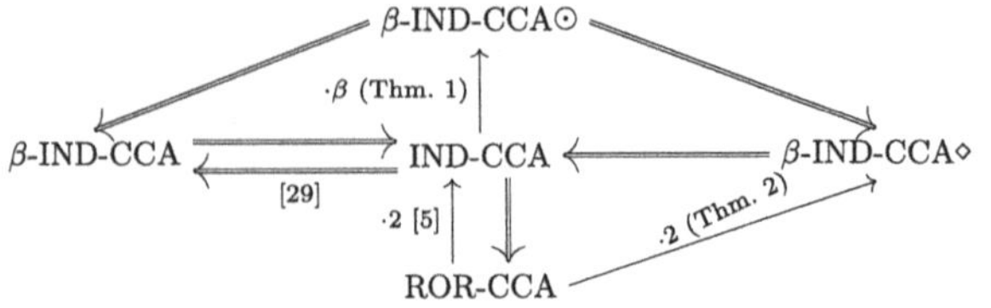

Fig. 4. Relations among the single-user single- and multi-bit notions of indistinguishability, with and without sender/transmission opening. (Double arrows = tight.)

both $\mathcal{S}$ and $\mathcal{T}$ for the latter). The notions β-IND-CCA and IND-CCA are tightly equivalent absent opening (i.e. the reduction loss = 1 in both directions) [29, Thm. 1]. Thus it is the reveal of messages and randomness, as opposed to the additional challenge bits, that gives the notions their strength, as the proof of tight equivalence fails in the presence of sender or transmission openings.

For transmission openings, we are able to show an almost tight equivalence to IND-CCA, losing only a factor 2 in one direction, while being trivially tight in the other direction. We conclude that transmission openings are of little interest in the a priori indistinguishability setting, adding at most a marginal strength.

Theorem 2 is inspired by BY12's proof of equivalence of IND-CPA and SSO-CPA⋄ and shows that β-IND-CCA⋄ is implied by ROR-CCA within a factor 2 (see the full version [11] for the proof). Recall that ROR-CCA also implies IND-CCA within a factor 2 [5], leaving open the possibility that β-IND-CCA⋄ and IND-CCA are in fact tightly equivalent (Open Problem 3, see also Fig. 4).

Open Problem 3. *Are* IND-CCA *and* β-IND-CCA⋄ *tightly equivalent?*

Theorem 2. *Let* $\mathsf{PKE}[\lambda]$ *be given. Then there is a type-preserving black-box reduction* $\mathbb{B}_{\mathrm{ror}}$ *such that, for all* $\mathbb{A}_\diamond$,

$$\mathsf{Adv}^{\beta\text{-ind-cca}\diamond}_{\mathsf{PKE}[\lambda]}(\mathbb{A}_\diamond) \le 2 \cdot \mathsf{Adv}^{\text{ror-cca}}_{\mathsf{PKE}[\lambda]}(\mathbb{B}_{\mathrm{ror}}) .$$

The runtime of $\mathbb{B}_{\mathrm{ror}}$ *is upper bounded by that of* $\mathbb{A}_\diamond$ *plus some small overhead.*

3.4 A Posteriori Indistinguishability with Selective Opening (ISO)

A posteriori indistinguishability, as described in Sect. 3.2, is defined relative to a message sampler M: rather than choosing challenge messages m_0 and m_1, the adversary is allowed to affect the sampling through input α. During a subsequent challenge phase, the adversary receives either the originally sampled message(s) or a resampled version thereof. The concept lends itself well to modelling opening attacks: the resampling can be refined to conditional resampling, thus ensuring consistency with the opening and avoiding that the challenge bit leaks trivially. Moreover, unlike a priori indistinguishability, the experiment poses no limitations on which ciphertexts may be opened, while simultaneously retaining the preferred single-challenge-bit structure.

Experiment $\mathsf{Exp}^{\kappa\text{-iso-cca}\circledast}_{\mathsf{PKE}[\lambda],\mathsf{M},\mathsf{S}}(\mathbb{A})$

$b \leftarrow\!\!\$\ \{0,1\}$
$\mathsf{challenged} \leftarrow \mathsf{false}$
$q \leftarrow 0, s \leftarrow \epsilon$
$\mathsf{pm} \leftarrow\!\!\$\ \mathsf{PKE.Pm}(\lambda)$
$\forall_{i\in[\kappa]}(\mathsf{pk}_i, \mathsf{sk}_i) \leftarrow\!\!\$\ \mathsf{PKE.Kg}(\mathsf{pm})$
$\hat{b} \leftarrow\!\!\$\ \mathbb{A}^{\mathcal{E},\mathcal{C},\mathcal{D},(\mathcal{T},)\mathcal{S},\mathcal{R}}(\mathsf{pk}_1, \ldots, \mathsf{pk}_\kappa)$
return $b = \hat{b}$

Oracle $\mathcal{D}(i, c)$

if $c \in \mathcal{C}_i$: **return** $\lightning$
$m \leftarrow \mathsf{PKE.Dec}_{\mathsf{sk}_i}(c)$
return m

Oracle $\mathcal{E}(i, \alpha)$

if $\mathsf{challenged}$: **return** $\lightning$
$q \leftarrow q + 1$
$\mathtt{K} \xleftarrow{\frown} i, \mathtt{A} \xleftarrow{\frown} \alpha$
$m \leftarrow\!\!\$\ \mathsf{M}_{\langle s \rangle}(\alpha)$
$\mathtt{L} \xleftarrow{\frown} |m|, \mathtt{M}^0 \xleftarrow{\frown} m$
$r \leftarrow\!\!\$\ \mathsf{PKE.Rnd}(\mathsf{pm})$
$c \leftarrow \mathsf{PKE.Enc}_{\mathsf{pk}_i}(m; r)$
$\mathtt{R} \xleftarrow{\frown} r, \mathcal{C}_i \xleftarrow{\cup} c$
return c

Oracle $\mathcal{C}$

if $\mathsf{challenged}$: **return** $\lightning$
$\mathsf{challenged} \leftarrow \mathsf{true}$
for $j \in [q]$:
  if $\mathtt{K}[j] \in \mathcal{I} : \mathcal{J} \xleftarrow{\cup} j$
$\mathtt{M}^1 \leftarrow\!\!\$\ \mathsf{S}(\mathtt{A}, \mathtt{L}, \mathcal{J}, \mathtt{M}^0[\mathcal{J}])$
return $\mathtt{M}^b$

Oracle $\mathcal{T}(j)$

if $\mathsf{challenged}$: **return** $\lightning$
$\mathcal{J} \xleftarrow{\cup} j$
return $\mathtt{M}^0[j]$

Oracle $\mathcal{S}(j)$

if $\mathsf{challenged}$: **return** $\lightning$
$\mathcal{J} \xleftarrow{\cup} j$
return $(\mathtt{M}^0[j], \mathtt{R}[j])$

Oracle $\mathcal{R}(i)$

if $\mathsf{challenged}$: **return** $\lightning$
$\mathcal{I} \xleftarrow{\cup} i$
return sk_i

Fig. 5. A posteriori indistinguishability (indistinguishability SOA) with bi-opening.

When formalizing an ISO notion, how messages get sampled (and resampled) plays an important role and different abstractions are possible, as surveyed in the full version. Our notion of ISO-CCA⊛ uses BY12's idea of a fixed, stateful sampling algorithm M, which on adversarial input α outputs a single message. We generalize BY12's notion by, in addition to sender and transmission opening, also allowing receiver opening and chosen ciphertext attacks. Furthermore, we make a syntactical distinction between the message sampler M and its resampler S. An adversary $\mathbb{A}$'s advantage (against a given PKE) will be relative to both this message sampler M and resampler S, as made explicit in Definition 3 below. This definition simultaneously serves to define weaker notions such as κ-ISO-CPA⋄, κ-ISO-CCA⋆, etc., by changing which oracles the adversary has access to.

Definition 3. *The* κ-ISO-CCA⊛ *advantage* $\mathsf{Adv}^{\kappa\text{-iso-cca}\circledast}_{\mathsf{PKE}[\lambda],\mathsf{M},\mathsf{S}}(\mathbb{A})$ *of an adversary* $\mathbb{A}$ *against public key encryption scheme* $\mathsf{PKE}[\lambda]$*, relative to message sampler* M *and resampler* S*, is the distinguishing advantage against the game* $\mathsf{Exp}^{\kappa\text{-iso-cca}\circledast}_{\mathsf{PKE}[\lambda],\mathsf{M},\mathsf{S}}(\mathbb{A})$ *(see Fig. 5).*

A run of the game proceeds in two stages. In the first stage, the adversary has access to its encryption oracle $\mathcal{E}$, as well as to any of its auxiliary oracles (to open and decrypt). Each encryption query will result in a single challenge ciphertext and the game keeps track of the corresponding encrypted messages (across queries) in the list $\mathtt{M}^0$. The opening oracle(s) will reveal some of $\mathtt{M}^0$, either directly through $\mathcal{T}$ or $\mathcal{S}$ or indirectly through $\mathcal{R}$; the shorthand $\mathtt{M}^0[\mathcal{J}]$ indicates the opened messages. The second stage commences once the adversary calls its challenge oracle $\mathcal{C}$, which blocks access to all oracles apart from $\mathcal{D}$; the flag $\mathsf{challenged}$ enforces the access control. The challenge oracle itself creates a full list of resampled messages $\mathtt{M}^1$ using resampler S and returns either the real or resampled list, depending on the challenge bit.

To avoid trivial wins, $\mathtt{M}^1$ needs to be consistent with $\mathtt{M}^0$ relative to what an adversary trivially learns about the latter: the opening oracles reveal $\mathtt{M}^0[\mathcal{J}]$ (and $\mathcal{J}$); the queries α, collected in $\mathtt{A}$, carry information about the distribution; and we usually assume that ciphertext lengths leak message lengths, collected in the list $\mathtt{L}$. Hence, the resampler S is given the input $(\mathtt{A}, \mathtt{L}, \mathcal{J}, \mathtt{M}^0[\mathcal{J}])$ to facilitate conditional resampling.

Ideally, the resampler S samples from exactly the same distribution as M, conditioned on S's input. Let $\mathring{\mathsf{S}}$ be this ideal, not necessarily efficient, resampler.

Definition 4 (Resampling error). *Let M be a stateful sampling algorithm with ideal resampler $\mathring{\mathsf{S}}$, and S be a resampling algorithm. Let $\ell \in \mathbb{Z}_{>0}$ correspond to the number of M calls, and define the support* $\mathrm{Supp}_{\ell,\lambda}(\mathsf{M})$ *as the set of all tuples $(\mathtt{A}, \mathtt{L}, \mathcal{J}, \mathtt{M}^0[\mathcal{J}])$ subject to $|\mathtt{A}| = |\mathtt{L}| = \ell$ that may occur, i.e. there exists an adversary $\mathbb{A}$ and PKE scheme $\mathsf{PKE}[\lambda]$ such that the probability that $\mathsf{Exp}^{\kappa\text{-iso-cca}\circledast}_{\mathsf{PKE}[\lambda],\mathsf{M},\mathsf{S}}(\mathbb{A})$ results in $(\mathtt{A}, \mathtt{L}, \mathcal{J}, \mathtt{M}^0[\mathcal{J}])$ being input to S is non-zero. For $(\mathtt{A}, \mathtt{L}, \mathcal{J}, \mathtt{M}^0[\mathcal{J}]) \in \mathrm{Supp}_{\ell,\lambda}(\mathsf{M})$, let $\delta_{\mathring{\mathsf{S}},\mathsf{S}}(\mathtt{A}, \mathtt{L}, \mathcal{J}, \mathtt{M}^0[\mathcal{J}])$ be the statistical distance between $\mathring{\mathsf{S}}(\mathtt{A}, \mathtt{L}, \mathcal{J}, \mathtt{M}^0[\mathcal{J}])$ and $\mathsf{S}(\mathtt{A}, \mathtt{L}, \mathcal{J}, \mathtt{M}^0[\mathcal{J}])$. The* resampling error *of S is*

$$\epsilon^{\ell}_{\mathring{\mathsf{S}},\mathsf{S}}(\lambda) = \max_{(\mathtt{A},\mathtt{L},\mathcal{J},\mathtt{M}^0[\mathcal{J}])\in \mathrm{Supp}_{\ell,\lambda}(\mathsf{M})} \delta_{\mathring{\mathsf{S}},\mathsf{S}}(\mathtt{A}, \mathtt{L}, \mathcal{J}, \mathtt{M}^0[\mathcal{J}]) .$$

Remark 2. Although BY12 mention the requirement that resampling should result in a distribution statistically close to the ideal conditional resampler, their formalization differs in a number of aspects. Firstly, they define ideal resampling algorithmically with respect to the coins of the original samplers; our approach is more abstract and simply accepts that the relevant conditional distribution is well-defined. Secondly, they define ideal resampling on inputs outside $\mathrm{Supp}_{\ell,\lambda}(\mathsf{M})$ to yield $\perp$ and expect a resampler to behave the same; we do not pose any demands on the resampler in that case (consequently, their resampler must be able to distinguish $\mathrm{Supp}_{\ell,\lambda}(\mathsf{M})$ whereas ours does not). Thirdly, they define the resampling error in terms of a game played by an unbounded adversary, thus hiding the dependency on ℓ. As any statistical distance can be realized as distinguishing advantage by an unbounded adversary—and no unbounded adversary can do any better—their advantage would be more akin to taking the supremum over $\ell \in \mathbb{Z}_{>0}$ of $\epsilon^{\ell}_{\mathring{\mathsf{S}},\mathsf{S}}(\lambda)$. Finally, their distinguishing game randomly samples parameters according to the PKE scheme at hand, making their advantage essentially an expectation of the resampling error over the choice of said parameters.

Compared to BY12, our definition of resampling error Definition 4 has the benefit of being easier to work with, by avoiding unbounded adversaries that interact in a resampling experiment, and connecting instead to the intuitive language of statistical distance. Due to the slightly different choices made, somewhat surprisingly the definitions appear technically incomparable; we leave open the task of convincing consolidation of the concept of conditional resamplability, especially in relation to the notion of efficient conditional resamplability (see the "Asymptotic interpretation" paragraph in the full version [11]).

Lemma 1. *Let* $\mathsf{PKE}[\lambda]$ *and* κ-ISO-CCA⊛ *adversary* $\mathbb{A}$, *making at most* ℓ $\mathcal{E}$-*queries, be given. Let* M *be a message sampler with ideal resampler* $\mathring{\mathsf{S}}$ *and let* S *be an arbitrary resampler. Then*

$$\left|\mathsf{Adv}^{\kappa\text{-iso-cca}\circledast}_{\mathsf{PKE}[\lambda],\mathsf{M},\mathsf{S}}(\mathbb{A}) - \mathsf{Adv}^{\kappa\text{-iso-cca}\circledast}_{\mathsf{PKE}[\lambda],\mathsf{M},\mathring{\mathsf{S}}}(\mathbb{A})\right| \leq \epsilon^{\ell}_{\mathring{\mathsf{S}},\mathsf{S}}(\lambda)$$

ISO Implies IND. We present a concrete variation of BY12's result that ISO security implies IND security [10, Thm. 4.3]. Specifically, we show that, for a suitably chosen message sampler (see Lemma 2), κ-ISO-CCA⋆ implies κ-IND-CCA⋆ with only a factor 2 loss (the CPA case follows from the reduction's type-preservation). In contrast, BY12 only showed that single-sample κ-IND-CPA◇ implies single challenge IND-CPA (with a factor 2 loss), thus our result is both tighter for multi-challenge situations and more general by allowing additional oracles , (see the full version [11] for the proof and asymptotic interpretation) .

Conversely, general separations in the form of counterexamples are known (see Sect. 4 for details), indicating that a posteriori indistinguishability is strictly stronger than a priori indistinguishability in the presence of receiver openings.

Lemma 2. *Let* $\mathsf{M}_{\langle s\rangle}$ *be the sampler that as input* α *only takes message pairs* (m_0, m_1) *subject to both* $|m_0| = |m_1|$ *and* $m_0 \neq m_1$. *On first invocation (when* $s = \varepsilon$*), it draws* $s \leftarrow_{\$} \{0,1\}$ *and, on all invocations, on input* $\alpha = (m_0, m_1)$, *it returns* m_s. *Let* $\mathring{\mathsf{S}}$ *be its ideal resampler.*

Consider S *that on input* $(\mathtt{A}, \mathtt{L}, \mathcal{J}, \mathtt{M}^0[\mathcal{J}])$, *first checks whether* $\mathtt{M}^0[\mathcal{J}]$ *is non-empty. If so, it contains at least one opened* m_s *drawn from* (m_0, m_1) *satisfying* $m_0 \neq m_1$, *and* S *sets* $s' \leftarrow s$; *otherwise it draws* $s' \leftarrow_{\$} \{0,1\}$. *Finally,* S *sets and returns* $\mathtt{M}^1 \leftarrow \mathtt{A}_{s'}$, *where* $\mathtt{A}$ *is interpreted as* $(\mathtt{A}_0, \mathtt{A}_1)$ *based on the special form of the* α. *Then* $\mathsf{S} = \mathring{\mathsf{S}}$.

Theorem 3. *Let* $\mathsf{PKE}[\lambda]$ *be given and let* $\mathsf{M}_{\langle s\rangle}$ *be as given in Lemma 2. Then there is a type-preserving black-box reduction* $\mathbb{B}_{\text{iso}}$ *such that, for all* $\mathbb{A}_{\text{ind}}$,

$$\mathsf{Adv}^{\kappa\text{-ind-cca}\star}_{\mathsf{PKE}[\lambda]}(\mathbb{A}_{\text{ind}}) \leq 2 \cdot \mathsf{Adv}^{\kappa\text{-iso-cca}\star}_{\mathsf{PKE}[\lambda],\mathsf{M},\mathring{\mathsf{S}}}(\mathbb{B}_{\text{iso}}).$$

The runtime of $\mathbb{B}_{\text{iso}}$ *is upper bounded by that of* $\mathbb{A}_{\text{ind}}$.

Experiment $\mathsf{Exp}^{\kappa\text{-sso-cca}\circledast}_{\mathsf{PKE}[\lambda],\mathsf{M},\mathsf{Sim}}(\mathbb{A},\mathbb{D})$

$b \leftarrow\!\!\$ \{0,1\}$
$s \leftarrow \varepsilon$
$\mathsf{pm} \leftarrow\!\!\$ \mathsf{PKE.Pm}(\lambda)$
$\forall_{i\in[\kappa]} (\mathsf{pk}_i, \mathsf{sk}_i) \leftarrow\!\!\$ \mathsf{PKE.Kg}(\mathsf{pm})$
if $b = 0$:
  $\mathsf{out} \leftarrow\!\!\$ \mathbb{A}^{\mathcal{E},\mathcal{D},\mathcal{S},\mathcal{R},\mathcal{T}}(\mathsf{pk}_1,\ldots,\mathsf{pk}_\kappa)$
  for $j \in [|\mathtt{K}|]$:
    if $\mathtt{K}[j] \in \mathcal{I} : \mathcal{J} \xleftarrow{\cup} j$
else :
  $\mathsf{out} \leftarrow\!\!\$ \mathsf{Sim}^{\mathcal{E},\mathcal{T}}(\mathsf{pm})$
$\hat{b} \leftarrow\!\!\$ \mathbb{D}(\mathsf{pm}, \mathtt{A}, \mathtt{M}, \mathcal{J}, \mathsf{out})$
return $b = \hat{b}$

Oracle $\mathcal{E}(i,\alpha)$

$\mathtt{K} \xleftarrow{\frown} i, \mathtt{A} \xleftarrow{\frown} \alpha$
$m \leftarrow\!\!\$ \mathsf{M}_{\langle s\rangle}(\alpha)$
$\mathtt{M} \xleftarrow{\frown} m$
$r \leftarrow\!\!\$ \mathsf{PKE.Rnd}(\mathsf{pm})$
$c \leftarrow \mathsf{PKE.Enc}_{\mathsf{pk}_i}(m; r)$
$\mathtt{R} \xleftarrow{\frown} r, \mathcal{C}_i \xleftarrow{\cup} c$
if $b = 0$: **return** c
else : **return** $|m|$

Oracle $\mathcal{D}(i,c)$

if $c \in \mathcal{C}_i$: **return** $\lightning$
$m \leftarrow \mathsf{PKE.Dec}_{\mathsf{sk}_i}(c)$
return m

Oracle $\mathcal{T}(j)$

$\mathcal{J} \xleftarrow{\cup} j$
return $\mathtt{M}[j]$

Oracle $\mathcal{S}(j)$

$\mathcal{J} \xleftarrow{\cup} j$
return $(\mathtt{M}[j], \mathtt{R}[j])$

Oracle $\mathcal{R}(i)$

$\mathcal{I} \xleftarrow{\cup} i$
return sk_i

Fig. 6. κ-SSO-CCA⊛ security game, for which a distinguisher $\mathbb{D}$ is tasked with guessing whether it received the view of adversary $\mathbb{A}$ playing the real game or a simulated view (by Sim).

Remark 3. Given that (κ,β)-IND-CCA⊛ is implied by κ-IND-CCA⋆ with a β, we may conclude that κ-ISO-CCA⋆ implies (κ,β)-IND-CCA⊛ with a $2{\cdot}\beta$ security loss. In fact, a tighter reduction that loses only a factor 2 is possible by starting from κ-ISO-CCA⊛ (instead of κ-ISO-CCA⋆ as in Theorem 3), see the full version for details.

3.5 A Posteriori Simulatability with Selective Opening (SSO)

As explained in Sect. 3.2, the main idea of a posteriori simulatability is to have a simulator Sim simulate the computations of $\mathbb{A}$ without seeing the ciphertexts, thus capturing the idea that the ciphertexts leak nothing about the plaintexts. Unlike the ISO notion from the previous section, for SSO the relevant security game does not contain a conditional resampling phase, making the notion suitable when such resampling is problematic. A potential downside is that the presence of simulators and distinguishers can complicate reductions compared to indistinguishability-based alternatives.

In the CPA setting, with either sender or receiver opening SSO-CPA is known to be strictly stronger (and therefore harder to achieve) than ISO-CPA [27], and so we place a posteriori simulatability above a priori indistinguishability in our hierarchy (Fig. 1). With only transmission openings present, the notion is implied by a priori indistinguishability with only a factor 2 tightness loss [10], see Sect. 4.

On the other hand, in the CCA setting the relationship between a posteriori simulatability and a posteriori indistinguishability remains largely open: in particular, while we conjecture that SSO-CCA implies ISO-CCA with any

Experiment $\mathsf{Exp}^{\kappa\text{-sso}'\text{-cca}\circledast}_{\mathsf{PKE}[\lambda],\mathsf{M},\mathsf{Sim}}(\mathbb{A},\mathbb{D})$	Oracle $\mathcal{E}(i,\alpha)$	Oracle $\mathcal{R}'(i)$
$b \leftarrow\$ \{0,1\}$	$\mathtt{K} \xleftarrow{\frown} i, \mathtt{A} \xleftarrow{\frown} \alpha$	$\mathcal{I} \xleftarrow{\cup} i$
$s \leftarrow \varepsilon$	$m \leftarrow\$ \mathsf{M}_{\langle s \rangle}(\alpha)$	**for** $j \in [\lvert\mathtt{K}\rvert]$:
$\mathsf{pm} \leftarrow\$ \mathsf{PKE.Pm}(\lambda)$	$\mathtt{M} \xleftarrow{\frown} m$	**if** $\mathtt{K}[j] = i$:
$\forall_{i\in[\kappa]}(\mathsf{pk}_i, \mathsf{sk}_i) \leftarrow\$ \mathsf{PKE.Kg}(\mathsf{pm})$	$r \leftarrow\$ \mathsf{PKE.Rnd}(\mathsf{pm})$	$\mathtt{L} \xleftarrow{\frown} \mathtt{M}[j]$
if $b = 0$:	$c \leftarrow \mathsf{PKE.Enc}_{\mathsf{pk}_i}(m; r)$	**return** $\mathtt{L}$
$\mathsf{out} \leftarrow\$ \mathbb{A}^{\mathcal{E},\mathcal{D},\mathcal{S},\mathcal{R},\mathcal{T}}(\mathsf{pk}_1, \ldots, \mathsf{pk}_\kappa)$	$\mathtt{R} \xleftarrow{\frown} r, \mathcal{C}_i \xleftarrow{\cup} c$	
else : $\mathsf{out} \leftarrow\$ \mathsf{Sim}^{\mathcal{E},\mathcal{R}',\mathcal{T}}(\mathsf{pm})$	**if** $b = 0$: **return** c	
$\hat{b} \leftarrow\$ \mathbb{D}(\mathsf{pm}, \mathtt{K}, \mathtt{A}, \mathtt{M}, \mathcal{I}, \mathcal{J}, \mathsf{out})$	**else if** $i \in \mathcal{I}$:	
return $b = \hat{b}$	**return** m	
	else : **return** $\lvert m \rvert$	

Fig. 7. An alternative κ-SSO′-CCA$\circledast$ security game, where the simulator Sim's behaviour is bound by additional direct inputs (by the game) to the distinguisher $\mathbb{D}$. The simulator has access to its $\mathcal{T}$ oracle whenever the adversary has access to $\mathcal{S}$ or $\mathcal{T}$ ($\diamond$, $\odot$, and $\circledast$ notions) and to $\mathcal{R}'$ whenever $\mathbb{A}$ has access to $\mathcal{R}$ ($\star$ and $\circledast$ notions).

(matching) openings (see Fig. 9), a proof thereof has to the best of our knowledge yet to appear, see Open Problem 5.

Our formalization (Fig. 6) is based on BY12's SSO-CPA$\odot$ notion, where we added multiple users, receiver and thus bi-openings, as well as a CCA oracle. The joint advantage of adversary $\mathbb{A}$ and distinguisher $\mathbb{D}$ is therefore relative to the stateful, single-message sampler M (see Sect. 3.4) as well as simulator Sim.

Definition 5. *The* κ-SSO-CCA$\circledast$ *advantage* $\mathsf{Adv}^{\kappa\text{-sso-cca}\circledast}_{\mathsf{PKE}[\lambda],\mathsf{M},\mathsf{Sim}}(\mathbb{A},\mathbb{D})$ *of an adversary* $\mathbb{A}$ *and distinguisher* $\mathbb{D}$ *against public key encryption scheme* $\mathsf{PKE}[\lambda]$*, relative to message sampler* M *and simulator* Sim*, is the distinguishing advantage against the game* $\mathsf{Exp}^{\kappa\text{-sso-cca}\circledast}_{\mathsf{PKE}[\lambda],\mathsf{M},\mathsf{Sim}}(\mathbb{A},\mathbb{D})$ *(see Fig. 6).*

And so our formalization of SSO comes with three players: adversary $\mathbb{A}$, simulator Sim, and distinguisher $\mathbb{D}$. In the real game ($b = 0$), $\mathbb{A}$ gets access to the public keys and all oracles, and the encryption oracle $\mathcal{E}$ returns encryptions of the sampled messages. Once the adversary is content, it halts with some output out. Intuitively, $\mathbb{A}$'s goal is to make it as easy as possible for $\mathbb{D}$ to guess correctly, and without loss of generality $\mathbb{A}$ will simply output its view, i.e. the transcript of its interactions with the game as well as its internal randomness.

In the ideal game ($b = 1$), the game instead calls Sim who does not get access to the ciphertexts, and whose goal is to fool the distinguisher, and so Sim will want to do everything in its power to make out look like it originated from an adversary who did have access to the real ciphertexts. Since we usually assume that ciphertexts leak message lengths, the simulator does receive message lengths (in place of ciphertexts) to facilitate its job; additionally, it can open individual messages through the transmission opening oracle. The sender and receiver oracles are not present as, in the ideal game, there are no keys to be opened, nor is there any randomness sampled by the encryption oracle.

Eventually, $\mathbb{D}$ makes a decision on whether out was produced by someone with access to the real ciphertexts and opening oracles or not, halting with a guess $\hat{b} = 0$ for "real", or $\hat{b} = 1$ for "ideal". Crucially, the distinguisher receives all the sampled messages $\mathtt{M}$ directly from the experiment, in addition to the real parameters pm, sampler inputs $\mathtt{A}$ and list of opened challenges $\mathcal{J}$.

Remark 4. The strength of the notion is governed by which of these additional inputs $\mathbb{D}$ receives directly from the game, as those inputs effectively bind the simulator to be honest. For instance, denying the distinguisher access to the list $\mathcal{J}$ of opened challenges yields a vacuous notion: a simulator could run a copy of the experiment with $\mathbb{A}$ and, whenever $\mathbb{A}$ makes an $\mathcal{E}$-query, Sim would call its own $\mathcal{E}$-oracle, immediately open that challenge using $\mathcal{T}$ to receive the underlying message, and then simply encrypt that message to obtain a ciphertext to return to $\mathbb{A}$ (and eventually Sim uses $\mathbb{A}$'s out as output). Conditioned on only pm, $\mathtt{A}$, and $\mathtt{M}$, this simulator's out will be identically distributed to that of a real adversary.

For receiver openings, our mechanism only provides the distinguisher with the indices of the messages that were opened as a logical consequence of revealing private keys. Instead, one could provide the distinguisher directly with the list $\mathcal{I}$ of the opened keys [27], plus the information ($\mathtt{K}$) needed to identify which ciphertexts were encrypted under which key (for past single-shot, stateless vector sampling formalizations, restrictions on $\mathcal{E}$ typically made $\mathtt{K}$ superfluous). In the case of bi-openings, one would then provide both the list $\mathcal{I}$ and $\mathcal{J}$ to an adversary [41]. For completeness, we have included the alternative notion κ-SSO′-CCA⊛ in Fig. 7, that captures this finer-grained mechanism in the context of adaptive, stateful sampling.

Considering sender openings only, Bellare, Hofheinz and Yilek [7] opt for another mechanism: their advantage statement is parameterized by the number of openings allowed and both the adversary and simulator are restricted to making at most that many openings (the restriction on the number of openings made by the simulator is not made explicit in the published versions [7,30], but follows from one of the full versions [8]). Inspired by this mechanism, one could in our formalism replace the distinguisher's input $\mathcal{J}$ by only the cardinality $|\mathcal{J}|$ of said list; effectively, it allows the simulator a bit more freedom to deviate from what an adversary is doing, but not enough to render the notion vacuous as above.

Not providing $\mathbb{D}$ with the parameters pm gives an alternative, weaker notion of SSO [49]: since the simulator is now free to produce the parameters itself, it opens for strategies that e.g. involve inserting trapdoors in pm. Conversely, providing the public keys pk_i to the distinguisher takes away the ability for a simulator to use 'fake' keys in its output out; in that case, for the notion to make sense, Sim would have to be provided the pk_i as input, as well as oracle access to $\mathcal{R}$, furthermore the list $\mathcal{I}$ of corrupted parties would then be a secondary additional input to the distinguisher. We let our notion of a posteriori simulatability be one in which $\mathbb{D}$, and thus also Sim, are given pm (matching BY12), but not the pk_i.

Remark 5. A further weakening of SSO⊛ (and SSO⋆) is possible by restricting adversarial access to the challenge oracle $\mathcal{E}$ on already corrupted key handles, by adding a line to the top of $\mathcal{E}$ that, whenever $i \in \mathcal{I}$, immediately return $\lightning$; we denote this notion by SSO*. Past definitions of SSO⋆ often implicitly included this restriction by virtue of being staged and using stateless vector sampling: for instance, an adversary would have a single shot to receive a vector of challenge ciphertexts after which it could non-adaptively corrupt a set of keys [27].

There is no obvious reason for such a restriction, although intuitively challenging on an already corrupted key handle seems of little benefit to an adversary as the messages involved are not considered confidential: the call's corresponding index j is guaranteed to end up in $\mathcal{J}$, so a simulator Sim can access the message as well. Yet, the newly sampled message can depend on the sampler's state, and corrupting a private key possibly allows an adversary to trigger a subsequent call to the sampler that reveals information about its state relating to past, unopened messages. Curiously, for NCE we will soon see (Definition 6) that the restriction is inevitable and, as a consequence, we can only show that NCE implies this weaker, restricted version of SSO.

Open Problem 4. *How do notions of* SSO, SSO′, *and* SSO* *relate?*

SSO Implies ISO. A posteriori simulatability with selective opening implies a posteriori indistinguishability with selective opening in the CPA-setting, as shown by BY12 for transmission and sender openings [10, Theorem 3.3]. We next provide a concrete, updated statement to include receiver and bi-openings. Our proof corrects a subtle mistake in BY12's original, as explained inline, see the full version [11] (which also features an asymptotic interpretation).

Theorem 4. *Let* $\mathsf{PKE}[\lambda]$ *be given, and let* M *be a sampler with ideal resampler* $\mathring{\mathsf{S}}$*. Then, for any adversary* $\mathbb{A}_{\text{iso}}$ *playing* $\mathsf{Exp}^{\kappa\text{-iso-cpa}⊛}_{\mathsf{PKE}[\lambda],\mathsf{M},\mathring{\mathsf{S}}}(\cdot)$ *and making at most* q *challenge queries, there exist (non black-box) type-preserving reduction* $\mathbb{B}_{\text{sso}}$ *and distinguisher* $\mathbb{D}_{\text{sso}}$ *such that, for all simulators* Sim*,*

$$\mathsf{Adv}^{\kappa\text{-iso-cpa}⊛}_{\mathsf{PKE}[\lambda],\mathsf{M},\mathring{\mathsf{S}}}(\mathbb{A}_{\text{iso}}) \leq 2 \cdot \mathsf{Adv}^{\kappa\text{-sso-cpa}⊛}_{\mathsf{PKE}[\lambda],\mathsf{M},\mathsf{Sim}}(\mathbb{B}_{\text{sso}}, \mathbb{D}_{\text{sso}}),$$

The combined runtime of $\mathbb{B}_{\text{sso}}$ *and* $\mathbb{D}_{\text{sso}}$ *is upper bounded by twice that of* $\mathbb{A}_{\text{iso}}$ *plus that of one call to* $\mathring{\mathsf{S}}$ *and some small overhead.*

The proof of Theorem 4 does not carry over to the CCA setting, as the distinguisher $\mathbb{D}_{\text{sso}}$ would have to provide a simulation of the decryption oracle $\mathcal{D}$ to $\mathbb{A}^2_{\text{iso}}$ without access to the private keys or any oracles itself (indeed, already for weaker notions like PCA, CVA, etc., the proof breaks down). Whether SSO-CCA implies ISO-CCA with either kind of opening remains open, captured in Open Problem 5.

Open Problem 5. *Does* SSO-CCA *imply* ISO-CCA *in the presence of sender, receiver, or transmission opening?*

SSO⋆ is unachievable (without programming). Our formalization of SSOis multi-challenge, which allows for non-trivial relations between sampled messages through stateful sampling. Yang et al. [49] showed κ-SSO-CPA⋆ to be unachievable in the non-programmable random oracle model, in the sense that private keys would have to be at least as long as the total number of plaintext bits to be encrypted [49, Thm. 3.1]. Thus, κ-SSO-CPA⊛, κ-SSO-CCA⋆, and κ-SSO-CCA⊛ must all be similarly unachievable. This mirrors Nielsen's earlier impossibility of non-interactive NCE in the non-programmable oracle model [43], see Sect. 3.6.

Intuitively, the impossibility works as follows: the adversary $\mathbb{A}$, who wants to help distinguisher $\mathbb{D}$, commits to the public keys and challenge ciphertexts using the (non-programmable) random oracle. Then, it communicates the commitment, i.e. the digest of the random oracle, to $\mathbb{D}$, through the set of opened key handles, $\mathcal{I}$ (as $\mathcal{I}$ is given to $\mathbb{D}$ in their experiment, cf. Fig. 7). This is done by opening key number i iff the digest at position i has bit value 1. Then, $\mathbb{D}$ can recompute the commitment and check that it matches the form of $\mathcal{I}$. This strategy is hard to simulate, as it would require a simulator to commit to the ciphertexts before opening the corresponding messages. With the ability to program the random oracle, the commitment can be delayed until after opening. The analysis relies on the uniformity of the random oracle and combinatorial bounds on the possible ways to choose the various cryptographic objects: for private keys larger than the number of bits encrypted, the analysis fails, leading to the stated requirement. The strategy puts a lower bound on the number of users in the system: concretely, if the random oracle output length is h, Yang et al. set $\kappa = h+1$. Yang et al.'s impossibility involved a notion of SSO in which the simulator was allowed to produce the parameters itself, cf. Remark 4; it implies impossibility for stronger notions where the simulator has less freedom.

3.6 A Priori Simulatability with Selective Opening (NCE)

As explained in Sect. 3.2, a priori simulatability captures the idea that knowledge of a message should not be a prerequisite for producing ciphertexts that can pass off as encryptions of it, or in other words: irrespective of m, a simulator (without access to m) should be able to create a ciphertext c that cannot be distinguished from a real encryption of m.

Our formalization tasks a simulator Sim with simulating the view of adversary $\mathbb{A}$, taking on the role of game rather than player. This has the benefit of involving no message samplers: single messages are simply chosen by the adversary and given to the encryption oracle, who receives a (real or simulated) encryption in return. This mechanism makes a transmission oracle superfluous, as $\mathbb{A}$ always knows what message a challenge was supposed to encrypt; we therefore exclude the $\mathcal{T}$ oracle from Fig. 8.

Definition 6. *The* κ-NCE-CCA⊛ *advantage* $\mathsf{Adv}^{\kappa\text{-nce-cca}\circledast}_{\mathsf{PKE}[\lambda],\mathsf{Sim}}(\mathbb{A})$ *of an adversary* $\mathbb{A}$ *against public key encryption scheme* $\mathsf{PKE}[\lambda]$*, relative to simulator* Sim*, is the distinguishing advantage against the game* $\mathsf{Exp}^{\kappa\text{-nce-cca}\circledast}_{\mathsf{PKE}[\lambda],\mathsf{Sim}}(\mathbb{A})$ *(see Fig. 8).*

Experiment $\mathsf{Exp}^{\kappa\text{-nce-cca}\circledast}_{\mathsf{PKE}[\lambda],\mathsf{Sim}}(\mathbb{A})$

$b \leftarrow\!\!\$ \{0,1\}$
$\mathcal{O}_b \leftarrow (\mathcal{E}_b, \mathcal{D}_b, \mathcal{S}_b, \mathcal{R}_b)$
$s \leftarrow \varepsilon, q \leftarrow 0$
$\mathsf{pm} \leftarrow\!\!\$ \mathsf{PKE.Pm}(\lambda)$
if $b = 0$:
  $\forall_{i \in [\kappa]} (\mathsf{pk}_i, \mathsf{sk}_i) \leftarrow\!\!\$ \mathsf{PKE.Kg}(\mathsf{pm})$
else :
  $\forall_{i \in [\kappa]} \mathsf{pk}_i \leftarrow\!\!\$ \mathsf{Sim}_{\langle s \rangle}(\mathsf{Ini}, \mathsf{pm})$
$\hat{b} \leftarrow\!\!\$ \mathbb{A}^{\mathcal{O}_b}(\mathsf{pm}, \mathsf{pk}_1, \ldots, \mathsf{pk}_\kappa)$
return $b = \hat{b}$

Oracle $\mathcal{E}_0(i, m)$

if $i \in \mathcal{I}$: **return** $\lightning$
$r \leftarrow\!\!\$ \mathsf{PKE.Rnd}(\mathsf{pm})$
$c \leftarrow \mathsf{PKE.Enc}_{\mathsf{pk}_i}(m; r)$
$\mathtt{R} \xleftarrow{\frown} r$
$\mathcal{C}_i \xleftarrow{\cup} c$
return c

Oracle $\mathcal{E}_1(i, m)$

if $i \in \mathcal{I}$: **return** $\lightning$
$q \leftarrow q + 1$
$c \leftarrow\!\!\$ \mathsf{Sim}_{\langle s \rangle}(\mathsf{Enc}, i, |m|)$
$\mathtt{M} \xleftarrow{\frown} m, \mathtt{M}_i \xleftarrow{\frown} (q, m)$
$\mathcal{C}_i \xleftarrow{\cup} c$
return c

Oracle $\mathcal{D}_0(i, c)$

if $c \in \mathcal{C}_i$: **return** $\lightning$
$m \leftarrow \mathsf{PKE.Dec}_{\mathsf{sk}_i}(c)$
return m

Oracle $\mathcal{D}_1(i, c)$

if $c \in \mathcal{C}_i$: **return** $\lightning$
$m \leftarrow\!\!\$ \mathsf{Sim}_{\langle s \rangle}(\mathsf{Dec}, i, c)$
return m

Oracle $\mathcal{S}_0(j)$

$r \leftarrow \mathtt{R}[j]$
return r

Oracle $\mathcal{S}_1(j)$

$m \leftarrow \mathtt{M}[j]$
$r \leftarrow\!\!\$ \mathsf{Sim}_{\langle s \rangle}(\mathsf{Sen}, j, m)$
return r

Oracle $\mathcal{R}_0(i)$

$\mathcal{I} \xleftarrow{\cup} i$
return sk_i

Oracle $\mathcal{R}_1(i)$

$\mathcal{I} \xleftarrow{\cup} i$
$\mathsf{sk}_i \leftarrow\!\!\$ \mathsf{Sim}_{\langle s \rangle}(\mathsf{Rec}, i, \mathtt{M}_i)$
return sk_i

Fig. 8. The NCE experiment. Middle column = real, right column = ideal.

The oracles of Fig. 8 each come in two variants: one "real" (for $b = 0$), and one simulated, or "ideal" ($b = 1$). The real encryption, decryption, and opening oracles behave as expected: in particular, the real challenge encryption oracle simply encrypts the chosen message and returns the ciphertext.

Ideal oracles, meanwhile, call the corresponding subroutine of Sim. For the encryption oracle, Sim is asked to produce a ciphertext (under the relevant key handle) seeing only the length of the message. The message (or messages) is later revealed to Sim in the event that an opening oracle is called. To avoid trivial wins by the adversary, in the case of an $\mathcal{S}$ call Sim must come up with randomness such that re-encrypting the message produces the same ciphertext; similarly, in the case of $\mathcal{R}$ it should provide a private key such that decrypting *any* of the ciphertexts previously provided as a challenge under the corresponding key handle yields the correct message.

In our previous notions (Sect. 3.3–3.5), $\mathbb{A}$ was free to continue challenging a key handle i after the key had been opened. For NCE, such behaviour must be restricted, lest the notion becomes trivially unachievable. To see how, consider an adversary that calls $\mathcal{R}_b(i)$, receiving private key $\widetilde{\mathsf{sk}}_i$, followed by $\mathcal{E}_b(i,m)$ for a uniformly at random chosen message m of pre-determined length, receiving ciphertext c, and subsequently the adversary outputs $\hat{b}=0$ iff $m = \mathsf{PKE.Dec}_{\widetilde{\mathsf{sk}}_i}(c)$. In the $b=0$ world, the decryption check is guaranteed to succeed (assuming perfect correctness) so $\hat{b}=0$ is guaranteed; yet, in the $b=1$ world, m is information-theoretically hidden from Sim beyond its length $|m|$, thus the decryption check will hold with probability at most $2^{-|m|}$, yielding a significant distinguishing advantage of $1-2^{-|m|}$.

Even when a simulator would be allowed to program a random oracle, the adversary above is troublesome. Realistically, Sim's only hope to fool $\mathbb{A}$ is to program the random oracle for the calls that $\mathbb{A}$ makes to perform the check $m = \mathsf{PKE.Dec}_{\widetilde{\mathsf{sk}}_i}(c)$. In order to do so successfully, Sim would somehow have to learn m based on the queries $\mathbb{A}$ makes, but herein lies the rub: consider the sequence of oracle calls that honest decryption would make, and suppose there is a first oracle call whose input allows Sim to extract non-trivial information about m. Then that non-trivial information is already extractable from the answers Sim itself has provided so far, creating a complication (as m's contents would still have been information-theoretically hidden up to then based on prior calls). Essentially, even when Sim is allowed to program, it still ends up having to bootstrap its own knowledge of m (which is impossible).

As in previous sections, Sim is stateful, and we again allow it (in the ideal game) to produce the public keys but not the parameters: as with SSO (cf. Remark 4), the notion is meaningful even when the parameters are generated by Sim. Restricting the simulator by disallowing the generation of its own pm yields a potentially stronger notion and, as it matches the formalism of SSO better, is our preferred option.

Remark 6. Our formalization employs stateful simulators; earlier formalizations of NCE often consider NCE schemes to be tuples of algorithms extended to include a faking and an opening algorithm. For example, Hazay et al. [27] define the algorithms $\mathsf{PKE.Enc}^*$ and $\mathsf{PKE.Open}$ such that any ciphertext produced by $\mathsf{PKE.Enc}^*$ (on input the public key and message length) may be opened using $\mathsf{PKE.Open}$ (on input the message, the public and private keys, a trapdoor produced by $\mathsf{PKE.Enc}^*$, and the ciphertext to be opened). In our nomenclature, this corresponds to a simulator with precisely prescribed state and behaviour, potentially strengthening the notion without clear benefits. (Hazay et al. further strengthen their notion by insisting the simulator uses an externally, honestly generated public key of which it only learns the private key when running $\mathsf{PKE.Open}$, but not yet when running $\mathsf{PKE.Enc}^*$.)

NCE Implies SSO. We next show (Theorem 5) how a priori simulatability (NCE) tightly implies a posteriori simulatability (SSO) in the presence of bi-openings, see the full version [11] for the proof and asymptotic interpretation. The reduction comes with a crucial caveat though: due to our NCE notion's restriction that opened keys cannot subsequently be challenged, the notion of SSO implied by NCE is weakened to one that makes the same restriction.

Theorem 5. *Let* SSO* *be defined as* SSO*(Fig. 6), except that a query* $\mathcal{E}(i,\alpha)$ *with* $i \in \mathcal{I}$ *leads to the immediate return of* $\lightning$. *Let* $\mathsf{PKE}[\lambda]$ *be given, then there exists a type-preserving black-box reduction* $\mathbb{B}_{\text{nce}}$ *(with black-box access to* $\mathbb{A}_{\text{sso}}, \mathbb{D}_{\text{sso}}$*, and* M *to be quantified later) such that for all* NCE *simulators* $\mathsf{Sim}_{\text{nce}}$*, there is a (black-box)* SSO *simulator* $\mathsf{Sim}_{\text{sso}}$ *such that for all adversaries* $\mathbb{A}_{\text{sso}}$*, message samplers* M*, and distinguishers* $\mathbb{D}_{\text{sso}}$*,*

$$\mathsf{Adv}^{\kappa\text{-sso}^*\text{-cca}\circledast}_{\mathsf{PKE}[\lambda],\mathsf{M},\mathsf{Sim}_{\text{sso}}}(\mathbb{A}_{\text{sso}}, \mathbb{D}_{\text{sso}}) = \mathsf{Adv}^{\kappa\text{-nce-cca}\circledast}_{\mathsf{PKE}[\lambda],\mathsf{Sim}_{\text{nce}}}(\mathbb{B}_{\text{nce}}) .$$

The runtime of $\mathbb{B}_{\text{nce}}$ *is upper bounded by that of* $\mathbb{A}_{\text{sso}}$ *and* $\mathbb{D}_{\text{sso}}$ *combined, plus that of running* M q_e *times, where* q_e *is the number of oracle calls made by* $\mathbb{A}_{\text{sso}}$ *to* $\mathcal{E}$*. The runtime of* $\mathsf{Sim}_{\text{SSO}}$ *is upper bounded by* q *times that of* $\mathsf{Sim}_{\text{nce}}$*, where* q *is the total number of oracle calls made by* $\mathbb{A}_{\text{sso}}$ *to* $\mathcal{E}$, $\mathcal{D}$, $\mathcal{T}$, $\mathcal{S}$, *and* $\mathcal{R}$*, and* $\mathsf{Sim}_{\text{SSO}}$ *additionally calls its* $\mathcal{T}$ *oracle* $|\mathcal{J}|$ *times, where* $|\mathcal{J}|$ *is the total number of opened challenge ciphertexts.*

Remark 7. The restriction on $i \notin \mathcal{I}$ for $\mathcal{E}(i,\alpha)$-calls appears unfortunate and is largely an artefact of our modelling choice to allow an adversary adaptive oracle access to challenge encryptions. Clearly, our theorem suffices to show that (our notion of) NCE tightly implies the more customary staged, single-shot version of SSO (with stateless vector-sampling), as there the game only allows corruptions after the challenge. For instance, implications similar to ours were previously shown for sender openings [20, Lemma 1] and receiver openings [27, Theorem 4.4] (based on variants of NCE⊙ and NCE⋆, respectively). However, both those results use a staged SSO notion; moreover, both results use a single-key single-shot NCE notion, resulting in a reduction loss linear in the number of challenge ciphertexts (i.e. equal to the length of the vector of messages being sampled). In comparison, our result is tighter and more general and seems to resolve an open problem identified by BY12, who imagine that the general NCE⊛ (referred to as "MPC definition" by BY12) implies both SSO⊙ and SSO⋆.

The proof of Theorem 5 can readily be adapted to use the ($i \notin \mathcal{I}$)-restricted variant of SSO′ (Fig. 7) as target notion, if so desired. However, whether NCE suffices to imply (unrestricted) SSO we leave open (Open Problem 6).

Open Problem 6. *Does* NCE *imply* SSO *(no restriction) and if so, how tightly?*

NCE⋆ is unachievable (without programming). Just like κ-SSO-CPA⋆, κ-NCE-CPA⋆ is unachievable in the non-programmable random oracle model (in the sense that private keys would have to be at least as long as the total number of plaintext bits to be encrypted), as first shown by Nielsen [43]. Since κ-NCE-CPA⋆ implies κ-SSO-CPA⋆, this impossibility also follows from the (later) impossibility of κ-SSO-CPA⋆ [49] (see Sect. 3.5).

Intuitively, Nielsen's proof is combinatorial in nature. There are at most $2^{|\mathsf{sk}|}$ possible decryptions of each ciphertext (one for each key); since chosen messages are independent of the private keys, if the messages are chosen from a set significantly larger than $2^{|\mathsf{sk}|}$, then it becomes likely that the chosen message is not in the set of possible decryptions for the simulated ciphertext.

The unachievability of κ-NCE-CPA⊛, κ-NCE-CCA⋆, and κ-NCE-CCA⊛ in the non-programmable random oracle model follows.

4 Relations

The road to understand the relations between the various notions presented in Sect. 3 has been long and winding, and as we have seen with the various open problems, the journey is still ongoing. We provide overviews of known relations in the CPA and CCA settings in Fig. 9. Here, bold arrows highlight results new to the current work, while purple dashed arrows represent relations that have yet to be formally established, but that mirror other known results.

We stress that Fig. 9 reflects asymptotic interpretations of the various notions as, historically, these relations have primarily been considered asymptotically. The implications and separations are given relative to classes of samplers/simulators in that case. For instance, an implication such as SSO-CPA⊙ $\Rightarrow$ ISO-CPA⊙ should be interpreted that, for all efficient PKE, if for the class of all efficient samplers SSO-CPA⊙ security holds, then ISO-CPA⊙ security also holds for the class of all samplers with efficient resamplability. For this particular implication, one can instead show the more concrete statement that for any efficient PKE and sampler with efficient resamplability, SSO-CPA⊙ security with respect to that sampler implies ISO-CPA⊙ security with respect to the same sampler. In addition to the trivial, 'drop-an-oracle' concrete implications, we provided concrete counterparts for the "downwards" implications in Sect. 3.

In contrast, we leave the remaining (non-trivial) results using their original asymptotic phrasing, unless explicitly stated otherwise. In addition to (full) implications as explained above, these results include partial implications and various kinds of separations. A partial implication IND-CPA $\Rightarrow$ SSO-CPA⊙ states that for all efficient PKE, if IND-CPA security holds, then for all samplers in some class, SSO-CPA⊙ security holds (the partiality of the implication may also restrict the class of PKE). Separations show that implications cannot be proven, for instance IND-CPA $\not\Rightarrow$ SSO-CPA⊙ would indicate that there exists an efficient IND-CPA-secure scheme and some efficient sampler for which SSO-CPA⊙ security does not hold. From a strict, logical perspective, such a separation has to be conditional on the existence of an efficient IND-CPA-secure scheme to begin with. Often separations only have a partial scope, for instance by showing that they only hold for efficient PKE with certain properties, or when considering black-box reductions only.

Finally, we encounter some semi-separations, in the sense that partial security of one notion is insufficient to establish an impliciation. For instance, Cor. 1's semi-separation ISO-CCA⊙ $\not\Rightarrow$ SSO-CPA⊙ indicates that there plausibly exists an efficient PKE for which ISO-CCA⊙ security holds with respect to some strict subclass of message samplers, yet SSO-CPA⊙ security with respect to some relevant class of message samplers does not.

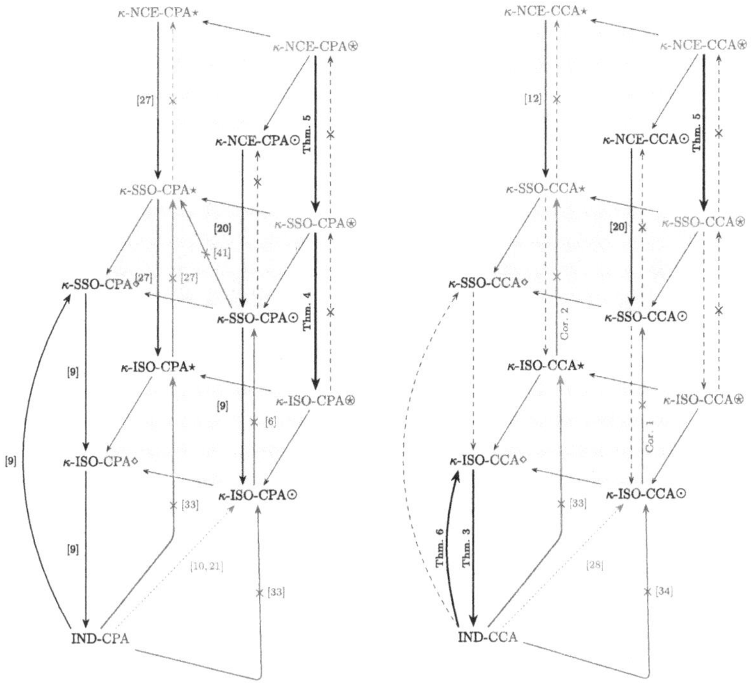

Fig. 9. Known and conjectured relations in the CPA and CCA settings. Highlighted in red are notions known to be unachievable in the standard model, and in blue notions for which standard model achievability remains open. Slim arrows (without references) are trivial, bold arrows highlight implications shown for the first time here, and violet dashed arrows are open problems (shown as the relation one would expect based on known results). Finally, green dotted arrows represent conditional implications. (Color figure online)

We discuss some further relations including hybridization and other related notions in the full version [11].

Remark 8. Formalizations often differ between works in subtle but important ways (for instance the order of quantifiers or the exact interfaces of adversaries, simulators and distinguishers), and the implications and separations given in Fig. 9 should therefore be interpreted as going between families of notions, in the sense that there is for instance a formalization of SSO-CPA⊙ known to imply a formalization of ISO-CPA⊙; or the other way around, that some formalization of ISO-CPA⊙ cannot imply some formalization of SSO-CPA⊙. Consequently, one should take some care when interpreting the figure, as arrows may not trivially compose. To alleviate some of these complications, we provided concrete, more systematic versions of several known implications in Sect. 3 with updated proofs, and our asymptotic interpretations clarify which implications do hold and between which formalizations subtleties arise, see the full version [11]. One striking example where composition is not straightforward is our reduction from

NCE to SSO (Theorem 5), as it requires challenging compromised key handles to be disallowed also in the SSO experiment, as it is in the NCE experiment. Thus, implications from NCE to notions further down the hierarchy also do not immediately follow without putting similar restrictions on each notion.

Downward Implications. The hierarchical structure between the different philosophies presented in Fig. 1 (from a priori indistinguishability up to a priori simulatability) is well-established in the CPA setting, as follows from the asymptotic interpretations of Theorem 5 (NCE implies SSO [20,26,27]), Theorem 4 (SSO implies ISO [9]), and Theorem 3 (ISO implies INS [9]), respectively. The main caveat that we uncovered is that NCE only implies a slightly restricted version of our more general SSO notion, although it still suffices to imply the older SSO version (with a stateless vector sampler, see the full version [11]). Various separation results, to be discussed below, reinforce the hierarchy by ruling out that 'lower' notions are in fact equivalent to the corresponding 'higher' one (with the noticeable exception of CPA$\diamond$, for which IND, ISO and SSO are all equivalent). By contrast, the CCA hierarchy currently contains a gap as far as implications go, i.e. whether SSO-CCA security implies ISO-CCA security in the presence of openings (Open Problem 5).

IND Partially Implies ISO$\odot$. There are classes of message samplers for which IND-CPA does imply κ-ISO-CPA$\odot$: Fuchsbauer et al. [21] showed that these include samplers inducing product distributions (i.e. independent message sampling), Markov distributions, and more generally any graph-induced message distribution for which the underlying directed graph can be traversed in polynomial time (for a certain definition of "traversed"). Heuer later showed that the result transfers to the CCA setting [28]; extending to receiver openings remains open. These partial implications appear as green dotted arrows in Fig. 9.

Open Problem 7. *For which classes of message samplers does* IND-CPA *security imply* κ-ISO-CPA$\star$ *or even* κ-ISO-CPA$\circledast$ *security? How about for* CCA*?*

IND Implies Notions of SOA with Transmission Openings. As shown by BY12, IND-CPA implies κ-SSO-CPA$\diamond$, and when starting from κ-IND-CPA, the reduction is furthermore tight [10, Thm. 4.1]. As we will show momentarily, for ISO a similar implication holds also in the CCA setting, which follows from a reduction to multi-user real-or-random indistinguishability (Theorem 6, see the full version [11] for the proof and asymptotic interpretation).

For SSO, it is unclear whether a similar implication holds in the CCA setting; a straightforward upgrade of BY12's proof runs into technical difficulties with simulating access to a decryption oracle (i.e. the simulator would not have access to a decryption oracle, and we cannot rule out the possibility that an adversary could somehow convince the distinguisher that it does have access to one).

Open Problem 8. *Does* IND-CCA *security imply* SSO-CCA$\diamond$ *security?*

Theorem 6. *Let* $\mathsf{PKE}[\lambda]$ *be given, let* $q \in \mathbb{Z}_{>0}$*, and let* M *be a sampler with ideal resampler* $\mathring{\mathsf{S}}$*. Then there is a reduction* $\mathbb{B}_{\mathrm{ror}}$ *such that for any adversary* $\mathbb{A}_{\mathrm{iso}}$ *making at most* q *challenge oracle calls,*

$$\mathsf{Adv}^{\kappa\text{-iso-cca}\diamond}_{\mathsf{PKE}[\lambda],\mathsf{M},\mathring{\mathsf{S}}}(\mathbb{A}_{\mathrm{iso}}) = 2 \cdot \mathsf{Adv}^{\kappa\text{-ror-cca}}_{\mathsf{PKE}[\lambda]}(\mathbb{B}_{\mathrm{ror}})\,.$$

The runtime of $\mathbb{B}_{\mathrm{ror}}$ *is upper bounded by that of* $\mathbb{A}_{\mathrm{iso}}$*, plus that of running* M q *times and* $\mathring{\mathsf{S}}$ *once, and some small overhead.*

IND Does Not Imply ISO (with Sender or Receiver Openings). Standard IND-CCA security implies neither ISO-CPA⊙ nor κ-ISO-CPA⋆ in general: Hofheinz et al. [33,34] showed that IND-CCA does not imply a closely related notion of threshold ISO-CPA⊙ security, for which the adversary gets a number of encrypted shares of a secret and must uncover the secret. Meanwhile, ISO-CPA⊙ does imply threshold ISO-CPA⊙, establishing a separation. Adapting the strategy to the receiver opening setting via an analogous notion of receiver-threshold security (in which each share is encrypted under a random public key rather than a single, fixed public key), they were able to likewise establish a separation from IND-CCA to κ-ISO-CPA⋆ [33].

As actually developed use cases of SOA-notions are rare, the separations above simultaneously support our belief in the notions' usefulness in the context of threshold security, where IND-CCA is insufficient.

ISO Does Not Imply SSO (with Sender or Receiver Openings). Bellare et al. [6], generalizing an earlier result due to Hofheinz [7,30], showed that no *committing* PKE scheme (i.e. one that implies a computationally binding non-interactive commitment scheme) can achieve SSO-CPA⊙, even when message samplers are restricted to independently sampled uniform bitstrings. (Hofheinz only showed that there exists a sampler relative to which such schemes cannot be proven SSO-CPA⊙-secure via black-box reductions to standard cryptographic assumptions.) Since there are IND-CCA schemes that are committing, for instance the Cramer–Shoup encryption scheme [16], they concluded that IND-CCA cannot imply SSO-CPA⊙. As explained above, Heuer [28] lifted an earlier result in the CPA setting [21] to the CCA setting, and thereby showed that for many message samplers, including those that sample independently (i.e. that infer product distributions), IND-CCA does imply ISO-CCA⊙.

Combining the two results, we see that for a large class of message samplers, IND-CCA implies ISO-CCA⊙ while being separated from SSO-CPA⊙ (even when restricted to that same class of message samplers). Thus we reach a semi-separation (previously a full separation was observed in the CPA setting only [6]):

Corollary 1. *Class restricted* ISO-CCA⊙ *security does not imply (class restricted)* SSO-CPA⊙ *security.*

Turning to receiver openings, Bellare et al. [6] also identified a feature called decryption verifiability, which captures that anyone given a tuple consisting of public key, private key, ciphertext and message, should be able to verify that the ciphertext is an honest encryption of the message (for some definition of "honest"). They showed that no scheme that is decryption verifiable can be SSO-CPA$\star$ secure, even for independent, uniform sampling. Since many natural IND-CPA schemes are decryption verifiable, for instance ElGamal [19], a separation is established.

Both their results (committing schemes do not achieve SSO-CPA$\odot$; decryption verifiable schemes do not achieve κ-SSO-CPA$\star$) build on the same underlying proof idea as the impossibility of SSO$\star$, already discussed in Sect. 3.5: the adversary computes the hash of the challenge ciphertexts, and communicates the digest to the distinguisher using the set of opened indices ($\mathcal{J}$ for $\odot$; $\mathcal{I}$ for $\star$); for any scheme that satisfies the respective property, no efficient simulator can provide a convincing simulation of this strategy.

However, with the standard model impossibility of κ-SSO-CPA$\star$ in hand, combined with the existence of schemes achieving κ-ISO-CCA$\star$ in the standard model (under reasonable computational assumptions, see the full version [11]), we can reach a stronger conclusion (previously only shown for the CPA setting [27]):

Corollary 2. κ-ISO-CCA$\star$ *security does not imply* κ-SSO-CPA$\star$ *security.*

The separation above leaves room for partial implications, where κ-SSO-CPA$\star$ is implied for restricted classes of message samplers (that are not captured by the impossibility). Furthermore, that impossibility result itself relies on the ability of an adversary to use the index set of corrupted challenges ($\mathcal{J}$) or keys ($\mathcal{I}$) to 'communicate' with the distinguisher. Using a formalization of κ-SSO-CPA$\star$ where only the cardinality of those sets is passed directly to the distinguisher would require re-examination of those impossibility results (to determine whether they can be ported to the new formalization).

Technically, the situation is still partly open for bi-opening, as no scheme has yet been shown to achieve κ-ISO-CPA$\circledast$ in the standard model; any such scheme would immediately lead to a separation, namely that κ-ISO-CPA$\circledast$ security does not imply κ-SSO-CPA$\circledast$ security, either in part (if the scheme only achieves CPA) or in full (if it also achieves CCA).

SSO and NCE. Remarkably, whether SSO and NCE are separated or equivalent appears largely open, beyond the logical consequences of various unachievability results for both SSO$\star$ and NCE$\star$ in the standard model.

Camenisch et al. [12] claim that NCE$\star$ is strictly stronger than notions of SSO$\star$, however this claim was based on the former being unachievable in the standard model, and the belief that the latter was achievable in the standard model. With neither achievable in the standard model, their relation becomes less relevant from a logical perspective (unless perhaps in an idealized model, such as the programmable random oracle).

Hazay et al. [27] gave a separation from κ-SSO-CPA$\star$ to κ-NCE-CPA$\star$, however their algorithmic formalization of NCE was stronger than our Definition 6, cf. Remark 6: in particular, and unlike our formalization, their NCE simulator was not allowed to produce the public keys (while their SSO simulator was). This technicality turns out to be central to their separation result.

Open Problem 9. *Which plausibly achievable notions of* SSO *imply notions of NCE in general and which are separated? When neither notion is achievable in the standard model, which relations can be drawn in (specific) idealized models?*

Acknowledgement. The authors would like to thank Joseph Jaeger for many helpful comments and discussions.

References

1. Bader, C., Hofheinz, D., Jager, T., Kiltz, E., Li, Y.: Tightly-secure authenticated key exchange. In: Dodis, Y., Nielsen, J.B. (eds.) TCC 2015. LNCS, vol. 9014, pp. 629–658. Springer, Heidelberg (2015). https://doi.org/10.1007/978-3-662-46494-6_26
2. Bader, C., Jager, T., Li, Y., Schäge, S.: On the impossibility of tight cryptographic reductions. In: Fischlin, M., Coron, J.-S. (eds.) EUROCRYPT 2016. LNCS, vol. 9666, pp. 273–304. Springer, Heidelberg (2016). https://doi.org/10.1007/978-3-662-49896-5_10
3. Beaver, D., Haber, S.: Cryptographic protocols provably secure against dynamic adversaries. In: Rueppel, R.A. (ed.) EUROCRYPT 1992. LNCS, vol. 658, pp. 307–323. Springer, Heidelberg (1993). https://doi.org/10.1007/3-540-47555-9_26
4. Bellare, M., Boldyreva, A., Micali, S.: Public-key encryption in a multi-user setting: security proofs and improvements. In: Preneel, B. (ed.) EUROCRYPT 2000. LNCS, vol. 1807, pp. 259–274. Springer, Heidelberg (2000). https://doi.org/10.1007/3-540-45539-6_18
5. Bellare, M., Desai, A., Pointcheval, D., Rogaway, P.: Relations among notions of security for public-key encryption schemes. In: Krawczyk, H. (ed.) CRYPTO 1998. LNCS, vol. 1462, pp. 26–45. Springer, Heidelberg (1998). https://doi.org/10.1007/BFb0055718
6. Bellare, M., Dowsley, R., Waters, B., Yilek, S.: Standard security does not imply security against selective-opening. In: Pointcheval, D., Johansson, T. (eds.) EUROCRYPT 2012. LNCS, vol. 7237, pp. 645–662. Springer, Heidelberg (2012). https://doi.org/10.1007/978-3-642-29011-4_38
7. Bellare, M., Hofheinz, D., Yilek, S.: Possibility and impossibility results for encryption and commitment secure under selective opening. In: Joux, A. (ed.) EUROCRYPT 2009. LNCS, vol. 5479, pp. 1–35. Springer, Heidelberg (2009). https://doi.org/10.1007/978-3-642-01001-9_1
8. Bellare, M., Yilek, S.: Encryption schemes secure under selective opening attack. Cryptology ePrint Archive, Report 2009/101 (original full version) (2009). https://eprint.iacr.org/2009/101, version 20090302:083605
9. Bellare, M., Yilek, S.: Encryption schemes secure under selective opening attack. Cryptology ePrint Archive, Report 2009/101 (2009). https://eprint.iacr.org/2009/101

10. Bellare, M., Yilek, S.: Encryption schemes secure under selective opening attack. Cryptology ePrint Archive, Report 2009/101 (updated full version) (2012). https://eprint.iacr.org/2009/101, version 20120923:212424
11. Brunetta, C., Heum, H., Stam, M.: SoK: public key encryption with openings. Cryptology ePrint Archive, Report 2023/1337 (2023). https://eprint.iacr.org/2023/1337
12. Camenisch, J., Lehmann, A., Neven, G., Samelin, K.: UC-secure non-interactive public-key encryption. In: Kópf, B., Chong, S. (eds.) CSF 2017 Computer Security Foundations Symposium (2017)
13. Canetti, R.: Universally composable security: a new paradigm for cryptographic protocols. Cryptology ePrint Archive, Report 2000/067 (2000). https://eprint.iacr.org/2000/067
14. Canetti, R., Feige, U., Goldreich, O., Naor, M.: Adaptively secure multi-party computation. In: 28th ACM STOC, pp. 639–648. ACM Press, May 1996. https://doi.org/10.1145/237814.238015
15. Canetti, R., Krawczyk, H., Nielsen, J.B.: Relaxing chosen-ciphertext security. In: Boneh, D. (ed.) CRYPTO 2003. LNCS, vol. 2729, pp. 565–582. Springer, Heidelberg (2003). https://doi.org/10.1007/978-3-540-45146-4_33
16. Cramer, R., Shoup, V.: A practical public key cryptosystem provably secure against adaptive chosen ciphertext attack. In: Krawczyk, H. (ed.) CRYPTO 1998. LNCS, vol. 1462, pp. 13–25. Springer, Heidelberg (1998). https://doi.org/10.1007/BFb0055717
17. Das, A., Dutta, S., Adhikari, A.: Indistinguishability against chosen ciphertext verification attack revisited: the complete picture. In: Susilo, W., Reyhanitabar, R. (eds.) ProvSec 2013. LNCS, vol. 8209, pp. 104–120. Springer, Heidelberg (2013). https://doi.org/10.1007/978-3-642-41227-1_6
18. Dwork, C., Naor, M., Reingold, O., Stockmeyer, L.J.: Magic functions. In: 40th FOCS, pp. 523–534. IEEE Computer Society Press, October 1999. https://doi.org/10.1109/SFFCS.1999.814626
19. ElGamal, T.: A public key cryptosystem and a signature scheme based on discrete logarithms. In: Blakley, G.R., Chaum, D. (eds.) CRYPTO 1984. LNCS, vol. 196, pp. 10–18. Springer, Heidelberg (1984)
20. Fehr, S., Hofheinz, D., Kiltz, E., Wee, H.: Encryption schemes secure against chosen-ciphertext selective opening attacks. In: Gilbert, H. (ed.) EUROCRYPT 2010. LNCS, vol. 6110, pp. 381–402. Springer, Heidelberg (2010). https://doi.org/10.1007/978-3-642-13190-5_20
21. Fuchsbauer, G., Heuer, F., Kiltz, E., Pietrzak, K.: Standard security does imply security against selective opening for Markov distributions. In: Kushilevitz, E., Malkin, T. (eds.) TCC 2016. LNCS, vol. 9562, pp. 282–305. Springer, Heidelberg (2016). https://doi.org/10.1007/978-3-662-49096-9_12
22. Gellert, K., Jager, T., Lyu, L., Neuschulten, T.: On fingerprinting attacks and length-hiding encryption. In: Galbraith, S.D. (ed.) CT-RSA 2022. LNCS, vol. 13161, pp. 345–369. Springer, Cham (2022). https://doi.org/10.1007/978-3-030-95312-6_15
23. Goldreich, O.: Foundations of Cryptography: Basic Tools, vol. 1. Cambridge University Press, Cambridge (2001)
24. Goldwasser, S., Micali, S.: Probabilistic encryption and how to play mental poker keeping secret all partial information. In: 14th ACM STOC, pp. 365–377. ACM Press, May 1982. https://doi.org/10.1145/800070.802212

25. Han, S., Liu, S., Gu, D.: Almost tight multi-user security under adaptive corruptions and leakages in the standard model. In: Hazay, C., Stam, M. (eds.) EUROCRYPT 2023, Part III. LNCS, vol. 14006, pp. 132–162. Springer, Heidelberg (2023). https://doi.org/10.1007/978-3-031-30620-4_5
26. Hara, K., Kitagawa, F., Matsuda, T., Hanaoka, G., Tanaka, K.: Simulation-based receiver selective opening CCA secure PKE from standard computational assumptions. In: Catalano, D., De Prisco, R. (eds.) SCN 2018. LNCS, vol. 11035, pp. 140–159. Springer, Cham (2018). https://doi.org/10.1007/978-3-319-98113-0_8
27. Hazay, C., Patra, A., Warinschi, B.: Selective opening security for receivers. In: Iwata, T., Cheon, J.H. (eds.) ASIACRYPT 2015. LNCS, vol. 9452, pp. 443–469. Springer, Heidelberg (2015). https://doi.org/10.1007/978-3-662-48797-6_19
28. Heuer, F.: On the selective opening security of public-key encryption. Doctoral thesis, Ruhr-Universität Bochum, Universitätsbibliothek (2017)
29. Heum, H., Stam, M.: Tightness subtleties for multi-user PKE notions. In: Paterson, M.B. (ed.) IMACC 2021. LNCS, vol. 13129, pp. 75–104. Springer, Cham (2021). https://doi.org/10.1007/978-3-030-92641-0_5
30. Hofheinz, D.: Possibility and impossibility results for selective decommitments. J. Cryptol. **24**(3), 470–516 (2011). https://doi.org/10.1007/s00145-010-9066-x
31. Hofheinz, D., Kiltz, E.: Secure hybrid encryption from weakened key encapsulation. In: Menezes, A. (ed.) CRYPTO 2007. LNCS, vol. 4622, pp. 553–571. Springer, Heidelberg (2007). https://doi.org/10.1007/978-3-540-74143-5_31
32. Hofheinz, D., Müller-Quade, J., Steinwandt, R.: On modeling IND-CCA security in cryptographic protocols. Cryptology ePrint Archive, Report 2003/024 (2003). https://eprint.iacr.org/2003/024
33. Hofheinz, D., Rao, V., Wichs, D.: Standard security does not imply indistinguishability under selective opening. In: Hirt, M., Smith, A. (eds.) TCC 2016. LNCS, vol. 9986, pp. 121–145. Springer, Heidelberg (2016). https://doi.org/10.1007/978-3-662-53644-5_5
34. Hofheinz, D., Rupp, A.: Standard versus selective opening security: separation and equivalence results. In: Lindell, Y. (ed.) TCC 2014. LNCS, vol. 8349, pp. 591–615. Springer, Heidelberg (2014). https://doi.org/10.1007/978-3-642-54242-8_25
35. Huang, Z., Lai, J., Han, S., Lyu, L., Weng, J.: Anonymous public key encryption under corruptions. In: Agrawal, S., Lin, D. (eds.) ASIACRYPT 2022, Part III. LNCS, vol. 13793, pp. 423–453. Springer, Heidelberg (2022). https://doi.org/10.1007/978-3-031-22969-5_15
36. Huang, Z., Liu, S., Mao, X., Chen, K.: Non-malleability under selective opening attacks: implication and separation. In: Malkin, T., Kolesnikov, V., Lewko, A.B., Polychronakis, M. (eds.) ACNS 2015. LNCS, vol. 9092, pp. 87–104. Springer, Cham (2015). https://doi.org/10.1007/978-3-319-28166-7_5
37. Jager, T., Kiltz, E., Riepel, D., Schäge, S.: Tightly-secure authenticated key exchange, revisited. In: Canteaut, A., Standaert, F.-X. (eds.) EUROCRYPT 2021. LNCS, vol. 12696, pp. 117–146. Springer, Cham (2021). https://doi.org/10.1007/978-3-030-77870-5_5
38. Jager, T., Stam, M., Stanley-Oakes, R., Warinschi, B.: Multi-key authenticated encryption with corruptions: reductions are lossy. In: Kalai, Y., Reyzin, L. (eds.) TCC 2017. LNCS, vol. 10677, pp. 409–441. Springer, Cham (2017). https://doi.org/10.1007/978-3-319-70500-2_14
39. Joye, M., Quisquater, J.-J., Yung, M.: On the power of misbehaving adversaries and security analysis of the original EPOC. In: Naccache, D. (ed.) CT-RSA 2001. LNCS, vol. 2020, pp. 208–222. Springer, Heidelberg (2001). https://doi.org/10.1007/3-540-45353-9_16

40. Küsters, R., Tuengerthal, M.: Joint state theorems for public-key encryption and digital signature functionalities with local computation. In: Sabelfeld, A. (ed.) CSF 2008 Computer Security Foundations Symposium, pp. 270–284. IEEE Computer Society Press (2008). https://doi.org/10.1109/CSF.2008.18
41. Lai, J., Yang, R., Huang, Z., Weng, J.: Simulation-based bi-selective opening security for public key encryption. In: Tibouchi, M., Wang, H. (eds.) ASIACRYPT 2021. LNCS, vol. 13091, pp. 456–482. Springer, Cham (2021). https://doi.org/10.1007/978-3-030-92075-3_16
42. Lee, Y., Lee, D.H., Park, J.H.: Tightly CCA-secure encryption scheme in a multi-user setting with corruptions. DCC **88**(11), 2433–2452 (2020). https://doi.org/10.1007/s10623-020-00794-z
43. Nielsen, J.B.: Separating random oracle proofs from complexity theoretic proofs: the non-committing encryption case. In: Yung, M. (ed.) CRYPTO 2002. LNCS, vol. 2442, pp. 111–126. Springer, Heidelberg (2002). https://doi.org/10.1007/3-540-45708-9_8
44. Okamoto, T., Pointcheval, D.: REACT: rapid enhanced-security asymmetric cryptosystem transform. In: Naccache, D. (ed.) CT-RSA 2001. LNCS, vol. 2020, pp. 159–174. Springer, Heidelberg (2000). https://doi.org/10.1007/3-540-45353-9_13
45. Shamir, A.: How to share a secret. Commun. Assoc. Comput. Mach. **22**(11), 612–613 (1979). https://doi.org/10.1145/359168.359176
46. Shannon, C.E.: Communication theory of secrecy systems. Bell Syst. Techn. J. **28**(4), 656–715 (1949)
47. Tezcan, C., Vaudenay, S.: On hiding a plaintext length by preencryption. In: Lopez, J., Tsudik, G. (eds.) ACNS 2011. LNCS, vol. 6715, pp. 345–358. Springer, Heidelberg (2011). https://doi.org/10.1007/978-3-642-21554-4_20
48. Watanabe, Y., Shikata, J., Imai, H.: Equivalence between semantic security and indistinguishability against chosen ciphertext attacks. In: Desmedt, Y.G. (ed.) PKC 2003. LNCS, vol. 2567, pp. 71–84. Springer, Heidelberg (2003). https://doi.org/10.1007/3-540-36288-6_6
49. Yang, R., Lai, J., Huang, Z., Au, M.H., Xu, Q., Susilo, W.: Possibility and impossibility results for receiver selective opening secure PKE in the multi-challenge setting. In: Moriai, S., Wang, H. (eds.) ASIACRYPT 2020. LNCS, vol. 12491, pp. 191–220. Springer, Cham (2020). https://doi.org/10.1007/978-3-030-64837-4_7

Dynamic Collusion Functional Encryption and Multi-Authority Attribute-Based Encryption

Rachit Garg[2], Rishab Goyal[1(✉)], and George Lu[2]

[1] UW-Madison, Madison, USA
rishab@cs.wisc.edu
[2] UT Austin, Austin, USA

Abstract. Functional Encryption (FE) is a powerful notion of encryption which enables computations and partial message recovery of encrypted data. In FE, each decryption key is associated with a function f such that decryption recovers the function evaluation $f(m)$ from an encryption of m. Informally, security states that a user with access to function keys $\mathsf{sk}_{f_1}, \mathsf{sk}_{f_2}, \ldots$ (and so on) can only learn $f_1(m), f_2(m), \ldots$ (and so on) but nothing more about the message. The system is said to be q-bounded collusion resistant if the security holds as long as an adversary gets access to at most $q = q(\lambda)$ decryption keys.

However, until very recently, all these works studied bounded collusion resistance in a *static model*, where the collusion bound q was a global system parameter. While the static model has led to many great applications, it has major drawbacks. Recently, Agrawal et al. (Crypto 2021) and Garg et al. (Eurocrypt 2022) introduced the *dynamic model* for bounded collusion resistance, where the collusion bound q was a fluid parameter, not globally set, but chosen by each encryptor. The dynamic model enabled harnessing many virtues of the static model, while avoiding its various drawbacks. In this work, we provide a generic compiler to upgrade any FE scheme from the static model to the dynamic model.

We also extend our techniques to multi-authority attribute-based encryption (MA-ABE). We show that bounded collusion MA-ABE supporting predicates that can be represented as an efficient computational secret sharing (CSS) scheme can be built from minimal assumptions. Efficient CSS schemes are known for access structures whose characteristic function can be computed by a polynomial-size monotone circuit under the existence of one-way functions [Yao89, unpublished]. Thus, our MA-ABE construction is the first MA-ABE scheme from standard assumptions for predicates beyond polynomial-size monotone boolean formula. Our construction also satisfies full adaptive security in the Random Oracle Model.

1 Introduction

Functional Encryption (FE) [SW05,BSW11] is a powerful generalization of public-key encryption [DH76] which enables fine-grained access over encrypted

Research supported by Wisconsin Alumni Research Foundation.

Q. Tang and V. Teague (Eds.): PKC 2024, LNCS 14604, pp. 69–104, 2024.
https://doi.org/10.1007/978-3-031-57728-4_3

data. In such systems, a setup algorithm produces a master public-secret key pair $(\mathsf{mpk}, \mathsf{msk})$, where the master public key is made public and the master secret key is retained by an authority. Using mpk, any user can encrypt data m to produce a ciphertext ct. On the other hand, the authority can use the master secret key to generate partial decryption keys for authorized users, where the decryption key sk_f for a function f enables the key holder to compute the function output $f(m)$ from the ciphertext encrypting data m while learning nothing else about m.

The notion of "learning nothing else about m" is formalized in one of two ways – indistinguishability (IND) or simulation (SIM) based security. The intuition behind them can be jointly understood as follows. The attacker receives a challenge ciphertext ct encrypting a message m along with a polynomial number (say q) of decryption keys $\mathsf{sk}_{f_1}, \ldots, \mathsf{sk}_{f_q}$ for functions $f_1, \ldots, f_q$. In the case of SIM-security, an attacker cannot distinguish this from a 'simulated' distribution of keys and ciphertext where only the function evaluation $f_1(m), \ldots, f_q(m)$ are available to the simulator, and *not* the entire message. While in IND-security, an attacker cannot distinguish it from when the ciphertext ct encrypts another message m' where $f_i(m) = f_i(m')$ for all q functions.

Over the last several years, functional encryption has been extensively studied and shown to remarkably useful (irrespective of the underlying security model, IND/SIM) for numerous applications across cryptography and beyond. Depending upon the message space and function space supported, it defines a new encryption system with appropriate fine-grained access control. For example, public-key encryption can be viewed as FE with only the identity function, identity-based encryption (IBE) [Sha84,Coc01,BF01] can be viewed as FE with *point* functions, etc.

Bounded Collusions. In this work, we study functional encryption in the widely popular bounded collusion model [SS10,GVW12]. The bounded collusion model states that the FE system is guaranteed to be secure so long as the attacker does not receive more than q decryption keys. The parameter q is referred to as the collusion bound. The bounded collusion model has been highly successful and very well-studied leading to numerous positive as well as negative results (see [DKXY02,SS10,GLW12,GVW12,AR17,Agr17,ISV+17, AS17,GKW18,CVW+18,AV19,WFL19] and references therein), and improving understanding of the complexity of designing FE more generally. Moreover, it captures the essence of security needed for many applications, and can be built from *low tech assumptions* such as public-key encryption in most cases. Thus, FE in the bounded collusion model overcomes the extremely high cost needed for full collusion resistance [GGH+13,JLS21,JLS22] (both in terms of cryptographic assumptions and concrete practical efficiency), and bypasses known impossibilities [AGVW13]. Furthermore, it readily gives solutions that are provably post-quantum secure, unlike fully collusion resistant FE where current solutions are either known to be post-quantum insecure [JLS21,JLS22] or have only conjectured security [WW21,GP21,BDGM20,DQV+21].

Until very recently, FE in the bounded collusion model was formalized as the collusion bound q being declared at the time of system setup, restricting it to be fixed for the entire lifetime of the FE system. This introduces an undesirable inflexibility as whenever more than q corruptions occur, the system becomes useless since no security is guaranteed! Moreover, the sizes of all system parameters grew polynomially with q, including all the public and secret keys.

In recent works by Agrawal et al. [AMVY21] and Garg et al. [GGLW22], this limitation in the existing formalization of bounded collusion model was explored. They observed that this inflexibility is simply an artefact of existing formalizations of the bounded collusion model, and not a true barrier. They referred to the existing models as *static bounded collusion model* (henceforth called the static model), and introduced a stronger yet more natural corruption model called the *dynamic bounded collusion model* (henceforth dynamic model).

In the dynamic model, the setup algorithm no longer needs a maximum collusion bound q! It removes this inflexibility by letting an encryptor *dynamically* decide the number of colluding users against which it desires protection. That is, an encryptor selects the collusion bound q for each ciphertext ct at encryption time. And, crucially, a secure FE system in the dynamic model provides a fine-grained "per-ciphertext guarantee", which says a ciphertext ct generated for collusion level q is guaranteed to be secure so long as the attacker does not receive more than q decryption keys. In other words, an encryptor can select different collusion levels while a decryption key holder can decrypt it all the same. As a consequence, in the dynamic model, only the size of the ciphertexts grows with q, while everything else is independent of q.

This new formalization preserves all the desirable features (such as low tech assumptions, concrete efficiency, post-quantum security etc.) while giving much better flexibility for applications. [AMVY21, GGLW22] designed FE schemes for circuits in the dynamic model assuming the minimum and necessary[1] assumption of identity-based encryption (IBE). And, [AMVY21] also extended them to succinct FE schemes for circuits, and FE schemes for Turing Machines (TMs) and Nondeterministic Logspace (NL) by leveraging the hardness of learning with errors (LWE) assumption [Reg05].

A recurring theme in their constructions is to perform careful surgery of existing FE schemes secure in the static model to upgrade to the dynamic model. In a few words, the core idea in these works is to open up existing (static) FE constructions and exploit the key space compression offered by IBE to encode the collusion bound more efficiently in each ciphertext rather than the master public key. On a technical level, the existing FE constructions and their proofs in the dynamic model are not more challenging compared to the static model, but they definitely are far more complicated to describe due to the intrinsic adaptivity offered by dynamic model.[2]

[1] See [AMVY21, §7] for more details about minimality of IBE.

[2] Briefly, this is because existing constructions [AMVY21, GGLW22, AKM+22] have to redo all the work done for proving security in the static model and then patch it to

This leads to an interesting predicament – static model is well understood and weaker, but constructions are comparatively easier to design; while dynamic model is newer and stronger, but constructions are technically more cumbersome to design. Ideally, we want to design FE in the dynamic model but as simply as have been designing them in the static model so far. Thus, it likely suggests that we have two pathways:

A. Stick with static model for an initial feasibility result, and later circle back to the (static) construction to make it dynamic à la the surgery approach [AMVY21,GGLW22].
B. Adopt the dynamic model as the primary corruption model, and develop a holistic approach.

While B would be a better choice scientifically, it might be too much to ask for. Even historically, in similar situations, we have observed pathway A is more likely to be taken. E.g., CPA vs CCA security, generic group vs standard model, composite vs prime order bilinear groups, random oracle vs standard model etc. In all the aforementioned situations, the community more often adopted the easier to design security model as a first step, and later strengthened it to the stronger model.

Static to Dynamic Generically. This leads to the first question we ask:

Q- *Can we generically upgrade any FE in the static model to dynamic model without changing the function/message class?*

A bit more philosophically, the question we ask is whether the two aforementioned pathways be unified? Somewhat surprisingly, we answer affirmatively! In this work, we show:

Informal Theorem 1. *Assuming IBE, an FE scheme secure in the static model can be transformed into a secure FE scheme in the dynamic model.*

A bit formally, we show that a statically secure FE scheme, protecting against collusions of size $\leq \lambda$, can be lifted to an FE scheme that protects from dynamic collusions. Given IBE is a necessary assumption (see [AMVY21, §7]), thus the above theorem is the best one can hope for. We view our result to follow along the lines of similar (pseudo-)generic transformations known for other comparable models in the literature (such as for CPA-to-CCA [NY90,KW19], composite-to-prime-order-pairings [Fre10,Lew12,OT10,Att14], etc.). This reduces the task of building an FE scheme in the general dynamic model to a comparatively easier target of building a λ-bounded collusion FE scheme. In fact our procedure works for both uniform and non-uniform models of computation, which in turn lends to new FE results in the dynamic model as mere corollaries [GSW21,Wee21] (further discussed in the main body).

make it secure in the dynamic model. And, there is no compiler that can generically upgrade static model to dynamic model.

While in the future, there might be scenarios when a direct construction for a particular function class might be more advantageous, our transformation would remain a good starting point. More importantly, it serves as a good foundation and clear indication that FE in the dynamic model is as easy/hard as in the static model for that function-message space.

1.1 Multi-Authority Attribute-Based Encryption

While FE has been a great abstraction to study encryption over the last few decades, it has its own limitations. One well-known limitation is the need of a central trusted authority necessary for generating and issuing decryption keys. There has been a long line of works focussed on mitigating this centralization issue starting with the works of Chase, Chow, Lewko, and Waters [Cha07,CC09,LW11]. They introduced the notion of decentralization for attribute-based encryption (ABE) systems, commonly referred to as "multi-authority" attribute-based encryption (MA-ABE).

Recall in ABE, each ciphertext ct encrypts the payload m under an access policy ϕ, and a decryption key sk_x is associated with an attribute $\mathbf{x}$.[3] The functionality ensures, given such a ciphertext-key pair, one can learn payload m so long as $\phi(\mathbf{x}) = 1$. While security states that the payload is hidden so long as an attacker receives decryption keys for only unsatisfying attributes.

In an MA-ABE system, anyone can become a key issuing authority. There is no longer one master authority, but multiple individual authorities each controlling only a portion of the attribute space. Without loss of generality, consider attributes to be n-bit strings with n key authorities where the ith authority controls the ith bit of the attribute and gives a partial decryption key for just that attribute bit (say $\mathsf{sk}_b^{(i)}$ denotes partial key from authority i for bit b).

During decryption, a user combines partial decryption keys $\mathsf{sk}_{x_1}^{(1)}, \ldots, \mathsf{sk}_{x_n}^{(n)}$ associated with the same global user identifier GID (necessary for avoiding a *mix&match* attack[4]) to decrypt the ciphertext so long as $\phi(\mathbf{x} = (x_1, \ldots, x_n)) = 1$. Security is still required to hold against users who possess an arbitrary number of unauthorized secret keys, with an additional challenge that some subset of the authorities could now be corrupted as well. What makes MA-ABE so desirable in practice is this significantly stronger corruption model where key authorities can now be corrupted too. Over the last decade, there have been numerous attempts with varying levels of success (see [Cha07,CC09,LW11,WFL19,OT20,AGT21,

3 Note that we are sticking with the ciphertext-policy variant of attribute-based encryption, as is the norm while defining multi-authority ABE.

4 It is well understood that since the key authorities are completely decentralized and work independently, multiple partial decryption keys for the same attribute bit can be combined arbitrarily with partial keys from other key authorities. Briefly, the issue is partial decryption keys for different users from two independent authorities can be used together. To get around this, Chase [Cha07] introduced the concept of using unique public global identifiers for each distinct user as a "linchpin" for tying partial keys together.

DKW21, DKW23] to name a few and references therein for complete history) in building MA-ABE schemes, with mostly investigating in the highly popular (by now standardized) GID-model.

In this work, we design MA-ABE with bounded collusion resistance and, following the theme of our work, we formally define it in the dynamic (as well as static) model. Very briefly, we say an MA-ABE scheme is (statically) q-bounded collusion secure: if an attacker that can corrupt an arbitrary set of key authorities in addition to receiving partial decryption keys from all honest key authorities on at most q unique GIDs, cannot guess the message (so long as the partial decryption keys for any particular GID does not satisfy the challenge predicate ϕ). In a few words, the restriction is not on corrupting the key authorities, but only on the number of honest partial keys an attacker can see. The dynamic model can be similarly defined by delaying the choice of collusion bound to the encryptor instead.

We show that, in the bounded collusion setting, MA-ABE supporting any predicate that can be represented as an efficient computational secret sharing (CSS) scheme can be built from general low tech assumptions. A bit formally, we show:

Informal Theorem 2. *Assuming public-key encryption, there exists an MA-ABE scheme for efficient CSS predicates secure in the static model, in the Random Oracle Model (ROM).*

In an unpublished work (mentioned in [Bei11], see also Vinod et al. [VNS+03]), Yao showed an efficient computational secret-sharing scheme for access structures whose characteristic function can be computed by a polynomial-size monotone circuit under the existence of one-way functions. Thus, by combining with Yao's secret sharing scheme, we obtain an MA-ABE scheme for monotone circuits in the static model from plain public-key encryption.

Corollary 1. *Assuming public-key encryption, there exists an MA-ABE scheme for polynomial-depth monotone circuits secure in the static model, in the Random Oracle Model (ROM).*

The most expressive state of the art MA-ABE scheme in the fully collusion resistant model [LW11] only supports monotone formulae (i.e., log-depth circuits), thus we can support a much more general class at the cost of relatively weaker security model. Moreover, our construction satisfies full adaptive security where the attacker can corrupt authorities and keys adaptively in any arbitrary order. Prior to our work, there were only two MA-ABE constructions [WFL19, DKW23] that achieved full adaptive security. Both these schemes support encrypting access policies computable using an $\mathbf{NC}^1$ circuit, where Datta et al. [DKW23] gave a fully collusion resistant scheme under standard pairing-based assumptions, while Wang et al. [WFL19] gave a bounded collusion scheme under DDH/LWE assumption. Our scheme supports encrypting polynomial-depth monotone circuits, while relying on a minimal assumption of public-key encryption. Somewhat interestingly (though not surprisingly), we can prove security of our construction in the standard model (without ROM) if we stick to a super selective model. Since we do not formally prove it in the current version, we simply state it as an interesting observation.

Observation 1. *Assuming public-key encryption, there exists an MA-ABE scheme for polynomial-depth monotone circuits secure in the super-selective static model.*

Finally, following the theme of our work, we also construct and prove an MA-ABE scheme in the dynamic collusion model. Here, we show:

Informal Theorem 3. *Assuming identity-based encryption, there exists an MA-ABE scheme for polynomial-depth monotone circuits in the* dynamic *collusion model (in ROM).*

We can make the same observation as above about proving security in the standard model (without ROM). It is an interesting problem to remove the dependence on ROM for proving full adaptive security. We quickly remind the reader that IBE is a necessary assumption (see [AMVY21, §7] for more details).

Lastly, we remark that due to the minimal nature of assumptions needed for our MA-ABE results, they can be instantiated from post-quantum assumptions such as LWE [Reg05, GPV08] or even LPN [Ale03, DGHM18]. This gives us the first post-quantum MA-ABE scheme (though in the bounded collusion model) for predicates beyond DNF, and the very first MA-ABE scheme from the hardness of learning parity with noise (LPN) assumption.

2 Technical Overview

The overview is split into two parts. First, we discuss our design of a generic accumulator for functional encryption systems. We show that such an accumulator is the main technical barrier that separates static and dynamic collusion models. In the second part, we look at how to build a multi-authority attribute-based encryption system for polynomial-sized monotone circuits.

Part I: The FE Accumulator

Consider the problem of succinctly representing 2^λ pairs of FE master keys $(\mathsf{mpk}_i, \mathsf{msk}_i)$ for $i \leq 2^\lambda$ using only polynomial space, i.e. $\mathsf{poly}(\lambda)$ space to store all 2^λ key pairs. That is, you are given a functional encryption system $\mathsf{FE} = (\mathsf{Setup}, \mathsf{Enc}, \mathsf{KeyGen}, \mathsf{Dec})$ for some message-function space $\mathcal{M}, \mathcal{F}$. Without loss of generality, suppose the $\mathsf{FE.Setup}$ algorithm takes λ bits of randomness. Thus, $\mathsf{FE.Setup}$ outputs 2^λ possible master public-secret key pairs, one for each randomness value. The problem is to come up with a compressed representation, say $(\mathsf{MPK}, \mathsf{MSK})$, of these 2^λ key pairs $(\mathsf{mpk}_i, \mathsf{msk}_i)$ with the following properties:

Succinctness. $|\mathsf{MPK}|, |\mathsf{MSK}| = \mathsf{poly}(\lambda)$, i.e. they have fixed polynomial size.
Functionality. There exist efficient algorithms $\mathsf{ENC}, \mathsf{KEYGEN}, \mathsf{DEC}$ such that $\mathsf{ENC}(\mathsf{MPK}, i, \cdot)$, $\mathsf{KEYGEN}(\mathsf{MSK}, i, \cdot)$, $\mathsf{DEC}(\mathsf{SK}_f, i, \cdot)$ gave similar functionality as $\mathsf{Enc}(\mathsf{mpk}_i, \cdot)$, $\mathsf{KeyGen}(\mathsf{msk}_i, \cdot)$, $\mathsf{Dec}(\mathsf{sk}_{f,i}, \cdot)$.
(Here $\mathsf{SK}_f, \mathsf{sk}_{f,i}$ corresponding to a function decryption key.)

Here the second property can be defined formally, but intuitively it just says that $(\mathsf{MPK}, \mathsf{MSK})$ along with these algorithms simulate the same functionality/behavior of actually using the original versions of the FE keys.

Interestingly, designing such an accumulatable version of FE is the main technical hurdle for closing the gap between bounded collusion FE schemes in the static vs dynamic models. All prior works in the dynamic model [AMVY21, GGLW22, AKM+22] essentially design their own versions of such an accumulatable FE system and use it, either explicitly or implicitly, to build an FE scheme in the dynamic model. Garg et al. [GGLW22] make it most explicit, and define a new object called Tagged Functional Encryption (Tagged FE).

Formally, a tagged FE system contains the same four algorithms – Setup, Enc, KeyGen, Dec. That is, as in regular static model FE scheme, Setup takes the collusion bound q as an input. The main difference as follows: each ciphertext $\mathsf{ct}_{m,\mathsf{tag}_1}$ and secret key $\mathsf{sk}_{f,\mathsf{tag}_2}$ are now additionally associated with a tag value, tag_1 and tag_2 (respectively), in addition to a message m and a function f. The decryption correctness states that $\mathsf{Dec}(\mathsf{sk}_{f,\mathsf{tag}_2}, \mathsf{ct}_{m,\mathsf{tag}_1})$ is equal to $f(m)$ *iff* $\mathsf{tag}_1 = \mathsf{tag}_2$, otherwise it outputs $\perp$. For security, it should be the case that regular FE security holds for all tag values where an attacker make less than q key queries. It is crucial that the attacker is allowed to make an unrestricted number of key queries on as many tag values that it wants. Basically, for tag values where the collusion bound is not exceeded, FE security should still hold even if collusion bound is exceeded on other tag values.

It is straightforward to see that tagged FE is simply an accumulated version of an FE scheme in the static model. The point is tagged FE enables a succinct representation of an exponential number of static model FE key pairs, and we mentioned before, this captures the main technical challenge to design FE in the dynamic model. Note that the setup of a tagged FE system still takes the collusion bound as input. Later we discuss how tagged FE can be upgraded genericaly in a black-box way to dynamic model FE. For now, we focus on building tagged FE from any static model FE scheme.

Our Accumulation Compiler. The main technical component of our first result is a generic compiler to succinctly represent an exponential number of FE keys in polynomial space. That is, a generic compiler to go from static model FE to tagged FE.

Our first main observation is that a tagged FE is simply an identity-based static FE scheme. That is, one could visualize tagged FE as a generalization of static model FE similar to how IBE is a generalization of plain PKE. Recall in IBE, each ciphertext and function key is associated with an identity (or simply a 'tag' value). Thus, it seems like all we need to do is find a generic mechanism to embed identities/tags in both the secret keys and ciphertexts of a tagged FE scheme.

Coincidentally, a similar problem was solved in an unrelated context of building registration-based encryption [GHMR18, GHM+19, GV20]. Although the motivation behind registration-based encryption was to solve the key-escrow problem, one could very easily visualize it as a mechanism to accumulate a large number of independently sampled PKE public keys into a short commitment where each public key is associated with an identity (and, so is the corresponding secret key as well). And, an encryptor only needs the short commitment to encrypt the message for any particular identity. Internally, these encryption schemes rely on the beautiful line of works studying non-black-box IBE constructions from simpler assumptions [DG17b, DG17a].

Our idea is to use these non-black-box techniques for compressing static model FE schemes. Looking within all these existing constructions, we notice that the usage of PKE in these prior works ([DG17b, DG17a, GHMR18, GHM+19] to name a few) is not essential. Rather we view this overall line of work as providing a beautiful mechanism to embed identities in any type of FE, and not just in plain PKE. While embedding identities in fully collusion resistant FE schemes does not seem to be useful for any new applications, we find that embedding identities is very useful for bounded collusion FE. For us, this gives a simple and generic approach to dynamic model FE. We believe that our re-visualization of Döttling-Garg [DG17b, DG17a] garbling-based tree compression techniques to beyond PKE will find more applications in the future.

Focussing on static model FE as the base encryption system and combining it with the garbling-based compression techniques, we prove the following:

Informal Theorem 4. *Assuming IBE*[5]*, there exists a generic compiler for building tagged FE from static model FE.*

From Static Model to Tagged FE via Garbling. The core technical idea behind the non-black-box garbling techniques [DG17b, DG17a] was to delegate computation of actual ciphertext computation to the decryption algorithm via a sequence of cascaded garbled circuits [Yao82]. Abstractly, there is a sequence of λ garbled circuits where the ith garbled circuit gives as output the wire labels for the $(i+1)^{th}$ garbled circuit. The last garbled circuit is special as the it performs the actual delegated computation of the real ciphertext. This basic abstract representation is not enough on its own as the wire keys for the $(i+1)^{th}$ garbled circuit (the ones that are part of the ith circuit's output) have to be encrypted such that only half of them are revealed during the actual decryption. This last part is crucial for security as it ensures all the garbled circuits can be simulated properly.

In this work, we use one-time signature with encryption (OTSE) for hiding wire labels in the above approach. They were introduced for building IBE generically from plain PKE via garbling [DGHM18]. In short, an OTSE scheme is a

[5] Looking ahead, we actually use One-Time Signature with Encryption (OTSE) introduced in [DGHM18].

one-time signature scheme that is equipped with an encryption and decryption algorithm. Encryption is performed w.r.t. a verification key vk and a pair of message bit and index (i, b). The resulting ciphertext can be decrypted using any signature σ for some string x so long as the bit b matches corresponding bit in x (i.e., $m[i] = b$). Formally, a ciphertext ct is associated with an index-bit pair (i, b), and decryption works given a signature σ for any x such that $x[i] = b$. Combining OTSE with garbled circuits is sufficient for designing a generic accumulation compiler.

To give a quick overview, we start with a simpler goal. Suppose we only want *compress* and *embed* N independent instantiations of a static model FE scheme (referred to as base FE scheme for ease of exposition) into a tagged FE scheme. That is, all the parameter sizes should grow only as $\mathsf{poly}(\lambda, \log N)$, but now the running time of the setup and key generation algorithms can be large (say $\mathsf{poly}(\lambda, N)$). The core idea is as follows:

Setup: Sample N random key pairs $(\mathsf{mpk}_i, \mathsf{msk}_i)$ for base FE (using a PRF key K for generating randomness). Hash all N public keys to a short digest h using a Merkle tree. Set digest h as the short master public key mpk and PRF key K as the short master secret key msk.

Encrypt: Use the garbling technique describe above. It defers the base FE encryption to the decryption phase. It does this by generating a sequence of garbled circuits $C_1, \ldots, C_\lambda$. The final circuit C_λ outputs the base FE encryption under the correct key $\mathsf{mpk}_{\mathsf{tag}}$, while the intermediate circuits perform step-by-step verification of the root-to-leaf path where at each step only one bit of the tag value tag is read and verified.
Now as discussed above, all the garbled wire keys have to be encrypted (using OTSE). This enforces the decryptor to run the final garbled circuit only on $\mathsf{mpk}_{\mathsf{tag}}$. (Clearly, the setup has to be modified to ensure the hash tree is compatible with OTSE, and msk needs to contain OTSE signing keys.)

Key generation: It generates a decryption key for base FE w.r.t. master key $\mathsf{msk}_{\mathsf{tag}}$, and a sequence of OTSE signatures $\sigma_1, \ldots, \sigma_\lambda$ such that they enable evaluation of the intermediate garbled circuits along the appropriate root-to-leaf path.

Decrypt: Use the root-to-leaf path (in the form of OTSE signatures) to iteratively run garbled circuits from the ciphertext. It obtains the wire keys corresponding to the key $\mathsf{mpk}_{\mathsf{tag}}$, and then computes the base FE ciphertext w.r.t. $\mathsf{mpk}_{\mathsf{tag}}$ using the last garbled circuit. Decrypted the base FE ciphertext by using the corresponding base FE decryption key.

The above overview omits a lot of details, but the main intuition is that the root value of the Merkle tree serves as a short commitment to the sequence of N master public keys, and each leaf node can be succinctly opened w.r.t. the root node. Now, to encrypt a message for the tag^{th} base FE system (i.e., under key $\mathsf{mpk}_{\mathsf{tag}}$), the encryptor needs to search the entire Merkle tree to obtain the corresponding public key from the root node. But it cannot perform this search operation given only the root value, thus it defers it to the decryption phase by generating a sequence of garbled circuits. We suggest the reader to the main body for a formal description.

Note that this readily gives the following lemma:

Informal Lemma 1. *Assuming OTSE and garbled circuits, for any $N, q > 0$, there exists an explicit compiler from a static q-bounded collusion FE scheme to a q-bounded tagged FE scheme with tag space $[N]$.*

The above approach relies on the setup algorithm being able to explicitly hash down all the N master public keys, thus seems useful for compression of a polynomial sized sequence of master public keys only. However, prior works in this space [GKW16, DG17b, DG17a, GHMR18] have shown that a slightly more intricate design can be used to compress an exponential number of master keys too. The core trick is to use a simple lazy sampling technique where the setup algorithm uses a PRF key to deterministically generate the hash tree at the time of key generation instead. This enables deferring the setup algorithm's work to the key generator which only needs to open the tree along a particular path at a time. The usage of PRFs is essential for consistency (in turn security). More details are provided later in Sect. 5.

From Tagged FE to Dynamic Model via Combinatorics. It turns out that the main technical challenge in building FE in the dynamic model is captured in the tagged FE framework. And, tagged FE is powerful enough to build dynamic model FE via black-box transformations that only need simple combinatorial ideas used numerous times over the last decade in FE research. Briefly, Garg et al. [GGLW22] showed that the load balancing trick by Ananth and Vaikuntanathan [AV19] and powers-of-two technique by Goldwasser et al. [GKP+13] are sufficient to get dynamic model FE from tagged FE. Due to the non-cryptographic (combinatorial) nature of the techniques, this gives a simple black-box transformation that is oblivious to the underlying cryptography (and even the model of computation). Let us look at them one-by-one.

STEP 1. Consider the static model FE scheme to satisfy a special property called 'fast key generation'. The property says the running times of the setup and key generation algorithms grow as $\mathsf{poly}(\lambda, \log q)$. The collusion bound q is still a global system parameter, but it does not affect algorithms generating keys too much. It turns out the "powers-of-two trick" [GKP+13] can lift such static model FE schemes to the dynamic model. The core idea is to set up λ parallel static model FE systems with geometrically increasing collusion bounds from $q = 2, 4, \ldots, 2^{\lambda}$. The master keys and decryption keys are generated for each of the λ parallel systems. The point is the encryptor actually selects exactly one of these λ systems to encrypt. The choice depends on the desired level of collusion security q (i.e., select the $\lceil \log q \rceil^{th}$ static FE system for encryption). The security and correctness follow by design, while the 'fast key generation' property ensures efficiency.

STEP 2. The last missing piece is to translate a tagged FE scheme into a static FE scheme with *fast key generation*. The intuition here is (inspired from [AV19]) to visualize the collusion bound as a security "load" on the system. And, distribute the security "load" of q users into $O(q)$ buckets, each with a maximum security load of just λ users. The idea is to view each bucket as a separate tag value with collusion bound λ, and each decryption key gets tossed in one of those 'tag' buckets at random. Since tagged FE succinctly represents all $O(q)$ buckets within a single FE system, thus tagged FE gives a static FE scheme with desired poly-log dependence property via load balancing.

The above combinatorial ideas have appeared throughout the literature, especially in the bounded collusion regime. Prior works in the dynamic model [AMVY21, GGLW22, AKM+22] have made them even more explicit to separate the cryptographic part from the combinatorial part. In this work, we show that the cryptographic component can be generically executed.

An Alternate and Simpler Approach for Accumulating FE

In the above overview so far, we have explained our main technical idea for accumulating FE schemes. The technical centerpiece of our accumulator is to use a sequence of λ garbled circuits to generate a "tagged" ciphertext during decryption by using delegation of computation.

It turns out one can perform this "tagging" operation using just a single garbled circuit rather than a sequence of λ garbled circuits. The idea is to simply use the deferred encryption technique developed by Goyal et al. [GKW16]. While in the main body we still stick to the above OTSE approach for instantiating our accumulator, we describe the simpler alternate idea below for completeness and improved future designs.

During setup, we sample an IBE key pair $(\mathsf{mpk}, \mathsf{msk})$ as well as a PRF seed s. The master public key consists of mpk, and rest everything is kept secret. To encrypt a message m under a tag tag, the encryptor constructs a circuit that takes as input an FE master public key X and outputs $\mathsf{BFE.Enc}(X, m)$ – an encryption of m using X as the FE master public key.[6] The encryptor garbles this circuit and obtains a garbled circuit G and 2ℓ garbled circuit wires $\{w_{i,0}, w_{i,1}\}_{i\in[\ell]}$ where ℓ denotes the length of the FE public key. Finally, the encryptor outputs the garbled circuit G and 2ℓ IBE encryptions $\{\mathsf{ct}_{i,b} = \mathsf{IBE.Enc}(\mathsf{mpk}, (\mathsf{tag}, i, b), w_{i,b})\}_{i\in[\ell], b\in\{0,1\}}$.

To generate a secret key for function f corresponding to the tag tag, the key generator first samples an FE key pair as $(\mathsf{mpk}_{\mathsf{tag}}, \mathsf{msk}_{\mathsf{tag}}) \leftarrow \mathsf{BFE.Setup}(1^\lambda; \mathsf{PRF}(s, \mathsf{tag}))$. Next, it generates ℓ IBE secret keys as

$$\{\mathsf{IBE.sk}_{\mathsf{tag},i} \leftarrow \mathsf{IBE.KeyGen}(\mathsf{msk}, (\mathsf{tag}, i, \mathsf{mpk}_{\mathsf{tag}}[i]))\}_{i\in[\ell]}$$

That is, it generates one IBE secret key for each identity in $(\mathsf{tag}, 1, \mathsf{mpk}_{\mathsf{tag}}[1]), \ldots, (\mathsf{tag}, \ell, \mathsf{mpk}_{\mathsf{tag}}[\ell])$. In other words, it encodes the FE master public key inside the IBE keys. Further, the key generator samples an FE key as

[6] We ignore the random coins used during encryption for simplicity, however they can be easily hardwired inside such a circuit.

$\mathsf{BFE.KeyGen}(\mathsf{msk}_{\mathsf{tag}}, f)$, and include this along with the ℓ IBE keys as part of the final tagged secret key. In order to decrypt the ciphertext, a user proceeds in two steps. First, it recovers the wire labels as $\mathsf{IBE.Dec}(\mathsf{IBE.sk}_{\mathsf{tag},i}, \mathsf{ct}_{i,\mathsf{mpk}_{\mathsf{tag}}[i]})$, and runs the garbled circuit G on these wire labels to recover the actual function output. The correctness follows directly from correctness of garbling, untagged FE scheme, and IBE.

The proof of security also follows via a simple sequence of garbled circuits. First, one can use PRF security to argue that the PRF output is indistinguishable from a truly random function. Once we replace all PRF outputs with truly random values, then in the next hybrid we can use IBE security to replace half of the IBE ciphertexts from encryptions of real wire keys to IBE encryptions of zero strings. This can be done because for each unique tag string tag, only one FE master key $\mathsf{mpk}_{\mathsf{tag}}$ is sampled. Thus, at most half of the IBE ciphertexts in the challenge ciphertexts can be decrypted using available IBE secret keys. Next, we can use simulation security of the garbling scheme to replace the garbled circuit G with a simulated circuit that is generated using a randomly generated FE encryption of challenge message m. Finally, we can use bounded collusion FE security of the underlying untagged FE scheme to finish the proof, since the adversary only learns a single FE ciphertext (inside the simulated garbled circuit) and a bounded number of FE secret keys for the corresponding tagged FE instance.

As mentioned earlier, in the main body, we present our FE accumulator using OTSE as a starting point. The above direct scheme is a simpler alternate approach.

Part II: MA-ABE from Simple Assumptions.

In multi-authority ABE, there are n key authorities where the ith authority generates its local keys $\mathsf{pk}_u, \mathsf{sk}_u$. An encryptor picks a subset U of authorities under whose public keys $\{\mathsf{pk}_u\}_{u \in U}$ it encrypts a message μ along with policy ϕ. For our MA-ABE construction, we consider the class of all predicates that can be represented as an efficient computational secret sharing (CSS) scheme.

Secret Sharing. Recall in an efficient CSS for n parties, there is a dealer algorithm that given a secret s and a description of an access structures $\mathcal{A}$, runs in polynomial time, outputs a set of n shares $\mathsf{sh}_1, \ldots, \mathsf{sh}_n$.[7] More importantly, there is a reconstruction algorithm that given a subset of shares $\{\mathsf{sh}_i\}_{i \in T}$, for some set $T \subseteq [n]$, outputs the reconstructed secret s so long as $T \in \mathcal{A}$ (i.e., T is an authorized set). The secret sharing scheme is secure if the secret s is computationally hidden from every group of *unauthorized* parties.

Getting back to MA-ABE, we view our encryptor to receive the policy ϕ as the description of an access structure $\mathcal{A}$ (for which efficient CSS exists) along with a mapping $\rho : [n] \to U$ from the party index to authority index (recall U is

[7] In some formalisms, the dealer outputs a public share sh_0 as well which is said to be available to all parties. For simplicity, we consider it to be a part of each party's share since it does not affect the asymptotic efficiency too much.

the set of authorities used by encryptor). That is, $\rho(i)$ tells the index of authority from the set $U := \{u_1, \ldots, u_\ell\}$, for some $\ell > 0$, that controls the attribute for the ith party. For simplicity, consider that the number of authorities and parties (as defined by $\mathcal{A}$) is the same (say n), and ρ is simply the identity function.

During key generation, each authority receives a global identifier GID and it outputs a partial predicate key $\mathsf{sk}_{\mathsf{GID},u}$. One should read this as if a user receives a predicate key from authority u, then it is authorized to receive the uth share from the shares generated by the CSS. Lastly, during decryption, a user combines all the partial predicate keys it obtained $\{\mathsf{sk}_{\mathsf{GID},u}\}_{u \in T}$, for some set $T \subseteq [n]$, to decrypt the ciphertext, and outputs the message μ as long as T corresponds to an authorized set w.r.t. $\mathcal{A}$.

MA-ABE for CSS. Our starting point is the Sahai-Seyalioglu [SS10] construction for 1-bounded collusion FE. Clearly, the same construction can be directly extended to a 1-bounded collusion ABE scheme. Briefly, the idea is:

Setup: Sample $2n$ PKE public-secret key pairs $\mathsf{pk}_{i,b}, \mathsf{sk}_{i,b}$. Keep all public and all secret PKE keys as the master public and secret key, respectively.

Encrypt: To encrypt a message μ for predicate C, garble the circuit $\mathsf{Test}_{C,\mu}$ which on input an attribute $\mathbf{x}$ outputs μ *iff* $C(\mathbf{x}) = 1$. Encrypt each wire key $w_{i,b}$ under key $\mathsf{pk}_{i,b}$, and release garbled circuit with encrypted wire keys as the ciphertext.

Key generation: For attribute $\mathbf{x}$, the predicate key simply contains n PKE secret keys sk_{i,x_i}.

Decrypt: Decrypt the encrypt wire keys, and use it to evaluate the garbled circuit.

It might seem that Sahai-Seyalioglu scheme readily gives a multi-authority ABE scheme. The idea might be to have the ith authority generate two PKE key pairs $\mathsf{pk}_{i,b}, \mathsf{sk}_{i,b}$ for $b \in \{0, 1\}$. Note that this way the predicate key generation can also be distributed very easily. *Unfortunately, this is not the case!* The problem is the garbled circuit security crucially relies on only half of the wire labels to ever be revealed, but in MA-ABE setting, an attacker can corrupt key authorities. This completes breaks down extending this to the multi-authority setting.

Our idea is to make this basic approach compliant with the multi-authority model. The problem was if an attacker can corrupt key authorities, then garbled circuits does not provide the right protection. However, there is a simple fix – efficient CSS. In a few words, our idea is to replace garbled circuits with CSS, and rely on secrecy of CSS instead of garbling security. Formally, we do as follows:

Authority setup: Sample a single PKE public-secret key pair $\mathsf{pk}_u, \mathsf{sk}_u$.

Encrypt:
To encrypt a message μ for access structure $\mathcal{A}$, compute a CSS of μ for $\mathcal{A}$ as $\mathsf{sh}_1, \ldots, \mathsf{sh}_n$. Simply encrypt share sh_u under key pk_u.

Key generation: The predicate key is simply sk_u.

Decrypt: Decrypt the encrypted shares and use them to reconstruct the message.

Amazingly, this simple construction gives us a 1-bounded MA-ABE for efficient CSS from just public key encryption. The idea is simply to use semantic security to hide all unauthorized shares, and then use secrecy of CSS to hide the message. The remaining goal is to upgrade to q-bounded security (i.e., static model), and dynamic model eventually.

To that end, we revisit the simple strategy to go from 1-bounded collusion to q-bounded collusion for plain ABE. The idea there is to use repetition and add enough redundancy in the system. Concretely, one runs a large polynomial number of 1-bounded ABE systems in parallel, and a predicate key contains 1-bounded ABE predicate keys for a 'small' subset of them. The encryptor then threshold secret shares the message μ where each share is independently encrypted under each 1-bounded ABE system. By setting up the parameters carefully, this gives us security in the static model for ABE.

The question is whether we can replay a similar strategy in the multi-authority setting to mirror a similar collusion bound amplification. While this might seem natural, it is not immediately clear. The concern is two-fold:

1. In multi-authority setting, each authority works fully independently and asynchronously. Forget security, just for correctness it is essential that each authority selects the same subset of 1-bounded MA-ABE for a particular user. How can such a subset be computed?
2. Moreover, a core idea in the collusion bound amplification is to use a standard probabilistic argument [GVW12] that says randomly chosen subsets of small size will not have a large combined pairwise intersection. How can we use a probabilistic argument when some of the key authorities can get corrupted? (That is, their choices of subsets might not be truly random.)

Both these issues have simple solutions, but they are conflicting. The problem is to solve the first issue, we need to make the subset selection process deterministic. But, having the subsets be deterministically selected seems problematic for using a standard probabilistic argument such as cover-freeness.

We notice that if the adversary commits to all its corruptions at the beginning, then we could use an (almost) perfect hash function to deterministically select these subsets. Simply set the subset to be the hash of GID. (Recall an almost perfect hash function from $\{0,1\}^* \to [\mathsf{poly}(n)]$ maps n inputs to $\mathsf{poly}(n)$ numbers such that there are no collisions.) The construction now is very simple – each authority selects the subset of 1-bounded systems to use depending upon $H(\mathsf{GID})$. This solves both the above issues since $H(\mathsf{GID})$ is deterministic (and out of adversary's hand) as well as it has nice pairwise intersection property due to our assumption of it being a perfect hash function. It turns out a careful analysis of above approach could be used to prove super-selective security of our MA-ABE scheme in the static model. This is due to the fact that PRFs can be mostly used to design such near-perfect hash functions in the super-selective setting.

However, perfect hashes do not exist if the attacker gets to see the hash key! Moreover, even collision resistant hash functions are not good enough as the digest size needs to be very small so that the encryptor can enumerate over all possible digest values. This is due to the fact that the encryptor in the above strategy has to encrypt a secret share for each possible digest value. While this might seem like a tricky problem to bypass, it turns out modeling the hash function as a random oracle gives us the desired property. A (non-programmable) ROM is sufficient to show that an attacker cannot find q distinct GIDs where a special combinatorial property does not hold. We discuss this further in the full version.

The above ideas can be formalized to design an MA-ABE for CSS in the static model, and it can be very easily extended to the dynamic model. We discuss this in Sect. 6.3, but briefly remark here. Our approach is to first extend the above construction to a tagged version of MA-ABE. This can be done quite simply by relying on IBE as the only change would be that an encryptor uses IBE encryption to encrypt the secret shares where the identity is set to be the corresponding tag value. Next, by relying on the combinatorial ideas, discussed previously for the FE accumulator, we can upgrade its security to hold in the dynamic collusion model too.

3 Preliminaries

Notations. Let PPT denote probabilistic polynomial-time. For any integer $q \geq 2$, we let $\mathbb{Z}_q$ denote the ring of integers modulo q. We denote the set of all positive integers upto n as $[n] := \{1, \ldots, n\}$. For any finite set S, $x \leftarrow S$ denotes a uniformly random element x from the set S. Similarly, for any distribution $\mathcal{D}$, $x \leftarrow \mathcal{D}$ denotes an element x drawn from distribution $\mathcal{D}$. The distribution $\mathcal{D}^n$ is used to represent a distribution over vectors of n components, where each component is drawn independently from the distribution $\mathcal{D}$. Two distributions $\mathcal{D}_1$ and $\mathcal{D}_2$, parameterized by security parameter λ, are said to be computationally indistinguishable, represented by $\mathcal{D}_1 \approx_c \mathcal{D}_2$, if for all PPT adversaries $\mathcal{A}$, $\Pr[\mathcal{A}(x) = 1 : x \leftarrow \mathcal{D}_1] - \Pr[\mathcal{A}(x) = 1 : x \leftarrow \mathcal{D}_2] \leq \mathsf{negl}(\lambda)$.

Due to space constraints, basic cryptographic preliminaries are provided later in the full version.

4 Functional Encryption: Definitions

In this section, we revisit the notion of functional encryption (FE) in the bounded setting [SS10, GVW12]. Recent works of [AMVY21, GGLW22] proposed a collusion bound in the dynamic setting where the scheme's setup and key generation algorithms are independent of the collusion bound and instead, we can specify the collusion bound during encryption. We follow the formal security definitions from [GGLW22] almost verbatim and describe them below.

4.1 Static Collusion Model

Syntax. Let $\mathcal{M} = \{\mathcal{M}_n\}_{n\in\mathbb{N}}$, $\mathcal{R} = \{\mathcal{R}_n\}_{n\in\mathbb{N}}$ be families of sets, and $\mathcal{F} = \{\mathcal{F}_n\}$ a family of functions, where for all $n \in \mathbb{N}$ and $f \in \mathcal{F}_n$, $f : \mathcal{M}_n \to \mathcal{R}_n$. We will also assume that for all $n \in \mathbb{N}$, the set $\mathcal{F}_n$ contains an *empty function* $\epsilon_n : \mathcal{M}_n \to \mathcal{R}_n$. As in [BSW11], the empty function is used to capture information that intentionally leaks from the ciphertext.

A bounded functional encryption scheme FE for a family of function classes $\{\mathcal{F}_n\}_{n\in\mathbb{N}}$, message spaces $\{\mathcal{M}_n\}_{n\in\mathbb{N}}$ and collusion bound $q(\lambda)$ consists of four polynomial-time algorithms $(\mathsf{Setup}, \mathsf{Enc}, \mathsf{KeyGen}, \mathsf{Dec})$ with following semantics:

$\mathsf{Setup}(1^\lambda, 1^n, 1^q) \to (\mathsf{mpk}, \mathsf{msk})$. The setup algorithm takes as input the security parameter λ, the functionality index n[8] and the collusion bound 1^q. It outputs the master public-secret key pair $(\mathsf{mpk}, \mathsf{msk})$.

$\mathsf{Enc}(\mathsf{mpk}, m \in \mathcal{M}_n) \to \mathsf{ct}$. The encryption algorithm takes as input the master public key mpk and a message $m \in \mathcal{M}_n$ and outputs a ciphertext ct.

$\mathsf{KeyGen}(\mathsf{msk}, f \in \mathcal{F}_n) \to \mathsf{sk}_f$. The key generation algorithm takes as input the master secret key msk and a function $f \in \mathcal{F}_n$ and outputs sk_f.

$\mathsf{Dec}(\mathsf{sk}_f, \mathsf{ct}) \to y \in \mathcal{R}_n$. The decryption algorithm takes as input a ciphertext ct and a secret key sk_f and outputs a value $y \in \mathcal{R}_n$.

Correctness and Efficiency. A functional encryption scheme FE is said to be correct if for all $\lambda, n, q \in \mathbb{N}$, functions $f \in \mathcal{F}_n$, messages $m \in \mathcal{M}_n$ and $(\mathsf{mpk}, \mathsf{msk}) \leftarrow \mathsf{Setup}(1^\lambda, 1^n, 1^q)$, we have that

$$\Pr\left[\mathsf{Dec}(\mathsf{KeyGen}(\mathsf{msk}, f), \mathsf{Enc}(\mathsf{mpk}, m)) = f(m)\right] = 1.$$

And, it is said to be efficient if the running time of the algorithms is a fixed polynomial in the parameters λ, n and q.

Static Bounded Collusion Security. This is formally captured via the following 'simulation based' security definition as follows.

Definition 4.1 (static-bounded-collusion simulation-security). *A functional encryption scheme* FE *is said to be* statically-bounded-collusion simulation-secure *if there exists a stateful PPT simulator* $\mathsf{Sim} = (\mathsf{S}_0, \mathsf{S}_1, \mathsf{S}_2, \mathsf{S}_3)$ *such that for every stateful PPT adversary* $\mathcal{A}$*, the following distributions are computationally indistinguishable:*

$$\left\{ \mathcal{A}^{O(\cdot)}(\mathsf{ct}) : \begin{array}{c} (1^n, 1^q) \leftarrow \mathcal{A}(1^\lambda) \\ (\mathsf{mpk}, \mathsf{msk}) \leftarrow \mathsf{Setup}(1^\lambda, 1^n, 1^q) \\ m \leftarrow \mathcal{A}^{\mathsf{KeyGen}(\mathsf{msk}, \cdot)}(\mathsf{mpk}) \\ \mathsf{ct} \leftarrow \mathsf{Enc}(\mathsf{mpk}, m) \\ O(\cdot) = \mathsf{KeyGen}(\mathsf{msk}, \cdot) \end{array} \right\}_{\lambda\in\mathbb{N}} \approx_c \left\{ \mathcal{A}^{O(\cdot)}(\mathsf{ct}) : \begin{array}{c} (1^n, 1^q) \leftarrow \mathcal{A}(1^\lambda) \\ (\mathsf{mpk}, \mathsf{st}_0) \leftarrow \mathsf{S}_0(1^\lambda, 1^n, 1^q) \\ m \leftarrow \mathcal{A}^{\mathsf{S}_1(\mathsf{st}_0, \cdot)}(\mathsf{mpk}) \\ (\mathsf{ct}, \mathsf{st}_2) \leftarrow \mathsf{S}_2(\mathsf{st}_1, \Pi^m) \\ O(\cdot) = \mathsf{S}_3^{U_m(\cdot)}(\mathsf{st}_2, \cdot) \end{array} \right\}_{\lambda\in\mathbb{N}}$$

whenever the following admissibility constraints and properties are satisfied:

[8] One could additionally consider the setup algorithm to take as input a sequence of functionality indices where the function class and message space are characterized by all such indices (e.g., having input length and circuit depth as functionality indices). For ease of notation, we keep a single functionality index in the above definition.

- S_1 *and* S_3 *are stateful in that after each invocation, they updates their states* st_1 *and* st_3 *(respectively) which is carried over to its next invocation.*
- Π^m *contains a list of functions* f_i *queried by* $\mathcal{A}$ *in the pre-challenge phase along with the their output on the challenge message* m*. That is, if* f_i *is the* i*-th function queried by* $\mathcal{A}$ *to oracle* S_1 *and* q_{pre} *be the number of queries* $\mathcal{A}$ *makes before outputting* m*, then* $\Pi^m = \big((f_1, f_1(m)), \ldots, (f_{q_{\mathsf{pre}}}, f_{q_{\mathsf{pre}}}(m))\big)$.
- $\mathcal{A}$ *makes at most* q *total key generation queries.*
- S_3*, for each queried function* f_i*, makes a single query to its message oracle* U_m *on the same* f_i*, and gets output as* $f_i(m)$*.*

4.2 Dynamic Collusion Model

In the "dynamic" bounded collusion model [AMVY21, GGLW22], the scheme is no longer tied to a single collusion bound q fixed a-priori at the system setup, but instead the encryptor could choose the amount of collusion resilience it wants. Thus, this changes the syntax of the setup and encryption algorithm when compared to the static setting from above:

$\mathsf{Setup}(1^\lambda, 1^n) \to (\mathsf{mpk}, \mathsf{msk})$. The setup algorithm takes as input the security parameter λ and the functionality index n (in unary). It outputs the master public-secret key pair $(\mathsf{mpk}, \mathsf{msk})$.

$\mathsf{Enc}(\mathsf{mpk}, m \in \mathcal{M}_n, 1^q) \to \mathsf{ct}$. The encryption algorithm takes as input the master public key mpk, a message $m \in \mathcal{M}_n$, and it takes the desired collusion bound q as an input. It outputs a ciphertext ct.

Efficiency. The runtime of $\mathsf{Setup}, \mathsf{KeyGen}$ is polynomial in λ, n. While rest of the algorithms can run in time polynomial in λ, n, q.

Dynamic Bounded Collusion Security. We define a 'simulation based' security notion similar to the static security definition (Definition 4.1).

Definition 4.2 (dynamic-bounded-collusion simulation-security). *A functional encryption scheme* $\mathsf{FE} = (\mathsf{Setup}, \mathsf{Enc}, \mathsf{KeyGen}, \mathsf{Dec})$ *is said to be* dynamically-bounded-collusion *simulation-secure if there exists a stateful PPT simulator* Sim *such that for every stateful PPT adversary* $\mathcal{A}$*, the following distributions are computationally indistinguishable:*

$$\left\{ \mathcal{A}^{O(\cdot)}(\mathsf{ct}) : \begin{array}{c} 1^n \leftarrow \mathcal{A}(1^\lambda) \\ (\mathsf{mpk}, \mathsf{msk}) \leftarrow \mathsf{Setup}(1^\lambda, 1^n) \\ (m, 1^q) \leftarrow \mathcal{A}^{\mathsf{KeyGen}(\mathsf{msk}, \cdot)}(\mathsf{mpk}) \\ \mathsf{ct} \leftarrow \mathsf{Enc}(\mathsf{mpk}, m, 1^q) \\ O(\cdot) = \mathsf{KeyGen}(\mathsf{msk}, \cdot) \end{array} \right\}_{\lambda \in \mathbb{N}} \approx_c \left\{ \mathcal{A}^{O(\cdot)}(\mathsf{ct}) : \begin{array}{c} 1^n \leftarrow \mathcal{A}(1^\lambda) \\ \mathsf{mpk} \leftarrow \mathsf{Sim}(1^\lambda, 1^n) \\ (m, 1^q) \leftarrow \mathcal{A}^{\mathsf{Sim}(\cdot)}(\mathsf{mpk}) \\ \mathsf{ct} \leftarrow \mathsf{Sim}(\Pi^m, 1^q) \\ O(\cdot) = \mathsf{Sim}^{U_m(\cdot)}(\cdot) \end{array} \right\}_{\lambda \in \mathbb{N}}$$

whenever the admissibility constraints and properties, as defined in Definition 4.1, are satisfied.

4.3 Tagged Functional Encryption

Next, we recall the notion of tagged FE from [GGLW22]. Tagged FE intuitively represents a succinct collection of an exponential number of instances of a FE scheme, where each instance is denoted by a tag $\mathsf{tag} \in \mathcal{I}_z$ ($|\mathcal{I}_z|$ is the total number of FE instances bundled together). A tagged bounded functional encryption scheme FE for a family of function classes $\{\mathcal{F}_n\}_{n\in\mathbb{N}}$, message spaces $\{\mathcal{M}_n\}_{n\in\mathbb{N}}$ and tag spaces $\mathcal{I} = \{\mathcal{I}_z\}_{z\in\mathbb{N}}$ consists of four polynomial-time algorithms (Setup, Enc, KeyGen, Dec) with the following semantics.

$\mathsf{Setup}(1^\lambda, 1^n, 1^z, 1^q) \to (\mathsf{mpk}, \mathsf{msk})$. In addition to the normal inputs taken by a static-bounded FE scheme, the setup also takes in a tag space index z, which fixes a tag space $\mathcal{I}_z$.

$\mathsf{Enc}(\mathsf{mpk}, \mathsf{tag} \in \mathcal{I}_z, m \in \mathcal{M}_n) \to \mathsf{ct}$. The encryption also takes in a tag $\mathsf{tag} \in \mathcal{I}_z$ to bind to the ciphertext.

$\mathsf{KeyGen}(\mathsf{msk}, \mathsf{tag} \in \mathcal{I}_z, f \in \mathcal{F}_n) \to \mathsf{sk}_{\mathsf{tag},f}$. The key generation also binds the secret keys to a fixed tag $\mathsf{tag} \in \mathcal{I}_z$.

$\mathsf{Dec}(\mathsf{sk}_{\mathsf{tag},f}, \mathsf{ct}) \to \mathcal{R}_n$. The decryption algorithm has syntax identical to a non-tagged scheme.

Definition 4.3 (Correctness). *We say the scheme is correct if for all $\lambda, n \in \mathbb{N}, z, q \in \mathsf{poly}(\lambda)$, functions $f \in \mathcal{F}_n$, messages $m \in \mathcal{M}_n$ and $\mathsf{tag} \in \mathcal{I}_z$, we have that for $(\mathsf{mpk}, \mathsf{msk}) \leftarrow \mathsf{Setup}(1^\lambda, 1^n, 1^z, 1^q)$, the following holds true,*

$$\Pr\left[\mathsf{Dec}(\mathsf{KeyGen}(\mathsf{msk}, \mathsf{tag}, f), \mathsf{Enc}(\mathsf{mpk}, \mathsf{tag}, m)) = f(m)\right] = 1.$$

where the probability is taken over the coins of setup, key generation and encryption algorithms.

Definition 4.4 (tagged-static-bounded-collusion simulation-security). *For any choice of parameters $\lambda, n, q, z \in \mathbb{N}$, consider the following list of stateful oracles $\mathsf{S}_0, \mathsf{S}_1, \mathsf{S}_2$ where these oracles simulate the FE setup, key generation, and encryption algorithms respectively, and all three algorithms share and update the same global state of the simulator. Here the attacker interacts with the execution environment $\mathcal{E}$, and the environment makes queries to the simulator oracles. Formally, the simulator oracles and the environment are defined below:*

$\mathsf{S}_0(1^\lambda, 1^n, 1^z, 1^q)$ *generates the simulated master public key* mpk *of the system, and initializes the global state* st *of the simulator which is used by the next two oracles.*

$\mathsf{S}_1(\cdot,\cdot,\cdot)$, *upon a call to generate secret key on a function-tag-value tuple $(f_i, \mathsf{tag}_i, \mu_i)$, where the function value is either $\mu_i = \perp$ (signalling that the adversary has not yet made any encryption query on tag tag_i), or $(m^{\mathsf{tag}_i}, \mathsf{tag}_i)$ has already been queried for encryption (for some message m^{tag_i}), and $\mu_i = f_i(m^{\mathsf{tag}_i})$, the oracle outputs a simulated key $\mathsf{sk}_{f_i,\mathsf{tag}_i}$.*

$\mathsf{S}_2(\cdot,\cdot)$, *upon a call to generate ciphertext on a tag-list tuple $(\mathsf{tag}_i, \Pi^{m^{\mathsf{tag}_i}})$, where the list $\Pi^{m^{\mathsf{tag}_i}}$ is a possibly empty list of the form $\Pi^{m^{\mathsf{tag}_i}} = (f_1^{\mathsf{tag}_i}, f_1^{\mathsf{tag}_i}(m^{\mathsf{tag}_i})), \ldots, (f_{q_{\mathsf{pre}}}^{\mathsf{tag}_i}, f_{q_{\mathsf{pre}}}^{\mathsf{tag}_i}(m^{\mathsf{tag}_i}))$ (that is, contains the list of function-value pairs for which the adversary has already received a secret key for), the oracle outputs a simulated ciphertext $\mathsf{ct}_{\mathsf{tag}_i}$.*

$\mathcal{E}^{\mathsf{S}_1,\mathsf{S}_2}(\cdot,\cdot)$, *receives two types of queries – secret key query and encryption query.* *Upon a secret key query on a function-tag pair* (f_i, tag_i), *if* $(m^{\mathsf{tag}_i}, \mathsf{tag}_i)$ *has already been queried for encryption (for some message* m^{tag_i}*) then* $\mathcal{E}$ *queries key oracle* S_1 *on tuple* $(f_i, \mathsf{tag}_i, \mu_i = f_i(m^{\mathsf{tag}_i}))$, *otherwise it adds* (f_i, tag_i) *to the its local state, and queries* S_1 *on tuple* $(f_i, \mathsf{tag}_i, \mu_i = \perp)$. *And, it simply forwards oracle's simulated key* $\mathsf{sk}_{f_i,\mathsf{tag}_i}$ *to the adversary.*
Upon a ciphertext query on a message-tag pair (m_i, tag_i), *if the adversary made an encryption query on the same tag* tag_i *previously, then the query is disallowed (that is, at most one message query per every unique tag is permitted). Otherwise, it computes a (possibly empty) list of function-value pairs of the form* $\Pi^{m_i} = \left((f_1^{\mathsf{tag}_i}, f_1^{\mathsf{tag}_i}(m^{\mathsf{tag}_i})), \ldots, (f_{q_{\mathsf{pre}}}^{\mathsf{tag}_i}, f_{q_{\mathsf{pre}}}^{\mathsf{tag}_i}(m^{\mathsf{tag}_i}))\right)$ *where* $(f_j^{\mathsf{tag}_i}, \mathsf{tag}_i)$ *are stored in* $\mathcal{E}$*'s local state, and removes all such pairs* $(f_j^{\mathsf{tag}_i}, \mathsf{tag}_i)$ *from its local state.* $\mathcal{E}$ *then queries ciphertext oracle* S_2 *on tuple* $(\mathsf{tag}_i, \Pi^{m_i})$, *and simply forwards oracle's simulated ciphertext* $\mathsf{ct}_{\mathsf{tag}_i}$ *to the adversary.*

A tagged functional encryption scheme $\mathsf{FE} = (\mathsf{Setup}, \mathsf{Enc}, \mathsf{KeyGen}, \mathsf{Dec})$ *is said to be tagged-statically-bounded-collusion simulation-secure if there exists a stateful PPT simulator* $\mathsf{Sim} = (\mathsf{S}_0, \mathsf{S}_1, \mathsf{S}_2)$ *such that for every stateful* admissible *PPT adversary* $\mathcal{A}$, *the following distributions are computationally indistinguishable:*

$$\left\{ \mathcal{A}^{\mathsf{KeyGen}(\mathsf{msk},\cdot,\cdot),\mathsf{Enc}(\mathsf{mpk},\cdot,\cdot)}(\mathsf{mpk}) : \begin{array}{c} (1^n, 1^q, 1^z) \leftarrow \mathcal{A}(1^\lambda) \\ (\mathsf{mpk}, \mathsf{msk}) \leftarrow \mathsf{Setup}(1^\lambda, 1^n, 1^z, 1^q) \end{array} \right\}_{\lambda \in \mathbb{N}}$$

$$\approx_c$$

$$\left\{ \mathcal{A}^{\mathcal{E}^{\mathsf{S}_1,\mathsf{S}_2}(\cdot,\cdot)}(\mathsf{mpk}) : \begin{array}{c} (1^n, 1^q, 1^z) \leftarrow \mathcal{A}(1^\lambda) \\ \mathsf{mpk} \leftarrow \mathsf{S}_0(1^\lambda, 1^n, 1^z, 1^q) \end{array} \right\}_{\lambda \in \mathbb{N}}$$

where $\mathcal{A}$ *is an admissible adversary if:*

- $\mathcal{A}$ *makes at most one encryption query per unique tag (that is, if the adversary made an encryption query on some tag* tag_i *previously, then making another encryption query for the same tag is disallowed)*
- $\mathcal{A}$ *makes at most* q *queries combined to the key generation oracles in the above experiments for all tags* tag_i *such that it also submitted an encryption query for tag* tag_i.

Tagged FE to Dynamic Collusion Resistance. Garg et al. [GGLW22] proved that the notion of tagged FE captures the essence behind dynamic collusion resistance. Below we restate one of their main results.

Theorem 4.1 ([GGLW22, **Paraphrased, Theorems 3.1 and 5.1**]). *If* tgfe *is a tagged statically* λ*-bounded collusion simulation-secure FE scheme (as per Definition 4.4), then it can be upgraded into a dynamic bounded collusion simulation-secure FE scheme (as per Definition 4.2) via a black-box transformation.*

It turns out the same black-box transformation also works for multi-authority attribute-based encryption. We get the following theorem as a simple extension.

Theorem 4.2. *If* tgMAABE *is a tagged statically* λ*-bounded collusion-secure multi-authority attribute-based encryption scheme, then it can be upgraded into a dynamic bounded collusion-secure multi-authority attribute-based encryption scheme via the GGLW black-box transformation.*

5 From Static to Dynamic Collusion Model Generically

In this section, we show how to upgrade any statically bounded collusion FE scheme for function class $\mathcal{F}$ to dynamically bounded collusion FE scheme for the same function class $\mathcal{F}$. Our transformation is fully generic, but it is not black-box since we rely on the use of garbled circuits where we garble the encryption circuit for the underlying statically secure FE scheme.

High Level Sketch. We start with the simple observation from the previous section that to design a dynamically bounded collusion FE scheme for function class $\mathbb{F}$, it is sufficient to design a *tagged* FE scheme for function class $\mathcal{F}$. This is due to the black-box GGLW compiler that upgrades a tagged FE scheme to be dynamically secure. So, we design a generic compiler that builds a *tagged* FE scheme for function class $\mathcal{F}$ from any statically secure FE scheme for function class $\mathbb{F}$. Combining the generic compiler with the GGLW black-box compiler, we obtain a dynamically secure FE scheme for function class $\mathcal{F}$.

A bit more concretely, we design a tagged FE accumulator which accumulates 2^z many instances of a statically secure FE scheme to a tagged FE scheme for tag space $\mathcal{I}_z = \{0,1\}^z$. Our compiler preserves the bound on the number of key generation queries that can be made on a particular tag. That is, if we start with a q-bounded static FE scheme, we obtain a q-bounded tagged FE scheme. Our accumulator is inspired from the recent success in usage of garbling techniques [DG17a] for designing identity-based encryption, registration-based encryption and more [DG17b, DG17a, BLSV18, GHMR18, GHM+19, GV20].

In the aforementioned list of works, a central component of the design was to combine garbled circuits with a nearly equivalent set of core primitive such as chameleon hash functions, one time signatures with encryption (OTSE), batch encryption, etc. A key idea was to use this combination to conceptually enable delegation of encryption keys to the leaves of a Merkle tree. Our starting point for the tagged FE accumulator is to use a similar delegation trick to delegate an exponential number of FE keys to a unique leaf of the Merkle tree. We build our tagged FE by relying on compact one-time signature with encryption (OTSE), which were initially introduced in [DG17a] to build IBE.

Below we provide our construction for tagged FE accumulator. We remark that our accumulator supports accumulating static FE for uniform models of computation as well.

5.1 Tagged FE Accumulator

Ingredients. Let $\mathsf{BFE} = (\mathsf{BFE.Setup}, \mathsf{BFE.Enc}, \mathsf{BFE.KeyGen}, \mathsf{BFE.Dec})$ be a q-bounded FE scheme for function space $\mathcal{F}$ and message space $\mathcal{M}$, and let

$\mathsf{OTSE} = (\mathsf{SSetup}, \mathsf{SGen}, \mathsf{SSign}, \mathsf{SEnc}, \mathsf{SDec})$ be an OTSE scheme. Let PRF be a pseudorandom function with key size λ, inputs to be any bit string of length $\leq z$ bits, and outputs 2λ bits of output. We use PRF_1 and PRF_2 to denote the first λ and last λ bits of the output, respectively.[9] That is, $\mathsf{PRF}(s \in \{0,1\}^\lambda, v \in \{0,1\}^{\leq z}) = \mathsf{PRF}_1(s,v)||\mathsf{PRF}_2(s,v)$.

Below we provide our tagged FE scheme for function space $\mathcal{F}$ and message space $\mathcal{M}$ with tag space $\mathcal{I}_z = \{0,1\}^z$. We remark that $\mathcal{F}$ could be specifying any uniform/non-uniform model of computation.

$\mathsf{NodeGen}(pp, v, s)$

Input: OTSE parameter pp, node index $v \in \{0,1\}^{z' \leq z}$, seed $s \in \{0,1\}^\lambda$
Output: OTSE verification key vk_v, signature σ_v, auxiliary value x_v

1. Let $(\mathsf{vk}_w, \mathsf{sk}_w) \leftarrow \mathsf{SGen}(\mathsf{pp}; \mathsf{PRF}_1(s,w))$ for $w \in \{v, v||0, v||1\}$.
2. Set $x_v = \mathsf{vk}_{v||0}||vk_{v||1}$ and $\sigma_v = \mathsf{SSign}(\mathsf{pp}, \mathsf{sk}_v, x_v)$.
3. Output $(\mathsf{vk}_v, \sigma_v, x_v)$.

Fig. 1. Routine NodeGen

$\mathsf{Setup}(1^\lambda, 1^n, 1^z, 1^q) \rightarrow (\mathsf{mpk}, \mathsf{msk})$. It samples a PRF seed $s \leftarrow \{0,1\}^\lambda$. Let ℓ be the length of BFE.mpk corresponding to parameters λ, n, q. It samples parameters $\mathsf{pp} \leftarrow \mathsf{SSetup}(1^\lambda, \ell)$.[10] Compute the root parameters as $(\mathsf{vk}_\epsilon, \sigma_\epsilon, x_\epsilon) \leftarrow \mathsf{NodeGen}(\mathsf{pp}, \epsilon, s)$ (routine NodeGen described in Fig. 1).
It outputs the master key pair as $\mathsf{mpk} = (\mathsf{pp}, \mathsf{vk}_\epsilon), \mathsf{msk} = s$.

$\mathsf{KeyGen}(\mathsf{msk} = s, \mathsf{tag} \in \{0,1\}^z, f \in \mathcal{F}_n) \rightarrow \mathsf{sk}_{f,\mathsf{tag}}$. Let v_j denote the j-bit prefix of tag, i.e. $v_j = \mathsf{tag}[1:j]$ for $j \in [0,z]$. Note that $v_0 = \epsilon$ and $v_z = \mathsf{tag}$.
The key generator first computes $(\mathsf{vk}_{v_j}, \sigma_{v_j}, x_{v_j}) \leftarrow \mathsf{NodeGen}(\mathsf{pp}, v_j, s)$ for $j \in [0, z-1]$. It computes $(\mathsf{vk}_{\mathsf{tag}}, \sigma_{\mathsf{tag}}, \mathsf{BFE.mpk}_{\mathsf{tag}}, \mathsf{BFE.sk}_{\mathsf{tag},f}) \leftarrow \mathsf{LeafGen}(\mathsf{pp}, \mathsf{tag}, s, f)$ (routine LeafGen described in Fig. 2).
It outputs $\mathsf{sk}_{f,\mathsf{tag}} = (\{(\sigma_{v_j}, x_{v_j})\}_{j \in [0,z-1]}, \sigma_{\mathsf{tag}}, \mathsf{BFE.mpk}_{\mathsf{tag}}, \mathsf{BFE.sk}_{\mathsf{tag},f})$.

$\mathsf{Enc}(\mathsf{mpk}, \mathsf{tag}, m) \rightarrow \mathsf{ct}$. It parses mpk as above. Let v_j denote the j-bit prefix of tag for $j \in [z]$, and $\ell = |\mathsf{BFE.mpk}|$. Let $\mathsf{T}[m,r]$ be a circuit as described in Fig. 3.
The encryptor first garbles $\mathsf{T}[m,r]$ as $(\tilde{\mathsf{T}}, \mathsf{e_T}) \leftarrow \mathsf{GC.Garble}(1^\lambda, \mathsf{T}[m,r])$ for uniform randomness r, and next it garbles $\mathsf{Q}[\mathsf{pp}, 0, \ell, \mathsf{e_T}, \mathsf{r_T}]$ for uniform randomness $\mathsf{r_T}$ as follows (see Fig. 4 for details) – $(\tilde{\mathsf{Q}}^{(z)}, \mathsf{e}_{\mathsf{Q}}^{(z)}) \leftarrow$

[9] We assume, w.l.o.g., that the setup algorithms for BFE and OTSE take λ-bits as input.
[10] Recall from the succinctness property of OTSE, the length of the verification key $|\mathsf{vk}|$ is some polynomial in λ and independent of ℓ.

LeafGen(pp, v, s, f)

Input: OTSE parameters pp, leaf index $v \in \{0,1\}^z$, seed $s \in \{0,1\}^\lambda$, function $f \in \mathcal{F}_n$
Output: OTSE verification key vk_v, signature σ_v, public key of vth instance $\mathsf{BFE.mpk}_v$, secret key $\mathsf{BFE.sk}_{v,f}$

1. Let $(\mathsf{vk}_v, \mathsf{sk}_v) \leftarrow \mathsf{SGen}(\mathsf{pp}; \mathsf{PRF}_1(s,v))$.
2. Compute $(\mathsf{BFE.mpk}_v, \mathsf{BFE.msk}_v) \leftarrow \mathsf{BFE.Setup}(1^\lambda; \mathsf{PRF}_2(s,v))$ (i.e., v^{th} instance of base FE scheme with fixed randomness $\mathsf{PRF}_2(s,v)$).
3. Sample $\mathsf{BFE.sk}_{v,f} \leftarrow \mathsf{BFE.KeyGen}(\mathsf{BFE.msk}_v, f)$, and compute $\sigma_v = \mathsf{SSign}(\mathsf{pp}, \mathsf{sk}_v, \mathsf{BFE.mpk}_v)$.
4. Output $(\mathsf{vk}_v, \sigma_v, \mathsf{BFE.mpk}_v, \mathsf{BFE.sk}_{v,f})$.

Fig. 2. Routine LeafGen

$\mathsf{GC.Garble}(1^\lambda, \mathsf{Q}[\mathsf{pp}, 0, \ell, \mathsf{e_T}, \mathsf{r_T}])$.

Next, for $j = z-1, \ldots, 0$, it garbles a sequence of circuits as

$$(\tilde{\mathsf{Q}}^{(j)}, \mathsf{e}_\mathsf{Q}^{(j)}) \leftarrow \mathsf{GC.Garble}(1^\lambda, \mathsf{Q}[\mathsf{pp}, \mathsf{tag}_{j+1}, \ell', \mathsf{e}_\mathsf{Q}^{(j+1)}, \mathsf{r}_\mathsf{Q}^{(j+1)}]),$$

where ℓ' be $|\mathsf{vk}_\epsilon|$, $\mathsf{r}_\mathsf{Q}^{(j+1)}$ is uniform randomness. Finally, it parses $\mathsf{e}_\mathsf{Q}^{(0)} = \{Y_{\iota,0}, Y_{\iota,1}\}_{\iota\in[\ell']}$, and outputs $\mathsf{ct} = \left(\tilde{\mathsf{y}}^{(0)}, \tilde{\mathsf{Q}}^{(0)}, \ldots, \tilde{\mathsf{Q}}^{(z)}, \tilde{\mathsf{T}}\right)$, where $\tilde{\mathsf{y}}^{(0)} = \{Y_{\iota,\mathsf{y}_\iota}\}_{\iota\in[\ell']}$ and y_ι denote the ιth bit of vk_ϵ.

Leaf Encryption Circuit $\mathsf{T}[m,r](\mathsf{BFE.mpk})$

Input: Leaf public key BFE.mpk, **Output:** Ciphertext ct.
Constant: message m, randomness r.

1. Compute and output $\mathsf{ct} = \mathsf{BFE.Enc}(\mathsf{BFE.mpk}, m; r)$.

Fig. 3. Circuit T

Internal Encryption Circuit $\mathsf{Q}[\mathsf{pp}, \beta, \ell', \mathsf{e}, \mathsf{r}](\mathsf{vk})$

Input: OTSE verification key vk, **Output:** Encrypted labels $\hat{\mathsf{e}}^\beta$.
Constants: OTSE parameters pp, bit β, no of labels ℓ', wire labels $\mathsf{e} = \{(Y_{\iota,0}, Y_{\iota,1})\}_{\iota\in[\ell']}$, randomness $\mathsf{r} = \{(r_{\iota,0}, r_{\iota,1})\}_{\iota\in[\ell']}$.

1. Output $\{\mathsf{SEnc}(\mathsf{pp}, (\mathsf{vk}, \beta\cdot\ell' + \iota, b), Y_{\iota,b}; r_{\iota,b})\}_{\iota\in[\ell'], b\in\{0,1\}}$.

Fig. 4. Circuit Q

$\mathsf{Dec}(\mathsf{sk}_{\mathsf{tag},f}, \mathsf{ct})$. It parses the key and ciphertext as above. Recall that we use v_j to denote the j-bit prefix of tag, $\ell = |\mathsf{BFE.mpk}|$ and ℓ' as length of OTSE verification key. It simply runs the following iterative procedure for decryption where it first runs the garbled circuit to recover encrypted wire labels, and then decrypt half of the wire labels, and then continue this until it recovers an FE ciphertext under the public key associated for the leaf node corresponding to tag. Concretely, it does as follows:

1. For $j = 0$ to $z - 1$:
   (a) $\{\hat{\mathsf{e}}^{(j)}_{\iota,b}\}_{\iota\in[\ell'],b\in\{0,1\}} \leftarrow \mathsf{GC.Eval}(\tilde{\mathsf{Q}}^{(j)}, \tilde{\mathsf{y}}^{(j)})$.
   (b) $\tilde{\mathsf{y}}^{(j+1)} \leftarrow \left\{\mathsf{SDec}(\mathsf{pp}, (\mathsf{vk}_{v_j}, \sigma_{v_j}, x_{v_j}), \hat{\mathsf{e}}^{(j)}_{\iota,(x_{v_j})_\iota})\right\}_{\iota\in[\ell']}$.
2. Evaluate $\{\hat{\mathsf{e}}^{(z)}_{\iota,b}\}_{\iota\in[\ell],b\in\{0,1\}} \leftarrow \mathsf{GC.Eval}(\tilde{\mathsf{Q}}^{(z)}, \tilde{\mathsf{y}}^{(z)})$, and let pk_ι denote the ιth bit of $\mathsf{BFE.mpk}_{\mathsf{tag}}$.
3. Decrypt $\mathsf{y}^{\mathsf{T}} = \left\{\mathsf{SDec}\left(\mathsf{pp}, \left(\mathsf{vk}_{\mathsf{tag}}, \sigma_{\mathsf{tag}}, \mathsf{BFE.mpk}_{\mathsf{tag}}\right), \hat{\mathsf{e}}^{(z)}_{\iota,\mathsf{pk}_\iota}\right)\right\}_{\iota\in[\ell]}$.
4. Finally, output $\mathsf{BFE.Dec}(\mathsf{BFE.sk}_{\mathsf{tag},f}, \mathsf{ct}_{\mathsf{BFE}})$ where $\mathsf{ct}_{\mathsf{BFE}} = \mathsf{Eval}(\tilde{\mathsf{T}}, \mathsf{y}^{\mathsf{T}})$.

Correctness and Efficiency. We say the scheme is correct if it satisfies Definition 4.3. By correctness of the garbling scheme, we have that $\tilde{\mathsf{Q}}^{(0)}$, when run on garbled input $\tilde{\mathsf{y}}^{(0)}$ computes $Q[\mathsf{pp}, 0, \ell, \cdot](\mathsf{vk}_\epsilon)$ and outputs encrypted labels to $\tilde{\mathsf{Q}}^{(1)}$. By correctness of the OTSE encryption scheme, we can decrypt the labels corresponding to tag_1 to compute $\tilde{y}^{(1)}$. Similarly, iteratively calling the correctness of garbling and the signature scheme, we compute the garbled inputs to circuit $\tilde{\mathsf{T}}$ corresponding to $\mathsf{BFE.mpk}_{\mathsf{tag}}$. Thus, eventually it computes $\mathsf{ct}_{\mathsf{BFE}} \leftarrow \mathsf{T}[m](\mathsf{BFE.mpk}_{\mathsf{tag}})$ by correctness of garbling, and by the correctness of the tag^{th} instance of BFE scheme, we get $\mathsf{BFE.Dec}(\mathsf{BFE.sk}_{\mathsf{tag},f}, \mathsf{BFE.Enc}(\mathsf{BFE.mpk}_{\mathsf{tag}}, m)) = f(m)$.

The different algorithms Setup, KeyGen run polynomial in λ, z, n, q and this can be seen easily from the construction. Encryption algorithm runs polynomial in λ, z, n, q and the message m that is chosen during encryption time. Crucially, we observe here that our tagged FE accumulator is agnostic to the model of computation of the base BFE scheme. Thus if the base scheme BFE can support uniform models of computation, so can our transformation.

5.2 Security

Theorem 5.1. *If* PRF *is a secure pseudorandom function,* GC *is a secure garbling scheme,* OTSE *is a secure one-time signature with encryption scheme,* BFE $=$ (BFE.Setup, BFE.Enc, BFE.KeyGen, BFE.Dec) *is a bounded-collusion simulation-secure FE scheme (as per Definition 4.1), then the above scheme is a tagged-statically-bounded-collusion simulation-secure FE scheme (as per Definition 4.4).*

Proof. The proof strategy is inspired from the proof of adaptive security of identity-based encryption from [DG17a]. Let us start by discussing the similarities that we can use in our proof of security. The initial idea used in the IBE setting was to successively simulate garbled circuits one-by-one inside the challenge ciphertext using a sequence of hybrid proof steps, where first they switch the use of an actual PRF with a truly random function by making the challenger store state. And, next they simulate the garbled circuits since once half of the wire keys are ever decryptable for any garbled circuit in the sequence, and this is guaranteed by the security of the one-time signature with encryption scheme since the signatures created binds to the entire sequence of tree nodes which can be opened on any path. This strategy enables simulation of every garbled circuit until the challenger wants to simulate the last garbled circuit $T[m, r]$ which contains the actual message. Using the same strategy as above, this garbled circuit can also be simulated using just the encryption of message m under randomness r.

At this point, our proof and the [DG17a] proof diverge since in the case of IBE, the attacker never receives the secret key corresponding to the final ciphertext, thus security follows from security of public-key encryption. However, in our case an attacker can get a bounded number of function keys that enable decryption for the corresponding FE ciphertext. But this is only a minor technical issue and we can get around this using simulation security of the base FE scheme. Thus, by using simulation security of base (untagged) FE, we can simulate this ciphertext and simulate the garbled circuit using the simulated FE ciphertext instead. For completeness, we provide a full proof of security later in the full version. □

5.3 Central Theorem

Finally, by combining the above theorem (Theorem 5.1) with Theorem 4.1, we get our central theorem as follows.

Theorem 5.2. *If* IBE *is a secure IBE scheme and* BFE *is a λ-bounded collusion simulation-secure FE scheme (as per Definition 4.1), then there exists a dynamic bounded collusion simulation-secure FE scheme (as per Definition 4.2). And, the dynamic FE scheme can be obtained via a non-black-box transformation from the static FE scheme.*

As discussed in [AMVY21], dynamic bounded collusion FE schemes imply IBE for most basic function classes, thus the above theorem is unconditional, and we could simplify it as follows.

Corollary 5.1. *If* BFE *is a λ-bounded collusion simulation-secure FE scheme (as per Definition 4.1), then there exists a dynamic bounded collusion simulation-secure FE scheme (as per Definition 4.2) obtained via a non-black-box transformation.*

This immediately leads to new results by combining with [GSW21, Wee21].

Corollary 5.2. *If* IBE *is a secure IBE scheme, then there exists a dynamic-bounded collusion simulation-secure ABE scheme for Turing Machines.*

Corollary 5.3. *If Learning with Errors assumption is hard, then there exists a dynamic-bounded collusion simulation-secure ABE scheme for DFAs in the secret-key-selective setting.*

6 Multi-Authority ABE: Tagged and Dynamic Collusion

The second result in our paper is a multi-authority attribute-based encryption scheme (MA-ABE) in the bounded collusion model for efficient computational secret sharing schemes (CSS). We show that our construction enjoys dynamic collusion property. We obtain our result via the tagged FE framework that we discussed in Sect. 4.3. We start by recalling the notion of access structures and MA-ABE.

6.1 Definition and Preliminaries

Access Structures and Computational Secret-Sharing. We recall the concepts of access structures and computational secret-sharing schemes (CSSS). We follow the notation from prior works [GPSW06,LW11].

Definition 6.1 (Access Structures). *Let $\{P_i\}_{i\in[n]}$ be a set of parties. A collection $\mathbb{A} \subseteq 2^{\{P_1,\ldots,P_n\}}$ is monotone if $\forall B, C$: if $B \in \mathbb{A}$ and $B \subseteq C$, then $C \in \mathbb{A}$. An access structure (respectively, monotone access structure) is a collection (respectively, monotone collection) $\mathbb{A}$ of non-empty subsets of $\{P_i\}_{i\in[n]}$. The sets in $\mathbb{A}$ are called the authorized sets, and the sets not in $\mathbb{A}$ are called the unauthorized sets.*

As in prior works, attributes will play the role of parties and we will only consider monotone access structures. We observe that more general access structures can be (inefficiently) realized with our techniques by letting the negation of an attribute be a separate attribute (this doubles the total number of attributes).

Definition 6.2 (Computational Secret-Sharing Schemes (CSSS)). *A computational secret sharing scheme Π over a set of parties $\mathcal{P}$ contains two polynomial time algorithms:*

$\mathsf{Share}(1^\lambda, 1^\ell, \mathbb{A}, \rho, s) \rightarrow \{\mathsf{sh}_i\}_{i\leq n}$. *The dealer algorithm takes as input the access structure $\mathbb{A}$ and share mapping function $\rho : [n] \rightarrow [\ell]$ along with the secret $s \in \{0,1\}^\lambda$ and number of parties ℓ. It outputs n shares.*

$\mathsf{Recon}(\{\mathsf{sh}_i\}_{i\in T}) \rightarrow s$. *The reconstruction algorithm takes as input a subset of shares $\{sh_i\}_{i\in T}$ for some subset $T \subseteq [n]$, and outputs a reconstructed share s if the set of corresponding parties make up an authorized set.*

Correctness. A CSS scheme is said to be correct if for every $\lambda \in \mathbb{N}$, every supported access structure $(\mathbb{A}, \rho)$ and number of corresponding parties ℓ, every *authorized* set of users $U \in \mathbb{A}$, every secret $s \in \{0,1\}^\lambda$, the following holds:

$$\Pr\left[\mathsf{Recon}(\{\mathsf{sh}_i\}_{i:\rho(i)\in U}) = s \ :\ \{\mathsf{sh}_i\}_i \leftarrow \mathsf{Share}(1^\lambda, 1^\ell, \mathbb{A}, \rho, s)\right] = 1.$$

Security. In terms of security, we say CSS satisfy secrecy if the any set of unauthorized shares hide the secret.

Definition 6.3 (CSS secrecy). *A CSS scheme for access structure* $(\mathbb{A}, \rho)$ *satisfies secrecy if there exists a polynomial-time simulator* Sim *such that for every supported access structure* $(\mathbb{A}, \rho)$ *and number of corresponding parties* ℓ*, every unauthorized subset* $U \notin \mathbb{A}$*, every secret* $s \in \{0,1\}^\lambda$*, the following distributions are computationally indistinguishable:*

$$\left\{\mathsf{Sim}\left(1^\lambda, 1^\ell, \mathbb{A}, U\right)\right\}_\lambda \approx_c \left\{\{\mathsf{sh}_i\}_{i:\rho(i)\in U} \ : \ \{\mathsf{sh}_i\}_{i\in[n]} \leftarrow \mathsf{Share}(1^\lambda, 1^\ell, \mathbb{A}, \rho, s)\right\}_\lambda.$$

Syntax of MA-ABE. A MA-ABE scheme for a CSS schemes consists of the following PPT algorithms.

$\mathsf{GSetup}(1^\lambda) \to \mathsf{crs}$. The setup algorithm takes as input the security parameter λ, and outputs common reference string crs. (We assume that crs includes the space of attribute authorities $\mathcal{AU}$ and the space of global identifiers of users $\mathcal{GID}$, and every algorithm receives crs as an implicit input.)

$\mathsf{ASetup}(\mathsf{crs}, u) \to (\mathsf{pk}_u, \mathsf{sk}_u)$. The authority setup algorithm takes as input crs and authority $u \in \mathcal{AU}$, and outputs an authority key pair.

$\mathsf{KeyGen}(\mathsf{GID}, \mathsf{sk}_u) \to \mathsf{sk}_{\mathsf{GID},u}$. The key generation algorithm takes as input a global identifier $\mathsf{GID} \in \mathcal{GID}$ and sk_u for an authority $u \in \mathcal{AU}$. It outputs the corresponding secret key.

$\mathsf{Enc}((\mathbb{A}, \rho), \{\mathsf{pk}_u\}, \mu) \to \mathsf{ct}$. The encryption algorithm takes in a message μ, a CSSS access structure $(\mathbb{A}, \rho)$. Here, the set $\{\mathsf{pk}_u\}$ denotes all public keys corresponding to the authorities which are specified by the access structure $\mathbb{A}$. It outputs a ciphertext ct. (We assume that the ciphertext implicitly contains $(\mathbb{A}, \rho)$. We consider any access structure that is imposed by some polynomial-sized monotone circuit and ρ is its share-labeling function.)

$\mathsf{Dec}(\mathsf{ct}, \{\mathsf{sk}_{\mathsf{GID},u}\}) \to \mu \cup \perp$. The decryption algorithm takes as input a ciphertext ct and secret keys issued for different attributes by the respective authorities. It outputs a message μ, or $\perp$ if decryption fails.

Correctness. A MA-ABE scheme is said to be correct if for every $\lambda \in \mathbb{N}$, any set U of attribute authorities, any CSSS access structure $(\mathbb{A}, \rho)$ defined over set U, $\mathsf{GID} \in \mathcal{GID}$, message μ, and a set of authorized parties $S \subset U$ which satisfy $\mathbb{A}$, the following holds:

$$\Pr\left[\mathsf{Dec}(\mathsf{ct}, \{\mathsf{sk}_{\mathsf{GID},u}\}_{u\in S}) = \mu : \begin{array}{l} \mathsf{crs} \leftarrow \mathsf{GSetup}(1^\lambda) \\ (\mathsf{pk}_u, \mathsf{sk}_u) \leftarrow \mathsf{ASetup}(\mathsf{crs}, u) \ \forall u \in U \\ \mathsf{sk}_{\mathsf{GID},u} \leftarrow \mathsf{KeyGen}(\mathsf{GID}, \mathsf{sk}_u) \ \forall u \in U \\ \mathsf{ct} \leftarrow \mathsf{Enc}((\mathbb{A}, \rho), \{\mathsf{pk}_u\}_u, \mu)) \end{array}\right] = 1.$$

Security. In terms of security, we say MA-ABE is fully secure if the IND-CPA security holds even if the attacker corrupts some of the authorities as well as corrupts secret keys generated by honest authorities *as long as* there is no combination of secret keys and corrupt authorities that are authorized to decrypt the challenge ciphertext.

Definition 6.4 (MA-ABE **full security**). *A* MA-ABE *scheme is fully secure if for every stateful admissible PPT adversary $\mathcal{A}$, there exists a negligible function* $\mathsf{negl}(\cdot)$ *such that for all $\lambda \in \mathbb{N}$, the following holds*

$$\Pr\left[\mathcal{A}^{O(\cdot,\cdot)}(\mathsf{ct}) = b : \begin{array}{l} \mathsf{crs} \leftarrow \mathsf{GSetup}(1^\lambda), \mathcal{C} = \emptyset, \mathcal{N} = \emptyset, b \leftarrow \{0,1\} \\ (U, (\mathbb{A}, \rho), (\mu_0, \mu_1)) \leftarrow \mathcal{A}^{O(\cdot,\cdot)}(1^\lambda, \mathsf{crs}) \\ \mathsf{ct} \leftarrow \mathsf{Enc}((\mathbb{A}, \rho), \{\mathsf{pk}_u\}_{u \in U}, \mu_b)) \end{array}\right] \leq \frac{1}{2} + \mathsf{negl}(\lambda),$$

where $O(\cdot,\cdot)$ is a stateful *oracle that receives four types of queries and responds as follows:*

$(\mathsf{AuthGen}, \mathsf{u})$. *$\mathcal{A}$ submits an authority $u \notin \mathcal{C} \cup \mathcal{N}$. O samples $(\mathsf{pk}_u, \mathsf{sk}_u) \leftarrow \mathsf{ASetup}(\mathsf{crs}, u)$, sets $\mathcal{N} := \mathcal{N} \cup \{u\}$, stores $(u, \mathsf{pk}_u, \mathsf{sk}_u)$ in its state, and outputs pk_u to $\mathcal{A}$.*

$(\mathsf{Corrupt}, \mathsf{u})$. *$\mathcal{A}$ submits an authority $u \in \mathcal{N}$. O sets $\mathcal{N} := \mathcal{N} \setminus \{u\}$, $\mathcal{C} := \mathcal{C} \cup \{u\}$, and sends sk_u from its state to $\mathcal{A}$.*

$(\mathsf{Register}, (\mathsf{u}, \mathsf{pk}_\mathsf{u}))$. *$\mathcal{A}$ submits an authority $u \notin \mathcal{C} \cup \mathcal{N}$ with key pk_u. O sets $\mathcal{C} := \mathcal{C} \cup \{u\}$, stores $(u, \mathsf{pk}_u, \bot)$ in its state.*

$(\mathsf{KeyGen}, (\mathsf{u}, \mathsf{GID}))$. *$\mathcal{A}$ submits an authority $u \in \mathcal{N}$ with identifier* GID. *O samples $\mathsf{sk}_{\mathsf{GID},u} \leftarrow \mathsf{KeyGen}(\mathsf{GID}, \mathsf{sk}_u)$ where $(u, \mathsf{pk}_u, \mathsf{sk}_u)$ is in its state, stores (u, GID) as well in its internal state, and sends $\mathsf{sk}_{\mathsf{GID},u}$ to $\mathcal{A}$.*

And, the adversary $\mathcal{A}$ is admissible as long as for each unique identifier GID *queried by $\mathcal{A}$, the set of authorities $\mathcal{C} \cup \{u : (u, \mathsf{GID})$ was queried$\}$ is not an authorized set.*

Definition 6.5 (MA-ABE **static collusion security**). *An MA-ABE scheme is static collusion-bounded secure if the* GSetup *algorithm takes in an additional parameter q (the collusion bound) and in the security game, $\mathcal{A}$ specifies 1^q at the beginning, and is admissible if it correctly guesses b* and *the number of unique identifiers* GID *for which $\mathcal{A}$ submits* KeyGen *queries is $\leq q$.*

Definition 6.6 (MA-ABE **dynamic collusion security**). *An MA-ABE scheme is dynamic collusion-bounded secure if the* Enc *algorithm takes in an additional parameter q (the collusion bound) and in the security game, $\mathcal{A}$ specifies 1^q during the "challenge" phase, and is admissible if it correctly guesses b* and *the number of unique identifiers* GID *for which $\mathcal{A}$ submits* KeyGen *queries is $\leq q$.*

6.2 Statically Secure MA-ABE for CSS Schemes

Ingredients. Let $\mathsf{IBE} = (\mathsf{IBE.Setup}, \mathsf{IBE.KeyGen}, \mathsf{IBE.Enc}, \mathsf{IBE.Dec})$ be an identity based encryption scheme and $\Pi = (\mathsf{Share}, \mathsf{Recon})$ be a secure CSS scheme, and $\mathcal{H}$ be a hash function modelled as a random oracle. Below we provide our construction for a statically secure MA-ABE scheme.

We want to point out that our construction can be instantiated from the minimal assumption of public key encryption. The reason we use IBE in our construction instead is for an easier exposition and, as we discuss later, because it results in a tagged MA-ABE scheme quite easily.

$\mathsf{GSetup}(1^\lambda, 1^q) \to \mathsf{crs}$. Our global parameters simply specify the domain and range of a random oracle, which grows with collusion bound q.
- Let $\mathcal{H}$ be a hash function from $\mathcal{GID} \times [q\lambda] \to [q^2]$.
- Output global parameters $\mathsf{crs} = (\lambda, q, \mathcal{H})$.

$\mathsf{ASetup}(\mathsf{crs}, u) \to (\mathsf{pk}_u, \mathsf{sk}_u)$. Each authority independently generates an IBE key pair, which encryptors later use to generate ciphertext components.
- $(\mathsf{ibe.mpk}_u, \mathsf{ibe.msk}_u) \leftarrow \mathsf{IBE.Setup}(1^\lambda, \mathcal{ID} = ([q\lambda] \times [q^2]))$.
- Output $\mathsf{pk}_u = \mathsf{ibe.mpk}_u$, $\mathsf{sk}_u = \mathsf{ibe.msk}_u$.

$\mathsf{KeyGen}(\mathsf{GID}, \mathsf{sk}_u) \to \mathsf{sk}_{\mathsf{GID},u}$. A secret key consists of $q \cdot \lambda$ IBE keys, where each IBE key is randomly drawn from disjoint space of size q^2. Effectively, our keyspace is partitioned into $q\lambda$ intervals of size $[q^2]$. For each interval, it deterministically samples a random identity from $[q^2]$ for each $i \in [q\lambda]$ according to the random oracle on the GID.
- For $i \in [q\lambda]$, compute $\mathsf{ibe.sk}_{u,\mathsf{GID},i} \leftarrow \mathsf{IBE.KeyGen}(\mathsf{sk}_u, \mathsf{ID}_{\mathsf{GID},i})$ where $\mathsf{ID}_{\mathsf{GID},i} = (i, \mathcal{H}(\mathsf{GID}, i))$.
- Output $\mathsf{sk}_{\mathsf{GID},u} = \{\mathsf{ibe.sk}_{u,\mathsf{GID},i}\}_{i \in [q\lambda]}$.

$\mathsf{Enc}((\mathbb{A}, \rho), \{\mathsf{pk}_u\}_{u \in U}, \mu) \to \mathsf{ct}$. To encrypt, we simply *additively* secret share our message into $q\lambda$ shares $\mu_1, \mu_2, \ldots \mu_{q\lambda}$ (as the keyspace is partitioned). Then each secret share is itself secret shared via the CSS access structure $(\mathbb{A}, \rho)$ q^2 times, and encrypted resulting share under the identity corresponding to the authority and slot.
- Let $\mu_1, \mu_2, \ldots \mu_{q\lambda}$ be an additive N-of-N secret sharing of μ. (That is, $\mu = \oplus_i \mu_i$.)
- For all $i \in [q\lambda]$ and $\mathsf{id} \in [q^2]$,
  - Compute shares $\{\mathsf{sh}_{i,\mathsf{id},j}\}_j \leftarrow \mathsf{Share}(1^\lambda, 1^{|U|}, \mathbb{A}, \rho, \mu_i)$
  - For all $u \in U$, compute $\mathsf{ct}_{u,i,\mathsf{id}} \leftarrow \mathsf{IBE.Enc}(\mathsf{pk}_u, (i, \mathsf{id}), \{\mathsf{sh}_{i,\mathsf{id},j}\}_{j:\rho(j)=u})$.[11]
- Output $\mathsf{ct} = ((\mathbb{A}, \rho), \{\mathsf{ct}_{u,i,\mathsf{id}}\}_{u,i,\mathsf{id}})$.

$\mathsf{Dec}(\mathsf{ct}, \{\mathsf{sk}_{\mathsf{GID},u}\}_{u \in S}) \to \mu$. To decrypt, for each of the $q\lambda$ intervals, we simply recover the corresponding secret share μ_i for exactly one of the q^2 CSS schemes as determined by the random oracle on the GID. To recover the final message, we simply add our message shares together.
- Parse $\mathsf{ct} = ((\mathbb{A}, \rho), \{\mathsf{ct}_{u,i,\mathsf{id}}\}_{u,i,\mathsf{id}})$, and $\mathsf{sk}_{\mathsf{GID},u} = \{\mathsf{ibe.sk}_{u,\mathsf{GID},i}\}_i$.
- For each $i \in [q\lambda]$,
  - For each $u \in S$, recover $\{\mathsf{sh}_{i,\mathcal{H}(\mathsf{GID},i),j}\}_{j:\rho(j)=u} = \mathsf{IBE.Dec}((\mathsf{sk}_{u,\mathsf{GID},i}, \mathsf{ct}_{u,i,\mathcal{H}(\mathsf{GID},i)})$.
  - Recover $\mu_i = \mathsf{Recon}(\{\mathsf{sh}_{i,\mathcal{H}(\mathsf{GID},i),j}\}_{j:\rho(j) \in S})$.
- Output $\mu = \oplus_{i \in [q\lambda]} \mu_i$.

[11] Recall that IBE supports encryptions of unbounded length messages via hybrid encryption.

Correctness and Efficiency. The correctness of the scheme follows from the correctness of IBE scheme and the reconstruction property of CSS. Note that by reconstruction property of CSS, we have that in every honestly computed ciphertext, for each additive share μ_i and its corresponding CSS shares $\{\mathsf{sh}_{i,\mathsf{id},j}\}_j$, we have that $\mathsf{Recon}(\{\mathsf{sh}_{i,\mathcal{H}(\mathsf{GID},i),j}\}_{\rho(j)\in S})$ for every set S that is authorized for CSS access structure $(\mathcal{A}, \rho)$. Combining this with the fact that the IBE decryption part of the above decryption procedure recovers $\{\mathsf{sh}_{i,\mathcal{H}(\mathsf{GID},i),j}\}_{\rho(j)=u}$ whenever $\mathsf{id} = \mathcal{H}(\mathsf{GID}, i)$ using the IBE secret key $\mathsf{ibe.sk}_{u,\mathsf{GID},i}$. Since a set of authorized secret keys for a particular GID contains all such IBE keys for $i \in [q\lambda]$ and $u \in S$ where S is the set of authorized attributes, thus the decryption correctness follows by combining above facts.

Next, the efficiency of the scheme follows directly from the efficiency of the IBE system. Each user's attribute key contains a fixed number $(q\lambda)$ of IBE secret keys, while the ciphertext contains $q^3 \cdot \lambda \cdot |U|$ IBE ciphertexts. Thus, the secret keys and ciphertexts are fixed polynomial in the collusion bound q. Since the goal is to design a statically secure MA-ABE scheme, thus it satisfies the required efficiency condition.

Security. The main intuition behind the security proof can be explained in two steps.

1. First, observe that $\mathcal{H}$ is modelled as a random oracle and an admissible adversary does not make key generation queries for honest authorities on more than q distinct global identifiers. Thus, for each index $i \in [q\lambda]$, the number of IBE identities for which a secret key will get generated is at most q. Note that there are q^2 possible identities for index i. Now, information-theoretically, we can show that there will exist at least one index i^* such that for all q queried $\mathsf{GID}_1, \ldots, \mathsf{GID}_q$ identifiers, their corresponding hash values $\mathcal{H}(\mathsf{GID}_1, i^*), \ldots, \mathcal{H}(\mathsf{GID}_q, i^*)$ are all pairwise distinct (i.e., their are no collisions). This no-collision property for queried identifiers is crucial in the next step of the proof.
2. Second, note that we secret share the message μ using a N-of-N secret sharing scheme into $q\lambda$ shares $\{\mu_i\}_i$. Thus, to prove IND-CPA security, it is sufficient to show that one of these shares is computationally hidden. Once we prove this, then the security follows directly from the secrecy of secret sharing.

   At this point, we can use the no-collision property of the queried identifiers. That is, we know that there exists an i^* where all q queried $\mathsf{GID}_1, \ldots, \mathsf{GID}_q$ identifiers are uniquely hashed. Now recall that for each i, we do a second level of secret sharing for each share μ_i where we use the CSS to secret share each μ_i independently q^2 times. That is, for each possible hash value $\mathsf{id} \in [q^2]$, we do a fresh secret sharing of μ_i for each i. By the admissibility constraint on the attacker, we have that for every queried GID the attacker does not have a set of authorized keys. This, combined with the no-collision property, gives us that there cannot be a hash value $\mathsf{id} \in [q^2]$ where the attacker has enough CSS shares to reconstruct μ_i. Thus, by using CSS secrecy property for each sharing (for $\mathsf{id} \in [q^2]$) and security of IBE scheme (which is applied for hiding all unauthorized CSS shares), we get that μ_{i^*} is computationally hidden. This gives us our result.

Formally, we prove the following.

Theorem 6.1. *If* IBE *is a secure IBE scheme and* Π *is a secure CSS scheme, then the above scheme is a statically secure bounded-collusion MA-ABE scheme as per Definition 6.5 in the random oracle model where the adversary makes all queries in the pre-challenge phase.*

Due to space constraints, we provide the full proof in the full version. Moreover, we also discuss how it can be combined with a random oracle based non-committing encryption scheme to handle queries in the post-challenge phase.

6.3 Making It Tagged and Handling Dynamic Collusion

Tagged MA-ABE. While the above MA-ABE construction is a statically secure scheme, it can be made a tagged MA-ABE scheme quite easily. The central idea is to simply use the tag as an additional component of the identity space. Concretely, the encryption and key generation algorithms can be updated as follows.

$\mathsf{KeyGen}(\mathsf{tag}, \mathsf{GID}, \mathsf{sk}_u) \to \mathsf{sk}_{\mathsf{GID},u}$.] A secret key consists of $q \cdot \lambda$ IBE keys computed as follows:
  - For $i \in [q\lambda]$, compute $\mathsf{ibe.sk}_{u,\mathsf{tag},\mathsf{GID},i} \leftarrow \mathsf{IBE.KeyGen}(\mathsf{sk}_u, \mathsf{ID}_{\mathsf{tag},\mathsf{GID},i})$ where $\mathsf{ID}_{\mathsf{tag},\mathsf{GID},i} = (\mathsf{tag}, i, \mathcal{H}(\mathsf{GID}, i))$.
  - Output $\mathsf{sk}_{\mathsf{tag},\mathsf{GID},u} = \{\mathsf{ibe.sk}_{u,\mathsf{tag},\mathsf{GID},i}\}_{i \in [q\lambda]}$.

$\mathsf{Enc}(\mathsf{tag}, (\mathbb{A}, \rho), \{\mathsf{pk}_u\}_{u \in U}, \mu) \to \mathsf{ct}$. It is identical to the encryption algorithm as before, except the IBE encryption algorithm specifies tag as an additional part of the identity. Below we highlight the main change.
  - For all $i \in [q\lambda]$ and $\mathsf{id} \in [q^2]$,
    - For all $u \in U$, compute $\mathsf{ct}_{u,i,\mathsf{id}} \leftarrow \mathsf{IBE.Enc}(\mathsf{ibe.mpk}_u, (\mathsf{tag}, i, \mathsf{id}), \{\mathsf{sh}_{i,\mathsf{id},j}\}_{\rho(j)=u})$.

The correctness, efficiency, and proof of security are similar to that of the untagged scheme.

Fully Dynamically Bounded Collusion Secure. Finally, combining it with Theorem 4.2, we get our final result.

Theorem 6.2. *If* IBE *is a secure IBE scheme and* Π *is a secure CSS scheme, then there exists a dynamically secure bounded-collusion MA-ABE scheme in the random oracle model.*

References

Agr17. Agrawal, S.: Stronger security for reusable garbled circuits, general definitions and attacks. In: Katz, J., Shacham, H. (eds.) CRYPTO 2017. LNCS, vol. 10401, pp. 3–35. Springer, Cham (2017). https://doi.org/10.1007/978-3-319-63688-7_1

AGT21. Agrawal, S., Goyal, R., Tomida, J.: Multi-party functional encryption. In: Nissim, K., Waters, B. (eds.) TCC 2021, Part II. LNCS, vol. 13043, pp. 224–255. Springer, Cham (2021). https://doi.org/10.1007/978-3-030-90453-1_8

AGVW13. Agrawal, S., Gorbunov, S., Vaikuntanathan, V., Wee, H.: Functional encryption: new perspectives and lower bounds. In: Canetti, R., Garay, J.A. (eds.) CRYPTO 2013. LNCS, vol. 8043, pp. 500–518. Springer, Heidelberg (2013). https://doi.org/10.1007/978-3-642-40084-1_28

AKM+22. Agrawal, S., Kitagawa, F., Modi, A., Nishimaki, R., Yamada, S., Yamakawa, T.: Bounded functional encryption for turing machines: adaptive security from general assumptions. In: Kiltz, E., Vaikuntanathan, V. (eds.) TCC 2022, Part I. LNCS, vol. 13747, pp. 618–647. Springer, Cham (2022). https://doi.org/10.1007/978-3-031-22318-1_22

Ale03. Alekhnovich, M.: More on average case vs approximation complexity. In: 44th Annual IEEE Symposium on Foundations of Computer Science. Proceedings (2003)

AMVY21. Agrawal, S., Maitra, M., Vempati, N.S., Yamada, S.: Functional encryption for turing machines with dynamic bounded collusion from LWE. In: Malkin, T., Peikert, C. (eds.) CRYPTO 2021. LNCS, vol. 12828, pp. 239–269. Springer, Cham (2021). https://doi.org/10.1007/978-3-030-84259-8_9

AR17. Agrawal, S., Rosen, A.: Functional encryption for bounded collusions, revisited. In: Kalai, Y., Reyzin, L. (eds.) TCC 2017. LNCS, vol. 10677, pp. 173–205. Springer, Cham (2017). https://doi.org/10.1007/978-3-319-70500-2_7

AS17. Agrawal, S., Singh, I.P.: Reusable garbled deterministic finite automata from learning with errors. In: Chatzigiannakis, I., Indyk, P., Kuhn, F., Muscholl, A. (eds.) ICALP (2017)

Att14. Attrapadung, N.: Dual system encryption via doubly selective security: framework, fully secure functional encryption for regular languages, and more. In: Nguyen, P.Q., Oswald, E. (eds.) EUROCRYPT 2014. LNCS, vol. 8441, pp. 557–577. Springer, Heidelberg (2014). https://doi.org/10.1007/978-3-642-55220-5_31

AV19. Ananth, P., Vaikuntanathan, V.: Optimal bounded-collusion secure functional encryption. In: Hofheinz, D., Rosen, A. (eds.) TCC 2019. LNCS, vol. 11891, pp. 174–198. Springer, Cham (2019). https://doi.org/10.1007/978-3-030-36030-6_8

BDGM20. Brakerski, Z., Döttling, N., Garg, S., Malavolta, G.: Factoring and pairings are not necessary for IO: Circular-secure LWE suffices. Cryptology ePrint Archive (2020)

Bei11. Beimel, A.: Secret-sharing schemes: a survey. In: Chee, Y.M., Guo, Z., Ling, S., Shao, F., Tang, Y., Wang, H., Xing, C. (eds.) IWCC 2011. LNCS, vol. 6639, pp. 11–46. Springer, Heidelberg (2011). https://doi.org/10.1007/978-3-642-20901-7_2

BF01. Boneh, D., Franklin, M.: Identity-based encryption from the Weil pairing. In: Kilian, J. (ed.) CRYPTO 2001. LNCS, vol. 2139, pp. 213–229. Springer, Heidelberg (2001). https://doi.org/10.1007/3-540-44647-8_13

BHR12. Bellare, M., Hoang, V.T., Rogaway, P.: Foundations of garbled circuits. In: CCS 2012 (2012)

BLSV18. Brakerski, Z., Lombardi, A., Segev, G., Vaikuntanathan, V.: Anonymous IBE, leakage resilience and circular security from new assumptions. In: Nielsen, J.B., Rijmen, V. (eds.) EUROCRYPT 2018. LNCS, vol. 10820, pp. 535–564. Springer, Cham (2018). https://doi.org/10.1007/978-3-319-78381-9_20

BSW11. Boneh, D., Sahai, A., Waters, B.: Functional encryption: definitions and challenges. In: Ishai, Y. (ed.) TCC 2011. LNCS, vol. 6597, pp. 253–273. Springer, Heidelberg (2011). https://doi.org/10.1007/978-3-642-19571-6_16

CC09. Chase, M., Chow, S.S.M.: Improving privacy and security in multi-authority attribute-based encryption. In: ACM Conference on Computer and Communications Security, pp. 121–130 (2009)

Cha07. Chase, M.: Multi-authority attribute based encryption. In: TCC, pp. 515–534 (2007)

Coc01. Cocks, C.: An identity based encryption scheme based on quadratic residues. In: Honary, B. (ed.) Cryptography and Coding 2001. LNCS, vol. 2260, pp. 360–363. Springer, Heidelberg (2001). https://doi.org/10.1007/3-540-45325-3_32

CVW+18. Chen, Y., Vaikuntanathan, V., Waters, B., Wee, H., Wichs, D.: Traitor-tracing from LWE made simple and attribute-based. In: Beimel, A., Dziembowski, S. (eds.) TCC 2018. LNCS, vol. 11240, pp. 341–369. Springer, Cham (2018). https://doi.org/10.1007/978-3-030-03810-6_13

DG17a. Döttling, N., Garg, S.: From selective IBE to Full IBE and selective HIBE. In: Kalai, Y., Reyzin, L. (eds.) TCC 2017. LNCS, vol. 10677, pp. 372–408. Springer, From selective ibe to full ibe and selective hibe (2017). https://doi.org/10.1007/978-3-319-70500-2_13

DG17b. Döttling, N., Garg, S.: Identity-based encryption from the Diffie-Hellman assumption. In: Katz, J., Shacham, H. (eds.) CRYPTO 2017. LNCS, vol. 10401, pp. 537–569. Springer, Cham (2017). https://doi.org/10.1007/978-3-319-63688-7_18

DGHM18. Döttling, N., Garg, S., Hajiabadi, M., Masny, D.: New constructions of identity-based and key-dependent message secure encryption schemes. In: Abdalla, M., Dahab, R. (eds.) PKC 2018. LNCS, vol. 10769, pp. 3–31. Springer, Cham (2018). https://doi.org/10.1007/978-3-319-76578-5_1

DH76. Diffie, W., Hellman, M.E.: New directions in cryptography (1976)

DKW21. Datta, P., Komargodski, I., Waters, B.: Decentralized multi-authority ABE for DNFs from LWE. In: Canteaut, A., Standaert, F.-X. (eds.) EUROCRYPT 2021, Part I. LNCS, vol. 12696, pp. 177–209. Springer, Cham (2021). https://doi.org/10.1007/978-3-030-77870-5_7

DKW23. Datta, P., Komargodski, I., Waters, B.: Fully Adaptive Decentralized Multi-Authority ABE. In: Hazay, C., Stam, M. (eds.) EUROCRYPT 2023, Part III. LNCS, vol. 14006, pp. 447–478. Springer, Cham (2023). https://doi.org/10.1007/978-3-031-30620-4_15

DKXY02. Dodis, Y., Katz, J., Xu, S., Yung, M.: Key-insulated public key cryptosystems. In: Knudsen, L.R. (ed.) EUROCRYPT 2002. LNCS, vol. 2332, pp. 65–82. Springer, Heidelberg (2002). https://doi.org/10.1007/3-540-46035-7_5

DQV+21. Devadas, L., Quach, W., Vaikuntanathan, V., Wee, H., Wichs, D.: Succinct LWE sampling, random polynomials, and obfuscation. In: Nissim, K., Waters, B. (eds.) TCC 2021, Part II. LNCS, vol. 13043, pp. 256–287. Springer, Succinct lwe sampling, random polynomials, and obfuscation (2021). https://doi.org/10.1007/978-3-030-90453-1_9

Fre10. Freeman, D.M.: Converting pairing-based cryptosystems from composite-order groups to prime-order groups. In: Gilbert, H. (ed.) EUROCRYPT 2010. LNCS, vol. 6110, pp. 44–61. Springer, Heidelberg (2010). https://doi.org/10.1007/978-3-642-13190-5_3

GGH+13. Garg, S., Gentry, C., Halevi, S., Raykova, M., Sahai, A., Waters, B.: Candidate indistinguishability obfuscation and functional encryption for all circuits. In: FOCS (2013)

GGLW22. Garg, R., Goyal, R., Lu, G., Waters, B.: Dynamic collusion bounded functional encryption from identity-based encryption. In: Dunkelman, O., Dziembowski, S. (eds.) EUROCRYPT 2022. LNCS, vol. 13276, pp. 736–763. Springer, Cham (2022). https://doi.org/10.1007/978-3-031-07085-3_25. https://ia.cr/2021/847

GHM+19. Garg, S., Hajiabadi, M., Mahmoody, M., Rahimi, A., Sekar, S.: Registration-based encryption from standard assumptions. In: Lin, D., Sako, K. (eds.) PKC 2019. LNCS, vol. 11443, pp. 63–93. Springer, Cham (2019). https://doi.org/10.1007/978-3-030-17259-6_3

GHMR18. Garg, S., Hajiabadi, M., Mahmoody, M., Rahimi, A.: Registration-based encryption: removing private-key generator from IBE. In: Beimel, A., Dziembowski, S. (eds.) TCC 2018. LNCS, vol. 11239, pp. 689–718. Springer, Cham (2018). https://doi.org/10.1007/978-3-030-03807-6_25

GKP+13. Goldwasser, S., Kalai, Y.T., Popa, R.A., Vaikuntanathan, V., Zeldovich, N.: How to run turing machines on encrypted data. In: Canetti, R., Garay, J.A. (eds.) CRYPTO 2013. LNCS, vol. 8043, pp. 536–553. Springer, Heidelberg (2013). https://doi.org/10.1007/978-3-642-40084-1_30

GKW16. Goyal, R., Koppula, V., Waters, B.: Semi-adaptive security and bundling functionalities made generic and easy. In: Hirt, M., Smith, A. (eds.) TCC 2016, Part II. LNCS, vol. 9986, pp. 361–388. Springer, Heidelberg (2016). https://doi.org/10.1007/978-3-662-53644-5_14

GKW18. Goyal, R., Koppula, V., Waters, B.: Collusion resistant traitor tracing from learning with errors. In: STOC (2018)

GLW12. Goldwasser, S., Lewko, A., Wilson, D.A.: Bounded-collusion IBE from key homomorphism. In: Cramer, R. (ed.) TCC 2012. LNCS, vol. 7194, pp. 564–581. Springer, Heidelberg (2012). https://doi.org/10.1007/978-3-642-28914-9_32

GP21. Gay, R., Pass, R.: Indistinguishability obfuscation from circular security. In: Proceedings of the 53rd Annual ACM SIGACT Symposium on Theory of Computing, pp. 736–749 (2021)

GPSW06. Goyal, V., Pandey, O., Sahai, A., Waters, B.: Attribute-based encryption for fine-grained access control of encrypted data. In: Juels, A., Wright, R.N., De Capitani di Vimercati, S. (eds.) Proceedings of the 13th ACM Conference on Computer and Communications Security, CCS 2006, Alexandria, VA, USA, Ioctober 30–November 3, 2006, pp. 89–98. ACM (2006)

GPV08. Gentry, C., Peikert, C., Vaikuntanathan, V.: Trapdoors for hard lattices and new cryptographic constructions. In: STOC, pp. 197–206 (2008)

GSW21. Goyal, R., Syed, R., Waters, B.: Bounded collusion ABE for TMs from IBE. In: Tibouchi, M., Wang, H. (eds.) ASIACRYPT 2021. LNCS, vol. 13093, pp. 371–402. Springer, Cham (2021). https://doi.org/10.1007/978-3-030-92068-5_13

GV20. Goyal, R., Vusirikala, S.: Verifiable registration-based encryption. In: Micciancio, D., Ristenpart, T. (eds.) CRYPTO 2020. LNCS, vol. 12170, pp. 621–651. Springer, Cham (2020). https://doi.org/10.1007/978-3-030-56784-2_21

GVW12. Gorbunov, S., Vaikuntanathan, V., Wee, H.: Functional encryption with bounded collusions via multi-party computation. In: Safavi-Naini, R., Canetti, R. (eds.) CRYPTO 2012. LNCS, vol. 7417, pp. 162–179. Springer, Heidelberg (2012). https://doi.org/10.1007/978-3-642-32009-5_11

ISV+17. Itkis, G., Shen, E., Varia, M., Wilson, D., Yerukhimovich, A.: Bounded-collusion attribute-based encryption from minimal assumptions. In: Fehr, S. (ed.) PKC 2017. LNCS, vol. 10175, pp. 67–87. Springer, Heidelberg (2017). https://doi.org/10.1007/978-3-662-54388-7_3

JLS21. Jain, A., Lin, H., Sahai, A.: Indistinguishability obfuscation from well-founded assumptions. In: STOC (2021)

JLS22. Jain, A., Lin, H., Sahai, A.: Indistinguishability Obfuscation from LPN over $\mathbb{F}_p$, DLIN, and PRGs in NC^0. In: Dunkelman, O., Dziembowski, S. (eds.) EUROCRYPT 2022, Part I. LNCS, vol. 13275, pp. 670–699. Springer, Cham (2022). https://doi.org/10.1007/978-3-031-06944-4_23

KW19. Koppula, V., Waters, B.: Realizing chosen ciphertext security generically in attribute-based encryption and predicate encryption. In: Boldyreva, A., Micciancio, D. (eds.) CRYPTO 2019. LNCS, vol. 11693, pp. 671–700. Springer, Cham (2019). https://doi.org/10.1007/978-3-030-26951-7_23

Lew12. Lewko, A.: Tools for simulating features of composite order bilinear groups in the prime order setting. In: Pointcheval, D., Johansson, T. (eds.) EUROCRYPT 2012. LNCS, vol. 7237, pp. 318–335. Springer, Heidelberg (2012). https://doi.org/10.1007/978-3-642-29011-4_20

LW11. Lewko, A., Waters, B.: Decentralizing attribute-based encryption. In: Paterson, K.G. (ed.) EUROCRYPT 2011. LNCS, vol. 6632, pp. 568–588. Springer, Heidelberg (2011). https://doi.org/10.1007/978-3-642-20465-4_31

NY90. Naor, M., Yung, M.: Public-key cryptosystems provably secure against chosen ciphertext attacks. In: STOC, pp. 427–437 (1990)

OT10. Okamoto, T., Takashima, K.: Fully secure functional encryption with general relations from the decisional linear assumption. In: Rabin, T. (ed.) CRYPTO 2010. LNCS, vol. 6223, pp. 191–208. Springer, Heidelberg (2010). https://doi.org/10.1007/978-3-642-14623-7_11

OT20. Okamoto, T., Takashima, K.: Decentralized attribute-based encryption and signatures. IEICE Trans. Fundam. Electron. Commun. Comput. Sci. **103**(1), 41–73 (2020)

Reg05. Regev, O.: On lattices, learning with errors, random linear codes, and cryptography. In: STOC (2005)

Sha84. Shamir, A.: Identity-based cryptosystems and signature schemes. In: Blakley, G.R., Chaum, D. (eds.) CRYPTO 1984. LNCS, vol. 196, pp. 47–53. Springer, Heidelberg (1985). https://doi.org/10.1007/3-540-39568-7_5

SS10. Sahai, A., Seyalioglu, H.: Worry-free encryption: functional encryption with public keys. In: CCS (2010)

SW05. Sahai, A., Waters, B.: Fuzzy identity-based encryption. In: Cramer, R. (ed.) EUROCRYPT 2005. LNCS, vol. 3494, pp. 457–473. Springer, Heidelberg (2005). https://doi.org/10.1007/11426639_27

VNS+03. Vinod, V., Narayanan, A., Srinathan, K., Rangan, C.P., Kim, K.: On the power of computational secret sharing. In: Johansson, T., Maitra, S. (eds.) INDOCRYPT 2003. LNCS, vol. 2904, pp. 162–176. Springer, Heidelberg (2003). https://doi.org/10.1007/978-3-540-24582-7_12

Wee21. Wee, H.: ABE for DFA from LWE against bounded collusions, revisited. In: Nissim, K., Waters, B. (eds.) TCC 2021. LNCS, vol. 13043, pp. 288–309. Springer, Cham (2021). https://doi.org/10.1007/978-3-030-90453-1_10

WFL19. Wang, Z., Fan, X., Liu, F.-H.: FE for inner products and its application to decentralized ABE. In: Lin, D., Sako, K. (eds.) PKC 2019. LNCS, vol. 11443, pp. 97–127. Springer, Cham (2019). https://doi.org/10.1007/978-3-030-17259-6_4

WW21. Wee, H., Wichs, D.: Candidate obfuscation via oblivious LWE sampling. In: Canteaut, A., Standaert, F.-X. (eds.) EUROCRYPT 2021, Part III. LNCS, vol. 12698, pp. 127–156. Springer, Cham (2021). https://doi.org/10.1007/978-3-030-77883-5_5

Yao82. Yao, A.C.: Protocols for secure computations. In: FOCS (1982)

Yao86. Yao, A.: How to generate and exchange secrets. In: FOCS (1986)

Public-Key Encryption with Keyword Search in Multi-user, Multi-challenge Setting under Adaptive Corruptions

Yunhao Ling[1], Kai Zhang[2], Jie Chen[1(✉)], Qiong Huang[3,4], and Haifeng Qian[1]

[1] Shanghai Key Laboratory of Trustworthy Computing, East China Normal University, Shanghai 200062, China
s080001@e.ntu.edu.sg

[2] College of Computer Science and Technology, Shanghai University of Electric Power, Shanghai 201306, China

[3] College of Mathematics and Informatics, South China Agricultural University, Guangzhou 510642, China

[4] Guangzhou Key Laboratory of Intelligent Agriculture, Guangzhou 510642, China

Abstract. In the past decade, much progress has been made on proposing encryption schemes with multi-user security. However, no known work aims at constructing a Public-key Encryption with Keyword Search (PEKS) scheme that is secure in multi-user setting. PEKS is a well-known primitive to solve the problem of searching over encrypted data. In this paper, we fill the gap. For more realistic multi-user scenario, we consider a strong security notion. Specifically, the adversary can adaptively corrupt some users' secret keys, and can adaptively request searchable ciphertexts of related keywords under different public keys as well as trapdoors of related keywords under different secret keys. We present two multi-user PEKS schemes both under simple assumptions in the standard model to achieve this strong security notion.

Technically, our first scheme is a variation of the Lewko-Waters identity-based encryption scheme, and our second scheme is a variation of the Wee identity-based encryption scheme. However, we need to prove that the presented public key encryption schemes are secure in the multi-user, multi-challenge setting under adaptive corruptions. We modify the dual system encryption methodology to meet the goal. In particular, the security loss is constant.

Keywords: Searchable encryption · public key encryption · keyword search · multi-user setting · tight security

1 Introduction

Security Reduction and Tight Security. The security reduction shows that if there exists an adversary $\mathcal{A}$ attacking the scheme Π in time t with success probability $\epsilon_{\mathcal{A}}$, then immediately imply an efficient algorithm $\mathcal{B}$ breaking the underlying hard problem in time roughly t with success probability $\epsilon_{\mathcal{A}}/L$. We

Q. Tang and V. Teague (Eds.): PKC 2024, LNCS 14604, pp. 105–126, 2024.
https://doi.org/10.1007/978-3-031-57728-4_4

refer to L as security loss, and a tight reduction is one where the security loss is constant, i.e. $L = \mathcal{O}(1)$.

In general, L is a large polynomial in the number of users and ciphertexts in the deployed system. As a result, when instantiate the scheme Π, we have to consider how many public keys and ciphertexts the system will be used, but it is possible that they are not clear at deployment time. More importantly, we must increase the size of the group in order to compensate for the security loss [14], which in turn increases the running time and storage consumption of the implementation. Therefore, achieving constant security loss is desired. In this way, we can select optimal parameters to instantiate the scheme Π. We say that a scheme is tightly secure if the reduction is tight.

Multi-user, Multi-challenge Setting under Adaptive Corruptions. In the real world, there are many users, each with a public key, and the encrypted data is sent to each other. A cryptographic scheme should presume to be deployed in multi-user system. However, the traditional CPA/CCA security notion is defined in Single-User, Single-Challenge (SUSC) setting where one public key is generated (i.e., one receiver) and one ciphertext can be requested by the adversary. Clearly, it does not cover practical attacks [6]. In a real multi-user system, many public/secret key pairs are generated, and many ciphertexts are produced. The adversary may reveal some secret keys, and can intercept encryptions of related messages under different public keys. The knowledge usually gives more powerful to the adversary to implement its attack. Therefore, in order to capture the attack, it is natural to consider and use multi-user, multi-challenge setting under adaptive corruptions [5,22,23,29].

Roughly speaking, the multi-user, multi-challenge setting models the fact that the adversary, seeing all public keys, can obtain many ciphertexts under different public keys, and the adaptive corruptions models the fact that the adversary can corrupt a number of users' secret keys. We emphasize that *permitting adaptive corruptions is also important to build a multi-user cryptosystem*, since in the real world, the attacker may take full control of some users' secret keys probably due to poor key management or hack attack, and in particular, we can never restrict the attacker on revealing which users' secret keys.

Public-key Encryption with Keyword Search. Public-key Encryption with Keyword Search (PEKS) [8] is a well-known primitive to solve the problem of searching over encrypted data. In the PEKS system, there are many data owners and a receiver. Any data owner can encrypt keywords with the receiver's public key, and then attaches the resulting searchable ciphertexts to encrypted data. The receiver can generate trapdoors using his/her secret key and the selected keywords, and sends these trapdoors to the server to retrieve encrypted data. With trapdoors, the server tests whether the keywords underlying encrypted data are equal to those selected keywords. If they match, it sends the corresponding encrypted data to the receiver.

There have been many efforts [15,32,33,36] to introduce various query, advanced security requirements, efficiency improvements and expansions. Meanwhile, PEKS has found use as a tool for providing and enhancing privacy in a variety of settings from encrypted e-mail system to electronic medical records and outsourced cloud storage.

However, PEKS is defined in single-user setting. Data owners may want to share encrypted data with multi-user receivers, thus designing a multi-user PEKS system more realistic. More importantly, multi-user PEKS system has broader application scenarios than single-user one. So the question now is, can we design such a system?

Problem and Goal. In the past decade, much progress [5,18,23,24,29,31] has been made on proposing encryption schemes with multi-user security, yet no known work aims at constructing a PEKS scheme that is secure in multi-user setting. Actually, the task is quite challenging.

Normally, single-user security implies multi-user security. However, the general reduction [6] tells us that it will arise a multiplicative security loss $\mathcal{O}(\mu q_C)$, where μ is the number of users and q_C is the number of ciphertexts per user. The problem is that *large security loss will lead to low efficiency*, and it should be emphasized that unlike many classical public key encryption algorithms which can achieve tight reductions in SUSC setting, such as ElGamal encryption algorithm, the reduction of PEKS schemes is *generally* non-tight even in SUSC setting, for example, the original PEKS scheme [8] suffers from a security loss of $\mathcal{O}(q_H q_T)$, where q_H is the number of hash query and q_T is the number of trapdoor query. Consequently, the security loss of the scheme [8] will be *at least* $\mathcal{O}(q_H q_T \mu q_C)$ in multi-user, multi-challenge setting under adaptive corruptions. A typical setting is that $q_H = 2^{60}$, $q_T = 2^{30}$, $q_C = 2^{30}$. Assume to achieve 128-bits security level, and consider that there are $\mu = 2^{30}$ users with public keys, which is possible, for instance, Facebook has about three billion users. Instead of selecting a security parameter that provides 128-bits security level, one needs to pick a security parameter that provides at least 278-bits security level. Since exponentiation in a r-bit group takes time roughly $\mathcal{O}(r^3)$ [6,14], the efficiency of the scheme [8] is, of course, heavily decreased.

In this paper, our goal is to propose multi-user PEKS. To this end, we consider a strong security notion defined in multi-user, multi-challenge setting under adaptive corruptions. We are particularly interested in obtaining constant security loss.

The Challenge. Abdalla et al. [1] proved that any anonymous Identity-Based Encryption (IBE) scheme can be transformed into a secure PEKS scheme. One may try to find an anonymous IBE scheme that is secure in "strong-enough" setting, and then transform it into a secure multi-user PEKS scheme. What is "strong-enough" setting? Intuitively, multi-user, multi-challenge setting under adaptive corruptions in PEKS is corresponding to Multi-Instance, Multi-Challenge (MIMC) setting under adaptive corruptions in anonymous IBE, in the sense that each user possesses an anonymous IBE instance.

One may attempt to improve anonymous IBE schemes [10,35] from Single-Instance, Single-Challenge (SISC) setting to MIMC setting under adaptive corruptions. However, even in simpler SISC setting, the security loss is linear in the number of secret keys queried by the adversary.

Recently, state-of-the-art anonymous IBE schemes in MIMC setting [13,19,20] have appeared. However, they forbade the adversary from corrupting master secret keys. We note that not having adaptive corruptions is far from sufficient to build a multi-user encryption system. Beyond that, they achieved almost tight security, that is, $L = \mathcal{O}(\lambda)$. Although this security loss is much better than security loss that is linear in the number of the adversary's query, the ultimate goal is to realize constant security loss.

Therefore, the following question arises naturally:

Can we obtain a multi-user PEKS scheme that is tightly secure in multi-user, multi-challenge setting under adaptive corruptions?

1.1 Our Results

In this work, we answer the above question affirmatively. For more realistic multi-user setting, we present two Multi-User PEKS (MU-PEKS) schemes both under simple assumptions in the standard model. Our constructions rely on asymmetric composite-order bilinear groups [9,30]. Table 1 compares efficiency and properties between our MU-PEKS schemes.

We define a strong security notion, introduced by Definition 8. Informally, the adversary can adaptively corrupt some users' secret keys, and can adaptively request searchable ciphertexts of related keywords under different public keys, *as well as trapdoors of related keywords under different secret keys.* It is worth noting that this security notion is more complex than the security notion of public key encryption in multi-user setting, since the adversary can additionally acquire trapdoors generated by different users. We are thus subject to more restrictions in the simulation.

We prove that the presented schemes achieve the strong security notion. In particular, the security loss is constant.

Table 1. Comparing Efficiency and Properties between our MU-PEKS schemes. Column $|\mathsf{pk}|$, $|\mathsf{ct}|$, $|\mathsf{td}|$ show the size of public keys, searchable ciphertexts and trapdoors, respectively. Column T_{Enc}, T_{Trapdoor} and T_{Test} show encryption cost, trapdoor generation cost and test cost, respectively. E_{G_N}, E_{H_N} and E_T refer to exponentiations on group G_N, H_N and G_T, respectively, and P refers to pairings. MUMC$_\mathrm{C}$ represents multi-user, multi-challenge setting under adaptive corruptions.

Scheme	$\|\mathsf{pk}\|$		$\|\mathsf{ct}\|$		$\|\mathsf{td}\|$	T_{Enc}		T_{Trapdoor}	T_{Test}	MUMC$_\mathrm{C}$	Security loss	Randomized trapdoors
	G_N	G_T	G_N	G_T	H_N	E_{G_N}	E_T	E_{H_N}	P			
Section 4	2	1	2	2	2	3	1	2	2	✓	$\mathcal{O}(1)$	✓
Section 5	1	1	1	2	1	1	1	1	1	✓	$\mathcal{O}(1)$	✗

Our Approach. The dual system methodology, exploited by Waters [34], is a powerful tool and has been employed to construct many adaptively secure IBE schemes [14,26,30]. We observe that the dual system methodology can effectively address the adaptive adversary by deferring the deployment of the parameters. More specifically, the parameters are not fixed during the setup phase, but only appear in response to the adversary's query. *This can permit us to deal with adaptive corruptions.* However, applying the dual system methodology to prove our schemes will encounter several challenges.

(a) In the proof, the dual system methodology is required to hide the message, but which is not our goal. The goal is to hide the keyword, i.e. the identity in IBE.
(b) In order to mask a master secret key for hiding the message, the dual system methodology introduces the entropy in all secret keys. However, if the simulator sends the master secret key to the adversary, with those secret keys the adversary can immediately distinguish the game. We note that this is why those anonymous IBE schemes in MIMC setting [13,19,20] forbid the adversary from acquiring any master secret key. Thus, the dual system methodology cannot directly handle adaptive corruptions.
(c) The dual system methodology uses information-theoretic arguments to introduce entropy, and the reduction cannot be tight.

We need to modify the dual system methodology in order for our proof. We begin by asymmetric composite-order bilinear groups (G_N, H_N, G_T) whose order N is the product of two primes p_1, p_2. Let g_i, h_i denote generators of order p_i in G_N and H_N, respectively, for $i = 1, 2$.

The First MU-PEKS Scheme. The first MU-PEKS scheme is obtained by modifying the non-anonymous Lewko-Waters IBE scheme [30], presented as follows.

$$\begin{aligned} \mathsf{pk} &:= (g_1^x, g_1^y, e(g_1, h_1)^\alpha), \quad \mathsf{sk} := (x, y, \alpha), \\ \mathsf{ct} &:= (U, V, W, \delta) = (g_1^r, g_1^{(x\mathsf{w}+y)r}, e(g_1, h_1)^{\alpha r} \cdot \delta, \delta), \\ \mathsf{td}_\mathsf{w} &:= (A, B) = (h_1^s, h_1^\alpha \cdot h_1^{(x\mathsf{w}+y)s}), \end{aligned}$$

For more details, please refer to Sect. 4. The test algorithm is performed by testing whether $e(U, B)/e(V, A) \cdot \delta = W$, requiring two pairing operations. To prove the security, it suffices to show that the keywords in searchable ciphertexts are hidden from the adversary.

We have the following intuitions.

- *Hiding keywords.* In the proof, we need to hide the keyword w in the searchable ciphertext, rather than the value δ, which is the goal of the dual system methodology, so the proof strategy is very different from the dual system methodology. The key point is that we only introduce G_{p_2}-components into searchable ciphertexts and then the entropy into these searchable ciphertexts, but never introduce H_{p_2}-components and entropy into trapdoors.

- *Addressing adaptive corruptions.* We defer the deployment of the parameters to handle adaptive corruptions. Concretely, the parameters are deployed in G_{p_2} and appear only in the searchable ciphertext query. Notably, the simulator knows all parameters in G_{p_1}, which are used to create the real system, and thus it can answer all secret keys and all trapdoors queried by the adversary. We note that we never introduce the entropy to the trapdoors, hence the simulator can send users' secret keys to the adversary even given the trapdoors.
- *Tighter reduction.* Instead of relying on information-theoretic arguments, we utilize computational assumptions and their self-reducibility properties to introduce the entropy, realizing tighter reduction. We note that we never introduce H_{p_2}-components into the trapdoors, allowing us to avoid the use of information-theoretic arguments.

Our proof idea is presented as follows. Throughout this paper, we will draw boxes to highlight the differences.

(1) We can replace

$$\{g_1^r, g_1^{(x\mathsf{w}+y)r}, e(g_1, h_1)^{\alpha r} \cdot \delta, \delta\}$$

with

$$\{g_1^r \boxed{\cdot g_2^{\hat{r}}}, (g_1^r \boxed{\cdot g_2^{\hat{r}}})^{x\mathsf{w}+y}, e(g_1^r \boxed{\cdot g_2^{\hat{r}}}, h_1^{\alpha}) \cdot \delta, \delta\}$$

Intuitively, this should follow from the $\mathbf{SD}_{p_1 \mapsto p_1 p_2}^{G_N}$ assumption (Definition 1), which says that $g_1^r \approx_c g_1^r \cdot g_2^{\hat{r}}$. We note that the terms in G_{p_2} only appear in the query of searchable ciphertext, and they are not fixed in advance. This is critical for us to adaptively deal with the adversary.

In the next, we will introduce the entropy to the searchable ciphertext.

(2) We can replace

$$\{g_1^r \cdot g_2^{\hat{r}}, g_1^{(x\mathsf{w}+y)r} \cdot g_2^{x\mathsf{w}\hat{r}+y\hat{r}}, e(g_1^r \cdot g_2^{\hat{r}}, h_1^{\alpha}) \cdot \delta, \delta\}$$

with

$$\{g_1^r \cdot g_2^{\hat{r}}, g_1^{(x\mathsf{w}+y)r} \cdot g_2^{x\mathsf{w}\hat{r}+y\hat{r}} \boxed{\cdot g_2^{\hat{z}}}, e(g_1^r \cdot g_2^{\hat{r}}, h_1^{\alpha}) \cdot \delta, \delta\}$$

Intuitively, this should follow from the $\mathbf{DDH}_{p_2}^{G_N}$ assumption (Definition 3), which says that $(g_2^{\hat{r}}, g_2^{y\hat{r}}) \approx_c (g_2^{\hat{r}}, g_2^{y\hat{r}+\hat{z}})$. At this point, we obtain a random $g_2^{\hat{z}}$ uniformly distributed in G_{p_2}. Proving the security becomes relatively easy.

As to multi-challenge setting, we can produce fresh instances (cf. Definition 5) to simulate each searchable ciphertext, analogue to [6,25].

Remark 1. We select the above scheme as our first scheme, as randomized trapdoors are more general and very useful for some expansions of PEKS, such as Public-key Authenticated Encryption with Keyword Search (PAEKS) [15,27,32].

In addition to ensure security of searchable ciphertext, PAEKS is required to guarantee security of trapdoor. We can expand the first scheme to obtain a PAEKS scheme with multi-user security, and the construction is presented as follows.

$$\begin{aligned}\mathsf{pk}_\sigma &:= (g_1^{x_\sigma}, g_1^{y_\sigma}, h_1^{k_\sigma}, e(g_1,h_1)^{\alpha_\sigma}), \quad \mathsf{sk}_\sigma := (x_\sigma, y_\sigma, k_\sigma, \alpha_\sigma),\\ \mathsf{pk}_\rho &:= (g_1^{x_\rho}, g_1^{y_\rho}, h_1^{k_\rho}, e(g_1,h_1)^{\alpha_\rho}), \quad \mathsf{sk}_\rho := (x_\rho, y_\rho, k_\rho, \alpha_\rho),\\ \mathsf{ct} &:= (U,V,W,\delta) = (g_1^r, g_1^{(x_\rho \mathsf{w} + y_\rho k_\sigma)r}, e(g_1,h_1)^{\alpha_\rho r}\cdot\delta, \delta),\\ \mathsf{td}_\mathsf{w} &:= (A,B) = (h_1^s, h_1^{\alpha_\rho}\cdot h_1^{(x_\rho \mathsf{w} + k_\sigma y_\rho)s}).\end{aligned}$$

where $(\mathsf{pk}_\sigma, \mathsf{sk}_\sigma)$ represents the sender's pubic/secret key pair and $(\mathsf{pk}_\rho, \mathsf{sk}_\rho)$ represents the receiver's pubic/secret key pair. The test algorithm is performed by testing whether $e(U,B)/e(V,A)\cdot\delta = W$, requiring two pairing operations. Since PAEKS in multi-user setting is not our goal, we omit the details.

The Second MU-PEKS Scheme. In the second MU-PEKS scheme, the trapdoor is deterministic, but the public/secret key pair, the searchable ciphertext and the trapdoor are shorter. This scheme is obtained by modifying Wee's anonymous IBE scheme [35], presented as follows.

$$\begin{aligned}\mathsf{pk} &:= (g_1^x, e(g_1,h_1)^\alpha), \quad \mathsf{sk} := (x,\alpha),\\ \mathsf{ct} &:= (V,W,\delta) = (g_1^{(x+\mathsf{w})r}, e(g_1,h_1)^{\alpha r}\cdot\delta, \delta),\\ \mathsf{td}_\mathsf{w} &:= h_1^{\frac{\alpha}{x+\mathsf{w}}},\end{aligned}$$

For more details, please refer to Sect. 5. The test algorithm is performed by testing whether $e(V, \mathsf{td}_\mathsf{w})\cdot\delta = W$, requiring only one pairing operation. To prove the security, it suffices to show that the keywords in searchable ciphertexts are hidden from the adversary.

The proof idea is analogous to that of the first MU-PEKS scheme, and is presented as below.

(1) We can replace

$$\{g_1^{(x+\mathsf{w})r}, e(g_1,h_1)^{\alpha r}\cdot\delta, \delta\}$$

with

$$\{(g_1^r \boxed{\cdot g_2^{\hat r}})^{x+\mathsf{w}}, e(g_1^r \boxed{\cdot g_2^{\hat r}}, h_1^\alpha)\cdot\delta, \delta\}$$

Intuitively, this should follow from the $\mathbf{SD}^{G_N}_{p_1\mapsto p_1p_2}$ assumption (Definition 1), which says that $g_1^r \approx_c g_1^r\cdot g_2^{\hat r}$. We note that the terms in G_{p_2} only appear in the query of searchable ciphertext, and they are not fixed in advance. This is critical for us to adaptively deal with the adversary.

As before, we will introduce the entropy to the searchable ciphertext.

(2) We can replace

$$\{g_1^{(x+\mathrm{w})r} \cdot g_2^{x\hat{r}+\mathrm{w}\hat{r}}, e(g_1^r \cdot g_2^{\hat{r}}, h_1^{\alpha}) \cdot \delta, \delta\}$$

with

$$\{g_1^{(x+\mathrm{w})r} \cdot g_2^{x\hat{r}+\mathrm{w}\hat{r}} \boxed{\cdot g_2^{\hat{z}}}, e(g_1^r \cdot g_2^{\hat{r}}, h_1^{\alpha}) \cdot \delta, \delta\}$$

Intuitively, this should follow from the $\mathbf{DDH}_{p_2}^{G_N}$ assumption (Definition 3), which says that $(g_2^{\hat{r}}, g_2^{x\hat{r}}) \approx_c (g_2^{\hat{r}}, g_2^{x\hat{r}+\hat{z}})$. At this point, we obtain a random $g_2^{\hat{z}}$ uniformly distributed in G_{p_2}. Proving the security becomes relatively easy.

As to multi-challenge setting, we can produce fresh instances (cf. Definition 5) to simulate each searchable ciphertext, analogue to [6,25].

Remark 2. We choose the Lewko-Waters IBE construction [30] and Wee IBE construction [35] as our candidates, since they are adaptively secure IBE schemes in composite-order bilinear groups *with essentially optimal parameters.*

1.2 Discussion

Inspired by the dual-system methodology, we handle the adaptive adversary by deferring the deployment of the parameters and making use of asymmetric composite-order bilinear groups, and it is observed that the simulator can answer all query made by the adversary since it knows the parameters in G_{p_1}. Our approach opens up a new way to address adaptive corruptions. In fact, many public key encryption schemes with functionality employed bilinear pairings, for example, proxy re-encryption [2,3,7,16]. We believe that they will benefit from the approach in designing a multi-user encryption scheme with tight security.

Open Problem. Although asymmetric composite-order bilinear groups provide us with a more intuitive way to design the scheme, it is desirable to obtain corresponding prime-order constructions of the scheme. Prime-order groups can offer more efficient and compact instantiations. For instance, for the same 128-bit security level, Attrapadung [4] pointed out that group elements in composite-order groups are more than 12 times larger than those in prime-order groups. Meanwhile, Guillevic [21] reported that bilinear pairings are 254 times slower in composite-order than in prime-order groups. The researchers [12,17,28] commonly present a scheme based on composite-order groups for intuition, and then employ techniques [4,11,19,20] that simulate composite-order groups in prime-order groups to obtain the prime-order construction for practicality. Unfortunately, these techniques do not work for our schemes. When using the techniques, in our prime-order construction, our keywords will not only appear in so-called normal space but also in so-called semi-functional space, but the entropy is introduced only in the semi-functional space. Thus, there is insufficient entropy to hide the keywords. It seems that the technique in [20] can provide sufficient entropy when k is set to 1. However, the problem is that those terms in the group

G also appear in the group H, and hence we cannot use certain computational assumptions, e.g. SXDH assumption, to provide the entropy, and the reduction cannot be tight. Therefore, we leave an open problem to find a new technique for simulating composite-order groups in prime-order groups in order to transform our MU-PEKS schemes to the prime-order versions in a general way.

Organization. We review necessary preliminary background in Sect. 2. Section 3 introduces the definition of MU-PEKS. In Sect. 4, we present the first MU-PEKS scheme. In Sect. 5, we give the second MU-PEKS scheme.

2 Preliminaries

Let S be a finite set. The notation $s \stackrel{\$}{\leftarrow} S$ means that s is picked uniformly at random from a finite set S. We use $\approx_c$ to denote two distributions being computationally indistinguishable. By PPT, we denote a probabilistic polynomial-time algorithm.

2.1 Asymmetric Composite-Order Bilinear Groups

Our constructions rely on asymmetric composite-order bilinear groups [12,35]. The group generator GrpGen is an algorithm that takes as the security parameter 1^λ and outputs a group description $\mathbb{G} = (N = p_1 p_2, G_N, H_N, G_T, e)$, where p_1 and p_2 are distinct $\Theta(\lambda)$-bit primes, G_N, H_N and G_T are cyclic groups of order N, and $e : G_N \times H_N \to G_T$ is a non-degenerate bilinear map. The group G_N can be written as $G_N = G_{p_1} G_{p_2}$, where G_{p_1} and G_{p_2} are subgroups of G_N of order p_1 and p_2, respectively. Moreover, we use g_1, g_2 to denote random generators for the subgroups G_{p_1}, G_{p_2}. The definition $H_N = H_{p_1} H_{p_2}$ and the notations H_{p_1}, H_{p_2}, h_1, h_2 are analogous.

Cryptographic Assumptions. In this paper, we use the following cryptographic assumptions.

Definition 1 ($\mathbf{SD}^{G_N}_{p_1 \mapsto p_1 p_2}$). *We say that ($p_1 \mapsto p_1 p_2$)-subgroup decision assumption in the group G_N, denoted by $\mathbf{SD}^{G_N}_{p_1 \mapsto p_1 p_2}$, holds if for all PPT adversaries $\mathcal{A}$, the following advantage function is negligible in λ.*

$$\mathsf{Adv}_{\mathcal{A}}^{\mathbf{SD}^{G_N}_{p_1 \mapsto p_1 p_2}}(1^\lambda) := |\Pr[\mathcal{A}(\mathbb{G}, D, T_0) = 1] - \Pr[\mathcal{A}(\mathbb{G}, D, T_1) = 1]|$$

where $\mathbb{G} \leftarrow \mathsf{GrpGen}(1^\lambda)$, $D =: (g_1, g_{\{1,2\}}, h_1, h_{\{1,2\}})$, $g_{\{1,2\}} \stackrel{\$}{\leftarrow} G_{p_1} G_{p_2}$, $h_{\{1,2\}} \stackrel{\$}{\leftarrow} H_{p_1} H_{p_2}$ *and* $T_0 \stackrel{\$}{\leftarrow} \boxed{G_{p_1}}$, $T_1 \stackrel{\$}{\leftarrow} \boxed{G_{p_1} G_{p_2}}$.

Definition 2 ($\mathbf{SD}^{H_N}_{p_1 \mapsto p_1 p_2}$). *We say that ($p_1 \mapsto p_1 p_2$)-subgroup decision assumption in the group H_N, denoted by $\mathbf{SD}^{H_N}_{p_1 \mapsto p_1 p_2}$, holds if for all PPT adversaries $\mathcal{A}$, the following advantage function is negligible in λ.*

$$\mathsf{Adv}_{\mathcal{A}}^{\mathbf{SD}^{H_N}_{p_1 \mapsto p_1 p_2}}(1^\lambda) := |\Pr[\mathcal{A}(\mathbb{G}, D, T_0) = 1] - \Pr[\mathcal{A}(\mathbb{G}, D, T_1) = 1]|$$

where $\mathbb{G} \leftarrow \mathsf{GrpGen}(1^\lambda)$, $D =: (g_1, g_{\{1,2\}}, h_1, h_{\{1,2\}})$, $g_{\{1,2\}} \xleftarrow{\$} G_{p_1}G_{p_2}$, $h_{\{1,2\}} \xleftarrow{\$} H_{p_1}H_{p_2}$ *and* $T_0 \xleftarrow{\$} \boxed{H_{p_1}}$, $T_1 \xleftarrow{\$} \boxed{H_{p_1}H_{p_2}}$.

Definition 3 ($\mathbf{DDH}_{p_2}^{G_N}$). *We say that p_2-subgroup Diffie-Hellman assumption in the group G_N, denoted by $\mathbf{DDH}_{p_2}^{G_N}$, holds if for all PPT adversaries $\mathcal{A}$, the following advantage function is negligible in λ.*

$$\mathsf{Adv}_{\mathcal{A}}^{\mathbf{DDH}_{p_2}^{G_N}}(1^\lambda) := |\Pr[\mathcal{A}(\mathbb{G}, D, T_0) = 1] - \Pr[\mathcal{A}(\mathbb{G}, D, T_1) = 1]|,$$

where $\mathbb{G} \leftarrow \mathsf{GrpGen}(1^\lambda)$, $D =: (g_1, g_2, g_2^a, g_2^b, h_1, h_2)$ *and* $T_0 := \boxed{g_2^{ab}}$, $T_1 := \boxed{g_2^{ab+c}}$, $a, b, c \xleftarrow{\$} \mathbb{Z}_N$.

Definition 4 ($\mathbf{DDH}_{p_2}^{H_N}$). *We say that p_2-subgroup Diffie-Hellman assumption in the group H_N, denoted by $\mathbf{DDH}_{p_2}^{H_N}$, holds if for all PPT adversaries $\mathcal{A}$, the following advantage function is negligible in λ.*

$$\mathsf{Adv}_{\mathcal{A}}^{\mathbf{DDH}_{p_2}^{G_N}}(1^\lambda) := |\Pr[\mathcal{A}(\mathbb{G}, D, T_0) = 1] - \Pr[\mathcal{A}(\mathbb{G}, D, T_1) = 1]|,$$

where $\mathbb{G} \leftarrow \mathsf{GrpGen}(1^\lambda)$, $D =: (g_1, g_2, h_1, h_2, h_2^a, h_2^b)$ *and* $T_0 := \boxed{h_2^{ab}}$, $T_1 := \boxed{h_2^{ab+c}}$, $a, b, c \xleftarrow{\$} \mathbb{Z}_N$.

Rerandomization. In order to simulate all searchable ciphertexts once, we need the following efficient algorithms to re-randomize the $\mathbf{DDH}_{p_2}^{G_N}$ problem instance. These algorithms are built by self-reducibility properties of the assumption. We refer the reader to [6] for more details.

Definition 5 (Rerandomization).

– *Given an instance $(\mathbb{G}, D, T)$ of $\mathbf{DDH}_{p_2}^{G_N}$ where either $T := g_2^{ab}$ or $T := g_2^{ab+c}$, we can produce $(g_2^{a'}, g_2^{b'}, T')$ by running algorithm $\mathsf{ReRand}_{a,b,T}^{\mathbf{DDH}_{p_2}^{G_N}}$:*

$$(g_2^{a'}, g_2^{b'}, T') \leftarrow \mathsf{ReRand}_{a,b,T}^{\mathbf{DDH}_{p_2}^{G_N}}(g_2, g_2^a, g_2^b, T).$$

We can also produce $(g_2^{b'}, T')$ by running algorithm $\mathsf{ReRand}_{b,T}^{\mathbf{DDH}_{p_2}^{G_N}}$:

$$(g_2^{b'}, T') \leftarrow \mathsf{ReRand}_{b,T}^{\mathbf{DDH}_{p_2}^{G_N}}(g_2, g_2^a, g_2^b, T).$$

3 Definition of MU-PEKS

We introduce the definition of MU-PEKS. In a MU-PEKS system, there are many users, each with a public key, and encrypted data can be sent to any user.

Definition 6 (Syntax of MU-PEKS). *A MU-PEKS is composed of the following five PPT algorithms:*

$\mathsf{Setup}(1^\lambda) \rightarrow \mathsf{pp}$. *On input the security parameter* 1^λ, *the setup algorithm outputs a public parameter* pp.
$\mathsf{KeyGen}(\mathsf{pp}) \rightarrow (\mathsf{pk}, \mathsf{sk})$. *On input the public parameter* pp, *the key generation algorithm outputs a public/secret key pair* $(\mathsf{pk}, \mathsf{sk})$.
$\mathsf{Enc}(\mathsf{pk}, \mathsf{w}) \rightarrow \mathsf{ct}$. *On input the receiver's public key* pk *and a keyword* w, *the encryption algorithm outputs a searchable ciphertext* ct *of the keyword* w.
$\mathsf{Trapdoor}(\mathsf{sk}, \mathsf{w}) \rightarrow \mathsf{td_w}$. *On input the receiver's secret key* sk *and a keyword* w, *the trapdoor generation algorithm outputs a trapdoor* $\mathsf{td_w}$ *of the keyword* w.
$\mathsf{Test}(\mathsf{ct}, \mathsf{td_w}) \rightarrow 0/1$. *On input a searchable ciphertext* ct *and a trapdoor* $\mathsf{td_w}$, *the test algorithm outputs output* 1 *or* 0.

Definition 7 (Correctness). *For any* $\lambda \in \mathbb{N}$, *any keyword* $\mathsf{w}, \mathsf{w}' \in \mathcal{KW}$, *if* $\mathsf{w} = \mathsf{w}'$, *we require that*

$$\Pr\left[1 \leftarrow \mathsf{Test}(\mathsf{ct}, \mathsf{td_w}) \;\middle|\; \begin{array}{c} \mathsf{pp} \leftarrow \mathsf{Setup}(1^\lambda) \\ (\mathsf{pk}, \mathsf{sk}) \leftarrow \mathsf{KeyGen}(\mathsf{pp}) \\ \mathsf{ct} \leftarrow \mathsf{Enc}(\mathsf{pk}, \mathsf{w}') \\ \mathsf{td_w} \leftarrow \mathsf{Trapdoor}(\mathsf{sk}, \mathsf{w}) \end{array} \right] = 1.$$

And if $\mathsf{w} \neq \mathsf{w}'$, *we require that*

$$\Pr\left[0 \leftarrow \mathsf{Test}(\mathsf{ct}, \mathsf{td_w}) \;\middle|\; \begin{array}{c} \mathsf{pp} \leftarrow \mathsf{Setup}(1^\lambda) \\ (\mathsf{pk}, \mathsf{sk}) \leftarrow \mathsf{KeyGen}(\mathsf{pp}) \\ \mathsf{ct} \leftarrow \mathsf{Enc}(\mathsf{pk}, \mathsf{w}') \\ \mathsf{td_w} \leftarrow \mathsf{Trapdoor}(\mathsf{sk}, \mathsf{w}) \end{array} \right] = 1 - \mathsf{negl}(\lambda).$$

Security Notion. For MU-PEKS, we define indistinguishability of searchable ciphertexts in multi-user, multi-challenge setting under adaptive corruptions, denoted by $\mathsf{IND\text{-}MUMC_C}$.

Definition 8 (Indistinguishability of searchable ciphertexts in multi-user, multi-challenge setting under adaptive corruptions). *For all PPT adversaries* $\mathcal{A}$, *we define the advantage function*

$$\mathsf{Adv}^{\mathsf{IND\text{-}MUMC_C}}_{\mathrm{MU\text{-}PEKS},\mathcal{A}}(1^\lambda, \mu) = \Pr\left[\beta = \beta' \;\middle|\; \begin{array}{c} \beta \xleftarrow{\$} \{0,1\} \\ \mathsf{pp} \leftarrow \mathsf{Setup}(1^\lambda) \\ (\mathsf{pk}_1, \mathsf{sk}_1) \leftarrow \mathsf{KeyGen}(\mathsf{pp}) \\ \dots \\ (\mathsf{pk}_\mu, \mathsf{sk}_\mu) \leftarrow \mathsf{KeyGen}(\mathsf{pp}) \\ \beta' \leftarrow \mathcal{A}^{\mathsf{O_{sk}}, \mathsf{O_{ct}}, \mathsf{O_{td}}}(1^\lambda, \mathsf{pp}, \mathsf{pk}_1, \dots, \mathsf{pk}_\mu) \end{array} \right] - \frac{1}{2},$$

where oracles $\mathsf{O_{sk}}$, $\mathsf{O_{ct}}$ *and* $\mathsf{O_{td}}$ *work as follows*

- $\mathsf{O_{sk}}$: *On input an index* i, *the oracle returns* sk_i *and updates* $Q_{\mathsf{sk}} = Q_{\mathsf{sk}} \cup \{i\}$.
- $\mathsf{O_{ct}}$: *On input an index* i^* *and two keywords* w_0^*, w_1^*, *the oracle returns* $\mathsf{ct}^* \leftarrow \mathsf{Enc}(\mathsf{pk}_{i^*}, \mathsf{w}_\beta^*)$ *and updates* $Q_{i^*} = Q_{i^*} \cup \{i^*\}$ *and* $Q_{\mathsf{ct}} = Q_{\mathsf{ct}} \cup \{(i^*, \mathsf{w}_0^*), (i^*, \mathsf{w}_1^*)\}$.

- O_{td} : *On input an index* i *and a keyword* w, *the oracle returns* $\mathsf{td}_{\mathsf{w}} \leftarrow \mathsf{Trapdoor}(\mathsf{sk}_i, \mathsf{w})$ *and updates* $Q_{\mathsf{td}} = Q_{\mathsf{td}} \cup \{(i, \mathsf{w})\}$.

We say that a MU-PEKS scheme is $\mathsf{IND\text{-}MUMC_C}$ *secure if for all PPT adversary* $\mathcal{A}$ *the advantage function* $\mathsf{Adv}^{\mathsf{IND\text{-}MUMC_C}}_{\text{MU-PEKS},\mathcal{A}}(1^\lambda, \mu)$ *is negligible in* λ, μ *and* $Q_{i^*} \cap Q_{\mathsf{sk}} = \emptyset$, $Q_{\mathsf{ct}} \cap Q_{\mathsf{td}} = \emptyset$.

4 The First MU-PEKS Scheme

4.1 Construction

Our first MU-PEKS scheme is described as follows.

$\mathsf{Setup}(1^\lambda)$. On input 1^λ, this algorithm runs $\mathbb{G} := (N = p_1p_2, G_N, H_N, G_T, e) \leftarrow \mathsf{GrpGen}(1^\lambda)$, picks random generators g_1 and h_1 of G_{p_1} and H_{p_1}, respectively, and outputs

$$\mathsf{pp} := (\mathbb{G}, g_1, h_1).$$

$\mathsf{KeyGen}(\mathsf{pp})$. On input the public parameter pp, this algorithm picks $x, y, \alpha \stackrel{\$}{\leftarrow} \mathbb{Z}_N$, and outputs

$$\mathsf{pk} := (g_1^x, g_1^\alpha, e(g_1, h_1)^\alpha) \quad \text{and} \quad \mathsf{sk} := (x, y, \alpha).$$

$\mathsf{Enc}(\mathsf{pk}, \mathsf{w})$. On input the receiver's public key pk and a keyword $\mathsf{w} \in \mathcal{KW}$, this algorithm picks $r \stackrel{\$}{\leftarrow} \mathbb{Z}_N$ and $\delta \stackrel{\$}{\leftarrow} G_T$, computes

$$U := g_1^r, \quad V := g_1^{(x\mathsf{w}+y)r}, \quad W := e(g_1, h_1)^{\alpha r} \cdot \delta$$

and outputs

$$\mathsf{ct} := (U, V, W, \delta).$$

$\mathsf{Trapdoor}(\mathsf{sk}, \mathsf{w})$. On input the receiver's secret key sk and a keyword $\mathsf{w} \in \mathcal{KW}$, this algorithm picks $s \stackrel{\$}{\leftarrow} \mathbb{Z}_N$, computes

$$A := h_1^s, \quad B := h_1^\alpha \cdot h_1^{(x\mathsf{w}+y)s}$$

and outputs

$$\mathsf{td}_{\mathsf{w}} := (A, B).$$

$\mathsf{Test}(\mathsf{ct}, \mathsf{td}_{\mathsf{w}})$. On input a trapdoor td_{w} and a searchable ciphertext ct, this algorithm tests whether

$$\frac{e(U, B)}{e(V, A)} \cdot \delta = W.$$

If so, return 1; otherwise return 0.

Correctness. For any $\mathsf{w}, \mathsf{w}' \in \mathbb{Z}_N$, $\mathsf{ct} \leftarrow \mathsf{Enc}(\mathsf{pk}, \mathsf{w}')$ and $\mathsf{td}_{\mathsf{w}} \leftarrow \mathsf{Trapdoor}(\mathsf{sk}, \mathsf{w})$, we have that

$$\frac{e(U, B)}{e(V, A)} = \frac{e(g_1^r, h_1^\alpha \cdot h_1^{(x\mathsf{w}+y)s})}{e(g_1^{(x\mathsf{w}'+y)r}, h_1^s)} = e(g_1, h_1)^{\alpha r} \cdot e(g_1, h_1)^{xsr(\mathsf{w}-\mathsf{w}')}$$

Thus, the correctness is straightforward.

4.2 Security Proof

As for security, we establish the following result.

Theorem 1. *For any PPT adversary $\mathcal{A}$ sending at most q_{sk}, q_{ct} and q_{td} queries to O_{sk}, O_{ct} and O_{td}, respectively, there exist $\mathcal{B}_1$, $\mathcal{B}_2$ such that*

$$\mathsf{Adv}^{\mathsf{IND\text{-}MUMC_C}}_{\mathrm{MU\text{-}PEKS},\mathcal{A}}(1^\lambda,\mu) \le \mathsf{Adv}^{\mathbf{SD}^{G_N}_{p_1\mapsto p_1p_2}}_{\mathcal{B}_1}(\lambda) + \mathsf{Adv}^{\mathbf{DDH}^{G_N}_{p_2}}_{\mathcal{B}_2}(\lambda) + \mu q_{\mathsf{ct}}/2^{\Theta(\lambda)}.$$

Proof. We define the advantage function of any PPT adversary $\mathcal{A}$ in Game_x as

$$\mathsf{Adv}^{\mathsf{Game}_x}_{\mathcal{A}}(\lambda).$$

We name the various forms of ciphertext used in the proof in Table 2, where the $\mathsf{Type}\,0$ ciphertext is exactly real searchable ciphertext.

Table 2. Various forms of ciphertext used in the proof.

	ct
$\mathsf{Type}\,0$	$(g_1^r,\quad g_1^{(x\mathsf{w}+y)r},\quad e(g_1^r,h_1^\alpha)\cdot\delta,\quad \delta)$
$\mathsf{Type}\,1$	$(g_1^r\boxed{\cdot g_2^{\hat{r}}},\quad (g_1^r\boxed{\cdot g_2^{\hat{r}}})^{x\mathsf{w}+y},\quad e(g_1^r\boxed{\cdot g_2^{\hat{r}}},h_1^\alpha)\cdot\delta,\quad —)$
$\mathsf{Type}\,2$	$(—,\quad g_1^{(x\mathsf{w}+y)r}\cdot g_2^{(x\mathsf{w}+y)\hat{r}}\boxed{\cdot g_2^{\hat{z}}},\quad —,\quad —)$

Note: A dash (—) means the same as in the above.

We will complete the proof by establishing the following sequence of lemmas.

Game_0: is the real game. In this game, all ciphertexts given to the adversary $\mathcal{A}$ are $\mathsf{Type}\,0$ ciphertexts. We have that

$$\mathsf{Adv}^{\mathsf{IND\text{-}MUMC_C}}_{\mathrm{MU\text{-}PEKS},\mathcal{A}}(1^\lambda,\mu) = \mathsf{Adv}^{\mathsf{Game}_0}_{\mathcal{A}}(\lambda).$$

Game_1: is identical to Game_0 except that all ciphertexts given to the adversary $\mathcal{A}$ are $\mathsf{Type}\,1$ ciphertexts.

Lemma 1 ($\mathsf{Game}_0 \approx_c \mathsf{Game}_1$). *For any PPT adversary $\mathcal{A}$,*

$$\left|\mathsf{Adv}^{\mathsf{Game}_0}_{\mathcal{A}}(\lambda) - \mathsf{Adv}^{\mathsf{Game}_1}_{\mathcal{A}}(\lambda)\right| \le \mathsf{Adv}^{\mathbf{SD}^{G_N}_{p_1\mapsto p_1p_2}}_{\mathcal{B}_1}(\lambda).$$

Proof. Given an instance $(\mathbb{G}, D, T)$ of the $\mathbf{SD}^{G_N}_{p_1\mapsto p_1p_2}$ problem where either $T \xleftarrow{\$} G_{p_1}$ or $T \xleftarrow{\$} G_{p_1}G_{p_2}$, $\mathcal{B}_1$ sets

$$\mathsf{pp} := (\mathbb{G}, g_1, h_1).$$

For any $i \in [\mu]$, $\mathcal{B}_1$ picks $x_i, y_i, \alpha_i \xleftarrow{\$} \mathbb{Z}_N$ and produces

$$\mathsf{pk}_i := (g_1^{x_i}, g_1^{y_i}, e(g_1,h_1)^{\alpha_i}) \quad \text{and} \quad \mathsf{sk}_i := (x_i, y_i, \alpha_i).$$

Finally, $\mathcal{B}_1$ picks $\beta \xleftarrow{\$} \{0,1\}$ and sends pp and pk_1, ..., pk_μ to $\mathcal{A}$.

- O_{sk}: Given an index i, $\mathcal{B}_1$ returns x_i, y_i, α_i and updates $Q_{\mathsf{sk}} = Q_{\mathsf{sk}} \cup \{i\}$, where Q_{sk} is an initially empty set.
- O_{ct}: Given an index i^* and two keywords w_0^*, w_1^*, $\mathcal{B}_1$ picks $r' \xleftarrow{\$} \mathbb{Z}_N$ and $\delta^* \xleftarrow{\$} G_T$, computes

$$U^* := T^{r'}, \quad V^* := T^{(x_{i^*}\mathsf{w}_\beta^* + y_{i^*})r'}, \quad W^* := e(U^*, h_1^{\alpha_{i^*}}) \cdot \delta^*$$

and outputs

$$\mathsf{ct}^* := (U^*, V^*, W^*, \delta^*).$$

Update $Q_{i^*} = Q_{i^*} \cup \{i^*\}$, $Q_{\mathsf{ct}} = Q_{\mathsf{ct}} \cup \{(i^*, \mathsf{w}_0^*), (i^*, \mathsf{w}_1^*)\}$, where both Q_{i^*} and Q_{ct} are initially empty sets. We clarify that it is a properly distributed ciphertext for $\mathsf{Type}\,0$ or $\mathsf{Type}\,1$. To see this, we observe that the ciphertext is formed as

$$\left\{ \begin{matrix} (g_1^{t_1} \cdot g_2^{t_2})^{r'}, & (g_1^{t_1} \cdot g_2^{t_2})^{(x_{i^*}\mathsf{w}_\beta^* + y_{i^*})r'} \\ e((g_1^{t_1} \cdot g_2^{t_2})^{r'}, h_1^{\alpha_{i^*}}) \cdot \delta^*, & \delta^* \end{matrix} \right\},$$

that is,

$$\left\{ \begin{matrix} g_1^{t_1 r'} \cdot g_2^{t_2 r'}, & (g_1^{t_1 r'} \cdot g_2^{t_2 r'})^{x_{i^*}\mathsf{w}_\beta^* + y_{i^*}} \\ e(g_1^{t_1 r'} \cdot g_2^{t_2 r'}, h_1^{\alpha_{i^*}}) \cdot \delta^*, & \delta^* \end{matrix} \right\},$$

where we write $T = g_1^{t_1} g_2^{t_2}$ and implicitly set $r = t_1 r'$, $\hat{r} = t_2 r'$. We note that r' mod p_1 is independent from r' mod p_2 due to the Chinese Remainder Theorem. If $T \xleftarrow{\$} G_{p_1}$, which means $t_2 = 0$, the ciphertext is properly distributed as a $\mathsf{Type}\,0$ ciphertext. If $T \xleftarrow{\$} G_{p_1} G_{p_2}$, the ciphertext is properly distributed as a $\mathsf{Type}\,1$ ciphertext. Thus, we can conclude that all ciphertexts are properly distributed ciphertexts for $\mathsf{Type}\,0$ or $\mathsf{Type}\,1$.
- O_{td}: Given an index i and a keyword w, $\mathcal{B}_1$ picks $s \xleftarrow{\$} \mathbb{Z}_N$, computes

$$A := h_1^s, \quad B := h_1^{\alpha_i} \cdot h_1^{(x_i \mathsf{w} + y_i)s}$$

and outputs

$$\mathsf{td}_{\mathsf{w}} := (A, B).$$

Update $Q_{\mathsf{td}} = Q_{\mathsf{td}} \cup \{(i, \mathsf{w})\}$, where Q_{td} is an initially empty set.

Eventually, $\mathcal{A}$ returns β'. $\mathcal{B}_1$ outputs 1 if $\beta = \beta'$; otherwise, output 0.

Game_2: is identical to Game_1 except that all ciphertexts given to the adversary $\mathcal{A}$ are $\mathsf{Type}\,2$ ciphertexts.

Lemma 2 ($\mathsf{Game}_1 \approx_c \mathsf{Game}_2$). *For any PPT adversary $\mathcal{A}$,*

$$\left| \mathsf{Adv}_{\mathcal{A}}^{\mathsf{Game}_1}(\lambda) - \mathsf{Adv}_{\mathcal{A}}^{\mathsf{Game}_2}(\lambda) \right| \leq \mathsf{Adv}_{\mathcal{B}_2}^{\mathbf{DDH}_{p_2}^{G_N}}(\lambda).$$

Proof. Given an instance $(\mathbb{G}, D, T)$ of the $\mathbf{DDH}_{p_2}^{G_N}$ problem where either $T = g_2^{ab}$ or $T = g_2^{ab+c}$, $\mathcal{B}_2$ sets

$$\mathsf{pp} := (\mathbb{G}, g_1, h_1).$$

For any $i \in [\mu]$, $\mathcal{B}_2$ picks $x_i, y_i, \alpha_i \xleftarrow{\$} \mathbb{Z}_N$, produces

$$\mathsf{pk}_i := (g_1^{x_i}, g_1^{y_i}, e(g_1, h_1)^{\alpha_i}) \quad \text{and} \quad \mathsf{sk}_i := (x_i, y_i, \alpha_i),$$

and runs

$$(g_2^{a_i}, g_2^{b_i}, T_i) \leftarrow \mathsf{ReRand}_{a,b,T}^{\mathbf{DDH}_{p_2}^{G_N}}(g_2, g_2^a, g_2^b, T).$$

$\mathcal{B}_2$ implicitly defines $y_i \ mod \ p_2 = a_i$ (in the group G_N), where we use the fact that y_i mod p_1 is independent from y_i mod p_2 due to the Chinese Remainder Theorem. Finally, $\mathcal{B}_2$ picks $\beta \xleftarrow{\$} \{0, 1\}$ and sends pp and pk_1, ..., pk_μ to $\mathcal{A}$.

- O_{sk}: is the same as that in Lemma 2.
- O_{ct}: Given an index i^* and two keywords w_0^*, w_1^*, $\mathcal{B}_2$ picks $r \xleftarrow{\$} \mathbb{Z}_N$ and $\delta^* \xleftarrow{\$} G_T$, runs

$$(g_2^{b'_{i^*}}, T'_{i^*}) \leftarrow \mathsf{ReRand}_{b,T}^{\mathbf{DDH}_{p_2}^{G_N}}(g_2, g_2^{a_{i^*}}, g_2^{b_{i^*}}, T_{i^*}),$$

  computes

$$U^* := g_1^r \cdot g_2^{b'_{i^*}}, \quad V^* := g_1^{(x_{i^*}\mathsf{w}_\beta^* + y_{i^*})r} \cdot (g_2^{b'_{i^*}})^{x_{i^*}\mathsf{w}_\beta^*} \cdot T'_{i^*}, \quad W^* := e(U^*, h_1^{\alpha_{i^*}}) \cdot \delta^*,$$

  where we implicitly set $\hat{r} = b'_{i^*}$, and outputs

$$\mathsf{ct}^* := (U^*, V^*, W^*, \delta^*).$$

  Update $Q_{i^*} = Q_{i^*} \cup \{i^*\}$, $Q_{\mathsf{ct}} = Q_{\mathsf{ct}} \cup \{(i^*, \mathsf{w}_0^*), (i^*, \mathsf{w}_1^*)\}$, where both Q_{i^*} and Q_{ct} are initially empty sets. We clarify that it is a properly distributed ciphertext for $\mathsf{Type\,1}$ or $\mathsf{Type\,2}$. To see this, we observe that the ciphertext is formed as

$$\left\{ \begin{array}{ll} g_1^r \cdot g_2^{b'_{i^*}}, & g_1^{(x_{i^*}\mathsf{w}_\beta^* + y_{i^*})r} \cdot (g_2^{b'_{i^*}})^{x_{i^*}\mathsf{w}_\beta^*} \cdot g_2^{a_{i^*}b'_{i^*} + c'_{i^*}} \\ & e(g_1^r \cdot g_2^{b'_{i^*}}, h_1^{\alpha_{i^*}}) \cdot \delta^*, \quad \delta^* \end{array} \right\},$$

  that is,

$$\left\{ \begin{array}{ll} g_1^r \cdot g_2^{b'_{i^*}}, & g_1^{(x_{i^*}\mathsf{w}_\beta^* + y_{i^*})r} \cdot (g_2^{b'_{i^*}})^{x_{i^*}\mathsf{w}_\beta^* + a_{i^*}} \cdot g_2^{c'_{i^*}} \\ & e(g_1^r \cdot g_2^{b'_{i^*}}, h_1^{\alpha_{i^*}}) \cdot \delta^*, \quad \delta^* \end{array} \right\},$$

  where we implicitly set $\hat{z} = c'_{i^*}$. If $T = g_2^{ab}$, which means $c'_{i^*} = 0$, then the ciphertext is properly distributed as a $\mathsf{Type\,1}$ ciphertext. If $T = g_2^{ab+c}$, then the ciphertext is properly distributed as a $\mathsf{Type\,2}$ ciphertext. Thus, we can conclude that all ciphertexts are properly distributed ciphertexts for $\mathsf{Type\,1}$ or $\mathsf{Type\,2}$.
- O_{td}: is the same as that in Lemma 2.

Eventually, $\mathcal{A}$ returns β'. $\mathcal{B}_2$ outputs 1 if $\beta = \beta'$; otherwise, output 0.

Lemma 3. *For any PPT adversary* $\mathcal{A}$,

$$\mathsf{Adv}_{\mathcal{A}}^{\mathsf{Game}_2}(\lambda) = \mu q_{\mathsf{ct}}/2^{\Theta(\lambda)}.$$

Proof. In the Game_2, it is observed that each $\mathsf{Type\,2}$ ciphertext has a fresh $g_2^{\hat{z}}$ that is uniform in G_{p_2}, and the quantity has $\log p_2 = \Theta(\lambda)$ bits of min-entropy. The keyword w thus is independent from the adversary $\mathcal{A}$'s view. We can conclude that all keywords in searchable ciphertexts are independent from the adversary $\mathcal{A}$'s view.

5 The Second MU-PEKS Scheme

5.1 Construction

Our second MU-PEKS scheme is described as follows.

$\mathsf{Setup}(1^\lambda)$. On input 1^λ, this algorithm runs $\mathbb{G} := (N = p_1p_2, G_N, H_N, G_T, e) \leftarrow \mathsf{GrpGen}(1^\lambda)$, picks random generators g_1 and h_1 of G_{p_1} and H_{p_1}, respectively, and outputs

$$\mathsf{pp} := (\mathbb{G}, g_1, h_1).$$

$\mathsf{KeyGen}(\mathsf{pp})$. On input the public parameter pp, this algorithm picks $x, y, \alpha \xleftarrow{\$} \mathbb{Z}_N$, and outputs

$$\mathsf{pk} := (g_1^x, e(g_1, h_1)^\alpha) \quad \text{and} \quad \mathsf{sk} := (x, \alpha).$$

$\mathsf{Enc}(\mathsf{pk}, \mathsf{w})$. On input the receiver's public key pk and a keyword $\mathsf{w} \in \mathcal{KW}$, this algorithm picks $r \xleftarrow{\$} \mathbb{Z}_N$ and $\delta \xleftarrow{\$} G_T$, computes

$$V := g_1^{(x+\mathsf{w})r}, \quad W := e(g_1, h_1)^{\alpha r} \cdot \delta,$$

and outputs

$$\mathsf{ct} := (V, W, \delta).$$

$\mathsf{Trapdoor}(\mathsf{sk}, \mathsf{w})$. On input the receiver's secret key sk and a keyword $\mathsf{w} \in \mathcal{KW}$, this algorithm picks $s \xleftarrow{\$} \mathbb{Z}_N$, computes and outputs

$$\mathsf{td}_\mathsf{w} := h_1^{\frac{\alpha}{x+\mathsf{w}}},$$

$\mathsf{Test}(\mathsf{ct}, \mathsf{td}_\mathsf{w})$. On input a trapdoor td_w and a searchable ciphertext ct, this algorithm tests whether

$$e(V, \mathsf{td}_\mathsf{w}) \cdot \delta = W.$$

If so, return 1; otherwise return 0.

Correctness. For any $\mathsf{w}, \mathsf{w}' \in \mathbb{Z}_N$, $\mathsf{ct} \leftarrow \mathsf{Enc}(\mathsf{pk}, \mathsf{w}')$ and $\mathsf{td}_\mathsf{w} \leftarrow \mathsf{Trapdoor}(\mathsf{sk}, \mathsf{w})$, we have that

$$e(V, \mathsf{td}_\mathsf{w}) = e(g_1^{(x+\mathsf{w}')r}, h_1^{\frac{\alpha}{x+\mathsf{w}}}) = e(g_1, h_1)^{\frac{(x+\mathsf{w}')\alpha r}{x+\mathsf{w}}}$$

Thus, the correctness is straightforward.

5.2 Security Proof

As for security, we establish the following result.

Theorem 2. *For any PPT adversary $\mathcal{A}$ sending at most q_{sk}, q_{ct} and q_{td} queries to O_{sk}, O_{ct} and O_{td}, respectively, there exist $\mathcal{B}_1$, $\mathcal{B}_2$ such that*

$$\mathsf{Adv}^{\mathsf{IND\text{-}MUMCc}}_{\text{MU-PEKS},\mathcal{A}}(1^\lambda,\mu) \le \mathsf{Adv}^{\mathbf{SD}^{G_N}_{p_1\mapsto p_1p_2}}_{\mathcal{B}_1}(\lambda) + \mathsf{Adv}^{\mathbf{DDH}^{G_N}_{p_2}}_{\mathcal{B}_2}(\lambda) + \mu q_{\mathsf{ct}}/2^{\Theta(\lambda)}.$$

Proof. As before, we define the advantage function of any PPT adversary $\mathcal{A}$ in Game_x as

$$\mathsf{Adv}^{\mathsf{Game}_x}_{\mathcal{A}}(\lambda).$$

We name the various forms of ciphertext used in the proof in Table 3, where the $\mathsf{Type}\,0$ ciphertext is exactly real searchable ciphertext.

Table 3. Various forms of ciphertext used in the proof.

	ct
Type 0	$(g_1^{(x+\mathsf{w})r},\quad e(g_1,h_1)^{\alpha r}\cdot\delta,\quad \delta)$
Type 1	$((g_1^r\boxed{\cdot g_2^{\hat{r}}})^{x+\mathsf{w}},\quad e(g_1^r\boxed{\cdot g_2^{\hat{r}}},h_1^{\alpha})\cdot\delta,\quad —)$
Type 2	$(g_1^{(x+\mathsf{w})r}\cdot g_2^{(x+\mathsf{w})\hat{r}}\boxed{\cdot g_2^{\hat{z}}},\quad —,\quad —)$

Note: A dash (—) means the same as in the above.

We will complete the proof by establishing the following sequence of lemmas.

Game_0: is the real game. In this game, all ciphertexts given to the adversary $\mathcal{A}$ are $\mathsf{Type}\,0$ ciphertexts. We have that

$$\mathsf{Adv}^{\mathsf{IND\text{-}MUMCc}}_{\text{MU-PEKS},\mathcal{A}}(1^\lambda,\mu) = \mathsf{Adv}^{\mathsf{Game}_0}_{\mathcal{A}}(\lambda).$$

Game_1: is identical to Game_0 except that all ciphertexts given to the adversary $\mathcal{A}$ are $\mathsf{Type}\,1$ ciphertexts.

Lemma 4 ($\mathsf{Game}_0 \approx_c \mathsf{Game}_1$)**.** *For any PPT adversary $\mathcal{A}$,*

$$\left|\mathsf{Adv}^{\mathsf{Game}_0}_{\mathcal{A}}(\lambda) - \mathsf{Adv}^{\mathsf{Game}_1}_{\mathcal{A}}(\lambda)\right| \le \mathsf{Adv}^{\mathbf{SD}^{G_N}_{p_1\mapsto p_1p_2}}_{\mathcal{B}_1}(\lambda).$$

Proof. Given an instance $(\mathbb{G}, D, T)$ of the $\mathbf{SD}^{G_N}_{p_1\mapsto p_1p_2}$ problem where either $T \xleftarrow{\$} G_{p_1}$ or $T \xleftarrow{\$} G_{p_1}G_{p_2}$, $\mathcal{B}_1$ sets

$$\mathsf{pp} := (\mathbb{G}, g_1, h_1).$$

For any $i \in [\mu]$, $\mathcal{B}_1$ picks $x_i, \alpha_i \xleftarrow{\$} \mathbb{Z}_N$ and produces

$$\mathsf{pk}_i := (g_1^{x_i}, e(g_1,h_1)^{\alpha_i}) \quad \text{and} \quad \mathsf{sk}_i := (x_i, \alpha_i).$$

Finally, $\mathcal{B}_1$ picks $\beta \xleftarrow{\$} \{0,1\}$ and sends pp and pk_1, ..., pk_μ to $\mathcal{A}$.

- $\mathsf{O_{sk}}$: Given an index i, $\mathcal{B}_1$ returns x_i, α_i and updates $Q_{\mathsf{sk}} = Q_{\mathsf{sk}} \cup \{i\}$, where Q_{sk} is an initially empty set.
- $\mathsf{O_{ct}}$: Given an index i^* and two keywords w_0^*, w_1^*, $\mathcal{B}_1$ picks $r' \xleftarrow{\$} \mathbb{Z}_N$ and $\delta^* \xleftarrow{\$} G_T$, computes

$$V^* := T^{(x_{i^*}+\mathsf{w}_\beta^*)r'}, \quad W^* := e(T^{r'}, h_1^{\alpha_{i^*}}) \cdot \delta^*$$

and outputs

$$\mathsf{ct}^* := (V^*, W^*, \delta^*).$$

Update $Q_{i^*} = Q_{i^*} \cup \{i^*\}$, $Q_{\mathsf{ct}} = Q_{\mathsf{ct}} \cup \{(i^*, \mathsf{w}_0^*), (i^*, \mathsf{w}_1^*)\}$, where both Q_{i^*} and Q_{ct} are initially empty sets. We clarify that it is a properly distributed ciphertext for $\mathsf{Type\,0}$ or $\mathsf{Type\,1}$. To see this, we observe that the ciphertext is formed as

$$\left\{ (g_1^{t_1} \cdot g_2^{t_2})^{(x_{i^*}+\mathsf{w}_\beta^*)r'}, \quad e((g_1^{t_1} \cdot g_2^{t_2})^{r'}, h_1^{\alpha_{i^*}}) \cdot \delta^*, \quad \delta^* \right\},$$

that is,

$$\left\{ g_1^{(x_{i^*}+\mathsf{w}_\beta^*)t_1 r'} \cdot g_2^{(x_{i^*}+\mathsf{w}_\beta^*)t_2 r'}, \quad e(g_1^{t_1 r'} \cdot g_2^{t_2 r'}, h_1^{\alpha_{i^*}}) \cdot \delta^*, \quad \delta^* \right\},$$

where we write $T = g_1^{t_1} g_2^{t_2}$ and implicitly set $r = t_1 r'$, $\hat{r} = t_2 r'$. We note that $r' \bmod p_1$ is independent from $r' \bmod p_2$ due to the Chinese Remainder Theorem. If $T \xleftarrow{\$} G_{p_1}$, which means $t_2 = 0$, the ciphertext is properly distributed as a $\mathsf{Type\,0}$ ciphertext. If $T \xleftarrow{\$} G_{p_1} G_{p_2}$, the ciphertext is properly distributed as a $\mathsf{Type\,1}$ ciphertext. Thus, we can conclude that all ciphertexts are properly distributed ciphertexts for $\mathsf{Type\,0}$ or $\mathsf{Type\,1}$.
- $\mathsf{O_{td}}$: Given an index i and a keyword w, $\mathcal{B}_1$ picks $s \xleftarrow{\$} \mathbb{Z}_N$, computes and outputs

$$\mathsf{td_w} := h_1^{\frac{\alpha_i}{x_i+\mathsf{w}}}.$$

Update $Q_{\mathsf{td}} = Q_{\mathsf{td}} \cup \{(i, \mathsf{w})\}$, where Q_{td} is an initially empty set.

Eventually, $\mathcal{A}$ returns β'. $\mathcal{B}_1$ outputs 1 if $\beta = \beta'$; otherwise, output 0.

$\mathsf{Game_2}$: is identical to $\mathsf{Game_1}$ except that all ciphertexts given to the adversary $\mathcal{A}$ are $\mathsf{Type\,2}$ ciphertexts.

Lemma 5 ($\mathsf{Game_1} \approx_c \mathsf{Game_2}$). *For any PPT adversary $\mathcal{A}$,*

$$\left| \mathsf{Adv}_{\mathcal{A}}^{\mathsf{Game_1}}(\lambda) - \mathsf{Adv}_{\mathcal{A}}^{\mathsf{Game_2}}(\lambda) \right| \le \mathsf{Adv}_{\mathcal{B}_2}^{\mathbf{DDH}_{p_2}^{G_N}}(\lambda).$$

Proof. Given an instance $(\mathbb{G}, D, T)$ of the $\mathbf{DDH}_{p_2}^{G_N}$ problem where either $T = g_2^{ab}$ or $T = g_2^{ab+c}$, $\mathcal{B}_2$ sets

$$\mathsf{pp} := (\mathbb{G}, g_1, h_1).$$

For any $i \in [\mu]$, $\mathcal{B}_2$ picks $x_i, \alpha_i \xleftarrow{\$} \mathbb{Z}_N$, produces

$$\mathsf{pk}_i := (g_1^{x_i}, e(g_1, h_1)^{\alpha_i}) \quad \text{and} \quad \mathsf{sk}_i := (x_i, \alpha_i),$$

and runs

$$(g_2^{a_i}, g_2^{b_i}, T_i) \leftarrow \mathsf{ReRand}_{a,b,T}^{\mathbf{DDH}_{p2}^{G_N}}(g_2, g_2^a, g_2^b, T).$$

$\mathcal{B}_2$ implicitly defines $x_i \ mod\ p_2 = a_i$ (in the group G_N), where we use the fact that x_i mod p_1 is independent from x_i mod p_2 due to the Chinese Remainder Theorem. Finally, $\mathcal{B}_2$ picks $\beta \xleftarrow{\$} \{0,1\}$ and sends pp and pk_1, ..., pk_μ to $\mathcal{A}$.

- O_{sk}: is the same as that in Lemma 2.
- O_{ct}: Given an index i^* and two keywords w_0^*, w_1^*, $\mathcal{B}_2$ picks $r \xleftarrow{\$} \mathbb{Z}_N$ and $\delta^* \xleftarrow{\$} G_T$, runs

$$(g_2^{b'_{i^*}}, T'_{i^*}) \leftarrow \mathsf{ReRand}_{b,T}^{\mathbf{DDH}_{p2}^{G_N}}(g_2, g_2^{a_{i^*}}, g_2^{b_{i^*}}, T_{i^*}),$$

  computes

$$V^* := g_1^{(x_{i^*}\mathsf{w}_\beta^* + y_{i^*})r} \cdot (g_2^{b'_{i^*}})^{x_{i^*}\mathsf{w}_\beta^*} \cdot T'_{i^*}, \quad W^* := e(g_1^r \cdot g_2^{b'_{i^*}}, h_1^{\alpha_{i^*}}) \cdot \delta^*,$$

  where we implicitly set $\hat{r} = b'_{i^*}$, and outputs

$$\mathsf{ct}^* := (V^*, W^*, \delta^*).$$

  Update $Q_{i^*} = Q_{i^*} \cup \{i^*\}$, $Q_{\mathsf{ct}} = Q_{\mathsf{ct}} \cup \{(i^*, \mathsf{w}_0^*), (i^*, \mathsf{w}_1^*)\}$, where both Q_{i^*} and Q_{ct} are initially empty sets. We clarify that it is a properly distributed ciphertext for Type 1 or Type 2. To see this, we observe that the ciphertext is formed as

$$\left\{ g_1^{(x_{i^*}+\mathsf{w}_\beta^*)r} \cdot (g_2^{b'_{i^*}})^{\mathsf{w}_\beta^*} \cdot g_2^{a_{i^*}b'_{i^*}+c'_{i^*}}, \quad e(g_1^r \cdot g_2^{b'_{i^*}}, h_1^{\alpha_{i^*}}) \cdot \delta^*, \quad \delta^* \right\},$$

  that is,

$$\left\{ g_1^{(x_{i^*}+\mathsf{w}_\beta^*)r} \cdot (g_2^{b'_{i^*}})^{\mathsf{w}_\beta^*+a_{i^*}} \cdot g_2^{c'_{i^*}}, \quad e(g_1^r \cdot g_2^{b'_{i^*}}, h_1^{\alpha_{i^*}}) \cdot \delta^*, \quad \delta^* \right\},$$

  where we implicitly set $\hat{z} = c'_{i^*}$. If $T = g_2^{ab}$, which means $c'_{i^*} = 0$, then the ciphertext is properly distributed as a Type 1 ciphertext. If $T = g_2^{ab+c}$, then the ciphertext is properly distributed as a Type 2 ciphertext. Thus, we can conclude that all ciphertexts are properly distributed ciphertexts for Type 1 or Type 2.
- O_{td}: is the same as that in Lemma 2.

Eventually, $\mathcal{A}$ returns β'. $\mathcal{B}_2$ outputs 1 if $\beta = \beta'$; otherwise, output 0.

Lemma 6. *For any PPT adversary $\mathcal{A}$,*

$$\mathsf{Adv}_{\mathcal{A}}^{\mathsf{Game}_2}(\lambda) = \mu q_{\mathsf{ct}}/2^{\Theta(\lambda)}.$$

Proof. In the Game_2, it is observed that each $\mathsf{Type\,2}$ ciphertext has a fresh $g_2^{\hat{z}}$ that is uniform in G_{p_2}, and the quantity has $\log p_2 = \Theta(\lambda)$ bits of min-entropy. The keyword w thus is independent from the adversary $\mathcal{A}$'s view. We can conclude that all keywords in searchable ciphertexts are independent from the adversary $\mathcal{A}$'s view.

Acknowledgements. We want to thank Tongchen Shen for his useful advice. We also thank all anonymous reviewers of PKC 2024 for their helpful comments. Yunhao Ling, Jie Chen, Haifeng Qian were supported by National Natural Science Foundation of China (61972156, 62372180), National Key Research and Development Program of China (2018YFA0704701), Innovation Program of ShanghaiMunicipal Education Commission (2021-01-07-00-08-E00101), and the "Digital Dilk Road" Shanghai International Joint lab of Trustworthy Intelligent Software (22510750100). Kai Zhang was supported by National Natural Science Foundation of China (No. 62372285), and Shanghai Rising-Star Program (No. 22QA1403800). Qiong Huang was supported by National Natural Science Foundation of China (No. 62272174), Major Program of Guangdong Basic and Applied Research (2019B030302008), and Science and Technology Program of Guangzhou (2024A04J6542).

References

1. Abdalla, M., et al.: Searchable encryption revisited: consistency properties, relation to anonymous IBE, and extensions. In: Shoup, V. (ed.) CRYPTO 2005. LNCS, vol. 3621, pp. 205–222. Springer, Heidelberg (2005). https://doi.org/10.1007/11535218_13
2. Ateniese, G., Benson, K., Hohenberger, S.: Key-private proxy re-encryption. In: Fischlin, M. (ed.) CT-RSA 2009. LNCS, vol. 5473, pp. 279–294. Springer, Heidelberg (2009). https://doi.org/10.1007/978-3-642-00862-7_19
3. Ateniese, G., Fu, K., Green, M., Hohenberger, S.: Improved proxy re-encryption schemes with applications to secure distributed storage. ACM Trans. Inf. Syst. Secur. **9**(1), 1–30 (2006). https://doi.org/10.1145/1127345.1127346
4. Attrapadung, N.: Dual system encryption framework in prime-order groups via computational pair encodings. In: Cheon, J.H., Takagi, T. (eds.) ASIACRYPT 2016. LNCS, vol. 10032, pp. 591–623. Springer, Heidelberg (2016). https://doi.org/10.1007/978-3-662-53890-6_20
5. Bader, C., Hofheinz, D., Jager, T., Kiltz, E., Li, Y.: Tightly-secure authenticated key exchange. In: Dodis, Y., Nielsen, J.B. (eds.) TCC 2015. LNCS, vol. 9014, pp. 629–658. Springer, Heidelberg (2015). https://doi.org/10.1007/978-3-662-46494-6_26
6. Bellare, M., Boldyreva, A., Micali, S.: Public-key encryption in a multi-user setting: security proofs and improvements. In: Preneel, B. (ed.) EUROCRYPT 2000. LNCS, vol. 1807, pp. 259–274. Springer, Heidelberg (2000). https://doi.org/10.1007/3-540-45539-6_18
7. Blaze, M., Bleumer, G., Strauss, M.: Divertible protocols and atomic proxy cryptography. In: Nyberg, K. (ed.) EUROCRYPT 1998. LNCS, vol. 1403, pp. 127–144. Springer, Heidelberg (1998). https://doi.org/10.1007/BFb0054122
8. Boneh, D., Di Crescenzo, G., Ostrovsky, R., Persiano, G.: Public key encryption with keyword search. In: Cachin, C., Camenisch, J.L. (eds.) EUROCRYPT 2004.

LNCS, vol. 3027, pp. 506–522. Springer, Heidelberg (2004). https://doi.org/10.1007/978-3-540-24676-3_30
9. Boneh, D., Goh, E.-J., Nissim, K.: Evaluating 2-DNF formulas on ciphertexts. In: Kilian, J. (ed.) TCC 2005. LNCS, vol. 3378, pp. 325–341. Springer, Heidelberg (2005). https://doi.org/10.1007/978-3-540-30576-7_18
10. De Caro, A., Iovino, V., Persiano, G.: Fully secure anonymous HIBE and secret-key anonymous IBE with short ciphertexts. In: Joye, M., Miyaji, A., Otsuka, A. (eds.) Pairing 2010. LNCS, vol. 6487, pp. 347–366. Springer, Heidelberg (2010). https://doi.org/10.1007/978-3-642-17455-1_22
11. Chen, J., Gay, R., Wee, H.: Improved dual system ABE in prime-order groups via predicate encodings. In: Oswald, E., Fischlin, M. (eds.) EUROCRYPT 2015. LNCS, vol. 9057, pp. 595–624. Springer, Heidelberg (2015). https://doi.org/10.1007/978-3-662-46803-6_20
12. Chen, J., Gong, J., Kowalczyk, L., Wee, H.: Unbounded ABE via bilinear entropy expansion, revisited. In: Nielsen, J.B., Rijmen, V. (eds.) EUROCRYPT 2018. LNCS, vol. 10820, pp. 503–534. Springer, Cham (2018). https://doi.org/10.1007/978-3-319-78381-9_19
13. Chen, J., Gong, J., Weng, J.: Tightly secure IBE under constant-size master public key. In: Fehr, S. (ed.) PKC 2017. LNCS, vol. 10174, pp. 207–231. Springer, Heidelberg (2017). https://doi.org/10.1007/978-3-662-54365-8_9
14. Chen, J., Wee, H.: Fully, (almost) tightly secure IBE and dual system groups. In: Canetti, R., Garay, J.A. (eds.) CRYPTO 2013. LNCS, vol. 8043, pp. 435–460. Springer, Heidelberg (2013). https://doi.org/10.1007/978-3-642-40084-1_25
15. Cheng, L., Meng, F.: Public key authenticated encryption with keyword search from LWE. In: ESORICS 2022, pp. 303–324 (2022). https://doi.org/10.1007/978-3-031-17140-6_15
16. Cohen, A.: What about bob? The inadequacy of CPA security for proxy reencryption. In: Lin, D., Sako, K. (eds.) PKC 2019. LNCS, vol. 11443, pp. 287–316. Springer, Cham (2019). https://doi.org/10.1007/978-3-030-17259-6_10
17. Datta, P., Komargodski, I., Waters, B.: Fully adaptive decentralized multi-authority ABE. In: Hazay, C., Stam, M. (eds.) EUROCRYPT 2023, vol. 14006. pp. 447–478 (2023). https://doi.org/10.1007/978-3-031-30620-4_15
18. Gay, R., Hofheinz, D., Kiltz, E., Wee, H.: Tightly CCA-secure encryption without pairings. In: Fischlin, M., Coron, J.-S. (eds.) EUROCRYPT 2016. LNCS, vol. 9665, pp. 1–27. Springer, Heidelberg (2016). https://doi.org/10.1007/978-3-662-49890-3_1
19. Gong, J., Chen, J., Dong, X., Cao, Z., Tang, S.: Extended nested dual system groups, revisited. In: Cheng, C.-M., Chung, K.-M., Persiano, G., Yang, B.-Y. (eds.) PKC 2016. LNCS, vol. 9614, pp. 133–163. Springer, Heidelberg (2016). https://doi.org/10.1007/978-3-662-49384-7_6
20. Gong, J., Dong, X., Chen, J., Cao, Z.: Efficient IBE with tight reduction to standard assumption in the multi-challenge setting. In: Cheon, J.H., Takagi, T. (eds.) ASIACRYPT 2016. LNCS, vol. 10032, pp. 624–654. Springer, Heidelberg (2016). https://doi.org/10.1007/978-3-662-53890-6_21
21. Guillevic, A.: Comparing the pairing efficiency over composite-order and prime-order elliptic curves. In: Jacobson, M., Locasto, M., Mohassel, P., Safavi-Naini, R. (eds.) ACNS 2013. LNCS, vol. 7954, pp. 357–372. Springer, Heidelberg (2013). https://doi.org/10.1007/978-3-642-38980-1_22
22. Han, S., Liu, S., Gu, D.: Key encapsulation mechanism with tight enhanced security in the multi-user setting: impossibility result and optimal tightness. In: Tibouchi,

M., Wang, H. (eds.) ASIACRYPT 2021. LNCS, vol. 13091, pp. 483–513. Springer, Cham (2021). https://doi.org/10.1007/978-3-030-92075-3_17
23. Han, S., Liu, S., Wang, Z., Gu, D.: Almost tight multi-user security under adaptive corruptions from LWE in the standard model. In: Handschuh, H., Lysyanskaya, A. (eds.) CRYPTO 2023, vol. 14085, pp. 682–715 (2023). https://doi.org/10.1007/978-3-031-38554-4_22
24. Hofheinz, D.: Adaptive partitioning. In: Coron, J.-S., Nielsen, J.B. (eds.) EUROCRYPT 2017. LNCS, vol. 10212, pp. 489–518. Springer, Cham (2017). https://doi.org/10.1007/978-3-319-56617-7_17
25. Hofheinz, D., Jager, T.: Tightly secure signatures and public-key encryption. In: Safavi-Naini, R., Canetti, R. (eds.) CRYPTO 2012. LNCS, vol. 7417, pp. 590–607. Springer, Heidelberg (2012). https://doi.org/10.1007/978-3-642-32009-5_35
26. Hofheinz, D., Koch, J., Striecks, C.: Identity-based encryption with (almost) tight security in the multi-instance, multi-ciphertext setting. In: Katz, J. (ed.) PKC 2015. LNCS, vol. 9020, pp. 799–822. Springer, Heidelberg (2015). https://doi.org/10.1007/978-3-662-46447-2_36
27. Huang, Q., Li, H.: An efficient public-key searchable encryption scheme secure against inside keyword guessing attacks. Inf. Sci. **403–404**, 1–14 (2017). https://doi.org/10.1016/j.ins.2017.03.038
28. Kowalczyk, L., Wee, H.: Compact adaptively secure ABE for NC^1 from k-Lin. J. Cryptol. **33**, 954–1002 (2020). https://doi.org/10.1007/s00145-019-09335-x
29. Lee, Y., Lee, D.H., Park, J.H.: Tightly CCA-secure encryption scheme in a multi-user setting with corruptions. Des. Codes Crypt. **8**(11), 2433–2452 (2020). https://doi.org/10.1007/s10623-020-00794-z
30. Lewko, A., Waters, B.: New techniques for dual system encryption and fully secure HIBE with short ciphertexts. In: Micciancio, D. (ed.) TCC 2010. LNCS, vol. 5978, pp. 455–479. Springer, Heidelberg (2010). https://doi.org/10.1007/978-3-642-11799-2_27
31. Libert, B., Joye, M., Yung, M., Peters, T.: Concise multi-challenge CCA-secure encryption and signatures with almost tight security. In: Sarkar, P., Iwata, T. (eds.) ASIACRYPT 2014. LNCS, vol. 8874, pp. 1–21. Springer, Heidelberg (2014). https://doi.org/10.1007/978-3-662-45608-8_1
32. Liu, Z.Y., Tseng, Y.F., Tso, R., Mambo, M., Chen, Y.C.: Public-key authenticated encryption with keyword search: cryptanalysis, enhanced security, and quantum-resistant instantiation. In: ASIACCS 2022, pp. 423–436 (2022). https://doi.org/10.1145/3488932.3497760
33. Wang, B., Song, W., Lou, W., Hou, Y.T.: Inverted index based multi-keyword public-key searchable encryption with strong privacy guarantee. In: INFOCOM 2015, pp. 2092–2100 (2015). https://doi.org/10.1109/INFOCOM.2015.7218594
34. Waters, B.: Dual system encryption: realizing fully secure IBE and HIBE under simple assumptions. In: Halevi, S. (ed.) CRYPTO 2009. LNCS, vol. 5677, pp. 619–636. Springer, Heidelberg (2009). https://doi.org/10.1007/978-3-642-03356-8_36
35. Wee, H.: Déjà Q: encore! Un petit IBE. In: Kushilevitz, E., Malkin, T. (eds.) TCC 2016. LNCS, vol. 9563, pp. 237–258. Springer, Heidelberg (2016). https://doi.org/10.1007/978-3-662-49099-0_9
36. Xu, P., Jin, H., Wu, Q., Wang, W.: Public-key encryption with fuzzy keyword search: a provably secure scheme under keyword guessing attack. IEEE Trans. Comput. **62**(11), 2266–2277 (2013). https://doi.org/10.1109/TC.2012.215

Compact Selective Opening Security from LWE

Dennis Hofheinz(✉), Kristina Hostáková, Julia Kastner, Karen Klein, and Akin Ünal

Department of Computer Science, ETH Zurich, Zurich, Switzerland
{hofheinz,kristina.hostakova,julia.kastner,karen.klein, akin.uenal}@inf.ethz.ch

Abstract. Selective opening (SO) security is a security notion for public-key encryption schemes that captures security against adaptive corruptions of senders. SO security comes in chosen-plaintext (SO-CPA) and chosen-ciphertext (SO-CCA) variants, neither of which is implied by standard security notions like IND-CPA or IND-CCA security.

In this paper, we present the first SO-CCA secure encryption scheme that combines the following two properties: (1) it has a constant ciphertext expansion (i.e., ciphertexts are only larger than plaintexts by a constant factor), and (2) its security can be proven from a standard assumption. Previously, the only known SO-CCA secure encryption scheme achieving (1) was built from an ad-hoc assumption in the RSA regime.

Our construction builds upon LWE, and in particular on a new and surprisingly simple construction of compact lossy trapdoor functions (LTFs). Our LTF can be converted into an "all-but-many LTF" (or ABM-LTF), which is known to be sufficient to obtain SO-CCA security. Along the way, we fix a technical problem in that previous ABM-LTF-based construction of SO-CCA security.

1 Introduction

Selective Opening Security. Selective opening (SO) security [5,19] is a security notion for public-key encryption that models adaptive corruptions of senders. For instance, consider a scenario in which a number of small devices send data (such as measurements) to a single receiver. Each device encrypts its messages using the public key of the receiver. However, each single sending device can be also corrupted, in which case an adversary may learn its complete internal state.

More abstractly, SO security considers a scenario in which an adversary gets a number of ciphertexts (for messages jointly chosen from an adversarially chosen message distribution), and can then ask for *openings* of a subset of those ciphertexts. Here, an opening yields both the encrypted messages *and* the used

This work was partially supported by ERC Project PREP-CRYPTO 724307.

Supplementary Information The online version contains supplementary material available at https://doi.org/10.1007/978-3-031-57728-4_5.

Q. Tang and V. Teague (Eds.): PKC 2024, LNCS 14604, pp. 127–160, 2024.
https://doi.org/10.1007/978-3-031-57728-4_5

encryption random coins. After providing these openings, we require that the unopened ciphertexts remain secure, in the sense that the adversary does not obtain any information about the corresponding unopened messages that does not follow from the opened messages. This latter property is somewhat tedious to formalize, and several concrete SO security notions have been proposed in the literature; see [9] for an overview.

The Hardness of Obtaining SO Security. Curiously, SO security does not follow from standard security notions such as semantic security [4,34,35]. Indeed, while there are a number of constructions of SO-secure schemes (e.g., [5,7,12,20,22, 27,32,33,36,38]), the most efficient of those schemes are still considerably less efficient than state-of-the-art IND-CCA-secure encryption schemes. To be more precise: when aiming at SO security against chosen-ciphertext attacks (i.e., SO-CCA security), then all known constructions except the one from [32] suffer from large ciphertexts with a super-constant ciphertext/message size ratio. The only exception, [32], is tied to the RSA regime, and relies on an ad-hoc and non-standard assumption.[1] One reason for this inefficiency is that SO security does not appear to permit hybrid encryption techniques (notwithstanding positive results in idealized computational models [30,31]).

Outside the standard model, it is possible to achieve tight and very compact SO secure PKE constructions [43] by using random oracles. However, these constructions are not post-quantum, as they rely on group-based assumptions.

Our Goal. Our goal in this work will be to provide an SO-CCA secure public-key encryption scheme with compact ciphertexts (i.e., with a constant ciphertext/message size ratio) from the LWE assumption. Obviously, more compact ciphertexts are always desirable, but in a setting like the SO application sketched above (with many small devices sending data to a base station), keeping transmitted messages compact seems particularly desirable. To achieve our goal, we will follow the high-level approach of [32,38], and construct an SO-CCA secure scheme from a variant of lossy trapdoor functions.

Lossy Trapdoor Functions. A lossy trapdoor function (LTF [46]), is a family of functions f_{ek} parameterized by an evaluation key ek, and such that the following holds:

- If ek is chosen using an "injective key generation algorithm" $\mathsf{LTF.IGen}$, then f_{ek} is invertible using a trapdoor also output by $\mathsf{LTF.IGen}$ alongside ek.
- But if ek is chosen using a "lossy key generation algorithm" $\mathsf{LTF.LGen}$ (that does not output any trapdoors alongside ek), then f_{ek} is highly non-injective.
- The keys ek output by $\mathsf{LTF.IGen}$ are computationally indistinguishable from those output by $\mathsf{LTF.LGen}$.

[1] Specifically, [32] assumes in a very strong sense that the Paillier encryption scheme is *not* multiplicatively homomorphic.

This indistinguishability of injective and lossy keys ek already implies one-wayness of the function f_{ek}, and hence LTFs imply trapdoor one-way functions (TD-OWFs). In particular, all applications of TD-OWFs are also applications of LTFs. However, from a theoretical perspective, LTFs seem to be more powerful objects than TD-OWFs as LTFs imply collision-resistant hash functions which is not known to be implied (in a black-box way) from TD-OWFs.

From a practical perspective, LTFs are also a convenient way to obtain lossy encryption [5,45], deterministic encryption [10], or chosen-ciphertext-secure encryption [41,46], possibly secure even against selective openings [32]. There are also several concrete constructions of LTFs from number-theoretic assumptions, including from Decisional Diffie-Hellman [46] (or related group-based assumptions [21]), the Decisional Composite Residuosity (DCR) assumption [21] (or other RSA-related assumptions [3,8,21,28,37]), and even from the Learning With Errors (LWE) assumption [1,6,12,18,38,46].

Properties of LTFs. There are two particularly interesting quantitative properties of an LTF in view of our SO application: its expansion, and its lossiness. To explain these attributes of an LTF, let us simplify things a bit and assume that inputs and outputs of f_{ek} are bits, i.e., we have $f_{ek} : \{0,1\}^\nu \to \{0,1\}^\mu$. Then we may call the fraction $\chi = \mu/\nu$ the (multiplicative) "expansion" of the LTF. Of course, $\chi \geq 1$ because at least with injective keys, f_{ek} is injective.

We may also define the "lossiness" of f_{ek} for lossy keys ek as $\ell = \nu - \log_2 |\mathcal{IG}|$, where $\mathcal{IG} := f_{ek}(\{0,1\}^\nu)$ is the actual image of the function. Intuitively, ℓ denotes the average number of input bits that are lost by evaluating f_{ek} with a lossy key. We can also define the "relative lossiness" of f_{ek} as $L = \ell/\nu$. In view of applications, of course a larger (relative) lossiness, and a smaller expansion are desirable. For instance, in encryption applications, typically $y := f_{ek}(x)$ (for a random x) is part of the ciphertext, and entropy from x is used to hide a message to be encrypted. Hence, the ciphertext grows with $|y| = \mu$ (and thus with χ), and generally a larger ℓ means more entropy in x (when ek is lossy), and thus a larger potential message.[2]

Achieving large (relative) lossiness with a small expansion seems to be difficult. With one exception, all known group-based LTFs [21,46] process the preimage in a bitwise fashion (which results in large outputs). The one exception is the group-based LTF from [18], which achieves large lossiness and optimal expansion asymptotically, but uses several abstractions and is comparatively involved to evaluate. Known lattice-based LTFs either also process their input bitwise [46], suffer from a relatively small relative lossiness [1,6,12,38], or are again comparatively complex to evaluate [18].[3] The situation in the RSA regime is somewhat

[2] Of course, in many encryption applications, hybrid encryption is possible, and thus x only needs to have enough entropy (even given y) that a symmetric encryption key can be extracted. However, in certain applications like selective-opening security, hybrid encryption does not seem to be useful, and thus a larger lossiness leads to larger messages.

[3] We note that while this may seem promising, it is also not possible to boost relative lossiness generically, e.g., by repetition [47].

brighter: some RSA-based LTFs achieve a constant relative lossiness *and* a constant expansion simultaneously.[4]

It also seems hard to construct RSA-based LTFs with additional properties, and in particular "all-but-many LTFs" (ABM-LTFs [12,32,38]). Such ABM-LTFs are particularly useful to obtain selective-opening security. However, the only ABM-LTF construction in the RSA regime [32] relies on an ad-hoc and nonstandard assumption related to the *absence* of multiplicative homomorphisms in the Paillier encryption scheme [42].[5]

Our Contribution. To obtain our goal of compact SO-CCA secure encryption, we first construct a conceptually extremely simple LTF from LWE that achieves both constant relative lossiness (arbitrarily close to 1) *and* a constant expansion. Building on ideas from [12,38], we also extend our LTF to an ABM-LTF. We use this ABM-LTF to construct a public-key encryption scheme that combines the following properties:

- it is chosen-ciphertext selective-opening secure,
- it has a constant ciphertext expansion (i.e., ciphertexts are larger than plaintexts only by a constant factor),
- its security is based on a standard assumption (in this case: LWE).

We stress that our main claim regarding this ABM-LTF is conceptual simplicity and efficiency. Indeed, while it seems plausible that existing works (such as [13,23], when combined with [12,38]) yield an asymptotically similar result, our construction is simple and efficient.

1.1 Technical Overview

In this section, we will give more details on our ideas and techniques, and in particular on the application of our LTF on selective-opening secure encryption.

Starting Point: LWE Trapdoors. Assume a modulus $q \in \mathbb{Z}$, dimensions $n, m \in \mathbb{N}$ with $m \gg n$, and a uniformly distributed matrix $\mathbf{A} \in \mathbb{Z}_q^{m \times n}$. Let $\mathfrak{D} \subset \mathbb{Z}_q$ be a set of short "noise values", i.e., of values $e \in \mathbb{Z}_q$ with $|e| \ll q$. The function $g_{\mathbf{A}}$ with

$$g_{\mathbf{A}}(\mathbf{s}, \mathbf{e}) = \mathbf{A}\mathbf{s} + \mathbf{e}$$

(for $\mathbf{s} \in \mathbb{Z}_q^n$ and short $\mathbf{e} \in \mathfrak{D}^m$) is injective with high probability over the choice of $\mathbf{A}$. In fact, $g_{\mathbf{A}}$ is efficiently invertible with a suitable trapdoor $\tau_{\mathbf{A}}$ that can be generated alongside $\mathbf{A}$, e.g., as in [40].

[4] It is not easy to give a more quantitative comparison, since all mentioned LTF constructions offer tradeoffs regarding efficiency, relative lossiness, and compactness.

[5] It would seem promising to construct LTFs and ABM-LTFs from suitable homomorphic encryption schemes, and in particular from "Rate-1 FHE schemes" [13,23], using the blueprint of [29] and [12,38]. This may indeed lead to asymptotically compact LTFs and ABM-LTFs with large lossiness, but the corresponding constructions have an involved evaluation procedure and will require huge parameters to play out their asymptotic properties.

It has been noted before that, for suitable choices of q, n, m, and "shortness" of vectors, the function $g_{\mathbf{A}}$ above is already a lossy trapdoor function [1,6,38,44]. Indeed, setting up $\mathbf{A}' = \mathbf{BD} + \mathbf{E}$ for "very flat" $\mathbf{D} \in \mathbb{Z}_q^{k \times n}$ with $k \ll n$ and short $\mathbf{E} \in \mathfrak{D}^{m \times n}$ leads to a highly non-injective $g_{\mathbf{A}'}$ [25]. The corresponding matrices $\mathbf{A}'$ are computationally indistinguishable from uniformly random $\mathbf{A}$ under the LWE assumption and can hence be used as lossy keys.

Unfortunately, since $m \gg n$, this $g_{\mathbf{A}}$ has large images $g_{\mathbf{A}}(\mathbf{s}, \mathbf{e}) \in \mathbb{Z}_q^m$ for relatively small preimages $(\mathbf{s}, \mathbf{e}) \in \mathbb{Z}_q^n \times \mathfrak{D}^m$, and thus a large expansion of around $\log_2 q$ for typical parameters. This is particularly problematic in settings in which q is large (i.e., superpolynomial), e.g., [38].[6]

Our Basic Lossy Trapdoor Function. We first borrow an idea that has been used in the context of dual-mode commitments [16] (and later found use also in lossy encryption schemes [27,45]). In a nutshell, we can convert any publicly re-randomizable encryption scheme $(\mathsf{Gen}, \mathsf{Enc}, \mathsf{Dec})$ into a lossy commitment or encryption scheme as follows. The public key is $pk = (c_0 = \mathsf{Enc}(0), c_1 = \mathsf{Enc}(1))$, and to encrypt a message $b \in \{0, 1\}$, we simply output a re-randomized version of c_b. This yields a fresh encryption of b, which Dec can decrypt as usual. Lossy (public) keys are of the form $pk' = (c_0 = \mathsf{Enc}(0), c_1 = \mathsf{Enc}(0))$, such that encryptions are *always* fresh 0-encryptions.

This trick easily scales to larger message spaces when assuming (additively) homomorphic encryption. For instance, we can publish $pk = c_1 = \mathsf{Enc}(1)$ and compute a fresh encryption of any M homomorphically (as a re-randomized version of $M \cdot c_1$). In our setting, we can implement the encryption scheme $(\mathsf{Gen}, \mathsf{Enc}, \mathsf{Dec})$ with a dual version of Regev's encryption (as done in [45]), and omit the final re-randomization step. This yields a deterministic encryption scheme, which we can immediately interpret as a lossy trapdoor function.[7]

After resolving a few technical obstacles[8], we obtain the following scheme. Injective keys are of the form

$$ek = \mathbf{C} = \mathbf{AS} + \mathbf{E} + \mathbf{G}$$

for suitably-sized uniform $\mathbf{A}$, short $\mathbf{E}$, and the "gadget matrix" $\mathbf{G}$ from [40]. For this overview, it is only important that $\mathbf{G}$ allows for an efficiently computable "bit

[6] It is tempting to rely on $\mathbf{e}$ (and not $\mathbf{s}$) as a means to transport information. In particular, making $\mathfrak{D}$ larger improves expansion (since preimages carry more information). However, at least with the arguments above, we can only argue that information about $\mathbf{s}$ (not $\mathbf{e}$) is lost in lossy mode, i.e., with $\mathbf{A}' = \mathbf{BD} + \mathbf{E}$. Hence, making $\mathfrak{D}$ larger improves expansion, but at the same time hurts (relative) lossiness.

[7] This is similar to [29], who interpret lossy encryption schemes as lossy trapdoor functions (by deriving encryption random coins deterministically from the encrypted message). Our setting is considerably simpler, however, since our final encryption scheme is deterministic.

[8] For instance, in (dual) Regev encryption, noise terms in ciphertexts grow with homomorphic computations. This is a problem with large factors M as above, but can be avoided by the use of a "gadget matrix" [40]. Furthermore, we are using a more economic, "batched" version of (dual) Regev encryption as with [2].

decomposition" operation $\mathbf{G}^{-1} : \mathbb{Z}_q^m \to \{0,1\}^{m\lceil \log_2 q \rceil}$ that satisfies $\mathbf{G} \cdot \mathbf{G}^{-1}(\mathbf{z}) = \mathbf{z}$ for all $\mathbf{z}$.

This $\mathbf{C}$ can be viewed as an economic dual-Regev encryption of $\mathbf{G}$. In this context, it is also helpful to point out that $\mathbf{S}$ will be a "very flat" matrix (with many more columns than rows). Together with the fact that $\mathbf{E}$ is short (i.e., has a small norm), this means that the encryption randomness in this encryption is much smaller (in, say, overall bitsize) than the encrypted message. In the upcoming lossiness analysis, this will be crucial and enable an argument similar to the one in [29].

In order to evaluate the resulting LTF g_{ek} on an input $\mathbf{x}$, we encode $\mathbf{x}$ as $\tilde{\mathbf{x}} = \begin{pmatrix} \mathbf{0} \\ c \cdot \mathbf{x} \end{pmatrix}$ for a suitable constant c and then simply compute

$$g_{ek}(\mathbf{x}) = \mathbf{C} \cdot \mathbf{G}^{-1}(\tilde{\mathbf{x}}) = \mathbf{A}\left(\mathbf{S} \cdot \mathbf{G}^{-1}(\tilde{\mathbf{x}})\right) + \mathbf{E} \cdot \mathbf{G}^{-1}(\tilde{\mathbf{x}}) + \tilde{\mathbf{x}}.$$

This is an economic dual-Regev encryption of $\mathbf{x}$ from which $\mathbf{x}$ can be retrieved using a decryption key (that incorporates trapdoor information about $\mathbf{A}$). This evaluation can also be viewed as a variant of the LWE-based LTF from [46], however with a different encoding $\tilde{\mathbf{x}}$ of inputs. This encoding, along with its "flattening" $\mathbf{G}^{-1}(\tilde{\mathbf{x}})$, essentially allows to use a [46]-like evaluation strategy on non-short input vectors $\mathbf{x}$ while containing noise growth.

Lossy keys, however, are of the form

$$ek' = \mathbf{C}' = \mathbf{AS} + \mathbf{E},$$

and their indistinguishability from injective keys readily follows from LWE. When evaluating $g_{ek'}$ with such lossy keys ek', we obtain

$$g_{ek'}(\mathbf{x}) = \mathbf{C} \cdot \mathbf{G}^{-1}(\tilde{\mathbf{x}}) = \mathbf{A}\left(\mathbf{S} \cdot \mathbf{G}^{-1}(\tilde{\mathbf{x}})\right) + \mathbf{E} \cdot \mathbf{G}^{-1}(\tilde{\mathbf{x}}),$$

which leaks information about $\mathbf{x}$ only through the terms $\mathbf{S} \cdot \mathbf{G}^{-1}(\tilde{\mathbf{x}})$ and $\mathbf{E} \cdot \mathbf{G}^{-1}(\tilde{\mathbf{x}})$. But the former of these terms will be a vector that has much fewer entries than $\mathbf{x}$ (due to the "very flat" nature of $\mathbf{S}$), and the latter term is a small-norm vector. A careful analysis (in Sect. 3 and Appendix B) will indeed show that any constant relative lossiness $L < 1$ (with constant expansion) can be achieved by setting q, n, m up as suitable polynomials in the security parameter. Larger values of q enable a relative lossiness even closer to 1 (see Appendix B for details), which also implies quantitative improvements for certain LTF applications (see [47]).

Extension to All-But-Many Lossy Trapdoor Functions. We will now sketch how to use methods from [12,38] to convert our LTF into an "all-but-many LTF" (ABM-LTF). In a nutshell, ABM-LTFs are *tagged* LTFs (i.e., LTFs in which evaluation also takes as input a tag t) that are lossy or injective depending on that tag. It should be hard to generate lossy tags without a trapdoor, while it should be easy to publicly sample injective tags.[9]

[9] Moreover, random tags should be injective with high probability, and it should even be possible to explain any tag (injective or not) as having been randomly sampled.

Tags will be of the form $t = (t_c, t_a)$ with a core part t_c and an auxiliary part t_a, and will be lossy if and only if $t_c = F_K(t_a)$ for a pseudorandom function (PRF) F with a key $K = (K_i)_{i=1}^{\lambda} \in \{0,1\}^\lambda$ that is encrypted (bit-wise) in the LTF overall key. More specifically, our ABM-LTF evaluation key will be of the form

$$ek = (\mathbf{C}_i)_{i=1}^{\lambda} = (\mathbf{A}\mathbf{S}_i + \mathbf{E}_i + K_i \cdot \mathbf{G})_{i=1}^{\lambda},$$

i.e., consist of bit-wise encryptions (with independent $\mathbf{S}_i, \mathbf{E}_i$) of the bits of K. We have chosen to encrypt the K_i in this wasteful fashion to enable fully homomorphic computations with the K_i. In fact, these encryptions can be viewed as ciphertexts of the "dual GSW" fully homomorphic encryption scheme [24,39]. Hence, we can publicly derive ciphertexts that encrypt the result of the binary "test" function $T(K,t)$ with $T(K,(t_c,t_a)) = 0$ if and only if $t_c = F_K(t_a)$ (and $T(K,(t_c,t_a)) = 1$ otherwise).

To evaluate this ABM-LTF on a tag $t = (t_c, t_a)$ and input $\mathbf{x}$, we first (deterministically, using fully homomorphic operations) compute a ciphertext

$$\mathbf{C}_t = \mathbf{A}\mathbf{S}_t + \mathbf{E}_t + T(K,t) \cdot \mathbf{G}$$

and then evaluate $g_{ek,t}(x) = \mathbf{C}_t \cdot \mathbf{G}^{-1}(\tilde{\mathbf{x}})$ for $\tilde{\mathbf{x}} = \begin{pmatrix} \mathbf{0} \\ c \cdot \mathbf{x} \end{pmatrix}$, as with our LTF. Observe that random tags (t_c, t_a) lead to injective LTF keys, and lossy tags (of the form $(F_K(t_a), t_a)$) can be generated using the PRF key K as trapdoor.

We provide full details in Sect. 4.

Achieving Selective-Opening Security. Plugging both our LTF and ABM-LTF above in the construction of [32], however, yields the first SO-CCA secure encryption scheme with constant ciphertext expansion. We provide a full analysis in Sect. 5. Since the lossiness of our ABM-LTF is significantly larger than that of the (similarly LWE-based) ABM-LTFs from [12,38], we end up with a conceptually simpler encryption scheme.[10] As a side note, we also identify and fix a minor problem in the original SO-CCA security proof of [32] (which is also inherited by [12,38]) along the way, see Sect. 5, "Mending a gap in [32]". We admit that while the resulting scheme significantly improves in efficiency upon [12,38], it is still not overly practical. Like [12,38], we rely on FHE computations, and the resulting ciphertext expansion is constant but still considerably larger than the (moderate) expansion of the involved LTF and ABM-LTF (see Appendix B for a detailed and more quantitative discussion). However, we also believe that our ideas may open the door to further improvements, e.g., for more efficient transformations from LTFs to ABM-LTFs.

[10] For instance, the treatment of leakage through noise terms in [38] is quite involved, which causes also a more complex construction. In our case, the involved error terms leak little information (relative to the ABM-LTF input), and we can afford a simpler construction and analysis.

2 Preliminaries

2.1 Notation

We denote by $x \xleftarrow{\$} \mathfrak{D}$ for a distribution $\mathfrak{D}$ that x is sampled at random according to $\mathfrak{D}$. For a set X we denote by $x \xleftarrow{\$} X$ that x is sampled uniformly at random from X. We denote by $x := y$ that x is deterministically assigned the value y.

For a vector $\mathbf{x} = (x_1, \ldots, x_n) \in \mathbb{Z}^n$ and $c \geq 0$, we use the following notation:

$$\mathbf{x} \text{ div } c := \left(\left\lfloor \frac{x_1}{c} \right\rceil, \ldots, \left\lfloor \frac{x_n}{c} \right\rceil \right),$$

where $\lfloor \frac{x_i}{c} \rceil := \lfloor \frac{x_i}{c} + \frac{1}{2} \rfloor$.

Definition 1 (Infinity-Norm). *Let $\mathbf{x} = (x_1, \ldots, x_n)^\top \in \mathbb{R}^n$ and $\mathbf{A} \in \mathbb{R}^{m \times n}$. The ∞-**norm** of $\mathbf{x}$ is given by $||\mathbf{x}||_\infty := \max_{i \in [n]} |x_i|$. The corresponding operator norm of $\mathbf{A}$ is given by $||\mathbf{A}||_\infty := \max_{\substack{\mathbf{x} \in \mathbb{R}^n \\ \mathbf{x} \neq 0}} \frac{||\mathbf{A}\mathbf{x}||_\infty}{||\mathbf{x}||_\infty}$.*

Proposition 1 ([26]). *For $\mathbf{A} = (a_{i,j})_{i,j} \in \mathbb{R}^{m \times n}$, $||\mathbf{A}||_\infty = \max_{i \in [m]} \sum_{j=1}^{n} |a_{i,j}|$.*

In particular, if $\mathbf{A} \in \{-1, 0, 1\}^{m \times n}$, we get $||\mathbf{A}||_\infty \leq n$.

Further, we have $||\mathbf{A}^T||_\infty \leq m \cdot ||\mathbf{A}||_\infty$ for any matrix $\mathbf{A} \in \mathbb{R}^{m \times n}$.

Definition 2 (Discrete Gaussian Distribution). *For $\mathbf{x} \in \mathbb{R}^m$ and $\sigma > 0$, set $\rho_\sigma(\mathbf{x}) := \exp\left(-\pi \cdot ||\mathbf{x}||_2^2 \cdot \sigma^{-2}\right)$. Then, the series $\rho_\sigma(\mathbb{Z}^m) = \sum_{\mathbf{x} \in \mathbb{Z}^m} \rho_\sigma(\mathbf{x})$ converges.*

*The **discrete Gaussian distribution** D_σ^m with deviation σ is the probability distribution over $\mathbb{Z}^m$ that assigns to each integer vector $\mathbf{x}$ the probability $D_\sigma^m(\mathbf{x}) := \rho_\sigma(\mathbf{x}) / \rho_\sigma(\mathbb{Z}^m)$.*

Remark 1. D_σ^m is subgaussian with parameter σ. For each $t > 0$, we have

$$\Pr_{\mathbf{e} \xleftarrow{\$} D_\sigma^m} [||\mathbf{e}||_\infty > t] \leq 2m \cdot \exp\left(-\pi \frac{t^2}{\sigma^2}\right).$$

Further, we have for each $t > 0$

$$\Pr_{\mathbf{E} \xleftarrow{\$} D_\sigma^{m \times N}} [||\mathbf{E}||_\infty > N \cdot t] \leq 2mN \cdot \exp\left(-\pi \frac{t^2}{\sigma^2}\right).$$

By setting $t = \sqrt{\lambda} \cdot \sigma$, we therefore get

$$\Pr_{\mathbf{E} \xleftarrow{\$} D_\sigma^{m \times N}} \left[||\mathbf{E}||_\infty > \sqrt{\lambda} \cdot \sigma \cdot N\right] \leq 2mN \cdot \exp(-\pi \cdot \lambda).$$

2.2 LWE-Based Trapdoors

Definition 3 (Decisional Learning With Errors Assumption). *Let* $n \in \mathbb{N}, m \in \mathsf{poly}(n)$ *and* $q = q(n) \in \mathbb{N}, \alpha = \alpha(n) \in (0,1)$. *The* ***decisional learning with errors assumption*** $\mathsf{LWE}_{n,q,\alpha,m}$ *states that the advantage of each PPT adversary in distinguishing the matrix distributions*

$$(\mathbf{A},\mathbf{b}) \text{ and } (\mathbf{A},\mathbf{A}\mathbf{s}+\mathbf{e} \mod q),$$

for $\mathbf{A} \xleftarrow{\$} \mathbb{Z}_q^{m\times n}, \mathbf{s} \xleftarrow{\$} \mathbb{Z}_q^n, \mathbf{e} \xleftarrow{\$} D_{\alpha q}^m, \mathbf{b} \xleftarrow{\$} \mathbb{Z}_q^m$, *is negligible in* n. *Given an adversary* $\mathcal{A}$, *we denote by* $\mathsf{Adv}_{\mathsf{LWE},\mathcal{A}}^{n,q,\alpha,m}(\lambda)$ *its advantage in distinguishing LWE samples from uniformly random matrices i.e.*

$$\mathsf{Adv}_{\mathsf{LWE},\mathcal{A}}^{n,q,\alpha,m}(\lambda) := \Bigg| \Pr_{\mathbf{A}\xleftarrow{\$}\mathbb{Z}_q^{m\times n},\mathbf{b}\xleftarrow{\$}\mathbb{Z}_q^m}[\mathcal{A}(\mathbf{A},\mathbf{b})=1] - \Pr_{\mathbf{A}\xleftarrow{\$}\mathbb{Z}_q^{m\times n},\mathbf{s}\xleftarrow{\$}\mathbb{Z}_q^n,\mathbf{e}\xleftarrow{\$}D_{\alpha q}^m}[\mathcal{A}(\mathbf{A},\mathbf{A}\mathbf{s}+\mathbf{e} \bmod q)=1]\Bigg|.$$

Definition 4 (Gadget Matrix). *Let* $n, q \in \mathbb{N}$. *By* $\mathbf{G}_{n,q} \in \mathbb{Z}_q^{n\times(n\cdot\lceil\log_2 q\rceil)}$ *we denote the* ***gadget matrix*** *(for* n *and* q*) that is given by*

$$\mathbf{G}_{n,q} = \begin{pmatrix} 1\,2\,\ldots\,2^{\lceil\log_2 q\rceil-1} & & & \\ & 1\,2\,\ldots\,2^{\lceil\log_2 q\rceil-1} & & \\ & & \ddots & \\ & & & 1\,2\,\ldots\,2^{\lceil\log_2 q\rceil-1} \end{pmatrix}.$$

Since each number $a \in \{0,\ldots,q-1\}$ *has a binary decomposition* $a = b_0\cdot 1 + b_1\cdot 2 + \ldots + b_{\lceil\log_2 q\rceil-1}\cdot 2^{\lceil\log_2 q\rceil-1}$ *over the integers, for each* $\mathbf{y}\in\mathbb{Z}_q^n$ *there is a binary vector* $\mathbf{x}\in\{0,1\}^{n\cdot\lceil\log_2 q\rceil}$ *s.t.*

$$\mathbf{y} = \mathbf{G}_{n,q}\cdot\mathbf{x}.$$

This vector $\mathbf{x}$ *is uniquely determined by* $\mathbf{y}$ *and we set* $\mathbf{G}_{n,q}^{-1}(\mathbf{y}) := \mathbf{x}$. *Given* $\mathbf{y}$, $\mathbf{G}_{n,q}^{-1}(\mathbf{y})$ *can be computed efficiently. If* $\mathbf{B} = (\mathbf{b}_1|\ldots|\mathbf{b}_N)$ *is an* $m\times N$*-matrix, then we define* $\mathbf{G}_{n,q}^{-1}(\mathbf{B})$ *as*

$$\mathbf{G}_{n,q}^{-1}(\mathbf{B}) = (\mathbf{G}_{n,q}^{-1}(\mathbf{b}_1)|\ldots|\mathbf{G}_{n,q}^{-1}(\mathbf{b}_N)) \in \{0,1\}^{\lceil\log_2 q\rceil m\times N}.$$

In general, we will omit the subscripts n, q *and simply write* $\mathbf{G}$ *and* $\mathbf{G}^{-1}$ *instead of* $\mathbf{G}_{n,q}$ *and* $\mathbf{G}_{n,q}^{-1}$ *when* n, q *can be deduced from the current context.*

Lemma 1. *Let* $n, q\in\mathbb{N}$ *with* $q \geq 8$. *For each* $\mathbf{y}\in\mathbb{Z}_q^{n\cdot\lceil\log_2 q\rceil}$, *there is at most one pair* $(\mathbf{s},\mathbf{e})\in\mathbb{Z}_q^n\times\mathbb{Z}^{n\cdot\lceil\log_2 q\rceil}$ *with* $||\mathbf{e}||_\infty < \frac{q}{2\cdot\lceil\log_2 q\rceil}$ *s.t.*

$$\mathbf{y} = \mathbf{G}^T\mathbf{s}+\mathbf{e} \mod q.$$

There is a PPT algorithm that, given $\mathbf{y}\in\mathbb{Z}_q^{n\cdot\lceil\log_2 q\rceil}$, *can output such a pair* $(\mathbf{s},\mathbf{e})$ *if it exists.*

A proof of Lemma 1 is given in [40]. Additionally, a proof can be found in Appendix A.1.

Definition 5 (Trapdoor Sampling and Inversion). *Let $\mathfrak{R}$ be the distribution over $\{-1, 0, +1\}$ that draws $b_1, b_2 \xleftarrow{\$} \{0, 1\}$ and outputs $b_1 - b_2$.*

The LWE-based trapdoor scheme of Micciancio & Peikert [40] works as follows:

GenTrap: *Given numbers $n, \overline{u}, q \in \mathbb{N}$,* GenTrap *sets $w := n\lceil\log_2 q\rceil$ and $u := \overline{u}+w$. It samples $\overline{\mathbf{B}} \xleftarrow{\$} \mathbb{Z}_q^{\overline{u}\times n}$, $\mathbf{R} \xleftarrow{\$} \mathfrak{R}^{w\times\overline{u}}$ and outputs the trapdoor $\mathbf{R}$ and the $u \times n$-matrix*

$$\mathbf{B} := \begin{pmatrix} \overline{\mathbf{B}} \\ \mathbf{G}_{n,q}^T - \mathbf{R}\overline{\mathbf{B}} \end{pmatrix} = \begin{pmatrix} \mathbf{I}_{\overline{u}} & \mathbf{0} \\ -\mathbf{R} & \mathbf{G}_{n,q}^T \end{pmatrix} \cdot \begin{pmatrix} \overline{\mathbf{B}} \\ \mathbf{I}_n \end{pmatrix} \mod q.$$

Eval: *Given $\mathbf{B} \in \mathbb{Z}_q^{u\times n}, \mathbf{s} \in \mathbb{Z}_q^n$ and $\mathbf{e} \in \mathbb{Z}^u$,* Eval *outputs*

$$\mathbf{y} := \mathbf{B}\mathbf{s} + \mathbf{e} \mod q.$$

Invert: *Given $\mathbf{B} \in \mathbb{Z}_q^{u\times n}, \mathbf{y} \in \mathbb{Z}_q^u$ and a trapdoor $\mathbf{R} \in \{-1, 0, 1\}^{w\times\overline{u}}$,* Invert *computes*

$$\widehat{\mathbf{y}} := \begin{pmatrix} \mathbf{R} & \mathbf{I}_w \end{pmatrix} \cdot \mathbf{y} \mod q.$$

It uses the algorithm of Lemma 1 to find $\widehat{\mathbf{s}} \in \mathbb{Z}_q^n$ and $\widehat{\mathbf{e}} \in \mathbb{Z}^w$ s.t.

$$\widehat{\mathbf{y}} = \mathbf{G}^T \cdot \widehat{\mathbf{s}} + \widehat{\mathbf{e}} \mod q$$

and outputs

$$\mathbf{s} := \widehat{\mathbf{s}} \text{ and } \mathbf{e} = \mathbf{y} - \mathbf{B}\mathbf{s} \mod q.$$

Lemma 2. *Let $n, \overline{u}, q \in \mathbb{N}$. Set $w := n\lceil\log_2 q\rceil$ and $u := \overline{u} + w$.*

1. *For $(\mathbf{R}, \mathbf{B}) \xleftarrow{\$}$ GenTrap$(n, \overline{u}, q)$, the statistical distance of $\mathbf{B}$ and $U(\mathbb{Z}_q^{u\times n})$ is bounded by $\leq \frac{w}{2}\sqrt{q^n/2^{\overline{u}}}$.*
   If we have $\overline{u} \geq w + 2(n + \log_2(w) - 1)$, then the statistical distance is $\leq 2^{-n}$.
2. *For each $\mathbf{R} \in \{-1, 0, 1\}^{w\times\overline{u}}$, we have $||\mathbf{R}||_\infty \leq \overline{u}$.*
3. *Let $\mathbf{s} \in \mathbb{Z}_q^n, \mathbf{e} \in \mathbb{Z}^u$ and $(\mathbf{R}, \mathbf{B}) \xleftarrow{\$}$ GenTrap$(n, \overline{u}, q)$. The algorithm* Invert$(\mathbf{B}, \mathbf{B}\mathbf{s} + \mathbf{e} \bmod q, \mathbf{R})$ *computes $(\mathbf{s}, \mathbf{e})$ if*

$$||\mathbf{e}||_\infty < \frac{q}{2 \cdot \log_2(q) \cdot (\overline{u} + 1)}.$$

Proof. The first claim follows from the Leftover Hash Lemma for matrices. The second point is a consequence of Proposition 1, and the last point follows from Lemma 1. A more detailed proof of the first claim can be found in [40].

2.3 Fully Homomorphic Encryption from Lattices

Lemma 3 (Barrington's Theorem). *Let $C : \{0,1\}^\eta \to \{0,1\}$ be a circuit of depth d that only consists of "NAND" gates. Then, there is a branching program of length 4^d that computes the same functionality as C. I.e., there is a function $\iota : [4^d] \to [\eta]$ and permutations $\sigma_{i,j} \in S_5, i \in [4^d], j \in \{0,1\}$, s.t. we have for each $\mathbf{x} \in \{0,1\}^\eta$*

$$C(x_1, \ldots, x_\eta) = 1 \iff \sigma_{4^d, x_{\iota(4^d)}} \circ \cdots \circ \sigma_{1, x_{\iota(1)}}(1) = 1.$$

There is a polynomial time algorithm that – given a description of C – outputs ι and $(\sigma_{i,j})_{i \in [4^d], j \in \{0,1\}}$.

We will now introduce a fully homomorphic encryption (FHE) scheme that is mainly known as *dual GSW* [24,39]. However, we note that the dual GSW FHE scheme is actually very close to the FHE scheme of Brakerski & Vaikuntanathan [14] (up to applications of the inverse of the gadget matrix).

We will in the following only describe the encryption and the homomorphic evaluation algorithm of the dual GSW FHE scheme (since we will not need the key generation and decryption algorithm for our lossy trapdoor functions).

Definition 6 (Dual GSW FHE). *Let $q, n, m \in \mathbb{N}$ and $\alpha > 0$. Set $N := m \cdot \lceil \log_2 q \rceil$. The dual GSW FHE scheme consists of the following two algorithms:*

FHE.Enc: *Given a public key $\mathbf{A} \in \mathbb{Z}_q^{m \times n}$ and a message $\mu \in \{0,1\}$,* FHE.Enc *samples $\mathbf{E} \xleftarrow{\$} D_{\alpha q}^{m \times N}$, $\mathbf{S} \xleftarrow{\$} \mathbb{Z}_q^{n \times N}$ and outputs the ciphertext*

$$\mathbf{C} := \mathbf{A}\mathbf{S} + \mathbf{E} + \mu \mathbf{G} \mod q \in \mathbb{Z}_q^{m \times N}.$$

FHE.Eval: *We first describe how* FHE.Eval *evaluates negations, additions and multiplications:*

Negations: FHE.Eval *negates the message of a ciphertext $\mathbf{C}_\mu \in \mathbb{Z}_q^{m \times N}$ by computing*

$$\mathbf{C}_{\neg\mu} := \mathbf{G} - \mathbf{C}_\mu \mod q.$$

Additions: *Given two ciphertexts $\mathbf{C}_{\mu_1}, \mathbf{C}_{\mu_2} \in \mathbb{Z}_q^{m \times N}$,* FHE.Eval *adds their messages by*

$$\mathbf{C}_{\mu_1 + \mu_2} := \mathbf{C}_{\mu_1} + \mathbf{C}_{\mu_2} \mod q.$$

Multiplications: *Given two ciphertexts $\mathbf{C}_{\mu_1}, \mathbf{C}_{\mu_2} \in \mathbb{Z}_q^{m \times N}$,* FHE.Eval *multiplies their messages by*

$$\mathbf{C}_{\mu_1 \cdot \mu_2} := \mathbf{C}_{\mu_1} \cdot \mathbf{G}^{-1}(\mathbf{C}_{\mu_2}) \mod q$$

where $\mathbf{G}^{-1}(\mathbf{B})$ of an $m \times N$-matrix $\mathbf{B} = (\mathbf{b}_1 | \ldots | \mathbf{b}_N)$ is the binary $N \times N$-matrix

$$\mathbf{G}^{-1}(\mathbf{B}) = (\mathbf{G}^{-1}(\mathbf{b}_1) | \ldots | \mathbf{G}^{-1}(\mathbf{b}_N)).$$

If FHE.Eval *is given* η *input ciphertexts* $\mathbf{C}_1, \ldots, \mathbf{C}_\eta$ *and a circuit* $C : \{0,1\}^\eta \rightarrow \{0,1\}$ *of depth* d *that only consists of "NAND" gates, then* FHE.Eval *converts* C *to a branching program of length* $4d$*, which is described by a function* $\iota : [4^d] \rightarrow [\eta]$ *and permutations* $\sigma_{i,\mu} \in S_5, i \in [4d], \mu \in \{0,1\}$ *(see Lemma 3). For* $i, j \in [5]$*,* FHE.Eval *sets*

$$\mathbf{Q}_{i,j}^{(0)} := \begin{cases} \mathbf{G}_{m,q}, & \text{if } i = j, \\ \mathbf{0} \in \mathbb{Z}_q^{m \times N}, & \text{if } i \neq j. \end{cases}$$

Additionally, it computes negations $\mathbf{C}_{\neg i} := \mathbf{G} - \mathbf{C}_i$ *of the inputs for* $i = 1, \ldots, \eta$*.*
For $h = 1, \ldots, 4^d$ *and* $i, j \in [5]$*,* FHE.Eval *computes* $\mathbf{Q}_{i,j}^{(h)}$ *by setting*

$$\mathbf{Q}_{i,j}^{(h)} := \mathbf{C}_{\iota(h)} \cdot \mathbf{G}^{-1}\left(\mathbf{Q}^{(h-1)}_{\sigma_{h,1}^{-1}(i),j}\right) + \mathbf{C}_{\neg\iota(h)} \cdot \mathbf{G}^{-1}\left(\mathbf{Q}^{(h-1)}_{\sigma_{h,0}^{-1}(i),j}\right).$$

Finally, it outputs the result

$$\mathsf{FHE.Eval}(C, \mathbf{C}_1, \ldots, \mathbf{C}_\eta) := \mathbf{Q}_{1,1}^{(4^d)}.$$

Similar to Brakerski & Vaikuntanathan [14], we define the **noise** *of an* $m \times N$*-matrix* $\mathbf{C} \in \mathbb{Z}_q^{m \times N}$ *under a public key* $\mathbf{A} \in \mathbb{Z}_q^{m \times n}$ *and a message* $\mu \in \{0,1\}$ *by*

$$\mathsf{noise}_{\mathbf{A},\mu}(\mathbf{C}) := \min\left\{ ||\mathbf{C} - \mathbf{AS} - \mu\mathbf{G} \mod q||_\infty \mid \mathbf{S} \in \mathbb{Z}_q^{n \times N} \right\}$$

where we interpret $\mathbf{C} - \mathbf{AS} - \mu\mathbf{G} \mod q$ *as a real matrix in* $[\frac{-q}{2}, \frac{q}{2})^{m \times N}$*.*

Remark 2. Note, that we gave the scheme FHE above without a key generation or a decryption algorithm. This is, because we wanted to keep its definition simple and seperate it from Definition 5.

In our ABM-LTF scheme, we will use the algorithm GenTrap to generate the matrix $\mathbf{A}$ as a public key for FHE together with the trapdoor $\mathbf{R}$ as secret key. In fact, by using GenTrap for key generation, we get a full encryption scheme:

If $\overline{u} \geq w + 2(n + \log_2(w) - 1)$, $\mathbf{A}$ is close to a uniformly random matrix and the ciphertexts of FHE are indistinguishable from random as we will show in the next lemma. Further, with the trapdoor $\mathbf{R}$ it is possible to decrypt a given ciphertext with sufficiently small noise (we show this in Lemma 5 that can be found in Appendix A.2.).

Lemma 4. *Let* $q, n, m \in \mathbb{N}$ *and* $\alpha > 0$*. Set* $N := m \cdot \lceil \log_2 q \rceil$*.*

1. *For each* $b \in \{0,1\}$*, if* $\mathbf{A} \xleftarrow{\$} \mathbb{Z}_q^{m \times n}$ *is drawn uniformly at random, then for each algorithm* $\mathcal{A}$ *with time complexity* t *there is an LWE-distinguisher* $\mathcal{B}$ *with time complexity* $t + \mathsf{poly}(n, m, \log_2 q)$ *s.t.*

$$\left| \Pr_{\mathbf{C} \xleftarrow{\$} \mathsf{FHE.Enc}(\mathbf{A}, b)}[\mathcal{A}(\mathbf{C}) = 1] - \Pr_{\mathbf{C} \xleftarrow{\$} \mathbb{Z}_q^{m \times N}}[\mathcal{A}(\mathbf{C}) = 1] \right| \leq N \cdot \mathsf{Adv}_{\mathsf{LWE},\mathcal{B}}^{n,q,\alpha,m}(\lambda).$$

2. *Let* $\mathbf{A} \in \mathbb{Z}_q^{m\times n}$*,* $\mu_1, \ldots, \mu_\eta \in \{0,1\}$ *and let* $C : \{0,1\}^\eta \to \{0,1\}$ *be a circuit consisting of "NAND" gates of depth* d*. Let* $\mathbf{C}_1, \ldots, \mathbf{C}_\eta \in \mathbb{Z}_q^{m\times N}$ *and compute*

$$\mathbf{C} := \mathsf{FHE.Eval}(C, \mathbf{C}_1, \ldots, \mathbf{C}_\eta).$$

We have

$$\mathsf{noise}_{\mathbf{A},C(\mu_1,\ldots,\mu_\eta)}(\mathbf{C}) \leq 2 \cdot 4^d \cdot N \cdot \max_{i\in[\eta]} (\mathsf{noise}_{\mathbf{A},\mu_i}(\mathbf{C}_i)) .$$

We will give a proof of this lemma in Appendix A.2.

2.4 Lossy Trapdoor Functions

Definition 7 (Lossy trapdoor function). *A* lossy trapdoor function *(LTF)* LTF *with domain* $\mathcal{D}$ *and range* $\mathcal{RG}$ *consists of the following algorithms:*

Key generation. $\mathsf{LTF.IGen}(1^\lambda)$ *yields an evaluation key* ek *and an inversion key* ik*.*
Evaluation. $\mathsf{LTF.Eval}(ek, x)$ *(with* $x \in \mathcal{D}$*) yields an image* $y \in \mathcal{RG}$*. Write* $y = f_{ek}(x)$*.*
Inversion. $\mathsf{LTF.Invert}(ik, y)$ *outputs a preimage* x*. Write* $x = f_{ik}^{-1}(y)$*.*
Lossy key generation. $\mathsf{LTF.LGen}(1^\lambda)$ *outputs an evaluation key* ek'*.*

We consider the following properties of LTF*:*

Correctness. *We require for* $(ek, ik) \xleftarrow{\$} \mathsf{LTF.IGen}(1^\lambda)$*,* $x \in \mathcal{D}$*, that* $f_{ik}^{-1}(f_{ek}(x)) = x$ *with all-but-negligible probability over the random coins used by* $\mathsf{LTF.IGen}$*.*
Expansion. *We define the expansion of* LTF *as* $\chi := \log_2 |\mathcal{RG}| / \log_2 |\mathcal{D}|$*.*
Lossiness. *We say that* LTF *is* ℓ*-lossy if for* $ek' \xleftarrow{\$} \mathsf{LTF.LGen}(1^\lambda)$*, with all-but-negligible probability the image set* $f_{ek'}(\mathcal{D})$ *is of size at most* $|\mathcal{D}|/2^\ell$*. We define the relative lossiness as* $L := \ell / \log_2 |\mathcal{D}|$*.*
Indistinguishability. *We require that the first output of* $\mathsf{LTF.IGen}(1^\lambda)$ *is indistinguishable from the output of* $\mathsf{LTF.LGen}(1^\lambda)$*, i.e., for any PPT* $\mathcal{A}$

$$\mathsf{Adv}^{\mathsf{ind}}_{\mathsf{LTF},\mathcal{A}}(\lambda) := \left|\Pr\left[\mathcal{A}(1^\lambda, ek) = 1\right] - \Pr\left[\mathcal{A}(1^\lambda, ek') = 1\right]\right|$$

is negligible, for $(ek, ik) \xleftarrow{\$} \mathsf{LTF.IGen}(1^\lambda)$*,* $ek' \xleftarrow{\$} \mathsf{LTF.LGen}(1^\lambda)$*.*

LTF *is an* ℓ*-lossy LTF with expansion* χ *if it satisfies above properties for* ℓ*,* χ*.*

2.5 All-But-Many Lossy Trapdoor Functions (ABM-LTF)

We recall the definition of All-But-Many Lossy-Trapdoor-Function (ABM-LTF) put forward by Hofheinz [32].

Definition 8 (ABM-LTF [32]). *An* all-but-many lossy trapdoor function ABM *with domain* $\mathcal{D}$ *and range* $\mathcal{RG}$ *consists of four PPT algorithms* ($\mathsf{ABM.Gen}$, $\mathsf{ABM.Eval}$, $\mathsf{ABM.Invert}$, $\mathsf{ABM.LTag}$) *with the following syntax:*

$\mathsf{ABM.Gen}(1^\lambda)$: *On input the security parameter, outputs an evaluation key ek, an inversion key ik, and a tag key tk. The evaluation key ek defines a set* $\mathcal{T} = \mathcal{T}_\mathsf{c} \times \{0,1\}^*$ *that contains the disjoint sets of* lossy tags $\mathcal{T}_\mathsf{loss} \subseteq \mathcal{T}$ *and* injective tags $\mathcal{T}_\mathsf{inj} \subseteq \mathcal{T}$. *Tags are of the form* $t = (t_c, t_a)$, *where* $t_c \in \mathcal{T}_\mathsf{c}$ *is the* core part *of the tag, and* $t_a \in \{0,1\}^*$ *is the* auxiliary part *of the tag.*

$\mathsf{ABM.Eval}(ek, t, x)$: *On input an evaluation key ek, a tag* $t \in \mathcal{T}$ *and a preimage* $x \in \mathcal{D}$, *outputs an image* $y \in \mathcal{RG}$.

$\mathsf{ABM.Invert}(ik, t, y)$: *On input an inversion key ik, a tag* $t \in \mathcal{T}_\mathsf{inj}$ *and an image* y, *outputs a preimage* $x \in \mathcal{D}$.

$\mathsf{ABM.LTag}(tk, t_a)$: *On input the tag key tk and auxiliary part of the tag* $t_a \in \{0,1\}^*$, *outputs a core tag* $t_c \in \mathcal{T}_\mathsf{c}$ *such that the tag* $t := (t_c, t_a) \in \mathcal{T}_\mathsf{loss}$.

We consider the following properties of ABM*:*

Correctness. *We require for* $(ek, ik, tk) \xleftarrow{\$} \mathsf{ABM.Gen}(1^\lambda)$, $t \in \mathcal{T}_\mathsf{inj}$, *and* $x \in \mathcal{D}$ *that with all-but-negligible probability over the choice of the random coins used by* ABM.Gen *we have* $\mathsf{ABM.Invert}(ik, t, (\mathsf{ABM.Eval}(ek, t, x))) = x$.

Expansion. *We define the expansion of* ABM *as* $\chi := \log_2 |\mathcal{RG}| / \log_2 |\mathcal{D}|$.

Lossiness. *We say that* ABM *is* ℓ*-lossy if for* $(ek, ik, tk) \xleftarrow{\$} \mathsf{ABM.Gen}(1^\lambda)$, *and all lossy tags* $t \in \mathcal{T}_\mathsf{loss}$, *with all-but negligible probability the image set* $\{\mathsf{ABM.Eval}(ek, t, x) \mid x \in \mathcal{D}\}$ *is of size at most* $|\mathcal{D}|/2^\ell$. *We define the relative lossiness as* $L := \ell / \log_2 |\mathcal{D}|$.

Indistinguishability. *We require that even multiple lossy tags are indistinguishable from random tags. I.e.,*

$$\mathsf{Adv}^{\mathsf{ind}}_{\mathsf{ABM},\mathcal{A}}(\lambda) := \left| \Pr[\mathcal{A}(1^\lambda, ek)^{\mathsf{ABM.LTag}(tk,\cdot)} = 1] - \Pr[\mathcal{A}(1^\lambda, ek)^{\mathcal{O}_{\mathcal{T}_\mathsf{c}}(\cdot)} = 1] \right|$$

is negligible for all PPT $\mathcal{A}$, *where* $(ek, ik, tk) \xleftarrow{\$} \mathsf{ABM.Gen}(1^\lambda)$, *and* $\mathcal{O}_{\mathcal{T}_\mathsf{c}}(\cdot)$ *returns a uniform and independent core tag* $t_c \xleftarrow{\$} \mathcal{T}_\mathsf{c}$ *at each new query and consistently returns the same* t_c *if given query* t_a *occurs more than once.*

Evasiveness. *We require that non-injective tags are hard to find, even given multiple lossy tags, and an oracle* isLossy *that on input of a tag returns* 1 *if the tag is lossy and* 0 *if not. I.e.,*

$$\mathsf{Adv}^{\mathsf{eva}}_{\mathsf{ABM},\mathcal{A}}(\lambda) := \Pr[\mathcal{A}(1^\lambda, ek)^{\mathsf{ABM.LTag}(tk,\cdot),\mathsf{isLossy}(tk,\cdot)} \in \mathcal{T} \setminus \mathcal{T}_\mathsf{inj}]$$

is negligible with $(ek, ik, tk) \xleftarrow{\$} \mathsf{ABM.Gen}(1^\lambda)$, *and for any PPT algorithm* $\mathcal{A}$ *that never outputs tags obtained through oracle queries (i.e.,* $\mathcal{A}$ *never outputs tags* $t = (t_c, t_a)$, *where* t_c *has been obtained by an oracle query* t_a*).*

ABM *is an* ℓ*-lossy ABM-LTF with expansion* χ *if it satisfies the above properties for* ℓ *and* χ.

For the application of IND-SO-CCA security, we need a slight variant of ABM-LTFs. Concretely, we require that values that are revealed during a ciphertext opening can be explained as uniformly chosen "without ulterior motive," if only their distribution is uniform. (This is called "invertible sampling" by Damgård & Nielsen [15].)

Definition 9 (Efficiently samplable and explainable). *A finite set S is* efficiently samplable and explainable *if any element of S can be explained as the result of a uniform sampling. Formally, there are PPT algorithms* Samp_S, Expl_S, *such that*

1. $\mathsf{Samp}_S(1^\lambda)$ *uniformly samples from S, and*
2. *for any $s \in S$,* $\mathsf{Expl}_S(s)$ *outputs random coins for* Samp *that are uniformly distributed among all random coins R with* $\mathsf{Samp}_S(1^\lambda; R) = s$.

Definition 10 (ABM-LTF with explainable tags [32]). *An ABM-LTF has* explainable tags *if the core part of tags is efficiently samplable and explainable. Formally, if we write $\mathcal{T} = \mathcal{T}_\mathsf{c} \times \mathcal{T}_\mathsf{a}$, where $\mathcal{T}_\mathsf{c}$ and $\mathcal{T}_\mathsf{a}$ denote the core and auxiliary parts of tags, then $\mathcal{T}_\mathsf{c}$ is efficiently samplable and explainable.*

2.6 Lossy Authenticated Encryption

Since the construction by Hofheinz [32] follows a hybrid approach, we require a suitable symmetric encryption scheme (we use the same definition as [32]):

Definition 11 (Lossy authenticated encryption). *A* lossy authenticated encryption scheme $\mathsf{LAE} = (\mathsf{E}, \mathsf{D})$ *with key space $\{0,1\}^{2\kappa}$ and message space $\{0,1\}^\kappa$ for some $\kappa = \kappa(\lambda)$ consists of the following two PPT algorithms:*

Encryption. $\mathsf{E}(K, msg)$, *for a key $K \in \{0,1\}^{2\kappa}$ and a message $msg \in \{0,1\}^\kappa$, outputs a (symmetric) ciphertext* ct.

Decryption. $\mathsf{D}(K, \mathsf{ct})$, *for a key $K \in \{0,1\}^{2\kappa}$ and a (symmetric) ciphertext* ct, *outputs a message $msg \in \{0,1\}^\kappa$ or $\bot$. (In the latter case, we say that* D *rejects* ct.*)*

We require the following:

Correctness. *We have* $\mathsf{D}(K, \mathsf{E}(K, msg)) = msg$ *for all $K \in \{0,1\}^{2\kappa}$ and $msg \in \{0,1\}^\kappa$.*

Authentication. *For an adversary $\mathcal{A}$, we let* $\mathsf{Adv}^{\mathsf{auth}}_{\mathsf{LAE},\mathcal{A}}(\lambda)$ *denote the probability that $\mathcal{A}$ succeeds in the following experiment:*
1. *$\mathcal{A}$, on input 1^λ, chooses a message $msg \in \{0,1\}^\kappa$, and gets an encryption* $\mathsf{ct} = \mathsf{E}(K, msg)$ *of msg under a freshly chosen key $K \xleftarrow{\$} \{0,1\}^{2\kappa}$.*
2. *$\mathcal{A}$ gets (many-time) oracle access to a decryption oracle $\mathsf{D}(K, \cdot)$ with hard-wired key K.*
3. *$\mathcal{A}$ wins iff it manages to submit a decryption query* $\mathsf{ct}' \neq \mathsf{ct}$ *to* D *that is not rejected (i.e., for which* $\mathsf{D}(K, \mathsf{ct}') \neq \bot$*).*

We require that $\mathsf{Adv}^{\mathsf{auth}}_{\mathsf{LAE},\mathcal{A}}(\lambda)$ *is negligible for every PPT $\mathcal{A}$. We say that* LAE *is statistically secure if this holds even for inefficient $\mathcal{A}$.*

Lossiness. *For $msg \in \{0,1\}^\kappa$, let $\mathcal{D}_{msg}$ be the distribution of $\mathsf{E}(K, msg)$ (for random $K \xleftarrow{\$} \{0,1\}^{2\kappa}$). We require that for any two $msg, msg' \in \{0,1\}^\kappa$, the distributions $\mathcal{D}_{msg}$ and $\mathcal{D}_{msg'}$ are identical. (That is, when K is unknown, a ciphertext reveals no information about the plaintext.)*

Statistically secure lossy authenticated encryption schemes exist unconditionally. For instance, if we parse $K = (K_1, K_2) \in (\{0,1\}^\kappa)^2$, we can set $\mathsf{E}(K, msg) = (\rho, \tau) = (msg \oplus K_1, \mathsf{MAC}(K_2, \rho))$ for a message authentication code MAC that is strongly existentially unforgeable under one-time chosen-message attacks.

2.7 Selective Opening Security

We use the following definitions from [32]:

Definition 12 (Efficiently re-samplable). *Let $N = N(\lambda) > 0$, $\kappa = \kappa(\lambda)$, and let* dist *be a joint distribution over* $(\{0,1\}^\kappa)^N$. *We say that* dist *is* efficiently re-samplable *if there is a PPT algorithm* $\mathsf{ReSamp}_{\mathsf{dist}}$ *such that for any $\mathcal{I} \subseteq [N]$ and any partial vector* $\mathbf{msg}'_{\mathcal{I}} := (msg'^{(i)})_{i\in\mathcal{I}} \in (\{0,1\}^\kappa)^{|\mathcal{I}|}$, $\mathsf{ReSamp}_{\mathsf{dist}}(\mathbf{msg}'_{\mathcal{I}})$ *samples from the distribution* dist, *conditioned on $msg^{(i)} = msg'^{(i)}$ for all $i \in \mathcal{I}$.*

We recall the definition of IND-SO-CCA security. In this game, the adversary first gets to specify a distribution from which message vectors will be sampled along with a resampling algorithm. Then it will be provided with a vector of ciphertexts encrypting a vector of messages drawn from the distribution specified earlier. It then selects a set of indices $\mathcal{I}$ to be opened by the challenger (indicated by running the adversary with the input `select`). The challenger opens the indicated ciphertexts (by revealing the random coins used during encryption along with the messages), and either provides the adversary with the initially encrypted message vector, or with a message vector that has been resampled (with the restriction that the opened messages are the same). This phase of the adversary is triggered with the input `output`. The output of this phase is the adversary's decision bit, i.e. whether it believes that the message vector it received is the encrypted one (indicated by 0) or whether it received a resampled vector (indicated by 1). The adversary wins if it guessed correctly.

Definition 13 (IND-SO-CCA security). *A PKE scheme* $\mathsf{PKE} = (\mathsf{PKE.Gen}, \mathsf{PKE.Enc}, \mathsf{PKE.Dec})$ *is* IND-SO-CCA secure *iff for every polynomially bounded functions $N = N(\lambda) > 0$ and $\kappa = \kappa(\lambda)$, and every stateful PPT adversary $\mathcal{A}$, the function*

$$\mathsf{Adv}^{\mathsf{cca\text{-}so}}_{\mathsf{PKE},\mathcal{A}}(\lambda) := \left|\Pr\left[\mathsf{Exp}^{\mathsf{ind\text{-}so\text{-}cca}}_{\mathsf{PKE},\mathcal{A},N}(\lambda) = 1\right] - \frac{1}{2}\right|$$

is negligible. Here, the experiment $\mathsf{Exp}^{\mathsf{ind\text{-}so\text{-}cca}}_{\mathsf{PKE},\mathcal{A},N}(\lambda)$ *is defined as follows:*

Experiment $\mathsf{Exp}^{\mathsf{ind\text{-}so\text{-}cca}}_{\mathsf{PKE},\mathcal{A},N}$
$b \xleftarrow{\$} \{0,1\}$
$(pk, sk) \xleftarrow{\$} \mathsf{PKE.Gen}(1^\lambda)$
$(\mathsf{dist}, \mathsf{ReSamp}_{\mathsf{dist}}) \xleftarrow{\$} \mathcal{A}^{\mathsf{PKE.Dec}(sk,\cdot)}(pk)$
$\mathbf{msg}_0 := (msg^{(i)})_{i\in[N]} \xleftarrow{\$} \mathsf{dist}$
$\mathbf{R} := (R^{(i)})_{i\in[N]} \xleftarrow{\$} (\mathcal{R}_{\mathsf{PKE.Enc}})^N$
$\mathbf{C} := (C^{(i)})_{i\in[N]} := (\mathsf{PKE.Enc}(pk, msg^{(i)}; R^{(i)}))_{i\in[N]}$
$\mathcal{I} \xleftarrow{\$} \mathcal{A}^{\mathsf{PKE.Dec}(sk,\cdot)}(\mathtt{select}, \mathbf{C})$
$\mathbf{msg}_1 := \mathsf{ReSamp}_{\mathsf{dist}}(\mathbf{msg}_{\mathcal{I}})$
$\mathsf{out}[\mathcal{A}] \xleftarrow{\$} \mathcal{A}^{\mathsf{PKE.Dec}(sk,\cdot)}(\mathtt{output}, (msg^{(i)}, R^{(i)})_{i\in\mathcal{I}}, \mathbf{msg}_b)$
return $(\mathsf{out}[\mathcal{A}] = b)$

We only allow adversaries $\mathcal{A}$ that

- *always output efficiently re-samplable distributions* dist *over* $(\{0,1\}^{\kappa})^N$ *with corresponding efficient re-sampling algorithms* $\mathsf{ReSamp}_{\mathsf{dist}}$,
- *never submit a received challenge ciphertext* $C^{(i)}$ *to their decryption oracle* $\mathsf{PKE.Dec}(sk,\cdot)$, *and*
- *always produce binary final output* $\mathsf{out}[\mathcal{A}]$.

3 Lossy Trapdoor Function Construction

In this section, we define our LTF construction which is based on the dual version of Regev's encryption scheme. As discussed in the introduction, injective evaluation keys of our LTF can be seen as economic dual-Regev encryptions of the gadget matrix $\mathbf{G}$ (as defined in Definition 4), while lossy keys are encryptions of 0. The indistinguishability of injective and lossy keys then follows from LWE.

To evaluate our LTF on an input $\mathbf{x}$ under the evaluation key $ek = \mathbf{C}$, one computes $\mathbf{C}\cdot\mathbf{G}^{-1}(\tilde{\mathbf{x}})$, where $\tilde{\mathbf{x}} := \begin{pmatrix}\mathbf{0}\\ c\cdot\mathbf{x}\end{pmatrix}$. Hence, in the injective mode, the image is an encryption of $\tilde{\mathbf{x}}$ (i.e., $\mathbf{A}\cdot\mathbf{s}+\mathbf{e}+\tilde{\mathbf{x}}$ for some $\mathbf{s}$ and small $\mathbf{e}$), and $\mathbf{x}$ can be obtained using the public key $\mathbf{A}$ and its trapdoor. In the lossy mode, in constrast, the image has the form $\mathbf{A}\cdot\mathbf{s}+\mathbf{e}$, where only $\mathbf{s}=\mathbf{S}\cdot\mathbf{G}^{-1}(\tilde{\mathbf{x}})$ and $\mathbf{e}=\mathbf{E}\cdot\mathbf{G}^{-1}(\tilde{\mathbf{x}})$ leak information about $\mathbf{x}$. Now since $\mathbf{S}$ is "very flat" and $\mathbf{E}$ has small norm, we can argue that $\mathbf{A}\cdot\mathbf{s}+\mathbf{e}$ loses a lot of entropy of $\mathbf{x}$.

Although it is natural to think about the evaluation key ek being a dual-Regev ciphertext, it will be more convenient to view ek as a dual-GSW ciphertext (i.e., dual-GSW encryption of 1 in the injective case and dual-GSW encryption of 0 in the lossy case) in the formal LTF description and proofs. Looking ahead to Sect. 4, this view will help us to convert the LTF construction into a ABM-LTF construction, where we make use of the fully homomorphic properties of the dual-GSW encryption scheme.

Let n, m, q and α be the LWE parameters. As in the previous section, we denote $w := n\lceil\log q\rceil$ and $N := m\lceil\log q\rceil$. The domain $\mathcal{D}$ of our LTF is $\mathbb{Z}_p^{\overline{m}}$ with $p<q$ and $\overline{m}<m$; for convenience, let $u := m-\overline{m}$ and $c := \lfloor q/p\rfloor$. Our LTF construction is defined as follows:

$\mathsf{LTF.IGen}(1^{\lambda})$: On input the security parameter, proceed as follows:

1. Define $\mathbf{A} := \begin{pmatrix}\overline{\mathbf{A}}\\ \underline{\mathbf{A}}\end{pmatrix}\in\mathbb{Z}_q^{m\times n}$, where $(\mathbf{R},\overline{\mathbf{A}})\xleftarrow{\$}\mathsf{GenTrap}(n,u-w,q)$ and $\underline{\mathbf{A}}\xleftarrow{\$}\mathbb{Z}_q^{\overline{m}\times n}$.
2. Let $\mathbf{C}$ be the Dual-GSW encryption of 1; that is
   (a) Sample $\mathbf{S}\xleftarrow{\$}\mathbb{Z}_q^{n\times N}$ and $\mathbf{E}\xleftarrow{\$}D_{\alpha q}^{m\times N}$.
   (b) Set $\mathbf{C} := \mathbf{A}\mathbf{S}+\mathbf{E}+\mathbf{G}\in\mathbb{Z}_q^{m\times N}$.
3. Output (ek, ik), where $ek := \mathbf{C}$, $ik := (\mathbf{R},\mathbf{A})$.

$\mathsf{LTF.Eval}(ek,\mathbf{x})$: On input the evaluation key $ek=\mathbf{C}$ and $\mathbf{x}\in\mathbb{Z}_p^{\overline{m}}\subset\mathbb{Z}_q^{\overline{m}}$, output
$$\mathbf{y} := \mathbf{C}\cdot\mathbf{G}^{-1}\begin{pmatrix}\mathbf{0}\\ c\cdot\mathbf{x}\end{pmatrix}\in\mathbb{Z}_q^{m}.$$

$\mathsf{LTF.Invert}(ik,\mathbf{y})$: On input the inversion key ik and image $\mathbf{y}$, proceed as follows:

1. Parse $ik = \left(\mathbf{R}, \mathbf{A} = \begin{pmatrix} \overline{\mathbf{A}} \\ \underline{\mathbf{A}} \end{pmatrix}\right)$, where $\overline{\mathbf{A}} \in \mathbb{Z}_q^{u \times n}$ and $\underline{\mathbf{A}} \in \mathbb{Z}_q^{\overline{m} \times n}$, and $\mathbf{y} = \begin{pmatrix} \overline{\mathbf{y}} \\ \underline{\mathbf{y}} \end{pmatrix}$, where $\overline{\mathbf{y}} \in \mathbb{Z}_q^u$ and $\underline{\mathbf{y}} \in \mathbb{Z}_q^{\overline{m}}$.
2. Compute $(\mathbf{s}, \mathbf{e}) := \mathsf{Invert}(\overline{\mathbf{A}}, \overline{\mathbf{y}}, \mathbf{R})$
3. Output $\mathbf{x} \in \mathbb{Z}_p^{\overline{m}}$ defined as $\mathbf{x} := (\underline{\mathbf{y}} - \underline{\mathbf{A}}\mathbf{s} \bmod q) \operatorname{div} c$.

$\mathsf{LTF.LGen}(1^\lambda)$: On input the security parameter, proceed as follows:
1. Let $\mathbf{A} \xleftarrow{\$} \mathbb{Z}_q^{m \times n}$.
2. Let $\mathbf{C}$ be the Dual-GSW encryption of 0; that is
   (a) Sample $\mathbf{S} \xleftarrow{\$} \mathbb{Z}_q^{n \times N}$ and $\mathbf{E} \xleftarrow{\$} D_{\alpha q}^{m \times N}$.
   (b) Set $\mathbf{C} := \mathbf{A}\mathbf{S} + \mathbf{E} \in \mathbb{Z}_q^{m \times N}$.
3. Output $ek' := \mathbf{C}$.

We now prove that the construction from above is an LTF with constant expansion. For interpretation of the parameter bounds and to see that arbitrary constant relative lossiness can be achieved, we refer to Appendix B.1.

Theorem 1. *Assuming hardness of* $\mathsf{LWE}_{n,q,\alpha,m}$*, the LTF construction* $\mathsf{LTF} = (\mathsf{LTF.IGen}, \mathsf{LTF.Eval}, \mathsf{LTF.Invert}, \mathsf{LTF.LGen})$ *is an* ℓ*-lossy LTF with constant expansion for parameters that satisfy the following constraints:*

$$\log q = O(\log p), \quad m = O(\overline{m}), \quad 2^{-n} = \mathsf{negl}(\lambda), \quad u \geq 2(w + n + \log(w) - 1),$$
$$\alpha < \frac{1}{\sqrt{\lambda} \cdot 2 \cdot N \max\{N, p\}}, \quad \ell = \overline{m} \log(p) - n \log q - m \log(2N\sqrt{\lambda}\alpha q + 1).$$

In particular, for any PPT adversary $\mathcal{A}$*, there exists an LWE-distinguisher* $\mathcal{B}$ *that runs in about the same time as* $\mathcal{A}$*, such that*

$$\mathsf{Adv}^{\mathsf{ind}}_{\mathsf{LTF},\mathcal{A}}(\lambda) \leq 2^{-n} + 2 \cdot N \cdot \mathsf{Adv}^{n,q,\alpha,m}_{\mathsf{LWE},\mathcal{B}}(\lambda).$$

Proof. In the following we prove each property of our ABM-LTF separately.
Constant expansion. Our LTF constructed from Dual-GSW, achieves constant expansion. For $\mathbf{x} \in \mathbb{Z}_p^{\overline{m}}$, we get $\mathbf{y} := \mathsf{LTF.Eval}(ek, \mathbf{x}) \in \mathbb{Z}_q^m$. Hence, the expansion χ can be computed as

$$\chi = \frac{m \cdot \lceil \log q \rceil}{\overline{m} \cdot \lceil \log p \rceil} = \frac{O(\overline{m}) \cdot O(\log p)}{\overline{m} \cdot \lceil \log p \rceil} = O(1).$$

Correctness. Let $(ek, ik) \xleftarrow{\$} \mathsf{LTF.IGen}(1^\lambda)$, $\mathbf{x} \in \mathbb{Z}_p^{\overline{m}}$ and $\mathbf{y} := \mathsf{LTF.Eval}(ek, \mathbf{x})$. We know that $ik = (\mathbf{R}, \mathbf{A})$, where $\mathbf{A} = \begin{pmatrix} \overline{\mathbf{A}} \\ \underline{\mathbf{A}} \end{pmatrix}$, $\mathbf{R}$ is a trapdoor for $\overline{\mathbf{A}}$ and $\mathbf{y}$ can be expressed as

$$\mathbf{y} := \mathbf{C} \cdot \mathbf{G}^{-1} \begin{pmatrix} \mathbf{0} \\ c \cdot \mathbf{x} \end{pmatrix} \mod q,$$

where $\mathbf{C}$ is a Dual-GSW encryption of 1, i.e., $\mathbf{C} = \mathbf{A} \cdot \mathbf{S} + \mathbf{E} + \mathbf{G}$. Setting $\mathbf{s} := \mathbf{S} \cdot \mathbf{G}^{-1}\begin{pmatrix} \mathbf{0} \\ c \cdot \mathbf{x} \end{pmatrix}$ and $\mathbf{e} := \begin{pmatrix} \overline{\mathbf{e}} \\ \underline{\mathbf{e}} \end{pmatrix} := \mathbf{E} \cdot \mathbf{G}^{-1}\begin{pmatrix} \mathbf{0} \\ c \cdot \mathbf{x} \end{pmatrix}$, we can express $\mathbf{y}$ as

$$\mathbf{y} = \begin{pmatrix} \overline{\mathbf{y}} \\ \underline{\mathbf{y}} \end{pmatrix} = \begin{pmatrix} \overline{\mathbf{A}}\mathbf{s} + \overline{\mathbf{e}} \\ \underline{\mathbf{A}}\mathbf{s} + \underline{\mathbf{e}} + c \cdot \mathbf{x} \end{pmatrix} \mod q.$$

Since $\mathbf{G}^{-1}\begin{pmatrix} \mathbf{0} \\ c \cdot \mathbf{x} \end{pmatrix}$ is a binary vector and $\mathbf{E} \xleftarrow{\$} D_{\alpha q}^{m \times N}$, we know that with all-but-negligible probability

$$||\overline{\mathbf{e}}||_\infty \leq ||\mathbf{e}||_\infty \leq ||\mathbf{E}||_\infty \leq N \cdot \sqrt{\lambda} \cdot \alpha q,$$

where the last inequality stems from Remark 1. Hence, by Lemma 2, with all-but-negligible probability $\mathsf{Invert}(\overline{\mathbf{A}}, \overline{\mathbf{y}}, \mathbf{R})$ returns $\mathbf{s}$ and $\overline{\mathbf{e}}$ whenever

$$||\overline{\mathbf{e}}||_\infty \leq N \cdot \sqrt{\lambda} \cdot \alpha q < q/(2 \cdot \log(q) \cdot (u - w + 1)).$$

Having $\mathbf{s}$, and hence $\underline{\mathbf{A}}\mathbf{s}$, one can compute $\mathbf{x}$ from $\underline{\mathbf{y}}$ as

$$(\underline{\mathbf{y}} - \underline{\mathbf{A}}\mathbf{s}) \text{ div } c = (\underline{\mathbf{A}}\mathbf{s} + \underline{\mathbf{e}} + c \cdot \mathbf{x} - \underline{\mathbf{A}}\mathbf{s}) \text{ div } c = (\underline{\mathbf{e}} + c \cdot \mathbf{x}) \text{ div } c = \mathbf{x},$$

where the last equality holds if $||\mathbf{e}||_\infty < c/2$.

Thus, the correctness property is satisfied for any parameters such that

$$N \cdot \sqrt{\lambda} \cdot \alpha q < \min\left\{\frac{q}{2 \cdot \log(q) \cdot (u - w + 1)}, \frac{c}{2}\right\}.$$

Since $N \geq m \log(q) \geq (u - w + 1) \log(q)$, the above inequality is satisfied if

$$\alpha < \min\left\{\frac{1}{\sqrt{\lambda} \cdot 2 \cdot N^2}, \frac{c}{q \cdot \sqrt{\lambda} \cdot 2 \cdot N}\right\} \leq \frac{1}{\sqrt{\lambda} \cdot 2 \cdot N \max\{N, p\}}.$$

Lossiness. In order to show that our LTF construction is ℓ-lossy, we need to prove that for $ek' \xleftarrow{\$} \mathsf{LTF.LGen}(1^\lambda)$, with all-but-negligible probability, the image set $\{\mathsf{LTF.Eval}(ek', \mathbf{x}) \mid \mathbf{x} \in \mathcal{D}\}$ is of size at most $|\mathcal{D}|/2^\ell$.

Let $\mathbf{y}$ be an arbitrary element in $\mathsf{LTF.Eval}(ek', \mathcal{D})$. Since $ek' = \mathbf{C}$ is lossy (i.e., $\mathbf{C} = \mathbf{AS} + \mathbf{E}$), setting $\mathbf{s}$ and $\mathbf{e}$ as in the correctness proof above, we can now express $\mathbf{y}$ as $\mathbf{y} = \mathbf{As} + \mathbf{e} \mod q$. Since $\mathbf{s} \in \mathbb{Z}_q^n$ and $||\mathbf{e}||_\infty \leq ||\mathbf{E}||_\infty \leq N \cdot \sqrt{\lambda} \cdot \alpha q$ with all-but-negligible probability, we obtain

$$|\{\mathsf{LTF.Eval}(ek', \mathbf{x}) \mid \mathbf{x} \in \mathcal{D}\}| \leq q^n \cdot (2 \cdot N \cdot \sqrt{\lambda} \cdot \alpha q + 1)^m$$

with all-but-negligible probability. On the other hand, we have $|\mathcal{D}| = p^{\overline{m}}$. Hence, we obtain ℓ-lossiness if we choose parameters such that

$$q^n \cdot (2 \cdot N \cdot \sqrt{\lambda} \cdot \alpha q + 1)^m \leq \frac{p^{\overline{m}}}{2^\ell}.$$

Indistinguishability. The fact that the first output $ek = \mathbf{AS} + \mathbf{E} + \mathbf{G}$ of $\mathsf{LTF.IGen}(1^\lambda)$ is indistinguishable from the output $ek' = \mathbf{AS}+\mathbf{E}$ of $\mathsf{LTF.LGen}(1^\lambda)$ follows straight-forward from Lemma 2 and the $\mathsf{LWE}_{n,q,\alpha,m}$ assumption. Formally, we can proceed by defining a series of game hops, where we denote by one_i the event that the adversary $\mathcal{A}$ outputs 1 in the i-th game.

Game 1: This is the game, where the adversary $\mathcal{A}$ receives an injective evaluation key ek.

Game 2: The game is defined as Game 1, except that the injective evaluation key ek is generated differently. Concretely, the generation of the matrix $\mathbf{A}$ in step 1 of $\mathsf{LTF.IGen}$ is replaced by sampling $\mathbf{A}$ uniformly at random, i.e., $\mathbf{A} \xleftarrow{\$} \mathbb{Z}_q^{m\times n}$. Since $\mathsf{GenTrap}$ is called with $u-w$ and we assume that $u \geq 2(w+n+\log(w)-1)$, we can apply Lemma 2 to argue that the statistical distance between the matrix $\mathbf{A}$ generated as in Game 1 and matrix $\mathbf{A}$ chosen uniformly at random as in Game 2 is 2^{-n} and hence $|\Pr[\mathsf{one}_2] - \Pr[\mathsf{one}_1]| \leq 2^{-n}$.

Game 3: In this game, the adversary $\mathcal{A}$ receives a uniformly random matrix $\mathbf{C} \xleftarrow{\$} \mathbb{Z}_q^{m\times N}$ instead of an injective evaluation key ek. We have by Lemma 4 $|\Pr[\mathsf{one}_3] - \Pr[\mathsf{one}_2]| \leq N \cdot \mathsf{Adv}_{\mathsf{LWE},\mathcal{B}_1}^{n,q,\alpha,m}(\lambda)$, for an LWE-distinguisher $\mathcal{B}_1$ that runs in about the same time as $\mathcal{A}$.

Game 4: This is the game, where the adversary $\mathcal{A}$ receives a lossy evaluation key ek'. Again, by Lemma 4, we have $|\Pr[\mathsf{one}_4] - \Pr[\mathsf{one}_3]| \leq N \cdot \mathsf{Adv}_{\mathsf{LWE},\mathcal{B}_2}^{n,q,\alpha,m}(\lambda)$, for an LWE-distinguisher $\mathcal{B}_2$ that runs in about the same time as $\mathcal{A}$.

Combining these bounds, we obtain

$$\mathsf{Adv}_{\mathsf{LTF},\mathcal{A}}^{\mathsf{ind}}(\lambda) = |\mathsf{one}_1 - \mathsf{one}_4| \leq 2^{-n} + 2 \cdot N \cdot \mathsf{Adv}_{\mathsf{LWE},\mathcal{B}}^{n,q,\alpha,m}(\lambda)$$

for an LWE-distinguisher $\mathcal{B}$ that runs in about the same time as $\mathcal{A}$.

4 All-But-Many Lossy Trapdoor Function Construction

Using the methods from [12,38], we now convert the LTF construction into an ABM-LTF. That is, our ABM-LTF tags are of the form $t = (t_c, t_a) \in \{0,1\}^\lambda \times \{0,1\}^*$ and are lossy if and only if $t_c = \mathsf{PRF}_K(t_a)$, for a pseudorandom function PRF and key $K \in \{0,1\}^\lambda$. The evaluation key of the ABM-LTF then consists of λ dual-GSW ciphertexts, each of which encrypts one bit of the PRF key K. During ABM-LTF evaluation, we make use of the full homomorphism of the dual-GSW encryption scheme and evaluate the PRF through homomorphic computations on the encrypted key bits.

To this end, we need to assume a PRF family $\mathsf{PRF}\colon \{0,1\}^\lambda \times \{0,1\}^* \to \{0,1\}^\lambda$, such that for each fixed input $t_a \in \{0,1\}^*$, the map $K \mapsto \mathsf{PRF}(K, t_a)$ can be computed by a circuit of NAND-gates of depth $d \in O(\log \lambda)$. We can instantiate such a PRF family using the LWE-based PRF construction of Boneh et al. [11] by first hashing the input using a collision resistant hash function.

The domain $\mathcal{D}$ of our ABM-LTF is the same as for the LTF, namely $\mathbb{Z}_p^{\overline{m}}$ with $p < q$ and $\overline{m} < m$. As in the previous sections, let n, m, q and α be the LWE parameters and let us denote $w = n\lceil \log q\rceil$ and $N = m\lceil \log q\rceil$, $u := m - \overline{m}$ and $c := \lfloor q/p \rfloor$. We define our ABM-LTF as follows:

$\mathsf{ABM.Gen}(1^\lambda)$: On input the security parameter, proceed as follows:

1. Define $\mathbf{A} := \begin{pmatrix} \overline{\mathbf{A}} \\ \underline{\mathbf{A}} \end{pmatrix} \in \mathbb{Z}_q^{m \times n}$, for $(\mathbf{R}, \overline{\mathbf{A}}) \xleftarrow{\$} \mathsf{GenTrap}(n, u - w, q)$ and $\underline{\mathbf{A}} \xleftarrow{\$} \mathbb{Z}_q^{\overline{m} \times n}$.
2. Sample a PRF key $K = (K[i])_{i \in [\lambda]} \xleftarrow{\$} \{0,1\}^\lambda$.
3. For each $i \in [\lambda]$, let $\mathbf{C}_i$ be the Dual-GSW encryption of $K[i]$; that is
   (a) Sample $\mathbf{S}_i \xleftarrow{\$} \mathbb{Z}_q^{n \times N}$ and $\mathbf{E}_i \xleftarrow{\$} D_{\alpha q}^{m \times N}$.
   (b) Set $\mathbf{C}_i := \mathbf{A}\mathbf{S}_i + \mathbf{E}_i + K[i] \cdot \mathbf{G} \in \mathbb{Z}_q^{m \times N}$.
4. Output (ek, ik, tk), where $ek := (\mathbf{C}_i)_{i \in [\lambda]}$, $ik := (\mathbf{R}, \mathbf{A})$, $tk := K$.

The tag space is $\mathcal{T} = \{0,1\}^\lambda \times \{0,1\}^*$, i.e., $\mathcal{T}_\mathsf{c} = \{0,1\}^\lambda$. The lossy tags are $\mathcal{T}_\mathsf{loss} = \{(t_c, t_a) \mid t_c = \mathsf{PRF}_K(t_a)\}$ and injective tags are $\mathcal{T}_\mathsf{inj} = \mathcal{T} \setminus \mathcal{T}_\mathsf{loss}$.

$\mathsf{ABM.LTag}(t_a, K)$: On input an auxiliary tag $t_a \in \{0,1\}^*$ and a PRF key $K \in \{0,1\}^\lambda$, output a core tag $t_c := \mathsf{PRF}_K(t_a)$.

$\mathsf{ABM.Eval}(ek, t, \mathbf{x})$: On input the evaluation key $ek = (\mathbf{C}_i)_{i \in [\lambda]}$, tag $t = (t_c, t_a) \in \mathcal{T}$ and $\mathbf{x} \in \mathbb{Z}_p^{\overline{m}} \subset \mathbb{Z}_q^{\overline{m}}$, proceed as follows

1. Let RC_t be a circuit consisting of "NAND" gates of depth d computing the function $f_\mathsf{RC}(\cdot, t)$ defined as
$$f_\mathsf{RC}(K, t) := \begin{cases} 0, & \text{if } t_c = \mathsf{PRF}_K(t_a), \\ 1, & \text{otherwise.} \end{cases}$$
2. Using the FHE scheme, evaluate RC_t on the PRF key in its encrypted form, i.e., $\mathbf{C}_t \leftarrow \mathsf{FHE.Eval}(\mathsf{RC}_t, (\mathbf{C}_i)_{i \in [\lambda]})$.
3. Output $\mathbf{y} := \mathbf{C}_t \cdot \mathbf{G}_{m,q}^{-1} \begin{pmatrix} \mathbf{0} \\ c \cdot \mathbf{x} \end{pmatrix} \in \mathbb{Z}_q^m$.

$\mathsf{ABM.Invert}(ik, \mathbf{y}, t)$:

1. Parse $ik = \left(\mathbf{R}, \mathbf{A} = \begin{pmatrix} \overline{\mathbf{A}} \\ \underline{\mathbf{A}} \end{pmatrix}\right)$, where $\overline{\mathbf{A}} \in \mathbb{Z}_q^{u \times n}$ and $\underline{\mathbf{A}} \in \mathbb{Z}_q^{\overline{m} \times n}$, $\mathbf{y} = \begin{pmatrix} \overline{\mathbf{y}} \\ \underline{\mathbf{y}} \end{pmatrix}$, where $\overline{\mathbf{y}} \in \mathbb{Z}_q^u$ and $\underline{\mathbf{y}} \in \mathbb{Z}_q^{\overline{m}}$, and $t = (t_c, t_a)$.
2. Compute $(\mathbf{s}_t, \mathbf{e}_t) := \mathsf{Invert}(\overline{\mathbf{A}}, \overline{\mathbf{y}}, \mathbf{R})$.
3. Output $\mathbf{x} \in \mathbb{Z}_p^{\overline{m}}$ defined as $\mathbf{x} := (\underline{\mathbf{y}} - \underline{\mathbf{A}}\mathbf{s}_t \mod q) \text{ div } c$.

We now prove that the construction from above is an ABM-LTF with constant expansion. For interpretation of the parameter bounds and to see that arbitrarily large constant relative lossiness $L := \ell / \log_2 |\mathcal{D}|$ can be achieved, we refer to Appendix B.2.

Theorem 2. *Assuming hardness of* $\mathsf{LWE}_{n,q,\alpha,m}$ *and the security of* PRF, *the construction* $\mathsf{ABM} = (\mathsf{ABM.Gen}, \mathsf{ABM.Eval}, \mathsf{ABM.Invert}, \mathsf{ABM.LTag})$ *is an* ℓ*-lossy ABM-LTF with constant expansion for parameters that satisfy the following constraints:*

$$\log q = O(\log p), \quad m = O(\overline{m}), \quad 2^{-n} = \mathsf{negl}(\lambda), \quad d \in O(\log \lambda),$$
$$\alpha < \frac{1}{\sqrt{\lambda} \cdot 4^{d+1} \cdot N^2 \max\{N, p\}}, \quad u \geq 2(w + n + \log(w) - 1),$$
$$\ell = \overline{m} \log(p) - n \log(q) - m \log(\alpha q \cdot \sqrt{\lambda} \cdot 4^{d+1} \cdot N^2 + 1).$$

In particular, for any PPT adversary $\mathcal{A}_{\mathsf{ind}}$, there exists an LWE-distinguisher $\mathcal{B}$ and a PRF-distinguisher $\mathcal{C}$ that run in about the same time as $\mathcal{A}_{\mathsf{ind}}$, such that

$$\mathsf{Adv}^{\mathsf{ind}}_{\mathsf{ABM},\mathcal{A}_{\mathsf{ind}}}(\lambda) \le 2^{-n+1} + 2 \cdot \lambda \cdot N \cdot \mathsf{Adv}^{n,q,\alpha,m}_{\mathsf{LWE},\mathcal{B}}(\lambda) + \mathsf{Adv}^{\mathsf{ind}}_{\mathsf{PRF},\mathcal{C}}(\lambda),$$

where $\mathsf{Adv}^{\mathsf{ind}}_{\mathsf{PRF},\mathcal{C}}$ denotes the advantage of $\mathcal{C}$ in the PRF security experiment. Moreover, for any PPT adversary $\mathcal{A}_{\mathsf{eva}}$, there exists an LWE-distinguisher $\mathcal{B}$ and a PRF-distinguisher $\mathcal{C}$ that run in about the same time as $\mathcal{A}_{\mathsf{eva}}$, such that

$$\mathsf{Adv}^{\mathsf{eva}}_{\mathsf{ABM},\mathcal{A}_{\mathsf{eva}}}(\lambda) \le 2^{-n} + \lambda \cdot N \cdot \mathsf{Adv}^{n,q,\alpha,m}_{\mathsf{LWE},\mathcal{B}}(\lambda) + \mathsf{Adv}^{\mathsf{ind}}_{\mathsf{PRF},\mathcal{C}}(\lambda) + \frac{Q}{2^\lambda},$$

where Q denotes the number of queries $\mathcal{A}_{\mathsf{eva}}$ made to $\mathsf{isLossy}$ *oracle.*

Proof. The proof of constant expansion is exactly the same as for our LTF construction (see proof of Theorem 1).
Correctness. Let $(ek, ik, tk) \xleftarrow{\$} \mathsf{ABM.Gen}(1^\lambda)$, $t = (t_c, t_a) \in \mathcal{T}_{\mathsf{inj}}$, $\mathbf{x} \in \mathbb{Z}_p^{\overline{m}}$ and $\mathbf{y} := \mathsf{ABM.Eval}(ek, t, \mathbf{x})$. We know that $tk = K$ is the PRF key and $ik = (\mathbf{R}, \mathbf{A})$, where $\mathbf{A} = \begin{pmatrix} \overline{\mathbf{A}} \\ \underline{\mathbf{A}} \end{pmatrix}$, $\mathbf{R}$ is a trapdoor for $\overline{\mathbf{A}}$. Moreover, $\mathbf{y}$ can be expressed as $\mathbf{y} := \mathbf{C}_t \cdot \mathbf{G}^{-1} \begin{pmatrix} \mathbf{0} \\ c \cdot \mathbf{x} \end{pmatrix} \mod q$, where $\mathbf{C}_t$ is an encryption of $\mathsf{RC}_t(K)$ with noise bounded by Lemma 4 as

$$\mathsf{noise}_{\mathbf{A},\mathsf{RC}_t(K)}(\mathbf{C}_t) \le 2 \cdot 4^d \cdot N \cdot \max_{i \in [\eta]} (\mathsf{noise}_{\mathbf{A},\mu_i}(\mathbf{C}_i)) =: B.$$

Since t is injective (i.e., $t_c \neq \mathsf{PRF}_K(t_a)$), we know that $\mathsf{RC}_t(K) = 1$, and thus there exist $\mathbf{S}_t$ and $\mathbf{E}_t$ with $||\mathbf{E}_t||_\infty \le B$ such that $\mathbf{C}_t = \mathbf{A} \cdot \mathbf{S}_t + \mathbf{E}_t + \mathbf{G}$. Setting $\mathbf{s}_t := \mathbf{S}_t \cdot \mathbf{G}^{-1} \begin{pmatrix} \mathbf{0} \\ c \cdot \mathbf{x} \end{pmatrix}$ and $\mathbf{e}_t := \begin{pmatrix} \overline{\mathbf{e}}_t \\ \underline{\mathbf{e}}_t \end{pmatrix} := \mathbf{E}_t \cdot \mathbf{G}^{-1} \begin{pmatrix} \mathbf{0} \\ c \cdot \mathbf{x} \end{pmatrix}$, we can now express $\mathbf{y}$ as $\mathbf{y} = \begin{pmatrix} \overline{\mathbf{y}} \\ \underline{\mathbf{y}} \end{pmatrix} = \begin{pmatrix} \overline{\mathbf{A}}\mathbf{s}_t + \overline{\mathbf{e}}_t \\ \underline{\mathbf{A}}\mathbf{s}_t + \underline{\mathbf{e}}_t + c \cdot \mathbf{x} \end{pmatrix} \mod q$. Since $\mathbf{G}^{-1} \begin{pmatrix} \mathbf{0} \\ c \cdot \mathbf{x} \end{pmatrix}$ is a binary vector, we know that $||\mathbf{e}_t||_\infty \le ||\mathbf{E}_t||_\infty \le B$. Hence, by Lemma 2, $\mathsf{Invert}(\overline{\mathbf{A}}, \overline{\mathbf{y}}, \mathbf{R})$ returns $\mathbf{s}_t$ and $\overline{\mathbf{e}}_t$ whenever $B < q/(2 \cdot \log(q) \cdot (u - w + 1))$. Having $\mathbf{s}_t$, and hence $\underline{\mathbf{A}}\mathbf{s}_t$, one can compute $\mathbf{x}$ from $\underline{\mathbf{y}}$ as

$$(\underline{\mathbf{y}} - \underline{\mathbf{A}}\mathbf{s}_t) \text{ div } c = (\underline{\mathbf{A}}\mathbf{s}_t + \underline{\mathbf{e}}_t + c \cdot \mathbf{x} - \underline{\mathbf{A}}\mathbf{s}_t) \text{ div } c = (\underline{\mathbf{e}}_t + c \cdot \mathbf{x}) \text{ div } c = \mathbf{x},$$

where the last equality holds if $||\mathbf{e}_t||_\infty < c/2$. Thus, we obtain correctness if

$$B < \min\left\{\frac{q}{2 \cdot \log(q) \cdot (u - w + 1)}, \frac{c}{2}\right\}. \tag{1}$$

Since $\mathbf{C}_i = \mathbf{A}\mathbf{S}_i + \mathbf{E}_i + K[i] \cdot \mathbf{G}$ with $\mathbf{E}_i \xleftarrow{\$} D^{m \times N}_{\alpha q}$, we have $\mathsf{noise}_{\mathbf{A},K[i]}(\mathbf{C}_i) = ||\mathbf{E}_i||_\infty \le N \cdot \sqrt{\lambda} \cdot \alpha q$ for all $i \in [\lambda]$ with all-but-negligible (in λ) probability, and therefore the correctness property is satisfied for any parameters such that

$$2 \cdot 4^d \cdot N^2 \cdot \alpha q \cdot \sqrt{\lambda} < \min\left\{\frac{q}{2 \cdot \log(q) \cdot (u - w + 1)}, \frac{c}{2}\right\};$$

in particular if $\alpha < \min\left\{\frac{1}{\sqrt{\lambda}\cdot 4^{d+1}\cdot N^3}, \frac{c}{q\cdot\sqrt{\lambda}\cdot 4^{d+1}\cdot N^2}\right\} \leq \frac{1}{\sqrt{\lambda}\cdot 4^{d+1}\cdot N^2 \max\{N,p\}}$.

Lossiness. In order to show that ABM is ℓ-lossy, we need to prove that for $(ek, ik, tk) \xleftarrow{\$} \mathsf{ABM.Gen}(1^\lambda)$ and all lossy tags $t = (t_c, t_a) \in \mathcal{T}_{\mathsf{loss}}$, with all-but-negligible probability the image set $\{\mathsf{ABM.Eval}(ek, t, \mathbf{x}) \mid \mathbf{x} \in \mathcal{D}\}$ is of size at most $|\mathcal{D}|/2^\ell$.

Let t be lossy and $\mathbf{y} := \mathbf{C}_t \cdot \mathbf{G}^{-1}\begin{pmatrix}\mathbf{0}\\ c\cdot\mathbf{x}\end{pmatrix} \mod q$, be an arbitrary element in $\{\mathsf{ABM.Eval}(ek, t, \mathbf{x}) \mid \mathbf{x} \in \mathcal{D}\}$. Since t is lossy (i.e., $t_c = \mathsf{PRF}_K(t_a)$), we know that $\mathsf{RC}_t(K) = 0$, and thus there exist $\mathbf{S}_t$ and $\mathbf{E}_t$ with $||\mathbf{E}_t||_\infty \leq B$ such that $\mathbf{C}_t = \mathbf{A}\cdot\mathbf{S}_t + \mathbf{E}_t$. Setting $\mathbf{s}_t := \mathbf{S}_t\cdot\mathbf{G}^{-1}\begin{pmatrix}\mathbf{0}\\ c\cdot\mathbf{x}\end{pmatrix}$ and $\mathbf{e}_t := \mathbf{E}_t\cdot\mathbf{G}^{-1}\begin{pmatrix}\mathbf{0}\\ c\cdot\mathbf{x}\end{pmatrix}$, we can now express $\mathbf{y}$ as $\mathbf{y} = \mathbf{A}\mathbf{s}_t + \mathbf{e}_t \mod q$. Since $\mathbf{s}_t \in \mathbb{Z}_q^n$ and $||\mathbf{e}_t||_\infty \leq ||\mathbf{E}_t||_\infty \leq B$, we obtain

$$\begin{aligned}|\{\mathsf{ABM.Eval}(ek, t, \mathbf{x}) \mid \mathbf{x} \in \mathcal{D}\}| &\leq q^n \cdot (2B+1)^m \\ &\leq q^n \cdot \left(4^{d+1}\cdot N^2 \cdot \alpha q \cdot \sqrt{\lambda} + 1\right)^m\end{aligned}$$

with all-but-negligible probability. On the other hand, we have $|\mathcal{D}| = p^{\overline{m}}$. Hence, we obtain ℓ-lossiness if we choose parameters such that

$$q^n \cdot \left(\alpha q \cdot \sqrt{\lambda} \cdot 4^{d+1} \cdot N^2 + 1\right)^m \leq \frac{p^{\overline{m}}}{2^\ell}.$$

Indistinguishability. The proof very closely follows the proof of indistinguishability of the GSW-based scheme of Libert et al. [38, Lemma 14].

Let $\mathcal{A}$ be a PPT adversary and let us fix $(ek, ik, tk) \xleftarrow{\$} \mathsf{ABM.Gen}(1^\lambda)$. We proceed by defining a series of game hops, where we denote by one_i the event that the adversary $\mathcal{A}$ outputs 1 in the i-th game.

Game 1: $\mathcal{A}$ is given ek and interacts with the tag oracle $\mathsf{ABM.LTag}(tk, \cdot)$ that on input an auxiliary tag t_a outputs $t_c := \mathsf{PRF}_K(t_a)$ for $K = tk$.

Game 2: The game is defined as Game 1, except that the adversary $\mathcal{A}$ is given a differently generated evaluation key. Concretely, the generation of the matrix $\mathbf{A}$ in step 1 of ABM.Gen is replaced by sampling $\mathbf{A}$ uniformly at random, i.e., $\mathbf{A} \xleftarrow{\$} \mathbb{Z}_q^{m\times n}$. Since GenTrap is called with $u - w$ and we assume that $u \geq 2(w + n + \log(w) - 1)$, we can apply Lemma 2 to argue that the statistical distance between the matrix $\mathbf{A}$ generated as in Game 1 and matrix $\mathbf{A}$ chosen uniformly at random as in Game 2 is 2^{-n} and hence $|\Pr[\mathsf{one}_2] - \Pr[\mathsf{one}_1]| \leq 2^{-n}$.

Game 3: In this game, the evaluation key given to $\mathcal{A}$ is generated by sampling independent and uniform matrices $\mathbf{C}_i \xleftarrow{\$} \mathbb{Z}_q^{m\times N}$, $i \in [\lambda]$. The rest of the game is defined as Game 2. Indistinguishability of Game 3 from Game 2 follows from Lemma 4 by a standard hybrid argument: For $j \in \{0, \ldots, \lambda\}$, let G_j denote the distribution of $\{\mathbf{C}_i\}_{i\in\lambda}$ defined as follows

$$\begin{aligned}\mathbf{C}_i &\xleftarrow{\$} \mathsf{FHE.Enc}(\mathbf{A}, b_i), \text{ for } i \in [1, \lambda - j] \\ \mathbf{C}_i &\xleftarrow{\$} \mathbb{Z}_q^{m\times N}, \text{ for } i \in [\lambda - j + 1, \lambda].\end{aligned}$$

By Lemma 4 there exists an LWE-distinguisher $\mathcal{B}_1$ that runs in about the same time as $\mathcal{A}$ such that the advantage of the adversary $\mathcal{A}$ to distinguish G_j from G_{j+1}, for every $j \in \{0, \ldots, \lambda - 1\}$ is upper bounded by $N \cdot \mathsf{Adv}^{n,q,\alpha,m}_{\mathsf{LWE},\mathcal{B}_1}(\lambda)$. By triangular inequality, the advantage of the adversary $\mathcal{A}$ to distinguish G_0 from G_λ is upper bounded by $\lambda \cdot N \cdot \mathsf{Adv}^{n,q,\alpha,m}_{\mathsf{LWE},\mathcal{B}_1}(\lambda)$. It follows $|\Pr[\mathsf{one}_3] - \Pr[\mathsf{one}_2]| \leq \lambda \cdot N \cdot \mathsf{Adv}^{n,q,\alpha,m}_{\mathsf{LWE},\mathcal{B}_1}(\lambda)$.

Game 4: Compared to Game 3, the only change is in the oracle available to the adversary. The oracle $\mathsf{ABM.LTag}(tk, \cdot)$ is now replaced by the oracle $\mathcal{O}_{\mathcal{T}_\mathsf{c}}(\cdot)$ that returns a uniform and independent core tag $t_c \xleftarrow{\$} \mathcal{T}_\mathsf{c}$ at each new query and consistently returns the same t_c if the given query t_a occurs more than once.

Let us construct a PRF distinguisher $\mathcal{C}$ that uses $\mathcal{A}$ to win the PRF game. $\mathcal{C}$ first samples independent and uniform matrices $\{\mathbf{C}_i\}_{i \in [\lambda]}$ and sends them as ek to $\mathcal{A}$. When $\mathcal{A}$ makes a call t_a to its tag oracle, the distinguisher $\mathcal{C}$ forwards t_a to the PRF challenger and relays the reply back to $\mathcal{A}$. The distinguisher $\mathcal{C}$ outputs whatever $\mathcal{A}$ outputs.

If the PRF challenger is returning PRF values, the view of $\mathcal{A}$ is the same as in Game 3 as $\mathcal{C}$ always replies with $\mathsf{PRF}_{K^*}(t_a)$ when queried on t_a. Otherwise the view of $\mathcal{A}$ is the same as in Game 4 because $\mathcal{C}$ always replies with a random value when queried on t_a. Hence $|\Pr[\mathsf{one}_4] - \Pr[\mathsf{one}_3]| \leq \mathsf{Adv}^{\mathsf{ind}}_{\mathsf{PRF},\mathcal{C}}(\lambda)$.

Game 5: This game is defined as Game 4 except that we change back how matrices $\mathbf{C}_i$ are generated. They are not sampled uniformly at random any more, but according to step 3 of the $\mathsf{ABM.Gen}$ algorithm. By a similar argument as for the indistinguishability of Game 2 and Game 3, we conclude that there exists an LWE-distinguisher $\mathcal{B}_2$ that runs in about the same time as $\mathcal{A}$ such that $|\Pr[\mathsf{one}_5] - \Pr[\mathsf{one}_4]| \leq \lambda \cdot N \cdot \mathsf{Adv}^{n,q,\alpha,m}_{\mathsf{LWE},\mathcal{B}_2}(\lambda)$.

Game 6: The game is defined as Game 5 except that the adversary gets ek that was generated via $\mathsf{ABM.Gen}$. This, in particular, means that $\overline{\mathbf{A}}$ is not sampled uniformly at random as in Game 5 but via $\mathsf{GenTrap}(n, u - w, q)$. Again by Lemma 2, we know that the statistical distance between the two matrices is 2^{-n} and hence $|\Pr[\mathsf{win}_6] - \Pr[\mathsf{win}_5]| \leq 2^{-n}$.

To conclude, we have

$$\mathsf{Adv}^{\mathsf{ind}}_{\mathsf{ABM},\mathcal{A}}(\lambda) = |\mathsf{one}_1 - \mathsf{one}_6| \leq 2^{-n+1} + 2 \cdot \lambda \cdot N \cdot \mathsf{Adv}^{n,q,\alpha,m}_{\mathsf{LWE},\mathcal{B}}(\lambda) + \mathsf{Adv}^{\mathsf{ind}}_{\mathsf{PRF},\mathcal{C}}(\lambda)$$

for some LWE-distinguisher $\mathcal{B}$ and some PRF distinguisher $\mathcal{C}$ that run in about the same time as $\mathcal{A}$.

Evasiveness. The proof very closely follows the proof of evasiveness of the GSW-based scheme of Libert et al. [38, Lemma 13].

Let $\mathcal{A}$ be a PPT adversary and let $(ek, ik, tk) \xleftarrow{\$} \mathsf{ABM.Gen}(1^\lambda)$. We proceed by defining a series of game hops, where we denote by win_i the event that the adversary wins the i-th game, i.e., $\mathcal{A}$ outputs a tag $t^* = (t_c^*, t_a^*) \in \mathcal{T} \setminus \mathcal{T}_{\mathsf{inj}}$ that has not been obtained through a query to the $\mathsf{ABM.LTag}$ oracle.

Game 1: This game corresponds to the evasiveness experiment as of Definition 8. Namely, the adversary $\mathcal{A}$ is given ek and interacts with the tag oracle $\mathsf{ABM.LTag}(tk, \cdot)$ that on input an auxiliary tag t_a outputs $t_c := \mathsf{PRF}_K(t_a)$ for $K = tk$. Moreover, $\mathcal{A}$ has access to the $\mathsf{isLossy}(tk, \cdot)$ oracle that on input

$t = (t_c, t_a)$ returns 1 iff $t_c = \mathsf{PRF}_K(t_a)$ and 0 otherwise. We have $\mathsf{Adv}^{\mathsf{eva}}_{\mathsf{ABM},\mathcal{A}}(\lambda) = \Pr[\mathsf{win}_1]$.

Game 2: The game is defined as Game 1, except that the adversary $\mathcal{A}$ is given a differently generated evaluation key. Concretely, the generation of the matrix $\mathbf{A}$ in step 1 of ABM.Gen is replaced by sampling $\mathbf{A}$ uniformly at random, i.e., $\mathbf{A} \xleftarrow{\$} \mathbb{Z}_q^{m\times n}$. Since GenTrap is called with $u - w$ and we assume that $u \geq 2(w + n + \log(w) - 1)$, by Lemma 2 we have $|\Pr[\mathsf{win}_2] - \Pr[\mathsf{win}_1]| \leq 2^{-n}$.

Game 3: In this game, the evaluation key given to $\mathcal{A}$ is generated by sampling independent and uniform matrices $\mathbf{C}_i \xleftarrow{\$} \mathbb{Z}_q^{m\times N}$. The rest of the game is defined as Game 2. By Lemma 4 and a hybrid argument (similar to the argument justifying the switch from Game 2 to Game 3 in the proof of the indistinguishability property above), there exists an LWE-distinguisher $\mathcal{B}$ that runs in about the same time as $\mathcal{A}$ such that $|\Pr[\mathsf{win}_3] - \Pr[\mathsf{win}_2]| \leq \lambda \cdot N \cdot \mathsf{Adv}^{n,q,\alpha,m}_{\mathsf{LWE},\mathcal{B}}(\lambda)$.

Game 4: Compared to Game 3, the only changes are in the oracles available to the adversary. Namely, instead of returning $t_c := \mathsf{PRF}_K(t_a)$ at each query $\mathsf{ABM.LTag}(tk, t_a)$, the ABM.LTag oracle returns $t_c := R(t_a) \in \{0,1\}^\lambda$, where R is a random function lazily defined by sampling a uniform λ-bit string at each new query $t_a \in \{0,1\}^*$. At each query $\mathsf{isLossy}(tk, t)$, the oracle outputs 1 iff $t_c = R(t_a)$ for $t = (t_c, t_a)$, and 0 otherwise. Given that R is a truly random function, $\Pr[\mathsf{win}_4] = \frac{Q}{2^\lambda}$, where Q is the number of queries to the $\mathsf{isLossy}(tk, \cdot)$ oracle. We now show that $|\Pr[\mathsf{win}_4] - \Pr[\mathsf{win}_3]|$ is bounded by the probability of breaking the security of the PRF.

Let us construct a PRF distinguisher $\mathcal{C}$ that uses $\mathcal{A}$ to win the PRF game. The distinguisher $\mathcal{C}$ first samples independent and uniform matrices $\{\mathbf{C}_i\}_{i\in[\lambda]}$ and sends them as ek to $\mathcal{A}$. When $\mathcal{A}$ makes a call t_a to $\mathsf{ABM.LTag}(tk, \cdot)$, the distinguisher $\mathcal{C}$ forwards t_a to the PRF challenger and relays the reply back to $\mathcal{A}$. When $\mathcal{A}$ makes a call $t = (t_c, t_a)$ to $\mathsf{isLossy}(tk, \cdot)$, the distinguisher $\mathcal{C}$ forwards t_a to the PRF challenger. If the reply equals t_c, $\mathcal{C}$ replies to $\mathcal{A}$ with 1. Otherwise $\mathcal{C}$ replies with 0. Once $\mathcal{A}$ outputs a tag $t = (t_c, t_a)$, $\mathcal{C}$ submits t_a to its challenger. If the reply equals t_c, $\mathcal{C}$ outputs 1. Otherwise $\mathcal{C}$ outputs 0.

If the PRF challenger is returning PRF values, the view of $\mathcal{A}$ is the same as in Game 3 as $\mathcal{C}$ always replies with $\mathsf{PRF}_{K^*}(t_a)$ when queried on t_a. Otherwise the view of $\mathcal{A}$ is the same as in Game 4 because $\mathcal{C}$ always replies with a random value when queried on t_a. Hence the advantage $\mathsf{Adv}^{\mathsf{ind}}_{\mathsf{PRF},\mathcal{C}}(\lambda)$ of the distinguisher $\mathcal{C}$ is at least $|\Pr[\mathsf{win}_4] - \Pr[\mathsf{win}_3]|$ as required.

To summarize, we have

$$\mathsf{Adv}^{\mathsf{eva}}_{\mathsf{ABM},\mathcal{A}}(\lambda) \leq 2^{-n} + \lambda \cdot N \cdot \mathsf{Adv}^{n,q,\alpha,m}_{\mathsf{LWE},\mathcal{B}}(\lambda) + \mathsf{Adv}^{\mathsf{ind}}_{\mathsf{PRF},\mathcal{C}}(\lambda) + \frac{Q}{2^\lambda}.$$

Remark 3. Note that the core tag space $\mathcal{T}_\mathsf{c} = \{0,1\}^\lambda$ is efficiently samplable and explainable. Hence ABM is an ABM-LTF with explainable tags according to Definition 10.

Alg. $\mathsf{PKE.Gen}(1^\lambda)$	**Alg.** $\mathsf{PKE.Enc}(pk, msg)$	**Alg.** $\mathsf{PKE.Dec}(sk, C)$
$(ek', ik') \xleftarrow{\$} \mathsf{LTF.IGen}(1^\lambda)$	parse $pk =: (ek', ek, h)$	parse $sk =: (ik', ek, h)$,
$(ek, ik, tk) \xleftarrow{\$} \mathsf{ABM.Gen}(1^\lambda)$	$x \xleftarrow{\$} \{0,1\}^n$	$\quad C =: (\mathsf{ct}, y', t_c, y)$
$h \xleftarrow{\$} \mathcal{UH}$	$K := h(x)$	$x \xleftarrow{\$} f_{ik'}^{-1}(y')$
$pk := (ek', ek, h)$	$\mathsf{ct} \xleftarrow{\$} \mathsf{E}(K, msg)$	if $y \neq f_{ek,(t_c,y')}(x)$
$sk := (ik', ek, h)$	$y' := f_{ek'}(x)$	$\quad$ return $\perp$
return (pk, sk)	$t_c := \mathsf{Samp}_{\mathcal{T}_c}(1^\lambda; R_{t_c})$	$K := h(x)$
	$y := f_{ek,(t_c,y')}(x)$	$msg \xleftarrow{\$} \mathsf{D}(K, \mathsf{ct})$
	$C := (\mathsf{ct}, y', t_c, y)$	return msg
	return C	

Fig. 1. The construction of IND-SO-CCA secure encryption by Hofheinz [32].

5 IND-SO-CCA Security from ABM-LTFs

Having our ABM-LTF construction at hand, we are now prepared to present a IND-SO-CCA secure PKE with compact ciphertexts which is the main goal of our paper. To this end, let us recall the construction of IND-SO-CCA secure PKE based on ABM-LTFs by Hofheinz [32] which we follow. We require the following ingredients:

1. an LTF $\mathsf{LTF} = (\mathsf{LTF.IGen}, \mathsf{LTF.Eval}, \mathsf{LTF.Invert}, \mathsf{LTF.LGen})$ with domain $\{0,1\}^n$ (as in Definition 7) that is ℓ'-lossy,
2. an ABM-LTF with explainable tags $\mathsf{ABM} = (\mathsf{ABM.Gen}, \mathsf{ABM.Eval}, \mathsf{ABM.Invert}, \mathsf{ABM.LTag})$ with domain $\{0,1\}^n$ and tag set $\mathcal{T} = \mathcal{T}_c \times \{0,1\}^*$ (as in Definition 10) that is ℓ-lossy,
3. a family $\mathcal{UH}$ of universal hash functions $h : \{0,1\}^n \to \{0,1\}^{2\kappa}$ for some $\kappa = \kappa(\lambda)$, so that for any $f : \{0,1\}^n \to \{0,1\}^{2n-(\ell+\ell')}$, it holds that $\mathsf{SD}\left((h, f(x), h(x)); (h, f(x), U)\right) = O(2^{-\lambda})$, where $h \xleftarrow{\$} \mathcal{UH}$, $x \xleftarrow{\$} \{0,1\}^n$, and $U \xleftarrow{\$} \{0,1\}^{2\kappa}$, and
4. a statistically secure lossy authenticated encryption scheme $\mathsf{LAE} = (\mathsf{E}, \mathsf{D})$ (see Definition 11) with 2κ-bit keys K, κ-bit messages msg, and ciphertexts of size 2κ.

Remark 4. The requirement in Item 3 above can be fulfilled for n linear in λ due to the Leftover Hash Lemma. We detail this in Appendix B.3

The PKE scheme from [32] $\mathsf{PKE} = (\mathsf{PKE.Gen}, \mathsf{PKE.Enc}, \mathsf{PKE.Dec})$ works as shown in Fig. 1.

We give a brief intuition of how the scheme works. The LTF and the ABM-LTF are used to "encrypt" a hash-pre-image of a symmetric key. The key is then used to encrypt the message using the LAE scheme. This allows for switching the LTF to lossy mode, and the ABM-LTF to lossy tags for the challenge ciphertexts in the security proof, allowing the reduction to ultimately switch the symmetric keys to random keys that are unrelated to the remaining ciphertext components.

Mending a Gap in [32]. We rewrite the proof instead of using the one from the original work, as there is a gap in the original work. In particular, in Game 7 of the original work, the keys of the lossy authenticated encryption scheme used for generating challenge ciphertexts are switched to truly random keys. The proof does not mention however how challenge ciphertexts that were generated like this can be opened, as the preimage x of the key K would need to be revealed. We close this gap by introducing an additional game where the preimages x of the keys are resampled using an inefficient opening algorithm. When the keys are switched to random, we continue to use this inefficient opening algorithm to output preimages x matching the key K as well as the LTF and ABM-LTF images y' and y. This change means that all following games are inefficient, and we need to rely on statistical security for the game hops after this game.

Theorem 3. *If* LTF *is an LTF,* ABM *an ABM-LTF with explainable tags,* $\mathcal{UH}$ *an UHF family as described, and* LAE *a statistically secure lossy authenticated encryption scheme, then* PKE *is IND-SO-CCA secure. In particular, for every IND-SO-CCA adversary* $\mathcal{A}$ *on* PKE*, there exist adversaries* $\mathcal{B}$*,* $\mathcal{C}$*, and* $\mathcal{F}$ *of roughly same complexity as* $\mathcal{A}$*, and unbounded adversary* $\mathcal{E}$ *such that*

$$\begin{aligned}\mathsf{Adv}^{\mathsf{cca\text{-}so}}_{\mathsf{PKE},\mathcal{A}}(\lambda) \leq & \mathsf{Adv}^{\mathsf{ind}}_{\mathsf{ABM},\mathcal{B}}(\lambda) + \mathsf{Adv}^{\mathsf{eva}}_{\mathsf{ABM},\mathcal{C}}(\lambda) + \mathsf{Adv}^{\mathsf{ind}}_{\mathsf{LTF},\mathcal{F}}(\lambda) \\ & + N \cdot \mathsf{Adv}^{\mathsf{auth}}_{\mathsf{LAE},\mathcal{E}}(\lambda) + O(N/2^{\lambda}). \end{aligned} \tag{2}$$

Remark 5. While the reduction depends on the number N of challenge ciphertexts, these dependencies only appear in statistical terms (when using the unconditionally secure lossy authenticated encryption from Sect. 2).

Remark 6. We note that when instantiated with our construction of an LTF and an ABM-LTF from sections Sects. 3 and 4, respectively, we achieve constant expansion, i.e. the ciphertext size is only by a constant factor larger than the plaintext size.

We now turn to the proof of Theorem 3.

Proof. The proof largely follows [27,32,46]. Assume $N = N(\lambda) > 0$ and an IND-SO-CCA adversary $\mathcal{A}$ that makes exactly $q_{\mathsf{PKE.Dec}}$ decryption queries, where $q_{\mathsf{PKE.Dec}} = q_{\mathsf{PKE.Dec}}(\lambda)$ is a suitable polynomial. We proceed in games, and start with the real IND-SO-CCA experiment $\mathsf{Exp}^{\mathsf{ind\text{-}so\text{-}cca}}_{\mathsf{PKE},\mathcal{A},N}$ as **Game** 1. An overview of how the game works can be seen in Definition 13 and the implementations of the algorithms used to generate keys, encrypt the challenges, respond to decryption queries, and open ciphertexts can be found in Fig. 2. If we denote with one_i the output of Game i, we get

$$\left| \Pr\left[\mathsf{one}_1\right] - \frac{1}{2} \right| = \mathsf{Adv}^{\mathsf{cca\text{-}so}}_{\mathsf{PKE},\mathcal{A}}(\lambda). \tag{3}$$

In **Game** 2 we make a change to how the decryption oracle handles decryption queries with a tag that has been *copied* from a challenge ciphertext. We say that a tag (t_c, y') is copied if it occurs already in $C^{(i)}$ for some i. We reject decryption queries $C = (\mathsf{ct}, y', t_c, y)$ if (t_c, y') is copied, but y is not the same as in the challenge ciphertext that it was copied from (see Fig. 2 for details). For copied tags where y was copied as well, we use the key $K^{(i)}$ from the challenge ciphertext to decrypt ct. (That way, neither y nor y' have to be inverted when processing decryption queries with copied tag.)

Since y' uniquely determines x (and thus y) at this point, these changes are purely conceptual, and we have

$$\Pr[\mathsf{one}_2] = \Pr[\mathsf{one}_1]. \tag{4}$$

In **Game** 3, we output random coins for the tag generation via $R_{t_c} \xleftarrow{\$} \mathsf{Expl}_{\mathcal{T}_c}(1^\lambda, t_c)$ instead of the random coins that were used to sample t_c originally (see Fig. 2). Since $\mathcal{T}_c$ is efficiently samplable and explainable, we get

$$\Pr[\mathsf{one}_3] = \Pr[\mathsf{one}_2]. \tag{5}$$

In **Game** 4, we generate the ABM tags used in the challenge ciphertexts $C^{(i)}$ as lossy tags, see Fig. 2. A straightforward reduction shows

$$|\Pr[\mathsf{one}_4] - \Pr[\mathsf{one}_3]| = \mathsf{Adv}^{\mathsf{ind}}_{\mathsf{ABM},\mathcal{B}}(\lambda) \tag{6}$$

for a suitable adversary $\mathcal{B}$ on ABM's indistinguishability.

In **Game** 5, we switch from using the inversion key ik' to invert y' and obtain $x = f^{-1}_{ik'}(y')$ and then checking that $f_{ek,(t_c,y')}(x) = y$ to using the inversion key ik of ABM and then checking consistency using LTF. These changes can be seen in Fig. 2. (Note that by the changes from Game 2, we may assume that the tag (t_c, y') is fresh.) By the correctness properties of LTF and ABM, these procedures yield the same results, *unless* the adversary submits a decryption query with a non-injective, non-copied tag. We thus need to bound $\Pr[\mathsf{bad}_{\mathsf{ninj}}]$, where $\mathsf{bad}_{\mathsf{ninj}}$ denotes the event that $\mathcal{A}$ submits a decryption query with a non-injective ABM tag $t = (t_c, y')$ that is not copied. However, the evasiveness property of ABM guarantees that

$$|\Pr[\mathsf{one}_5] - \Pr[\mathsf{one}_4]| \leq \Pr[\mathsf{bad}_{\mathsf{ninj}}] \leq \mathsf{Adv}^{\mathsf{eva}}_{\mathsf{ABM},\mathcal{C}}(\lambda) \tag{7}$$

is negligible, where $\mathcal{C}$ is a suitable adversary against the evasiveness property of ABM. (Concretely, $\mathcal{C}$ simulates Game 4 using the oracle $\mathsf{ABM.LTag}(tk, \cdot)$, and for each decryption query with non-copied tag checks whether this tag is lossy (using the oracle $\mathsf{isLossy}(\cdot)$). If $\mathcal{C}$ finds a non-copied lossy tag, it outputs this tag.)

In **Game** 6, we generate LTF's evaluation key ek' as a lossy key, via $ek' \xleftarrow{\$} \mathsf{LTF.LGen}(1^\lambda)$ (see Fig. 3). Since in Game 5, LTF's inversion key ik' is never used, a straightforward reduction shows

$$|\Pr[\mathsf{one}_5] - \Pr[\mathsf{one}_6]| = \mathsf{Adv}^{\mathsf{ind}}_{\mathsf{LTF},\mathcal{F}}(\lambda) \tag{8}$$

for a suitable PPT adversary on LTF's indistinguishability.

In **Game** 7 we sample x for the opened ciphertexts through an inefficient opening algorithm Opener that given K, y, y' outputs x s.t. $h(x) = K$, $f_{ek'}(x) = y'$, $f_{ek,(t_c,y')}(x) = y$ (see Fig. 3). (It is here that our proof diverges from that of [32]). The opening algorithm Opener can for example be implemented as follows:

$\underline{\mathsf{PKE.Gen}(1^\lambda)}$

$(ek', ik') \xleftarrow{\$} \mathsf{LTF.IGen}(1^\lambda)$
$(ek, ik, tk) \xleftarrow{\$} \mathsf{ABM.Gen}(1^\lambda)$
$h \xleftarrow{\$} \mathcal{UH}$
$pk := (ek', ek, h)$
$sk := (ik', ek, h)$
return (pk, sk)

$\underline{\mathsf{Open}(\mathcal{I})}$

for $i \in \mathcal{I}$
  $R_{t_c}^{(i)\prime} \xleftarrow{\$} \mathsf{Expl}(t_c^{(i)})$
return $\mathbf{R} = (x^{(i)}, R_{\mathsf{LAE}}^{(i)}, R_{t_c}^{(i)\prime})_{i \in \mathcal{I}}$
return $\mathbf{R} = (x^{(i)}, R_{\mathsf{LAE}}^{(i)}, R_{t_c}^{(i)})_{i \in \mathcal{I}}$ //until $\boxed{2}$

$\underline{\mathsf{PKE.Enc}(pk, msg^{(i)}; R^{(i)} = (x^{(i)}, R_{\mathsf{LAE}}^{(i)}, R_{t_c}^{(i)}))}$

parse $pk =: (ek', ek, h)$
$K^{(i)} := h(x^{(i)})$
$\mathsf{ct}^{(i)} := \mathsf{E}(K^{(i)}, msg^{(i)}; R_{\mathsf{LAE}}^{(i)})$
$y^{(i)\prime} := f_{ek'}(x^{(i)})$
$t_c^{(i)} := \mathsf{Samp}_{\mathcal{T}_c}(1^\lambda; R_{t_c}^{(i)})$ //until 3
$t_c^{(i)} \leftarrow \mathsf{ABM.LTag}(tk, y^{(i)\prime})$
$y^{(i)} := f_{ek,(t_c^{(i)}, y^{(i)\prime})}(x^{(i)})$
$C^{(i)} := (\mathsf{ct}^{(i)}, y^{(i)\prime}, t_c^{(i)}, y^{(i)})$
return $C^{(i)}$

$\underline{\mathsf{PKE.Dec}(sk, C)}$

if $\exists i \colon C^{(i)} = C$
  return $\perp$
parse $sk =: (ik', ek, h)$,
  $C =: (\mathsf{ct}, y', t_c, y)$
$\boxed{\text{if } \exists i \colon C^{(i)} = (\mathsf{ct}^{(i)}, y^{(i)\prime}, t_c^{(i)}, y^{(i)}):}$
    $\boxed{(t_c, y') = (t_c^{(i)}, y^{(i)\prime})}$
  $\boxed{\text{if } y \neq y^{(i)}}$
    $\boxed{\text{return } \perp}$
  $\boxed{K := K^{(i)}}$
$\boxed{\text{else}}$
  if $t_c \in \mathsf{ABM.LTag}(tk, y')$
    $\mathsf{bad_{ninj}} = 1$
    return $\perp$
  $x := f^{-1}_{ik,(t_c,y')}(y)$
  if $f_{ek'}(x) \neq y'$
    return $\perp$
  $x := f^{-1}_{ik'}(y')$ //until 4
  if $y \neq f_{ek,(t_c,y')}(x)$ //until 4
    return $\perp$ //until 4
  $K := h(x)$
$msg := \mathsf{D}(K, \mathsf{ct})$
return msg

Fig. 2. Handling of encryption, decryption and opening in the games **Game** 1, $\boxed{\textbf{Game 2}}$, **Game 3**, **Game 4**, **Game 5**

First compute the set $\mathbf{X}_{K,y,y'} := \{x \mid h(x) = K, f_{ek,t_c,y'}(x) = y, f_{ek'}(x) = y'\}$ of possible values for x, then sample $x^{(i)\prime} \xleftarrow{\$} \mathbf{X}_{K,y,y'}$ uniformly at random.

It is easy to see that it holds that $\forall x \in \{0,1\}^n$

$$\Pr_{x' \xleftarrow{\$} \{0,1\}^n} [x' = x] = \Pr_{\substack{x'' \xleftarrow{\$} \{0,1\}^n \\ x' \xleftarrow{\$} \mathbf{X}_{h(x''), f_{ek,(t_c,y')}(x''), f_{ek'}(x'')}}} [x' = x]$$

and thus

$$\Pr[\mathsf{one}_7] = \Pr[\mathsf{one}_6]. \tag{9}$$

In **Game** 8, we compute the keys K used during encryption as independently and truly random keys $K \in \{0,1\}^{2\kappa}$, instead of setting $K = h(x)$ (see Fig. 3). (Note that by our rules from Game 2, this also means that upon a decryption query with a copied tag (t_c, y'), that same random key K used during encryption is used to decrypt.)

To justify our change, observe that in Game 7, all evaluations $y' = f_{ek'}(x)$, resp. $y = f_{ek,(t_c,y')}(x)$ that $\mathcal{A}$ receives in the challenge ciphertexts are made

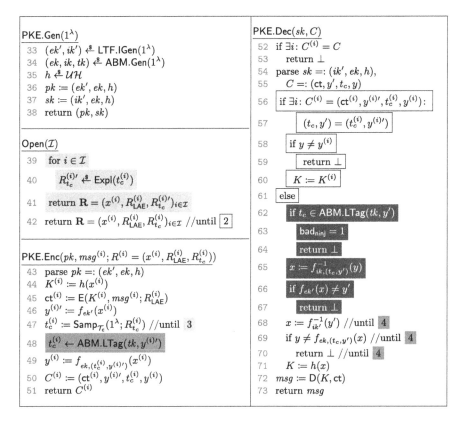

```
PKE.Gen(1^λ)
  (ek', ik') <-$ LTF.IGen(1^λ) //until 5
  [ ek' <-$ LTF.LGen(1^λ) ]
  (ek, ik, tk) <-$ ABM.Gen(1^λ)
  h <-$ UH
  pk := (ek', ek, h)
  sk := (ik', ek, h)
  return (pk, sk)

Open(I)
  for i ∈ I
    R_{t_c}^{(i)'} <-$ Expl(t_c^{(i)})
    x^{(i)'} <-$ Opener(K^{(i)}, y, y')
  return R = (x^{(i)'}, R_LAE^{(i)}, R_{t_c}^{(i)'})_{i∈I}
  return R = (x^{(i)}, R_LAE^{(i)}, R_{t_c}^{(i)'})_{i∈I}

PKE.Enc(pk, msg^{(i)}; R^{(i)} = (x^{(i)}, R_LAE^{(i)}, R_{t_c}^{(i)}))
  parse pk =: (ek', ek, h)
  K^{(i)} := h(x^{(i)}) // until 7
  K^{(i)} <-$ {0,1}^{2κ}
  ct^{(i)} := E(K^{(i)}, msg^{(i)}; R_LAE^{(i)})
  y^{(i)'} := f_{ek'}(x^{(i)})
  t_c^{(i)} <-$ ABM.LTag(tk, y^{(i)'})
  y^{(i)} := f_{ek,(t_c^{(i)}, y^{(i)'})}(x^{(i)})
  C^{(i)} := (ct^{(i)}, y^{(i)'}, t_c^{(i)}, y^{(i)})
  return C^{(i)}

PKE.Dec(sk, C)
  if ∃i: C^{(i)} = C
    return ⊥
  parse sk =: (ik', ek, h),
    C =: (ct, y', t_c, y)
  if ∃i: C^{(i)} = (ct^{(i)}, y^{(i)'}, t_c^{(i)}, y^{(i)}):
       (t_c, y') = (t_c^{(i)}, y^{(i)'})
       if i ∉ I
         return ⊥
    if y ≠ y^{(i)}
      return ⊥
    K := K^{(i)}
  else
    x := f^{-1}_{ik,(t_c,y')}(y)
    if f_{ek'}(x) ≠ y'
      return ⊥
    K := h(x)
  msg := D(K, ct)
  return msg
```

Fig. 3. Handling of encryption, decryption and opening in the games **Game** 5, **Game 6**, **Game 7**, **Game 8**, **Game 9**

with respect to lossy keys, resp. tags. In particular, at this point, the values $h(x)$ generated during encryption of *msg* are statistically close to uniform, *even given* y' *and* y. This is due to the requirement we made in Item 3. Hence, the difference between Game 7 and Game 8 is only statistical:

$$|\Pr[\mathsf{one}_8] - \Pr[\mathsf{one}_7]| \leq O(N/2^\lambda). \tag{10}$$

Finally, in **Game** 9, we reject all decryption queries with copied tags (t_c, y') (even if also y is copied from the same challenge ciphertext) unless said ciphertext has been opened (see Fig. 3). A difference to Game 8 only occurs if $\mathcal{A}$ manages to submit a decryption query $(\mathsf{ct}, y', t_c, y)$ with the following properties:

- the values t_c, y', y are all copied from the same previous unopened challenge ciphertext $C^{(i)}$, and
- ct decrypts correctly to some message under the key K used in that challenge ciphertext $C^{(i)}$.

Let us call $\mathsf{bad}_{\mathsf{auth}}$ the event that $\mathcal{A}$ places such a decryption query. We can bound the probability that $\mathsf{bad}_{\mathsf{auth}}$ occurs using LAE's authentication property. Namely, a hybrid argument over all challenge ciphertexts shows that

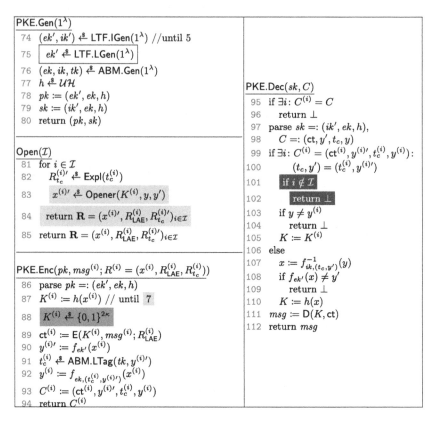

$$|\Pr[\mathsf{one}_9] - \Pr[\mathsf{one}_8]| \le \Pr[\mathsf{bad}_{\mathsf{auth}}] \le N \cdot \mathsf{Adv}^{\mathsf{auth}}_{\mathsf{LAE},\mathcal{E}}(\lambda) \tag{11}$$

for an adversary $\mathcal{E}$ that simulates Game 8, and embeds its own challenge ciphertext as one of the IND-SO-CCA challenge ciphertexts of Game 8.

Now observe that in Game 9, $\mathcal{A}$ receives only lossy LAE ciphertexts made with independently random keys K (that are never used again for any decryption queries). The message vectors $\mathbf{msg}_0$ and $\mathbf{msg}_1$ from $\mathsf{Exp}^{\mathsf{ind\text{-}so\text{-}cca}}_{\mathsf{PKE},\mathcal{A}}$ are thus identically distributed (even given $\mathcal{A}$'s view), and we finally obtain

$$\Pr[\mathsf{one}_9] = \frac{1}{2}. \tag{12}$$

Taking (Eq. (3)–Eq. (12)) together shows (Eq. (2)).

Acknowledgements. We would like to thank the anonymous reviewers for their helpful feedback.

References

1. Alwen, J., Krenn, S., Pietrzak, K., Wichs, D.: Learning with rounding, revisited. In: Canetti, R., Garay, J.A. (eds.) CRYPTO 2013, Part I. LNCS, vol. 8042, pp. 57–74. Springer, Heidelberg (2013). https://doi.org/10.1007/978-3-642-40041-4_4
2. Applebaum, B., Cash, D., Peikert, C., Sahai, A.: Fast cryptographic primitives and circular-secure encryption based on hard learning problems. In: Halevi, S. (ed.) CRYPTO 2009. LNCS, vol. 5677, pp. 595–618. Springer, Heidelberg (2009). https://doi.org/10.1007/978-3-642-03356-8_35
3. Auerbach, B., Kiltz, E., Poettering, B., Schoenen, S.: Lossy trapdoor permutations with improved lossiness. In: Matsui, M. (ed.) CT-RSA 2019. LNCS, vol. 11405, pp. 230–250. Springer, Cham (2019). https://doi.org/10.1007/978-3-030-12612-4_12
4. Bellare, M., Dowsley, R., Waters, B., Yilek, S.: Standard security does not imply security against selective-opening. In: Pointcheval, D., Johansson, T. (eds.) EUROCRYPT 2012. LNCS, vol. 7237, pp. 645–662. Springer, Heidelberg (2012). https://doi.org/10.1007/978-3-642-29011-4_38
5. Bellare, M., Hofheinz, D., Yilek, S.: Possibility and impossibility results for encryption and commitment secure under selective opening. In: Joux, A. (ed.) EUROCRYPT 2009. LNCS, vol. 5479, pp. 1–35. Springer, Heidelberg (2009). https://doi.org/10.1007/978-3-642-01001-9_1
6. Bellare, M., Kiltz, E., Peikert, C., Waters, B.: Identity-based (lossy) trapdoor functions and applications. In: Pointcheval, D., Johansson, T. (eds.) EUROCRYPT 2012. LNCS, vol. 7237, pp. 228–245. Springer, Heidelberg (2012). https://doi.org/10.1007/978-3-642-29011-4_15
7. Bellare, M., Waters, B., Yilek, S.: Identity-based encryption secure against selective opening attack. In: Ishai, Y. (ed.) TCC 2011. LNCS, vol. 6597, pp. 235–252. Springer, Heidelberg (2011). https://doi.org/10.1007/978-3-642-19571-6_15
8. Benhamouda, F., Herranz, J., Joye, M., Libert, B.: Efficient cryptosystems from 2^k-th power residue symbols. J. Cryptol. **30**(2), 519–549 (2017). https://doi.org/10.1007/s00145-016-9229-5

9. Böhl, F., Hofheinz, D., Kraschewski, D.: On definitions of selective opening security. In: Fischlin, M., Buchmann, J., Manulis, M. (eds.) PKC 2012. LNCS, vol. 7293, pp. 522–539. Springer, Heidelberg (2012). https://doi.org/10.1007/978-3-642-30057-8_31
10. Boldyreva, A., Fehr, S., O'Neill, A.: On notions of security for deterministic encryption, and efficient constructions without Random Oracles. In: Wagner, D. (ed.) CRYPTO 2008. LNCS, vol. 5157, pp. 335–359. Springer, Heidelberg (2008). https://doi.org/10.1007/978-3-540-85174-5_19
11. Boneh, D., Lewi, K., Montgomery, H., Raghunathan, A.: Key homomorphic PRFs and their applications. In: Canetti, R., Garay, J.A. (eds.) CRYPTO 2013, Part I. LNCS, vol. 8042, pp. 410–428. Springer, Heidelberg (2013). https://doi.org/10.1007/978-3-642-40041-4_23
12. Boyen, X., Li, Q.: All-but-many lossy trapdoor functions from lattices and applications. In: Katz, J., Shacham, H. (eds.) CRYPTO 2017, Part III. LNCS, vol. 10403, pp. 298–331. Springer, Cham (2017). https://doi.org/10.1007/978-3-319-63697-9_11
13. Brakerski, Z., Döttling, N., Garg, S., Malavolta, G.: Leveraging linear decryption: rate-1 fully-homomorphic encryption and time-lock puzzles. In: Hofheinz, D., Rosen, A. (eds.) TCC 2019, Part II. LNCS, vol. 11892, pp. 407–437. Springer, Cham (2019). https://doi.org/10.1007/978-3-030-36033-7_16
14. Brakerski, Z., Vaikuntanathan, V.: Lattice-based FHE as secure as PKE. In: Proceedings of the 5th Conference on Innovations in Theoretical Computer Science, ITCS 2014, pp. 1–12. ACM, New York (2014). https://doi.org/10.1145/2554797.2554799
15. Damgård, I., Nielsen, J.B.: Improved non-committing encryption schemes based on a general complexity assumption. In: Bellare, M. (ed.) CRYPTO 2000. LNCS, vol. 1880, pp. 432–450. Springer, Heidelberg (2000). https://doi.org/10.1007/3-540-44598-6_27
16. Damgård, I., Nielsen, J.B.: Perfect hiding and perfect binding universally composable commitment schemes with constant expansion factor. In: Yung, M. (ed.) CRYPTO 2002. LNCS, vol. 2442, pp. 581–596. Springer, Heidelberg (2002). https://doi.org/10.1007/3-540-45708-9_37
17. Dodis, Y., Reyzin, L., Smith, A.: Fuzzy extractors: how to generate strong keys from biometrics and other noisy data. In: Cachin, C., Camenisch, J.L. (eds.) EUROCRYPT 2004. LNCS, vol. 3027, pp. 523–540. Springer, Heidelberg (2004). https://doi.org/10.1007/978-3-540-24676-3_31
18. Döttling, N., Garg, S., Ishai, Y., Malavolta, G., Mour, T., Ostrovsky, R.: Trapdoor hash functions and their applications. In: Boldyreva, A., Micciancio, D. (eds.) CRYPTO 2019, Part III. LNCS, vol. 11694, pp. 3–32. Springer, Cham (2019). https://doi.org/10.1007/978-3-030-26954-8_1
19. Dwork, C., Naor, M., Reingold, O., Stockmeyer, L.J.: Magic functions. In: 40th FOCS, October 1999, pp. 523–534. IEEE Computer Society Press (1999). https://doi.org/10.1109/SFFCS.1999.814626
20. Fehr, S., Hofheinz, D., Kiltz, E., Wee, H.: Encryption schemes secure against chosen-ciphertext selective opening attacks. In: Gilbert, H. (ed.) EUROCRYPT 2010. LNCS, vol. 6110, pp. 381–402. Springer, Heidelberg (2010). https://doi.org/10.1007/978-3-642-13190-5_20
21. Freeman, D.M., Goldreich, O., Kiltz, E., Rosen, A., Segev, G.: More constructions of lossy and correlation-secure trapdoor functions. In: Nguyen, P.Q., Pointcheval, D. (eds.) PKC 2010. LNCS, vol. 6056, pp. 279–295. Springer, Heidelberg (2010). https://doi.org/10.1007/978-3-642-13013-7_17

22. Fujisaki, E.: All-but-many encryption. In: Sarkar, P., Iwata, T. (eds.) ASIACRYPT 2014. LNCS, vol. 8874, pp. 426–447. Springer, Heidelberg (2014). https://doi.org/10.1007/978-3-662-45608-8_23
23. Gentry, C., Halevi, S.: Compressible FHE with applications to PIR. In: Hofheinz, D., Rosen, A. (eds.) TCC 2019. LNCS, vol. 11892, pp. 438–464. Springer, Cham (2019). https://doi.org/10.1007/978-3-030-36033-7_17
24. Gentry, C., Sahai, A., Waters, B.: Homomorphic encryption from learning with errors: Conceptually-simpler, asymptotically-faster, attribute-based. In: Canetti, R., Garay, J.A. (eds.) CRYPTO 2013, Part I. LNCS, vol. 8042, pp. 75–92. Springer, Heidelberg (Aug 2013). https://doi.org/10.1007/978-3-642-40041-4_5
25. Goldwasser, S., Kalai, Y.T., Peikert, C., Vaikuntanathan, V.: Robustness of the learning with errors assumption. In: Yao, A.C.C. (ed.) ICS 2010, January 2010, pp. 230–240. Tsinghua University Press (2010)
26. Gustafsson, B.: Scientific Computing. TCSE, vol. 17. Springer, Cham (2018). https://doi.org/10.1007/978-3-319-69847-2
27. Hemenway, B., Libert, B., Ostrovsky, R., Vergnaud, D.: Lossy encryption: constructions from general assumptions and efficient selective opening chosen ciphertext security. In: Lee, D.H., Wang, X. (eds.) ASIACRYPT 2011. LNCS, vol. 7073, pp. 70–88. Springer, Heidelberg (2011). https://doi.org/10.1007/978-3-642-25385-0_4
28. Hemenway, B., Ostrovsky, R.: Extended-DDH and lossy trapdoor functions. In: Fischlin, M., Buchmann, J., Manulis, M. (eds.) PKC 2012. LNCS, vol. 7293, pp. 627–643. Springer, Heidelberg (May 2012). https://doi.org/10.1007/978-3-642-30057-8_37
29. Hemenway, B., Ostrovsky, R.: Building lossy trapdoor functions from lossy encryption. In: Sako, K., Sarkar, P. (eds.) ASIACRYPT 2013, Part II. LNCS, vol. 8270, pp. 241–260. Springer, Heidelberg (2013). https://doi.org/10.1007/978-3-642-42045-0_13
30. Heuer, F., Jager, T., Kiltz, E., Schäge, S.: On the selective opening security of practical public-key encryption schemes. In: Katz, J. (ed.) PKC 2015. LNCS, vol. 9020, pp. 27–51. Springer, Heidelberg (2015). https://doi.org/10.1007/978-3-662-46447-2_2
31. Heuer, F., Poettering, B.: Selective opening security from simulatable data encapsulation. In: Cheon, J.H., Takagi, T. (eds.) ASIACRYPT 2016, Part II. LNCS, vol. 10032, pp. 248–277. Springer, Heidelberg (2016). https://doi.org/10.1007/978-3-662-53890-6_9
32. Hofheinz, D.: All-but-many lossy trapdoor functions. In: Pointcheval, D., Johansson, T. (eds.) EUROCRYPT 2012. LNCS, vol. 7237, pp. 209–227. Springer, Heidelberg (2012). https://doi.org/10.1007/978-3-642-29011-4_14
33. Hofheinz, D., Jager, T., Rupp, A.: Public-key encryption with simulation-based selective-opening security and compact ciphertexts. In: Hirt, M., Smith, A. (eds.) TCC 2016, Part II. LNCS, vol. 9986, pp. 146–168. Springer, Heidelberg (2016). https://doi.org/10.1007/978-3-662-53644-5_6
34. Hofheinz, D., Rao, V., Wichs, D.: Standard security does not imply indistinguishability under selective opening. In: Hirt, M., Smith, A. (eds.) TCC 2016, Part II. LNCS, vol. 9986, pp. 121–145. Springer, Heidelberg (2016). https://doi.org/10.1007/978-3-662-53644-5_5
35. Hofheinz, D., Rupp, A.: Standard versus selective opening security: separation and equivalence results. In: Lindell, Y. (ed.) TCC 2014. LNCS, vol. 8349, pp. 591–615. Springer, Heidelberg (2014). https://doi.org/10.1007/978-3-642-54242-8_25

36. Huang, Z., Liu, S., Qin, B.: Sender-equivocable encryption schemes secure against chosen-ciphertext attacks revisited. In: Kurosawa, K., Hanaoka, G. (eds.) PKC 2013. LNCS, vol. 7778, pp. 369–385. Springer, Heidelberg (2013). https://doi.org/10.1007/978-3-642-36362-7_23
37. Kiltz, E., O'Neill, A., Smith, A.: Instantiability of RSA-OAEP under chosen-plaintext attack. In: Rabin, T. (ed.) CRYPTO 2010. LNCS, vol. 6223, pp. 295–313. Springer, Heidelberg (2010). https://doi.org/10.1007/978-3-642-14623-7_16
38. Libert, B., Sakzad, A., Stehlé, D., Steinfeld, R.: All-but-many lossy trapdoor functions and selective opening chosen-ciphertext security from LWE. In: Katz, J., Shacham, H. (eds.) CRYPTO 2017, Part III. LNCS, vol. 10403, pp. 332–364. Springer, Cham (2017). https://doi.org/10.1007/978-3-319-63697-9_12
39. Mahadev, U.: Classical homomorphic encryption for quantum circuits. In: Thorup, M. (ed.) 59th FOCS, October 2018, pp. 332–338. IEEE Computer Society Press (2018). https://doi.org/10.1109/FOCS.2018.00039
40. Micciancio, D., Peikert, C.: Trapdoors for lattices: simpler, tighter, faster, smaller. In: Pointcheval, D., Johansson, T. (eds.) EUROCRYPT 2012. LNCS, vol. 7237, pp. 700–718. Springer, Heidelberg (2012). https://doi.org/10.1007/978-3-642-29011-4_41
41. Mol, P., Yilek, S.: Chosen-ciphertext security from slightly lossy trapdoor functions. In: Nguyen, P.Q., Pointcheval, D. (eds.) PKC 2010. LNCS, vol. 6056, pp. 296–311. Springer, Heidelberg (2010). https://doi.org/10.1007/978-3-642-13013-7_18
42. Paillier, P.: Public-key cryptosystems based on composite degree residuosity classes. In: Stern, J. (ed.) EUROCRYPT 1999. LNCS, vol. 1592, pp. 223–238. Springer, Heidelberg (1999). https://doi.org/10.1007/3-540-48910-X_16
43. Pan, J., Zeng, R.: Compact and tightly selective-opening secure public-key encryption schemes. In: Agrawal, S., Lin, D. (eds.) Advances in Cryptology, ASIACRYPT 2022, vol. 13793, pp. 363–393. Springer Nature Switzerland, Cham (2022). https://doi.org/10.1007/978-3-031-22969-5_13
44. Peikert, C.: Public-key cryptosystems from the worst-case shortest vector problem: extended abstract. In: Mitzenmacher, M. (ed.) 41st ACM STOC, May/June 2009, pp. 333–342. ACM Press (2009). https://doi.org/10.1145/1536414.1536461
45. Peikert, C., Vaikuntanathan, V., Waters, B.: A framework for efficient and composable oblivious transfer. In: Wagner, D. (ed.) CRYPTO 2008. LNCS, vol. 5157, pp. 554–571. Springer, Heidelberg (2008). https://doi.org/10.1007/978-3-540-85174-5_31
46. Peikert, C., Waters, B.: Lossy trapdoor functions and their applications. In: Ladner, R.E., Dwork, C. (eds.) 40th ACM STOC, May 2008, pp. 187–196. ACM Press (2008). https://doi.org/10.1145/1374376.1374406
47. Pietrzak, K., Rosen, A., Segev, G.: Lossy functions do not amplify well. In: Cramer, R. (ed.) TCC 2012. LNCS, vol. 7194, pp. 458–475. Springer, Heidelberg (2012). https://doi.org/10.1007/978-3-642-28914-9_26
48. Regev, O.: On lattices, learning with errors, random linear codes, and cryptography. In: Gabow, H.N., Fagin, R. (eds.) 37th ACM STOC, May 2005, pp. 84–93. ACM Press (2005). https://doi.org/10.1145/1060590.1060603

Multi-hop Fine-Grained Proxy Re-encryption

Yunxiao Zhou[1,2], Shengli Liu[2,3](✉), and Shuai Han[1,2](✉)

[1] School of Cyber Science and Engineering, Shanghai Jiao Tong University, Shanghai 200240, China
cloudzhou@sjtu.edu.cn

[2] State Key Laboratory of Cryptology, P.O. Box 5159, Beijing 100878, China
dalen17@sjtu.edu.cn

[3] Department of Computer Science and Engineering, Shanghai Jiao Tong University, Shanghai 200240, China
slliu@sjtu.edu.cn

Abstract. Proxy re-encryption (PRE) allows a proxy to transform a ciphertext intended for Alice (delegator) to another ciphertext intended for Bob (delegatee) without revealing the underlying message. Recently, a new variant of PRE, namely fine-grained PRE (FPRE), was proposed in [Zhou et al., Asiacrypt 2023]. Generally, FPRE is designed for a function family $\mathcal{F}$: each re-encryption key $\mathsf{rk}_{A\to B}^{f}$ is associated with a function $f \in \mathcal{F}$, and with $\mathsf{rk}_{A\to B}^{f}$, a proxy can transform Alice's ciphertext encrypting m to Bob's ciphertext encrypting $f(m)$. However, their scheme only supports single-hop re-encryption and achieves only CPA security.

In this paper, we formalize *multi-hop* FPRE (mFPRE) that supports multi-hop re-encryptions in the fine-grained setting, and propose two mFPRE schemes achieving CPA security and stronger HRA security (security against honest re-encryption attacks), respectively.

- For multi-hop FPRE, we formally define its syntax and formalize a set of security notions including CPA security, HRA security, undirectionality and ciphertext unlinkablity. HRA security is stronger and more reasonable than CPA security, and ciphertext unlinkablity blurs the proxy relations among a chain of multi-hop re-encryptions, hence providing better privacy. We establish the relations between these security notions.
- Our mFPRE schemes support fine-grained re-encryptions for bounded linear functions and have security based on the learning-with-errors (LWE) assumption in the standard model. In particular, one of our schemes is HRA secure and enjoys all the aforementioned desirable securities. To achieve CPA security and HRA security for mFPRE, we extend the framework of [Jafargholi et al., Crypto 2017] and the technique of the [Fuchsbauer et al., PKC 2019].

1 Introduction

Proxy re-encryption (PRE) extends the functionality of public-key encryption with re-encryption capability [4]. Let $(pk^{(A)}, sk^{(A)})$ and $(pk^{(B)}, sk^{(B)})$ be Alice

Q. Tang and V. Teague (Eds.): PKC 2024, LNCS 14604, pp. 161–192, 2024.
https://doi.org/10.1007/978-3-031-57728-4_6

and Bob's public and secret keys, respectively. Then Alice can generate a re-encryption key $\mathsf{rk}_{A\to B}$ with her key pair $(pk^{(A)}, sk^{(A)})$ and Bob's public key $pk^{(B)}$, and issue $\mathsf{rk}_{A\to B}$ to a proxy. Later her proxy is able to transform Alice's ciphertext $ct^{(A)}$ encrypting a message m to Bob's ciphertext $ct^{(B)}$ encrypting the same message, but the proxy cannot learn any information about m from $ct^{(A)}$, $ct^{(B)}$ and $\mathsf{rk}_{A\to B}$. Since its introduction, PRE has found a variety of applications, like email forwarding systems [4], secure distributed file systems [3], digital rights management systems [19] and block chain systems.

If the re-encryption key $\mathsf{rk}_{A\to B}$ can implement ciphertext transform not only from Alice to Bob, but also vice verse, then the PRE scheme is a *bidirectional* one. In contrast, if $\mathsf{rk}_{A\to B}$ does not support ciphertext transformation from Bob to Alice, then the PRE scheme is a *unidirectional* one. Note that the unidirectional property captures a more precise re-encryption authorization than the bidirectional property. Meanwhile, a unidirectional PRE can support bidirectional re-encryption authorization by issuing both $\mathsf{rk}_{A\to B}$ and $\mathsf{rk}_{B\to A}$ to a proxy. Therefore, unidirectional PRE is more welcome. However, designing unidirectional PREs is more challenging than its bidirectional siblings. In this paper, we focus on unidirectional PRE.

After transformation from $ct^{(A)}$ to $ct^{(B)}$ with $\mathsf{rk}_{A\to B}$, if the resulting $ct^{(B)}$ cannot be further transformed, the PRE scheme is a *single-hop* one. Otherwise, the resulting $ct^{(B)}$ can be further transformed to Charlie's ciphertext $ct^{(C)}$ with $\mathsf{rk}_{B\to C}$ (and so on), then the PRE scheme becomes a *multi-hop* one. Multi-hop PRE schemes support ciphertext transformation chains and provide re-encryption services in a more convenient way.

Fine-Grained Proxy Re-encryption. Traditionally, PRE provides an all-or-nothing authorization with which either the receiver can decrypt the transformed ciphertext to obtain the whole message m, or it learns nothing about m. Recently, PRE was further extended to support fine-grained re-encryption authorization in [21], and this variant PRE is named *fine-grained* PRE (FPRE). In an FPRE scheme, the re-encryption key $\mathsf{rk}^f_{A\to B}$ is further equipped with a function f which captures the precise re-encryption ability granted to a proxy. With $\mathsf{rk}^f_{A\to B}$, the proxy can transform Alice's ciphertext $ct^{(A)}$ encrypting a message m to Bob's ciphertext $ct^{(B)}$ encrypting $f(m)$ under $pk^{(B)}$. The recent work in [21] constructed a single-hop unidirectional FPRE scheme w.r.t. bounded linear functions, and proved its CPA security based on the learning-with-errors (LWE) assumption. However, there are two limitations in the FPRE scheme [21].

- The scheme only supports single-hop re-encryption. Suppose that Alice's ciphertext $ct^{(A)}$ has been transformed to a re-encrypted ciphertext $ct^{(B)}$ for Bob. Now Bob wants to forward the underlying message to Charlie, but he can not ask his proxy to do the ciphertext transformation for him due to the single-hop limitation of the FPRE. Thus, he has to decrypt $ct^{(B)}$ to recover the message and encrypt that message under Charlie's public key by himself. The decrypt-then-encrypt operation imposes extra working load to Bob. With a multi-hop FPRE scheme, this job becomes easy. Bob can simply forward the ciphertext $ct^{(B)}$ to his proxy and his proxy will be in charge of the ciphertext transformation.

- The scheme only achieves CPA security. In their CPA model, the adversary is not allowed to learn any re-encryptions from the target user to corrupted users. This is not reasonable. Consider such a scenario: Alice has sent a ciphertext $ct^{(A)}$ to her proxy and her proxy has transformed $ct^{(A)}$ to a re-encrypted ciphertext $ct^{(B)}$ for Bob. Now Bob is corrupted by an adversary. Later, Alice receives a new ciphertext $ct^{*(A)}$, and it is natural to require that the adversary learns nothing about the underlying message of $ct^{*(A)}$. However, this desired security cannot be guaranteed by CPA security since in the CPA model, the adversary is not allowed to learn any re-encryptions from the target user Alice to a corrupted user Bob.

  In fact, obtaining re-encryptions from the target user to a corrupted user is the so-called honest re-encryption attacks (HRA) [6]. When taking HRA attacks into account, the CPA security is lifted to HRA security. As demonstrated in [6], HRA security is more reasonable than CPA security.

The above two limitations lead to an interesting question:

Can we construct a multi-hop fine-grained PRE scheme, preferably also achieving HRA security?

Related Works on Multi-hop PRE Schemes. There already exist some unidirectional multi-hop PRE schemes in the literature. Chandran et al. [5] designed the first multi-hop unidirectional PRE scheme from program obfuscation and showed the selective obfuscation-based security of their schemes from the LWE assumption. Phong et al. [17] proposed a multi-hop PRE scheme with selective CPA security. However, their scheme is interactive, i.e., the re-encryption key generation algorithm requires both user i and user j's secret keys. Lai et al. [13] proposed a multi-hop PRE scheme achieving selective CCA security from indistinguishability obfuscation (iO). However, iO is a theoretical tool and far from being practical. Fan et al. [8] presented a latticed-based scheme, achieving selective tag-based CCA (tbCCA) security, but proxy relations (i.e., challenge graph of the adversary) are restricted to tree structure. Note that the tbCCA security and the HRA security are not comparable since tbCCA security model does not capture honest re-encryption attacks. Later, Fuchsbauer et al. [9] improved Chandran et al.'s scheme [5] to HRA security based on LWE. At the same time, they presented another multi-hop unidirectional scheme constructed from fully homomorphic encryption [10] and also achieved HRA security from LWE on the ideal lattices and circular-security assumption. Recently, Miao et al. [15] proposed a generic construction of multi-hop PRE with selective HRA security, and presented instantiations based on the decisional Diffie-Hellman (DDH) assumption.

All the existing multi-hop PRE schemes do not consider the fine-grained re-encryption, so the multi-hop *fine-grained* PRE with HRA security is still missing.

Our Contributions. In this work, we propose the first *multi-hop fine-grained* PRE scheme from LWE in the standard model.

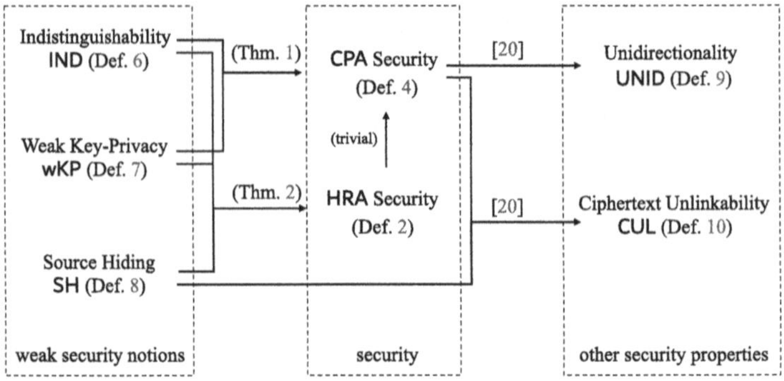

Fig. 1. Security notions of multi-hop FPRE and their relations, where [20] is the full version of this paper.

- *Formal Definitions for Multi-hop Fine-Grained PRE and Its Securities.* We formalize multi-hop fine-grained PRE (mFPRE) that supports multiple re-encryptions in the fine-grained setting. We also present the formal CPA and HRA security notions for multi-hop FPRE. In addition, we define unidirectionality (UNID) and ciphertext unlinkability (CUL) for mFPRE. The CUL security guarantees that the chain of multi-hop re-encryptions does not leak information about proxy relations among them, and hence provide better privacy. Moreover, we prove that UNID is implied by CPA, and CUL is implied by CPA and a weak security notion named source-hiding (SH).
- *Generic Framework for Achieving CPA and HRA Security for Multi-hop FPRE.* We extend the framework in [12] and adapt the techniques in [9] to the multi-hop FPRE setting for achieving (adaptive) CPA and HRA security. More precisely, we first define three weaker security notions including indistinguishability (IND), weak key-privacy (wKP) and source-hiding (SH). Then, we show that the CPA security of multi-hop FPRE is implied by IND and wKP, and the HRA security is implied by IND, wKP and SH. For proxy relations being chains or trees, our reduction only loses a quasi-polynomial factor. Note that the chain and tree topology have good applications in encrypted cloud storage, encrypted email forwarding, etc., as noted by [9].
- *Construction of Multi-hop FPRE from LWE.* We propose two unidirectional multi-hop FPRE schemes, including a CPA secure mFPRE_1 and an HRA secure mFPRE_2, for bounded linear functions[1]. More precisely, we prove that our first scheme mFPRE_1 has IND and wKP securities and hence achieves CPA

[1] Here "bounded" mean that the coefficients are of bounded norm. We note that the existing (single-hop) FPRE schemes [21] are also w.r.t. bounded linear functions.

security and UNID security, and prove that our second scheme mFPRE_2 has IND, wKP and SH securities and hence achieves HRA security, UNID security and CUL security. Both of the schemes are based on the LWE assumption in the standard model.

We refer to Fig. 1 for an overview of the security notions for multi-hop FPRE and their relations established in this work, and refer to Table 1 for a comparison of our schemes with known multi-hop unidirectional PRE schemes.

Table 1. Comparison of multi-hop unidirectional PRE schemes. The column **Standard Model?** asks whether the security is proved in the standard model. The column **Adaptive Corruptions?** asks whether all the security notions support adaptive corruptions. The column **Security** shows the type of security that the scheme achieves, where "HRA" refers to security against honest re-encryption attacks [6], and "tbCCA" refers to tag-based CCA [8] which is incomparable with HRA and restricts the proxy relations (i.e., challenge graph) to tree structure. The column **UNID** shows whether the scheme has unidirectionality. The column **CUL** shows whether the scheme has ciphertext unlinkability. The column **Assumption** shows the assumptions that the security of the scheme is based on, where "iO" refers to indistinguishability obfuscation. The column **Post Quantum?** asks whether the scheme is based on a post-quantum assumption. The column **Fine-Grained?** asks whether the scheme supports fine-grained re-encryptions. The column **Maximum Hops** shows the maximum re-encryption hops that the scheme supports, where "poly-log" refers to $\mathsf{poly}(\log \lambda)$, "sub-linear" refers to λ^{ε} with $0 < \varepsilon < 1$ in the security parameter λ, and "unbounded*" means that the PRE scheme in [15] can support any number of re-encryptions, but at the cost that the ciphertext length grows linearly with the number of re-encryptions. "–" means that no proof or discussion is provided.

PRE Scheme	Standard Model?	Adaptive Corruptions?	Security	UNID	CUL	Assumption	Post Quantum?	Fine-Grained?	Maximum Hops
FL19 [8]	✓	×	tbCCA	✓	–	LWE	✓	–	poly-log
LHAM20 [14]	✓	×	CCA	✓	–	iO	×	–	–
MPW23 [15]	✓	×	HRA	✓	–	DDH	×	–	unbounded*
FKKP19 [9]+ CCLNX14 [5]	✓	✓	HRA	✓	✓	LWE	✓	–	sub-linear
FKKP19 [9] +Gen09 [10]	✓	✓	HRA	✓	✓	LWE over ideal lattice + circular security	✓	–	–
mFPRE_1	✓	✓	CPA	✓	–	LWE	✓	✓	sub-linear
mFPRE_2	✓	✓	HRA	✓	✓	LWE	✓	✓	sub-linear

Technical Overview. Below we give a high-level overview of our multi-hop fine-grained PRE (mFPRE) scheme. We will first review the single-hop FPRE scheme proposed in [21]. Then we will explain how we realize multi-hop re-encryptions and how we achieve HRA security. For simplicity, we do not specify the dimensions of matrices/vectors.

Recap: The Single-Hop FPRE Scheme in [21] and Its Limitations. We give a brief description of the single-hop scheme in [21]. For user i, its public key $pk^{(i)}$ consists of two matrices $\mathbf{A}_1^{(i)} = \binom{\overline{\mathbf{A}}_1^{(i)}}{\underline{\mathbf{A}}_1^{(i)}}$ and $\mathbf{A}_2^{(i)} = \binom{\overline{\mathbf{A}}}{\underline{\mathbf{A}}_2^{(i)}}$, and its secret key $sk^{(i)}$ contains a trapdoor $\mathbf{T}^{(i)}$ of $\overline{\mathbf{A}}_1^{(i)}$.[2] Here the upper part of $\mathbf{A}_2^{(i)}$ is a (fixed) matrix $\overline{\mathbf{A}}$ generated by a trusted setup and shared by all users, as required by the security of the scheme [21].

The ciphertexts of their scheme have two levels. The first-level/second-level ciphertext $ct_1^{(i)}/ct_2^{(i)}$ of user i is generated using $\mathbf{A}_1^{(i)}/\mathbf{A}_2^{(i)}$ in $pk^{(i)}$ according to the dual Regev encryption scheme [18], namely for level $b \in \{1, 2\}$,

$$ct_b^{(i)} = \mathbf{A}_b^{(i)}\mathbf{s} + \mathbf{e} + \begin{pmatrix} \mathbf{0} \\ \lfloor q/2 \rfloor \mathbf{m} \end{pmatrix} = \begin{pmatrix} \overline{\mathbf{A}}_b^{(i)}\mathbf{s} + \overline{\mathbf{e}} \\ \underline{\mathbf{A}}_b^{(i)}\mathbf{s} + \underline{\mathbf{e}} + \lfloor q/2 \rfloor \cdot \mathbf{m} \end{pmatrix}, \tag{1}$$

where $\mathbf{s}$ and $\mathbf{e} = \binom{\overline{\mathbf{e}}}{\underline{\mathbf{e}}}$ are sampled according to a noise distribution χ.

To realize fine-grained re-encryptions w.r.t. a linear function $f_{\mathbf{M}} : \mathbf{m} \mapsto \mathbf{M} \cdot \mathbf{m}$, the re-encryption key is defined as $\mathsf{rk}_{i \to j}^{f_{\mathbf{M}}} := \left(\mathbf{R} \,\middle|\, \begin{smallmatrix} \mathbf{0} \\ \mathbf{M} \end{smallmatrix}\right)$, where $\mathbf{R}$ is a small norm matrix satisfying

$$\mathbf{R}\overline{\mathbf{A}}_1^{(i)} = \mathbf{A}_2^{(j)}\mathbf{S} + \mathbf{E} - \left(\begin{smallmatrix} \mathbf{0} \\ \mathbf{M} \end{smallmatrix}\right)\underline{\mathbf{A}}_1^{(i)} \tag{2}$$

with matrices $\mathbf{S}, \mathbf{E}$ following the noise distribution χ. Such $\mathbf{R}$ can be efficiently found by using the pre-image sampling algorithm $\mathsf{SamplePre}$ in [11] with the help of the trapdoor $\mathbf{T}^{(i)}$ of $\overline{\mathbf{A}}_1^{(i)}$ contained in $sk^{(i)}$ (cf. see Footnote 2). Now with $\mathsf{rk}_{i \to j}^{f_{\mathbf{M}}}$, user i's first-level ciphertext $ct_1^{(i)}$ of $\mathbf{m}$ can be converted to user j's second-level ciphertext $ct_2^{(j)}$ of the linear function $\mathbf{M} \cdot \mathbf{m}$ via multiplication

$$\begin{aligned} ct_2^{(j)} &:= \mathsf{rk}_{i \to j}^{f_{\mathbf{M}}} \cdot ct_1^{(i)} = \left(\mathbf{R} \,\middle|\, \begin{smallmatrix} \mathbf{0} \\ \mathbf{M} \end{smallmatrix}\right) \cdot \begin{pmatrix} \overline{\mathbf{A}}_1^{(i)}\mathbf{s} + \overline{\mathbf{e}} \\ \underline{\mathbf{A}}_1^{(i)}\mathbf{s} + \underline{\mathbf{e}} + \lfloor q/2 \rfloor \cdot \mathbf{m} \end{pmatrix} \\ &= \underbrace{\left(\mathbf{R}\overline{\mathbf{A}}_1^{(i)} + \left(\begin{smallmatrix} \mathbf{0} \\ \mathbf{M} \end{smallmatrix}\right)\underline{\mathbf{A}}_1^{(i)}\right)}_{=\mathbf{A}_2^{(j)}\mathbf{S}+\mathbf{E} \text{ by (2)}} \cdot \mathbf{s} + \mathbf{R}\overline{\mathbf{e}} + \left(\begin{smallmatrix} \mathbf{0} \\ \mathbf{M}\underline{\mathbf{e}} \end{smallmatrix}\right) + \left(\begin{smallmatrix} \mathbf{0} \\ \lfloor q/2 \rfloor \cdot \mathbf{M}\mathbf{m} \end{smallmatrix}\right) \\ &= \mathbf{A}_2^{(j)} \underbrace{\mathbf{S}\mathbf{s}}_{:=\mathbf{s}'} + \underbrace{\mathbf{E}\mathbf{s} + \mathbf{R}\overline{\mathbf{e}} + \left(\begin{smallmatrix} \mathbf{0} \\ \mathbf{M}\underline{\mathbf{e}} \end{smallmatrix}\right)}_{:=\mathbf{e}'} + \left(\begin{smallmatrix} \mathbf{0} \\ \lfloor q/2 \rfloor \cdot \mathbf{M}\mathbf{m} \end{smallmatrix}\right). \end{aligned} \tag{3}$$

Though a first-level ciphertext $ct_1^{(i)}$ can be re-encrypted to a second-level ciphertext $ct_2^{(j)}$, a second-level ciphertext $ct_2^{(j)}$ cannot be re-encrypted furthermore (no matter to first- or second-level ciphertexts), as explained below.

- To enable further re-encryptions of $ct_2^{(j)}$ to another user (say user k), user j need to compute a re-encryption key $\mathsf{rk}_{j \to k}^{f_{\mathbf{M}'}}$ similar to (2), and in particular, user j need to compute a small-norm $\mathbf{R}$ satisfying

$$\mathbf{R}\overline{\mathbf{A}} = \mathbf{A}_b^{(k)}\mathbf{S} + \mathbf{E} - \left(\begin{smallmatrix} \mathbf{0} \\ \mathbf{M}' \end{smallmatrix}\right)\underline{\mathbf{A}}_2^{(j)} \quad \text{for some } b \in \{1, 2\}, \tag{4}$$

  where $\overline{\mathbf{A}}$ is the upper part of $\mathbf{A}_2^{(j)}$.

[2] With the trapdoor $\mathbf{T}^{(i)}$ of $\overline{\mathbf{A}}_1^{(i)}$, one can use the pre-image sampling algorithm $\mathsf{SamplePre}$ developed in [11] to sample a small-norm $\mathbf{R}$ such that $\mathbf{R} \cdot \overline{\mathbf{A}}_1^{(i)} = \mathbf{B}$ holds, given any $\mathbf{B}$.

- Note that $\overline{\mathbf{A}}$ is chosen by a trusted setup, so user j has no trapdoor of $\overline{\mathbf{A}}$. This is crucial to the security of their single-hop scheme [21], since their security proof needs to embed an LWE instance to $\overline{\mathbf{A}}$. But without knowing a trapdoor of $\overline{\mathbf{A}}$, user j *cannot* generate a $\mathbf{R}$ satisfying (4).[3]

Overall, it is the security that limits the scheme in [21] serving only for *single-hop* re-encryptions.

ACHIEVING MULTI-HOP RE-ENCRYPTIONS. Note that in the single-hop scheme [21], the ciphertexts $ct_1^{(i)}, ct_2^{(i)}$ of two levels have an almost identical form (i.e., the dual Regev encryption) except for the matrix ($\mathbf{A}_1^{(i)}$ or $\mathbf{A}_2^{(i)}$) used in the encryption. The first-level ciphertext $ct_1^{(i)}$ can be re-encrypted since user i has the trapdoor of $\overline{\mathbf{A}}_1^{(i)}$, while the second-level ciphertext $ct_2^{(i)}$ cannot since user i does not have the trapdoor of $\overline{\mathbf{A}}$.

To enable multi-hop re-encryptions, the public key $pk^{(i)}$ in our scheme contains only one matrix $\mathbf{A}^{(i)} = \binom{\overline{\mathbf{A}}^{(i)}}{\underline{\mathbf{A}}^{(i)}}$, and the secret key $sk^{(i)}$ is the trapdoor $\mathbf{T}^{(i)}$ of $\overline{\mathbf{A}}^{(i)}$. (So our scheme has a transparent setup in contrast to [21].) The ciphertexts $ct^{(i)}$ in our scheme stick to $\mathbf{A}^{(i)}$ during encryption, i.e.,

$$ct^{(i)} = \mathbf{A}^{(i)}\mathbf{s} + \mathbf{e} + \begin{pmatrix} \mathbf{0} \\ \lfloor q/2 \rfloor \mathbf{m} \end{pmatrix}.$$

The re-encryption key $\mathsf{rk}_{i \to j}^{f_{\mathbf{M}}} := \left(\mathbf{R} \,\middle|\, \begin{smallmatrix} \mathbf{0} \\ \mathbf{M} \end{smallmatrix}\right)$ in our scheme generates the small norm $\mathbf{R}$ according to

$$\mathbf{R}\overline{\mathbf{A}}^{(i)} = \mathbf{A}^{(j)}\mathbf{S} + \mathbf{E} - \binom{\mathbf{0}}{\mathbf{M}}\underline{\mathbf{A}}^{(i)}.$$

In a nutshell, we discard the subscripts 1, 2 in our scheme.

Similar to the analysis (3), in our scheme, user i's ciphertext $ct^{(i)} = \mathbf{A}^{(i)}\mathbf{s} + \mathbf{e} + \binom{\mathbf{0}}{\lfloor q/2 \rfloor \cdot \mathbf{m}}$ of message $\mathbf{m}$ can be translated to user j's ciphertext with

$$ct^{(j)} := \mathsf{rk}_{i \to j}^{f_{\mathbf{M}}} \cdot ct^{(i)} = \mathbf{A}^{(j)} \underbrace{\mathbf{S}\mathbf{s}}_{:=\mathbf{s}'} + \underbrace{\mathbf{E}\mathbf{s} + \mathbf{R}\bar{\mathbf{e}} + \binom{\mathbf{0}}{\mathbf{M}\underline{\mathbf{e}}}}_{:=\mathbf{e}'} + \binom{\mathbf{0}}{\lfloor q/2 \rfloor \cdot \underbrace{\mathbf{M} \cdot \mathbf{m}}_{=f_{\mathbf{M}}(\mathbf{m})}}. \tag{5}$$

Now in our scheme, user j owns the trapdoor $\mathbf{T}^{(j)}$ of $\overline{\mathbf{A}}^{(j)}$ in its secret key, so it is able to generate $\mathsf{rk}_{j \to k}^{f_{\mathbf{M}'}} := \left(\mathbf{R}' \,\middle|\, \begin{smallmatrix} \mathbf{0} \\ \mathbf{M}' \end{smallmatrix}\right)$ by sampling a small norm $\mathbf{R}'$ satisfying

$$\mathbf{R}'\overline{\mathbf{A}}^{(j)} = \mathbf{A}^{(k)}\mathbf{S}' + \mathbf{E}' - \binom{\mathbf{0}}{\mathbf{M}'}\underline{\mathbf{A}}^{(j)}.$$

[3] Otherwise, assuming that user j can generate a $\mathbf{R}$ satisfying (4) without knowing a trapdoor of $\overline{\mathbf{A}}$, then anyone (including user k) can generate such $\mathbf{R}$ and thus $\mathsf{rk}_{j \to k}^{f_{\mathbf{M}'}}$ without the help of user j. In this case, user k can translate all ciphertexts $ct_2^{(j)}$ intended for j to ciphertexts $ct_b^{(k)}$ ($b \in \{1, 2\}$) encrypted under $pk^{(k)}$ by itself, and then decrypt the re-encrypted ciphertexts using $sk^{(k)}$ to learn information about the message underlying $ct_2^{(j)}$, violating the confidentiality of encryption scheme.

Consequently, with $\mathsf{rk}_{j\to k}^{f_{\mathbf{M}'}}$, the re-encryption $ct^{(j)} = \mathbf{A}^{(j)}\mathbf{s}' + \mathbf{e}' + \binom{\mathbf{0}}{\lfloor q/2 \rfloor \cdot \mathbf{M}\cdot\mathbf{m}}$ generated by (5) can be further re-encrypted to user k's ciphertext

$$ct^{(k)} := \mathsf{rk}_{j\to k}^{f_{\mathbf{M}'}} \cdot ct^{(j)} = \mathbf{A}^{(k)} \underbrace{\mathbf{S}'\mathbf{s}'}_{:=\mathbf{s}''} + \underbrace{\mathbf{E}'\mathbf{s}' + \mathbf{R}'\overline{\mathbf{e}'} + \binom{\mathbf{0}}{\mathbf{M}'\underline{\mathbf{e}'}}}_{:=\mathbf{e}''} + \binom{\mathbf{0}}{\lfloor q/2 \rfloor \cdot \underbrace{\mathbf{M}' \cdot (\mathbf{M}\mathbf{m})}_{=f_{\mathbf{M}'}(f_{\mathbf{M}}(\mathbf{m}))}},$$

which encrypts $f_{\mathbf{M}'}(f_{\mathbf{M}}(\mathbf{m})) := \mathbf{M}' \cdot \mathbf{M} \cdot \mathbf{m}$. In this way, the re-encryptions can be further extended with $ct^{(i)} \xrightarrow{\mathsf{rk}_{i\to j}^{f_{\mathbf{M}}}} ct^{(j)} \xrightarrow{\mathsf{rk}_{j\to k}^{f_{\mathbf{M}'}}} ct^{(k)} \xrightarrow{\mathsf{rk}_{k\to w}^{f_{\mathbf{M}''}}} \cdots$, and thus we achieve *multi-hop* fine-grained PRE for linear functions. Note that the norm of the errors $\mathbf{e}, \mathbf{e}', \mathbf{e}'', \cdots$ increases as the re-encryption continues, so to guarantee the correctness of decryption, the re-encryption can go on until the norm of errors reaches $\lfloor q/4 \rfloor$. In fact, our multi-hop FPRE scheme supports constant hops of re-encryptions under polynomial modulus q and supports sub-linear hops of re-encryptions under sub-exponential modulus q.

Overall, since user j has the trapdoor $\mathbf{T}^{(j)}$ of $\overline{\mathbf{A}}^{(j)}$ in our scheme, this rescues our scheme from single-hop, but at the same time, it incurs an issue: we cannot embed an LWE instance to $\overline{\mathbf{A}}^{(j)}$ in the security proof. To avoid this issue, the scheme in [21] prohibits user j from having the trapdoor of both matrices in public key, which in turn limits it to supporting only single-hop re-encryption. To address this issue, we need new techniques to prove security for our mFPRE.

Below we will first show the high-level ideas of the selective CPA security proof of our scheme, and then explain how we upgrade the selective security to adaptive security by adapting the framework of [9,12] to the fine-grained setting, and explain how we achieve the stronger HRA security.

Selective CPA Security of Our Scheme. We give a high-level overview of the selective CPA security proof of our scheme. Roughly speaking, the (adaptive) CPA security asks the hardness of determining whether a ciphertext ct^* under $pk^{(i^*)}$ encrypts $\mathbf{m}_0$ or $\mathbf{m}_1$, even if an adversary $\mathcal{A}$ can get re-encryption keys $\{\mathsf{rk}_{i\to j}^{f}\}$ and secret keys $\{sk^{(i)}\}$ of some users. To prevent trivial attacks, $\mathcal{A}$ cannot corrupt the target user i^*, and cannot obtain a chain of re-encryption keys from i^* to some corrupted user j. Selective CPA security is weaker as it requires $\mathcal{A}$ to declare the target user i^* and the tuples (i, j) for which $\mathcal{A}$ wants to obtain the corresponding $\{\mathsf{rk}_{i\to j}^{f}\}$ at the beginning of the game.

The main ideas for the selective CPA security proof are: we first change the generations of re-encryption keys $\{\mathsf{rk}_{i\to j}^{f}\}$ so that it does not involve $sk^{(i^*)}$, and then the indistinguishability of ct^* essentially follows from the CPA security of the dual Regev encryption scheme (based on LWE). More precisely,

- **Step 1. Simulating the generation of $\{\mathsf{rk}_{i\to j}^{f}\}$ without knowing** $sk^{(i^*)}$. Let us take an (acyclic) chain of re-encryption keys $\mathsf{rk}_{i^*\to j_1}^{f_1}, \mathsf{rk}_{j_1\to j_2}^{f_2}, \cdots, \mathsf{rk}_{j_{d-1}\to j_d}^{f_{d-1}}$ as example to show how we simulate them in a computationally indistinguishable way without using $sk^{(i^*)}$.

Observe that only the generation of $\mathsf{rk}_{i^* \to j_1}^{f_1}$ involves $sk^{(i^*)}$, where the trapdoor $sk^{(i^*)} = \mathbf{T}^{(i^*)}$ of $\overline{\mathbf{A}}^{(i^*)}$ is used to sample $\mathbf{R}$ satisfying

$$\mathbf{R}\overline{\mathbf{A}}^{(i^*)} = \mathbf{A}^{(j_1)}\mathbf{S} + \mathbf{E} - \binom{0}{\mathbf{M}}\underline{\mathbf{A}}^{(i^*)}.$$

Thus we need an indistinguishable way to sample it without trapdoor $\mathbf{T}^{(i^*)}$.

If we can embed an LWE instance to $\mathbf{A}^{(j_1)}\mathbf{S} + \mathbf{E}$ in the above equation, then it can be replaced by a uniform $\mathbf{U}$, and consequently, we have

$$\mathbf{R}\overline{\mathbf{A}}^{(i^*)} = \mathbf{A}^{(j_1)}\mathbf{S} + \mathbf{E} - \binom{0}{\mathbf{M}}\underline{\mathbf{A}}^{(i^*)} \overset{c}{\approx} \mathbf{U} - \binom{0}{\mathbf{M}}\underline{\mathbf{A}}^{(i^*)} \equiv \mathbf{U}.$$

As a result, we are able to sample $\mathbf{R}$ such that $\mathbf{R}\overline{\mathbf{A}}^{(i^*)} \equiv \mathbf{U}$ by simply choosing it according to a proper discrete Gaussian distribution.[4] However, we cannot embed the LWE instance, since the trapdoor of $\mathbf{A}^{(j_1)}$ is needed to generate $\mathsf{rk}_{j_1 \to j_2}^{f_2}$. This is exactly the issue we mentioned before.

To solve the problem without sacrificing the capability of multi-hop re-encryptions, we simulate the chain of re-encryption keys in reverse order. We will first change the generation of the very last $\mathsf{rk}_{j_{d-1} \to j_d}^{f_{d-1}}$ in the chain as follows. Since $\mathsf{rk}_{j_{d-1} \to j_d}^{f_{d-1}}$ lies in the very end of the chain, we do not need to generate re-encryption key from user j_d to any other users. Moreover, this chain starting from i^* contains only uncorrupted users to avoid trivial attacks. Consequently, the secret key $sk^{(j_d)}$ of user j_d is in fact not needed in the experiment, and now we can embed an LWE instance to $\mathbf{A}^{(j_d)}\mathbf{S} + \mathbf{E}$ such that

$$\mathbf{R}\overline{\mathbf{A}}^{(j_{d-1})} = \mathbf{A}^{(j_d)}\mathbf{S} + \mathbf{E} - \binom{0}{\mathbf{M}}\underline{\mathbf{A}}^{(j_{d-1})} \overset{c}{\approx} \mathbf{U} - \binom{0}{\mathbf{M}}\underline{\mathbf{A}}^{(j_{d-1})} \equiv \mathbf{U}.$$

Then $\mathbf{R}$ can be simply sampled following the proper discrete Gaussian distribution so that $\mathbf{R}\overline{\mathbf{A}}^{(j_{d-1})} \equiv \mathbf{U}$.

After the changing of $\mathsf{rk}_{j_{d-1} \to j_d}^{f_{d-1}}$, the secret key $sk^{(j_{d-1})}$ of user j_{d-1} is no longer involved, and thus through a similar analysis, we can then embed an LWE instance to $\mathbf{A}^{(j_{d-1})}\mathbf{S} + \mathbf{E}$ so that the $\mathbf{R}$ in the second last $\mathsf{rk}_{j_{d-2} \to j_{d-1}}^{f_{d-2}}$ can be sampled following discrete Gaussian. By changing the re-encryption keys one by one, we can eventually simulate all re-encryption keys in the chain by simply sampling them according to discrete Gaussian, without $sk^{(i^*)}$.

More generally, the re-encryption keys $\{\mathsf{rk}_{i \to j}^{f}\}$ queried by $\mathcal{A}$ might not be a chain. Nevertheless, we can simulate them in a similar way, roughly by processing all the chains simultaneously and for each chain in reverse order.

- **Step 2. Computationally hiding $\mathbf{m}_0/\mathbf{m}_1$ in $ct^{(i^*)}$.** After Step 1, $sk^{(i^*)}$ is not used at all, and thus for the challenge ciphertext $ct^{(i^*)} = \mathbf{A}^{(i^*)}\mathbf{s} + \mathbf{e} + \binom{\mathbf{0}}{\lfloor q/2 \rfloor \mathbf{m}_\beta}$ ($\beta \in \{0,1\}$), we can embed an LWE instance to $\mathbf{A}^{(i^*)}\mathbf{s} + \mathbf{e}$, so that the underlying message $\mathbf{m}_\beta$ is hidden to the adversary $\mathcal{A}$.

[4] By [11], if $\mathbf{R}$ follows a proper discrete Gaussian distribution, then $\mathbf{R}\overline{\mathbf{A}}^{(i^*)}$ is statistically close to the uniform distribution $\mathbf{U}$.

Overall, this proof strategy works only in the selective setting, as it requires to know the tuples (i, j) for which $\mathcal{A}$ wants to obtain $\{\mathsf{rk}^f_{i\to j}\}$ in advance, so that they can be properly simulated (i.e., in reverse order for each chain).

To achieve adaptive security, if we guess the tuples (i, j) that $\mathcal{A}$ wants to query at the beginning of game, it will incur a security loss as large as $O(2^{\mathfrak{n}^2})$ with $\mathfrak{n}$ the number of users. To reduce the security loss of adaptive security, we extend the frameworks in [9,12] to multi-hop FPRE, as explained below.

ACHIEVING ADAPTIVE SECURITY WITH JAFARGHOLI ET AL.'S FRAMEWORK. Jafargholi et al. [12] proposed a generic framework for upgrading selective security to adaptive security with a more fine-grained analysis. Later, Fuchsbauer et al. [9] applied the framework of [12] to the security of (traditional) PRE. In this work, we extend the framework of Jafargholi et al. [12] and the techniques of Fuchsbauer et al. [9] to our multi-hop FPRE.

Roughly speaking, the main observations are: although in the above selective proof strategy, we need the whole information (denoted by w) about the tuples (i, j) that $\mathcal{A}$ wants to query for re-encryption keys, only part of the information (denoted by u) is used in simulating the intermediate hybrids. For example, in the proof strategy shown above, Step 1 consists of many hybrids, while in each hybrid we only change the generation of a single re-encryption key in the chain, so a small amount of information u will be sufficient for the reduction to the LWE assumption; in Step 2, the information of $u := i^*$ is sufficient for the reduction. It is shown in [12] that the security loss in such cases can be limited to the maximum size of the information u used across any two successive hybrids, which might be much smaller than the size of w.

To apply their techniques [9,12], we abstract two useful yet weaker security notions for our multi-hop FPRE, including indistinguishability (IND) and weak key-privacy (wKP), and then establish a theorem by reducing the adaptive CPA security to IND and wKP with a smaller security loss. Concretely, the two weaker notions exactly correspond to Step 1 and Step 2 in the above proof strategy.

Weak Key-Privacy (wKP). It stipulates that the re-encryption key $\mathsf{rk}^f_{i\to j}$ honestly generated by $sk^{(i)}$ can be indistinguishably changed to a simulated one generated without $sk^{(i)}$ in the view of adversary who gets no secret keys $sk^{(i)}$.

Indistinguishability (IND). It requires the indistinguishability of ciphertext for adversary who gets no re-encryption keys $\mathsf{rk}^f_{i\to j}$ and no secret keys $sk^{(i)}$.

The theorem showing adaptive CPA security based on IND and wKP for our multi-hop FPRE is proved in a similar way as [9,12]. For an arbitrary adversary who can obtain re-encryption keys $\{\mathsf{rk}^f_{i\to j}\}$ for arbitrary tuples (i, j), the security loss of adaptive CPA security is $\mathfrak{n}^{O(\mathfrak{n})}$ in contrast to the naive guessing strategy $O(2^{\mathfrak{n}^2})$. In many realistic scenarios like key rotation for encrypted cloud storage or forwarding of encrypted mail, as demonstrated in [9], the proxy relations are in fact *trees, chains or low-depth graphs*. In these situations, an adversary can only obtain $\{\mathsf{rk}^f_{i\to j}\}$ for tuples (i, j) that form trees, chains or low-depth graphs, and the security loss is only quasi-polynomial $\mathfrak{n}^{O(\log \mathfrak{n})}$.

Achieving HRA Security. Security against honest re-encryption attacks (HRA) was first introduced by Cohen [6] and is a security notion stronger and more reasonable than CPA. Compared with CPA security, HRA also allows the adversary $\mathcal{A}$ to obtain re-encryptions of ciphertexts from the target user i^* to *corrupted* users, as long as the ciphertexts to be re-encrypted are honestly generated and are not (re-encryptions of) the challenge ciphertext ct^*. Note that HRA security is stronger than CPA: in the CPA experiment, $\mathcal{A}$ cannot obtain a chain of re-encryption keys from i^* to corrupted users in order to prevent trivial attacks, and thus cannot generate re-encryptions from i^* to corrupted users by itself.

In order to achieve HRA security, we need to enhance our aforementioned CPA proof strategy with a new computationally indistinguishable method for simulating the generation of re-encryptions of ciphertexts from the target user i^* to corrupted users without using $sk^{(i^*)}$. Note that the re-encryptions from i^* to corrupted users might be a chain $ct^{(i^*)} \to ct^{(j_1)} \to ct^{(j_2)} \to \cdots \to ct^{(j_d)}$, the generation of which involves a chain of re-encryption keys $\mathsf{rk}^{f_1}_{i^* \to j_1}, \mathsf{rk}^{f_2}_{j_1 \to j_2}, \cdots, \mathsf{rk}^{f_{d-1}}_{j_{d-1} \to j_d}$. However, we cannot use similar techniques as the CPA security proof strategy to replace this chain of re-encryption keys with simulated ones, since the involved users $j_1, j_2, \cdots, j_d$ might be corrupted by $\mathcal{A}$.

To bypass this problem, we will simulate the generation of the chain of re-encryptions $ct^{(i^*)} \to ct^{(j_1)} \to ct^{(j_2)} \to \cdots \to ct^{(j_d)}$ directly, without using any of the re-encryption keys $\mathsf{rk}^{f_1}_{i^* \to j_1}, \mathsf{rk}^{f_2}_{j_1 \to j_2}, \cdots, \mathsf{rk}^{f_{d-1}}_{j_{d-1} \to j_d}$, thus also without using $sk^{(i^*)}$. To this end, we abstract a (weak) security notion called source-hiding (SH) for multi-hop FPRE, by adapting the techniques in [9, 12].

Source-Hiding (SH). It stipulates that the honestly generated re-encryption $ct^{(i)} \to ct^{(j)}$ by using $\mathsf{rk}^{f}_{i \to j}$ can be indistinguishably changed to a simulated one generated without $\mathsf{rk}^{f}_{i \to j}$.

The SH security is exactly what we need to upgrade our CPA security proof strategy to HRA security: roughly speaking, by the SH security, we can change all re-encryptions $ct^{(i)} \to ct^{(j)}$ queried by $\mathcal{A}$ to simulated ones without using re-encryption keys (thus $sk^{(i^*)}$ is not involved); then by the wKP security, we can change all re-encryption keys $\{\mathsf{rk}^{f}_{i \to j}\}$ queried by $\mathcal{A}$ to simulated ones without using $sk^{(i^*)}$; finally, by the IND security, the challenge ciphertext ct^* of the target user i^* hides the underlying message.

For achieving *adaptive* HRA security for multi-hop FPRE, we also extend the framework of Jafargholi et al. [12] and the techniques of Fuchsbauer et al. [9], and establish a theorem by reducing the adaptive HRA security to IND, wKP and SH, with similar security loss.

Finally, we give a high-level overview of our second multi-hop FPRE scheme which additionally satisfies SH security. More precisely, we augment each ciphertext with a level $v \in \mathbb{N}$, and use different noise distribution χ_v for the generation of ciphertexts of different levels. Namely, the v-level ciphertext of user i is now generated by

$$ct_v^{(i)} := \mathbf{A}^{(i)}\mathbf{s} + \mathbf{e} + \binom{\mathbf{0}}{\lfloor q/2 \rfloor \mathbf{m}} \quad \text{with } \mathbf{s} \text{ and } \mathbf{e} \text{ following } \chi_v. \tag{6}$$

Moreover, we randomize the generation of re-encryption $ct_v^{(i)} \to ct_{v+1}^{(j)}$ with $\mathsf{rk}_{i \to j}^{f_{\mathbf{M}}}$ by adding noises, i.e., choosing $\tilde{\mathbf{s}}$ and $\tilde{\mathbf{e}}$ according to χ_{v+1} and computing

$$\begin{aligned} ct_{v+1}^{(j)} &:= \mathsf{rk}_{i \to j}^{f_{\mathbf{M}}} \cdot ct_v^{(i)} + \boxed{\mathbf{A}^{(j)}\tilde{\mathbf{s}} + \tilde{\mathbf{e}}} \\ &= \mathbf{A}^{(j)} \underbrace{\mathbf{S}\mathbf{s}}_{:=\mathbf{s}'} + \underbrace{\mathbf{E}\mathbf{s} + \mathbf{R}\bar{\mathbf{e}} + \binom{\mathbf{0}}{\mathbf{M}\underline{\mathbf{e}}}}_{:=\mathbf{e}'} + \binom{\mathbf{0}}{\lfloor q/2 \rfloor \cdot \underbrace{\mathbf{M} \cdot \mathbf{m}}_{=f_{\mathbf{M}}(\mathbf{m})}} + \boxed{\mathbf{A}^{(j)}\tilde{\mathbf{s}} + \tilde{\mathbf{e}}} \quad (7) \\ &= \mathbf{A}^{(j)}(\boxed{\tilde{\mathbf{s}}} + \mathbf{s}') + (\boxed{\tilde{\mathbf{e}}} + \mathbf{e}') + \binom{\mathbf{0}}{\lfloor q/2 \rfloor \cdot \mathbf{M} \cdot \mathbf{m}}, \quad (8) \end{aligned}$$

where (7) follows from (5). By choosing the noise distribution χ_v carefully, we can ensure that $\boxed{\tilde{\mathbf{s}}}$ smudges $\mathbf{s}'$ and $\boxed{\tilde{\mathbf{e}}}$ smudges $\mathbf{e}'$. Consequently, the honestly generated re-encryption $ct_{v+1}^{(j)}$ in (8) is statistically indistinguishable from a freshly generated $(v+1)$-level ciphertext of user j that encrypts $\mathbf{M} \cdot \mathbf{m}$ according to (6), without using $\mathsf{rk}_{i \to j}^{f_{\mathbf{M}}}$. This shows the SH security of this scheme. Similar to our first scheme, this scheme also achieves IND and wKP securities, thus achieving adaptive HRA security via the generic theorem.

Interestingly, we also show that the SH security together with the CPA security (or HRA security) imply *ciphertext unlinkability* (CUL), which can blur the proxy relations in a chain of multi-hop re-encryptions in a more complex setting.

Relations to Existing Works. Finally, we summarize the results already known in the non-fine-grained setting or in the single-hop fine-grained setting, and the results that are novel in our work.

The weaker security notions IND, wKP, SH were originally defined by Fuchsbauer et al. [9] for (non-fine-grained) PRE. Fuchsbauer et al. [9] also established two theorems showing adaptive CPA security based on IND and wKP and showing adaptive HRA security based on IND, wKP and SH, respectively, for (non-fine-grained) PRE, building upon the framework of Jafargholi et al. [12].

The notion of single-hop FPRE and its CUL security were recently introduced by Zhou et al. [21], where they also formally proved the relation that CPA implies UNID for single-hop FPRE.

In our work, we propose the concept of multi-hop FPRE to support multi-hop fine-grained re-encryptions, and formalize a set of security notions CPA, HRA, IND, wKP, SH, UNID, CUL in the multi-hop fine-grained setting. Moreover, we establish several useful relations between these security notions for multi-hop FPRE, by adapting the two theorems in [9] and the relation in [21] to our multi-hop FPRE. Besides, we show the relation that SH + CPA $\Rightarrow$ CUL holds for our multi-hop FPRE, which is for the first time established for PRE (no matter in which setting). Furthermore, we construct two multi-hop FPRE schemes from LWE, and prove their IND, wKP and SH securities based on the LWE assumption in the standard model, which are novel in our work. According to the relations we established (i.e., Theorem 1 and Theorem 2), the two multi-hop FPRE schemes achieves adaptive CPA and adaptive HRA securities, respectively.

2 Preliminaries

Notations. Let $\lambda \in \mathbb{N}$ denote the security parameter throughout the paper, and all algorithms, distributions, functions and adversaries take 1^λ as an implicit input. If x is defined by y or the value of y is assigned to x, we write $x := y$. For $i, j \in \mathbb{N}$ with $i < j$, define $[i, j] := \{i, i+1, ..., j\}$ and $[j] := \{1, 2, ..., j\}$. For a set $\mathcal{X}$, denote by $x \leftarrow_\$ \mathcal{X}$ the procedure of sampling x from $\mathcal{X}$ uniformly at random. If $\mathcal{D}$ is distribution, $x \leftarrow_\$ \mathcal{D}$ means that x is sampled according to $\mathcal{D}$. All our algorithms are probabilistic unless stated otherwise. We use $y \leftarrow_\$ \mathcal{A}(x)$ to define the random variable y obtained by executing algorithm $\mathcal{A}$ on input x. If $\mathcal{A}$ is deterministic we write $y \leftarrow \mathcal{A}(x)$. "PPT" abbreviates probabilistic polynomial-time. Denote by negl some negligible function. By $\Pr_i[\cdot]$ we denote the probability of a particular event occurring in game G_i.

For random variables X and Y, the min-entropy of X is defined as $\mathbf{H}_\infty(X) := -\log(\max_x \Pr[X = x])$, and the statistical distance between X and Y is defined as $\Delta(X, Y) := \frac{1}{2} \cdot \sum_x |\Pr[X = x] - \Pr[Y = x]|$. If $\Delta(X, Y) = \mathsf{negl}(\lambda)$, we say that X and Y are statistically indistinguishable (close), and denote it by $X \approx_s Y$.

Let $n, m, m', q \in \mathbb{N}$, and let $\mathbf{A} \in \mathbb{Z}_q^{m \times n}$, $\mathbf{v} \in \mathbb{Z}_q^n$, $\mathbf{B} \in \mathbb{Z}_q^{m' \times n}$. Define the lattice $\Lambda(\mathbf{A}) := \{\mathbf{A}\mathbf{x} \mid \mathbf{x} \in \mathbb{Z}^n\}$, the q-ary lattice $\Lambda_q(\mathbf{A}) := \{\mathbf{A}\mathbf{x} \mid \mathbf{x} \in \mathbb{Z}_q^n\} + q\mathbb{Z}^m$, its "orthogonal" lattice $\Lambda_q^\perp(\mathbf{A}) := \{\mathbf{x} \in \mathbb{Z}^m \mid \mathbf{x}^\top \mathbf{A} = \mathbf{0} \mod q\}$, and the "shifted" lattice $\Lambda_q^{\mathbf{v}}(\mathbf{A}) := \{\mathbf{r} \in \mathbb{Z}^m \mid \mathbf{r}^\top \mathbf{A} = \mathbf{v}^\top \mod q\}$, which can be further extended to $\Lambda_q^{\mathbf{B}}(\mathbf{A}) := \{\mathbf{R} \in \mathbb{Z}^{m' \times m} \mid \mathbf{R}\mathbf{A} = \mathbf{B} \mod q\}$. Let $\|\mathbf{v}\|$ (resp., $\|\mathbf{v}\|_\infty$) denote its ℓ_2 (resp., infinity) norm. For a matrix $\mathbf{A}$, we define $\|\mathbf{A}\|$ (resp., $\|\mathbf{A}\|_\infty$) as the largest ℓ_2 (resp., infinity) norm of $\mathbf{A}$'s rows. A distribution χ is B-bounded if its support is limited to $[-B, B]$. Let $\mathbb{Z}_q$ be the ring of integers modulo q, and its elements are represented by the integers in $(-q/2, q/2]$.

Due to space limitations, we present lattice backgrounds in the full version [20], where we recall the definitions of discrete Gaussian, LWE assumption, and the $\mathsf{TrapGen}$, Invert, $\mathsf{SamplePre}$ algorithms introduced in [1,11,16].

3 Multi-hop Fine-Grained PRE

In this section, we formalize a new primitive called *Multi-Hop Fine-Grained PRE* (mFPRE), by extending the concept of single-hop FPRE proposed in [21] to support multi-hop of re-encryptions. Compared with (traditional) PRE, FPRE allows fine-grained delegations, by associating re-encryption key $\mathsf{rk}_{i \to j}^f$ with a function f to support the conversion of user i's ciphertext $ct^{(i)}$ encrypting message m to user j's ciphertext $ct^{(j)}$ encrypting the function value $f(m)$. Moreover, in contrast to single-hop FPRE, our multi-hop FPRE supports multiple re-encryptions, namely, user j's re-encrypted ciphertext $ct^{(j)}$ encrypting $f(m)$ can be further re-encrypted to user k's ciphertext $ct^{(k)}$ encrypting $f'(f(m))$ with the help of another $\mathsf{rk}_{j \to k}^{f'}$, and as forth. These multiple re-encryptions can be correctly decrypted to the corresponding function values, as long as the number of re-encryption hops does not exceed the maximum level.

As for security, we formalize the CPA and HRA security for multi-hop FPRE. To achieve both security, we adapt the framework proposed in [9,12] to fine-grained setting and establish two theorems reducing CPA and HRA to a set of weaker security notions, including indistinguishablity (IND), weak key-privacy (wKP) and source-hiding (SH), for multi-hop FPRE. Furthermore, we introduce some other security properties including unidirectionality (UNID) and ciphertext unlinkability (CUL) for multi-hop FPRE. See Fig. 1 in introduction for an overview of the relations between these security notions.

3.1 Syntax of Multi-hop FPRE and Its CPA and HRA Security

Definition 1 (Multi-Hop Fine-Grained PRE). *Let $\mathcal{F}$ be a family of functions from $\mathcal{M}$ to $\mathcal{M}$, where $\mathcal{M}$ is a message space. A multi-hop fine-grained proxy re-encryption (multi-hop FPRE) scheme for function family $\mathcal{F}$ is associated with a maximum level $L \in \mathbb{N}$ and defined with a tuple of PPT algorithms* $\mathsf{mFPRE} = (\mathsf{KGen}, \mathsf{FReKGen}, \mathsf{Enc}, \mathsf{FReEnc}, \mathsf{Dec})$.

- $(pk, sk) \leftarrow_{\$} \mathsf{KGen}$: *The key generation algorithm outputs a pair of public key and secret key (pk, sk).*
- $\mathsf{rk}^f_{i \to j} \leftarrow_{\$} \mathsf{FReKGen}(pk^{(i)}, sk^{(i)}, pk^{(j)}, f)$: *Taking as input a public-secret key pair $(pk^{(i)}, sk^{(i)})$, another public key $pk^{(j)}$ and a function $f \in \mathcal{F}$, the fine-grained re-encryption key generation algorithm outputs a fine-grained re-encryption key $\mathsf{rk}^f_{i \to j}$ that allows re-encrypting ciphertexts intended to i into ciphertexts encrypted for j.*
- $ct_v \leftarrow_{\$} \mathsf{Enc}(pk, m, v)$: *Taking as input pk, a message $m \in \mathcal{M}$ and a level $v \in [0, L]$, the encryption algorithm outputs a v-level ciphertext ct_v.*
- $ct^{(j)}_{v+1} \leftarrow_{\$} \mathsf{FReEnc}(\mathsf{rk}^f_{i \to j}, ct^{(i)}_v, v)$: *Taking as input a re-encryption key $\mathsf{rk}^f_{i \to j}$ and a ciphertext $ct^{(i)}_v$ intended for i and its level $v \in [0, L-1]$, the fine-grained re-encryption algorithm outputs a $(v+1)$-level ciphertext $ct^{(j)}_{v+1}$ re-encrypted for j. We denote it by $ct^{(i)}_v \xrightarrow{\mathsf{rk}^f_{i \to j}} ct^{(j)}_{v+1}$.*
- $m \leftarrow \mathsf{Dec}(sk, ct)$: *Taking as input a secret key sk and a ciphertext ct, the deterministic decryption algorithm outputs a message m.*

Correctness. *For all $m \in \mathcal{M}, v \in [0, L]$, $(pk, sk) \leftarrow_{\$} \mathsf{KGen}$, $ct_v \leftarrow_{\$} \mathsf{Enc}(pk, m, v)$, it holds that $\mathsf{Dec}(sk, ct_v) = m$.*

Fine-Grained L-Hop Correctness. *For all $m \in \mathcal{M}$, user indices $i_0, i_1, \cdots, i_L$, functions $f_1, \cdots, f_L \in \mathcal{F}$, $(pk^{(i_j)}, sk^{(i_j)}) \leftarrow_{\$} \mathsf{KGen}$ with $j \in [0, L]$, 0-level ciphertext $ct^{(i_0)}_0 \leftarrow_{\$} \mathsf{Enc}(pk^{(i_0)}, m, 0)$ and re-encryption hops $ct^{(i_0)}_0 \xrightarrow{\mathsf{rk}^{f_1}_{i_0 \to i_1}} ct^{(i_1)}_1 \xrightarrow{\mathsf{rk}^{f_2}_{i_1 \to i_2}} \cdots \xrightarrow{\mathsf{rk}^{f_L}_{i_{L-1} \to i_L}} ct^{(i_L)}_L$, where each $\mathsf{rk}^{f_j}_{i_{j-1} \to i_j} \leftarrow_{\$} \mathsf{FReKGen}(pk^{(i_{j-1})}, sk^{(i_{j-1})}, pk^{(i_j)}, f_j)$ and each $ct^{(i_j)}_j \leftarrow_{\$} \mathsf{FReEnc}(\mathsf{rk}^{f_j}_{i_{j-1} \to i_j}, ct^{(i_{j-1})}_{j-1}, j-1)$, it holds that for all $j \in [L]$,*

$$\mathsf{Dec}(sk^{(i_j)}, ct^{(i_j)}_j) = f_j(f_{j-1}(\dots f_1(m))).$$

CPA Security. Below we formalize the indistinguishability of ciphertexts under chosen-plaintext attacks (CPA) for multi-hop FPRE.

Definition 2 (CPA Security for Multi-hop FPRE). *A multi-hop FPRE scheme* mFPRE *is* CPA *secure, if for any PPT adversary* $\mathcal{A}$ *and any polynomial* $\mathfrak{n}$, *it holds that* $\mathsf{Adv}^{\mathsf{CPA}}_{\mathsf{mFPRE},\mathcal{A},\mathfrak{n}}(\lambda) := \big|\Pr[\mathsf{Exp}^{\mathsf{CPA}}_{\mathsf{mFPRE},\mathcal{A},\mathfrak{n}} \Rightarrow 1] - \frac{1}{2}\big| \leq \mathsf{negl}(\lambda)$, *where the experiment* $\mathsf{Exp}^{\mathsf{CPA}}_{\mathsf{mFPRE},\mathcal{A},\mathfrak{n}}$ *is defined in Fig. 2.*

$\underline{\mathsf{Exp}^{\mathsf{CPA}}_{\mathsf{mFPRE},\mathcal{A},\mathfrak{n}}}$:
For $i \in [\mathfrak{n}]$: $(pk^{(i)}, sk^{(i)}) \leftarrow_\$ \mathsf{KGen}$
$\mathcal{Q}_{rk} := \emptyset$ //record re-encryption key queries
$\mathcal{Q}_c := \emptyset$ //record corruption queries
$i^* := \perp$ //record challenge user
$(i^*, m_0, m_1, v, st) \leftarrow_\$ \mathcal{A}^{\mathcal{O}_{\mathrm{ReKey}}(\cdot,\cdot,\cdot),\mathcal{O}_{\mathrm{Cor}}(\cdot)}(\{pk^{(i)}\}_{i\in[\mathfrak{n}]})$
If $(i^* \in \mathcal{Q}_c)$ or $\mathsf{CheckTA}(i^*, \mathcal{Q}_{rk}, \mathcal{Q}_c) = 1$:
  Return $b \leftarrow_\$ \{0,1\}$ //avoid **TA1**, **TA2**
$\beta \leftarrow_\$ \{0,1\}$
$ct^*_v \leftarrow_\$ \mathsf{Enc}(pk^{(i^*)}, m_\beta, v)$
$\beta' \leftarrow_\$ \mathcal{A}^{\mathcal{O}_{\mathrm{ReKey}}(\cdot,\cdot,\cdot),\mathcal{O}_{\mathrm{Cor}}(\cdot)}(st, ct^*_v)$
If $\beta' = \beta$: Return 1; Else: Return 0

$\underline{\mathcal{O}_{\mathrm{ReKey}}(i,j,f)}$: //re-encryption key queries
If $\mathsf{CheckTA}(i^*, \mathcal{Q}_{rk} \cup \{(i,j)\}, \mathcal{Q}_c) = 1$:
  Return $\perp$ //avoid **TA2**
$\mathcal{Q}_{rk} := \mathcal{Q}_{rk} \cup \{(i,j)\}$
$\mathsf{rk}^f_{i\to j} \leftarrow_\$ \mathsf{FReKGen}(pk^{(i)}, sk^{(i)}, pk^{(j)}, f)$
Return $\mathsf{rk}^f_{i\to j}$

$\underline{\mathcal{O}_{\mathrm{Cor}}(i)}$: //corruption queries
If $i = i^*$: Return $\perp$ //avoid **TA1**
If $\mathsf{CheckTA}(i^*, \mathcal{Q}_{rk}, \mathcal{Q}_c \cup \{i\}) = 1$:
  Return $\perp$ //avoid **TA2**
$\mathcal{Q}_c := \mathcal{Q}_c \cup \{i\}$
Return $sk^{(i)}$

$\underline{\mathsf{CheckTA}(i^*, \mathcal{Q}_{rk}, \mathcal{Q}_c)}$: //check **TA2**
If $\exists\ (i^*, j_1), (j_1, j_2), \ldots, (j_{t-1}, j_t) \in \mathcal{Q}_{rk}$
  s.t. $j_t \in \mathcal{Q}_c$ for some $t \geq 1$:
  Return 1
Else: Return 0

Fig. 2. The CPA security experiment $\mathsf{Exp}^{\mathsf{CPA}}_{\mathsf{mFPRE},\mathcal{A},\mathfrak{n}}$ for mFPRE. Here CheckTA is a sub-procedure used to check the trivial attacks.

Remark 1 (On the formalization of CPA *security and discussion on trivial attacks).* We formalize the CPA security by defining the experiment $\mathsf{Exp}^{\mathsf{CPA}}_{\mathsf{mFPRE},\mathcal{A},\mathfrak{n}}$ in Fig. 2. More precisely, we consider a multi-user setting, and the adversary $\mathcal{A}$ is allowed to make two kinds of oracle queries *adaptively*:

- through $\mathcal{O}_{\mathrm{ReKey}}(i,j,f)$ query, $\mathcal{A}$ can get re-encryption keys $\mathsf{rk}^f_{i\to j}$, and
- through $\mathcal{O}_{\mathrm{Cor}}(i)$ query, $\mathcal{A}$ can corrupt user i and obtain its secret key $sk^{(i)}$.

We stress that the adversary can issue multiple $\mathcal{O}_{\mathrm{ReKey}}(i,j,f)$ queries, even for the same delegator i and same delegatee j, thus achieving *multiple delegations*. At some point, $\mathcal{A}$ outputs a challenge user i^*, a pair of messages (m_0, m_1) as well as a level v, and receives a challenge ciphertext ct^*_v which encrypts m_β under $pk^{(i^*)}$ at level v, where β is the challenge bit that $\mathcal{A}$ aims to guess.

To prevent trivial attacks from $\mathcal{A}$, we keep track of two sets: $\mathcal{Q}_c$ records the corrupted users, and $\mathcal{Q}_{rk}$ records the tuples (i,j) that $\mathcal{A}$ obtains a re-encryption key $\mathsf{rk}^f_{i\to j}$. Based on that, there are two kinds of trivial attacks **TA1-TA2** to obtain information about the plaintext underlying the challenge ciphertext ct^*_v.

TA1: $i^* \in \mathcal{Q}_c$, i.e., $\mathcal{A}$ corrupts user i^* and obtains its secret key $sk^{(i^*)}$. In this case, $\mathcal{A}$ can decrypt ct_v^* directly via $\mathsf{Dec}(sk^{(i^*)}, ct_v^*)$ and recover m_β.

TA2: $\exists (i^*, j_1), (j_1, j_2), \ldots, (j_{t-1}, j_t) \in \mathcal{Q}_{rk}$ s.t. $j_t \in \mathcal{Q}_c$ for some $t \geq 1$, i.e., $\mathcal{A}$ gets a chain of re-encryption keys $\mathsf{rk}^{f_1}_{i^* \to j_1}, \mathsf{rk}^{f_2}_{j_1 \to j_2}, \ldots, \mathsf{rk}^{f_t}_{j_{t-1} \to j_t}$ starting from the challenge user i^* and ending at some corrupted user j_t for whom $\mathcal{A}$ ever obtains its secret key $sk^{(j_t)}$. In this case, $\mathcal{A}$ can re-encrypt ct_v^* via $ct_v^* \xrightarrow{\mathsf{rk}^{f_1}_{i^* \to j_1}} ct_{v+1}^{(j_1)} \xrightarrow{\mathsf{rk}^{f_2}_{j_1 \to j_2}} \cdots \xrightarrow{\mathsf{rk}^{f_t}_{j_{t-1} \to j_t}} ct_{v+t}^{(j_t)}$, then simply decrypt $ct_{v+t}^{(j_t)}$ with $sk^{(j_t)}$ to obtain a function of m_β. This kind of trivial attacks is checked by the algorithm $\mathsf{CheckTA}$ defined in Fig. 2 throughout the experiment.

As such, we exclude the above trivial attacks in the CPA experiment.

We note that in contrast to the CPA security for PRE defined in [9], our CPA security does not provide a re-encryption oracle for re-encrypting ciphertexts from the challenge user i^* to uncorrupted users $j \notin \mathcal{Q}_c$. This is because in our CPA experiment, $\mathcal{A}$ can obtain re-encryption keys from i^* to $j \notin \mathcal{Q}_c$ through the $\mathcal{O}_{\text{ReKey}}$ oracle and do re-encryption itself for such ciphertexts.

HRA Security. Next we formalize the indistinguishability of ciphertexts under honest-re-encryption attacks (HRA) for multi-hop FPRE. Originally, HRA was first introduced by Cohen [6] as a stronger and more reasonable security notion than CPA for PRE. Below we adapt HRA security to the fine-grained setting for mFPRE. Compared with the CPA security, HRA also allows the adversary to have access to a re-encryption oracle $\mathcal{O}_{\text{ReEnc}}$, through which the adversary can learn re-encryptions of ciphertexts from the challenge user i^* to *corrupted* users $j \in \mathcal{Q}_c$, as long as the queried ciphertexts are honestly generated and different from (all derivatives of) the challenge ciphertext ct_v^*.

Definition 3 (HRA **Security for Multi-Hop FPRE).** *A multi-hop FPRE scheme* mFPRE *is* HRA *secure, if for any PPT adversary* $\mathcal{A}$ *and any polynomial* $\mathfrak{n}$, *it holds that* $\mathsf{Adv}^{\mathsf{HRA}}_{\mathsf{mFPRE},\mathcal{A},\mathfrak{n}}(\lambda) := \left| \Pr[\mathsf{Exp}^{\mathsf{HRA}}_{\mathsf{mFPRE},\mathcal{A},\mathfrak{n}} \Rightarrow 1] - \frac{1}{2} \right| \leq \mathsf{negl}(\lambda)$, *where the experiment* $\mathsf{Exp}^{\mathsf{HRA}}_{\mathsf{mFPRE},\mathcal{A},\mathfrak{n}}$ *is defined in Fig. 3.*

Remark 2 (On the formalization of HRA *security and discussion on trivial attacks).* We formalize the HRA security by defining the experiment $\mathsf{Exp}^{\mathsf{HRA}}_{\mathsf{mFPRE},\mathcal{A},\mathfrak{n}}$ in Fig. 3. More precisely, we consider a multi-user setting, and the adversary $\mathcal{A}$ is allowed to make four kinds of oracle queries *adaptively*:

- through $\mathcal{O}_{\text{ReKey}}(i, j, f)$ query, $\mathcal{A}$ can get re-encryption keys $\mathsf{rk}^f_{i \to j}$;
- through $\mathcal{O}_{\text{Cor}}(i)$ query, $\mathcal{A}$ can corrupt user i and obtain its secret key $sk^{(i)}$;
- through $\mathcal{O}_{\text{Enc}}(i, m, v)$ query, $\mathcal{A}$ can obtain honestly generated ciphertexts, which are indexed by counters ctr and can be further re-encrypted through $\mathcal{O}_{\text{ReEnc}}$ query;
- through $\mathcal{O}_{\text{ReEnc}}(i, j, f, k)$ query, $\mathcal{A}$ can obtain re-encryptions of honestly generated ciphertexts (including the challenge ciphertext ct_v^* to be defined later, as well as the re-encrypted ciphertexts output by $\mathcal{O}_{\text{ReEnc}}$ previously), where k is the index of the honestly generated ciphertext to be re-encrypted and i, j, f specify the re-encryption key $\mathsf{rk}^f_{i \to j}$ to be used.

$\mathsf{Exp}^{\mathsf{HRA}}_{\mathsf{mFPRE},\mathcal{A},\mathsf{n}}$:
For $i \in [\mathsf{n}]$: $(pk^{(i)}, sk^{(i)}) \leftarrow_\$ \mathsf{KGen}$
$\mathcal{Q}_{rk} := \emptyset$ //record re-encryption key queries
$\mathcal{Q}_c := \emptyset$ //record corruption queries
$i^* := \perp$ //record challenge user
$\mathcal{L} := \perp$ //record honestly generated ciphertexts
$\mathcal{L}^* := \perp$ //record derivatives of the challenge ciphertext
$\mathsf{ctr} := 0$ //index of honestly generated ciphertexts
$(i^*, m_0, m_1, v, st) \leftarrow_\$ \mathcal{A}^{\mathcal{O}_{\text{ReKey}}(\cdot,\cdot,\cdot),\mathcal{O}_{\text{Cor}}(\cdot),\mathcal{O}_{\text{Enc}}(\cdot,\cdot,\cdot),\mathcal{O}_{\text{ReEnc}}(\cdot,\cdot,\cdot,\cdot)}(\{pk^{(i)}\}_{i\in[\mathsf{n}]})$
If $(i^* \in \mathcal{Q}_c)$ or $\mathsf{CheckTA}(i^*, \mathcal{Q}_{rk}, \mathcal{Q}_c) = 1$:
  Return $b \leftarrow_\$ \{0,1\}$ //avoid **TA1**, **TA2**
$\beta \leftarrow_\$ \{0,1\}$
$\mathsf{ctr} := \mathsf{ctr} + 1$
$ct_v^* \leftarrow_\$ \mathsf{Enc}(pk^{(i^*)}, m_\beta, v)$
$\mathcal{L} := \mathcal{L} \cup \{(\mathsf{ctr}, i^*, (ct_v^*, v))\}$
$\mathcal{L}^* := \mathcal{L}^* \cup \{(\mathsf{ctr}, i^*)\}$ //index of challenge ciphertext
$\beta' \leftarrow_\$ \mathcal{A}^{\mathcal{O}_{\text{ReKey}}(\cdot,\cdot,\cdot),\mathcal{O}_{\text{Cor}}(\cdot),\mathcal{O}_{\text{Enc}}(\cdot,\cdot,\cdot),\mathcal{O}_{\text{ReEnc}}(\cdot,\cdot,\cdot,\cdot)}(st, ct_v^*)$
If $\beta' = \beta$: Return 1; Else: Return 0

$\mathcal{O}_{\text{ReKey}}(i, j, f)$: //re-encryption key queries
  If $\mathsf{CheckTA}(i^*, \mathcal{Q}_{rk} \cup \{(i,j)\}, \mathcal{Q}_c) = 1$:
    Return $\perp$ //avoid **TA2**
  $\mathcal{Q}_{rk} := \mathcal{Q}_{rk} \cup \{(i,j)\}$
  $\mathsf{rk}^f_{i\to j} \leftarrow_\$ \mathsf{FReKGen}(pk^{(i)}, sk^{(i)}, pk^{(j)}, f)$
  Return $\mathsf{rk}^f_{i\to j}$

$\mathcal{O}_{\text{Cor}}(i)$: //corruption queries
  If $\exists(\cdot, i) \in \mathcal{L}^*$: Return $\perp$ //avoid **TA1**, **TA3**
  If $\mathsf{CheckTA}(i^*, \mathcal{Q}_{rk}, \mathcal{Q}_c \cup \{i\}) = 1$:
    Return $\perp$ //avoid **TA2**
  $\mathcal{Q}_c := \mathcal{Q}_c \cup \{i\}$
  Return $sk^{(i)}$

$\mathcal{O}_{\text{Enc}}(i, m, v)$: //honest encryption queries
  $\mathsf{ctr} := \mathsf{ctr} + 1$
  $ct_v^{(i)} \leftarrow_\$ \mathsf{Enc}(pk^{(i)}, m, v)$
  $\mathcal{L} := \mathcal{L} \cup \{(\mathsf{ctr}, i, (ct_v^{(i)}, v))\}$
  Return $(\mathsf{ctr}, ct_v^{(i)})$

$\mathcal{O}_{\text{ReEnc}}(i, j, f, k)$: //honest re-encryption queries
  If $(k, i) \in \mathcal{L}^*$ and $j \in \mathcal{Q}_c$:
    Return $\perp$ //avoid **TA3**
  Retrieve $(k, i, (ct', v'))$ from $\mathcal{L}$:
    If fails, return $\perp$
  $\mathsf{rk}^f_{i\to j} \leftarrow_\$ \mathsf{FReKGen}(pk^{(i)}, sk^{(i)}, pk^{(j)}, f)$
  $ct^{(j)}_{v'+1} \leftarrow_\$ \mathsf{FReEnc}(\mathsf{rk}^f_{i\to j}, ct', v')$
  $\mathsf{ctr} := \mathsf{ctr} + 1$
  $\mathcal{L} := \mathcal{L} \cup \{(\mathsf{ctr}, j, (ct^{(j)}_{v'+1}, v'+1))\}$
  If $(k, i) \in \mathcal{L}^*$: $\mathcal{L}^* := \mathcal{L}^* \cup \{(\mathsf{ctr}, j)\}$
  Return $(\mathsf{ctr}, ct^{(j)}_{v'+1})$

$\mathsf{CheckTA}(i^*, \mathcal{Q}_{rk}, \mathcal{Q}_c)$: //check **TA2**
  If $\exists\ (i^*, j_1), (j_1, j_2), \ldots, (j_{t-1}, j_t) \in \mathcal{Q}_{rk}$
    s.t. $j_t \in \mathcal{Q}_c$ for some $t \geq 1$:
    Return 1
  Else: Return 0

Fig. 3. The HRA security experiment $\mathsf{Exp}^{\mathsf{HRA}}_{\mathsf{mFPRE},\mathcal{A},\mathsf{n}}$ for mFPRE. Here the oracles $\mathcal{O}_{\text{ReKey}}$, $\mathcal{O}_{\text{Cor}}$ and the sub-procedure CheckTA are the same as those in Fig. 2.

At some point, $\mathcal{A}$ outputs a challenge user i^*, a pair of messages (m_0, m_1) as well as a level v, and receives a challenge ciphertext ct_v^* which encrypts m_β under $pk^{(i^*)}$ at level v, where β is the challenge bit that $\mathcal{A}$ aims to guess.

Similar to the CPA security, we also exclude the two trivial attacks **TA1-TA2** as defined in Remark 1, from which $\mathcal{A}$ can trivially obtain information about the plaintext m_β underlying the challenge ciphertext ct_v^*. Moreover, there is an additional trivial attack **TA3** to obtain information about m_β.

TA3: Via $\mathcal{O}_{\text{ReEnc}}$ queries, $\mathcal{A}$ obtains a chain of re-encryptions $ct_v^* \xrightarrow{\mathcal{O}_{\text{ReEnc}}} ct_{v+1}^{(j_1)} \xrightarrow{\mathcal{O}_{\text{ReEnc}}} \cdots \xrightarrow{\mathcal{O}_{\text{ReEnc}}} ct_{v+t}^{(j_t)}$ starting from the challenge ciphertext ct_v^* and ending at ciphertext $ct_{v+t}^{(j_t)}$ of some corrupted user $j_t \in \mathcal{Q}_c$ from whom $\mathcal{A}$ ever obtains its secret key $sk^{(j_t)}$. In this case, $\mathcal{A}$ can use $sk^{(j_t)}$ to decrypt $ct_{v+t}^{(j_t)}$ to trivially obtain a function of m_β.

To exclude this additional trivial attack, we keep track of a set $\mathcal{L}^*$ to record (index of) the challenge ciphertext ct_v^* as well as all honestly generated re-encryptions of ct_v^* output by $\mathcal{O}_{\text{ReEnc}}$.

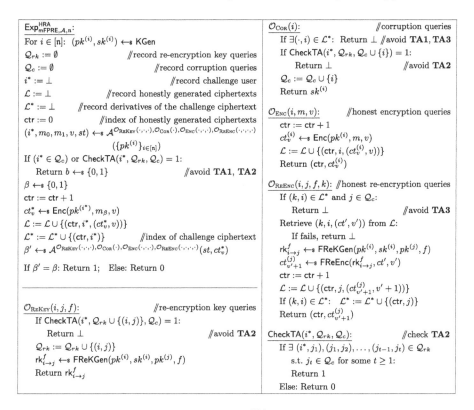

3.2 Achieving CPA and HRA Security for Multi-hop FPRE from Weaker Security Notions: IND, wKP and SH

Our CPA and HRA security for multi-hop FPRE formalized in the previous subsection are defined in an *adaptive* manner, where the adversary $\mathcal{A}$ can designate the challenge user i^* and make all oracle queries adaptively, including corruption queries $\mathcal{O}_{\text{COR}}$, re-encryption key queries $\mathcal{O}_{\text{REKEY}}$, and honest encryption queries $\mathcal{O}_{\text{ENC}}$ and honest re-encryption queries $\mathcal{O}_{\text{REENC}}$ in the case of HRA. Accordingly, the tuples (i, j) for which $\mathcal{A}$ obtains a re-encryption key $\mathsf{rk}^f_{i \to j}$ (i.e., the set $\mathcal{Q}_{rk}$ in Fig. 2 and Fig. 3) are adaptively determined by $\mathcal{A}$ and form a complex directed graph. In the case of HRA, the tuples (i, j) for which $\mathcal{A}$ makes a re-encryption query $\mathcal{O}_{\text{REENC}}(i, j, \cdot, \cdot)$ form another complex directed graph.

One possible way to achieve adaptive CPA/HRA security is first proving a selective version of CPA/HRA security, and then reducing the adaptive security to the selective counterpart via a guessing strategy. The selective CPA/HRA security means that $\mathcal{A}$ has to declare the graphs for re-encryption keys/re-encryptions at the beginning of the experiment, and thus it is relatively easy to prove selective security in general. However, the price is a considerably large security loss $O(2^{\mathsf{n}^2})$ incurred by the guessing of the graphs.

To reduce the security loss of adaptive security, Jafargholi et al. [12] proposed a generic framework for upgrading selective security to adaptive security with a more fine-grained analysis. Later, Fuchsbauer et al. [9] applied the framework of [12] to the CPA/HRA security of (traditional) PRE.

In this subsection, we will extend the framework of Jafargholi et al. [12] further to the CPA and HRA security of our multi-hop fine-grained PRE, by adapting the techniques of Fuchsbauer et al. [9] to the fine-grained setting. More precisely, we will first defined three weaker security notions, including indistinguishability (IND), weak key-privacy (wKP) and source-hiding (SH), to our multi-hop FPRE, and then establish two theorems showing CPA, HRA security of our multi-hop FPRE based on these weaker security notions. The formalization of the weaker security notions and the proofs of the theorems are mainly adapted from [9,12].

Now we present the formal definitions of IND, wKP, SH for multi-hop FPRE.

Indistinguishability. The IND security of multi-hop FPRE considers the indistinguishability of ciphertexts in a single-user and multi-challenge setting, where the adversary is given no re-encryption keys compared with the CPA security.

Definition 4 (IND Security). *A multi-hop FPRE scheme* mFPRE *is* IND *secure, if for any PPT adversary $\mathcal{A}$, it holds that* $\mathsf{Adv}^{\mathsf{IND}}_{\mathsf{mFPRE},\mathcal{A}}(\lambda) := |\Pr[\mathsf{Exp}^{\mathsf{IND}}_{\mathsf{mFPRE},\mathcal{A}} \Rightarrow 1] - \frac{1}{2}| \leq \mathsf{negl}(\lambda)$, *where the experiment* $\mathsf{Exp}^{\mathsf{IND}}_{\mathsf{mFPRE},\mathcal{A}}$ *is defined in Fig. 4.*

Weak Key-Privacy. The original key-privacy for PREs was introduced in [2]. In [9], weak key-privacy was introduced and it requires the indistinguishability between the re-encryption key $\mathsf{rk}_{0 \to j}$ from user 0 to user j and the re-encryption key $\mathsf{rk}_{1 \to j}$ from user 1 to user j. Below we adapt it to our multi-hop FPRE, by

$\mathsf{Exp}^{\mathsf{IND}}_{\mathsf{mFPRE},\mathcal{A}}$:	
$(pk, sk) \leftarrow_\$ \mathsf{KGen}$	$\underline{\mathcal{O}_{\text{CHAL}}(m_0, m_1, v)}$:
$\beta \leftarrow_\$ \{0,1\}$	$ct_v \leftarrow_\$ \mathsf{Enc}(pk, m_\beta, v)$
$\beta' \leftarrow_\$ \mathcal{A}^{\mathcal{O}_{\text{CHAL}}(\cdot,\cdot,\cdot)}(pk)$	Return ct_v
If $\beta' = \beta$: Return 1; Else: Return 0	

Fig. 4. The indistinguishability experiment $\mathsf{Exp}^{\mathsf{IND}}_{\mathsf{mFPRE},\mathcal{A}}$ for mFPRE.

requiring the existence of a PPT algorithm $\mathsf{FReKGen}^*$ which can simulate the generation of re-encryption keys $\mathsf{rk}^f_{0\to j}$ without the secret key of source user 0.

Definition 5 (wKP **Security).** *A multi-hop FPRE scheme* mFPRE *has weak key privacy (*wKP *security), if there exists a PPT simulation algorithm* $\mathsf{FReKGen}^*$*, s.t. for any PPT adversary* $\mathcal{A}$ *and any polynomial* $\mathfrak{n}$*, it holds that* $\mathsf{Adv}^{\mathsf{wKP}}_{\mathsf{mFPRE},\mathcal{A},\mathfrak{n}}(\lambda) := |\Pr[\mathsf{Exp}^{\mathsf{wKP}}_{\mathsf{mFPRE},\mathcal{A},\mathfrak{n}} \Rightarrow 1] - \frac{1}{2}| \leq \mathsf{negl}(\lambda)$*, where* $\mathsf{Exp}^{\mathsf{wKP}}_{\mathsf{mFPRE},\mathcal{A},\mathfrak{n}}$ *is defined in Fig. 5.*

$\mathsf{Exp}^{\mathsf{wKP}}_{\mathsf{mFPRE},\mathcal{A},\mathfrak{n}}$:	$\underline{\mathcal{O}_{\text{REKEY}}(j \in [\mathfrak{n}], f)}$: //user 0 is always the source user
For $i \in [0, \mathfrak{n}]$: $(pk^{(i)}, sk^{(i)}) \leftarrow_\$ \mathsf{KGen}$	If $\beta = 0$: //real re-encryption key
$\beta \leftarrow_\$ \{0,1\}$	$\mathsf{rk}^f_{0\to j} \leftarrow_\$ \mathsf{FReKGen}(pk^{(0)}, sk^{(0)}, pk^{(j)}, f)$
$\beta' \leftarrow_\$ \mathcal{A}^{\mathcal{O}_{\text{REKEY}}(\cdot,\cdot)}(\{pk^{(i)}\}_{i\in[0,\mathfrak{n}]})$	Else: //simulated re-encryption key
	$\mathsf{rk}^f_{0\to j} \leftarrow_\$ \mathsf{FReKGen}^*(pk^{(0)}, pk^{(j)}, f)$
If $\beta' = \beta$: Return 1; Else: Return 0	Returns $\mathsf{rk}^f_{0\to j}$

Fig. 5. The weak key-privacy experiment $\mathsf{Exp}^{\mathsf{wKP}}_{\mathsf{mFPRE},\mathcal{A},\mathfrak{n}}$ for mFPRE.

Source-Hiding. Roughly speaking, source-hiding (SH) requires the indistinguishability between freshly-encrypted ciphertexts (via Enc) and re-encrypted ciphertexts (via FReEnc), even if the adversary has all secret keys and re-encryption keys. SH security can help us upgrade CPA security to HRA security for FPRE.

Definition 6 (SH **Security).** *A multi-hop FPRE scheme* mFPRE *has the property of source-hiding (*SH *security), if for any (unbounded) adversary* $\mathcal{A}$*, it holds that* $\mathsf{Adv}^{\mathsf{SH}}_{\mathsf{mFPRE},\mathcal{A}}(\lambda) := |\Pr[\mathsf{Exp}^{\mathsf{SH}}_{\mathsf{mFPRE},\mathcal{A}} \Rightarrow 1] - \frac{1}{2}| \leq \mathsf{negl}(\lambda)$*, where experiment* $\mathsf{Exp}^{\mathsf{SH}}_{\mathsf{mFPRE},\mathcal{A}}$ *is defined in Fig. 6.*

Achieving CPA and HRA Security for Multi-Hop FPRE. Now we are ready to present two theorems showing (adaptive) CPA and HRA of multi-hop FPRE assuming the weak security notions IND, wKP and SH. The theorems are essentially applications of the framework of Jafargholi et al. [12] and adaptions of the techniques of Fuchsbauer et al. [9] to multi-hop FPRE. We refer to the full version [20] for their proofs, as they almost verbatim follow [9,12].

$\underline{\mathsf{Exp}^{\mathsf{SH}}_{\mathsf{mFPRE},\mathcal{A}}}$:	$\underline{\mathcal{O}_{\text{ENC}}(m, v)}$: //honestly generated ciphertext of user 0
$(pk^{(0)}, sk^{(0)}) \leftarrow_{\$} \mathsf{KGen}$	$\mathsf{ctr} := \mathsf{ctr} + 1$
$(pk^{(1)}, sk^{(1)}) \leftarrow_{\$} \mathsf{KGen}$	$ct_v^{(0)} \leftarrow_{\$} \mathsf{Enc}(pk^{(0)}, m, v)$
$\mathcal{Q}_f := \perp$ //record functions	$\mathcal{L} := \mathcal{L} \cup \{(\mathsf{ctr}, m, (ct_v^{(0)}, v))\}$
$\mathcal{L} := \perp$ //record honestly generated ciphertexts	Return $(\mathsf{ctr}, ct_v^{(0)})$
$\mathsf{ctr} := 0$ //index of honestly generated ciphertexts	
$\beta \leftarrow_{\$} \{0,1\}$	$\underline{\mathcal{O}_{\text{CHAL}}(k, f)}$: //challenge oracle
$\beta' \leftarrow_{\$} \mathcal{A}^{\mathcal{O}_{\text{REKEY}}(\cdot), \mathcal{O}_{\text{ENC}}(\cdot,\cdot), \mathcal{O}_{\text{CHAL}}(\cdot,\cdot)}(pk^{(0)}, sk^{(0)}, pk^{(1)}, sk^{(1)})$	Retrieve $(k, m, (ct_v^{(0)}, v))$ from $\mathcal{L}$:
	If fails, return $\perp$
If $\beta' = \beta$: Return 1; Else: Return 0	If $\beta = 0$: //re-encrypted ciphertext
	If $f \notin \mathcal{Q}_f$: $\mathsf{rk}^f_{0\to1} \leftarrow_{\$} \mathsf{FReKGen}(pk^{(0)}, sk^{(0)}, pk^{(1)}, f)$
$\underline{\mathcal{O}_{\text{REKEY}}(f)}$: //re-key from user 0 to user 1 on function f	$ct_{v+1}^{(1)} \leftarrow_{\$} \mathsf{FReEnc}(\mathsf{rk}^f_{0\to1}, ct_v^{(0)}, v)$
$\mathsf{rk}^f_{0\to1} \leftarrow_{\$} \mathsf{FReKGen}(pk^{(0)}, sk^{(0)}, pk^{(1)}, f)$	Else: //freshly-encrypted ciphertext
$\mathcal{Q}_f := \mathcal{Q}_f \cup \{f\}$	$ct_{v+1}^{(1)} \leftarrow_{\$} \mathsf{Enc}(pk^{(1)}, f(m), v+1)$
Return $\mathsf{rk}^f_{0\to1}$	Return $ct_{v+1}^{(1)}$

Fig. 6. The source-hiding experiment $\mathsf{Exp}^{\mathsf{SH}}_{\mathsf{mFPRE},\mathcal{A}}$ for mFPRE.

To state the theorems precisely, we consider an adversary $\mathcal{A}$ in the CPA/HRA security experiment, and define some notations. If we view users $[\mathfrak{n}]$ as vertices and re-encryption keys $\mathsf{rk}^f_{i\to j}$ that $\mathcal{A}$ obtains through $\mathcal{O}_{\text{REKEY}}$ queries as an edge from i to j, then it forms a directed graph. We define the subgraph that is reachable from the challenge user i^* as *the challenge graph* of $\mathcal{A}$, denoted by G. For the challenge graph G, if we denote by δ the outdegree (i.e., the maximum outdegree over all vertices) and d the depth, then the challenge graph is in the graph class $\mathcal{G}(\mathfrak{n}, \delta, d)$ of all graphs with $\mathfrak{n}$ vertices, outdegree δ and depth d.

In the full version [20], we further define the pebbling time complexity τ and space complexity σ for the class $\mathcal{G}(\mathfrak{n}, \delta, d)$, respectively, according to [9,12].

Theorem 1 (IND + wKP ⇒ CPA for Multi-Hop FPRE). *If a multi-hop FPRE scheme* mFPRE *has both* IND *and* wKP *security, then it is* CPA *secure.*

More precisely, for any PPT adversary $\mathcal{A}$ against the CPA *security with challenge graph G in $\mathcal{G}(\mathfrak{n}, \delta, d)$ whose pebbling time complexity is τ and space complexity is σ, there exist PPT algorithms $\mathcal{B}$ and $\mathcal{B}'$ s.t.* $\mathsf{Adv}^{\mathsf{CPA}}_{\mathsf{mFPRE},\mathcal{A},\mathfrak{n}}(\lambda) \le (2 \cdot \mathsf{Adv}^{\mathsf{IND}}_{\mathsf{mFPRE},\mathcal{B}} + 2\tau \cdot \mathsf{Adv}^{\mathsf{wKP}}_{\mathsf{mFPRE},\mathcal{B}',\delta}) \cdot \mathfrak{n}^{\sigma+\delta+1}$.

Theorem 2 (IND + wKP + SH ⇒ HRA for Multi-Hop FPRE). *If a multi-hop FPRE scheme* mFPRE *has* IND, wKP *and* SH *security simultaneously, then it is* HRA *secure.*

More precisely, for any PPT adversary $\mathcal{A}$ against the HRA *security with challenge graph G in $\mathcal{G}(\mathfrak{n}, \delta, d)$ whose pebbling time complexity is τ and space complexity is σ, there exist PPT algorithms $\mathcal{B}, \mathcal{B}'$ and $\mathcal{B}''$ s.t.* $\mathsf{Adv}^{\mathsf{HRA}}_{\mathsf{mFPRE},\mathcal{A},\mathfrak{n}}(\lambda) \le (2 \cdot \mathsf{Adv}^{\mathsf{IND}}_{\mathsf{mFPRE},\mathcal{B}} + 2\tau \cdot \mathsf{Adv}^{\mathsf{wKP}}_{\mathsf{mFPRE},\mathcal{B}',\delta}) \cdot \mathfrak{n}^{\sigma+\delta+1} + 2\mathfrak{n}(\mathfrak{n}-1)L \cdot \mathsf{Adv}^{\mathsf{SH}}_{\mathsf{mFPRE},\mathcal{B}''}$*, where L is the maximum level supported by* mFPRE.[5]

[5] We note that Theorem 2 has slightly different parameters than the corresponding theorem (i.e., Theorem 6) in [9]. This is because we use slightly different proof strategy than [9] when reducing to SH, in order to change all re-encrypted ciphertexts to freshly generated ciphertexts. We refer to the full version [20] for more details.

Note that the security loss of Theorem 1 and Theorem 2 is dominating by $2\tau \cdot \mathfrak{n}^{\sigma+\delta+1}$ and $2\mathfrak{n}(\mathfrak{n}-1)L$.

- For an arbitrary adversary $\mathcal{A}$ with an arbitrary challenge graph G, according to the bounds given in [9], we have the pebbling time complexity $\tau \le (2\delta)^d$, the space complexity $\sigma \le \mathfrak{n}$, the outdegree $\delta \le \mathfrak{n}$ and the depth $d \le \mathfrak{n}$. Moreover, L is (at most) a polynomial in $\mathfrak{n}$. Consequently, the security loss for arbitrary adversary $\mathcal{A}$ is $\mathfrak{n}^{O(\mathfrak{n})}$.
- In many realistic scenarios like key rotation for encrypted cloud storage or forwarding of encrypted mail, as demonstrated in [9], the proxy relations are in fact *trees, chains or low-depth graphs*, so does the challenge graph G. In these situations, according to the bounds given in [9], we have the pebbling time complexity $\tau = O(1)^{\log \mathfrak{n}}$, the space complexity $\sigma = O(\log \mathfrak{n})$ and the outdegree δ = constant, and consequently, the security loss is only quasi-polynomial $\mathfrak{n}^{O(\log \mathfrak{n})}$.

3.3 Other Security Notions for Multi-hop FPRE: UNID and CUL

In this subsection, we formalize two additional security notions for multi-hop FPRE, namely unidirectionality (UNID) and ciphertext unlinkability (CUL), by adapting the formalization in [21] defined for single-hop FPRE.

Unidirectionality. Intuitively, unidirectionality (UNID) means that the proxy ability in one direction does not imply the proxy ability in the other direction.

$\mathsf{Exp}^{\mathsf{UNID}}_{\mathsf{mFPRE},\mathcal{A},\mathfrak{n}}$:
For $i \in [\mathfrak{n}]$: $(pk^{(i)}, sk^{(i)}) \leftarrow_\$ \mathsf{KGen}$
$\mathcal{Q}_{rk} := \emptyset$ //record re-encryption key queries
$\mathcal{Q}_{c} := \emptyset$ //record corruption queries
$i^* := \bot, j^* := \bot$ //record challenge users
$(i^*, j^*, f, st) \leftarrow_\$ \mathcal{A}^{\mathcal{O}_{\text{ReKey}}(\cdot,\cdot,\cdot),\mathcal{O}_{\text{Cor}}(\cdot)}(\{pk^{(i)}\}_{i\in[\mathfrak{n}]})$
If $(i^* = j^*)$ or $(i^* \in \mathcal{Q}_c)$ or $\mathsf{CheckTA}(i^*, j^*, \mathcal{Q}_{rk}, \mathcal{Q}_c) = 1$:
  Return 0 //avoid **TA1′, TA2′, TA3′, TA4′**
$\mathsf{rk}^f_{j^*\to i^*} \leftarrow_\$ \mathsf{FReKGen}(pk^{(j^*)}, sk^{(j^*)}, pk^{(i^*)}, f)$
$\mathcal{Q}_{rk} := \mathcal{Q}_{rk} \cup \{(j^*, i^*)\}$
$(f', \mathsf{rk}^{f'}_{i^*\to j^*}) \leftarrow_\$ \mathcal{A}^{\mathcal{O}_{\text{ReKey}}(\cdot,\cdot,\cdot),\mathcal{O}_{\text{Cor}}(\cdot)}(st, \mathsf{rk}^f_{j^*\to i^*})$
If f' does not have output diversity:
  Return $\bot$ //avoid **TA5′**
//check the functionality of $\mathsf{rk}^{f'}_{i^*\to j^*}$ in the following way
$m \leftarrow_\$ \mathcal{M}$, $ct_0^{(i^*)} \leftarrow_\$ \mathsf{Enc}(pk^{(i^*)}, m, 0)$
$ct_1^{(j^*)} \leftarrow_\$ \mathsf{FReEnc}(\mathsf{rk}^{f'}_{i^*\to j^*}, ct_0^{(i^*)}, 0)$
If $\mathsf{Dec}(sk^{(j^*)}, ct_1^{(j^*)}) = f'(m)$:
  Return 1
Else: Return 0

$\mathcal{O}_{\text{ReKey}}(i, j, f)$:
If $\mathsf{CheckTA}(i^*, j^*, \mathcal{Q}_{rk} \cup \{(i,j)\}, \mathcal{Q}_c) = 1$:
  Return $\bot$ //avoid **TA3′, TA4′**
$\mathcal{Q}_{rk} := \mathcal{Q}_{rk} \cup \{(i,j)\}$
$\mathsf{rk}^f_{i\to j} \leftarrow_\$ \mathsf{FReKGen}(pk^{(i)}, sk^{(i)}, pk^{(j)}, f)$
Return $\mathsf{rk}^f_{i\to j}$

$\mathcal{O}_{\text{Cor}}(i)$:
If $i = i^*$: Return $\bot$ //avoid **TA2′**
If $\mathsf{CheckTA}(i^*, j^*, \mathcal{Q}_{rk}, \mathcal{Q}_c \cup \{i\}) = 1$:
  Return $\bot$ //avoid **TA3′, TA4′**
$\mathcal{Q}_c := \mathcal{Q}_c \cup \{i\}$
Return $sk^{(i)}$

$\mathsf{CheckTA}(i^*, j^*, \mathcal{Q}_{rk}, \mathcal{Q}_c)$: //avoid **TA3′, TA4′**
If $\exists\ (i^*, j_1), (j_1, j_2), \ldots, (j_{t-1}, j_t) \in \mathcal{Q}_{rk}$
  s.t. $(j_t \in \mathcal{Q}_c)$ or $(j_t = j^*)$ for some $t \ge 1$:
  Return 1
Else: Return 0

Fig. 7. The Unidirectionality security experiment $\mathsf{Exp}^{\mathsf{UNID}}_{\mathsf{mFPRE},\mathcal{A},\mathfrak{n}}$ for mFPRE, where "output diversity" is defined as $\Pr[m_0, m_1 \leftarrow_\$ \mathcal{M} : f'(m_0) \ne f'(m_1)] \ge 1/\mathsf{poly}(\lambda)$ (see the full version [20] for more details).

Definition 7 (Unidirectionality for Multi-Hop FPRE). *A multi-hop FPRE scheme* mFPRE *is unidirectional (*UNID *secure), if for any PPT adversary* $\mathcal{A}$ *and any polynomial* $\mathfrak{n}$*, it holds that* $\mathsf{Adv}^{\mathsf{UNID}}_{\mathsf{mFPRE},\mathcal{A},\mathfrak{n}}(\lambda) := \Pr[\mathsf{Exp}^{\mathsf{UNID}}_{\mathsf{mFPRE},\mathcal{A},\mathfrak{n}} \Rightarrow 1] \leq \mathsf{negl}(\lambda)$*, where the experiment* $\mathsf{Exp}^{\mathsf{UNID}}_{\mathsf{mFPRE},\mathcal{A},\mathfrak{n}}$ *is defined in Fig. 7.*

In the full version [20], we give some explanations of the UNID security definition and discuss the trivial attacks **TA1′-TA5′**, and then show that the UNID security is implied by the CPA security for multi-hop FPRE.

Ciphertext Unlinkability. In real scenarios, re-encryption relations between ciphertexts often imply the proxy connections between users. Therefore, it is desirable to hide the relations/connections, which is captured by the property ciphertext unlinkability (CUL). We formalize CUL for multi-hop FPRE by requiring the indistinguishability between a chain of re-encrypted ciphertexts $ct_0^{(i_0)} \xrightarrow{\mathsf{rk}^{f_1}_{i_0\to i_1}} ct_1^{(i_1)} \xrightarrow{\mathsf{rk}^{f_2}_{i_1\to i_2}} \cdots \xrightarrow{\mathsf{rk}^{f_L}_{i_{L-1}\to i_L}} ct_L^{(i_L)}$ generated by FReEnc and a set of freshly and independently encrypted ciphertexts $(ct_0^{(i_0)}, ct_1^{(i_1)}, \ldots, ct_L^{(i_L)})$ generated by Enc.

Definition 8 (Ciphertext Unlinkability for Multi-Hop PRE). *A multi-hop FPRE scheme* mFPRE *has ciphertext unlinkability (*CUL*), if for any PPT adversary* $\mathcal{A}$ *and any polynomial* $\mathfrak{n}$*, it holds that* $\mathsf{Adv}^{\mathsf{CUL}}_{\mathsf{mFPRE},\mathcal{A},\mathfrak{n}}(\lambda) := \left|\Pr[\mathsf{Exp}^{\mathsf{CUL}}_{\mathsf{mFPRE},\mathcal{A},\mathfrak{n}} \Rightarrow 1] - \frac{1}{2}\right| \leq \mathsf{negl}(\lambda)$*, where the experiment* $\mathsf{Exp}^{\mathsf{CUL}}_{\mathsf{mFPRE},\mathcal{A},\mathfrak{n}}$ *is defined in Fig. 8.*

In the full version [20], we give some explanations of the CUL security definition and discuss the trivial attacks **TA1″-TA2″**. We note that CUL security is similar to the SH security (cf. Definition 6) as they both capture the indistinguishability of re-encrypted ciphertexts and freshly generated ciphertexts. However, CUL security is defined in a much more realistic setting compared with the SH security: CUL considers a setting of multiple users while SH deals with only two users, and moreover, CUL protects the unlinkability of a chain of L re-encrypted ciphertexts with L the maximum level of mFPRE, while SH considers only chains of two ciphertexts. Nevertheless, in the full version [20], we show that the CUL security is implied by the SH + CPA security.

Remark 3 (Post-compromise Security). In [7], Davidson et al. proposed post-compromise security (PCS) for PRE, which considers the scenario where PRE serves for key rotation and guarantees that security still exists after the compromise of past secret keys. More concretely, suppose that Alice has stored some encrypted data and wants to update her public key from pk to pk'. To this end, she can generate an update token (i.e., a re-encryption key from pk to pk'), and re-encrypts the encrypted data using the token. In such scenario, PCS ensures that an adversary cannot distinguish which of two adversarially-chosen ciphertexts a re-encryption was created from, even when given the old secret key (i.e., the sk corresponding to pk) and the update token. Davidson et al. [7] also discussed the relations between PCS and other security notions of PRE, and proved that HRA together with SH imply PCS for (non-fine-grained) PRE.

$\underline{\mathsf{Exp}^{\mathsf{CUL}}_{\mathsf{mFPRE},\mathcal{A},\mathfrak{n}}}$:
For $i \in [\mathfrak{n}]$: $(pk^{(i)}, sk^{(i)}) \overset{\$}{\leftarrow} \mathsf{KGen}$
$\mathcal{Q}_{rk} := \emptyset$ //record re-encryption key queries
$\mathcal{Q}_{c} := \emptyset$ //record corruption queries
$\mathcal{Q}_{u} := \emptyset$ //record challenge users
$\left(\{i_j\}_{j\in[0,L]}, \begin{pmatrix}(\{f_j\}_{j\in[L]}, m) \\ (m_0, m_1, \ldots, m_L)\end{pmatrix}, st\right) \overset{\$}{\leftarrow} \mathcal{A}^{\mathcal{O}_{\text{ReKey}}(\cdot,\cdot,\cdot),\mathcal{O}_{\text{Cor}}(\cdot)}\left(\{pk^{(i)}\}_{i\in[\mathfrak{n}]}\right)$
$\mathcal{Q}_u := \{i_j\}_{j\in[0,L]}$ //update challenge users
If $(\exists j \in [0, L]$ s.t. $i_j \in \mathcal{Q}_c)$ or $\mathsf{CheckTA}(\mathcal{Q}_u, \mathcal{Q}_{rk}, \mathcal{Q}_c) = 1$:
  Return $b \overset{\$}{\leftarrow} \{0,1\}$ //avoid **TA1″**, **TA2″**
$\beta \overset{\$}{\leftarrow} \{0,1\}$
If $\beta = 0$:
  $ct_0^{(i_0)} \overset{\$}{\leftarrow} \mathsf{Enc}(pk^{(i_0)}, m, 0)$
  For $j \in [L]$: //re-encrypted ciphertexts
    $\mathsf{rk}^{f_j}_{i_{j-1}\to i_j} \overset{\$}{\leftarrow} \mathsf{FReKGen}(pk^{(i_{j-1})}, sk^{(i_{j-1})}, pk^{(i_j)}, f_j)$
    $ct_j^{(i_j)} \overset{\$}{\leftarrow} \mathsf{FReEnc}(\mathsf{rk}^{f_j}_{i_{j-1}\to i_j}, ct^{(i_{j-1})}, j-1)$
If $\beta = 1$:
  For $j \in [0, L]$: //independently generated ciphertexts
    $ct_j^{(i_j)} \overset{\$}{\leftarrow} \mathsf{Enc}(pk^{(i_j)}, m_j, j)$
$\beta' \overset{\$}{\leftarrow} \mathcal{A}^{\mathcal{O}_{\text{ReKey}}(\cdot,\cdot,\cdot),\mathcal{O}_{\text{Cor}}(\cdot)}(st, \{\mathsf{rk}^{f_j}_{i_{j-1}\to i_j}\}_{j\in[L]}, \{ct_j^{(i_j)}\}_{j\in[0,L]})$
If $\beta' = \beta$: Return 1; Else: Return 0

$\underline{\mathcal{O}_{\text{ReKey}}(i, j, f)}$: //re-encryption key queries
  If $\mathsf{CheckTA}(\mathcal{Q}_u, \mathcal{Q}_{rk} \cup \{(i,j)\}, \mathcal{Q}_c) = 1$:
    Return $\perp$ //avoid **TA2″**
  $\mathcal{Q}_{rk} := \mathcal{Q}_{rk} \cup \{(i,j)\}$
  $\mathsf{rk}^{f}_{i\to j} \overset{\$}{\leftarrow} \mathsf{FReKGen}(pk^{(i)}, sk^{(i)}, pk^{(j)}, f)$
  Return $\mathsf{rk}^{f}_{i\to j}$

$\underline{\mathcal{O}_{\text{Cor}}(i)}$: //corruption queries
  If $i \in \mathcal{Q}_u$: Return $\perp$ //avoid **TA1″**
  If $\mathsf{CheckTA}(\mathcal{Q}_u, \mathcal{Q}_{rk}, \mathcal{Q}_c \cup \{i\}) = 1$:
    Return $\perp$ //avoid **TA2″**
  $\mathcal{Q}_c := \mathcal{Q}_c \cup \{i\}$
  Return $sk^{(i)}$

$\underline{\mathsf{CheckTA}(\mathcal{Q}_u, \mathcal{Q}_{rk}, \mathcal{Q}_c)}$: //check **TA2″**
  If $\exists\, i^* \in \mathcal{Q}_u$ and
    $\exists\, (i^*, j_1), (j_1, j_2), \ldots, (j_{t-1}, j_t) \in \mathcal{Q}_{rk}$
    s.t. $j_t \in \mathcal{Q}_c$ for some $t \geq 1$:
    Return 1
  Else: Return 0

Fig. 8. The Ciphertext Unlinkability security experiment $\mathsf{Exp}^{\mathsf{CUL}}_{\mathsf{mFPRE},\mathcal{A},\mathfrak{n}}$ for mFPRE.

Following [7], we can extend PCS for our multi-hop FPRE, by requiring the indistinguishability between fine-grained re-encryptions of two adversarially chosen ciphertexts, even if the adversary can obtain the old secret key and the fine-grained re-encryption key used to perform the re-encryption. Moreover, similar to [7], we can also show that $\mathsf{HRA} + \mathsf{SH} \Rightarrow$ PCS holds for our multi-hop FPRE. The formalization of PCS and the proof of $\mathsf{HRA} + \mathsf{SH} \Rightarrow$ PCS for multi-hop FPRE are straightforward based on [7], and we will not elaborate on them.

4 Constructions of Multi-hop Fine-Grained PRE Scheme

In this section, we present two constructions of multi-hop fine-grained PRE (mFPRE) schemes, including a CPA secure scheme mFPRE_1 and an HRA secure scheme mFPRE_2, from the LWE assumptions.

4.1 The CPA Secure Multi-hop FPRE Scheme mFPRE_1

Parameters. Let $\mathsf{pp}_{\mathsf{LWE}} = (p, q, n, N, L, \ell, \gamma, \Delta, \chi)$ be LWE-related parameters that meet the following conditions:

- $p, q, n, N, L, \ell, \gamma, \Delta \in \mathbb{N}$, where $q := p^2$, $\gamma \geq O(\sqrt{n \log q}) \cdot \omega(\sqrt{\log n})$;
- χ is a B-bounded distribution, where B satisfies $\gamma \cdot \omega(\log n) \leq B < \min\{p/2, q/(10N)\}$ and $(nB + NB + \ell\Delta)^L B < \min\{p/2, q/(10N)\}$.

More precisely, we describe two settings of parameter in Table 2, one for constant hops ($L = c$) and under polynomial modulus q, while the other for sub-linear

Table 2. Concrete parameters setting, where λ denotes the security parameter and c denotes an arbitrary constant.

Parameters	p	q	n	N	L	ℓ	γ	Δ	B
Settings (L = constant)	λ^{2c+1}	λ^{4c+2}	λ	λ	c	λ	$\sqrt{\lambda}(\log\lambda)^2$	λ	$\sqrt{\lambda}(\log\lambda)^4$
Settings (L = sub-linear)	$2^{\sqrt{\lambda}}$	$2^{2\sqrt{\lambda}}$	λ	λ	$c\cdot\sqrt[3]{\lambda}$	λ	$\sqrt{\lambda}(\log\lambda)^2$	λ	$\sqrt{\lambda}(\log\lambda)^4$

hops ($L = c\cdot\sqrt[3]{\lambda}$) under sub-exponential modulus q. For simplicity, we assume that all algorithms of our scheme mFPRE_1 take $\mathsf{pp}_{\mathsf{LWE}}$ as an implicit input.

Bounded Linear Function Family. The message space is $\mathcal{M} := \mathbb{Z}_p^{\ell}$. Define the family of bounded linear functions $\mathcal{F}_{\text{lin}}$ from $\mathcal{M}$ to $\mathcal{M}$ over $\mathbb{Z}_p$ as follows:

$$\mathcal{F}_{\text{lin}} = \left\{ \begin{array}{l} f_{\mathbf{M}} : \mathbb{Z}_p^{\ell} \to \mathbb{Z}_p^{\ell} \\ \quad \mathbf{m} \mapsto \mathbf{M}\cdot\mathbf{m} \bmod p \end{array} \;\middle|\; \mathbf{M}\in\mathbb{Z}_p^{\ell\times\ell}, \|\mathbf{M}\|_{\infty} \le \Delta \right\}. \tag{9}$$

LWE-Based Multi-hop FPRE Scheme mFPRE_1**.** Let $\mathsf{TrapGen}$, $\mathsf{SamplePre}$, Invert be the PPT algorithms introduced in [1,11,16]. Our LWE-based multi-hop FPRE scheme $\mathsf{mFPRE}_1 = (\mathsf{KGen}, \mathsf{FReKGen}, \mathsf{Enc}, \mathsf{FReEnc}, \mathsf{Dec})$ for the bounded linear function family $\mathcal{F}_{\text{lin}}$ defined in (9) is shown in Fig. 9.

$\underline{(pk, sk) \leftarrow_{\$} \mathsf{KGen}:}$
$(\overline{\mathbf{A}} \in \mathbb{Z}_q^{N\times n}, \mathbf{T}) \leftarrow \mathsf{TrapGen}(1^n, 1^N)$
$\underline{\mathbf{A}} \leftarrow_{\$} \mathbb{Z}_q^{\ell\times n}$
$pk := \mathbf{A} = \binom{\overline{\mathbf{A}}}{\underline{\mathbf{A}}} \in \mathbb{Z}_q^{(N+\ell)\times n}$
$sk := \mathbf{T}$
Return (pk, sk)

$\underline{\mathsf{rk}_{i\to j}^{f_{\mathbf{M}}} \leftarrow_{\$} \mathsf{FReKGen}(pk^{(i)} = \mathbf{A}^{(i)}, sk^{(i)} = \mathbf{T}^{(i)}, pk^{(j)} = \mathbf{A}^{(j)}, f_{\mathbf{M}} \in \mathcal{F}_{\text{lin}}):}$
$\mathbf{S} \leftarrow_{\$} \chi^{n\times n}$, $\mathbf{E} \leftarrow_{\$} \chi^{(N+\ell)\times n}$
Parse $\mathbf{A}^{(i)} = \binom{\overline{\mathbf{A}}^{(i)}}{\underline{\mathbf{A}}^{(i)}}$
$\mathbf{R} \in \mathbb{Z}^{(N+\ell)\times N} \leftarrow_{\$} \mathsf{SamplePre}\left(\mathbf{T}^{(i)}, \overline{\mathbf{A}}^{(i)}, \mathbf{A}^{(j)}\mathbf{S} + \mathbf{E} - \binom{\mathbf{0}}{\mathbf{M}}\underline{\mathbf{A}}^{(i)}, \gamma\right)$
$\mathsf{rk}_{i\to j}^{f_{\mathbf{M}}} := \left(\mathbf{R} \;\middle|\; \begin{matrix}\mathbf{0}\\ \mathbf{M}\end{matrix}\right) \in \mathbb{Z}_p^{(N+\ell)\times(N+\ell)}$ //$\mathbf{M}$ is the description of $f_{\mathbf{M}}$
Return $\mathsf{rk}_{i\to j}^{f_{\mathbf{M}}}$

$\underline{ct_v \leftarrow_{\$} \mathsf{Enc}(pk = \mathbf{A}, \mathbf{m} \in \mathcal{M}, v \in [0, L]):}$
$\mathbf{s} \leftarrow_{\$} \chi^n$, $\mathbf{e} \leftarrow_{\$} \chi^{N+\ell}$
$ct_v := \mathbf{A}\mathbf{s} + \mathbf{e} + \binom{\mathbf{0}}{p\mathbf{m}} \in \mathbb{Z}_q^{N+\ell}$

$\underline{ct_{v+1}^{(j)} \leftarrow \mathsf{FReEnc}(\mathsf{rk}_{i\to j}^{f_{\mathbf{M}}} \in \mathbb{Z}_p^{(N+\ell)\times(N+\ell)}, ct_v^{(i)} \in \mathbb{Z}_q^{N+\ell}, v \in [0, L-1]):}$
$ct_{v+1}^{(j)} := \mathsf{rk}_{i\to j}^{f_{\mathbf{M}}} \cdot ct_v^{(i)} \in \mathbb{Z}_q^{N+\ell}$
Return $ct_{v+1}^{(j)}$

$\underline{\mathbf{m} \leftarrow \mathsf{Dec}(sk = \mathbf{T}, ct \in \mathbb{Z}_q^{N+\ell}):}$
Parse $ct = \binom{\overline{ct} \in \mathbb{Z}_q^N}{\underline{ct} \in \mathbb{Z}_q^{\ell}}$
$(\mathbf{s}, \overline{\mathbf{e}}) \leftarrow_{\$} \mathsf{Invert}(\mathbf{T}, \overline{ct})$
$\tilde{\mathbf{m}} = (\tilde{m}_1, \ldots, \tilde{m}_{\ell}) := \underline{ct} - \underline{\mathbf{A}}\mathbf{s}$
For $i \in [\ell]$: $m_i := \lceil \tilde{m}_i / p \rfloor$
Return $\mathbf{m} = (m_1, m_2, \ldots, m_{\ell})$

Fig. 9. The LWE-based Multi-Hop FPRE scheme mFPRE_1 for $\mathcal{F}_{\text{lin}}$.

Correctness. Let $pk = \mathbf{A}$ and $sk = \mathbf{T}$. For a v-level ciphertext ct_v generated by $\mathsf{Enc}(pk, \mathbf{m}, v)$, we have $ct_v = \binom{\overline{ct_v}}{\underline{ct_v}} = \binom{\overline{\mathbf{A}}\mathbf{s}+\overline{\mathbf{e}}}{\underline{\mathbf{A}}\mathbf{s}+\underline{\mathbf{e}}+p\mathbf{m}}$, where $\mathbf{e} = \binom{\overline{\mathbf{e}}}{\underline{\mathbf{e}}} \leftarrow_{\$} \chi^{N+\ell}$ and the upper part is an LWE instance of $\overline{\mathbf{A}}$. Since $\overline{\mathbf{e}}$ is B-bounded with $B < q/(10N)$, $\|\overline{\mathbf{e}}\| \le \sqrt{N}\,\|\overline{\mathbf{e}}\|_{\infty} \le \sqrt{N}B < q/(10\cdot\sqrt{N})$. Then by the property of Invert (cf. the full version [20]), $(\mathbf{s}, \overline{\mathbf{e}})$ can be correctly recovered via $(\mathbf{s}, \overline{\mathbf{e}}) \leftarrow \mathsf{Invert}(\mathbf{T}, \overline{ct_v})$. Thus according to the decryption algorithm $\mathsf{Dec}(sk, ct_v)$, we get $\tilde{\mathbf{m}} = \underline{ct_v} - \underline{\mathbf{A}}\mathbf{s} = \underline{\mathbf{e}} + p\mathbf{m}$, and by parsing $\underline{\mathbf{e}} = (e_1, \ldots, e_{\ell})^{\top}$, we have that $\tilde{m}_i = e_i + pm_i$ for all

$i \in [\ell]$. Moreover, since $\underline{\mathbf{e}}$ is B-bounded with $B < p/2$, each $|e_i| \leq B < p/2$. Consequently, $\lceil \tilde{m}_i/p \rfloor = m_i$ and Dec can recover $\mathbf{m}$ correctly from ct_v.

Fine-Grained L-Hop Correctness. For $ct_0^{(i)} \xrightarrow{\mathsf{rk}_{i\to j}^{f_{\mathbf{M}_1}}} ct_1^{(j)}$, where $ct_0^{(i)} \leftarrow_\$ \mathsf{Enc}(pk^{(i)}, \mathbf{m}, 0)$, $\mathsf{rk}_{i\to j}^{f_{\mathbf{M}_1}} \leftarrow_\$ \mathsf{FReKGen}(pk^{(i)}, sk^{(i)}, pk^{(j)}, f_{\mathbf{M}_1})$ and $ct_1^{(j)} \leftarrow_\$ \mathsf{FReEnc}(\mathsf{rk}_{i\to j}^{f_{\mathbf{M}_1}}, ct_0^{(i)}, 0)$, we will show that the decryption of $ct_1^{(j)}$ results in $f_{\mathbf{M}_1}(\mathbf{m}) = \mathbf{M}_1\mathbf{m}$. More precisely, let $\mathsf{rk}_{i\to j}^{\mathbf{M}_1} := \left(\mathbf{R}_1 \;\middle|\; {}^{\mathbf{0}}_{\mathbf{M}_1}\right)$, we have

$$\begin{aligned}
ct_1^{(j)} &:= \left(\mathbf{R}_1 \;\middle|\; \begin{matrix}\mathbf{0}\\ \mathbf{M}_1\end{matrix}\right) \cdot ct_0^{(i)} = \left(\mathbf{R}_1 \;\middle|\; \begin{matrix}\mathbf{0}\\ \mathbf{M}_1\end{matrix}\right) \cdot \left(\begin{pmatrix}\overline{\mathbf{A}}^{(i)}\\ \underline{\mathbf{A}}^{(i)}\end{pmatrix} \mathbf{s}_0 + \begin{pmatrix}\overline{\mathbf{e}_0}\\ \underline{\mathbf{e}_0}\end{pmatrix} + \begin{pmatrix}\mathbf{0}\\ p\mathbf{m}\end{pmatrix} \right)\\
&= \left(\mathbf{R}_1\overline{\mathbf{A}}^{(i)} + \begin{pmatrix}\mathbf{0}\\ \mathbf{M}_1\end{pmatrix}\underline{\mathbf{A}}^{(i)}\right) \cdot \mathbf{s}_0 + \mathbf{R}_1\overline{\mathbf{e}_0} + \begin{pmatrix}\mathbf{0}\\ \mathbf{M}_1\underline{\mathbf{e}_0}\end{pmatrix} + \begin{pmatrix}\mathbf{0}\\ p\cdot\mathbf{M}_1\mathbf{m}\end{pmatrix}\\
&= \left(\mathbf{A}^{(j)}\mathbf{S} + \mathbf{E}\right) \cdot \mathbf{s}_0 + \mathbf{R}_1\overline{\mathbf{e}_0} + \begin{pmatrix}\mathbf{0}\\ \mathbf{M}_1\underline{\mathbf{e}_0}\end{pmatrix} + \begin{pmatrix}\mathbf{0}\\ p\cdot\mathbf{M}_1\mathbf{m}\end{pmatrix}\\
&= \mathbf{A}^{(j)} \underbrace{\mathbf{S}\mathbf{s}_0}_{:=\mathbf{s}_1} + \underbrace{\mathbf{E}\mathbf{s}_0 + \mathbf{R}_1\overline{\mathbf{e}_0} + \begin{pmatrix}\mathbf{0}\\ \mathbf{M}_1\underline{\mathbf{e}_0}\end{pmatrix}}_{:=\mathbf{e}_1} + \begin{pmatrix}\mathbf{0}\\ p\cdot \underbrace{\mathbf{M}_1\mathbf{m}}_{=f_{\mathbf{M}_1}(\mathbf{m})}\end{pmatrix},
\end{aligned} \tag{10}$$

where $\mathbf{s}_0 \leftarrow_\$ \chi^n$, $\mathbf{e}_0 = \begin{pmatrix}\overline{\mathbf{e}_0}\\ \underline{\mathbf{e}_0}\end{pmatrix} \leftarrow_\$ \chi^{N+\ell}$, $\mathbf{S} \leftarrow_\$ \chi^{n\times n}$, $\mathbf{E} \leftarrow_\$ \chi^{(N+\ell)\times n}$. Here the second last equality follows from the fact that $\mathbf{R}_1$ generated by $\mathbf{R}_1 \leftarrow_\$ \mathsf{SamplePre}(\mathbf{T}^{(i)}, \overline{\mathbf{A}}^{(i)}, \mathbf{A}^{(j)}\mathbf{S}+\mathbf{E}-\binom{\mathbf{0}}{\mathbf{M}_1}\underline{\mathbf{A}}^{(i)}, \gamma)$ satisfies $\mathbf{R}_1\overline{\mathbf{A}}^{(i)} = \mathbf{A}^{(j)}\mathbf{S}+\mathbf{E}-\binom{\mathbf{0}}{\mathbf{M}_1}\underline{\mathbf{A}}^{(i)}$ and $\|\mathbf{R}_1\|_\infty \leq \gamma\cdot\omega(\log n)$ according to the property of $\mathsf{SamplePre}$ (cf. the full version [20]). Besides, $\|\mathbf{R}_1\|_\infty \leq \gamma\cdot\omega(\log n)$ implies that $\|\mathbf{R}_1\|_\infty \leq B$ due to $\gamma\cdot\omega(\log n) \leq B$. Now that $\mathbf{S}, \mathbf{E}, \mathbf{R}_1, \mathbf{s}_0, \mathbf{e}_0$ are all B-bounded and $\mathbf{M}_1$ is Δ-bounded, so we have $\|\mathbf{s}_1\|_\infty \leq nB^2$ and $\|\mathbf{e}_1\|_\infty \leq (nB+NB+\ell\Delta)B < \min\{p/2, q/(10N)\}$. Then by a similar argument as that for correctness, since $\|\mathbf{e}_1\|_\infty < q/(10N)$ and $\|\mathbf{e}_1\|_\infty < p/2$, Dec recovers $f_{\mathbf{M}_1}(\mathbf{m}) = \mathbf{M}_1\mathbf{m}$ from $ct_1^{(j)}$.

Next suppose that $ct_1^{(j)}$ is further re-encrypted to $ct_2^{(k)}$, i.e., $ct_1^{(j)} \xrightarrow{\mathsf{rk}_{j\to k}^{f_{\mathbf{M}_2}}} ct_2^{(k)}$, where $\mathsf{rk}_{j\to k}^{f_{\mathbf{M}_2}} \leftarrow_\$ \mathsf{FReKGen}(pk^{(j)}, sk^{(j)}, pk^{(k)}, f_{\mathbf{M}_2})$ and $ct_2^{(k)} \leftarrow_\$ \mathsf{FReEnc}(\mathsf{rk}_{j\to k}^{f_{\mathbf{M}_2}}, ct_1^{(j)}, 1)$, we will show that the decryption of $ct_2^{(k)}$ results in $f_{\mathbf{M}_2}(f_{\mathbf{M}_1}(\mathbf{m})) = \mathbf{M}_2\cdot\mathbf{M}_1\cdot\mathbf{m}$. By a similar analysis as above, let $\mathsf{rk}_{j\to k}^{f_{\mathbf{M}_2}} := \left(\mathbf{R}_2 \;\middle|\; {}^{\mathbf{0}}_{\mathbf{M}_2}\right)$, we have

$$\begin{aligned}
ct_2^{(k)} &:= \left(\mathbf{R}_2 \;\middle|\; \begin{matrix}\mathbf{0}\\ \mathbf{M}_2\end{matrix}\right) \cdot ct_1^{(j)} = \left(\mathbf{R}_2 \;\middle|\; \begin{matrix}\mathbf{0}\\ \mathbf{M}_2\end{matrix}\right) \cdot \left(\begin{pmatrix}\overline{\mathbf{A}}^{(j)}\\ \underline{\mathbf{A}}^{(j)}\end{pmatrix} \mathbf{s}_1 + \begin{pmatrix}\overline{\mathbf{e}_1}\\ \underline{\mathbf{e}_1}\end{pmatrix} + \begin{pmatrix}\mathbf{0}\\ p\mathbf{M}_1\mathbf{m}\end{pmatrix} \right)\\
&= \mathbf{A}^{(k)} \underbrace{\mathbf{S}\mathbf{s}_1}_{:=\mathbf{s}_2} + \underbrace{\mathbf{E}\mathbf{s}_1 + \mathbf{R}_2\overline{\mathbf{e}_1} + \begin{pmatrix}\mathbf{0}\\ \mathbf{M}_2\underline{\mathbf{e}_1}\end{pmatrix}}_{:=\mathbf{e}_2} + \begin{pmatrix}\mathbf{0}\\ p\cdot \underbrace{\mathbf{M}_2\mathbf{M}_1\mathbf{m}}_{=f_{\mathbf{M}_2}(f_{\mathbf{M}_1}(\mathbf{m}))}\end{pmatrix},
\end{aligned}$$

where $\mathbf{S} \leftarrow_\$ \chi^{n\times n}$ and $\mathbf{E} \leftarrow_\$ \chi^{(N+\ell)\times n}$. Similarly, we know that $\mathbf{S}, \mathbf{E}, \mathbf{R}_2$ are B-bounded and $\mathbf{M}_2$ is Δ-bounded. Together with the fact that $\|\mathbf{s}_1\|_\infty \leq nB^2 \leq (nB+NB+\ell\Delta)B$ and $\|\mathbf{e}_1\|_\infty \leq (nB+NB+\ell\Delta)B$, it follows that $\|\mathbf{s}_2\|_\infty \leq (nB+NB+\ell\Delta)nB^2$ and $\|\mathbf{e}_2\|_\infty \leq (nB+NB+\ell\Delta)^2B < \min\{p/2, q/(10N)\}$.

Again, with a similar argument as that for correctness, the decryption algorithm Dec recovers $f_{\mathbf{M}_2}(f_{\mathbf{M}_1}(\mathbf{m})) = \mathbf{M}_2\mathbf{M}_1\mathbf{m}$ from $ct_2^{(k)}$.

As the re-encryption proceeds, after L hops of re-encryption under $f_{\mathbf{M}_1}, f_{\mathbf{M}_2}, \cdots, f_{\mathbf{M}_L}$, we get an L-level ciphertext $ct_L^{(\eta)}$ and it satisfies

$$ct_L^{(\eta)} = \mathbf{A}^{(\eta)}\mathbf{s}_L + \mathbf{e}_L + \begin{pmatrix} \mathbf{0} \\ p \cdot \underbrace{\mathbf{M}_L \cdots \mathbf{M}_2\mathbf{M}_1\mathbf{m}}_{=f_{\mathbf{M}_L}(\cdots f_{\mathbf{M}_2}(f_{\mathbf{M}_1}(\mathbf{m})))} \end{pmatrix},$$

where $\|\mathbf{s}_L\|_\infty \le (nB + NB + \ell\Delta)^{L-1}nB^2$ and $\|\mathbf{e}_L\|_\infty \le (nB + NB + \ell\Delta)^L B < \min\{p/2, q/(10N)\}$. Consequently, the function value $f_{\mathbf{M}_L}(\cdots f_{\mathbf{M}_2}(f_{\mathbf{M}_1}(\mathbf{m}))) = \mathbf{M}_L \cdots \mathbf{M}_2\mathbf{M}_1\mathbf{m}$ can be recovered from $ct_L^{(\eta)}$ by the decryption algorithm Dec.

Below we show the IND security and wKP security of our scheme mFPRE_1 via the following two theorems. Then together with Theorem 1 (IND + wKP $\Rightarrow$ CPA) in Subsect. 3.2, it yields the CPA security of our scheme mFPRE_1.

Theorem 3 (**IND Security of** mFPRE_1). *Assume that the* $\mathsf{LWE}_{n,q,\chi,N+\ell}$*-assumption holds, then the scheme* mFPRE_1 *proposed in Fig. 9 has* IND *security. More precisely, for any PPT adversary* $\mathcal{A}$ *that make at most* Q_{chal} *queries to* $\mathcal{O}_{\text{CHAL}}$*, there exists a PPT algorithm* $\mathcal{B}$ *against the LWE assumption s.t.* $\mathsf{Adv}^{\mathsf{IND}}_{\mathsf{mFPRE}_1,\mathcal{A}}(\lambda) \le Q_{chal} \cdot \mathsf{Adv}^{\mathsf{LWE}}_{[n,q,\chi,N+\ell],\mathcal{B}}(\lambda)$.

Proof of Theorem 3. We prove the theorem via two games G_0 and G_1.

Game G_0: This is the IND experiment (cf. Fig. 4). Let Win denote the event that $\beta' = \beta$. By definition, $\mathsf{Adv}^{\mathsf{IND}}_{\mathsf{mFPRE}_1,\mathcal{A}}(\lambda) = |\Pr_0[\mathsf{Win}] - \frac{1}{2}|$.

Let $(pk = \mathbf{A}, sk = \mathbf{T})$. In this game, the challenger chooses a random bit $\beta \leftarrow_\$ \{0,1\}$ and answers $\mathcal{A}$'s $\mathcal{O}_{\text{CHAL}}$ queries $(\mathbf{m}_0, \mathbf{m}_1, v)$ with $ct_v \leftarrow_\$ \mathsf{Enc}(pk, \mathbf{m}_\beta, v)$, i.e., $ct_v := \mathbf{As} + \mathbf{e} + \binom{\mathbf{0}}{p\mathbf{m}_\beta}$ for $\mathbf{s} \leftarrow_\$ \chi^n, \mathbf{e} \leftarrow_\$ \chi^{N+\ell}$.

Game G_1: It is the same as G_0, except that, when answering $\mathcal{O}_{\text{CHAL}}(\mathbf{m}_0, \mathbf{m}_1, v)$ queries, the challenger returns a uniformly sampled $ct_v \leftarrow_\$ \mathbb{Z}_q^{N+\ell}$ to $\mathcal{A}$. Clearly, now the challenge bit β is completely hidden to $\mathcal{A}$, thus $\Pr_0[\mathsf{Win}] = \frac{1}{2}$.

It is not hard to see that the $ct_v \leftarrow_\$ \mathsf{Enc}(pk, \mathbf{m}_\beta, v)$ in G_1 is indistinguishable from the $ct_v \leftarrow_\$ \mathbb{Z}_q^{N+\ell}$ in G_1 based on the LWE assumption. Formally, we have the following claim with proof appeared in the full version [20].

Claim 1. $\big|\Pr_0[\mathsf{Win}] - \Pr_1[\mathsf{Win}]\big| \le Q_{chal} \cdot \mathsf{Adv}^{\mathsf{LWE}}_{[n,q,\chi,N+\ell],\mathcal{B}}(\lambda)$.

Finally, taking all things together, Theorem 3 follows. □

Theorem 4. (**wKP Security of** mFPRE_1). *Assume that the* $\mathsf{LWE}_{n,q,\chi,N+\ell}$*-assumption holds, then the scheme* mFPRE_1 *proposed in Fig. 9 has* wKP *security. More precisely, for any PPT adversary* $\mathcal{A}$ *that makes at most* Q_{rk} *queries to* $\mathcal{O}_{\text{REKEY}}$ *and for any polynomial* $\mathfrak{n}$*, there exists a PPT algorithm* $\mathcal{B}$ *against the LWE assumption s.t.* $\mathsf{Adv}^{\mathsf{wKP}}_{\mathsf{mFPRE}_1,\mathcal{A},\mathfrak{n}}(\lambda) \le \mathfrak{n} \cdot nQ_{rk} \cdot \mathsf{Adv}^{\mathsf{LWE}}_{[n,q,\chi,N+\ell],\mathcal{B}}(\lambda) + \mathsf{negl}(\lambda)$.

Proof of Theorem 4. We prove the theorem via a sequence of games G_0-G_2, where G_0 is the wKP experiment, and in G_2, $\mathcal{A}$ has a negligible advantage.

Game G_0: This is the wKP experiment (cf. Fig. 5). Let Win denote the event that $\beta' = \beta$. By definition, $\mathsf{Adv}^{\mathsf{wKP}}_{\mathsf{mFPRE}_1,\mathcal{A},\mathfrak{n}}(\lambda) = |\Pr_0[\mathsf{Win}] - \frac{1}{2}|$.

Let $pk^{(i)} = \mathbf{A}^{(i)}, sk^{(i)} = \mathbf{T}^{(i)}$ denote the public key and secret key of user $i \in [0, \mathfrak{n}]$. In this game, the challenger chooses a random bit $\beta \leftarrow_\$ \{0,1\}$ and answers $\mathcal{A}$'s $\mathcal{O}_{\text{ReKey}}$ queries $(j \in [\mathfrak{n}], f_{\mathbf{M}} \in \mathcal{F}_{\text{lin}})$ as follows:

- If $\beta = 0$, the challenger returns $\mathsf{rk}^{f_{\mathbf{M}}}_{0\to j} \leftarrow_\$ \mathsf{FReKGen}(\mathbf{A}^{(0)}, \mathbf{T}^{(0)}, \mathbf{A}^{(j)}, f_{\mathbf{M}})$. More precisely, it samples $\mathbf{S} \leftarrow_\$ \chi^{n\times n}, \mathbf{E} \leftarrow_\$ \chi^{(N+\ell)\times n}$, $\mathbf{R} \leftarrow_\$ \mathsf{SamplePre}(\mathbf{T}^{(0)}, \overline{\mathbf{A}}^{(0)}, \mathbf{A}^{(j)}\mathbf{S} + \mathbf{E} - \binom{\mathbf{0}}{\mathbf{M}}\underline{\mathbf{A}}^{(0)}, \gamma)$, and returns $\mathsf{rk}^{f_{\mathbf{M}}}_{0\to j} := \left(\mathbf{R} \,\middle|\, \begin{smallmatrix}\mathbf{0}\\ \mathbf{M}\end{smallmatrix}\right)$ to $\mathcal{A}$.
- If $\beta = 1$, the challenger invokes $\mathsf{rk}^{f_{\mathbf{M}}}_{0\to j} \leftarrow_\$ \mathsf{FReKGen}^*(\mathbf{A}^{(0)}, \mathbf{A}^{(j)}, f_{\mathbf{M}})$ which is defined as $\mathsf{FReKGen}^*$: $\mathbf{R} \leftarrow_\$ D_{\mathbb{Z}^{(N+\ell)\times N},\gamma}$ and $\mathsf{rk}^{f_{\mathbf{M}}}_{0\to j} := \left(\mathbf{R} \,\middle|\, \begin{smallmatrix}\mathbf{0}\\ \mathbf{M}\end{smallmatrix}\right)$. Then the challenger returns $\mathsf{rk}^{f_{\mathbf{M}}}_{0\to j}$ to $\mathcal{A}$.

Game $\mathsf{G}_{0.t}, t \in [0, \mathfrak{n}]$: It is the same as G_0, except for the reply to $\mathcal{A}$'s $\mathcal{O}_{\text{ReKey}}(j, f_{\mathbf{M}})$ query when $\beta = 0$:

- For $j \le t$, the challenger uniformly samples $\mathbf{U} \leftarrow_\$ \mathbb{Z}_q^{(N+\ell)\times n}$ and invokes $\mathbf{R} \leftarrow_\$ \mathsf{SamplePre}(\mathbf{T}^{(0)}, \overline{\mathbf{A}}^{(0)}, \mathbf{U}, \gamma)$ to get $\mathsf{rk}^{f_{\mathbf{M}}}_{0\to j} := \left(\mathbf{R} \,\middle|\, \begin{smallmatrix}\mathbf{0}\\ \mathbf{M}\end{smallmatrix}\right)$.
- For $j > t$, the challenger answers the query just like G_0, that is, $\mathbf{R} \leftarrow_\$ \mathsf{SamplePre}\left(\mathbf{T}^{(0)}, \overline{\mathbf{A}}^{(0)}, \mathbf{A}^{(j)}\mathbf{S} + \mathbf{E} - \binom{\mathbf{0}}{\mathbf{M}}\underline{\mathbf{A}}^{(0)}, \gamma\right)$ with $\mathbf{S} \leftarrow_\$ \chi^{n\times n}, \mathbf{E} \leftarrow_\$ \chi^{(N+\ell)\times n}$.

Clearly, $\mathsf{G}_{0.0}$ is identical to G_0. Thus, we have $\Pr_0[\mathsf{Win}] = \Pr_{0.0}[\mathsf{Win}]$.

Below we show the computational indistinguishability between $\mathsf{G}_{0.t-1}$ and $\mathsf{G}_{0.t}$ based on the LWE assumption.

Claim 2. For all $t \in [\mathfrak{n}]$, $|\Pr_{0.t-1}[\mathsf{Win}] - \Pr_{0.t}[\mathsf{Win}]| \le nQ_{rk} \cdot \mathsf{Adv}^{\mathsf{LWE}}_{[n,q,\chi,N+\ell],\mathcal{B}}(\lambda)$.

Proof. Firstly, we construct a PPT adversary $\mathcal{B}'$ against the nQ_{rk}-$\mathsf{LWE}_{n,q,\chi,N+\ell}$-assumption, such that $|\Pr_{0.t-1}[\mathsf{Win}] - \Pr_{0.t}[\mathsf{Win}]| \le \mathsf{Adv}^{nQ_{rk}\text{-}\mathsf{LWE}}_{[n,q,\chi,N+\ell],\mathcal{B}'}(\lambda)$. Then by a standard hybrid argument, we have $\mathsf{Adv}^{nQ_{rk}\text{-}\mathsf{LWE}}_{[n,q,\chi,N+\ell],\mathcal{B}'}(\lambda) \le nQ_{rk} \cdot \mathsf{Adv}^{\mathsf{LWE}}_{[n,q,\chi,N+\ell],\mathcal{B}}(\lambda)$ and the claim follows.

Algorithm $\mathcal{B}'$. Given a challenge $(\mathbf{A}, \mathbf{Z})$, $\mathcal{B}'$ wants to distinguish $\mathbf{Z} = \mathbf{AS} + \mathbf{E}$ from $\mathbf{Z} \leftarrow_\$ \mathbb{Z}_q^{(N+\ell)\times nQ_{rk}}$, where $\mathbf{A} \leftarrow_\$ \mathbb{Z}_q^{(N+\ell)\times n}$, $\mathbf{S} \leftarrow_\$ \chi^{n\times nQ_{rk}}$, $\mathbf{E} \leftarrow_\$ \chi^{(N+\ell)\times nQ_{rk}}$.

$\mathcal{B}'$ is constructed by simulating $\mathsf{G}_{0.t-1}/\mathsf{G}_{0.t}$ for $\mathcal{A}$ as follows. Firstly, $\mathcal{B}'$ sets $pk^{(t)} := \mathbf{A}^{(t)} := \mathbf{A}$ directly for the user t, and invokes KGen honestly to generate $(pk^{(i)}, sk^{(i)})$ for all other users $i \in [0, \mathfrak{n}] \setminus \{t\}$. In particular, $\mathcal{B}'$ owns $sk^{(0)} = \mathbf{T}^{(0)}$. $\mathcal{B}'$ sends $\{pk^{(i)}\}_{i\in[0,\mathfrak{n}]}$ to $\mathcal{A}$. Then $\mathcal{B}'$ chooses a random bit $\beta \leftarrow_\$ \{0,1\}$ and parses $\mathbf{Z} = (\mathbf{Z}_1 \mid \cdots \mid \mathbf{Z}_{Q_{rk}}) \in \mathbb{Z}_q^{(N+\ell)\times nQ_{rk}}$ with each $\mathbf{Z}_k \in \mathbb{Z}_q^{(N+\ell)\times n}$ for $k \in [Q_{chal}]$. On receiving an $\mathcal{O}_{\text{ReKey}}(j \in [\mathfrak{n}], f_{\mathbf{M}})$ query from $\mathcal{A}$, if $\beta = 1$, $\mathcal{B}'$ invokes $\mathsf{FReKGen}^*$ to get $\mathsf{rk}^{f_{\mathbf{M}}}_{0\to j}$ and returns it to $\mathcal{A}$, the same as $\mathsf{G}_{0.t-1}$ and $\mathsf{G}_{0.t}$. Otherwise, i.e., $\beta = 0$, $\mathcal{B}'$ answers the $\mathcal{O}_{\text{ReKey}}(j \in [\mathfrak{n}], f_{\mathbf{M}})$ query in the following way:

- For $j \le t-1$, $\mathcal{B}'$ samples $\mathbf{U} \leftarrow_{\$} \mathbb{Z}_q^{(N+\ell)\times n}$ and invokes $\mathbf{R} \leftarrow_{\$} \mathsf{SamplePre}(\mathbf{T}^{(0)}, \overline{\mathbf{A}}^{(0)}, \mathbf{U}, \gamma)$ to get $\mathsf{rk}_{0\to j}^{f_{\mathbf{M}}} := \left(\mathbf{R} \,\middle|\, \begin{smallmatrix}\mathbf{0}\\ \mathbf{M}\end{smallmatrix}\right)$, the same as $\mathsf{G}_{0.t-1}$ and $\mathsf{G}_{0.t}$.
- For $j = t$, suppose that this is the k-th $\mathcal{O}_{\text{REKEY}}$ query with $k \in [Q_{rk}]$, $\mathcal{B}'$ makes use of $\mathbf{Z}_k$ to invoke $\mathbf{R} \leftarrow_{\$} \mathsf{SamplePre}(\mathbf{T}^{(0)}, \overline{\mathbf{A}}^{(0)}, \mathbf{Z}_k - \left(\begin{smallmatrix}\mathbf{0}\\ \mathbf{M}\end{smallmatrix}\right)\underline{\mathbf{A}}^{(0)}, \gamma)$ to get $\mathsf{rk}_{0\to t}^{f_{\mathbf{M}}} := \left(\mathbf{R} \,\middle|\, \begin{smallmatrix}\mathbf{0}\\ \mathbf{M}\end{smallmatrix}\right)$.
  In the case of $\mathbf{Z} = \mathbf{A}\mathbf{S} + \mathbf{E}$, by parsing $\mathbf{S} = (\mathbf{S}_1 \mid \cdots \mid \mathbf{S}_{Q_{rk}}) \in \mathbb{Z}_q^{n\times nQ_{rk}}$ with each $\mathbf{S}_k \in \mathbb{Z}_q^{n\times n}$ and parsing $\mathbf{E} = (\mathbf{E}_1 \mid \cdots \mid \mathbf{E}_{Q_{rk}}) \in \mathbb{Z}_q^{(N+\ell)\times nQ_{rk}}$ with each $\mathbf{E}_k \in \mathbb{Z}_q^{(N+\ell)\times n}$, we have $\mathbf{Z}_k = \mathbf{A}\mathbf{S}_k + \mathbf{E}_k = \mathbf{A}^{(t)}\mathbf{S}_k + \mathbf{E}_k$ for $\mathbf{S}_k \leftarrow_{\$} \chi^{n\times n}$ and $\mathbf{E}_k \leftarrow_{\$} \chi^{(N+\ell)\times n}$, and consequently, $\mathcal{B}'$'s simulation is identical to $\mathsf{G}_{0.t-1}$.
  In the case of $\mathbf{Z} \leftarrow_{\$} \mathbb{Z}_q^{(N+\ell)\times nQ_{rk}}$, we have that $\mathbf{Z}_k$ is uniformly distributed over $\mathbb{Z}_q^{(N+\ell)\times n}$, so $\mathcal{B}'$'s simulation is identical to $\mathsf{G}_{0.t}$.
- For $j > t$, $\mathcal{B}'$ samples $\tilde{\mathbf{S}} \leftarrow_{\$} \chi^{n\times n}, \tilde{\mathbf{E}} \leftarrow_{\$} \chi^{(N+\ell)\times n}$, $\mathbf{R} \leftarrow_{\$} \mathsf{SamplePre}(\mathbf{T}^{(0)}, \overline{\mathbf{A}}^{(0)}, \mathbf{A}^{(j)}\tilde{\mathbf{S}} + \tilde{\mathbf{E}} - \left(\begin{smallmatrix}\mathbf{0}\\ \mathbf{M}\end{smallmatrix}\right)\underline{\mathbf{A}}^{(0)}, \gamma)$ to get $\mathsf{rk}_{0\to j}^{f_{\mathbf{M}}} := \left(\mathbf{R} \,\middle|\, \begin{smallmatrix}\mathbf{0}\\ \mathbf{M}\end{smallmatrix}\right)$, the same as $\mathsf{G}_{0.t-1}$ and $\mathsf{G}_{0.t}$.

Finally, $\mathcal{B}'$ receives β' from $\mathcal{A}$ and outputs 1 to its own challenger if and only if $\beta' = \beta$.

Now we analyze the advantage of $\mathcal{B}'$. Overall, $\mathcal{B}'$ simulates $\mathsf{G}_{0.t-1}$ for $\mathcal{A}$ in the case $\mathbf{Z} = \mathbf{A}\mathbf{S} + \mathbf{E}$ while simulates $\mathsf{G}_{0.t}$ for $\mathcal{A}$ in the case $\mathbf{Z} \leftarrow_{\$} \mathbb{Z}_q^{(N+\ell)\times nQ_{rk}}$. Thus $\mathcal{B}'$ successfully distinguishes $\mathbf{Z} = \mathbf{A}\mathbf{S} + \mathbf{E}$ from $\mathbf{Z} \leftarrow_{\$} \mathbb{Z}_q^{(N+\ell)\times nQ_{rk}}$ as long as the probability that $\beta' = \beta$ in $\mathsf{G}_{0.t-1}$ differs non-negligibly from that in $\mathsf{G}_{0.t}$. Consequently, we have $\mathsf{Adv}_{[n,q,\chi,N+\ell],\mathcal{B}'}^{nQ_{rk}\text{-}\mathsf{LWE}}(\lambda) \ge \left|\Pr_{0.t-1}[\mathsf{Win}] - \Pr_{0.t}[\mathsf{Win}]\right|$. ∎

Game G_1: It's the same as G_0, except for the reply to $\mathcal{A}$'s $\mathcal{O}_{\text{REKEY}}(j, f_{\mathbf{M}})$ query when $\beta = 0$:

- For all $j \in [\mathfrak{n}]$, the challenger samples $\mathbf{U} \leftarrow_{\$} \mathbb{Z}_q^{(N+\ell)\times n}$ and uses $\mathbf{U}$ to invoke $\mathbf{R} \leftarrow_{\$} \mathsf{SamplePre}(\mathbf{T}^{(0)}, \overline{\mathbf{A}}^{(0)}, \mathbf{U}, \gamma)$, and returns $\mathsf{rk}_{0\to j}^{f_{\mathbf{M}}} := \left(\mathbf{R} \,\middle|\, \begin{smallmatrix}\mathbf{0}\\ \mathbf{M}\end{smallmatrix}\right)$ to $\mathcal{A}$.

Clearly, $\mathsf{G}_1 = \mathsf{G}_{0.\mathfrak{n}}$ and $\Pr_1[\mathsf{Win}] = \Pr_{0.\mathfrak{n}}[\mathsf{Win}]$.

Game G_2: It's the same as G_1, except for the reply to $\mathcal{A}$'s $\mathcal{O}_{\text{REKEY}}(j, f_{\mathbf{M}})$ query when $\beta = 0$. The challenger samples $\mathbf{R}$ by $\mathbf{R} \leftarrow_{\$} D_{\mathbb{Z}^{(N+\ell)\times N},\gamma}$, instead of invoking $\mathbf{R} \leftarrow_{\$} \mathsf{SamplePre}\left(\mathbf{T}^{(0)}, \overline{\mathbf{A}}^{(0)}, \mathbf{U} \leftarrow_{\$} \mathbb{Z}_q^{(N+\ell)\times n}, \gamma\right)$ as in G_1.

Since $\gamma \ge O(\sqrt{n \log q}) \cdot \omega(\sqrt{\log n})$, according to the indistinguishability of preimage-sampling $\mathsf{SamplePre}$ (as recalled in the full version [20]), G_2 is statistically close to G_1. Thus we have $\left|\Pr_1[\mathsf{Win}] - \Pr_2[\mathsf{Win}]\right| \le \mathsf{negl}(\lambda)$.

Finally, note that in G_2, the challenger's reply to $\mathcal{A}$'s $\mathcal{O}_{\text{REKEY}}$ query in the case $\beta = 0$ is identical to that in the case $\beta = 1$. Thus the challenge bit β is completely hidden to $\mathcal{A}$, and we have $\Pr_2[\mathsf{Win}] = \frac{1}{2}$.

Taking all things together, Theorem 4 follows. □

By plugging Theorem 3 (IND security) and Theorem 4 (wKP security) into Theorem 1 (IND + wKP ⇒ CPA) in Subsect. 3.2, we have the following corollary showing the CPA security of mFPRE_1 based on the LWE assumption.

Corollary 1 (CPA Security of mFPRE_1). *Assume that the $\mathsf{LWE}_{n,q,\chi,N+\ell}$-assumption holds, then the scheme mFPRE_1 proposed in Fig. 9 is CPA secure. More precisely, for any PPT adversary $\mathcal{A}$ that makes at most Q_{rk} queries to $\mathcal{O}_{\text{ReKey}}$ and forms a challenge graph G (i.e., subgraph reachable from the vertex of challenge user) in $\mathcal{G}(\mathfrak{n}, \delta, d)$, for any polynomial $\mathfrak{n}$, there exists a PPT algorithm $\mathcal{B}$ against the LWE assumption s.t.*

$$\mathsf{Adv}^{\mathsf{CPA}}_{\mathsf{mFPRE}_1,\mathcal{A},\mathfrak{n}} \leq (2\tau \cdot n\mathfrak{n}Q_{rk} + 2) \cdot \mathfrak{n}^{\sigma+\delta+1} \cdot \mathsf{Adv}^{\mathsf{LWE}}_{[n,q,\chi,N+\ell],\mathcal{B}}(\lambda) + \mathsf{negl}(\lambda),$$

where δ denotes the outdegree, d the depth, τ the pebbling time complexity and σ space complexity for the class $\mathcal{G}(\mathfrak{n}, \delta, d)$, respectively.

4.2 The HRA Secure Multi-hop FPRE Scheme mFPRE_2

Parameters. Let $\mathsf{pp}_{\mathsf{LWE}} = (p, q, n, N, L, \ell, \gamma, \Delta, \chi, \{\chi_v\}_{v\in[0,L]})$ be LWE-related parameters that meet the following conditions:

- $p, q, n, N, L, \ell, \gamma, \Delta \in \mathbb{N}$, where $q := p^2$, $\gamma \geq O(\sqrt{n \log q}) \cdot \omega(\sqrt{\log n})$;
- χ is a B-bounded distribution, where B satisfies $\gamma \cdot \omega(\log n) \leq B$.
- For each $v \in [0, L]$, χ_v is the uniform distribution over $[-B_v, B_v]$, where B_v satisfies $B_v \geq 2^{\sqrt[3]{\lambda}} \cdot (nB + NB + \ell\Delta)B_{v-1}$ for $v \geq 1$ and $B_L \leq \min\{p/4, q/(20N)\}$.

More precisely, we describe two settings of parameter in Table 3, one for constant hops ($L = c$) and the other for sub-linear hops ($L = c \cdot \sqrt[3]{\lambda}$), both under sub-exponential modulus q. For simplicity, we assume that all algorithms of our scheme mFPRE_2 take $\mathsf{pp}_{\mathsf{LWE}}$ as an implicit input.

Table 3. Concrete parameters setting, where λ denotes the security parameter and c denotes an arbitrary constant.

Parameters	p	q	n	N	L	ℓ	γ	Δ	B	B_v ($v \in [0, L]$)
Settings (L = constant)	$2^{\sqrt{\lambda}}$	$2^{2\sqrt{\lambda}}$	λ	λ	c	λ	$\sqrt{\lambda}(\log \lambda)^2$	λ	$\sqrt{\lambda}(\log \lambda)^4$	$(\lambda^2 \cdot 2^{\sqrt[3]{\lambda}+1})^{v+1}$
Settings (L = sub-linear)	$2^{\lambda^{3/4}}$	$2^{2\lambda^{3/4}}$	λ	λ	$c \cdot \sqrt[3]{\lambda}$	λ	$\sqrt{\lambda}(\log \lambda)^2$	λ	$\sqrt{\lambda}(\log \lambda)^4$	$(\lambda^2 \cdot 2^{\sqrt[3]{\lambda}+1})^{v+1}$

LWE-Based Multi-hop FPRE Scheme mFPRE_2. Our LWE-based FPRE scheme $\mathsf{mFPRE}_2 = (\mathsf{KGen}, \mathsf{FReKGen}, \mathsf{Enc}, \mathsf{FReEnc}, \mathsf{Dec})$ is also for the bounded linear function family $\mathcal{F}_{\text{lin}}$ defined in (9) in Subsect. 4.1, and is shown in Fig. 10.

The analysis for the correctness and fine-grained L-hop correctness of mFPRE_2 are similar to those for mFPRE_1. Due to space limitations, we postpone the formal analysis to the full version [20].

$\underline{(pk, sk) \leftarrow\!\!\$\ \mathsf{KGen}:}$
$(\overline{\mathbf{A}} \in \mathbb{Z}_q^{N\times n}, \mathbf{T}) \leftarrow \mathsf{TrapGen}(1^n, 1^N)$
$\underline{\mathbf{A}} \leftarrow\!\!\$\ \mathbb{Z}_q^{\ell\times n}$
$pk := \mathbf{A} = \binom{\overline{\mathbf{A}}}{\underline{\mathbf{A}}} \in \mathbb{Z}_q^{(N+\ell)\times n}$
$sk := \mathbf{T}$
Return (pk, sk)

$\underline{\mathsf{rk}_{i\to j}^{f_{\mathbf{M}}} \leftarrow\!\!\$\ \mathsf{FReKGen}(pk^{(i)} = \mathbf{A}^{(i)}, sk^{(i)} = \mathbf{T}^{(i)}, pk^{(j)} = \mathbf{A}^{(j)}, f_{\mathbf{M}} \in \mathcal{F}_{\text{lin}}):}$
$\mathbf{S} \leftarrow\!\!\$\ \chi^{n\times n}, \mathbf{E} \leftarrow\!\!\$\ \chi^{(N+\ell)\times n}$
Parse $\mathbf{A}^{(i)} = \binom{\overline{\mathbf{A}}^{(i)}}{\underline{\mathbf{A}}^{(i)}}$
$\mathbf{R} \in \mathbb{Z}^{(N+\ell)\times N} \leftarrow\!\!\$\ \mathsf{SamplePre}\left(\mathbf{T}^{(i)}, \overline{\mathbf{A}}^{(i)}, \mathbf{A}^{(j)}\mathbf{S} + \mathbf{E} - \binom{\mathbf{0}}{\mathbf{M}}\underline{\mathbf{A}}^{(i)}, \gamma\right)$
$\mathsf{rk}_{i\to j}^{f_{\mathbf{M}}} := \left(\mathbf{R} \,\middle|\, \begin{matrix}\mathbf{0}\\ \mathbf{M}\end{matrix}\right) \in \mathbb{Z}_p^{(N+\ell)\times(N+\ell)}$ //$\mathbf{M}$ is the description of $f_{\mathbf{M}}$
Return $\mathsf{rk}_{i\to j}^{f_{\mathbf{M}}}$

$\underline{ct_v \leftarrow\!\!\$\ \mathsf{Enc}(pk = \mathbf{A}, \mathbf{m} \in \mathcal{M}, v \in [0, L]):}$
$\mathbf{s} \leftarrow\!\!\$\ \chi_v^n, \mathbf{e} \leftarrow\!\!\$\ \chi_v^{N+\ell}$
$ct_v := \mathbf{A}\mathbf{s} + \mathbf{e} + \binom{\mathbf{0}}{p\mathbf{m}} \in \mathbb{Z}_q^{N+\ell}$

$\underline{ct_{v+1}^{(j)} \leftarrow\!\!\$\ \mathsf{FReEnc}(\mathsf{rk}_{i\to j}^{f_{\mathbf{M}}} \in \mathbb{Z}_p^{(N+\ell)\times(N+\ell)},}$
$\underline{pk^{(j)} = \mathbf{A}^{(j)}, ct_v^{(i)} \in \mathbb{Z}_q^{N+\ell}, v \in [0, L-1]):}$
$\hat{ct}_{v+1}^{(j)} := \mathsf{rk}_{i\to j}^{f_{\mathbf{M}}} \cdot ct_v^{(i)} \in \mathbb{Z}_q^{N+\ell}$
$\mathbf{s} \leftarrow\!\!\$\ \chi_{v+1}^n, \mathbf{e} \leftarrow\!\!\$\ \chi_{v+1}^{N+\ell}$
$ct_{v+1}^{(j)} := \hat{ct}_v^{(j)} + \mathbf{A}^{(j)}\mathbf{s} + \mathbf{e} \in \mathbb{Z}_q^{N+\ell}$
Return $ct_{v+1}^{(j)}$

$\underline{\mathbf{m} \leftarrow \mathsf{Dec}(sk = \mathbf{T}, ct \in \mathbb{Z}_q^{N+\ell}):}$
Parse $ct = \binom{\overline{ct} \in \mathbb{Z}_q^N}{\underline{ct} \in \mathbb{Z}_q^\ell}$
$(\mathbf{s}, \overline{\mathbf{e}}) \leftarrow\!\!\$\ \mathsf{Invert}(\mathbf{T}, \overline{ct})$
$\tilde{\mathbf{m}} = (\tilde{m}_1, \ldots, \tilde{m}_\ell) := \underline{ct} - \underline{\mathbf{A}}\mathbf{s}$
For $i \in [\ell]$: $m_i := \lceil \tilde{m}_i / p \rfloor$
Return $\mathbf{m} = (m_1, m_2, \ldots, m_\ell)$

Fig. 10. The LWE-based Multi-Hop FPRE scheme mFPRE_2 for $\mathcal{F}_{\text{lin}}$. For ease of reading, we emphasize different parts with the CPA secure scheme mFPRE_1 in gray boxes.

Next, we show the IND security, wKP security and SH security of mFPRE_2 via the following three theorems. Then together with Theorem 2 (IND + wKP + SH $\Rightarrow$ HRA) in Subsect. 3.2, it yields the HRA security of our scheme mFPRE_2.

Theorem 5 (IND **Security of** mFPRE_2)**.** *Assume that the* $\mathsf{LWE}_{n,q,\chi_i,N+\ell}$*-assumption holds for all* $i \in [0, L]$*, then the scheme* mFPRE_2 *proposed in Fig. 10 has* IND *security. More precisely, for any PPT adversary* $\mathcal{A}$ *that make at most* Q_{chal} *queries to* $\mathcal{O}_{\text{CHAL}}$*, there exist PPT algorithms* $\mathcal{B}_0, \ldots, \mathcal{B}_L$ *against the LWE assumptions such that* $\mathsf{Adv}_{\mathsf{mFPRE}_2,\mathcal{A}}^{\mathsf{IND}}(\lambda) \le Q_{chal} \cdot \sum_{i=0}^{L} \mathsf{Adv}_{[n,q,\chi_i,N+\ell],\mathcal{B}_i}^{\mathsf{LWE}}(\lambda)$.

We refer to the full version [20] for the proof of Theorem 5.

Theorem 6 (wKP **Security of** mFPRE_2)**.** *Assume that the* $\mathsf{LWE}_{n,q,\chi,N+\ell}$*-assumption holds, then the scheme* mFPRE_2 *proposed in Fig. 10 has* wKP *security. More precisely, for any PPT adversary* $\mathcal{A}$ *that makes at most* Q_{rk} *queries to* $\mathcal{O}_{\text{REKEY}}$ *and for any polynomial* $\mathfrak{n}$*, there exists a PPT algorithm* $\mathcal{B}$ *against the LWE assumption s.t.* $\mathsf{Adv}_{\mathsf{mFPRE}_2,\mathcal{A},\mathfrak{n}}^{\mathsf{wKP}}(\lambda) \le \mathfrak{n} \cdot nQ_{rk} \cdot \mathsf{Adv}_{[n,q,\chi,N+\ell],\mathcal{B}}^{\mathsf{LWE}}(\lambda) + \mathsf{negl}(\lambda)$.

Note that the KGen and FReKGen algorithms of scheme mFPRE_2 are the same as those of mFPRE_1 in Subsect. 4.1, so does the wKP security. Consequently, the proof of Theorem 6 is identical to that for Theorem 4 and we omit it.

Theorem 7 (SH **Security of** mFPRE_2)**.** *The scheme* mFPRE_2 *proposed in Fig. 10 has* SH *security. More precisely, for any (unbounded) adversary* $\mathcal{A}$*, we have* $\mathsf{Adv}_{\mathsf{mFPRE}_2,\mathcal{A}}^{\mathsf{SH}}(\lambda) \le \mathsf{negl}(\lambda)$.

We refer to the full version [20] for the proof of Theorem 7.

By plugging Theorem 5 (IND security), Theorem 6 (wKP security) and Theorem 7 (SH security) into Theorem 2 (IND + wKP + SH $\Rightarrow$ HRA) in

Subsect. 3.2, we have the following corollary showing the HRA security of our scheme mFPRE_2 based on the LWE assumption.

Corollary 2 (HRA **Security of** mFPRE_2). *Assume that the* $\mathsf{LWE}_{n,q,\chi,N+\ell}$*-assumption and the* $\mathsf{LWE}_{n,q,\chi_i,N+\ell}$*-assumption hold for all* $i \in [0, L]$*, then the scheme* mFPRE_2 *proposed in Fig. 10 is* HRA *secure. More precisely, for any PPT adversary* $\mathcal{A}$ *that makes at most* Q_{rk} *queries to* $\mathcal{O}_{\text{ReKey}}$ *and forms a challenge graph* G *(i.e., subgraph reachable from the vertex of challenge user) in* $\mathcal{G}(\mathfrak{n}, \delta, d)$*, for any polynomial* $\mathfrak{n}$*, there exists PPT algorithms* $\mathcal{B}_0, \ldots, \mathcal{B}_L$ *and* $\mathcal{B}$ *against the LWE assumption s.t.*

$$\mathsf{Adv}^{\mathsf{HRA}}_{\mathsf{mFPRE}_2,\mathcal{A},\mathfrak{n}} \leq \left(2\sum_{i=0}^{L} \mathsf{Adv}^{\mathsf{LWE}}_{[n,q,\chi_i,N+\ell],\mathcal{B}_i}(\lambda) + 2\tau \cdot n\mathfrak{n}Q_{rk} \cdot \mathsf{Adv}^{\mathsf{LWE}}_{[n,q,\chi,N+\ell],\mathcal{B}}(\lambda)\right) \cdot \mathfrak{n}^{\sigma+\delta+1} + \mathsf{negl}(\lambda),$$

where δ *denotes the outdegree,* d *the depth,* τ *the pebbling time complexity and* σ *space complexity for the class* $\mathcal{G}(\mathfrak{n}, \delta, d)$*, respectively.*

Acknowledgments. We would like to thank the reviewers for their valuable comments and helpful suggestions. Yunxiao Zhou, Shengli Liu and Shuai Han were partially supported by the National Key R&D Program of China under Grant 2022YFB2701500, National Natural Science Foundation of China (Grant Nos. 61925207, 62372292), Guangdong Major Project of Basic and Applied Basic Research (2019B030302008), and Young Elite Scientists Sponsorship Program by China Association for Science and Technology (YESS20200185).

References

1. Ajtai, M.: Generating hard instances of lattice problems (extended abstract). In: 28th ACM STOC, pp. 99–108. ACM Press, May 1996
2. Ateniese, G., Benson, K., Hohenberger, S.: Key-private proxy re-encryption. In: Fischlin, M. (ed.) CT-RSA 2009. LNCS, vol. 5473, pp. 279–294. Springer, Heidelberg (2009). https://doi.org/10.1007/978-3-642-00862-7_19
3. Ateniese, G., Fu, K., Green, M., Hohenberger, S.: Improved proxy re-encryption schemes with applications to secure distributed storage. In: NDSS 2005. The Internet Society, February 2005
4. Blaze, M., Bleumer, G., Strauss, M.: Divertible protocols and atomic proxy cryptography. In: Nyberg, K. (ed.) EUROCRYPT 1998. LNCS, vol. 1403, pp. 127–144. Springer, Heidelberg (1998). https://doi.org/10.1007/BFb0054122
5. Chandran, N., Chase, M., Liu, F.-H., Nishimaki, R., Xagawa, K.: Re-encryption, functional re-encryption, and multi-hop re-encryption: a framework for achieving obfuscation-based security and instantiations from lattices. In: Krawczyk, H. (ed.) PKC 2014. LNCS, vol. 8383, pp. 95–112. Springer, Heidelberg (2014). https://doi.org/10.1007/978-3-642-54631-0_6
6. Cohen, A.: What about Bob? The inadequacy of CPA security for proxy reencryption. In: Lin, D., Sako, K. (eds.) PKC 2019. LNCS, vol. 11443, pp. 287–316. Springer, Cham (2019). https://doi.org/10.1007/978-3-030-17259-6_10
7. Davidson, A., Deo, A., Lee, E., Martin, K.: Strong post-compromise secure proxy re-encryption. In: Jang-Jaccard, J., Guo, F. (eds.) ACISP 2019. LNCS, vol. 11547, pp. 58–77. Springer, Cham (2019). https://doi.org/10.1007/978-3-030-21548-4_4

8. Fan, X., Liu, F.-H.: Proxy re-encryption and re-signatures from lattices. In: Deng, R.H., Gauthier-Umaña, V., Ochoa, M., Yung, M. (eds.) ACNS 2019. LNCS, vol. 11464, pp. 363–382. Springer, Cham (2019). https://doi.org/10.1007/978-3-030-21568-2_18
9. Fuchsbauer, G., Kamath, C., Klein, K., Pietrzak, K.: Adaptively secure proxy re-encryption. In: Lin, D., Sako, K. (eds.) PKC 2019. LNCS, vol. 11443, pp. 317–346. Springer, Cham (2019). https://doi.org/10.1007/978-3-030-17259-6_11
10. Gentry, C.: Fully homomorphic encryption using ideal lattices. In: Mitzenmacher, M. (ed.) 41st ACM STOC, pp. 169–178. ACM Press, May/June 2009
11. Gentry, C., Peikert, C., Vaikuntanathan, V.: Trapdoors for hard lattices and new cryptographic constructions. In: Ladner, R.E., Dwork, C. (eds.) 40th ACM STOC, pp. 197–206. ACM Press, May 2008
12. Jafargholi, Z., Kamath, C., Klein, K., Komargodski, I., Pietrzak, K., Wichs, D.: Be adaptive, avoid overcommitting. In: Katz, J., Shacham, H. (eds.) CRYPTO 2017. LNCS, vol. 10401, pp. 133–163. Springer, Cham (2017). https://doi.org/10.1007/978-3-319-63688-7_5
13. Lai, J., Huang, Z., Au, M.H., Mao, X.: Constant-size CCA-secure multi-hop unidirectional proxy re-encryption from indistinguishability obfuscation. In: Susilo, W., Yang, G. (eds.) ACISP 2018. LNCS, vol. 10946, pp. 805–812. Springer, Cham (2018). https://doi.org/10.1007/978-3-319-93638-3_49
14. Lai, J., Huang, Z., Au, M.H., Mao, X.: Constant-size CCA-secure multi-hop unidirectional proxy re-encryption from indistinguishability obfuscation. Theor. Comput. Sci. **847**, 1–16 (2020). https://www.sciencedirect.com/science/article/pii/S0304397520305302
15. Miao, P., Patranabis, S., Watson, G.J.: Unidirectional updatable encryption and proxy re-encryption from DDH. In: Boldyreva, A., Kolesnikov, V. (eds.) PKC 2023, Part II. LNCS, vol. 13941, pp. 368–398. Springer, Cham (2023). https://doi.org/10.1007/978-3-031-31371-4_13
16. Micciancio, D., Peikert, C.: Trapdoors for lattices: simpler, tighter, faster, smaller. In: Pointcheval, D., Johansson, T. (eds.) EUROCRYPT 2012. LNCS, vol. 7237, pp. 700–718. Springer, Heidelberg (2012). https://doi.org/10.1007/978-3-642-29011-4_41
17. Phong, L.T., Wang, L., Aono, Y., Nguyen, M.H., Boyen, X.: Proxy re-encryption schemes with key privacy from LWE. Cryptology ePrint Archive, Report 2016/327 (2016). https://eprint.iacr.org/2016/327
18. Regev, O.: On lattices, learning with errors, random linear codes, and cryptography. In: Gabow, H.N., Fagin, R. (eds.) 37th ACM STOC, pp. 84–93. ACM Press, May 2005
19. Smith, T.: DVD Jon: Buy DRM-less tracks from apple iTunes (2005). https://www.theregister.com/2005/03/18/itunes_pymusique/
20. Zhou, Y., Liu, S., Han, S.: Multi-hop fine-grained proxy re-encryption. Cryptology ePrint Archive, 2024/055 (2024). https://eprint.iacr.org/2024/055
21. Zhou, Y., Liu, S., Han, S., Zhang, H.: Fine-grained proxy re-encryption: definitions & constructions from LWE. In: Guo, J., Steinfeld, R. (eds.) ASIACRYPT 2023, Part VI. LNCS, vol. 14443, pp. 199–231. Springer, Cham (2023). https://doi.org/10.1007/978-981-99-8736-8_7

Quantum CCA-Secure PKE, Revisited

Navid Alamati[1] and Varun Maram[2(✉)]

[1] VISA Research, Foster City, USA
nalamati@visa.com
[2] SandboxAQ, London, United Kingdom
varun.maram@sandboxaq.com

Abstract. Security against chosen-ciphertext attacks (CCA) concerns privacy of messages *even* if the adversary has access to the decryption oracle. While the classical notion of CCA security seems to be strong enough to capture many attack scenarios, it falls short of preserving the privacy of messages in the presence of *quantum* decryption queries, i.e., when an adversary can query a superposition of ciphertexts.

Boneh and Zhandry (CRYPTO 2013) defined the notion of quantum CCA (qCCA) security to guarantee privacy of messages in the presence of *quantum* decryption queries. However, their construction is based on an exotic cryptographic primitive (namely, identity-based encryption with security against *quantum* queries), for which only one instantiation is known. In this work, we comprehensively study qCCA security for public-key encryption (PKE) based on both generic cryptographic primitives and concrete mathematical assumptions, yielding the following results:

- We show that key-dependent message secure encryption (along with PKE) is sufficient to realize qCCA-secure PKE. This yields the first construction of qCCA-secure PKE from the LPN assumption.
- We prove that hash proof systems imply qCCA-secure PKE, which results in the first instantiation of PKE with qCCA security from (isogeny-based) group actions.
- We extend the notion of adaptive TDFs (ATDFs) to the quantum setting by introducing *quantum* ATDFs, and we prove that quantum ATDFs are sufficient to realize qCCA-secure PKE. We also show how to instantiate quantum ATDFs from the LWE assumption.
- We show that a single-bit qCCA-secure PKE is sufficient to realize a multi-bit qCCA-secure PKE by extending the completeness of bit encryption for CCA security to the quantum setting.

Keywords: Quantum CCA security · Key-Dependent Message security · hash proof systems, quantum adaptive TDFs · One-Way To Hiding lemma

---

V. Maram—Work done while the author was at ETH Zürich and an intern at VISA Research.

Q. Tang and V. Teague (Eds.): PKC 2024, LNCS 14604, pp. 193–226, 2024.
https://doi.org/10.1007/978-3-031-57728-4_7

1 Introduction

Security against chosen-ciphertext attacks (CCA) concerns privacy of messages against adversaries whose power is beyond eavesdropping. In a CCA-secure public-key encryption (PKE) scheme, encryptions of two adverserially chosen messages are computationally indistinguishable *even* if the adversary has access to the decryption oracle [NY90,DDN91,RS92]. CCA security is considered to be the *de facto* notion of security for PKE [Sho98], and there has been a long line of works studying CCA security from various cryptographic assumptions (e.g., [CS02,PW08,RS09,KMP14,KW19,KMT19, HLLG19,HKW20,ADMP20]).

Quantum CCA Security. While the classical notion of CCA security seems to be strong enough to capture many attack scenarios, it falls short of preserving the privacy of messages in the presence of *quantum* decryption queries, i.e., when an adversary can query a superposition of ciphertexts and receive a superposition of their decryptions. To capture such attack scenarios, Boneh and Zhandry [BZ13b] defined the notion of quantum CCA (IND-qCCA, or qCCA for short) security, and as they pointed out, issuing quantum decryption queries (and the notion of qCCA in general) capture the security of a natural model of ubiquitous quantum computing environment where users encrypt messages on a quantum computer.

Comparing qCCA to (classical) CCA security, Boneh and Zhandry showed that there exist PKE schemes that satisfy (post-quantum) CCA security but those schemes can be immediately broken under qCCA attacks, concluding that qCCA security is stronger than CCA security. In terms of instantiations, they demonstrated a construction of qCCA-secure PKE from an identity-based encryption (IBE) scheme with selective security against *quantum* (secret key) queries (by relying on the generic transformation of [BCHK07]). They showed how to realize qCCA security from the learning with errors (LWE) assumption by observing that the LWE-based IBE scheme of [ABB10] can be shown to satisfy selective security against quantum queries.

However, despite considerable progress in the area of quantum cryptography in recent years (e.g., [FKS+13,BJSW16,RZ21,KNY21,BCKM21,MY22b, AQY22]), to the best of our knowledge, the aforementioned blueprint of Boneh and Zhandry remains the *only* way of realizing qCCA-secure PKE from either generic or concrete assumptions in the *standard* model after nearly a decade; it is worth pointing out that a line of recent works, namely [XY19,LW21,SGX23], do provide generic constructions of qCCA-secure PKE albeit in the *idealized* quantum random oracle model (QROM).

This is in contrast with the (classical) CCA-secure PKE for which we have a variety of constructions from concrete (post-quantum) assumptions such as learning parity with noise (LPN) or variants of isogeny-based group actions (e.g., variants of CSIDH [CLM+18]). Thus we ask the following natural question:

Can we construct qCCA-secure PKE from a wider class of concrete assumptions such as LPN or isogeny-based group actions?

Furthermore, in the past two decades, there has been remarkable progress on building CCA-secure PKE (in a black-box manner) from generic assumptions starting from hash proof systems [CS02] and lossy/correlated-secure/adaptive trapdoor functions (TDFs) [PW08, RS09, KMO10] to more recent ones based on circular security and injective trapdoor functions [KW19, KMT19, HKW20]. On the other hand, the only generic cryptographic primitive which is known to imply qCCA-secure PKE is IBE with security against *quantum* queries. Therefore, even in terms of generic cryptographic assumptions, qCCA security is much less understood compared to its classical counterpart. This is despite the fact that for many other cryptographic primitives (e.g., symmetric-key primitives, digital signatures, passively secure PKE, etc.), the gap between classical and quantum security is little to none [Zha12, BZ13a, BZ13b]. In particular, in case of symmetric-key encryption (SKE), qCCA security has already been shown to be implied by (post-quantum) CCA-secure SKE (or by the minimal assumption of post-quantum one-way functions) [BZ13b]. This leads to the following question:

Can we build qCCA-secure PKE from the same set of cryptographic primitives (or a subset thereof) that imply CCA-secure PKE?

On a related note, it has long been known that bit encryption is complete for CCA security [Ms09]. Specifically, given a *single-bit* CCA-secure PKE one can construct a *multi-bit* PKE with CCA security. However, such an implication is not known for quantum CCA security. So we ask the following pertinent question:

Is bit encryption complete for quantum CCA-secure PKE?

Quantum Security for Adaptive TDFs. In 2010, Kiltz *et al.* [KMO10] introduced the notion of *adaptive* trapdoor functions, which can be viewed as a "deterministic" form of CCA-secure PKE. Informally, a trapdoor function is said to be adaptive if it remains one way even if the adversary is given access to an inversion oracle. The authors of [KMO10] demonstrated a construction of CCA-secure PKE from adaptive TDFs. They also showed how adaptive TDFs can be constructed from lossy or correlated-secure TDFs. This motivates us to ask the following question:

Does there exist a quantum analog of adaptive TDFs that imply qCCA-secure PKE?

1.1 Our Contributions

We answer the questions described above in the affirmative by presenting the following results, narrowing the gap between CCA and qCCA security for PKE. In particular, our results for qCCA essentially match what is known for CCA security in terms of generic cryptographic primitives, while also yielding new instantiations of qCCA security from a variety of mathematical assumptions. We refer to the full version of our paper for a diagram that provides a simplified overview of our results.

Quantum CCA Security from Hash Proof Systems. We prove that the CCA-secure PKE construction of Cramer and Shoup [CS02] from hash proof systems also satisfies *quantum* CCA security if the underlying hash proof system satisfies post-quantum security. Coupled with the hash proof system construction of [ADMP20] from variants of CSIDH, our result yields the first construction of qCCA-secure PKE from isogeny-based group actions.

Quantum CCA Security from KDM-Secure SKE and PKE. We show that the CCA-secure PKE construction of Kitagawa *et al.* [KMT19] from PKE and a key-dependent message secure[1] SKE also satisfies *quantum* CCA security if the underlying primitives satisfy post-quantum security. By plugging in the KDM-secure SKE construction of [ACPS09] from LPN, our result yields the first construction of qCCA-secure PKE from the LPN assumption. Along the way, we also prove that the KEM-DEM[2] "hybrid" encryption of [CS03] results in a qCCA-secure PKE if (1) the underlying KEM is qCCA-secure and, (2) the underlying DEM offers (post-quantum) one-time authenticated encryption security with respect to *classical* queries only.

Completeness of Bit Encryption for qCCA Security. We demonstrate the quantum analogue of completeness of bit encryption for CCA security by showing that single-bit qCCA-secure PKE is sufficient to realize multi-bit PKE with qCCA security. Our result extends the framework of [HLW12] to the quantum setting without any additional assumption.

Quantum Adaptive TDFs. We extend the notion of adaptive TDFs (ATDFs) to the quantum setting by introducing the notion of *quantum* ATDFs. We also extend the result of Kiltz *et al.* [KMO10] to the quantum setting by showing that quantum ATDFs are sufficient to realize qCCA-secure PKE. In addition, in terms of constructions, we describe how to build quantum adaptive TDFs from (post-quantum) correlated-product TDFs, which in turn yields an instantiation from the LWE assumption [PW08, RS09, MP13].

Remark 1. We emphasize that all the above constructions are *classical PKE schemes* in the sense that they can be implemented on classical computers; this is in contrast to so-called *quantum PKE schemes* constructed in recent works such as [MY22a, Col23, GSV23, BMW23] which inherently require quantum machinery, e.g., requiring public keys to be quantum states. We essentially share the same goal as [BZ13b] – namely, to construct classical cryptosystems which remain secure when eventually implemented on quantum computers wherein adversaries potentially get quantum decryption access to such devices.

---

[1] Informally, key-dependent message (KDM) secure encryption guarantees the privacy of a message even if it is some function of the secret key.

[2] Key Encapsulation Mechanism and Data Encapsulation Mechanism, respectively.

Remark 2. Quantum CCA security restricts the adversary to *classical* challenge messages (but still allowing *quantum* decryption queries; see Definition 1 in Sect. 2). Recently, Chevalier *et al.* [CEV22] introduced a new quantum security notion that captures indistinguishability under quantum chosen-ciphertext attacks (i.e., qIND-qCCA security), where the indistinguishability of ciphertexts holds even for quantum superpositions of messages. They also show that qIND-qCCA secure PKE can be realized from any qCCA-secure PKE. Hence, by plugging in their lifting theorem in our above results, we get new constructions of qIND-qCCA secure PKE from a variety of generic cryptographic primitives as well as concrete post-quantum assumptions.

1.2 Technical Overview

We now provide a simplified technical overview of our results. For the ease of exposition, we focus on a particular construction as a warm-up example. We begin by recalling the construction of CCA-secure PKE from *correlated-product* trapdoor functions (CP-TDFs) in [RS09], and next we prove its *quantum* CCA security (while relying on the post-quantum security of the underlying CP-TDF). Looking ahead, even though we show in Sect. 5 that CP-TDFs imply the stronger notion of quantum adaptive TDFs (which in turn are sufficient to realize qCCA security), for this overview we aim to highlight the main aspects of extending the classical CCA security proofs of [RS09] to the quantum setting. It is worth pointing out that the following analysis can be extended in a straightforward fashion to prove qCCA security of the LWE-based PKE construction in [BZ13b] that relies on *quantum* selective-secure IBE.

Informally speaking, a CP-TDF is a family of trapdoor functions $\{f_{\mathsf{ek}}\}_{\mathsf{ek}\in\mathcal{K}}$ such that the following family $\{f_{\mathsf{ek}_1,\ldots,\mathsf{ek}_t}\}_{(\mathsf{ek}_1,\ldots,\mathsf{ek}_t)\in\mathcal{K}^t}$ defined by

$$f_{\mathsf{ek}_1,\ldots,\mathsf{ek}_t}(x) = (f_{\mathsf{ek}_1}(x), \ldots, f_{\mathsf{ek}_t}(x))$$

is also one-way, i.e., one-wayness is guaranteed even if one uses the same input (but independently chosen evaluation keys). The PKE construction of [RS09] from CP-TDFs proceeds as follows. The public key consists of t pairs of (random) functions $(f_{\mathsf{ek}_1^0}, f_{\mathsf{ek}_1^1}), \ldots, (f_{\mathsf{ek}_t^0}, f_{\mathsf{ek}_t^1})$, where each ek_i^b is sampled from $\mathcal{K}$, and the secret key consists of the trapdoors $(\mathsf{td}_1^0, \mathsf{td}_1^1), \ldots, (\mathsf{td}_t^0, \mathsf{td}_t^1)$, where each td_i^b is a trapdoor corresponding to $f_{\mathsf{ek}_i^b}$. To encrypt a bit m,[3] first generate $(\mathsf{vk}, \mathsf{sk})$ for a one-time signature $(\mathsf{Sign}, \mathsf{Ver})$ such that $\mathsf{vk} = (\mathsf{vk}_1, \ldots, \mathsf{vk}_t) \in \{0,1\}^t$, then choose a random input x and compute the following:

$$\forall i \in [t] : y_i = f_{\mathsf{ek}_i^{\mathsf{vk}_i}}(x), \quad \mathsf{ct}_1 = \mathsf{m} \oplus h(x), \quad \mathsf{ct}_2 \leftarrow \mathsf{Sign}(\mathsf{sk}, (y_1, \ldots, y_t, \mathsf{ct}_1)),$$

where h is a hard-core predicate of $f_{\mathsf{ek}_1,\ldots,\mathsf{ek}_t}$, and output $(\mathsf{vk}, y_1, \ldots, y_t, \mathsf{ct}_1, \mathsf{ct}_2)$. To decrypt such a ciphertext, check $\mathsf{Ver}(\mathsf{vk}, ((y_1, \ldots, y_t, \mathsf{ct}_1)), \mathsf{ct}_2) = 0$. If so, return $\perp$. Otherwise, for every $i \in [t]$, invert y_i using $\mathsf{td}_i^{\mathsf{vk}_i}$ to obtain x_i. If $x_1 = x_2 = \cdots = x_k$, output $h(x_1) \oplus \mathsf{ct}_1$; otherwise, output $\perp$.

[3] [RS09] later showed how to extend their construction to encrypt multi-bit messages.

To sketch the CCA security proof of the above PKE construction in [RS09], consider the following distinguisher $\mathcal{D}$ where $\mathcal{D}$ gets t functions $f_{\mathsf{ek}_1}, \ldots, f_{\mathsf{ek}_t}$ along with t values $y_1^* = f_{\mathsf{ek}_1}(x^*), \ldots, y_t^* = f_{\mathsf{ek}_t}(x^*)$ for a uniformly random x^*, and a challenge bit b which is either $h(x^*)$ or a random bit. $\mathcal{D}$ can simulate the CCA security game for $\mathcal{A}$ by first generating $(\mathsf{vk}^*, \mathsf{sk}^*)$ for one-time signature, and computing the public key $(f_{\mathsf{ek}_1^0}, f_{\mathsf{ek}_1^1}), \ldots, (f_{\mathsf{ek}_t^0}, f_{\mathsf{ek}_t^1})$ to be sent to $\mathcal{A}$ as follows: first, $\mathcal{D}$ sets

$$\forall i \in [t] : f_{\mathsf{ek}_i^{\mathsf{vk}_i^*}} := f_{\mathsf{ek}_i},$$

and then for the remaining part of the public key, $\mathcal{D}$ samples $\mathsf{ek}_i^{1-\mathsf{vk}_i^*}$ along with the corresponding $\mathsf{td}_i^{1-\mathsf{vk}_i^*}$. Now observe that $\mathcal{D}$ can answer any of $\mathcal{A}$'s decryption queries by using the trapdoor $\mathsf{td}_i^{1-\mathsf{vk}_i^*}$ for some index i such that $\mathsf{vk}_i \neq \mathsf{vk}_i^*$. The challenge ciphertext is later computed as $\mathsf{ct}^* = (\mathsf{vk}^*, y_1^*, \ldots, y_t^*, \mathsf{ct}_1^*, \mathsf{ct}_2^*)$ where $\mathsf{ct}_1^* = \mathsf{m} \oplus b$ for a random message $\mathsf{m} \in \{0,1\}$ and $\mathsf{ct}_2^* \leftarrow \mathsf{Sign}(\mathsf{sk}^*, (y_1^*, \ldots, y_t^*, \mathsf{ct}_1^*))$. As before, $\mathcal{D}$ can respond to the rest of $\mathcal{A}$'s decryption queries while responding $\perp$ when the query is equal to ct^*. If $\mathcal{A}$ later guesses the message m correctly, $\mathcal{D}$ outputs that $b = h(x^*)$; otherwise, $\mathcal{D}$ outputs that b is a random bit.

Observe that $\mathcal{D}$ perfectly simulates the decryption algorithm above *only* when $\mathsf{vk} \neq \mathsf{vk}^*$ since otherwise $\mathcal{D}$ does not have access to the corresponding trapdoor for decryption. However, as argued in [RS09], the probability that $\mathcal{A}$ makes a query $\overline{\mathsf{ct}} = (\mathsf{vk}^*, y_1, \ldots, y_t, \mathsf{ct}_1, \mathsf{ct}_2)$ with $\mathsf{Ver}(\mathsf{vk}^*, ((y_1, \ldots, y_t, \mathsf{ct}_1)), \mathsf{ct}_2) = 1$ is negligible thanks to the unforgeability of $(\mathsf{Sign}, \mathsf{Ver})$. So if $\mathcal{A}$ makes such a query $\overline{\mathsf{ct}}$, then a signature forger simulating the CCA security game towards $\mathcal{A}$ can use $\overline{\mathsf{ct}}$ to break the unforgeability of $(\mathsf{Sign}, \mathsf{Ver})$.

Coming to the qCCA setting however (see Definition 1 in Sect. 2 for a formal definition of qCCA security for PKE), where $\mathcal{A}$ can ask for the decryption of a quantum superposition of different ciphertexts, it is quite possible that ciphertexts $\overline{\mathsf{ct}}$ of the above form that induce a signature forgery are among the superposition. Therefore, if we want to repeat the *same* reduction above, it is not clear how a signature forger can "extract" $\overline{\mathsf{ct}}$-based forgeries from $\mathcal{A}$'s quantum queries. This brings us to the main tool we employ in our qCCA security proofs in this paper: the (generalized) One-Way To Hiding (OW2H) lemma [AHU19]. Informally, the lemma states that given two oracles $G, H : \mathcal{X} \to \mathcal{Y}$ whose outputs differ with respect to a set of inputs S, and an algorithm A that has *quantum* access to either G or H, the probability that A can distinguish between G and H is essentially bounded by the square root of the probability when measuring a random quantum oracle query made by A results in a classical state in S.

To resolve the issue above in the quantum setting, we use the OW2H lemma as follows. Let G be the original decryption oracle that $\mathcal{A}$ has quantum access to in the qCCA security game. We modify G to obtain a *new* quantum decryption oracle H which rejects (i.e., returns $\perp$) ciphertexts $\overline{\mathsf{ct}}$ of the above form; the difference set S described above precisely includes such ciphertexts $\overline{\mathsf{ct}}$. Now note that $\mathcal{D}$ can simulate the modified decryption oracle H towards $\mathcal{A}$ *even in the quantum setting* using the same CCA simulation strategy described above while simply rejecting ciphertexts $\overline{\mathsf{ct}}$ that contain vk^* as above.[4] In our qCCA security proof, we argue that $\mathcal{A}$'s winning probability in the original qCCA security game (where it has access to G) changes by at most a negligible amount when it has access to H instead. Here we invoke the OW2H lemma to show the quantum indistinguishability of oracles G and H by bounding the probability when measuring a random decryption query made by $\mathcal{A}$ to H results in a ciphertext $\overline{\mathsf{ct}} \in S$ that induces a signature forgery. This follows straightforwardly from the *classical* unforgeability of the one-time signature scheme. Namely, in the corresponding reduction, a signature forger simulates quantum access to H towards $\mathcal{A}$ and randomly measures one of $\mathcal{A}$'s decryption queries; if the measurement results in $\overline{\mathsf{ct}}$, then the forger succeeds. We remark that the reason we only require *classical* security from the signature is that, the forger queries a *classical* message to its one-time signing oracle (as opposed to querying messages in superposition, which is accounted for by the definition of *quantum* security of signatures in [BZ13b]) to obtain a signature $\mathsf{ct}_2^* \leftarrow \mathsf{Sign}(\mathsf{sk}^*, (y_1^*, \ldots, y_t^*, \mathsf{ct}_1^*))$, when computing the challenge ciphertext.

This is a common theme across most of our qCCA security proofs, i.e., we extend the classical CCA security proofs of PKE constructions considered in this paper to the quantum CCA setting by first identifying the modifications made to the decryption oracle in the classical CCA analysis and then arguing about the quantum indistinguishability between these oracles in our qCCA analysis by relying on the generalized OW2H lemma.[5] However, it is not always easy to bound the probability of "measuring a decryption query to S" when applying the OW2H lemma in our qCCA analysis, in contrast to our proof sketch above where we relied on the unforgeability of a one-time signature. For instance, as we will see later, we show that single-bit qCCA secure PKE implies multi-bit qCCA secure PKE by extending the framework of [HLW12] to the quantum setting, and bounding the measurement probability requires another *"nested"* application of the OW2H lemma, which introduces further subtleties in the proof.

On a related note, the original version of the OW2H lemma (introduced in [Unr14]) handled only *random* oracles G and H, and found widespread use in proving security of cryptosystems in the Quantum Random Oracle Model (QROM) [BDF+11]. Later, [AHU19] introduced a generalized version of the OW2H lemma which not only allowed G and H to have an arbitrary output distribution but also allowed the distinguisher's auxiliary input to be arbitrarily correlated with G, H, and the difference set S. This allows us to apply the generalized OW2H lemma in our qCCA security proofs with respect to quantum decryption oracles, which are *not* synonymous with random oracles. To the best of our knowledge, our results include the *first* application of the OW2H lemma in the context of proving quantum CCA security of PKE schemes in the

[4] Note that since $\mathcal{D}$ can *classically* implement the decryption function corresponding to H, it can also implement the function as a quantum-accessible oracle.

[5] Sometimes such changes are made *implicitly* to the decryption oracle, as was the case in the CCA security proof of [RS09] sketched above; but we have to make these modifications more explicit in our qCCA proofs in order to apply the OW2H lemma.

standard model. This is in contrast to relying on, arguably, more complicated techniques such as the *compressed oracle* framework introduced in [Zha19], which was used to analyze qCCA security of PKE schemes obtained from the *Fujisaki-Okamoto transformation* [FO13] (in QROM). In fact, the (q)CCA security proof in [Zha19] was later found to have some subtle gaps in it [DFMS22]. Furthermore, [Unr20] showed a framework for *formally* verifying post-quantum security proofs of cryptosystems that involve applications of the OW2H lemma; this can be seen as evidence of the relative simplicity of the OW2H proof technique.

Remark 3. We remark that we chose to present the toy example above (for qCCA security) for the sake of brevity and providing intuition, since otherwise explaining our main results (e.g., based on hash proof systems or KDM security) would require recalling a rather lengthy preliminary background. We refer to Sects. 3–5 for our detailed results.

Remark 4. We note that one might use other well-known techniques (for example, the Gentle Measurement Lemma; see [BBC+21, Theorem 1], an adaptation of [BBBV97, Theorem 3.3]) to show the indistinguishability of the quantum decryption oracles G and H in the above overview. We chose to use the OW2H lemma because of its relative simplicity and that it does not result in a significant loss in security proofs, as evidenced by the widespread usage of this technique in analyzing CCA security of some proposals (in the QROM) in the NIST standardization process for post-quantum cryptography. Hence, one of the technical contributions of this paper is finding a novel application for the OW2H lemma (a popular QROM proof technique) in the *standard* model, in order to establish the quantum CCA security of various standard model PKE constructions.

2 Preliminaries

Notations. For a positive integer n, we denote $[n]$ to be the set $\{1, 2, \ldots, n\}$. We denote $\lambda \in \mathbb{N}$ to be the security parameter, unless stated otherwise. For a finite set S, we write $x \leftarrow S$ to denote that x is uniformly at random sampled from S, unless stated otherwise. $x \parallel y$ denotes their concatenation. $|x|$ denotes bit-length of the encoding of x. For probabilistic algorithms we use $y \leftarrow \mathcal{A}(x)$ to denote a (randomized) output of $\mathcal{A}$ on input x; we also sometimes specify the randomness r used in $\mathcal{A}$ as $y \leftarrow \mathcal{A}(x; r)$. We omit writing λ when it is clear from context. The value of $(x \stackrel{?}{=} y)$ is defined to be 1 if $x = y$ and 0 otherwise.[6]

Quantum(-accessible) Oracles. We refer the reader to [NC00] for the basics of quantum computation and information. Here we recall a basic and useful fact about quantum computation.

> **Fact:** *Any classical computation can also be implemented on a quantum computer, and also any function that has an efficient classical algorithm can be implemented efficiently as a quantum-accessible oracle.*

[6] We cover some essential definitions in this section. We refer to the full version of our paper for the remaining preliminary background material.

Given an algorithm $\mathcal{A}$ and a (classical) function $O : \{0,1\}^m \to \{0,1\}^n$, we use $\mathcal{A}^{|O\rangle}$ to denote that $\mathcal{A}$ has *quantum* access to an oracle implementing O. To be more precise, $\mathcal{A}^{|O\rangle}$ can make standard superposition queries $\sum_{x,z} \psi_{x,z} |x, z\rangle$ to the quantum oracle $|O\rangle$ and gets as a response $\sum_{x,z} \psi_{x,z} |x, z \oplus O(x)\rangle$; here x and z are arbitrary m-bit and n-bit strings respectively. (We omit the "ket" notation in $\mathcal{A}^{|O\rangle}$, and instead just write $\mathcal{A}^O$ when it is clear from context.)

Lemma 1 (Generalized OW2H [AHU19, **Theorem 3**]**).** *Let $\mathcal{S} \subseteq \mathcal{X}$ be a random subset. Let $G, H : \mathcal{X} \to \mathcal{Y}$ be random oracles satisfying $G(x) = H(x)$ for every $x \notin \mathcal{S}$. Let z be a random bit string. ($\mathcal{S}, G, H, z$ may have arbitrary joint distribution.) Let A be a quantum oracle algorithm making at most q quantum queries to its corresponding oracle (either G or H). Let B^H be an oracle algorithm that on input z does the following: picks $i \leftarrow \{1, \ldots, q\}$, runs $A^H(z)$ until (just before) the i-th query, measures all query input registers in the computational basis, and outputs the set $\mathcal{T} = \{t_1, \ldots, t_{|\mathcal{T}|}\}$ of measurement outcomes (if A makes less than i queries, the measurement outcomes are taken to be $\perp \notin \mathcal{X}$). Let,*

$$
\begin{aligned}
P_{\text{left}} &= \Pr[1 \leftarrow A^H(z)] \\
P_{\text{right}} &= \Pr[1 \leftarrow A^G(z)] \\
P_{\text{guess}} &= \Pr[\mathcal{S} \cap \mathcal{T} \neq \emptyset : \mathcal{T} \leftarrow B^H(z)]
\end{aligned}
$$

Then, $|P_{\text{left}} - P_{\text{right}}| \leq 2q\sqrt{P_{\text{guess}}}$. The same result also holds with B^G instead of B^H in the definition of P_{guess}.

qCCA-Secure PKE. We define the formal syntax of a PKE scheme in the full version of our paper. Now let $\varepsilon : \mathbb{N} \mapsto [0,1]$ be a function. We say that $\mathsf{PKE} = (\mathsf{Gen}, \mathsf{Enc}, \mathsf{Dec})$ is ε-almost-all-keys correct if we have

$$\Pr_{(\mathsf{pk},\mathsf{sk})\leftarrow\mathsf{Gen}(1^\lambda)}[\exists(\mathsf{m},\mathsf{r}) \text{ s.t. } \mathsf{Dec}(\mathsf{sk}, \mathsf{Enc}(\mathsf{pk}, \mathsf{m}; \mathsf{r}) \neq \mathsf{m})] \leq \varepsilon(\lambda).$$

(We also call key-pairs $(\mathsf{pk}, \mathsf{sk})$ under which the above decryption error occurs as "erroneous".)

Definition 1. *A PKE scheme* $\mathsf{PKE} = (\mathsf{Gen}, \mathsf{Enc}, \mathsf{Dec})$ *is said to be* qCCA *secure if for every QPT adversary $\mathcal{A}$, the following quantity $\mathbf{Adv}^{\text{qCCA}}_{\mathsf{PKE},\mathcal{A}}$ is negligible:*

$$\mathbf{Adv}^{\text{qCCA}}_{\mathsf{PKE},\mathcal{A}} = \left| \Pr\left[b = b' : \begin{array}{c} (pk, sk) \leftarrow \mathsf{Gen}(1^\lambda); b \leftarrow \{0,1\} \\ (m_0, m_1, st) \leftarrow \mathcal{A}^{|O_\perp(sk,\cdot)\rangle}(pk) \\ ct^* \leftarrow \mathsf{Enc}(pk, m_b); b' \leftarrow \mathcal{A}^{|O_{ct^*}(sk,\cdot)\rangle}(ct^*, st) \end{array} \right] - \frac{1}{2} \right|$$

where the function $O_{\tilde{ct}}(sk, \cdot)$ (with $\tilde{ct} \in \{ct^*, \perp\}$) is defined as

$$O_{\tilde{ct}}(sk, ct) = \begin{cases} \perp & \text{if } ct = \tilde{ct} \\ \mathsf{Dec}(sk, ct) & \text{otherwise.} \end{cases}$$

In the above definition, we require the messages m_0 *and* m_1 *to be of the same length; also* st *is some arbitrary state information.* $\mathcal{A}$ *has access to* $|O_\perp(\mathsf{sk},\cdot)\rangle$ *(resp.* $|O_{\mathsf{ct}^*}(\mathsf{sk},\cdot)\rangle$*) in the* pre-challenge phase *(resp.* post-challenge phase*);* ct^* *is computed in the* challenge phase. *(As in the qCCA security definition for encryption in [BZ13b], we also encode* $\perp$ *to be a bit-string outside the message space* $\mathcal{M}$ *in order to properly define the result "*$z \oplus \perp$*" in the output register of* $|O_{\tilde{\mathsf{ct}}}(\mathsf{sk},\cdot)\rangle$ *described above.)*

The notion of CCA security for PKE schemes differs from Definition 1 in the fact that the adversary $\mathcal{A}$ has *classical* access to $O_\perp(\mathsf{sk},\cdot)$ and $O_{\mathsf{ct}^*}(\mathsf{sk},\cdot)$.

3 Quantum CCA Security from Hash Proof Systems

Cramer and Shoup [CS02] introduced the notion of *hash proof systems*, which provides a generic framework to construct CCA-secure PKE. In this section, we show how one can also obtain *quantum* CCA-secure PKE from hash proof systems while relying on the *same* statistical (i.e., universality and smoothness) and computational[7] properties that were used for building CCA-secure PKE. By plugging in the hash proof system construction of [ADMP20] from isogeny-based group actions (e.g., CSIDH), we obtain the first realization of qCCA-secure PKE from isogeny-based assumptions.

We begin by recalling the definition of universal hash proof systems (also known as *projective* hash functions) as in [CS02, ADMP20].

Definition 2. *Let* $\Lambda : K \times \Sigma \to \Gamma$ *be an efficiently computable function, and let* $L \subset \Sigma$. *Also, let* $\alpha : K \to S$ *be a projection function. We say that the tuple* $\Pi = (\Lambda, K, S, \Sigma, \Gamma, L)$ *is a universal hash proof system if the following holds:*

- Samplability: *There exist efficient algorithms to sample from* Σ *and from* K. *In addition, there exists an efficient algorithm to sample from* L *along with a witness* w *that proves membership in* L.
- Subset Membership Problem: *If* $\sigma_0 \leftarrow L$ *and* $\sigma_1 \leftarrow \Sigma \setminus L$, *it holds that* σ_0 *is computationally indistinguishable from* σ_1, *i.e., for any PPT distinguisher* $\mathcal{D}$, *the following is negligible:*

$$\mathbf{Adv}^{\mathrm{SMP}}_{(\Sigma,L),\mathcal{D}} = \left| \Pr\left[b' = b : b \leftarrow \{0,1\}; \sigma_0 \leftarrow L, \sigma_1 \leftarrow \Sigma \setminus L, b' \leftarrow \mathcal{D}(\sigma_b)\right] - \frac{1}{2} \right|.$$

- Projective Evaluation: *There exists an efficient algorithm* $\mathsf{ProjEval}$ *such that for any* $k \in K$ *and any* $\sigma \in L$ *with membership witness* w, *we have*

$$\mathsf{ProjEval}(\alpha(k), \sigma, w) = \Lambda(k, \sigma).$$

- Universality: Π *is said to be* ε*-universal if for any* $\sigma \in \Sigma \setminus L$, $s \in S$, *and* $\gamma \in \Gamma$, *we have*

$$\Pr_{k \leftarrow K}[\Lambda(k,\sigma) = \gamma \mid \alpha(k) = s] \le \varepsilon.$$

[7] The only difference is that we require the computational properties to hold in the presence of QPT adversaries (i.e., post-quantum security).

Universality*$_2$ *and Smoothness. We recall two stronger notions for universal hash proof systems, namely universality$_2$ and smoothness, as in [CS02].

- *Universality*$_2$*:* A hash proof system $\Pi = (\Lambda, K, S, \Sigma, \Gamma, L)$ is ε-universal$_2$ if for any $\sigma, \sigma^* \in \Sigma$ such that $\sigma \in \Sigma \setminus (L \cup \{\sigma^*\})$, for any $s \in S$ and $\gamma, \gamma^* \in \Gamma$, we have

$$\Pr_{k \leftarrow K}[\Lambda(k, \sigma) = \gamma \mid \alpha(k) = s \wedge \Lambda(k, \sigma^*) = \gamma^*] \leq \varepsilon.$$

- *Smoothness:* A hash proof system $\Pi = (\Lambda, K, S, \Sigma, \Gamma, L)$ is ε-smooth if for any $\sigma \in \Sigma \setminus L$, $k \leftarrow K$ and $\gamma \leftarrow \Gamma$, the statistical distance between $(\alpha(k), \sigma, \Lambda(k, \sigma))$ and $(\alpha(k), \sigma, \gamma)$ is at most ε.

As in [CS02], we also define an *extended* hash proof system with a tuple of the form $\Pi = (\Lambda, K, S, \Sigma \times E, \Gamma, L \times E)$ associated with a finite set E (where E is going to be used for encoding messages). The only difference between an extended and an "ordinary" hash proof system is that to compute $\Lambda(k, \sigma, e)$ for $\sigma \in L$ and $e \in E$, the $\mathsf{ProjEval}$ algorithm takes as input $\alpha(k) \in S$, $\sigma \in L$, $e \in E$ and a witness w, i.e., $\mathsf{ProjEval}(\alpha(k), \sigma, e, w) = \Lambda(k, \sigma, e)$.

Construction. We recall the construction of CCA-secure PKE from universal (and smooth) hash proof systems [CS02]. We then proceed to show that the same construction also results in qCCA-secure PKE, assuming the post-quantum security of the underlying hash proof system.

Let $\Pi = (\Lambda, K, S, \Sigma, \Gamma, L)$ be an ε'-*smooth* hash proof system, and also let $\alpha : K \to S$ be its projection function. Let $\hat{\Pi} = (\hat{\Lambda}, \hat{K}, \hat{S}, \Sigma \times \Gamma, \hat{\Gamma}, L \times \Gamma)$ be an extended hash proof system with ε-*universality*$_2$, with $\hat{\alpha} : \hat{K} \to \hat{S}$ being the corresponding projection function. Consider the scheme $\mathsf{PKE} = (\mathsf{Gen}, \mathsf{Enc}, \mathsf{Dec})$ with message space Γ based on Π and $\hat{\Pi}$ as follows (note that we require Γ to be an abelian group wherein elements can be efficiently added and subtracted):

$\mathsf{Gen}(1^\lambda)$: Sample $k \leftarrow K$, $\hat{k} \leftarrow \hat{K}$, and compute $s = \alpha(k)$, $\hat{s} = \hat{\alpha}(\hat{k})$. Output

$$\mathsf{pk} = (s, \hat{s}), \quad \mathsf{sk} = (k, \hat{k}).$$

$\mathsf{Enc}(\mathsf{pk} = (s, \hat{s}), \mathsf{m})$: Sample $\sigma \in L$ with its witness w. Output $(\sigma, e, \hat{\gamma})$ where

$$\gamma = \mathsf{ProjEval}(s, \sigma, w), \quad e = \mathsf{m} + \gamma \in \Gamma, \quad \hat{\gamma} = \widehat{\mathsf{ProjEval}}(\hat{s}, \sigma, e, w).$$

$\mathsf{Dec}(\mathsf{sk}, \mathsf{ct} = (\sigma, e, \hat{\gamma}))$: Compute $\bar{\gamma} = \hat{\Lambda}(\hat{k}, \sigma, e)$. If $\hat{\gamma} = \bar{\gamma}$ do the following, else output $\perp$: compute $\gamma = \Lambda(k, \sigma) \in \Gamma$ and output $\mathsf{m} = e - \gamma \in \Gamma$.

Theorem 1. *If Π is a* ε'-smooth *hash proof system and $\hat{\Pi}$ is a* ε-universal$_2$ *extended hash proof system, for negligible ε' and ε, then* PKE *is qCCA secure.*

At a high level, the proof proceeds similarly to that of [CS02] but the main difference is that in [CS02], the original Dec oracle is replaced with an alternative oracle, and then the ε-universality$_2$ property of $\hat{\Pi}$ is invoked in order to argue the (classical) indistinguishability of decryption oracles. In our case, we argue the *quantum* indistinguishability of these decryption oracles by relying on the generalized OW2H lemma [AHU19] (also referred to as "Lemma 1" in the rest of this paper, as formally defined in Sect. 2), in addition to the *statistical* ε-universality$_2$ property of $\hat{\Pi}$.

Proof. Let $\mathcal{A}$ be any QPT adversary that breaks the qCCA security of PKE (see Definition 1) while making q quantum decryption queries, with q_{pre}/q_{post} decryption queries in the pre/post-challenge phase. Consider the following sequence of games.

Game 1: This is essentially the same as the qCCA game except for some minor changes.[8]

- Sample $k \leftarrow K$ and $\hat{k} \leftarrow \hat{K}$ and compute $s = \alpha(k)$, $\hat{s} = \hat{\alpha}(\hat{k})$. Set $\mathsf{pk} = (s, \hat{s})$ and $\mathsf{sk} = (k, \hat{k})$. Generate $\sigma^* \in L$ along with a corresponding witness w^*, and sample a random bit $b \leftarrow \{0, 1\}$.
- Forward pk to $\mathcal{A}$ and respond to $\mathcal{A}$'s quantum decryption queries using the description of $\mathsf{Dec}(\mathsf{sk}, \cdot)$ above, i.e., given a ciphertext $|\mathsf{ct}\rangle = |\sigma, e, \hat{\gamma}\rangle$ in the computational basis, compute $\bar{\gamma} = \hat{\Lambda}(\hat{k}, \sigma, e)$ and if $\hat{\gamma} = \bar{\gamma}$ then compute $\gamma = \Lambda(k, \sigma)$ and output $\mathsf{m} = e - \gamma$. Otherwise, output $\perp$.
- After receiving $(\mathsf{m}_0, \mathsf{m}_1)$ from $\mathcal{A}$, output $\mathsf{ct}^* = (\sigma^*, e^*, \hat{\gamma}^*)$ where

$$\gamma^* = \mathsf{ProjEval}(s, \sigma^*, w^*), \quad e^* = \mathsf{m}_b + \gamma^*, \quad \hat{\gamma}^* = \widehat{\mathsf{ProjEval}}(\hat{s}, \sigma^*, e^*, w^*).$$

- Respond to $\mathcal{A}$'s quantum decryption queries in the normal way as above, but this time making sure to reject ciphertexts that are equal to ct^* (i.e., given a ciphertext $|\mathsf{ct}\rangle = |\mathsf{ct}^*\rangle$, return $\perp$.)
- $\mathcal{A}$ terminates with an output $b' \in \{0, 1\}$.

Game 2: In this game, we modify the way $\mathsf{ct}^* = (\sigma^*, e^*, \hat{\gamma}^*)$ is computed. Specifically, instead of using pk to encrypt m_b, we use $\mathsf{sk} = (k, \hat{k})$ as follows:

$$\gamma^* = \Lambda(k, \sigma^*), \quad e^* = \mathsf{m}_b + \gamma^*, \quad \hat{\gamma}^* = \hat{\Lambda}(\hat{k}, \sigma^*, e^*).$$

Game 3: In this game, we sample σ^* uniformly from $\Sigma \setminus L$, instead of L. Note that we do not need a corresponding witness "w^*" as we are not using the ProjEval function (which requires a witness as input) anymore to encrypt m_b.

Game 4a: In this game, we modify the decryption oracle in the *pre-challenge* phase as follows: in addition to rejecting a ciphertext $(\sigma, e, \hat{\gamma})$ if $\hat{\Lambda}(\hat{k}, \sigma, e) \neq \hat{\gamma}$, the modified oracle also rejects the ciphertext if $\sigma \notin L$.

Game 4b: Here we modify the decryption oracle in the *post-challenge* phase as follows: in addition to rejecting a ciphertext $(\sigma, e, \hat{\gamma})$ if $\hat{\Lambda}(\hat{k}, \sigma, e) \neq \hat{\gamma}$, the modified oracle also rejects the ciphertext if $\sigma \notin L$.[9]

[8] Specifically, (σ^*, w^*) is generated in the *pre-challenge phase* (which is going to be used in the challenge phase). However, this change does not affect $\mathcal{A}$'s view.

[9] As usual, ciphertexts equal to the challenge ciphertext ct^* will also be rejected.

Game 5: In this game, we modify the challenge phase as follows: instead of computing γ^* as $\gamma^* = \Lambda(k, \sigma^*)$, we sample γ^* uniformly from Γ.

We define $W^{(j)}$, for $j \in \{1, 2, 3, 4a, 4b, 5\}$, to be the event that $\mathcal{A}$ succeeds in guessing the bit b (i.e., $b' = b$) in Game j. By definition, we have

$$\mathbf{Adv}^{\mathrm{qCCA}}_{\mathsf{PKE},\mathcal{A}} = \left| \Pr[W^{(1)}] - \frac{1}{2} \right|.$$

We now have the following in the subsequent games.

Lemma 2. $\Pr[W^{(1)}] = \Pr[W^{(2)}]$.

Proof. Note that since $\sigma^* \in L$ (where w^* is the corresponding witness), by the projective evaluation property we have $\gamma^* = \mathsf{ProjEval}(s, \sigma^*, w^*) = \Lambda(k, \sigma^*)$ and $\hat{\gamma}^* = \widehat{\mathsf{ProjEval}}(\hat{s}, \sigma^*, e^*, w^*) = \hat{\Lambda}(\hat{k}, \sigma^*, e^*)$.

Lemma 3. *There exists a distinguisher $\mathcal{D}$ that solves the subset membership problem of Π (and $\hat{\Pi}$) such that* $|\Pr[W^{(2)}] - \Pr[W^{(3)}]| = 2 \cdot \mathbf{Adv}^{\mathrm{SMP}}_{(\Sigma,L),\mathcal{D}}$.

Proof. The description of $\mathcal{D}$ is as follows: on input $\sigma^* \in \Sigma$, the distinguisher $\mathcal{D}$ samples $\mathsf{sk} = (k, \hat{k}) \leftarrow K \times \hat{K}$ and forwards the corresponding public key $\mathsf{pk} = (\alpha(k), \hat{\alpha}(\hat{k}))$ to the qCCA adversary $\mathcal{A}$. It then samples $b \leftarrow \{0, 1\}$ and answers $\mathcal{A}$'s quantum decryption queries as in Game 2 using sk. When $\mathcal{A}$ provides $(\mathsf{m}_0, \mathsf{m}_1)$, the distinguisher $\mathcal{D}$ computes the challenge ciphertext as follows: it computes $\gamma^* = \Lambda(k, \sigma^*)$ using sk. Next, $\mathcal{D}$ computes $e^* = \mathsf{m}_b + \gamma^*$ and $\hat{\gamma}^* = \hat{\Lambda}(\hat{k}, \sigma^*, e^*)$, and forwards $(\sigma^*, e^*, \hat{\gamma}^*)$ to $\mathcal{A}$. The distinguisher $\mathcal{D}$ proceeds to respond to $\mathcal{A}$'s quantum decryption queries again as in Game 2 using sk while making sure to reject ciphertexts equal to ct^*. Finally, when $\mathcal{A}$ terminates with a bit b', the distinguisher $\mathcal{D}$ outputs 1 if $b = b'$ and outputs 0 otherwise. It is easy to see that $\mathcal{D}$ perfectly simulates Game 2 (respectively, Game 3) if $\sigma^* \in L$ (respectively, $\sigma^* \in \Sigma \setminus L$). Therefore, we have

$$|\Pr[W^{(2)}] - \Pr[W^{(3)}]| = 2 \cdot \mathbf{Adv}^{\mathrm{SMP}}_{(\Sigma,L),\mathcal{D}}.$$

Lemma 4. $|\Pr[W^{(3)}] - \Pr[W^{(4a)}]| \leq 2q_{pre}\sqrt{\varepsilon}$.

Proof. Here we use Lemma 1 to bound $|\Pr[W^{(3)}] - \Pr[W^{(4a)}]|$. In the context of applying Lemma 1, let A be a quantum oracle algorithm which receives as input the hash proof systems Π and $\hat{\Pi}$ along with the random values $k \leftarrow K$ and $\hat{k} \leftarrow \hat{K}$ (namely, the secret key $\mathsf{sk} = (k, \hat{k})$); i.e., $z = ((\Pi, \hat{\Pi}), (k, \hat{k}))$. A also has quantum access either to the original decryption oracle $G := \mathsf{Dec}(\mathsf{sk}, \cdot)$ used in Game 3 or to the modified decryption oracle H used in Game 4a. Note that the outputs of oracles G and H differ with respect to the set of ciphertexts $S = \{\mathsf{ct} = (\sigma, e, \hat{\gamma}) | \sigma \notin L \wedge \hat{\Lambda}(\hat{k}, \sigma, e) = \hat{\gamma}\}$. Next, A proceeds to perfectly simulate either Game 3 or Game 4a towards the qCCA adversary $\mathcal{A}$ (depending on whether it has access to G or H) as follows: A first samples $b \leftarrow \{0, 1\}$ and forwards the public key $(s, \hat{s}) = (\alpha(k), \hat{\alpha}(\hat{k}))$ to $\mathcal{A}$. Then A *strictly* uses its quantum oracle (i.e., G or H) to answer $\mathcal{A}$'s queries in the pre-challenge phase; i.e., A does not use the secret key $(k, \hat{k})$ *directly* for decryption here. To compute the challenge ciphertext $\mathsf{ct}^* = (\sigma^*, e^*, \hat{\gamma}^*)$ in the challenge phase, A uses the private keys k and $\hat{k}$ for encrypting m_b just as in Game 3 (and 4a) above. Finally, A proceeds to answer the rest of $\mathcal{A}$'s quantum decryption queries in the post-challenge phase as in Game 3, this time using the secret key $(k, \hat{k})$ (and *not* the oracles G or H), while at the same time rejecting ciphertexts that are equal to ct^*. Finally A outputs 1 if and only if $\mathcal{A}$ outputs $b' = b$.

Observe that in the context of Lemma 1, $\Pr[W^{(3)}] = \Pr[1 \leftarrow A^G(z)]$ and $\Pr[W^{(4a)}] = \Pr[1 \leftarrow A^H(z)]$. Thus, we have $|\Pr[W^{(3)}] - \Pr[W^{(4a)}]| \leq 2q_{pre}\sqrt{P_{\text{guess}}}$ where P_{guess} is the probability of the event when measurement of a random quantum decryption query made by $\mathcal{A}$ in the pre-challenge phase of Game 4a results in a ciphertext $(\sigma, e, \hat{\gamma}) \in S$.

In order to bound the probability P_{guess} in Game 4a, we first condition on fixed hash proof systems Π and $\hat{\Pi}$, as well as fixed values of k, $\hat{s}$, and $\mathcal{A}$'s random coins. These values completely determine the public key received by $\mathcal{A}$ in Game 4a, the quantum decryption queries made by $\mathcal{A}$ in the *pre-challenge phase*, the corresponding responses of the decryption oracle (note that in Game 4a, the decryption oracle rejects ciphertexts $(\sigma, e, \hat{\gamma})$ when $\sigma \notin L$; hence, when $\sigma \in L$, we only need the keys k and $\hat{s}$ for decryption), and the values m_0 and m_1 chosen by $\mathcal{A}$ in the challenge phase. Now consider any ciphertext $\mathsf{ct} = (\sigma, e, \hat{\gamma})$ which is a result of measuring any quantum decryption query made by $\mathcal{A}$ in the pre-challenge phase. If E is an event in this conditional probability space, then we denote the associated probability of the event in this space as $\Pr_{\text{cond}}[E]$. In the next step, we want to bound the following quantity:

$$\Pr_{\text{cond}}[(\sigma, e, \hat{\gamma}) \in S] = \Pr_{\text{cond}}[\sigma \notin L \wedge \hat{\Lambda}(\hat{k}, \sigma, e) = \hat{\gamma}] \leq \Pr_{\text{cond}}[\hat{\Lambda}(\hat{k}, \sigma, e) = \hat{\gamma} \mid \sigma \notin L]$$

In this conditional probability space where σ, e, and $\hat{\gamma}$ are fixed, along with the other values fixed above, note that $\hat{k}$ is still uniformly distributed over $\hat{K}$ conditioned on $\hat{\alpha}(\hat{k}) = \hat{s}$. Hence, from the ε-universality$_2$ property of $\hat{\Pi}$, we have $\Pr_{\text{cond}}[\hat{\Lambda}(\hat{k}, \sigma, e) = \hat{\gamma} \mid \sigma \notin L] \leq \varepsilon$. Thus, from a simple averaging argument over this conditional probability space, it follows that $P_{\text{guess}} \leq \varepsilon$ in Game 4a. Therefore, it follows that

$$|\Pr[W^{(3)}] - \Pr[W^{(4a)}]| \leq 2q_{pre}\sqrt{P_{\text{guess}}} \leq 2q_{pre}\sqrt{\varepsilon}.$$

Lemma 5. $|\Pr[W^{(4a)}] - \Pr[W^{(4b)}]| \leq 2q_{post}\sqrt{\varepsilon}$.

Proof. We again use Lemma 1 as above to bound $|\Pr[W^{(4a)}] - \Pr[W^{(4b)}]|$. We first simulate the pre-challenge phase of Game 4a (and 4b) as follows: let A_{pre} be an algorithm which receives as input the hash proof systems Π and $\hat{\Pi}$ along with a randomly chosen $\mathsf{sk} = (k, \hat{k})$ generated as in Game 4a above. A_{pre} samples $b \leftarrow \{0, 1\}$ and forwards $\mathsf{pk} = (s, \hat{s}) = (\alpha(k), \hat{\alpha}(\hat{k}))$ to $\mathcal{A}$. It responds to $\mathcal{A}$'s quantum decryption queries in the pre-challenge phase as in Game 4a using sk: for any $\mathsf{ct} = (\sigma, e, \hat{\gamma})$, it returns $\perp$ whenever $\sigma \notin L$ (note that A_{pre} need not be efficient); otherwise, it returns $\mathsf{Dec}(\mathsf{sk}, \mathsf{ct})$. After receiving $(\mathsf{m}_0, \mathsf{m}_1)$ from $\mathcal{A}$, the algorithm A_{pre} computes $\mathsf{ct}^* = (\sigma^*, e^*, \hat{\gamma}^*)$ using sk as in Game 4a (and 4b) above. It then forwards ct^* to $\mathcal{A}$. In addition, in the context of applying Lemma 1, A_{pre} forwards the input $z = ((\Pi, \hat{\Pi}), (\mathsf{pk}, \mathsf{sk}), \mathsf{ct}^*, b)$ to a quantum oracle algorithm A_{post}. The algorithm A_{post} also has quantum access either to the corresponding post-challenge decryption oracle $G = \mathsf{Dec}(\mathsf{sk}, \cdot)$ in Game 4a (which also rejects ciphertexts equal to ct^*) or to the modified post-challenge decryption oracle H in Game 4b. Note that the outputs of G and H differ with respect to the set $S = \{\mathsf{ct} = (\sigma, e, \hat{\gamma}) | \mathsf{ct} \neq \mathsf{ct}^* \wedge \sigma \notin L \wedge \hat{\Lambda}(\hat{k}, \sigma, e) = \hat{\gamma}\}$. Next, A_{post} proceeds to simulate the post-challenge phase of Game 4a or Game 4b towards $\mathcal{A}$ (depending on whether it has access to G or H) by forwarding $\mathcal{A}$'s quantum decryption queries to its own oracle (i.e., G or H) and returning the corresponding output. Finally, A_{post} outputs 1 if and only if $\mathcal{A}$ outputs $b' = b$.

Observe that $\Pr[W^{(4a)}] = \Pr[1 \leftarrow A^G_{post}(z)]$ and $\Pr[W^{(4b)}] = \Pr[1 \leftarrow A^H_{post}(z)]$. By applying Lemma 1 we have $|\Pr[W^{(4a)}] - \Pr[W^{(4b)}]| \leq 2q_{post}\sqrt{P_{\text{guess}}}$ where P_{guess} is essentially the probability of the event when measurement of a random quantum decryption query made by $\mathcal{A}$ in the post-challenge phase of Game 4b results in a non-challenge ciphertext $\mathsf{ct} = (\sigma, e, \hat{\gamma}) \in S$.

In order to bound the probability P_{guess} in Game 4b, we condition on fixed hash proof systems Π and $\hat{\Pi}$, fixed values of k, $\hat{s}$, and $\mathcal{A}$'s random coins as in our analysis of the pre-challenge phase in the previous lemma. Moreover, we also condition on the fixed values of b and σ^* in the challenge phase (which determine γ^* and e^*) as well as a fixed value of $\hat{\gamma}^* = \hat{\Lambda}(\hat{k}, \sigma^*, e^*)$. These values completely determine all of the quantum decryption queries made by $\mathcal{A}$ in the *post-challenge phase* and the corresponding responses of the decryption oracle in Game 4b. Now consider any ciphertext $\mathsf{ct} = (\sigma, e, \hat{\gamma})$ which is a result of the measurement of any quantum decryption query made by $\mathcal{A}$ in the post-challenge phase. Using the same notation of $\Pr_{\text{cond}}[\cdot]$ as in the proof of the previous lemma to denote conditional probabilities, we want to bound:

$$\begin{aligned} \Pr_{\text{cond}}[(\sigma, e, \hat{\gamma}) \in S] &= \Pr_{\text{cond}}[(\sigma, e, \hat{\gamma}) \neq (\sigma^*, e^*, \hat{\gamma}^*) \wedge \sigma \notin L \wedge \hat{\Lambda}(\hat{k}, \sigma, e) = \hat{\gamma}] \\ &\leq \Pr_{\text{cond}}[\hat{\Lambda}(\hat{k}, \sigma, e) = \hat{\gamma} \mid (\sigma, e, \hat{\gamma}) \neq (\sigma^*, e^*, \hat{\gamma}^*) \wedge \sigma \notin L]. \end{aligned}$$

If $(\sigma, e) = (\sigma^*, e^*)$, then since $(\sigma, e, \hat{\gamma}) \neq (\sigma^*, e^*, \hat{\gamma}^*)$ we have $\hat{\Lambda}(\hat{k}, \sigma, e) \neq \hat{\gamma}$ with certainty; that is, $\Pr_{\text{cond}}[\hat{\Lambda}(\hat{k}, \sigma, e) = \hat{\gamma} \mid (\sigma, e, \hat{\gamma}) \neq (\sigma^*, e^*, \hat{\gamma}^*) \wedge \sigma \notin L] = 0$.

On the other hand, if $(\sigma, e) \neq (\sigma^*, e^*)$, then in this conditional probability space where σ, e, and $\hat{\gamma}$ are fixed, along with the other values fixed above, note that $\hat{k}$ is uniformly distributed conditioned on $\hat{\alpha}(\hat{k}) = \hat{s}$ *and* $\hat{\Lambda}(\hat{k}, \sigma^*, e^*) = \hat{\gamma}^*$. Thus, by the ε-universality$_2$ property of $\hat{\Pi}$, we have

$$\Pr_{\text{cond}}[\hat{\Lambda}(\hat{k}, \sigma, e) = \hat{\gamma} \mid (\sigma, e, \hat{\gamma}) \neq (\sigma^*, e^*, \hat{\gamma}^*) \wedge \sigma \notin L] \leq \varepsilon.$$

By a simple averaging argument, it follows that $P_{\text{guess}} \leq \varepsilon$, which implies

$$|\Pr[W^{(4a)}] - \Pr[W^{(4b)}]| \leq 2q_{post}\sqrt{P_{\text{guess}}} \leq 2q_{post}\sqrt{\varepsilon}.$$

Remark 5. Note that in our application of the OW2H lemma above (and also in the rest of our qCCA security proofs below), we first make an explicit distinction between the "pre-challenge" and "post-challenge" decryption oracles and then apply the OW2H lemma *separately* to the respective oracles. The reason is that the OW2H lemma, in its current form, is not directly applicable to *stateful* oracles (which is the case for decryption oracles in the qCCA security game). Nevertheless, we believe that a one-shot application of a "stateful"-version of the OW2H lemma will still not lead to improved security bounds compared to our two-fold application of the plain OW2H lemma.

Lemma 6. $|\Pr[W^{(4b)}] - \Pr[W^{(5)}]| \leq \varepsilon'$.

Proof. We construct a (potentially inefficient) distinguisher $\mathcal{D}'$ as follows: on input the hash proof systems Π, $\hat{\Pi}$ and a tuple $(\alpha(k), \sigma^*, \gamma^*)$ where $\sigma^* \leftarrow \Sigma \setminus L$, $k \leftarrow K$ and an element $\gamma^* \in \Gamma$ (where $\mathcal{D}'$ is supposed to determine whether $\gamma^* = \Lambda(k, \sigma^*)$ or $\gamma^* \leftarrow \Gamma$), the distinguisher $\mathcal{D}'$ first samples $\hat{k} \leftarrow \hat{K}$ and forwards $\mathsf{pk} = (\alpha(k), \hat{\alpha}(\hat{k}))$ to $\mathcal{A}$. It then samples $b \leftarrow \{0,1\}$ and proceeds to answer $\mathcal{A}$'s queries as in Game 4b (and 5) as follows: for any $\mathsf{ct} = (\sigma, e, \hat{\gamma})$, return $\perp$ whenever $\sigma \notin L$. Otherwise, compute $\bar{\gamma} = \hat{\Lambda}(\hat{k}, \sigma, e)$ and check if $\bar{\gamma} = \hat{\gamma}$. If not, output $\perp$. Otherwise, find a witness w corresponding to $\sigma \in L$ and compute $\gamma = \mathsf{ProjEval}(\alpha(k), \sigma, w)$, and return $\mathsf{m} = e - \gamma$.[10] In the challenge phase, when $\mathcal{A}$ provides $(\mathsf{m}_0, \mathsf{m}_1)$, the distinguisher $\mathcal{D}'$ computes $\mathsf{ct}^* = (\sigma^*, e^*, \hat{\gamma}^*)$ as follows: it computes $e^* = \mathsf{m}_b + \gamma^*$ and $\hat{\gamma}^* = \hat{\Lambda}(\hat{k}, \sigma^*, e^*)$ using $\hat{k}$. Next, $\mathcal{D}'$ proceeds to respond to the rest of $\mathcal{A}$'s queries as in the pre-challenge phase while rejecting ciphertexts equal to ct^*. Finally, when $\mathcal{A}$ terminates with a bit b', the distinguisher $\mathcal{D}'$ outputs 1 if $b = b'$ and outputs 0 otherwise. Observe that $\mathcal{D}'$ perfectly simulates Game 4b or Game 5 (depending on its input). Therefore, by the ε'-smoothness property of Π, it follows that the statistical distance between $(\alpha(k), \sigma^*, \gamma^* = \Lambda(k, \sigma^*))$ and $(\alpha(k), \sigma^*, \gamma^* \leftarrow \Gamma)$ is bounded by ε', as required.

Lemma 7. $\Pr[W^{(5)}] = 1/2$.

Proof. The lemma follows by observing that the view of $\mathcal{A}$ is independent of b.

By putting together all of the above bounds, it follows that

$$\mathbf{Adv}^{\text{qCCA}}_{\mathsf{PKE},\mathcal{A}} \leq 2 \cdot \mathbf{Adv}^{\text{SMP}}_{(\Sigma,L),\mathcal{D}} + 2q\sqrt{\varepsilon} + \varepsilon',$$

which establishes the qCCA security of PKE.

[10] For a *fixed* $\sigma \in L$, finding a corresponding witness w may not be efficient. However, note that $\mathcal{D}'$ is potentially inefficient since our proof relies on a *statistical* property of hash proof systems: namely, ε'-smoothness (Definition 2).

Quantum CCA-Secure PKE from Isogeny-Based Group Actions. We remark that an ε'-smooth and ε-universal$_2$ hash proof system (where ε' and ε are negligible) can be generically constructed from a 1/2-universal hash proof system by relying on the leftover hash lemma (as shown by [CS02]), and for the above construction one can take Γ to be the group of (fixed-length) bit strings with xor operation. Thus, all one needs to realize qCCA-secure PKE is a 1/2-universal hash proof system. In particular, by relying the hash proof system construction of [ADMP20], Theorem 1 immediately yields a quantum CCA-secure PKE from isogeny-based group actions (e.g., CSIDH).[11]

4 qCCA Security from PKE and KDM-Secure SKE

Kitagawa *et al.* [KMT19] showed how to realize CCA-secure KEM/PKE given any CPA-secure KEM/PKE and any SKE scheme with one-time KDM security (for projection functions). In this section, we prove that their construction also satisfies qCCA security while relying on (post-quantum security of) the same building blocks.

4.1 Quantum CCA-Secure KEM

We recall the KEM construction of [KMT19] from the following building blocks (see the full version of our paper for formal definitions of their corresponding security notions):

- a CPA-secure KEM $\mathsf{KEM} = (\mathsf{Gen}, \mathsf{Encaps}, \mathsf{Decaps})$,
- a one-time KDM secure SKE (for projection functions) $\mathsf{SKE} = (\mathsf{K}, \mathsf{E}, \mathsf{D})$,
- a target-collision resistant hash function $\mathsf{Hash} = (\mathsf{HGen}, \mathsf{H})$[12],

These building blocks are required to have the following properties:[13]

- The session key space of KEM and the randomness space of Encaps are $\{0,1\}^{4\lambda}$ and $\{0,1\}^{\lambda}$, respectively. The secret key space of SKE is $\{0,1\}^{n}$ and plaintext space is $\{0,1\}^{n\cdot\lambda+\ell}$. The range of H is $\{0,1\}^{\lambda}$.
- The size of the range of $\mathsf{Decaps}(\mathsf{sk},\cdot)$ (excluding $\bot$) for any sk in the support of $\mathsf{Gen}(1^{\lambda})$ is at most 2^{λ}.

Consider the scheme $\overline{\mathsf{KEM}} = (\overline{\mathsf{Gen}}, \overline{\mathsf{Encaps}}, \overline{\mathsf{Decaps}})$ described in Fig. 1 and Fig. 2. Correctness of $\overline{\mathsf{KEM}}$ can be verified as in [KMT19]. We proceed to prove the quantum CCA security of $\overline{\mathsf{KEM}}$ via the following theorem.

[11] We note that the transformation of Cramer and Shoup [CS02] to construct a negligibly smooth and universal hash proof system from a 1/2-universal hash proof system is also valid in a *quantum* setting since it neither requires a computational assumption nor does it involve interacting with an oracle. Namely, the transformation of [CS02] is entirely *statistical*, and only relies on simple statistical techniques/lemmas, e.g., parallelization and the leftover hash lemma (Sect. 3.5 of [CS02]).

[12] Target collision-resistance can be realized from any one-way function [Rom90].

[13] These requirements can be assumed without loss of generality as in [KMT19].

$\overline{\mathsf{Gen}}(1^\lambda)$:	$\overline{\mathsf{Encaps}}(\mathsf{PK} = (\mathsf{pk}^0, \mathsf{pk}^1, (\mathbf{a}_i)_{i\in[n]}, \mathbf{c}, \mathsf{hk}))$:
$(\mathsf{pk}^\mathsf{b}, \mathsf{sk}^\mathsf{b}) \leftarrow \mathsf{Gen}(1^\lambda)$ for $\mathsf{b} \in \{0,1\}$ $\mathbf{a}_i, \mathbf{c} \leftarrow \{0,1\}^{4\lambda}$ for $i \in [n]$ $\mathsf{hk} \leftarrow \mathsf{HGen}(1^\lambda)$ $\mathsf{PK} := (\mathsf{pk}^0, \mathsf{pk}^1, (\mathbf{a}_i)_{i\in[n]}, \mathbf{c}, \mathsf{hk})$ $\mathsf{SK} := (\mathsf{sk}^0, \mathsf{PK})$ return $(\mathsf{PK}, \mathsf{SK})$	$\forall (i, \mathsf{b}) \in [n] \times \{0,1\}$: $\mathbf{r}_i^\mathsf{b} \leftarrow \{0,1\}^\lambda$, $(\mathsf{ct}_i^\mathsf{b}, \mathbf{k}_i^\mathsf{b}) \leftarrow \mathsf{Encaps}(\mathsf{pk}^\mathsf{b}; \mathbf{r}_i^\mathsf{b})$ $\mathbf{s} = (s_1, \ldots, s_n) \leftarrow \mathsf{K}(1^\lambda)$, $\boldsymbol{\kappa} \leftarrow \{0,1\}^\ell$ $\mathsf{ct}_{\mathsf{SKE}} \leftarrow \mathsf{E}(\mathbf{s}, (\mathbf{r}_i^{s_i})_{i\in[n]} \parallel \boldsymbol{\kappa})$ $\mathbf{h} := \mathsf{H}(\mathsf{hk}, (\mathsf{ct}_i^0, \mathsf{ct}_i^1)_{i\in[n]} \parallel \mathsf{ct}_{\mathsf{SKE}})$ $\mathbf{t}_i := \mathbf{k}_i^{s_i} + s_i \cdot (\mathbf{a}_i + \mathbf{c} \cdot \mathbf{h})$ $(\forall i \in [n])$ $\mathsf{CT} := ((\mathsf{ct}_i^0, \mathsf{ct}_i^1, \mathbf{t}_i)_{i\in[n]}, \mathsf{ct}_{\mathsf{SKE}})$ return $(\mathsf{CT}, \boldsymbol{\kappa})$

Fig. 1. Algorithms $\overline{\mathsf{Gen}}$ and $\overline{\mathsf{Encaps}}$. (The arithmetic is done over $\mathrm{GF}(2^{4\lambda})$ and $\mathbf{h}$ is interpreted as an element of $\{0,1\}^{4\lambda}$)

$\overline{\mathsf{Decaps}}(\mathsf{SK} = (\mathsf{sk}^0, \mathsf{PK}), \mathsf{CT} = ((\mathsf{ct}_i^0, \mathsf{ct}_i^1, \mathbf{t}_i)_{i\in[n]}, \mathsf{ct}_{\mathsf{SKE}}))$:

$\mathbf{h} := \mathsf{H}(\mathsf{hk}, (\mathsf{ct}_i^0, \mathsf{ct}_i^1)_{i\in[n]} \parallel \mathsf{ct}_{\mathsf{SKE}})$.
For each $i \in [n]$: if $\mathsf{Decaps}(\mathsf{sk}^0, \mathsf{ct}_i^0) = \mathbf{t}_i$, set $s_i = 0$. Otherwise set $s_i = 1$.
$((\mathbf{r}_i^{s_i})_{i\in[n]} \parallel \boldsymbol{\kappa}) := \mathsf{D}(\mathbf{s}, \mathsf{ct}_{\mathsf{SKE}})$

If the following holds return $\boldsymbol{\kappa}$. Otherwise return $\perp$.
$\forall i \in [n]$: $\mathsf{Encaps}(\mathsf{pk}^{s_i}; \mathbf{r}_i^{s_i}) = (\mathsf{ct}_i^{s_i}, \mathbf{t}_i - s_i \cdot (\mathbf{a}_i + \mathbf{c} \cdot \mathbf{h}))$

Fig. 2. Algorithm $\overline{\mathsf{Decaps}}$.

Theorem 2. *Let* KEM, SKE, *and* Hash *be as described above with security against QPT adversaries. If* KEM *is almost-all-keys correct*[14] *then* $\overline{\mathsf{KEM}}$ *is qCCA secure.*

Proof. Let $\mathcal{A}$ be any QPT adversary that breaks the qCCA security of $\overline{\mathsf{KEM}}$ while making q quantum decapsulation queries. Let KEM be ε-almost-all-keys correct. Our proof proceeds with a similar sequence of games as in [KMT19]. For the sake of completeness, we provide the descriptions of the games as follows.

Game 1: This is essentially identical to qCCA game for $\overline{\mathsf{KEM}}$ except for a few changes in the ordering.

- Set $\mathsf{PK} = (\mathsf{pk}^0, \mathsf{pk}^1, (\mathbf{a}_i)_{i\in[n]}, \mathbf{c}, \mathsf{hk})$, $\mathsf{SK} = (\mathsf{sk}^0, \mathsf{PK})$, and then compute the ciphertext $\hat{\mathsf{CT}} = ((\hat{\mathsf{ct}}_i^0, \hat{\mathsf{ct}}_i^1, \hat{\mathbf{t}}_i)_{i\in[n]}, \hat{\mathsf{ct}}_{\mathsf{SKE}})$ as follows:
  1. Sample $(\mathsf{pk}^\mathsf{b}, \mathsf{sk}^\mathsf{b}) \leftarrow \mathsf{Gen}(1^\lambda)$ for $\mathsf{b} \in \{0,1\}$, and $\mathbf{c} \leftarrow \{0,1\}^{4\lambda}$.
  2. Sample $\hat{\mathbf{s}} \leftarrow \mathsf{K}(1^\lambda)$, $\hat{\boldsymbol{\kappa}}_1 \leftarrow \{0,1\}^\ell$, $\hat{\mathbf{r}}_i^\mathsf{b} \leftarrow \{0,1\}^{4\lambda}$ $(\forall (i, \mathsf{b}) \in [n] \times \{0,1\})$.
  3. Compute $\hat{\mathsf{ct}}_{\mathsf{SKE}} \leftarrow \mathsf{E}(\hat{\mathbf{s}}, (\hat{\mathbf{r}}_i^{\hat{s}_i})_{i\in[n]} \parallel \hat{\boldsymbol{\kappa}}_1)$.

[14] This correctness notion is analogous to the almost-all-keys correctness defined for PKE schemes in Sect. 2; see the full version of our paper for a formal definition of the corresponding notion for KEMs.

4. Compute $(\hat{\mathsf{ct}}_i^{\mathsf{b}}, \hat{\mathbf{k}}_i^{\mathsf{b}}) \leftarrow \mathsf{Encaps}(\mathsf{pk}^{\mathsf{b}}; \hat{\mathbf{r}}_i^{\mathsf{b}})$ for $(i, \mathsf{b}) \in [n] \times \{0,1\}$.
5. Compute $\mathsf{hk} \leftarrow \mathsf{HGen}(1^\lambda)$ and $\hat{\mathbf{h}} = \mathsf{H}(\mathsf{hk}, (\hat{\mathsf{ct}}_i^0, \hat{\mathsf{ct}}_i^1)_{i\in[n]} \parallel \hat{\mathsf{ct}}_{\mathsf{SKE}})$.
6. Sample $\mathbf{a}_i \leftarrow \{0,1\}^{4\lambda}$ for $i \in [n]$.
7. Compute $\hat{\mathbf{t}}_i = \hat{\mathbf{k}}_i^{\hat{s}_i} + \hat{s}_i \cdot (\mathbf{a}_i + \mathbf{c} \cdot \hat{\mathbf{h}})$ for $i \in [n]$.

- Sample a random key $\hat{\boldsymbol{\kappa}}_0 \leftarrow \{0,1\}^\ell$ and a bit $b \leftarrow \{0,1\}$, and run $\mathcal{A}(\mathsf{PK}, \hat{\mathsf{CT}}, \hat{\boldsymbol{\kappa}}_b)$. The adversary $\mathcal{A}$ may now start making quantum decapsulation queries.
- Decapsulation queries are answered as follows. We describe the response for any ciphertext $|\mathsf{CT}\rangle = |((\mathsf{ct}_i^0, \mathsf{ct}_i^1, \mathbf{t}_i)_{i\in[n]}, \mathsf{ct}_{\mathsf{SKE}})\rangle$ in the computational basis; the response to ciphertexts in a superposition follows in a standard way. If $\mathsf{CT} = \hat{\mathsf{CT}}$ output $\perp$. If $\mathsf{Decaps}(\mathsf{sk}^0, \mathsf{ct}_i^0) = \mathbf{t}_i$, set $s_i = 0$. Else, set $s_i = 1$ (for each $i \in [n]$). Set $\mathbf{h} = \mathsf{H}(\mathsf{hk}, (\mathsf{ct}_i^0, \mathsf{ct}_i^1)_{i\in[n]} \parallel \mathsf{ct}_{\mathsf{SKE}})$. Next, compute $((\mathbf{r}_i^{s_i})_{i\in[n]} \parallel \boldsymbol{\kappa}) := \mathsf{D}(\mathbf{s}, \mathsf{ct}_{\mathsf{SKE}})$. If for each $i \in [n]$ it holds that $\mathsf{Encaps}(\mathsf{pk}^{s_i}; \mathbf{r}_i^{s_i}) = (\mathsf{ct}_i^{s_i}, \mathbf{t}_i - s_i \cdot (\mathbf{a}_i + \mathbf{c} \cdot \mathbf{h}))$, return $\boldsymbol{\kappa}$. Otherwise return $\perp$.
- $\mathcal{A}$ finally outputs a bit $b' \in \{0,1\}$.

For the sake of convenience, we define the following sets:

$$S_0 := \{j \in [n] \mid \hat{s}_j = 0\}, \qquad S_1 := [n] \setminus S_0.$$

Game 2: We modify the decapsulation oracle as follows: if a ciphertext $|\mathsf{CT}\rangle = |((\mathsf{ct}_i^0, \mathsf{ct}_i^1, \mathbf{t}_i)_{i\in[n]}, \mathsf{ct}_{\mathsf{SKE}})\rangle$ satisfies $\mathbf{h} = \mathsf{H}(\mathsf{hk}, (\mathsf{ct}_i^0, \mathsf{ct}_i^1)_{i\in[n]} \parallel \mathsf{ct}_{\mathsf{SKE}}) = \hat{\mathbf{h}}$, the modified oracle returns $\perp$.

Game 3: We modify how $\mathbf{a}_i$'s for the positions $i \in S_0$ are generated: for every $i \in S_0$, we generate $\mathbf{a}_i$ as $\mathbf{a}_i = \hat{\mathbf{k}}_i^0 - \hat{\mathbf{k}}_i^1 - \mathbf{c} \cdot \hat{\mathbf{h}}$.

Game 4: We modify the decapsulation oracle as follows: if a (non-challenge) ciphertext satisfies $\mathbf{h} = \mathsf{H}(\mathsf{hk}, (\mathsf{ct}_i^0, \mathsf{ct}_i^1)_{i\in[n]} \parallel \mathsf{ct}_{\mathsf{SKE}}) = \hat{\mathbf{h}}$, return $\perp$ (same as in Games 2 and 3). Otherwise, the quantum oracle uses an alternative decapsulation algorithm $\overline{\mathsf{AltDecaps}}$ and an alternative secret key SK' described below.

$\overline{\mathsf{AltDecaps}}$ takes $\mathsf{SK}' := (\mathsf{sk}^1, \mathsf{PK})$ and CT as input, and proceeds identically to $\overline{\mathsf{Decaps}}(\mathsf{SK}, \mathsf{CT})$ except when computing the s_i's; we instead do the following:[15]

$$\forall i \in [n]: \qquad s_i = \begin{cases} 1 \text{ if } \mathsf{Decaps}(\mathsf{sk}^1, \mathsf{ct}_i^1) = \mathbf{t}_i - \mathbf{a}_i - \mathbf{c} \cdot \mathbf{h}, \\ 0 \text{ otherwise.} \end{cases}$$

Game 5: We modify how $\mathbf{a}_i$'s for the positions $i \in S_1$ are generated. For every $i \in S_1$, we generate $\mathbf{a}_i$ as $\mathbf{a}_i = \hat{\mathbf{k}}_i^0 - \hat{\mathbf{k}}_i^1 - \mathbf{c} \cdot \hat{\mathbf{h}}$. Due to this change, for every $i \in [n]$ we have $\hat{\mathbf{t}}_i = \hat{\mathbf{k}}_i^0$, irrespective of whether $\hat{s}_i$ is 0 or 1. Thus, in this game, only the value of $\hat{\mathsf{ct}}_{\mathsf{SKE}}$ is dependent on $\hat{\mathbf{s}}$.

Game 6: In this game, we generate $\hat{\mathsf{ct}}_{\mathsf{SKE}}$ in the challenge ciphertext $\hat{\mathsf{CT}}$ as $\hat{\mathsf{ct}}_{\mathsf{SKE}} \leftarrow \mathsf{E}(\hat{\mathbf{s}}, 0^{n\cdot\lambda+\ell})$. In this game, $\hat{\mathsf{ct}}_{\mathsf{SKE}}$ has no information on the bit b.

We now define $W^{(j)}$, for $j \in [6]$, to be the event when $\mathcal{A}$ succeeds in guessing the bit b (i.e., $b' = b$) in Game j. By definition, we have

$$\mathbf{Adv}_{\mathsf{KEM},\mathcal{A}}^{\mathrm{qCCA}} = \left| \Pr[W^{(1)}] - 1/2 \right|.$$

[15] Note that we no longer require sk^0 in this modified decapsulation oracle.

Remark 6. In Lemmas 8-12 below, we argue the indistinguishability of certain hybrids. We remark that the proofs of these lemmas are (almost) identical to those of [KMT19] and we briefly mention them to provide more context. The main technical part (namely Lemma 13) is where the proof significantly differs from its classical counterpart, which will appear subsequently.

Lemma 8. $|\Pr[W^{(2)}] - \Pr[W^{(3)}]| = 2 \cdot \mathbf{Adv}^{\text{mCPA}}_{\mathsf{KEM},n,\mathcal{B}^3_{cpa}}$ *for some QPT adversary* $\mathcal{B}^3_{cpa}$.

Proof (Sketch). In [KMT19, Lemma 2], an (essentially) equivalent result is shown but in the context of CCA security of $\overline{\mathsf{KEM}}$. In their reduction, a PPT adversary breaks CPA security of KEM by simulating (the CCA analogue of) Games 2 and 3 towards the underlying CCA adversary for $\overline{\mathsf{KEM}}$. It can be easily verified that their reduction can also be extended to the qCCA setting, because one can simulate the decapsulation oracles of Games 2 and 3 in quantum superposition given access to the secret key SK. As mentioned in Sect. 2, note that *any* function (in our case, $\overline{\mathsf{Decaps}}(\mathsf{SK}, \cdot)$) that has an efficient classical algorithm, can also be implemented efficiently as a quantum-accessible oracle.

Lemma 9. $|\Pr[W^{(3)}] - \Pr[W^{(4)}]| \leq 2\varepsilon + n \cdot 2^{-\lambda+1}$.

Proof (Sketch). In [KMT19, Lemma 3], it is shown that unless the public key PK generated at the start of the CCA game for $\overline{\mathsf{KEM}}$ is "bad" in a certain sense, the *classical* decapsulation oracles in (the CCA analogues of) Games 3 and 4 (namely, $\overline{\mathsf{Decaps}}(\mathsf{SK}, \cdot)$ and $\overline{\mathsf{AltDecaps}}(\mathsf{SK}', \cdot)$) are *identical.* It was also shown in [KMT19, Lemma 3] that the probability of choosing such a "bad" PK is bounded by $2\varepsilon + n \cdot 2^{-\lambda+1}$.

The analysis in [KMT19, Lemma 3] also applies to the qCCA setting. This is because the distribution of "bad" PKs at the start of the (q)CCA game (for $\overline{\mathsf{KEM}}$) is not in any way affected by the fact that whether the adversary $\mathcal{A}$ has quantum access to the corresponding decapsulation oracle in the rest of the game. Based on [KMT19, Lemma 3], if PK is not "bad", then for *any* ciphertext CT we must have $\overline{\mathsf{Decaps}}(\mathsf{SK}, \mathsf{CT}) = \overline{\mathsf{AltDecaps}}(\mathsf{SK}', \mathsf{CT})$; this means that provided PK is not "bad", the quantum decapsulation oracles in Games 3 and 4 are *identical.*

Lemma 10. $|\Pr[W^{(4)}] - \Pr[W^{(5)}]| = 2 \cdot \mathbf{Adv}^{\text{mCPA}}_{\mathsf{KEM},n,\mathcal{B}^4_{cpa}}$ *for some QPT adversary* $\mathcal{B}^4_{cpa}$.

Proof (Sketch). A similar reasoning to that of Lemma 8 applies here as well.

Lemma 11. $|\Pr[W^{(5)}] - \Pr[W^{(6)}]| = 2 \cdot \mathbf{Adv}^{\text{KDM}}_{\mathsf{SKE},\mathcal{P},\mathcal{B}_{kdm}}$ *for some QPT adversary* $\mathcal{B}_{kdm}$ *that makes a single KDM query.*

Proof (Sketch). In [KMT19, Lemma 5], an (essentially) equivalent result is shown for CCA security of $\overline{\mathsf{KEM}}$, wherein a PPT adversary breaks the one-time KDM security of SKE by simulating (the CCA analogue of) Games 5 and 6 towards the underlying CCA adversary for $\overline{\mathsf{KEM}}$. By a simple extension to the qCCA setting, it is easy to see that the reduction can also simulate the decapsulation oracles of Games 5 and 6 in quantum superposition towards $\mathcal{A}$ as it generates the corresponding secret key SK' by itself. (Note that the "alternative" secret key SK' is used to compute $\overline{\mathsf{AltDecaps}}(\mathsf{SK}',\cdot)$ in Games 5 and 6.)

Lemma 12. $\Pr[W^{(6)}] = 1/2$.

Proof (Sketch). In Game 6, the view of $\mathcal{A}$ is completely independent of the bit b (irrespective of whether it has quantum access to the decapsulation oracle).

We now focus on the main ingredient of the proof, which is to bound the quantity $|\Pr[W^{(1)}] - \Pr[W^{(2)}]|$. As mentioned earlier, here's where the proof differs significantly from its *classical* counterpart in [KMT19, Lemma 1]. Namely, in the qCCA setting, we argue about the *quantum* indistinguishability of the decapsulation oracles in Games 1 and 2 using Lemma 1, while following a similar "deferred analysis" approach as in [KMT19].

Lemma 13. *There exist QPT adversaries $\mathcal{B}_{tcr}$, $\mathcal{B}^1_{cpa}$, $\mathcal{B}^2_{cpa}$, and $\mathcal{B}'_{cpa}$ satisfying*

$$|\Pr[W^{(1)}] - \Pr[W^{(2)}]| \leq 2q\sqrt{\mathsf{Adv} + 10\varepsilon + n\cdot 2^{-4\lambda+1} + n\cdot 2^{-\lambda+1}}$$

where $\mathsf{Adv} = \mathbf{Adv}^{\mathrm{TCR}}_{\mathsf{Hash},\mathcal{B}_{tcr}} + 2\cdot(\mathbf{Adv}^{\mathrm{mCPA}}_{\mathsf{KEM},n,\mathcal{B}^1_{cpa}} + \mathbf{Adv}^{\mathrm{mCPA}}_{\mathsf{KEM},n,\mathcal{B}^2_{cpa}} + \mathbf{Adv}^{\mathrm{mCPA}}_{\mathsf{KEM},n,\mathcal{B}'_{cpa}})$.

Proof. Following the terminology of [KMT19], we call a decapsulation query $\mathsf{CT} = ((\mathsf{ct}^0_i, \mathsf{ct}^1_i, \mathbf{t}_i)_{i\in[n]}, \mathsf{ct}_{\mathsf{SKE}})$ of $\mathcal{A}$ in Game j (for some $j \in [4]$) *hash-bad* if

$$\mathbf{h} = \mathsf{H}(\mathsf{hk}, (\mathsf{ct}^0_i, \mathsf{ct}^1_i)_{i\in[n]} \parallel \mathsf{ct}_{\mathsf{SKE}}) = \hat{\mathbf{h}} \quad \text{and} \quad \overline{\mathsf{Decaps}}(\mathsf{SK},\mathsf{CT}) \neq \bot,$$

such that $\mathsf{CT} \neq \hat{\mathsf{CT}}$. Observe that the outputs of decapsulation oracles of Games 1 and 2 differ *exactly* in these hash-bad queries. We also categorize a hash-bad decapsulation query $\mathsf{CT} = ((\mathsf{ct}^0_i, \mathsf{ct}^1_i, \mathbf{t}_i)_{i\in[n]}, \mathsf{ct}_{\mathsf{SKE}})$ into the following two types:

- Type 1: $(\mathsf{ct}^0_i, \mathsf{ct}^1_i)_{i\in[n]} \parallel \mathsf{ct}_{\mathsf{SKE}} \neq (\hat{\mathsf{ct}}^0_i, \hat{\mathsf{ct}}^1_i)_{i\in[n]} \parallel \hat{\mathsf{ct}}_{\mathsf{SKE}}$
- Type 2: $(\mathsf{ct}^0_i, \mathsf{ct}^1_i)_{i\in[n]} \parallel \mathsf{ct}_{\mathsf{SKE}} = (\hat{\mathsf{ct}}^0_i, \hat{\mathsf{ct}}^1_i)_{i\in[n]} \parallel \hat{\mathsf{ct}}_{\mathsf{SKE}}$

We rely on Lemma 1 to bound the term $|\Pr[W^{(1)}] - \Pr[W^{(2)}]|$ as follows. First, let A be a quantum oracle algorithm which receives as input a public key $\mathsf{PK} = (\mathsf{pk}^0, \mathsf{pk}^1, (\mathbf{a}_i)_{i\in[n]}, \mathbf{c}, \mathsf{hk})$, the "real" encapsulated key $\hat{\kappa}_1 \in \{0,1\}^\ell$ and a challenge ciphertext $\hat{\mathsf{CT}} = ((\hat{\mathsf{ct}}^0_i, \hat{\mathsf{ct}}^1_i, \hat{\mathbf{t}}_i)_{i\in[n]}, \hat{\mathsf{ct}}_{\mathsf{SKE}})$ as generated in Game 1 above. A has quantum access either to the decapsulation oracle $G := \overline{\mathsf{Decaps}}(\mathsf{SK},\cdot)$ used in Game 1 (which also rejects ciphertexts equal to $\hat{\mathsf{CT}}$) or to the modified decapsulation oracle H used in Game 2. A proceeds to simulate either Game 1 or 2 towards $\mathcal{A}$ as follows: A samples a random key $\hat{\kappa}_0 \leftarrow \{0,1\}^\ell$ and a bit $b \leftarrow \{0,1\}$, and forwards $(\mathsf{PK}, \hat{\mathsf{CT}}, \hat{\kappa}_b)$ to $\mathcal{A}$. Then A responds to $\mathcal{A}$'s quantum decapsulation queries using its oracle (i.e., G or H). A outputs 1 iff $b' = b$.

By applying Lemma 1, it follows that $\Pr[W^{(1)}] = \Pr[1 \leftarrow A^G(z)]$ and $\Pr[W^{(2)}] = \Pr[1 \leftarrow A^H(z)]$. Thus we have $|\Pr[W^{(1)}] - \Pr[W^{(2)}]| \leq 2q\sqrt{P_{\text{guess}}}$

where P_{guess} is essentially the probability of the event when measurement of a random quantum decapsulation query made by $\mathcal{A}$ in Game 2 would result in a *hash-bad* ciphertext CT ($\neq \hat{\mathsf{CT}}$) defined above; i.e., $G(\mathsf{CT}) \neq H(\mathsf{CT})$.

For $(j, \mathsf{b}) \in [4] \times [2]$, let $M_j^{(\mathsf{b})}$ be the event that the measurement of a random i-th quantum decapsulation query made by $\mathcal{A}$ in Game j (where $i \leftarrow [q]$) results in a type b hash-bad ciphertext. (Note that $\Pr[M_2^{(1)}] + \Pr[M_2^{(2)}] = P_{\text{guess}}$.)

Based on Lemma 1, we have

$$|\Pr[W^{(1)}] - \Pr[W^{(2)}]| \leq 2q\sqrt{\Pr[M_2^{(1)}] + \Pr[M_2^{(2)}]}.$$

Observe that a type 1 hash-bad query can be used to break the target collision resistance of Hash. To see this, we construct a QPT adversary $\mathcal{B}_{tcr}$ such that $\Pr[M_2^{(1)}] = \mathbf{Adv}^{\text{TCR}}_{\mathsf{Hash},\mathcal{B}_{tcr}}$. First $\mathcal{B}_{tcr}$ generates the values $(\hat{\mathsf{ct}}_i^0, \hat{\mathsf{ct}}_i^1)_{i\in[n]}$ and $\hat{\mathsf{ct}}_{\mathsf{SKE}}$ by itself as in Game 2 and forwards $(\hat{\mathsf{ct}}_i^0, \hat{\mathsf{ct}}_i^1)_{i\in[n]} \parallel \hat{\mathsf{ct}}_{\mathsf{SKE}}$ to its TCR challenger (with respect to Hash). After obtaining a key hk from its challenger, $\mathcal{B}_{tcr}$ forwards the public key PK (which includes hk) along with the values $\hat{\mathsf{CT}}$, $\hat{\boldsymbol{\kappa}}_b$ to $\mathcal{A}$. Next, $\mathcal{B}_{tcr}$ samples $i \leftarrow [q]$ and proceeds to simulate the quantum decapsulation oracle of Game 2 towards $\mathcal{A}$. Observe that this is possible because $\mathcal{B}_{tcr}$ generates the secret key SK by itself. $\mathcal{B}_{tcr}$ then measures the i-th decapsulation query of $\mathcal{A}$ and forwards the measurement to its TCR challenger.

It remains to bound $\Pr[M_2^{(2)}]$. For type 2 hash-bad queries we have $\mathsf{CT} \neq \hat{\mathsf{CT}}$, and hence there exists a position $j \in [n]$ such that $\mathbf{t}_j \neq \hat{\mathbf{t}}_j$. For a type 2 hash-bad ciphertext $\mathsf{CT} = ((\hat{\mathsf{ct}}_i^0, \hat{\mathsf{ct}}_i^1, \mathbf{t}_i)_{i\in[n]}, \hat{\mathsf{ct}}_{\mathsf{SKE}})$, we define $S_{\mathsf{CT}} = \{j \in [n] \mid \mathbf{t}_j \neq \hat{\mathbf{t}}_j\}$. As in the proof of [KMT19, Lemma 1], we have the following for positions $i \in S_{\mathsf{CT}}$ *conditioned* on pk^0 and pk^1 not resulting in decapsulation errors:

- If $\hat{s}_i = 0$ (i.e., $i \in S_{\mathsf{CT}} \cap S_0$), then $\mathbf{t}_i - \mathbf{a}_i - \mathbf{c} \cdot \hat{\mathbf{h}} = \hat{\mathbf{k}}_i^1$, where $\hat{\mathbf{k}}_i^1$ is the encapsulated key corresponding to $\hat{\mathsf{ct}}_i^1$.
- If $\hat{s}_i = 1$ (i.e., $i \in S_{\mathsf{CT}} \cap S_1$), then $\mathbf{t}_i = \hat{\mathbf{k}}_i^0$, where $\hat{\mathbf{k}}_i^0$ is the encapsulated key corresponding to $\hat{\mathsf{ct}}_i^0$.

Consider the following categorization of type 2 queries into two sub-types:

- Type 2a: There exists a position $i \in S_{\mathsf{CT}} \cap S_0$.
- Type 2b: There exists a position $i \in S_{\mathsf{CT}} \cap S_1$.

For $j \in \{2, 3, 4\}$ and $\mathsf{b} \in \{2a, 2b\}$, let $M_j^{(\mathsf{b})}$ be the event that the measurement of a random i-th quantum query of $\mathcal{A}$ in Game j (where $i \leftarrow [q]$) results in a type b hash-bad decapsulation query. First, we have $\Pr[M_2^{(2)}] \leq \Pr[M_2^{(2a)}] + \Pr[M_2^{(2b)}]$. Towards bounding $\Pr[M_2^{(2)}]$, we first show that there exists a QPT adversary $\mathcal{B}_{cpa}^1$ that breaks the CPA security of KEM and satisfies

$$\Pr[M_2^{(2a)}] \leq 2 \cdot \mathbf{Adv}^{\text{mCPA}}_{\mathsf{KEM},n,\mathcal{B}_{cpa}^1} + 4\varepsilon + n \cdot 2^{-4\lambda}.$$

The description of $\mathcal{B}_{cpa}^1$ is as follows: on input $(\mathsf{pk}', (\hat{\mathsf{ct}}_i', \hat{\mathbf{k}}_{i,\beta}'))$ where the bit β is $\mathcal{B}_{cpa}^1$'s challenge bit, $\mathcal{B}_{cpa}^1$ first runs $\hat{\mathbf{s}} \leftarrow \mathsf{K}(1^\lambda)$, and sets $\mathsf{pk}^1 := \mathsf{pk}'$ and

$\hat{\mathsf{ct}}_i^1 := \hat{\mathsf{ct}}_i'$ for the positions $i \in S_0$. Next, $\mathcal{B}_{cpa}^1$ generates the remaining values of PK, SK, $\hat{\mathsf{CT}}$, and $\hat{\kappa}_b$ by itself as in Game 2 and forwards $(\mathsf{PK}, \hat{\mathsf{CT}}, \hat{\kappa}_b)$ to $\mathcal{A}$. Next, $\mathcal{B}_{cpa}^1$ samples $i \leftarrow [q]$ and proceeds to simulate the quantum decapsulation oracle of Game 2 towards $\mathcal{A}$ until the i-th decapsulation query; $\mathcal{B}_{cpa}^1$ measures the i-th query and checks if it is a type 2a hash-bad query CT.

- If the measurement results in a type 2a query $\mathsf{CT} = ((\hat{\mathsf{ct}}_i^0, \hat{\mathsf{ct}}_i^1, \mathbf{t}_i)_{i\in[n]}, \hat{\mathsf{ct}}_{\mathsf{SKE}})$, $\mathcal{B}_{cpa}^1$ checks if there is a position $i \in S_{\mathsf{CT}} \cap S_0$ such that $\mathbf{t}_i - \mathbf{a}_i - \mathbf{c} \cdot \hat{\mathbf{h}} = \hat{\mathbf{k}}_{i,\beta}'$. If so, $\mathcal{B}_{cpa}^1$ sets $\beta' = 1$. Otherwise, it sets $\beta' = 0$.
- If the measurement does not result in a type 2a query, then $\mathcal{B}_{cpa}^1$ sets $\beta' = 0$.

Finally, $\mathcal{B}_{cpa}^1$ terminates with the output β'.

Observe that $\mathcal{B}_{cpa}^1$ simulates Game 2 towards $\mathcal{A}$ (regardless of the challenge bit β) until the i-th quantum decapsulation query. Hence, the probability that the measurement of the i-th decapsulation query made by $\mathcal{A}$ results in a type 2a query is $\Pr[M_2^{(2a)}]$. Now recall from the above observation that conditioned on pk^0 and pk^1 not resulting in decapsulation errors, if the measurement results in a type 2a query $\mathsf{CT} = ((\hat{\mathsf{ct}}_i^0, \hat{\mathsf{ct}}_i^1, \mathbf{t}_i)_{i\in[n]}, \hat{\mathsf{ct}}_{\mathsf{SKE}})$, then $\mathbf{t}_i - \mathbf{a}_i - \mathbf{c} \cdot \hat{\mathbf{h}} = \hat{\mathbf{k}}_i^1$ holds for positions $i \in S_{\mathsf{CT}} \cap S_0$. Since $\mathcal{B}_{cpa}^1$ embeds each of its given challenge ciphertexts $\hat{\mathsf{ct}}_i'$ as $\hat{\mathsf{ct}}_i^1$ for the positions $i \in S_0$, if $\beta = 1$ (i.e., the keys $\hat{\mathbf{k}}_{i,\beta}'$ given to $\mathcal{B}_{cpa}^1$ are "real" encapsulated keys with respect to $\hat{\mathsf{ct}}_i'$), then we have $\hat{\mathbf{k}}_i^1 = \hat{\mathbf{k}}_{i,1}'$ for the positions $i \in S_0$. Thus, if $\beta = 1$, then there is at least one position $i \in S_{\mathsf{CT}} \cap S_0$ for which $\mathbf{t}_i - \mathbf{a}_i - \mathbf{c} \cdot \hat{\mathbf{h}} = \hat{\mathbf{k}}_i^1 = \hat{\mathbf{k}}_{i,1}'$ holds, and $\mathcal{B}_{cpa}^1$ outputs $\beta' = 1$ (conditioned on pk^0 and pk^1 not resulting in decapsulation errors). If we denote E to be the event that the sampled public keys pk^0 and pk^1 do result in decapsulation errors, then we have $\Pr[\beta' = 1 | \beta = 1 \wedge \neg E] = \Pr[M_2^{(2a)} | \neg E]$.

Similarly, if $\beta = 0$, then the keys $\hat{\mathbf{k}}_{i,0}'$ for every $i \in [n]$ are chosen uniformly from $\{0,1\}^{4\lambda}$ and are completely independent of $\mathcal{A}$'s view. Thus, the probability that there exists $i \in S_{CT} \cap S_0$ for which $\mathbf{t}_i - \mathbf{a}_i - \mathbf{c} \cdot \hat{\mathbf{h}} = \hat{\mathbf{k}}_{i,0}'$ holds (and $\mathcal{B}_{cpa}^1$ outputs $\beta' = 1$ when $\beta = 0$) is at most $n \cdot 2^{-4\lambda}$ by a union bound. Therefore, we have $\Pr[\beta' = 1 | \beta = 0] \leq n \cdot 2^{-4\lambda}$. It follows that

$$2 \cdot \mathbf{Adv}^{\mathrm{mCPA}}_{\mathsf{KEM},n,\mathcal{B}_{cpa}^1} = |\Pr[\beta' = 1 | \beta = 1] - \Pr[\beta' = 1 | \beta = 0]|.$$

Since KEM is ε-all-keys correct, we have $\Pr[E] \leq 2\varepsilon$. By a routine calculation we have

$$\begin{aligned}\Pr[\beta' = 1 | \beta = 1] &\geq \Pr[\beta' = 1 | \beta = 1 \wedge \neg E] - 2\varepsilon = \Pr[M_2^{(2a)} | \neg E] - 2\varepsilon \\ &\geq (\Pr[M_2^{(2a)}] - 2\varepsilon) - 2\varepsilon = \Pr[M_2^{(2a)}] - 4\varepsilon,\end{aligned}$$

and hence it follows that $2 \cdot \mathbf{Adv}^{\mathrm{mCPA}}_{\mathsf{KEM},n,\mathcal{B}_{cpa}^1} \geq \Pr[M_2^{(2a)}] - 4\varepsilon - n \cdot 2^{-4\lambda}$.

Next, we show how to bound $\Pr[M_2^{(2b)}]$. Here we use a "deferred analysis" approach, as in the proof of [KMT19, Lemma 1]. By triangle inequality we have

$$\Pr[M_2^{(2b)}] \leq \sum_{j \in \{2,3\}} \left| \Pr[M_j^{(2b)}] - \Pr[M_{j+1}^{(2b)}] \right| + \Pr[M_4^{(2b)}].$$

Here, with essentially the same argument as in the proof of Lemma 8, we have $|\Pr[M_2^{(2b)}] - \Pr[M_3^{(2b)}]| = 2 \cdot \mathbf{Adv}^{\mathrm{mCPA}}_{\mathsf{KEM},n,\mathcal{B}^2_{cpa}}$ for a QPT adversary $\mathcal{B}^2_{cpa}$. To be more specific, in the reduction, $\mathcal{B}^2_{cpa}$ samples a query index $i \leftarrow [q]$ and runs in exactly the same way as $\mathcal{B}^3_{cpa}$ in the proof of Lemma 8, until the i-th query made by $\mathcal{A}$; $\mathcal{B}^2_{cpa}$ instead measures the i-th query and returns 1 if and only if the measurement results in a type 2b hash-bad query CT, which can be checked since $\mathcal{B}^2_{cpa}$ has access to sk^0 (to check if $\overline{\mathsf{Decaps}}(\mathsf{SK}, \mathsf{CT}) \neq \perp$).

Similarly, with the same argument as in the proof of Lemma 9, we have $|\Pr[M_3^{(2b)}] - \Pr[M_4^{(2b)}]| \leq 2\varepsilon + n \cdot 2^{-\lambda+1}$. Finally, we show that there exists a QPT adversary $\mathcal{B}'_{cpa}$ that breaks the CPA security of KEM and satisfies

$$\Pr[M_4^{(2a)}] \leq 2 \cdot \mathbf{Adv}^{\mathrm{mCPA}}_{\mathsf{KEM},n,\mathcal{B}'_{cpa}} + 4\varepsilon + n \cdot 2^{-4\lambda}.$$

The description of $\mathcal{B}'_{cpa}$ is quite similar to that of $\mathcal{B}^1_{cpa}$ above: on input $(\mathsf{pk}', (\hat{\mathsf{ct}}'_i, \hat{\mathbf{k}}'_{i,\beta}))$, $\mathcal{B}'_{cpa}$ first runs $\hat{\mathbf{s}} \leftarrow \mathsf{K}(1^\lambda)$, and sets $\mathsf{pk}^0 = \mathsf{pk}'$ and $\hat{\mathsf{ct}}^0_i = \hat{\mathsf{ct}}'_i$ for positions $i \in S_1$. Next, $\mathcal{B}'_{cpa}$ generates the remaining values of PK, SK, $\hat{\mathsf{CT}}$, and $\hat{\kappa}_b$ by itself as in Game 4, and forwards $(\mathsf{PK}, \hat{\mathsf{CT}}, \hat{\kappa}_b)$ to $\mathcal{A}$. Next, $\mathcal{B}'_{cpa}$ samples $i \leftarrow [q]$ and simulates the quantum decapsulation oracle with respect to $\overline{\mathsf{AltDecaps}}(\mathsf{SK}', \cdot)$ in Game 4 towards $\mathcal{A}$ (note that $\mathcal{B}'_{cpa}$ has access to sk^1 which is sufficient to compute $\overline{\mathsf{AltDecaps}}(\mathsf{SK}', \cdot)$) until the i-th decapsulation query; $\mathcal{B}'_{cpa}$ measures the i-th query (and does *not* check if it is a type 2b query since $\mathcal{B}'_{cpa}$ does not have sk^0). Let the measured query be $\mathsf{CT} = ((\mathsf{ct}^0_i, \mathsf{ct}^1_i, \mathbf{t}_i)_{i \in [n]}, \mathsf{ct}_{\mathsf{SKE}})$. Finally, $\mathcal{B}'_{cpa}$ checks if there exists a position $i \in S_{\mathsf{CT}} \cap S_1$ such that $\mathbf{t}_i = \hat{\mathbf{k}}'_{i,\beta}$. If so, $\mathcal{B}'_{cpa}$ outputs $\beta' = 1$. Otherwise it outputs $\beta' = 0$.

As in the analysis of $\mathcal{B}^1_{cpa}$, observe that $\mathcal{B}'_{cpa}$ simulates Game 4 towards $\mathcal{A}$ (regardless of the challenge bit β) until the i-th quantum decapsulation query. Hence, the probability that the measurement of the i-th decapsulation query of $\mathcal{A}$ results in a type 2b query is $\Pr[M_2^{(2b)}]$. Recall from the above observation that conditioned on pk^0 and pk^1 not resulting in decapsulation errors, if the measurement results in a type 2b query $\mathsf{CT} = ((\hat{\mathsf{ct}}^0_i, \hat{\mathsf{ct}}^1_i, \mathbf{t}_i)_{i \in [n]}, \hat{\mathsf{ct}}_{\mathsf{SKE}})$, then $\mathbf{t}_i = \hat{\mathbf{k}}^0_i$ holds for positions $i \in S_{\mathsf{CT}} \cap S_1$. Since $\mathcal{B}'_{cpa}$ embeds each of its given challenge ciphertexts $\hat{\mathsf{ct}}'_i$ as $\hat{\mathsf{ct}}^0_i$ for the positions $i \in S_1$, if $\beta = 1$ then we have $\hat{\mathbf{k}}^0_i = \hat{\mathbf{k}}'_{i,1}$ for the positions $i \in S_1$. Thus, if $\beta = 1$ then there is at least one position $i \in S_{\mathsf{CT}} \cap S_1$ for which $\mathbf{t}_i = \hat{\mathbf{k}}^0_i = \hat{\mathbf{k}}'_{i,1}$ holds, and $\mathcal{B}^1_{cpa}$ outputs $\beta' = 1$ (conditioned on pk^0 and pk^1 not resulting in decapsulation errors). Let E denote the event that the sampled KEM public keys pk^0 and pk^1 do result in decapsulation errors, then we have $\Pr[\beta' = 1 | \beta = 1 \wedge \neg E] = \Pr[M_4^{(2b)} | \neg E]$.

Similarly, if $\beta = 0$, then the keys $\hat{\mathbf{k}}'_{i,0}$ for every $i \in [n]$ are chosen uniformly from $\{0,1\}^{4\lambda}$ and are completely independent of $\mathcal{A}$'s view. Thus, the probability that there exists $i \in S_{\mathsf{CT}} \cap S_1$ for which $\mathbf{t}_i = \hat{\mathbf{k}}'_{i,0}$ holds (and $\mathcal{B}'_{cpa}$ outputs $\beta' = 1$ when $\beta = 0$) is at most $n \cdot 2^{-4\lambda}$ by a union bound. Therefore, we have $\Pr[\beta' = 1 | \beta = 0] \leq n \cdot 2^{-4\lambda}$.

By a routine calculation as in the one for $\mathcal{B}^1_{cpa}$'s advantage above, we have[16]

$$2 \cdot \mathbf{Adv}^{\mathrm{mCPA}}_{\mathsf{KEM},n,\mathcal{B}'_{cpa}} \geq \Pr[M_4^{(2b)}] - 4\varepsilon - n \cdot 2^{-4\lambda}.$$

The desired bound in the lemma is obtained by putting the obtained bounds together, as required.

In the full version of our paper, we prove that qCCA-secure KEM implies qCCA-secure PKE by showing that the "hybrid" encryption (KEM-DEM) framework of Cramer and Shoup [CS03] results in a qCCA-secure PKE if a qCCA-secure KEM is composed with a *classical* (post-quantum) one-time authenticated encryption scheme.[17]

5 Quantum Adaptive Trapdoor Functions

In 2010, Kiltz *et al.* [KMO10] introduced the notion of *adaptive* TDFs (ATDFs) and they showed how to realize CCA-secure PKE from ATDFs. Informally, a TDF is said to be adaptive if it remains one way even if the adversary is given access to an inversion oracle. In this work, we introduce a *quantum* analogue of ATDFs, namely quantum ATDFs (qATDFs), which require one-wayness to hold even if the adversary has *quantum* access to an inversion oracle. In the first part, we formally define qATDFs and prove that they imply qCCA-secure PKE. Later, we show how qATDFs can be constructed from (post-quantum) correlated-product TDFs [RS09] or lossy TDFs [PW08], which in turn can be constructed from the LWE assumption.

Definition 3. *A trapdoor function* $\mathsf{TDF} = (\mathsf{Gen}, \mathsf{Eval}, \mathsf{Invert})$ *satisfies quantum adaptive security if for every QPT inverter* $\mathcal{A}$ *we have*

$$\mathbf{Adv}^{\mathrm{qATDF}}_{\mathcal{A}} = \Pr\left[x = x' : \begin{array}{c}(\mathit{ek}, \mathsf{td}) \leftarrow \mathsf{Gen}(1^\lambda); x \leftarrow \{0,1\}^\lambda \\ y^* \leftarrow \mathsf{Eval}(\mathit{ek}, x); x' \leftarrow \mathcal{A}^{|O_{y^*}(\mathsf{td},\cdot)\rangle}(\mathit{ek}, y^*)\end{array}\right] \leq \mathrm{negl}$$

where the function $O_{y^*}(\mathsf{td}, \cdot)$ *is defined as*

$$O_{y^*}(\mathsf{td}, y) = \begin{cases} \bot & \text{if } y = y^* \\ \mathsf{Invert}(\mathsf{td}, y) & \text{otherwise.} \end{cases}$$

(Similar to Definition 1, we also encode $\bot$ *to be a bitstring outside* $\{0,1\}^\lambda$ *in order to properly define the result "*$z \oplus \bot$*" in the output register of* $|O_{y^*}(\mathsf{td}, \cdot)\rangle$ *described above.)*

[16] It is worth pointing out that in the bounds obtained on the classical CCA analogue of "$\Pr[M_4^{(2b)}]$" in [KMT19, Lemma 1], there is a "$(1/q)$" multiplicative factor, since in their reduction, the CPA adversary (with respect to KEM) chooses one of $\mathcal{A}$'s decapsulation queries uniformly at random. However, we do not have such a factor in our bounds since by applying Lemma 1, we are already measuring one of $\mathcal{A}$'s decapsulation queries uniformly at random; i.e., this "random guessing" is accounted for in the definition of "P_{guess}" $= \Pr[M_4^{(2b)}]$.

[17] Such a scheme is implied by post-quantum one-way functions.

Note that adaptive one-wayness for TDFs defined in [KMO10] differs from Definition 3 only in the fact that $\mathcal{A}$ has *classical* access to the oracle $O_{y^*}(\mathsf{td}, \cdot)$. It's not hard to extend the separation result in [BZ13b, Subsection 4.1] to TDFs, which implies that our notion of qATDFs is *strictly* stronger than ATDFs.

5.1 Quantum CCA Security from Quantum ATDFs

Kiltz *et al.* [KMO10] showed a construction of *classically* CCA-secure PKE from any ATDF. We prove that the *same* construction results in a qCCA-secure PKE if the underlying ATDF satisfies quantum security. To be more specific, [KMO10] constructs a *single-bit* CCA-secure PKE from an ATDF and then relies on the "single-bit to multi-bit" compiler of [Ms09, HLW12]. In the quantum setting, we follow the same blueprint to first build a single-bit qCCA secure PKE from a qATDF, and then we show that the "single-bit to multi-bit" compiler of [HLW12] also extends to qCCA-secure PKE in the full version of our paper.

Let $\mathsf{TDF} = (\mathsf{Gen}, \mathsf{Eval}, \mathsf{Invert})$ be a TDF and $\mathrm{GL}(\cdot)$ be the corresponding Goldreich-Levin hardcore bit [GL89][18]. We construct a single-bit PKE scheme $\mathsf{PKE} = (\mathsf{Gen}, \mathsf{Enc}, \mathsf{Dec})$ as follows:

$\mathsf{Gen}(1^\lambda)$: Run $(\mathsf{ek}, \mathsf{td}) \leftarrow \mathsf{Gen}(1^\lambda)$, and set $(\mathsf{pk}, \mathsf{sk}) := (\mathsf{ek}, \mathsf{td})$. Return $(\mathsf{pk}, \mathsf{sk})$.
$\mathsf{Enc}(\mathsf{pk}, \mathsf{m})$: For $i = 1, \ldots, \lambda$, do:
$x \leftarrow \{0,1\}^\lambda$; $h \leftarrow \mathrm{GL}(x)$; if $h = \mathsf{m}$, return $\mathsf{Eval}(\mathsf{pk}, x)||0$.
Return $\mathsf{m}||1$.
$\mathsf{Dec}(\mathsf{sk}, \mathsf{ct})$: Parse $\mathsf{ct} \rightarrow (\mathsf{ct}_1||b)$ with $b \in \{0,1\}$. If $b = 1$, return ct_1, else return $\mathrm{GL}(\mathsf{Invert}(\mathsf{sk}, \mathsf{ct}_1))$.

Theorem 3. *If* TDF *is a qATDF, then* PKE *is a (single-bit) qCCA secure PKE.*

Proof. Let $\mathcal{A}$ be any QPT adversary that breaks the qCCA security of PKE while making q quantum decryption queries, where q_{pre}/q_{post} denotes the number of queries in the pre/post-challenge phase. Consider the following games:

Game 1: This is essentially the same as the qCCA game with respect to PKE, except for some changes in the setup.[19]

- Generate $(\mathsf{ek}, \mathsf{td}) \leftarrow \mathsf{Gen}(1^\lambda)$, and set $(\mathsf{pk}, \mathsf{sk}) := (\mathsf{ek}, \mathsf{td})$. Then for all $i \in [\lambda]$, generate tuples $\big((y_i, h_i)\big)_{i \in [\lambda]}$ where $y_i = \mathsf{Eval}(\mathsf{pk}, x_i)$ for uniformly random $x_i \leftarrow \{0,1\}^\lambda$ and $h_i = \mathrm{GL}(x_i)$. Also sample a random bit $b \leftarrow \{0,1\}$.

[18] It is not hard to see that the Goldreich-Levin theorem relating the one-wayness of a TDF to the hardcore bit security also applies when the TDF inverter and the bit distinguisher have *quantum* access to the corresponding TDF inversion oracle. This is because the probability-theoretic analysis in the original Goldreich-Levin theorem [GL89] is agnostic of any oracle access (be it classical or quantum) that the inverter and distinguisher have; the oracles would only be needed to ensure that the inverter can properly simulate the distinguisher's view.

[19] We "pre-compute" the randomness $(x_i)_{i \in [\lambda]}$ (used to encrypt $\mathcal{A}$'s chosen messages in the challenge phase) already in the *pre-challenge* phase. But this does not affect $\mathcal{A}$'s view in any way compared to the original qCCA game.

- Forward pk to the adversary $\mathcal{A}$ and respond to $\mathcal{A}$'s quantum decryption queries in the normal way using the description of $\mathsf{Dec}(\mathsf{sk}, \cdot)$ above.
- After receiving a pair of messages $(\mathsf{m}_0, \mathsf{m}_1)$ from $\mathcal{A}$, find the least $i^* \in [\lambda]$ such that $h_{i^*} = \mathsf{m}_b$. If no such i^* exists, compute the challenge ciphertext ct^* as $\mathsf{ct}^* := \mathsf{m}_b \parallel 1$; otherwise, set $\mathsf{ct}^* := y_{i^*} \parallel 0$.
- Again respond to $\mathcal{A}$'s quantum decryption queries in the normal way as above, but this time making sure to reject ciphertexts that are equal to ct^*.
- $\mathcal{A}$ then terminates with an output $b' \in \{0, 1\}$.

Game 2a: In this game, we modify the decryption oracle *post-challenge phase* such that it rejects ciphertexts (i.e., returns $\perp$) that are equal to $(y_i \parallel 0)$ for some $i \in [\lambda]$, in addition to rejecting ciphertexts equal to ct^*.[20]

Game 2b: In this game, we modify the decryption oracle *pre-challenge phase* such that it also rejects ciphertexts that are equal to $(y_i \parallel 0)$ for some $i \in [\lambda]$.

Game 3: In this game, we sample $h_i \leftarrow \{0, 1\}$, instead of "$h_i = \mathrm{GL}(x_i)$".

Game 4: During the computation of challenge ciphertext ct^*, when no $i^* \in [\lambda]$ satisfying $h_{i^*} = \mathsf{m}_b$ exists, we set $\mathsf{ct}^* := \perp$ (instead of "$\mathsf{ct}^* := \mathsf{m}_b \parallel 1$").

Now let's define $W^{(j)}$, for $j \in \{1, 2a, 2b, 3, 4\}$, to be the event when $\mathcal{A}$ succeeds in guessing the bit b (i.e., $b' = b$) in Game j. By definition, we have

$$\mathbf{Adv}^{\mathrm{qCCA}}_{\mathsf{PKE},\mathcal{A}} = \left| \Pr[W^{(1)}] - \frac{1}{2} \right|.$$

Quantum CCA security of the scheme PKE follows from the following lemmas.

Lemma 14. $|\Pr[W^{(1)}] - \Pr[W^{(2a)}]| \leq 2q_{post}\sqrt{\frac{\lambda}{2^{\lambda-1}}}$.

Proof. Here we use Lemma 1 to bound $|\Pr[W^{(1)}] - \Pr[W^{(2a)}]|$. We simulate the pre-challenge phase of Game 1 (and 2a) using a QPT algorithm A_{pre} which first receives as input a pair $(\mathsf{pk}, \mathsf{sk})$ and $((y_i, h_i))_{i \in [\lambda]}$ as generated in Game 1 (and 2a) above. A_{pre} proceeds to simulate the pre-challenge phase (using sk to respond to $\mathcal{A}$'s quantum decryption queries). After computing ct^*, (by applying Lemma 1) A_{pre} forwards the input $z = (((\mathsf{pk}, \mathsf{sk}), ((y_i, h_i))_{i \in [\lambda]}), \mathsf{ct}^*, b)$ to the oracle algorithm A_{post}. The algorithm A_{post} has quantum access either to the corresponding post-challenge decryption oracle $G := \mathsf{Dec}(\mathsf{sk}, \cdot)$ in Game 1 (which also rejects ciphertexts equal to ct^*) or to the modified post-challenge decryption oracle H in Game 2a (which additionally rejects non-challenge ciphertexts of the form $|c\rangle \in \{|y_i \parallel 0\rangle \mid i \in [\lambda]\}$). Note that the outputs of oracles G and H differ with respect to the set $S = \{\mathsf{ct} = (y_i \parallel 0) \mid i \in [\lambda] \wedge \mathsf{ct} \neq \mathsf{ct}^*\}$. Next, A_{post} proceeds to simulate the post-challenge phase of Game 1 or Game 2a towards $\mathcal{A}$ depending on whether it has access to G or H respectively by forwarding $\mathcal{A}$'s

[20] In contrast to qCCA security proofs in earlier sections (e.g., Sect. 3) here we're first modifying the decryption oracle in the post-challenge phase followed by the pre-challenge phase. This step is crucial in our analysis as will be seen later on.

quantum decryption queries to its own oracle (i.e., G or H) and returning the corresponding output. Finally, A_{post} outputs 1 if the output of $\mathcal{A}$ is b.

Observe that $\Pr[W^{(1)}] = \Pr[1 \leftarrow A^G_{post}(z)]$ and $\Pr[W^{(2a)}] = \Pr[1 \leftarrow A^H_{post}(z)]$. Thus we have $|\Pr[W^{(1)}] - \Pr[W^{(2a)}]| \leq 2q_{post}\sqrt{P_{\text{guess}}}$ where P_{guess} denotes the probability of the event when measurement of a random quantum decryption query made by $\mathcal{A}$ in the post-challenge phase of Game 1 results in a non-challenge ciphertext $\mathsf{ct} := (\mathsf{ct}_1 \parallel b) \in S$ ($b \in \{0,1\}$). To bound $P_{\text{guess}} := \Pr[(\mathsf{ct}_1 \parallel b) \in S]$, we consider $b = 0$ (if $b = 1$, the corresponding probability is zero). Now we have

$$\begin{aligned}\Pr[(\mathsf{ct}_1 \parallel 0) \in S] &\leq \Pr[\exists i \in [\lambda] \text{ s.t. } \mathsf{ct}_1 = y_i \wedge \mathsf{ct} \neq \mathsf{ct}^*] \\ &\leq \Pr[\exists i \in [\lambda] \text{ s.t. } \mathsf{ct}_1 = y_i \mid \mathsf{ct} \neq \mathsf{ct}^*].\end{aligned}$$

Consider the case when $\mathsf{ct}^* = y_{i^*} \parallel 0$ for some $i^* \in [\lambda]$. This means that for $i < i^*$, we have $\mathrm{GL}(x_i) = 1 - \mathsf{m}_b$. Here we use a *statistical* fact that conditioning on $\mathrm{GL}(x_i) = 1 - \mathsf{m}_b$ reduces the min-entropy of x_i by one bit. Hence, $\mathcal{A}$'s view in the post-challenge phase of Game 1 is independent of the values $((y_i, h_i))_{i^* < i \leq \lambda}$ (as well as the corresponding x_i's) and *conditionally* independent of the values $((y_i, h_i))_{1 \leq i < i^*}$, conditioned on $\mathrm{GL}(x_i) = 1 - \mathsf{m}_b$ (because the decryption oracle in Game 1 *does not* use the "y_i" values to reject ciphertexts yet). Therefore, to analyze $\Pr[\exists i \in [\lambda] \text{ s.t. } \mathsf{ct}_1 = y_i \mid \mathsf{ct}_1 \neq y_{i^*}]$, it's easier to consider the values $((y_i, h_i))_{i \in [\lambda]}$ being generated (with an appropriate distribution following the conditional independence noted above) *after* measuring $\mathcal{A}$'s decryption query to ct. Observe that after measurement, each x_i for $1 \leq i < i^*$ (resp., for $i^* < i \leq \lambda$) is sampled independently from an entropy source of $\lambda - 1$ bits (resp., λ bits). Moreover, since $\mathsf{Eval}(\mathsf{pk}, \cdot)$ is a bijection, the probability that any y_i ($i \in [\lambda]$) coincides with the measured ct_1 is at most $1/2^{\lambda-1}$. Hence by applying a union bound, we obtain that $\Pr[\exists i \in [\lambda] \text{ s.t. } \mathsf{ct}_1 = y_i \mid \mathsf{ct}_1 \neq y_{i^*}] \leq (\lambda - 1) \cdot \frac{1}{2^{\lambda-1}}$.

Similarly, if $\mathsf{ct}^* = \mathsf{m}_b \parallel 1$ we have $\mathrm{GL}(x_i) = 1 - \mathsf{m}_b$ for all $i \in [\lambda]$. Hence, $\mathcal{A}$'s view in the post-challenge phase of Game 1 is *conditionally* independent of the values $((y_i, h_i))_{i \in [\lambda]}$, conditioned on $\mathrm{GL}(x_i) = 1 - \mathsf{m}_b$. This time, after measuring $\mathcal{A}$'s random decryption query to ct, we have each x_i ($i \in [\lambda]$) to be sampled independently from an entropy source of $\lambda - 1$ bits. Therefore, by a similar analysis as above, we have $\Pr[\exists i \in [\lambda] \text{ s.t. } \mathsf{ct}_1 = y_i \mid \mathsf{ct} \neq (\mathsf{m}_b \parallel 1)] \leq \lambda \cdot \frac{1}{2^{\lambda-1}}$. Hence, from an averaging argument, we finally obtain that $P_{\text{guess}} \leq \lambda \cdot \frac{1}{2^{\lambda-1}}$.

Lemma 15. $|\Pr[W^{(2a)}] - \Pr[W^{(2b)}]| \leq 2q_{pre}\sqrt{\frac{\lambda}{2^\lambda}}$.

Proof. We again use Lemma 1 as above to bound $|\Pr[W^{(2a)}] - \Pr[W^{(2b)}]|$. Let A be a quantum oracle algorithm which receives as input a pair $(\mathsf{pk}, \mathsf{sk})$ and $((y_i, h_i))_{i \in [\lambda]}$ as generated in Game 2a (and 2b) above; $z = ((\mathsf{pk}, \mathsf{sk}), \langle (y_i, h_i) \rangle_{i \in [\lambda]})$. A also has quantum access to either the corresponding pre-challenge decryption oracle $G := \mathsf{Dec}(\mathsf{sk}, \cdot)$ in Game 2a or to the oracle H in Game 2b (which rejects ciphertexts $|c\rangle \in \{|y_i \parallel 0\rangle \mid i \in [\lambda]\}$). Note that the outputs of oracles G and H differ with respect to the set $S = \{\mathsf{ct} = (y_i \parallel 0) \mid i \in [\lambda]\}$. Using its input z, A proceeds to simulate either Game 2a or 2b towards $\mathcal{A}$

depending on whether it has access to G or H, respectively. It is worth mentioning that A responds to $\mathcal{A}$'s quantum decryption queries in the pre-challenge phase using its own oracle (i.e., G or H), while in the post-challenge phase, A uses the secret key sk for quantum decryption while rejecting ciphertexts equal to $(y_i \parallel 0)$ for some $i \in [\lambda]$ or equal to ct^*. Finally A outputs 1 if and only if the output of $\mathcal{A}$ equals b.

Similar to the previous case, we have $|\Pr[W^{(2a)}] - \Pr[W^{(2b)}]| \leq 2q_{pre}\sqrt{P_{\text{guess}}}$ where P_{guess} is essentially the probability of the event when measurement of a random quantum decryption query made by $\mathcal{A}$ in the pre-challenge phase of Game 2a results in a ciphertext $(\mathsf{ct}_1 \parallel b) \in S$ $(b \in \{0,1\})$. To bound P_{guess}, note that $\mathcal{A}$'s view in the pre-challenge phase of Game 2a is completely independent of the values $((y_i, h_i))_{i\in[\lambda]}$ (as well as the corresponding x_i's) because these values are *only* used starting from the challenge phase. Hence to analyze the term $\Pr[(\mathsf{ct}_1 \parallel b) \in S]$, it's easier to consider the values $((y_i, h_i))_{i\in[\lambda]}$ being generated *after* measuring $\mathcal{A}$'s decryption query to $(\mathsf{ct}_1 \parallel b)$. In the rest of this analysis, we consider $b = 0$ (if $b = 1$, the corresponding probability is zero). After measurement, each x_i $(i \in [\lambda])$ is sampled independently from an entropy source of λ bits. Since $\mathsf{Eval}(\mathsf{pk}, \cdot)$ is a bijection, the probability that any y_i coincides with the measured ct_1 is $1/2^\lambda$. By applying a union bound, we get $P_{\text{guess}} \leq \lambda \cdot 2^{-\lambda}$.

Remark 7. If we modify the decryption oracle in the pre-challenge phase first followed by the post-challenge phase, then we cannot use a similar argument as in the proof of Lemma 14 to claim that $\mathcal{A}$'s view in the post-challenge phase is (conditionally) independent of the values $((y_i, h_i))_{i\in[\lambda]}$ (and that we can generate the values $((y_i, h_i))_{i\in[\lambda]}$ *after* measuring $\mathcal{A}$'s decryption query in post-challenge phase). To see this, note that because of our prior modification to the decryption oracle in pre-challenge phase, the values $((y_i, h_i))_{i\in[\lambda]}$ are implicitly generated to be used to reject ciphertexts, and hence $\mathcal{A}$'s view in the pre-challenge (and post-challenge) phase would then depend on these values.

Lemma 16. *There exists a QPT hardcore-bit distinguisher $\mathcal{D}$ with respect to $GL(\cdot)$ such that* $|\Pr[W^{(2b)}] - \Pr[W^{(3)}]| = 2 \cdot \mathbf{Adv}^{\text{hcDist}}_{GL,\mathcal{D}}$.

Proof. The description of $\mathcal{D}$ is as follows: It gets as input $(\mathsf{ek}, ((y_i, h_i))_{i\in[\lambda]})$ where $y_i = \mathsf{Eval}(\mathsf{ek}, x_i)$ for $x_i \leftarrow \{0,1\}^\lambda$, and either $h_i = \mathrm{GL}(x_i)$ or $h_i \leftarrow \{0,1\}$; D also has quantum access to an oracle O implementing the function $\mathsf{Invert}(\mathsf{td}, \cdot)$ but which also rejects inputs equal to y_i (i.e., returns $\perp$) for some $i \in [\lambda]$. $\mathcal{D}$ then proceeds to simulate either Game 2b or Game 3 by forwarding ek to $\mathcal{A}$ and responding to $\mathcal{A}$'s quantum decryption queries as in Game 2b (and 3) using the oracle O. $\mathcal{D}$ also uses $((y_i, h_i))_{i\in[\lambda]})$ to compute the challenge ciphertext ct^* (after first sampling a bit $b \leftarrow \{0,1\}$). Finally, when $\mathcal{A}$ terminates with a bit b', $\mathcal{D}$ outputs 1 if $b = b'$ and outputs 0 otherwise.

Observe that $\Pr[1 \leftarrow \mathcal{D}(\mathsf{ek}, ((y_i, h_i))_{i\in[\lambda]}) | h_i = \mathrm{GL}(x_i)] = \Pr[W^{(2b)}]$ and $\Pr[1 \leftarrow \mathcal{D}(\mathsf{ek}, ((y_i, h_i))_{i\in[\lambda]}) | h_i \leftarrow \{0,1\}] = \Pr[W^{(3)}]$. Therefore, we have

$$|\Pr[W^{(2b)}] - \Pr[W^{(3)}]| = 2 \cdot \mathbf{Adv}^{\text{hcDist}}_{\text{GL},\mathcal{D}}.$$

Lemma 17. $|\Pr[W^{(3)}] - \Pr[W^{(4)}]| \leq 2^{-\lambda}$.

Proof. Note that Games 3 and 4 proceed identically unless there does not exist an $i^* \in [\lambda]$ such that $h_{i^*} = \mathsf{m}_b$, which happens with probability $2^{-\lambda}$.

Lemma 18. $\Pr[W^{(4)}] = 1/2$.

Proof. In Game 4, note that $\mathcal{A}$'s view is completely independent of the bit b.

5.2 Quantum ATDFs from Correlated-Product TDFs

In this section, we show that the ATDF construction of Kiltz *et al.* [KMO10] from correlated-product TDFs (CP-TDFs) satisfies *quantum* security if the underlying CP-TDF is post-quantum secure, i.e., we prove that (post-quantum) CP-TDFs are sufficient to realize quantum ATDFs. We recall the definition of CP-TDFs from [RS09].

Definition 4. *A trapdoor function* $\mathsf{TDF} = (\mathsf{Gen}, \mathsf{Eval}, \mathsf{Invert})$ *is one-way under t-correlated-product (i.e., t-CP-TDF) if for every QPT inverter* $\mathcal{A}$*, it holds that*

$$\mathbf{Adv}^{\mathrm{CPOW}}_{\mathsf{TDF},\mathcal{A}} = \Pr[x' = x : x' \leftarrow \mathcal{A}((ek_i)_{i\in[t]}, \mathbf{y}^*)] \leq \mathrm{negl},$$

where $(ek_i, \mathsf{td}_i) \leftarrow \mathsf{Gen}(1^\lambda)$ *for* $i \in [t]$, $x \leftarrow \{0,1\}^\lambda$, *and* $\mathbf{y}^* = (\mathsf{Eval}(ek_i, x))_{i\in[t]}$.

Let $\mathsf{TDF} = (\mathsf{Gen}, \mathsf{Eval}, \mathsf{Invert})$ be a TDF with fixed output length $n = n(\lambda)$. Now we recall the construction of ATDF $\overline{\mathsf{TDF}} = (\overline{\mathsf{Gen}}, \overline{\mathsf{Eval}}, \overline{\mathsf{Invert}})$ from TDF in [KMO10] as follows:

$\overline{\mathsf{Gen}}(1^\lambda)$: Let $(\mathsf{ek}_0, \mathsf{td}_0) \leftarrow \mathsf{Gen}(1^\lambda)$. Sample $(\mathsf{ek}_i^b, \mathsf{td}_i^b) \leftarrow \mathsf{Gen}(1^\lambda)$ for $i \in [n]$ and $b \in \{0,1\}$. Output $(\mathsf{ek}, \mathsf{td})$ where

$$\mathsf{ek} := (\mathsf{ek}_0, ((\mathsf{ek}_i^0, \mathsf{ek}_i^1))_{i\in[n]}), \quad \mathsf{td} := (\mathsf{td}_0, ((\mathsf{td}_i^0, \mathsf{td}_i^1))_{i\in[n]}).$$

$\overline{\mathsf{Eval}}(\mathsf{ek}, x)$: Output $(\mathsf{Eval}(\mathsf{ek}_0, x) \parallel \mathsf{Eval}(\mathsf{ek}_1^{\mathsf{b}_1}, x) \parallel \ldots \parallel \mathsf{Eval}(\mathsf{ek}_n^{\mathsf{b}_n}, x))$, where b_i denotes the i-th bit of $\mathsf{b} := \mathsf{Eval}(\mathsf{ek}_0, x)$ for $i \in [n]$.

$\overline{\mathsf{Invert}}(\mathsf{td}, y)$: Parse $y \rightarrow (\mathsf{b} \parallel y_1 \parallel \ldots \parallel y_n)$. Let $x \leftarrow \mathsf{Invert}(\mathsf{td}_0, \mathsf{b})$. Return x if $x = \mathsf{Invert}(\mathsf{td}_i^{\mathsf{b}_i}, y_i)$ for all $i \in [n]$. Otherwise, return $\perp$.

Theorem 4. *If* TDF *is an* $(n+1)$*-CP-TDF, then* $\overline{\mathsf{TDF}}$ *is a quantum ATDF.*

Proof. We provide a sketch since the proof follows closely to that of [KMO10, Theorem 3]. Given any efficient inverter $\mathcal{A}$ breaking the adaptive one-wayness of $\overline{\mathsf{TDF}}$, they describe an efficient inverter $\mathcal{B}$ breaking the one-wayness under $(n+1)$-correlated-product of TDF. In their reduction, $\mathcal{B}$ simulates the adaptive one-wayness game with respect to $\overline{\mathsf{TDF}}$ towards $\mathcal{A}$ since it is able to (classically) implement the $\overline{\mathsf{TDF}}$ inversion functionality using some trapdoor information. It's easy to see that their reduction can be extended to the *quantum* setting since $\mathcal{B}$ can also simulate this $\overline{\mathsf{TDF}}$ inversion oracle in quantum superposition using the same trapdoor information (we're using the fact, mentioned in Sect. 2, that any function which has an efficient classical algorithm computing it can be implemented efficiently as a quantum-accessible oracle).

Quantum ATDF from LWE. We briefly describe two ways to instantiate quantum ATDFs from the LWE assumption. For the first approach, recall that Rosen and Segev [RS09] showed lossy TDFs imply TDFs with correlated security. By pluggin the LWE-based lossy TDF construction of [PW08] and relying on our construction of quantum ATDFs from TDFs with correlated security, we get an instantiation of quantum ATDFs from the LWE assumption. An alternative (and more efficient) approach is to rely on the LWE-based TDF construction of [MP13] (which also satisfies correlated security), which in turn yields a construction of quantum ATDF from LWE (based on our generic transformation).

References

[ABB10] Agrawal, S., Boneh, D., Boyen, X.: Efficient lattice (H)IBE in the standard model. In: Gilbert, H. (ed.) EUROCRYPT 2010. LNCS, vol. 6110, pp. 553–572. Springer, Heidelberg (2010). https://doi.org/10.1007/978-3-642-13190-5_28

[ACPS09] Applebaum, B., Cash, D., Peikert, C., Sahai, A.: Fast cryptographic primitives and circular-secure encryption based on hard learning problems. In: Halevi, S. (ed.) CRYPTO 2009. LNCS, vol. 5677, pp. 595–618. Springer, Heidelberg (2009)

[ADMP20] Alamati, N., De Feo, L., Montgomery, H., Patranabis, S.: Cryptographic group actions and applications. In: Moriai, S., Wang, H. (eds.) ASIACRYPT 2020. Part II, volume 12492 of LNCS, pp. 411–439. Springer, Heidelberg (2020)

[AHU19] Ambainis, A., Hamburg, M., Unruh, D.: Quantum security proofs using semi-classical oracles. In: Boldyreva, A., Micciancio, D. (eds.) CRYPTO 2019. Part II, volume 11693 of LNCS, pp. 269–295. Springer, Heidelberg (2019)

[AQY22] Ananth, P., Qian, L., Yuen, H.: Cryptography from pseudorandom quantum states. In: Dodis, Y., Shrimpton, T. (eds.) CRYPTO 2022. Part I, volume 13507 of LNCS, pp. 208–236. Springer, Heidelberg (2022)

[BBBV97] Bennett, C.H., Bernstein, E., Brassard, G., Vazirani, U.: Strengths and weaknesses of quantum computing. SIAM J. Comput. **26**(5), 1510–1523 (1997)

[BBC+21] Bhaumik, R., et al.: QCB: efficient quantum-secure authenticated encryption. In: Tibouchi, M., Wang, H. (eds.) ASIACRYPT 2021. Part I, volume 13090 of LNCS, pp. 668–698. Springer, Heidelberg (2021)

[BCHK07] Boneh, D., Canetti, R., Halevi, S., Katz, J.: Chosen-ciphertext security from identity-based encryption. SIAM J. Comput. **36**(5), 1301–1328 (2007)

[BCKM21] Bartusek, J., Coladangelo, A., Khurana, D., Ma, F.: On the round complexity of secure quantum computation. In: Malkin, T., Peikert, C. (eds.) CRYPTO 2021. LNCS, vol. 12825, pp. 406–435. Springer, Cham (2021). https://doi.org/10.1007/978-3-030-84242-0_15

[BDF+11] Boneh, D., Dagdelen, Ö., Fischlin, M., Lehmann, A., Schaffner, C., Zhandry, M.: Random oracles in a quantum world. In: Lee, D.H., Wang, X. (eds.) ASIACRYPT 2011. LNCS, vol. 7073, pp. 41–69. Springer, Heidelberg (2011). https://doi.org/10.1007/978-3-642-25385-0_3

[BJSW16] Broadbent, A., Ji, Z., Song, F., Watrous, J.: Zero-knowledge proof systems for QMA. In: Dinur, I., editor, 57th FOCS, pp. 31–40. IEEE Computer Society Press (2016)

[BMW23] Barooti, K., Malavolta, G., Walter, M.: A simple construction of quantum public-key encryption from quantum-secure one-way functions. Cryptology ePrint Archive, Report 2023/306 (2023). https://eprint.iacr.org/2023/306

[BZ13a] Boneh, D., Zhandry, M.: Quantum-secure message authentication codes. In: Johansson, T., Nguyen, P.Q. (eds.) EUROCRYPT 2013. LNCS, vol. 7881, pp. 592–608. Springer, Heidelberg (2013)

[BZ13b] Boneh, D., Zhandry, M.: Secure signatures and chosen ciphertext security in a quantum computing world. In: Canetti, R., Garay, J.A. (eds.) CRYPTO 2013. LNCS, vol. 8043, pp. 361–379. Springer, Heidelberg (2013). https://doi.org/10.1007/978-3-642-40084-1_21

[CEV22] Chevalier, C., Ebrahimi, E., Vu, Q.H.: On security notions for encryption in a quantum world. In: Isobe, T., Sarkar, S., editors, INDOCRYPT 2022, vol. 13774 of LNCS, pp. 592–613. Springer (2022). https://doi.org/10.1007/978-3-031-22912-1_26

[CLM+18] Castryck, W., Lange, T., Martindale, C., Panny, L., Renes, J.: CSIDH: an efficient post-quantum commutative group action. In: Peyrin, T., Galbraith, S. (eds.) ASIACRYPT 2018. Part III, volume 11274 of LNCS, pp. 395–427. Springer, Heidelberg (2018)

[Col23] Coladangelo, A.: Quantum trapdoor functions from classical one-way functions. Cryptology ePrint Archive, Report 2023/282 (2023). https://eprint.iacr.org/2023/282

[CS02] Cramer, R., Shoup, V.: Universal hash proofs and a paradigm for adaptive chosen ciphertext secure public-key encryption. In: Knudsen, L.R., editor, EUROCRYPT 2002, volume 2332 of LNCS, pp. 45–64. Springer, Heidelberg (2002). https://doi.org/10.1007/3-540-46035-7_4

[CS03] Cramer, R., Shoup, V.: Design and analysis of practical public-key encryption schemes secure against adaptive chosen ciphertext attack. SIAM J. Comput. **33**(1), 167–226 (2003)

[DDN91] Dolev, D., Dwork, C., Naor, M.: Non-malleable cryptography (extended abstract). In: 23rd ACM STOC, pp. 542–552. ACM Press (1991)

[DFMS22] Don, J., Fehr, S., Majenz, C., Schaffner, C.: Online-extractability in the quantum random-oracle model. In: Dunkelman, O., Dziembowski, S., editors, EUROCRYPT 2022, Part III, vol. 13277 of LNCS, pp. 677–706. Springer, Heidelberg (2022). https://doi.org/10.1007/978-3-031-07082-2_24

[FKS+13] Fehr, S., Katz, J., Song, F., Zhou, H.-S., Zikas, V.: Feasibility and completeness of cryptographic tasks in the quantum world. In: Sahai, A. (ed.) TCC 2013. LNCS, vol. 7785, pp. 281–296. Springer, Heidelberg (2013). https://doi.org/10.1007/978-3-642-36594-2_16

[FO13] Fujisaki, E., Okamoto, T.: Secure integration of asymmetric and symmetric encryption schemes. J. Cryptol. **26**(1), 80–101 (2013)

[GL89] Goldreich, O., Levin, L.A.: A hard-core predicate for all one-way functions. In 21st ACM STOC, pp. 25–32. ACM Press (1989)

[GSV23] Grilo, A.B., Sattath, O., Vu, Q.-H.: Encryption with quantum public keys. Cryptology ePrint Archive, Report 2023/345 (2023). https://eprint.iacr.org/2023/345

[HKW20] Hohenberger, S., Koppula, V., Waters, B.: Chosen ciphertext security from injective trapdoor functions. In: Micciancio, D., Ristenpart, T. (eds.) CRYPTO 2020. Part I, volume 12170 of LNCS, pp. 836–866. Springer, Heidelberg (2020). https://doi.org/10.1007/978-3-030-56784-2_28

[HLLG19] Han, S., Liu, S., Lyu, L., Dawu, G.: Tight leakage-resilient CCA-security from quasi-adaptive hash proof system. In: Boldyreva, A., Micciancio, D. (eds.) CRYPTO 2019. Part II, volume 11693 of LNCS, pp. 417–447. Springer, Heidelberg (2019). https://doi.org/10.1007/978-3-030-26951-7_15

[HLW12] Hohenberger, S., Lewko, A.B., Waters, B.: Detecting dangerous queries: a new approach for chosen ciphertext security. In: Pointcheval, D., Johansson, T. (eds.) EUROCRYPT 2012. LNCS, vol. 7237, pp. 663–681. Springer, Heidelberg (2012)

[KMO10] Kiltz, E., Mohassel, P., O'Neill, A.: Adaptive trapdoor functions and chosen-ciphertext security. In: Gilbert, H. (ed.) EUROCRYPT 2010. LNCS, vol. 6110, pp. 673–692. Springer, Heidelberg (2010). https://doi.org/10.1007/978-3-642-13190-5_34

[KMP14] Kiltz, E., Masny, D., Pietrzak, K.: Simple chosen-ciphertext security from low-noise LPN. In: Krawczyk, H. (ed.) PKC 2014. LNCS, vol. 8383, pp. 1–18. Springer, Heidelberg (2014). https://doi.org/10.1007/978-3-642-54631-0_1

[KMT19] Kitagawa, F., Matsuda, T., Tanaka, K.: CCA security and trapdoor functions via key-dependent-message security. In: Boldyreva, A., Micciancio, D. (eds.) CRYPTO 2019. Part III, volume 11694 of LNCS, pp. 33–64. Springer, Heidelberg (2019). https://doi.org/10.1007/978-3-030-26954-8_2

[KNY21] Kitagawa, F., Nishimaki, R., Yamakawa, T.: Secure software leasing from standard assumptions. In: Nissim, K., Waters, B. (eds.) TCC 2021. Part I, volume 13042 of LNCS, pp. 31–61. Springer, Heidelberg (2021). https://doi.org/10.1007/978-3-030-90459-3_2

[KW19] Koppula, V., Waters, B.: Realizing chosen ciphertext security generically in attribute-based encryption and predicate encryption. In: Boldyreva, A., Micciancio, D. (eds.) CRYPTO 2019. Part II, volume 11693 of LNCS, pp. 671–700. Springer, Heidelberg (2019). https://doi.org/10.1007/978-3-030-26951-7_23

[LW21] Liu, X., Wang, M.: QCCA-secure generic key encapsulation mechanism with tighter security in the quantum random oracle model. In: Garay, J. (ed.) PKC 2021. Part I, volume 12710 of LNCS, pp. 3–26. Springer, Heidelberg (2021). https://doi.org/10.1007/978-3-030-75245-3_1

[MP13] Micciancio, D., Peikert, C.: Hardness of SIS and LWE with small parameters. In: Canetti, R., Garay, J.A. (eds.) CRYPTO 2013. Part I, volume 8042 of LNCS, pp. 21–39. Springer, Heidelberg (2013). https://doi.org/10.1007/978-3-642-40041-4_2

[Ms09] Myers, S., Shelat, A.: Bit encryption is complete. In: 50th FOCS, pp. 607–616. IEEE Computer Society Press (2009)

[MY22a] Morimae, T., Yamakawa, T.: One-Wayness in quantum cryptography. Cryptology ePrint Archive, Report 2022/1336 (2022). https://eprint.iacr.org/2022/1336

[MY22b] Morimae, T., Yamakawa, T.: Quantum commitments and signatures without one-way functions. In: Dodis, Y., Shrimpton, T. (eds.) CRYPTO 2022. Part I, volume 13507 of LNCS, pp. 269–295. Springer, Heidelberg (2022). https://doi.org/10.1007/978-3-031-15802-5_10

[NC00] Nielsen, M., Chuang, I.: Quantum Computation and Quantum Information. Cambridge University Press, Cambridge (2000)

[NY90] Naor, M., Yung, M.: Public-key cryptosystems provably secure against chosen ciphertext attacks. In: 22nd ACM STOC, pp. 427–437. ACM Press (1990)

[PW08] Peikert, C., Waters, B.: Lossy trapdoor functions and their applications. In: Ladner, R.E., Dwork, C., editors, 40th ACM STOC, pp. 187–196. ACM Press (2008)

[Rom90] Rompel, J.: One-way functions are necessary and sufficient for secure signatures. In: 22nd ACM STOC, pp. 387–394. ACM Press (1990)

[RS92] Rackoff, C., Simon, D.R.: Non-interactive zero-knowledge proof of knowledge and chosen ciphertext attack. In: Feigenbaum, J. (ed.) CRYPTO'91. LNCS, vol. 576, pp. 433–444. Springer, Heidelberg (1992). https://doi.org/10.1007/3-540-46766-1_35

[RS09] Rosen, A., Segev, G.: Chosen-ciphertext security via correlated products. In: Reingold, O. (ed.) TCC 2009. LNCS, vol. 5444, pp. 419–436. Springer, Heidelberg (2009). https://doi.org/10.1007/978-3-642-00457-5_25

[RZ21] Roberts, B., Zhandry, M.: Franchised quantum money. In: Tibouchi, M., Wang, H. (eds.) ASIACRYPT 2021. Part I, volume 13090 of LNCS, pp. 549–574. Springer, Heidelberg (2021). https://doi.org/10.1007/978-3-030-92062-3_19

[SGX23] Shan, T., Ge, J., Xue, R.: Qcca-secure generic transformations in the quantum random oracle model. In: Boldyreva, A., Kolesnikov, V., editors, PKC 2023, Part I, volume 13940 of LNCS, pp. 36–64. Springer (2023). https://doi.org/10.1007/978-3-031-31368-4_2

[Sho98] Shoup, V.: Why chosen ciphertext security matters (1998). IBM TJ Watson Research Center

[Unr14] Unruh, D.: Revocable quantum timed-release encryption. In: Nguyen, P.Q., Oswald, E. (eds.) EUROCRYPT 2014. LNCS, vol. 8441, pp. 129–146. Springer, Heidelberg (2014). https://doi.org/10.1007/978-3-642-55220-5_8

[Unr20] Unruh, D.: Post-quantum verification of Fujisaki-Okamoto. In: Moriai, S., Wang, H. (eds.) ASIACRYPT 2020. Part I, volume 12491 of LNCS, pp. 321–352. Springer, Heidelberg (2020). https://doi.org/10.1007/978-3-030-64837-4_11

[XY19] Xagawa, K., Yamakawa, T.: (Tightly) QCCA-secure key-encapsulation mechanism in the quantum random oracle model. In: Ding, J., Steinwandt, R. (eds.) Post-Quantum Cryptography - 10th International Conference. PQCrypto 2019, pp. 249–268. Springer, Heidelberg (2019). https://doi.org/10.1007/978-3-030-25510-7_14

[Zha12] Zhandry, M.: How to construct quantum random functions. In: 53rd FOCS, pp. 679–687. IEEE Computer Society Press (2012)

[Zha19] Zhandry, M.: How to record quantum queries, and applications to quantum indifferentiability. In: Boldyreva, A., Micciancio, D. (eds.) CRYPTO 2019. Part II, volume 11693 of LNCS, pp. 239–268. Springer, Heidelberg (2019). https://doi.org/10.1007/978-3-030-26951-7_9

Parameter-Hiding Order-Revealing Encryption Without Pairings

Cong Peng[1], Rongmao Chen[2](✉), Yi Wang[2], Debiao He[1](✉), and Xinyi Huang[3]

[1] Key Laboratory of Aerospace Information Security and Trusted Computing, Ministry of Education, School of Cyber Science and Engineering, Wuhan University, Wuhan, China
cpeng@whu.edu.cn, hedebiao@163.com

[2] School of Computer, National University of Defense Technology, Changsha, China
{chromao,wangyi14}@nudt.edu.cn

[3] The Hong Kong University of Science and Technology (Guangzhou), Guangzhou, China
xinyi@ust.hk

Abstract. Order-Revealing Encryption (ORE) provides a practical solution for conducting range queries over encrypted data. Achieving a desirable privacy-efficiency tradeoff in designing ORE schemes has posed a significant challenge. At Asiacrypt 2018, Cash et al. proposed Parameter-hiding ORE (pORE), which specifically targets scenarios where the data distribution shape is known, but the underlying parameters (such as mean and variance) need to be protected. However, existing pORE constructions rely on impractical bilinear maps, limiting their real-world applicability. In this work, we propose an alternative and efficient method for constructing pORE using identification schemes. By leveraging the map-invariance property of identification schemes, we eliminate the need for pairing computations during ciphertext comparison. Specifically, we instantiate our framework with the pairing-free Schnorr identification scheme and demonstrate that our proposed pORE scheme reduces ciphertext size by approximately 31.25% and improves encryption and comparison efficiency by over two times compared to the current state-of-the-art pORE construction. Our work provides a more efficient alternative to existing pORE constructions and could be viewed as a step towards making pORE a viable choice for practical applications.

Keywords: Order-revealing encryption · Property-preserving hash · Identification scheme · Range query

1 Introduction

In recent years, there has been a growing interest in developing cryptographic tools that offer both security and efficiency in supporting computations on encrypted data. This is particularly relevant in light of the increasing need

Q. Tang and V. Teague (Eds.): PKC 2024, LNCS 14604, pp. 227–256, 2024.
https://doi.org/10.1007/978-3-031-57728-4_8

for encrypted databases. Order-Revealing Encryption (ORE) [6,8] is a special encryption scheme[1] where the ciphertexts reveal the order of the underlying plaintexts. This feature is highly valuable in practice as it allows clients to delegate range queries on encrypted data to (potentially) untrusted servers while ensuring data privacy and confidentiality. In fact, ORE has been utilized in proposals of specific outsourced database systems, including CryptDB [35], Cipherbase [2], and TrustedDB [3]. The practical applications of ORE extend beyond databases and into various other areas, including secure computation, privacy-preserving machine learning, and more. As such, ORE has become an increasingly important tool and has spurred further research.

In an ORE scheme, the order of plaintext is revealed via a comparison algorithm, denoted by Cmp. Specifically, for two ciphertexts c_i and c_j (w.r.t. the messages m_i and m_j), the comparison result $\mathsf{Cmp}(c_i, c_j)$ equals to the predicate function $\mathcal{O}(m_i, m_j)$ defined as:

$$\mathcal{O}(m_i, m_j) = \begin{cases} 1, & \text{if } m_i > m_j \\ -1, & \text{if } m_i < m_j \\ 0, & \text{otherwise.} \end{cases} \tag{1}$$

On the Leakage of ORE. Ideally, the "best-possible" security for ORE should reveal nothing about the plaintext but only their order. Such *ideal leakage* profile, denoted by $\mathcal{L}_0$, is defined as follows,

$$\mathcal{L}_0(m_1, \cdots, m_q) := (\forall 1 \leq i, j \leq q, \mathbf{1}(m_i < m_j)). \tag{2}$$

To show such an ideal ORE is achievable in principle, Boneh et al. [8] proposed a construction based on multilinear maps. Unfortunately, current multilinear maps are quite inefficient, and thus such ORE is too impractical for real-world application. Hence, since then there have been various efforts to relax the security requirements of ORE to develop efficient schemes. Below we will introduce several notable constructions that are closely related to our work.

Chenette et al. [12] proposed a much more efficient ORE (CLWW ORE) but with more information leakage than ideal ones. Precisely, in their construction, the most significant differing bit $\mathsf{msdb}(m_i, m_j)$ of plaintexts would be additionally revealed. Their leakage profile, called *CLWW leakage*, is defined as

$$\mathcal{L}_2(m_1, \cdots, m_q) := (\forall 1 \leq i, j \leq q, \mathbf{1}(m_i < m_j), \mathsf{msdb}(m_i, m_j)). \tag{3}$$

More details about the CLWW ORE will be provided in Sect. 1.2. Lewi and Wu [30] presented an improved version of the above CLWW ORE which leaks strictly less. They constructed a practical, small-domain ORE scheme with best-possible security and extended it to large-domain ORE by block-wise encryption, which leaks the position of the first different block, and thus allows a practitioner to set performance-security tradeoff by tuning the block size.

Unfortunately, a series of work [9,14,19,32] have demonstrated that even hypothetical ideal ORE schemes are insecure for various use cases. This holds

[1] It was called efficiently-orderable encryption in [6].

true even when the scheme only reveals the order of the plaintexts and nothing more. The inherent issue lies in the fact that the mere knowledge of the order of plaintexts can disclose a significant amount of information about the underlying data. For instance, in cases where the data is uniformly selected from the entire domain, even an ideal ORE scheme will inadvertently leak the most significant bits. In fact, the aforementioned attacks reveal that when the adversary possesses a strong estimate of the prior distribution from which the data is drawn, achieving meaningful security is impossible.

Parameter-Hiding ORE. Given the aforementioned attacks against ORE, Cash et al. [10] turned to consider specific scenarios (more details are referred to Appendix A) where the adversary lacks a strong estimate of the prior distribution of the data. For such a case, Cash et al. proposed a new notion, called *parameter-hiding ORE* (pORE), aiming at protecting some information about the underlying data distribution. In particular, Cash et al. [10] mainly consider a ORE scheme with so-called *smoothed CLWW leakage* which is defined as follows:

$$\begin{aligned}\mathcal{L}_1(m_1, \cdots, m_q) :=& (\forall 1 \le i, j, k \le q, \mathbf{1}(m_i < m_j), \\ & \mathbf{1}(\mathsf{msdb}(m_i, m_j) = \mathsf{msdb}(m_i, m_k))),\end{aligned} \tag{4}$$

and show how to convert it into parameter-hiding ORE by composing with a linear function: for any plaintext m, it is computed as $\alpha m + \beta$ before being encrypted, where α, β are the same across all plaintexts and are sampled as part of the secret key.

Cash et al. [10] proposed a pORE construction using a new primitive called Property-Preserving Hash (PPH). PPH enables the comparison key holder to detect whether the preimage of two hash values satisfies a given predicate $\mathcal{P}$, such as $\mathcal{P}(x, y) = 1$ if $x = y + 1$. A concrete pairing-based instance of PPH was proposed by Cash et al. [10] to construct the pORE scheme. In particular, Cash et al.'s ORE scheme requires $O(4n^2)$ pairings for each comparison between n bits message. To reduce the computational overhead, Cash et al. fixed the random permutation to achieve $O(n)$ comparison overhead, but with a slightly more leakage $\mathcal{L}_1'$ (still smoothed CLWW leakage):

$$\begin{aligned}\mathcal{L}_1'(m_1, \cdots, m_q) :=& (\forall 1 \le i, j, k, l \le q, \mathbf{1}(m_i < m_j), \\ & \mathbf{1}(\mathsf{msdb}(m_i, m_j) = \mathsf{msdb}(m_k, m_l))).\end{aligned} \tag{5}$$

Compared to $\mathcal{L}_1$, $\mathcal{L}_1'$ reveals extra information, i.e. whether $\mathsf{msdb}(m_i, m_j)$ equals to $\mathsf{msdb}(m_k, m_l))$ even when $i \neq k$. For example, two sets $\{0, 4, 5, 10, 11\}$ and $\{1, 2, 3, 5, 6\}$ are distinguishable with $\mathcal{L}_1'$ leakage since $\mathsf{msdb}(4, 5) = \mathsf{msdb}(10, 11)$ and $\mathsf{msdb}(2, 3) \neq \mathsf{msdb}(5, 6)$. But, two sets $\{0, 4, 5, 10, 11\}$ and $\{1, 2, 3, 4, 5\}$ are also indistinguishable with $\mathcal{L}_1$ leakage.

Motivating Question. As highlighted by Bogatov et al. [4], Cash et al.'s ORE scheme suffers from two limitations that render it impractical. One of these limitations is the use of bilinear maps, which incurs significant computational costs—orders of magnitude higher than other efficient ORE schemes. Motivated by this observation and the specific leakage properties of pORE, our objective is to explore the feasibility of enhancing the efficiency of Cash et al.'s construction while preserving the same level of leakage. Specifically, we aim to address the following question:

Is it possible to design a parameter-hiding order-revealing encryption scheme without pairings?

1.1 Our Contributions

In this work, we provide an affirmative answer to the above question by designing a new pairing-free PPH scheme to improve the efficiency of the state-of-the-art pORE construction [10].

Our main contributions can be summarized as follows.

- We formally define a special type of identification schemes which is of additional property called *map-invariance*, due to which we manage to design a generic construction of PPH schemes. We then formally prove that our PPH construction is restricted-chosen-input secure with respect to the predicate $\mathcal{P}$ where $\mathcal{P}(x, y) = \pm 1$ if and only if $x = y \pm 1$.
- We then provide a generic construction of ORE with smoothed CLWW leakage $\mathcal{L}_1$ from identification protocols, and prove that the proposed scheme is $\mathcal{L}_1$-non-adaptive-simulation secure with respect to the predicate $\mathcal{O}(x, y)$, which is defined as $\mathcal{O}(x, y) = \pm 1$ if and only if $x > y$ or $x < y$. Instanced with Schnorr identification, we presented an ORE scheme, which can be converted to parameter-hiding ORE via Cash et al.'s framework [10].
- We implement our instanced ORE schemes and perform a comprehensive comparison with existing construction (see Table 1). The results demonstrate that our scheme outperforms the current parameter-hiding ORE [10] at the same security level, in which the ciphertext length reduced more than 31.25%, the encryption efficiency increased by nearly 2.6 times and the comparison efficiency increased by more than 3 times.

As also mentioned by Lewi and Wu [30], the leakage inherent in any ORE scheme renders the primitive not always suitable for applications requiring a high level of security. Nevertheless, since it is up to a practitioner to trade off security and performance constraints, we hope our more efficient realization of the pORE scheme could help practitioners make well-informed decisions regarding its suitability for specific applications, especially when the data distribution shape is public, but the underlying parameters (such as mean and variance) need to be protected.

1.2 Technique Overview

First, we provide an overview of our design idea for PPH. To better illustrate how our idea works, we start with recalling Chenette et al.'s construction [12], followed by Cash et al.'s scheme to explain how PPH could be used to reduce the leakage. Thereafter, we illustrate our design idea of pairing-free PPH schemes.

Table 1. Comparison with existing ORE schemes with smoothed CLWW leakage. λ is the security parameter, n is the bit-length of the plaintext; $|\mathbb{G}_1|$ and $|\mathbb{G}_2|$ is the size of elements in groups $\mathbb{G}_1$ and $\mathbb{G}_2$, respectively; PM_1, PM_2 and BP is the group exponentiation in $\mathbb{G}_1$ and $\mathbb{G}_2$ and the bilinear pairing operation, respectively; PRF is the pseudorandom function operation. ORE* refers to the ORE scheme with fixed permutation.

ORE Scheme	Ciphertext size	Encryption cost	Comparison Cost	Leakage
Cash et al.'s ORE [10]	$2n\|\mathbb{G}_1\| + 2n\|\mathbb{G}_2\|$	$2n\mathsf{PM}_1 + 2n\mathsf{PM}_2 + 3n\mathsf{PRF}$	$4n^2\mathsf{BP}$	$\mathcal{L}_1$
Cash et al.'s ORE* [10]	$2n\|\mathbb{G}_1\| + 2n\|\mathbb{G}_2\|$	$2n\mathsf{PM}_1 + 2n\mathsf{PM}_2 + 3n\mathsf{PRF}$	$4n\mathsf{BP}$	$\mathcal{L}_1'$
Our Sch-ORE	$4n\|\mathbb{G}_1\| + 3n\|\mathbb{Z}_p\|$	$6n\mathsf{PM}_1 + 5n\mathsf{PRF}$	$8n^2\mathsf{PM}_1 + 2n\mathsf{PRF}$	$\mathcal{L}_1$
Our Sch-ORE*	$4n\|\mathbb{G}_1\| + 3n\|\mathbb{Z}_p\|$	$6n\mathsf{PM}_1 + 5n\mathsf{PRF}$	$8n\mathsf{PM}_1 + 2n\mathsf{PRF}$	$\mathcal{L}_1'$

CLWW ORE [12]**.** In CLWW ORE scheme [12], the encryption process involves splitting a n-bits plaintext m into n values by concatenating each bit of m with all more significant bits, and the resulting value is then processed through a keyed pseudorandom function F with the secret key k. The output of the PRF is numerically added to the next less significant bit. More precisely, the resulting ciphertext c consists of $\{u_1, \cdots, u_n\}$:

$$u_i = \mathcal{E}(k, m, i) = F(k, i||m_{[:i-1]}||0^{n-i+1}) + m_{[i]} \mod M, \forall\ i \in [n]$$

where $m_{[i]}$ denotes the i-th bit of m, $m_{[:i]}$ denotes the first i-bits of m and 0^i denotes the i-length zero bit-string[2]. To compare two ciphertexts, the comparator needs to find the smallest index i at which the two sequences occur different values. Denote the ciphertext w.r.t. m' as $c' = \{u_1', \cdots, u_n'\}$. Then, the comparator judges $m > m'$ if $u_i = u_i' + 1 \mod M$ (or $m < m'$ if $u_i = u_i' - 1 \mod M$). If not found, it means $m = m'$. Obviously, the first index i for which $u_i = u_i' \pm 1$ leaks the information $\mathsf{msdb}(m, m')$.

Reducing CLWW ORE Leakage via PPH. The scheme by Cash et al. [10] improves the leakage of the above CLWW ORE. Their scheme builds upon the CLWW construction, but incorporates a permutation step for the list of PRF outputs, as finding a pair that differs by one is sufficient. However, solely permuting the outputs is not adequate for reducing leakage, as an adversary can still deduce the number of common elements between two ciphertexts.

To the end, Cash et al. [10] introduced a new primitive, called *property-preserving hash* (PPH) to "hash" the elements of the CLWW ORE ciphertexts before outputting them. The most essential property of PPH is the randomized output which means that the same element hashed twice will result in different hashes, due to which the adversary is unable to determine the number of common elements between two ciphertexts, thereby preventing the identification of the location of the differing bit.

[2] In Chenette et al.'s work, they took M to be the minimum value, i.e. $M = 3$, making the ciphertext size only $\lceil n \cdot \log_2 3 \rceil$ bits.

Pairing-Based PPH [10]. The main difficulty of constructing PPH lies in the fact that how to randomize the hash output while still preserve the main property of the input. In [10], Cash et al. proposed a concrete construction of PPH based on bilinear pairings. Precisely, for each input u_i, the hash output consists of the following elements

$$\left(g_1^{r_0}, g_1^{r_0 \cdot H(s,u_i)}, g_2^{r_1}, g_2^{r_1 \cdot H(s,u_i+1)}\right)$$

where $e : \mathbb{G}_1 \times \mathbb{G}_2 \rightarrow \mathbb{G}_T$ is a bilinear pairing, $g_1 \in \mathbb{G}_1$ and $g_2 \in \mathbb{G}_2$ are the generators of the prime order q. One could note that due to two freshly chosen randomness $r_0, r_1 \in \mathbb{Z}_q^*$, both u_i and $u_i + 1$ are hidden in the uniformly distributed hash outputs. As shown in Fig. 1, for another input u'_j which has the hash output:

$$\left(g_1^{r'_0}, g_1^{r'_0 \cdot H(s,u'_j)}, g_2^{r'_1}, g_2^{r'_1 \cdot H(s,u'_j+1)}\right),$$

the comparison algorithm computes

$$e\left(g_1^{r_0 \cdot H(s,u_i)}, g_2^{r'_1}\right) \stackrel{?}{=} e\left(g_1^{r_0}, g_2^{r'_1 \cdot H(s,u'_j+1)}\right)$$

to test whether $u_i = u'_j + 1$. A similar computation could be performed to test whether $u_i = u'_j - 1$ or not.

Our Efficient PPH from Schnorr Identification. In this work, we provide a new approach to construct PPH. In the following description, we consider the predicate $\mathcal{P}$ defined as follows:

$$\mathcal{P}(x, y) = \begin{cases} 1, & \text{if } x = y + 1 \\ -1, & \text{if } x = y - 1 \\ 0, & \text{otherwise.} \end{cases} \tag{6}$$

For a more intuitive understanding, here we illustrate our main idea by introducing the concrete PPH based on Schnorr identification. Figure 1 depicts our core idea via a rough comparison with Cash et al.'s pairing-based PPH construction.

Schnorr Identification. The Schnorr scheme is simply described as: Given an cyclic group $\mathbb{G} = \langle g \rangle$ of the prime order p, the secret key is $\mathsf{sk} := x \leftarrow_\$ \mathbb{Z}_p^*$ and the public key is $\mathsf{pk} := (g, y = g^x) \in \mathbb{G}^2$. The prover generates the commitment $\mathsf{cmt} := w = g^{r_0}$ with a random integer $r_0 \in \mathbb{Z}_p^*$ and the response $\mathsf{rsp} := z = r_0 - \xi \cdot x$ where $\xi \in \mathbb{Z}_p^*$ is the verifier's challenge. The verifier checks whether $w = g^z \cdot y^\xi$ holds to decide acceptance or rejection.

A New PPH without Pairings. In our PPH, the encryptor (who computes PPH in the underlying ORE) generates two key-pairs $(x_0, y_0 := g^{x_0})$ and $(x_1, y_1 := g^{x_1})$, hides u_i into the identification response $z_0 := H(s, u_i) \cdot r_0 - x_0 \cdot \xi$ and $z_1 := H(s, u_i+1) \cdot r_1 - x_1 \cdot \xi$ with the same challenge $\xi \leftarrow_\$ \mathbb{Z}_p^*$ and two randomness $r_0, r_1 \leftarrow_\$ \mathbb{Z}_p^*$ respectively. Then, the encryptor computes the output of the PPH:

$$h_i := \{g^{r_1}, y_0^{r_1}, z_0, \xi, g^{r_0}, y_1^{r_0}, z_1\}, \text{w.r.t. } u_i. \tag{7}$$

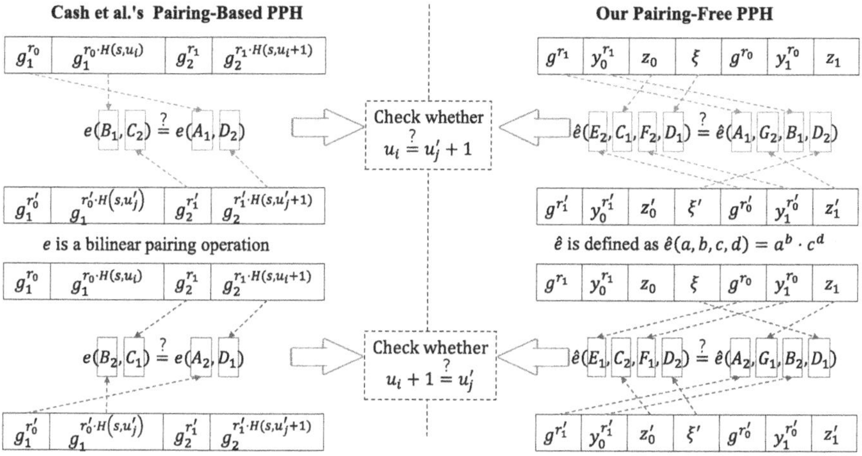

Fig. 1. Visual description of two PPHs.

For comparison with $h'_j := \{g^{r'_1}, y_0^{r'_1}, z'_0, \xi', g^{r'_0}, y_1^{r'_0}, z'_1\}$ w.r.t. u'_j, one can utilize the commitment recovery algorithm to check the predicate $\mathcal{P}(u_i, u'_j)$ as follows:

$$(g^{r'_1})^{z_0} \cdot (y_0^{r'_1})^{\xi} \stackrel{?}{=} (g^{r_0})^{z'_1} \cdot (y_1^{r_0})^{\xi'},$$

to test whether $u_i = u'_j + 1$, equivalent to check $g^{r_0 \cdot r'_1 \cdot H(s,u_i)} \stackrel{?}{=} g^{r_0 \cdot r'_1 \cdot H(s,u'_j+1)}$. A similar computation could be performed to test whether $u_i = u'_j - 1$ or not.

In fact, the value u_i is hidden in two responses z_0 and z_1 with independent random integers r_0 and r_1. Based on the security of Schnorr identification, it is known that r_0, r_1, x_0, x_1 would not be revealed. Thus, the security of PPH holds. Based on the binding property of commitments, one could determine that two equal commitment values are related to the same message.

Generalization from Specific Identifications. Inspired by the above concrete PPH construction, we formalize a new property named *map-invariance* for identification protocols, and show how to generically construct PPH from specific identification with map-invariance. Thereafter, we show that our generic PPH construction achieves restricted-chosen-input security which is crucial for ORE schemes with smoothed CLWW leakage that could be extended to parameter-hiding ORE schemes with Cash et al.'s approach [10, Section 4].

1.3 Related Work

In this section, we survey some literature on order-revealing and order-preserving encryption, as well as the existing work on secure range query protocols.

Order-Preserving Encryption. Prior to ORE, Agrawal et al. [1] first introduced the notion of *order-preserving encryption (OPE)*, which can encrypt numeric data and order ciphertexts with the numerical comparison operator.

Subsequently, Boldyreva et al. [5] formalized the ideal security definition for OPE, which states that ciphertexts should only reveal the order of plaintexts without any other information leakages, similar to the ideal security definition for ORE. However, Boldyreva et al. [5] showed that this "best-possible" security cannot be achieved in stateless and immutable OPE schemes. They also showed that any OPE scheme with ideal security will make the ciphertext length grow exponentially with the plaintext length. Since then, a number of OPE schemes have been proposed such as [6,23,24,34,36]. To achieve the ideal security, Popa et al. [34] proposed a mutable OPE scheme that constructs a stateful binary tree on plaintexts and an interactive protocol for path-based ciphertext updates. Unfortunately, due to the constraint on the ciphertext space, most OPE constructions are vulnerable to various inference attacks, as demonstrated by Naveed et al. [32], where attackers can recover partial bits of plaintexts.

Secure Range Query Protocols. From OPE/ORE schemes, the general idea is to modify all comparison operators to the ORE comparison algorithm in some data structures optimized for range queries, e.g., the B+ tree working on top of an ORE scheme [4]. In ORE/OPE-based applications, one mostly considers the snapshot attacker [19,32], who can observe all the database contents at one time instant. This makes designers more inclined to focus on leakage from fixed datasets and minimize the information available to adversaries through reconstruction. Undisputedly, leakage from adaptive queries can lead to additional privacy issues for clients and servers. In this scenario, the adversarial model mainly discusses leakage-abuse attacks based on different datasets, such as those based on access-pattern leakage [18,22,29], search-pattern leakage [27,31], volumetric leakage [17,22]. Approaches that help protect against such an attacker include searchable symmetric encryption (SSE) [13,15], Oblivious RAM [11], response-hiding constructions [21,28]. These schemes are more secure than OPE/ORE schemes, although they still leak some information, and in general, are more expensive to compute. As shown in Bogatov et al.'s comparative evaluation [4] of ORE and other secure range-query protocols, the ORE-based approach is provably I/O optimal and can potentially be extended by using another data structure with ORE.

2 Preliminaries

Let $\lambda \in \mathbb{N}$ be the security parameter and write $\mathsf{negl}(\lambda)$ to denote a negligible function w.r.t. λ and $\mathsf{poly}(\lambda)$ to denote a polynomial function w.r.t. λ. Let $[n]$ denote the set of integers $\{1, 2, \cdots, n\}$ for $n \in \mathbb{N}$. For a bit string $b = b_1 b_2 \cdots b_n$, let $b_{[:i]} = b_1 b_2 \cdots b_i$ denote the first i bits of b in the bit string representing and 0^i denote a i-length zero string in the bit string representing. For two bit strings b and b', we write $\mathsf{msdb}(b, b')$ to denote the most significant different bit of them. For a given set U, we let $u \leftarrow_\$ U$ denote the uniform sampling from U. For any bit strings $x, y \in \{0,1\}^*$, we write $x||y$ to denote the concatenation of x and y. If $\mathcal{P}$ is a predicate on x, $\mathbf{1}(\mathcal{P}(x))$ means the indicator function for $\mathcal{P}$, that is $\mathbf{1}(\mathcal{P}(x)) = 1$ if and only if $\mathcal{P}(x) = 1$.

2.1 Keyed Hash Function

Let $F : \mathcal{K} \times \mathcal{X} \to \mathcal{Y}$ be a keyed hash function family [20]. Here $\mathcal{K}$ is the key space of F, $\mathcal{X}$ is the domain of F and $\mathcal{Y}$ is the range of F.

Definition 1 (Collision Resistance). *Given a fixed security parameter λ, a keyed hash function family $F : \mathcal{K} \times \mathcal{X} \to \mathcal{Y}$ is collision resistant if for any efficient adversary $\mathcal{A}$, its advantage*

$$\mathsf{Adv}^{\mathsf{COL}}_{F,\mathcal{A}}(\lambda) := \Pr\left[(x, x') \leftarrow \mathcal{A} : F(k, x) = F(k, x') \wedge x \neq x'\right]$$

is negligible.

Definition 2 (Pseudorandom [16]). *Given a fixed security parameter λ, a keyed hash function family $F : \mathcal{K} \times \mathcal{X} \to \mathcal{Y}$ is pseudorandom if for any efficient adversary $\mathcal{A}$, its advantage*

$$\begin{aligned}\mathsf{Adv}^{\mathsf{PRF}}_{F,\mathcal{A}}(\lambda) := \big|&\Pr\left[k \leftarrow_{\$} \mathcal{K} : \mathcal{A}^{F(k,\cdot)}(\lambda) = 1\right] - \\ &\Pr\left[f \leftarrow_{\$} \mathsf{Funs}(\mathcal{X}, \mathcal{Y}) : \mathcal{A}^{f(\cdot)}(\lambda) = 1\right]\big|\end{aligned}$$

is negligible, where $\mathsf{Funs}(\mathcal{X}, \mathcal{Y})$ is the set of all functions from $\mathcal{X}$ to $\mathcal{Y}$.

Definition 3 (Entropy Smoothing). *Given a fixed security parameter λ, a keyed hash function family $F : \mathcal{K} \times \mathcal{X} \to \mathcal{Y}$ is entropy smoothing if for any efficient adversary $\mathcal{A}$, its advantage*

$$\begin{aligned}\mathsf{Adv}^{\mathsf{ES}}_{F,\mathcal{A}}(\lambda) := |&\Pr\left[k \leftarrow_{\$} \mathcal{K}, \delta \leftarrow_{\$} \mathcal{X} : \mathcal{A}(\lambda, k, F(k, \delta)) = 1\right] - \\ &\Pr\left[k \leftarrow_{\$} \mathcal{K}, h \leftarrow_{\$} \mathcal{Y} : \mathcal{A}(\lambda, k, h) = 1\right]|\end{aligned}$$

is negligible.

2.2 Property-Preserving Hash

In this section, we recall the syntax and security of a basic tool, called *Property-Preserving Hash (PPH)* [10], which is essentially the simplified variant of property-preserving encryption schemes [33]. In the PPH scheme, a hash key hk is a necessary input to calculate the hash value. The difference is that a test key tk can be used to determine whether two different hash values $\{h, h'\}$ with respect to two distinct messages $\{x, y\}$ satisfy an associated property $\mathcal{P}$.

Definition 4 (Property-Preserving Hash). *A property-preserving hash scheme is a tuple of polynomial-time algorithms Γ = ($\mathsf{PPH.KeyGen}$, $\mathsf{PPH.Hash}$, $\mathsf{PPH.Test}$) defined as follows:*

- $(\mathsf{par}, \mathsf{hk}, \mathsf{tk}) \leftarrow \mathsf{PPH.KeyGen}(1^\lambda)$: *The key generation algorithm is a randomized algorithm that takes as input a security parameter λ and outputs the system parameters par, the hash key hk and the test key tk. These implicitly define the input domain DSet and the output range HSet of the hash algorithm.*

– $h \leftarrow \mathsf{PPH.Hash}(\mathsf{hk}, u)$: *The hash evaluation algorithm is a randomized algorithm that takes as input a hash key* hk *and a message* $u \in \mathsf{DSet}$, *and outputs a hash value* $h \in \mathsf{HSet}$.
– $b \leftarrow \mathsf{PPH.Test}(\mathsf{tk}, h, h')$: *The hash test algorithm is a deterministic algorithm that takes as input a test key* tk *and two hash values* $(h, h') \in \mathsf{HSet}^2$ *and outputs a bit* $b \in \{0, 1\}$.

Correctness of PPH Schemes. For a predicate $\mathcal{P}$, the PPH scheme Γ is *computationally correct* if the following advantage

$$\mathsf{Adv}^{\mathsf{COR}}_{\Gamma,\mathcal{P},\mathcal{A}}(\lambda) := \Pr\left[\begin{array}{c|l} \mathsf{Test}(\mathsf{tk}, h, h') & (\mathsf{par},\mathsf{hk},\mathsf{tk}) \leftarrow \mathsf{KeyGen}(1^\lambda), \\ \neq \mathcal{P}(x, y) & x, y \leftarrow \mathcal{A}^{\mathsf{Hash}(\mathsf{hk},\cdot)}(\mathsf{tk}), \\ & h \leftarrow \mathsf{Hash}(\mathsf{hk}, x), \\ & h' \leftarrow \mathsf{Hash}(\mathsf{hk}, y), \end{array}\right]$$

is negligible for any efficient PPT adversary $\mathcal{A}$ which can query the Hash oracle with any inputs in DSet.

Security of PPH Schemes. For a predicate $\mathcal{P}$, the PPH scheme Γ is *restricted-chosen-input secure* if the following advantage

$$\mathsf{Adv}^{\mathsf{PPH}}_{\Gamma,\mathcal{P},\mathcal{A}}(\lambda) := 2\Pr\left[b = b' \;\middle|\; \begin{array}{l} (\mathsf{par},\mathsf{hk},\mathsf{tk}) \leftarrow \mathsf{KeyGen}(1^\lambda), \\ x^* \leftarrow \mathcal{A}(\mathsf{tk}), \\ h_0 \leftarrow \mathsf{Hash}(\mathsf{hk}, x^*), \\ h_1 \leftarrow_\$ \mathsf{HSet}, b \leftarrow_\$ \{0, 1\}, \\ b' \leftarrow \mathcal{A}^{\mathsf{Hash}(\mathsf{hk},\cdot)}(\mathsf{tk}, x^*, h_b), \end{array}\right] - 1$$

is negligible for any efficient PPT adversary $\mathcal{A}$ which can query the Hash oracle with restricted inputs $x \in \mathsf{DSet}$ satisfying $\mathcal{P}(x, x^*) = 0$.

2.3 Parameter-Hiding ORE

In this part, we review the syntax and security of parameter-hiding ORE (pORE) schemes formalized by Cash et al. [10].

Definition 5 (Parameter-Hiding ORE). *For a predicate* $\mathcal{O}$ *defined over a well-ordered domain* $\mathcal{D}$, *a parameter-hiding ORE scheme is a tuple of polynomial-time algorithms* $\Pi = (\mathsf{ORE.KGen}, \mathsf{ORE.Enc}, \mathsf{ORE.Cmp})$ *defined as follows:*

– $(\mathsf{par}, \mathsf{msk}, \mathsf{ck}) \leftarrow \mathsf{ORE.KGen}(1^\lambda)$: *The key generation algorithm is a randomized algorithm that takes as input a security parameter* λ *and outputs the system parameters* par, *the master secret key* msk *and the comparison key* ck. *We remark* par *is an implicit input of following algorithms.*
– $c \leftarrow \mathsf{ORE.Enc}(\mathsf{msk}, m)$: *The encryption algorithm is a randomized algorithm that takes as input the master secret key* msk *and a message* $m \in \mathcal{D}$, *and outputs a ciphertext* c.
– $b \leftarrow \mathsf{ORE.Cmp}(\mathsf{ck}, c, c')$: *The comparison algorithm is a deterministic algorithm that takes as input the comparison key* ck *and two ciphertexts* c *(w.r.t. the plaintext* m*) and* c' *(w.r.t. the plaintext* m'*), and outputs a flag* b.

Correctness of ORE Schemes. For a predicate $\mathcal{O}$, the ORE scheme Π is *computationally correct* if the following advantage

$$\mathsf{Adv}^{\mathsf{COR}}_{\Pi,\mathcal{O},\mathcal{A}}(\lambda) := \Pr\left[\begin{array}{c|l} \mathsf{Cmp}(\mathsf{ck}, c, c') & (\mathsf{par}, \mathsf{msk}, \mathsf{ck}) \leftarrow \mathsf{KGen}(1^\lambda) \\ \neq \mathcal{O}(m, m') & c \leftarrow \mathsf{Enc}(\mathsf{msk}, m) \\ & c' \leftarrow \mathsf{Enc}(\mathsf{msk}, m') \end{array}\right]$$

is negligible for any efficient adversary $\mathcal{A}$.

Security of ORE Schemes. The ORE scheme is non-adaptive simulation-based secure with the leakage function $\mathcal{L}(\cdot)$, if there exists a polynomial-size simulator $\mathcal{S}$ to construct a non-adaptive experiment $\mathsf{Sim}^{\mathsf{ORE}}_{\mathcal{A},\mathcal{L},\mathcal{S}}(\lambda)$ which is computationally indistinguishable from the real non-adaptive experiment $\mathsf{Real}^{\mathsf{ORE}}_{\mathcal{A}}(\lambda)$ for any PPT adversary $\mathcal{A}$. Experiments are described in Fig. 2.

$\underline{\mathsf{Real}^{\mathsf{ORE}}_{\mathcal{A}}(\lambda)}$:

1: $(\mathsf{par}, \mathsf{msk}, \mathsf{ck}) \leftarrow \mathsf{ORE.KGen}(1^\lambda)$;
2: $(m_1, \cdots, m_q) \leftarrow \mathcal{A}$;
3: **for** $1 \leq i \leq q$ **do**
4: $\quad c_i \leftarrow \mathsf{ORE.Enc}(\mathsf{msk}, m_i)$;
5: **return** $(c_1, \cdots, c_q)$;

$\underline{\mathsf{Sim}^{\mathsf{ORE}}_{\mathcal{A},\mathcal{L},\mathcal{S}}(\lambda)}$:

1: $\mathsf{st}_{\mathcal{S}} \leftarrow \mathcal{S}(\lambda)$;
2: $(m_1, \cdots, m_q) \leftarrow \mathcal{A}$;
3: $(c_1, \cdots, c_q) \leftarrow \mathcal{S}(\mathsf{st}_{\mathcal{S}}, \mathcal{L}(m_1, \cdots, m_q))$;
4: **return** $(c_1, \cdots, c_q)$;

Fig. 2. Experiments $\mathsf{Real}^{\mathsf{ORE}}_{\mathcal{A}}(\lambda)$ and $\mathsf{Sim}^{\mathsf{ORE}}_{\mathcal{A},\mathcal{L},\mathcal{S}}(\lambda)$.

3 Identification Schemes with Map-Invariance

In this section, we recall the definition of canonical identification schemes described in [26]. Then, we formalize a type of identification protocols with map-invariance property and give an instance from Schnorr Identification.

3.1 Formal Definitions

Definition 6 (Canonical Identification Scheme). *A canonical identification scheme* ID *is defined as a tuple of algorithms* $\mathsf{ID} := (\mathsf{Setup}, \mathsf{IGen}, \mathsf{P}, \mathsf{V})$ *with system parameter space* $\mathcal{SP}$, *public key space* $\mathcal{PK}$, *commitment space* $\mathcal{W}$, *randomness space* $\mathcal{R}$, *challenge space* $\mathcal{CH}$ *and response space* $\mathcal{Z}$.

- $\mathsf{par} \leftarrow \mathsf{Setup}(1^\lambda)$: *Taking security parameter* λ *as input, it outputs system parameters* $\mathsf{par} \in \mathcal{SP}$.
- $(\mathsf{sk}, \mathsf{pk}) \leftarrow \mathsf{IGen}(\mathsf{par})$: *Taking system parameters* par *as input, it outputs a secret and public key pair* $(\mathsf{sk}, \mathsf{pk})$.
- *The prover algorithm* $\mathsf{P} = (\mathsf{Com}, \mathsf{Rsp})$ *consists of two algorithms:*
    - $(\mathsf{cmt}, \mathsf{st}) \leftarrow \mathsf{Com}(\mathsf{par}, \mathsf{sk}; \mathsf{rnd})$: *Taking system parameters* par *and secret key* sk *as inputs, it outputs commitment* $\mathsf{cmt} \in \mathcal{W}$ *and state* st. *Here we explicitly write the randomness* $\mathsf{rnd} \in \mathcal{R}$ *in the input.*
    - $\mathsf{rsp} \leftarrow \mathsf{Rsp}(\mathsf{par}, \mathsf{sk}, \mathsf{st}, \mathsf{ch})$: *Taking system parameters* par, *secret key* sk, *state* st *and challenge* $\mathsf{ch} \in \mathcal{CH}$ *as inputs, it outputs a response* rsp.
- $b \leftarrow \mathsf{V}(\mathsf{par}, \mathsf{pk}, \mathsf{tr})$: *Taking system parameters* par, *the public key* pk *and the transcript* $\mathsf{tr} = (\mathsf{cmt}, \mathsf{ch}, \mathsf{rsp})$ *as inputs, and outputs a bit* $b \in \{0, 1\}$. *If the verifier accepts,* $b = 1$; *Otherwise,* $b = 0$.

The identification works as follows: The prover first publishes its public key pk and sends a commitment cmt to the verifier. Then, the verifier randomly chooses a challenge ch from the challenge space $\mathcal{CH}$ and sends it to the prover. After receiving the challenge, the prover computes a response rsp and sends it to the verifier. Finally, the verifier makes a decision (acceptance or rejection) based on the public key and the conversation transcript.

Below, we discuss some properties of commitments in special identification schemes, which are crucial to our efficient PPH constructions.

Definition 7 (Commitment-Independency). *An identification scheme* ID *is commitment-independent if for* $\mathsf{par} \leftarrow \mathsf{Setup}(1^\lambda)$, $(\mathsf{sk}, \mathsf{pk}) \leftarrow \mathsf{IGen}(\mathsf{par})$, $(\mathsf{cmt}, \mathsf{st}) \leftarrow \mathsf{Com}(\mathsf{par}, \mathsf{sk}; \mathsf{rnd})$ *and any* $\mathsf{rnd}, \mathsf{rnd}' \in \mathcal{R}$, *following conditions holds:*

- *the value of* $(\mathsf{cmt}, \mathsf{st})$ *is uniquely determined by system parameter* par *and randomness* rnd, *and independent of the secret key* sk *and the public key* pk;
- $\mathsf{Com}_1(\mathsf{par}, \mathsf{sk}; \mathsf{rnd}) = \mathsf{Com}_1(\mathsf{par}, \mathsf{sk}; \mathsf{rnd}')$ *if and only if* $\mathsf{rnd} = \mathsf{rnd}'$, *where algorithm* Com_1 *only returns the first element of the output of algorithm* Com *(i.e.,* cmt*).*

Definition 8 (Commitment-Recoverability [25]). *An identification scheme* ID *is commitment-recoverable if for* $\mathsf{par} \leftarrow \mathsf{Setup}(1^\lambda)$, $(\mathsf{sk}, \mathsf{pk}) \leftarrow \mathsf{IGen}(\mathsf{par})$, *any* $\mathsf{ch} \in \mathcal{CH}$, *and any* $\mathsf{rsp} \in \mathcal{Z}$, *there exists a unique commitment* $\mathsf{cmt} \in \mathcal{W}$ *such that* $\mathsf{V}(\mathsf{par}, \mathsf{pk}, \mathsf{cmt}, \mathsf{ch}, \mathsf{rsp}) = 1$. *And, the unique commitment* cmt *can be publicly computed by a commitment recovery algorithm* Rec, *i.e.,*

$$\mathsf{cmt} = \mathsf{Rec}(\mathsf{par}, \mathsf{pk}, \mathsf{ch}, \mathsf{rsp}).$$

Definition 9 (Commitment-Augmentability [7]). *An identification scheme* ID *is augmentable if for* $\mathsf{par} \leftarrow \mathsf{Setup}(1^\lambda)$, $(\mathsf{sk}, \mathsf{pk}) \leftarrow \mathsf{IGen}(\mathsf{par})$ *and* $(\mathsf{cmt}, \mathsf{st}) \leftarrow \mathsf{Com}(\mathsf{par}, \mathsf{sk}; \mathsf{rnd})$, *there exists an* append algorithm Apd *that takes as input* cmt *and randomness* $\mathsf{rnd}' \in \mathcal{R}$ *and outputs* cmt' *satisfying*

$$\mathsf{cmt}' \leftarrow \mathsf{Com}_1(\mathsf{par}, \mathsf{sk}; \mathsf{rnd} \cdot \mathsf{rnd}'),$$

where $\cdot$ *is the operation defined over* $\mathcal{R}$.

Definition 10 (Response-Indistinguishability). *An identification scheme* ID *is response-indistinguishable if for any PPT adversary* $\mathcal{A}$*, the advantage of* $\mathcal{A}$ *winning the game* $\mathsf{IND}^{\mathsf{RSP}}_{\mathsf{ID},\mathcal{A}}(\lambda)$*, defined as* $\mathsf{Adv}^{\mathsf{RSP}}_{\mathsf{ID},\mathcal{A}}(\lambda) = 2\Pr\left[\mathsf{IND}^{\mathsf{RSP}}_{\mathsf{ID},\mathcal{A}}(\lambda) = 1\right] - 1$*, is negligible (Fig. 3).*

Game $\mathsf{IND}^{\mathsf{RSP}}_{\mathsf{ID},\mathcal{A}}(\lambda)$:

1: $\mathsf{par} \leftarrow \mathsf{Setup}(1^\lambda)$; $(\mathsf{sk}, \mathsf{pk}) \leftarrow \mathsf{IGen}(\mathsf{par})$; $\mathsf{rnd} \leftarrow_\$ \mathcal{R}$;
2: $(\mathsf{cmt}, \mathsf{st}) \leftarrow \mathsf{Com}(\mathsf{par}, \mathsf{sk}; \mathsf{rnd})$; $\mathsf{ch} \leftarrow_\$ \mathcal{CH}$;
3: $\mathsf{rsp}_0 \leftarrow \mathsf{Rsp}(\mathsf{par}, \mathsf{sk}, \mathsf{st}, \mathsf{ch})$; $\mathsf{rsp}_1 \leftarrow_\$ \mathcal{Z}$;
4: $b \leftarrow_\$ \{0,1\}; b' \leftarrow \mathcal{A}(\mathsf{par}, \mathsf{sk}, \mathsf{ch}, \mathsf{rsp}_b)$
5: **return** $b \stackrel{?}{=} b'$

Fig. 3. Game $\mathsf{IND}^{\mathsf{RSP}}_{\mathsf{ID},\mathcal{A}}(\lambda)$ for indistinguishability on response.

If the commitment-independency property holds, the commit algorithm can be denoted as $(\mathsf{cmt}, \mathsf{st}) \leftarrow \mathsf{Com}(\mathsf{par}; \mathsf{rnd})$. If the commitment-recoverability property holds, the verifier algorithm V checks whether cmt equals to $\mathsf{Rec}(\mathsf{par}, \mathsf{pk}, \mathsf{ch}, \mathsf{rsp})$.

We now define a new property, called map-invariance, meaning that the verification equation $\mathsf{cmt} = \mathsf{Rec}(\mathsf{par}, \mathsf{pk}, \mathsf{ch}, \mathsf{rsp})$ holds even after permuting the public key and the commitment using the same randomness.

Definition 11 (Map-Invariance). *An identification scheme* ID *is of map-invariance if following conditions hold:*

- *The identification scheme* ID *is correct, commitment-independent, commitment-recoverable, commitment-augmentable and response-indistinguishable.*
- *There exist two mapping algorithms* ParMap *that takes as input* par *and* rnd' *and outputs* rpar*, and* PkMap *that takes as input* pk *and* rnd' *and outputs* rpk*, such that*

$$\Pr\left[\mathsf{Apd}(\mathsf{cmt}, \mathsf{rnd}') \neq \mathsf{Rec}(\mathsf{rpar}, \mathsf{rpk}, \mathsf{ch}, \mathsf{rsp}) \;\middle|\; \begin{array}{l} \mathsf{par} \leftarrow \mathsf{Setup}(1^\lambda), \\ (\mathsf{sk}, \mathsf{pk}) \leftarrow \mathsf{IGen}(\mathsf{par}), \\ \mathsf{rnd}, \mathsf{rnd}' \leftarrow_\$ \mathcal{R}, \mathsf{ch} \leftarrow_\$ \mathcal{CH}, \\ (\mathsf{cmt}, \mathsf{st}) \leftarrow \mathsf{Com}(\mathsf{par}; \mathsf{rnd}), \\ \mathsf{rsp} \leftarrow \mathsf{Rsp}(\mathsf{par}, \mathsf{sk}, \mathsf{st}, \mathsf{ch}), \\ \mathsf{rpar} \leftarrow \mathsf{ParMap}(\mathsf{par}, \mathsf{rnd}'), \\ \mathsf{rpk} \leftarrow \mathsf{PkMap}(\mathsf{pk}, \mathsf{rnd}') \end{array}\right]$$

is negligible, and for $\mathsf{par} \leftarrow \mathsf{Setup}(1^\lambda)$, $(\mathsf{sk}, \mathsf{pk}) \leftarrow \mathsf{IGen}(\mathsf{par})$ *and* $\mathsf{rnd}' \leftarrow_\$ \mathcal{R}$*, following two distributions are computationally indistinguishable.*

$$\left\{(\mathsf{par}, \mathsf{pk}, \mathsf{rpar}_0, \mathsf{rpk}_0) \;\middle|\; \begin{array}{l} \mathsf{rpar}_0 \leftarrow \mathsf{ParMap}(\mathsf{par}, \mathsf{rnd}') \\ \mathsf{rpk}_0 \leftarrow \mathsf{PkMap}(\mathsf{pk}, \mathsf{rnd}') \end{array}\right\},$$

$$\left\{(\mathsf{par}, \mathsf{pk}, \mathsf{rpar}_1, \mathsf{rpk}_1) \;\middle|\; \begin{array}{l} \mathsf{rpar}_1 \leftarrow_\$ \mathcal{SP} \\ \mathsf{rpk}_1 \leftarrow_\$ \mathcal{PK} \end{array}\right\}.$$

3.2 An Instance from Schnorr Identification

Let $\mathbb{G} = \langle g \rangle$ be a cyclic group with the generator g of the prime order p. For the IGen execution, it randomly selects an integer $\mathsf{sk} := x \leftarrow_\$ \mathbb{Z}_p^*$ and computes the public key $\mathsf{pk} := y = g^x \in \mathbb{G}$. The prover generates a commitment $\mathsf{cmt} := w = g^r \in \mathbb{G}$ with a random integer $\mathsf{rnd} := r \leftarrow_\$ \mathbb{Z}_p^*$. Then, the verifier picks up a random challenge $\mathsf{ch} := e \leftarrow_\$ \mathbb{Z}_p$. The prover computes the response $\mathsf{rsp} := z = r - e \cdot x \mod p$. The verifier checks whether $w = g^z \cdot y^e$ holds. The algorithms $\mathsf{Com}, \mathsf{Rsp}, \mathsf{Rec}$ are defined as follows:

Schnorr Identification:

1: $\mathsf{par} := g \leftarrow_\$ \mathbb{G}, \mathsf{sk} := x \leftarrow_\$ \mathbb{Z}_p^*, \mathsf{pk} := y = g^x \in \mathbb{G}$;
2: $(\mathsf{cmt}, \mathsf{st}) := (w = g^r, r) \leftarrow \mathsf{Com}(\mathsf{par}; \mathsf{rnd})$
3: $\mathsf{ch} := e \leftarrow_\$ \mathbb{Z}_p$
4: $\mathsf{rsp} := z \leftarrow \mathsf{Rsp}(\mathsf{par}, \mathsf{sk}, \mathsf{st}, \mathsf{ch}) = r - e \cdot x \mod p$
5: $\mathsf{cmt}' := w' \leftarrow \mathsf{Rec}(\mathsf{par}, \mathsf{pk}, \mathsf{ch}, \mathsf{rsp}) = g^z \cdot y^e \in \mathbb{G}$

Theorem 1. *The Schnorr identification is of map-invariance under the decisional Diffie-Hellman (DDH) assumption.*

Proof. One can note that the commitment w is independent of the secret key x and $g^r = g^{r'}$ if and only if $r = r'$ for any $r, r' \in \mathbb{Z}_p^*$. The commitment space is the group $\mathbb{G}$ of prime order p and the challenge space is $\mathbb{Z}_p$. So, only one group element can be recovered by Rec with the input instance (g, y, e, z) and equals to the prover's commitment w.

With a new randomness $\mathsf{rnd}' := r'$, the maps Apd, ParMap and PkMap are defined as follows:

$$\begin{aligned} w' &:= w^{r'} \leftarrow \mathsf{Apd}(w, r'), \\ \mathsf{rpar} &= g^{r'} \leftarrow \mathsf{ParMap}(g, r'), \\ \mathsf{rpk} &= y^{r'} \leftarrow \mathsf{PkMap}(y, r'). \end{aligned} \tag{8}$$

Obviously, the output of algorithm Apd can be derived from $\mathsf{Com}(\mathsf{par}; \mathsf{rnd} \cdot \mathsf{rnd}')$. We claim that $\mathsf{Apd}(\mathsf{cmt}, \mathsf{rnd}') = \mathsf{Rec}(\mathsf{rpar}, \mathsf{rpk}, \mathsf{ch}, \mathsf{rsp})$ holds with overwhelming probability, as $\mathsf{Apd}(\mathsf{cmt}, \mathsf{rnd}') = g^{r \cdot r'}$ and $\mathsf{Rec}(\mathsf{rpar}, \mathsf{rpk}, \mathsf{ch}, \mathsf{rsp}) = g^{r' \cdot z} y^{r' \cdot e} = g^{r \cdot r'}$.

Since r is uniformly distributed in $\mathbb{Z}_p^*$, the response $\mathsf{rsp}_0 := z_0 = r - e \cdot x$ is also uniformly distributed in $\mathbb{Z}_p^*$. While $\mathsf{rsp}_1 := z_1 \leftarrow_\$ \mathbb{Z}_p^*$ is uniformly sampled from $\mathbb{Z}_p^*$, no adversary can distinguish z_0 and z_1 with non-negligible advantage.

Finally, if a PPT adversary $\mathcal{A}$ can distinguish $(\mathsf{par}, \mathsf{pk}, \mathsf{rpar}_0, \mathsf{rpk}_0)$ and $(\mathsf{par}, \mathsf{pk}, \mathsf{rpar}_1, \mathsf{rpk}_1)$ with the probability ϵ, we can build an adversary $\mathcal{B}$ to break the DDH problem as follows: Let (g, g^a, g^b, Z) be a DDH instance, $\mathcal{B}$ simulates two tuples as

$$\mathsf{par} = g, \mathsf{pk} = g^a, \mathsf{rpar}_0 = g^{b \cdot v_0}, \mathsf{rpk}_0 = Z^{v_0}, \mathsf{rpar}_1 = g^{b \cdot v_1}, \mathsf{rpk}_1 = h$$

where v_0, v_1 are randomly sampled from $\mathbb{Z}_p^*$ and h is randomly sampled from $\mathbb{G}$. If $Z = g^{ab}$, the simulation $(\mathsf{rpar}_0, \mathsf{rpk}_0)$ is indistinguishable from $(\mathsf{rpar}_1, \mathsf{rpk}_1)$, and thus the adversary $\mathcal{A}$ has probability $\frac{1}{2} + \frac{\epsilon}{2}$ of guessing the correct tuple. If $Z \neq g^{ab}$, the adversary only has probability $\frac{1}{2}$ of guessing the correct tuple. So, the advantage of solving the DDH problem is $\frac{\epsilon}{2}$.

4 PPH from Schnorr Identification

In this section, we show how to construct a PPH scheme from identification schemes with map-invariance.

4.1 Generic PPH Construction

Let identification scheme $\mathsf{ID} := (\mathsf{Setup}, \mathsf{IGen}, \mathsf{Com}, \mathsf{Rsp}, \mathsf{Rec}, \mathsf{Apd}, \mathsf{ParMap}, \mathsf{PkMap})$ with system parameter space $\mathcal{SP}$, public key space $\mathcal{PK}$, commitment space $\mathcal{W}$, randomness space $\mathcal{R}$, challenge space $\mathcal{CH}$ and response space $\mathcal{Z}$. Below, we describe the generic PPH construction $\Gamma = (\mathsf{PPH.KeyGen}, \mathsf{PPH.Hash}, \mathsf{PPH.Test})$.

- $\mathsf{PPH.KeyGen}(1^\lambda)$: On input a security parameter λ, it generates $\mathsf{par}_{\mathsf{ID}} \leftarrow \mathsf{Setup}(1^\lambda)$ and two key pairs $(\mathsf{sk}_i, \mathsf{pk}_i)$ $(i \in \{0,1\})$ by the key generation algorithm $\mathsf{IGen}(\mathsf{par}_{\mathsf{ID}})$. Define two keyed hash functions $H_r : \{0,1\}^\lambda \times \{0,1\}^* \rightarrow \mathcal{R}$ and $H_c : \{0,1\}^\lambda \times \{0,1\}^* \rightarrow \mathcal{CH}$, satisfying collision resistance and pseudorandom-function property. Then, it randomly chooses two keys $s, \kappa \leftarrow_\$ \{0,1\}^\lambda$. Finally, it returns the system parameter as $\mathsf{par}_{\mathsf{PPH}} = (\mathsf{par}_{\mathsf{ID}}, H_r, H_c)$, the hash key as $\mathsf{hk} = (s, \kappa, \mathsf{sk}_0, \mathsf{sk}_1, \mathsf{pk}_0, \mathsf{pk}_1)$ and the test key as $\mathsf{tk} = \kappa$, where $\mathsf{par}_{\mathsf{PPH}}$ is an implicit input of other algorithms.
- $\mathsf{PPH.Hash}(\mathsf{hk}, u)$: On input the hash key hk, a message u, it computes the values $\hat{u}_0 \leftarrow H_r(s, u)$, $\hat{u}_1 \leftarrow H_r(s, u+1)$ and samples randomness $r_0, r_1 \leftarrow_\$ \mathcal{R}$. Then, it generates the commitments $(\mathsf{cmt}_i, \mathsf{st}_i) \leftarrow \mathsf{Com}(\mathsf{par}_{\mathsf{ID}}; \hat{u}_i \cdot r_i)$, computes the challenge $\mathsf{ch} \leftarrow H_c(\kappa, \hat{u}_0 || \hat{u}_1 || \mathsf{cmt}_0 || \mathsf{cmt}_1)$ and the responses $\mathsf{rsp}_i \leftarrow \mathsf{Rsp}(\mathsf{par}_{\mathsf{ID}}, \mathsf{sk}_i, \mathsf{st}_i, \mathsf{ch})$ for $i \in \{0,1\}$. [3] It computes

$$\mathsf{rpar}_0 \leftarrow \mathsf{ParMap}(\mathsf{par}_{\mathsf{ID}}, r_1), \mathsf{rpk}_0 \leftarrow \mathsf{PkMap}(\mathsf{pk}_0, r_1),$$

$$\mathsf{rpar}_1 \leftarrow \mathsf{ParMap}(\mathsf{par}_{\mathsf{ID}}, r_0), \mathsf{rpk}_1 \leftarrow \mathsf{PkMap}(\mathsf{pk}_1, r_0),$$

  and encodes the challenge by $\mathsf{ech} = \mathsf{ch} \oplus H_c(\kappa, \mathsf{rsp}_0 || \mathsf{rsp}_1)$. Finally, it outputs the hash value $h := \{\mathsf{rpar}_0, \mathsf{rpar}_1, \mathsf{rpk}_0, \mathsf{rpk}_1, \mathsf{ech}, \mathsf{rsp}_0, \mathsf{rsp}_1\} \in \mathcal{SP}^2 \times \mathcal{PK}^2 \times \mathcal{CH} \times \mathcal{Z}^2$.
- $\mathsf{PPH.Test}(\mathsf{tk}, h, h')$: On input the test key tk and two hash values

$$h = \{\mathsf{rpar}_0, \mathsf{rpar}_1, \mathsf{rpk}_0, \mathsf{rpk}_1, \mathsf{ech}, \mathsf{rsp}_0, \mathsf{rsp}_1\},$$

$$h' = \{\mathsf{rpar}'_0, \mathsf{rpar}'_1, \mathsf{rpk}'_0, \mathsf{rpk}'_1, \mathsf{ech}', \mathsf{rsp}'_0, \mathsf{rsp}'_1\},$$

[3] Note that $(\mathsf{ch}, \mathsf{rsp}_i)$ is a signature of the message $\hat{u}_0 || \hat{u}_1$ with respect to the public key pk_i, while the secret key is sk_i and the randomness is $\hat{u}_i \cdot r_i$.

it recovers the challenges $\mathsf{ch} = \mathsf{ech} \oplus H_c(\kappa, \mathsf{rsp}_0||\mathsf{rsp}_1)$ and $\mathsf{ch}' = \mathsf{ech}' \oplus H_c(\kappa, \mathsf{rsp}'_0||\mathsf{rsp}'_1)$. Finally, it outputs a flag $b = 1$ if $\mathsf{rec}_0 = \mathsf{rec}'_1$, or $b = -1$ if $\mathsf{rec}_1 = \mathsf{rec}'_0$, otherwise $b = 0$.

$$\begin{cases} \mathsf{rec}_0 \leftarrow \mathsf{Rec}(\mathsf{rpar}'_0, \mathsf{rpk}'_0, \mathsf{ch}, \mathsf{rsp}_0), \\ \mathsf{rec}'_1 \leftarrow \mathsf{Rec}(\mathsf{rpar}_1, \mathsf{rpk}_1, \mathsf{ch}', \mathsf{rsp}'_1), \\ \mathsf{rec}_1 \leftarrow \mathsf{Rec}(\mathsf{rpar}'_1, \mathsf{rpk}'_1, \mathsf{ch}, \mathsf{rsp}_1), \\ \mathsf{rec}'_0 \leftarrow \mathsf{Rec}(\mathsf{rpar}_0, \mathsf{rpk}_0, \mathsf{ch}', \mathsf{rsp}'_0), \end{cases}$$

Correctness. For the predicate $\mathcal{P}$ (in Eq. 6), correctness depends on whether $\mathsf{PPH.Test}(\mathsf{tk}, h, h')$ equals to $\mathcal{P}(x, y)$ for any $x, y \in \mathsf{DSet}$. See Theorem 2 for detailed proof.

Theorem 2. *The proposed PPH scheme Γ is computationally correct under the collision-resistance property of the hash function H_r and the map-invariance property of the identification* ID.

Proof. By the map-invariance property, the identification ID is commitment-augmentable and commitment-independent. So,

$$\begin{cases} \mathsf{rec}_0 = \mathsf{Com}_1(\mathsf{par}_{\mathsf{ID}}; \hat{u}_0 \cdot r_0 \cdot r'_1), \\ \mathsf{rec}_1 = \mathsf{Com}_1(\mathsf{par}_{\mathsf{ID}}; \hat{u}_1 \cdot r_1 \cdot r'_0), \\ \mathsf{rec}'_0 = \mathsf{Com}_1(\mathsf{par}_{\mathsf{ID}}; \hat{u}'_0 \cdot r_1 \cdot r'_0), \\ \mathsf{rec}'_1 = \mathsf{Com}_1(\mathsf{par}_{\mathsf{ID}}; \hat{u}'_1 \cdot r_0 \cdot r'_1), \end{cases}$$

If $\mathsf{rec}_0 = \mathsf{rec}'_1$, then $\hat{u}_0 = \hat{u}'_1$ by the commitment-independency of ID. If a PPT adversary $\mathcal{A}$ finds two values x, y such that both $\mathcal{P}(x, y) \neq 1$ and $\mathsf{rec}_0 = \mathsf{rec}'_1$ hold, $H_r(s, x) = H_r(s, y + 1)$ holds with the state $x \neq y + 1$. Clearly, we can build an adversary $\mathcal{B}$ to break the collision-resistance property of H_r with solution $(x, y + 1)$. So,

$$\Pr\left[\mathcal{P}(x, y) \neq 1 \,|\, \mathsf{Test}(\mathsf{tk}, h, h') = 1\right] \leq \mathsf{Adv}^{\mathsf{COL}}_{H_r}$$

Similarly, one can prove

$$\Pr\left[\mathcal{P}(x, y) \neq -1 \,|\, \mathsf{Test}(\mathsf{tk}, h, h') = -1\right] \leq \mathsf{Adv}^{\mathsf{COL}}_{H_r}$$

If $\mathsf{Test}(\mathsf{tk}, h, h') = 0$, it ensures that $H_r(s, x) \neq H_r(s, y + 1)$ and $H_r(s, x) \neq H_r(s, y-1)$, which leads to the fact $x \neq y \pm 1$. Thus, the advantage $\mathsf{Adv}^{\mathsf{COR}}_{\Gamma,\mathcal{P},\mathcal{A}}(\lambda) \leq \mathsf{Adv}^{\mathsf{COL}}_{H_r}$ is negligible and the scheme Γ is correct.

4.2 Security Analysis

Theorem 3. *Assume the hash function family H_r is pseudorandom, H_c is entropy smoothing and the identification* ID *is of map-invariance, the proposed PPH scheme Γ is restricted-chosen-input secure.*

Proof. We define a sequence of games as follows:

- Game G_0: This is the real game. Specifically, the challenger generates the hash key hk and tk, samples $h_1 \leftarrow_\$ \mathsf{HSet}$, and computes challenge hash value $h_0 \leftarrow \mathsf{PPH.Hash}(\mathsf{hk}, x^*)$ where $x^* \in \mathsf{DSet}$ is chosen by $\mathcal{A}$. The challenger picks up a random bit $b \leftarrow_\$ \{0,1\}$ and sends h_b to $\mathcal{A}$. The adversary $\mathcal{A}$ guesses a bit b'. If $b = b'$, the game outputs 1.
- Game G_1: The pseudorandom function H_r with key s in algorithm $\mathsf{PPH.Hash}$ is replaced by a uniformly random function $f^* : \{0,1\}^* \to \mathcal{R}$.
- Game G_2: The challenge ch in algorithm $\mathsf{PPH.Hash}$ is uniformly sampled from $\mathcal{CH}$.
- Game G_3: The responses $\mathsf{rsp}_0, \mathsf{rsp}_1$ in algorithm $\mathsf{PPH.Hash}$ are uniformly sampled from $\mathcal{Z}^3$.
- Game G_4: $\mathsf{rpar}_0, \mathsf{rpar}_1, \mathsf{rpk}_0, \mathsf{rpk}_1$ in algorithm $\mathsf{PPH.Hash}$ are uniformly sampled from $\mathcal{SP}^2 \times \mathcal{PK}^2$, instead of computing via ParMap and PkMap.

Note that in G_4, all the elements of hash value h_0 are uniformly sampled from appropriate space, and the oracle does not provide any extra information about the bit b. Clearly, the advantage of adversary $\mathcal{A}$ in game G_4 is 0.

Lemma 1. $\mathsf{G}_0 \approx \mathsf{G}_1$ *under the pseudorandom property of the hash function* H_r.

Proof (Proof of Lemma 1). Assume $\mathcal{A}$ is a PPT adversary that can distinguish G_0 and G_1 with non-negligible probability. We can build an adversary $\mathcal{B}$ to break the pseudorandom property of H_r as follows.

$\mathcal{B}$ simulates the PPH security game as prescribed for $\mathcal{A}$, except that the computation of $\hat{u}_0$ and $\hat{u}_1$ in algorithm $\mathsf{PPH.Hash}$ relies on the oracle in the PRF game. When the oracle is $H_r(s,\cdot)$, $\mathcal{B}$ simulates G_0. When the oracle is f^*, $\mathcal{B}$ simulates G_1. So, we have

$$|\Pr[\mathsf{G}_0 = 1] - \Pr[\mathsf{G}_1 = 1]| \leq \mathsf{Adv}_{H_r}^{\mathsf{PRF}}.$$

Lemma 2. $\mathsf{G}_1 \approx \mathsf{G}_2$ *under the commitment-independency of identification scheme and the entropy smoothing property of hash function* H_c.

Proof (Proof of Lemma 2). Consider game G_1' that is the same as G_1 except that the challenge ch in algorithm $\mathsf{PPH.Hash}$ is computed by $H_c(\kappa, \delta)$ where δ is uniformly sampled from $\mathcal{R}^2 \times \mathcal{W}^2$.

First, we claim that $\mathsf{G}_1 = \mathsf{G}_1'$. In G_1, since $\hat{u}_0$ and $\hat{u}_1$ are generated via random function, these two elements can be viewed as one uniform sampling from $\mathcal{R}^2$. Note that the identification scheme is commitment-independent. In H_1, given fixed system parameters $\mathsf{par}_{\mathsf{ID}}$, the value of cmt_i is determined by randomness $\hat{u}_i \cdot r_i$ for $i \in \{0,1\}$. Since $\hat{u}_i \cdot r_i$ is uniformly distributed over $\mathcal{R}$, cmt_i is uniformly distributed over $\mathcal{W}$.

Then, we claim that $\mathsf{G}_1' \approx \mathsf{G}_2$. Let Q denote the number of hash value queries by adversary $\mathcal{A}$. W.l.o.g., we assume every query made by adversary $\mathcal{A}$ is valid so that the oracle would not return $\perp$. Thus, the oracle would invoke the algorithm $\mathsf{PPH.Hash}$ Q times in G_1'.

Let $\mathsf{G}_{1,0}'$ be the same as G_1' except that challenge ch^* in h_0 is randomly sampled from $\mathcal{CH}$. For $i \in \{1, \cdots, Q\}$, let $\mathsf{G}_{1,i}'$ be the same as $\mathsf{G}_{1,i-1}'$ except that challenge ch in the hash value of the i-th query is randomly sampled from $\mathcal{CH}$. Clearly, $\mathsf{G}'_{1,Q} = \mathsf{G}_2$.

Assume $\mathcal{A}$ is a PPT adversary that can distinguish G'_1 and $\mathsf{G}'_{1,0}$ with non-negligible probability. We can build an adversary $\mathcal{B}$ to break the entropy smoothing property of H_c as follows. $\mathcal{B}$ receives (k, g) from the challenger in the game of entropy smoothing, and sets $\kappa = k$ and $\mathsf{ch}^* = g$. The rest of the simulation is the same as G'_1. When $g = H_c(k, \delta)$ and $\delta \leftarrow_\$ \mathcal{R}^2 \times \mathcal{W}^2$, $\mathcal{B}$ simulates G'_1. When $g \leftarrow_\$ \mathcal{CH}$, $\mathcal{B}$ simulates $\mathsf{G}'_{1,0}$. Similarly, one can prove $\mathsf{G}'_{1,i-1} \approx \mathsf{G}'_{1,i}$ for $i \in \{1, \cdots, Q\}$.

Lemma 3. $\mathsf{G}_2 \approx \mathsf{G}_3$ *under the indistinguishability of response.*

Proof (Proof of Lemma 3). Let game G'_2 be the same as G_2 except that response rsp_0 in algorithm $\mathsf{PPH.Hash}$ is randomly sampled from $\mathcal{Z}$. Let Q be the number of hash value queries by adversary $\mathcal{A}$. Let $\mathsf{G}_{2,0}$ be the same as G_2 except that response rsp_0^* in h_0 is randomly sampled from $\mathcal{Z}$. For $i \in \{1, \cdots, Q\}$, let $\mathsf{G}_{2,i}$ be the same as $\mathsf{G}_{2,i-1}$ except that response rsp_0 in the hash value of the i-th query is randomly sampled from $\mathcal{Z}$. Clearly, $\mathsf{G}_{2,Q} = \mathsf{G}'_2$.

We claim that $\mathsf{G}_2 \approx \mathsf{G}_{2,0}$. Assume that $\mathcal{A}$ can distinguish G_2 and $\mathsf{G}_{2,0}$ with non-negligible probability, we can build an adversary $\mathcal{B}$ to break the indistinguishability of response as follows. The adversary $\mathcal{B}$ receives par, sk, ch and rsp_b from challenger in game $\mathsf{IND}_{\mathsf{ID}}^{\mathsf{RSP}}$, and uses them to simulate game G_2 for $\mathcal{A}$. In particular, $\mathsf{par}_{\mathsf{ID}}$ and sk_0 in algorithm $\mathsf{PPH.KeyGen}$ are set as par and sk respectively. When computing hash value h_0, challenge ch^* is set as ch and rsp_0^* is set as rsp_b. If rsp_b is computed via algorithm Rsp, $\mathcal{B}$ simulates game G_2. Otherwise, rsp_b is randomly sampled from $\mathcal{Z}$ and $\mathcal{B}$ simulates game $\mathsf{G}_{2,0}$. Similarly, one can prove $\mathsf{G}_{2,i-1} \approx \mathsf{G}_{2,i}$ for $i \in \{1, \cdots, Q\}$.

Let game G''_2 be the same as G'_2 except that response rsp_1 in algorithm $\mathsf{PPH.Hash}$ is randomly sampled from $\mathcal{Z}$. Note that G_3 is the same as G''_2 except that response rsp_2 in algorithm $\mathsf{PPH.Hash}$ is randomly sampled from $\mathcal{Z}$. Using same strategy, one can prove $\mathsf{G}'_2 \approx \mathsf{G}''_2$ and $\mathsf{G}''_2 \approx \mathsf{G}_3$.

Lemma 4. $\mathsf{G}_3 \approx \mathsf{G}_4$ *under the map-invariance of identification scheme.*

Proof (Proof of Lemma 4). Let game G'_3 be the same as G_3 except that rpar_0 and rpk_0 in algorithm $\mathsf{PPH.Hash}$ are uniformly sampled from $\mathcal{SP} \times \mathcal{PK}$. Let Q be the number of hash value queries by adversary $\mathcal{A}$. Let $\mathsf{G}_{3,0}$ be the same as G_3 except that rpar_0^* and rpk_0^* in h_0 are uniformly sampled from $\mathcal{SP} \times \mathcal{PK}$. For $i \in \{1, \cdots, Q\}$, let $\mathsf{G}_{3,i}$ be the same as $\mathsf{G}_{3,i-1}$ except that rpar_0 and rpk_0 in the hash value of the i-th query are randomly sampled from $\mathcal{SP} \times \mathcal{PK}$. Clearly, $\mathsf{G}_{3,Q} = \mathsf{G}'_3$.

We claim that $\mathsf{G}_3 \approx \mathsf{G}_{3,0}$. If there exists a PPT adversary $\mathcal{A}$ that can distinguish G_3 and $\mathsf{G}_{3,0}$ with overwhelming probability, we can build a PPT adversary $\mathcal{B}$ to distinguish the distributions of rpar_0^* and rpk_0^* in G_3 and $\mathsf{G}_{3,0}$.

The adversary $\mathcal{B}$ receives an instance of $(\mathsf{par}_{\mathsf{ID}}, \mathsf{rpar}, \mathsf{rpk})$ and simulates the game G_3 as prescribed for $\mathcal{A}$ using $\mathsf{par}_{\mathsf{ID}}$. In particular, $\mathcal{B}$ sets $\mathsf{rpar}_0^* = \mathsf{rpar}$ and $\mathsf{rpk}_0^* = \mathsf{rpk}$. If rpar and rpk are computed via algorithms ParMap and PkMap,

$\mathcal{B}$ simulates G_3. If rpar and rpk are randomly sampled from $\mathcal{SP}$ and $\mathcal{PK}$, $\mathcal{B}$ simulates $\mathsf{G}_{3,0}$. Similarly, one can prove $\mathsf{G}_{3,i-1} \approx \mathsf{G}_{3,i}$ for $i \in \{1, \cdots, Q\}$.

Let game G_3'' be the same as G_3' except that rpar_1 and rpk_1 in algorithm $\mathsf{PPH.Hash}$ are uniformly sampled from $\mathcal{SP} \times \mathcal{PK}$. Clearly, $\mathsf{G}_3'' = \mathsf{G}_4$ Similarly, one can prove that $\mathsf{G}_3' \approx \mathsf{G}_3''$ under the map-invariance of identification scheme.

To sum up, the advantage of $\mathcal{A}$ is

$$\mathsf{Adv}^{\mathsf{PPH}}_{\Gamma,\mathcal{P},\mathcal{A}} \leq \mathsf{Adv}^{\mathsf{PRF}}_{H_r} + (Q+1)(\mathsf{Adv}^{\mathsf{ES}}_{H_c} + 3(\mathsf{Adv}^{\mathsf{RSP}}_{\mathsf{ID}} + \mathsf{Adv}^{\mathsf{MI}}_{\mathsf{ID}})).$$

Thus, the proposed PPH scheme Γ is restricted-chosen-input secure.

4.3 PPH Instance from Schnorr Identification

The instanced PPH construction Γ based on the Schnorr identification ID with commitment space $\mathbb{G}$, randomness space $\mathbb{Z}_p^*$ and challenge space $\mathbb{Z}_p$ is described formally in Fig. 4.

5 The Proposed Parameter-Hiding ORE

In this part, based on our proposed generic PPH schemes from identification schemes, we optimize Cash et al.'s scheme by eliminating bilinear mappings. Finally, we follow the security analysis of previous works [10] to prove the security of our scheme.

5.1 From PPH to Parameter-Hiding ORE

Below, we follow Cash et al's framework [10] to construct a generic parameter-hiding ORE scheme. The first step is to construct ORE with smoothed CLWW leakage based on PPH. Here, consider the same leakage profile $\mathcal{L}_1$ (see Eq. 4) as [10]. By definition, it is clear that the ORE construction only leaks the order of underlying plaintexts and the statement whether $\mathsf{msdb}(m_i, m_j)$ and $\mathsf{msdb}(m_i, m_k)$ are the same.

Let $\Gamma = (\mathsf{PPH.KeyGen}, \mathsf{PPH.Hash}, \mathsf{PPH.Test})$ be a PPH scheme with respect to the predicate $\mathcal{P}$, the generic ORE construction is given as follows:

- $\mathsf{ORE.KGen}(1^\lambda)$: On input a security parameter λ, it runs $\mathsf{PPH.KeyGen}(1^\lambda)$ to generate $(\mathsf{par}_{\mathsf{PPH}}, \mathsf{hk}, \mathsf{tk})$. Let $F : \mathcal{K} \times ([n] \times \{0,1\}^n) \to \{0,1\}^\lambda$ be a pseudorandom hash function family. It picks $k \leftarrow_\$ \mathcal{K}$. Define the encoding function $\mathcal{E}(k, m, i) = F(k, i||m_{[:i-1]}||0^{n-i+1}) + m_{[i]} \in \{0,1\}^\lambda$. Then, it outputs the master secret key $\mathsf{msk} = (\mathsf{hk}, k)$ and the comparison key $\mathsf{ck} = \mathsf{tk}$. For brevity, the system parameters $\mathsf{par} = \{\mathsf{par}_{\mathsf{PPH}}, \mathcal{E}\}$ are implicit inputs of other algorithms.

$\mathsf{PPH.KeyGen}(1^\lambda)$

Pick keyed hash functions $H_r : \{0,1\}^\lambda \times \{0,1\}^* \to \mathbb{Z}_p^*$ and $H_c : \{0,1\}^\lambda \times \{0,1\}^* \to \mathbb{Z}_p$.
$g \leftarrow_\$ \mathbb{G}$, $s, \kappa, x_0, x_1 \leftarrow_\$ \mathbb{Z}_p$
$y_0 := g^{x_0}$, $y_1 := g^{x_1}$
$\mathsf{par}_{\mathsf{PPH}} := \{g, H_r, H_c\}$
$\mathsf{hk} := \{s, \kappa, x_0, x_1, g, y_0, y_1\}$, $\mathsf{tk} := \{\kappa\}$
return $(\mathsf{par}_{\mathsf{PPH}}, \mathsf{hk}, \mathsf{tk})$

$\mathsf{PPH.Hash}(\mathsf{hk}, u)$

$\{s, \kappa, x_0, x_1, g, y_0, y_1\} \leftarrow \mathsf{hk}$
$\hat{u}_0 \leftarrow H_r(s, u)$, $\hat{u}_1 \leftarrow H_r(s, u+1)$
$r_0, r_1 \leftarrow_\$ \mathbb{Z}_p$, $w_0 := g^{\hat{u}_0 \cdot r_0}$, $w_1 := g^{\hat{u}_1 \cdot r_1}$
$\xi \leftarrow H_c(\hat{u}_0 || \hat{u}_1 || w_0 || w_1)$
$z_0 := \hat{u}_0 \cdot r_0 - \xi \cdot x_0$, $z_1 := \hat{u}_1 \cdot r_1 - \xi \cdot x_1$
$\hat{g}_0 := g^{r_1}$, $\hat{y}_0 := y_0^{r_1}$, $\hat{g}_1 := g^{r_0}$, $\hat{y}_1 := y_1^{r_0}$
$\hat{\xi} := \xi \oplus H_c(\kappa || z_0 || z_1)$
return $H := \{\hat{g}_0, \hat{g}_1, \hat{y}_0, \hat{y}_1, \hat{\xi}, z_0, z_1\}$

$\mathsf{PPH.Test}(\mathsf{tk}, h, h')$

$\{\hat{g}_0, \hat{g}_1, \hat{y}_0, \hat{y}_1, \hat{\xi}, z_0, z_1\} \leftarrow h$
$\{\hat{g}'_0, \hat{g}'_1, \hat{y}'_0, \hat{y}'_1, \hat{\xi}', z'_0, z'_1\} \leftarrow h'$
$\xi := \hat{\xi} \oplus H_c(\kappa || z_0 || z_1)$, $\xi' := \hat{\xi}' \oplus H_c(\kappa || z'_0 || z'_1)$
$\mathsf{rec}_0 := (\hat{g}'_0)^{z_0} \cdot (\hat{y}'_0)^{\xi}$, $\mathsf{rec}'_1 := (\hat{g}_1)^{z'_1} \cdot (\hat{y}_1)^{\xi'}$
if $\mathsf{rec}_0 = \mathsf{rec}'_1$ **then**
    return 1
$\mathsf{rec}_1 := (\hat{g}'_1)^{z_1} \cdot (\hat{y}'_1)^{\xi}$, $\mathsf{rec}'_0 := (\hat{g}_0)^{z'_0} \cdot (\hat{y}_0)^{\xi'}$
if $\mathsf{rec}_1 = \mathsf{rec}'_0$ **then**
    return -1
return 0

Fig. 4. The instanced PPH construction based on the Schnorr identification ID.

- ORE.Enc(msk, m): On input msk and a n bits message m, it randomly selects a permutation $\pi : [n] \to [n]$ and computes

$$\begin{cases} u_i = \mathcal{E}(k, m, \pi(i)), \\ h_i \leftarrow \mathsf{PPH.Hash}(\mathsf{hk}, u_i), \end{cases} \forall i \in [n]$$

Finally, it outputs the ciphertext

$$\vec{c} := \{h_1, \cdots, h_n\} \in \mathcal{SP}^{2n} \times \mathcal{PK}^{2n} \times \mathcal{CH}^n \times \mathcal{Z}^{2n}.$$

- ORE.Cmp(ck, $\vec{c}, \vec{c'}$): On input the comparison key ck and two ciphertexts $(\vec{c}, \vec{c'})$, it computes

$$b_{ij} \leftarrow \mathsf{PPH.Test}(\mathsf{ck}, h_i, h'_j), \ \forall i, j \in [n]$$

and stops when $b_{ij} \neq 0$. If it stops with $b_{ij} = 1$, it outputs 1 to indicate that $m > m'$; else if it stops with $b_{ij} = -1$, it outputs -1 to indicate that $m > m'$. If there does not exist i, j such that $b_{ij} \neq 0$, it outputs 0 to indicate that $m = m'$.

The above description differs from the original construction [10] mainly in that the predicate corresponding to PPH adds an additional case, i.e. $\mathcal{P}(x, y) = -1$ if and only if $x < y$. In the original construction, the predicate is defined as $\mathcal{P}(x, y) = 1$ if and only if $x > y$, which results in that it needs to execute $\mathsf{PPH.Test}$ algorithm twice for each c_i, c'_j, i.e. $\mathsf{PPH.Test}(\mathsf{ck}, h_i, h'_j)$ and $\mathsf{PPH.Test}(\mathsf{ck}, h'_j, h_i)$. But, our generic PPH construction only needs to execute $\mathsf{PPH.Test}$ algorithm once for each h_i, h'_j.

Correctness. For the predicate $\mathcal{O}$ (in Eq. 1), correctness depends on whether $\mathsf{ORE.Cmp}(\mathsf{ck}, c, c')$ equals to $\mathcal{O}(m, m')$ for any $m, m' \in \mathcal{D}$. See Theorem 4 for detailed proof.

Theorem 4. *The proposed ORE scheme Π is computationally correct under the pseudorandom property of the hash function F and the computational correctness of the PPH scheme Γ.*

Proof. If the PPH scheme Γ is computationally correct, b_{ij} equals to $\mathcal{P}(u_i, u'_j)$ with overwhelming probability. Considering the first case $\mathcal{O}(m, m') = 1$, there must be two indexes (i, j) satisfying $\pi(i) = \pi'(j')$ and $\mathcal{P}(u_i, u'_j) = 1$, since the function F with the key s outputs deterministic results. Here,

$$\begin{aligned}
&\mathcal{E}(k, m, \pi(i)) = \mathcal{E}(k, m', \pi'(j)) + 1 \Rightarrow \\
&F(k, \pi(i)||m_{[:\pi(i)-1]}||0^{n-\pi(i)+1}) + m_{[\pi(i)]} \\
=&F(k, \pi'(j)||m'_{[:\pi'(j)-1]}||0^{n-\pi'(j)+1}) + m'_{[\pi'(j)]} + 1.
\end{aligned}$$

As long as there is no indexes (i', j') satisfying $\mathcal{P}(u_{i'}, u'_{j'}) = -1$, $\mathsf{ORE.Cmp}(\mathsf{ck}, c, c')$ must output 1. For all $(i', j') \neq (i, j)$, we have

$$\Pr\left[\mathcal{P}(u_{i'}, u'_{j'}) = -1\right] \leq 1 - \left(1 - \frac{n}{2^\lambda}\right)^n$$

In this case, the probability of $\mathsf{ORE.Cmp}$ $(\mathsf{ck}, c, c') \neq \mathcal{O}(m, m')$ is negligible. Similarly, one can prove this probability is also negligible in the case $\mathcal{O}(m, m') = -1$ and $\mathcal{O}(m, m') = 0$. Thus, the proposed ORE scheme Π is correct.

Security. The proof of Theorem 5 is similar to Theorem 12 in [10], so we omit the details here.

Theorem 5. *Given a secure pseudorandom function F, if the underlying PPH scheme Γ is restricted-chosen-input secure, the generic ORE scheme is $\mathcal{L}_1$-non-adaptive-simulation secure.*

Starting from Cash et al.'s framework, one can easily construct pORE schemes from identification-based PPH schemes. For instance with identification schemes, the hash key and the test key are modified by $\mathsf{hk} := \{s, \kappa, \mathsf{sk}_0, \mathsf{sk}_1, \mathsf{pk}_0, \mathsf{pk}_1\}$ and $\mathsf{tk} := \{\kappa\}$, respectively. For each $i \in [n]$, the hash value h_i is composed of $\{\mathsf{rpar}_{i,0}, \mathsf{rpar}_{i,1}, \mathsf{rpk}_{i,0}, \mathsf{rpk}_{i,1}, \mathsf{ech}_i, \mathsf{rsp}_{i,0}, \mathsf{rsp}_{i,1}\}$. Clearly, the ciphertext $\vec{c}$ belongs to the space $\mathcal{SP}^{2n} \times \mathcal{PK}^{2n} \times \mathcal{CH}^n \times \mathcal{Z}^{2n}$ and the comparison algorithm Cmp needs to perform n^2 times Hash algorithms, equivalent to $4n^2$ times Rec operations.

5.2 ORE Instance from Schnorr Identification

Now, from Schnorr identification, we construct an efficient ORE scheme, named $\mathsf{Sch\text{-}ORE}$, without bilinear pairings in Fig. 5. The master secret key consists of two randomness $s, \kappa \leftarrow_\$ \mathbb{Z}_p$, two secret keys $x_0, x_1 \leftarrow_\$ \mathbb{Z}_p$ and public keys $\{g, y_0, y_1\} \in \mathbb{G}$, while the comparison key is only the randomness κ. For each bit-wise hash value h_i, its size is $4|\mathbb{G}| + 3|\mathbb{Z}_p|$. For the comparison algorithm, at most $8n^2$ group exponentiation operations are required to compare two ciphertexts with respect to any messages. Essentially, our ORE scheme uses two group exponentiation operations to replace one bilinear pairing operation. Theoretically, the comparison efficiency can be improved by about 3 to 4 times with the same security level.

Improving Efficiency with $\mathcal{L}_1'$ Leakage. Cash et al. [10] proposed the optimization idea of fixing the permutation π in msk to replace randomized permutation in $\mathsf{PPH.Hash}$ algorithm. The optimization point is that it only executes the $\mathsf{PPH.Test}$ algorithm on the same index, i.e. $i = j$, in the comparison algorithm. Combined with our optimization points, each comparison algorithm requires $8n$ times group exponentiation operations, but it can lead to a weaker leakage $\mathcal{L}_1'$ (in Eq. 5). Compared to $\mathcal{L}_1$ (in Eq. 4), $\mathcal{L}_1'$ reveals extra information that $\mathbf{1}(\mathsf{msdb}(m_i, m_j) = \mathsf{msdb}(m_k, m_l))$ even when $i \neq k$. According to Theorem 12 in [10], it can still be confirmed that our $\mathsf{Sch\text{-}ORE}$ is $\mathcal{L}_1'$-non-adaptive-simulation secure if Γ is restricted-chosen-input secure and F is a secure pseudorandom function.

6 Experimental Evaluation

In order to evaluate the performance of our parameter-hiding ORE scheme, we built and evaluated an implementation with instantiated components[4] Then, we describe the comparison results with Cash et al.'s ORE scheme [10] in the aspect of storage and computation costs under different plaintext bit-lengths.

Instantiating Primitives. Our implementation is written in C language. We instantiate the necessary keyed hash function using SHA-256. We use GMP library to implement multi-precision integer arithmetic and PBC library to

[4] Our implementation is available at https://github.com/cpeng-crypto/pORE.

$\mathsf{ORE.KGen}(1^\lambda)$

Pick keyed hash functions $H_r : \{0,1\}^\lambda \times \{0,1\}^* \to \mathbb{Z}_p^*$ and $H_c : \{0,1\}^\lambda \times \{0,1\}^* \to \mathbb{Z}_p$.
$g \leftarrow_\$ \mathbb{G}$, $s, \kappa, x_0, x_1 \leftarrow_\$ \mathbb{Z}_p$
$y_0 := g^{x_0}$, $y_1 := g^{x_1}$
$\mathsf{par}_{\mathsf{PPH}} := \{g, H_r, H_c\}$
$\mathsf{hk} := \{s, \kappa, x_0, x_1, g, y_0, y_1\}$, $\mathsf{tk} := \{\kappa\}$
$k \leftarrow_\$ \mathcal{K}$
$\mathcal{E}(k, m, i) := F(k, i||m_{[:i-1]}||0^{n-i+1}) + m_{[i]}$
$\mathsf{par} := (\mathsf{par}_{\mathsf{PPH}}, \mathcal{E})$, $\mathsf{msk} := (\mathsf{hk}, k)$, $\mathsf{ck} := \mathsf{tk}$
return $(\mathsf{par}, \mathsf{msk}, \mathsf{ck})$

$\mathsf{ORE.Enc}(\mathsf{msk}, m)$

$\{s, \kappa, x_0, x_1, g, y_0, y_1, k\} \leftarrow \mathsf{msk}$
$\pi : [n] \to [n]$
for $i \in [n]$ **do**
    $r_{i,0}, r_{i,1} \leftarrow_\$ \mathbb{Z}_p^*$
    $u_i := \mathcal{E}(k, m, \pi(i))$
    $\hat{u}_{i,0} \leftarrow H_r(s, u_i)$, $\hat{u}_{i,1} \leftarrow H_r(s, u_i + 1)$
    $w_{i,0} := g^{\hat{u}_{i,0} \cdot r_{i,0}}$, $w_{i,1} := g^{\hat{u}_{i,1} \cdot r_{i,1}}$
    $\xi_i \leftarrow H_c(\hat{u}_{i,0}||w_{i,0}||\hat{u}_{i,1}||w_{i,1})$
    $z_{i,0} := \hat{u}_{i,0} \cdot r_{i,0} - \xi_i \cdot x_0$
    $z_{i,1} := \hat{u}_{i,1} \cdot r_{i,1} - \xi_i \cdot x_1$
    $\hat{g}_{i,0} := g^{r_{i,1}}$, $\hat{y}_{i,0} := y_0^{r_{i,1}}$, $\hat{g}_{i,1} := g^{r_{i,0}}$, $\hat{y}_{i,1} := y_1^{r_{i,0}}$
    $\hat{\xi}_i := \xi_i \oplus H_c(\kappa||z_{i,0}||z_{i,1})$
    $h_i := \{\hat{g}_{i,0}, \hat{y}_{i,0}, \hat{g}_{i,1}, \hat{y}_{i,1}, \hat{\xi}_i, z_{i,0}, z_{i,1}\}$
$\vec{c} := \{h_1, \cdots, h_n\}$;
return $\vec{c}$

$\mathsf{ORE.Cmp}(\mathsf{ck}, \vec{c}, \vec{c}')$

$\{h_1, \cdots, h_n\} \leftarrow \vec{c}$, $\{h_1', \cdots, h_n'\} \leftarrow \vec{c}'$
$\{\hat{g}_{i,0}, \hat{y}_{i,0}, \hat{g}_{i,1}, \hat{y}_{i,1}, \hat{\xi}_i, z_{i,0}, z_{i,1}\} \leftarrow h_i$
$\{\hat{g}_{j,0}', \hat{y}_{j,0}', \hat{g}_{j,1}', \hat{y}_{j,1}', \hat{\xi}_j', z_{j,0}', z_{j,1}'\} \leftarrow h_j'$
for $i \in [n], j \in [n]$ **do**
    $\xi_i := \hat{\xi}_i \oplus H_c(\kappa||z_{i,0}||z_{i,1})$
    $\xi_j' := \hat{\xi}_j' \oplus H_c(\kappa||z_{j,0}'||z_{j,1}')$
    $\mathsf{rec}_{i,j,0} := (\hat{g}_{j,0}')^{z_{i,0}} \cdot (\hat{y}_{j,0}')^{\xi_i}$, $\mathsf{rec}_{i,j,1}' := (\hat{g}_{i,1})^{z_{j,1}'} \cdot (\hat{y}_{i,1})^{\xi_j'}$
    if $\mathsf{rec}_{i,j,0} = \mathsf{rec}_{i,j,1}'$ **then** ▷ check $u_i = u_j' + 1$?
        return $b_{ij} = 1$
    $\mathsf{rec}_{i,j,1} = (\hat{g}_{j,1}')^{z_{i,1}} \cdot (\hat{y}_{j,1}')^{\xi_i}$, $\mathsf{rec}_{i,j,0}' = (\hat{g}_{i,0})^{z_{j,0}'} \cdot (\hat{y}_{i,0})^{\xi_j'}$
    if $\mathsf{rec}_{i,j,1} = \mathsf{rec}_{i,j,0}'$ **then** ▷ check $u_i + 1 = u_j'$?
        return $b_{ij} = -1$
return $b = 0$

Fig. 5. Sch-ORE scheme, the instanced ORE construction based on the Schnorr identification.

Table 2. Ciphertext size in KB and running time in milliseconds of ORE schemes with different message bit-length n in $\{8, 16, 24, 32, 48, 64\}$.ORE* refers to the ORE scheme with fixed permutation.

n	Scheme	Ciphertext size (KB)	Encryption cost (ms)	Comparison Cost (ms)	Leakage
8	Cash et al.'s ORE [10]	2.50	43.52	487.17	$\mathcal{L}_1$
	Cash et al.'s ORE* [10]	2.50	43.52	60.91	$\mathcal{L}'_1$
	Our Sch-ORE	1.72	16.71	151.06	$\mathcal{L}_1$
	Our Sch-ORE	**1.72**	**16.71**	**19.81**	$\mathcal{L}'_1$
16	Cash et al.'s ORE [10]	5.00	87.04	1948.67	$\mathcal{L}_1$
	Cash et al.'s ORE* [10]	5.00	87.04	121.97	$\mathcal{L}'_1$
	Our Sch-ORE	3.44	33.42	602.14	$\mathcal{L}_1$
	Our Sch-ORE	**3.44**	**33.42**	**39.62**	$\mathcal{L}'_1$
24	Cash et al.'s ORE [10]	7.50	130.56	4384.51	$\mathcal{L}_1$
	Cash et al.'s ORE* [10]	7.50	130.56	182.69	$\mathcal{L}'_1$
	Our Sch-ORE	5.16	50.12	1353.23	$\mathcal{L}_1$
	Our Sch-ORE	**5.16**	**50.12**	**59.43**	$\mathcal{L}'_1$
32	Cash et al.'s ORE [10]	10.00	174.08	7794.69	$\mathcal{L}_1$
	Cash et al.'s ORE* [10]	10.00	174.08	243.58	$\mathcal{L}'_1$
	Our Sch-ORE	6.88	66.83	2404.32	$\mathcal{L}_1$
	Our Sch-ORE	**6.88**	**66.83**	**79.24**	$\mathcal{L}'_1$
48	Cash et al.'s ORE [10]	15.00	261.12	17538.05	$\mathcal{L}_1$
	Cash et al.'s ORE* [10]	15.00	261.12	365.38	$\mathcal{L}'_1$
	Our Sch-ORE	10.31	100.25	5406.56	$\mathcal{L}_1$
	Our Sch-ORE	**10.31**	**100.25**	**118.85**	$\mathcal{L}'_1$
64	Cash et al.'s ORE [10]	20.00	348.16	31178.75	$\mathcal{L}_1$
	Cash et al.'s ORE* [10]	20.00	348.16	487.17	$\mathcal{L}'_1$
	Our Sch-ORE	13.75	133.67	9608.83	$\mathcal{L}_1$
	Our Sch-ORE	**13.75**	**133.67**	**158.47**	$\mathcal{L}'_1$

implement bilinear pairings. Notice that there is no need to use bilinear pairing operation in our schemes, but to ensure fairness, we uniformly use the $\mathbb{G}_1$ group of bilinear pairing as the cyclic group $\mathbb{G}$ in our schemes. We believe this provides a more balanced comparison of the performance tradeoffs between Cash et al.'s scheme and our new scheme.

Security Parameters. All evaluations were performed with the bilinear pairing parameter set "*d159.param*" under the security parameter $\lambda = 80$ bits. In such case, Symmetric eXternal Diffie-Hellman (SXDH) assumption holds, which is the basis for the security of parameter-hiding ORE in [10]. Specifically, the size of elements in $\mathbb{G}_1$ and $\mathbb{G}_2$ is $|\mathbb{G}_1| = 40$ bytes and $|\mathbb{G}_2| = 120$ bytes, respectively.

The size of elements in $\mathbb{Z}_q^*$ is $|\mathbb{Z}_q^*| = 20$ bytes. Note that elements in group $\mathbb{G}_2$ need only be 3 times longer than elements in group $\mathbb{G}_1$.

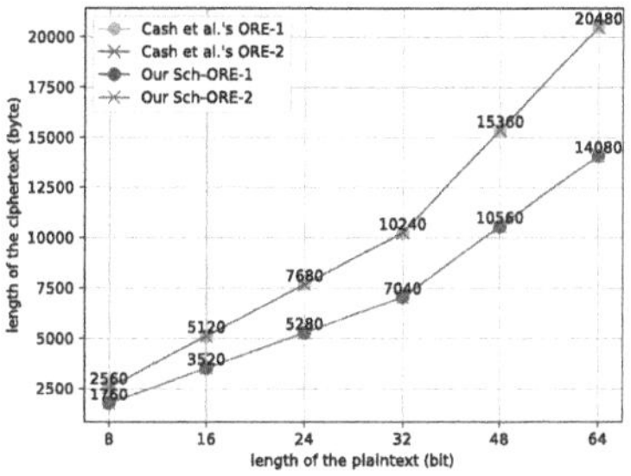

(a) Ciphertext size in ORE

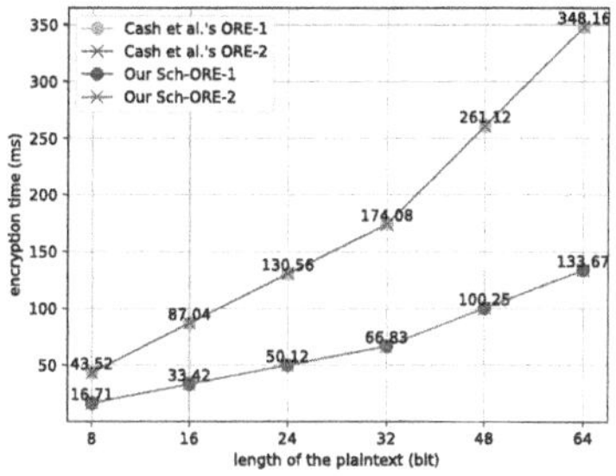

(b) Encryption time in ORE

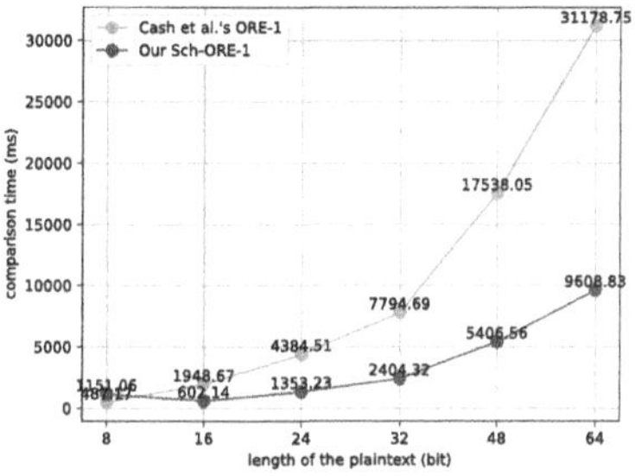

(c) Comparison time in ORE with randomized permutations

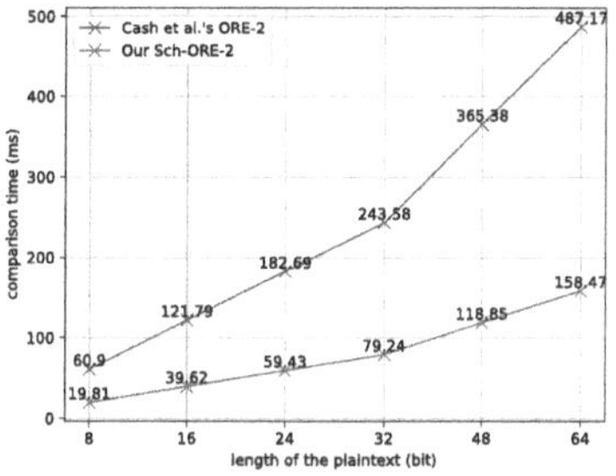

(d) Comparison time in ORE with fixed permutations

Fig. 6. Performance comparison

Benchmarks and Evaluation. All experiments are executed on a desktop with Intel(R) Core(TM) i5-10500 CPU @ 3.10GHz, 16GB RAM and Ubuntu 18.04 LTS. Although both Cash et al.'s scheme and our scheme are easily parallelizable, we do not exploit parallelism in our benchmarks. We report detailed comparisons in Table 2 for different plaintext bit-length $n \in \{8, 16, 24, 32, 48, 64\}$. As expected, our protocol shows a significant performance improvement for each bit-length. For a more intuitive presentation, we divide into these results into three categories for comparison.

Ciphertext Size. As shown in Fig. 6(a), ciphertexts encrypted with random permutation or fixed permutation have the same bit length for the same plaintext length. For n bits plaintext, our Sch-ORE scheme costs $4n|\mathbb{G}_1| + 3n|\mathbb{Z}_p| \approx 220n$ bytes. Compared to Cash et al.'s ORE [10], our Sch-ORE scheme can reduce the ciphertext size by about 31.25%. However, the ciphertext expansion ratio is still large, for example, the ciphertext size reaches 13.75 KB at 64-bit plaintext length.

Encryption Efficiency. For encrypted n-bit messages, roughly $6n$ $\mathbb{G}_1$ group exponentiation operations need to be computed in Sch-ORE scheme while $2n$ $\mathbb{G}_1$ group exponentiation and $2n$ $\mathbb{G}_2$ group exponentiation operations in [10]. In contrast, $\mathbb{G}_2$ is an elliptic curve point group over $\mathbb{F}_{p^3}$, which is nearly 7 times less efficient in terms of point multiplication than the elliptic curve point group $\mathbb{G}_2$ over $\mathbb{F}_p$. As shown in Fig. 6(b), for the whole encryption algorithm, our scheme is almost 2.6 times faster than Cash et al.'s ORE [10].

Comparison Efficiency. In Fig. 6(c) and 6(d), we evaluate the comparative efficiency of various ORE schemes. It show that in the case of randomized permutations, the comparison time consumption grows rapidly with the increase of plaintext bits, but for fixed permutations, it grows more slowly. Clearly, the comparative efficiency of random permutations is n times slower than that of fixed permutations. Besides, in both modes, our Sch-ORE is more than 3 times faster than ORE in [10]. For 64-bit plaintext, it needs 158 ms for a single comparison.

To sum up, our Sch-ORE scheme performs better than other parameter-hiding ORE at the same security level and leakage, in which the ciphertext length is reduced by more than 31.25%, the encryption efficiency increased by nearly 2.6 times and the comparison efficiency increased by more than 3 times.

7 Conclusion

In this paper, we proposed an efficient and secure construction for parameter-hiding order-revealing encryption (pORE). Our approach relies on the map-invariance property for identification protocols, which enables us to develop a generic construction of property-preserving hash (PPH) schemes. Using our PPH scheme, we presented a new parameter-hiding ORE that outperforms existing state-of-the-art constructions. Specifically, we instantiated our framework with the pairing-free Schnorr identification scheme and demonstrated that our proposed pORE scheme achieves a reduction in ciphertext size of approximately 31.25%, while improving encryption and comparison efficiency by more than two times.

Our work offers a practical and secure alternative to existing pORE constructions. As future work, it is interesting to instant our ID schemes (with map-variance) from other hardness assumptions. For example, it seems like that one could construct ID scheme based on isogeny-related assumptions for post-quantum pORE. Note that it is difficult to extend previous construction for post-quantum security due to the need of pairing computation for comparison, while our work enables more potential for constructing pORE with better security and efficiency.

Acknowlegements. We thank the anonymous reviewers for their helpful discussion and feedback. The work was supported by the National Key Research and Development Program of China (No. 2022YFB3102400), the National Natural Science Foundation of China (Nos. U21A20466, 62325209, 62272350,62122092, 62032005, 62202485), and the Major Program(JD) of Hubei Province (No. 2023BAA027).

A More on the Leakage of Different ORE Schemes

As shown by Cash et al. [10], $\mathcal{L}_1$ leaks less information than the leakage caused by CLWW ORE ($\mathcal{L}_2$) and Lewi-Wu ORE. Below we will provide more details about these leakage profiles.

Smoothed CLWW Leakage. Considering the set $\{0, 4, 5, 10, 11\}$ in 4-bit plaintext space, it can be viewed as leaves of a 4-level full binary tree. In Fig. 7, the ideal leakage $\mathcal{L}_0$ refers to the numeric order-relation. After removing the irrelevant leaves/nodes, the CLWW leakage $\mathcal{L}_2$ refers to the subtree structure, in which grey points mean the position of msdb and green nodes mean unleaked msdb. Note that for some plaintexts such as $\{2, 6, 7, 12, 13\}$, it would also have equivalent subtree w.r.t. $\{0, 4, 5, 10, 11\}$. While for other plaintexts such as $\{1, 2, 3, 5, 6\}$, there are significant differences between the two subtree structures, and these two plaintext sequences are distinguishable by the leakage $\mathcal{L}_2$ of the ciphertext alone. Moreover, the comparator can know from the ciphertext that $m_i = 4$ has the bit form "01-0", where "-" indicates the unknown bits. Considering the leakage $\mathcal{L}_1$ which leaks the equality pattern of msdb, while the comparator can infer additional information (i.e., msdb(0,4) < msdb(5, 11)), green nodes in subtrees are unknown to the comparator as the positions of msdb are not determined. Also, the position of gray nodes can be moved up or down. So, one can see that

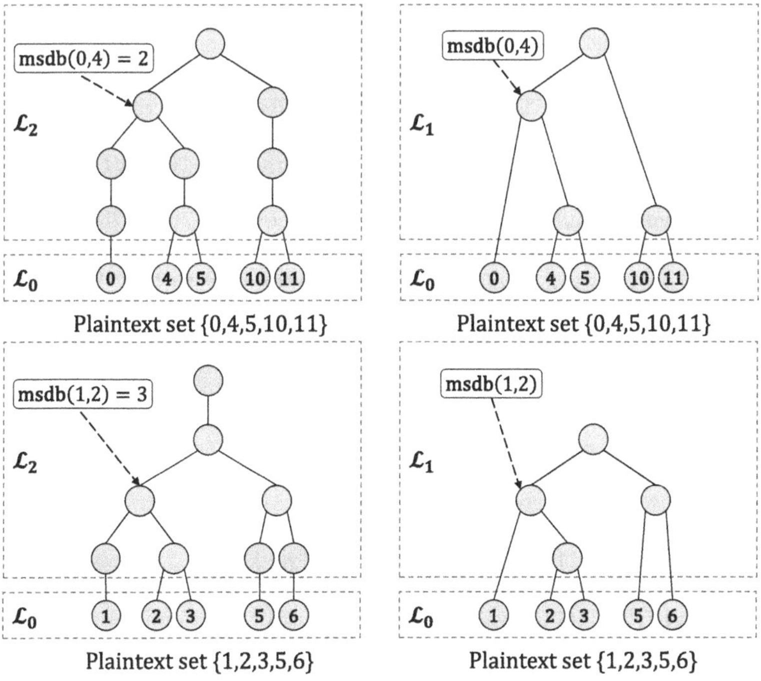

Fig. 7. Comparison of different leakage profiles.

$\{0, 4, 5, 10, 11\}$ and $\{1, 2, 3, 5, 6\}$ leak the same information under $\mathcal{L}_1$. Note that inspired by the block-wise encryption [30], Cash et al. [10] also demonstrated that an enhanced level of leakage $\mathcal{L}_1$ can be achieved by encrypting message blocks instead of individual bits.

Specific Applications of pORE. Cash et al. [10] show that pORE is particularly suitable for specific scenarios where the adversary lacks a strong estimate of the prior distribution of the data. In many settings, data often follows a known type of distribution, as exemplified by Cash et al. [10], where various physical, biological, and financial quantities approximate a normal distribution due to the central limit theorem. In these scenarios, the database entries are independently drawn from a distribution with a known "shape" (e.g., normal, uniform, Laplace, etc.), but the adversary does not possess the mean and variance information necessary to determine the shifting and scaling factors. Consequently, pORE can be employed to effectively conceal both the shifting and scaling information. Notably, it has been observed by Cash et al. [10] that CLWW ORE [12] and Lewis-Wu ORE [30] fail to achieve shift hiding and scale hiding simultaneously. Nonetheless, as acknowledged by Cash et al. [10], pORE specifically guarantees security when the sensitivity lies solely in the scale and shift of the underlying plaintext distributions, and it may not be sufficient in scenarios where the shape of the distribution itself is highly sensitive or when there are correlations with other available data that could be exploited by an attacker.

References

1. Agrawal, R., Kiernan, J., Srikant, R., Xu, Y.: Order preserving encryption for numeric data. In: Proceedings of the 2004 ACM SIGMOD International Conference on Management of Data, pp. 563–574 (2004)
2. Arasu, A., et al.: Orthogonal security with cipherbase. In: CIDR (2013)
3. Bajaj, S., Sion, R.: Trusteddb: a trusted hardware-based database with privacy and data confidentiality. IEEE Trans. Knowl. Data Eng. **26**(3), 752–765 (2013)
4. Bogatov, D., Kollios, G., Reyzin, L.: A comparative evaluation of order-revealing encryption schemes and secure range-query protocols. Proc. VLDB Endow. **12**(8), 933–947 (2019)
5. Boldyreva, A., Chenette, N., Lee, Y., O'Neill, A.: Order-preserving symmetric encryption. In: Joux, A. (ed.) EUROCRYPT 2009. LNCS, vol. 5479, pp. 224–241. Springer, Heidelberg (2009). https://doi.org/10.1007/978-3-642-01001-9_13
6. Boldyreva, A., Chenette, N., O'Neill, A.: Order-preserving encryption revisited: improved security analysis and alternative solutions. In: Rogaway, P. (ed.) CRYPTO 2011. LNCS, vol. 6841, pp. 578–595. Springer, Heidelberg (2011). https://doi.org/10.1007/978-3-642-22792-9_33
7. Boneh, D., Kogan, D., Woo, K.: Oblivious pseudorandom functions from isogenies. In: Moriai, S., Wang, H. (eds.) ASIACRYPT 2020. LNCS, vol. 12492, pp. 520–550. Springer, Heidelberg (2020). https://doi.org/10.1007/978-3-030-64834-3_18
8. Boneh, D., Lewi, K., Raykova, M., Sahai, A., Zhandry, M., Zimmerman, J.: Semantically secure order-revealing encryption: multi-input functional encryption without obfuscation. In: Oswald, E., Fischlin, M. (eds.) EUROCRYPT 2015, Part II. LNCS, vol. 9057, pp. 563–594. Springer, Heidelberg (2015). https://doi.org/10.1007/978-3-662-46803-6_19

9. Cash, D., Grubbs, P., Perry, J., Ristenpart, T.: Leakage-abuse attacks against searchable encryption. In: Proceedings of the 22nd ACM SIGSAC Conference on Computer and Communications Security, pp. 668–679 (2015)
10. Cash, D., Liu, F.H., O'Neill, A., Zhandry, M., Zhang, C.: Parameter-hiding order revealing encryption. In: Peyrin, T., Galbraith, S. (eds.) ASIACRYPT 2018, Part I. LNCS, vol. 11272, pp. 181–210. Springer, Heidelberg (2018). https://doi.org/10.1007/978-3-030-03326-2_7
11. Chang, Z., Xie, D., Li, F.: Oblivious ram: a dissection and experimental evaluation. Proc. VLDB Endow. **9**(12), 1113–1124 (2016)
12. Chenette, N., Lewi, K., Weis, S.A., Wu, D.J.: Practical order-revealing encryption with limited leakage. In: Peyrin, T. (ed.) FSE 2016. LNCS, vol. 9783, pp. 474–493. Springer, Heidelberg (2016). https://doi.org/10.1007/978-3-662-52993-5_24
13. Demertzis, I., Papadopoulos, S., Papapetrou, O., Deligiannakis, A., Garofalakis, M.: Practical private range search revisited. In: Proceedings of the 2016 International Conference on Management of Data, pp. 185–198 (2016)
14. Durak, F.B., DuBuisson, T.M., Cash, D.: What else is revealed by order-revealing encryption? In: Proceedings of the 2016 ACM SIGSAC Conference on Computer and Communications Security, pp. 1155–1166 (2016)
15. Faber, S., Jarecki, S., Krawczyk, H., Nguyen, Q., Rosu, M.C., Steiner, M.: Rich queries on encrypted data: beyond exact matches. In: Pernul, G., Ryan, P.Y.A., Weippl, E.R. (eds.) ESORICS 2015, Part II. LNCS, vol. 9327, pp. 123–145. Springer, Heidelberg (2015). https://doi.org/10.1007/978-3-319-24177-7_7
16. Goldreich, O., Goldwasser, S., Micali, S.: How to construct random functions. J. ACM (JACM) **33**(4), 792–807 (1986)
17. Grubbs, P., Lacharité, M.S., Minaud, B., Paterson, K.G.: Pump up the volume: practical database reconstruction from volume leakage on range queries. In: Lie, D., Mannan, M., Backes, M., Wang, X. (eds.) ACM CCS 2018, pp. 315–331. ACM Press (2018). https://doi.org/10.1145/3243734.3243864
18. Grubbs, P., Lacharité, M.S., Minaud, B., Paterson, K.G.: Learning to reconstruct: statistical learning theory and encrypted database attacks. In: 2019 IEEE Symposium on Security and Privacy, pp. 1067–1083. IEEE Computer Society Press (2019). https://doi.org/10.1109/SP.2019.00030
19. Grubbs, P., Sekniqi, K., Bindschaedler, V., Naveed, M., Ristenpart, T.: Leakage-abuse attacks against order-revealing encryption. In: 2017 IEEE Symposium on Security and Privacy, pp. 655–672. IEEE Computer Society Press (2017). https://doi.org/10.1109/SP.2017.44
20. Hirose, S.: Collision-resistant and pseudorandom function based on Merkle-Damgård hash function. In: Park, J.H., Seo, S.H. (eds.) ICISC 2021. LNCS, vol. 13218, pp. 325–338. Springer, Cham (2022). https://doi.org/10.1007/978-3-031-08896-4_17
21. Kamara, S., Moataz, T.: Computationally volume-hiding structured encryption. In: Ishai, Y., Rijmen, V. (eds.) EUROCRYPT 2019, Part II. LNCS, vol. 11477, pp. 183–213. Springer, Heidelberg (2019). https://doi.org/10.1007/978-3-030-17656-3_7
22. Kellaris, G., Kollios, G., Nissim, K., O'Neill, A.: Generic attacks on secure outsourced databases. In: Weippl, E.R., Katzenbeisser, S., Kruegel, C., Myers, A.C., Halevi, S. (eds.) ACM CCS 2016, pp. 1329–1340. ACM Press (2016). https://doi.org/10.1145/2976749.2978386
23. Kerschbaum, F.: Frequency-hiding order-preserving encryption. In: Ray, I., Li, N., Kruegel, C. (eds.) ACM CCS 2015, pp. 656–667. ACM Press (2015). https://doi.org/10.1145/2810103.2813629

24. Kerschbaum, F., Schröpfer, A.: Optimal average-complexity ideal-security order-preserving encryption. In: Ahn, G.J., Yung, M., Li, N. (eds.) ACM CCS 2014, pp. 275–286. ACM Press (2014). https://doi.org/10.1145/2660267.2660277
25. Kiltz, E., Lyubashevsky, V., Schaffner, C.: A concrete treatment of Fiat-Shamir signatures in the quantum random-oracle model. In: Nielsen, J., Rijmen, V. (eds.) EUROCRYPT 2018. LNCS, vol. 10822, pp. 552–586. Springer, Cham (2018). https://doi.org/10.1007/978-3-319-78372-7_18
26. Kiltz, E., Masny, D., Pan, J.: Optimal security proofs for signatures from identification schemes. In: Robshaw, M., Katz, J. (eds.) CRYPTO 2016. LNCS, vol. 9815, pp. 33–61. Springer, Heidelberg (2016). https://doi.org/10.1007/978-3-662-53008-5_2
27. Kornaropoulos, E.M., Papamanthou, C., Tamassia, R.: The state of the uniform: attacks on encrypted databases beyond the uniform query distribution. In: 2020 IEEE Symposium on Security and Privacy, pp. 1223–1240. IEEE Computer Society Press (2020). https://doi.org/10.1109/SP40000.2020.00029
28. Kornaropoulos, E.M., Papamanthou, C., Tamassia, R.: Response-hiding encrypted ranges: revisiting security via parametrized leakage-abuse attacks. In: 2021 IEEE Symposium on Security and Privacy, pp. 1502–1519. IEEE Computer Society Press (2021). https://doi.org/10.1109/SP40001.2021.00044
29. Lacharité, M.S., Minaud, B., Paterson, K.G.: Improved reconstruction attacks on encrypted data using range query leakage. In: 2018 IEEE Symposium on Security and Privacy, pp. 297–314. IEEE Computer Society Press (2018). https://doi.org/10.1109/SP.2018.00002
30. Lewi, K., Wu, D.J.: Order-revealing encryption: new constructions, applications, and lower bounds. In: Weippl, E.R., Katzenbeisser, S., Kruegel, C., Myers, A.C., Halevi, S. (eds.) ACM CCS 2016, pp. 1167–1178. ACM Press (2016). https://doi.org/10.1145/2976749.2978376
31. Markatou, E.A., Tamassia, R.: Full database reconstruction with access and search pattern leakage. In: Lin, Z., Papamanthou, C., Polychronakis, M. (eds.) ISC 2019. LNCS, vol. 11723, pp. 25–43. Springer, Heidelberg (2019). https://doi.org/10.1007/978-3-030-30215-3_2
32. Naveed, M., Kamara, S., Wright, C.V.: Inference attacks on property-preserving encrypted databases. In: Ray, I., Li, N., Kruegel, C. (eds.) ACM CCS 2015, pp. 644–655. ACM Press (2015). https://doi.org/10.1145/2810103.2813651
33. Pandey, O., Rouselakis, Y.: Property preserving symmetric encryption. In: Pointcheval, D., Johansson, T. (eds.) EUROCRYPT 2012. LNCS, vol. 7237, pp. 375–391. Springer, Heidelberg (2012). https://doi.org/10.1007/978-3-642-29011-4_23
34. Popa, R.A., Li, F.H., Zeldovich, N.: An ideal-security protocol for order-preserving encoding. In: 2013 IEEE Symposium on Security and Privacy, pp. 463–477. IEEE Computer Society Press (2013). https://doi.org/10.1109/SP.2013.38
35. Popa, R.A., Redfield, C.M., Zeldovich, N., Balakrishnan, H.: Cryptdb: protecting confidentiality with encrypted query processing. In: Proceedings of the Twenty-Third ACM Symposium on Operating Systems Principles, pp. 85–100 (2011)
36. Teranishi, I., Yung, M., Malkin, T.: Order-preserving encryption secure beyond one-wayness. In: Sarkar, P., Iwata, T. (eds.) ASIACRYPT 2014, Part II. LNCS, vol. 8874, pp. 42–61. Springer, Heidelberg (2014). https://doi.org/10.1007/978-3-662-45608-8_3

Chosen-Ciphertext Secure Dual-Receiver Encryption in the Standard Model Based on Post-quantum Assumptions

Laurin Benz[2,3](✉), Wasilij Beskorovajnov[1], Sarai Eilebrecht[1], Roland Gröll[1], Maximilian Müller[1], and Jörn Müller-Quade[2,3]

[1] FZI Research Center for Information Technology, Karlsruhe, Germany
{beskorovajnov,eilebrecht,groell,m.mueller}@fzi.de
[2] Karlsruhe Institute of Technology, Karlsruhe, Germany
joern.mueller-quade,laurin.benz@kit.edu
[3] KASTEL Security Research Labs, Karlsruhe, Germany

Abstract. Dual-receiver encryption (DRE) is a special form of public key encryption (PKE) that allows a sender to encrypt a message for two recipients. Without further properties, the difference between DRE and PKE is only syntactical. One such important property is soundness, which requires that no ciphertext can be constructed such that the recipients decrypt to different plaintexts. Many applications rely on this property in order to realize more complex protocols or primitives. In addition, many of these applications explicitly avoid the usage of the random oracle, which poses an additional requirement on a DRE construction. We show that all of the IND-CCA2 secure standard model DRE constructions based on post-quantum assumptions fall short of augmenting the constructions with soundness and describe attacks thereon.

We then give an overview over all applications of IND-CCA2 secure DRE, group them into generic (i. e., applications using DRE as black-box) and non-generic applications and demonstrate that all generic ones require either soundness or public verifiability.

Conclusively, we identify the gap of sound and IND-CCA2 secure DRE constructions based on post-quantum assumptions in the standard model. In order to fill this gap we provide two IND-CCA2 secure DRE constructions based on the standard post-quantum assumptions, Normal Form Learning With Errors (NLWE) and Learning Parity with Noise (LPN).

Keywords: Dual-receiver encryption (DRE) · Soundness · Hybrid Encryption · NLWE · LPN · Post-Quantum · IND-CCA2 · Standard Model

1 Introduction

Dual-receiver encryption (DRE) may be seen as a special case of Broadcast encryption (BE), where the number of recipients is constrained to two. Chow, Franklin, and Zhang [18] and Diament et al. [22] showed that DRE has plenty of applications, which impose different requirements on the used scheme. For some

Q. Tang and V. Teague (Eds.): PKC 2024, LNCS 14604, pp. 257–288, 2024.
https://doi.org/10.1007/978-3-031-57728-4_9

applications the chosen plaintext attack (CPA) security is sufficient, whereas others require the stronger adaptive chosen ciphertext attack (CCA2) security. Furthermore, some applications require very specific DRE constructions using for example bilinear pairings. In this work we call such applications non-generic, as they make calls on internals routines of the employed DRE construction, preventing the use of DRE in a black-box manner within these applications.

Nevertheless, plenty of applications use DRE in a black-box manner and require only the property of soundness, for example [4,8,18,20,23,43,47]. This property requires that no adversary, even with knowledge of the secret keys of both recipients, is able to create a ciphertext that decrypts to two different plaintexts when decrypting with the secret keys of the recipients. Note that many of these applications are explicitly avoiding the use of the random oracle, which carries over to the employed DRE construction.

All standard model CCA2 secure DRE constructions based on post-quantum (PQ) assumptions [36,53] are lattice-based and, as we show in this work, surprisingly fail at providing the soundness property. Moreover, Brendel et al. [14] mentions that amongst others, a CCA2 secure and sound PQ-instantiation did not yet appear in the literature. Thus, the aim of this work is to provide such DRE constructions, and therefore close this gap.

Contribution and Outline. Firstly, we conduct a literature review on—to the best of our knowledge—all applications requiring a sound CCA2 secure DRE in order to categorize them into generic and non-generic. Each application is explained shortly in Sect. 3.

- We identify the following generic applications requiring soundness: applications of CCA2 secure binding encryption [43], plaintext awareness via key registration [31], protocols for deniable authentication (DA) [23,47], non-malleable commitments [19], and PKE schemes with non-interactive opening (PKENO) [20].
- The remaining applications are identified as non-generic: combined encryption schemes [22], protocols for secure group key management [12], tripartite key exchange [46], and schemes of dual receiver proxy re-encryption [9,39].

Secondly, we conduct another literature review on—to the best of our knowledge—all constructions of CCA2 secure DRE in the standard model that may be used in a post-quantum setting and whether these constructions satisfy the soundness property. We present and explain our results in depth in Sect. 4. Our observation is that right now all of IND-CCA2 secure constructions are based on lattices and lack the soundness property.

Finally, in Sect. 5, we give efficient lattice- and LPN-based constructions in the standard model for IND-CCA2 secure and sound DRE schemes based on the hybrid encryption construction by Boyen, Izabachène, and Li [11] and the PKE construction by Kiltz, Masny, and Pietrzak [34], which can be used in any of the generic applications.

Moreover, we would like to point out that the employed trapdoor function in our lattice-based construction is from Micciancio and Peikert [41] and its ring and module variant was already implemented by Bert et al. [6,7]. We therefore expect that our constructions are readily usable in prototypical implementations of generic applications from Sect. 3.

2 Preliminaries

Notations: For a positive integer k, $[k]$ denotes the set $\{1, 2, \dots, k\}$. We define the set of integers modulo $q > 1$ by $\mathbb{Z}_q$ and the modular operation $(x \bmod q)$ as mapping the integer x into $[-q/2, q/2)$. Column-vectors are written as **bold** lower-case letters (e. g., $\mathbf{v}$) and row-vectors are transposed column-vectors (e. g., $\mathbf{v}^\top$). The standard scalar product of the vectors $\mathbf{x}$ and $\mathbf{y}$ of the same dimension is denoted by $\langle \mathbf{x}, \mathbf{y} \rangle$. We denote matrices by **bold** upper-case letters (e. g., $\mathbf{A}$). The concatenation of two vectors $\mathbf{v}_1$, $\mathbf{v}_2$ is denoted by $(\mathbf{v}_1, \mathbf{v}_2)$. By $\mathbf{v}[i]$ we refer to the i-th element of a vector $\mathbf{v}$ and $\mathbf{a}_i$ is the i-th column vector of a matrix $\mathbf{A}$. The Euclidean norm of a vector $\mathbf{v}$ is written as $\|\mathbf{v}\|$, its Hamming weight is denoted by $\|\mathbf{v}\|_w$, and $|x|$ is the absolute value of a scalar x. Let S be an arbitrary set. By $s \leftarrow\$ S$, we define the uniformly sampling of an element from S. If χ is a probability distribution, $x \leftarrow \chi$ denotes sampling an element according to the distribution. For a probabilistic algorithm R we denote by $y \leftarrow R(\mathbf{x})$ the result of one execution of R with input $\mathbf{x}$. If an algorithm $\mathcal{A}$ has access to an oracle $\mathcal{O}$, we write $\mathcal{A}^{\mathcal{O}}$. Our security parameter will always be called λ. We call a function $\texttt{negl} : \mathbb{N} \to \mathbb{R}$ *negligible* in λ, if for each positive integer k there exists an integer k_0 such that for all $\lambda > k_0 : |\texttt{negl}(\lambda)| < \lambda^{-k}$.

2.1 Definitions

We adapt the definition of DRE from Chow, Franklin, and Zhang [18] to a broader setting without the use of a common reference string (CRS). In many applications of DRE, the sender does not encrypt a message to two independent recipients. Instead, the sender interprets themselves as one of the recipients and encrypts the message under their own public key, too. Thus, we refer to the two receiving parties as receiver R and sender S with key pairs (sk^R, pk^R) and (sk^S, pk^S), respectively.

Definition 1 (DRE). A public-key *dual-receiver encryption* scheme $\text{DRE} = (\texttt{gen}, \texttt{enc}, \texttt{dec})$ consists of the following algorithms:

- $\texttt{gen}(1^\lambda)$: The randomized *key generation* algorithm takes as input a unary encoding of the security parameter λ and outputs a public/secret key pair (pk, sk). We write (sk^R, pk^R) and (sk^S, pk^S) for the key pairs of two independent users.
- $\texttt{enc}(pk^R, pk^S, \mathbf{m})$: The randomized *encryption algorithm* takes as input two public keys pk^R and pk^S and a message $\mathbf{m}$, and outputs a ciphertext $\mathbf{c}$.
- $\texttt{dec}(sk^i, pk^R, pk^S, \mathbf{c})$: The deterministic *decryption algorithm* takes one of the secret keys $sk^i (i \in \{R, S\})$, two public keys pk^R, pk^S, and a ciphertext $\mathbf{c}$ as input, and outputs a message $\mathbf{m}^i$ (which may be the special symbol $\bot$); we write $\mathbf{m}^i = \texttt{dec}(sk^i, pk^R, pk^S, \mathbf{c})$.

The usual IND-CCA2 security is somewhat different for a DRE scheme defined in Definition 2. However, when a DRE scheme already satisfies the soundness property from Definition 3 then the definition of $\text{IND-CCA2}_{\text{DRE}}$ collapses to the standard definition of IND-CCA2.

Definition 2 ($\text{IND-CCA2}_{\text{DRE}}$). A DRE scheme is said to be indistinguishable under adaptive chosen ciphertext attack ($\text{IND-CCA2}_{\text{DRE}}$ secure), if any probabilistic polynomial time (PPT) algorithm $\mathcal{A}$ wins the $\text{IND-CCA2}_{\text{DRE}}$ game in Fig. 1 with probability at most $\frac{1}{2} + \texttt{negl}(\lambda)$, i.e.,

$$\mathsf{Adv}_{\text{DRE},\mathcal{A}}^{\text{IND-CCA2}_{\text{DRE}}}(\lambda) := \left| \mathbb{P}\left[\mathsf{Exp}_{\text{DRE},\mathcal{A}}^{\text{IND-CCA2}_{\text{DRE}}}(\lambda) = 1\right] - \frac{1}{2} \right| \leq \texttt{negl}(\lambda).$$

$$\mathsf{Adv}_{\text{DRE},\mathcal{A}}^{\text{IND-CCA2}_{\text{DRE}}}(\lambda) := \left| \mathbb{P}\left[\mathsf{Exp}_{\text{DRE},\mathcal{A}}^{\text{IND-CCA2}_{\text{DRE}}}(\lambda) = 1\right] - \frac{1}{2} \right| \leq \texttt{negl}(\lambda).$$

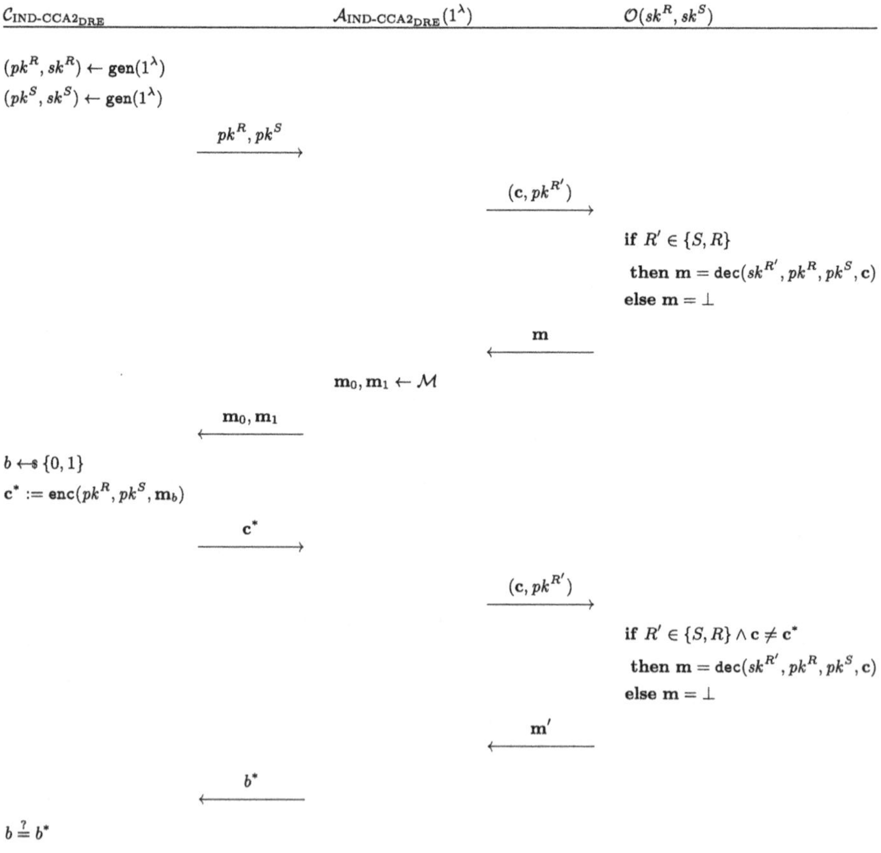

Fig. 1. Depiction of the $\text{IND-CCA2}_{\text{DRE}}$ game.

$$\mathsf{Adv}_{\mathcal{E},\mathcal{A}}^{\mathrm{sound}}(\lambda) := \mathbb{P}\left[\mathsf{Exp}_{\mathcal{E},\mathcal{A}}^{\mathrm{sound}}(\lambda) = 1\right] \leq \mathsf{negl}(\lambda).$$

$\mathcal{C}_{\mathrm{sound}}$ $\hspace{10cm}$ $\mathcal{A}_{\mathrm{sound}}$

$(pk^R, sk^R) \leftarrow \mathsf{gen}(1^\lambda)$

$(pk^R, sk^S) \leftarrow \mathsf{gen}(1^\lambda)$

$$\xrightarrow{\quad (pk^R, pk^S, sk^R, sk^S) \quad}$$

$$\xleftarrow{\quad c \quad}$$

$\mathsf{dec}(sk^R, pk^R, pk^S, c) \overset{?}{\neq} \mathsf{dec}(sk^S, pk^R, pk^S, c)$

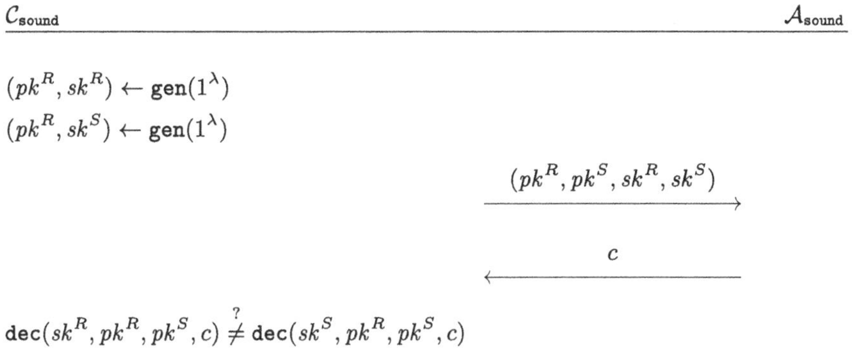

Fig. 2. Depiction of the soundness game.

The most important property of a DRE scheme is that of soundness, which states that every ciphertext will be decrypted to the same message from both parties, even if it was maliciously made. Without this property every PKE scheme can also be used as a DRE scheme, simply by encrypting the message for both parties independently.

Definition 3 (Soundness for DRE [18]). Consider the experiment $\mathsf{Exp}_{\mathcal{E},\mathcal{A}}^{\mathrm{sound}}$ from Fig. 2 for a DRE scheme $\mathcal{E}$ and a PPT algorithm $\mathcal{A}$. A DRE scheme $\mathcal{E}$ satisfies soundness if for any $\mathcal{A}$ we have that $\mathsf{Adv}_{\mathcal{E},\mathcal{A}}^{\mathrm{sound}}$ is negligible in λ, i.e.,

$$\mathsf{Adv}_{\mathcal{E},\mathcal{A}}^{\mathrm{sound}}(\lambda) := \mathbb{P}\left[\mathsf{Exp}_{\mathcal{E},\mathcal{A}}^{\mathrm{sound}}(\lambda) = 1\right] \leq \mathsf{negl}(\lambda).$$

We will be constructing DRE schemes with the help of the hybrid encryption paradigm. For our constructions we require the following symmetric primitives and the according security definitions.

Definition 4 (SKE). A secret-key encryption (SKE) scheme is a pair of algorithms $\mathsf{SKE} = (\mathsf{SKE.enc}, \mathsf{SKE.dec})$ with key space $\mathcal{K}_{\mathrm{ske}}$ and ciphertext space $\mathcal{C}_{\mathrm{ske}}$ with:

- $\mathsf{SKE.enc}(dk, \mathbf{m})$: The deterministic *encryption algorithm* takes as input a key $dk \in \mathcal{K}_{\mathrm{ske}}$ and a message $\mathbf{m}$, and outputs a ciphertext $\mathbf{c}$.
- $\mathsf{SKE.dec}(dk, \mathbf{c})$: The deterministic *decryption algorithm* takes as input a key $dk \in \mathcal{K}_{\mathrm{ske}}$ and a ciphertext $\mathbf{c}$, and outputs a message $\mathbf{m}'$ (which may be the special symbol $\perp$)

We require that for all $dk \in \mathcal{K}_{\mathrm{ske}}$ it holds that

$$\mathbf{m} = \mathsf{SKE.dec}(dk, \mathsf{SKE.enc}(dk, \mathbf{m})).$$

Definition 5 (OT-IND). A SKE scheme SKE is said to be one-time indistinguishable (OT-IND secure), if any PPT algorithm $\mathcal{A}$ wins the OT-IND game in Fig. 3 with probability at most $\frac{1}{2} + \mathtt{negl}(\lambda)$, i. e.,

$$\mathsf{Adv}^{\text{OT-IND}}_{\text{SKE},\mathcal{A}}(\lambda) := \left| \mathbb{P}\left[\mathsf{Exp}^{\text{OT-IND}}_{\text{SKE},\mathcal{A}}(\lambda) = 1\right] - \frac{1}{2} \right| \leq \mathtt{negl}(\lambda) .$$

$\mathcal{C}_{\texttt{OT-IND}}$		$\mathcal{A}_{\texttt{OT-IND}}(1^\lambda)$
	$\xleftarrow{\quad m \quad}$	
$dk \leftarrow\$ \mathcal{K}_{\mathsf{ske}}$ $b \leftarrow\$ \{0,1\}$ $\phi_0 \leftarrow \mathtt{SKE.enc}(dk, m)$ $\phi_1 \leftarrow\$ \mathcal{C}_{\mathsf{ske}}$		
	$\xrightarrow{\quad \phi_b \quad}$	
	$\xleftarrow{\quad b' \quad}$	
$b \stackrel{?}{=} b'$		

Fig. 3. Depiction of the OT-IND game.

A hash function is a function $\mathtt{H} : \{0,1\}^* \to \{0,1\}^\ell$ mapping bit strings of any length to bit strings of a fixed length ℓ.

Definition 6 (Collision Resistance). A family of hash functions $\{\mathtt{H}_k\}_{k \in K}$ is said to be collision resistant (CR) if for all PPT algorithms $\mathcal{A}$ the advantage $\mathsf{Adv}^{\text{CR}}_{\mathtt{H},\mathcal{A}}(\lambda)$ is negligibly small, where

$$\mathsf{Adv}^{\text{CR}}_{\mathtt{H},\mathcal{A}}(\lambda) := \mathbb{P}\left[k \leftarrow\$ K, (\mathbf{x}, \mathbf{x}') \leftarrow \mathcal{A}(1^\lambda, \mathtt{H}_k) : \mathbf{x} \neq \mathbf{x}' \text{ and } \mathtt{H}(\mathbf{x}) = \mathtt{H}(\mathbf{x}')\right] .$$

We need to look at keyed hash functions, as for every fixed hash function there exists an adversary with a collision hard coded by the pigeonhole principle. Still, in a slight abuse of notation we will speak of a "collision resistant hash function", by which we mean a function sampled uniformly from a collision resistant hash function family.

Definition 7 (MAC). A message authentication code (MAC) scheme MAC with key space $\mathcal{K}_{\text{mac}}$ consists of the two algorithms $\mathtt{MAC} = (\mathtt{MAC.sign}, \mathtt{MAC.ver})$, where

- $\mathtt{MAC.sign}(mk, \mathbf{m})$: The randomized *signing algorithm* takes as input a signing key $mk \in \mathcal{K}_{\text{mac}}$ and a message $\mathbf{m}$, and outputs a tag σ.

- $\texttt{MAC.ver}(mk, \mathbf{m}, \sigma)$: The deterministic *verification algorithm* takes as input a signing key $mk \in \mathcal{K}_{\text{ske}}$, a message $\mathbf{m}$ and a tag σ, and outputs 1 if $\sigma \leftarrow \texttt{MAC.sign}(mk, \mathbf{m})$ and 0 otherwise.

Definition 8 (OT-SUF). A message authentication code scheme MAC is said to be one-time strongly unforgeable (OT-SUF secure) if any PPT algorithm $\mathcal{A}$ wins the OT-SUF game in Fig. 4 with at most negligible probability, i. e.,

$$\mathsf{Adv}^{\text{OT-SUF}}_{\texttt{MAC},\mathcal{A}}(\lambda) := \mathbb{P}\left[\mathsf{Exp}^{\text{OT-SUF}}_{\texttt{MAC},\mathcal{A}}(\lambda) = 1\right] \leq \texttt{negl}(\lambda)\,.$$

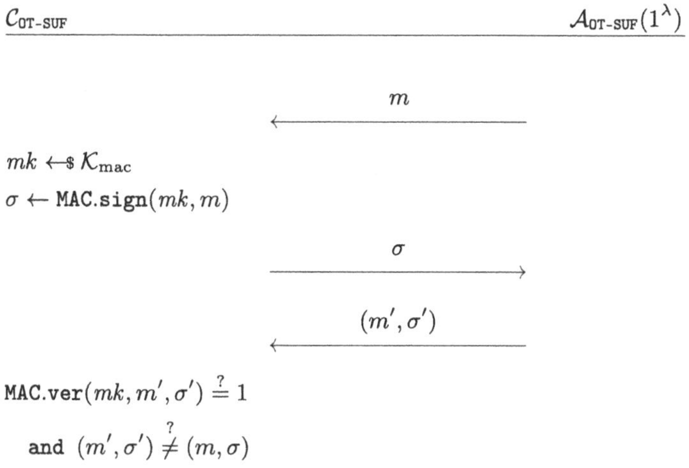

Fig. 4. Depiction of the OT-SUF game.

We use a key derivation function $\texttt{KDF} : \mathcal{K} \to \{0,1\}^n$ with key-space $\mathcal{K}$ in order to generate the SKE- and MAC-keys from a short seed. We require for a KDF function to be IND secure according to Definition 9.

Definition 9 (IND KDF [11]). A key derivation function KDF is said to be IND secure if for all PPT algorithms $\mathcal{A}$ the advantage $\mathsf{Adv}^{\text{IND}}_{\texttt{KDF},\mathcal{A}}(\lambda)$ is negligibly small, where

$$\mathsf{Adv}^{\text{IND}}_{\texttt{KDF},\mathcal{A}}(\lambda) := \left|\mathbb{P}\left[\mathcal{A}(1^\lambda, \texttt{KDF}(\mathbf{k})) = 1\right] - \mathbb{P}\left[\mathcal{A}(1^\lambda, \mathbf{r}) = 1\right]\right|$$

for $\mathbf{k} \leftarrow\!\$\ \mathcal{K}$ and $\mathbf{r} \leftarrow\!\$\ \{0,1\}^n$.

2.2 Assumptions and Lemmas

The following assumptions and lemmas are required in our proofs.

Definition 10 (NLWE Problem [11]). Let $n = n(\lambda), m = m(\lambda), q = q(\lambda)$ be integers and χ be an error distribution. The advantage of a PPT adversary $\mathcal{A}$ for the (normal-form) $\mathsf{NLWE}_{n,m,q,\chi}$ problem, denoted by $\mathsf{Adv}_{\mathcal{A}}^{\mathsf{NLWE}_{n,m,q,\chi}}(\lambda)$, is defined as

$$\mathsf{Adv}_{\mathcal{A}}^{\mathsf{NLWE}_{n,m,q,\chi}}(\lambda) := \left|\mathbb{P}\left[\mathcal{A}(\mathbf{A}, \mathbf{s}^\top\mathbf{A} + \mathbf{e}^\top) = 1\right] - \mathbb{P}\left[\mathcal{A}(\mathbf{A}, \mathbf{b}^\top) = 1\right]\right|,$$

where $\mathbf{A} \leftarrow\!\!\$\, \mathbb{Z}_q^{n\times m}, \mathbf{s} \leftarrow \chi^n$ and $\mathbf{e} \leftarrow \chi^m$. The $\mathsf{NLWE}_{n,m,q,\chi}$ problem is hard if $\mathsf{Adv}_{\mathcal{A}}^{\mathsf{NLWE}_{n,m,q,\chi}}$ is negligible in λ for all PPT adversaries $\mathcal{A}$

Applebaum et al. [3, Lemma 2] proved that NLWE is equivalent to the standard form of LWE where the LWE secret $\mathbf{s}$ is sampled from $\mathbb{Z}_q^n$ instead of χ^n.

Let Ber_p denote the Bernoulli distribution with parameter p, so $x \leftarrow \mathrm{Ber}_p$ is the random variable over $\{0, 1\}$ with $\mathbb{P}[x = 1] = p$.

Definition 11 (LPN Problem [34]). Let $n = n(\lambda), m = m(\lambda) \geq n$ as well as $0 \leq p = p(\lambda) \leq \frac{1}{2}$ be the Bernoulli parameter. The advantage of a PPT adversary $\mathcal{A}$ for the $\mathsf{LPN}_{n,m,p}$ problem, denoted by $\mathsf{Adv}_{\mathcal{A}}^{\mathsf{LPN}_{n,m,p}}(\lambda)$, is defined as

$$\mathsf{Adv}_{\mathcal{A}}^{\mathsf{LPN}_{n,m,p}}(\lambda) := \left|\mathbb{P}\left[\mathcal{A}(\mathbf{A}, \mathbf{s}^\top\mathbf{A} + \mathbf{e}^\top) = 1\right] - \mathbb{P}\left[\mathcal{A}(\mathbf{A}, \mathbf{b}^\top) = 1\right]\right|,$$

where $\mathbf{A} \leftarrow\!\!\$\, \mathbb{Z}_2^{n\times m}, \mathbf{s} \leftarrow\!\!\$\, \mathbb{Z}_2^n$ and $\mathbf{e} \leftarrow \mathrm{Ber}_p^m$. The $\mathsf{LPN}_{n,m,p}$ problem is hard if $\mathsf{Adv}_{\mathcal{A}}^{\mathsf{LPN}_{n,m,p}}$ is negligible in λ for all PPT adversaries $\mathcal{A}$.

The LPN assumption is equivalent to the hardness of decoding a random linear code, and it is believed to be post-quantum secure just like LWE. We also need two extended dual version of the LPN assumption, called Knapsack Learning Parity with Noise (KLPN) and Extended Knapsack Learning Parity with Noise (EKLPN).

Definition 12 (KLPN Problem [34]). Let $n = n(\lambda), m = m(\lambda) \geq 2n$ and $0 \leq p = p(\lambda) \leq \frac{1}{2}$ be the Bernoulli parameter. The advantage of a PPT adversary $\mathcal{A}$ for the $\mathsf{KLPN}_{n,m,p}$ problem, denoted by $\mathsf{Adv}_{\mathcal{A}}^{\mathsf{KLPN}_{n,m,p}}(\lambda)$, is defined as

$$\mathsf{Adv}_{\mathcal{A}}^{\mathsf{KLPN}_{n,m,p}}(\lambda) := \left|\mathbb{P}[\mathcal{A}(\mathbf{A}, \mathbf{A}\mathbf{E}) = 1] - \mathbb{P}[\mathcal{A}(\mathbf{A}, \mathbf{B}) = 1]\right|,$$

where $\mathbf{A}, \mathbf{B} \leftarrow\!\!\$\, \mathbb{Z}_2^{n\times m}$ and $\mathbf{E} \leftarrow \mathrm{Ber}_p^{m\times m}$.

Definition 13 (EKLPN Problem [34]). Let $n = n(\lambda), m = m(\lambda) \geq 2n$ and $0 \leq p = p(\lambda) \leq \frac{1}{2}$ be the Bernoulli parameter. The advantage of a PPT adversary $\mathcal{A}$ for the $\mathsf{EKLPN}_{n,m,p}$ problem, denoted by $\mathsf{Adv}_{\mathcal{A}}^{\mathsf{EKLPN}_{n,m,p}}(\lambda)$, is defined as

$$\mathsf{Adv}_{\mathcal{A}}^{\mathsf{EKLPN}_{n,m,p}}(\lambda) := \left|\mathbb{P}\left[\mathcal{A}(\mathbf{A}, \mathbf{A}\mathbf{E}, \mathbf{z}, \mathbf{z}^\top\mathbf{E}) = 1\right] - \mathbb{P}\left[\mathcal{A}(\mathbf{A}, \mathbf{B}, \mathbf{z}, \mathbf{z}^\top\mathbf{E}) = 1\right]\right|,$$

where $\mathbf{A}, \mathbf{B} \leftarrow\!\!\$\, \mathbb{Z}_2^{n\times m}, \mathbf{E} \leftarrow \mathrm{Ber}_p^{m\times m}$ and $\mathbf{z} \leftarrow \mathrm{Ber}_p^m$.

There is a reduction from EKLPN and KLPN to LPN by Kiltz, Masny, and Pietrzak [34] that states:

Lemma 1 ([34]). *For all algorithms $\mathcal{B}$ and $\mathcal{B}'$ there exist algorithms $\mathcal{A}$ and $\mathcal{A}'$ that run in roughly the same time as $\mathcal{B}$, respectively $\mathcal{B}'$, and* $\mathsf{Adv}_{\mathcal{A}}^{\mathsf{LPN}_{m-n,m,p}} \geq \frac{1}{m}\mathsf{Adv}_{\mathcal{B}}^{\mathsf{KLPN}_{n,m,p}}$ *as well as* $\mathsf{Adv}_{\mathcal{A}}^{\mathsf{LPN}_{m-n,m,p}} \geq \frac{1}{2m}\mathsf{Adv}_{\mathcal{B}}^{\mathsf{EKLPN}_{n,m,p}}$.

We also need efficient codes, which exist by the following lemma.

Lemma 2 ([33]). *For any rate $0 < R < 1$, there exists a binary linear error-correcting code family which is polynomial time constructible, encodable and decodable and can decode up to $\lfloor \frac{\delta n}{2} \rfloor$ errors where $\delta \approx \frac{1}{2}(1-R)$.*

To carry out attacks against the soundness property of DRE schemes from the literature (Sect. 4), we need to construct a carefully chosen malicious LWE secret, called $\mathbf{s}_2$ in the following lemma.

Lemma 3. *For all $\mathbf{d} \in \mathbb{Z}_q^n \setminus \{0\}$ and $\mathbf{s}_1 \in \mathbb{Z}_q^n$ there exists $\mathbf{s}_2 \in \mathbb{Z}_q^n$ such that*

$$\langle \mathbf{d}, \mathbf{s}_1 - \mathbf{s}_2 \rangle \notin \left[-\frac{q}{4}, \frac{q}{4}\right).$$

Moreover, this $\mathbf{s}_2$ can be found efficiently.

Proof. Choose an index i such that $\mathbf{d}[i] \neq 0$. If there exists $x \in \mathbb{Z}_q$ such that $\mathbf{d}[i] \cdot x \mod q \notin \left[-\frac{q}{4}, \frac{q}{4}\right)$ we can set $\mathbf{s}_2[i] = \mathbf{s}_1[i] - x$ and $\mathbf{s}_2[j] = \mathbf{s}_1[j]$ for all $j \in [n] \setminus \{i\}$. It then follows that $\langle \mathbf{d}, \mathbf{s}_1 - \mathbf{s}_2 \rangle = \mathbf{d}[i] \cdot x \notin \left[-\frac{q}{4}, \frac{q}{4}\right)$, proving the lemma. To see that such an x exists let $m \in \mathbb{N}_0$ be minimal such that $\mathbf{d}[i] \cdot 2^m \notin \left[-\frac{q}{4}, \frac{q}{4}\right)$. As m is minimal we know that $\mathbf{d}[i] \cdot 2^{\max(0, m-1)} \in \left[-\frac{q}{4}, \frac{q}{4}\right)$, and thus $\mathbf{d}[i] \cdot 2^m \in \left[-\frac{q}{2}\frac{q}{2}\right)$. Therefore, $\mathbf{d}[i] \cdot 2^m$ is not affected by the modulus and $x = 2^m$ satisfies the constraint.

This x can be found in $\log q$ steps. □

3 Applications of Dual-Receiver Encryption

In the following, we describe—to the best of our knowledge—all applications that are reportedly realized with a CCA2 secure DRE scheme.

This section is structured as follows: Firstly, we describe all applications that generically require a sound DRE scheme. Then we briefly describe, for the sake of completeness, two remaining generic applications where a CCA2 secure and sound DRE construction is either unnecessarily strong or requires a reformulation and an additional proof in the CRS model. Finally, we describe the remaining non-generic applications.

3.1 Applications of CCA2 Secure DRE with Soundness

Applications of Binding Encryption. Binding Encryption schemes are a special case of Broadcast Encryption [27], where the property of strong or weak decryption consistency is guaranteed. DRE in turn is a special case of a binding encryption scheme with only two recipients. The definitions of (partial) soundness and (weak) strong decryption consistency are syntactically equivalent when constrained to the special case of two recipients. Conclusively, one may therefore use a binding encryption scheme constrained to two recipients with a suitable level of decryption consistency in any DRE scenario. This means that the most efficient construction of binding encryption by Noh et al. [43] is basically an IND-CPA DRE scheme with soundness as it guarantees strong decryption consistency.

In some cases, a DRE scheme can also be extended to a binding encryption scheme. Consider the case that a sound DRE scheme is scalable for up to n receivers, which is the case with our constructions in Sect. 5. Then the DRE scheme becomes a binding encryption scheme and can therefore be used for all of its applications. These observations are somewhat simple but surprisingly have not yet been mentioned in the literature.

Plaintext Awareness via Key Registration (PAvKR). One variant of plaintext-awareness is *plaintext-awareness via key registration* introduced by Herzog, Liskov, and Micali [31]. In this notion, both sender and receiver need a public/private-key pair. These key pairs are registered via a key registration authority that ensures that the owner of a public key has knowledge of the private key. DRE is a natural way to utilize such an authority to achieve PA.

PAvKR can be used to enforce the Dolev-Yao model [24]. It is a formal proof model in which automated theorem provers like TAMARIN [40] can be used.

Deniable Authenticated Key Exchange. DRE is used in [23,47] to implement a special case of deniable authentication (DA) introduced by Dwork, Naor, and Sahai [26] called on-line deniability, which captures the fact that deniability should also apply when one of the parties cooperates with a third party during the protocol. Dodis et al. [23] proposed an asymmetric key exchange protocol for symmetric keys called key exchange with incriminating abort (KEIA), which is a weak form of a deniable key exchange protocol. Roughly said, KEIA enables deniability if the key exchange protocol is terminated successfully. Once a shared key is established, deniability is guaranteed, even if corruptions occur later on. An IND-CCA2 secure and sound DRE scheme is used together with non-committing encryption by Canetti et al. [16] to realize a key exchange with incriminating abort functionality $\mathcal{F}_{keia}$ in the generalized universal composability (GUC) framework by Canetti et al. [15]. The soundness property is mandatory, as it allows to simulate specific actions with either S's or R's secret key.

PKE with Non-interactive Opening. The notion of public-key encryption with non-interactive opening (PKENO) by Damgård et al. [20] allows a receiver of a message to publicly open, when the encryption is interpreted as a commitment scheme, a received ciphertext to its plaintext without the necessity to interact with the sender. As stated by Chow, Franklin, and Zhang [18], a DRE trivially implies a one-time PKENO: The encrypting party takes the public keys of both receivers and sends $c = \texttt{enc}(pk^R, pk^T, \mathbf{m})$ to both receivers. One of the two receivers can then prove the validity of the ciphertext c by revealing $\mathbf{m}$ and its secret key.

3.2 Applications of DRE with Public Verifiability

Some applications require the property of public verifiability for ciphertexts of a DRE scheme, which is another property of DRE beside soundness. This property requires the existence of a public algorithm verifying the validity of a given DRE ciphertext.

Threshold Decryption. Chow, Franklin, and Zhang [18] describe that a publicly verifiable DRE scheme can be augmented with a secret sharing protocol that distributes one of the receiver's secret key among n parties in order to enable the threshold decryption scenario with a distributed so-called supervision party. We are not aware of any literature that explores these kinds of constructions any further.

Public-Key Encryption with Plaintext Equality Test (PET). Chow, Franklin, and Zhang [18] note that each publicly verifiable DRE enables the notion of PET introduced by Yang et al. [52]. This allows one to check if any two independent ciphertexts encrypt the same message by providing an additional public test functionality. However, to the best of our knowledge, all the established DRE constructions that are used in PET realizations so far are based on bilinear pairings.

3.3 Applications of CPA secure DRE and the CRS Model

There are two generic applications that differ substantially from the others in regard to their requirements on the DRE or the model they are proven secure within.

Completely Non-malleable DRE. Due to the impossibility results of the existence of a non-interactive completely non-malleable PKE that can be proven secure with a black-box simulation in the standard model from Fischlin [28]. Chow, Franklin, and Zhang [18] propose two constructions of a completely non-malleable DRE (CNM-DRE) scheme in the CRS model. This property requires that any adversary obtaining a ciphertext $\mathbf{c}$ without knowing the corresponding plaintext $\mathbf{m}$ is not able to create a ciphertext $\mathbf{c}^*$ and a (new) key pair such that the message $\mathbf{m}^*$ encrypted in $\mathbf{c}^*$ under this key pair is related to $\mathbf{m}$ in some way.

CNM-DRE schemes can be utilized to construct *dual-receiver non-malleable commitments* (DR-NMC). These are generalizations of normal commitment schemes introduced by Crescenzo, Ishai, and Ostrovsky [19] and enable the possibility of committing to a message in a non-malleable sense for two independent receivers such that both receivers are able to open the commitment and know that the other party obtained the same de-committed message. We leave it open for future work to check our constructions in regard to this security definition.

Construction of Secure Channels. A new security notion, called sender-binding chosen plaintext attack (SB-CPA), for a variant of PKE, namely sender-binding encryption (SBE), was introduced by Beskorovajnov et al. [8]. The reasoning behind this notion is a definition of minimal security for the public-key part of the encryption when used in conjunction with authenticated channels in order to realize a universally composable secure channel. The authors show that an IND-CPA secure and sound DRE can be used to construct an SB-CPA secure SBE when a key registration with knowledge (KRK) is available. Benz et al. [5] showed that the results carry over to the hybrid encryption or the key exchange setting by utilizing a CPA secure dual-receiver key encapsulation mechanism (KEM). Our constructions from Sect. 5 can be easily simplified to provide this lower security than CCA2 without losing the soundness property. Moreover, we note that our constructions can be easily adapted to provide a CPA secure dual-receiver KEM with soundness because they are constructed with the help of the hybrid encryption paradigm.

3.4 Non-generic Applications

In this section, we briefly introduce non-generic applications of DRE. We denote that the use of DRE in these applications may be generalizable by finding a property that correctly describes the application's requirements on a DRE construction. However, we are not aware of any such property in the literature and therefore argue that declaring these applications non-generic at this point in time is justified. Securely modifying the use of DRE in these applications in order to make them generic is out of scope and left as an open question. Finally, all the following applications are build upon bilinear pairings inside the employed DRE construction.

Useful Security Puzzles. Computational puzzles can be used to protect servers from resource-heavy client requests. That is, a client has to solve a computationally expensive task which is easily verifiable by the server. However, we call a puzzle *not useful* if for example its only purpose is to rate-limit a client. In the work of Diament et al. [22], there are two scenarios with *useful* security puzzles proposed. In the first scenario, a file server can utilize DRE to rate-limit clients requesting encrypted files by outsourcing a huge part of the decryption to the clients. In another scenario, security puzzles might be used for DDoS protection in a TLS-like protocol. Note that this work has been revised in [21].

Combined Encryption Schemes. DRE is utilized to construct combined encryption schemes in [18] and [21,22]. In the latter two works, the scheme can be used for signing and encryption at the same time. Meanwhile the former construction offers the possibility to use a DRE and PKE scheme with the same keys.

Secure Group Key Management. The concept of secure group communication (SGC) allows a group of users to communicate such that only members of the group can decrypt messages. For this purpose, the group shares a secret called the group key. The most crucial problem is to solve the management of this group key. In SGC, new members can join, and existing members may leave the group. However, new members must not read old messages (backward secrecy), and ex-users are not allowed to decrypt messages after leaving the group (forward secrecy). Hence, the group key must be changed after each entry or exit. This process is called rekeying.

One possible way to manage group keys is to use *key graphs* [49]. BR and Amberker [12] use the DRE scheme of Diament et al. [22] to manage such a key graph and thus to enable SGC.

Tripartite Key Exchange. The protocols for authenticated key exchange (AKE) are used to share a key among multiple parties via unauthenticated channels. A special case is the three-party AKE (3KE). One of the special properties of a 3KE is called *maximal-exposure-resilience* (MEX-resilience). It roughly captures the fact that no information about the session key is exposed, even if an adversary is able to obtain any non-trivial combination of keys, that is, not all parties are completely corrupted.

Suzuki and Yoneyama [46] utilize a modified version of a DRE KEM construction from Chow, Franklin, and Zhang [18] to realize an *exposure-resilient* one-round 3KE in the standard model with the help of bilinear pairings. During the protocol, each party samples a random nonce and broadcasts it to the two other parties. Afterwards, each party aggregates the three plaintexts and derives a shared key via a pseudo-random key derivation function (KDF).

Dual-Receiver Proxy Re-Encryption (DR-PRE). The general notion of proxy re-encryption (PRE) from Blaze, Bleumer, and Strauss [9] and Mambo and Okamoto [39] allows one to transform a ciphertext that has been encrypted for one user into a ciphertext for a different party. In the case of dual-receiver proxy re-encryption (DR-PRE), a ciphertext encrypted for a single user, called the delegator, can be converted into a ciphertext so that it can be decrypted by two independent users, called the delegatees.

Originally, this task had to be done for each delegatee individually with different PREs and re-encryption keys. Patil and BR [44] however use DRE to accomplish this task with a dedicated DR-PRE construction. Both delegatees can decrypt the resulting ciphertext with their respective secret key. In this way computational and bandwidth costs can be saved.

4 Related Work on Post-quantum DRE Constructions

In this section, we present all related works for post-quantum IND-CCA2$_{\mathrm{DRE}}$ secure DRE constructions in the standard model, that are [36,53]. For both of these works, we show that they do not fulfill the soundness property.

We also consider constructions of broadcast encryption schemes as such constructions may be applied to the DRE setting and may have the property of strong decryption consistency that is equivalent to soundness, cf. the discussion from Sect. 3.1. Belonging to the list of broadcast encryption constructions that do not mention strong decryption consistency, there are six (identity-based) BE schemes [13,29,32,38,48,51], one IND-CPA construction [10] and four generic constructions from Libert, Paterson, and Quaglia [35]. One exception is the binding encryption construction from Noh et al. [43], which explicitly proves the decryption consistency property. However, this construction is only IND-CPA secure.

For the sake of completeness, we also denote that there are four DRE schemes which are based on post-quantum assumptions satisfying the soundness property. However, they are only IND-CPA secure. The first is from a Master's Thesis by Gegier [30], which presents a generic construction of a DRE KEM from any deterministic PKE and trapdoor functions with hardcore functions. The second is from a Master's Thesis by Müller [42], which presents a lattice-based direct construction of a DRE PKE. The third and fourth are two McEliece-based constructions by Beskorovajnov et al. [8].

4.1 IND-CCA2 Secure DRE Schemes Without Soundness

There are two IND-CCA2$_{\mathrm{DRE}}$ secure DRE schemes in the standard model, one by Zhang et al. [53] and one by Liu et al. [36]. The constructions differ roughly only in the choice of hash functions. In this subsection, we will show that these schemes do not satisfy the soundness property due to the lack of structure checks. In order to explain the attack on the soundness of these schemes, we abstract the two schemes into one abstract template that covers both schemes:

- The parameters χ and χ' denote LWE error distributions.
- OTS $= (\mathsf{KGen}_{\mathrm{OTS}}, \mathsf{Sig}_{\mathrm{OTS}}, \mathsf{Vfy}_{\mathrm{OTS}})$ is a strongly unforgeable one-time signature scheme (see [53, Appendix B] for a definition).
- $\mathbf{H}^R, \mathbf{H}^S$ are matrices generated by deterministic functions whose computation includes parts of the public key and a hash function depending on a verification key of OTS. These functions differ among both schemes, but are well-defined.
- The algorithm `SampleLeft` which occurs in line 4 of Fig. 6 outputs on input $(\mathbf{C}^R, \mathbf{d}_i, sk^R, s')$ a vector $\mathbf{v}_i$ such that $\mathbf{C}^R\mathbf{v}_i = \mathbf{d}_i$. The vector $\mathbf{d}_i$ is the i-th column vector of the matrix $\mathbf{D}$ which is sampled uniformly random, part of the CRS of this scheme, and used as LWE-Matrix to disguise the message.

We omit the details of the key generation here. Roughly, a LWE-Matrix and a corresponding trapdoor is generated in it.

Let us construct an adversary $\mathcal{A}$ which breaks the soundness property with probability 1. It creates a ciphertext $\mathbf{c}$ such that R decrypts 0 as the first bit of the message, whereas S obtains 1.

First, $\mathcal{A}$ obtains the public keys $\mathbf{A}^R$ and $\mathbf{A}^S$ (the secret keys are not needed for this attack). $\mathcal{A}$ runs $(vk, sk) \leftarrow \mathsf{KGen}_{\mathrm{OTS}}$ and creates the LWE-matrices $\mathbf{C}^i = \left[\mathbf{A}^i \middle| \mathbf{H}^i\right]$ for $i \in \{R, S\}$ where $\mathbf{H}_i$ are deterministic evaluations of some hash functions and other public information. Recall that $\mathbf{d}_1$ is the first column

$\mathsf{enc}(\mathbf{A}^R, \mathbf{A}^S, \mathbf{m} \in \{0,1\}^n)$

$\mathbf{s} \leftarrow\!\$\ \mathbb{Z}_q^n, \mathbf{e}_{\mathrm{msg}} \leftarrow \chi^n, \mathbf{e}^R, \mathbf{e}^S \leftarrow \chi'^{2m}$
$(vk, sk) \leftarrow \mathsf{KGen}_{\mathrm{OTS}}(1^\lambda)$
$\mathbf{C}^R = [\mathbf{A}^R | \mathbf{H}^R]$
$\mathbf{C}^S = [\mathbf{A}^S | \mathbf{H}^S]$
$\mathbf{c}^R = (\mathbf{C}^R)^\top \mathbf{s} + \mathbf{e}^R \in \mathbb{Z}_q^{2m}$
$\mathbf{c}^S = (\mathbf{C}^S)^\top \mathbf{s} + \mathbf{e}^S \in \mathbb{Z}_q^{2m}$
$\mathbf{c}_{\mathrm{msg}} = \mathbf{D}^\top \mathbf{s} + \mathbf{e}_{\mathrm{msg}} + \lceil q/2 \rceil \mathbf{m} \in \mathbb{Z}_q^n$
$\sigma \leftarrow \mathsf{Sig}_{\mathrm{OTS}}(sk, (\mathbf{c}^R, \mathbf{c}^S, \mathbf{c}_{\mathrm{msg}}))$
return $\mathbf{c} = (\mathbf{c}^R, \mathbf{c}^S, \mathbf{c}_{\mathrm{msg}}, \sigma)$

$\mathsf{dec}(sk^R, \mathbf{A}^R, \mathbf{A}^S, \mathbf{c})$

if $\mathsf{Vfy}_{\mathrm{OTS}}(vk, (\mathbf{c}^R, \mathbf{c}^S, \mathbf{c}_{\mathrm{msg}}), \sigma) == \mathrm{false}$
  return $\perp$
for $i \in [n]$
  $\mathbf{v}_i \leftarrow \mathtt{SampleLeft}(\mathbf{A}^R, \mathbf{H}^R, \mathbf{d}_i, sk^R, s')$
$\mathbf{V}^R = [\mathbf{v}_1 \dots \mathbf{v}_n]$
  // It holds $\mathbf{C}^R \mathbf{V}^R = \mathbf{D}$
$\mathbf{m}' = \mathbf{c}_{\mathrm{msg}} - (\mathbf{V}^R)^\top \mathbf{c}^R \ (\overset{!}{\approx} \lceil q/2 \rceil \mathbf{m})$
$\mathbf{m} \leftarrow$ Round each element of $\mathbf{m}'$
return m

Fig. 5. An abstract template of [36, 53].

vector of $\mathbf{D}$. Sample $\mathbf{s}^R \leftarrow\!\$\ \mathbb{Z}_q^n$ and use Lemma 3 to choose $\mathbf{s}^S \in \mathbb{Z}_q^n$ such that $\langle \mathbf{d}_1, \mathbf{s}^R - \mathbf{s}^S \rangle \notin [-\frac{q}{4}, \frac{q}{4})$. The vector d_1 is not equal to zero with overwhelming probability since it was sampled from $\mathbb{Z}_q^n$ uniformly at random. Now, $\mathcal{A}$ can construct a malicious ciphertext part $\mathbf{c}'$ as follows:

Challenger C		**Adversary $\mathcal{A}$**
$(pk^R, sk^R) \leftarrow \mathsf{KGen}(1^\lambda)$ $(pk^S, sk^S) \leftarrow \mathsf{KGen}(1^\lambda)$		
	$\xrightarrow[sk^R,\ sk^S]{pk^R = \mathbf{A}^R,\ pk^S = \mathbf{A}^S}$	
		$(vk, sk) \leftarrow \mathsf{KGen}_{\mathrm{OTS}}(1^\lambda)$ $\mathbf{C}^R = [\mathbf{A}^R \mid \mathbf{H}^R]$ $\mathbf{C}^S = [\mathbf{A}^S \mid \mathbf{H}^S]$ $\mathbf{s}^R \leftarrow\!\$\ \mathbb{Z}_q^n$ Choose $\mathbf{s}^S \leftarrow\!\$\ \mathbb{Z}_q^n$: $\langle \mathbf{d}, \mathbf{s}^R - \mathbf{s}^S \rangle \notin [-\frac{q}{4}, \frac{q}{4})$ $\mathbf{c}' = \begin{bmatrix} (\mathbf{C}^R)^\top \cdot \mathbf{s}^R \\ (\mathbf{C}^S)^\top \cdot \mathbf{s}^S \\ \mathbf{D}^\top \cdot \mathbf{s}^R \end{bmatrix}$ $\sigma \leftarrow \mathsf{Sig}_{\mathrm{OTS}}(sk, \mathbf{c}')$
	$\xleftarrow{\mathbf{c} = (vk, \mathbf{c}', \sigma)}$	

Fig. 6. Soundness attack against the schemes of [36, 53].

$$\mathbf{c}' = \begin{pmatrix} \mathbf{c}^R \\ \mathbf{c}^S \\ \mathbf{c}^{\mathrm{msg}} \end{pmatrix} = \begin{bmatrix} (\mathbf{C}^R)^\top \cdot \mathbf{s}^R \\ (\mathbf{C}^S)^\top \cdot \mathbf{s}^S \\ \mathbf{D}^\top \cdot \mathbf{s}^R \end{bmatrix} \in \mathbb{Z}_q^{2m+n}.$$

Note that we implicitly choose $\mathbf{e}^R, \mathbf{e}^S = \mathbf{0}^m$ and $\mathbf{e}^{\mathrm{msg}}, \mathbf{m} = 0^n$. To finish the encryption, $\mathcal{A}$ runs $\sigma \leftarrow \mathsf{Sig}_{\mathrm{OTS}}(sk, \mathbf{c}')$ and returns the ciphertext $\mathbf{c} = (vk, \mathbf{c}', \sigma)$. A sketch of this game is given in Fig. 5.

Let us discuss the respective decryptions. Since R does not use the malformed ciphertext part $\mathbf{c}^S$ in the decryption algorithm and the signature σ is valid, R decrypts 0^n as its message and thus 0 as the first bit. Now consider the decryption algorithm in the view of S, restricted to the first bit of $\mathbf{m}$. First, the signature check is successful since $\mathcal{A}$ made an honest signature. Next, $\mathtt{SampleLeft}(\mathbf{A}^S, \mathbf{H}^S, \mathbf{d}_1, sk^S, s')$ returns $\mathbf{v}_1$ such that $\mathbf{C}^S\mathbf{v}_1 = \mathbf{d}_1$. According to line 6 of the decryption algorithm from Fig. 6, S obtains $\mathbf{m}'[1] = \mathbf{c}^{\mathrm{msg}}[1] - \mathbf{v}_1^\top \mathbf{c}^S = \langle \mathbf{d}_1, \mathbf{s}^R \rangle - \mathbf{v}_1^\top (\mathbf{C}^S)^\top \cdot \mathbf{s}^S = \langle \mathbf{d}_1, \mathbf{s}^R \rangle - \mathbf{d}_1^\top \mathbf{s}^S = \langle \mathbf{d}_1, \mathbf{s}^R - \mathbf{s}^S \rangle \notin \left[-\frac{q}{4}, \frac{q}{4}\right)$ and hence decrypts 1 as first bit. Thus, R and S decrypt different messages from the same ciphertext which breaks the soundness property.

4.2 Identity-Based DRE Schemes Without Soundness

We now discuss identity-based DRE (IB-DRE) schemes. In identity based encryption (IBE), public information, such as an email address, called *identity*, is used for encryption instead of traditional public keys. Decryption is still performed with the help of a secret key. Such a secret key is attained from a key generation algorithm that takes a *master secret key* and an identity as input.

There are three works constructing post-quantum secure identity-based DRE schemes in the literature [36,37,53]. Zhang et al. [53] propose a generic construction, which is instantiated in the more recent work of Liu et al. [36]. Here, an additional primitive called *lattice-based programmable hash functions* is used. Liu et al. [37] use an injective map and a homomorphic computation technique due to Yamada [50].

Due to the huge storage costs of public parameters, IB-DRE schemes are impracticable in their current state. For example, in the recent work from Liu et al. [37], 70 public key matrices are demanded, leading to storage cost of approximately 1.2GB for a choice of $n = 284$ (as suggested by Micciancio and Peikert [41]). Besides the huge storage costs, none of the three IB-DRE schemes satisfies the soundness property. From a structural perspective, all of these schemes use the same ideas as the schemes from Sect. 4.1 for encryption, and the decryption algorithm does not contain any soundness tests as well. Hence, an adversary can inject different LWE-secrets $\mathbf{s}$ in the encryption.

For an attack against the schemes of Liu et al. [37], we refer to Sect. 4.1 since the attacks are very similar. The attack on the schemes of Liu et al. [36] is slightly more involved and is discussed in Appendix A of the full version.

5 IND-CCA2$_{\text{DRE}}$ Secure and Sound Hybrid DRE

Section 3 and Sect. 4 show that there is a need for efficient, post-quantum and IND-CCA2$_{\text{DRE}}$ secure and sound constructions of DRE schemes in the standard model. In the following we present two constructions that meet this need.

For both constructions we need a full-rank difference encoding FRD[1] as well as a hash function $\mathtt{H} : \{0,1\}^* \to \mathbb{Z}_q^n \setminus \{0\}$, a secret-key encryption system SKE, a message authentication code MAC and a key derivation function KDF.

5.1 NLWE-Based Construction

By adapting the NLWE-based hybrid construction from Boyen, Izabachène, and Li [11] we are able to straightforwardly construct an NLWE-based DRE construction with soundness. As usual, $\mathcal{D}_{\mathbb{Z},\alpha q}$ denotes the discrete Gaussian distribution.

In our description in Fig. 7 we only show the decryption for R, the decryption for S works exactly the same with swapped party identifiers.

Theorem 1. *The DRE* $\Sigma_{\mathtt{LWE\text{-}DRE}} = (\mathtt{gen}, \mathtt{enc}, \mathtt{dec})$ *is correct.*

The correctness proof carries over from the correctness of [11] since our construction does not change anything intrinsic.

Theorem 2. *The DRE* $\Sigma_{\mathtt{LWE\text{-}DRE}} = (\mathtt{gen}, \mathtt{enc}, \mathtt{dec})$ *is sound as in Definition 3.*

The basic idea is a statistical one: for a given matrix $\mathbf{A}$, the LWE tuple $(\mathbf{s}, \mathbf{e})$ in $\mathbf{s}^\top\mathbf{A} + \mathbf{e}$ is unique with overwhelming probability, see for example the work of Zhang et al. [54]. Therefore, even for maliciously created ciphertexts, both parties will recover the same $\mathbf{s}$.

Proof. Assume the scheme is not sound. Then there exists an adversary $\mathcal{A}$ with non-negligible advantage $\mathsf{Adv}_{\mathcal{E},\mathcal{A}}^{\text{dre-sound}}$ as in Definition 3. Thus, given two public keys $pk^R = (\mathbf{A}^R, \mathbf{A}_1^R)$ and $pk^S = (\mathbf{A}^S, \mathbf{A}_1^S)$, the adversary $\mathcal{A}$ returns with non-negligible advantage a valid ciphertext $\mathbf{c}$ such that $\mathtt{dec}(sk^R, pk^S, pk^R, \mathbf{c}) \neq \mathtt{dec}(sk^S, pk^S, pk^R, \mathbf{c})$.

At least one party has to accept the ciphertext as otherwise both parties would return $\perp$. Thus, we can assume without loss of generality that R outputs a message and therefore all checks are valid. In particular, we have $\left\|\mathbf{c}_1^{S^\top} - (\mathbf{s}^R)^\top(\mathbf{A}_1^S + \mathtt{FRD}(\mathtt{H}(\mathbf{c}_0))\mathbf{G})\right\| \leq \alpha q\sqrt{2m\overline{m}} \cdot \omega(\sqrt{\log n})$, where $\mathbf{s}^R$ is the vector that R recovered in step 5. This means that $\mathbf{c}_1^{S^\top} = (\mathbf{s}^R)^\top(\mathbf{A}_1^S + \mathtt{FRD}(\mathtt{H}(\mathbf{c}_0))\mathbf{G}) + (\mathbf{e}_1')^\top$ with $\|\mathbf{e}_1'\| \leq \alpha q\sqrt{2m\overline{m}} \cdot \omega(\sqrt{\log n})$. Similarly, we have $\mathbf{c}_0^{S^\top} = (\mathbf{s}^R)^\top\mathbf{A}^S + (\mathbf{e}_0')^\top$ with $\|\mathbf{e}_0'\| \leq \alpha q\sqrt{m}$.

[1] A FRD is a function $\mathtt{FRD} : \mathbb{Z}_q^n \to \mathbb{Z}_q^{n\times n}$ such that for any $x, y \in \mathbb{Z}_q^n, x \neq y$ we have $\mathtt{FRD}(x) - \mathtt{FRD}(y)$ is invertible over $\mathbb{Z}_q^{n\times n}$. See the work of Agrawal, Boneh, and Boyen [2] for an example of such functions.

$\mathsf{gen}(1^\lambda)$

$\mathbf{A} \leftarrow\!\!\$\ \mathbb{Z}_q^{n\times m}, \mathbf{R} \leftarrow \mathcal{D}_{\mathbb{Z},\omega(\sqrt{\log n})}^{m\times \overline{m}}$

$\mathbf{A}_1 = \mathbf{A}\cdot\mathbf{R}$

return $(pk, sk) := ((\mathbf{A}, \mathbf{A}_1), \mathbf{R})$

$\mathsf{enc}(pk^R, pk^S, \mathbf{M})$

parse $pk^R = (\mathbf{A}^R, \mathbf{A}_1^R)$

parse $pk^S = (\mathbf{A}^S, \mathbf{A}_1^S)$

$\mathbf{k} \leftarrow\!\!\$\ \{0,1\}^n$

$(dk, mk) := \mathtt{KDF}(\mathbf{k})$

$\bar{\mathbf{s}} \leftarrow \mathcal{D}_{\mathbb{Z},\alpha q}^m$, $\mathbf{s} := \mathbf{k}\cdot\lfloor\frac{q}{2}\rfloor + \bar{\mathbf{s}}$

$\mathbf{e}_0^R, \mathbf{e}_0^S \leftarrow \mathcal{D}_{\mathbb{Z},\alpha q}^m$

$\mathbf{c}_0 = (\mathbf{s}^\top\mathbf{A}^R + \mathbf{e}_0^R, \mathbf{s}^\top\mathbf{A}^S + \mathbf{e}_0^S)$

$\mathbf{e}_1^R, \mathbf{e}_1^S \leftarrow \mathcal{D}_{\mathbb{Z},s}^{\overline{m}}$,
where $s^2 = (\|\mathbf{e}_0\|^2 + m(\alpha q)^2)\cdot\omega(\sqrt{\log n})$

$\mathbf{c}_1 = (\mathbf{s}^\top(\mathbf{A}_1^R + \mathtt{FRD}(\mathtt{H}(\mathbf{c}_0))\mathbf{G}) + \mathbf{e}_1^R,$
$\mathbf{s}^\top(\mathbf{A}_1^S + \mathtt{FRD}(\mathtt{H}(\mathbf{c}_0))\mathbf{G}) + \mathbf{e}_1^S)$

$\phi := \mathtt{SKE.enc}(dk, \mathbf{M})$

$\sigma := \mathtt{MAC.sign}(mk, (\mathbf{c}_0, \mathbf{c}_1, \phi))$

return $\mathbf{c} = (\mathbf{c}_0, \mathbf{c}_1, \phi, \sigma)$

$\mathsf{dec}(sk^R, pk^R, pk^S, \mathbf{C})$

parse $pk^R = (\mathbf{A}^R, \mathbf{A}_1^R)$

parse $pk^S = (\mathbf{A}^S, \mathbf{A}_1^S)$

parse $sk^R = (\mathbf{R}^R)$

parse $\mathbf{C} = (\mathbf{c}_0^R, \mathbf{c}_0^S, \mathbf{c}_1^R, \mathbf{c}_1^S, \phi, \sigma)$

$(\mathbf{s}, \mathbf{e}_0^R, \mathbf{e}_1^R) \leftarrow \mathtt{Invert}(\mathbf{R},$
$\left[\mathbf{A}^R \mid \mathbf{A}_1^R + \mathtt{FRD}(\mathtt{H}(\mathbf{c}_0^R))\mathbf{G}\right], (\mathbf{c}_0^R, \mathbf{c}_1^R))$

if $\left\|\mathbf{e}_0^R\right\| > \alpha q\sqrt{m}$ output $\perp$

if $\left\|\mathbf{e}_1^R\right\| > \alpha q\sqrt{2m\overline{m}}\cdot\omega(\sqrt{\log n})$ output $\perp$

if $\left\|(\mathbf{c}_0^S)^\top - \mathbf{s}^\top\mathbf{A}^S\right\| > \alpha q\sqrt{m}$ output $\perp$

if $\left\|(\mathbf{c}_1^S)^\top - \mathbf{s}^\top(\mathbf{A}_1^S + \mathtt{FRD}(\mathtt{H}(\mathbf{c}_0))\mathbf{G})\right\| >$
$\alpha q\sqrt{2m\overline{m}}\cdot\omega(\sqrt{\log n})$ output $\perp$

for $i \in [m]$ **do**

$$\mathbf{k}[i] = \begin{cases} 0, & \mathbf{s}[i] \in [-\frac{q}{4}, \frac{q}{4}) \\ 1, & \mathbf{s}[i] \notin [-\frac{q}{4}, \frac{q}{4}) \end{cases}$$

if $\|\mathbf{s} - \mathbf{k}\| > \alpha q\sqrt{n}$ output $\perp$

$(dk, mk) = \mathtt{KDF}(\mathbf{k})$

if $1 == \mathtt{MAC.Vfy}(mk, (\mathbf{c}_0, \mathbf{c}_1, \phi), \sigma)$

return $\mathbf{M} = \mathtt{SKE.dec}(dk, \phi)$

else return $\mathbf{M} = \perp$

Fig. 7. Description of $\Sigma_{\mathtt{LWE\text{-}DRE}} = (\mathsf{gen}, \mathsf{enc}, \mathsf{dec})$.

By Micciancio and Peikert [41, Theorem 5.4] this means that S recovers $\mathbf{s}^R$ as well, succeeds with all checks and thus both parties recover the same $\mathbf{k}$, as well as the same $(dk,\ mk)$ because the KDF is deterministic.

Finally, as our decryption algorithm as well as our verification algorithm are deterministic, it follows that both parties recover the same $\mathbf{M}$. □

Theorem 3. *The DRE* $\Sigma_{\mathtt{LWE\text{-}DRE}} = (\mathsf{gen}, \mathsf{enc}, \mathsf{dec})$ *is IND-CCA2*$_{DRE}$*-secure as in Definition 2 if* $NLWE_{n,m,q,D_{\mathbb{Z},\alpha q}}$ *is hard, and SKE, MAC, H, KDF are all secure w. r. t. Definitions 5, 6, 8 and 9.*

To prove this we adapt the proof of Boyen, Izabachène, and Li [11, Theorem 1]. Thus, for a more in-depth discussion we refer interested reader to that paper. Starting with the IND-CCA2$_{\text{DRE}}$ game, we slowly replace parts of our scheme until we arrive at a game where any adversary cannot do better than guessing because the supposedly encrypted message is in fact only a random ciphertext. Our assumptions make sure that no adversary can differentiate the games with more than negligible probability and so this proves that our construction is indeed secure.

Proof. We start by giving a small overview of the games. Game 1 to 3 change the decryption oracle to make it easier for us to adapt the public keys in Game 4. Those changes aim to make sure that the adversary does not query ciphertexts using the challenge "tag" $\texttt{FRD}(\texttt{H}(\mathbf{c}_0^*))$. This in turn allows us to replace the binding parts $\mathbf{c}_0$ and $\mathbf{c}_1$ of $\mathbf{k}$ by randomness in Game 5 and 6. Now, Game 7 replaces this key $\mathbf{k}$ by randomness as well, and finally in Game 8 we replace the message encryption ϕ by a random ciphertext.

As usual, we denote by $\mathbb{P}[S_i]$ the probability, that the adversary outputs 1 in Game i.

Game 0: This game follows the IND-CCA2-DRE game. Here, $\mathcal{A}$ gets two independently generated public keys, makes decryption queries to the oracle which can be honestly answered using the secret keys. After that, $\mathcal{A}$ submits two messages M_0, M_1 of equal length, after which the challenge ciphertext is computed by $\mathbf{c}^* = \texttt{enc}(pk^R, pk^S, M_b)$ for $b \leftarrow_\$ \{0,1\}$. The adversary $\mathcal{A}$ can now make further queries provided that the used public key is from the set $\{R, S\}$ and $\mathbf{c} \neq \mathbf{c}^*$. Finally, $\mathcal{A}$ outputs b' and the game returns 1 if $b = b'$. By definition, we have

$$\mathbb{P}[S_0] = \mathbb{P}\left[\mathsf{Exp}_{\text{DRE},\mathcal{A}}^{\text{IND-CCA2}_{\text{DRE}}}(\lambda) = 1\right].$$

Game 1: We now precompute $\mathbf{c}_0^*$ before sending the two generated public keys to $\mathcal{A}$. More specifically, steps 3 to 7 of the encoding in Fig. 7 are now done before sending the public keys to $\mathcal{A}$. As the precomputed $\mathbf{c}_0^*$ is already unavailable to $\mathcal{A}$ until $\mathbf{c}^*$ is released and nothing else changed we get

$$\mathbb{P}[S_1] = \mathbb{P}[S_0].$$

Game 2: This is identical to Game 1 except for the decryption oracle, which now rejects ciphertexts with $\texttt{H}(\mathbf{c}_0) = \texttt{H}(\mathbf{c}_0^*)$ in the first phase as well as ciphertexts with $\mathbf{c}_0 \neq \mathbf{c}_0^*$ and $\texttt{H}(\mathbf{c}_0) = \texttt{H}(\mathbf{c}_0^*)$ in the second phase. Using [11, Lemma 4] we get (for Q_1 being the number of decryption queries in the first phase)[2]

$$|\mathbb{P}[S_2] - \mathbb{P}[S_1]| \leq \frac{Q_1}{q^n} + \mathsf{Adv}_{\texttt{H},\mathcal{B}_1(\lambda)}^{\text{CR}}.$$

Game 3: We now additionally forbid all decryption queries with $\mathbf{c}_0 = \mathbf{c}_0^*$ after the challenge ciphertext has been released. We can bound the probability that $\mathcal{A}$ submits a valid decryption query $\mathbf{c} = (\mathbf{c}_0^*, \mathbf{c}_1, \phi, \sigma) \neq \mathbf{c}^*$ by two sub-events: (1) NoBind: a different key $\mathbf{k} \neq \mathbf{k}^*$ is associated to $\mathbf{c}_0^*$.

[2] Notice that Q_2 in [11, Lemma 4] is not needed: The reduction algorithm $\mathcal{B}_1$ always wins if a collision occurs.

(2) Forge: the key $\mathbf{k}^*$ from $\mathbf{c}^*$ was used for $\mathbf{c}$.
Our definition of $\mathbf{c}_0$ (step 7 of Fig. 7) and the uniqueness of LWE samples[3] proves that $\mathbb{P}[\text{NoBind}]$ is negligible, and thus

$$|\mathbb{P}[S_4] - \mathbb{P}[S_3]| \leq \mathbb{P}[\text{Forge}_3] + \texttt{negl}(\lambda).$$

Game 4: We adapt the generation of both public keys, calculating $\mathbf{c}_0^*$ before setting $\mathbf{A}_1^R = \mathbf{A}^R\mathbf{R}^R - \texttt{FRD}(\texttt{H}(\mathbf{c}_0^*))\mathbf{G}$ and $\mathbf{A}_1^S = \mathbf{A}^S\mathbf{R}^S - \texttt{FRD}(\texttt{H}(\mathbf{c}_0^*))\mathbf{G}$. As $\mathbf{A}^S$ and $\mathbf{A}^R$ are both uniformly random, the distribution of the public keys in Game 3 and Game 4 are statistically close. Also, the decryption oracle can handle the same set of decryption queries as in Game 3. Indeed, given $\mathbf{c} = (\mathbf{c}_0, \mathbf{c}_1, \phi, \sigma)$ we have

$$\begin{aligned}\mathbf{c}_1 &= \left(\mathbf{s}^\top(\mathbf{A}_1^R + \texttt{FRD}(\texttt{H}(\mathbf{c}_0))\mathbf{G}) + \mathbf{e}_1^R, \mathbf{s}^\top(\mathbf{A}_1^S + \texttt{FRD}(\texttt{H}(\mathbf{c}_0))\mathbf{G}) + \mathbf{e}_1^S\right)\\ &= \left(\mathbf{s}^\top(\mathbf{A}^R\mathbf{R}^R + (\texttt{FRD}(\texttt{H}(\mathbf{c}_0)) - \texttt{FRD}(\texttt{H}(\mathbf{c}_0^*)))\mathbf{G}) + \mathbf{e}_1^R,\right.\\ &\qquad \left.\mathbf{s}^\top(\mathbf{A}^S\mathbf{R}^S + (\texttt{FRD}(\texttt{H}(\mathbf{c}_0)) - \texttt{FRD}(\texttt{H}(\mathbf{c}_0^*)))\mathbf{G}) + \mathbf{e}_1^S\right).\end{aligned}$$

As for all $\texttt{H}(\mathbf{c}_0) \neq \texttt{H}(\mathbf{c}_0^*)$ the difference $\texttt{FRD}(\texttt{H}(\mathbf{c}_0)) - \texttt{FRD}(\texttt{H}(\mathbf{c}_0^*))$ is invertible by the definition of FRD, the trapdoor $\mathbf{R}^S$ or $\mathbf{R}^R$ can be used to decrypt the queries. The case $\texttt{H}(\mathbf{c}_0) = \texttt{H}(\mathbf{c}_0^*)$ was already rejected in Game 3 and so we get

$$|\mathbb{P}[S_4] - \mathbb{P}[S_3]| \leq \texttt{negl}(\lambda) \quad \text{and} \quad |\mathbb{P}[\text{Forge}_4] - \mathbb{P}[\text{Forge}_3]| \leq \texttt{negl}(\lambda).$$

Game 5: Here, instead of honestly generating $\mathbf{c}_0^*$ and $\mathbf{c}_1^*$, we draw $\mathbf{c}_1^* \leftarrow\$ \mathbb{Z}_q^{2m}$ and $\tilde{\mathbf{c}_0^*}^R, \tilde{\mathbf{c}_0^*}^S \leftarrow\$ \mathbb{Z}_q^m$ and set $\mathbf{c}_0^* = (\tilde{\mathbf{c}_0^*}^R + (\mathbf{k}^* \cdot \lfloor q/2 \rfloor)^\top \mathbf{A}^R, \tilde{\mathbf{c}_0^*}^S + (\mathbf{k}^* \cdot \lfloor q/2 \rfloor)^\top \mathbf{A}^S)$. We can then use [11, Lemma 5] to reduce this game-step to the NLWE-assumption with the only adaption being that we replace the definition of $(\mathbf{c}_1^*)^\top = (\mathbf{c}_0^*)^\top \mathbf{R} + \mathbf{v}^\top$ by $(\mathbf{c}_1^*)^\top = ((\mathbf{c}_0^{*R})^\top \mathbf{R}^R + \mathbf{v}^{R^\top}, (\mathbf{c}_0^{*S})^\top \mathbf{R}^S + \mathbf{v}^{S^\top})$. This results in

$$\begin{aligned}|\mathbb{P}[S_5] - \mathbb{P}[S_4]| &\leq \mathsf{Adv}_{\mathcal{B}_2}^{\mathsf{NLWE}_{n,m,q,\chi}}(\lambda) \quad \text{as well as}\\ |\mathbb{P}[\text{Forge}_5] - \mathbb{P}[\text{Forge}_4]| &\leq 2\mathsf{Adv}_{\mathcal{B}_2'}^{\mathsf{NLWE}_{n,m,q,\chi}}(\lambda).\end{aligned}$$

Game 6: We now replace $\mathbf{c}_0^*$ of Game 5 with $\mathbf{c}_0^* \leftarrow\$ \mathbb{Z}_q^{2m}$. As $\tilde{\mathbf{c}_0^*}$ was only used to generate $\mathbf{c}_0^*$ and acted as a one-time-pad, the distributions of both games are identical and thus

$$\mathbb{P}[S_6] = \mathbb{P}[S_5] \quad \text{and} \quad \mathbb{P}[\text{Forge}_6] = \mathbb{P}[\text{Forge}_5].$$

Game 7: Instead of generating the signing key dk^* and the MAC key mk^* using the KDF, we just draw them from the key spaces of SKE and MAC uniformly.

[3] See for example [54, Lemma 6].

As $\mathbf{k}^*$ is independent of $\mathbf{c}^*$ since Game 6, this change can be reduced to the security of the KDF. More specifically, using [11, Lemma 6] we can show that

$$|\mathbb{P}[S_7] - \mathbb{P}[S_6]| \leq \mathsf{Adv}^{\mathrm{IND}}_{\mathsf{KDF},\mathcal{B}'_3}(\lambda) \quad \text{as well as}$$
$$|\mathbb{P}[\mathrm{Forge}_7] - \mathbb{P}[\mathrm{Forge}_6]| \leq 2\mathsf{Adv}^{\mathrm{IND}}_{\mathsf{KDF},\mathcal{B}'_3}(\lambda).$$

But as mk^* is now uniformly sampled and independent of $\mathbf{c}_0^*, \mathbf{c}_1^*$ and ϕ^*, $\mathbb{P}[\mathrm{Forge}_7]$ can straightforwardly be bound by the security of the MAC using [11, Lemma 7] to arrive at

$$\mathbb{P}[\mathrm{Forge}_7] \leq Q_2 \cdot \mathsf{Adv}^{\mathrm{OT\text{-}SUF}}_{\mathsf{MAC},\mathcal{B}_4}(\lambda).$$

Game 8: Last but not least we replace the encrypted message ϕ^* of the challenge ciphertext by a random ciphertext. As dk^* is independently and randomly chosen, a straightforward reduction shows

$$|\mathbb{P}[S_8] - \mathbb{P}[S_7]| \leq \mathsf{Adv}^{\mathrm{OT\text{-}IND}}_{\mathsf{SKE},\mathcal{B}_5}(\lambda).$$

We note that in Game 8 the challenge ciphertext is independent of the chosen value b, and thus the adversary has no advantage in winning Game 8. Using our assumptions we finally see that the winning probability between all games only changes negligible, and thus

$$\mathsf{Adv}^{\mathrm{IND\text{-}CCA2_{DRE}}}_{\mathrm{DRE},\mathcal{A}}(\lambda) \leq \frac{1}{2} + \mathtt{negl}(\lambda),$$

which finishes the proof. □

5.2 Code-Based Construction of a Sound and IND-CCA2$_{\mathrm{DRE}}$ Secure DRE

We adapt the LPN-based PKE from Kiltz, Masny, and Pietrzak [34] to create an IND-CCA2$_{\mathrm{DRE}}$ secure DRE scheme with soundness. The double trapdoor technique employed by the authors allows us to convert their PKE into a DRE construction, while actually reducing the public key by one matrix and only slightly increasing the ciphertext size.

We note here that Boyen, Izabachène, and Li [11] adapted the scheme of Kiltz, Masny, and Pietrzak [34] as well to create an IND-CCA2 secure hybrid encryption scheme based on LPN, which shares the symmetric part of our scheme.

As before only the decryption for R is described in Fig. 8, but the decryption for S works exactly the same with swapped party identifiers. Also, everything happens in $\mathbb{Z}_2$, and so the operations "+" and "−" can be used interchangeably.

In this scheme we use a constant $0 < c < 1/4$ defining the Bernoulli parameter $p = \sqrt{c/m}$ and the bounding parameter $\beta = 2\sqrt{cm}$. Additionally, we use an efficient binary linear error-correcting code $\mathbf{G} : \mathbb{Z}_2^n \to \mathbb{Z}_2^m$ correcting up to αm errors for $4c < \alpha < 1$, which exists by Lemma 2.

$\texttt{gen}(1^\lambda)$

$\mathbf{A} \leftarrow\!\!\$\ \mathbb{Z}_2^{n\times m}, \mathbf{R} \leftarrow \mathrm{Ber}_p^{m\times m}$
$\mathbf{A}_1 = \mathbf{A}\cdot\mathbf{R}$
$\textbf{return}\ (pk, sk) := ((\mathbf{A}, \mathbf{A}_1), \mathbf{R})$

$\texttt{enc}(pk^R, pk^S, \mathbf{M})$

parse $pk^R = (\mathbf{A}^R, \mathbf{A}_1^R)$
parse $pk^S = (\mathbf{A}^S, \mathbf{A}_1^S)$
$\mathbf{s} \leftarrow\!\!\$\ \{0,1\}^n$
$(dk, mk) := \mathtt{KDF}(\mathbf{s})$
$\mathbf{e}^R, \mathbf{e}^S \leftarrow \mathrm{Ber}_p^m$
$\mathbf{c}_0 = (\mathbf{s}^\top\mathbf{A}^R + \mathbf{e}^R, \mathbf{s}^\top\mathbf{A}^S + \mathbf{e}^S)$
$\mathbf{T}^R, \mathbf{T}^S \leftarrow \mathrm{Ber}_p^{m\times m}$
$\mathbf{c}_1 = \big(\mathbf{s}^\top(\mathbf{A}_1^R + \mathtt{FRD}(\mathtt{H}(\mathbf{c}_0))\mathbf{G}) + (\mathbf{e}^R)^\top\mathbf{T}^R,$
$\mathbf{s}^\top(\mathbf{A}_1^S + \mathtt{FRD}(\mathtt{H}(\mathbf{c}_0))\mathbf{G}) + (\mathbf{e}^S)^\top\mathbf{T}^S\big)$
$\phi := \mathtt{SKE.enc}(dk, \mathbf{M})$
$\sigma := \mathtt{MAC.sign}(mk, (\mathbf{c}_0, \mathbf{c}_1, \phi))$
$\textbf{return}\ \mathbf{c} = (\mathbf{c}_0, \mathbf{c}_1, \phi, \sigma)$

$\texttt{dec}(sk^R, pk^R, pk^S, \mathbf{C})$

parse $pk^R = (\mathbf{A}^R, \mathbf{A}_1^R)$
parse $pk^S = (\mathbf{A}^S, \mathbf{A}_1^S)$
parse $sk^R = (\mathbf{R}^R)$
parse $\mathbf{C} = (\mathbf{c}_0^R, \mathbf{c}_0^S, \mathbf{c}_1^R, \mathbf{c}_1^S, \phi, \sigma)$
$\mathbf{c}_t^R := \mathbf{c}_1^R - \mathbf{c}_0^R\mathbf{R}^R$
$\mathbf{s} := \mathtt{decode}_\mathbf{G}\left(\mathbf{c}_t^R\right)\cdot \mathtt{FRD}(\mathtt{H}(\mathbf{c}_0))^{-1}$
if $\left\|\mathbf{c}_0^R - \mathbf{s}^\top\mathbf{A}^R\right\|_w > \beta$ **output** $\perp$
if $\left\|\mathbf{c}_0^S - \mathbf{s}^\top\mathbf{A}^S\right\|_w > \beta$ **output** $\perp$
if $\left\|\mathbf{c}_1^R - \mathbf{s}^\top(\mathbf{A}_1^R + \mathtt{FRD}(\mathtt{H}(\mathbf{c}_0))\mathbf{G})\right\|_w > \frac{\alpha m}{2}$
if $\left\|\mathbf{c}_1^S - \mathbf{s}^\top(\mathbf{A}_1^S + \mathtt{FRD}(\mathtt{H}(\mathbf{c}_0))\mathbf{G})\right\|_w > \frac{\alpha m}{2}$
$(dk, mk) = \mathtt{KDF}(\mathbf{s})$
if $1 == \mathtt{MAC.Vfy}(mk, (\mathbf{c}_0, \mathbf{c}_1, \phi), \sigma)$
return $\mathbf{M} = \mathtt{SKE.dec}(dk, \phi)$
else return $\mathbf{M} = \perp$

Fig. 8. Description of $\Sigma_{\texttt{LPN-DRE}} = (\texttt{gen}, \texttt{enc}, \texttt{dec})$

Theorem 4. *The DRE* $\Sigma_{\texttt{LPN-DRE}} = (\texttt{gen}, \texttt{enc}, \texttt{dec})$ *is correct.*

Proof. As the same parameters are used, the proof of [34, Theorem 1] shows that

$$\mathop{\mathbb{P}}_{\mathbf{e}\leftarrow\mathrm{Ber}_p^m}\left[\|\mathbf{e}\|_w > \beta\right] < 2^{-\Theta(\sqrt{m})} \tag{1}$$

as well as

$$\mathop{\mathbb{P}}_{\mathbf{T}\leftarrow\mathrm{Ber}_p^{m\times m}}\left[\|\mathbf{Te}\|_w > \frac{\alpha m}{2} \mid \|\mathbf{e}\|_w \leq \beta\right] < 2^{-\Theta(m)}. \tag{2}$$

Thus, for a properly generated ciphertext, it holds with overwhelming probability $1 - 2^{\Theta(\sqrt{m})}$ for $i \in \{R, S\}$ that

$$\left\|\mathbf{e}^i\right\|_w \leq \beta \ \wedge\ \left\|(\mathbf{e}^i)^\top\mathbf{T}^i\right\|_w \leq \frac{\alpha m}{2} \ \wedge\ \left\|(\mathbf{e}^i)^\top\mathbf{R}^i\right\|_w \leq \frac{\alpha m}{2}.$$

In this case, by the error correction property of the code $\mathbf{G}$, the correct $\mathbf{s}$ is recovered from $\mathbf{c}_t^R = \mathbf{s}^\top\mathtt{FRD}(\mathtt{H}(\mathbf{c}_0))\mathbf{G} + (\mathbf{e}^R)^\top(\mathbf{T}^R - \mathbf{R}^R)$ as the error term satisfies $\left\|(\mathbf{e}^R)^\top(\mathbf{T}^R - \mathbf{R}^R)\right\|_w \leq \alpha m$ by Equation (2). Also, all decryption checks succeed and thus the correct message $\mathbf{M}$ is recovered by the determinism of $\mathtt{KDF}$, $\mathtt{MAC.Vfy}$ and $\mathtt{SKE.dec}$. □

Theorem 5. *The DRE* $\Sigma_{\texttt{LPN-DRE}} = (\texttt{gen}, \texttt{enc}, \texttt{dec})$ *is sound as in Definition 3.*

The proof is similar to proof 2 but this time we use the decoding properties of $\mathbf{G}$ for the uniqueness of $\mathbf{s}$.

Proof. Assume the scheme is not sound. Then there exists an adversary $\mathcal{A}$ whose advantage $\mathsf{Adv}^{\text{dre-sound}}_{\mathcal{E},\mathcal{A}}$ is non-negligible, where the advantage is defined as in Definition 3. Thus, given two public keys $pk^R = (\mathbf{A}^R, \mathbf{A}_1^R), pk^S = (\mathbf{A}^S, \mathbf{A}_1^S)$, the adversary $\mathcal{A}$ returns with non-negligible advantage a valid ciphertext $\mathbf{c}$ with $\texttt{dec}(sk^R, pk^S, pk^R, \mathbf{c}) \neq \texttt{dec}(sk^S, pk^S, pk^R, \mathbf{c})$.

At least one party has to accept the ciphertext as otherwise both parties would return $\perp$. Thus, we can assume without loss of generality that R outputs a message and therefore the decryption checks are valid. In particular, we have $\left\|\mathbf{c}_1^S - (\mathbf{s}^R)^\top(\mathbf{A}_1^S + \texttt{FRD}(\texttt{H}(\mathbf{c}_0))\mathbf{G})\right\|_w \leq \frac{\alpha m}{2}$, where $\mathbf{s}^R$ is the vector that R recovered in step 6. This means that $\mathbf{c}_1^S = (\mathbf{s}^R)^\top(\mathbf{A}_1^S + \texttt{FRD}(\texttt{H}(\mathbf{c}_0))\mathbf{G}) + (\mathbf{e}_1')^\top$ with $\|\mathbf{e}_1'\|_w \leq \frac{\alpha m}{2}$. Similarly, we have $\mathbf{c}_0^S = (\mathbf{s}^R)^\top\mathbf{A}^S + (\mathbf{e}_0')^\top$ with $\|\mathbf{e}_0'\|_w \leq \beta$.

Therefore, it holds that $\mathbf{c}_t^S = \mathbf{c}_1^S - \mathbf{c}_0^S\mathbf{R}^S = \mathbf{s}^R\texttt{FRD}(\texttt{H}(c_0))\mathbf{G} + (\mathbf{e}_1')^\top - (\mathbf{e}_0')^\top\mathbf{R}^S$. As $\|\mathbf{e}_1'\|_w \leq \frac{\alpha m}{2}$ we only need to show $\left\|(\mathbf{e}_0')^\top\mathbf{R}^S\right\|_w \leq \frac{\alpha m}{2}$. Indeed, the decoding property of $\mathbf{G}$ guarantees the correct decoding of $\mathbf{s}$ if the inequality holds, and as $\texttt{KDF}, \texttt{MAC.Vfy}$ and $\texttt{SKE.dec}$ are deterministic, both parties will decrypt the same message $\mathbf{M}$.

To show that $\left\|(\mathbf{e}_0')^\top\mathbf{R}\right\|_w \leq \frac{\alpha m}{2}$ with overwhelming probability, notice first that $\#\{\mathbf{e} \in \mathbb{Z}_2^m \mid \|\mathbf{e}\|_w \leq \beta\} = \sum_{i=0}^{\beta}\binom{m}{i} \leq 2^{\log(m)\mathcal{O}(\sqrt{m})}$ because $\beta = \Theta(\sqrt{m})$. Thus, taking the union bound over all $\mathbf{e} \in \mathbb{Z}_2^m$ with $\|\mathbf{e}\|_w \leq \beta$ we get

$$\mathop{\mathbb{P}}_{\mathbf{R}^S}\left[\forall \mathbf{e}, \|\mathbf{e}\|_w \leq \beta : \left\|\mathbf{e}^\top\mathbf{R}^S\right\|_w \leq \frac{\alpha m}{2}\right] \geq 1 - 2^{\Theta(m)}$$

using Equation (2) as desired, which finishes the proof.

Theorem 6. *The DRE* $\Sigma_{\texttt{LPN-DRE}} = (\texttt{gen}, \texttt{enc}, \texttt{dec})$ *is IND-CCA2*$_{DRE}$*-secure as in Definition 2 if* $LPN_{n,m,p}$ *is hard, and* $\texttt{SKE}, \texttt{MAC}, \texttt{H}, \texttt{KDF}$ *are all secure w.r.t. Definitions 5, 6, 8 and 9.*

To prove this we use ideas of Boyen, Izabachène, and Li [11, Theorem 1] and Kiltz, Masny, and Pietrzak [34, Theorem 2]. Therefore, this proof shares its structure with proof 3, and for faster understanding, games that differ from aforementioned proof are highlighted by underscoring them.

Proof. **Game 0:** This game follows the IND-CCA2-DRE game. So again, $\mathcal{A}$ gets two independently generated public keys, makes decryption queries to the oracle which can be honestly answered using the secret keys. After that, $\mathcal{A}$ submits two messages M_0, M_1 of equal length, after which the challenge ciphertext is computed by $\mathbf{c}^* = \texttt{enc}(pk^R, pk^S, M_b)$ for $b \leftarrow\$ \{0,1\}$. The adversary $\mathcal{A}$ can now make further queries provided that the used public key is from the set $\{R, S\}$ and $\mathbf{c} \neq \mathbf{c}^*$. Finally, $\mathcal{A}$ outputs b' and the game returns 1 if $b = b'$. By definition, we have

$$\mathbb{P}[S_0] = \mathbb{P}\left[\mathsf{Exp}^{\text{IND-CCA2}_{\text{DRE}}}_{\text{DRE},\mathcal{A}}(\lambda) = 1\right].$$

Game 1: In this game, $\mathbf{c}_0^*$ is precomputed before sending the two generated public keys to $\mathcal{A}$. More specifically, steps 3 to 6 of the encoding in Fig. 8 are now done before sending the public keys to $\mathcal{A}$. As the precomputed $\mathbf{c}_0^*$ is already unavailable to $\mathcal{A}$ until $\mathbf{c}^*$ is released and nothing else changed we get

$$\mathbb{P}[S_1] = \mathbb{P}[S_0].$$

Game 2: This is identical to Game 1 except for the decryption oracle, which now rejects ciphertexts with $\mathtt{H}(\mathbf{c}_0) = \mathtt{H}(\mathbf{c}_0^*)$ in the first phase as well as ciphertexts with $\mathbf{c}_0 \neq \mathbf{c}_0^*$ and $\mathtt{H}(\mathbf{c}_0) = \mathtt{H}(\mathbf{c}_0^*)$ in the second phase. Using [11, Lemma 4] we get (for Q_1 being the number of decryption queries in the first phase)

$$|\mathbb{P}[S_2] - \mathbb{P}[S_1]| \leq \frac{Q_1}{q^n} + \mathsf{Adv}_{\mathtt{H},\mathcal{B}_1(\lambda)}^{\mathrm{CR}}.$$

Game 3: We now additionally forbid all decryption queries with $\mathbf{c}_0 = \mathbf{c}_0^*$ after the challenge ciphertext has been released. We can bound the probability that $\mathcal{A}$ submits a valid decryption query $\mathbf{c} = (\mathbf{c}_0^*, \mathbf{c}_1, \phi, \sigma) \neq \mathbf{c}^*$ by two sub-events:
(1) NoBind: a different key $\mathbf{s} \neq \mathbf{s}^*$ is associated to $\mathbf{c}_0^*$.
(2) Forge: the key $\mathbf{s}^*$ from $\mathbf{c}^*$ was used for $\mathbf{c}$.
Our definition of $\mathbf{c}_0$ (step 6 of Fig. 8) and the uniqueness of LPN samples[4] proves that $\mathbb{P}[\text{NoBind}]$ is negligible, and thus

$$|\mathbb{P}[S_4] - \mathbb{P}[S_3]| \leq \mathbb{P}[\text{Forge}_3] + \mathtt{negl}(\lambda).$$

Game 4: Our goal again is to set $\mathbf{A}_1^R = \mathbf{A}^R\mathbf{R}^R - \mathtt{FRD}(\mathtt{H}(\mathbf{c}_0^*))\mathbf{G}$ as well as $\mathbf{A}_1^S = \mathbf{A}^S\mathbf{R}^S - \mathtt{FRD}(\mathtt{H}(\mathbf{c}_0^*))\mathbf{G}$. Because of the low noise rate of the private keys, $\mathbf{A}_1^R$ and $\mathbf{A}_1^S$ are only computationally indistinguishable from uniformly random matrices based on the KLPN problem (whereas those matrices were statistically close to uniform in our LWE construction from Sect. 5.1). To solve this we split this game into multiple smaller steps. The idea is to use the double trapdoor already present in the DRE scheme because of the (sound) encryption for both parties to first adapt sk^R and then sk^S. In the process we also adapt $\mathbf{c}^*$ so that later we can use an LPN sample to hide the challenge bit. A recap of the changes can be found before Game 5.

Game 4.1: All decryption queries are answered using sk^S. By the soundness property of our construction (see Theorem 5) we have

$$|\mathbb{P}[S_{4.1}] - \mathbb{P}[S_3]| \leq \mathtt{negl}(\lambda) \text{ and } |\mathbb{P}[\text{Forge}_{4.1}] - \mathbb{P}[\text{Forge}_3]| \leq \mathtt{negl}(\lambda).$$

Game 4.2: We replace $\mathbf{A}_1^R$ by a random matrix. This can be reduced to the KLPN assumption: Assume we have a distinguisher $\mathcal{D}$ between Game 4.1 and 4.2. Our attacker $\mathcal{A}_1$ on KLPN gets $(\mathbf{A}, \mathbf{B})$ and has to decide whether $\mathbf{B} \leftarrow\!\!\$\, \mathbb{Z}_2^{n\times m}$ or $\mathbf{B} = \mathbf{AE}$ for $\mathbf{A} \leftarrow\!\!\$\, \mathbb{Z}_2^{n\times m}$ and $\mathbf{E} \leftarrow \mathrm{Ber}_p^{m\times m}$. It simulates Game 4.1 but instead of generating $\mathbf{A}^R$ and $\mathbf{A}_1^R$ it sets $\mathbf{A}^R := \mathbf{A}$ and $\mathbf{A}_1^R := \mathbf{B}$. As sk^R is not used anymore this does not change the decryption

[4] See for example [25, Lemma 3.2].

capabilities of the oracle, and so if $\mathbf{B} \leftarrow\$ \mathbb{Z}_2^{n\times m}$ this perfectly simulates Game 4.2, while if $\mathbf{B} = \mathbf{AE}$ this perfectly simulates Game 4.1. Thus, the advantage of $\mathcal{A}_1$ is that of $\mathcal{D}$, and so we have

$$|\mathbb{P}[S_{4.2}] - \mathbb{P}[S_{4.1}]| \le \mathsf{Adv}_{\mathcal{A}_1}^{\mathsf{KLPN}_{n,m,p}}(\lambda).$$

For the Forge probabilities, the adversary $\mathcal{A}_2$ follows the same game as above, but for every decryption query $\mathbf{c} = (\mathbf{c}_0^*, \mathbf{c}_1, \phi, \sigma) \neq \mathbf{c}^*$ it checks if $\mathtt{MAC.Vfy}(mk^*, (\mathbf{c}_0, \mathbf{c}_1, \phi), \sigma) = 1$. In this case, it outputs 1 to the KLPN challenger, otherwise it replies with $\perp$ to the decryption query. If this never happens $\mathcal{A}_2$ outputs a random bit. As in [11, Lemma 5] this results in

$$|\mathbb{P}[\text{Forge}_{4.2}] - \mathbb{P}[\text{Forge}_{4.1}]| \le 2\mathsf{Adv}_{\mathcal{A}_2}^{\mathsf{KLPN}_{n,m,p}}(\lambda).$$

Game 4.3: In this game $\mathbf{A}_1^R = \mathbf{B}$ is replaced by $\mathbf{A}_1^R = \mathbf{B} - \mathtt{FRD}(\mathtt{H}(\mathbf{c}_0^*))\mathbf{G}$ for $\mathbf{B} \leftarrow\$ \mathbb{Z}_2^{n\times m}$. As $\mathbf{B}$ is a one time pad this does not change the distributions, and so

$$\mathbb{P}[S_{4.3}] = \mathbb{P}[S_{4.2}] \quad \text{and} \quad \mathbb{P}[\text{Forge}_{4.3}] = \mathbb{P}[\text{Forge}_{4.2}].$$

Game 4.4: We now replace $\mathbf{A}_1^R = \mathbf{B} - \mathtt{FRD}(\mathtt{H}(\mathbf{c}_0^*))$ by our secret key trapdoor $\mathbf{A}_1^R = \mathbf{A}^R\mathbf{R}^R - \mathtt{FRD}(\mathtt{H}(\mathbf{c}_0^*))\mathbf{G}$. We also adapt $\mathbf{c}_1^{*R}$ such that instead of sampling $\mathbf{T}^R$ and honestly generating $\mathbf{c}_1^{*R}$ we instead replace it by $\mathbf{c}_1^{*R} := \mathbf{s}^\top(\mathbf{A}_1^R + \mathtt{FRD}(\mathtt{H}(\mathbf{c}_0^*))\mathbf{G}) + (\mathbf{e}^R)^\top\mathbf{R}^R$. Similar to Game 4.2 this can be reduced to the EKLPN assumption. For this, assume that there is a distinguisher $\mathcal{D}$ between Game 4.4 and 4.3. The adversary $\mathcal{A}_3$ on EKLPN gets $(\mathbf{A}, \mathbf{B}, \mathbf{z}, \mathbf{u})$ and has to decide whether $\mathbf{B} \leftarrow\$ \mathbb{Z}_2^{n\times m}$ or $\mathbf{B} = \mathbf{AE}$ for $\mathbf{A} \leftarrow \mathbb{Z}_2^{n\times m}, \mathbf{E} \leftarrow \text{Ber}_p^{m\times m}, \mathbf{z} \leftarrow \text{Ber}_p^m$ and $\mathbf{u} = \mathbf{z}^\top\mathbf{E}$. It then simulates Game 4.3 but sets $\mathbf{A}^R := \mathbf{A}, \mathbf{A}_1^R := \mathbf{B}, \mathbf{c}_0^{*R} := \mathbf{s}^\top\mathbf{A}^R + \mathbf{z}$ and $\mathbf{c}_1^{*R} := \mathbf{s}^\top(\mathbf{A}_1^R + \mathtt{FRD}(\mathtt{H}(\mathbf{c}_0^*))\mathbf{G}) + \mathbf{u}$.
Now, if $\mathbf{B} \leftarrow\$ \mathbb{Z}_2^{n\times m}$ this perfectly simulates Game 4.3 because $\mathbf{E}$ and $\mathbf{T}^R$ have the same distribution and both are not used outside of the error generation, whereas if $\mathbf{B} = \mathbf{AE}$ the construction perfectly simulates Game 4.4. As before, together this gives us

$$|\mathbb{P}[S_{4.4}] - \mathbb{P}[S_{4.3}]| \le \mathsf{Adv}_{\mathcal{A}_3}^{\mathsf{EKLPN}_{n,m,p}}(\lambda) \quad \text{and}$$
$$|\mathbb{P}[\text{Forge}_{4.4}] - \mathbb{P}[\text{Forge}_{4.3}]| \le 2\mathsf{Adv}_{\mathcal{A}_4}^{\mathsf{EKLPN}_{n,m,p}}(\lambda).$$

Game 4.5: Decryption is now always done via sk^R instead of sk^S. The decryption oracle can still handle the same set of decryption queries. Indeed, given a valid $\mathbf{c} = (\mathbf{c}_0, \mathbf{c}_1, \phi, \sigma)$ we have

$$\begin{aligned}\mathbf{c}_1^{R^\top} &= \mathbf{s}^\top(\mathbf{A}_1^R + \mathtt{FRD}(\mathtt{H}(\mathbf{c}_0))\mathbf{G}) + (\mathbf{e}^R)^\top\mathbf{T}^R \\ &= \mathbf{s}^\top(\mathbf{A}^R\mathbf{R}^R + (\mathtt{FRD}(\mathtt{H}(\mathbf{c}_0)) - \mathtt{FRD}(\mathtt{H}(\mathbf{c}_0^*)))\mathbf{G}) + (\mathbf{e}^R)^\top\mathbf{T}^R.\end{aligned}$$

As for all $\mathtt{H}(\mathbf{c}_0) \neq \mathtt{H}(\mathbf{c}_0^*)$ the difference $\mathtt{FRD}(\mathtt{H}(\mathbf{c}_0)) - \mathtt{FRD}(\mathtt{H}(\mathbf{c}_0^*))$ is invertible by the definition of $\mathtt{FRD}$, the trapdoor $\mathbf{R}^R$ can be used to decrypt the queries. The case $\mathtt{H}(\mathbf{c}_0) = \mathtt{H}(\mathbf{c}_0^*)$ was already rejected from Game 3 on. Also, by the soundness the difference between using sk^R or sk^S is negligible, and so we get

$$|\mathbb{P}[S_{4.5}] - \mathbb{P}[S_{4.4}]| \leq \mathtt{negl}(\lambda) \text{ and } |\mathbb{P}[\text{Forge}_{4.5}] - \mathbb{P}[\text{Forge}_{4.4}]| \leq \mathtt{negl}(\lambda).$$

Game 4.6: We repeat Game 4.2-Game 4.4 with sk^S. This results in $\mathbf{A}_1^S = \mathbf{A}^S\mathbf{R}^S - \mathtt{FRD}(\mathtt{H}(\mathbf{c}_0^*))$ and $\mathbf{c}_1^{*S} := \mathbf{s}^\top(\mathbf{A}_1^S + \mathtt{FRD}(\mathtt{H}(\mathbf{c}_0^*))\mathbf{G}) + (\mathbf{e}^S)^\top\mathbf{R}^S$ with probability differences

$$|\mathbb{P}[S_{4.6}] - \mathbb{P}[S_{4.5}]| \leq \mathsf{Adv}_{\mathcal{A}_5}^{\mathsf{KLPN}_{n,m,p}}(\lambda) + \mathsf{Adv}_{\mathcal{A}_6}^{\mathsf{EKLPN}_{n,m,p}}(\lambda) \quad \text{and}$$
$$\mathbb{P}[\text{Forge}_{4.6}] - \mathbb{P}[\text{Forge}_{4.5}] \leq 2\mathsf{Adv}_{\mathcal{A}_7}^{\mathsf{KLPN}_{n,m,p}}(\lambda) + 2\mathsf{Adv}_{\mathcal{A}_8}^{\mathsf{EKLPN}_{n,m,p}}(\lambda).$$

After Game 4.6 we have (for $i \in \{R, S\}$) $\mathbf{A}_1^i + \mathtt{FRD}(\mathtt{H}(\mathbf{c}_0^*))\mathbf{G} = \mathbf{A}^i\mathbf{R}^i$, and thus at this point the scheme differs in the following way from the original scheme[5]:

- $(pk^i, sk^i) = ((\mathbf{A}^i, \mathbf{A}_1^i), \mathbf{R}^i)$ where $\mathbf{A}^i \leftarrow\$ \mathbb{Z}_2^{n\times m}, \mathbf{R}^i \leftarrow \mathrm{Ber}_p^{m\times m}$ and then $\mathbf{A}_1^i := \mathbf{A}^i\mathbf{R}^i - \mathtt{FRD}(\mathtt{H}(\mathbf{c}_0^*))\mathbf{G}$
- $\mathbf{c}_0^* = (\mathbf{s}^\top\mathbf{A}^R + \mathbf{e}^R, \mathbf{s}^\top\mathbf{A}^S + \mathbf{e}^S)$
- $\mathbf{c}_1^* = \left(\mathbf{s}^\top\mathbf{A}^R\mathbf{R}^R + (\mathbf{e}^R)^\top\mathbf{R}^R, \mathbf{s}^\top\mathbf{A}^S\mathbf{R}^S + (\mathbf{e}^S)^\top\mathbf{R}^S\right)$.

Game 5: Instead of honestly generating $\mathbf{c}_0^*$ and $\mathbf{c}_1^*$, we draw both $\mathbf{c}_0^{*R} \leftarrow\$ \mathbb{Z}_2^m$ and $\mathbf{c}_0^{*S} \leftarrow\$ \mathbb{Z}_2^m$ and set $\mathbf{c}_1^{*R} := \mathbf{c}_0^{*R}\mathbf{R}^R$ as well as $\mathbf{c}_1^{*S} := \mathbf{c}_0^{*S}\mathbf{R}^S$. This game step can be reduced to the LPN problem. So assume that there is a distinguisher $\mathcal{D}$ between Game 5 and 4.6. Let $\mathcal{A}_9$ be an adversary to the LPN[6] problem who gets $((\mathbf{A}^1, \mathbf{A}^2), (\mathbf{u}^1, \mathbf{u}^2))$ where $\mathbf{u}^i \leftarrow\$ \mathbb{Z}_2^m$ or $\mathbf{u}^i = \mathbf{s}^\top\mathbf{A}^i + \mathbf{e}^i$ for $\mathbf{A}^i \leftarrow\$ \mathbb{Z}_2^{n\times m}$ and $\mathbf{e}^i \leftarrow \mathrm{Ber}_p^m$. It simulates Game 4.6 but sets $\mathbf{c}_0^{*R} = \mathbf{u}^1$, $\mathbf{c}_0^{*S} = \mathbf{u}^2$, $\mathbf{c}_1^{*R} = \mathbf{u}^1\mathbf{R}^R$ and $\mathbf{c}_1^{*S} = \mathbf{u}^2\mathbf{R}^S$.
Now if $\mathbf{u}^i = \mathbf{s}^\top\mathbf{A}^i + \mathbf{e}^i$ this perfectly simulates Game 4.6 by our previous comment, whereas if $\mathbf{u}^i \leftarrow\$ \mathbb{Z}_2^m$ this simulates Game 5. As before that means we have

$$|\mathbb{P}[S_5] - \mathbb{P}[S_{4.6}]| \leq \mathsf{Adv}_{\mathcal{A}_9}^{\mathsf{LPN}_{n,2m,p}}(\lambda) \quad \text{as well as}$$
$$|\mathbb{P}[\text{Forge}_5] - \mathbb{P}[\text{Forge}_{4.6}]| \leq 2\mathsf{Adv}_{\mathcal{A}_{10}}^{\mathsf{LPN}_{n,2m,p}}(\lambda).$$

Game 6: Instead of generating the signing key dk^* and the $\mathtt{MAC}$ key mk^* using the $\mathtt{KDF}$, we just draw them from the key spaces of $\mathtt{SKE}$ and $\mathtt{MAC}$ uniformly. As $\mathbf{s}^*$ is independent of $\mathbf{c}^*$ since Game 5, this change can be reduced to the security of the $\mathtt{KDF}$. More specifically, using [11, Lemma 6] we can show that

$$|\mathbb{P}[S_6] - \mathbb{P}[S_5]| \leq \mathsf{Adv}_{\mathtt{KDF},\mathcal{B}'_3}^{\mathrm{IND}}(\lambda) \quad \text{as well as}$$
$$|\mathbb{P}[\text{Forge}_6] - \mathbb{P}[\text{Forge}_5]| \leq 2\mathsf{Adv}_{\mathtt{KDF},\mathcal{B}'_3}^{\mathrm{IND}}(\lambda).$$

---

[5] As $\mathbf{c}_0^*$ is calculated after $\mathbf{A}^i$ is generated but before $\mathbf{A}_1^i$ is generated, it can be used to calculate $\mathbf{A}_1^i$.

[6] Notice that this is actually an $\mathrm{LPN}_{n,2m,p}$ sample.

But as mk^* is now uniformly sampled and independent of $\mathbf{c}_0^*, \mathbf{c}_1^*$ and ϕ^*, $\mathbb{P}[\text{Forge}_6]$ can straightforwardly be bound by the security of the MAC using [11, Lemma 7] to arrive at

$$\mathbb{P}[\text{Forge}_6] \leq Q_2 \cdot \mathsf{Adv}_{\mathtt{MAC},\mathcal{B}_4}^{\text{OT-SUF}}(\lambda).$$

Game 7: Last but not least we replace the encrypted message ϕ^* of the challenge ciphertext by a random ciphertext. As dk^* is independently and randomly chosen, a straightforward reduction shows

$$|\mathbb{P}[S_7] - \mathbb{P}[S_6]| \leq \mathsf{Adv}_{\mathtt{SKE},\mathcal{B}_5}^{\text{OT-IND}}(\lambda)$$

We note that in Game 7 the challenge ciphertext is independent of the chosen value b, and thus the adversary has no advantage in winning Game 7. Using our assumptions we finally see that the winning probability between all games only changes negligible, and thus

$$\mathsf{Adv}_{\text{DRE},\mathcal{A}}^{\text{IND-CCA2}_{\text{DRE}}}(\lambda) \leq \frac{1}{2} + \mathtt{negl}(\lambda),$$

which finishes the proof. □

We discuss further observations that might be of independent interest in Sect. 6.

6 Discussion

Secure parameters for our schemes from Sect. 5 as well as their resulting sizes can be found in Appendix B of the full version of this paper.

Modular Hybrid Encryption: Boyen, Izabachène, and Li [11] mention that proving the security of the KEM-part in their construction is left for future work. Solving this task would be in fact an interesting result, which might lead to more efficient IND-CCA2 constructions of PKE or DRE in the standard model. For DRE, however, additional assumptions, such as correlated product security [45], are required as encrypting the same secret twice might in general counteract the one-wayness property as shown by Rosen and Segev [45] for the RSA one-way function. Our observation is that the security of the KEM part in the hybrid construction from Boyen, Izabachène, and Li [11] has to be weaker than the replayable chosen ciphertext attack (RCCA) security, which is defined for a PKE by Canetti, Krawczyk, and Nielsen [17] and adapted to the KEM definition from Abe, Gennaro, and Kurosawa [1]. In lattice- or LPN-based trapdoor functions an adversary may always manipulate the error such that the inversion outputs an $\mathbf{x} \neq \perp$. Consider having a validity oracle that on input $\mathbf{c}$ checks whether the ciphertext decrypts to $\perp$. Note that the decryption oracle from the RCCA-Game returning `test` is such an oracle. Then the adversary may obtain the error vector by manipulating $\mathbf{c}$ and testing, whether the RCCA oracle returns `test`.

Partial Soundness. There are corner cases where a weaker variant of soundness is sufficient, i. e., partial soundness or weak decryption consistency, which are equivalent when constrained to two recipients. This allows one party to decrypt the ciphertext to a valid message while the other party outputs $\perp$. The formal definitions can be found in Beskorovajnov et al. [8] and Noh et al. [43].

If one for example skips either step 8 or 9 (but not both) of the decryption in the NLWE-based construction of Sect. 5.1 (only checking the error of either $\mathbf{c}_0^S$ or $\mathbf{c}_1^S$) one gets a slightly more efficient partially sound DRE. Thus, while an attacker cannot create a valid ciphertext encrypting different messages to S and R, they can create a ciphertext which S decrypts to a valid message while R outputs $\perp$. Indeed, one can achieve this by creating a valid ciphertext and adding a big enough error term to either $\mathbf{c}_0^S$ or $\mathbf{c}_1^S$ such that S does not accept the ciphertext, whereas R accepts and decrypts the ciphertext because it does not check this error. Partial soundness still holds because of the injectivity of the LWE function.

7 Conclusion

We observe that the literature of IND-CCA2$_{\mathrm{DRE}}$ secure DRE constructions in the standard model based on post-quantum assumptions lacks constructions that guarantee soundness. However, most of the literature around applications that employ DRE in a generic way require this exact property. Our main result comprises two constructions that fill this gap.

We point out that applications identified by us as non-generic in Sect. 3.4 may be abstracted further in future work in order to use a DRE in a black-box manner. Finally, we note that a DRE construction based on a post-quantum assumption with public verifiability and soundness, which is required by applications from Sect. 3.2, is still an open question.

Acknowledgements. We thank the PKC 2024 anonymous reviewers for their valuable feedback. The work presented in this paper has been supported by Helmholtz Information, Program "Engineering Digital Futures", Topic "Engineering secure Systems".

References

1. Abe, M., Gennaro, R., Kurosawa, K.: Tag-KEM/DEM: A New Framework for Hybrid Encryption, Cryptology ePrint Archive, Report 2005/027 (2017). https://eprint.iacr.org/2005/027
2. Agrawal, S., Boneh, D., Boyen, X.: Efficient lattice (H)IBE in the standard model. In: Gilbert, H. (ed.) EUROCRYPT 2010. LNCS, vol. 6110, pp. 553–572. Springer, Heidelberg (2010). https://doi.org/10.1007/978-3-642-13190-5_28
3. Applebaum, B., Cash, D., Peikert, C., Sahai, A.: Fast cryptographic primitives and circular-secure encryption based on hard learning problems. In: Halevi, S. (ed.) CRYPTO 2009. LNCS, vol. 5677, pp. 595–618. Springer, Heidelberg (2009). https://doi.org/10.1007/978-3-642-03356-8_35

4. Bellare, M., Rogaway, P.: Optimal asymmetric encryption. In: De Santis, A. (ed.) EUROCRYPT 1994. LNCS, vol. 950, pp. 92–111. Springer, Heidelberg (1995). https://doi.org/10.1007/BFb0053428
5. Benz, L., Beskorovajnov, W., Eilebrecht, S., Müller-Quade, J., Ottenhues, A., Schwerdt, R.: Sender-binding Key Encapsulation. In: Boldyreva, A., Kolesnikov, V. (eds.) PKC 2023, Part I. LNCS, vol. 13940, pp. 744–773. Springer, Cham (2023). https://doi.org/10.1007/978-3-031-31368-4_26
6. Bert, P., Eberhart, G., Prabel, L., Roux-Langlois, A., Sabt, M.: Implementation of lattice trapdoors on modules and applications. In: Cheon, J.H., Tillich, J.-P. (eds.) PQCrypto 2021 2021. LNCS, vol. 12841, pp. 195–214. Springer, Cham (2021). https://doi.org/10.1007/978-3-030-81293-5_11
7. Bert, P., Fouque, P.-A., Roux-Langlois, A., Sabt, M.: Practical implementation of ring-SIS/LWE based signature and IBE. In: Lange, T., Steinwandt, R. (eds.) PQCrypto 2018. LNCS, vol. 10786, pp. 271–291. Springer, Cham (2018). https://doi.org/10.1007/978-3-319-79063-3_13
8. Beskorovajnov, W., Gröll, R., Müller-Quade, J., Ottenhues, A., Schwerdt, R.: A new security notion for PKC in the standard model: weaker, simpler, and still realizing secure channels. In: Hanaoka, G., Shikata, J., Watanabe, Y. (eds.) PKC 2022. LNCS, vol. 13178, pp. 316–344. Springer, Heidelberg (2022). https://doi.org/10.1007/978-3-030-97131-1_11
9. Blaze, M., Bleumer, G., Strauss, M.: Divertible protocols and atomic proxy cryptography. In: Nyberg, K. (ed.) EUROCRYPT 1998. LNCS, vol. 1403, pp. 127–144. Springer, Heidelberg (1998). https://doi.org/10.1007/BFb0054122
10. Boneh, D., Kim, S., Nikolaenko, V.: Lattice-based DAPS and generalizations: self-enforcement in signature schemes. In: Gollmann, D., Miyaji, A., Kikuchi, H. (eds.) ACNS 2017. LNCS, vol. 10355, pp. 457–477. Springer, Cham (2017). https://doi.org/10.1007/978-3-319-61204-1_23
11. Boyen, X., Izabachène, M., Li, Q.: Secure hybrid encryption in the standard model from hard learning problems. In: Cheon, J.H., Tillich, J.-P. (eds.) PQCrypto 2021 2021. LNCS, vol. 12841, pp. 399–418. Springer, Cham (2021). https://doi.org/10.1007/978-3-030-81293-5_21
12. Purushothama, B.R., Amberker, B.: Secure group key management scheme based on dual receiver cryptosystem. In: AsiaPKC 2013, pp. 45-50. ACM Press (2013). https://doi.org/10.1145/2484389.2484399
13. Brakerski, Z., Vaikuntanathan, V.: Lattice-Inspired Broadcast Encryption and Succinct Ciphertext-Policy ABE, Cryptology ePrint Archive, Report 2020/191 (2020). https://eprint.iacr.org/2020/191
14. Brendel, J., Fiedler, R., Günther, F., Janson, C., Stebila, D.: Post-quantum asynchronous deniable key exchange and the signal handshake. In: Hanaoka, G., Shikata, J., Watanabe, Y. (eds.) PKC 2022, Part II. LNCS, vol. 13178, pp. 3–34. Springer, Cham (2022). https://doi.org/10.1007/978-3-030-97131-1_1
15. Canetti, R., Dodis, Y., Pass, R., Walfish, S.: Universally composable security with global setup. In: Vadhan, S.P. (ed.) TCC 2007. LNCS, vol. 4392, pp. 61–85. Springer, Heidelberg (2007). https://doi.org/10.1007/978-3-540-70936-7_4
16. Canetti, R., Feige, R., Goldreich, O., Naor, M.: Adaptively secure multi-party computation. In: 28th ACM STOC, pp. 639–648. ACM Press (1996). https://doi.org/10.1145/237814.238015
17. Canetti, R., Krawczyk, H., Nielsen, J.B.: Relaxing chosen-ciphertext security. In: Boneh, D. (ed.) CRYPTO 2003. LNCS, vol. 2729, pp. 565–582. Springer, Heidelberg (2003). https://doi.org/10.1007/978-3-540-45146-4_33

18. Chow, S.S.M., Franklin, M., Zhang, H.: Practical dual-receiver encryption. In: Benaloh, J. (ed.) CT-RSA 2014. LNCS, vol. 8366, pp. 85–105. Springer, Cham (2014). https://doi.org/10.1007/978-3-319-04852-9_5
19. Crescenzo, G.D., Ishai, Y., Ostrovsky, R.: Non-interactive and non-malleable commitment. In: 30th ACM STOC, pp. 141–150. ACM Press (1998). https://doi.org/10.1145/276698.276722
20. Damgård, I., Hofheinz, D., Kiltz, E., Thorbek, R.: Public-key encryption with non-interactive opening. In: Malkin, T. (ed.) CT-RSA 2008. LNCS, vol. 4964, pp. 239–255. Springer, Heidelberg (2008). https://doi.org/10.1007/978-3-540-79263-5_15
21. Diament, T., Lee, H.K., Keromytis, A.D., Yung, M.: The efficient dual receiver cryptosystem and its applications. Int. J. Network Secur. **13**(3), 135–151 (2011). https://doi.org/10.7916/D81R7100
22. Diament, T., Lee, H.K., Keromytis, A.D., Yung, M.: The dual receiver cryptosystem and its applications. In: Atluri, V., Pfitzmann, B., McDaniel, P. (eds.) ACM CCS 2004, pp. 330–343. ACM Press (2004). https://doi.org/10.1145/1030083.1030128
23. Dodis, Y., Katz, J., Smith, A., Walfish, S.: Composability and on-line deniability of authentication. In: Reingold, O. (ed.) TCC 2009. LNCS, vol. 5444, pp. 146–162. Springer, Heidelberg (2009). https://doi.org/10.1007/978-3-642-00457-5_10
24. Dolev, D., Yao, A.: On the security of public key protocols. IEEE Trans. Inf. Theory **29**(2), 198–208 (1983). https://doi.org/10.1109/TIT.1983.1056650
25. Döttling, N.: Cryptography based on the Hardness of Decoding. Ph.D. thesis, Karlsruhe, Karlsruher Institut für Technologie (KIT), Diss., 2014 (2014)
26. Dwork, C., Naor, M., Sahai, A.: Concurrent zero-knowledge. J. ACM **51**(6), 851–898 (2004). https://doi.org/10.1145/1039488.1039489
27. Fiat, A., Naor, M.: Broadcast encryption. In: Stinson, D.R. (ed.) CRYPTO 1993. LNCS, vol. 773, pp. 480–491. Springer, Heidelberg (1994). https://doi.org/10.1007/3-540-48329-2_40
28. Fischlin, M.: Completely non-malleable schemes. In: Caires, L., Italiano, G.F., Monteiro, L., Palamidessi, C., Yung, M. (eds.) ICALP 2005. LNCS, vol. 3580, pp. 779–790. Springer, Heidelberg (2005). https://doi.org/10.1007/11523468_63
29. Ge, A., Wei, P.: Identity-based broadcast encryption with efficient revocation. In: Lin, D., Sako, K. (eds.) PKC 2019. LNCS, vol. 11442, pp. 405–435. Springer, Cham (2019). https://doi.org/10.1007/978-3-030-17253-4_14
30. Gegier, K.: On Novel Constructions of Dual Receiver Key Encapsulation Mechanisms Based on Deterministic Encryption. M.A. thesis, Karlsruhe Institute of Technology (KIT) (2020)
31. Herzog, J., Liskov, M., Micali, S.: Plaintext awareness via key registration. In: Boneh, D. (ed.) CRYPTO 2003. LNCS, vol. 2729, pp. 548–564. Springer, Heidelberg (2003). https://doi.org/10.1007/978-3-540-45146-4_32
32. Jinman, Z., Qin, C.: Hierarchical identity-based broadcast encryption scheme on lattices. In: 2011 Seventh International Conference on Computational Intelligence and Security, pp. 944–948. IEEE (2011). https://doi.org/10.1109/CIS.2011.212
33. Justesen, J.: Class of constructive asymptotically good algebraic codes. IEEE Trans. Inf. Theory **18**(5), 652–656 (1972). https://doi.org/10.1109/TIT.1972.1054893
34. Kiltz, E., Masny, D., Pietrzak, K.: Simple chosen-ciphertext security from low-noise LPN. In: Krawczyk, H. (ed.) PKC 2014. LNCS, vol. 8383, pp. 1–18. Springer, Heidelberg (2014). https://doi.org/10.1007/978-3-642-54631-0_1

35. Libert, B., Paterson, K.G., Quaglia, E.A.: Anonymous broadcast encryption: adaptive security and efficient constructions in the standard model. In: Fischlin, M., Buchmann, J., Manulis, M. (eds.) PKC 2012. LNCS, vol. 7293, pp. 206–224. Springer, Heidelberg (2012). https://doi.org/10.1007/978-3-642-30057-8_13
36. Liu, Y., Zhang, D., Deng, Y., Li, B.: (Identity-based) dual receiver encryption from lattice-based programmable hash functions with high min-entropy. Cybersecurity **2**(1), 1–15 (2019). https://doi.org/10.1186/s42400-019-0034-y
37. Liu, Y., Wang, L., Shen, X., Li, L.: New constructions of identity-based dual receiver encryption from lattices. Entropy **22**(6) (2020). https://doi.org/10.3390/e22060599
38. Ma, F., Zhandry, M.: Encryptor Combiners: A Unified Approach to Multiparty NIKE, (H)IBE, and Broadcast Encryption, Cryptology ePrint Archive, Report 2017/152 (2017). https://eprint.iacr.org/2017/152
39. Mambo, M., Okamoto, E.: Proxy cryptosystems: delegation of the power to decrypt ciphertexts. IEICE Trans. Fundam. Electron. Commun. Comput. Sci. **80**(1), 54–63 (1997)
40. Meier, S., Schmidt, B., Cremers, C., Basin, D.: The TAMARIN prover for the symbolic analysis of security protocols. In: Sharygina, N., Veith, H. (eds.) CAV 2013. LNCS, vol. 8044, pp. 696–701. Springer, Heidelberg (2013). https://doi.org/10.1007/978-3-642-39799-8_48
41. Micciancio, D., Peikert, C.: Trapdoors for lattices: simpler, tighter, faster, smaller. In: Pointcheval, D., Johansson, T. (eds.) EUROCRYPT 2012. LNCS, vol. 7237, pp. 700–718. Springer, Heidelberg (2012). https://doi.org/10.1007/978-3-642-29011-4_41
42. Müller, M.: On the Applicability of Dual-Receiver Encryption in a Post-Quantum World. M.A. thesis, Karlsruhe Institute of Technology (KIT) (2021)
43. Noh, G., Hong, D., Kwon, J.O., Jeong, I.R.: A strong binding encryption scheme from lattices for secret broadcast. IEEE Commun. Lett. **16**(6), 781–784 (2012). https://doi.org/10.1109/LCOMM.2012.041112.112495
44. Patil, S.M., BR, P.: DR-PRE: dual receiver proxy re-encryption scheme. Inf. Secur. J. Global Perspective **29**(2), 62–72 (2020). https://doi.org/10.1080/19393555.2020.1715515
45. Rosen, A., Segev, G.: Chosen-ciphertext security via correlated products. In: Reingold, O. (ed.) TCC 2009. LNCS, vol. 5444, pp. 419–436. Springer, Heidelberg (2009). https://doi.org/10.1007/978-3-642-00457-5_25
46. Suzuki, K., Yoneyama, K.: Exposure-resilient one-round tripartite key exchange without random oracles. In: Jacobson, M., Locasto, M., Mohassel, P., Safavi-Naini, R. (eds.) ACNS 2013. LNCS, vol. 7954, pp. 458–474. Springer, Heidelberg (2013). https://doi.org/10.1007/978-3-642-38980-1_29
47. Unger, N., Goldberg, I.: Improved strongly deniable authenticated key exchanges for secure messaging. PoPETs **2018**(1), 21–66 (2018). https://doi.org/10.1515/popets-2018-0003
48. Wang, J., Bi, J.: Lattice-Based Identity-Based Broadcast Encryption, IACR ePrint Archive, Report 2010/288 (2010). https://eprint.iacr.org/2010/288
49. Wong, C.K., Gouda, M., Lam, S.S.: Secure group communications using key graphs. IEEE/ACM Trans. Networking **8**(1), 16–30 (2000). https://doi.org/10.1109/90.836475
50. Yamada, S.: Adaptively secure identity-based encryption from lattices with asymptotically shorter public parameters. In: Fischlin, M., Coron, J.-S. (eds.) EUROCRYPT 2016. LNCS, vol. 9666, pp. 32–62. Springer, Heidelberg (2016). https://doi.org/10.1007/978-3-662-49896-5_2

51. Yang, C., Zheng, S., Wang, L., Lu, X., Yang, Y.: Hierarchical identity-based broadcast encryption scheme from LWE. J. Commun. Networks **16**(3), 258–263 (2014). https://doi.org/10.1109/JCN.2014.000045
52. Yang, G., Tan, C.H., Huang, Q., Wong, D.S.: Probabilistic public key encryption with equality test. In: Pieprzyk, J. (ed.) CT-RSA 2010. LNCS, vol. 5985, pp. 119–131. Springer, Heidelberg (2010). https://doi.org/10.1007/978-3-642-11925-5_9
53. Zhang, D., Zhang, K., Li, B., Lu, X., Xue, H., Li, J.: Lattice-based dual receiver encryption and more. In: Susilo, W., Yang, G. (eds.) ACISP 2018. LNCS, vol. 10946, pp. 520–538. Springer, Cham (2018). https://doi.org/10.1007/978-3-319-93638-3_30
54. Zhang, J., Yu, Y., Fan, S., Zhang, Z.: Improved lattice-based CCA2-secure PKE in the standard model. Sci. Chin. Inf. Sci. **63**(182101), 1–22 (2020). https://doi.org/10.1007/s11432-019-9861-3

Homomorphic Encryption

SoK: Learning with Errors, Circular Security, and Fully Homomorphic Encryption

Daniele Micciancio[1(✉)] and Vinod Vaikuntanathan[2]

[1] UC San Diego, La Jolla, CA, USA
daniele@cs.ucsd.edu
[2] MIT, Cambridge, MA, USA

Abstract. All known constructions of fully homomorphic encryption (FHE) schemes from the learning with errors (LWE) assumption require the encryption schemes to be circular secure. A long-standing open problem in the study of FHE schemes is to demonstrate evidence for their circular security. In this work, we systematize the flavors of circular security required for a number of FHE constructions, formulate circular security conjectures, show search-to-decision reductions for them, and pose several open problems.

1 Introduction

The celebrated notions of semantic security and indistinguishability of encryption schemes, first postulated by Goldwasser and Micali [33], assume that the message to be encrypted cannot depend on the private decryption key. Indeed, the dangers of encrypting messages that the adversary cannot herself come up with was already pointed out in their work [33, Section 5.1]. Nearly two decades later, Black, Rogaway and Shrimpton [8] initiated the formal study of security of encryption schemes with key-dependent messages, or KDM security, which requires that encryption schemes remain semantically secure—equivalently, IND-CPA secure—in the presence of ciphertexts that encrypt functions of the private decryption key. It is not hard to construct encryption schemes which are secure in the standard sense of indistinguishability, but completely insecure in the presence of encryptions of key-dependent messages.[1] So, KDM security is certainly a theoretically non-trivial notion. Moreover, while KDM security may seem at first an esoteric concern, it arises both naturally—in the context of full disk encryption where the private keys on disk may inadvertently get encrypted under themselves, and in the symbolic analysis of protocols [1,8,47]—and by design—in the context of certain anonymous credential systems [18].

[1] Indeed, consider a (private-key) encryption scheme where the encryption algorithm works as normal, except it checks if its input message is the private key, and if so, acts as the identity function outputting the private key. In the presence of the encryption of the private key, this scheme is clearly insecure. However, security is maintained in the absence of any such circular encryption.

Q. Tang and V. Teague (Eds.): PKC 2024, LNCS 14604, pp. 291–321, 2024.
https://doi.org/10.1007/978-3-031-57728-4_10

In 2009, circular security[2] found a new, prominent application: the construction of Fully Homomorphic Encryption (FHE) schemes, namely, encryption schemes that allow one to perform arbitrary computations on encrypted data. It is this latter application, namely circular security in the context of fully homomorphic encryption, that is the focus of this paper. While the functional and security requirements of FHE do not explicitly require circular security, Gentry's bootstrapping procedure (underlying his first candidate FHE proposal [29] and a long sequence of follow up works, e.g., see [3, 10, 12, 16, 17, 20, 23, 25, 31, 36]) makes essential use of circular security. More specifically, an encryption system that can support computation of arbitrary polynomial-size circuits, for a fixed set of encryption parameters, is called a *fully homomorphic* encryption (FHE) scheme. In contrast, a weaker type of homomorphic encryption is called *leveled* homomorphic if for every depth parameter d (which is polynomial in a security parameter), there is a set of encryption parameters that support computation of depth-$\leq d$ circuits. The point is, in leveled homomorphic encryption schemes, the size of the encryption parameters grow with d, and can only support homomorphic evaluation of circuits of depth at most d.

The first candidate construction of an FHE scheme was proposed by Gentry [29]. Starting from the work of Brakerski and Vaikuntanathan [16], we have several *leveled HE* schemes [3, 10, 12, 17, 20, 31, 36] whose security is based on the hardness of the learning with errors (LWE) problem, even with a polynomial modulus [17]. However, to this date, rather frustratingly, the only way we know to make them fully homomorphic goes via Gentry's bootstrapping procedure which requires making public a circular encryption of the private key. Even the plain semantic security of one of these encryption schemes seems to require circular-type assumptions [36].

Embarrassingly, more than a decade later, we still do not know how to prove the circular security of any of these leveled HE schemes short of simply assuming it. Indeed, the only constructions of (pure, or non-leveled) FHE schemes we know, with the exception of a construction based on indistinguishability obfuscation (IO) (namely, [19], instantiated with the IO candidates of [39, 40]), require assuming circular security. The situation has gotten steadily worse: while circular security assumptions for all the FHE schemes listed above have a similar flavor, the technical details are often different due to the different encryption schemes and/or the different encoding of the private key that each variant of each scheme demands. Even formulating the exact circular security assumption often requires first defining the homomorphic encryption scheme, and then expressing the assumption *in terms of it.* This makes the assumptions hard to understand and study, and has had downstream consequences. First, the standard that one expects with new hardness assumptions in cryptography is that they are followed with adequate cryptanalysis, including the description of challenge

[2] In this work, we will use the terms KDM security and circular security interchangeably, although the latter has been used in the literature to refer to encrypting some representation of the private key itself, whereas the former refers to more complex functions of the private key.

instances much like the RSA challenge [41] or the Darmstadt Lattice Crypto challenge [22]. Unfortunately, such "due diligence" has not been followed for the various circular security assumptions and indeed, a major bottleneck in doing so is the lack of even a systematic understanding of *what* these assumptions are. Secondly, versions of circular secure LWE were formulated in the context of building indistinguishability obfuscation [26,58], and claimed to be similar to FHE assumptions, but then broken shortly after [38]. This again is arguably due to a lack of systematic understanding of circular security assumptions.

In this paper, we take a *first step* to remedy this situation. The primary goal of this paper is to formulate (one or more) LWE circular security assumptions, just at the level of the LWE problem, and show that known FHE schemes can be proved secure based on such an assumption. This has the following advantages:

1. It provides a simple, concrete assumption (similar to LWE) that can be understood and investigated without having to fully describe an FHE scheme.
2. Such an effort potentially allows us to reduce the security of multiple FHE constructions to a single assumption (or a small set of assumptions), possibly in an efficient manner, relating the concrete security of several FHE schemes to the concrete security of the assumption.
3. If different assumptions are needed by different schemes, a systematic study lets us investigate possible reductions between assumptions, allowing to compare the strength of the assumption underlying different encryption schemes.
4. It offer a basis to generate concrete challenges, similar to Darmstadt lattice challenges (see `latticechallenge.org`).
5. It allows us to consider simpler, possibly weaker circular security assumptions, not necessarily enough to build FHE, but perhaps allowing a reduction to standard LWE or worst-case lattice problems.

Our concrete contributions are as follows.

1. We put forth a circular security conjecture called quadratic circular LWE or, succinctly, circLWE.
2. We show several properties of circLWE including: the proof of a weaker version, namely linear circular LWE, under the standard LWE assumption; a search to decision reduction; and a proof of security of a stronger variant that we call clique-circLWE where there are k keys each of which is encrypted with all other keys, under our basic circLWE assumption.
3. We prove the security of several representative FHE schemes [3,10,25,31,36] under circLWE.
4. We observe that the LWE circular security assumptions underlying the encryption schemes of [10,31] are essentially the same, namely circLWE (see Sect. 3 for a precise definition). This is a testament to the robust applicability of the assumption, and is enabled by an elegant perspective on GSW ciphertexts (originally developed in a sequence of talks by the first author as well as in [51]).
5. Even within a single encryption scheme (such as [10]), slightly different ways of encoding and encrypting the secret key seem to require different assump-

tions. Nevertheless, we show that circLWE implies the circular security of both variants, a further testament to the robustness of circLWE.
6. As an interesting direction for future research, we pose the question of whether one can show a worst-case to average-case reduction for circLWE, possibly under non-standard worst-case lattice assumptions.

The long-term challenge of this line of research is to prove circLWE from the standard LWE assumption or even the worst-case hardness of lattice problems. However, if this problem turns out to be intractable, we advocate making progress towards it by, e.g. showing a worst-case to average-case reduction starting from potentially new worst-case lattice assumptions.

To conclude, we clarify the *non-goals* of this paper. The quest to systematize the study of circular security of FHE schemes, as initiated in this paper, is a fundamental theoretical quest, one that will shed light on the security of essentially all the FHE constructions. Keeping this in mind, we study a subset of the FHE schemes, the foundational ones, focusing on LWE-based constructions, and, occasionally, making small changes to the schemes as required by our proofs.[3] We note that our results are not *directly* applicable to Ring-LWE and other variants of practical interest. Indeed, extending our results to a wider class of FHE schemes requires additional research. In particular, it requires not only adapting the results and proofs presented in this paper to the more challenging ring setting, but also investigate types of circular security information (e.g., automorphisms keys) that are specific to Ring-LWE. Still, these are extensions that can hopefully be informed by the techniques in our paper, and we leave them as an open problem.

Related Work: Circular-Secure Encryption Schemes. Constructing a circular secure encryption scheme was open until the work of Boneh, Halevi, Hamburg and Ostrovsky [9]. Several constructions have appeared since then under essentially all standard cryptographic assumptions [4,6,13,14]. None of these results, however, seem to imply the sort of circular security needed for FHE schemes.

Related Work: Counterexamples to Circular Security. A separate line of research has tried to extend the trivial counterexample from the first paragraph of the introduction to more demanding settings. For example, is there a *bit-wise* encryption scheme that is semantically secure yet circular *insecure*? Is there an encryption scheme that is insecure in the presence of key cycles of length ≥ 2? Neither question seems to have an obvious answer, yet we know sophisticated constructions that demonstrate that the answer to both is "yes" [7,34,35,42,43].

Organization of the Paper. The rest of the paper is organized as follows. In Sect. 2, we provide basic definitions and notation. Next, in Sect. 3, we formulate a number of conjectures that capture a circular secure variant of the LWE

[3] For example, we may use discrete Gaussian encryption noise with larger parameters than the original papers, or slightly different error distributions. These should be interpreted as artifacts of our proof techniques.

problem, and provide reductions between them. Finally, in Sect. 4, we analyze a representative set of FHE schemes.

2 Preliminaries

We write $\mathbb{Z}$ and $\mathbb{R}$ for the sets of integers and real numbers, respectively, and $\mathbb{Z}_p, \mathbb{R}_p$ for the integer and real numbers modulo $p \in \mathbb{Z}$, typically represented as values in the interval $[0, p)$ or $[-p/2, p/2)$. We write $\lfloor x \rfloor$, $\lceil x \rceil$ or $\lfloor x \rceil$ for the result of rounding $x \in \mathbb{R}$ down, up or to the closest integer, rounding up in case of a tie. We also define the *modulus switching* operation

$$\lfloor x \rceil_q = \left\lfloor \frac{q}{p} \cdot x \right\rceil$$

which maps any $\mathbf{x} \in \mathbb{Z}_p$ (or, more generally $\mathbf{x} \in \mathbb{R}_p$) to an element of $\mathbb{Z}_q$ (resp. $\mathbb{R}_q$). The input modulus p is implicitly defined by the domain of $x \in \mathbb{R}_p$, and we write $\lfloor x \pmod{p} \rceil_q$ when p is not clear from the context. We let $\mathbb{R}^+$, resp. $\mathbb{Z}^+$, denote the set of all non-negative reals, resp. integers.

We use bold lowercase letters $\mathbf{x}, \mathbf{y}$ for (column) vectors, and bold uppercase $\mathbf{X}, \mathbf{Y}$ for matrices. The transpose of a matrix $\mathbf{X}$ is denoted by $\mathbf{X}^t$. Row vectors are written using matrix transpose notation $\mathbf{x}^t$. We write $[\mathbf{X}_1, \ldots, \mathbf{X}_n]$ for (horizontal) concatenation of matrices with the same number of rows, and $(\mathbf{X}_1, \ldots, \mathbf{X}_n) = [\mathbf{X}_1^t, \ldots, \mathbf{X}_n^t]^t$ for (vertical) stacking of matrices. Unless stated otherwise, the coordinates of a vector are denoted by $\mathbf{x} = (x_1, \ldots, x_n)$. Similarly, $\mathbf{X} = [\mathbf{x}_1, \ldots, \mathbf{x}_n]$ for the columns of a matrix.

The inner product of two vectors is written either as $\langle \mathbf{x}, \mathbf{y} \rangle = \sum_i x_i y_i$, or using matrix transpose notation $\mathbf{x}^t \cdot \mathbf{y}$. The tensor product between two matrices $\mathbf{X} \in \mathbb{Z}^{n_0 \times k_0}$ and $\mathbf{Y} \in \mathbb{Z}^{n_1 \times k_1}$ is the matrix $\mathbf{X} \otimes \mathbf{Y} \in \mathbb{Z}^{n_0 n_1 \times k_0 k_1}$ obtained by replacing each entry $x_{i,j}$ with a scaled copy $x_{i,j} \cdot \mathbf{Y}$ of $\mathbf{Y}$.

We say that $\mathbf{x}$ is a short vector in $\mathbb{Z}^n$ or $\mathbb{R}^n$ if $\|\mathbf{x}\|$ is small, with respect to some norm, e.g., $\|\mathbf{x}\|_2 = \sqrt{\sum_i x_i^2}$, or $\|\mathbf{x}\|_\infty = \max_i |x_i|$. All the statements in this paper can be analyzed using any choice of norm, producing essentially the same results, with a small difference in the concrete norm bound. By default, when we use the expression $\|\mathbf{x}\|$ without further qualifiers, we will mean the Euclidean norm of $\mathbf{x}$.

The Gaussian Distribution. The Gaussian, or the normal, distribution over $\mathbb{R}^n$, centered at $\mathbf{c} \in \mathbb{R}^n$ and parameterized by a standard deviation $\sigma \in \mathbb{R}^+$, is defined by the following probability density function:

$$\forall \mathbf{x} \in \mathbb{R}^n : \quad \mathcal{N}_\sigma(\mathbf{x}) = \frac{1}{\sigma} \cdot e^{-\pi \|\mathbf{x} - \mathbf{c}\|^2 / \sigma^2}$$

Similarly, the discrete Gaussian distribution χ_σ is defined as the restriction of $\mathcal{N}_\sigma$ to $\mathbb{Z}^n$, i.e., the discrete random variable over $\mathbb{Z}^n$ that outputs $\mathbf{x} \in \mathbb{Z}^n$ with probability $\mathcal{N}_\sigma(\mathbf{x}) / \sum_{\mathbf{y} \in \mathbb{Z}^n} \mathcal{N}_\sigma(\mathbf{y})$.

Cryptographic Primitives. All asymptotic statements are with respect to a security parameter λ, which is implicitly given as input to all algorithms and associated sets. So, for example, a key generation algorithm Gen is simply defined as an efficiently samplable distribution over a set of keys $\mathcal{K}$. By this we mean that $\mathsf{Gen}(\lambda)$ is a probabilistic algorithm that, on input λ, runs in time polynomial in λ, and outputs a key from a set of bit-strings $\mathcal{K}(\lambda)$ which may also depend on λ. Events (e.g., describing security or correctness properties) are similarly parametrized by λ, and the probability of an event defines a function $f(\lambda) \in [0,1]$. A probability (function) $f(\lambda)$ is *negligible* if $f(\lambda) < 1/\lambda^c$ for every constant c and all large enough values of λ. A probability $f(\lambda)$ is *overwhelming* if $1 - f(\lambda)$ is negligible.

Definition 1. *A private key encryption scheme* $\mathsf{SKE} = (\mathsf{Gen}, \mathsf{Enc}, \mathsf{Dec})$ *with message space* $\mathcal{M}$*, key space* $\mathcal{K}$ *and ciphertext space* $\mathcal{C}$*, is a triple of (probabilistic polynomial time) algorithms* $\mathsf{Gen}\colon \mathcal{K}$ *(key generation),* $\mathsf{Enc}\colon \mathcal{K} \times \mathcal{M} \to \mathcal{C}$ *(encryption) and* $\mathsf{Dec}\colon \mathcal{K} \times \mathcal{C} \to \mathcal{M}$ *(decryption), such that* $\mathsf{Dec}_k(\mathsf{Enc}_k(m)) = m$ *for all messages* $m \in \mathcal{M}$ *and keys* $k \in \mathcal{K}$*. The correctness condition* $\mathsf{Dec}_k(\mathsf{Enc}_k(m)) = m$ *can be relaxed to hold only with overwhelming probability, over the choice of the key* k *and the encryption randomness.*

Homomorphic public-key encryption schemes can be constructed generically from any homomorphic private-key encryption scheme [57]. So, for simplicity, *we focus on the case of secret-key encryption.* All definitions and constructions are easily extended to the public-key setting. Still, we define security of private-key encryption in the presence of some public information $\mathsf{Pub}(k)$ about the secret key. This is useful to model the evaluation key used by some homomorphic operations, as well as bootstrapping. It can also be used to model certain forms of leakage resilience, like circular security. The standard notion of security for private-key encryption is obtained by letting Pub output nothing.

Definition 2. *Let* $\mathsf{SKE} = (\mathsf{Gen}, \mathsf{Enc}, \mathsf{Dec})$ *be a private-key encryption scheme, and* $\mathsf{Pub}\colon \mathcal{K} \to \mathcal{P}$ *a (possibly randomized, efficiently computable) function from the set of keys* $\mathcal{K}$ *to some set* $\mathcal{P}$*. The scheme* SKE *satisfies* indistinguishability under chosen plaintext attack *(IND-CPA security for short) in the presence of public information* Pub *if any efficient (probabilistic polynomial time) adversary* $\mathcal{A}$ *can only achieve a negligible advantage in the following game, parametrized by a bit* $b \in \{0,1\}$*: after generating parameters* $k \leftarrow \mathsf{Gen}$*,* $p \leftarrow \mathsf{Pub}(k)$*, the adversary* $b' \leftarrow \mathcal{A}^{O_b(\cdot,\cdot)}(p)$ *is run on input* p *and with access to a (probabilistic) oracle* $O_b(m_0, m_1) = \mathsf{Enc}_k(m_b)$ *that on input a pair of messages* $m_0, m_1 \in \mathcal{M}$*, computes the encryption of the message selected by the bit* b*. Upon termination, the adversary outputs a bit* b'*, with the goal of correctly guessing the value of* b*. The adversary's advantage*[4] *is defined as* $\mathsf{Adv}(\mathcal{A}) = |\Pr\{b' = 1 \mid b = 0\} - \Pr\{b' = 1 \mid b = 1\}|$.

[4] More refined notions of advantage that better capture the quantitative notion of "bit-security" are proposed in [53]. Here we use the traditional definition of advantage, which is simpler, and still adequate for our purposes.

As an important special case, we consider *circular-secure* (private-key) encryption schemes, i.e., schemes satisfying security with respect to adversaries that are given, as auxiliary information, an encryption of the secret key k under itself. Notice that in order to encrypt a key k, one must first encode k as a sequence $\psi(k) \in \mathcal{M}^w$ of elements from the message space. The encryption function is extended to $\mathcal{M}^w$ componentwise, setting $\mathsf{Enc}_k(m_1, \ldots, m_w) = (\mathsf{Enc}_k(m_1), \ldots, \mathsf{Enc}_k(m_w))$.

Definition 3. *Let* $(\mathsf{Gen}, \mathsf{Enc}, \mathsf{Dec}, \mathsf{Pub})$ *be an encryption scheme with message space* $\mathcal{M}$*, key space* $\mathcal{K}$ *and public information* Pub*, and let* $\psi\colon \mathcal{K} \to \mathcal{M}^w$ *be an (efficiently computable) encoding function. The encryption scheme is* ψ*-circular IND-CPA secure in the presence of* Pub *if it is IND-CPA secure with respect to the extended public information*[5] $\widehat{\mathsf{Pub}}(k) = (\mathsf{Pub}(k), \mathsf{Enc}_k(\psi(k)))$.

2.1 The Learning with Errors Problem (with Side Information)

The Learning With Errors (LWE) problem is an injective version of the Short Integer Solution (SIS) problem [2,52]. Its (average-case) computational hardness was proved by Regev in [56] based on the conjectured hardness of solving several standard lattice problems in the worst case, with further improvements in [15,54].

In this paper, we use the following matrix version [30,55] of LWE. The definition is parametrized by a secret distribution $\mathcal{S}$, which is typically set to either the uniform distribution over $\mathcal{S} = \mathbb{Z}_q^n$, or the same as the error distribution $\mathcal{S} = \chi^n$, which is equivalent to uniform secrets by the results of [4,46], or to uniformly random binary vectors $\mathcal{S} = \{0,1\}^n$. The latter choice is often made for efficiency reasons, and is theoretically justified by the results of [11,15,32,48].

Definition 4 (Learning With Errors (LWE) Distribution). *The LWE distribution with parameters* n, k, w, q*, a secret distribution* $\mathcal{S}$ *over* $\mathbb{Z}$ *and an error distribution* χ *over* $\mathbb{Z}^w$*, is given by* $[\mathbf{A}, \mathbf{AS} + \mathbf{E}]$ *where* $\mathbf{A} \leftarrow \mathbb{Z}_q^{w\times n}$, $\mathbf{S} \leftarrow \mathcal{S}^{n\times k}$ *and* $\mathbf{E} \leftarrow \chi^{w\times k}$.

In order to study the security of homomorphic encryption schemes, we parameterize the LWE hardness assumption by a public information function Pub, similarly to Definition 2. The standard LWE assumption is given by setting $\mathsf{Pub}(\mathbf{S}) = \perp$.

Definition 5 *Let* $\mathsf{Pub}(\mathbf{S})$ *be any efficiently computable, possibly randomized function of the LWE secret* $\mathbf{S}$*. The* Decisional LWE problem *with public information* Pub *is the computational problem of distinguishing between the following two distributions:*

[5] Here we are starting from an encryption scheme that already includes a Pub function (e.g., to provide a public key or other side information), and extend it to include an encryption cycle. When starting from a simple private-key encryption scheme, $\mathsf{Pub}(k)$ outputs nothing, and $\widehat{\mathsf{Pub}}(k) = \mathsf{Enc}_k(\psi(k))$ is just a circular encryption of the key.

- $(\mathsf{Pub}(\mathbf{S}), [\mathbf{A}, \mathbf{AS} + \mathbf{E}])$ *where* $\mathbf{A} \leftarrow \mathbb{Z}_q^{w \times n}$, $\mathbf{S} \leftarrow \mathcal{S}^{n \times k}$ *and* $\mathbf{E} \leftarrow \chi^{w \times k}$.
- $(\mathsf{Pub}(\mathbf{S}), [\mathbf{A}, \mathbf{B}])$ *where* $\mathbf{A} \leftarrow \mathbb{Z}_q^{w \times n}$, $\mathbf{S} \leftarrow \mathcal{S}^{n \times k}$ *and* $\mathbf{B} \leftarrow \mathbb{Z}_q^{w \times k}$.

The decisional LWE assumption postulates that the decisional LWE problem is hard to solve with non-negligible advantage for any probabilistic polynomial-time distinguisher.

One may also give a slightly stronger definition which requires the distribution $(\mathsf{Pub}(\mathbf{S}), [\mathbf{A}, \mathbf{AS} + \mathbf{E}])$ to be indistinguishable from $(\mathbf{P}, [\mathbf{A}, \mathbf{B}])$, where $\mathbf{P}, \mathbf{A}, \mathbf{B}$ are all chosen uniformly at random. Most of the results in this paper hold also for this stronger definition, but this is not needed for the application to circular security and fully homomorphic encryption.

Note that when $\mathsf{Pub}(\mathbf{S}) = \perp$ (or, more generally, when Pub provides independent public information $[\mathsf{Pub}(\mathbf{s}_1), \ldots, \mathsf{Pub}(\mathbf{s}_k)]$ about each column of $\mathbf{S}$), one may assume $k = 1$, and prove the hardness for any k by a standard hybrid argument [55]. However, the same does not generally hold true in the presence of global information $\mathsf{Pub}(\mathbf{S})$ about the whole secret matrix $\mathbf{S}$.

On the LWE Secret and Noise Distributions. Since LWE is an average-case problem, its computational hardness depends on the specific distributions $\mathcal{S}$ and χ used in the definition. Still, the hardness of LWE is fairly robust both with respect to the secret key distribution $\mathcal{S}$ (via *leakage resilience* results [11, 15,32,48]) and the error distribution χ. The main requirement on the noise distribution χ is that it should output small numbers, and the strength of the hardness assumption is often quantified by the ratio $q/|\chi|$ between the errors and the ciphertext modulus.

We state below a useful theorem on LWE with binary secrets [48].

Lemma 1 (Hardness of Binary-Secret LWE, adapted from *[48]***).** *Assume the hardness of the decisional LWE problem with modulus*[6] q*, uniform secrets* $\mathbf{s} \in \mathbb{Z}_q^{n'}$*,* $n+1$ *samples, and discrete Gaussian noise* χ_σ *is hard, for some* $q \leq 2^{n^{O(1)}}$*,* $\sigma \geq \omega(\sqrt{\log n})$*, and* $n \geq 2n' \log_2 q$*. Then, the Decisional LWE problem with binary secrets* $\mathbf{s} \in \{0,1\}^n$*, polynomially many samples, and discrete Gaussian noise* $\chi_{\sigma \cdot \sqrt{n'}}$ *is also hard.*

A common technique to "smooth out" differences between error distributions is *noise flooding*, i.e., the addition of random noise r to the LWE matrix $\mathbf{B}$, so that the error becomes $\chi + r$. If r is random and sufficiently larger than χ, then $\chi' = \chi + r$ becomes essentially independent of χ. Clearly, this technique (as well as many other methods to reduce between different versions of LWE) has the side effect of increasing the amount of error. However, one can usually compensate for the larger error χ' by using a correspondingly larger modulus q.

[6] To be precise, [48] proves this result for odd moduli q, and then explains in [48, Footnote 2] how to adapt the result to even moduli using modulo switching. Technically using modulus switching requires a small increase in the LWE modulus q when going from uniform to binary secrets, but, for simplicity, we ignore this technicality.

We state a version of the noise-flooding lemma below, adapted from [5] (where it is stated with respect to the uniform, rather than the Gaussian, distribution).

Lemma 2 (Noise-flooding Lemma, adapted from *[5, Lemma 1]***).** *Let $n \in \mathbb{Z}$ and let $\mathcal{E}$ be a set of vectors $\mathbb{R}^n$. Let $\mathbf{e} \in \mathcal{E}$. Then, the statistical distance between the distributions $\mathcal{N}_\sigma$ and $\mathbf{e}+\mathcal{N}_\sigma$ is $O(||\mathbf{e}||/\sigma)$. Similarly for the discrete Gaussian distribution χ_σ, as long as $\sigma = \omega(\sqrt{\log n})$.*

2.2 LWE Encryption

The LWE problem can be used to define a family of randomized functions, parametrized by n, k, w, q and indexed by the keys $\mathbf{S} \leftarrow \mathcal{S}^{n\times k}$, which, on input a matrix $\mathbf{X} \in \mathbb{Z}_q^{w\times k}$, chooses $\mathbf{A} \leftarrow \mathbb{Z}_q^{w\times n}$ and $\mathbf{E} \leftarrow \chi^{w\times k}$ at random, and outputs

$$\mathsf{LWE}_{\mathbf{S}}(\mathbf{X};\mathbf{A},\mathbf{E}) \stackrel{\text{def}}{=} [\mathbf{A}, \mathbf{X}+\mathbf{E}-\mathbf{AS}] \in \mathbb{Z}_q^{w\times(n+k)}. \tag{1}$$

We write $\mathsf{LWE}_{\mathbf{S}}(\mathbf{X})$ for the output distribution obtained by choosing $\mathbf{A}$ and $\mathbf{E}$ at random, and computing $\mathsf{LWE}_{\mathbf{S}}(\mathbf{X};\mathbf{A},\mathbf{E})$. Similarly, one can define an (approximate) inversion algorithm that, given a key $\mathbf{S}$ and a ciphertext $[\mathbf{A},\mathbf{B}] \in \mathbb{Z}_q^{w\times(n+k)}$, outputs:

$$\mathsf{LWE}_{\mathbf{S}}^{-1}([\mathbf{A},\mathbf{B}]) \stackrel{\text{def}}{=} [\mathbf{A},\mathbf{B}] \cdot \begin{bmatrix}\mathbf{S}\\ \mathbf{I}\end{bmatrix} = \mathbf{AS}+\mathbf{B} \in \mathbb{Z}_q^{w\times k}. \tag{2}$$

Notice that $(\mathsf{LWE}, \mathsf{LWE}^{-1})$ is not quite an encryption scheme because it only satisfies an approximate version of the correctness condition

$$\mathsf{LWE}_{\mathbf{S}}^{-1}(\mathsf{LWE}_{\mathbf{S}}(\mathbf{X})) = \mathbf{AS}+\mathbf{B} = \mathbf{X}+\mathbf{E} \approx \mathbf{X}$$

up to a small additive error $\mathbf{E}$. In order to get a proper encryption scheme, LWE is combined with an error correcting code, as described next.

For simplicity, we focus on linear codes defined by a single (so-called *gadget*) vector $\mathbf{g} \in \mathbb{Z}_p^w$, where p is a plaintext modulus possibly different from q, as these are the codes most commonly used in lattice-based cryptography. Using $\mathbf{g}$ as a gadget, a message $\mathbf{M} \in \mathbb{Z}_p^{h\times k}$ is encoded componentwise as $\mathbf{M}\otimes\mathbf{g}$, i.e., by replacing each entry $m_{i,j}$ by the vector $m_{i,j}\cdot\mathbf{g}$. Sometimes it is convenient to express the encoding $\mathbf{M}\otimes\mathbf{g}$ as a matrix product, rather than a tensor. This is easily done by letting $\mathbf{G}=\mathbf{I}\otimes\mathbf{g}$, and observing that

$$\mathbf{G}\cdot\mathbf{M} = (\mathbf{I}\otimes\mathbf{g})\cdot(\mathbf{M}\otimes(1)) = (\mathbf{IM})\otimes(\mathbf{g}\cdot(1)) = \mathbf{M}\otimes\mathbf{g}.$$

(Notice that when using matrix product, the message $\mathbf{M}$ is multiplied by $\mathbf{G}$ on the left.)

Gadget vectors $\mathbf{g}$ are required to satisfy the primitivity condition $\gcd(p,\mathbf{g}) = 1$, so that the encoding function is injective, and $m_{i,j}$ can be recovered from $m_{i,j}\cdot\mathbf{g}$. The encoding is rounded to a matrix $\lfloor\mathbf{M}\otimes\mathbf{g}\rceil_q$ in $\mathbb{Z}_q^{hw\times k}$ before applying the LWE function, producing the ciphertext

$$\mathbf{g}\text{-}\mathsf{LWE}_{q,\mathbf{S}}(\mathbf{M};\mathbf{A},\mathbf{E}) \stackrel{\text{def}}{=} \mathsf{LWE}_{\mathbf{S}}\left(\lfloor\mathbf{M}\otimes\mathbf{g}\rceil_q\right) \in \mathbb{Z}_q^{hw\times(n+k)}. \tag{3}$$

For brevity, we omit the ciphertext modulus when $q = p$ and the gadget vector when $\mathbf{g} = (1)$, and simply write $\mathbf{g}\text{-}\mathsf{LWE}_{\mathbf{S}}$ or $\mathsf{LWE}_{q,\mathbf{S}}$, noting that this is consistent with the notation $\mathsf{LWE}_{\mathbf{S}}$ used for the plain (unencoded) LWE function defined in Eq. (1). We also write $\mathbf{g}\text{-}\mathsf{LWE}_{q,\mathbf{S}}(\mathbf{M}; \mathcal{E})$ for the set of $\mathbf{g}$-LWE ciphertexts with error in the set $\mathcal{E}$ (and any matrix $\mathbf{A}$), or an arbitrary element of that set.

We will not be concerned with the decryption algorithm, as it plays no role in the definition of security.[7] For completeness, we only briefly mention that ciphertexts $\mathbf{C} = \mathbf{g}\text{-}\mathsf{LWE}_{\mathbf{S}}(\mathbf{M})$ can be decrypted by computing the matrix $\mathbf{M} \in \mathbb{Z}_p^{h\times k}$ such that the encoding $\mathbf{M} \otimes \mathbf{g}$ is closest to $\mathbf{X} = \frac{p}{q} \cdot \mathsf{LWE}_{\mathbf{S}}^{-1}(\mathbf{C})$.

Besides *encoding*, and *decoding* (as used for encryption and decryption), gadget vectors $\mathbf{g} \in \mathbb{Z}_p^w$ have one more *inversion* algorithm that on input any $x \in \mathbb{Z}_p$ outputs a *short* integer (row) vector $\mathbf{g}^{-t}(x) \in \mathbb{Z}^{1\times w}$ such that $\mathbf{g}^{-t}(x) \cdot \mathbf{g} = x \pmod p$. More generally, for any $\mathbf{M} \in \mathbb{Z}_p^{h\times k}$ and $\mathbf{T} \in \mathbb{Z}_p^{l\times h}$, the encoding and inversion operations satisfy

$$(\mathbf{g}^{-t}(\mathbf{T})) \cdot (\mathbf{M} \otimes \mathbf{g}) = \mathbf{TM} \pmod p$$

where, as usual, $\mathbf{g}^{-t}(\cdot)$ is extended to vectors and matrices componentwise. Sometimes it is convenient to use the output of $\mathbf{g}^{-t}(x)$ in column form, which we write as $\mathbf{g}^{-1}(x)$. More generally, for any matrix $\mathbf{X}$, we have $\mathbf{g}^{-1}(\mathbf{X}) \stackrel{\text{def}}{=} (\mathbf{g}^{-t}(\mathbf{X}^t))^t$. Following [3,51], this function is used to define the following homomorphic operation that plays a fundamental role in our presentation of LWE encryption and FHE.

Definition 6 *For any gadget* $\mathbf{g} \pmod p$, *message* $\mathbf{M} \pmod p$, *ciphertext* $\mathbf{C} \in \mathbf{g}\text{-}\mathsf{LWE}_{q,\mathbf{S}}(\mathbf{M})$ *and matrix* $\mathbf{T} \in \mathbb{Z}_p^{l\times h}$, *define the* gadget product

$$\mathbf{T} \odot \mathbf{C} \stackrel{def}{=} \mathbf{g}^{-t}(\mathbf{T}) \cdot \mathbf{C} \in \mathsf{LWE}_{q,\mathbf{S}}(\mathbf{TM}) \tag{4}$$

where the vector $\mathbf{g}$ *is implicitly specified by the type of ciphertext* $\mathbf{C}$.

This operation multiplies a message $\mathbf{M}$ encrypted under $\mathbf{g}$-LWE by a matrix $\mathbf{T}$, producing as a result an *unencoded* LWE encryption of $\mathbf{TM}$. Products encoded under any (possibly different) gadget $\mathbf{h} \pmod p$ can be computed as

$$\begin{aligned}\mathbf{T} \overset{\mathbf{h}}{\circledcirc} \mathbf{C} \stackrel{\text{def}}{=} (\mathbf{T} \otimes \mathbf{h}) \odot \mathbf{C} &\in \mathsf{LWE}_{q,\mathbf{S}}((\mathbf{T} \otimes \mathbf{h})\mathbf{M}) \\ &= \mathsf{LWE}_{q,\mathbf{S}}(\mathbf{TM} \otimes \mathbf{h}) = \mathbf{h}\text{-}\mathsf{LWE}_{q,\mathbf{S}}(\mathbf{TM}).\end{aligned}$$

As a special case, we write $\mathbf{T} \circledcirc \mathbf{C} \stackrel{\text{def}}{=} \mathbf{T} \overset{\mathbf{g}}{\circledcirc} \mathbf{C}$ for the operation of applying $\mathbf{T}$ to a $\mathbf{g}$-LWE ciphertext without changing the encoding gadget $\mathbf{g}$, and $\mathbf{h} \circ \mathbf{C} \stackrel{\text{def}}{=} \mathbf{I} \overset{\mathbf{h}}{\circledcirc} \mathbf{C}$ for the operation of changing the encoding gadget from $\mathbf{g}$ to $\mathbf{h}$ without modifying the message.

[7] This is for valid encryption schemes, satisfying the standard correctness condition $\mathsf{Dec}_s(\mathsf{Enc}_s(m)) = m$. For "approximate" encryption schemes where $\mathsf{Dec}_s(\mathsf{Enc}_s(m)) \approx m$, see [44,45]. We only consider valid encryption schemes in this paper.

2.3 Key Switching

As we show in this section, the gadget product operation $\odot$ can be used to define a "functional" key switching procedure that changes the key under which a ciphertext is encrypted, while at the same time multiplying the message by a given integer matrix $\mathbf{T}$ on the *right*. (Notice that this is different from the gadget product $\mathbf{T}\odot$, which multiplies the message by $\mathbf{T}$ on the *left*.) Plain key switching is a special case where $\mathbf{T} = \mathbf{I}$ is the identity function.

Definition 7. *For any two keys* $\mathbf{S} \in \mathbb{Z}^{n\times k}$ *and* $\tilde{\mathbf{S}} \in \mathbb{Z}^{\tilde{n}\times\tilde{k}}$, *gadget* $\mathbf{g} \in \mathbb{Z}_q^w$, *and matrix* $\mathbf{T} \in \mathbb{Z}^{\tilde{k}\times k}$ *with (small) integer entries, define the* switching key *generation algorithm*

$$\mathbf{g}\text{-LWE}_{\tilde{\mathbf{S}}\to\mathbf{S}}(\mathbf{T};\mathbf{A},\mathbf{E}) \stackrel{def}{=} \mathbf{g}\text{-LWE}_{\mathbf{S}}\left(\begin{bmatrix}\tilde{\mathbf{S}}\\ \mathbf{I}\end{bmatrix}\mathbf{T};\mathbf{A},\mathbf{E}\right), \tag{5}$$

and similarly for $\mathbf{g}\text{-LWE}_{\tilde{\mathbf{S}}\to\mathbf{S}}(\mathbf{T})$, *etc.*

We refer to ciphertexts of the form $\mathbf{g}\text{-LWE}_{\tilde{\mathbf{S}}\to\mathbf{S}}(\mathbf{T})$ as *switching keys*, as they can be used to map encryptions of $\mathbf{M}$ under $\tilde{\mathbf{S}}$ to encryptions of $\mathbf{MT}$ under $\mathbf{S}$ as shown in the next theorem. Indeed, they correspond exactly to switching keys in [10,12,16].

Theorem 1. *For any keys* $\mathbf{S} \in \mathbb{Z}_{n\times k}$, $\tilde{\mathbf{S}} \in \mathbb{Z}_{\tilde{n}\times\tilde{k}}$, *gadget* $\mathbf{g} \in \mathbb{Z}_q^w$, *matrix* $\mathbf{T} \in \mathbb{Z}^{\tilde{k}\times k}$ *with (small) integer entries, switching key*

$$\mathbf{W} \in \mathbf{g}\text{-LWE}_{\tilde{\mathbf{S}}\to\mathbf{S}}(\mathbf{T};\mathcal{F}),$$

possibly different plaintext modulus p, *gadget* $\mathbf{h} \in \mathbb{Z}_p^{\tilde{w}}$, *message* $\mathbf{M} \in \mathbb{Z}_p^{\tilde{h}\times k}$, *and ciphertext* $\mathbf{C} \in \mathbf{h}\text{-LWE}_{q,\tilde{\mathbf{S}}}(\mathbf{M};\mathcal{E})$ *we have*

$$\mathbf{C}\odot\mathbf{W} \in \mathbf{h}\text{-LWE}_{q,\mathbf{S}}(\mathbf{MT};\mathcal{E}'),$$

where $\mathcal{E}' = \mathcal{E}\cdot\mathbf{T} + \mathbf{g}^{-t}(\mathbf{C})\,\mathcal{F}$.

Proof. This follows by a simple calculation:

$$\begin{aligned}
\mathbf{C}\odot\mathbf{W} &= \mathbf{C}\odot\mathbf{g}\text{-LWE}_{\mathbf{S}}\left(\begin{bmatrix}\tilde{\mathbf{S}}\\ \mathbf{I}\end{bmatrix}\mathbf{T};\mathcal{F}\right)\\
&= \mathsf{LWE}_{q,\mathbf{S}}\left(\mathbf{C}\begin{bmatrix}\tilde{\mathbf{S}}\\ \mathbf{I}\end{bmatrix}\mathbf{T};\mathbf{g}^{-t}(\mathbf{C})\cdot\mathcal{F}\right)\\
&= \mathsf{LWE}_{q,\mathbf{S}}((\tfrac{q}{p}\mathbf{M}\otimes\mathbf{h}+\mathcal{E})\mathbf{T};\mathbf{g}^{-t}(\mathbf{C})\cdot\mathcal{F})\\
&= \mathsf{LWE}_{q,\mathbf{S}}(\tfrac{q}{p}(\mathbf{MT})\otimes\mathbf{h};\mathcal{E}\cdot\mathbf{T}+\mathbf{g}^{-t}(\mathbf{C})\cdot\mathcal{F})\\
&= \mathbf{h}\text{-LWE}_{q,\mathbf{S}}(\mathbf{MT};\mathcal{E}')
\end{aligned}$$

where $\mathcal{E}' = \mathcal{E}\cdot\mathbf{T} + \mathbf{g}^{-t}(\mathbf{C})\cdot\mathcal{F}$ is small because $\mathcal{E}$, $\mathbf{T}$, $\mathbf{g}^{-t}(\mathbf{C})$ and $\mathcal{F}$ are all small.

Using the fact that switching keys are just regular g-LWE ciphertexts (of carefully crafted, key-dependent messages), it is easy to see that switching keys can be combined both by pointwise addition and function composition:

$$\text{g-LWE}_{\mathbf{S}\to\mathbf{S}'}(\mathbf{T}_0) + \text{g-LWE}_{\mathbf{S}\to\mathbf{S}'}(\mathbf{T}_1) = \text{g-LWE}_{\mathbf{S}\to\mathbf{S}'}(\mathbf{T}_0 + \mathbf{T}_1)$$
$$\text{g-LWE}_{\mathbf{S}'\to\mathbf{S}''}(\mathbf{T}_0) \circledcirc \text{g-LWE}_{\mathbf{S}\to\mathbf{S}'}(\mathbf{T}_1) = \text{g-LWE}_{\mathbf{S}\to\mathbf{S}''}(\mathbf{T}_0 \cdot \mathbf{T}_1)$$

This turns out to be a *very interesting* insight: GSW ciphertexts [31] *are* switching keys where the transformation $\mathbf{T} = m\mathbf{I}$ is a scalar matrix representing the message m, and the observation above shows how to do additive and multiplicative homomorphisms on GSW ciphertexts. For more details, we refer the reader to Sect. 4.2.

2.4 Gadgets

We conclude this section with a brief discussion of the gadget vectors most commonly used in lattice cryptography. We will be primarily concerned with the "power base" gadget

$$\mathbf{pow}(b) \stackrel{\text{def}}{=} (1, b, b^2, \ldots, b^{w-1}) \in \mathbb{Z}_p^w$$

for $p = b^w$, possibly equal to the ciphertext modulus q. In fact, both for simplicity and historical reasons, most theoretical papers use the "power-of-two" gadget $\mathbf{pow}(2)$, i.e., the special case where $b = 2$. Efficient (bounded distance) decoding algorithms (used for decryption) are given in [50] (for $p = b^w$) and [27] (for arbitrary p). More relevant for this work is the gadget inversion algorithm $\mathbf{pow}(b)^{-t}(x)$ which outputs the (signed) base b representation of x. Randomized (subgaussian) inversion algorithms, with somewhat better average error growth, are given in [3,28].

The power gadget $\mathbf{pow}(b)$ is most commonly used with a plaintext modulus $p = q$ equal to the LWE ciphertext modulus. Another important special case is when $b = p$, and $\mathbf{g} = (1) \in \mathbb{Z}_p^1$ is the trivial vector. This is typically used with a fixed plaintext modulus p much smaller than the ciphertext modulus q. (E.g., $p = 2$ to encrypt single bits $m \in \{0, 1\}$.) The decoding algorithm for this gadget is just a simple rounding operation to the closest integer modulo p. Inversion is just as simple: $\mathbf{g}^{-t}(x) = x \bmod p$ outputs the signed integer representative of x in $[-p/2, \ldots, p/2)$, or a centered binary random variable taking as possible value the representative(s) of $x \pmod p$ in $(-p, \ldots, p)$.

Several other gadgets are often used in practice, to provide better efficiency, parallelism, or useful tradeoffs between ciphertext size and error growth. These include power gadgets $\mathbf{pow}(b)$ with a large base $b \approx \sqrt{p}$ or $b \approx p^{1/3}$ (so that $\mathbf{g}$ has only two or three coordinates), and the Residue Number System (RNS) gadget, which uses a highly composite $p = \prod_i p_i$ and represents integers $x \in \mathbb{Z}_p$ as $(x \bmod p_1, \ldots, x \bmod p_k)$ using the Chinese Reminder Theorem. These are also most commonly used with $p = q$.

3 Circular LWE Conjectures

We describe the *quadratic circular LWE* assumption, called $\mathsf{circLWE}$, using notation from Sect. 2. Let $\mathbf{g}$ be any gadget in dimension w and define the quadratic function

$$\psi_{\mathbf{g}}(\mathbf{s}) = \mathbf{g}^{-1}(\mathbf{s}, 1) \otimes \mathbf{g}^{-1}(\mathbf{s}, 1) \in \mathbb{Z}_q^{((n+1)w)^2}$$

The vector $\mathbf{g}$ is usually the power-of-two gadget $\mathbf{pow}(2)$ and $w = \lceil \log_2 q \rceil$ We omit the subscript and simply write $\psi(\mathbf{s})$ instead of $\psi_{\mathbf{g}}(\mathbf{s})$ when $\mathbf{g}$ is clear from the context, or unimportant.

The $\mathbf{g}$-$\mathsf{circLWE}$ assumption says that the decisional LWE problem with public information $\mathsf{Pub}(\mathbf{s}) = \mathbf{g}\text{-}\mathsf{LWE}_{\mathbf{s}}(\psi_{\mathbf{g}}(\mathbf{s}))$ (see Definition 5) is computationally hard. More specifically, parametrizing the definition by the LWE noise distributions used to compute $\mathsf{Pub}(\mathbf{s})$ and the LWE samples, $\mathbf{g}$-$\mathsf{circLWE}[\xi, \Xi]$ says that no probabilistic polynomial-time distinguisher $\mathcal{D}$ can distinguish between the following two distributions with non-negligible advantage, for any $\ell = \mathsf{poly}(n)$:

- $(\mathbf{g}\text{-}\mathsf{LWE}_{\mathbf{s}}(\psi(\mathbf{s}); \Xi), \mathbf{g}\text{-}\mathsf{LWE}_{\mathbf{s}}(\mathbf{0}^{\ell}; \xi))$ where $\mathbf{s} \leftarrow \mathbb{Z}_q^n$.
- $(\mathbf{g}\text{-}\mathsf{LWE}_{\mathbf{s}}(\psi(\mathbf{s}); \Xi), \mathbf{U})$ where $\mathbf{s} \leftarrow \mathbb{Z}_q^n$ and $\mathbf{U} \leftarrow \mathbb{Z}_q^{\ell w \times (n+1)}$.

We omit ξ and Ξ when they are both equal to the standard LWE error[8] (discrete Gaussian) distribution $\chi_{\sqrt{n}}$. Naturally, $\mathbf{g}$-$\mathsf{circLWE}$ reduces to $\mathbf{g}$-$\mathsf{circLWE}[\chi_\sigma, \chi_{\sigma'}]$ for larger $\sigma > \sqrt{n}$ simply by adding more Gaussian noise to both $\mathsf{Pub}(\mathbf{s})$ and the LWE samples.

As above, we will refer to the $\mathbf{g}$-$\mathsf{circLWE}$ assumption when $\mathbf{g} = \mathbf{pow}(2)$ as simply $\mathsf{circLWE}$. Our main conjecture is that the $\mathsf{circLWE}$ assumption is true under the decisional LWE assumption.

Main Conjecture 1 *The* $\mathsf{circLWE}$ *assumption (i.e., Definition 5 with side information* $\mathsf{Pub}(\mathbf{s}) = \mathbf{g}\text{-}\mathsf{LWE}_{\mathbf{s}}(\psi_{\mathbf{g}}(\mathbf{s}))$*) is true assuming that the decisional LWE assumption (i.e., Definition 5 with* $\mathsf{Pub}(\mathbf{s}) = \bot$*) is true.*

3.1 How About *Linear Circular LWE?*

One may wonder about a variant of the above assumption that asks to encrypt only the bits of the secret key. That is, letting

$$\phi(\mathbf{s}) := \phi_{\mathbf{g}}(\mathbf{s}) = \mathbf{g}^{-1}(\mathbf{s}) \in \mathbb{Z}_q^{(n+1)w} ,$$

is it the case that LWE with side information $\mathsf{Pub}(\mathbf{s}) = \mathbf{g}\text{-}\mathsf{LWE}_{\mathbf{s}}(\phi(\mathbf{s}))$ is hard, i.e.,

$$(\mathbf{g}\text{-}\mathsf{LWE}_{\mathbf{s}}(\phi(\mathbf{s})), \mathbf{g}\text{-}\mathsf{LWE}_{\mathbf{s}}(\mathbf{0}^{\ell})) \approx_c (\mathbf{g}\text{-}\mathsf{LWE}_{\mathbf{s}}(\phi(\mathbf{s})), \mathbf{U})?$$

[8] This is the smallest error for which the LWE problem is known to be as hard as worst case lattice problems [56].

We call this the linear circular LWE assumption. We show that the linear circular LWE assumption is true under the decisional LWE assumption. We remark that variants of this statement were known when the key is not decomposed into bits (i.e., when $\phi(\mathbf{s}) = \mathbf{s}$ and $\mathsf{Pub}(\mathbf{s}) = \mathbf{g}\text{-}\mathsf{LWE}_{\mathbf{s}}(\mathbf{s})$). E.g., [4] shows that assuming LWE, Regev's encryption is secure given as auxiliary encryption any affine function over the secret key. However, our result does not follow from [4] because the binary decomposition function $\phi_{\mathbf{g}}(\mathbf{s}) = \mathbf{g}^{-1}(\mathbf{s})$ is not linear (or even affine) in $\mathbf{s}$. So, to the best of our knowledge, the statement below is new.

Theorem 2. *Let $q = 2^k$ be a power of 2, and $\mathbf{g} = (1, 2, 4, \ldots, 2^{k-1})$ be the powers-of-two gadget vector. The linear circular LWE assumption (i.e., Definition 5 with public information $\mathsf{Pub}(\mathbf{s}) = \mathbf{g}\text{-}\mathsf{LWE}_{\mathbf{s}}(\phi_{\mathbf{g}}(\mathbf{s}))$) with secret dimension $n \geq 2n' \log_2 q$ and discrete Gaussian noise distribution $\xi = \Xi = \chi_{\sigma\sqrt{n}}$ is true assuming the hardness of decisional LWE (i.e., Definition 5 with $\mathsf{Pub}(\mathbf{s}) = \perp$) with secret dimension n' and discrete Gaussian noise χ_σ.*

Proof. We actually prove a slightly stronger property, showing that

$$(\mathbf{g}\text{-}\mathsf{LWE}_{\mathbf{s}}(\phi(\mathbf{s})), \mathbf{g}\text{-}\mathsf{LWE}_{\mathbf{s}}(\mathbf{0})) \in \mathbb{Z}_q^{(kn+kw)\times(n+1)}$$

is indistinguishable from a uniformly random matrix $(\mathbf{U}_0, \mathbf{U}_1)$ modulo q, where the $\mathbf{g}\text{-}\mathsf{LWE}$ ciphertexts use discrete Gaussian noise $\chi_{\sigma\sqrt{n}}$. We proceed in steps, giving a sequence of reductions, starting from the standard decisional LWE problem and ending with the linear circular LWE assumption. First, we use Lemma 1 to reduce the standard decisional LWE problem (with a uniformly random secret $\mathbf{s} \in \mathbb{Z}_q^{n'}$ and discrete Gaussian noise χ_σ) to the decisional LWE problem with a random binary secret $\mathbf{s}_0 \in \{0,1\}^n$, modulus q, and $kn + kw$ many samples. This is the only step of our proof that changes/increases the LWE dimension and noise. All the remaining steps preserve the error distribution and are very efficient. So, from this point on, we fix the LWE noise vector $\mathbf{e} \leftarrow \chi_{\sigma\sqrt{n}}^{kn+kw}$ and omit it from the notation.

Next, we reduce LWE with binary secret to the problem of distinguishing

$$\begin{bmatrix} \mathbf{g}\text{-}\mathsf{LWE}_{\mathbf{s}_0}(\mathbf{s}_0) \\ \mathbf{g}\text{-}\mathsf{LWE}_{\mathbf{s}_0}(\mathbf{0}) \end{bmatrix} = \mathbf{g}\text{-}\mathsf{LWE}_{\mathbf{s}_0}\left(\begin{bmatrix} \mathbf{s}_0 \\ \mathbf{0} \end{bmatrix}\right) = [\mathbf{A}', \mathbf{b}] \tag{6}$$

from the uniform distribution over $\mathbb{Z}_q$. Let $[\mathbf{A}, \mathbf{b}]$ be the input LWE distribution (with binary secret $\mathbf{s}_0$ and error $\mathbf{e}$), and map it to $[\mathbf{A}', \mathbf{b}] = [\mathbf{A}, \mathbf{b}] + \left[\begin{bmatrix} \mathbf{I} \\ \mathbf{O} \end{bmatrix} \otimes \mathbf{g}, \mathbf{0}\right]$. This transformation clearly maps the uniform distribution to the uniform distribution. On the other hand, $\left[\begin{bmatrix} \mathbf{I} \\ \mathbf{O} \end{bmatrix} \otimes \mathbf{g}, \mathbf{0}\right]$ is a noiseless $\mathbf{g}\text{-}\mathsf{LWE}_{\mathbf{s}_0}$ encryption of $(\mathbf{s}_0, \mathbf{0})$. So, if $[\mathbf{A}, \mathbf{b}]$ is an LWE instance, then $[\mathbf{A}', \mathbf{b}]$ is a random $\mathbf{g}\text{-}\mathsf{LWE}_{\mathbf{s}_0}$ encryption of $(\mathbf{s}_0, \mathbf{0})$, i.e., it is distributed according to (6), with the same error $\mathbf{e}$.

Next map $\mathbf{s}_0$ to a random key $\mathbf{s} = \sum_i 2^i \mathbf{s}_i \in \mathbb{Z}_q^n$ with binary decomposition $\mathbf{s}_i \in \{0,1\}^n$. We want to map (6) to

$$\mathsf{g\text{-}LWE}_{\mathbf{s}_0}\left(\begin{bmatrix} \mathbf{g}^{-1}(\mathbf{s}) \\ \mathbf{0} \end{bmatrix}\right) = \mathsf{g\text{-}LWE}_{\mathbf{s}_0}\left(\begin{bmatrix} \mathbf{s}_0 \\ \mathbf{s}_1 \\ \vdots \\ \mathbf{s}_k \\ \mathbf{0} \end{bmatrix}\right) = [\mathbf{A}', \mathbf{b}']. \tag{7}$$

This is done simply by picking $\mathbf{s}_1, \ldots, \mathbf{s}_k \in \{0,1\}^n$ uniformly at random, and adding $\mathbf{s}_i \otimes \mathbf{g}$ to the last column of (6), setting $\mathbf{b}' = \mathbf{b} + (\mathbf{0}, \mathbf{s}_1, \ldots, \mathbf{s}_k, \mathbf{0}) \otimes \mathbf{g}$. This is correct because $[\mathbf{O}, \mathbf{s}_i \otimes \mathbf{g}]$ is a noiseless $\mathsf{g\text{-}LWE}$ encryption of $\mathbf{s}_i$. Moreover, this transformation maps the uniform distribution to the uniform distribution. So, it gives a valid reduction to the problem of distinguishing (7) from the uniform distribution.

Finally, we need to change the encryption key in (7) from $\mathbf{s}_0$ to $\mathbf{s}$. This is done by subtracting $\mathbf{A}' \sum_{i \geq 1} \mathbf{s}_i$ from $\mathbf{b}'$. Again, this maps the uniform distribution to itself, and distribution (7) to the target distribution

$$\left[\mathbf{A}', \mathbf{b}' - \mathbf{A}' \sum_{i \geq 1} \mathbf{s}_i\right] = \mathsf{g\text{-}LWE}_{\mathbf{s}}\left(\begin{bmatrix} \phi(\mathbf{s}) \\ \mathbf{0} \end{bmatrix}\right).$$

□

To be clear, the linear circular LWE assumption does not have any implications to constructing non-leveled fully homomorphic encryption as far as we know. Nevertheless, we view the fact that Theorem 2 is true as a positive sign for the resolution of Conjecture 1. Note also that a quadratic circular encryption contains a linear circular encryption as a subset. So, circLWE is at least as strong as the linear LWE assumption.

3.2 Search to Decision Reduction

The search-circLWE assumption states that given

$$(\mathsf{g\text{-}LWE}_{\mathbf{s}}(\psi(\mathbf{s})), [\mathbf{A}, \mathbf{A}\mathbf{s} + \mathbf{e}])$$

where $\mathbf{A} \leftarrow \mathbb{Z}_q^{w \times n}$, $\mathbf{s} \leftarrow \mathbb{Z}_q^n$ and $\mathbf{e} \leftarrow \chi^w$, it is hard for probabilistic polynomial-time algorithms to recover $\mathbf{s}$ except with negligible probability. It is trivial to see that circLWE implies search-circLWE. The goal of this section is to show the converse.

First, we need the following lemma which says that breaking the circLWE assumption for random secrets gives us a way to break circLWE for any secret. Such a worst-case to average-case reduction for LWE is elementary; however, it does not seem to be so for the circular LWE assumption.

Lemma 3. *There is an efficiently computable map that transforms the* circLWE *distribution* $[\text{g-LWE}_{\mathbf{s}}(\psi(\mathbf{s});\chi_\sigma), \text{g-LWE}_{\mathbf{s}}(\mathbf{0};\chi)]$ *for any (fixed) secret* $\mathbf{s}$*, to the distribution* $[\text{g-LWE}_{\mathbf{s}'}(\psi(\mathbf{s}');\chi_{\sigma'}), \text{g-LWE}_{\mathbf{s}'}(\mathbf{0});\chi]$ *with random secret* $\mathbf{s}' = \mathbf{s} + \mathbf{r} \bmod q$ *where* $\sigma' = \sigma \cdot 2^{\omega(\log\lambda)}$.

Moreover, the map transforms $[\text{g-LWE}_{\mathbf{s}}(\psi(\mathbf{s});\chi_\sigma), \mathbf{U}]$ *with a uniformly random* $\mathbf{U}$ *to* $[\text{g-LWE}_{\mathbf{s}'}(\psi(\mathbf{s}');\chi_{\sigma'}), \mathbf{U}]$.

Proof. Recall that g-LWE encryption is key-homomorphic, in the sense that there is an efficiently computable transformation that on input a ciphertext $[\mathbf{A}, \mathbf{b}] = \text{g-LWE}_{\mathbf{s}}(\mathbf{m})$ and an arbitrary vector $\mathbf{r}$, outputs a ciphertext

$$h_{\mathbf{r}}([\mathbf{A}, \mathbf{b}]) = [\mathbf{A}, \mathbf{b} - \mathbf{A}\mathbf{r}] \tag{8}$$

in $\text{g-LWE}_{\mathbf{s}+\mathbf{r}}(\mathbf{m})$. This transformation preserves the encryption error. So, if the input is a fresh $\text{g-LWE}_{\mathbf{s}}(\mathbf{m})$ ciphertext, the output is also distributed as a fresh encryption of $\mathbf{m}$ under the modified key $\mathbf{s} + \mathbf{r} \bmod q$.

We also use the fact that using auxiliary information $\mathbf{P} = \text{g-LWE}_{\mathbf{s}}(\psi(\mathbf{s}))$ as an evaluation key, it is possible to perform arbitrary homomorphic computations on $\text{g-LWE}_{\mathbf{s}}$ ciphertexts. More specifically, there is an efficiently computable function Eval that on input any function f and ciphertext $\mathbf{C} = \text{g-LWE}_{\mathbf{s}}(\mathbf{m})$, outputs a ciphertext

$$\mathsf{Eval}(\mathbf{P}, f, \mathbf{C}) \in \text{g-LWE}_{\mathbf{s}}(f(\mathbf{m})).$$

(Such an evaluation algorithm follows from the GSW encryption scheme, e.g. as presented in Sect. 4.2.) This transformation modifies the encryption noise, but the output distribution can be made statistically close to a fresh g-LWE encryption with larger noise parameters using the noise-flooding lemma; see Lemma 2.

Now, for any vector $\mathbf{r}$, consider the function

$$f_{\mathbf{r}}(\psi(\mathbf{x})) = \psi(\mathbf{x} + \mathbf{r}).$$

Notice that this function maps binary vectors to binary vectors, and can be represented as an arithmetic circuit. It follows that

$$\begin{aligned} h_{\mathbf{r}}(\mathsf{Eval}(\mathbf{P}, f_{\mathbf{r}}, \mathbf{C})) &= h_{\mathbf{r}}(\mathsf{Eval}(\mathbf{P}, f_{\mathbf{r}}, \text{g-LWE}_{\mathbf{s}}(\psi(\mathbf{s})))) \\ &= h_{\mathbf{r}}(\text{g-LWE}_{\mathbf{s}}(f_{\mathbf{r}}(\psi(\mathbf{s})))) \\ &= \text{g-LWE}_{\mathbf{s}+\mathbf{r}}(\psi(\mathbf{s}+\mathbf{r})). \end{aligned}$$

This allows to map the first component of the distribution $[\text{g-LWE}_{\mathbf{s}}(\psi(\mathbf{s});\chi_\sigma), \mathbf{W}]$ to $\text{g-LWE}_{\mathbf{s}+\mathbf{r}}(\psi(\mathbf{s}+\mathbf{r});\chi')$ for some noise distribution χ' to be determined. For the second component $\mathbf{W} = \text{g-LWE}_{\mathbf{s}}(\mathbf{0};\chi)$ (or uniformly random $\mathbf{W} = \mathbf{U}$) we simply output $h_{\mathbf{r}}(\mathbf{W})$, which preserves the error distribution χ.

It remains to analyze the noise-growth χ' resulting from the homomorphic computation. First, we note that the function $f_{\mathbf{r}}$ essentially performs addition (in parallel on its coordinates) by a constant vector $\mathbf{r}$ with entries in $\mathbb{Z}_q$ followed by a single multiplication. This can be implemented with a circuit of depth

$O(\log\log q)$. By [17,31], homomorphic evaluation of $f_{\mathbf{r}}$ increases the noise magnitude from $\sigma\sqrt{\lambda}$ to at most $\sigma\sqrt{\lambda}\cdot 2^{O(\log\log q)}\cdot \text{poly}(\lambda) = \sigma\cdot\text{poly}(\lambda,\log q)$. Since $\log q = \text{poly}(\lambda)$, the noise flooding lemma using a Gaussian with standard deviation $\sigma' = \sigma\cdot\text{poly}(\lambda,\log q)\cdot 2^{\omega(\log\lambda)}$ makes this into a Gaussian with standard deviation $\sigma' = \sigma\cdot 2^{\omega(\log\lambda)}$. □

The following corollary follows immediately from Lemma 3.

Corollary 1. *If there is a probabilistic polynomial-time distinguisher for* circLWE *that works for a non-negligible fraction of secrets* $\mathbf{s}\leftarrow\mathbb{Z}_q^n$*, then there is a probabilistic polynomial-time distinguisher that, for all secrets* $\mathbf{s}\in\mathbb{Z}_q^n$*, outputs* 1 *with overwhelming probability given* $(\text{g-LWE}_{\mathbf{s}}(\psi(\mathbf{s})), \text{g-LWE}_{\mathbf{s}}(\mathbf{0}^\ell))$ *and* 0 *with overwhelming probability given* $(\text{g-LWE}_{\mathbf{s}}(\psi(\mathbf{s})), \mathbf{U})$.

Finally, we state and prove our search to decision reduction for circLWE.

Theorem 3. *Let* λ *be a security parameter. If* search-circLWE *with parameters* n, q *and discrete Gaussian error distribution* χ_σ *is true, so is* circLWE *with parameters* n, q *and discrete Gaussian error distribution* $\chi_{\sigma'}$ *where* $\sigma' = \sigma\cdot 2^{\omega(\log\lambda)}$.

Proof. The proof goes along the same lines as the simple (non-sample-preserving) search to decision reduction for LWE [56, Section 4], with the only non-triviality being that the reduction needs to re-randomize the secret. This is handled by our Lemma 3. Details follow.

Let $[\text{g-LWE}_{\mathbf{s}}(\psi(\mathbf{s})), \text{g-LWE}_{\mathbf{s}}(\mathbf{0})]$ be the input to the search-circLWE problem. The goal is to recover $\mathbf{s}$. This is done by recovering $\mathbf{s}$ one coordinate s_i at a time, with the help of the (decisional) circLWE oracle. For any coordinate i, and guess $v\in\mathbb{Z}_q$ for the value of s_i, select some rows $[\mathbf{A},\mathbf{b}]$ from $\text{g-LWE}_{\mathbf{s}}(\mathbf{0})$, choose $\mathbf{a}$ uniformly at random, and compute $[\mathbf{A}',\mathbf{b}'] = [\mathbf{A}+\mathbf{a}\cdot\mathbf{e}_i^t, \mathbf{b}+\mathbf{a}\cdot v]$. Note that $\mathbf{A}'$ is always uniformly random. Moreover, if $s_i = v$, then $\mathbf{b}'$ follows that $\text{g-LWE}_{\mathbf{s}}(\mathbf{0})$ distribution. On the other hand, if $s_i\neq v$, then $\mathbf{b}'$ is uniformly random and independent of $\mathbf{A}'$. Applying Lemma 3 to $(\mathbf{P}, [\mathbf{A}',\mathbf{b}'])$ (where $\mathbf{P} = \text{g-LWE}_{\mathbf{s}}(\psi(\mathbf{s}))$) we can randomize the secret $\mathbf{s}'$, and use the (decision) circLWE oracle to determine if $s_i = v$ was the correct guess.

Trying all possible guesses $v \pmod q$ takes time polynomial in q. For larger moduli, assume $q = \prod_i p_i$ factors into a product of small primes, and determine the value of $v \pmod{p_i}$ for each p_i separately. A reduction for arbitrary modulus q is obtained using modulus switching. □

It is natural to ask if there is a tighter reduction from search to decision, along the lines of the sample-preserving search-to-decision reduction for LWE from the work of Micciancio and Mol [49]. We conjecture that this is possible.

Conjecture 2. There is a *sample-preserving* reduction from search-circLWE to (decisional) circLWE.

3.3 Key Cliques

A natural question to ask is whether circLWE implies security of LWE when given multiple key cycles. For example, given

$$(\text{g-LWE}_{\mathbf{s}_i}(\psi(\mathbf{s}_j)) : i, j \in [k])$$

for some $k > 1$, one could conjecture that the collection of $[\mathbf{A}_i, \mathbf{A}_i\mathbf{s}_i + \mathbf{e}_i]$ for all $i \in [k]$ are indistinguishable from random numbers $[\mathbf{A}_i, \mathbf{b}_i]$. We call this the k-circLWE assumption, which turns out to be equivalent to the circLWE assumption. We provide an informal statement as well as a sketch of the proof below.

Theorem 4 (Informal). circLWE *implies* k-circLWE *(i.e., Definition 5 with* $\text{Pub}(\mathbf{S}) = \{\text{g-LWE}_{\mathbf{s}_i}(\psi(\mathbf{s}_j))\}_{i,j}$*) for any* $k = \text{poly}(n)$.

Proof (sketch). The reduction gets $\text{g-LWE}_{\mathbf{s}}(\psi(\mathbf{s}))$, and computes

$$(\text{g-LWE}_{\mathbf{s}_i}(\psi(\mathbf{s}_j)) : i, j \in [k])$$

The reduction defines $\mathbf{s}_j$ implicitly to be $\mathbf{s} + \mathbf{r}_j$ where the reduction chooses and knows $\mathbf{r}_j \leftarrow \mathbb{Z}_q^n$. This can be done exactly as in the proof of Lemma 3: first, starting from $\text{g-LWE}_{\mathbf{s}}(\psi(\mathbf{s}))$, compute $\text{g-LWE}_{\mathbf{s}}(\psi(\mathbf{s} + \mathbf{r}_j))$ using homomorphic computation, and then change the secret using the function $h_{\mathbf{r}}$ from Eq. 8 to get $\text{g-LWE}_{\mathbf{s}+\mathbf{r}_i}(\psi(\mathbf{s} + \mathbf{r}_j))$. □

3.4 Other Gadgets

In this paper, we focus on the use of the power of two gadget $\mathbf{pow}(2)$, as this is the most commonly used in theoretical papers. Still, one may consider the circLWE assumption with respect to a different gadget vectors $\mathbf{h}$, i.e., given the encryption $\text{Pub}_{\mathbf{h}}(\mathbf{s}) = \mathbf{h}\text{-LWE}_{\mathbf{s}}(\psi_{\mathbf{h}}(\mathbf{s}))$ instead of $\text{Pub}_{\mathbf{g}}(\mathbf{s}) = \text{g-LWE}_{\mathbf{s}}(\psi_{\mathbf{g}}(\mathbf{s}))$. So, one may ask, how does the choice of the gadget $\mathbf{g}$ affect the circLWE assumption? Is there a way to map $\text{Pub}_{\mathbf{g}}(\mathbf{s})$ to $\text{Pub}_{\mathbf{h}}(\mathbf{s})$?

It is easy to map $\mathbf{C} = \text{g-LWE}_{\mathbf{s}}(\psi_{\mathbf{g}}(\mathbf{s}))$ to $\mathbf{h}\text{-LWE}_{\mathbf{s}}(\psi_{\mathbf{g}}(\mathbf{s}))$ simply by computing $\mathbf{h} \circ \mathbf{C} = (\mathbf{I} \otimes \mathbf{h}) \odot \mathbf{C}$. However, changing $\psi_{\mathbf{g}}$ into $\psi_{\mathbf{h}}$ inside the encryption seems harder. A natural approach is to use the homomorphic properties of the encryption scheme to change $\psi_{\mathbf{g}}$ into $\psi_{\mathbf{h}}$ by means of a homomorphic computation. We conjecture that this is possible (up to some parameter growth) and pose it as a problem to be addressed in future work.

4 Homomorphic Encryption Schemes

We describe a number of widely used fully homomorphic encryption (FHE) schemes along with their associated Pub functions. Our goal is not to be comprehensive, but rather to describe a set of representative examples of FHE schemes together with the circular security assumptions they rely on. For each scheme, we will describe the key generation and encryption algorithms, focusing on the

Pub function that captures the auxiliary information about the secret key that is revealed by the scheme. We do not describe the decryption function, the homomorphic operations or the bootstrapping procedure as they are not necessary for the purposes of analyzing security. For these algorithms, we point the reader to the original papers.

4.1 BV 2011, BGV 2012 and Brakerski 2012

We begin with the Brakerski-Vaikuntanathan scheme [16], the first leveled FHE scheme whose security was based on LWE. This was followed shortly after by Brakerki, Gentry and Vaikuntanathan [12] which improved one of the key techniques in [16], namely modulus switching. In a nutshell, rather than perform modulus switching once at the end of a homomorphic computation, [12] did modulus reduction at every step, resulting in a large efficiency gain. We focus here on a scheme by Brakerski [10], which further improved on this line of work by doing *implicit modulus switching.* A concrete consequence was a simpler scheme that used the same modulus throughout, whereas BV11 and BGV12 use switching keys to go between LWE ciphertexts under different moduli. Brakerski [10] also introduced a different method to homomorphically multiply ciphertexts than BV/BGV. But the methods are very similar, and, in particular, they use essentially the same evaluation keys. So, everything we say holds for either multiplication method, since it only depends on the value of the evaluation key, and not the details of the homomorphic multiplication algorithm.

Here we consider the (circular) private-key version from [10, Section 4] with the following algorithms:

- **Parameters:** The scheme uses an LWE dimension n and an integer modulus q, and the plaintext space is integers modulo the plaintext modulus $p = 2$. (This can be generalized to other $\mathbb{Z}_q$ and $\mathbb{Z}_p$ as long as p is sufficiently smaller than q.)
- **Key Generation:** The key generation algorithm Gen outputs a random vector $\mathbf{s} \leftarrow \mathbb{Z}_q^n$ as the private key.
- **The Pub Function:** $\mathsf{Pub}_{\mathsf{B12}}(\mathbf{s})$ outputs

$$\mathbf{g}\text{-}\mathsf{LWE}_{q,\mathbf{s}}\big(\mathbf{g}^{-1}(\mathbf{s},1) \otimes \mathbf{g}^{-1}(\mathbf{s},1)\big) \in \mathbb{Z}_q^{((n+1)^2 w^3)\times(n+1)}$$

  where $\mathbf{g} = \mathbf{pow}(2) \in \mathbb{Z}_q^w$ is the power-of-two gadget and $w = \lfloor \log_2 q \rfloor$ is the gadget dimension.
- **Encryption:** A message $m \in \mathbb{Z}_2$ is encrypted using the trivial gadget $\mathbf{g} := (1) \in \mathbb{Z}_2$ as

$$\mathsf{Enc}_{\mathbf{s}}(m) = \mathbf{g}\text{-}\mathsf{LWE}_{q,\mathbf{s}}(m) \ .$$

Theorem 5. *Under the* $\mathsf{circLWE}[\xi, \Xi]$ *assumption, the Brakerski (private key, fully homomorphic) encryption scheme [10, Section 4] with encryption noise* ξ *and auxiliary input function* $\mathsf{Pub}_{\mathsf{B12}}[\Xi]$ *is IND-CPA-secure.*

Proof. Let $\mathcal{A}$ be an adversary that breaks the IND-CPA security of the encryption scheme with auxiliary input function $\mathsf{Pub}_{\mathsf{B12}}$, and notice that $\mathsf{Pub}_{\mathsf{B12}}(\mathbf{s}; \Xi)$ equals precisely $\mathbf{g}\text{-}\mathsf{LWE}_{\mathbf{s}}(\psi_{\mathbf{g}}(\mathbf{s}); \Xi)$, the auxiliary information of our circular LWE assumption. We use $\mathcal{A}$ to break the $\mathsf{circLWE}$ problem. Recall that $\mathcal{A}$ has access to an encryption oracle $O_b(m_0, m_1)$ that on input a pair of messages m_0, m_1 returns a ciphertext $\mathsf{LWE}_{\mathbf{s}}(m_b) = (\mathbf{a}^t, \mathbf{a}^t\mathbf{s} + e + \lfloor m_b \rceil_q)$, for a fixed, randomly chosen $b \in \{0, 1\}$. The goal of the adversary is to guess the bit b. We use $\mathcal{A}$ to break the $\mathsf{circLWE}$ assumption as follows. Let $(\mathbf{C}, [\mathbf{A}, \mathbf{b}])$ be the $\mathsf{circLWE}$ input distribution, where $[\mathbf{A}, \mathbf{b}]$ has a sufficiently high number of row[9] and follows either the uniform or LWE distribution with noise $\mathbf{e} \leftarrow \xi$. Pick $x \leftarrow \{0, 1\}$ uniformly at random, run $\mathcal{A}(\mathbf{C})$ and every time $\mathcal{A}$ makes a call to the encryption oracle $O(m_0, m_1)$ reply with $(\mathbf{a}_i^t, b_i + \lfloor m_x \rceil_q)$ using one of the rows of $[\mathbf{A}, \mathbf{b}]$. When $\mathcal{A}$ terminates with output $y \in \{0, 1\}$, the $\mathsf{circLWE}$ distinguisher outputs $x + y \pmod 2$. Notice that if $\mathbf{b} = \mathbf{A}\mathbf{s} + \mathbf{e}$, then $O(m_0, m_1) = \mathsf{LWE}_{\mathbf{s}}(m_x; \mathbf{e})$ and $\mathcal{A}$ will correctly guess the random bit x with some non-negligible advantage. On the other hand, if $\mathbf{b}$ is chosen uniformly at random, then the output of $O(m_0, m_1)$ is statistically independent of x, and $\mathcal{A}$ will output x with probability exactly $1/2$. So, the $\mathsf{circLWE}$ distinguisher has essentially the same running time and distinguishing advantage (up to a factor 2) as $\mathcal{A}$. □

An Optimization. It is possible to reduce the size of the switching key by letting

$$\mathsf{Pub}_{\mathsf{B12opt}}(\mathbf{s}) := \mathbf{g}\text{-}\mathsf{LWE}_{q,\mathbf{s}}(\mathbf{g}^{-1}((\mathbf{s}, 1) \otimes (\mathbf{s}, 1))) \in \mathbb{Z}_q^{((n+1)^2 w^2) \times (n+1)},$$

i.e., taking the binary decomposition *after* tensoring the key, rather than before. This reduces the size of the switching key by a factor of $w = \lfloor \log_2 q \rfloor$ and is an optimization employed in most subsequent papers that build on [10], e.g., the Fan-Vercauteren ring variant [24]. If $\mathbf{s} \in \{0, 1\}^n$ is binary, the two Pub functions coincide. However, they are different for general secrets $\mathbf{s} \in \mathbb{Z}_q^n$.

It is clear that the one can prove the security of the resulting scheme just as in Theorem 5, using a variant of our $\mathsf{circLWE}$ assumption where the function $\psi(\mathbf{s}) = \mathbf{g}^{-1}(\mathbf{s}, 1) \otimes \mathbf{g}^{-1}(\mathbf{s}, 1)$ is replaced by $\psi'(\mathbf{s}) = \mathbf{g}^{-1}((\mathbf{s}, 1) \otimes (\mathbf{s}, 1))$. It is also tempting to assume that one can compute $\mathsf{Pub}_{\mathsf{B12opt}}(\mathbf{s}) = \mathbf{g}\text{-}\mathsf{LWE}_{\mathbf{s}}(\psi'(\mathbf{s}))$ from $\mathsf{Pub}_{\mathsf{B12}}(\mathbf{s}) = \mathbf{g}\text{-}\mathsf{LWE}_{\mathbf{s}}(\psi(\mathbf{s}))$, and, thereby, establish the security of the optimized scheme under the standard $\mathsf{circLWE}$ assumption, possibly at the cost of using larger parameters. The idea is to express the products $u \cdot v$ in $(\mathbf{s}, 1) \otimes (\mathbf{s}, 1)$ where u, v are elements of $(\mathbf{s}, 1)$ as a binary circuit that takes as input the bits of $v = \sum_i v_i 2^i$ and $u = \sum_i u_i 2^i$. Then, evaluate the circuit homomorphically on the encryptions of u_i, v_i (which are available from $\mathsf{Pub}_{\mathsf{B12}}(\mathbf{s})$) using the (leveled) homomorphic operations of the encryption scheme, producing as a result the encryption of the bits of $u \cdot v$, and concatenate them together to form $\mathsf{Pub}_{\mathsf{B12opt}}(\mathbf{s})$. The problem is that this approach produces encryptions of the bits in $\psi'(\mathbf{s})$ under the BV/BGV/B12 LWE encryption scheme with trivial gadget $\mathbf{g} = (1)$ and plaintext modulus $p = 2$,

[9] The number of rows may be fixed using a public key version of the encryption scheme.

while $\mathsf{Pub}_{\mathsf{B12opt}}(\mathbf{s})$ requires the output to be encrypted under $\mathbf{g} = \mathbf{pow}(2)$ and modulus $p = q$. So, it is unclear how to compute $\mathsf{Pub}_{\mathsf{B12opt}}(\mathbf{s})$ from $\mathsf{Pub}_{\mathsf{B12}}(\mathbf{s})$, and at this point the optimized scheme seems to require a different (and possibly stronger) assumption than $\mathsf{circLWE}$.

4.2 GSW 2013 and BV 2014

We next consider a different family of LWE-based encryption schemes that stem from the work of Gentry, Sahai and Waters [31]. Their work does not describe an explicit bootstrapping algorithm, rather it mentions that the scheme can be bootstrapped using general techniques, leading to an FHE scheme with quasi-polynomial modulus q. Brakerski and Vaikuntanathan [17] describe a new bootstrapping algorithm for the GSW scheme, leading to the first leveled FHE with a polynomial modulus q. This has been further simplified and optimized by Alperin-Sheriff and Peikert [3].

The Key-Switching Lens on GSW 2013 Ciphertexts. Focusing on the encryption scheme in [31, Section 3], we present a very different, but completely equivalent, view on GSW ciphertexts as switching keys in the Regev encryption scheme. We describe our version of GSW 2013 below, and go on to show that the ciphertexts thus generated are computationally equivalent to the ciphertexts in [31, Section 3].

- **Parameters:** The scheme uses an LWE dimension n and an integer (ciphertext) modulus q, and the plaintext space is $\mathcal{M} = \{0, 1\} \subset \mathbb{Z}_q$.
- **Key Generation:** The key generation algorithm Gen outputs a random vector $\mathbf{s} \leftarrow \mathbb{Z}_q^n$ as the private key.
- **Encryption:** The scheme uses the power gadget $\mathbf{g} = \mathbf{pow}(2) \in \mathbb{Z}_q^w$ in dimension $w = \lfloor \log_2 q \rfloor$.[10] A message $m \in \mathcal{M}$ is encrypted as

  $$\mathsf{Enc}_{\mathbf{s}}(m) = \mathbf{g}\text{-}\mathsf{LWE}_{\mathbf{s} \to \mathbf{s}}(m) \in \mathbb{Z}_q^{(n+1)w \times (n+1)}$$

  so ciphertexts are matrices.[11]

Before proceeding any further, we observe that these ciphertexts can be added and multiplied using the switching keys composition properties described at the end of Sect. 2.3. We leave it to the reader to verify that the properties are operationally identical to the homomorphic addition and multiplication of the GSW encryption scheme.

[10] [31] also mentions the possibility of using $\mathbf{g} = \mathbf{pow}(b)$ for some other basis b, or a CRT gadget $\mathbf{g} = \mathbf{crt}(\mathbf{p})$, though the scheme is only presented and analyzed for the specific case of $\mathbf{g} = \mathbf{pow}(2)$.

[11] The original GSW 2013 encryption scheme outputs a bit-decomposition of the mod-q matrix as the ciphertext. Here, we use an equivalent variant from [3] which outputs the mod-q matrix as-is.

We now show that these ciphertexts are exactly GSW 2013 ciphertexts. Let us first rewrite the ciphertext in the language of LWE.

$$\begin{aligned}\mathsf{Enc}_{\mathbf{s}}(m) &= \mathbf{g}\text{-}\mathsf{LWE}_{\mathbf{s}\to\mathbf{s}}(m) = \mathbf{g}\text{-}\mathsf{LWE}_{\mathbf{s}}\left(\begin{bmatrix}\mathbf{s}\\1\end{bmatrix} m\right) = \mathsf{LWE}_{\mathbf{s}}\left(\begin{bmatrix}\mathbf{s}\\1\end{bmatrix} m \otimes \mathbf{g}\right)\\ &= \left[\mathbf{A}, -\mathbf{A}\mathbf{s} + \mathbf{e} + \begin{bmatrix} m\mathbf{s}\otimes\mathbf{g}\\ m\mathbf{g}\end{bmatrix}\right]\end{aligned}$$

Now, writing $m\mathbf{s}\otimes\mathbf{g}$ as

$$m\mathbf{s}\otimes\mathbf{g} = (m\mathbf{I}_n \otimes \mathbf{g})(\mathbf{s}\otimes 1) = (m\mathbf{I}_n\otimes\mathbf{g})\mathbf{s}\ ,$$

we can write the ciphertext as

$$\begin{aligned}\left[\mathbf{A}, -\mathbf{A}\mathbf{s} + \mathbf{e} + \begin{bmatrix} m\mathbf{s}\otimes\mathbf{g}\\ m\mathbf{g}\end{bmatrix}\right] &= \begin{bmatrix}\mathbf{A}_1, & -(\mathbf{A}_1 - m\mathbf{I}_n\otimes\mathbf{g})\mathbf{s} + \mathbf{e}_1\\ \mathbf{A}_2, & -\mathbf{A}_2\mathbf{s} + \mathbf{e}_2 + m\mathbf{g}\end{bmatrix}\\ &= \begin{bmatrix}\mathbf{A}_1' + m\mathbf{I}_n\otimes\mathbf{g}, & -\mathbf{A}_1'\mathbf{s} + \mathbf{e}_1\\ \mathbf{A}_2, & -\mathbf{A}_2\mathbf{s} + \mathbf{e}_2 + m\mathbf{g}\end{bmatrix}\\ &= \begin{bmatrix}\mathbf{A}_1', & -\mathbf{A}_1'\mathbf{s} + \mathbf{e}_1\\ \mathbf{A}_2, & -\mathbf{A}_2\mathbf{s} + \mathbf{e}_2\end{bmatrix} + m\mathbf{I}_{n+1}\otimes\mathbf{g}\\ &= [\mathbf{A}, -\mathbf{A}\mathbf{s} + \mathbf{e}] + m\mathbf{I}_{n+1}\otimes\mathbf{g}\end{aligned}$$

The latter expression is exactly a GSW 2013 ciphertext, except that (following [3]) it is written as a mod-q matrix whereas GSW 2013 further do bit-decomposition to turn it into a 0-1 matrix.

The Pub **Function for GSW.** The $\mathsf{Pub}_{\mathsf{GSW13}}$ function encrypts the bits of each coordinate of the secret key $\mathbf{s}$ under the GSW encryption algorithm:

$$\mathsf{Pub}_{\mathsf{GSW13}}(\mathbf{s}) = \mathbf{g}\text{-}\mathsf{LWE}_{\mathbf{s}\to\mathbf{s}}(\mathbf{g}^{-1}(\mathbf{s})).$$

We recall that the GSW encryption scheme has message space $\{0,1\}$. So, the above expression should be interpreted as the concatenation of wn $\mathbf{g}\text{-}\mathsf{LWE}_{\mathbf{s}\to\mathbf{s}}$ ciphertexts, each encrypting one of the elements of $\mathbf{g}^{-1}(\mathbf{s}) \in \{0,1\}^{wn}$ independently.

Theorem 6. *Under the* $\mathsf{circLWE}[\xi, \chi_\sigma]$ *assumption, the GSW (private key, fully homomorphic) encryption scheme [31, Section 3] with encryption noise* ξ *and auxiliary input function* $\mathsf{Pub}_{\mathsf{GSW13}}[\chi_{\sigma'}]$ *is IND-CPA-secure, where* $\sigma' = \sqrt{w}\cdot\sigma$.

Proof. By definition

$$\mathsf{Pub}_{\mathsf{GSW13}}(\mathbf{s}) = \mathbf{g}\text{-}\mathsf{LWE}_{\mathbf{s}\to\mathbf{s}}(\mathbf{g}^{-1}(\mathbf{s})) = \mathbf{g}\text{-}\mathsf{LWE}_{\mathbf{s}}\left(\mathbf{g}^{-1}(\mathbf{s})\otimes\begin{bmatrix}\mathbf{s}\\1\end{bmatrix}\right).$$

This can be generated from

$$\mathsf{Pub}_{\mathsf{B12}}(\mathbf{s}; \Xi) = \mathbf{g}\text{-}\mathsf{LWE}_{\mathbf{s}}(\mathbf{g}^{-1}(\mathbf{s},1)\otimes\mathbf{g}^{-1}(\mathbf{s},1)\,;\Xi)$$

via additive homomorphisms with noise growth $O(\sqrt{\log q})$. More specifically, one can compute

$$\mathsf{Pub}_{\mathsf{GSW13}}(\mathbf{s}) = \mathbf{G} \circledcirc \mathsf{Pub}_{\mathsf{B12}}(\mathbf{s}; \Xi) \qquad \text{where} \quad \mathbf{G} = [\mathbf{I}, \mathbf{O}] \otimes (\mathbf{I} \otimes \mathbf{g}^t)$$

which, by the mixed product property of $\otimes$ and the definition of $\circledcirc$, is a $\mathbf{g}$-$\mathsf{LWE}_{\mathbf{s}}$ encryption of

$$\begin{aligned}
&([\mathbf{I}, \mathbf{O}] \otimes (\mathbf{I} \otimes \mathbf{g}^t)) \cdot \left(\mathbf{g}^{-1}\left(\begin{bmatrix}\mathbf{s}\\1\end{bmatrix}\right) \otimes \mathbf{g}^{-1}\left(\begin{bmatrix}\mathbf{s}\\1\end{bmatrix}\right)\right) \\
&= \left([\mathbf{I}, \mathbf{O}] \cdot \mathbf{g}^{-1}\left(\begin{bmatrix}\mathbf{s}\\1\end{bmatrix}\right)\right) \otimes \left((\mathbf{I} \otimes \mathbf{g}^t) \cdot \mathbf{g}^{-1}\left(\begin{bmatrix}\mathbf{s}\\1\end{bmatrix}\right)\right) \\
&= \mathbf{g}^{-1}(\mathbf{s}) \otimes \begin{bmatrix}\mathbf{s}\\1\end{bmatrix}.
\end{aligned}$$

This proves that $\mathsf{Pub}_{\mathsf{GSW13}})(\mathbf{s})$ encrypts the correct message. As for the encryption noise distribution, notice that if $\mathsf{Pub}_{\mathsf{B12}}(\mathbf{s})$ has discrete gaussian noise distribution Ξ then $\mathsf{Pub}_{\mathsf{GSW13}}(\mathbf{s})$ has noise distribution $\mathbf{g}^{-t}(\mathbf{G}) \cdot \Xi$. But, for any gadget $\mathbf{g}$, the gadget decompositions of the coordinates of the gadget vector are (trivially) the unit vectors $\mathbf{g}^{-t}(\mathbf{g}_i) = \mathbf{e}_i^t = [0, \ldots, 1, \ldots, 0] \in \{0,1\}^w$ with the 1 at position i. It follows that $\mathbf{g}^{-t}(\mathbf{G}) = [\mathbf{I} \otimes \mathbf{g}^{-t}(\mathbf{g}^t), \mathbf{O}]$ is a binary matrix with orthogonal rows of weight w. So, if Ξ follows the gaussian distribution χ_σ, then each coordinate of $\mathbf{g}^{-t}(\mathbf{G})\, \Xi$ is the sum of w independent gaussians χ_σ. So, $\mathbf{g}^{-t}(\mathbf{G})\, \Xi$ is also gaussian $\chi_{\sigma'}$ with parameter $\sigma' = \sqrt{w} \cdot \sigma$.

This is not enough to show that the IND-CPA security of GSW follows from the security of B12 because the encryption function is also different. Still, we can proceed similarly to the proof of Theorem 5 as follows. Let $\mathcal{A}$ be an adversary breaking the IND-CPA security of GSW, and let $(\mathsf{Pub}_{\mathsf{B12}}(\mathbf{s}), \mathbf{C})$ the input for the $\mathsf{circLWE}$ problem. Here $\mathbf{C} \in \mathbb{Z}_q^{* \times (n+1)}$ is a matrix with sufficiently many rows, and it is broken into chunks $\mathbf{C}_i \in \mathbb{Z}_q^{(n+1)w \times (n+1)}$, one for each encryption query to be made by $\mathcal{A}$. The goal is to determine if $\mathbf{C}$ follows the LWE or the uniformly random distribution. First we compute $\mathsf{Pub}_{\mathsf{GSW13}}(\mathbf{s})$ from $\mathsf{Pub}_{\mathsf{B12}}(\mathbf{s})$ as described above, and pick a bit $x \in \{0,1\}$ uniformly at random. Next, we run $\mathcal{A}$ on input $\mathsf{Pub}_{\mathsf{GSW13}}(\mathbf{s})$, and every time $\mathcal{A}$ makes an encryption query (m_0, m_1) we reply with $\mathbf{C}_i + m_x \mathbf{I} \otimes \mathbf{g}$, where i is a counter which is incremented after every query. If $\mathbf{C}$ is follows the LWE distribution (with secret $\mathbf{s}$), $\mathbf{C}_i + m_x \mathbf{I} \otimes \mathbf{g}$ is a GSW encryption of m_x, and $\mathcal{A}$ will have some advantage in guessing the value of the bit x. On the other hand, if $\mathbf{C}_i$ is uniformly random, $\mathcal{A}$ has no information about x and will guess it with probability exactly $1/2$. So, we can determine if $\mathbf{C}$ is LWE or uniform by checking if $\mathcal{A}$ outputs x. □

4.3 AP14 and GINX16

The work of Alperin-Sheriff and Peikert [3] builds on GSW 2013 and BV 2014, but uses a different bootstrapping procedure requiring a different encoding of the secret key. Several encoding methods are described in [3]. In the simplest (but least efficient) method each coordinate $s_i \in \mathbb{Z}_q$ of the secret key is encoded as a permutation matrix $\Pi_i \in \{0,1\}^{q \times q}$ such that $\Pi_i \mathbf{x}$ rotates the vector $\mathbf{x}$ by s_i positions. Then, the entries of Π_i (for each i) are encrypted using the GSW encryption function. Then a number of optimizations are considered. First, since each row of Π_i is a rotation of the previous row, there is no need to encrypt all $q \times q$ entries: it is enough to provide encryptions of the first row π_i, producing just q ciphertexts for each i. (For the other rows one can use rotations of those q ciphertexts.) Even more substantial savings can be obtained when $q = \prod_j q_j$ is a product of small primes. Then, one can use the isomorphism between $\mathbb{Z}_q$ and $\prod_j \mathbb{Z}_{q_j}$, map the secret key to a collection of values $s_{i,j} = s_i \pmod{q_j}$, and then encode each $s_{i,j} \in \mathbb{Z}_{q_j}$ as before as (the first row of) a permutation matrix in dimension q_j. Our proof and security analysis holds for all different variants of the encoding functions, as it operates on each vector individually. For concreteness, we consider the direct encoding of $x \in \mathbb{Z}_q$ as a q-dimensional binary vector. But the proof is immediately adapted to the case of composite $q = \prod_j q_j$, breaking $\mathbb{Z}_q$ into the product of smaller cycles.

In summary, the $\mathsf{Pub}_{\mathsf{AP14}}$ function encrypts a one-hot encoding of each coordinate $s_i \in \mathbb{Z}_q$ (or $s_{i,j} \in \mathbb{Z}_{q_j}$) of the secret key. For a number $x \in \mathbb{Z}_q$, let $e_x \in \{0,1\}^q$ denote the vector with 1 in the xth coordinate and 0 everywhere else. Extending the notation to vectors, for $\mathbf{s} \in \mathbb{Z}_q^n$, let $e_{\mathbf{s}} \in \{0,1\}^{nq}$ denote the vertical concatenation of the e_{s_i} for all i.

$$\mathsf{Pub}_{\mathsf{AP14}}(\mathbf{s}) = \mathsf{g}\text{-}\mathsf{LWE}_{\mathbf{s}\to\mathbf{s}}(e_{\mathbf{s}})$$

Theorem 7. *Under the* $\mathsf{circLWE}[\xi, \chi_\sigma]$ *assumption, the AP14 (private key, fully homomorphic) encryption scheme [3, Section 5] with encryption noise* ξ *and auxiliary input function* $\mathsf{Pub}_{\mathsf{AP14}}[\Xi]$ *is IND-CPA-secure for some efficiently samplable distribution* Ξ *with subgaussian parameter* $|\Xi| \le w^2\sqrt{n+1}\cdot\sigma$.

Proof. Since AP14 and GSW use the same encryption function, it is enough to show how to generate $\mathsf{Pub}_{\mathsf{AP14}}(\mathbf{s})$ from $\mathsf{Pub}_{\mathsf{GSW13}}(\mathbf{s})$. Then, security follows from the proof of Theorem 6. Recall that $\mathsf{Pub}_{\mathsf{GSW13}}(\mathbf{s}) = \mathsf{g}\text{-}\mathsf{LWE}_{\mathbf{s}\to\mathbf{s}}(\mathbf{x}^t)$ where $\mathbf{x}^t = \mathbf{g}^{-t}(\mathbf{s})$ is the bit decomposition of the secret key $\mathbf{s}$. Moreover, Theorem 6 shows that (starting from the $\mathsf{circLWE}[\xi, \chi_\sigma]$ auxiliary information) these ciphertexts can be computed with gaussian encryption noise $\chi_{\sigma'}$ for $\sigma' = \sqrt{w}\sigma$. Consider the function $\phi(x_1, \ldots, x_w)$ that takes the bits $x_i \in \{0,1\}$ of a number $x \in \mathbb{Z}_q$ and outputs its one-hot encoding e_x. For any $y = \sum_i 2^i y_i$ (with $y_i \in \{0,1\}$), the yth element of the one-hot encoding $e_x[y]$ can be written as $e_x[y] = \prod_{i=0}^{w} z_i$ where

$$\begin{aligned} z_i &= (y_i \cdot x_i + (1-y_i)\cdot(1-x_i)) \\ &= ((2y_i - 1)x_i + 1 - y_i) = \begin{cases} 1 \text{ if } x_i = y_i \\ 0 \text{ otherwise} \end{cases} \end{aligned}$$

Notice that $(2y_i - 1) = \pm 1$, and it is a known constant. So, the product $(2y_i - 1)x_i$ can be evaluated homomorphically on the encryption of x_i (provided by $\mathsf{Pub}_{\mathsf{GSW13}}(\mathbf{s})$) while preserving the error distribution $\pm\chi_{\sigma'} = \chi_{\sigma'}$. Moreover, all factors z_i in the product evaluate to either 0 or 1. So, the product can be evaluated using AP14 homomorphic multiplications. More specifically, if $\mathbf{C}_i = \textsf{g-LWE}_{\mathbf{s}\to\mathbf{s}}(z_i; \chi_{\sigma'})$ are the encryptions of the secret bits z_i computed as above, then an encryption of $e_x[y] = \prod_{i=1}^{w} z_i$ can be computed as the product

$$\mathbf{C}_1 \odot \mathbf{C}_2 \odot \cdots \odot \mathbf{C}_w.$$

By Theorem 1, evaluating this products left-to-right gives an encryption of $e_x[y]$ with an error which is the sum of at most w terms for the form $\mathbf{g}^{-t}(\mathbf{C}'_i) \cdot \chi_{\sigma'}$, where $\mathbf{C}'_i = \mathbf{C}_1 \odot \cdots \odot \mathbf{C}_{i-1}$ are the ciphertexts corresponding to the intermediate partial products. Since the rows of $\mathbf{g}^{-t}(\mathbf{C}'_i) \in \{0,1\}^{(n+1)w \times (n+1)w}$ have norm at most $\sqrt{w(n+1)}$, each error component has gaussian distribution of parameter (at most) $\sqrt{w(n+1)}\sigma' = w\sqrt{n+1}\sigma$. Adding up the errors for all (at most w) terms, we see that $e_x[y]$ is encrypted with gaussian noise $\chi_{\sigma''}$ of parameter at most $\sigma'' \le w^2\sqrt{n+1}\sigma$. We remark that while each $e_x[y]$ is encrypted using gaussian noise, these error distributions (for different indexes y) are not totally independent because they are obtained by taking different linear combinations of the same $\textsf{g-LWE}_{\mathbf{s}\to\mathbf{s}}(\mathbf{x}^t; \chi_{\sigma'})$. Independence (and a slightly better bound) can be achieved by evaluating the $\odot$ products using the subgaussian decomposition technique of [3]. □

We remark that the fact that auxiliary information noise Ξ in Theorem 7 is not a Gaussian is just an artifact of the proof, and using discrete gaussian noise $\chi_{\sigma''}$ with the same parameter $\sigma'' = w^2\sigma\sqrt{n+1}$ is only expected to improve the security of the scheme. Alternatively, a formal statement can be obtained by using noise flooding to map the error distribution Ξ resulting from the homomorphic evaluation process into a discrete gaussian, at the cost of substantially increasing the noise level.

Gama et al. [25, Section 7] give yet another bootstrapping procedure,[12] similar to AP14, but offering some advantages when the secret key has binary entries $\mathbf{s} \in \{0,1\}^n$. Arbitrary keys are mapped to binary ones by taking their binary decomposition. (See [51] for a comparison of the two methods and their relation to ring versions of the same schemes [21,23].) Since the bootstrapping key consists of the GSW encryption of the bits of the secret key $\mathbf{s}$, the Pub function is precisely the same as in the GSW scheme

$$\textsf{Pub}_{\textsf{GINX16}}(\mathbf{s}) = \textsf{Pub}_{\textsf{GSW13}}(\mathbf{s}).$$

So, it immediately follows from Theorem 6 that the scheme is secure under the circLWE assumption.

Theorem 8. *Under the* circLWE$[\xi, \chi_\sigma]$ *assumption, the (private key, fully homomorphic) GINX encryption scheme [25, Section 7] with encryption noise ξ and auxiliary input function* $\textsf{Pub}_{\textsf{GINX16}}[\chi_{\sqrt{w}\sigma}]$. *is IND-CPA-secure.*

[12] Gama et al. also present an abstract generalization of GSW, and present the scheme using a rather nonstandard notation. But the scheme is essentially the same as GSW. So, for simplicity we present it using standard LWE notation.

4.4 HAO15

Hiromasa, Abe and Okamoto [37, Section 3] proposed a homomorphic encryption scheme called MatrixGSW, a variant of GSW 2013 which encrypts matrices directly. The private key version of the scheme is defined as follows:

- **Parameters:** The scheme uses an LWE dimension n, an integer ciphertext modulus q, and the an integer k which defines the message space $\mathcal{M} = \{0,1\}^{k\times k} \subset \mathbb{Z}_q^{k\times k}$.
- **Key Generation:** The secret key generation algorithm Gen outputs a random $n \times k$ integer matrix with small entries $\mathbf{S} \leftarrow \mathbb{Z}_q^{n\times k}$.
- **Encryption:** The encryption of a message $\mathbf{M}$ is

$$\mathsf{Enc}_{\mathbf{S}}(\mathbf{M}) = \mathbf{g}\text{-}\mathsf{LWE}_{\mathbf{S}\to\mathbf{S}}(\mathbf{M})$$

  where $\mathbf{g} = \mathbf{pow}(2)$.

Interestingly, even without bootstrapping, the IND-CPA security of MatrixGSW does not seem to follow from the standard LWE assumption.[13] The security of (the public key version of) the scheme is claimed [37, Lemma 4] under an unspecified "circular security" assumption. Here we provide a sketch of the proof that the private-key encryption scheme is secure under the key clique assumption from Sect. 3.3.

Theorem 9 (Informal). *Under the key clique assumption from Sect. 3.3, the HAO15 encryption scheme [37] is IND-CPA secure.*

Proof (Sketch). Expanding the definition of $\mathsf{Enc}_{\mathbf{S}}$ we see that

$$\begin{aligned}\mathsf{Enc}_{\mathbf{S}}(\mathbf{M}) = \mathbf{g}\text{-}\mathsf{LWE}_{\mathbf{S}\to\mathbf{S}}(\mathbf{M}) &= \mathbf{g}\text{-}\mathsf{LWE}_{\mathbf{S}}\left(\begin{bmatrix}\mathbf{S}\\ \mathbf{I}\end{bmatrix}\mathbf{M}\right)\\ &= \begin{bmatrix}\mathbf{g}\text{-}\mathsf{LWE}_{\mathbf{S}}(\mathbf{SM})\\ \mathbf{g}\text{-}\mathsf{LWE}_{\mathbf{S}}(\mathbf{M})\end{bmatrix}\end{aligned}$$

The bottom part is just a $\mathbf{g}$-LWE encryption of the matrix $\mathbf{M}$ under $\mathbf{S} = [\mathbf{s}_1,\ldots,\mathbf{s}_k]$, and its security follows from the standard LWE assumption using a standard hybrid argument. For the top part, we show how to compute $\mathbf{C} = \mathbf{g}\text{-}\mathsf{LWE}_{\mathbf{S}}(\mathbf{SM})$ from the key clique $\mathbf{Q}_{i,j} = \mathbf{g}\text{-}\mathsf{LWE}_{\mathbf{s}_j}(\mathbf{s}_i)$. Let $m_{i,j}$ be the entries of the message $\mathbf{M}$. Then, the jth column of $\mathbf{C}$ can be written as

$$\mathbf{g}\text{-}\mathsf{LWE}_{\mathbf{s}_j}\left(\sum_i \mathbf{s}_i \cdot m_{i,j}\right) = \sum_i m_{i,j} \overset{\mathbf{g}}{\circledcirc} \mathbf{g}\text{-}\mathsf{LWE}_{\mathbf{s}_j}(\mathbf{s}_i) = \sum_i m_{i,j} \overset{\mathbf{g}}{\circledcirc} \mathbf{Q}_{i,j}.$$

[13] [37] claims that the private key (but not the public key) version of the encryption scheme is secure under the standard decisional LWE assumption, but without giving a proof. However, the claim is probably incorrect as private key homomorphic encryption schemes can be generically transformed into public key homomorphic schemes without additional security assumptions.

In fact, if $\mathbf{M}$ is a matrix with binary entries, then one can use a simple product $m_{i,j} \cdot \mathbf{Q}_{i,j}$ instead of $\overset{\mathbf{g}}{\circledcirc}$. This expression produces an encryption of $\mathbf{SM}$, but with a different error distribution than the standard encryption function. Still, one can guarantee IND-CPA security under the key clique assumption by adding a random encryption of 0 with flooding noise, and using the noise flooding lemma (Lemma 2). □

Combining this with Theorem 4 we get security under our circLWE assumption.

Corollary 2. *Under the* circLWE *assumption, the HAO15 encryption scheme [37] is IND-CPA secure.*

Acknowledgement. DM was supported by an Intel Cryptographic Frontiers grant, SAIT Global Research Cluster and NSF award CNS-1936703. VV was supported by a Simons Investigator Award, NSF CNS-2154149, DARPA under Agreement No. HR00112020023, a grant from the MIT-IBM Watson AI and a Thornton Family Faculty Research Innovation Fellowship from MIT. Any opinions, findings and conclusions or recommendations expressed in this material are those of the author(s) and do not necessarily reflect the views of the United States Government or DARPA.

References

1. Abadi, M., Rogaway, P.: Reconciling two views of cryptography (the computational soundness of formal encryption). J. Cryptol. **20**(3), 395 (2007). https://doi.org/10.1007/s00145-007-0203-0
2. Ajtai, M.: Generating hard instances of lattice problems. In: Symposium on Theory of Computing - STOC 1996, pp. 99–108. ACM (1996). https://doi.org/10.1145/237814.237838
3. Alperin-Sheriff, J., Peikert, C.: Faster bootstrapping with polynomial error. In: Garay, J.A., Gennaro, R. (eds.) CRYPTO 2014. LNCS, vol. 8616, pp. 297–314. Springer, Heidelberg (2014). https://doi.org/10.1007/978-3-662-44371-2_17
4. Applebaum, B., Cash, D., Peikert, C., Sahai, A.: Fast cryptographic primitives and circular-secure encryption based on hard learning problems. In: Halevi, S. (ed.) CRYPTO 2009. LNCS, vol. 5677, pp. 595–618. Springer, Heidelberg (2009). https://doi.org/10.1007/978-3-642-03356-8_35
5. Asharov, G., Jain, A., López-Alt, A., Tromer, E., Vaikuntanathan, V., Wichs, D.: Multiparty computation with low communication, computation and interaction via threshold FHE. In: Pointcheval, D., Johansson, T. (eds.) EUROCRYPT 2012. LNCS, vol. 7237, pp. 483–501. Springer, Heidelberg (2012). https://doi.org/10.1007/978-3-642-29011-4_29
6. Barak, B., Haitner, I., Hofheinz, D., Ishai, Y.: Bounded key-dependent message security. In: Gilbert, H. (ed.) EUROCRYPT 2010. LNCS, vol. 6110, pp. 423–444. Springer, Heidelberg (2010). https://doi.org/10.1007/978-3-642-13190-5_22
7. Bishop, A., Hohenberger, S., Waters, B.: New circular security counterexamples from decision linear and learning with errors. In: Iwata, T., Cheon, J.H. (eds.) ASIACRYPT 2015. LNCS, vol. 9453, pp. 776–800. Springer, Heidelberg (2015). https://doi.org/10.1007/978-3-662-48800-3_32

8. Black, J., Rogaway, P., Shrimpton, T.: Encryption-scheme security in the presence of key-dependent messages. In: Nyberg, K., Heys, H. (eds.) SAC 2002. LNCS, vol. 2595, pp. 62–75. Springer, Heidelberg (2003). https://doi.org/10.1007/3-540-36492-7_6
9. Boneh, D., Halevi, S., Hamburg, M., Ostrovsky, R.: Circular-secure encryption from decision Diffie-Hellman. In: Wagner, D. (ed.) CRYPTO 2008. LNCS, vol. 5157, pp. 108–125. Springer, Heidelberg (2008). https://doi.org/10.1007/978-3-540-85174-5_7
10. Brakerski, Z.: Fully homomorphic encryption without modulus switching from classical GapSVP. In: Safavi-Naini, R., Canetti, R. (eds.) CRYPTO 2012. LNCS, vol. 7417, pp. 868–886. Springer, Heidelberg (2012). https://doi.org/10.1007/978-3-642-32009-5_50
11. Brakerski, Z., Döttling, N.: Hardness of LWE on general entropic distributions. In: Canteaut, A., Ishai, Y. (eds.) EUROCRYPT 2020. LNCS, vol. 12106, pp. 551–575. Springer, Cham (2020). https://doi.org/10.1007/978-3-030-45724-2_19
12. Brakerski, Z., Gentry, C., Vaikuntanathan, V.: (Leveled) fully homomorphic encryption without bootstrapping. ACM Trans. Comput. Theory **6**(3), 13:1–13:36 (2014). https://doi.org/10.1145/2633600. (Prelim. version in ITCS 2012)
13. Brakerski, Z., Goldwasser, S.: Circular and leakage resilient public-key encryption under subgroup indistinguishability. In: Rabin, T. (ed.) CRYPTO 2010. LNCS, vol. 6223, pp. 1–20. Springer, Heidelberg (2010). https://doi.org/10.1007/978-3-642-14623-7_1
14. Brakerski, Z., Goldwasser, S., Kalai, Y.T.: Black-box circular-secure encryption beyond affine functions. In: Ishai, Y. (ed.) TCC 2011. LNCS, vol. 6597, pp. 201–218. Springer, Heidelberg (2011). https://doi.org/10.1007/978-3-642-19571-6_13
15. Brakerski, Z., Langlois, A., Peikert, C., Regev, O., Stehlé, D.: Classical hardness of learning with errors. In: Symposium on Theory of Computing - STOC 2013, pp. 575–584. ACM (2013). https://doi.org/10.1145/2488608.2488680
16. Brakerski, Z., Vaikuntanathan, V.: Efficient fully homomorphic encryption from (standard) LWE. SIAM J. Comput. **43**(2), 831–871 (2014). https://doi.org/10.1137/120868669. (Prelim. version in FOCS 2011)
17. Brakerski, Z., Vaikuntanathan, V.: Lattice-based FHE as secure as PKE. In: Innovations in Theoretical Computer Science - ITCS 2014, pp. 1–12. ACM (2014). https://doi.org/10.1145/2554797.2554799
18. Camenisch, J., Lysyanskaya, A.: An efficient system for non-transferable anonymous credentials with optional anonymity revocation. In: Pfitzmann, B. (ed.) EUROCRYPT 2001. LNCS, vol. 2045, pp. 93–118. Springer, Heidelberg (2001). https://doi.org/10.1007/3-540-44987-6_7
19. Canetti, R., Lin, H., Tessaro, S., Vaikuntanathan, V.: Obfuscation of probabilistic circuits and applications. In: Dodis, Y., Nielsen, J.B. (eds.) TCC 2015. LNCS, vol. 9015, pp. 468–497. Springer, Heidelberg (2015). https://doi.org/10.1007/978-3-662-46497-7_19
20. Cheon, J.H., Kim, A., Kim, M., Song, Y.: Homomorphic encryption for arithmetic of approximate numbers. In: Takagi, T., Peyrin, T. (eds.) ASIACRYPT 2017. LNCS, vol. 10624, pp. 409–437. Springer, Cham (2017). https://doi.org/10.1007/978-3-319-70694-8_15
21. Chillotti, I., Gama, N., Georgieva, M., Izabachène, M.: TFHE: fast fully homomorphic encryption over the torus. J. Cryptol. **33**(1), 34–91 (2020). https://doi.org/10.1007/s00145-019-09319-x
22. TU Darmstadt Lattice Challenge. https://www.latticechallenge.org/

23. Ducas, L., Micciancio, D.: FHEW: bootstrapping homomorphic encryption in less than a second. In: Oswald, E., Fischlin, M. (eds.) EUROCRYPT 2015. LNCS, vol. 9056, pp. 617–640. Springer, Heidelberg (2015). https://doi.org/10.1007/978-3-662-46800-5_24
24. Fan, J., Vercauteren, F.: Somewhat practical fully homomorphic encryption. IACR Cryptology ePrint Archive, p. 144 (2012). http://eprint.iacr.org/2012/144
25. Gama, N., Izabachène, M., Nguyen, P.Q., Xie, X.: Structural lattice reduction: generalized worst-case to average-case reductions and homomorphic cryptosystems. In: Fischlin, M., Coron, J.-S. (eds.) EUROCRYPT 2016. LNCS, vol. 9666, pp. 528–558. Springer, Heidelberg (2016). https://doi.org/10.1007/978-3-662-49896-5_19
26. Gay, R., Pass, R.: Indistinguishability obfuscation from circular security. In: Symposium on Theory of Computing - STOC 2021, pp. 736–749. ACM (2021). https://doi.org/10.1145/3406325.3451070
27. Genise, N., Micciancio, D.: Faster Gaussian sampling for trapdoor lattices with arbitrary modulus. In: Nielsen, J.B., Rijmen, V. (eds.) EUROCRYPT 2018. LNCS, vol. 10820, pp. 174–203. Springer, Cham (2018). https://doi.org/10.1007/978-3-319-78381-9_7
28. Genise, N., Micciancio, D., Polyakov, Y.: Building an efficient lattice gadget toolkit: Subgaussian sampling and more. In: Ishai, Y., Rijmen, V. (eds.) EUROCRYPT 2019. LNCS, vol. 11477, pp. 655–684. Springer, Cham (2019). https://doi.org/10.1007/978-3-030-17656-3_23
29. Gentry, C.: Fully homomorphic encryption using ideal lattices. In: Symposium on Theory of Computing - STOC 2009, pp. 169–178. ACM (2009). https://doi.org/10.1145/1536414.1536440
30. Gentry, C., Peikert, C., Vaikuntanathan, V.: Trapdoors for hard lattices and new cryptographic constructions. In: Symposium on Theory of Computing - STOC 2008, pp. 197–206. ACM (2008). https://doi.org/10.1145/1374376.1374407
31. Gentry, C., Sahai, A., Waters, B.: Homomorphic encryption from learning with errors: conceptually-simpler, asymptotically-faster, attribute-based. In: Canetti, R., Garay, J.A. (eds.) CRYPTO 2013. LNCS, vol. 8042, pp. 75–92. Springer, Heidelberg (2013). https://doi.org/10.1007/978-3-642-40041-4_5
32. Goldwasser, S., Kalai, Y.T., Peikert, C., Vaikuntanathan, V.: Robustness of the learning with errors assumption. In: Innovations in Computer Science - ICS 2010, pp. 230–240. Tsinghua University Press (2010). http://conference.iiis.tsinghua.edu.cn/ICS2010/content/papers/19.html
33. Goldwasser, S., Micali, S.: Probabilistic encryption. J. Comput. Syst. Sci. **28**(2), 270–299 (1984). https://doi.org/10.1016/0022-0000(84)90070-9
34. Goyal, R., Koppula, V., Waters, B.: Separating IND-CPA and circular security for unbounded length key cycles. In: Fehr, S. (ed.) PKC 2017. LNCS, vol. 10174, pp. 232–246. Springer, Heidelberg (2017). https://doi.org/10.1007/978-3-662-54365-8_10
35. Goyal, R., Koppula, V., Waters, B.: Separating semantic and circular security for symmetric-key bit encryption from the learning with errors assumption. In: Coron, J.-S., Nielsen, J.B. (eds.) EUROCRYPT 2017. LNCS, vol. 10211, pp. 528–557. Springer, Cham (2017). https://doi.org/10.1007/978-3-319-56614-6_18
36. Hiromasa, R., Abe, M., Okamoto, T.: Packing messages and optimizing bootstrapping in GSW-FHE. In: Katz, J. (ed.) PKC 2015. LNCS, vol. 9020, pp. 699–715. Springer, Heidelberg (2015). https://doi.org/10.1007/978-3-662-46447-2_31
37. Hiromasa, R., Abe, M., Okamoto, T.: Packing messages and optimizing bootstrapping in GSW-FHE. IEICE Trans. Fundam. Electron. Commun. Comput. Sci. **99-A**(1), 73–82 (2016). https://doi.org/10.1587/transfun.E99.A.73

38. Hopkins, S., Jain, A., Lin, H.: Counterexamples to new circular security assumptions underlying iO. In: Malkin, T., Peikert, C. (eds.) CRYPTO 2021. LNCS, vol. 12826, pp. 673–700. Springer, Cham (2021). https://doi.org/10.1007/978-3-030-84245-1_23
39. Jain, A., Lin, H., Sahai, A.: Indistinguishability obfuscation from well-founded assumptions. In: Symposium on Theory of Computing - STOC 2021, pp. 60–73. ACM (2021). https://doi.org/10.1145/3406325.3451093
40. Jain, A., Lin, H., Sahai, A.: Indistinguishability obfuscation from LPN over $\mathbb{F}_p$, DLIN, and PRGs in NC0. In: Dunkelman, O., Dziembowski, S. (eds.) Advances in Cryptology - EUROCRYPT 2022. LNCS, vol. 13275, pp. 670–699. Springer, Cham (2022). https://doi.org/10.1007/978-3-031-06944-4_23
41. Kaliski, B.: Announcement of RSA factoring challenge (1991). https://groups.google.com/u/1/g/sci.crypt/c/AA7M9qWWx3w/m/EkrsR69CDqIJ
42. Koppula, V., Ramchen, K., Waters, B.: Separations in circular security for arbitrary length key cycles. In: Dodis, Y., Nielsen, J.B. (eds.) TCC 2015. LNCS, vol. 9015, pp. 378–400. Springer, Heidelberg (2015). https://doi.org/10.1007/978-3-662-46497-7_15
43. Koppula, V., Waters, B.: Circular security separations for arbitrary length cycles from LWE. In: Robshaw, M., Katz, J. (eds.) CRYPTO 2016. LNCS, vol. 9815, pp. 681–700. Springer, Heidelberg (2016). https://doi.org/10.1007/978-3-662-53008-5_24
44. Li, B., Micciancio, D.: On the security of homomorphic encryption on approximate numbers. In: Canteaut, A., Standaert, F.-X. (eds.) EUROCRYPT 2021. LNCS, vol. 12696, pp. 648–677. Springer, Cham (2021). https://doi.org/10.1007/978-3-030-77870-5_23
45. Li, B., Micciancio, D., Schultz, M., Sorrell, J.: Securing approximate homomorphic encryption using differential privacy. In: Dodis, Y., Shrimpton, T. (eds.) Advanced in Cryptology - CRYPTO 2022. LNCS, vol. 13507, pp. 560–589. Springer, Cham (2022). https://doi.org/10.1007/978-3-031-15802-5_20
46. Micciancio, D.: Improving lattice based cryptosystems using the Hermite normal form. In: Silverman, J.H. (ed.) CaLC 2001. LNCS, vol. 2146, pp. 126–145. Springer, Heidelberg (2001). https://doi.org/10.1007/3-540-44670-2_11
47. Micciancio, D.: Computational soundness, co-induction, and encryption cycles. In: Gilbert, H. (ed.) EUROCRYPT 2010. LNCS, vol. 6110, pp. 362–380. Springer, Heidelberg (2010). https://doi.org/10.1007/978-3-642-13190-5_19
48. Micciancio, D.: On the hardness of learning with errors with binary secrets. Theory Comput. **14**(1), 1–17 (2018). https://doi.org/10.4086/toc.2018.v014a013
49. Micciancio, D., Mol, P.: Pseudorandom knapsacks and the sample complexity of LWE search-to-decision reductions. In: Rogaway, P. (ed.) CRYPTO 2011. LNCS, vol. 6841, pp. 465–484. Springer, Heidelberg (2011). https://doi.org/10.1007/978-3-642-22792-9_26
50. Micciancio, D., Peikert, C.: Trapdoors for lattices: simpler, tighter, faster, smaller. In: Pointcheval, D., Johansson, T. (eds.) EUROCRYPT 2012. LNCS, vol. 7237, pp. 700–718. Springer, Heidelberg (2012). https://doi.org/10.1007/978-3-642-29011-4_41
51. Micciancio, D., Polyakov, Y.: Bootstrapping in FHEW-like cryptosystems. In: Workshop on Encrypted Computing & Applied Homomorphic Cryptography - WAHC 2021, pp. 17–28. ACM (2021). https://doi.org/10.1145/3474366.3486924
52. Micciancio, D., Regev, O.: Worst-case to average-case reductions based on Gaussian measures. SIAM J. Comput. **37**(1), 267–302 (2007). https://doi.org/10.1137/S0097539705447360

53. Micciancio, D., Walter, M.: On the bit security of cryptographic primitives. In: Nielsen, J.B., Rijmen, V. (eds.) EUROCRYPT 2018. LNCS, vol. 10820, pp. 3–28. Springer, Cham (2018). https://doi.org/10.1007/978-3-319-78381-9_1
54. Peikert, C.: Public-key cryptosystems from the worst-case shortest vector problem. In: Symposium on Theory of Computing - STOC 2009, pp. 333–342. ACM (2009). https://doi.org/10.1145/1536414.1536461
55. Peikert, C., Vaikuntanathan, V., Waters, B.: A framework for efficient and composable oblivious transfer. In: Wagner, D. (ed.) CRYPTO 2008. LNCS, vol. 5157, pp. 554–571. Springer, Heidelberg (2008). https://doi.org/10.1007/978-3-540-85174-5_31
56. Regev, O.: On lattices, learning with errors, random linear codes, and cryptography. J. ACM **56**(6), 34:1–34:40 (2009). https://doi.org/10.1145/1568318.1568324
57. Rothblum, R.: Homomorphic encryption: from private-key to public-key. In: Ishai, Y. (ed.) TCC 2011. LNCS, vol. 6597, pp. 219–234. Springer, Heidelberg (2011). https://doi.org/10.1007/978-3-642-19571-6_14
58. Wee, H., Wichs, D.: Candidate obfuscation via oblivious LWE sampling. In: Canteaut, A., Standaert, F.-X. (eds.) EUROCRYPT 2021. LNCS, vol. 12698, pp. 127–156. Springer, Cham (2021). https://doi.org/10.1007/978-3-030-77883-5_5

Faster Amortized FHEW Bootstrapping Using Ring Automorphisms

Gabrielle De Micheli[1], Duhyeong Kim[2], Daniele Micciancio[1](✉), and Adam Suhl[1]

[1] UC San Diego, San Diego, USA
daniele@cs.ucsd.edu
[2] Intel Labs, Hillsboro, OR, USA

Abstract. Amortized bootstrapping offers a way to simultaneously refresh many ciphertexts of a fully homomorphic encryption scheme, at a total cost comparable to that of refreshing a single ciphertext. An amortization method for FHEW-style cryptosystems was first proposed by (Micciancio and Sorrell, ICALP 2018), who showed that the amortized cost of bootstrapping n FHEW-style ciphertexts can be reduced from $\tilde{O}(n)$ basic cryptographic operations to just $\tilde{O}(n^{\epsilon})$, for any constant $\epsilon > 0$. However, despite the promising asymptotic saving, the algorithm was rather impractical due to a large constant (exponential in $1/\epsilon$) hidden in the asymptotic notation. In this work, we propose an alternative amortized bootstrapping method with much smaller overhead, still achieving $O(n^{\epsilon})$ asymptotic amortized cost, but with a hidden constant that is only linear in $1/\epsilon$, and with reduced noise growth. This is achieved following the general strategy of (Micciancio and Sorrell), but replacing their use of the Nussbaumer transform, with a much more practical Number Theoretic Transform, with multiplication by twiddle factors implemented using ring automorphisms. A key technical ingredient to do this is a new "scheme switching" technique proposed in this paper which may be of independent interest.

Keywords: Fully homomorphic encryption · Ring LWE · amortized bootstrapping

1 Introduction

Fully Homomorphic Encryption (FHE) schemes support the evaluation of arbitrary programs on encrypted data. Since a first solution to the problem was proposed in [8], FHE has become both a central tool in the theory of cryptography, and an attractive cryptographic primitive to be used to secure privacy sensitive applications. Still, improving the efficiency of these schemes is a major obstacle to the use of FHE in practice, and a very active area of research.

All reasonably efficient currently known constructions of FHE are based on the "Ring Learning With Errors" (RingLWE) problem [19,22]. There are two main approaches to design FHE schemes based on Ring LWE: the one pioneered

Q. Tang and V. Teague (Eds.): PKC 2024, LNCS 14604, pp. 322–353, 2024.
https://doi.org/10.1007/978-3-031-57728-4_11

by the BGV cryptosystem and its variants (e.g., see [4,9,10]) and the one put forward by the FHEW cryptosystem and follow up work (e.g., see [3,5,7].) In BGV, ring operations are directly used to implement (componentwise) addition and multiplication of ciphertexts encrypting *vectors* of values. The ability to simultaneously work on all the components of a vector (at the cost of a single cryptographic operation) makes these schemes very powerful. The downside is that they also require fairly large parameters, leading to stronger security assumptions (namely, the hardness of approximating lattice problems within superpolynomial factors), a very slow bootstrapping procedure, and complex programming model. By constrast, in FHEW, ciphertexts are simple LWE encryptions (which offer native support only for homomorphic addition,) while Ring LWE is used only internally, to implement a special "functional bootstrapping" procedure that, given an encryption of m, produces a (bootstrapped) encryption of $f(m)$, for a given function f. The combination of linearly homomorphic LWE addition and functional bootstrapping still allows to perform arbitrary computations: for example, as originally done in [7], one can represent bits $x, y \in \{0,1\}$ as integers modulo 4, and then implement a (universal) NAND boolean gate as an addition followed by a (functional bootstrapping) rounding operation $\lfloor (x + y + 2 \bmod 4)/2 \rfloor$. The FHEW approach has several attractive features: (1) since bootstrapping is performed after every operation, gates can be arbitrarily composed, leading to a very simple and easy to use programming model; (2) since we only need to bootstrap basic LWE ciphertexts supporting a single homomorphic addition, the scheme can be instantiated with much smaller parameters; (3) in turn, this leads to weaker security assumptions (hardness of approximating lattice problems within polynomial factors), and substantially simpler and faster bootstrapping, orders of magnitude faster than BGV.

However, the lower speeds of BGV bootstrapping are largely compensated by its ability to encrypt and operate on many values (encrypted as a vector) at the same time, allowing, for example, to simultaneously bootstrap thousands of ciphertexts. This drastically reduces the *amortized* cost of BGV bootstrapping, making it preferable to FHEW in terms of overall performance in many settings.

In an effort to bridge the gap between the two approaches, a method to amortize FHEW bootstrapping was proposed in [21]. The suggested method consists in combining several (say n) FHEW/LWE input ciphertexts into a single RingLWE ciphertext, and then perform FHEW-style bootstrapping on a single RingLWE ciphertext. This results in a major asymptotic performance improvement, reducing the amortized cost of FHEW bootstrapping from $O(n)$ homomorphic multiplications to just $O(n^\epsilon)$, for any fixed constant $\epsilon > 0$. Unfortunately, the method of [21] is rather far from being practical, due in large part to a large constant $2^{O(1/\epsilon)}$ hidden in the asymptotic notation.

Challenges, Results and Techniques. In this paper we propose a variant of the bootstrapping procedure of [21] with similar asymptotics, but substantially smaller multiplicative overhead. In particular, we reduce the amortized cost of FHEW bootstrapping from $2^{O(1/\epsilon)} \cdot n^\epsilon$ to just $(1/\epsilon) \cdot n^\epsilon$. In other words, we achieve a similar asymptotic cost $O(n^\epsilon)$ (for any constant $\epsilon > 0$), but with an exponentially smaller constant hidden in the asymptotic notation.

The main challenge faced by [21] was the use of RingGSW registers to implement the homomorphic fourier transform required to bootstrap a RingLWE ciphertext. These registers, introduced in [7], encrypt messages in the exponent as X^m. This allows to implement homomorphic addition using some form of ciphertext multiplication $X^{m_0} \cdot X^{m_1} = X^{m_0+m_1}$, but other homomorphic operations required by FFT/NTT algorithms (like subtraction and constant multiplication by so-called "twiddle factors") are much harder, seemingly requiring homomorphic division and exponentiation on ciphertexts. This is addressed in [21] by using the Nussbaumer transform, a variant of the FFT/NTT algorithm that does not require multiplication by twiddle factors. Unfortunately, the use of the Nussbaumer transform in [21] also introduces a $2^{O(1/\epsilon)}$ factor in the running time, making the algorithm impractical.

Methods to perform homomorphic multiplication in the exponent (i.e., exponentiation by a constant) are known, using automorphisms, and have been used in connection to the bootstrapping of FHEW-like cryptosystems [3,15], but they only work for RingLWE ciphertexts, making them inapplicable to the RingGSW ciphertexts required by [21]. In this paper we introduce three technical innovations that allow to overcome these issues:

We introduce a new RingLWE-to-RingGSW "scheme switching" procedure, which allows us to transform RingLWE ciphertexts into equivalent RingGSW ones. The method is of independent interest and may find applications elsewhere. Note that a similar technique also appears in [14].

We design a new variant of the amortized FHEW bootstrapping of [21] that operates on RingLWE registers, rather than RingGSW. This allow us to implement multiplication by arbitrary twiddle factors using the automorphism techniques of [3,15], and instantiate the amortized FHEW bootstrapping framework with a standard (homomorphic) FFT/NTT computation, which carries a much smaller overhead. Then, when RingGSW registers are required, we resort to our scheme switching procedure to convert RingLWE to RingGSW on the fly.

We replace the power-of-two cyclotomic rings [7,15,21] and circulant rings [3] used by previous FHEW bootstrapping algorithms, with prime cyclotomics. This requires a new error analysis for prime cyclotomics, which we describe in this paper. (Error analysis for power-of-two cyclotomic and circulant rings is comparatively much easier.) This speeds up and simplifies various steps of our bootstrapping procedure, e.g., by supporting a standard radix 2 FFT (as opposed to the radix 3 Nussbaumer transform of [21]), and completely bypassing the problem that automorphisms only exists for invertible exponents [15].

One important problem that still remains open is that of reducing the noise growth in amortized FHEW bootstrapping. Just as in previous work [21], the ciphertext noise of our bootstrapping procedure increases multiplicatively at every level of the FFT/NTT computation. In order to keep the RingLWE noise (and underlying lattice inapproximability factors) polynomial, this requires to limit the recursive depth of the FFT/NTT algorithms to a constant. This is the reason why both [21] and our work only achieve $O(n^\epsilon)$ amortized complexity, rather than the $O(\log n)$ one would expect from a full ($O(\log n)$-depth) FFT algorithm. In practice, this limits the recursive depth to a small constant, typically just two levels or so. Further improving amortized FHEW bootstrapping, allowing the execution of a homomorphic FFT with $O(\log n)$ levels is left as an open problem.

Related and Concurrent Work: Ring automorphisms have been used in many other works aimed at improving the efficiency of lattice cryptography based on the RingLWE problem, most notably the evaluation of linear functions in HElib [13] and algebraic trace computations [2]. Our use of automorphisms is most closely related to [15], which recently used them to improve the performance of FHEW (sequential, non-amortized) bootstrapping. In a concurrent and independent work [11], an algorithm very similar to ours is presented. The algorithm achieves essentially the same results, improving the cost of amortized FHEW bootstrapping from $2^{O(1/\epsilon)} \cdot n^{1/\epsilon}$ to $(1/\epsilon) \cdot n^{1/\epsilon}$. The overall structure of the algorithm is very similar, using automorphisms to replace the Nussbaumer transform in [21] with a standard FFT. However, the algorithms differ in some technical details. For example, while [11] uses the circular rings [3], we use prime cyclotomics, which results in marginally smaller ciphertexts. Another difference is that while [11] extends the automorphism multiplication technique to work directly on RingGSW ciphertexts, we center our FFT algorithm aroung RingLWE registers (which are smaller than RingGSW by a factor 2) and convert them to RingGSW only when necessary using our new scheme switching technique. This allows us to exploit RLWE'-RGSW multiplications instead of RGSW-RGSW multiplications during the homomorphic inverse FFT, which gives a 2x performance improvement compared to RGSW key-switching as used in [11].

At Eurocrypt 2023, Liu and Wang introduced a new algebraic framework for batch homomorphic computation based on the tensoring of three rings [16]. Their new framework is also used in the context of bootstrapping algorithms [17] to improve the efficiency of the amortized bootstrapping algorithm following the Nussbaumer technique from [21], achieving an amortized bootstrapping cost of $\tilde{O}(1)$ FHE multiplications within a polynomial modulus. We compare our algorithm to theirs in Sect. 5.4.

More recently still, another line a work from Liu and Wang [18] (Asiacrypt 2023) obtained the asymptotic results of [16,17] while also achieving concrete efficiency by exploiting both BFV and LWE ciphertexts. Asymptotically, [18] requires a super-polynomial modulus whereas our work considers only polynomial modulus. Considering a super-polynomial modulus would allow to increase the recursive depth in our work but would unlikely be effective in practice.

2 Preliminaries

2.1 Cyclotomic Rings and Embeddings

Given a positive integer N, the Nth cyclotomic polynomial is defined as $\Phi_N(X) = \prod_{i \in \mathbb{Z}_N^*}(X - \omega_N^i)$ for $\omega_N = e^{2\pi i/N} \in \mathbb{C}$ the complex N^{th} principal root of unity.

The Nth cyclotomic ring is defined as $\mathcal{R}_N = \mathbb{Z}[X]/(\Phi_N(X))$. In this work, we will consider the dth cyclotomic ring modulo q, for d a power-of-2, defined as $\mathcal{R}_d = \mathbb{Z}_q[X]/\Phi_d(X) \simeq \mathbb{Z}_q^{\phi(d)}$. Each element of this ring corresponds to a polynomial $\mathbf{a} \in \mathcal{R}_d$ of degree less than $\phi(d)$ and with coefficients taken modulo q. There exist various ways of representing a ring element. One can first map the polynomial $\mathbf{a}(X) = \sum_{i \leq \phi(d)} a_i \cdot X^i$ to its vector of coefficients $(a_1, a_2 \cdots, a_{\phi(d)}) \in \mathbb{Z}_q^{\phi(d)}$. This is known as the coefficient embedding. The norm of any ring element then refers to the ℓ_2 norm of the corresponding vector in the coefficient embedding.

Another representation of a ring element is with its canonical embedding $\sigma : K \to \mathbb{C}^n$ which endows K, the dth cyclotomic number field, with a geometry. Note that the ring of integers of K corresponds to the dth cyclotomic ring $\mathbb{Z}[X]/\Phi_d(X)$. We know that K has exactly $\phi(d)$ ring homomorphisms, also called embeddings, $\sigma_i : K \to \mathbb{C}$. The canonical embedding is then defined as the map $\sigma(a) = (\sigma_i(a))_{i \in \mathbb{Z}_d^*}$ for $a \in K$. The norm usually considered when using the canonical embedding is the ℓ_∞ norm $||\sigma(a)||_\infty = \max_i |\sigma_i(a)|$. More generally, for any $a \in K$ and any $p \in [1, \infty]$, the ℓ_p norm is defined as $||a||_p = ||\sigma(p)||_p$. Since the σ_i are ring homomorphisms, we then have for any $a, b \in K$ the inequality $||a \cdot b||_p \leq ||a||_\infty \cdot ||b||_p$.

Working with prime cyclotomics, or more generally with non-power-of-two cyclotomics can be rather cumbersome, in particular, when considering the canonical embedding and not just the coefficient embedding. We know that any two embeddings are related to each other by a fixed linear transformation on $\mathbb{R}^d$. For power-of-2 cyclotomics, the transformation is even an isometry and thus the coefficient and canonical embeddings are equivalent up to a $\sqrt{d}$ factor. In this work, we will be working with both $\mathcal{R}_d$, the dth cyclotomic ring modulo q for which we will use the notation $\mathcal{R}_{in}$ and the qth cyclotomic modulo Q for a prime q and a positive integer $Q > 0$, which we will denote $\mathcal{R}_{reg}$. The latter is a prime cyclotomic ring where the two embeddings cannot be easily interchanged. This will affect the error growth analysis as we later explain in Sect. 3.2.

2.2 Encryption Schemes and Operations

We recall definitions and notations for the standard LWE encryption scheme used in the bootstrapping algorithm. We also extend our description to the ring version of LWE and introduce two related schemes, GadgetRLWE and RGSW, both used in our algorithm.

LWE: Consider some positive integers n and q. Let $\mathbf{sk} \leftarrow \chi$ be a secret key sampled from a distribution χ and $m \in \mathbb{Z}$ a message. The LWE encryption of the message m under the secret key $\mathbf{sk}$ is given by

$$\mathrm{LWE}_{q,\mathbf{sk}}(m) = [\mathbf{a}^T, b] \in \mathbb{Z}_q^{1 \times (n+1)},$$

where $\mathbf{a} \leftarrow \mathbb{Z}_q^n$, $b = -\mathbf{a} \cdot \mathbf{sk} + e + m \in \mathbb{Z}_q$ and $e \leftarrow \chi'$ is the error, sampled from a distribution χ', and ciphertexts are represented as *row* vectors.

RLWE: The ring version of LWE considers the ring $\mathcal{R}_q$. Let $\mathbf{sk} \leftarrow \chi$ be a secret key sampled from a distribution χ and $\mathbf{m} \in \mathcal{R}_q$ a message. The RLWE encryption of the message $\mathbf{m}$ under the secret key $\mathbf{sk}$ is given by

$$\text{RLWE}_{q,\mathbf{sk}}(\mathbf{m}) = [\mathbf{a}, \mathbf{b}] \in {\mathcal{R}_q}^{1\times 2},$$

where $\mathbf{a} \leftarrow \mathcal{R}_q$ and $\mathbf{b} = -\mathbf{a}\cdot\mathbf{sk} + \mathbf{e} + \mathbf{m}$ and $e_i \leftarrow \chi'$ for each coefficent e_i of the error. If context is clear, we do not specify the modulus q or the secret key $\mathbf{sk}$.

Gadget RLWE or RLWE'. Consider a gadget vector $\mathbf{v} = (v_0, v_1, \cdots, v_{k-1})$. Gadget RLWE or equivalently refered to as RLWE' is expressed as a vector of RLWE ciphertexts of the form

$$\text{RLWE}'_{\mathbf{sk}}(\mathbf{m}) = (\text{RLWE}_{\mathbf{sk}}(v_0\cdot\mathbf{m}), \text{RLWE}_{\mathbf{sk}}(v_1\cdot\mathbf{m}), \cdots, \text{RLWE}_{\mathbf{sk}}(v_{k-1}\cdot\mathbf{m})) \in R_q^{k\times 2}$$

i.e., matrices with k rows, each representing a basic RLWE ciphertext. We remark that RLWE ciphertext can be regarded as a special case of RLWE$'$ instantiated with a trivial gadget $\vec{v} = (1)$. So, anything we say about RLWE$'$ applies to RLWE as well.

RingGSW. Given a message $\mathbf{m} \in \mathcal{R}_q$, we define

$$\text{RGSW}_{\mathbf{sk}}(\mathbf{m}) = (\text{RLWE}'_{\mathbf{sk}}(\mathbf{sk}\cdot\mathbf{m}), \text{RLWE}'_{\mathbf{sk}}(\mathbf{m})) \in {\mathcal{R}_q}^{2k\times 2}.$$

We now summarize the operations that can be done with the different schemes presented above and focus in particular on the operations used in our algorithm. The main operation in our algorithm that serves as a building block for other operations is the scalar multiplication by arbitrary ring elements. In order to compute this multiplication, one uses RLWE' with gadget vector $\mathbf{v} = (v_0, v_1, \cdots, v_{k-1})$. The scalar multiplication is denoted as $\mathcal{R} \odot \text{RLWE}'$ and corresponds to $\odot : \mathcal{R} \times \text{RLWE}' \to \text{RLWE}$ defined as

$$\begin{aligned}\mathbf{t} \odot \text{RLWE}'_{\mathbf{sk}}(\mathbf{m}) &:= \sum_{i=0}^{k-1} \mathbf{t}_i \cdot \text{RLWE}_{\mathbf{sk}}(v_i\cdot\mathbf{m}) \\ &= \text{RLWE}_{\mathbf{sk}}\left(\sum_{i=0}^{k-1} v_i\cdot\mathbf{t}_i\cdot\mathbf{m}\right) = \text{RLWE}_{\mathbf{sk}}(\mathbf{t}\cdot\mathbf{m})\end{aligned}$$

where $\sum_i v_i\mathbf{t}_i = \mathbf{t}$ is the gadget decomposion of $\mathbf{t}$ into "short" vectors $\mathbf{t}_i$, for an appropriate notion of "short" depending on the gadget $\mathbf{v}$. Each operation performed with ciphertexts increases the error. When performing many of these operations, as in our bootstrapping algorithm, it is crucial to keep track of the error growth. More details will be given in Sect. 3.2. For now, we simply state that each error e_i in $\text{RLWE}_{\mathbf{sk}}(v_i\cdot\mathbf{m})$, after the scalar multiplication, becomes $\sum_{i=0}^{k-1}\mathbf{t}_i\cdot\mathbf{e}_i$.

The RLWE and RLWE$'$ schemes only support multiplication by constant values. In order to obtain multiplication by ciphertexts, we need to consider the

RGSW scheme. Let us now consider the multiplication $\star : \text{RLWE} \times \text{RGSW} \to \text{RLWE}$ defined as

$$\begin{aligned}\text{RLWE}_{\mathbf{sk}}(\mathbf{m}_1) \star \text{RGSW}_{\mathbf{sk}}(\mathbf{m}_2) &:= \mathbf{a} \odot \text{RLWE}'_{\mathbf{sk}}(\mathbf{sk} \cdot \mathbf{m}_2) + \mathbf{b} \odot \text{RLWE}'_{\mathbf{sk}}(\mathbf{m}_2) \\ &= \text{RLWE}_{\mathbf{sk}}(\mathbf{a} \cdot \mathbf{sk} \cdot \mathbf{m}_2 + \mathbf{b} \cdot \mathbf{m}_2) \\ &= \text{RLWE}_{\mathbf{sk}}(\mathbf{m}_1 \cdot \mathbf{m}_2 + \mathbf{e}_1 \cdot \mathbf{m}_2)\end{aligned}$$

for $\text{RLWE}(\mathbf{m}_1) := (\mathbf{a}, \mathbf{b})$. The output of this multiplication is an RLWE ciphertext encrypting the message $\mathbf{m}_1 \cdot \mathbf{m}_2 + \mathbf{e} \cdot \mathbf{m}_2$. The error thus additively increases by $\mathbf{e}_1 \cdot \mathbf{m}_2$. If the error term $\mathbf{e}_1 \cdot \mathbf{m}_2$ is sufficiently small, then this approximately results in an RLWE encryption of the product of the two messages. This multiplication can be extended to RLWE′ ciphertext multiplication $\star' : \text{RLWE}' \times \text{RGSW} \to \text{RLWE}'$ defined as

$$\begin{aligned}&\text{RLWE}'_{\mathbf{sk}}(\mathbf{m}_1) \star' \text{RGSW}_{\mathbf{sk}}(\mathbf{m}_2) \\ &:= (\text{RLWE}_{\mathbf{sk}}(v_0 \cdot \mathbf{m}_1) \star \text{RGSW}_{\mathbf{sk}}(\mathbf{m}_2), \cdots, \text{RLWE}_{\mathbf{sk}}(v_{k-1} \cdot \mathbf{m}_1) \star \text{RGSW}_{\mathbf{sk}}(\mathbf{m}_2)) \\ &\approx \text{RLWE}'_{\mathbf{sk}}(\mathbf{m}_1 \cdot \mathbf{m}_2).\end{aligned}$$

Each component $\text{RLWE}_{\mathbf{sk}}(v_i \cdot \mathbf{m}_1) \star \text{RGSW}_{\mathbf{sk}}(\mathbf{m}_2)$ of the result has the same error growth as a $\star$ operation in the RLWE $\star$ RGSW case. In particular, it includes an error term $\mathbf{e}_{1,i} \cdot \mathbf{m}_2$ that requires the second message $\mathbf{m}_2$ to be small.

The $\star'$ operation corresponds to k times the $\star$ operations, and thus a total of $2k$ $\odot$ operations.

2.3 Using Ring Automorphisms

Similarly as in [15], we use ring automorphisms to perform scalar multiplication with registers. Recall that an automorphism is a bijective maps from the ring $\mathcal{R}$ to itself such that for a given $t \in \mathbb{Z}_q^*$, we have $\mathbf{a}(X) \mapsto \mathbf{a}(X^t)$.

Automorphism in RLWE *and* RLWE′*:* Consider the following RLWE ciphertext $(\mathbf{a}(X), \mathbf{b}(X))$ which encrypts a given message $\mathbf{m}(X)$ under a certain key $\mathbf{sk}$, *i.e.*, $(\mathbf{a}(X), \mathbf{b}(X)) = \text{RLWE}_{\mathbf{sk}}(\mathbf{m}(X))$. We also consider a switching key $\mathbf{ak}_t = \text{RLWE}'_{\mathbf{sk}}(\mathbf{sk}(X^t))$, which is used to map ciphertexts $[\mathbf{a}, \mathbf{b}]$ from key $\mathbf{sk}(X^t)$ to $\mathbf{sk}$. Given an automorphism $\psi_t : \mathcal{R} \to \mathcal{R}$ such that $\mathbf{a}(X) \mapsto \mathbf{a}(X^t)$, we recall the procedure `Evalauto` given in [15]:

1. apply ψ_t to each of the RLWE components. One obtains $(\mathbf{a}(X^t), \mathbf{b}(X^t)) = \text{RLWE}_{\mathbf{sk}(X^t)}(\mathbf{m}(X^t))$
2. apply a key switching function $[\mathbf{a}, \mathbf{b}] \mapsto \mathbf{a} \odot \mathbf{ak}_t + [\mathbf{0}, \mathbf{b}]$ to obtain a ciphertext $\text{RLWE}_{\mathbf{sk}(X)}(\mathbf{m}(X^t))$

The same application can be done on RLWE′ ciphertexts. The only difference comes during the second step where we require k key switching, one for each RLWE ciphertext. The only $\mathcal{R} \odot \text{RLWE}'$ operation comes from key switching. Hence, for automorphism on RLWE, we have a single $\mathcal{R} \odot \text{RLWE}'$ operation and when considering automorphisms on RLWE′ we have k $\mathcal{R} \odot \text{RLWE}'$ operations, where k is the length of the gadget.

2.4 Homomorphic Operations on Registers

Following the FHEW framework, we use cryptographic registers that encrypt a $\mathbb{Z}_q$ element "in the exponent". In other words, a register storing $m \in \mathbb{Z}_q$ is an encryption of $X^m \in \mathcal{R}_{reg}$. In our algorithm, the encryption scheme will sometimes be RLWE′ and sometimes RGSW. Some operations require one scheme or the other. In order to perform some of these operations, we will need to scheme-switch from RLWE′ to RGSW. We describe our scheme-switching technique in Sect. 3.1. In our bootstrapping algorithm, we will primarily use three operations on registers, *i.e.*, either RLWE′ or RGSW ciphertexts. We have already mentioned these operations and recall them now:

- $\star'$: RLWE′ × RGSW → RLWE′ multiplications: this operation allows to multiply two ciphertexts, which in the exponent acts like and addition.
- Scheme-switching: this operation converts an RLWE′ register into an RGSW register.
- Automorphisms: this operation allows us to multiply the exponent of a RLWE′ ciphertext by some (known) value, and correponds to multiplication by a constant.

Note that automorphisms can only operate on RLWE′ registers, not an RGSW ones. (This is because RGSW does not directly support the key switching operation required by the second step of the homomorphic automorphic application algorithm. See Sect. 3.1 for details.) On the other hand, multiplication requires one of the two registers to be in RGSW format. The scheme switching operation is used to combine the two operations, keeping all registers in RLWE′ form, and convert them to RGSW only when required for multiplication.

In order to analyse the performance and the correctness of our algorithm we will analyse these three operations in terms of number of $\mathcal{R} \odot$ RLWE′ operations needed to compute them and the related error growth (see Table 2).

2.5 Standard and Primitive (Inverse) FFT

We only mention in this paper some relevant facts about FFT algorithms that are useful for our algorithm. Note that when refering to FFT and related algorithms, we actually refer to the Number Theoretic Transform (NTT) algorithm.

An FFT algorithm can either evaluate a polynomial at all N^{th} roots of unity for a given N or only the primitive ones. The former case is refered to as a standard/cyclic FFT whereas the latter case is called a primitive/cyclotomic FFT. In the case of a standard FFT, the inverse direction reconstructs from these evaluations a polynomial mod $X^N - 1$. When multiplying two polynomials $a(x)$ and $z(x)$ modulo a cyclotomic polynomial, using a standard FFT (and its inverse) requires a "final reduction" step to take polynomials modulo $(X^N - 1)$ to polynomials modulo $\Phi_N(X)$. This "final reduction" increases the multiplicative depth of the circuit and, in our case, prevents some useful optimizations (namely, using RLWE instead of RLWE′ in the last FFT layer as we will explain in Sect. 4.2). We can avoid the final reduction step by using a primitive/cyclotomic

FFT, which we recall only evaluates the polynomials at the primitive N^{th} roots of unity ω^i for $i \in \mathbb{Z}_N^*$. The inverse FFT then reconstructs from these evaluations a polynomial modulo the Nth cyclotomic polynomial $\Phi_N(X)$. We note however that, unlike with a standard FFT, the forward and inverse directions are not interchangeable. We focus the rest of the discussion on the case of power-of-two cyclotomics (which is the case we will use in this paper) where $N = d = 2^{\log_2 N}$, and $\phi(d) = d/2$. For the forward direction, let $0 \leq i < \phi(d) = d/2$, and ω be a primitive d^{th} root of unity. Then the Fourier coefficients $\hat{f} := (\hat{f}_0, \hat{f}_1, ..., \hat{f}_{d/2})$ of a polynomial $f(X) = \sum_{i=0}^{d/2-1} f_i \cdot X^i \pmod{X^{d/2}+1}$ are computed as

$$\hat{f}_i := \sum_{j=0}^{d/2-1} f_j \omega^{(2i+1)j},$$

and the inverse FFT of $\hat{f}$ can be computed as

$$\hat{\hat{f}}_\ell := \frac{2}{d} \cdot \sum_{i=0}^{d/2-1} \hat{f}_i \omega^{-(2i+1)\ell} = \frac{2}{d} \cdot \omega^{-\ell} \sum_{i=0}^{d/2-1} \hat{f}_i \omega^{-2i\ell}$$

for each $0 \leq \ell < d/2$ and output $\hat{\hat{f}}(X) = \sum_{i=0}^{d/2-1} \hat{\hat{f}}_i \cdot X^i$. It is easy to verify that these operations are inverses of each other, *i.e.*, $\hat{\hat{f}} = f$. The FFT also preserves both addition and multiplication, *i.e.*, $\hat{f} + \hat{g} = \widehat{f+g}$ and $\hat{f} \circ \hat{g} = \widehat{f \cdot g}$ where $\circ$ denotes the component-wise multiplication of input vectors. Moreover, one notices that the inverse operation can be computed as a standard/cyclic length-$\phi(d)$ FFT (using ω^{-2} as the $\phi(d)^{th}$ root of unity) followed by a multiplication by a power of ω.

In this work, we mainly focus on homomorphic computation of the inverse FFT (while the forward FFT is done in cleartext), so the constant multiplication by $2/d$ becomes a (minor) computational overhead. We can easily remove this overhead by moving the constant from the inverse FFT to the forward FFT. If we move the constant $2/d$, we get

$$\mathrm{FFT}(f)_i := \frac{2}{d} \cdot \hat{f}_i = \frac{2}{d} \cdot \sum_{j=0}^{d/2-1} f_j \omega^{(2i+1)j},$$

$$\mathrm{FFT}^{-1}(\mathrm{FFT}(f))_\ell := \frac{d}{2} \cdot \widehat{\mathrm{FFT}(f)}_\ell = \sum_{i=0}^{d/2-1} \mathrm{FFT}(f)_i \omega^{-(2i+1)\ell}.$$

In this case, FFT^{-1} is still the inverse of FFT and addition is preserved in the same manner. However, note that there is a slight difference in multiplication: $\mathrm{FFT}^{-1}(\mathrm{FFT}(f) \circ \hat{g}) = \mathrm{FFT}^{-1}(\mathrm{FFT}(f \cdot g)) = f \cdot g$.

In our algorithm, we will consider partial (primitive) FFT, denoted by PFT, where instead of reducing modulo $(X - \zeta)$ (*i.e.*, evaluating the polynomials at $X = \zeta$, we reduce modulo $(X^k - \zeta)$. In this reduction, an X^i term will not interact with an X^j term unless $i \equiv j \mod k$. Hence, an equivalent description of a partial FTT is doing k FFTs in parallel, each with $1/k$ as many terms. More precisely, one FFT will operate on the terms which are 0 modulo k, one FFT on just the terms that are 1 modulo k, and so on. This also applies to the inverse direction. In our algorithm, we will thus divide by $\phi(d)/k$ and not $\phi(d)$.

2.6 Summary of Notations

We summarize the notations used throughout the paper in Table 1. For simplicity of exposition, this paper uses a standard power-of-B gadget $(1, B, B^2, \ldots, B^{d_B-1})$. In practice, this can be replaced by a CRT gadget which typically supports more efficient implementation.

Table 1. Summary of notations used in the paper

	Notation	Description
Modulus	q_{plain}	Ciphertext modulus for standard LWE
	q	Prime ciphertext modulus for input RLWE ciphertext. Plaintext modulus for registers
	Q	Ciphertext modulus used in RLWE′ / RGSW registers
Rings	$\mathcal{R}_{in}$	dth cyclotomic ring (mod q), $\frac{\mathbb{Z}_q[x]}{\Phi_d(x)} \simeq \mathbb{Z}_q^{\phi(d)}$
	d	power-of-2 degree of $\mathcal{R}_{in}$
	$\mathcal{R}_{reg}$	qth prime cyclotomic ring mod Q used by the registers
FFT	k	degree at which we stop the partial FFT
	$\phi(d)$	the number of Plain-LWE ciphertexts that are packed into an RLWE ciphertext; the number of coefficients in an $\mathcal{R}_{in}$ element; the number of coefficients in the input polynomial of the FFT; the number of registers in any layer of the IFFT; the number of registers output by the IFFT
	$N = \phi(d)/k$	the number of degree-$(k-1)$ polynomials output by the partial FFT
	$\omega \in \mathbb{Z}_q$	a primitive (d/k)th root of unity in $\mathbb{Z}_q$ for use in the FFT
	r_i	radix for FFT layer
	ℓ	number of FFT layers
Secret keys	$\mathbf{s}_p \in \mathbb{Z}_{q_{plain}}^{n_{plain}+1}$	Plain LWE secret key
	$z \in \mathcal{R}_{in}$	RLWE secret key for the input (packed) RLWE ciphertext
	$s \in \mathcal{R}_{reg}$	RGSW secret key used for registers
Gadget decomposition	B	Base for the powers-of-B gadget used in registers
	d_B	$\lceil \log_B(Q) \rceil$, the length of the PowersOfB gadget
Error variance	$\sigma^2_{\odot}$	The (expected) factor by which an $\mathcal{R}_{reg}$ $\odot$ RLWE′ operation scales up the error variance in a ciphertext
	$\sigma^2_{\odot,RGSW}$	The resulting error variance of the $\odot$ operation on each RLWE′ component of RGSW($\mathbf{m}_2$)
	$\sigma^2_{\odot,eval\_key}$	The resulting error variance of the $\odot$ operation on the evaluation key with error variance $\sigma^2_{eval\_key}$
	$\sigma^2_{\odot,aut\_key}$	The resulting error variance of the $\odot$ operation on the automorphism key $\text{RLWE}'_{\mathbf{sk}}(\psi(\mathbf{sk}))$
	σ^2_{in}	The error variance of the input to an operation

3 Novel Techniques

In this section, we introduce some novel techniques related to scheme switching and error analaysis. We first introduce a new variant of scheme-switching. We then introduce an error analysis in the context of prime cyclotomics. Indeed, our algorithm will use a prime cyclotomic for the registers, whereas common FHE schemes use power-of-2 cyclotomic rings for which the error analysis differs.

3.1 RLWE$'$ to RGSW Scheme Switching

When an automorphism is applied to a ciphertext, it modifies both the encrypted message and the encryption key. (This applies to RLWE, RLWE' and RGSW ciphertexts alike.) Therefore, in order to use automorphisms to operate homomorphically on ciphertexts, one needs a method to switch back to the original key. For RLWE and RLWE' ciphertexts, this is provided by a standard key switching operation as described in the previous section. However, for RGSW encryption, this does not quite work. The reason is that a RGSW encryption can be interpreted as a pair of RLWE' ciphertexts encrypting $\mathbf{m}$ and $\mathbf{m} \cdot \mathbf{sk}$. The first component does not pose any problem, as it can be transformed using a standard RLWE' key switching operation. However, key switching cannot be directly applied to the second component, because it encrypts a *key-dependent* message $\mathbf{m} \cdot \mathbf{sk}$. So, RGSW key-switching would require not only to modify the encryption key, but also to change the message from $\mathbf{m} \cdot \mathbf{sk}$ to $\mathbf{m} \cdot \mathbf{sk'}$, where $\mathbf{sk'}$ is the new key. For this reason, key switching (and homomorphic automorphism evaluation), is directly applicable only to RLWE and RLWE' ciphertexts. On the other hand, RGSW ciphertexts are required to perform homomorphic multiplications when both multiplicands are encrypted. We address this problem by providing a method to convert RLWE' ciphertexts to RGSW ones, which we call *scheme switching*. Let us now describe how this is done.

Since $\mathrm{RGSW}_{\mathbf{sk}}(\mathbf{m}) = (\mathrm{RLWE}'_{\mathbf{sk}}(\mathbf{sk} \cdot \mathbf{m}), \mathrm{RLWE}'_{\mathbf{sk}}(\mathbf{m}))$ and we are given $\mathrm{RLWE}'_{\mathbf{sk}}(\mathbf{m})$, we just need a way to compute $\mathrm{RLWE}'_{\mathbf{sk}}(\mathbf{sk} \cdot \mathbf{m})$. To do so, we will use $\mathrm{RLWE}'_{\mathbf{sk}}(\mathbf{sk^2})$ given as part of the evaluation key. We will operate in parallel on each of the $\mathrm{RLWE}_{\mathbf{sk}}(v_i \cdot \mathbf{m})$ ciphertexts that make up the $\mathrm{RLWE}'_{\mathbf{sk}}(\mathbf{m})$ ciphertext, lifting each $\mathrm{RLWE}_{\mathbf{sk}}(v_i \cdot \mathbf{m})$ to $\mathrm{RLWE}_{\mathbf{sk}}(v_i \cdot \mathbf{sk} \cdot \mathbf{m})$. More precisely, for each $\mathrm{RLWE}_{\mathbf{sk}}(v_i \cdot \mathbf{m}) := (\mathbf{a}, \mathbf{b})$, we compute

$$\mathbf{a} \odot \mathrm{RLWE}'_{\mathbf{sk}}(\mathbf{sk}^2) + (\mathbf{b}, 0).$$

By regarding $(\mathbf{b}, 0)$ as a noiseless RLWE encryption of $\mathbf{b} \cdot \mathbf{sk}$ under the secret key $\mathbf{sk}$, this computation gives $\mathrm{RLWE}_{\mathbf{sk}}(\mathbf{a} \cdot \mathbf{sk}^2 + \mathbf{b} \cdot \mathbf{sk}) = \mathrm{RLWE}_{\mathbf{sk}}((\mathbf{a} \cdot \mathbf{sk} + \mathbf{b}) \cdot \mathbf{sk}) = \mathrm{RLWE}_{\mathbf{sk}}((v_i \cdot \mathbf{m} + \mathbf{e}) \cdot \mathbf{sk})$. Hence we do get $\mathrm{RLWE}_{\mathbf{sk}}(v_i \cdot \mathbf{sk} \cdot \mathbf{m})$ as desired, but with an additional error $\mathbf{e} \cdot \mathbf{sk}$ scaled up by $\mathbf{sk}$ from the input RLWE$'$ ciphertext error $\mathbf{e}$. We will choose the secret key $\mathbf{sk}$ with small norm (e.g., binary) so that this multiplicative error growth remains small. More details about the full error growth for this scheme switching will be given in Sect. 3.2.

When our scheme switching method is used in conjuction with key switching, it allows a small optimization. Say we are given a $\mathrm{RLWE}'_{\mathbf{sk'}}(\mathbf{m})$, and we want to turn it into a RGSW encryption under $\mathbf{sk}$. This can be done in two steps, by first performing key-switching to $\mathrm{RLWE}'_{\mathbf{sk}}(\mathbf{m})$, and then using the scheme switching key $\mathrm{RLWE}'_{\mathbf{sk}}(\mathbf{sk^2})$ to compute $\mathrm{RLWE}'_{\mathbf{sk}}(\mathbf{m} \cdot \mathbf{sk})$. The optimization consists in using a modified scheme switching key $\mathrm{RLWE}'_{\mathbf{sk}}(\mathbf{sk}' \cdot \mathbf{sk})$ to turn the input ciphertext (encrypted under $\mathbf{sk}'$) directly into $\mathrm{RLWE}'_{\mathbf{sk}}(\mathbf{m} \cdot \mathbf{sk})$, performing key switching $\mathbf{sk'} \rightarrow \mathbf{sk}$ and homomorphic multiplication by $\mathbf{sk}$ at the same time. Notice that the running time is about the same as before as we still need another key switching $\mathbf{sk'} \rightarrow \mathbf{sk}$ to compute the other component of the output

RGSW ciphertext. However, combining key switching and multiplication in a single operation allows to slightly reduce the noise growth. To give a more modular presentation, we ignore this optimization in the description of our algorithm.

3.2 Error Growth in Prime Cyclotomics

Analysing the error growth in bootstrapping algorithms is crucial for the correctness of the scheme as it allows to set the proper modulus sizes and show the implementation can be run with concrete parameters. It is a standard practice in lattice cryptography to estimate the error growth during homomoprhic operations under the heuristic assumption that the noise in ciphertexts behaves like independent gaussian (or subgaussian) random variables, with standard deviation that depends on the computation leading to the ciphertext. In order to fairly compare our algorithm to previous work, in this paper we use a similar technique and compute the total error estimation based on the error variance introduced by a single $\mathcal{R}_{reg} \odot \mathrm{RLWE}'$ operation. In previous works, where a power-of-2 cyclotomic is being used, this value is equal to $\frac{1}{12} d_B q B^2 \sigma^2_{\mathrm{input}}$ where B is the base for the power-of-B gadget, d_B is the length of the gadget and $\sigma^2_{\mathrm{input}}$ is the error variance of the input RLWE' ciphertext considered. Because $\mathcal{R}_{reg}$ is a prime cyclotomic, the analysis of this variance differs in our case as we do not directly have a bound on the ℓ_∞ norm in the canonical embedding of a ring element for which we know a bound on each coefficient. We thus propose the following theorem.

Theorem 1. *For an odd prime q and a positive integer Q, let $\mathcal{R}_{reg}$ be the qth cyclotomic ring modulo Q used for registers, and d_B be the length of the gadget decomposition. For an* RLWE′ *ciphertext defined over $\mathcal{R}_{reg}$, the error variance of the result of a single $\mathcal{R}_{reg} \odot$* RLWE′ *operation is bounded by*

$$\sigma^2_{\odot} \leq 2 d_B q \sigma^2_r \sigma^2_{input},$$

where σ^2_{input} is the error variance of the input RLWE′ *ciphertext, and σ^2_r is the variance of the gadget decomposition of the input $\mathcal{R}_{reg}$ ring element.*

Proof. We model an element $r \in \mathcal{R}_{reg}$ as sampled uniformly at random—this is a reasonable model because in our algorithm the $\mathcal{R}_{reg}$ elements always either come from a ciphertext (and hence are uniform) or are simply an integer constant (leading to even smaller error growth). The gadget decomposition of $r \in \mathcal{R}_{reg}$, denoted $\mathbf{G}^{-1}(r)$, then consists of d_B ring elements $r_1, \ldots, r_{d_B}$ (which we model as independently distributed). Note that we will use in our algorithm a balanced base-B digit decomposition but we leave the decomposition unspecified here for sake of generality. We model the error vector $\vec{e}_{\mathrm{RLWE}'} = (e_1, \ldots, e_{d_B})$ where each component is the error of each RLWE ciphertext in the input RLWE′ ciphertext, as independent random variables with variance $\sigma^2_{\mathrm{input}}$. The output error can then be computed as an inner product

$$e_{\mathrm{output}} = \langle \mathbf{G}^{-1}(r), \vec{e}_{\mathrm{RLWE}'} \rangle = \sum_{i=1}^{d_B} r_i \cdot e_i.$$

We will start by considering a single multiplication $v_i := r_i \cdot e_i \pmod{\Phi_q(X)}$. Recall that r_i and e_i are both ring elements of $\mathcal{R}_{reg}$, *i.e.*, polynomials of degree $q-2$ (as $\mathcal{R}_{reg} = \mathbb{Z}_Q[X]/(\Phi_q(X))$ and $\Phi_q(X) = 1 + X + \cdots + X^{q-1}$). We want to compute the variance of each coefficient of

$$v_i = (r_{i,0} + r_{i,1}X + \cdots + r_{i,q-2}X^{q-2}) \cdot (e_{i,0} + e_{i,1}X + \cdots + e_{i,q-2}X^{q-2}) \pmod{\Phi_q(X)}.$$

For simplicity of notation in the formulas below, we will consider r_i and e_i to be polynomials of degree $q-1$ (instead of $q-2$) with leading coefficients 0, *i.e.*, the trivial terms $r_{i,q-1} = e_{i,q-1} := 0$. By computing $r_i \cdot e_i \pmod{X^q - 1}$ first and then taking the result modulo $\Phi_q(X)$, we can easily obtain the ℓth coefficient of v_i, which we denote $v_i^{(\ell)}$, for $0 \le \ell \le q-2$. First, note that the ℓth coefficient of $v_i' := r_i \cdot e_i \pmod{X^q - 1}$ is given by $v_i'^{(\ell)} = \sum_{j=0}^{q-1} r_{i,j} \cdot e_{i,\ell-j}$, where the subscripts of e are defined modulo q, *i.e.*, $e_{i,\ell-j} := e_{i,q+\ell-j}$ if $\ell < j$. Then, since $X^{q-1} = -X^{q-2} - \cdots - 1 \bmod \Phi_q(X)$, the ℓth coefficient of v_i modulo $\Phi_q(X)$ is computed as $v_i^{(\ell)} = v_i'^{(\ell)} - v_i'^{(q-1)} = \sum_{j=0}^{q-1} r_{i,j} \cdot (e_{i,\ell-j} - e_{i,q-j-1})$. Let $X_{i,j}^{(\ell)} := r_{i,j} \cdot (e_{i,\ell-j} - e_{i,q-j-1})$ for $0 \le j \le q-1$ and hence $v_i^{(\ell)} = \sum_{j=0}^{q-1} X_{i,j}^{(\ell)}$. Since $r_{i,q-1} = 0$ is a constant value, we trivially have that $\mathsf{var}(X_{i,q-1}^{(\ell)}) = 0$. When $0 \le j \le q-2$, the variance of each $X_{i,j}^{(\ell)}$ equals to

$$\mathsf{var}(X_{i,j}^{(\ell)}) = \mathsf{var}(r_{i,j}) \cdot \mathsf{var}(e_{i,\ell-j} - e_{i,q-j-1}) = \begin{cases} \sigma_r^2 \sigma_{\text{input}}^2 & \text{if } j = 0 \text{ or } \ell + 1 \\ 2\sigma_r^2 \sigma_{\text{input}}^2 & \text{else} \end{cases}.$$

The first variance corresponds to the case where $\mathsf{var}(e_{i,\ell-j} - e_{i,q-j-1}) = \mathsf{var}(e_{i,\ell-j})$ as $e_{i,q-j-1} = 0$ when $j = 0$ or when $\mathsf{var}(e_{i,\ell-j} - e_{i,q-j-1}) = \mathsf{var}(e_{i,q-j-1})$ as $\mathsf{var}(e_{i,\ell-j}) = 0$ when $j = \ell + 1$. Since $\mathsf{var}\left(\sum_{j=0}^{q-1} X_{i,j}^{\ell}\right) = \sum_{j=0}^{q-1} \mathsf{var}(X_{i,j}^{(\ell)}) + 2\sum_{0 \le j < k < q} \mathsf{cov}(X_{i,j}^{(\ell)}, X_{i,k}^{(\ell)})$, it now suffices to compute the covariance of each pair. We will first consider the special case where $k = j + \ell + 1$ as it is the only case where common terms appear between $X_{i,j}^{(\ell)}$ and $X_{i,k}^{(\ell)}$. Indeed, we have that for $k = j + \ell + 1$,

$$X_{i,k}^{(\ell)} = r_{i,j+\ell+1} \cdot (e_{i,-j-1} - e_{i,q-j-\ell-2}),$$

where $e_{i,-j-1} = e_{i,q-j-1}$ also appears in $X_{i,j}^{(\ell)}$. However, due to the distributive property of covariance, it holds that[1]

$$\mathsf{cov}(X_{i,j}^{(\ell)}, X_{i,k}^{(\ell)}) = -\mathsf{cov}(r_{i,j} \cdot e_{i,q-j-1}, r_{i,j+\ell+1} \cdot e_{i,q-j-1}) = 0.$$

In all other cases we trivially have $\mathsf{cov}(X_{i,j}^{\ell}, X_{i,k}^{(\ell)}) = 0$ since $X_{i,j}^{\ell}$ and $X_{i,k}^{\ell}$ are independent. Note that there exist two j indices ($j = 0, \ell + 1$) satisfying

[1] In general, it holds that $\mathsf{cov}(XY, XZ) = E(X^2)E(Y)E(Z) - E(X)^2E(Y)E(Z)$ for any random variables X, Y and Z. Therefore, if $E(Y) = E(Z) = 0$, then $\mathsf{cov}(XY, XZ) = 0$.

$\mathsf{var}(X_{i,j}^{(\ell)}) = \sigma_r^2\sigma_{\text{input}}^2$ when $0 \le \ell < q-2$, while there exists only one such j index ($j=0$) when $\ell = q-2$. As a result, we obtain the variance of $v_i^{(\ell)}$ as

$$\mathsf{var}(v_i^{(\ell)}) = \sum_{j=0}^{q-1} \mathsf{var}(X_{i,j}^{(\ell)}) = \begin{cases} (2q-4)\sigma_r^2\sigma_{\text{input}}^2 & \text{if } 0 \le \ell < q-2 \\ (2q-3)\sigma_r^2\sigma_{\text{input}}^2 & \text{if } \ell = q-2 \end{cases}.$$

Finally, the variance of each coefficient of e_{output} denoted by $\sigma_\odot^2$ is bounded by $2d_B q\sigma_r^2\sigma_{\text{input}}^2$. □

Corollary 1. *For an odd prime q and a positivie integer Q, let $\mathcal{R}_{reg}$ be the qth cyclotomic ring modulo Q used for registers, and d_B be the length of a balanced base-B gadget decomposition with uniform coefficients in $[-B/2, B/2)$. For an* RLWE′ *ciphertext defined over $\mathcal{R}_{reg}$, the error variance of the result of a single $\mathcal{R}_{reg} \odot$* RLWE′ *operation is bounded by*

$$\sigma_\odot^2 \le \frac{B^2}{6} d_B q \sigma_{input}^2,$$

where σ_{input}^2 is the error variance of the input RLWE′ *ciphertext.*

Proof. If one considers a balanced base-B digit decomposition of $r \in \mathcal{R}_{reg}$ which consists of d_B ring elements $r_1, \ldots, r_{d_B}$ whose coefficients are each uniform in $[-B/2, B/2)$, then the variance of the gadget decomposition of the input $\mathcal{R}_{reg}$ ring element satisfies $\sigma_r^2 = B^2/12$. By replacing this value in the upper bound for $\sigma_\odot^2$ given in Theorem 1, we get $\sigma_\odot^2 \le \frac{B^2}{6} d_B q \sigma_{input}^2$. □

Remark 1. Note that the variance $\sigma_\odot^2$ considered for error analysis in power-of-2 cyclotomic is $\sigma_\odot^2 = \frac{B^2}{12} d_B N \sigma_{input}^2$, (see [15, Section 4.2]), where N is a power of two and the $2N^{th}$ cyclotomic ring is considered. Interestingly, our analysis for prime cyclotomic rings only shows a difference by a factor 2.

Error Growth in Previous Operations. We now describe the error growth for the main operations used in our algorithm as a function of $\sigma_\odot^2$.

RGSW × RLWE′ *Multiplication:* Recall that a multiplication between $\text{RLWE}'_{\mathbf{sk}}(\mathbf{m}_1)$ and $\text{RGSW}_{\mathbf{sk}}(\mathbf{m}_2) = (\text{RLWE}'_{\mathbf{sk}}(\mathbf{m}_2), \text{RLWE}'_{\mathbf{sk}}(\mathbf{sk} \cdot \mathbf{m}_2))$ is computed as $\mathbf{a} \odot \text{RLWE}'_{\mathbf{sk}}(\mathbf{sk} \cdot \mathbf{m}_2) + \mathbf{b} \odot \text{RLWE}'_{\mathbf{sk}}(\mathbf{m}_2)$ for each RLWE component $(\mathbf{a}, \mathbf{b})$ of $\text{RLWE}'_{\mathbf{sk}}(\mathbf{m}_1)$. From this description, we easily see that two $\odot$ computations are performed to which should be added the error coming from the RGSW ciphertext itself multiplicatively. Finally, as already mentioned when describing the operation, the error also additively increases by $\mathbf{e}_{\text{RLWE}'} \cdot \mathbf{m}_2$. Since $\mathbf{m}_2$ is a monomial, we simply add $\sigma_{\text{RLWE}'}^2$. Therefore, the total error variance is equal to $2\sigma_{\odot,RGSW}^2 + \sigma_{RLWE'}^2$ where $\sigma_{\odot,RGSW}^2$ denotes the resulting error variance of the $\odot$ operation on each RLWE′ component of $\text{RGSW}(\mathbf{m}_2)$.

RLWE'-to-RGSW Scheme Switching: Recall that the operation can be described as $(\mathbf{b}, 0) + \mathbf{a} \odot \mathrm{RLWE}'_{\mathbf{sk}}(\mathbf{sk}^2)$ for each RLWE component $(\mathbf{a}, \mathbf{b})$ of the input RLWE' ciphertext. There are two sources of error. Firstly, an additive error growth comes from the $\odot$ operation in $\mathbf{a} \odot \mathrm{RLWE}'_{\mathbf{sk}}(\mathbf{sk}^2)$. Since $\mathrm{RLWE}'_{\mathbf{sk}}(\mathbf{sk}^2)$ is a fresh encryption that comes from the evaluation key, the error variance is relatively small. We thus have an additive error growth with variance $\sigma^2_{\odot,eval\_key}$ which denotes the resulting error variance of the $\odot$ operation on the evaluation key with error variance $\sigma^2_{eval\_key}$.

Secondly, a multiplicative error growth comes from the fact that the existing error in the RLWE' ciphertext gets scaled by $\mathbf{sk}$. The secret key $\mathbf{sk}$ is not a scalar but rather a ring element and recall we work in a prime cyclotomic. We know the error variance scales by a factor of no more than $\ell_1(\mathbf{sk})$, where the norm is with respect to the canonical embedding for $\mathbf{sk}$.

Combining these two sources of error under the assumption that each coefficient of $\mathbf{sk}$ is binary/ternary, then the error variance of the output is $\ell_1(\mathbf{sk}) \cdot \sigma^2_{RLWE'} + \sigma^2_{\odot,eval\_key}$.

RLWE' Automorphism: Applying an automorphism ψ itself does not change the error. The following key-switching operation however introduces an additive error growth with variance $\sigma^2_{\odot,aut\_key}$ which denotes the resulting error variance of the $\odot$ operation on the automorphism key $\mathrm{RLWE}'_{\mathbf{sk}}(\psi(\mathbf{sk}))$.

We summarize these error growth in Table 2.

Table 2. Summary of register operations with $\mathcal{R} \odot \mathrm{RLWE}'$ opcount and error growth.

Operation	Computation (for each RLWE $(\mathbf{a}, \mathbf{b})$ of RLWE′)	$\odot$ ops	Error Variance
$\mathrm{RLWE}' \times \mathrm{RGSW}$	$\mathbf{a} \odot \mathrm{RLWE}'_{\mathbf{sk}}(\mathbf{s} \cdot \mathbf{m}_2) + \mathbf{b} \odot \mathrm{RLWE}'_{\mathbf{sk}}(\mathbf{m}_2)$	$2k$	$2\sigma^2_{\odot,RGSW} + \sigma^2_{RLWE'}$
SchemeSwitch	$\mathbf{a} \odot \mathrm{RLWE}'_{\mathbf{sk}}(\mathbf{sk}^2) + (\mathbf{b}, 0)$	k	$\ell_1(\mathbf{sk}) \cdot \sigma^2_{RLWE'} + \sigma^2_{\odot,eval\_key}$
Automorphism	$\psi(\mathbf{a}) \odot \mathrm{RLWE}'_{\mathbf{sk}}(\psi(\mathbf{sk})) + (0, \psi(\mathbf{b}))$	k	$\sigma^2_{RLWE'} + \sigma^2_{\odot,aut\_key}$

4 Description of the Algorithm

The overall algorithm, at a high level, can be subdivided into various steps:

- Step 1: a *packing* step takes as input $\phi(d)$ LWE ciphertexts and "combines" them into a single RLWE ciphertext $(\mathbf{a}, \mathbf{b}) \in \mathcal{R}_{in} \times \mathcal{R}_{in}$.
- Step 2: a *homomorphic decryption* of the RLWE ciphertext consists in computing (an encryption of) the ring element $(\mathbf{a} \cdot \mathbf{z} + \mathbf{b}) \in \mathcal{R}_{in}$, homomorphically, given (as a bootstrapping key) an encryption of $\mathbf{z}$.

- Step 3: an *msbExtract* step recovers the $\phi(d)$ LWE ciphertexts with reduced noise.

Step 1 and Step 3, except for the use of different rings, are very similar to previous work [21]. We describe the 3 steps in detail with a particular emphasis on Step 2 which is the main novelty of this paper.

4.1 Packing

The very first step of bootstrapping procedure consists in taking a set of LWE ciphertexts and pack them into a single RLWE ciphertext. More precisely, the packing algorithm takes as input $\phi(d)$ LWE ciphertexts encrypting messages $m_i \in \mathbb{Z}$ as well as an RLWE′ encryption RLWE′(s_i) of each coefficients of the plain LWE secret key $\mathbf{s}_p = (s_0, s_1, \cdots, s_{n_{plain}}) \in \mathbb{Z}_{q_{plain}}^{n_{plain}+1}$, in the dth cyclotomic ring with modulus q_{plain} and outputs $(\mathbf{a}, \mathbf{b}) \in \mathcal{R}_{in} \times \mathcal{R}_{in}$ encrypting the message $\mathbf{m}(X) = \sum_i m_i X^{i-1}$. The pseudo-code is given in Algorithm 1.

Algorithm 1. Ring packing

Input: $\phi(d)$ plain LWE ciphertexts $(\vec{a}_i, b_i) \in \mathbb{Z}_{q_{plain}}^{n_{plain}} \times \mathbb{Z}_{q_{plain}}$, RLWE′$(s_i)$
Output: RLWE ciphertext in $\mathcal{R}_{in}$.
for $0 \leq i < n_{plain}$ **do**
  let $r_i = a_{0,i} + a_{1,i}X + a_{2,i}X^2 + \cdots + a_{\phi(d)-1,i}X^{\phi(d)-1}$ in $(\mathcal{R}_{in})_{q_{plain}}$.
end for
$r' = (0, (b_0 + b_1 X + b_2 X^2 + \cdots + b_{\phi(d)-1} X^{\phi(d)-1}))$ ▷ (Noiseless RLWE′ ciphertext)
$ct \leftarrow r' + \sum_{i=0}^{n_{plain}-1} r_i \odot \text{RLWE}'(s_i)$
return $\text{ModSwitch}_{q_{plain} \to q}(ct)$

For simplicity, we first built a ring ciphertext ct modulo q_{plain} (i.e., the original input modulus) and then switch the modulus to q. Alternatively, one can directly compute a ring ciphertext modulo q by using a packing key $\{\text{RLWE}'(s_i)\}_i$ already encrypted under modulus q. The packing key may also use a different gadget (e.g., the power-of-two gadget, instead of powers-of-B) than other ciphertexts used later in the algorithm.

Since this part of the algorithm is essentially identical to previous work [21], we omit these details, and move on to the second step.

4.2 Linear Step

This step of the algorithm takes as input a single RLWE ciphertext $(\mathbf{a}, \mathbf{b}) \in \mathcal{R}_{in}{}^2$ and outputs $\phi(d)$ RLWE ciphertexts, each encrypting a coefficient of $(\mathbf{a} \cdot \mathbf{z} + \mathbf{b}) \in \mathcal{R}_{in}$ (recall that an element of $\mathcal{R}_{in}$ is a polynomial of degree $\phi(d)$). It can be further subdivided into two computations: a (homomorphic) polynomial multiplication between $\mathbf{a}$ and (an encryption of) $\mathbf{z}$, where each coefficient of the polynomials (describing the key $\mathbf{z}$, all intermediate results, and the final ring element) is a distinct ciphertext, and the addition of the ring element $\mathbf{b}$. We now provide a detailed explanation of these computations along with a pseudo-code of the various steps of the algorithm.

An FFT-Based Polynomial Multiplication. For this step, the algorithm uses a standard FFT-based method summarized in Fig. 1. More precisely, we perform the following steps:

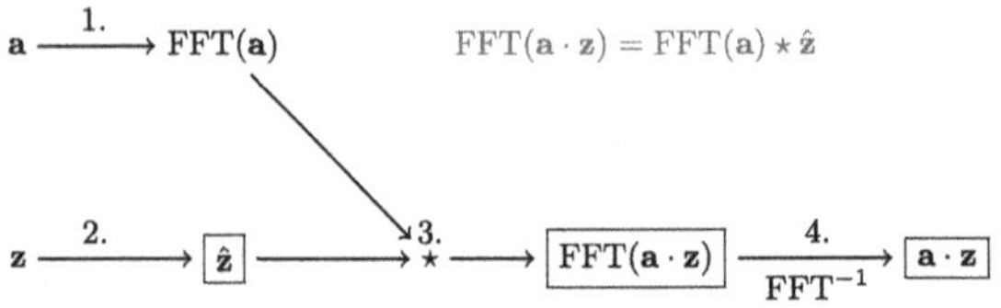

Fig. 1. High level description of the linear step of our algorithm. The notation $\star$ refers to pointwise multiplication. The boxed information refers to encrypted data where homomorphic operations are required. Each step i. is described in detail in the paper.

1. Compute a partial FFT of $\mathbf{a} \in \mathcal{R}_{in}$, *i.e.*, PFT($\mathbf{a}$) in cleartext form. Let $k-1$ be the degree of the polynomials outputted by PFT. Note that a full (non-partial) FFT would have $k=1$ as the algorithm recurses until the input polynomial is reduced modulo all $\phi(d)$ linear factors of $\Phi_d(X)$. When computing PFT, the algorithm outputs $\phi(d)/k$ polynomials of degree $k-1$ (and hence does not recurse all the way down to the linear factors). In other words, this corresponds to evaluating the CRT isomorphism
$$\frac{\mathbb{Z}_q[X]}{(X^{d/2}+1)} \simeq \left(\frac{\mathbb{Z}_q[X]}{(X^k-\zeta_0)}\right) \times \cdots \times \left(\frac{\mathbb{Z}_q[X]}{(X^k-\zeta_{\phi(d)/k-1})}\right)$$
where the ζ_i are the solutions to $(\zeta^k)^{\phi(d)} = -1$, namely the primitive (d/k)–th roots of unity modulo q. This step thus outputs a list of $\phi(d)/k$ polynomials $\{\tilde{\mathbf{a}}_i\}_{0\le i<\phi(d)/k}$, where each $\tilde{\mathbf{a}}_i = \mathbf{a} \mod (X^k-\zeta_i)$ is a polynomial with k coefficients. Note that this computation is done in the clear, and thus no homomorphic operations are needed.
Recall that when computing an inverse PFT, one must divide the polynomials $\tilde{\mathbf{a}}_i$ by $\phi(d)/k \pmod q$. In order to be able to compute this division in the clear rather than homomorphically, this step can be done now (Refer to Sect. 2.5). Hence the polynomials are updated to $\tilde{\mathbf{a}}_i \leftarrow \tilde{\mathbf{a}}_i/(\phi(d)/k) \pmod q$.
2. The evaluation key contains RGSW registers of PFT($\mathbf{z}$). Similarly as before, let $\tilde{\mathbf{z}}_i = \mathbf{z} \mod (X^k-\zeta_i)$, where each $\tilde{\mathbf{z}}_i$ is a polynomial with k coefficients. Let $\tilde{z}_i^{(j)}$ be the jth coefficient of $\tilde{\mathbf{z}}_i$. Then the evaluation key contains the list of RGSW $\left(X^{\tilde{z}_i^{(j)}}\right)$ for $0 \le i < \phi(d)/k$ and $0 \le j < k$.

3. We now want to homomorphically compute PFT($\mathbf{a} \cdot \mathbf{z}$) from PFT($\mathbf{a}$) and the RGSW registers of PFT($\mathbf{z}$). Note that the polynomial multiplication in $\mathcal{R}_{in}$ corresponds to component-wise multiplication in PFT representation, *i.e.*, $\text{PFT}(\mathbf{a} \cdot \mathbf{z}) = (\tilde{\mathbf{a}}_0 \cdot \tilde{\mathbf{z}}_0, \tilde{\mathbf{a}}_1 \cdot \tilde{\mathbf{z}}_1, ..., \tilde{\mathbf{a}}_{\phi(d)/k-1} \cdot \tilde{\mathbf{z}}_{\phi(d)/k-1})$. For ease of notation, let us fix i (we drop the subscript i) and consider a single multiplication of $\tilde{\mathbf{a}} := \sum_{j=0}^{k-1} \tilde{a}_j X^j$ and $\tilde{\mathbf{z}} := \sum_{j=0}^{k-1} \tilde{z}_j X^j$ modulo $(X^k - \zeta)$. More precisely, we want to homomorphically compute

$$(\tilde{a}_0 + \tilde{a}_1 X + \cdots + \tilde{a}_{k-1} X^{k-1})(\tilde{z}_0 + \tilde{z}_1 X + \cdots + \tilde{z}_{k-1} X^{k-1}) \mod (X^k - \zeta).$$

where each coefficient $\tilde{z}_j$ is encrypted as an RGSW register.

Each coefficient of the resulting product can be computed as follows. For $j = 0, \cdots, k-1$, the j-th coefficient of $\mathbf{v} := \tilde{\mathbf{a}} \cdot \tilde{\mathbf{z}}$ is equal to

$$v_j = \tilde{z}_0 \tilde{a}_j + \tilde{z}_1 \tilde{a}_{j-1} + \cdots + \tilde{z}_{j-1} \tilde{a}_1 + \tilde{z}_j \tilde{a}_0 + \zeta \left(\tilde{z}_{j+1} \tilde{a}_{k-1} + \tilde{z}_{j+2} \tilde{a}_{k-2} + \cdots + \tilde{z}_{k-1} \tilde{a}_{j+1} \right),$$

which corresponds to the inner product taken between the vector of coefficients $\vec{\mathbf{z}} = (\tilde{z}_0, \cdots, \tilde{z}_{k-1})$ of the polynomial $\tilde{\mathbf{z}}$ and the new vector $\vec{\mathbf{c}} = (\tilde{a}_j, \tilde{a}_{j-1}, \ldots, \tilde{a}_0, \zeta \tilde{a}_{k-1}, \ldots, \zeta \tilde{a}_{j+1})$. We emphasize again the fact that the coefficients of $\vec{\mathbf{c}}$ are in the clear, whereas the coefficients of $\vec{\mathbf{z}}$ are not. So, it is easy to multiply $\vec{\mathbf{c}}$ by ζ.

Without loss of generality, let us assume all the coefficents c_i of $\vec{\mathbf{c}}$ are nonzero and thus invertible. (Here we use the fact that q is a prime. So, all nonzero elements are invertible modulo q and multiplication (in the exponent) can be implemented using an automorphism of the prime cyclotomic ring.) Then we can compute the inner product in a telescoping manner as

$$v_j = \left(\left(\ldots \left(\left(\tilde{z}_0 c_0 c_1^{-1} + \tilde{z}_1 \right) c_1 c_2^{-1} + \tilde{z}_2 \right) c_2 c_3^{-1} + \ldots \right) c_{k-2} c_{k-1}^{-1} + \tilde{z}_{k-1} \right) c_{k-1}.$$

This will end up being the most efficient way to compute this inner product homomorphically.

Let us now explicit how one coefficient corresponding to a monomial X^j can be computed homomorphically (this computation will have to be repeated for all k coefficients of a single product as well as for all $\phi(d)/k$ pairs of $(\tilde{\mathbf{a}}_i, \tilde{\mathbf{z}}_i)$ polynomials).

a) Let *accum* be an RLWE′ register, initialized as $\text{RLWE}'\left(X^{\tilde{z}_0}\right)$ from the evaluation key.
b) For $j' \in [0, \ldots, k-2]$, update *accum* as follows:
   i. Apply the automorphism that sends X to $X^{c'_j c_{j'+1}^{-1}}$.
   ii. Do an RLWE′ × RGSW multiplication with $\text{RGSW}\left(X^{\tilde{z}_{j'+1}}\right)$ from the evaluation key.
c) Finally apply the automorphism sending X to $X^{c_{k-1}}$, yielding $\text{RLWE}'\left(X^{v_j}\right)$.

Since we repeat (a)-(c) for every coefficient of $\tilde{\mathbf{a}}_i \cdot \tilde{\mathbf{z}}_i$ for $1 \le i \le \phi(d)/k$, the output of this step consists of $\phi(d)$ RLWE′ registers of the form

$$\left\{ \text{RLWE}'\left(X^{\mathbf{v}_i^{(j)}} \right) \right\}_{0 \le i < \phi(d)/k, 0 \le j < k},$$

where $\mathbf{v}_i^{(j)}$ denotes the j-th coefficient of $\mathbf{v}_i := \tilde{\mathbf{a}}_i \cdot \tilde{\mathbf{z}}_i \pmod{X^k - \zeta_i}$. This procedure is illustrated in Fig. 2, and the corresponding pseudo-code for component-wise multiplication is given in Algorithm 2.

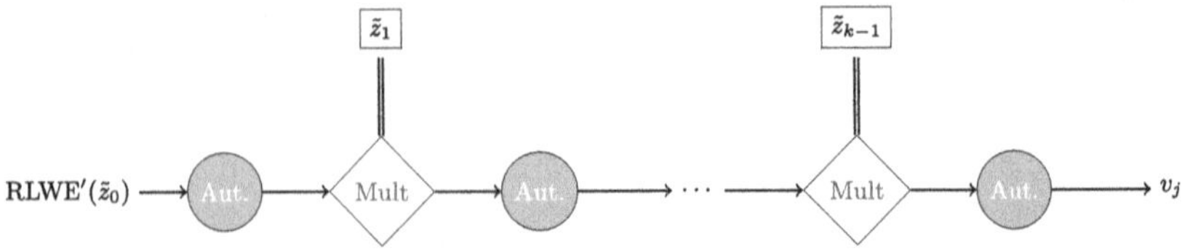

Fig. 2. Homomorphic computation of a X^j coefficient for pointwise multiplication. A single line corresponds to RLWE' ciphertexts and a double line to RGSW ciphertexts. Aut. stands for automorphisms and Mult. for multiplication. Boxed values are encrypted values.

Algorithm 2. Pointwise multiplication between polynomials $\tilde{\mathbf{a}}$ and $\tilde{\mathbf{z}}$.

Input: A set of degree-$(k-1)$ polynomials $\{\tilde{\mathbf{a}}_i\}_{0 \le i < N}$, $\{\mathrm{RGSW}(X^{\tilde{z}_i^{(j)}})\}_{0 \le i < N, 0 \le j < k}$ for $N := \phi(d)/k$, ω: the $2N$-th root of unity mod q
Output: $\phi(d)$ RLWE$'$ ciphertexts
REG $\leftarrow [0, \dots, 0]$
for all $0 \le i < N$ **do**
  $\zeta \leftarrow \omega^{2i+1}$
  Let $\vec{\tilde{\mathbf{a}}} = (\tilde{a}_{i,0}, \tilde{a}_{i,1}, \dots, \tilde{a}_{i,k-1})$ ▷ $\tilde{\mathbf{a}}_i := \sum_{j=0}^{k-1} \tilde{a}_{i,j} X^j$
  for all $0 \le j < k$ **do**
    $\vec{\mathbf{c}} \leftarrow (\tilde{a}_{i,j}, \tilde{a}_{i,j-1}, \dots, \tilde{a}_{i,0}, \zeta\tilde{a}_{i,k-1}, \zeta\tilde{a}_{i,k-2}, \dots \zeta\tilde{a}_{i,j+1})$
    $accum \leftarrow \mathrm{RLWE}'(X^{\tilde{z}_i^{(0)}})$
    for $j' \leftarrow 0, 1, \dots, k-2$ **do**
      $accum \leftarrow \mathrm{EvalAut}(accum,\ c_{j'} c_{j'+1}^{-1})$
      $accum \leftarrow \mathrm{MulRGSW}(\mathrm{RGSW}(\tilde{z}_i^{(j'+1)}), accum)$
    end for
    $accum \leftarrow \mathrm{EvalAut}(accum, c_{k-1})$ ▷ $accum = \mathrm{RGSW}(X^{(\tilde{\mathbf{a}}_i \cdot \tilde{\mathbf{z}}_i)^{(j)}})$
    $\mathrm{REG}[ik + j] \leftarrow accum$
  end for
end for
output REG ▷ Register of all coefficients of $\tilde{\mathbf{a}}_i \cdot \tilde{\mathbf{z}}_i$ for $0 \le i < N$

---

4. We now have the encryption of $\mathrm{PFT}(\mathbf{a} \cdot \mathbf{z})$. It remains to perform the inverse of PFT, denoted by PFT^{-1}, in order to recover the resulting polynomial product $\mathbf{a} \cdot \mathbf{z}$, more specifically RLWE encryptions of the coefficients of $\mathbf{a} \cdot \mathbf{z}$.

Recall from Sect. 2.5 that the inverse of a primitive FFT of length N (using a $2N$th root of unity ω) can be computed by first taking a standard FFT of length N using ω^{-2} as the Nth root of unity, then multiplying the ith term by

ω^{-i}. Moreover, a partial FFT of length $\phi(d)$ that reduces modulo $(X^k - \zeta)$ is equivalent to k full FFTs of length $N = \phi(d)/k$ done in parallel, and the same remains true for the inverse (see Sect. 2.5 for details about the equivalence). Hence, to homomorphically compute PFT^{-1}, we will

a) Split the $\phi(d)$ registers output by the pointwise multiplication step into k groups of size N: each group corresponds to the coefficients of the monomial X^j for $0 \le j \le k-1$ of all $\phi(d)/k$ polynomials.
b) Homomorphically perform a standard (not primitive) length-N FFT in the forward direction on each group of size N, using ω^{-2} as the Nth root of unity. Overall, this step corresponds to computing k FFTs. We refer the reader to Sect. 2.5 for more details on the equivalence between partial FFT modulo $X^k - \zeta$ and k-parallel standard FFT.
c) Multiply (homomorphically, via an automorphism) the ith output register in each group by ω^{-i}, for all i from 1 to $N-1$. More specifically, we apply the automorphism $X \mapsto X^{\omega^{-i}}$, corresponding to multiplication by ω^{-i} in the exponent, followed by a key switching operation.

The following algorithms provide pseudocodes for the above procedure to compute the homomorphic PFT^{-1}. More specifically, Algorithm 3 describes step (a) and then calls Algorithm 4 for each of the groups of registers. Algorithm 4 describes a primitive length-N (inverse) FFT for a single group of size N, consisting of a standard (cyclic) FFT (step (b)) as well as the multiplication by ω^{-i} (step (c)).

Algorithm 3. IFFT stage of bootstrapping (`BootstrapIFFT`)

```
 1: Input: a list of φ(d) registers REG, k, N, a list of radices {r_i}_{0≤i<ℓ}, and ω
Require: ω a primitive 2Nth root of unity mod q, ∏_{0≤i<ℓ} r_i = N, and kN = φ(d) =
    len(REG)
 2: for all 0 ≤ j < k do
 3:     REG[j, k+j, ..., (N−1)k+j] ← N-IFFT(REG[j, k+j, ..., (N−1)k+j], {r_i}, ω)
 4: end for
```

It remains to describe more precisely what happens in the (cyclic) FFT call, line 4 of Algorithm 4.

Recall that FFT is a recursive algorithm that follows the structure of a remainder tree, see the procedure **FFT** given in Algorithm 6. We will now focus on what happens in a single layer of the FFT as described in the second procedure `FFT Layer` in Algorithm 6.

At a single layer: Let r_i be the radix used for the i-th FFT layer for $0 \le i < \ell$. Then, for $R_i := \prod_{i \le i' < \ell} r_i$, the inputs to the i-th FFT layer are the coefficients of N/R_i polynomials modulo $(X^{R_i} - \omega'^j)$ (for varying values of j),

Algorithm 4. Primitive length-N IFFT for a single group of size N (`N-IFFT`)

1: **Input:** List of RLWE′ registers $\text{REG} = \{\text{RLWE}'(X^{(\tilde{\mathbf{a}}_i \cdot \tilde{\mathbf{z}}_i)^{(j)}})\}_{0 \leq i < N}$ for some fixed $0 \leq j < k$, list of radices $\{r_i\}_{0 \leq i < \ell}$, primitive $2N$th root of unity ω modulo q.
2: **Output:** list of RLWE registers $\text{REG} = \{\text{RLWE}(X^{(\mathbf{a}_i \cdot \mathbf{z}_i)^{(j)}})\}_{0 \leq i < N}$.
3: **let** $\omega' = \omega^{-2}$
4: $\text{REG} \leftarrow \text{FFT}(\text{REG}, \{r_i\}_{0 \leq i < \ell}, \omega')$ ▷ Step 4-(b)
5: **for** $i \leftarrow 1, \ldots N-1$ **do**
6: $\quad \text{REG}[i] \leftarrow \mathit{EvalAut}(\text{REG}[i], \omega^{-i})$ ▷ Step 4-(c)
7: **end for**
8: **return** REG

each with R_i coefficients.[2] Hence this corresponds to a total of N coefficients, *i.e.*, N registers. The outputs are the coefficients of N/R_{i+1} polynomials modulo $(X^{R_{i+1}} - \omega'^{j'})$ ranging over all j' such that $r_i \cdot j' \equiv j \mod N$. Note that the total number of coefficients remains the same, *i.e.*, we still have N registers.

Let us now consider a single input polynomial (out of N/R_i), *i.e.*, one of the nodes in the remainder tree, and describe what computations are needed to produce the children nodes. This subroutine is described in Algorithm 5, called `FFT Subroutine` and is repeated for every node (meaning polynomial) of the layer, hence N/R_i times. We illustrate the reduction of this polynomial via an example to better describe the operations needed in this subroutine.

Example 1. We describe in this example the reduction from an input polynomial to a single child node for the simple radix-2 FFT. Assume we have as input a polynomial of the form

$$g_0 + g_1X + g_2X^2 + g_3X^3 + g_4X^4 + g_5X^5 + g_6X^6 + g_7X^7$$

and we want to reduce it modulo $(X^2 - \zeta)$. Similarly as for pointwise multiplication, it is possible to compute the coefficient terms for each monomial X^j. In our example, we would have constant coefficient $g_0 + \zeta g_2 + \zeta^2 g_4 + \zeta^3 g_6$ and X coefficient $g_1 + \zeta g_3 + \zeta^2 g_5 + \zeta^3 g_7$. In the remainder tree, this operation would have to be repeated for r different values of ζ, in particular for this example, four different values.

The homomorphic circuit to perform this reduction is illustrated in Fig. 3. We recall that the input coefficients g_i (both in the example and in Fig. 3) correspond to registers, in particular RLWE′ ciphertexts. The main operations needed for a reduction are scheme-switching for most of the coefficients, multiplication by a power of ζ, which can be done using automorphisms, and addition which corresponds to RLWE′ × RGSW multiplications.

Remark 2. The scheme switches at the beginning of the circuit convert RLWE′ ciphertexts to RGSW ciphertexts for all coefficients except the last. As mentioned previously, the circuit for the same coefficients is performed for various

[2] When $i = 0$, it starts with a single input polynomial modulo $X^N - \omega^0$.

Algorithm 5. FFT Subroutine

1: **Input:** Radix r which divides R for $R \mid N$, index j, and RLWE$'$ ciphertexts $\{ct_i\}_{0 \le i < R}$ storing coefficients of a single polynomial mod $(x^R - \omega'^j)$

2: **Output:** r tuples each of which consists of index j' such that $r \cdot j' \equiv j \bmod N$, and R/r RLWE$'$ ciphertexts

3: **for all** $0 \le i < R - R/r$ **do**

4:     $ct_i \leftarrow SwitchToRGSW(ct_i)$

5: **end for**

6: **if** this is the final FFT layer **then**

7:     **for all** $R - R/r \le i < R$ **do**

8:         let $S = \frac{Q}{4}$ $\triangleright$ 4 is the plaintext modulus after bootstrapping

9:         $ct_i \leftarrow S \odot ct_i$ $\triangleright$ ct_i is now RLWE instead of RLWE$'$

10:     **end for**

11: **end if**

12: let $\{j'_0, ..., j'_{r-1}\}$ = the set of all j''s satisfying $rj' \equiv j \bmod N$

13: **for all** $0 \le v \le r - 1$ **do**

14:     let $\zeta = \omega'^{j'_v}$

15:     **for all** $0 \le i < R/r$ **do**

16:         $accum[v][i] \leftarrow ct_{R-R/r+i}$

17:         **for** $\kappa \leftarrow [2, 3, ..., r]$ **do**

18:             $accum[v][i] \leftarrow EvalAut(accum, \zeta)$

19:             $accum[v][i] \leftarrow MulRGSW(ct_{R-\kappa \cdot R/r+i}, accum)$

20:         **end for**

21:     **end for**

22: **end for**

23: **output** r tuples $(j'_v, accum[v])$ for $0 \le v < r$

Algorithm 6. Full radix-r standard FFT (FFT)

1: **procedure** FFT($\{REG\}, \{r_i\}_{0 \le i < \ell}, \omega'$)

2:     $state \leftarrow \{(N, REG)\}$ $\triangleright$ List of tuples

3:     **for** i in $[0, 1, ..., \ell - 1]$ **do**

4:         $state \leftarrow$ FFT LAYER($r_i, \omega', state$)

5:     **end for**

6:     **return** REG

7: **end procedure**

8: **procedure** FFT LAYER(r_i, ω', list of tuples)

9:     **Input:** N/R_i tuples of the form $(j, \{ct_{j,0}, ..., ct_{j,R_i-1}\})$, where each $ct_{j,v}$ is an RLWE$'$ ciphertext

10:         $\triangleright$ $ct_{j,v}$ represents the v-th coefficient of a polynomial mod $(X^{R_i} - \omega'^j)$

11:     **Output:** N/R_{i+1} tuples of the form $(j', \{ct_{j',0}, ..., ct_{j',R_{i+1}-1}\})$.

12:         $\triangleright$ Each input j has r_i corresponding outputs j' such that $r_i \cdot j' \equiv j \bmod N$.

13:         $\triangleright$ $ct_{j',v}$ represents the v-th coefficient of a polynomial mod $(x^{R_{i+1}} - \omega'^{j'})$

14:     **for all** $(j, \{ct_{j,0}, ..., ct_{j,R_i-1}\})$ in input **do**

15:         FFT_SUBROUTINE($\{ct_{j,0}, ..., ct_{j,R_i-1}\}, r_i, j, \omega'$)

16:     **end for**

17: **end procedure**

---

values of ζ. For all these cases, the scheme-switching operations need only to be performed once (as the coefficients do not change) and thus the cost is amortized.

Details of this subroutine are given in Algorithm 5. Algorithm 6 provides the pseudocode for all $\phi(d)$ registers (`FFT Layer`) as well as the full FFT algorithm where all layers are considered (`FFT`).

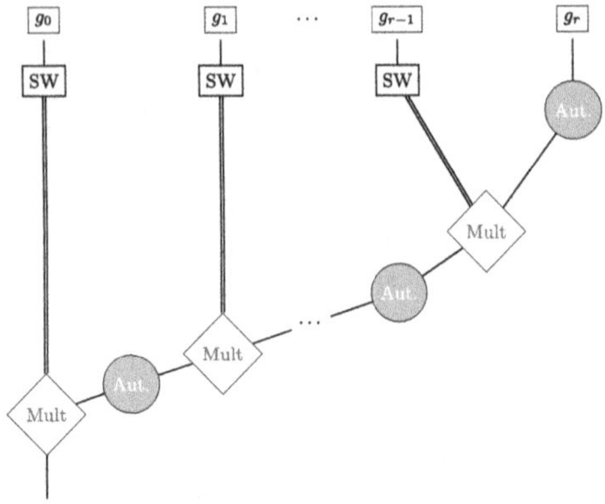

Fig. 3. One layer of FFT for a single input polynomial. A single line corresponds to RLWE ciphertexts and a double line to RGSW ciphertexts. SW stands for scheme-switching, Aut. for automorphisms and Mult for multiplication.

One can note from Algorithm 5 that the case of the last layer of the FFT slightly differs (see line 6). Indeed, it is possible to optimize the running-time of the FFT algorithm by modifying the nature of the elements considered in the very last layer of the FFT. Indeed, one can notice that the outputs of the IFFT only need to be RLWE ciphertexts, not RLWE$'$ ciphertexts. Hence, one can save operations by using RLWE registers instead of RLWE$'$ registers when possible. While RLWE cannot be scheme-switched to RGSW without blowing up the error, we can modify the last IFFT layer to use RLWE instead of RLWE$'$ for the registers that do not get scheme-switched (this corresponds to *accum* in Algorithm 5 or g_r in Fig. 3). Concretely, each of the $\phi(d)/r$ non-scheme-switched RLWE$'$ ciphertexts would be converted to RLWE by an $\mathcal{R} \odot$ RLWE$'$ operation with $\mathcal{R}$ element $\lceil Q/4 \rfloor$, where 4 is the plaintext modulus the msbExtract stage expects. This concludes the description of the homomorphic computation of $\mathbf{a} \cdot \mathbf{z}$. The output of this multiplicative step is thus $\phi(d)$ RLWE registers, each encrypting a coefficient of $\mathbf{a} \cdot \mathbf{z} \in \mathcal{R}_{in}$.

Adding b. From the previous step, we have obtained registers encoding the coefficients of $\mathbf{a} \cdot \mathbf{z}$. We also have the polynomial $\mathbf{b}$ in the clear. In order to obtain registers encoding the coefficients of $\mathbf{a} \cdot \mathbf{z} + \mathbf{b}$, we add $\mathbf{b}$ via fixed rotations, *i.e.*, scaling the ciphertext by a monomial. Concretely, to add a coefficient b_i to a register RLWE$(X^{(\mathbf{a} \cdot \mathbf{z})_i})$, we simply scale the RLWE ciphertext by X^{b_i} resulting in RLWE($X^{(\mathbf{a}\cdot\mathbf{z}+\mathbf{b})_i}$). Since X^{b_i} has norm 1, it does not increases the noise of the register. We thus now have $\phi(d)$ registers encoding the coefficients of $\mathbf{a}\cdot\mathbf{z}+\mathbf{b}$, as expected. This concludes the linear step of the algorithm.

4.3 msbExtract

The linear step outputs $\phi(d)$ RLWE registers each encrypting $\frac{Q}{4}X^{c_i}$, where each $c_i \in \mathbb{Z}_q$ is a noisy (un-rounded) decryption of the ith input ciphertext. We now operate separately on each register (and drop the subscript i) in order to recover from each register a plain-LWE encryption of $f(c)$, for some function f that applies rounding and allows for computation. Output ciphertexts have plaintext modulus 4; to compute NAND gates, it suffices for $f(c)$ to be 1 for $c \in [-q/8, 3q/8)$ and 0 elsewhere (we refer to [20] for more details). Focusing on a single register $(\mathbf{a}, \mathbf{b}) \in {\mathcal{R}_{reg}}^2$, we have

$$\mathbf{b}(X) = -\mathbf{a}(X)\cdot\mathbf{s}(X) + \mathbf{e}(X) + \frac{Q}{4}\mathbf{m}(X) \pmod{Q, \Phi_q(X)}$$

where $\mathbf{m}(X) = X^c$. Looking at a single coefficient of these polynomials, the ring product $\mathbf{a}(X)\cdot\mathbf{s}(X)$ will become a vector inner product between the coefficients of $\mathbf{s}$ and some permuted coefficients of $\mathbf{a}$. Because we use prime q, these polynomials have degree $\leq q-2$, and $X^{q-1} \equiv -1 - X - \cdots - X^{q-2}$. Note that, as for error growth, the fact that we consider prime cyclotomics instead of power-of-2 cyclotomics slightly changes the setting. We get for a single coefficient

$$\begin{aligned} b_i = &-a_i s_0 - a_{i-1}s_1 - \cdots - a_0 s_i - 0\cdot s_{i+1} - a_{q-2}s_{i+2} - a_{q-3}s_{i+3} - \cdots - a_{i+2}s_{q-2} \\ &+ a_{q-2}s_1 + a_{q-3}s_2 + \cdots + a_2 s_{q-3} + a_1 s_{q-2} + \frac{Q}{4}m_i + e_i \end{aligned}$$

which can be re-written as

$$\begin{aligned} \frac{Q}{4}m_i + e_i = b_i + \{&(a_i, a_{i-1}, \ldots, a_0, 0, a_{q-2}, a_{q-1}, \ldots, a_{i+2}) \\ &- (0, a_{q-2}, a_{q-1}, \ldots, a_1)\} \cdot (s_0, s_1 \ldots, s_{q-2}) \end{aligned}$$

For $0 \leq i \leq q-2$, letting $\vec{a_i}$ denote the above vector $(a_i, a_{i-1} - a_{q-2}, \ldots, a_{i+2} - a_1)$, we then have that $(\vec{a_i}, b_i)$ is an LWE encryption with noise e_i under secret key $\mathbf{s}_p = (s_0, \ldots, s_{q-2})$ of message m_i. Note that m_i is 1 if $c = i$, -1 if $c = q-1$, and 0 otherwise. To produce an encryption of $f(c)$, which should be 1 for $c \in (-q/8, 3q/8)$ and 0 elsewhere, we simply sum the relevant $(\vec{a_i}, b_i)$:

$$\sum_{i=\lceil 7q/8 \rceil}^{q-2} (\vec{a_i}, b_i) + \sum_{i=0}^{\lfloor 3q/8 \rfloor - 1} (\vec{a_i}, b_i)$$

taking care to ensure the number of summands is 3 mod 4, so that when $c = q-1$ the sum is 1 mod 4 as desired. (When $q \equiv 1 \bmod 8$, this will be the case for the summation written above.)

This gives us an LWE encryption with plaintext modulus 4 and ciphertext modulus Q under a key $\mathbf{s}_p \in \mathbb{Z}^{q-1}$. To conclude bootstrapping, we can keyswitch back to the orignal plain LWE secret key, and modulus switch back down to the original (much smaller than Q) ciphertext modulus.

5 Analysis

To evaluate the performance of our algorithm, we analyse its running-time as well as the error growth. We will first show that our homomorphic decryption procedure takes no more than $\mathcal{O}\left((k + r \cdot \ell)\phi(d)d_B\right)$ homomorphic operations.

5.1 Counting Homomorphic Operations

We will evaluate the efficiency of our algorithm by first measuring the time complexity in terms of the number of $\mathcal{R} \odot \mathrm{RLWE}'$ operations performed. We have already summarized in Sect. 3.2, Table 2 the number of $\mathcal{R} \odot \mathrm{RLWE}'$ operations needed for the main operations used in our scheme: scheme switching, automorphisms (with key switching) and $\mathrm{RGSW} \times \mathrm{RLWE}'$. We now describe the number of $\mathcal{R} \odot \mathrm{RLWE}'$ operations for the various steps of our algorithm.

Pointwise Multiplication. Based on the description given in Sect. 4.2, we have the following analysis. For a single coefficient X^j in the computation of the inner product, our algorithm performed k automorphisms and $(k-1)$ $\mathrm{RGSW} \times \mathrm{RLWE}'$ multiplications. Hence the number of $\mathcal{R} \odot \mathrm{RLWE}'$ operations per register is $(3k-2)d_B$. This computation needs to be repeated for all k coefficients of a single product and for $\phi(d)/k$ pairs of $(\tilde{\mathbf{a}}_i, \tilde{\mathbf{z}})$ polynomials. Thus the total number of $\mathcal{R} \odot \mathrm{RLWE}'$ operations for the entire pointwise multiplication algorithm is $(3k-2)\phi(d)d_B$.

Partial Inverse FFT. Based on the description given in Sect. 4.2, considering a single register and a single radix-r layer of FFT, the algorithm computes $(r-1)$ automorphisms, $(r-1)$ $\mathrm{RGSW} \times \mathrm{RLWE}'$ multiplications but only amortized $(1-1/r)$ scheme switches as explained in Sect. 4.2. Thus the total number of operations per layer is

$$\left((r-1) + 2(r-1) + \left(1 - \frac{1}{r}\right)\right)\phi(d)d_B = \left(3r - 2 - \frac{1}{r}\right)\phi(d)d_B.$$

Last Layer of IFFT Optimization: Recall that the outputs of the IFFT only need to be RLWE ciphertexts and not RLWE' ciphertexts. This allowed us to optimize the cost of the last layer of the IFFT by using RLWE registers instead of RLWE' registers when possible. By using this modification, the multiplications and automorphisms in this layer will use a factor of d_B fewer operations. Thus the total number of operations for the last layer is only

$$\left((r-1) + 2(r-1) + \frac{1}{r} + \left(1 - \frac{1}{r}\right)d_B\right)\phi(d) = \left(3r - 3 + \frac{1}{r} + d_B\left(1 - \frac{1}{r}\right)\right)\phi(d).$$

After the Last Layer: Recall that the very last step of the homomorphic partial IFFT is to multiply the ith output register in each group by ω^{-i}, via an automorphism that sends X to $X^{\omega^{-i}}$. Operation-wise, this corresponds to one automorphism per register. Since with the last-layer optimization the registers are RLWE instead of RLWE′, this corresponds to $\phi(d)$ operations in total.

Adding b. Recall that to add b_i to the register $\text{RLWE}(X^{(\mathbf{a}\cdot\mathbf{z})_i})$, we simply scaled the RLWE ciphertext by X^{b_i}. No $\mathcal{R} \odot \text{RLWE}'$ operations are involved (Table 3).

Table 3. Summary of $\mathcal{R} \odot \text{RLWE}'$ operation count.

Steps of the algorithm	$\mathcal{R} \odot \text{RLWE}'$ operations
Partial FFT of **a**	–
Pointwise multiplication	$(3k-2)\phi(d)d_B$
Partial IFFT (per layer)	$(3r-2-\frac{1}{r})\phi(d)d_B$
Last layer of IFFT	$(3r-3+\frac{1}{r}+d_B(1-\frac{1}{r}))\phi(d)$
Last IFFT step	$\phi(d)$
Adding **b**	–

5.2 Error Growth

We have already summarized in Table 2 the error growth coming from the scheme switching, automorphisms (with key switching) and RGSW × RLWE′ operations. We now describe the error growth resulting from the various steps of our algorithm based on the error variance for each of these operations and the operation count described in the previous section.

Pointwise Multiplication. Recall from the description given in Sect. 4.2 that the algorithm starts with an inital RLWE′ ciphertext, denoted as *accum*, which is a "fresh" ciphertext from the evaluation key with error variance $\sigma^2_{eval\_key}$. Each automorphism performed during pointwise multiplication adds $\sigma^2_{\odot,aut\_key}$ error variance, and each multiplication with a fresh RGSW ciphertext adds $2\sigma^2_{\odot,\text{RGSW}}$ error variance. Hence, the error variance after pointwise multiplication is $(3k-2)(\sigma^2_{\odot,aut\_key}+2\sigma^2_{\odot,\text{RGSW}})+\sigma^2_{eval\_key}$.

Inverse FFT. Again, recall that each automorphism adds $\sigma^2_{\odot,aut\_key}$ error variance. The output of schemeswitching has $\sigma^2_{sw}=\sigma^2_{\odot,eval\_key}+\ell_1(s)\sigma^2_{in}$ error variance. Let σ^2_{accum} be initialized as σ^2_{in}. Each automorphism and RGSW × RLWE′ multiplication (performed a total amount of $r-1$ times) updates the variance as $\sigma^2_{accum} \leftarrow \sigma^2_{accum}+\sigma^2_{\odot,aut\_key}$ and $\sigma^2_{accum} \leftarrow \sigma^2_{accum}+2\sigma^2_{\odot,sw}$ where $\sigma^2_{\odot,sw} \leq \frac{B^2}{6}d_B q\sigma^2_{sw}$. Hence, in total, the error variance after a radix-r layer becomes $\sigma^2_{in}+(r-1)(\sigma^2_{\odot,aut\_key}+2\sigma^2_{\odot,sw})$ for $\sigma^2_{\odot,sw} \leq \frac{B^2}{6}d_B q\sigma^2_{sw}$.

After Last Layer. Multiplying the ith output register in each group by ω^{-i} with an automorphism increases (additively) the error variance by $\sigma^2_{\odot,aut\_key}$.

Adding b. Scaling by a monomial does not increase the error. This result is summarized in Table 4.

Table 4. Summary of error growth.

Algorithms	Error growth
Partial FFT of **a**	–
Pointwise multiplication	$(3k-2)(\sigma^2_{\odot,aut\_key} + 2\sigma^2_{\odot,\mathrm{RGSW}}) + \sigma^2_{eval\_key}$
Partial IFFT (per layer)	$\sigma^2_{in} + (r-1)(\sigma^2_{\odot,aut\_key} + 2(\sigma^2_{\odot,eval\_key} + \ell_1(s)\sigma^2_{in}))$
Last IFFT step	$\sigma^2_{\odot,aut\_key}$
Adding **b**	–

5.3 Asymptotic Analysis

Let $\lambda = O(n)$ the be security level considered. We study the performance of our algorithm as λ increases, *i.e.*, when n tends to infinity. Recall that the other parameters used in our algorithm are $d_B = \lceil \log_B Q \rceil = O(\log n)$, the number of layers ℓ (*i.e.*, the multiplicative depth) and $k = r = \phi(d)^{1/\ell}$ (k is the degree at which we stop the partial FFT and r is the radix for an FFT layer).

Theorem 2. *Let $\phi(d) = O(n)$ be the number of packed ciphertexts and $q, Q =$ poly(n) the moduli of the rings considered. The total cost of bootstrapping (non-amortized) then corresponds to $O(n^{1+\frac{1}{\ell}} \cdot \log n \cdot \ell)$ homomorphic operations (in terms of the number of $\mathcal{R} \odot \mathrm{RLWE}'$ operations).*

Proof. The number of $\odot$ operations in the pointwise multiplication step is $(3k-2)\phi(d)d_B$ which asymptotically corresponds to $O(n^{1+\frac{1}{\ell}} \log n)$. Similarly, the inverse FFT requires $(3r - 2 - \frac{1}{r})\phi(d)d_B\ell$ operations (without including the last layer modification which asymptotically does not change the result) which asymptotically gives $O(n^{1+\frac{1}{\ell}} \cdot \log n \cdot \ell)$. □

Corollary 2. *The amortized cost per message is $O(n^{\frac{1}{\ell}} \cdot \log n \cdot \ell)$ homomorphic operations (in terms of the number of $\mathcal{R} \odot \mathrm{RLWE}'$ operations).*

Remark 3. Note that we can also reduce the total number of homomorphic operations in the case that we only need to pack less-than-$\phi(d)$ LWE ciphertexts, which we refer to sparse packing. Please refer to the full version of the paper [6] for the analysis on computational cost of the sparse packing case.

5.4 Comparison with Previous and Concurrent Work

Our algorithm can be compared to two lines of work: sequential bootstrapping algorithms such as FHEW/TFHE [5,7] and the amortized bootstrapping algorithms of [21] and [17] (as our algorithm performs asymptotically better than [16], we focus on the comparison with the follow-up work [17]). The asymptotic running times of the algorithms are reported in Table 5, and show that our algorithm is asymptotically much faster than both [5,7] (reducing the dependency on the main security parameter from linear $O(n)$ to just n^ϵ for arbitrary small $\epsilon = 1/\ell$), and [21] (reducing the dependency on ℓ from exponential 3^ℓ to linear $O(\ell)$.) While [17] is asymptotically faster, we now discuss why our algorithm is expected to outperform [17] for practical parameters.

Assume optimistically that the complexity of [17] is of the form $f(n, \ell) = 2^\ell \cdot \log(n)$, where ℓ is the recursive depth of the inverse FFT and n the ring dimension. The 2^ℓ term is inherited by the use of the Nussbaumer transform from [21], and $\log(n)$ is the "polylog" overhead. [17, section 7.3] sets $\ell = 5$, and, in fact, due to the use of the SIMD parallelization technique from [16], this is the smallest possible value of ℓ. On the other hand, the complexity of our algorithm is $g(n, \ell) = \ell \cdot n^{1/\ell}$, where ℓ can be set to any constant. To facilitate a more direct comparison to [17], consider setting $\ell = 5$ in our algorithm as well. Since noise growth of [17] and our algorithm depend in a similar way on the recursive depth ℓ, using the same value of ℓ should result in similar values of the ciphertext modulus Q and ring dimension n, for the same security level. So, for a fixed $\ell = 5$, basic operations in [17] and our work can be assumed to have roughly the same unit cost. The two algorithms can then be compared by checking when $f(n, 5) < g(n, 5)$. It is easy to check that the crossover point $f(n, 5) = g(n, 5)$ is given by ring dimension $n = 2^{40}$, which is well beyond any conceivable instantiation of lattice cryptography. While this is only a rough comparison, it should be clear that for any reasonable value of the ring dimension n, our algorithm can be expected to outperform the (asymptotically faster) algorithm of [17]. In other words, [17] suffers from the very same limitations that made [21] completely impractical. This is precisely the problem addressed in our work, where the overhead of [21] is reduced from 2^ℓ to just ℓ, making amortization much closer to practicality. We have already mentioned the work of Liu and Wang [18] who achieved the same asymptotic complexity as [16,17], but were able to make their bootstrapping scheme also efficient using BFV ciphertexts. As mentioned previously, their work differs by using a super-polynomial modulus. We refer to [18, Section 7] for detailed performance analysis, including timings.

Following previous work, performance in Table 5 is measured as the number of operations on cryptographic registers, and hides many important parameters that still have a big impact on the concrete performance of the algorithms in practice. In order to provide (still preliminary, but) more realistic estimates of the performance of the algorithm, we also evaluated the number of (integer) arithmetic operations required for concrete values of the parameters, with a target security level STD192. Next, we observe that since each NTT operation works on a q dimensional vector, it requires a number of arithmetic operation proportional

Table 5. Comparing asymptotic cost of various bootstrapping algorithms in terms of homomorphic operations, where ℓ corresponds to the recursive depth in each algorithm. For uniformity with previous work, performance is expressed as the number of RGSW $\times$ RGSW products, or equivalent operations. Alternatively, the number of basic $\mathcal{R} \odot$ RLWE$'$ products can be obtained by multiplying these figures by $O(\log n)$, the length of the gadget vector.

Scheme	Total cost	Number of messages	Amortized cost
FHEW	$\tilde{O}(n)$	1	$\tilde{O}(n)$
TFHE	$O(n)$	1	$O(n)$
[21]	$\tilde{O}(3^\ell \cdot n^{1+1/\ell})$	$O(n)$	$\tilde{O}(3^\ell \cdot n^{1/\ell})$
[17]	$\tilde{O}(n)$	$O(n)$	$\tilde{O}(1)$
[18]	$\tilde{O}(n)$	$O(n)$	$\tilde{O}(1)$
our work	$O(\ell \cdot n^{1+1/\ell})$	$O(n)$	$O(\ell \cdot n^{1/\ell})$

to $q \log q$. So, in the before-last column of Table 6 we estimate the total number of arithmetic operation as $NTT \times q \log q$. We used [15, Table 1] for the number of $\odot$ operations in FHEW-like schemes and recall that one can easily convert the number of $\odot$ products to the number of NTTs as each $\odot$ product requires $(d_B + 1)$ NTT operations. The reported number of $\odot$ multiplication for [21] comes from a non-public report provided to us by the authors. The before-last column for [21] was obtained using the smallest values of q, d_B in the table as a conservative lower bound. Finally, the last column of Table 6 reports the key size (number of RLWE' ciphertexts). The parameters and numbers provided in Table 6 are tentative, preliminary estimates only meant to provide some intuition about the potential performance of our algorithm. Still, they are enough to draw some general conclusions: our algorithm clearly outperforms previous methods for amortized FHEW bootstrapping, improving [21] by two orders of magnitude. When comparing with sequential bootstrapping methods, our algorithm is practical enough to offer comparable (potentially better) performance. But the improvement is not yet sufficiently marked to make its implementation and use attractive in practice.

Table 6. Comparing cost of various bootstrapping algorithm in terms of $\odot$ operations, number of NTTs performed and key size. The reported numbers for the amortized schemes are amortized over the number of packed ciphertexts. The parameter N is the ring dimension for registers (for us it is the same as q since q is prime in our algorithm).

FHEW-like schemes	n	q	N	$\log_2 Q$	B	d_B	$\odot$ mult.	NTTs	NTTs $\times q \log q$	# keys
FHEW-AP [7,20]	1024	1024	2048	54	2^{27}	2	3968	11,904	10^8	126 976
TFHE-GINX [5]	1024	1024	2048	54	2^{27}	2	4096	12288	10^8	4096
FHEW-improved [15]	1024	1024	2048	37	2^{13}	3	3074	12,296	10^8	3073
[21] (amortized)	–	–	2187	37	–	–	47844	–	$>10^9$	–
Ours (amortized)	1024	7681	7681	143	2^{71}	2	101	304	3×10^7	9728

6 Conclusion and Future Work

We present a novel amortized bootstrapping algorithm with much smaller overhead than prior amortized work, in particular smaller than in the algorithm presented by Micciancio and Sorrell in [21]. We make use of ring automorphisms to perform the multiplication by twiddle factors and replace the Nussbaumer transform with the more practical Number Theoretic Transform.

In order to properly evaluate the practicality of our algorithm, and accurately compare it with previous work, we considered implementing it within some mainstream FHE library, like OpenFHE [1]. However, the preliminary estimates in Sect. 5.4 and our initial implementation effort suggest that both the algorithm and the support offered by state-of-the-art FHE libraries may still not be adequate to deliver concrete improvements in practice. In fact, implementing our algorithm within OpenFHE (or similar libraries) raises a number of technical challenges. Most FHE libraries (incuding OpenFHE) currently only support power-of-two cyclotomic rings, which are the most widely used rings in lattice cryptography. However, our algorithm makes essential use of prime cyclotomics. Some support of cyclotomics other than powers-of-two is offered by the HElib library [12], as well some undocumented functions within the OpenFHE codebase. However, in both cases, the implementation is based on Bluestein FFT, which for technical reasons is limited to ciphertext moduli of size at most 27-bit. As a result, the use of a 143-bit modulus (as in the example parameters in Table 6) would carry at least a $\times 6$ slowdown, compared to sequential bootstrapping methods which can be directly implemented using standard 64-bit arithmetics. Still, our theoretical estimates in Sect. 5.4 show that amortized FHEW bootstrapping has the potential of being practical, and that, with proper library support and further optimizations, it can offer a practical alternative to sequential bootstrapping algorithms. We hope our work will provide a motivation to extend OpenFHE and other libraries with optimized support for prime (or arbitrary) cyclotomics, and promote further investigation and improvement of amortized FHEW bootstrapping algorithm.

Acknowledgement. Research supported in part by the Swiss National Science Foundation Early Postdoc Mobility Fellowship, Intel Cryptographic Frontiers award, NSF Award CNS-1936703, and SAIT Global Research Cluster.

References

1. Al Badawi, A., et al.: OpenFHE: open-source fully homomorphic encryption library. In: Proceedings of the 10th Workshop on Encrypted Computing & Applied Homomorphic Cryptography, pp. 53–63 (2022)
2. Alperin-Sheriff, J., Peikert, C.: Practical bootstrapping in quasilinear time. In: Canetti, R., Garay, J.A. (eds.) CRYPTO 2013. LNCS, vol. 8042, pp. 1–20. Springer, Heidelberg (2013). https://doi.org/10.1007/978-3-642-40041-4_1
3. Bonnoron, G., Ducas, L., Fillinger, M.: Large FHE gates from tensored homomorphic accumulator. In: Joux, A., Nitaj, A., Rachidi, T. (eds.) AFRICACRYPT 2018.

LNCS, vol. 10831, pp. 217–251. Springer, Cham (2018). https://doi.org/10.1007/978-3-319-89339-6_13
4. Brakerski, Z., Gentry, C., Vaikuntanathan, V.: (Leveled) fully homomorphic encryption without bootstrapping. ACM Trans. Comput. Theory **6**(3), 13:1–13:36 (2014). https://doi.org/10.1145/2633600
5. Chillotti, I., Gama, N., Georgieva, M., Izabachène, M.: TFHE: fast fully homomorphic encryption over the torus. J. Cryptol. **33**(1), 34–91 (2020)
6. DeMicheli, G., Kim, D., Micciancio, D., Suhl, A.: Faster amortized fhew bootstrapping using ring automorphisms. Cryptology ePrint Archive, Paper 2023/112 (2023). https://eprint.iacr.org/2023/112
7. Ducas, L., Micciancio, D.: FHEW: bootstrapping homomorphic encryption in less than a second. In: Oswald, E., Fischlin, M. (eds.) EUROCRYPT 2015. LNCS, vol. 9056, pp. 617–640. Springer, Heidelberg (2015). https://doi.org/10.1007/978-3-662-46800-5_24
8. Gentry, C.: A fully homomorphic encryption scheme. Stanford university (2009)
9. Gentry, C., Halevi, S., Smart, N.P.: Fully homomorphic encryption with polylog overhead. In: Pointcheval, D., Johansson, T. (eds.) EUROCRYPT 2012. LNCS, vol. 7237, pp. 465–482. Springer, Heidelberg (2012). https://doi.org/10.1007/978-3-642-29011-4_28
10. Gentry, C., Halevi, S., Smart, N.P.: Homomorphic evaluation of the AES circuit. In: Safavi-Naini, R., Canetti, R. (eds.) CRYPTO 2012. LNCS, vol. 7417, pp. 850–867. Springer, Heidelberg (2012). https://doi.org/10.1007/978-3-642-32009-5_49
11. Guimarães, A., Pereira, H.V.L., van Leeuwen, B.: Amortized bootstrapping revisited: simpler, asymptotically-faster, implemented. In: Guo, J., Steinfeld, R. (eds.) Advances in Cryptology – ASIACRYPT 2023. ASIACRYPT 2023. LNCS, vol. 14443, pp. 3–35. Springer, Singapore (2023). https://doi.org/10.1007/978-981-99-8736-8_1
12. Halevi, S., Shoup, V.: Algorithms in HElib. In: Garay, J.A., Gennaro, R. (eds.) CRYPTO 2014. LNCS, vol. 8616, pp. 554–571. Springer, Heidelberg (2014). https://doi.org/10.1007/978-3-662-44371-2_31
13. Halevi, S., Shoup, V.: Faster homomorphic linear transformations in HElib. In: Shacham, H., Boldyreva, A. (eds.) CRYPTO 2018. LNCS, vol. 10991, pp. 93–120. Springer, Cham (2018). https://doi.org/10.1007/978-3-319-96884-1_4
14. Kim, A., et al.: General bootstrapping approach for RLWE-based homomorphic encryption. IEEE Trans. Comput. (2023)
15. Lee, Y., et al.: Efficient FHEW bootstrapping with small evaluation keys, and applications to threshold homomorphic encryption. Cryptology ePrint Archive (2022)
16. Liu, F.H., Wang, H.: Batch bootstrapping I: a new framework for SIMD bootstrapping in polynomial modulus. In: Hazay, C., Stam, M. (eds.) Advances in Cryptology – EUROCRYPT 2023. EUROCRYPT 2023. LNCS, vol. 14006, pp. 321–352. Springer, Cham (2023). https://doi.org/10.1007/978-3-031-30620-4_11
17. Liu, F.H., Wang, H.: Batch bootstrapping II: bootstrapping in polynomial modulus only requires $\widetilde{O}(1)$ FHE multiplications in amortization. In: Hazay, C., Stam, M. (eds.) Advances in Cryptology – EUROCRYPT 2023. EUROCRYPT 2023. LNCS, vol. 14006, pp. 353–384. Springer, Cham (2023). https://doi.org/10.1007/978-3-031-30620-4_12
18. Liu, Z., Wang, Y.: Amortized functional bootstrapping in less than 7 ms, with $\widetilde{O}(1)$ polynomial multiplications. In: Guo, J., Steinfeld, R. (eds.) Advances in Cryptology – ASIACRYPT 2023. ASIACRYPT 2023. LNCS, vol. 14443, pp. 101–132. Springer, Singapore (2023). https://doi.org/10.1007/978-981-99-8736-8_4

19. Lyubashevsky, V., Peikert, C., Regev, O.: On ideal lattices and learning with errors over rings. J. ACM **60**(6), 43:1–43:35 (2013). https://doi.org/10.1145/2535925
20. Micciancio, D., Polyakov, Y.: Bootstrapping in FHEW-like cryptosystems. In: Proceedings of the 9th on Workshop on Encrypted Computing & Applied Homomorphic Cryptography, pp. 17–28 (2021)
21. Micciancio, D., Sorrell, J.: Ring packing and amortized FHEW bootstrapping. In: Chatzigiannakis, I., Kaklamanis, C., Marx, D., Sannella, D. (eds.) 45th International Colloquium on Automata, Languages, and Programming, ICALP 2018, 9–13 July 2018, Prague, Czech Republic. LIPIcs, vol. 107, pp. 100:1–100:14. Schloss Dagstuhl - Leibniz-Zentrum für Informatik (2018). https://doi.org/10.4230/LIPIcs.ICALP.2018.100
22. Stehlé, D., Steinfeld, R., Tanaka, K., Xagawa, K.: Efficient public key encryption based on ideal lattices. In: Matsui, M. (ed.) ASIACRYPT 2009. LNCS, vol. 5912, pp. 617–635. Springer, Heidelberg (2009). https://doi.org/10.1007/978-3-642-10366-7_36

Towards Practical Multi-key TFHE: Parallelizable, Key-Compatible, Quasi-linear Complexity

Hyesun Kwak, Seonhong Min, and Yongsoo Song(✉)

Seoul National University, Seoul, Republic of Korea
{hskwak,minsh,y.song}@snu.ac.kr

Abstract. Multi-key homomorphic encryption is a generalized notion of homomorphic encryption supporting arbitrary computation on ciphertexts, possibly encrypted under different keys. In this paper, we revisit the work of Chen, Chillotti and Song (ASIACRYPT 2019) and present yet another multi-key variant of the TFHE scheme.

The previous construction by Chen et al. involves a blind rotation procedure where the complexity of each iteration gradually increases as it continuously operates on ciphertexts under different keys. Hence, the complexity of gate bootstrapping grows quadratically with respect to the number of associated keys.

Our scheme is based on a new blind rotation algorithm which consists of two separate phases. We first split a given multi-key ciphertext into several single-key ciphertexts, take each of them as input to the blind rotation procedure, and obtain accumulators corresponding to individual keys. Then, we merge these single-key accumulators into a single multi-key accumulator. In particular, we develop a novel homomorphic operation between single-key and multi-key ciphertexts to instantiate our pipeline. Therefore, our construction achieves an almost linear time complexity since the gate bootstrapping is dominated by the first phase of blind rotation which requires only independent single-key operations. It also enjoys with great advantages of parallelizability and key-compatibility.

We implement the proposed scheme and provide its performance benchmark. For example, our 16-key gate bootstrapping takes about 5.65 s, which is 4.38x faster compared to the prior work.

Keywords: Homomorphic Encryption · Multi-Key Homomorphic Encryption · Fully Homomorphic Encryption over Torus

1 Introduction

Homomorphic encryption (HE) is a cryptosystem which allows us to evaluate arbitrary functions directly on encrypted data without decryption. For example, in a cloud environment, the user encrypts its message with its own key and send it

Q. Tang and V. Teague (Eds.): PKC 2024, LNCS 14604, pp. 354–385, 2024.
https://doi.org/10.1007/978-3-031-57728-4_12

to the cloud. The desired computations are executed in the cloud side and finally the user receive the ciphertext that encrypts the result of the computation without any information leakage. Due to such an attribute, it has been regarded as one of the promising solutions to process privacy-sensitive data such as financial or medical data. After the very first construction of HE by Gentry [16], a variety of HE schemes have been proposed such as BFV [3,15], GSW [17], BGV [4], TFHE [10] and CKKS [9].

However, the conventional HE technology has an intrinsic disadvantage in that the authority is concentrated to a single party, as it only supports operations between data encrypted under the same secret key. Thereby, the usage of HE is restricted to scenarios where all data owners commonly trust a party who owns the secret key. To resolve this problem, several variants of HE with distributed authority have been studied, such as threshold HE [1,25,27] and multi-key HE (MKHE) [6,7,12,22,26,28]. The former acts like a single-key HE by encrypting data under a jointly constructed public key and the latter supports operations between data encrypted with different secret keys. Although threshold HE is generally more efficient in ciphertext size and computation cost, no additional party can join the computation once the joint key is generated. On the other hand, MKHE allows each user to independently generate its own keys and join the computation. In this paper, we focus on the TFHE scheme [10], and its first and the only multi-key variant by Chen, Chillotti and Song (CCS19) [6].

TFHE is a well-known homomorphic encryption based on the *Learning with Errors* (LWE) [29] and Ring-LWE (RLWE) [23] problems. It allows us to perform arbitrary binary gate operations via a costly operation called the *gate bootstrapping* which mainly consists of three steps: linear combination, blind rotation and key-switching. In the first step, it computes a linear combination of input LWE ciphertexts corresponding to the gate to be evaluated. In the following blind rotation step, it homomorphically decrypts the resulting LWE ciphertext from the linear combination step over the exponent of a monomial using the *external product* operation. By multiplying this monomial to the *test polynomial* with pre-assigned coefficient and extracting the constant term, we obtain an LWE ciphertext with ring dimension encrypting the output of the gate. Finally, the key-switching step reduces the ciphertext dimension back to the LWE dimension.

The MK variant of TFHE follows the same pipeline although the blind rotation step is realized in a multi-key manner. During the blind rotation step in the original TFHE, it recursively evaluates the homomorphic MUX gates on the accumulator ACC via the external product that multiplies an RGSW ciphertext to an RLWE ciphertext. When it comes to the multi-key situation, the multiplicand of the external product is an MK-RLWE ciphertext whereas the multiplier is an RGSW ciphertext generated by a single party. In CCS19 [6], the authors designed an RGSW-like cryptosystem and a multiplication method called the *hybrid product* which has the same functionality to external product with faster speed and small noise growth. However, the time complexity of blind rotation step from hybrid product is quadratic with respect to the number of associated parties.

1.1 Our Contributions

In this paper, we construct an improved multi-key TFHE scheme with a blind rotation algorithm that is (1) asymptotically faster, (2) parallelizable, and (3) key-compatible with the single-key scheme. We refactored the blind rotation algorithm to first perform single-key multiplications and then merge the results into a multi-key ciphertext. During the party-wise computation, we only make use of a single-key multiplication and thus its time complexity is linear to the number of parties k. Merging the resulting ciphertexts of each party requires $O(k^2)$ time complexity since we perform k multi-key multiplications, nevertheless it is relatively fast compared to the party-wise blind rotation. Consequently, we achieve quasi-linear time complexity which is dominated by the party-wise blind rotation.

However, this cannot be actualized with the existing building blocks in prior work since they only support a multiplication between a fresh (structured) single-key encryption and a multi-key ciphertext. Hence we instantiate our idea by introducing a new homomorphic multiplication method called the *generalized external product.* This generalized external product can be regarded as an improvement of the hybrid product from CCS19, but it exploits the hybrid product as a building block. It multiplies a single-key RLEV ciphertext, which is upper half of the RGSW ciphertext, directly to an MK-RLWE ciphertext, and then 'relinearize' the resulting ciphertext with a quadratic key structure using the hybrid product. As a side contribution, we improve the performance of hybrid product from the observation that we can rearrange the order of operations and reduce the execution time in almost half. The noise variance is slightly smaller than the original algorithm as well.

With the improved hybrid product and the generalized external product, we finally realize the asymptotically faster MK-TFHE scheme. In the blind rotation step, we first execute the blind rotation party-wise with the temporary accumulators ACC'_i of RLEV ciphertexts for $1 \leq i \leq k$ in a single-key manner. Then we merge the ACC'_is into a single MK-RLWE ciphertext ACC using our generalized external product. Figure 1 depicts the blind rotation of CCS19 and our new algorithm.

We also remark that this party-wise blind rotation is parallelizable. Compared to the sequential multiplications in the blind rotation from CCS19, our algorithm can be executed party-wise in parallel and then merged sequentially. Furthermore, the bootstrapping key in our scheme is compatible to a single-party TFHE scheme [10] as well. Our scheme makes use of RGSW encryptions of the LWE secret key as blind rotation key, identical to the blind rotation key for the TFHE scheme with a single auxiliary key of the ring key.

Finally, we implement our multi-key variant of TFHE scheme and provide the basic benchmarks and the comparison between CCS19 and ours. For example, our experiment of 16-key gate bootstrapping demonstrates about 4.38x speedup without parallelization, and 52.60x speedup with parallelization over prior work.

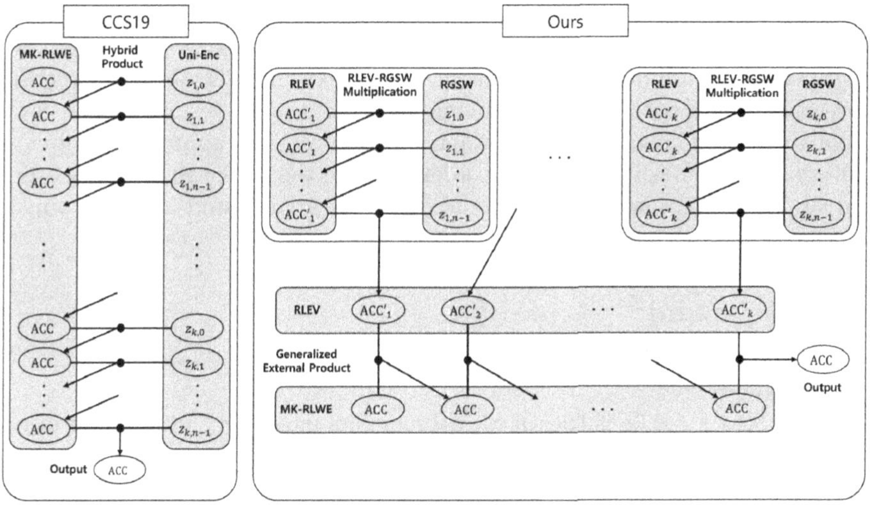

Fig. 1. High-level overview of the blind rotation algorithm of MK variant of TFHE from CCS19 and Ours.

1.2 Related Works

After López-Alt et al. [22] first proposed the concept of MKHE, there have been several follow-up studies to construct multi-key HE schemes. Clear and McGoldrick [12] constructed MKHE from GSW [17] by introducing a *masking system* where a ciphertext, encrypted under an individual key, is converted to be encrypted under a master secret key. Mukherjee and Wichs [26] simplified the masking system and build a two-round MPC protocol from the MKHE scheme. These schemes support a single-hop evaluation where participants must be determined at the start. The contemporary studies Peikert and Shiehian [28] constructed a multi-hop scheme from GSW [17] that supports dynamic computation on ciphertexts encrypted under additional keys by expanding the ciphertext to be encrypted under the union of the original set of keys and the additional keys.

Then, there have been several studies on MK variants of batched HE schemes. Chen, Zhang and Wang [8] built an MKHE scheme based on BGV [4] with a compact ciphertext extension. Chen, Dai, Kim and Song [7] presented multi-key variants of BFV [3,15] and CKKS [9] with quadratic complexity, and it was improved to have a linear complexity in a recent work of Kim et al. [19].

On the other hand, Brakerski and Perlman [5] presented an MK-LWE scheme whose bootstrapping process relies on the external product. A follow-up study by Chen, Chillotti and Song [6] improved its efficiency by introducing a hybrid product between single-key and multi-key encryptions and constructing an MK-variant of TFHE [10]. This is the most relevant work to ours, and its detailed description will be given in Sect. 3.

Recently, Klemsa et al. [20] proposed a variant of TFHE scheme for multiple parties, which is partially MK and partially Threshold. Its blind rotation keys are encrypted as n-out-of-n threshold HE ciphertexts under a joint key structure, while it encrypts data and key-switching keys in a multi-key manner in order to enhance the bootstrapping performance. However, this approach requires an additional communication round in order to make the public RGSW blind rotation key, and even few more additional communication round in order to make the scheme fully-dynamic.

2 Background

2.1 Notation

The real torus $\mathbb{T} = \mathbb{R}/\mathbb{Z}$ is the set of real numbers modulo 1. For a power-of-two integer N, we write $T = \mathbb{T}[X]/(X^N + 1)$. We denote vectors in lower-case bold (e.g. $\mathbf{a}$), and matrices in upper-case bold (e.g. $\mathbf{A}$). The inner product of two vectors $\mathbf{a}, \mathbf{b}$ is denoted by $\langle \mathbf{a}, \mathbf{b} \rangle$. For a positive integer k, we write $[k] = \{1, \ldots, k\}$.

We use $x \leftarrow S$ to denote that x is sampled uniformly from a set S. For a real $\alpha \geq 0$, ψ' denotes the Gaussian distribution of variance α^2. When sampling a polynomial from T, we use ψ to denote a distribution over T which samples N coefficients of the output polynomial independently from the Gaussian distribution of variance β^2 for a real $\beta \geq 0$.

2.2 LWE and RLWE Assumptions

The security of TFHE relies on the torus variants of LWE and RLWE assumptions [10].

Definition 1 (The LWE assumption). *Let n be a positive integer, $\alpha > 0$ a noise parameter, and χ' a key distribution over $\mathbb{Z}^n$. An LWE instance of a secret $\mathbf{z} \in \mathbb{Z}^n$ is a tuple $(b, \mathbf{a}) \in \mathbb{T}^{n+1}$ generated by $\mathbf{a} \leftarrow \mathbb{T}^n$, $e \leftarrow \psi'$ and $b = -\langle \mathbf{a}, \mathbf{z} \rangle + e \pmod 1$. The LWE assumption states that the LWE distribution of a secret $\mathbf{z} \leftarrow \chi'$ is computationally indistinguishable from the uniform distribution over $\mathbb{T}^{n+1}$.*

Definition 2 (The RLWE assumption). *Let N be a power of two, $\beta > 0$ a noise parameter, and χ a key distribution over R. An RLWE instance of a secret $s \in R = \mathbb{Z}[X]/(X^N + 1)$ is a pair $(b, a) \in T^2$ generated by $a \leftarrow T$, $e \leftarrow \psi$ and $b = -a \cdot s + e \pmod 1$. The RLWE assumption states that the RLWE distribution of a secret $s \leftarrow \chi$ is computationally indistinguishable from the uniform distribution over T^2.*

Under these assumptions, we can define the (R)LWE cryptosystem. An LWE ciphertext is a vector of torus elements, in a form of $(b, \mathbf{a}) \in \mathbb{T}^{n+1}$ and an RLWE ciphertext is a tuple $(b, a) \in T^2$. Now we introduce *phase*, a randomized encoding of (R)LWE ciphertexts. The phase for LWE ciphertext, $\varphi_{\mathbf{z}}(\cdot) : \mathbb{T}^{n+1} \to \mathbb{T}$ is defined by $\varphi_{\mathbf{z}}(b, \mathbf{a}) = b + \langle \mathbf{a}, \mathbf{z} \rangle \pmod 1$ and the phase for RLWE ciphertext $\varphi_s(\cdot) : T^2 \to T$ is defined by $\varphi_s(b, a) = b + a \cdot s \pmod 1$. We remark that the phase preserves the linear combinations between the (R)LWE ciphertexts.

2.3 Multi-key Homomorphic Encryption

MKHE is a variant of HE that enables computation on ciphertexts encrypted under different keys. It contains five PPT algorithms (Setup, KeyGen, Enc, Eval, Dec).

- **Setup**: $pp \leftarrow \texttt{Setup}(1^\lambda)$. Given the security parameter λ, set the public parameter set pp.
- **Key Generation**: $(\mathsf{sk}_i, \mathsf{pk}_i) \leftarrow \texttt{KeyGen}(i)$. A party i generates its secret key sk_i and public key pk_i.
- **Encryption**: $\mathsf{ct} \leftarrow \texttt{Enc}(\mathsf{pk}_i; m)$. A party i encrypts its message m with its public key pk_i and output a ciphertext ct.
- **Evaluation**: $\overline{\mathsf{ct}} \leftarrow \texttt{Eval}(\mathcal{C}, \mathsf{pk}_1, \ldots, \mathsf{pk}_k; \overline{\mathsf{ct}}_1, \ldots, \overline{\mathsf{ct}}_l)$. Given a circuit $\mathcal{C}$, ciphertexts $\overline{\mathsf{ct}}_1, \ldots, \overline{\mathsf{ct}}_l$, and public keys $\mathsf{pk}_1, \ldots, \mathsf{pk}_k$ of associated parties, output a ciphertext ct.
- **Decryption**: $m \leftarrow \texttt{Dec}(\mathsf{sk}_1, \ldots, \mathsf{sk}_k; \overline{\mathsf{ct}})$. Given a ciphertext $\overline{\mathsf{ct}}$ and secret keys $\mathsf{sk}_1, \ldots, \mathsf{sk}_k$ of associated parties, output a message m.

Let $\overline{\mathsf{ct}}_1, \ldots, \overline{\mathsf{ct}}_l$ be ciphertexts encrypting $m_1, \ldots, m_l$, respectively, and $\mathsf{pk}_1, \ldots, \mathsf{pk}_k$ be public keys of associated parties. An MKHE scheme is considered to be secure if its encryption is semantically secure. A valid MKHE scheme satisfies that

$$\texttt{Dec}(\mathsf{sk}_1, \ldots, \mathsf{sk}_k; \texttt{Eval}(\mathcal{C}, \mathsf{pk}_1, \ldots, \mathsf{pk}_k; \overline{\mathsf{ct}}_1, \ldots, \overline{\mathsf{ct}}_l)) = \mathcal{C}(m_1, \ldots, m_l)$$

with an overwhelming probability.

We also compare the MKHE to n out of n threshold HE as well. The key difference is that given the secret keys of each party s_i $(1 \le i \le k)$, MK ciphertexts are encrypted under a concatenated key structure of $(s_1, \ldots, s_k)$ whereas threshold ciphertexts are encrypted under a joint key structure $\sum_{i \in [k]} s_i$. Due to such key structure, MKHE scheme is less efficient than Threshold HE schemes, however it does not require any communications between the parties in the setup phase whereas Threshold HE scheme requires an additional communication in the setup phase. In addition, MKHE schemes are fully dynamic but Threshold HE schemes are not dynamic in general *i.e.,* any additional party cannot join the computation once the setup phase is completed.

2.4 Gadget Decomposition

A *gadget decomposition* is a map $h: \mathbb{T} \to \mathbb{Z}^d$ with a *gadget vector* $\mathbf{g} \in \mathbb{T}^d$ that satisfies $\|h(a)\|_\infty \le \delta$ and $|\langle h(a), \mathbf{g}\rangle - a| \le \epsilon$ for some small constants $\epsilon, \delta > 0$. It is a widely used technique to manage noise growth in HE schemes. The *digit decomposition* is an example of gadget decomposition corresponding to the gadget vector $\mathbf{g} = [B^{-1}, \ldots, B^{-d}] \in \mathbb{T}^d$, defined by $h(a) = (a_1, \ldots, a_d)$ where a_i is the ith-digit of a in base B. We can also balance the output $h(a)$ by decomposing a by $a = \sum_{p=1}^{d} a_i \cdot B^{-p}$ where $a_i \in (-B/2, B/2]$, which minimizes the decomposition error $|\langle h(a), \mathbf{g}\rangle - a|$.

The definition of a gadget decomposition is naturally extended to T as $h : T \to R^d$ by identifying an element of T to the vector of its coefficients in $\mathbb{T}^N$. In TFHE [10], the digit decomposition is used for an element in $\mathbb{T}$ and the balanced version for T.

2.5 RLEV and RGSW

In this section, we describe the RLEV [11] and RGSW [17] encryptions, and multiplication operations between ciphertexts of different types. For a gadget decomposition $h : T \to R^d$ corresponding to a gadget vector $\mathbf{g} \in \mathbb{T}^d$, we define encryption algorithms as follows:

- $\underline{\texttt{RLEV.Enc}(s; \mu)}$: Given a secret key s and a message $\mu \in R$, sample $\mathbf{a} \leftarrow T^d$ and $\mathbf{e} \leftarrow \psi^d$. return $\mathbf{C} \leftarrow [-s \cdot \mathbf{a} + \mathbf{e} + \mu \cdot \mathbf{g} \pmod 1), \mathbf{a}] \in T^{d \times 2}$.
- $\underline{\texttt{RGSW.Enc}(s; \mu)}$: Sample $\mathbf{a} \leftarrow T^{2d}$ and $\mathbf{e} \leftarrow \psi^{2d}$. Given a secret key s and a message $\mu \in R$, return $\overline{\mathbf{C}} \leftarrow [-s \cdot \mathbf{a} + \mathbf{e}, \mathbf{a}] + \mu \cdot \begin{bmatrix} \mathbf{g} & \mathbf{0} \\ \mathbf{0} & \mathbf{g} \end{bmatrix} \pmod 1 \in T^{2d \times 2}$.

We also define the phase of an RLEV encryption $\mathbf{C} = (\mathbf{b}, \mathbf{a}) \in T^{d \times 2}$ by $\varphi_s(\mathbf{C}) = \mathbf{b} + s \cdot \mathbf{a} \pmod 1$. Note that an RLEV encryption $\mathbf{C} \leftarrow \texttt{RLEV.Enc}(s; \mu)$ satisfies that $\varphi_s(\mathbf{C}) \approx \mu \cdot \mathbf{g} \pmod 1$.

Now we define three homomorphic multiplications between RLWE, RLEV and RGSW ciphertexts. For convenience, we generalize the definition of gadget decomposition to RLWE and RLEV ciphertexts by decomposing individual entries in T. For example, we write $h(\mathbf{c}) = (h(c_0), h(c_1)) \in R^{2d}$ for an RLWE ciphertext $\mathbf{c} = (c_0, c_1) \in T^2$, and $h(\mathbf{C}) = \begin{bmatrix} h(c_{0,0}) & h(c_{0,1}) \\ \vdots & \\ h(c_{d-1,0}) & h(c_{d-1,1}) \end{bmatrix} \in R^{d \times 2d}$ for an RLEV ciphertext $\mathbf{C} = \begin{bmatrix} c_{0,0} & c_{0,1} \\ \vdots & \\ c_{d-1,0} & c_{d-1,1} \end{bmatrix} \in T^{d \times 2}$.

Definition 3 (T-RLEV multiplication). *Let $\mathbf{C} \in T^{d \times 2}$ be an RLEV ciphertext and $c \in T$ be a torus polynomial. We define the T-RLEV multiplication $\odot : T \times T^{d \times 2} \to T^2$ as $c \odot \mathbf{C} = h(c) \cdot \mathbf{C} \pmod 1$.*

If $\mathbf{C}$ is an RLWE encryption of μ under s, then the T-RLWE multiplication outputs an RLWE ciphertext whose phase is

$$\varphi_s(c \odot \mathbf{C}) = \langle h(c), \varphi_s(\mathbf{C}) \rangle \approx \langle h(c), \mu \cdot \mathbf{g} \rangle \approx \mu \cdot c \pmod 1.$$

Definition 4 (RLWE-RGSW multiplication). *Let $\mathbf{c} \in T^2$ be an RLWE ciphertext and $\overline{\mathbf{C}} \in T^{2d \times 2}$ be an RGSW ciphertext. We define the RLWE-RGSW multiplication $\otimes : T^2 \times T^{2d \times 2} \to T^2$ as $\mathbf{c} \otimes \overline{\mathbf{C}} = h(\mathbf{c}) \cdot \overline{\mathbf{C}} \pmod 1$.*

Definition 5 (RLEV-RGSW multiplication). *Let* $\mathbf{C} \in T^{d\times 2}$ *be an RLEV ciphertext and* $\overline{\mathbf{C}} \in T^{2d\times 2}$ *be an RGSW ciphertext. The RLEV-RGSW multiplication* $\circledast : T^{d\times 2} \times T^{2d\times 2} \to T^{d\times 2}$ *is defined as* $\mathbf{C} \circledast \overline{\mathbf{C}} = h(\mathbf{C}) \cdot \overline{\mathbf{C}} \pmod 1$

If $\overline{\mathbf{C}}$ is RGSW encryption of μ under s, then the RLWE-RGSW multiplication outputs an RLWE ciphertext whose phase is

$$\varphi_s(\mathbf{c} \otimes \overline{\mathbf{C}}) = \langle h(\mathbf{c}), \varphi_s(\overline{\mathbf{C}}) \rangle \approx \langle h(\mathbf{c}), \mu \cdot (\mathbf{g}, s \cdot \mathbf{g}) \rangle \approx \mu \cdot \varphi_s(\mathbf{c}) \pmod 1.$$

The RLWE-RGSW multiplication is also called the *external product* [10]. Similarly, the RLWE-RGSW multiplication outputs an RLEV ciphertext whose phase is

$$\varphi_s(\mathbf{C} \circledast \overline{\mathbf{C}}) = h(\mathbf{C}) \cdot \varphi_s(\overline{\mathbf{C}}) \approx \langle h(\mathbf{C}), \mu \cdot (\mathbf{g}, s \cdot \mathbf{g}) \rangle \approx \mu \cdot \varphi_s(\mathbf{C}) \pmod 1.$$

3 Overview of Chen et al. (2019)

In 2016, Chillotti et al. [10] designed TFHE, which is a fully homomorphic encryption scheme based on the LWE and RLWE assumptions. The TFHE scheme can encrypt a single bit in each LWE ciphertext, and evaluate an arbitrary binary gate homomorphically using the "gate bootstrapping". The basic idea of TFHE bootstrapping is to homomorphically compute the phase of an LWE ciphertext on the exponent of a ring polynomial and extract the pre-assigned coefficient.

The gate bootstrapping of TFHE consists of three steps: linear combination, blind rotation and key-switching. Let $\mathbf{z} = (z_0, \ldots z_{n-1})$ be the LWE secret. Given LWE ciphertexts ct_1 and ct_2 such that $\varphi_{\mathbf{z}}(\mathsf{ct}_i) \approx \frac{1}{4} m_i \pmod 1$, the linear combination step computes an LWE ciphertext ct such that $\varphi_{\mathbf{z}}(\mathsf{ct}) \approx \frac{1}{2} m \pmod 1$ where m is the resulting bit of a binary operation between m_1 and m_2. In the next step, the ciphertext ct is scaled by $2N$ and converted into $(\tilde{b}, \tilde{\mathbf{a}} = (\tilde{a}_0, \ldots, \tilde{a}_{n-1}))$ such that $\tilde{b} + \langle \tilde{\mathbf{a}}, \mathbf{z} \rangle \approx N \cdot m \pmod{2N}$. The blind rotation algorithm initializes an "accumulator" as a trivial RLWE encryption $(v \cdot X^{\tilde{b}}, 0)$, where v is a fixed torus polynomial called the test vector, and then multiplies $X^{\tilde{a}_i z_i}$ recursively for $0 \le i < n$ using the external product to obtain an encryption of $v \cdot X^{\tilde{b} + \sum_{i=0}^{n-1} \tilde{a}_i z_i}$. The test vector v has pre-assigned coefficients so that we can extract an LWE ciphertext that is decryptable by the RLWE key into the constant term of the message polynomial of the output accumulator. Finally, the key-switching procedure is used to produce an LWE encryption of the same message under $\mathbf{z}$.

In 2019, Chen, Chillotti and Song [6] presented the first MK variant of TFHE (which we will refer to as CCS19 throughout the paper). Its gate bootstrapping follows a similar pipeline but uses MK variants of LWE and RLWE. The main challenge was to re-design the blind rotation algorithm in an MK manner, which requires substitution of the external product. To resolve the issue, the authors introduced a variant of RGSW (called "uni-encryption"), together with a dyadic operation (called "hybrid product") for multiplying a uni-encryption to an MK-RLWE ciphertext. In this section, we give a brief overview of CCS19.

3.1 Uni-Encryption and Hybrid Product

We first present basic setup and key generation algorithms, then describe *uni-encryption* and *hybrid product.* Uni-encryption is an RGSW-like single-key structured encryption scheme, while the hybrid product is a binary operation that takes its input as a pair of uni-encryption and MK-RLWE encryption and returns an MK-RLWE ciphertext. In general, an MK-RLWE ciphertext is in the form of $\overline{\mathsf{ct}} = (c_0, \ldots, c_k) \in T^{k+1}$ with an index set $\{1, \ldots, k\}$ of the associated parties. An MK-RLWE ciphertext corresponds to the concatenated secret key $\bar{\mathbf{s}} = (s_1, \ldots, s_k)$, and its phase is defined as $\varphi_{\bar{\mathbf{s}}}(\overline{\mathsf{ct}}) = c_0 + c_1 s_1 + \cdots + c_k s_k \pmod 1$.

• <u>`CCS.Setup`(1^λ)</u>: Given the security parameter λ, return the following parameters:

- An LWE dimension n, a key distribution χ' over $\mathbb{Z}^n$, an error parameter $\alpha > 0$.
- A base B' and a degree d' to set a gadget vector $\mathbf{g}' = [B'^{-1}, \ldots, B'^{-d'}]$ and a gadget decomposition $h' : \mathbb{T} \to \mathbb{Z}^{d'}$ for LWE.
- An RLWE dimension N, a key distribution χ over $R = \mathbb{Z}[X]/(X^N + 1)$, and an error parameter $\beta > 0$.
- A base B and a degree d to set a gadget vector $\mathbf{g} = [B^{-1}, \ldots, B^{-d}]$ and a gadget decomposition $h : T \to R^d$ for ring-based schemes.
- A CRS $\mathbf{a} \leftarrow T^d$.

We set the LWE error distribution ψ' as a Gaussian distribution over $\mathbb{R}$ of variance α^2, and the RLWE error distribution ψ as a distribution over T which samples N coefficients independently from a Gaussian distribution of variance β^2.

• <u>`CCS.KeyGen`(i)</u>: A party i generates its secret and public keys as follows:

- Sample an LWE secret key $\mathbf{z}_i = (z_{i,0}, \ldots, z_{i,n-1}) \leftarrow \chi'$.
- Sample an RLWE secret key $s_i = s_{i,0} + s_{i,1}X + \cdots + s_{i,N-1}X^{N-1} \leftarrow \chi$ and an error $\mathbf{e} \leftarrow \psi^d$. Compute $\mathbf{b}_i = -s_i \cdot \mathbf{a} + \mathbf{e} \pmod 1$ and set the public key as $\mathsf{pk}_i = \mathbf{b}_i$.

For simplicity, we write $s_0 = 1$ and $\mathbf{b}_0 = -\mathbf{a}$.

• <u>`CCS.UniEnc`$(s_i; \mu)$</u>: A party i samples $r_i \leftarrow \chi$, $\mathbf{f}_{i,1} \leftarrow T^d$, and $\mathbf{e}_1, \mathbf{e}_2 \leftarrow \psi^d$. Given a plaintext $\mu \in R$ and a secret s_i, return $\mathbf{d}_i = r_i \cdot \mathbf{a} + \mu \cdot \mathbf{g} + \mathbf{e}_1 \pmod 1$ and $\mathbf{F}_i = [\mathbf{f}_{i,0} | \mathbf{f}_{i,1}]$ where $\mathbf{f}_{i,0} = -s_i \cdot \mathbf{f}_{i,1} + r_i \cdot \mathbf{g} + \mathbf{e}_2 \pmod 1$.

• <u>`CCS.HbProd`$(\{\mathbf{b}_j\}_{j \in [k]}; \overline{\mathsf{ct}}, (\mathbf{d}_i, \mathbf{F}_i))$</u>: Given an MK-RLWE ciphertext $\overline{\mathsf{ct}} = (c_0, \ldots, c_k) \in T^{k+1}$, a uni-encryption $(\mathbf{d}_i, \mathbf{F}_i)$ of party i and the public keys $\{\mathbf{b}_j\}_{j \in [k]}$ of the parties associated with $\overline{\mathsf{ct}}$, compute and output an MK-RLWE ciphertext $\overline{\mathsf{ct}}'$ as follows:

1. For $0 \le j \le k$, let

$$\begin{aligned} u_j &= \langle h(c_j), \mathbf{d}_i \rangle, \\ v_j &= \langle h(c_j), \mathbf{b}_j \rangle, \\ w_{j,0} &= \langle h(v_j), \mathbf{f}_{i,0} \rangle, \\ w_{j,1} &= \langle h(v_j), \mathbf{f}_{i,1} \rangle. \end{aligned}$$

2. Output $\overline{\mathsf{ct}}' = (c'_0, \ldots, c'_k) \in T^{k+1}$ where

$$c'_j = \begin{cases} u_0 + \sum_{j=0}^{k} w_{j,0} \pmod 1 & \text{if } j = 0, \\ u_i + \sum_{j=0}^{k} w_{j,1} \pmod 1 & \text{if } j = i, \\ u_j & \text{otherwise;} \end{cases}$$

Below, we describe the correctness of the hybrid product. We refer the reader to [6] for a more detailed analysis. Suppose that $\overline{\mathsf{ct}}$ is an MK-RLWE ciphertext and $(\mathbf{d}_i, \mathbf{F}_i)$ is a uni-encryption of $\mu \in R$ of party i, and let $\overline{\mathsf{ct}}'$ be the resulting MK-RLWE ciphertext of the hybrid product algorithm. Then, we have

$$\begin{aligned} \varphi_{\overline{\mathbf{s}}}(\overline{\mathsf{ct}}') &\approx \sum_{j=0}^{k} \langle h(c_j), r_i \cdot \mathbf{a} + \mu \cdot \mathbf{g} \rangle \cdot s_j + \sum_{j=0}^{k} \langle h(v_j), r_i \cdot \mathbf{g} \rangle \pmod 1 \\ &\approx \mu \cdot \varphi_{\overline{\mathbf{s}}}(\overline{\mathsf{ct}}) + \sum_{j=0}^{k} \langle h(c_j), \mathbf{a} \cdot s_j \rangle \cdot r_i + \sum_{j=0}^{k} \langle h(c_j), \mathbf{b}_j \rangle \cdot r_i \pmod 1 \\ &\approx \mu \cdot \varphi_{\overline{\mathbf{s}}}(\overline{\mathsf{ct}}) \pmod 1. \end{aligned}$$

In other words, the phase of $\overline{\mathsf{ct}}$ is multiplied by μ with a small noise.

3.2 Gate Bootstrapping

We now describe the gate bootstrapping of CCS19 that is based on the uni-encryption and hybrid product algorithms. It requires additional generations of blind rotation and key-switching keys.

• $\underline{\texttt{CCS.BootKeyGen}(i)}$: Each party i generates and publishes a blind rotation key brk_i and a key-switching key ksk_i as follows:

- Generate $\mathsf{brk}_{i,j} = (\mathbf{d}_{i,j}, \mathbf{F}_{i,j}) \leftarrow \texttt{CCS.UniEnc}(s_i; z_{i,j})$ for $0 \le j < n$. Set the blind rotation key as $\mathsf{brk}_i = \{\mathsf{brk}_{i,j}\}_{0 \le j < n}$.
- Let $(s^*_{i,0}, \ldots, s^*_{i,N-1}) = (s_{i,0}, -s_{i,N-1}, \ldots, -s_{i,1})$. Sample $\mathbf{A}_{i,j} \leftarrow \mathbb{T}^{d' \times n}$ and $\mathbf{e}_{i,j} \leftarrow \psi'^{d'}$ for $0 \le j < N$, and let $\mathsf{ksk}_{i,j} = [\mathbf{b}_{i,j} | \mathbf{A}_{i,j}]$ where $\mathbf{b}_{i,j} = -\mathbf{A}_{i,j} \cdot \mathbf{z}_i + \mathbf{e}_{i,j} + s^*_{i,j} \cdot \mathbf{g}'$ (mod 1). Set the key-switching key as $\mathsf{ksk}_i = \{\mathsf{ksk}_{i,j}\}_{0 \le j < N}$.

• $\underline{\texttt{CCS.Enc}(\mathbf{z}_i; m)}$: A party i samples $\mathbf{a}_i \leftarrow \mathbb{T}^n$ and $e \leftarrow \psi'$. Given a message bit $m \in \{0, 1\}$ and its secret key $\mathbf{z}_i$, return the ciphertext $\mathsf{ct} = (b_i, \mathbf{a}_i)$ where $b_i = -\langle \mathbf{a}_i, \mathbf{z}_i \rangle + \frac{1}{4}m + e \pmod 1$.

• $\underline{\texttt{CCS.Dec}(\{\mathbf{z}_i\}_{i \in [k]}; \overline{\mathsf{ct}})}$: Given a ciphertext $\overline{\mathsf{ct}} \in \mathbb{T}^{kn+1}$ and secret keys $\{\mathbf{z}_i\}_{i \in [k]}$, return the bit $m \in \{0, 1\}$ which minimizes $|b + \sum_{i \in [k]} \langle \mathbf{a}_i, \mathbf{z}_i \rangle - \frac{1}{4}m|$.

A fresh encryption of CCS19 returns a usual (single-key) LWE ciphertext, but an MK-LWE ciphertext is generally written as a vector of the form

Algorithm 1. Blind Rotation of CCS [6]

Input: $\overline{\mathsf{ct}} = (b, \mathbf{a}_1, \ldots, \mathbf{a}_k), \{(\mathsf{pk}_i, \mathsf{brk}_i)\}_{i\in[k]}$
Output: ACC
Let $\tilde{b} := \lfloor 2Nb \rceil$, $\tilde{a}_{i,j} := \lfloor 2Na_{i,j} \rceil$ for $1 \le i \le k$, $0 \le j < n$
  and $v := -\frac{1}{8} \cdot (1 + X + \cdots + X^{N/2-1} - X^{N/2} - \cdots - X^{N-1})$.
$\mathsf{ACC} \leftarrow (v \cdot X^{\tilde{b}}, 0, \ldots, 0)$
for $1 \le i \le k$ **do**
  for $0 \le j < n$ **do**
    $\mathsf{ACC} \leftarrow \mathsf{ACC} + \mathtt{HbProd}(\{\mathsf{pk}_\ell\}_{\ell\in[k]}; (X^{\tilde{a}_{i,j}} - 1) \cdot \mathsf{ACC}, \mathsf{brk}_{i,j})$
  end for
end for

$\mathsf{ct} = (b, \mathbf{a}_1, \ldots, \mathbf{a}_k) \in \mathbb{T}^{kn+1}$ where k denotes the number of associated parties. It is decrypted using the concatenated key $\overline{\mathbf{z}} = (\mathbf{z}_1, \ldots, \mathbf{z}_k)$ of k parties, *i.e.*, $\varphi_{\overline{\mathbf{z}}}(\mathsf{ct}) = b + \sum_{i=1}^{k} \langle \mathbf{a}_i, \mathbf{z}_i \rangle \approx \frac{1}{4}m \pmod 1$. In the encryption phase, each party locally encrypts its message without knowing any information about other parties. The ciphertexts are extended before evaluation to be encrypted under the concatenated secret key of associated parties.

• $\underline{\mathtt{CCS.HomNAND}(\{(\mathsf{pk}_i, \mathsf{brk}_i, \mathsf{ksk}_i)\}_{i\in[k]}; \overline{\mathsf{ct}}_1, \overline{\mathsf{ct}}_2)}$: Given two ciphertexts $\overline{\mathsf{ct}}_1$, $\overline{\mathsf{ct}}_2$ and key-triple $\{(\mathsf{pk}_i, \mathsf{brk}_i, \mathsf{ksk}_i)\}_{i\in[k]}$ of associated parties, perform the following steps:

1. Compute $\overline{\mathsf{ct}} \leftarrow (\frac{5}{8}, 0, \ldots, 0) - \overline{\mathsf{ct}}_1 - \overline{\mathsf{ct}}_2 \pmod 1$.
2. Compute $\mathsf{ACC} \leftarrow \mathtt{CCS.BlindRotate}(\{(\mathsf{pk}_i, \mathsf{brk}_i)\}_{i\in[k]}; \overline{\mathsf{ct}})$ using the blind rotation algorithm (Algorithm 1).
3. Compute $\overline{\mathsf{ct}} \leftarrow (\frac{1}{8}, 0, \ldots, 0) + (b, \mathbf{a}_1, \ldots, \mathbf{a}_k) \pmod 1 \in \mathbb{T}^{kN+1}$ where b is the constant term of $\mathsf{ACC}[0]$ and $\mathbf{a}_i$ is the coefficient vector of $\mathsf{ACC}[i]$ for $i \in [k]$.
4. Perform the key-switching process: Compute $(b_i', \mathbf{a}_i') = \sum_{j=0}^{N-1} h'(a_{i,j}) \cdot \mathsf{ksk}_{i,j} \pmod 1$ for $i \in [k]$ and $b' = b + \sum_{i\in[k]} b_i'$. Return $\overline{\mathsf{ct}}' = (b', \mathbf{a}_1', \ldots, \mathbf{a}_k') \in \mathbb{T}^{kn+1}$.

4 Accelerating Multi-key TFHE

In this section, we present a new MK variant of the TFHE scheme. Our scheme is asymptotically faster than CCS19, and its bootstrapping procedure is parallelizable. In addition, its key structure is almost compatible with the original TFHE as each party only needs to publish a single auxiliary key. At the heart of our construction, we design a generalized external product to re-design the blind rotation algorithm.

Recall that the blind rotation algorithm (Algorithm 1) of CCS19 takes nk hybrid products to homomorphically multiply $X^{\tilde{a}_{i,j} z_{i,j}}$ to the accumulator. The hybrid product algorithm operates on multi-key ciphertexts and achieves linear complexity in terms of the number of parties involved. Thus, this linear complexity results in a quadratic overall complexity.

In our scheme, we minimize the cost of operations on MK ciphertexts and exploit single-key multiplication to reduce the overall complexity. This is based on our observation that an encryption of $X^{\langle \tilde{\mathbf{a}}_i, \mathbf{z}_i \rangle}$ for each $1 \le i \le k$ can be obtained in a 'single-key' manner since the secret $\mathbf{z}_i = (z_{i,0}, \ldots, z_{i,n-1})$ is related solely to party i. However, this approach cannot be achieved by known techniques in CCS19 since the hybrid product can only multiply a fresh single-key uni-encryption. To realize our framework, we introduce a novel homomorphic operation called the *generalized external product*, which enables us to multiply a single-key RLEV ciphertext to MK-RLWE accumulator. This operation does not require an input RLEV ciphertext to have a special structure like uni-encryption, so can be generally used for operation between possibly noisy ciphertexts.

In Sects. 4.1 and 4.2, we introduce our improved hybrid product and generalized external product as a building block. In Sect. 4.3, we describe the overall scheme.

4.1 Improved Hybrid Product

We present an improved hybrid product that enjoys better performance in terms of speed and noise growth. In the correctness proof of hybrid product in CCS19, we have

$$\sum_{j=0}^{k}(w_{j,0} + w_{j,1}s_i) = \sum_{j=1}^{k}\langle h(v_j), \mathbf{f}_{i,0} + s_i \cdot \mathbf{f}_{i,1}\rangle \approx \sum_{j=1}^{k}\langle h(v_j), r_i \cdot \mathbf{g}\rangle \approx r_i \cdot \sum_{j=0}^{k} v_j \pmod 1.$$

We observe that since

$$\sum_{j=1}^{k}\langle h(v_j), \mathbf{f}_{i,0} + s_i \cdot \mathbf{f}_{i,1}\rangle \approx \left\langle h\Big(\sum_{j=1}^{k} v_j\Big), \mathbf{f}_{i,0} + s_i \cdot \mathbf{f}_{i,1}\right\rangle,$$

the computation of $h(v_j)$ for $1 \le j \le k$ can be replaced by a single decomposition $h\big(\sum_{j=1}^{k} v_j\big)$. Below, we provide a formal description of the new hybrid product operation.

- $\underline{\texttt{NewHbProd}(\{\mathbf{b}_j\}_{j\in[k]}; \overline{\mathsf{ct}}, (\mathbf{d}_i, \mathbf{F}_i))}$: Given an MK-RLWE ciphertext $\overline{\mathsf{ct}} = (c_0, \ldots, c_k) \in T^{k+1}$, a uni-encryption $(\mathbf{d}_i, \mathbf{F}_i)$ of party i and the public keys $\{\mathbf{b}_j\}_{j\in[k]}$ of parties associated with $\overline{\mathsf{ct}}$, return an MK-RLWE ciphertext $\overline{\mathsf{ct}}'$ as follows:

1. Compute

$$u_j = \langle h(c_j), \mathbf{d}_i\rangle \quad (0 \le j \le k)$$
$$v = \sum_{j=0}^{k}\langle h(c_j), \mathbf{b}_j\rangle$$

2. Output $\overline{\mathsf{ct}}' = (c'_0, \ldots, c'_k) \in T^{k+1}$ where

$$c'_j = \begin{cases} u_0 + \langle h(v), \mathbf{f}_{i,0}\rangle \pmod 1 & \text{if } j = 0, \\ u_i + \langle h(v), \mathbf{f}_{i,1}\rangle \pmod 1 & \text{if } j = i, \\ u_j & \text{otherwise;} \end{cases}$$

Correctness. Let $\overline{\mathsf{ct}} = (c_0, \dots, c_k)$ be an MK-RLWE encryption and $(\mathbf{d}_i, \mathbf{F}_i)$ be a uni-encryption of μ of party i. The output $\overline{\mathsf{ct}}' = (c_0', \dots, c_k')$ satisfies that

$$\begin{aligned}
\varphi_{\overline{\mathbf{s}}}(\overline{\mathsf{ct}}') &= \sum_{j=0}^{k} \langle h(c_j), \mathbf{d}_i \rangle \cdot s_j + \langle h(v), \mathbf{f}_{i,0} \rangle + \langle h(v), \mathbf{f}_{i,1} \rangle \cdot s_i \\
&\approx \sum_{j=0}^{k} \langle h(c_j), r_i \cdot \mathbf{a} + \mu \cdot \mathbf{g} \rangle \cdot s_j + \langle h(v), \mathbf{f}_{i,0} + s_i \cdot \mathbf{f}_{i,1} \rangle \\
&\approx \mu \cdot \varphi_{\overline{\mathbf{s}}}(\overline{\mathsf{ct}}) + r_i \cdot \sum_{j=0}^{k} \langle h(c_j), s_j \cdot \mathbf{a} \rangle + r_i \cdot \sum_{j=0}^{k} \langle h(c_j), \mathbf{b}_j \rangle \\
&\approx \mu \cdot \varphi_{\overline{\mathbf{s}}}(\overline{\mathsf{ct}}) \pmod 1.
\end{aligned}$$

Performance. We estimate the number of $\langle h(\cdot), \cdot \rangle$, say gadget product, to analyze the time complexity. The hybrid product of CCS19 requires $4(k+1)$ gadget products to compute u_j, v_j, $w_{j,0}$, and $w_{j,1}$ for $0 \leq j \leq k$. Meanwhile, our algorithm takes only $2k+4$ gadget products in total.

Noise growth. As we compute $\langle h(v), \mathbf{f}_{i,0} \rangle$ and $\langle h(v), \mathbf{f}_{i,1} \rangle$ for $v = \sum_{j=0}^{k} \langle h(c_j), \mathbf{b}_j \rangle$ where it previously computed $\sum_{j=0}^{k} \langle h(v_j), \mathbf{f}_{i,0} \rangle$ and $\sum_{j=0}^{k} \langle h(v_j), \mathbf{f}_{i,1} \rangle$, the error introduced in this part has reduced by a factor of $k+1$. Nevertheless, the difference is negligibly small and thus the two hybrid product algorithms show similar error variance. We refer the reader to Sect. 5.2 for thorough noise analysis.

4.2 Generalized External Product

We introduce a new multiplication operation that multiplies an arbitrary single-key RLEV ciphertext to an MK-RLWE ciphertext. To understand the underlying idea, we first recall the external product: given an RLWE ciphertext $\mathbf{c}$ and an RGSW encryption $\overline{\mathbf{C}}$ of μ under the secret t, $\mathbf{c} \otimes \overline{\mathbf{C}}$ outputs an RLWE ciphertext with $\varphi_t(\mathbf{c} \otimes \overline{\mathbf{C}}) \approx \mu \cdot \varphi_t(\mathbf{c}) = \varphi_t(\mu \cdot \mathbf{c})$. Our key observation is that the external product can be comprehended as multiplying the message μ homomorphically to each component of $\mathbf{c}$.

Now let us 'generalize' the external product to the multi-key setting. Suppose that we are given an MK-RLWE ciphertext $\mathsf{ct} = (c_0, \dots, c_k)$ under the concatenated key $\overline{\mathbf{s}} = (1, s_1, \dots, s_k)$ and a single-key RLEV encryption $\mathbf{C}$ of μ under another key t_i of party i. Inspired by the external product, we aim to multiply μ to ct homomorphically. This goal can be achieved by executing $(k+1)$ T-RLEV multiplications: $c_j \odot \mathbf{C}$ for $0 \leq j \leq k$. However, the resulting ciphertext is not decryptable by $\mathbf{s}$, but it is encrypted under the tensor product of two keys, namely $(1, t) \otimes \overline{\mathbf{s}} = (\overline{\mathbf{s}}, t \cdot \overline{\mathbf{s}})$. To change the secret key back to $\overline{\mathbf{s}}$, we exploit the relinearization technique, which is used in a variety of HE schemes such as [3,4,9,15]. Let i-th party publish a relinearization key, a uni-encryption of t under the key s_i. Then we can obtain an MK-RLWE ciphertext $\overline{\mathsf{ct}}'$ with $\varphi_{\overline{\mathbf{s}}}(\overline{\mathsf{ct}}') \approx \mu \cdot \varphi_{\overline{\mathbf{s}}}(\overline{\mathsf{ct}})$ by multiplying t homomorphically to the corresponding components to $t \cdot \overline{\mathbf{s}}$ with hybrid product and adding it to the rest of the components. The exact algorithm is given below.

• $\underline{\texttt{ExtProd}(\{\mathbf{b}_j\}_{j\in[k]}, \mathsf{rlk}_i; \overline{\mathsf{ct}}, \mathbf{C}_i)}$: Given an MK-RLWE ciphertext $\overline{\mathsf{ct}}=(c_0,\ldots,c_k)\in T^{k+1}$, the public keys $\{\mathbf{b}_j\}_{j\in[k]}$ of parties associated with $\overline{\mathsf{ct}}$, an RLEV ciphertext $\mathbf{C}_i \in T^{d\times 2}$ and the relinearization key rlk_i of party $i\in[k]$, it returns an MK-RLWE ciphertext $\overline{\mathsf{ct}}'$ as follows:

1. Compute $(x_j, y_j) \leftarrow c_j \odot \mathbf{C}_i$ for $0 \le j \le k$. Let $\overline{\mathbf{x}} = (x_0, \ldots, x_k)$ and $\overline{\mathbf{y}} = (y_0, \ldots, y_k)$
2. Compute $\overline{\mathsf{ct}}' \leftarrow \texttt{NewHbProd}(\{\mathbf{b}_j\}_{j\in[k]}; \overline{\mathbf{y}}, \mathsf{rlk}_i) + \overline{\mathbf{x}}$ and return $\overline{\mathsf{ct}}'$.

Correctness. Suppose that $\overline{\mathsf{ct}} = (c_0, c_1 \ldots, c_k)$ is a MK-RLWE ciphertext under the secret $\overline{\mathbf{s}} = (s_1, \cdots, s_k)$ and $\mathbf{C}_i$ is an RLEV encryption of μ under the secret t_i. Now, $0 \le j \le k$, $(x_j, y_j) = c_j \odot \mathbf{C}_i$ satisfies $x_j \cdot t_i + y_j \approx \mu \cdot c_j$. Let $\overline{\mathsf{ct}}' = (c_0', \ldots, c_k') \leftarrow \texttt{NewHbProd}(\{\mathbf{b}_j\}_{j\in[k]}; \overline{\mathbf{y}}, \mathsf{rlk}_i) + \overline{\mathbf{x}}$ where $\mathsf{rlk}_i = \texttt{UniEnc}(s_i; t_i)$. Then we have

$$\varphi_{\overline{\mathbf{s}}}(\overline{\mathsf{ct}}') \approx \sum_{j=0}^{k} x_j s_j + t_i \cdot \sum_{j=0}^{k} y_j s_j = \sum_{j=0}^{k} (x_j + t_i y_j) \cdot s_j \approx \mu \cdot \sum_{j=0}^{k} c_j s_j = \mu \cdot \varphi_{\overline{\mathbf{s}}}(\overline{\mathsf{ct}}) \pmod 1$$

where $s_0 = 1$. Note that this algorithm is exact for any RGSW ciphertext $\overline{\mathbf{C}}$ as well, by replacing $c_j \odot \mathbf{C}_i$ to $(0, c_j) \otimes \overline{\mathbf{C}}$.

General-Purpose Utility. We remark that this generalized external product is a general-purpose multiplication in that it multiplies a commonly used single-key ciphertext to a multi-key ciphertext. Compared to the previous (R)GSW-like MKHEs [5,12,26,28] which construct multiplications on multi-key ciphertexts, CCS19 [6] and our scheme introduces multiplications, hybrid product and external product, between single-key and multi-key ciphertexts. These multiplications enable better performance in both time and memory. However, the hybrid product requires fresh uni-encryption of a multiplicand. For example, if one wants to evaluate arbitrary operations between uni-encryptions from the same party before they are multiplied to an MK ciphertext, they should be expanded to an MK-RGSW ciphertext and then evaluated via MK-RGSW operations. In contrast, our generalized external product enables us to perform arbitrary operations as a single-key ciphertext and then multiply the resulting RLEV or RGSW ciphertext to a multi-key ciphertext at any time, with the relinearization key generated once in the key generation phase.

Performance. In the first step of the external product, it executes $k + 1$ T-RLEV multiplications, which takes $2(k + 1)$ gadget products in total. Then in the second step, the new hybrid product consumes $2k + 4$ gadget products as explained in Sect. 4.1. To sum up, the external product requires $4k + 6$ gadget products.

Noise Growth. The error variance of our external product will be discussed in Sect. 5.2.

4.3 Our Scheme

In this section, we combine all building blocks to construct yet another MK-variant of TFHE. Similar to CCS19, our scheme shares the same blueprint for gate bootstrapping as TFHE. However, the major difference is that our blind rotation algorithm has a different structure consisting of two distinguished phases involving single-key and multi-key computation, respectively.

More precisely, the first phase of our blind rotation aims to perform blind rotation party-wise with the accumulator staying as a single-key ciphertext. In other words, we compute $X^{\langle \tilde{ba_i}, \mathbf{z}_i \rangle} (1 \le i \le k)$ simultaneously. In the second phase of blind rotation, we merge k accumulators, which are single-key RLEV encryptions of $X^{\langle \tilde{ba}_i, \mathbf{z}_i \rangle}$ under s_i, into a trivial MK-RLWE ciphertext of $v \cdot X^{\tilde{b}}$ under k secrets $s_1, \ldots, s_k$. This is achieved by using the generalized external product introduced in the previous section.

Below we provide a formal description of our MK-TFHE scheme. We remark that its setup, basic key generation and ciphertext structure are identical to that of CCS19.

- $\texttt{Setup}(1^\lambda)$: Given the security parameter λ, return the following parameters:
  - An LWE dimension n, a key distribution χ' over $\mathbb{Z}^n$, an error parameter $\alpha > 0$.
  - A base B' and a degree d' to set a gadget vector $\mathbf{g}' = [B'^{-1}, \ldots, B^{-d'}]$ and a gadget decomposition $h' : \mathbb{T} \to \mathbb{Z}^{d'}$ for LWE.
  - An RLWE dimension N, a key distribution χ over $R = \mathbb{Z}[X]/(X^N + 1)$, and an error parameter $\beta > 0$.
  - A base B and a degree d to set a gadget vector $\mathbf{g} = [B^{-1}, \ldots, B^{-d}]$ and a gadget decomposition $h : T \to R^d$ for ring-based schemes.
  - A CRS $\mathbf{a} \leftarrow T^d$.

- $\texttt{KeyGen}(i)$: A party i generates its secret and public keys as follows.
  - Sample an LWE secret key $\mathbf{z}_i = (z_{i,0}, \ldots, z_{i,n-1}) \leftarrow \chi'$.
  - Sample an RLWE secret key $s_i = s_{i,0} + s_{i,1}X + \cdots + s_{i,N-1}X^{N-1} \leftarrow \chi$ and an error $\mathbf{e} \leftarrow \psi^d$. Compute $\mathbf{b}_i = -s_i \cdot \mathbf{a} + \mathbf{e} \pmod 1$ and set the public key as $\mathsf{pk}_i = \mathbf{b}_i$.

- $\texttt{BootKeyGen}(i)$: A party i generates and publishes a blind rotation key brk_i, a relinearization key rlk_i and a key-switching key ksk_i as follows.
  - Sample $t_i \leftarrow \chi$ and generate $\mathsf{brk}_{i,j} \leftarrow \texttt{RGSW.Enc}(t_i; z_{i,j})$ for $0 \le j < n$. Set the blind rotation key $\mathsf{brk}_i = \{\mathsf{brk}_{i,j}\}_{0 \le j < n}$.
  - Generate the relinearization key $\mathsf{rlk}_i \leftarrow \texttt{CCS.UniEnc}(s_i; t_i)$.
  - Let $(s^*_{i,0}, \ldots, s^*_{i,N-1}) = (s_{i,0}, -s_{i,N-1}, \ldots, -s_{i,1})$. Sample $\mathbf{A}_{i,j} \leftarrow \mathbb{T}^{d' \times n}$ and $\mathbf{e}_{i,j} \leftarrow \psi'^{d'}$ for $0 \le j < N$, and let $\mathsf{ksk}_{i,j} = [\mathbf{b}_{i,j} | \mathbf{A}_{i,j}]$ where $\mathbf{b}_{i,j} = -\mathbf{A}_{i,j} \cdot \mathbf{z}_i + \mathbf{e}_{i,j} + s^*_{i,j} \cdot \mathbf{g}'$. Set the key-switching key $\mathsf{ksk}_i = \{\mathsf{ksk}_{i,j}\}_{0 \le j < N}$.

• $\texttt{Enc}(\mathbf{z}_i; m)$: A party i samples $\mathbf{a}_i \leftarrow \mathbb{T}^n$ and $e \leftarrow \psi'$. Given a message bit $m \in \{0,1\}$ and its secret key $\mathbf{z}_i$, return the ciphertext $\mathsf{ct} = (b_i, \mathbf{a}_i)$ where $b_i = -\langle \mathbf{a}_i, \mathbf{z}_i \rangle + \frac{1}{4}m + e \pmod 1$.

• $\texttt{Dec}(\{\mathbf{z}_i\}_{i\in[k]}; \overline{\mathsf{ct}})$: Given a ciphertext $\overline{\mathsf{ct}} \in \mathbb{T}^{kn+1}$ and secret keys $\{\mathbf{z}_i\}_{i\in[k]}$, return the bit $m \in \{0,1\}$ which minimizes $|b + \sum_{i\in[k]} \langle \mathbf{a}_i, \mathbf{z}_i \rangle - \frac{1}{4}m|$.

• $\texttt{HomNAND}(\{(\mathsf{pk}_i, \mathsf{brk}_i, \mathsf{rlk}_i, \mathsf{ksk}_i)\}_{i\in[k]}; \overline{\mathsf{ct}}_1, \overline{\mathsf{ct}}_2)$: Given two ciphertexts $\overline{\mathsf{ct}}_1$, $\overline{\mathsf{ct}}_2$ and key-quadruple $\{(\mathsf{pk}_i, \mathsf{brk}_i, \mathsf{rlk}_i, \mathsf{ksk}_i)\}_{i\in[k]}$ of associated parties, perform the following steps:

1. Compute $\overline{\mathsf{ct}} \leftarrow (\frac{5}{8}, 0, \ldots, 0) - \overline{\mathsf{ct}}_1 - \overline{\mathsf{ct}}_2 \pmod 1$.
2. Compute $\mathsf{ACC} \leftarrow \texttt{BlindRotate}(\{(\mathsf{pk}_i, \mathsf{brk}_i, \mathsf{rlk}_i)\}_{i\in[k]}; \overline{\mathsf{ct}})$ where $\texttt{BlindRotate}(\cdot)$ is the blind rotation algorithm in Algorithm 2.
3. Compute $\overline{\mathsf{ct}} \leftarrow (\frac{1}{8}, 0, \ldots, 0) + (b, \mathbf{a}_1, \ldots, \mathbf{a}_k) \pmod 1 \in \mathbb{T}^{kN+1}$ where b is the constant term of $\mathsf{ACC}[0]$ and $\mathbf{a}_i$ is the coefficient vector of $\mathsf{ACC}[i]$ for $i \in [k]$.
4. Perform the key-switching process: Compute $(b'_i, \mathbf{a}'_i) = \sum_{j=0}^{N-1} h'(a_{i,j}) \cdot \mathsf{ksk}_{i,j} \pmod 1$ for $i \in [k]$ and $b' = b + \sum_{i\in[k]} b'_i$. Return $\overline{\mathsf{ct}}' = (b', \mathbf{a}'_1, \ldots, \mathbf{a}'_k) \in \mathbb{T}^{kn+1}$.

Security. In the bootstrapping key generation, each party publishes the blind rotation key brk_i encrypting the elements of $\mathbf{z}_i$ under t_i, the relinearization key rlk_i encrypting t_i under s_i, and key-switching key ksk_i encrypting the coefficients of s_i under $\mathbf{z}_i$. As the previous TFHE [10] and multi-key TFHE [6] schemes, we require a circular security assumption along with the (R)LWE assumption to have our scheme semantically secure.

Correctness. We show that the output ACC of our blind rotation in Algorithm 2 is an MK-RLWE encryption of $v \cdot X^{\tilde{b}+\sum_{i=1}^{k}\langle \tilde{\mathbf{a}}_i, \mathbf{z}_i \rangle}$ under $\bar{\mathbf{s}}=(s_1, \ldots, s_k) \in T^k$. Initially, ACC is an MK-RLWE encryption of $v \cdot X^{\tilde{b}}$ under $\bar{\mathbf{s}}$ (line 3). In the i-th iteration of the first loop, it computes ACC'_i which is an RLEV encryption of $X^{\langle \tilde{\mathbf{a}}_i, \mathbf{z}_i \rangle}$ (line 5–8). In line 5, ACC'_i is initialized to a trivial RLEV encryption of $1 \in T$. Then for $0 \le j < n$ (line 6–8), ACC' is updated by $\mathsf{ACC}'_i + \left[(X^{\tilde{a}_{i,j}} - 1) \cdot \mathsf{ACC}'_i\right] \circledast \mathsf{brk}_{i,j}$ Since $\mathsf{brk}_{i,j}$ is the RGSW encryption of $z_{i,j}$, it implies that ACC'_i is multiplied by $X^{\tilde{a}_{i,j}}$ if $z_{i,j}=1$, or else $(z_{i,j}=0)$, stays the same. As a result, we get k different $\mathsf{ACC}'_i (1 \le i \le k)$ encrypting $X^{\langle \tilde{\mathbf{a}}_i, \mathbf{z}_i \rangle}$ under t_i. Finally, in the i-th iteration of the second loop (line 10–12), ACC is homomorphically multiplied by $X^{\langle \tilde{\mathbf{a}}_i, \mathbf{z}_i \rangle}$ with external product. Consequently, ACC is an MK-RLWE encryption of $v \cdot X^{\tilde{b}+\sum_{i=1}^{k}\langle \tilde{\mathbf{a}}_i, \mathbf{z}_i \rangle}$ under $\bar{\mathbf{s}}$.

Our new scheme provides an asymptotically faster NAND algorithm as we perform single-key, parallelizable operations in the first phase by which the time complexity is dominated. Furthermore, the bootstrapping keys are almost compatible with the single-key TFHE [10], which allows to perform multi-key evaluation from the original (single-key) TFHE scheme with a small number of auxiliary keys. We describe the advantages in detail below.

- **Performance.** As will be analyzed in Sect. 5.1, our blind rotation algorithm Algorithm 2 requires $O(nkd + k^2)$ gadget decompositions, while the blind

Algorithm 2. New Blind Rotation

Input: $\overline{\mathsf{ct}} = (b, \mathbf{a}_1, \ldots, \mathbf{a}_k), \{(\mathsf{pk}_i, \mathsf{brk}_i, \mathsf{rlk}_i)\}_{i\in[k]}$
Output: ACC

Let $\tilde{b} := \lfloor 2Nb \rceil$, $\tilde{a}_{i,j} := \lfloor 2Na_{i,j} \rceil$ for $1 \leq i \leq k$, $0 \leq j < n$
    and $v := -\frac{1}{8} \cdot (1 + X + \cdots + X^{N/2-1} - X^{N/2} - \cdots - X^{N-1})$.
$\mathsf{ACC} \leftarrow (v \cdot X^{\tilde{b}}, 0, \ldots, 0)$
for $1 \leq i \leq k$ **do**
    $\mathsf{ACC}'_i \leftarrow (\mathbf{g}, \mathbf{0}) \in T^{d\times 2}$
    for $0 \leq j < n$ **do**
        $\mathsf{ACC}'_i \leftarrow \mathsf{ACC}'_i + \left[(X^{\tilde{a}_{i,j}} - 1) \cdot \mathsf{ACC}'_i\right] \circledast \mathsf{brk}_{i,j}$
    end for
end for
for $1 \leq i \leq k$ **do**
    $\mathsf{ACC} \leftarrow \mathtt{ExtProd}(\{\mathsf{pk}_\ell\}_{\ell\in[k]}, \mathsf{rlk}_i; \mathsf{ACC}, \mathsf{ACC}'_i)$
end for

rotation algorithm Algorithm 1 of CCS19 requires $O(nk^2)$. In typical settings, n is much bigger than k, therefore the time complexity of our algorithm is quasi-linear to the number of parties.

- **Parallelization.** Our blind rotation generates k different single-key RLEV encryptions ACC'_i of $X^{\langle \tilde{\mathbf{a}}_i, \mathbf{z}_i \rangle}$ and then merge them into a single MK-RLWE ciphertext ACC by the generalized external product. Since ACC'_is are independently generated, we can evaluate them in parallel. However, merging the RLEV ciphertext cannot be parallelized since they should be sequentially multiplied, thus the time complexity of the parallelized algorithm becomes $O(nd + k^2)$.
- **Key Compatibility.** Recall that our scheme generates three bootstrapping keys: the blind rotation key brk_i, the relinearization rlk_i and the key-switching key ksk_i. We note that the blind rotation key and the key-switching key is identical to the single-key TFHE [10]. Thus, the single-key TFHE scheme can be easily expanded to the multi-key scheme with each party generating a key $\mathsf{rlk}_i = \mathtt{UniEnc}(s_i; t_i)(1 \leq i \leq k)$.

On the other hand, our scheme consumes two levels (one for each phase) so that the noise blows up to an extent which cannot be handled in the ring dimension $N = 1024$ used in CCS19. We use a larger ring dimension $N = 2048$ in spite of performance degradation, but still, it is negligible as the number of parties increases. We compare CCS19 and our scheme using $N = 1024$ and $N = 2048$, respectively, in Sect. 6.

4.4 Using Different Gadget Decompositions

So far we have used the same gadget decomposition h for elements in T, but in fact, different gadgets can be applied for different encryptions in our scheme. Let h_{lev} and h_{uni} be two different gadget decompositions corresponding to gadget vectors $\mathbf{g}_{lev}$ and $\mathbf{g}_{uni}$, respectively. In the external product, for example, we can use h_{lev} in T-RLEV multiplication (step 1) and use h_{uni} in the hybrid product (step 2). More precisely, let the input RLEV ciphertext $\mathbf{C}$ of μ under a secret s involve the gadget vector $\mathbf{g}_{lev}$ *i.e.*, $\mathbf{C} = (\mathbf{b} = -s \cdot \mathbf{a} + \mathbf{e} + \mu \cdot \mathbf{g}_{lev} \pmod 1, \mathbf{a})$, and compute the T-RLEV multiplication as

$$c \odot \mathbf{C} = (\langle h_{lev}(c), \mathbf{b}\rangle, \langle h_{lev}(c), \mathbf{a}\rangle) \pmod 1$$

for $c \in T$. Then it satisfies that

$$\varphi_s(c \odot \mathbf{C}) = \langle h_{lev}(c), \mathbf{b}\rangle + \langle h_{lev}(c), \mathbf{a}\rangle \cdot s \approx \langle h_{lev}(c), \mu \cdot \mathbf{g}_{lev}\rangle \approx \mu \cdot c \pmod 1.$$

In a similar argument, we can compute the hybrid product using the decomposition h_{uni} when the uni-encryption as input involves $\mathbf{g}_{uni}$.

In the rest of the paper, we use different gadget decompositions for RGSW, RLEV ciphertexts and uni-encryption respectively, each of which contains the corresponding gadget vector. We write $\{gsw, lev, uni\}$ by subscript to distinguish the gadget decompositions, i.e., h_{gsw} is the gadget decomposition corresponding to the gadget vector $\mathbf{g}_{gsw}$ of dimension d_{gsw}. The scheme using different gadget decompositions is provided in Appendix A.

4.5 Distributed Decryption

The decryption process of an MKHE scheme can be regarded as an interactive protocol between the parties associated with a ciphertext. To securely decrypt a ciphertext, a special functionality called the *distributed decryption* is used. Its functionality is presented in Fig. 2.

The parties are allowed to use any MPC protocol to realize the distributed decryption, but the most popular method involves the noise flooding technique [16]. In this approach, each i-th party publicly discloses $\mu_i := \langle \mathbf{a}_i, \mathbf{s}_i\rangle + e_i \pmod 1$ for some noise e_i sampled from a large error distribution. This allows the parties to recover the message by aggregating b and μ_i, and rounding it. This technique is generally applicable to various (R)LWE-based encryption schemes, such as CKKS, BGV or B/FV, which utilize large parameter sets. In contrary, the TFHE scheme has relatively tight parameters to provide the best performance, making the noise flooding technique potentially prone to a decryption failure.

To address this issue, Dahl et al. [13] recently introduced a distributed decryption technique tailored for the Threshold TFHE scheme, with communication overhead. In their approach, each participating party provides an additional blind rotation key with a larger dimension which can accommodate exponential errors during the setup phase. It is worth noting that this approach is directly applicable to the multi-key scenario, but can be more expensive compared to the threshold case. On other hand, the garbled circuit can also serve as the building block for the distributed decryption. Kraitsberg et al. [21] proposed a distributed decryption method of two-out-of-three threshold FV ciphertexts, which exploits a garbled circuit scheme for honest majority in a three party

Functionality Distributed decryption

Input: A multi-key LWE encryption $\overline{\text{ct}} = (b, \mathbf{a}_1, \ldots, \mathbf{a}_k)$ of the message m, secret key of each party $\mathbf{s}_1, \ldots, \mathbf{s}_k$.
Output: Message m

1. Each i-th party computes $\langle \mathbf{a}_i, \mathbf{s}_i \rangle$ locally.
2. All parties collaborate to securely decrypt the input ciphertext $\overline{\text{ct}}$ without any information leakage.
3. Distribute the decrypted result m to the parties.

Fig. 2. The distributed decryption functionality for TFHE.

setting. This approach can be naturally extended to the multi-key setting using the multi-party garbling [2], however, it would require quadratic communication costs with respect to the number of parties involved.

5 Performance Analysis

5.1 Time and Space Complexity

We remark that the hybrid product of CCS19 and our novel hybrid product require $4(k+1)$ and $2k+4$ uni-gadget products, respectively. Furthermore, the external product performs $k+1$ T-RLEV multiplications and one novel hybrid product to require $2(k+1)$ lev-gadget and $2k+4$ uni-gadget products. As the previous blind rotation in Algorithm 1 performs nk hybrid products of CCS19, it takes $4nk(k+1)$ uni-gadget products. In our novel blind rotation Algorithm 2, it performs nk RLEV-RGSW multiplications and k external products to have $2nkd_{lev}$ gsw-gadget, $2k(k+1)$ lev-gadget, and $k(2k+4)$ uni-gadget decompositions. Since the gadget decomposition takes by a factor of its degree, we have the complexity of about $O(nkd_{lev}d_{gsw} + k^2 d_{lev} + k^2 d_{uni})$. As the time complexity almost depends on $d_{lev}d_{gsw}$, we minimize $d_{lev}d_{gsw}$ when setting parameters in Sect. 6.

In the blind rotation, previous algorithm Algorithm 1 takes the blind rotation keys brk_i for $1 \leq i \leq k$ as input where brk_i consists of n uni-encryptions. However, our algorithm Algorithm 2 takes the blind rotation keys brk_i and the relinearization keys rlk_i for $1 \leq i \leq k$, where brk_i consists of n RGSW encryptions and rlk_i is a uni-encryption. Since a uni-encryption is in $T^{d \times 3}$ and an RGSW encryption is in $T^{2d \times 2}$, the size of the key used in our blind rotation is about $\frac{4}{3}$ times bigger than the previous one.

We remark that the blind rotation key size of our scheme can be reduced using key-compression methods for the TFHE scheme. For example, we can halve the size of the blind rotation key using the key compression method proposed by Kim et al. [18]. Or, we can replace the RGSW keys with uni-encryptions since the hybrid product is exact for a single party as well. However, there is a trade-off between the size of the key and the execution time for key-compression tricks in general.

5.2 Noise Growth

In this section, we provide an average-case noise analysis of homomorphic operations and analyze the noise growth from our gate bootstrapping procedure. We focus on the new blind rotation algorithm since other algorithms such as key-switching have been studied already in CCS19.

We start from introducing several assumptions and terminologies which we use in our analysis.

- For an RLEV encryption $\mathbf{C}$ of μ under secret s, the error of $\mathbf{C}$ is defined as $\mathsf{Err}(\mathbf{C}) = \varphi_s(\mathbf{C}) - \mu \cdot \mathbf{g}_{lev} \in T^{d_{lev}}$.
- For an RGSW encryption $\overline{\mathbf{C}}$ of μ under secret s, the error of $\overline{\mathbf{C}}$ is defined as $\mathsf{Err}(\overline{\mathbf{C}}) = \varphi_s(\overline{\mathbf{C}}) - \mu \cdot \begin{bmatrix} \mathbf{g} & \mathbf{0} \\ \mathbf{0} & \mathbf{g} \end{bmatrix} \in T^{2d_{gsw}}$.
- In our scheme, all entries of the error vector of an RLEV (RGSW) ciphertext have the same variance. Therefore, we use $\mathsf{VarErr}(\cdot)$ to denote the common variance of error components.
- For the gadget decomposition h with the gadget base B (a power-of-two) and the degree d, we define $\epsilon^2 = 1/(12B^{2d})$, the variance of uniform distribution over $(-\frac{1}{2}B^{-d}, \frac{1}{2}B^{-d}]$, and $V = \frac{1}{12}(B^2+2)$, the mean square of a uniform distribution over $\mathbb{Z}_B = \mathbb{Z} \cap (-B/2, B/2]$. We use $\{gsw, lev, uni\}$ as subscript to distinguish the variance and the mean square of specific gadget decompostions, e.g., we write ϵ_{gsw}, V_{gsw} for the gadget decomposition h_{gsw}.
- We assume that each component of an RLWE, RLEV, or RGSW ciphertext behaves as if it is a uniform random variable on T. Hence, the entries of the gadget decompositions are uniformly distributed over the set of polynomials of coefficients in $\mathbb{Z}_B$.

We provide the lemmas, corollaries and theorem on the error of the operations and algorithms used in CCS19 and our scheme. The proofs for the following lemmas, corollaries and theorem are given in Appendix B.

Lemma 1 (T-RLEV Multiplication). *Let c be a torus polynomial and $\mathbf{C}$ be an RLEV encryption of μ under secret s. Then $\mathbf{c} \leftarrow c \odot \mathbf{C}$ is an RLWE ciphertext such that $\varphi_s(\mathbf{c}) = \mu \cdot c + e \pmod 1$ for some error $e \in R$ whose variance is*

$$\mathit{Var}(e) = \|\mu\|_2^2 \epsilon_{lev}^2 + d_{lev} N V_{lev} \mathit{VarErr}(\mathbf{C}).$$

Lemma 2 (RLWE-RGSW Multiplication). *Let $\mathbf{c}$ be an RLWE ciphertext and $\overline{\mathbf{C}}$ an RGSW encryption of μ under secret s. Then $\mathbf{c}' \leftarrow \mathbf{c} \circledast \overline{\mathbf{C}}$ is an RLWE ciphertext such that $\varphi_s(\mathbf{c}') = \mu \cdot \varphi_s(\mathbf{c}) + e \pmod 1$ for some error $e \in R$ whose variance is*

$$\mathit{Var}(e) = (1 + N/2)\|\mu\|_2^2 \epsilon_{gsw}^2 + 2 d_{gsw} N V_{gsw} \mathit{VarErr}(\overline{\mathbf{C}}).$$

Corollary 1 (RLEV-RGSW Multiplication). *Let* $\mathbf{C}$ *be an RLEV ciphertext and* $\overline{\mathbf{C}}$ *be an RGSW encryption of* μ *under secret* s*. Then* $\mathbf{C}' \leftarrow \mathbf{C} \circledast \overline{\mathbf{C}}$ *is an RLEV ciphertext with* $\varphi_s(\mathbf{C}') = \mu \cdot \varphi_s(\mathbf{C}) + \mathbf{e}$ *for some error* $\mathbf{e} = \begin{bmatrix} e_1 \\ \vdots \\ e_{d_{lev}} \end{bmatrix} \in T^{d_{lev}}$ *with*

$$\mathit{Var}(e_i) = (1 + N/2)\|\mu\|_2^2 \epsilon_{gsw}^2 + 2d_{gsw} N V_{gsw} \mathit{VarErr}(\overline{\mathbf{C}}) (1 \le i \le d_{lev}).$$

We provide a noise analysis on the hybrid product and blind rotation algorithms in CCS19.

Lemma 3 (Hybrid Product). *Let* $\overline{\mathsf{ct}}$ *be an MK-RLWE ciphertext and* $(\mathbf{d}_i, \mathbf{F}_i)$ *be a uni-encryption of* μ *of party* i*. Then* $\overline{\mathsf{ct}}' \leftarrow \mathtt{HbProd}(\{\mathbf{b}_j\}_{j\in[k]}; \mathsf{ct}, (\mathbf{d}_i, \mathbf{F}_i))$ *is an MK-RLWE ciphertext such that* $\varphi_{\overline{\mathbf{s}}}(\overline{\mathsf{ct}}') = \mu \cdot \varphi_{\overline{\mathbf{s}}}(\overline{\mathsf{ct}}) + e \pmod 1$ *for some error* $e \in R$ *with*

$$\mathit{Var}(e) \approx \frac{k}{2}\|\mu\|_2^2 N^2 \epsilon_{uni}^2 + k d_{uni} N^2 V_{uni} \beta^2.$$

Corollary 2 (Blind Rotation of CCS19). *Let* ACC *be the resulting MK-RLWE ciphertext from the blind rotate algorithm 1. Then* $\varphi_{\overline{\mathbf{s}}}(\mathsf{ACC}) = X^{\sum_{i=1}^{k}\langle \tilde{\mathbf{a}}_i, \mathbf{z}_i\rangle + \tilde{b}} \cdot v + e \pmod 1$ *for some error* $e \in T$ *with*

$$\mathit{Var}(e) \approx \frac{k(k+1)}{8} n N^2 (\epsilon_{uni}^2 + 4 d_{uni} V_{uni} \beta^2).$$

Now, we provide a noise analysis of our new hybrid product and generalized external product and the blind rotation.

Lemma 4 (New Hybrid Product). *Let* $\overline{\mathsf{ct}}$ *be an MK-RLWE ciphertext and* $(\mathbf{d}_i, \mathbf{F}_i)$ *be a uni-encryption of* μ *of party* i*. Then* $\overline{\mathsf{ct}}' \leftarrow \mathtt{NewHbProd}(\{\mathbf{b}_j\}_{j\in[k]}; \mathsf{ct}, (\mathbf{d}_i, \mathbf{F}_i))$ *is an MK-RLWE ciphertext such that* $\varphi_{\overline{\mathbf{s}}}(\overline{\mathsf{ct}}') = \mu \cdot \varphi_{\overline{\mathbf{s}}}(\overline{\mathsf{ct}}) + e \pmod 1$ *for some error* $e \in R$ *with*

$$\mathit{Var}(e) \approx \frac{k}{2}\|\mu\|_2^2 N^2 \epsilon_{uni}^2 + k d_{uni} N^2 V_{uni} \beta^2.$$

Lemma 5 (Generalized External Product). *Let* $\overline{\mathsf{ct}}$ *be an MK-RLWE ciphertext,* $\mathbf{C}_i$ *be a single-key RLEV encryption of* μ *under secret key* t *and* $\mathsf{rlk}_i = (\mathbf{d}_i, \mathbf{F}_i)$ *be a uni-encryption of* t *of party* i*. Then* $\overline{\mathsf{ct}}' \leftarrow \mathtt{ExtProd}(\{\mathbf{b}_j\}_{j\in[k]}, \mathsf{rlk}_i; \overline{\mathsf{ct}}, \mathbf{C}_i)$ *is an MK-RLWE ciphertext such that* $\varphi_{\overline{\mathbf{s}}}(\overline{\mathsf{ct}}') = \mu \cdot \varphi_{\overline{\mathbf{s}}}(\overline{\mathsf{ct}}) + e \pmod 1$ *for some error* $e \in T$ *with*

$$\mathit{Var}(e) \approx (1 + kN/2)\left[\|\mu\|_2^2 \epsilon_{lev}^2 + d_{lev} N V_{lev} \mathit{VarErr}(\mathbf{C}_i)\right] + \frac{k}{4} N^3 \epsilon_{uni}^2 + k d_{uni} N^2 V_{uni} \beta^2.$$

Theorem 1 (Our Blind Rotation). *Let* ACC *be the resulting MK-RLWE ciphertext from our new blind rotation algorithm [2]. Then* $\varphi_{\overline{\mathbf{s}}}(\mathsf{ACC}) = X^{\sum_{i=1}^{k}\langle \tilde{\mathbf{a}}_i, \mathbf{z}_i\rangle + \tilde{b}} \cdot v + e \pmod 1$ *for some error* $e \in T$ *with*

$$\mathit{Var}(e) \approx \frac{k(k+1)}{8}\left[2 d_{lev} n N^3 V_{lev} \cdot \left(2 d_{gsw} V_{gsw} \beta^2 + \epsilon_{gsw}^2\right) + N^3 \epsilon_{uni}^2 + 4 d_{uni} N^2 V_{uni} \beta^2\right].$$

6 Implementation

We provide a proof-of-concept implementation of our MK-TFHE scheme and the previous work [6]. Note that in the implementation of CCS19, the underpinning algorithms for the original TFHE [10] such as external product are optimized, however the algorithms for the multi-key variant are not fully optimized. Since our algorithm exploits the algorithms from original TFHE, we implemented our scheme and CCS19 based in Julia for a fair comparison. All experiments were performed on a machine with Intel(R) Xeon(R) Platinum 8268 @ 2.90 GHz CPU and 192 GB RAM running Ubuntu 20.04.2 LTS. Our source code is available at https://github.com/SNUCP/MKTFHE.

Table 1 and Table 2 describe candidate parameter sets for our MK-TFHE scheme and CCS19, respectively. They achieve at least 110-bit of security level according to LWE-estimator [24] with the same LWE parameters in both schemes. However, we use different RLWE parameters as our scheme introduces high noise variance due to an additional level consumption in the generalized external product, which is intolerable by the conventional ring dimension N=1024 and the standard deviation $3.72 \cdot 10^{-9}$ of TFHE. Using a larger ring dimension N=2048 in our scheme, we then have smaller β=$4.63 \cdot 10^{-18}$ and accordingly implement high-precision torus arithmetic (64-bit). The five parameters sets from I to V in Table 1 supports up to 2, 4, 8, 16, and 32 parties. In Table 2, the first three parameter sets I′, II′, and III′ of CCS19 are introduced in the original paper [6] that support at most 2, 4, and 8 parties, respectively. We note that we changed the gadget base for parameter set I′, to guarantee the correct functionality of fully homomorphic encryption. To compare the performance under more parties, we additionally use the parameter set IV′ to evaluate the scheme on 16 parties, but could not find an appropriate parameter set that handles 32 parties in ring dimension $N = 1024$ of CCS19.

We make use of a well-known optimization technique with space-time tradeoff used in [10,14]. In the key-switching key generation step of party i, we publish LWE encryptions of $b \cdot s^*_{i,j} \cdot \mathbf{g}'$ for $0 \le j < n$ and $b \in \mathbb{Z} \cap (-B'/2, B'/2]$, instead of $s^*_{i,j} \cdot \mathbf{g}'$. With this technique, we do not need to perform any multiplication during the key-switching phase with $B' - 1$ times bigger key-switching key size.

Table 1. Recommended parameter settings for our scheme. n, α and N, β denote the dimension and the standard deviations for LWE and RLWE ciphertexts, respectively. B_{ksk} and d_{ksk} are the gadget decomposition parameter for key-switching key.

Set	LWE				RLWE		RGSW		RLEV		UniEnc	
	n	α	B'	d'	N	β	B	d	B	d	B	d
I	560	$3.05 \cdot 10^{-5}$	2^2	8	2048	$4.63 \cdot 10^{-18}$	2^{12}	3	2^6	2	2^{10}	3
II							2^8	5	2^8		2^6	7
III							2^9	4	2^6	3	2^4	8
IV							2^8	5				9
V							2^7	6	2^7		2^2	16

As mentioned in Sect. 5.1, we aim to minimize $d_{gsw} \cdot d_{lev}$ with smallest error variance possible. Let us recall the error analysis of our blind rotation given in Sect. 5.

$$\frac{k(k+1)}{8}\left[2d_{lev}nN^3V_{lev}\cdot\left(2d_{gsw}V_{gsw}\beta^2+\epsilon_{gsw}^2\right)+N^3\epsilon_{uni}^2+4d_{uni}N^2V_{uni}\beta^2\right]$$

We note that the effect of the uni-encryption on both the noise variance and the performance of the blind rotation is almost negligible, therefore we mainly focus on the parameters of RGSW and RLEV ciphertexts. As the error variance is dominated by $d_{lev}V_{lev}(d_{gsw}V_{gsw}\beta^2 + \epsilon_{gsw}^2)$, it follows that the gadget base and the gadget length of both RGSW and RLEV ciphertexts affect the final noise variance. However, the decomposition error of RLEV ciphertexts has little influence whereas that of RGSW ciphertexts has a great influence on the final noise. Based on this observation, our strategy to find the suitable parameter set is to set $d_{lev} \cdot d_{gsw}$ first, and then set the gadget base of RGSW ciphertexts according to d_{gsw} with small decomposition noise, followed by setting the gadget base of RLEV ciphertexts with regard to other parameters. Although the effect of the parameters for uni-encryptions are almost negligible to the time complexity, the final error variance, and even the space complexity, we chose the parameter achieving the least space complexity.

Table 2. Recommended parameter settings for CCS19 scheme.

Set	LWE				RLWE		UniEnc	
	n	α	B'	d'	N	β	B	d
I′	560	$3.05 \cdot 10^{-5}$	2^2	8	1024	$3.72 \cdot 10^{-9}$	2^8	3
II′							2^8	4
III′							2^6	5
IV′							2^2	12

We describe the performance of our scheme and of CCS19 in Table 3. Our scheme is slower when the number of parties is small due to a larger ring dimension $N = 2048$. However, our algorithmic improvements overwhelm its disadvantage and outperform the previous scheme. Finally, our experiments verify that the running time of our NAND algorithm is almost linear with the number of parties as expected, compared to quadratic growth of CCS19 (see Fig. 3). We also provide the execution time of our NAND and parallelized NAND algorithm and that of CCS19 in Table 3.

Table 3. The memory consumed by keys and the elapsed time of NAND algorithms in our scheme and the CCS19 scheme.

Ours						CCS19				
Set	brk	ksk	k	NAND	Parallelized	Set	brk	ksk	k	NAND
I	106 MB	109 MB	2	0.24 s	0.17 s	I′	40 MB	54 MB	2	0.24 s
II	176 MB	109 MB	2	0.38 s	0.25 s	II′	53 MB	54 MB	2	0.30 s
			4	0.88 s	0.27 s				4	0.89 s
III	141 MB	109 MB	2	0.41 s	0.30 s	III′	66 MB	54 MB	2	0.36 s
			4	1.02 s	0.33 s				4	1.01 s
			8	2.23 s	0.35 s				8	3.32 s
IV	176 MB	109 MB	2	0.49 s	0.37 s	IV′	159 MB	54MB	2	0.75 s
			4	1.22 s	0.39 s				4	2.16 s
			8	2.69 s	0.42 s				8	6.92 s
			16	5.65 s	0.47 s				16	24.72 s
V	212 MB	109 MB	2	0.58 s	0.44 s	-	-	-	-	-
			4	1.46 s	0.48 s					
			8	3.18 s	0.49 s					
			16	6.78 s	0.57 s					
			32	13.94 s	0.88 s					

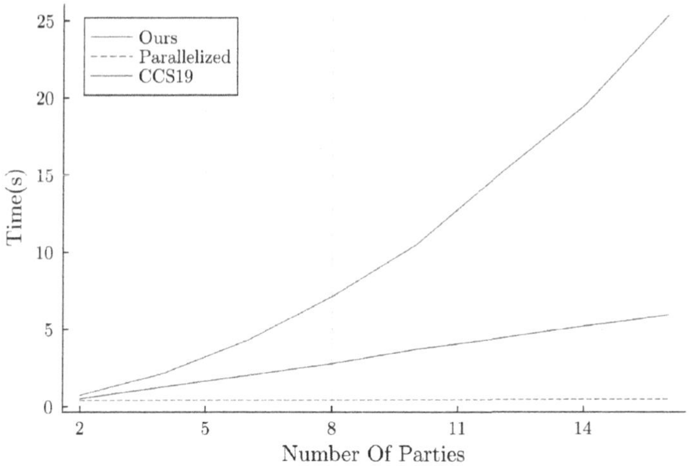

Fig. 3. The time elapsed in NAND algorithms of ours and CCS19 for parameter set IV and IV′, respectively.

Acknowledgement. This work was supported by Samsung Research Funding & Incubation Center of Samsung Electronics under Project Number SRFC-TB2103-01.

A Multi-key TFHE Variant Using Different Gadget Decompositions

We provide the algorithms of our new MK-TFHE scheme with different gadget decompositions. The encryption and decryption algorithms are the same as given in Sect. 4.3.

- `Setup`(1^λ): Given the security parameter λ, return the following parameters:

  - An LWE dimension n, a key distribution χ' over $\mathbb{Z}^n$, and an error variance $\alpha > 0$.
  - An RLWE dimension N, a key distribution χ over $R = \mathbb{Z}[X]/(X^N + 1)$, and an error variance $\beta > 0$.
  - A CRS $\mathbf{a} \leftarrow T^{d_{uni}}$.
  - 4 pairs of gadget decompositions and gadget vectors.
    - A gadget decomposition h_{ksk} of key-switching key and the corresponding gadget vector $\mathbf{g}_{ksk}$ with base B_{ksk} and degree d_{ksk}.
    - A gadget decomposition h_{gsw} of RGSW encryption and the corresponding gadget vector $\mathbf{g}_{gsw}$ with base B_{gsw} and degree d_{gsw}.
    - A gadget decomposition h_{lev} of RLEV encryption and the corresponding gadget vector $\mathbf{g}_{lev}$ with base B_{lev} and degree d_{lev}.
    - A gadget decomposition h_{uni} of uni-encryption and the corresponding gadget vector $\mathbf{g}_{uni}$ with base B_{uni} and degree d_{uni}.

- `KeyGen`(i): A party i generates its secret and public keys as follows.

  - Sample LWE secret key $\mathbf{z}_i = (z_{i,0}, \ldots, z_{i,n-1}) \leftarrow \chi$.
  - Sample RLWE secret key $s_i = s_{i,0} + s_{i,1}X + \cdots + s_{i,N-1}X^{N-1} \leftarrow \chi'$ and error $\mathbf{e} \leftarrow \psi^{d_{uni}}$. Compute $\mathbf{b}_i = -s_i \cdot \mathbf{a} + \mathbf{e} \pmod 1$ and set the public key as $\mathsf{pk}_i = \mathbf{b}_i$.

- `BootKeyGen`(i): A party i generates and publishes a blind rotation key brk_i, a relinearization key rlk_i and a key-switching key ksk_i as follows.

  - Sample $t_i \leftarrow \chi'$ and generate $\mathsf{brk}_{i,j} \leftarrow \texttt{RGSW.Enc}_{h_{gsw}}(t_i; z_{i,j})$ for $0 \le j < n$. Set the blind rotation key $\mathsf{brk}_i = \{\mathsf{brk}_{i,j}\}_{0 \le j < n}$.
  - Generate the relinearization key $\mathsf{rlk}_i \leftarrow \texttt{UniEnc}_{h_{uni}}(s_i; t_i)$.
  - Let $(s^*_{i,0}, \ldots, s^*_{i,N-1}) = (s_{i,0}, -s_{i,N-1}, \ldots, -s_{i,1})$. Sample $\mathbf{A}_{i,j} \leftarrow \mathbb{T}^{d_{ksk} \times n}$ and $\mathbf{e}_{i,j} \leftarrow \psi'^{d_{ksk}}$ for $0 \le j < N$, and let $\mathsf{ksk}_{i,j} = [\mathbf{b}_{i,j} | \mathbf{A}_{i,j}]$ where $\mathbf{b}_{i,j} = -\mathbf{A}_{i,j} \cdot \mathbf{s}_i + \mathbf{e}_{i,j} + s^*_{i,j} \cdot \mathbf{g}_{ksk}$. Set the key-switching key $\mathsf{ksk}_i = \{\mathsf{ksk}_{i,j}\}_{0 < N}$.

- `HomNAND`$(\{(\mathsf{pk}_i, \mathsf{brk}_i, \mathsf{rlk}_i, \mathsf{ksk}_i)\}_{i \in [k]}; \overline{\mathsf{ct}}_1, \overline{\mathsf{ct}}_2)$: Given two LWE ciphertexts $\overline{\mathsf{ct}}_1$, $\overline{\mathsf{ct}}_2$ and key-quadruple $\{(\mathsf{pk}_i, \mathsf{brk}_i, \mathsf{rlk}_i, \mathsf{ksk}_i)\}_{i \in [k]}$ of associated parties, perform the following steps:

1. Compute $\overline{\mathsf{ct}} \leftarrow (\frac{5}{8}, 0, \ldots, 0) - \overline{\mathsf{ct}}_1 - \overline{\mathsf{ct}}_2 \pmod 1$.
2. Compute $\overline{\mathsf{ct}} \leftarrow \texttt{BlindRotate}(\{(\mathsf{pk}_i, \mathsf{brk}_i, \mathsf{rlk}_i)\}_{i \in [k]}; \overline{\mathsf{ct}})$ where $\texttt{BlindRotate}(\cdot)$ is the blind rotation algorithm in Algorithm 3.

3. Compute $\overline{\mathsf{ct}} \leftarrow (\frac{1}{8}, 0, \ldots, 0) + \overline{\mathsf{ct}} \pmod 1$ and return $\mathsf{ct} = (b, \mathbf{a}_1, \ldots, \mathbf{a}_k) \in \mathbb{T}^{kN+1}$ where b is the constant term of $\overline{\mathsf{ct}}_0$ and $\mathbf{a}_i$ is the coefficient vector of $\overline{\mathsf{ct}}_i$ for $i \in [k]$.
4. Perform the key-switching process: Compute $(b_i', \mathbf{a}_i') = \sum_{j=0}^{N-1} h'(a_{i,j}) \cdot \mathsf{ksk}_{i,j} \pmod 1$ for $i \in [k]$ and $b' = b + \sum_{i \in [k]} b_i'$. Return $\mathsf{ct}' = (b', \mathbf{a}_1', \ldots, \mathbf{a}_k') \in \mathbb{T}^{kn+1}$.

Algorithm 3. New Blind Rotation using Different Gadget Decompositions

---

Input: $\overline{\mathsf{ct}} = (b, \mathbf{a}_1, \ldots, \mathbf{a}_k), \{(\mathsf{pk}_i, \mathsf{brk}_i, \mathsf{rlk}_i)\}_{i \in [k]}$
Output: ACC
1: Let $\tilde{b} := \lfloor 2Nb \rceil$, $\tilde{a}_{i,j} := \lfloor 2Na_{i,j} \rceil$ for $1 \le i \le k$, $0 \le j < n$
2: and $v := -\frac{1}{8} \cdot (1 + X + \cdots + X^{N/2-1} - X^{N/2} - \cdots - X^{N-1})$.
3: $\mathsf{ACC} \leftarrow (v \cdot X^{\tilde{b}}, 0, \ldots, 0)$
4: **for** $1 \le i \le k$ **do**
5: $\quad \mathsf{ACC}_i' \leftarrow (\mathbf{g}_{lev}, \mathbf{0})$
6: $\quad$**for** $0 \le j < n$ **do**
7: $\quad\quad \mathsf{ACC}_i' \leftarrow \mathsf{ACC}_i' + \left[(X^{\tilde{a}_{i,j}} - 1) \cdot \mathsf{ACC}_i'\right] \circledast_{h_{lev}} \mathsf{brk}_{i,j}$
8: $\quad$**end for**
9: **end for**
10: **for** $1 \le i \le k$ **do**
11: $\quad \mathsf{ACC} \leftarrow \mathtt{ExtProd}_{h_{lev}, h_{uni}}(\{\mathsf{pk}_\ell\}_{\ell \in [k]}, \mathsf{rlk}_i; \mathsf{ACC}, \mathsf{ACC}_i')$
12: **end for**

B Proofs for the Noise Analysis

First we define GdErr_{gsw}, GdErr_{lev} and GdErr_{uni}, the gadget decomposition error of h_{gsw}, h_{lev} and h_{uni} respectively.
Proof of Lemma 1 (T-RLEV Multiplication)

Proof. By definition, we have

$$\begin{aligned}\varphi_s(c \odot \mathbf{C}) &= \langle h_{lev}(c), \varphi_s(\mathbf{C})\rangle \\ &= \langle h_{lev}(c), \mu \cdot \mathbf{g}_{lev} + \mathsf{Err}(\mathbf{C})\rangle \\ &= \mu \cdot c + \mu \cdot \mathsf{GdErr}_{lev}(c) + \langle h_{lev}(c), \mathsf{Err}(\mathbf{C})\rangle \pmod 1.\end{aligned}$$

Therefore $e = \mu \cdot \mathsf{GdErr}_{lev}(c) + \langle h_{lev}(c), \mathsf{Err}(\mathbf{C})\rangle$. Since $h_{lev}(c)$ and $\mathsf{err}(\mathbf{C})$ are vectors of length d_{lev}, we get

$$\mathsf{Var}(e) = \|\mu\|_2^2 \epsilon_{lev}^2 + d_{lev} N V_{lev} \mathsf{VarErr}(\mathbf{C})$$

□

Proof of Lemma 2 (RLWE-RGSW Multiplication)

Proof. Let $\mathbf{c} = (b, a)$ and $\mathsf{Err}(\mathbf{C}) = \begin{bmatrix} \mathbf{e}_0 \\ \mathbf{e}_1 \end{bmatrix}$ where $\mathbf{e}_0, \mathbf{e}_1 \in T^{d_{gsw}}$. Then we can obtain

$$\begin{aligned}
\varphi_s(\mathbf{c} \otimes \overline{\mathbf{C}}) &= \left\langle h_{gsw}(\mathbf{c}), \varphi_s(\overline{\mathbf{C}}) \right\rangle \\
&= \langle h_{gsw}(b), \mu \cdot \mathbf{g}_{gsw} + \mathbf{e}_0 \rangle + \langle h_{gsw}(a), \mu \cdot s \cdot \mathbf{g}_{gsw} + \mathbf{e}_1 \rangle \\
&= \mu \cdot \varphi_s(\mathbf{c}) + \mu \cdot (\mathsf{GdErr}_{gsw}(b) + \mathsf{GdErr}_{gsw}(a)s) + \left\langle h_{gsw}(\mathbf{c}), \mathsf{Err}(\overline{\mathbf{C}}) \right\rangle \pmod 1.
\end{aligned}$$

Therefore, we can get the following error variance.

$$\mathsf{Var}(e) = (1 + N/2)\|\mu\|_2^2 \epsilon_{gsw}^2 + 2d_{gsw} N V_{gsw} \mathsf{VarErr}(\overline{\mathbf{C}}).$$

□

Proof of Corollary 1 (RLEV-RGSW Multiplication)

Proof. An RLEV ciphertext can be seen as a column vector of RLWE ciphertexts. Therefore, this corollary can be shown directly from the previous lemma. □

For efficiency, we prove Lemma 4 first, and then prove Lemma 3.

Proof of Lemma 4 (New Hybrid Product)

Proof. We shall use $\mathbf{e}_0 = \mathbf{0}$ and the same temporary variables as in the algorithm description for the easier notation. Let $\mathbf{u} = (u_0, \ldots, u_k)$ and $\mathbf{w} = (w_0, w_1)$. Then we have $\varphi_{\overline{\mathbf{s}}}(\overline{\mathsf{ct}}') = \varphi_{\overline{\mathbf{s}}}(\mathbf{u}) + \varphi_{s_i}(\mathbf{w}) \pmod 1$. The first term is

$$\begin{aligned}
\varphi_{\overline{\mathbf{s}}}(u) &= \sum_{j=0}^{k} \langle h_{uni}(c_j), r \cdot \mathbf{a} + \mu \cdot \mathbf{g}_{uni} + \mathbf{e}_{i,1} \rangle \cdot s_j \\
&= \mu \cdot \varphi_{\overline{\mathbf{s}}}(\overline{\mathsf{ct}}) + \mu \cdot \sum_{j=0}^{k} \mathsf{GdErr}_{uni}(c_j) \cdot s_j + r \cdot \sum_{j=0}^{k} \langle h_{uni}(c_j), s_j \cdot \mathbf{a} \rangle \\
&+ \sum_{j=0}^{k} \langle h_{uni}(c_j), \mathbf{e}_{i,1} \rangle \cdot s_j \pmod 1,
\end{aligned}$$

and the second term is

$$\begin{aligned}
\varphi_{s_i}(\mathbf{w}) &= \langle h_{uni}(v), \mathbf{F}_{i,0} \rangle + \langle h_{uni}(v), \mathbf{F}_{i,1} \rangle \cdot s_i \\
&= \langle h_{uni}(v), r \cdot \mathbf{g}_{uni} + \mathbf{e}_{i,2} \rangle \\
&= r \cdot v + r \cdot \mathsf{GdErr}_{uni}(v) + \langle h_{uni}(v), \mathbf{e}_{i,2} \rangle \pmod 1.
\end{aligned}$$

Now, from the fact that

$$\begin{aligned}
v + \sum_{j=0}^{k} \langle h_{uni}(c_j), s_j \cdot \mathbf{a} \rangle &= \sum_{j=0}^{k} (\langle h_{uni}(c_j), \mathbf{b}_j \rangle + \langle h_{uni}(c_j), s_j \cdot \mathbf{a} \rangle) \\
&= \sum_{j=1}^{k} \langle h_{uni}(c_j), \mathbf{e}_j \rangle \pmod 1,
\end{aligned}$$

it follows that $e = \varphi_{\overline{\mathbf{s}}}(\overline{\mathsf{ct}}') - \mu \cdot \varphi_{\overline{\mathbf{s}}}(\overline{\mathsf{ct}})$ is

$$\mu \cdot \sum_{j=0}^{k} \mathsf{GdErr}_{uni}(c_j) \cdot s_j + \sum_{j=0}^{k} \langle h_{uni}(c_j), \mathbf{e}_{i,1} \rangle \cdot s_j +$$

$$r \cdot \mathsf{GdErr}_{uni}(v) + \langle h_{uni}(v), \mathbf{e}_{i,2} \rangle + r \cdot \sum_{j=1}^{k} \langle h_{uni}(c_j), \mathbf{e}_j \rangle .$$

Therefore, we have

$$\begin{aligned} \mathsf{Var}(e) &= \|\mu\|_2^2 (1 + kN/2) N \epsilon_{uni}^2 + (1 + kN/2) d_{uni} N V_{uni} \beta^2 \\ &+ (N/2)\epsilon_{uni}^2 + d_{uni} N V_{uni} \beta^2 + k d_{uni} (N^2/2) V_{uni} \beta^2 \\ &\approx \frac{k}{2} \|\mu\|_2^2 N^2 \epsilon_{uni}^2 + k d_{uni} N^2 V_{uni} \beta^2 . \end{aligned}$$

□

Proof of Lemma 3 (Hybrid Product)

Proof. The only difference of the error variance of HbProd to the error variance NewHbProd is the error from $w_{j,0}$ and $w_{j,1}$'s, which is $k + 1$ times bigger than NewHbProd. Therefore, we get the error variance of

$$\begin{aligned} \mathsf{Var}(e) &= \|\mu\|_2^2 (1 + kN/2) N \epsilon_{uni}^2 + (1 + kN/2) d_{uni} N V_{uni} \beta^2 \\ &+ (k+1)(N/2)\epsilon_{uni}^2 + (k+1) d_{uni} N V_{uni} \beta^2 + k d_{uni} (N^2/2) V_{uni} \beta^2 \\ &\approx \frac{k}{2} \|\mu\|_2^2 N^2 \epsilon_{uni}^2 + k d_{uni} N^2 V_{uni} \beta^2 . \end{aligned}$$

□

Proof of Corollary 2 (Blind Rotation of CCS19)

Proof. We first analyze the line 6. Let $\overline{\mathbf{c}}_{i,j} = \mathtt{HbProd}(\{\mathsf{pk}_j\}_{j \in [k]}, (X^{\tilde{a}_{i,j}} - 1) \cdot \mathsf{ACC}, \mathsf{BK}_{i,j})$ and $\mathbf{e}_{i,j}$ be the error solely from the HbProd. Then,

$$\begin{aligned} \varphi_{\overline{\mathbf{s}}}(\mathsf{ACC} + \overline{\mathbf{c}}_{i,j}) &= \varphi_{\overline{\mathbf{s}}}(\mathsf{ACC}) + \varphi_{\overline{\mathbf{s}}}((X^{\tilde{a}_{i,j}} - 1) \cdot \mathsf{ACC}) + \mathbf{e}_{i,j} \\ &= \varphi_{\overline{\mathbf{s}}}(X^{\tilde{a}_{i,j} z_{i,j}} \cdot \mathsf{ACC}) + \mathbf{e}_{i,j} \pmod 1 . \end{aligned}$$

Note that during the i-th iteration, ACC should be regarded as a multi-key RLWE ciphertext with i parties since $i + 1, \ldots, k$-th indices remains zero. Therefore,

$$\begin{aligned} \mathsf{Var}(\mathbf{e}_{i,j}) &\approx \frac{i}{2} \|z_{i,j}\|_2^2 N^2 \epsilon_{uni}^2 + i d_{uni} N^2 V_{uni} \beta^2 \\ &= \frac{i}{4} N^2 \epsilon_{uni}^2 + i d_{uni} N^2 V_{uni} \beta^2 \end{aligned}$$

Since $X^{\tilde{a}_{i,j} z_{i,j}}$ is a monomial, the variance adds up every iteration in the inner loop (line 5–7) and therefore an error variance of $\frac{i}{4} n N^2 \epsilon_{uni}^2 + i d_{uni} n N^2 V_{uni} \beta^2$ is added for every iteration in the outer loop (line 4–8). Therefore we get the error variance of

$$\frac{k(k+1)}{8} nN^2(\epsilon_{uni}^2 + 4d_{uni}V_{uni}\beta^2).$$

□

Proof of Lemma 5 (Generalized External Product)

Proof. Let us follow the notations from the algorithm description. First, by Lemma 1 we obtain

$$\begin{aligned}\varphi_{\overline{\mathbf{s}}}(\overline{\mathbf{x}} + \overline{\mathbf{y}} \cdot t) = \sum_{j=0}^{k} (x_j + y_j \cdot t) \cdot s_j = \sum_{j=0}^{k} \varphi_t(c_j \odot \mathbf{C}_i) \cdot s_j \\ = \mu \cdot \varphi_{\overline{\mathbf{s}}}(\overline{\mathsf{ct}}) + \sum_{j=0}^{k} e_j \cdot s_j \pmod 1.\end{aligned}$$

where $e_j = \varphi_t(c_j \odot \mathbf{C}_i) - \mu \cdot c_j (0 \leq j \leq k) \pmod 1 \in T$ with variance

$$\mathsf{Var}(e_j) = \|\mu\|_2^2 \epsilon_{lev}^2 + d_{lev} N V_{lev} \mathsf{VarErr}(\mathbf{C}_i).$$

Let $\overline{\mathbf{y}}' = \texttt{NewHbProd}(\{\mathbf{b}_j\}_{j \in [k]}, \mathsf{ct}, \mathsf{rlk}_i)$. By Lemma 4, $\varphi_{\overline{\mathbf{s}}}(\overline{\mathbf{y}}') = t \cdot \varphi_{\overline{\mathbf{s}}}(\overline{\mathbf{y}}) + e'$ for some $e' \in T$ with variance

$$\begin{aligned}\mathsf{Var}(e') &\approx \frac{k}{2} \mathsf{Var}(\|t\|_2^2) N^2 \epsilon_{uni}^2 + k d_{uni} N^2 V_{uni} \beta^2 \\ &= \frac{k}{4} N^3 \epsilon_{uni}^2 + k d_{uni} N^2 V_{uni} \beta^2.\end{aligned}$$

Therefore, we get

$$\begin{aligned}\varphi_{\overline{\mathbf{s}}}(\overline{\mathsf{ct}}') = \varphi_{\overline{\mathbf{s}}}(\overline{\mathbf{x}}) + \varphi_{\overline{\mathbf{s}}}(\overline{\mathbf{y}}') = \varphi_{\overline{\mathbf{s}}}(\overline{\mathbf{x}}) + \varphi_{\overline{\mathbf{s}}}(\overline{\mathbf{y}}) \cdot t + e' \\ = \mu \cdot \varphi_{\overline{\mathbf{s}}}(\overline{\mathsf{ct}}) + \sum_{j=0}^{k} e_j \cdot s_j + e' \pmod 1.\end{aligned}$$

Therefore the variance of error $e = \sum_{j=0}^{k} e_j \cdot s_j + e'$ be

$$\begin{aligned}\mathsf{Var}(e) \approx (1 + kN/2) \left[\|\mu\|_2^2 \epsilon_{lev}^2 + d_{lev} N V_{lev} \mathsf{VarErr}(\mathbf{C}_i)\right] \\ + \frac{k}{4} N^3 \epsilon_{uni}^2 + k d_{uni} N^2 V_{uni} \beta^2.\end{aligned}$$

□

Proof of Theorem 1 (Our Blind Rotation)

Proof. We start from analyzing line 7 of the algorithm. By Corollary 1,

$$\begin{aligned}&\varphi_{t_i}(\mathsf{ACC}_i' + \left[(X^{\tilde{a}_{i,j}} - 1) \cdot \mathsf{ACC}_i'\right] \circledast \mathsf{BK}_{i,j}) \\ &= \varphi_{t_i}(\mathsf{ACC}_i') + \varphi_{t_i}(\left[(X^{\tilde{a}_{i,j}} - 1) \cdot \mathsf{ACC}_i'\right] \circledast \mathsf{BK}_{i,j}) \\ &= \varphi_{t_i}(X^{\tilde{a}_{i,j} z_{i,j}} \cdot \mathsf{ACC}_i') + \mathbf{e}_{i,j} \pmod 1\end{aligned}$$

for some $\mathbf{e}_{i,j} \in T^{d_{lev}}$ with the common variance of rows $(1+N/2)\|\mu z_{i,j}\|_2^2\epsilon_{gsw}^2 + 2d_{gsw}NV_{gsw}\mathsf{VarErr}(\mathsf{BK}_{i,j})$. Therefore, with each iteration within the for loop 6–8, the error variance increases by $V_{ACC} = (1+N)\epsilon_{gsw}^2 + 2d_{gsw}NV_{gsw}\beta^2$. Hence, the error variance of the resulting RLEV ciphertext ACC_i' of the for loop is $n \cdot ((1+N)\epsilon_{gsw}^2 + 2d_{gsw}NV_{gsw}\beta^2)$ with message $X^{\sum_{j=1}^{n} \tilde{a}_{i,j} z_{i,j}}$.

Note that only $0,\ldots,i$-th indices of the MK-RLWE ciphertext ACC are non-zero after the $i-th$ iteration of the for loop 4–10, hence it can be regarded as an MK-RLWE encryption of i parties. Now we let ACC_i be ACC after the `ExtProd`, then by the Lemma 5, we have

$$\varphi_{\bar{\mathbf{s}}}(\mathsf{ACC}_i) = X^{\langle \tilde{\mathbf{a}}_i, \mathbf{z}_i \rangle} \cdot \varphi_{\bar{\mathbf{s}}}(\mathsf{ACC}_{i-1}) + e_i (1 \le i \le k)$$

where

$$\mathsf{Var}(e_i) \approx (1+iN/2)\left[\epsilon_{lev}^2 + d_{lev}NV_{lev}V_{ACC}\right] + \frac{i}{4}N^3\epsilon_{uni}^2 + id_{uni}N^2V_{uni}\beta^2.$$

Since $X^{\tilde{\mathbf{a}}_i, \mathbf{z}_i}$ is a monomial, the error variance adds up every iteration and thus the error variance of the final output of our new blind rotation algorithm is

$$\frac{k(k+1)}{8}\left[2d_{lev}nN^3V_{lev} \cdot \left(2d_{gsw}V_{gsw}\beta^2 + \epsilon_{gsw}^2\right) + N^3\epsilon_{uni}^2 + 4d_{uni}N^2V_{uni}\beta^2\right].$$

□

References

1. Asharov, G., Jain, A., López-Alt, A., Tromer, E., Vaikuntanathan, V., Wichs, D.: Multiparty computation with low communication, computation and interaction via threshold fhe. In: Pointcheval, D., Johansson, T. (eds.) EUROCRYPT 2012. LNCS, vol. 7237, pp. 483–501. Springer, Heidelberg (2012). https://doi.org/10.1007/978-3-642-29011-4_29
2. Ben-Efraim, A.: On multiparty garbling of arithmetic circuits. In: Peyrin, T., Galbraith, S. (eds.) ASIACRYPT 2018. LNCS, vol. 11274, pp. 3–33. Springer, Cham (2018). https://doi.org/10.1007/978-3-030-03332-3_1
3. Brakerski, Z.: Fully homomorphic encryption without modulus switching from classical GapSVP. In: Safavi-Naini, R., Canetti, R. (eds.) CRYPTO 2012. LNCS, vol. 7417, pp. 868–886. Springer, Heidelberg (2012). https://doi.org/10.1007/978-3-642-32009-5_50
4. Brakerski, Z., Gentry, C., Vaikuntanathan, V.: (leveled) fully homomorphic encryption without bootstrapping. ACM Trans. Comput. Theory (TOCT) **6**(3), 1–36 (2014)
5. Brakerski, Z.: Fully homomorphic encryption without modulus switching from classical GapSVP. In: Safavi-Naini, R., Canetti, R. (eds.) CRYPTO 2012. LNCS, vol. 7417, pp. 868–886. Springer, Heidelberg (2012). https://doi.org/10.1007/978-3-642-32009-5_50
6. Chen, H., Chillotti, I., Song, Y.: Multi-key homomorphic encryption from TFHE. In: Galbraith, S.D., Moriai, S. (eds.) ASIACRYPT 2019. LNCS, vol. 11922, pp. 446–472. Springer, Cham (2019). https://doi.org/10.1007/978-3-030-34621-8_16

7. Chen, H., Dai, W., Kim, M., Song, Y.: Efficient multi-key homomorphic encryption with packed ciphertexts with application to oblivious neural network inference. In: Proceedings of the 2019 ACM SIGSAC Conference on Computer and Communications Security, pp. 395–412 (2019)
8. Chen, L., Zhang, Z., Wang, X.: Batched multi-hop multi-key FHE from ring-LWE with compact ciphertext extension. In: Kalai, Y., Reyzin, L. (eds.) TCC 2017. LNCS, vol. 10678, pp. 597–627. Springer, Cham (2017). https://doi.org/10.1007/978-3-319-70503-3_20
9. Cheon, J.H., Kim, A., Kim, M., Song, Y.: Homomorphic encryption for arithmetic of approximate numbers. In: Takagi, T., Peyrin, T. (eds.) ASIACRYPT 2017. LNCS, vol. 10624, pp. 409–437. Springer, Cham (2017). https://doi.org/10.1007/978-3-319-70694-8_15
10. Chillotti, I., Gama, N., Georgieva, M., Izabachène, M.: Faster fully homomorphic encryption: bootstrapping in less than 0.1 seconds. In: Cheon, J.H., Takagi, T. (eds.) ASIACRYPT 2016. LNCS, vol. 10031, pp. 3–33. Springer, Heidelberg (2016). https://doi.org/10.1007/978-3-662-53887-6_1
11. Chillotti, I., Ligier, D., Orfila, J.-B., Tap, S.: Improved programmable bootstrapping with larger precision and efficient arithmetic circuits for TFHE. In: Tibouchi, M., Wang, H. (eds.) ASIACRYPT 2021. LNCS, vol. 13092, pp. 670–699. Springer, Cham (2021). https://doi.org/10.1007/978-3-030-92078-4_23
12. Clear, M., McGoldrick, C.: Multi-identity and multi-key leveled FHE from learning with errors. In: Gennaro, R., Robshaw, M. (eds.) CRYPTO 2015. LNCS, vol. 9216, pp. 630–656. Springer, Heidelberg (2015). https://doi.org/10.1007/978-3-662-48000-7_31
13. Dahl, M., et al.: Noah's ark: Efficient threshold-FHE using noise flooding. In: Proceedings of the 11th Workshop on Encrypted Computing & Applied Homomorphic Cryptography, pp. 35–46 (2023)
14. Ducas, L., Micciancio, D.: FHEW: bootstrapping homomorphic encryption in less than a second. In: Oswald, E., Fischlin, M. (eds.) EUROCRYPT 2015. LNCS, vol. 9056, pp. 617–640. Springer, Heidelberg (2015). https://doi.org/10.1007/978-3-662-46800-5_24
15. Fan, J., Vercauteren, F.: Somewhat practical fully homomorphic encryption. IACR Cryptol. ePrint Arch. **2012**, 144 (2012)
16. Gentry, C.: Fully homomorphic encryption using ideal lattices. In: Proceedings of the forty-first Annual ACM Symposium on Theory of Computing, pp. 169–178 (2009)
17. Gentry, C., Sahai, A., Waters, B.: Homomorphic encryption from learning with errors: conceptually-simpler, asymptotically-faster, attribute-based. In: Canetti, R., Garay, J.A. (eds.) CRYPTO 2013. LNCS, vol. 8042, pp. 75–92. Springer, Heidelberg (2013). https://doi.org/10.1007/978-3-642-40041-4_5
18. Kim, A., et al.: General bootstrapping approach for RLWE-based homomorphic encryption. IEEE Trans. Comput. **73**, 86–96 (2023)
19. Kim, T., Kwak, H., Lee, D., Seo, J., Song, Y.: Asymptotically faster multi-key homomorphic encryption from homomorphic gadget decomposition. In: Proceedings of the 2023 ACM SIGSAC Conference on Computer and Communications Security, pp. 726–740 (2023)
20. Klemsa, J., Önen, M., Akın, Y.: A practical TFHE-based multi-key homomorphic encryption with linear complexity and low noise growth. In: Tsudik, G., Conti, M., Liang, K., Smaragdakis, G. (eds.) Computer Security. ESORICS 2023. LNCS, vol. 14344, pp. 3–23. Springer, Cham (2023). https://doi.org/10.1007/978-3-031-50594-2_1

21. Kraitsberg, M., Lindell, Y., Osheter, V., Smart, N.P., Talibi Alaoui, Y.: Adding distributed decryption and key generation to a Ring-LWE based CCA encryption scheme. In: Jang-Jaccard, J., Guo, F. (eds.) ACISP 2019. LNCS, vol. 11547, pp. 192–210. Springer, Cham (2019). https://doi.org/10.1007/978-3-030-21548-4_11
22. López-Alt, A., Tromer, E., Vaikuntanathan, V.: On-the-fly multiparty computation on the cloud via multikey fully homomorphic encryption. In: Proceedings of the Forty-fourth Annual ACM Symposium on Theory of Computing, pp. 1219–1234 (2012)
23. Lyubashevsky, V., Peikert, C., Regev, O.: On ideal lattices and learning with errors over rings. J. ACM (JACM) **60**(6), 1–35 (2013)
24. malb: lattice-estimator (2022). https://github.com/malb/lattice-estimator
25. Mouchet, C., Troncoso-Pastoriza, J., Bossuat, J.P., Hubaux, J.P.: Multiparty homomorphic encryption from ring-learning-with-errors. Proc. Priv. Enhanc. Technol. **2021**(4), 291–311 (2021)
26. Mukherjee, P., Wichs, D.: Two round multiparty computation via multi-key FHE. In: Fischlin, M., Coron, J.-S. (eds.) EUROCRYPT 2016. LNCS, vol. 9666, pp. 735–763. Springer, Heidelberg (2016). https://doi.org/10.1007/978-3-662-49896-5_26
27. Park, J.: Homomorphic encryption for multiple users with less communications. IEEE Access **9**, 135915–135926 (2021)
28. Peikert, C., Shiehian, S.: Multi-key FHE from LWE, revisited. In: Hirt, M., Smith, A. (eds.) TCC 2016. LNCS, vol. 9986, pp. 217–238. Springer, Heidelberg (2016). https://doi.org/10.1007/978-3-662-53644-5_9
29. Regev, O.: On lattices, learning with errors, random linear codes, and cryptography. J. ACM (JACM) **56**(6), 1–40 (2009)

Implementation

Fast and Simple Point Operations on Edwards448 and E448

Luying Li[1,2], Wei Yu[2,3](✉), and Peng Xu[1,4](✉)

[1] JinYinHu Laboratory, Wuhan 430040, China
liluying@pku.org.cn
[2] State Key Laboratory of Cryptology, P. O. Box 5159, Beijing 100878, China
[3] Key Laboratory of Cyberspace Security Defense, Institute of Information Engineering, Chinese Academy of Sciences, Beijing 100093, China
yuwei@iie.ac.cn, yuwei_1_yw@163.com
[4] Hubei Key Laboratory of Distributed System Security, School of Cyber Science and Engineering, Huazhong University of Science and Technology, Wuhan 430074, China
xupeng@mail.hust.edu.cn

Abstract. Since Edwards curves were introduced in elliptic curve cryptography, they have attracted a lot of attention. The twisted Edwards curves are defined by the equation $E_{a,d} : ax^2 + y^2 = 1 + dx^2y^2$. Twisted Edwards curve is the state-of-the-art for $a = -1$, and even for $a \neq -1$. E448 and Edwards448 are NIST standard curve in 2023 and TLS 1.3 standard curve in 2018. They both can be converted to $d = -1$, but can not be converted to $a = -1$ through isomorphism. The motivation of using a curve with $d = -1$ is that we want to improve the efficiency of E448, and Edwards448, especially to achieve a great saving in terms of the number of field multiplications (**M**) and field squarings (**S**). We propose new explicit formulas for point operations on these curves. Our full point addition only requires 8**M**, and mixed addition requires 7**M**. Our results applied on the Edward448 and E448 yield a clean and simple implementation and achieve a brand new speed record. The scalar multiplication on Edwards448 and E448 have the same cost of **M** and **S** as that on Edwards25519 per bit.

Keywords: Scalar multiplication · Addition · Doubling · Explicit formulas · Twisted Edwards curves · E448 · Edwards448

1 Introduction

Elliptic curve cryptography is one of the most popular cryptosystems. Because elliptic curve cryptography's shorter key length offers the same level of security as other public key cryptosystems with longer key lengths, it has been widely used in modern life since 2005. It is particularly well-liked in applications for mobile devices such as wireless and the internet of things.

The elliptic curves are the curves of genus one with a specified base point. In cryptography, the interest in elliptic curves is focused on their group structure.

Q. Tang and V. Teague (Eds.): PKC 2024, LNCS 14604, pp. 389–411, 2024.
https://doi.org/10.1007/978-3-031-57728-4_13

The points on the elliptic curve form an additive Abelian group. The scalar multiplication is an operation that continually adds the same point to itself repeatedly. In other words, scalar multiplication computes

$$nP = \underbrace{P + P + \cdots + P}_{n \text{ times}},$$

where n is a large positive integer known as the *scalar* and P is a point on an elliptic curve over the finite field. Elliptic curve cryptography is usually based on scalar multiplication on prime order cyclic subgroups of the elliptic curve point groups. Scalar multiplication is considered as the core operation in elliptic-curve cryptography. It is also the costliest part of some wildly used elliptic curve cryptography protocols, e.g. elliptic curve Diffie-Hellman key exchange and elliptic curve digital signature algorithm.

Compared to other elliptic curves, the Edwards curve in elliptic curve cryptography does not have such a long history. It was not until 2007 that this elliptic curve form was first explicitly proposed by Edwards [10]. In the same year, Bernstein and Lange introduced the Edwards curve into cryptography [3]. The importance of Edwards curves and their generalizations, especially the twisted Edwards curves, is beyond doubt. The twisted Edwards form is one of the three forms of curves recommended by NIST Special Publication 800-186 [7] over the finite field of large prime. The twisted Edwards curves Edwards25519 and Edwards448, also referred to as Ed25519 and Ed448, were recommended to be used in digital signature by NIST FIPS 186-5 [22], and Internet Engineering Task Force Request for Comments (IETF RFC) 8032 [19]; and were recommended to be employed in secure shell (SSH) protocol by IETF RFC 8709 [21]. The twisted Edwards curves are also employed in the Elliptic Curve Method (ECM) [2,6].

Ever since it was proposed, the scalar multiplication on the Edwards curve has become the leader in multi-scalar multiplication. Speeding up the scalar multiplications is one of the major challenges of elliptic curve cryptography. There are three main ways to improve the efficiency of scalar multiplication:

- Improving the point operations [18,25].
- Using efficient endomorphisms [13,14].
- Reducing the Hamming weight of the scalar, for example, non-adjacent form, window non-adjacent form, and double base chains [24].

In this paper, we investigate elliptic curve point arithmetic formulas on twisted Edwards curves for $d = -1$ to bridge the gap of previous works which focus on the general and $a = -1$ cases.

We provide two addition formulas on twisted Edwards curves in extended twisted Edwards coordinates. The *unified* addition formula, i.e., the point addition formula remains valid when two input points are equal, offers better side-channel resistance. The *unified* addition formula costs 8 field multiplications and one field multiplication with constant a, and the fast addition formula takes only 8 field multiplications, as fast as the addition formula for $a = -1$ on twisted Edwards curves [18].

The table below illustrates the state-of-the-art theoretical time costs of the unified addition, the mixed unified addition (where one coordinate is fixed as one in the unified addition formula), the fast addition ($P = Q$ may cause an exception), and the mixed addition of the fast addition. The **M**, **S**, and **D** denote field multiplication, field squaring, and field multiplication with a constant respectively (Table 1).

Table 1. The theoretical time cost of twisted Edwards curves

parameter	unified add	mixed unified add	fast add	mixed add
$a = -1$ [18]	$8\mathbf{M} + 1\mathbf{D}$	$7\mathbf{M} + 1\mathbf{D}$	$8\mathbf{M}$	$7\mathbf{M}$
$a \neq -1$ [18]	$9\mathbf{M} + 2\mathbf{D}$	$8\mathbf{M} + 2\mathbf{D}$	$9\mathbf{M} + 1\mathbf{D}$	$8\mathbf{M} + 1\mathbf{D}$
$d = -1$	$8\mathbf{M} + 1\mathbf{D}$	$7\mathbf{M} + 1\mathbf{D}$	$8\mathbf{M}$	$7\mathbf{M}$

The following problem is that the efficient doubling and tripling equations on $a = -1$ do not immediately yield good efficiency when $d = -1$. In order to solve this problem, we consider another set of projections of the extended twisted Edwards coordinates on $\mathbb{P}^2$ other than projective coordinates.

The remainder of this paper is organized as follows: in Sect. 2, we review twisted Edwards curves. Section 3 provides the unified addition formula. In Sect. 4, we provide the unified addition formulae with clearing denominators. In Sect. 5, we provide fast addition, doubling, and tripling formulae for further speedup. In Sect. 6, we analyze the exceptional cases of $2q$ and $4q$ order subgroups. In Sect. 7, we show the benefit of clearing denominators addition formulas in parallel environments and adapt the strategy of mixing different coordinates to obtain better efficiency for fast addition formulas. We draw our conclusions in Sect. 8.

2 Twisted Edwards Curve

The history of the Edwards curve family goes back to Euler's time. Euler studied an interesting curve $x^2 + y^2 + x^2y^2 = 1$. In his paper [11], Euler hinted at the explicit addition formula for this curve. Gauss explicitly stated this addition formula decades later.

In 2007, Edwards generalized the special curve $x^2 + y^2 + x^2y^2 = 1$ into the form

$$x^2 + y^2 = a^2 + a^2x^2y^2$$

and believed that this curve form deserves more attention than it had received at that time [10]. Edwards demonstrated that elliptic curves of this equation have the following addition law:

$$X = \frac{1}{a} \cdot \frac{xy' + yx'}{1 + xyx'y'}, \qquad Y = \frac{1}{a} \cdot \frac{yy' - xx'}{1 - xyx'y'}.$$

Edwards illustrated that it is a normal form of elliptic curves, i.e., every elliptic curve over algebraically closed field k is equivalent to $x^2 + y^2 = a^2 + a^2x^2y^2$ for some a. Thus, in a sense, this addition law can be employed for any elliptic curve.

Bernstein and Lange introduced this model and its addition law into elliptic curve cryptography, and proposed fast explicit formulas for addition, mixed addition, and doubling in projective coordinates [3]. Additionally, Bernstein and Lange expanded the addition law to a generalization form of the Edwards curve: $x^2 + y^2 = c^2(1 + dx^2y^2)$, and showed all the elliptic curves in the generalization form are isomorphic to curves $x^2 + y^2 = 1 + dx^2y^2$. When $c = 1$, they provided a $3\mathbf{M} + 4\mathbf{S}$ algorithm for the doubling formula and a $10\mathbf{M} + 1\mathbf{S} + 1\mathbf{D}$ algorithm for the addition formula.

Bernstein and Lange later introduced inverted Edwards coordinates [4] to further lower down the cost of performing group operations on Edwards curves. The doubling costs $3\mathbf{M} + 4\mathbf{S} + 1\mathbf{D}$, requires one more field multiplication with constant $2d$ when compared with [3]; and the addition costs $9\mathbf{M} + 1\mathbf{S} + 1\mathbf{D}$, saving one field multiplication.

In order to cover more curves over finite fields, Bernstein, Birkner, Joye, Lange, and Peters generalized the Edwards curves into twisted Edwards curves with a new parameter a

$$E_{a,d} : ax^2 + y^2 = 1 + dx^2y^2.$$

A twisted Edwards curve with $a = 1$ is an Edwards curve. Each twisted Edwards curve $E_{a,d}$ is a quadratic twist of the Edwards curve $E_{1,d/a}$. Meanwhile, every quadratic twist of a twisted Edwards curve is isomorphic to a twisted Edwards curve. Scalar multiplications on twisted Edwards curves cost almost as much as they do on Edwards curves. More specifically, the doubling costs $3\mathbf{M} + 4\mathbf{S} + 2\mathbf{D}$ and the addition costs $9\mathbf{M} + 1\mathbf{S} + 2\mathbf{D}$. They proved that their addition law on the twisted Edwards curve is complete when a is a square and d is a non-square [1]. In addition, the twisted Edwards model can save time for many curves that were already expressible as Edwards curves by clearing denominators i.e. computing the scalar multiplication on $E_{a,d}$ rather than $E_{1,d/a}$. They also employ the clearing denominators technique in the curve $E_{1,d/a}$.

Hisil, Wong, Carter, and Dawson proposed extended twisted Edwards coordinates on the twisted Edwards curve to obtain a more efficient addition formula [18]. They found that there are four addition laws on twisted Edwards curves. They discovered that the twisted Edwards curves with $a = -1$ have an $8\mathbf{M}$ addition formula and $8\mathbf{M} + 1\mathbf{D}$ unified addition formula. The corresponding mixed addition formulae save one multiplication each. As a corresponding cost, the doubling formula in extended twisted Edwards coordinates required $4\mathbf{M} + 4\mathbf{S} + 1\mathbf{D}$, one multiplication slower than the doubling formula in projective coordinates. In order to solve this problem, Hisil et al. introduced a strategy of mixing different coordinates [18]. Therefore, the majority of the doubling could be computed in projective coordinates.

Bernstein and Lange studied the twisted Edwards curves as curves in $\mathbb{P}^1 \times \mathbb{P}^1$ [5]. They showed that the curve

$$aX^2W^2 + Y^2Z^2 = Z^2W^2 + dX^2Y^2,$$

is nonsingular, where $(X : Z)$ and $(Y : W)$ are the representation of affine coordinates x and y in $\mathbb{P}^1$. They provided a set of two addition laws that can accept any pair of input points P_1, P_2 as input.

In [20], Kohel studied the symmetric model of twisted Edwards curves, including the extended twisted Edwards coordinates and $\mathbb{P}^1 \times \mathbb{P}^1$ model given by Bernstein and Lange. Kohel showed that a twisted Edwards curve using the extended twisted Edwards coordinates can be seen as the curve on $\mathbb{P}^3$, i.e., the curve is

$$E : dT^2 + Z^2 = aX^2 + Y^2, \qquad ZT = XY.$$

Kohel showed that the twisted Edwards curve on $\mathbb{P}^3$ can be regarded as the intersection of two symmetric surfaces. It follows that parameter d should have properties as parameter a, which inspired us to look for efficient point operations for special d. Meanwhile, when a is a non-square and d is a square, Kohel implied another complete addition law.

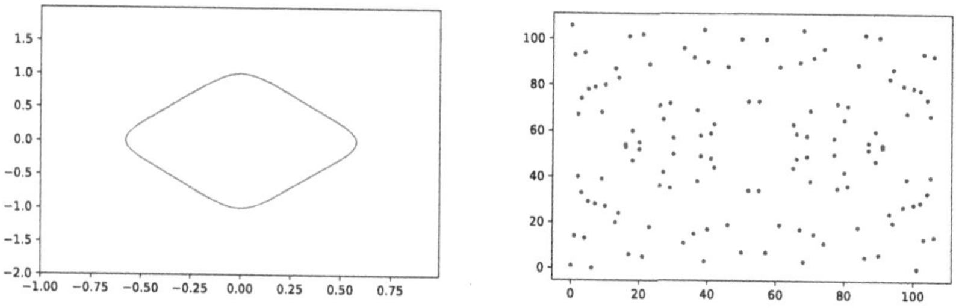

(a) Twisted Edwards curve $3x^2 + y^2 = 1 - 11x^2y^2$

(b) Rational points on twisted Edwards curve $3x^2 + y^2 = 1 - 11x^2y^2$ over finite field $\mathbb{F}_{107}$

2.1 Ed448 and E448

The most famous curves in the twisted Edwards curves are the Edwards25519 (Ed25519), Edwards448 (Ed448), and E448. The curve Edwards25519 is a twisted Edwards curve that is isomorphic to the Montgomery curve Curve25519. The curve Edwards448 is designed by Hamburg [16] and has been favored by the Internet Research Task Force Crypto Forum Research Group (IETF CFRG) ever since. The curve E448 is a twisted Edwards curve. It is birationally equivalent to the Montgomery curve Curve448, and is 4-isogenous to the curve Edwards448.

The curve Edwards25519 has parameter $a = -1$, Edwards448 and E448 have parameter $a = 1$ instead of $a = -1$. In the following paragraphs, we will describe how to convert Edwards448 and E448 to the relative curves with $d = -1$.

Let $E_{a,d}$ be a twisted Edwards curve. If there exists an element c in the finite field that satisfies $d = -c^2$, in other words, $-d$ is a square in the finite field, then there is an isomorphism between $E_{a,d}$ and the following curve:

$$E_{-a/d,-1} : -\frac{a}{d}x^2 + y^2 = 1 - x^2y^2.$$

The map from $E_{a,d}$ to $E_{-a/d,-1}$ is given by $(x, y) \mapsto (cx, y)$.

The parameters d in both Edwards448 and E448 satisfy the condition that $-d$ is a square in the finite field. Thus, they are isomorphic to $E_{-a/d,-1}$. The isomorphism between $E_{a,d}$ and $E_{-a/d,-1}$ allow us to use the curve $E_{-a/d,-1}$ to compute the scalar multiplication rather than $E_{a,d}$. More specifically, the parameters for Edwards448 are given as follows:

$$\begin{aligned} p &= 2^{448} - 2^{224} - 1, \\ a &= 1, \\ d &= -39081. \end{aligned}$$

It satisfies $-d = 39081$ is a square in $\mathbb{F}_p$. One of the square roots of $-d$ is

$$\begin{aligned} c = \sqrt{-d} = 0x&22d962fbeb24f7683bf68d722fa26aa0a1f1a7b8a5b8d54b64a2d78\backslash \\ &0968c14ba839a66f4fd6eded260337bf6aa20ce529642ef0f45572736. \end{aligned}$$

And the parameters for E448 are given as follows:

$$\begin{aligned} p &= 2^{448} - 2^{224} - 1, \\ a &= 1, \\ d &= 39082/39081, \end{aligned}$$

The curve E448 satisfies $-d = -39082/39081$ is a square in $\mathbb{F}_p$. One of the square roots of $-d$ is

$$\begin{aligned} c = \sqrt{-d} = 0x&54457070fb7967d346710750c9f632c2792bd08a0d9bc3791700015\backslash \\ &fcada1acc74ce0dd46445d2d8b81c730cd43d844a7e20c44e4b9a266c. \end{aligned}$$

2.2 Affine Addition and Doubling Laws on Twisted Edwards Curves

We recalled the addition laws given by Hisil, Wong, Carter, and Dawson [18]. Let (x_3, y_3) be the point $(x_1, y_1) + (x_2, y_2)$. x_3 has two representations:

$$\mathfrak{x}_0 = \frac{x_2y_1 + x_1y_2}{1 + dx_1x_2y_1y_2} \quad \text{and} \quad \mathfrak{x}_1 = \frac{x_1y_1 + x_2y_2}{y_1y_2 + ax_1x_2},$$

y_3 has two representations, too:

$$\mathfrak{y}_0 = \frac{y_1y_2 - ax_1x_2}{1 - dx_1x_2y_1y_2} \quad \text{and} \quad \mathfrak{y}_1 = \frac{x_1y_1 - x_2y_2}{x_1y_2 - x_2y_1}.$$

Thus, there are four different affine addition laws for twisted Edwards curves. They are respectively presented as follows:

$$(x_3, y_3) = (x_1, y_1)+(x_2, y_2) = \left(\frac{x_2y_1 + x_1y_2}{1 + dx_1x_2y_1y_2}, \frac{y_1y_2 - ax_1x_2}{1 - dx_1x_2y_1y_2}\right) = (\mathfrak{x}_0, \mathfrak{y}_0), \quad (1)$$

$$(x_3, y_3) = (x_1, y_1) + (x_2, y_2) = \left(\frac{x_2y_1 + x_1y_2}{1 + dx_1x_2y_1y_2}, \frac{x_1y_1 - x_2y_2}{x_1y_2 - x_2y_1}\right) = (\mathfrak{x}_0, \mathfrak{y}_1), \quad (2)$$

$$(x_3, y_3) = (x_1, y_1) + (x_2, y_2) = \left(\frac{x_1y_1 + x_2y_2}{y_1y_2 + ax_1x_2}, \frac{y_1y_2 - ax_1x_2}{1 - dx_1x_2y_1y_2}\right) = (\mathfrak{x}_1, \mathfrak{y}_0), \quad (3)$$

$$(x_3, y_3) = (x_1, y_1) + (x_2, y_2) = \left(\frac{x_1y_1 + x_2y_2}{y_1y_2 + ax_1x_2}, \frac{x_1y_1 - x_2y_2}{x_1y_2 - x_2y_1}\right) = (\mathfrak{x}_1, \mathfrak{y}_1). \quad (4)$$

The point $(0, 1)$ on $E_{a,d}$ is the identity element and $(0, -1)$ is a point of order 2. The negative of a point (x, y) is $(-x, y)$.

The addition law (1) is the first one found on twisted Edwards curves which was proposed by Bernstein, Birkner, Joey, Lange, and Peters in [1]. They pointed out that when a is a square and d is not a square, this addition law is complete. In [18], Hisil et al. studied the addition law (1) and (4) in detail.

In this paper, we study the addition laws (2) and (3). Since the expression of the addition law (2) is independent of a, (2) can perform efficiently even if a is large. The addition law (3) is another complete addition law implied by Kohel [20] and explicitly stated by Farashahi and Hosseini [12]. This addition law is complete if and only if d is a square and a is a nonsquare. But when the finite field $\mathbb{F}_p$ satisfies $p \equiv 3 \pmod 4$, $d = -1$ is a nonsquare. Thus, this addition law on Edwards448 is not complete. Later in Sect. 3, we will show this addition formula is unified when $d = -1$ is a nonsquare and a is a square.

Similar to (4), the addition law (2) has some exceptional cases even if a and d are carefully selected.

The following lemmas show that the exceptional cases would not occur when the scalar multiplication performs on the odd order subgroup.

Lemma 1 (Lemma 2 in [23]). *Let $P = (x_1, y_1)$, $Q = (x_2, y_2)$ be a pair of non-trivial exceptional points ($P \neq \pm Q$ and P, Q are points of odd prime order) on $E_{a,d}$. Then the following holds:*

$$\begin{aligned} x_1x_2y_1y_2 &\neq 0, \\ dx_1x_2y_1y_2 \pm 1 &\neq 0, \\ ax_1x_2 \pm y_1y_2 &\neq 0, \\ x_1y_2 \pm x_2y_1 &\neq 0, \\ x_1y_1 \pm x_2y_2 &\neq 0. \end{aligned}$$

Lemma 1 shows that when the elliptic curve scalar multiplication is performed on the subgroup of points of prime order, the addition law (3) and (2) are exception-free for distinct input points. By [1], the doubling law is

$$2(x_1, y_1) = (\frac{2x_1y_1}{1 + dx_1^2y_1^2}, \frac{y_1^2 - ax_1^2}{1 - dx_1^2y_1^2}) = (x_3, y_3). \quad (5)$$

2.3 Extended Twisted Edwards Coordinates

Recall the homogenous projective equation for twisted Edwards curves:

$$(aX^2 + Y^2)Z^2 = Z^4 + dX^2Y^2.$$

Hisil et al. introduced an auxiliary coordinate $T = XY/Z$ to represent a point (x, y) on twisted Edwards curves [18]. For all nonzero $\lambda \in K$, $(T : X : Y : Z) = (\lambda T : \lambda X : \lambda Y : \lambda Z)$ represents the affine point $(x, y) = (X/Z, Y/Z)$ in affine coordinates. Following the notation in [18], $\mathcal{E}^e$ was employed to denote the extended twisted Edwards coordinates.

However, under this definition, the points $(0 : 1 : 0)$ and $(1 : 0 : 0)$ will be invalid when they are extended to points in extended twisted Edwards coordinates. This problem can be fixed by another model of extended twisted Edwards coordinates proposed by Kohel [20]. Recall that Kohel revisited the twisted Edwards curve with the extended twisted Edwards coordinates by the projective closure.

$$Z^2 + dT^2 = aX^2 + Y^2, \qquad ZT = XY.$$

In this model, the twisted Edwards curve was considered as the intersection of two surfaces in $\mathbb{P}^3$.

The points $(0 : 1 : 0)$ and $(1 : 0 : 0)$ can be extended to $(\pm 1/\sqrt{d} : 0 : 1 : 0)$ and $(\pm\sqrt{a/d} : 1 : 0 : 0)$.

Specifically, in an algebraically closed field $\bar{k}$, each twisted Edwards curve has eight points that contain zero value coordinates. There are four points of order 4: $(\pm 1/\sqrt{d} : 0 : 1 : 0)$, $(0 : 1 : 0 : \pm\sqrt{a})$; three points of order 2: $(\pm\sqrt{a}/\sqrt{d} : 1 : 0 : 0)$ and $(0 : 0 : -1 : 1)$, and an identity point $(0 : 0 : 1 : 1)$. The point $(0 : 0 : 0 : 0)$ satisfies the equation in $\mathbb{P}^3$ but not satisfies that in $\mathbb{P}^2$. It should be ignored.

3 Unified Addition in $\mathcal{E}^e$ for $d = -1$

To prevent the protocols from simple power analysis, unified addition formulae are more favorable [23]. Let K be a finite field of odd characteristic. This section proposes a unified addition formula for $d = -1$ on the prime order subgroup of twisted Edwards curves over K.

3.1 The Unified Addition Law

The addition formulas are designed for $d = -1$ to obtain the speeding up on Edwards448, E448, and other twisted Edwards curves that satisfy $-d$ is a square. For the state-of-the-art formulas for other situations, please refer to [18].

In the following, we recall the addition law (3)

$$(x_3, y_3) = (x_1, y_1) + (x_2, y_2) = \left(\frac{x_1y_1 + x_2y_2}{y_1y_2 + ax_1x_2}, \frac{y_1y_2 - ax_1x_2}{1 - dx_1x_2y_1y_2} \right).$$

When a is a non-square and d is a square, this addition law has been proved as a complete addition law [12,20]. In the following parts, we will demonstrate that this formula is unified on the prime order subgroup for arbitrary a and d.

Lemma 2. *Let K be a finite field of odd characteristic. Let $E_{a,d}$ be a twisted Edwards curve defined over K. Let $P = (x_1, y_1)$ be a fixed point on $E_{a,d}$ and $Q = (x_2, y_2)$ be another point on $E_{a,d}$.*

- $1 - dx_1x_2y_1y_2 = 0$ *if and only if*

$$Q \in S_{P,1} = \left\{ \left(\frac{-1}{\sqrt{d}y_1}, \frac{-1}{\sqrt{d}x_1}\right), \left(\frac{1}{\sqrt{d}y_1}, \frac{1}{\sqrt{d}x_1}\right), \left(\frac{-1}{\sqrt{ad}x_1}, \frac{-\sqrt{a}}{y_1\sqrt{d}}\right), \left(\frac{1}{\sqrt{ad}x_1}, \frac{\sqrt{a}}{y_1\sqrt{d}}\right) \right\}$$

and $Q \in K^2$ is well-defined.

- $y_1y_2 + ax_1x_2 = 0$ *if and only if*

$$Q \in S_{P,2} = \left\{ \left(\frac{y_1}{\sqrt{a}}, -\sqrt{a}x_1\right), \left(\frac{-y_1}{\sqrt{a}}, \sqrt{a}x_1\right), \left(\frac{-1}{\sqrt{ad}x_1}, \frac{\sqrt{a}}{y_1\sqrt{d}}\right), \left(\frac{1}{\sqrt{ad}x_1}, \frac{-\sqrt{a}}{y_1\sqrt{d}}\right) \right\}$$

and $Q \in K^2$ is well-defined.

Proof. Since P and Q are points on $E_{a,d}$, x_1, y_1, x_2, and y_2 satisfy the equations $ax_1^2 + y_1^2 = 1 + dx_1^2y_1^2$ and $ax_2^2 + y_2^2 = 1 + dx_2^2y_2^2$. If $1 - dx_1x_2y_1y_2 = 0$ (resp. $y_1y_2 + ax_1x_2 = 0$), then combining these functions we have $Q \in S_{P,1}$ (resp. $Q \in S_{P,2}$).

Corollary 1. *Any points P and Q of odd order q would not induce the exceptional cases of the addition law (3). (3) is a unified addition law on prime order subgroup.*

Proof. If both P and Q are points of odd prime order q, then $P \pm Q$ are either 0 or of odd prime order too. Let $S_{1,P}$ and $S_{2,P}$ be defined as in Lemma 2. Then for any point P and point $Q \in S_{1,P} \bigcup S_{2,P}$, it can be computed that one of $Q + P$ and $Q - P$ is a point of order two or order four (in the extension of K where they exist). In contrast to earlier assumptions.

The projective form of it can be obtained as

$$\begin{aligned}(x_3, y_3) &= (X_1 : Y_1 : Z_1) + (X_2 : Y_2 : Z_2) \\ &= \left(\frac{X_1Y_1Z_2^2 + X_2Y_2Z_1^2}{(Y_1Y_2 + aX_1X_2)Z_1Z_2}, \frac{(Y_1Y_2 - aX_1X_2)Z_1Z_2}{Z_1^2Z_2^2 - dX_1X_2Y_1Y_2}\right).\end{aligned}$$

When $Z_1Z_2 \neq 0$, the addition law can be rewritten in extended twisted Edwards coordinates as

$$\begin{aligned}(x_3, y_3) &= (T_1 : X_1 : Y_1 : Z_1) + (T_2 : X_2 : Y_2 : Z_2) \\ &= \left(\frac{\frac{X_1Y_1}{Z_1}Z_2 + \frac{X_2Y_2}{Z_2}Z_1}{Y_1Y_2 + aX_1X_2}, \frac{Y_1Y_2 - aX_1X_2}{Z_1Z_2 - d\frac{X_1Y_1}{Z_1}\frac{X_2Y_2}{Z_2}}\right).\end{aligned}$$

When $Z_i \neq 0$, we have $T_i = X_iY_i/Z_i$. It turns to be

$$\begin{aligned}(x_3, y_3) &= (T_1 : X_1 : Y_1 : Z_1) + (T_2 : X_2 : Y_2 : Z_2)\\ &= \left(\frac{T_1Z_2 + T_2Z_1}{Y_1Y_2 + aX_1X_2}, \frac{Y_1Y_2 - aX_1X_2}{Z_1Z_2 - dT_1T_2}\right).\end{aligned}$$

All the points on twisted Edwards curves satisfying the Z-coordinates of it is zero have even order. In particular, for Edwards448 and E448, there are no points that have coordinate $Z = 0$ in $\mathcal{E}^e$ or $\mathcal{E}$. According to Lemma 1, when P and Q is a pair of non-trivial exceptional points on $E_{a,d}$, we have $T_1Z_2 + T_2Z_1 \neq 0$, $Y_1Y_2 + aX_1X_2 \neq 0$, $Y_1Y_2 - aX_1X_2 \neq 0$, and $Z_1Z_2 - dT_1T_2 \neq 0$. When $P = Q$ and P, Q have odd prime order, according to Corollary 1, the exceptional cases also would not happen when $Z_1Z_2 \neq 0$.

Then the unified addition formulae with $d = -1$ on extended twisted Edwards coordinates can be obtained as follows. Given two points $(T_1 : X_1 : Y_1 : Z_1)$ and $(T_2 : X_2 : Y_2 : Z_2)$ with $Z_1Z_2 \neq 0$, the point addition on $E_{a,-1}$ can be performed as $(T_1 : X_1 : Y_1 : Z_1) + (T_2 : X_2 : Y_2 : Z_2) = (T_3 : X_3 : Y_3 : Z_3)$, where

$$\begin{aligned}T_3 &= (T_1Z_2 + T_2Z_1)(Y_1Y_2 - aX_1X_2),\\ X_3 &= (T_1Z_2 + T_2Z_1)(Z_1Z_2 + T_1T_2),\\ Y_3 &= (Y_1Y_2 + aX_1X_2)(Y_1Y_2 - aX_1X_2),\\ Z_3 &= (Y_1Y_2 + aX_1X_2)(Z_1Z_2 + T_1T_2).\end{aligned} \tag{6}$$

3.2 The Unified Addition Formula

The addition formula can be performed with a $8\mathbf{M} + 1\mathbf{D}$ algorithm given by

$$\begin{aligned}m_1 \leftarrow 2Y_1 \cdot Y_2, \quad m_2 \leftarrow 2X_1 \cdot X_2, m_3 \leftarrow (T_1 + Z_1) \cdot (T_2 + Z_2),\\ m_4 \leftarrow (T_1 - Z_1) \cdot (T_2 - Z_2), \quad d_1 = a \cdot m_2, \quad a_1 = m_1 + d_1,\end{aligned}$$

$$a_2 = m_1 - d_1, \quad a_3 = m_3 + m_4, \quad a_4 = m_3 - m_4,$$

$$X_3 = a_3 \cdot a_4, \quad Y_3 = a_1 \cdot a_2, \quad Z_3 = a_1 \cdot a_3, \quad T_3 = a_2 \cdot a_4.$$

The $\mathbf{D}$ in this algorithm is a field multiplication with the constant value a.

A $7\mathbf{M} + 1\mathbf{D}$ mixed addition algorithm can be derived by setting $X_2 = 1$ or $Y_2 = 1$. If one of the input points is fixed, for example, assuming $(X_2 : Y_2 : T_2 : Z_2)$ is fixed, then the multiplication m_2 and the multiplication with constant d_1 can be combined in a single multiplication $2aX_2 \cdot X_1$ if $2a \cdot X_2$ is pre-computed. Then the cost of the addition becomes $8\mathbf{M}$ and the cost of the mixed addition becomes $7\mathbf{M}$. Since $1/39081$ is a large number in the finite field of Edwards448, this pre-computation is recommended when the formula is employed to compute the scalar multiplication on Edwards448.

Since this addition formula is unified on the prime order subgroup, it can be employed in protocols that require SPA protection.

4 Clearing Denominators and Scalar Multiplication in Parallel Environments

When Bernstein et al. [1] introduced the twisted Edwards curves, they used the clearing denominators technique to speed up the scalar multiplication of the Edwards curves

$$x^2 + y^2 = 1 + dx^2y^2$$

with parameters $d = \bar{d}/\bar{a}$, where $\bar{d}$ and $\bar{a}$ are small in K and $\bar{d}/\bar{a}$ is large. In projective coordinates, they proposed $10\mathbf{M} + 1\mathbf{S} + 3\mathbf{D}$ clearing denominators addition formula, where the $3\mathbf{D}$ are two multiplications by $\bar{a}$ and one by $\bar{d}$. As a comparison, the previous addition formula costs $10\mathbf{M} + 1\mathbf{S} + 1\mathbf{D}$, where the $\mathbf{D}$ is one multiplication by d. In inverted projective coordinates, they proposed $9\mathbf{M} + 1\mathbf{S} + 3\mathbf{D}$ clearing denominators addition formula, where the $3\mathbf{D}$ are two multiplications by $\bar{a}$ and one by $\bar{d}$. As a comparison, the previous addition formula costs $9\mathbf{M} + 1\mathbf{S} + 1\mathbf{D}$, where the $\mathbf{D}$ is one by d.

In the implementations, the ratio $\mathbf{D}/\mathbf{M}$ varies for different constants, different libraries, and different implement environments. For example, the multiplication with 10, and the multiplication with 1/10 are both denoted by $\mathbf{D}$, but in the former case, the ratio $\mathbf{D}/\mathbf{M}$ may close to 0, while in the latter case, this ratio may close to 1. When d and a are small in K, several field multiplications with a and d might be faster than one field multiplication with d/a.

Later in Sect. 7, we will show that clearing denominators formulae in particular suit the parallel environments.

4.1 Clearing Denominators for $d = -1$

For a twisted Edwards curve $E_{\bar{a}/\bar{d},-1}$, the addition formula can also be performed with a $8\mathbf{M} + 4\mathbf{D}$ algorithm given by

$$m_1 \leftarrow Y_1 \cdot Y_2, \quad m_2 \leftarrow X_1 \cdot X_2, \quad m_3 \leftarrow (T_1 + Z_1) \cdot (T_2 + Z_2),$$
$$m_4 \leftarrow (T_1 - Z_1) \cdot (T_2 - Z_2), \quad d_1 = 2\bar{d} \cdot m_1, \quad d_2 = 2\bar{a} \cdot m_2,$$
$$d_3 = \bar{d} \cdot m_3, \quad d_4 = \bar{d} \cdot m_4, \quad a_1 = d_1 + d_2,$$
$$a_2 = d_1 - d_2, \quad a_3 = d_3 + d_4, \quad a_4 = d_3 - d_4,$$
$$X_3 = a_3 \cdot a_4, \quad Y_3 = a_1 \cdot a_2, \quad Z_3 = a_1 \cdot a_3, \quad T_3 = a_2 \cdot a_4.$$

The $4\mathbf{D}$ in this algorithm is a field multiplication with the constant $2\bar{a}$, a field multiplication with the constant $2\bar{d}$, and two field multiplications with the constant $\bar{d}$.

4.2 Clearing Denominators for $a = -1$

For a twisted Edwards curve $E_{-1,\bar{d}/\bar{a}}$, the addition formula can also be performed with a $8\mathbf{M} + 4\mathbf{D}$ algorithm given by

$$m_1 \leftarrow (Y_1 - X_1) \cdot (Y_2 - X_2), \quad m_2 \leftarrow (Y_1 + X_1) \cdot (Y_2 + X_2),$$
$$m_3 \leftarrow T_1 \cdot T_2, \quad m_4 \leftarrow Z_1 \cdot Z_2, \quad d_1 = \bar{a} \cdot m_1, \quad d_2 = \bar{a} \cdot m_2,$$

$$d_3 = 2\bar{d} \cdot m_3, \quad d_4 = 2\bar{a} \cdot m_4,$$
$$a_1 = d_2 - d_1, \quad a_2 = d_4 - d_3, \quad a_3 = d_3 + d_4, \quad a_4 = d_1 + d_2,$$
$$X_3 = a_1 \cdot a_2, \quad Y_3 = a_3 \cdot a_4, \quad Z_3 = a_1 \cdot a_4, \quad T_3 = a_2 \cdot a_3.$$

The 4**D** in this algorithm is a field multiplication with the constant $2\bar{a}$, a field multiplication with the constant $2\bar{d}$, and two field multiplications with the constant $\bar{a}$.

5 Fast Formulae in $\mathcal{E}^e$

This section shows the fast addition, doubling, and tripling formulae on twisted Edwards curves with $d = -1$. The doubling and tripling in $\mathcal{E}^e$ are doubling and tripling from $\mathcal{E}$ to $\mathcal{E}^e$. In general, only one of the parameters a and d can be set as very tiny. Since the existing doubling, addition, and tripling formulas on the twisted Edwards curves all focus on the smaller a, they cannot achieve good efficiency for the case where d is smaller and a is larger. In this paper, we proposed new addition, doubling, and tripling formulas for this situation.

5.1 Fast Addition in $\mathcal{E}^e$ for $d = -1$

Similar to the unified addition formulae, the fast addition formulae can be obtained as follows. Given two points $(T_1 : X_1 : Y_1 : Z_1)$ and $(T_2 : X_2 : Y_2 : Z_2)$ with $Z_1 Z_2 \neq 0$, the point addition can be performed as $(T_1 : X_1 : Y_1 : Z_1) + (T_2 : X_2 : Y_2 : Z_2) = (T_3 : X_3 : Y_3 : Z_3)$, where

$$\begin{aligned} T_3 &= (X_2Y_1 + X_1Y_2)(T_1Z_2 - T_2Z_1) \\ X_3 &= (X_2Y_1 + X_1Y_2)(X_1Y_2 - X_2Y_1) \\ Y_3 &= (T_1Z_2 - T_2Z_1)(Z_1Z_2 + dT_1T_2) \\ Z_3 &= (X_1Y_2 - X_2Y_1)(Z_1Z_2 + dT_1T_2) \end{aligned}. \tag{7}$$

When $d = -1$, the addition formula can be performed with a 8**M** algorithm given by

$$m_1 \leftarrow 2X_1 \cdot Y_2, \quad m_2 \leftarrow 2X_2 \cdot Y_1, \quad m_3 \leftarrow (T_1 + Z_1) \cdot (-T_2 + Z_2),$$
$$m_4 \leftarrow (-T_1 + Z_1) \cdot (T_2 + Z_2), \quad a_1 = m_1 + m_2, \quad a_2 = m_1 - m_2,$$
$$a_3 = m_3 + m_4, \quad a_4 = m_3 - m_4,$$
$$X_3 = a_1 \cdot a_2, \quad Y_3 = a_3 \cdot a_4, \quad Z_3 = a_2 \cdot a_3, \quad T_3 = a_1 \cdot a_4.$$

A 7**M** mixed addition algorithm can be derived by setting $X_2 = 1$ or $Y_2 = 1$.

5.2 Modified Projective Coordinates $\mathcal{E}$

As we mentioned in Sect. 1, only one of the parameters a and d can reasonably be assumed to be very small. All the efficient doubling and tripling point formulae are based on the case where a is very small. Meanwhile, the doubling and tripling formulae on projective coordinates are more efficient than those on extended twisted Edwards coordinates.

This section introduces new modified projective coordinates to obtain the efficient doubling and tripling point formulae. All these formulae are as efficient as the existing projective formulae on twisted Edwards curves.

Recall that the extended twisted Edwards coordinates have four components: X, Y, Z, and T. Since $ZT = XY$, every three components can determine the value of the remaining ones. The modified projective coordinates are a projection of extended Edwards coordinates on $\mathbb{P}^2$, denoted by $\mathcal{E}$. It employs the components T, Y, and Z. Then the affine coordinates (x, y) can be recovered as $(x, y) = (\frac{T}{Y}, \frac{Y}{Z})$ by a point $(Y : T : Z)$ in $\mathcal{E}$. This representation is invalid if it represents the point at infinity or y-coordinate in affine form satisfies $y = 0$, which follows that $(x, y) = (\pm 1/\sqrt{a}, 0)$. By [1], $(\pm 1/\sqrt{a}, 0)$ and points at infinity are points of even order, would not appear in prime order subgroup scalar multiplication.

Given $(T : Y : Z)$ in $\mathcal{E}$ passing to $\mathcal{E}^e$ requires $3\mathbf{M} + 1\mathbf{S}$ by computing (TY, TZ, Y^2, YZ). Given $(T : X : Y : Z)$ in $\mathcal{E}^e$ passing to $\mathcal{E}$ is cost-free by simply ignoring X.

5.3 Doubling in $\mathcal{E}^e$

For any point $(T_1 : X_1 : Y_1 : Z_1)$ on the twisted Edwards curves, we have

$$aX_1^2 + Y_1^2 = Z_1^2 + dT_1^2, \quad Z_1T_1 = X_1Y_1.$$

As a result, the doubling formula (5) can be rewritten as

$$(x_3, y_3) = 2(x_1, y_1) = (\frac{2X_1Y_1}{Z_1^2 + dT_1^2}, \frac{Y_1^2 - aX_1^2}{Z_1^2 - dT_1^2}) = (\frac{2Z_1T_1}{Z_1^2 + dT_1^2}, \frac{2Y_1^2 - Z_1^2 - dT_1^2}{Z_1^2 - dT_1^2}) \tag{8}$$

This formula is *independent of* a. The point doubling can be performed as $2(X_1 : Y_1 : T_1 : Z_1) = (X_3 : Y_3 : T_3 : Z_3)$ where

$$\begin{aligned} X_3 &= 2Z_1T_1(Z_1^2 - dT_1^2), \\ Y_3 &= (Z_1^2 + dT_1^2)(2Y_1^2 - Z_1^2 - dT_1^2), \\ Z_3 &= (Z_1^2 + dT_1^2)(Z_1^2 - dT_1^2), \\ T_3 &= 2Z_1T_1(2Y_1^2 - Z_1^2 - dT_1^2). \end{aligned}$$

This formula can be performed with a $4\mathbf{M} + 4\mathbf{S} + 1\mathbf{D}$ algorithm as follows:

$$s_1 = T_1^2, \quad s_2 = Z_1^2, \quad s_3 = (T_1 + Z_1)^2 - s_1 - s_2, \quad s_4 = Y_1^2,$$

$$d_1 = d \cdot s_1, \quad a_1 = s_2 - d_1, \quad a_2 = s_2 + d_1, \quad a_3 = 2s_4 - a_2,$$

$$X_3 = s_3 \cdot a_1, \quad Y_3 = a_2 \cdot a_3, \quad Z_3 = a_1 \cdot a_2, \quad T_3 = s_3 \cdot a_3.$$

5.4 Tripling in $\mathcal{E}^e$

The tripling formula can be derived by computing $3P = 2P + P$. The following formulas compute $(X_3 : Y_3 : T_3 : Z_3) = 3(X_1 : Y_1 : T_1 : Z_1)$ in $11\mathbf{M} + 3\mathbf{S} + 1\mathbf{D}$, where $\mathbf{D}$ is one multiplication by d.

$$s_1 = dT_1^2, \quad s_2 = Y_1^2, \quad s_3 = Z_1^2, \quad a_1 = s_1 + s_3,$$
$$a_2 = s_3 - s_1, \quad m_1 = a_2 \cdot s_2, \quad m_2 = a_2 \cdot (a_1 - s_2), \quad m_3 = a_1 \cdot (2s_2 - a_1),$$
$$a_3 = m_3 + m_1, \quad a_4 = m_3 + m_2, \quad a_5 = m_3 - m_1, \quad a_6 = m_2 - m_3,$$
$$m_4 = Y \cdot a_4, \quad m_5 = Y \cdot a_6, \quad , m_6 = Z \cdot a_5, \quad m_7 = T \cdot a_3,$$
$$X_3 = m_6 \cdot m_7, \quad Y_3 = m_4 \cdot m_5, \quad Z_3 = m_4 \cdot m_6, \quad T_3 = m_5 \cdot m_7.$$

5.5 Doubling in $\mathcal{E}$

The point doubling on $\mathcal{E}$ formula can be performed with a $4\mathbf{M} + 3\mathbf{S} + 1\mathbf{D}$ algorithm as follows:

$$s_1 = T_1^2, \quad s_2 = Z_1^2, \quad s_3 = (T_1 + Z_1)^2 - s_1 - s_2, \quad s_4 = Y_1^2,$$
$$d_1 = d \cdot s_1, \quad a_1 = s_2 - d_1, \quad a_2 = s_2 + d_1, \quad a_3 = 2s_4 - a_2,$$
$$T_3 = s_3 \cdot a_3 \quad Y_3 = a_2 \cdot a_3, \quad Z_3 = a_1 \cdot a_2.$$

5.6 Tripling in $\mathcal{E}$

The tripling formula can be performed with a $9\mathbf{M}+3\mathbf{S}+1\mathbf{D}$ algorithm as follows:

$$s_1 = dT_1^2, \quad s_2 = Y_1^2, \quad s_3 = Z_1^2, \quad a_1 = s_1 + s_3,$$
$$a_2 = s_3 - s_1, \quad m_1 = a_2 \cdot s_2, \quad m_2 = a_2 \cdot (a_1 - s_2), \quad m_3 = a_1 \cdot (2s_2 - a_1),$$
$$a_3 = m_3 + m_1, \quad a_4 = m_3 + m_2, \quad a_5 = m_3 - m_1, \quad a_6 = m_2 - m_3,$$
$$T_3 = T_1 \cdot a_3 \cdot a_6 \quad Y_3 = Y_1 \cdot a_4 \cdot a_6, \quad Z_3 = Z_1 \cdot a_4 \cdot a_5.$$

These formulae of addition, doubling, and tripling in this section cost the same as $a = -1$. And the formulae of addition save a few field operations compared with unified addition formulae.

6 Exceptional Case Analysis and Handling Strategies

In this section, we explore scalar multiplication on $2q$-order and $4q$-order subgroups, in addition to q-order subgroups, motivated by three factors.

Firstly, while q-order subgroups are known for their favorable properties and high completeness, ensuring that a point precisely lies on a subgroup of order q is challenging. In contrast, on Edwards448 curves, points must belong to the $4q$-order group. This forms the primary motivation for our investigation.

Secondly, the structure of the (twisted) Edwards curve inherently includes small-order points, which may expose it to attacks exploiting small cofactors. These attacks manipulate the scalar multiplication from q-order subgroups to 2q-order or 4q-order subgroups. If scalar multiplication fails on the $2q$-order and $4q$-order subgroups, an attacker could gather information about the secret key. Therefore, studying scalar multiplication in these cases becomes essential for protecting sensitive information.

Thirdly, Hamburg proposed the decaf technique to address the small cofactor trap on the Edwards448 curve using point compression and decompression [15] (CRYPTO 2015). Decaf technology eliminates the requirement for scalar multiplications to operate solely on subgroups of prime order. Instead, scalar multiplications over $2q$-order and $4q$-order subgroups are permitted. These subgroups are treated as a prime order group. The differences are handled during compression and decompression. Cremers and Jackson thought decaf is an exciting proposal [9]. Achieving exceptional-free scalar multiplication on $2q$-order and $4q$-order subgroups holds significance for decaf. It is the final motivation for our investigation.

A straightforward solution for scalar multiplication on both the $2q$-order and $4q$-order subgroups is to utilize the $9\mathbf{M} + 2\mathbf{D}$ unified point addition formula proposed by Hisil et al. [18]. Here, one $\mathbf{D}$ corresponds to multiplication with a, while the other corresponds to multiplication with d.

It is worth noting that our isomorphism mapping preserves the fact that a is a square element and d is a non-square element. Consequently, the elliptic curve obtained through the isomorphism remains a complete Edwards curve. The unified point addition formula proposed by Hisil et al. [18] is complete in this case. This is also why we propose the $d = -1$ point operation algorithms instead of obtaining the elliptic curve with $a = -1$ by birational mapping or isogeny as in [15] and run the point operations on that curve.

In this section, we analyze the exceptional cases in our new point addition algorithm. We propose corresponding solutions to enhance efficiency on the $2q$-order and $4q$-order subgroups.

We detail the exceptional cases of $2q$-order and $4q$-order subgroups on $\mathcal{E}^e$ in the following lemma.

Lemma 3. *Let K be a finite field of odd characteristic. Let $E_{a,d}$ be a twisted Edwards curve defined over K. Let $P = (T_1 : X_1 : Y_1 : Z_1)$ be a fixed point on $E_{a,d}$. Let $Q = (T_2 : X_2 : Y_2 : Z_2)$ be another point on $E_{a,d}$. Let $R_1 = (0 : 1 : 0 : \sqrt{a})$. Assume that a is a square and $d = -1$ is a non-square.*

For the unified addition formula, we have

- $Y_1Y_2 + aX_1X_2 = 0$ *if and only if*

$$(T_2 : X_2 : Y_2 : Z_2) \in \{(-T_1 : Y_1/\sqrt{a} : -\sqrt{a}X_1 : Z_1), (-T_1 : -Y_1/\sqrt{a} : \sqrt{a}X_1 : Z_1)\} = \{P + R_1, P + 3R_1\}$$

- $Y_1Y_2 - aX_1X_2 = 0$ *if and only if*

$$(T_2 : X_2 : Y_2 : Z_2) \in \{(T_1 : -Y_1/\sqrt{a} : -\sqrt{a}X_1 : Z_1), (T_1 : Y_1/\sqrt{a} : \sqrt{a}X_1 : Z_1)\} = \{-P + R_1, -P + 3R_1\}$$

- $T_1Z_2 + Z_1T_2 = 0$ *if and only if*

$$\begin{aligned}(T_2 : X_2 : Y_2 : Z_2) \in &\{(-T_1 : Y_1/\sqrt{a} : -\sqrt{a}X_1 : Z_1), (-T_1 : -Y_1/\sqrt{a} : \sqrt{a}X_1 : Z_1), (-T_1 : -X_1 : Y_1 : Z_1), (-T_1 : X_1 : -Y_1 : Z_1)\}\\ =&\{P + R_1, P + 3R_1, -P, -P + 2R_1\}\end{aligned}$$

- $T_1T_2 + Z_1Z_2 = 0$ *would not occur.*

For the fast addition formula, we have

- $Y_1X_2 + X_1Y_2 = 0$ *if and only if*

$$\begin{aligned}(T_2 : X_2 : Y_2 : Z_2) \in &\{(-T_1 : -X_1 : Y_1 : Z_1), (-T_1 : X_1 : -Y_1 : Z_1)\}\\ =&\{-P, -P + 2R_1\}\end{aligned}$$

- $Y_1X_2 - X_1Y_2 = 0$ *if and only if*

$$\begin{aligned}(T_2 : X_2 : Y_2 : Z_2) \in &\{(T_1 : -X_1 : -Y_1 : Z_1), (T_1 : X_1 : Y_1 : Z_1)\}\\ =&\{P, P + 2R_1\}\end{aligned}$$

- $T_1Z_2 - Z_1T_2 = 0$ *if and only if*

$$\begin{aligned}(T_2 : X_2 : Y_2 : Z_2) \in &\{(T_1 : -Y_1/\sqrt{a} : -\sqrt{a}X_1 : Z_1), (T_1 : Y_1/\sqrt{a} : \sqrt{a}X_1 : Z_1), (T_1 : X_1 : Y_1 : Z_1), (T_1 : -X_1 : -Y_1 : Z_1)\}\\ =&\{-P + R_1, -P + 3R_1, P, P + 2R_1\}\end{aligned}$$

- $T_1T_2 - Z_1Z_2 = 0$ *would not occur.*

Proof. Similar to Lemma 1, these equivalences are derived from combing the equations. For example, when obtain the exceptional cases of $Y_1Y_2+aX_1X_2 = 0$, we combine $Y_1Y_2+aX_1X_2 = 0$ with $aX_1^2+Y_1^2 = Z_1^2+dT_1^2, aX_2^2+Y_2^2 = Z_2^2+dT_2^2$, $X_1Y_1 = Z_1T_1$, and $X_2Y_2 = Z_2T_2$. And we ignore the solution $(T_2 : X_2 : Y_2 : Z_2) = (0 : 0 : 0 : 0)$.

6.1 Unified Addition Formula on $2q$-Order Subgroup

We first handle the easier but crucial case, the unified addition formula performs on the subgroup of order $2q$. For curve Edwards448, we have the following corollary of Lemma 3:

Corollary 2. *For the cases that a is a square element and $d = -1$ is a non-square element, points P and Q in the subgroup of order $2q$ would not induce the exceptional cases of our unified addition formula. In particular, the finite field of Edwards448 and E448 satisfy this condition.*

Proof. If both $P = (T_1 : X_1 : Y_1 : Z_1)$ and $Q = (T_2 : X_2 : Y_2 : Z_2)$ are points in the subgroup of order $2q$. According to Lemma 3, if zero occurs in $P + Q$, then $Q = -P$ or $Q = -P + 2R_1$. In addition, since $Q = -P$ or $-P + 2R_1$, we have $Q \neq \pm P + \pm R_1$. Thus, $Y_1Y_2 \pm aX_1X_2 \neq 0$. If $Q = -P$, $P + Q$ is computed as

$$P + Q = (0, 0, (Y_1^2 - aX_1^2)(Y_1^2 + aX_1^2), (Y_1Y_2 - aX_1X_2)(Z_1^2 - T_1^2))$$

by our unified addition formula. Combined with the fact that $Y_1^2 + aX_1^2 = Z_1^2 - T_1^2$ and $(Y_1^2 - aX_1^2)(Y_1^2 + aX_1^2) = (Y_1Y_2 + aX_1X_2)(Y_1Y_2 - aX_1X_2) \neq 0$. We have

$$P + Q = (0, 0, 1, 1).$$

The result is equal to what it should be. Thus, $Q = -P$ will not induce an exceptional case. Similarly, $Q = -P + 2R_1$ will not induce exceptional cases.

Corollary 2 shows that our unified addition formula is complete on the $2q$-order subgroup.

6.2 Strategy for Single-Scalar Multiplication

The single-scalar multiplication computes kP for a scalar k and a fixed point P. Since our unified addition formula is complete on the $2q$-order subgroup, it is exceptional free when computing single-scalar multiplication on the $2q$-order subgroup. However, Lemma 3 shows that our unified addition formula is not complete on the $4q$-order subgroup.

As for our fast point addition formula, it yields exceptions on subgroups of order $2q$ and $4q$ on Edwards448. Even if the exception to doubling ($P = Q$) is ignored, still some cases need to be handled on Edwards448.

We handle these exceptional cases by reducing the scalar k modulo q first, limiting the scalar in $\{0, 1, \cdots, q-1\}$. And then eliminate the difference through equivalence classes, as the way decaf did. The justification for this operation is supported by two reasons. Firstly, this modulus operation is common in elliptic curve cryptography. For example, the EdDSA signature generation operation in IETF RFC 8032 reduced the scalar modulo q for efficiency reasons [19]. Secondly, we will show that the differences between points calculated with and without the modulus fall within the 4-torsion subgroup of E later. Therefore, when integrated with decaf's Edwards-only strategy, these two outcomes effectively represent the same point. The equivalence testing of $P = (T_1 : X_1 : Y_1 : Z_1)$ and $Q = (T_2 : X_2 : Y_2 : Z_2)$ can be made by checking whether

$$X_1Y_2 = Y_1X_2 \qquad \text{or} \qquad Y_1Y_2 = -aX_1X_2$$

as in ristretto [17]. Another solution is to test whether $4P = 4Q$ as mentioned in RFC 8032 [19].

If P is a point of order $4q$ or $2q$ on Edwards448 or E448, then we have $R_1 = mqP$, $m = 1, 3$, or $qP = 2R_1 = (0, -1)$, $R_1 \notin \{kP, k \in \mathbb{N}\}$. Assuming Q is an exceptional point of P in Lemma 3, then

$$Q = kP, \quad k \equiv 1, q-1 \mod q, \qquad \text{or} \qquad Q \notin \{kP, k \in \mathbb{N}\}$$

In single-scalar multiplication with scalar smaller than $q-1$, the case $(q-1)P+P$ would not occur; the case $P+P$ is not the exceptional case of the unified addition formula and performed by the doubling formula when employing the fast addition formula; and the case $Q \notin \{kP, k \in \mathbb{N}\}$ can be disregarded.

The modular equivalence $k' = k \mod q$ yields that $k - k' = mq$ with $m \in \mathbb{N}$. Since each of Edwards448 and E448 only contains one 4-torsion subgroup, and the size of it is 4. We have $kP - k'P = mqP \in E[4]$, where $E[4] = \{(0, \pm 1), (\pm 1/\sqrt{a}, 0)\}$ is the 4-torsion subgroup of E.

6.3 Strategy for Multi-scalar Multiplication

Since the scalars between the adding points are blinding, our strategy for single-scalar multiplication is invalid for multi-scalar multiplication.

We propose a new algorithm that combines our unified addition formula and the unified addition formula proposed by Hisil et al. [18] to speed up the point addition on multi-scalar multiplication on Edwards448 and E448.

Assuming that $P = (T_1 : X_1 : Y_1 : Z_1)$ and $Q = (T_2 : X_2 : Y_2 : Z_2)$ are the two inputs of our unified addition formula. The addition can be performed by the following algorithm:

In Algorithm 1, we first compute the value of X_1X_2, Y_1Y_2, and aX_1X_2. In Lemma 3, we analyzed the exceptional cases of our unified addition formula. Similar to $Q = -P$ or $-P+2R_1$, our unified addition formula runs correct when $Q = -P + R_1$ or $-P + 3R_1$ with $Q \neq P + R_1$ or $P + 3R_1$. The exceptional cases that remained to be concerned are $Q = P+R_1, P+3R_1$ with P in the subgroup of order $4q$ or 4. No matter what the order of P is, the exceptional cases $Q = P+R_1$ or $P+3R_1$ yield $Y_1Y_2+aX_1X_2 = 0$ by Lemma 3. Algorithm 1 compute the result by the unified addition formula proposed by Hisil et al. [18] in these cases. Since this addition formula has been proved to be complete [20], Algorithm 1 returns the correct answer in these cases. As for the case $Y_1Y_2+aX_1X_2 \neq 0$, the output of our unified addition formula is correct. Algorithm 1 employs our unified addition formula in this situation.

When $Y_1Y_2 + aX_1X_2 = 0$, our algorithm costs $9\mathbf{M} + 1\mathbf{D} + 1\mathbf{V}$, where $\mathbf{V}$ denotes the time cost of verifying whether $Y_1Y_2 + aX_1X_2 = 0$ or not. And when $Y_1Y_2 + aX_1X_2 \neq 0$, our algorithm costs $8\mathbf{M} + 1\mathbf{D} + 1\mathbf{V}$. Since $d = -1$, Hisil

---

Algorithm 1: Addition algorithm for multi-scalar multiplication

---

Data: $P = (T_1 : X_1 : Y_1 : Z_1)$ and $Q = (T_2 : X_2 : Y_2 : Z_2)$
Result: $(T_3 : X_3 : Y_3 : Z_3) = P + Q$

$m_1 \rightarrow Y_1 \cdot Y_2$; $m_2 \rightarrow X_1 \cdot X_2$; $d_1 \rightarrow a \cdot m_2$;
if $m_1 + d_1 \neq 0$ **then**
  $m_3 \rightarrow (T_1 + Z_1) \cdot (T_2 + Z_2)$; $m_3 \rightarrow (T_1 - Z_1) \cdot (T_2 - Z_2)$; $a_1 \rightarrow 2m_1 + 2d_1$; $a_2 \rightarrow 2m_1 - 2d_1$; $a_3 \rightarrow m_3 + m_4$; $a_4 \rightarrow m_3 - m_4$; $X_3 \rightarrow a_3 \cdot a_4$; $Y_3 \rightarrow a_1 \cdot a_2$; $Z_3 \rightarrow a_1 \cdot a_3$; $T_3 \rightarrow a_2 \cdot a_4$;
else
  $m_3 \rightarrow -T_1 \cdot T_2$; $m_4 \rightarrow Z_1 \cdot Z_2$; $m_5 \rightarrow (X_1 + Y_1) \cdot (X_2 + Y_2) - m_1 - m_2$; $a_2 \rightarrow m_4 - m_3$; $a_3 \rightarrow m_4 + m_3$; $a_4 \rightarrow m_1 - d_1$; $X_3 \rightarrow m_5 \cdot a_2$; $Y_3 \rightarrow a_3 \cdot a_4$; $Z_3 \rightarrow a_2 \cdot a_3$; $T_3 \rightarrow m_5 \cdot a_4$;
return $(T_3 : X_3 : Y_3 : Z_3)$

---

et al.'s unified addition formula costs $9\mathbf{M} + 1\mathbf{D}$. Thus, our algorithm costs one more $\mathbf{V}$ when $Y_1Y_2 + aX_1X_2 = 0$, and saves $1\mathbf{M} - 1\mathbf{V}$ when $Y_1Y_2 + aX_1X_2 \neq 0$. Since $Y_1Y_2 + aX_1X_2 = 0$ rarely occurs, our algorithm is competitive with Hisil et al.'s unified addition formula when there are no constant time requirements.

However, our new algorithm contains an if-else judgment, and the time cost varies in different conditional branches. Thus, the unified addition formula proposed by Hisil et al. [18] is a better choice for multi-scalar multiplication that requires side-channel assistance.

7 Fast Scalar Multiplication

7.1 Parallelization for Unified Addition Formulae

In [18], Hisil et al. noticed that their unified addition formula is highly parallelizable. Our unified addition formulae also maintain this good property.

In particular, when there are 4 processors can be employed, both of the $8\mathbf{M}+1\mathbf{D}$ unified addition formula and the $8\mathbf{M}+4\mathbf{D}$ clearing denominators unified addition formulas can be performed with effective 5-steps $2\mathbf{M} + 1\mathbf{D}$ algorithm as in Table 2.

As in Table 2, although both of the $8\mathbf{M}+1\mathbf{D}$ unified addition formula and the $8\mathbf{M} + 4\mathbf{D}$ unified addition formulae require $2\mathbf{M} + 1\mathbf{D}$ in a 4-processor parallel point operation, the latter may be faster than the former. For example, the parameter d in Edwards25519 is $d = 121665/121666$. It implies that $d = \bar{d}/\bar{a}$ where $\bar{d} = 121665$ and $\bar{a} = 121666$. Thus, the D in 4-processor parallel of Edwards25519 is a field multiplication by $d = 121665/121666$, and the D in 4-processor parallel of Edwards25519 with clearing denominator is about field multiplication by $2\bar{d} = 2 \cdot 121666 = 243332$.

Table 2. 4-Processor unified addition formulae

cost	step	Processor 1	Processor 2	Processor 3	Processor 4
	1	$a_1 \leftarrow T_1 + Z_1$	$a_2 \leftarrow T_2 + Z_2$	$a_3 \leftarrow T_1 - Z_1$	$a_4 \leftarrow T_2 - Z_2$
1M	2	$m_1 \leftarrow X_1 \cdot X_2$	$m_2 \leftarrow Y_1 \cdot Y_2$	$m_3 \leftarrow a_1 \cdot a_2$	$m_4 \leftarrow a_3 \cdot a_4$
1D	3	$d_1 \leftarrow 2m_1$	$d_2 \leftarrow 2a \cdot m_2$	idle	idle
	4	$a_1 \leftarrow d_1 + d_2$	$a_2 \leftarrow d_1 - d_2$	$a_3 \leftarrow m_3 + m_4$	$a_4 \leftarrow m_3 - m_4$
1M	5	$X_3 \leftarrow a_3 \cdot a_4$	$Y_3 \leftarrow a_1 \cdot a_2$	$Z_3 \leftarrow a_1 \cdot a_3$	$T_3 \leftarrow a_2 \cdot a_4$

(a) $d = -1$

cost	step	Processor 1	Processor 2	Processor 3	Processor 4
	1	$a_1 \leftarrow T_1 + Z_1$	$a_2 \leftarrow T_2 + Z_2$	$a_3 \leftarrow T_1 - Z_1$	$a_4 \leftarrow T_2 - Z_2$
1M	2	$m_1 \leftarrow X_1 \cdot X_2$	$m_2 \leftarrow Y_1 \cdot Y_2$	$m_3 \leftarrow a_1 \cdot a_2$	$m_4 \leftarrow a_3 \cdot a_4$
1D	3	$d_1 \leftarrow 2\bar{d}m_1$	$d_2 \leftarrow 2\bar{a} \cdot m_2$	$d_3 \leftarrow 2\bar{d}m_4$	$d_4 \leftarrow 2\bar{d}m_4$
	4	$a_1 \leftarrow d_1 + d_2$	$a_2 \leftarrow d_1 - d_2$	$a_3 \leftarrow d_3 + d_4$	$a_4 \leftarrow d_3 - d_4$
1M	5	$X_3 \leftarrow a_3 \cdot a_4$	$Y_3 \leftarrow a_1 \cdot a_2$	$Z_3 \leftarrow a_1 \cdot a_3$	$T_3 \leftarrow a_2 \cdot a_4$

(b) $d = -1$ with clearing denominators

cost	step	Processor 1	Processor 2	Processor 3	Processor 4
	1	$a_1 \leftarrow X_1 + Y_1$	$a_2 \leftarrow X_2 + Y_2$	$a_3 \leftarrow X_1 - Y_1$	$a_4 \leftarrow X_2 - Y_2$
1M	2	$m_1 \leftarrow a_3 \cdot a_4$	$m_2 \leftarrow a_1 \cdot a_2$	$m_3 \leftarrow T_1 \cdot T_2$	$m_4 \leftarrow Z_1 \cdot Z_2$
1D	3	$d_1 \leftarrow \bar{a}m_1$	$d_2 \leftarrow \bar{a} \cdot m_2$	$d_3 \leftarrow 2\bar{d}m_4$	$d_4 \leftarrow 2\bar{a}m_4$
	4	$a_1 \leftarrow d_2 - d_1$	$a_2 \leftarrow d_4 - d_3$	$a_3 \leftarrow d_3 + d_4$	$a_4 \leftarrow d_1 + d_2$
1M	5	$X_3 \leftarrow a_1 \cdot a_2$	$Y_3 \leftarrow a_3 \cdot a_4$	$Z_3 \leftarrow a_1 \cdot a_4$	$T_3 \leftarrow a_2 \cdot a_3$

(c) $a = -1$ with clearing denominators

7.2 Speedup by Mixing Different Coordinates

The mixing different coordinates technique in elliptic curve cryptography was first proposed by Cohen, Miyaji, and Ono to speed up the scalar multiplication on short Weierstrass curves [8]. Hisil et al. used this technique on twisted Edwards curves [18]. We also take this technique for the case $d = -1$.

Recall that given $(T : Y : Z)$ in $\mathcal{E}$ passing to $\mathcal{E}^e$ requires $3\mathbf{M} + 1\mathbf{S}$ by computing (TY, TZ, Y^2, YZ), and given $(T : X : Y : Z)$ in $\mathcal{E}^e$ passing to $\mathcal{E}$ is cost-free by simply ignoring X. When performing a scalar multiplication, the scalar multiplication can be speedup by employing the following strategies:

(1) If a point doubling or tripling is followed by another point doubling or tripling, one should employ the corresponding formula on $\mathcal{E}$.
(2) After each addition, the tripling scalar multiplication *should* be performed as early as possible.
(3) If a point doubling or tripling is followed by a point addition, please use $\mathcal{E}^e \leftarrow k\mathcal{E}, k = 2, 3$ and $\mathcal{E} \leftarrow \mathcal{E}^e + \mathcal{E}^e$ for the point doubling or tripling and the point addition.

The core idea is cutting down the number of computations of the coordinate X. Then, when $d = -1$, the cost of the doubling formula can be considered as $4\mathbf{M} + 3\mathbf{S}$; and the cost of the addition formula can be considered as $8\mathbf{M}$ (with one $\mathbf{M}$ more from the doubling formula to obtain X-coordinate for the input point of the addition and one $\mathbf{M}$ less since the X-coordinate output point can be ignored). For more details, please see [18] §4.

8 Conclusion

In this paper, we proposed efficient point operations on twisted Edwards curves $d = -1$. Two addition formulas are introduced, one of them is unified. Two unified addition formulas with clearing denominators are introduced to gain new speed records in the parallel environments.

The unified addition formula with $d = -1$ saves $1\mathbf{M} + 1\mathbf{D}$ compared with the general case in [18]. It is approximately 11.1% and 18.2% faster than the results in [18] under the assumptions $\mathbf{D}/\mathbf{M} \approx 0$ and $\mathbf{D}/\mathbf{M} \approx 1$, respectively. The faster addition formula costs only $8\mathbf{M}$, saving an additional $\mathbf{D}$ compared to our unified addition formula. Moreover, special doubling and tripling formulas are proposed. All of these formulae are as fast as the best-known results for $a = -1$.

Acknowledgments. The authors would like to thank the anonymous reviewers for many helpful comments and their helpful suggestions. This work was supported by the National Key R&D Program of China (Grant No. 2023YFB4503203), the National Natural Science Foundation of China (Grant No. 62272453 and 62272186), the Key Research Program of the Chinese Academy of Sciences (Grant No. ZDRW-XX-2022-1), and the Innovation Project of Jinyinhu Laboratory (Grant No. 2023JYH010103).

References

1. Bernstein, D.J., Birkner, P., Joye, M., Lange, T., Peters, C.: Twisted Edwards curves. In: Vaudenay, S. (ed.) AFRICACRYPT 2008. LNCS, vol. 5023, pp. 389–405. Springer, Heidelberg (2008). https://doi.org/10.1007/978-3-540-68164-9_26
2. Bernstein, D.J., Birkner, P., Lange, T., Peters, C.: ECM using Edwards curves. Math. Comput. **82**, 1139–1179 (2013)
3. Bernstein, D.J., Lange, T.: Faster addition and doubling on elliptic curves. In: Kurosawa, K. (ed.) ASIACRYPT 2007. LNCS, vol. 4833, pp. 29–50. Springer, Heidelberg (2007). https://doi.org/10.1007/978-3-540-76900-2_3
4. Bernstein, D.J., Lange, T.: Inverted Edwards coordinates. In: Boztaş, S., Lu, H.-F.F. (eds.) AAECC 2007. LNCS, vol. 4851, pp. 20–27. Springer, Heidelberg (2007). https://doi.org/10.1007/978-3-540-77224-8_4
5. Bernstein, D.J., Lange, T.: A complete set of addition laws for incomplete Edwards curves. J. Number Theory **131**(5), 858–872 (2011). https://doi.org/10.1016/j.jnt.2010.06.015, https://www.sciencedirect.com/science/article/pii/S0022314X10002155. Elliptic Curve Cryptography
6. Bouvier, C., Imbert, L.: Faster cofactorization with ECM using mixed representations. In: Kiayias, A., Kohlweiss, M., Wallden, P., Zikas, V. (eds.) PKC 2020. LNCS, vol. 12111, pp. 483–504. Springer, Cham (2020). https://doi.org/10.1007/978-3-030-45388-6_17

7. Chen, L., Moody, D., Regenscheid, A., Randall, K.: NIST special publication 800-186, recommendations for discrete logarithm-based cryptography: elliptic curve domain parameters. Technical report (2023). https://nvlpubs.nist.gov/nistpubs/SpecialPublications/NIST.SP.800-186.pdf
8. Cohen, H., Miyaji, A., Ono, T.: Efficient elliptic curve exponentiation using mixed coordinates. In: Ohta, K., Pei, D. (eds.) ASIACRYPT 1998. LNCS, vol. 1514, pp. 51–65. Springer, Heidelberg (1998). https://doi.org/10.1007/3-540-49649-1_6
9. Cremers, C., Jackson, D.: Prime, order please! Revisiting small subgroup and invalid curve attacks on protocols using Diffie-Hellman. In: 2019 IEEE 32nd Computer Security Foundations Symposium (CSF), pp. 78–7815. IEEE (2019)
10. Edwards, H.M.: A normal form for elliptic curves. Bull. Am. Math. Soc. **44**, 393–423 (2007). https://doi.org/10.1090/S0273-0979-07-01153-6
11. Euler, L.: Observationes de comparatione arcuum curvarum irrectificibilium. Novi commentarii academiae scientiarum Petropolitanae 58–84 (1761)
12. Farashahi, R.R., Hosseini, S.G.: Differential addition on twisted Edwards curves. In: Pieprzyk, J., Suriadi, S. (eds.) ACISP 2017. LNCS, vol. 10343, pp. 366–378. Springer, Cham (2017). https://doi.org/10.1007/978-3-319-59870-3_21
13. Galbraith, S.D., Lin, X., Scott, M.: Endomorphisms for faster elliptic curve cryptography on a large class of curves. In: Joux, A. (ed.) EUROCRYPT 2009. LNCS, vol. 5479, pp. 518–535. Springer, Heidelberg (2009). https://doi.org/10.1007/978-3-642-01001-9_30
14. Gallant, R.P., Lambert, R.J., Vanstone, S.A.: Faster point multiplication on elliptic curves with efficient endomorphisms. In: Kilian, J. (ed.) CRYPTO 2001. LNCS, vol. 2139, pp. 190–200. Springer, Heidelberg (2001). https://doi.org/10.1007/3-540-44647-8_11
15. Hamburg, M.: Decaf: eliminating cofactors through point compression. In: Gennaro, R., Robshaw, M. (eds.) CRYPTO 2015, Part I. LNCS, vol. 9215, pp. 705–723. Springer, Heidelberg (2015). https://doi.org/10.1007/978-3-662-47989-6_34
16. Hamburg, M.: Ed448-goldilocks, a new elliptic curve. Cryptology ePrint Archive, Report 2015/625 (2015). https://eprint.iacr.org/2015/625
17. de Valence, H., Grigg, J., Tankersley, G., Valsorda, F., Lovecruft, I.: The ristretto255 group. Technical report, IETF CFRG Internet Draft (2019)
18. Hisil, H., Wong, K.K.-H., Carter, G., Dawson, E.: Twisted Edwards curves revisited. In: Pieprzyk, J. (ed.) ASIACRYPT 2008. LNCS, vol. 5350, pp. 326–343. Springer, Heidelberg (2008). https://doi.org/10.1007/978-3-540-89255-7_20
19. Josefsson, S., Liusvaara, I.: Edwards-curve digital signature algorithm (EdDSA). RFC 8032 (2017). https://doi.org/10.17487/RFC8032, https://www.rfc-editor.org/info/rfc8032
20. Kohel, D.: Addition law structure of elliptic curves. J. Number Theory **131**(5), 894–919 (2011). https://doi.org/10.1016/j.jnt.2010.12.001
21. Miniero, L., Murillo, S.G., Pascual, V.: Guidelines for end-to-end support of the RTP control protocol (RTCP) in back-to-back user agents (B2BUAs). RFC 8079 (2017). https://doi.org/10.17487/RFC8079, https://www.rfc-editor.org/info/rfc8079
22. National Institute of Standards and Technology (NIST): Federal information processing standard (FIPS) 186-5, digital signature standard (DSS)
23. Sedlacek, V., Chi-Domínguez, J.-J., Jancar, J., Brumley, B.B.: A formula for disaster: a unified approach to elliptic curve special-point-based attacks. In: Tibouchi, M., Wang, H. (eds.) ASIACRYPT 2021. LNCS, vol. 13090, pp. 130–159. Springer, Cham (2021). https://doi.org/10.1007/978-3-030-92062-3_5

24. Yu, W., Musa, S.A., Li, B.: Double-base chains for scalar multiplications on elliptic curves. In: Canteaut, A., Ishai, Y. (eds.) EUROCRYPT 2020. LNCS, vol. 12107, pp. 538–565. Springer, Cham (2020). https://doi.org/10.1007/978-3-030-45727-3_18
25. Yu, W., Xu, G.: Pre-computation scheme of window τNAF for koblitz curves revisited. In: Canteaut, A., Standaert, F.-X. (eds.) EUROCRYPT 2021. LNCS, vol. 12697, pp. 187–218. Springer, Cham (2021). https://doi.org/10.1007/978-3-030-77886-6_7

Author Index

Q. Tang and V. Teague (Eds.): PKC 2024, LNCS 14604, p. 413, 2024.
https://doi.org/10.1007/978-3-031-57728-4

Printed in the United States
by Baker & Taylor Publisher Services